1 MONTH OF
FREE
READING

at

www.ForgottenBooks.com

By purchasing this book you are eligible for one month membership to ForgottenBooks.com, giving you unlimited access to our entire collection of over 1,000,000 titles via our web site and mobile apps.

To claim your free month visit:

www.forgottenbooks.com/free898532

ISBN 978-0-266-84746-5
PIBN 10898532

NEW YORK

IN THE

SPANISH-AMERICAN WAR

1898.

Part of the Report of the Adjutant-General of the
State for 1900.

IN THREE VOLUMES.

VOLUME II.

ALBANY:
JAMES B. LYON, STATE PRINTER.
1900.

VOLUME II.

TABLE OF CONTENTS.

NINTH REGIMENT, INFANTRY.

The ninth regiment, national guard, having volunteered its services, was one of the regiments selected in general orders, No. 8, general headquarters, state of New York, dated adjutant-general's office, Albany, April 27, 1898, to enter the service of the United States as a volunteer regiment.

The regiment at that time consisted of ten companies, and at once commenced recruiting to fill its companies and to organize two additional ones. Its prior history follows:

NINTH REGIMENT.

(First Brigade.)

Armory, 125 West Fourteenth street, New York city.

The actual date when this regiment was organized is not disclosed by the records; evidence is found that it existed as far back as the period of the war of 1812. In 1845 it appears to have been re-organized, but the present organization really dates from June, 1859. It entered the United States service for three years, being known in such service as the ninth New York state militia, and also as the eighty-third New York volunteers; was mustered in at Washington, D. C., June 8, 1861, and mustered out at New York city, June 23, 1864. It rendered the state service in the Orange riot, July 12, 1871; in the Railroad riots, in July, 1877; at the Switchmen's strike at Buffalo, in August, 1892, and during the Brooklyn Motormen's strike, in January, 1895.

The regiment received authority to place silver rings on the lances of its colors, engraved as follows:

On the national color:—Harper's Ferry, Va., July 4, 1861; Warrenton Junction, Va., April 6, 1862; Warrenton Junction, Va., April 16, 1862; North Fork River, Va., April 18, 1862; Rappahannock River, Va., May 5, 1862; Cedar Mountain, Va., August 9, 1862; Rappahannock River, Va., August 22, 1862; Rappahannock Station, Va., August 23, 1862; Thoroughfare Gap, Va., August 28, 1862; Bull Run, Va., August 30, 1862; Chantilly, Va., September

1, 1862; South Mountain, Md., September 14, 1862; Antietam, Md., September 17, 1862; Fredericksburg, Va., December 13, 1862; Pollock's Mill Creek, Va., April 29, 1863; Chancellorsville, Va., May 2 and 3, 1863; Gettysburg, Pa., July 1 to 4, 1863; Hagerstown, Md., July 12 and 13, 1863; Liberty, Va., November 21, 1863; Mine Run, Va., November 26 to December 2, 1863; Wilderness, Va., May 5 to 7, 1864; Spotsylvania Court House, Va., May 8, 1864; Piney Branch Church, Va., May 8, 1864; Laurel Hill, Va., May 10, 1864; Spotsylvania, Va., May 12, 1864; North Anna, Va., May 22, 1864; Totopotomoy, Va., May 27 to 31, 1864; Cold Harbor, Va., June 1 to 7, 1864.

On the state color:—Abolition riot, January 11 and 12, 1835; Great Fire, December 17, 1835; Orange riot, July 12, 1871; West Albany, July, 1877; Buffalo, August, 1892; Brooklyn, January, 1895.

Special orders, No. 72, A. G. O., May 1, 1898, ordered the regiment to report at the foot of Twenty-second street, North river, New York city, at noon of the 2d of May; there to embark for the Camp of Instruction, near Peekskill, and on arrival at the camp to report to Brigadier-General Peter C. Doyle, national guard, commanding the camp.   The order was duly carried out.

Under the provisions of general orders, No. 11, A. G. O., Albany, May 3, 1898, the regiment was at the camp fully organized as a twelve company regiment, and was mustered in the United States service as follows; companies A, D and M, May 17th; C, I and K, May 19th; B, E, G, H and L, May 20th; the field and staff, and company F, May 25th; the whole as the "ninth regiment, infantry, New York volunteers."

Under orders of the war department the regiment left Camp Townsend (Camp of Instruction heretofore), at 10 a. m., of May 24th; embarked on the steamer "Glen Island" for New York city, and after a short parade in the latter city it was transferred by ferry to Jersey City, N. J., where it embarked and left on trains of the Pennsylvania railroad for Camp George H. Thomas, Chicka-manga Park, Ga., the same day.   It arrived at the park in the forenoon of the 26th of May, and was assigned to the third army corps.

May 29th, it was assigned to the first brigade, second division of the same corps; the brigade consisting of the first regiment,

Arkansas; second regiment, Kentucky, and ninth regiment, New York volunteer infantry.

The regiment while at the park performed the usual camp routine of drills, rifle practice and guard duties.

The regiment returned to its home station via Cincinnati and Buffalo, leaving camp, September 13th, and arriving at New York city, September 16th, where it was quartered at the armory of the ninth regiment, national guard; receiving a furlough for thirty days, and where it was mustered out of the service of the United States, November 15, 1898.

Commissioned Officers.

COLONEL:

Goodman James Greene, May 18 to November 15, 1898.

LIEUTENANT-COLONEL:

Thomas B. Rand, May 2 to November 15, 1898.

MAJORS:

George T. Lorigan, May 2 to July 16, 1898.
Washington Willcocks, May 2 to November 15, 1898.
Godfrey A. S. Wieners, May 2 to November 15, 1898.

REGIMENTAL ADJUTANTS:

George J. Hardy, May 2 to June 12, 1898.
William A. Angus, July 23 to November 15, 1898.

BATTALION ADJUTANTS:

James T. Hardy, May 2 to November 25, 1898.
John M. Jones, May 21 to November 15, 1898.
Henry S. Kip, May 22 to November 15, 1898.

QUARTERMASTER:

John H. Ball, May 21 to November 15, 1898.

SURGEON:

Samuel D. Hubbard, May 2 to November 15, 1898.

ASSISTANT SURGEONS:

John B. L'Hommedieu, May 4 to September 8, 1898.
Albert W. Preston, May 15 to November 15, 1898.

CHAPLAIN:

Rowland S. Nichols, May 24 to November 15, 1898.

COMPANY A.

CAPTAIN:

Samuel S. O'Connor, May 2 to November 15, 1898.

FIRST LIEUTENANTS:

James M. O'Donnell, May 2 to July 30, 1898.
Michael J. Mahoney, July 30 to October 3, 1898.
James J. Walsh, October 28 to November 15, 1898.

SECOND LIEUTENANTS:

Michael J. Mahoney, May 17 to July 30, 1898.
Charles E. Hinckley, July 30 to October 17, 1898.
George J. Fritzmier, October 28 to November 15, 1898.

COMPANY B.

CAPTAINS:

Arthur M. Tompkins, May 2 to July 26, 1898.
James M. O'Donnell, July 30 to November 15, 1898,

FIRST LIEUTENANTS:

Herman C. Leonhardi, May 2 to July 22, 1898.
Charles A. Meyer, Jr., July 27 to July 30, 1898.
John C. Hegarty, August 5 to November 15, 1898.

SECOND LIEUTENANT:

Edwin W. Watkins, May 2 to November 15, 1898.

COMPANY C.

CAPTAIN:

Frederick J. Quinby, May 2 to November 15, 1898.

FIRST LIEUTENANT:

Emott Seward, Jr., May 2 to October 17, 1898.

SECOND LIEUTENANT:

Charles W. Seward, May 2 to September 16, 1898.

COMPANY D.

CAPTAINS:

John D. Walton, May 2, to July 14, 1898.
Charles A. Meyer, Jr., July 30 to November 15, 1898.

FIRST LIEUTENANT:

John F. Hendrickson, May 17 to November 15, 1898.

SECOND LIEUTENANT:

Joseph Beaumont, Jr., May 15 to November 15, 1898.

COMPANY E.

CAPTAIN:

Horace M. Graff, May 2 to November 15, 1898.

FIRST LIEUTENANT:

Addison McDougall, May 22 to November 15, 1898.

SECOND LIEUTENANTS:

David H. Miller, May 2 to July 22, 1898.
Charles Y. Judson, July 29 to November 15, 1898.

COMPANY F.

CAPTAINS:

Wesley E. Bryde, May 2 to July 18, 1898.
Frank H. Peck, July 22 to November 15, 1898.

FIRST LIEUTENANT:

Robert N. Mackin, May 2 to August 15, 1898.

SECOND LIEUTENANTS:

Frank H. Peck, June 3 to July 22, 1898.
William H. Smith, July 23 to November 15, 1898.

COMPANY G.

CAPTAIN:

Oscar D. Weed, May 2 to November 15, 1898.

FIRST LIEUTENANTS·

Abraham L. Willcocks, May 2 to August 3, 1898.
David H. Miller, July 22 to November 15, 1898.

SECOND LIEUTENANT:

James H. Lee, May 2 to November 15, 1898.

COMPANY H.

CAPTAIN:

Warner S. Young, May 2 to November 15, 1898.

FIRST LIEUTENANT:

Franklin D. L. Walker, May 2 to September 20, 1898.

SECOND LIEUTENANT:

Wallace S. Parker, May 2 to November 15, 1898.

NINTH REGIMENT, INFANTRY.

COMPANY I.

CAPTAIN:

Charles E. Kohlberger, May 2 to November 15, 1898.

FIRST LIEUTENANTS:

Charles A. Meyer, Jr., May 19 to July 27, 1898.
George J. Hardy, July 27 to November 15, 1898.

SECOND LIEUTENANT:

William F. J. Higgins, May 2 to November 15, 1898.

COMPANY K.

CAPTAINS:

William F. Morris, May 2 to August 3, 1898.
John J. Byrne, August 17 to November 15, 1898.

FIRST LIEUTENANTS:

John J. Byrne, May 2 to August 17, 1898.
James Lynch, August 20 to November 15, 1898.

SECOND LIEUTENANTS:

James Lynch, May 2 to August 20, 1898.
Edward J. Cullen, August 20 to November 15, 1898.

COMPANY L.

CAPTAIN:

C. Arthur Coan, May 2 to November 15, 1898.

FIRST LIEUTENANTS:

Emil J. Winterroth, May 20 to July 27, 1898.
Ulysses S. G. Croft, August 20 to November 15, 1898.

SECOND LIEUTENANTS

Ulysses S. G. Croft, May 2 to August 20, 1898.
William G. Romaine, August 20 to November 15, 1898.

COMPANY M.

CAPTAIN:

Thomas W. Timpson, May 2 to November 15, 1898.

FIRST LIEUTENANT:

Edwin D. Graff, May 2 to November 15, 1898.

SECOND LIEUTENANTS:

John C. Hegarty, May 2 to August 5, 1898.
James H. Farquharson, July 23 to November 15, 1898.

RECORDS OF THE OFFICERS AND ENLISTED MEN.

ABEL, WILLIAM.—Age, 24 years. Enlisted, May 2, 1898, at New York city, to serve two years; mustered in as private, Co. C, May 19, 1898; appointed wagoner, July 13, 1898; mustered out with company, November 15, 1898, at New York city.

ADAMS, CHARLES.—Age, — years. Enlisted, July 1, 1898, at New York city, to serve two years; mustered in as private, Co. C, same date; promoted corporal, September 9, 1898; mustered out with company, November 15, 1898, at New York city.

ADDISS, LORENZO C.—Age, 20 years. Enlisted, May 2, 1898, at New York city, to serve two years; mustered in as private, Co. H, May 20, 1898; promoted corporal, no date; discharged, September 5, 1898, at Huntsville, Ala.

ADLER, FREDERICK.—Age, 20 years. Enlisted, May 2, 1898, at New York city, to serve two years; mustered in as private, Co. L, May 20, 1898; deserted, September 7, 1898.

AFELD, OSCAR C.—Age, 23 years. Enlisted, May 2, 1898, at New York city, to serve two years; mustered in as private, Co. I, May 19, 1898; mustered out with company, November 15, 1898, at New York city.

AIKEN, JOSEPH R.—Age, 24 years. Enlisted, May 2, 1898, at New York city, to serve two years; mustered in as private, Co. B, May 20, 1898; mustered out with company, November 15, 1898, at New York city.

ALBERT, RAYMOND.—Age, 24 years. Enlisted, May 2, 1898, at New York city, to serve two years; mustered in as private, Co. E, May 20, 1898; mustered out with company, November 15, 1898, at New York city.

ALSWORTH, THOMAS.—Age, 30 years. Enlisted, May 2, 1898, at New York city, to serve two years; mustered in as private, Co. F, May 21, 1898; mustered out with company, November 15, 1898, at New York city.

AMES, CLYDE E.—Age, 26 years. Enlisted, May 2, 1898, at New York city, to serve two years; mustered in as artificer, Co. C, May 19, 1898; returned to ranks, August 13, 1898; deserted, August 18, 1898.

AMMON, CHARLES E.—Age, 21 years. Enlisted, May 2, 1898, at New York city, to serve two years; mustered in as sergeant, Co. G, May 20, 1898; mustered out with company, November 15, 1898, at New York city.

ANABLE, SHELDON B.—Age, 29 years. Enlisted, May 2, 1898, at New York city, to serve two years; mustered in as private, Co. M, May 17, 1898; promoted corporal, July 27, 1898; mustered out with company, November 15, 1898, at New York city.

ANDERSON, GEORGE.—Age, 21 years. Enlisted, May 2, 1898, at New York city, to serve two years; mustered in as private, Co. G, May 20, 1898; mustered out with company, November 15, 1898, at New York city.

ANDERSON, WILLIAM.—Age, 29 years. Enlisted, May 2, 1898, at New York city, to serve two years; mustered in as private, Co. B, May 20, 1898; promoted corporal, August 22, 1898; mustered out with company, November 15, 1898, at New York city.

ANGERER, CHARLES.—Age, 24 years. Enlisted, May 2, 1898, at New York city, to serve two years; mustered in as corporal, Co. M, May 17, 1898; mustered out with company, November 15, 1898, at New York city.

ANGUS, WILLIAM A.—Age, — years. Enrolled, July 23, 1898, at Camp Thomas, Ga., to serve two years; mustered in as first lieutenant, same date; appointed regimental adjutant, August 4, 1898; mustered out with regiment, November 15, 1898, at New York city, as first lieutenant and regimental adjutant; commissioned first lieutenant, July 30, 1898, with rank from same date, vice Leonhardi, discharged.

ARCHBOLD, ROBERT P.—Age, 21 years. Enlisted, May 2, 1898, at New York city, to serve two years; mustered in as private, Co. M, May 17, 1898; mustered out with company, November 15, 1898, at New York city.

ARENS, CHARLES R.—Age, 22 years. Enlisted, May 2, 1898, at New York city, to serve two years; mustered in as private, Co. L, May 20, 1898; mustered out with company, November 15, 1898, at New York city.

AREY, ARTHUR C.—Age, 24 years. Enlisted, May 2, 1898, at New York city, to serve two years; mustered in as private, Co. D, May 17, 1898; promoted corporal, July 27, 1898; discharged, October 12, 1898.

ARMAND, JULES.—Age, 25 years. Enlisted, May 2, 1898, at New York city, to serve two years; mustered in as private, Co. I, May 19, 1898; mustered out with company, November 15, 1898, at New York city.

ARMISTEAD, SAMUEL.—Age, 42 years. Enlisted, May 2, 1898, at New York city, to serve two years; mustered in as artificer, Co. G, May 20, 1898; mustered out with company, November 15, 1898, at New York city.

ARPE, FREDERICK.—Age, — years. Enlisted, July 6, 1898, at New York city, to serve two years; mustered in as private, Co. H, same date; mustered out with company, November 15, 1898, at New York city.

ASH, EDWIN.—Age, 34 years. Enlisted, May 2, 1898, at New York city, to serve two years; mustered in as private, Co. L, May 20, 1898; mustered out with company, November 15, 1898, at New York city.

ASHWORTH, WILLIAM N.—Age, — years. Enlisted, June 24, 1898, at New York city, to serve two years; mustered in as private, Co. L, same date; mustered out with company, November 15, 1898, at New York city.

AUGERMULLER, GEORGE E.—Age, 23 years. Enlisted, May 2, 1898, at New York city, to serve two years; mustered in as artificer, Co. K, May 19, 1898; mustered out with company, November 15, 1898, at New York city.

BAENISCH, CHARLES.—Age, — years. Enlisted, July 8, 1898, at New York city, to serve two years; mustered in as private, Co. H, same date; transferred to band, July 27, 1898; mustered out with regiment, November 15, 1898, at New York city.

BAETTCHER, JR., WILLIAM H.—Age, 19 years. Enlisted, May 2, 1898, at New York city, to serve two years; mustered in as private, Co. E, May 20, 1898; promoted corporal, September 7, 1898; mustered out with company, November 15, 1898, at New York city.

BAGLEY, LOUIS L.—Age, 27 years. Enlisted, May 2, 1898, at New York city, to serve two years; mustered in as quarter-master-sergeant, Co. G, May 20, 1898; discharged, October 19, 1898.

BAHNSEN, HENRY.—Age, — years. Enlisted, July 6, 1898, at New York city, to serve two years; mustered in as private, Co. L, same date; mustered out with company, November 15, 1898, at New York city.

BAILEY, FRANK.—Age, 28 years. Enlisted, May 2, 1898, at New York city, to serve two years; mustered in as private, Co. I, May 19, 1898; mustered out with company, November 15, 1898, at New York city.

BALDWIN, JUSTIN D.—Age, — years. Enlisted, June 23, 1898, at New York city, to serve two years; mustered in as private, Co. A, same date; mustered out with company, November 15, 1898, at New York city.

BALL, JOHN H.—Age, 36 years. Enrolled, May 21, 1898, at camp near Peekskill, to serve two years; mustered in as regimental quartermaster, May 21, 1898; mustered out, to date, November 15, 1898; commissioned captain and regimental quartermaster, May 21, 1898, with rank from same date, original.

BANKS, LEE.—Age, 27 years. Enlisted, May 2, 1898, at New York city, to serve two years; mustered in as corporal, Co. A, May 17, 1898; returned to ranks, August 28, 1898; promoted corporal, September 3, 1898; mustered out with company, November 15, 1898, at New York city.

BANZHAF, EDWIN J.—Age, 22 years. Enlisted, May 2, 1898, at New York city, to serve two years; mustered in as private, Co. G, May 21, 1898; promoted corporal, October 22, 1898; mustered out with com an November 15 1898 at New York ci .

BARCKLEY, CHESTER.—Age, — years.   Enlisted, July 11, 1898, at New York city, to serve two years; mustered in as private, Co. L, same date; transferred to band, July 27, 1898; mustered out with regiment, November 15, 1898, at New York city.

BARCLAY, FRANCIS J.—Age, — years.   Enlisted, June 23, 1898, at New York city, to serve two years; mustered in as private, Co. A, same date; mustered out with company, November 15, 1898, at New York city.

BARKAS, CHARLES.—Age, 21 years.   Enlisted, May 2, 1898, at New York city, to serve two years; mustered in as private, Co. C, May 19, 1898; mustered out with company, November 15, 1898, at New York city.   .

BARLOW, JOHN.—Age, 25 years.   Enlisted, May 2, 1898, at New York city, to serve two years; mustered in as private, Co. G, May 20, 1898; mustered out with company, November 15, 1898, at New York city.

BARNES, RUFUS K.—Age, 21 years.   Enlisted, May 2, 1898, at New York city, to serve two years; mustered in as private, Co. C, May 19, 1898; mustered out with company, November 15, 1898, at New York city.

BARRATT, EDGAR S.—Age, 27 years.   Enlisted, May 2, 1898, at New York city, to serve two years; mustered in as private, Co. C, May 19, 1898; discharged for disability, August 21, 1898.

BARRETT, GEORGE.—Age, 31 years.   Enlisted, May 2, 1898, at New York city, to serve two years; mustered in as private, Co. G, May 20, 1898; mustered out with company, November 15, 1898, at New York city.

BARRETT, MICHAEL J.—Age, 22 years.   Enlisted, May 2, 1898, at New York city, to serve two years; mustered in as private, Co. B, May 20, 1898; mustered out with company, November 15, 1898, at New York city.

BARRON, RICHARD.—Age, 24 years.   Enlisted, May 18, 1898, at New York city, to serve two years; mustered in as private, Co. I, May 19, 1898; mustered out with company, November 15, 1898, at New York city.

BARRY, DAVID A.—Age, 32 years. Enlisted, May 2, 1898, at New York city, to serve two years; mustered in as private, Co. M, May 17, 1898; mustered out with company, November 15, 1898, at New York city.

BARRY, EDWARD F.—Age, 24 years. Enlisted, May 2, 1898, at New York city, to serve two years; mustered in as private, Co. A, May 17, 1898; mustered out with company, November 15, 1898, at New York city.

BARRY, STEPHEN A.—Age, 22 years. Enlisted, May 2, 1898, at New York city, to serve two years; mustered in as private, Co. A, May 17, 1898; appointed wagoner, August 8, 1898; mustered out with company, November 15, 1898, at New York city.

BASSETT, JAMES.—Age, — years. Enlisted, June 23, 1898, at New York city, to serve two years; mustered in as private, Co. M, same date; mustered out with company, November 15, 1898, at New York city.

BATINSEY, JOSEPH.—Age, — years. Enlisted, July 5, 1898, at New York city, to serve two years; mustered in as private, Co. F, same date; mustered out with company, November 15, 1898, at New York city.

BAUMAN, LOUIS F.—Age, 34 years. Enlisted, May 2, 1898, at New York city, to serve two years; mustered in as private, Co. D, May 17, 1898; discharged, October 14, 1898.

BAUTZ, JOSEPH.—Age, — years. Enlisted, July 1, 1898, at New York city, to serve two years; mustered in as private, Co. I, same date; mustered out with company, November 15, 1898, at New York city.

BAVIER, JAMES M.—Age, 29 years. Enlisted, May 2, 1898, at New York city, to serve two years; mustered in as private, Co. A, May 17, 1898; mustered out with company, November 15, 1898, at New York city.

BEAUMONT, JR., JOSEPH.—Age, 24 years. Enlisted, May 2, 1898, at New York city, as corporal, to serve two years; mustered in as second lieutenant, Co. D, May 17, 1898; mustered out with company November 15, 1898, at New York city; commissioned second lieutenant, May 17, 1898, with rank from same date, original.

BEAUMONT, WILLIAM.—Age, 26 years. Enlisted, May 2, 1898, at New York city, to serve two years; mustered in as first sergeant, Co. D, May 17, 1898; mustered out with company, November 15, 1898, at New York city.

BECKER, LOUIS.—Age, 20 years. Enlisted, May 2, 1898, at New York city, to serve two years; mustered in as corporal, Co. B, May 20, 1898; mustered out with company, November 15, 1898, at New York city.

BECKER, SAMUEL.—Age, 19 years. Enlisted, May 2, 1898, at New York city, to serve two years; mustered in as private, Co. A, May 17, 1898; mustered out with company, November 15, 1898, at New York city.

BEDE, ADOLPHE.—Age, 42 years. Enlisted, May 2, 1898, at New York city, to serve two years; mustered in as musician, Co. G, May 20, 1898; mustered out with company, November 15, 1898, at New York city.

BELL, JOHN.—Age, 26 years. Enlisted, May 2, 1898, at New York city, to serve two years; mustered in as private, Co. K, May 19, 1898; mustered out with company, November 15, 1898, at New York city.

BELLER, CHARLES F.—Age, 24 years. Enlisted, May 2, 1898, at New York city, to serve two years; mustered in as private, Co. B, May 20, 1898; mustered out with company, November 15, 1898, at New York city.

BENDEL, GOTTLIB.—Age, 22 years. Enlisted, May 2, 1898, at New York city, to serve two years; mustered in as private, Co. I, May 19, 1898; mustered out with company, November 15, 1898, at New York city.

BENISH, FRANK.—Age, 24 years. Enlisted, May 16, 1898, at New York city, to serve two years; mustered in as private, Co. B, May 20, 1898; mustered out with company, November 15, 1898, at New York city.

BENNETT, HOWARD E.—Age, 20 years. Enlisted, May 2, 1898, at New York city, to serve two years; mustered in as private, Co. E, May 20, 1898; mustered out with company, November 15, 1898, at New York city.

BENOIT, RAOUL.—Age, 33 years. Enlisted, May 2, 1898, at New York city, to serve two years; mustered in as private, Co. H, May 20, 1898; discharged, October 17, 1898.

BENSON, EGBERT.—Age, 24 years. Enlisted, May 2, 1898, at New York city, to serve two years; mustered in as private, Co. M, May 17, 1898; promoted sergeant-major, October 19, 1898; mustered out with regiment, November 15, 1898, at New York city.

BERG, AUGUST.—Age, 21 years. Enlisted, May 2, 1898, at New York city, to serve two years; mustered in as private, Co. C, May 19, 1898; mustered out with company November 15, 1898, at New York city.

BERGIN, MARTIN F.—Age, 22 years. Enlisted, May 2, 1898, at New York city, to serve two years; mustered in as private, Co. K, May 19, 1898; mustered out with company, November 15, 1898 at New York city.

BERK, JOSEPH G.—Age, 22 years. Enlisted, May 2, 1898, at New York city, to serve two years; mustered in as private, Co. I, May 19, 1898; mustered out with company, November 15, 1898, at New York city.

BESLER, ADOLPH.—Age, 21 years. Enlisted, May 2, 1898, at New York city to serve two years; mustered in as private, Co. B, May 20, 1898; mustered out with company, November 15, 1898, at New York city.

BETTS, HARRY M.—Age, 22 years. Enlisted, May 2, 1898, at New York city, to serve two years; mustered in as private, Co. F, May 21, 1898; mustered out with company, November 15, 1898, at New York city.

BEVAN, SAMUEL H.—Age, 33 years. Enlisted, May 2, 1898, at New York city, to serve two years; mustered in as private, Co. D, May 17, 1898; promoted corporal, July 22, 1898; mustered out with company, November 15, 1898, at New York city.

BEYER, HENRY J.—Age, 21 years. Enlisted, May 2, 1898, at New York city, to serve two years; mustered in as private, Co. E, May 20, 1898; mustered out with company, November 15, 1898, at New York city.

BICKLER, CHARLES.—Age, 27 years. Enlisted, May 2, 1898, at New York city, to serve two years; mustered in as private, Co. I, May 19, 1898; mustered out with company, November 15, 1898, at New York city.

BISHOP, ROBERT T.—Age, 29 years. Enlisted May 2, 1898, at New York city, to serve two years; mustered in as private, Co. K, May 19, 1898; mustered out with company, November 15, 1898, at New York city.

BITTONG, HERMAN.—Age, 21 years. Enlisted May 2, 1898, at New York city, to serve two years; mustered in as private, Co. D, May 17, 1898; mustered out with company, November 15, 1898, at New York city.

BLACKBURN, THOMAS LEON.—Age, — years. Enlisted, June 30, 1898, at New York city, to serve two years; mustered in as private, Co. L, same date; mustered out with company, November 15, 1898, at New York city.

BLAKE, EDWARD J.—Age, 23 years. Enlisted, May 2, 1898, at New York city, to serve two years; mustered in as private, Co. C, May 19, 1898; discharged for disability, July 19, 1898.

BLAKE, JAMES.—Age, — years. Enlisted, June 23, 1898, at New York city, to serve two years; mustered in as private, Co. G, same date; died of typhoid fever, August 21, 1898, at New York city.

BLANC, EDWARD J.—Age, 24 years. Enlisted, May 2, 1898, at New York city, to serve two years; mustered in as private, Co. K, May 19, 1898; mustered out with company, November 15, 1898, at New York city.

BLANEY, EDWARD J.—Age, 21 years. Enlisted, May 2, 1898, at New York city, to serve two years; mustered in as private, Co. C, May 19, 1898; mustered out with company, November 15, 1898, at New York city.

BLUNT, JOHN H.—Age, 36 years. Enlisted, May 2, 1898, at New York city, to serve two years; mustered in as private, Co. K, May 19, 1898; mustered out with company, November 15, 1898, at New York city.

BODAMER, WILLIAM.—Age, 36 years. Enlisted, May 2, 1898, at New York city, to serve two years; mustered in as sergeant, Co. F, May 21, 1898; promoted quartermaster-sergeant, June 22. 1898; returned to ranks, October 14, 1898; mustered out with company, November 15, 1898, at New York city.

BOEHMCKE, RICHARD.—Age, — years. Enlisted, July 2, 1898, at New York city, to serve two years; mustered in as private, Co. M, same date; mustered out with company, November 15, 1898, at New York city.

BOGERT, JOHN.—Age, 23 years. Enlisted, May 2, 1898, at New York city, to serve two years; mustered in as corporal, Co. C, May 19, 1898; returned to ranks, June 16, 1898; mustered out with company, November 15, 1898, at New York city.

BOLES, EDWARD C.—Age, — years. Enlisted, June 24, 1898, at New York city, to serve two years; mustered in as private, Co. E, same date; mustered out with company, November 15, 1898, at New York city.

BOSCHE, ANDREW.—Age, 38 years. Enlisted, May 2, 1898, at New York city, to serve two years; mustered in as private, Co. C, May 19, 1898; mustered out with company, November 15, 1898, at New York city.

BOSSHARDT, EMIL.—Age, 25 years. Enlisted, May 2, 1898, at New York city, to serve two years; mustered in as private, Co. H, May 20, 1898; mustered out with company, November 15, 1898, at New York city.

BOSWELL, CHARLES S.—Age, 20 years. Enlisted, May 2, 1898, at New York city, to serve two years; mustered in as corporal, Co. B, May 20, 1898; mustered out with company, November 15, 1898, at New York city.

BOTT, HENRY.—Age, 26 years. Enlisted, May 2, 1898, at New York city, to serve two years; mustered in as sergeant, Co. I, May 19, 1898; mustered out with company, November 15, 1898, at New York city.

BOURNE, ALFRED A.—Age, 23 years. Enlisted, May 2, 1898, at New York city, to serve two years; mustered in as quarter-master-sergeant, Co. B, May 20, 1898; reduced to sergeant, at own request, no date; returned to ranks, September 5, 1898; mustered out with company, November 15, 1898, at New York city.

BOWMAN, WILLIAM.—Age, 25 years. Enlisted, May 2, 1898, at New York city, to serve two years; mustered in as private, Co. A, May 17, 1898; mustered out with company, November 15, 1898, at New York city.

BOYLAN, JAMES A.—Age, — years. Enlisted, June 25, 1898, at New York city, to serve two years; mustered in as private, Co. F, same date; mustered out with company, November 15, 1898, at New York city.

BOYLE, THOMAS J.—Age, 27 years. Enlisted, May 2, 1898, at New York city, to serve two years; mustered in as private, Co. M, May 17, 1898; mustered out with company, November 15, 1898, at New York city.

BRADY, BERNARD.—Age, — years. Enlisted, June 28, 1898, at New York city, to serve two years; mustered in as private, Co. F, same date; mustered out with company, November 15, 1898, at New York city.

BRANDOLPH, WILLIAM.—Age, 22 years. Enlisted, May 2, 1898, at New York city, to serve two years; mustered in as private, Co. L, May 20, 1898; promoted corporal, August 17, 1898; mustered out with company, November 15, 1898, at New York city.

BRANE, JR., JOHN D.—Age, 22 years. Enlisted, May 2, 1898, at New York city, to serve two years; mustered in as corporal, Co. A, May 17, 1898; promoted sergeant, October 27, 1898; mustered out with company, November 15, 1898, at New York city.

BRASSINGTON, JOHN C.—Age, 24 years. Enlisted, May 2, 1898, at New York city, to serve two years; mustered in as private, Co. D, May 17, 1898; mustered out with company, November 15, 1898, at New York city.

BRAUER, ARCHIE M.—Age, 20 years. Enlisted, May 2, 1898, at New York city, to serve two years; mustered in as private, Co. G, May 20, 1898; mustered out with company, November 15, 1898, at New York city.

BRAUER, SAMUEL.—Age, 21 years. Enlisted, May 2, 1898, at New York city, to serve two years; mustered in as private, Co. F, May 21, 1898; mustered out with company, November 15, 1898, at New York city.

BRAUN, CHARLES.—Age, 25 years. Enlisted, May 2, 1898, at New York city, to serve two years; mustered in as private, Co. I, May 19, 1898; promoted corporal, July 27, 1898; mustered out with company, November 15, 1898, at New York city.

BRAUN, RICHARD.—Age, 21 years. Enlisted, May 2, 1898, at New York city, to serve two years; mustered in as private, Co. C, May 19, 1898; mustered out with company, November 15, 1898, at New York city.

BRAWLEY, JR., JOHN J.—Age, 21 years. Enlisted, May 2, 1898, at New York city, to serve two years; mustered in as private, Co. B, May 20, 1898; promoted corporal, August 22, 1898; mustered out with company, November 15, 1898, at New York city.

BRENNAN, CHARLES J.—Age, — years. Enlisted, June 29, 1898, at New York city, to serve two years; mustered in as private, Co. D, same date; mustered out with company, November 15, 1898, at New York city.

BRENNAN, THOMAS.—Age, — years. Enlisted, June 30, 1898, at New York city, to serve two years; mustered in as private, Co. C, same date; mustered out with company, November 15, 1898, at New York city.

BRENNAN, WILLIAM J.—Age, 22 years. Enlisted, May 16, 1898, at New York city, to serve two years; mustered in as private, Co. D, May 17, 1898; mustered out with company, November 15, 1898, at New York city.

BRESLIN, THOMAS.—Age, — years. Enlisted, July 6, 1898, at New York city, to serve two years; mustered in as private, Co. E, same date; mustered out with company, November 15, 1898, at New York city.

BRETTHAUER, CHARLES H.—Age, 19 years. Enlisted, May 2, 1898, at New York city, to serve two years; mustered in as private, Co. I, May 19, 1898; mustered out with company, November 15, 1898, at New York city.

BRIEN, ROBERT L.—Age, 22 years. Enlisted, May 2, 1898, at New York city, to serve two years; mustered in as private, Co. A, May 17, 1898; mustered out with company, November 15, 1898, at New York city.

BRINKMAN, GEORGE WILLIAM.—Age, 24 years. Enlisted, May 2, 1898, at New York city, to serve two years; mustered in as private, Co. A, May 17, 1898; transferred to Co. B, July 27, 1898; mustered out with company, November 15, 1898, at New York city.

BRISTOL, CLARENCE B.—Age, 27 years. Enlisted, May 2, 1898, at New York city, to serve two years; mustered in as private, Co. H, May 20, 1898; mustered out with company, November 15, 1898, at New York city.

BRITT, WILLIAM F.—Age, 35 years. Enlisted, May 2, 1898, at New York city, to serve two years; mustered in as private, Co. D, May 17, 1898; mustered out with company, November 15, 1898, at New York city.

BROAD, HENRY J.—Age, 38 years. Enlisted, May 2, 1898, at New York city, to serve two years; mustered in as private, Co. E, May 20, 1898; mustered out with company, November 15, 1898, at New York city.

BRODERICK, JAMES J.—Age, 22 years. Enlisted, May 2, 1898, at New York city, to serve two years; mustered in as quarter-master-sergeant, Co. H, May 20, 1898; mustered out with company, November 15, 1898, at New York city.

BROOKS, HERBERT.—Age, 18 years. Enlisted, May 2, 1898, at New York city, to serve two years; mustered in as private, Co. K, May 19, 1898; mustered out with company, November 15, 1898, at New York city.

BROSS, EDWARD.—Age, 19 years. Enlisted, May 2, 1898, at New York city, to serve two years; mustered in as private, Co. L, May 20, 1898; mustered out with company, November 15, 1898, at New York city.

BROWN, ALBERT A.—Age, — years. Enlisted, July 1, 1898, at New York city, to serve two years; mustered in as private, Co. I, same date; mustered out with company, November 15, 1898, at New York city.

BROWN, ARTHUR J.—Age, 29 years. Enlisted, May 2, 1898, at New York city, to serve two years; mustered in as private, Co. A, May 17, 1898; promoted corporal, July 27, 1898; mustered out with company, November 15, 1898, at New York city.

BROWN, DOUGLAS A.—Age, — years. Enlisted, August 12, 1898, at Camp Thomas, Ga., to serve two years; mustered in as private, Co. D, same date; discharged, October 13, 1898.

BROWN, FREDERICK.—Age, 28 years. Enlisted, May 2, 1898, at New York city, to serve two years; mustered in as private, Co. B, May 20, 1898; mustered out with company, November 15, 1898, at New York city.

BROWN, LUKE, F.—Age, — years. Enlisted, July 1, 1898, at New York city, to serve two years; mustered in as private, Co. M, same date; mustered out with company, November 15, 1898, at New York city.

BROWN, WALTER H.—Age, 23 years. Enlisted, May 2, 1898, at New York city, to serve two years; mustered in as private, Co. D, May 17, 1898; promoted corporal, July 27, 1898; discharged, October 12, 1898.

BROWNE, GEORGE J.—Age, 19 years. Enlisted, May 2, 1898, at New York city, to serve two years; mustered in as musician, Co. B, May 20, 1898; deserted, June 27, 1898, at Camp Thomas, Chickamauga Park, Ga.

BRUNE, WILLIAM.—Age, — years. Enlisted, July 7, 1898, at New York city, to serve two years; mustered in as private, Co. K, same date; mustered out with company, November 15, 1898, at New York city.

BRUNNER, JOSEPH J.—Age, — years. Enlisted, June 23, 1898, at New York city, to serve two years; mustered in as private, Co. M, same date; mustered out with company, November 15, 1898, at New York city.

BRYDE, WESLEY E.—Age, 38 years. Enrolled, May 2, 1898, at New York city, to serve two years; mustered in as captain, Co. F, May 21, 1898; discharged, July 21, 1898, at Camp Thomas, Chickamauga Park, Ga.; commissioned captain, May 21, 1898, with rank from same date, original.

BRYSON, EDWARD.—Age, — years. Enlisted, June 30, 1898, at New York city, to serve two years; mustered in as private, Co. D, same date; mustered out with company, November 15, 1898, at New York city.

BUCKBEE, HENRY H.—Age, 27 years. Enlisted, May 2, 1898, at New York city, to serve two years; mustered in as private, Co. L, May 20, 1898; promoted sergeant-major, May 28, 1898; returned to ranks and transferred to Co. C, July 3, 1898; promoted corporal, August 10, 1898; mustered out with company, November 15, 1898, at New York city.

BUDENBENDER, GEORGE W.—Age, — years. Enlisted, May 21, 1898, at camp near Peekskill, to serve two years; mustered in as musician, Co. K, same date; mustered out with company, November 15, 1898, at New York city.

BUGG, DOUGLAS B.—Age, 21 years. Enlisted, May 2, 1898, at New York city, to serve two years; mustered in as private, Co. G, May 20, 1898; mustered out with company, November 15, 1898, at New York city.

BUHR, JOHN E.—Age 24 years. Enlisted May 2, 1898, at New York city, to serve two years; mustered in as corporal, Co. F, May 21, 1898; died of disease, August 25, 1898, in Leiter Hospital, Chickamauga, Ga.

BULINGER, GEORGE A.—Age, 27 years. Enlisted, May 2, 1898, at New York city, to serve two years; mustered in as private, Co. A, May 17, 1898; mustered out with company, November 15, 1898, at New York city.

BULSKI, JOSEPH M.—Age, — years. Enlisted, June 27, 1898, at New York city, to serve two years; mustered in as private, Co. D, same date; mustered out with company, November 15, 1898, at New York city.

BUQUET, EDWARD.—Age, 32 years. Enlisted, May 2, 1898, at New York city, to serve two years; mustered in as sergeant, Co. K, May 19, 1898; mustered out with company, November 15, 1898, at New York city.

BURCH, GEORGE.—Age, 22 years. Enlisted, May 2, 1898, at New York city, to serve two years; mustered in as private, Co. E, May 20, 1898; mustered out with company, November 15, 1898, at New York city.

BURDOCK, THEODORE.—Age, 34 years. Enlisted, May 2, 1898, at New York city, to serve two years; mustered in as private, Co. M, May 17, 1898; mustered out with company, November 15, 1898, at New York city.

BURHAUS, WILLETS C.—Age, 28 years. Enlisted, May 2, 1898, at New York city, to serve two years; mustered in as first sergeant, Co. F, May 21, 1898; reduced to sergeant, August 5, 1898; returned to ranks, September 5, 1898; mustered out with company, November 15, 1898, at New York city.

BURKE, JOHN R.—Age, 24 years. Enlisted, May 2, 1898, at New York city, to serve two years; mustered in as private, Co. A, May 17, 1898; mustered out with company, November 15' 1898, at New York city.

BURKE THOMAS F.—Age, 32 years. Enlisted, May 2, 1898, at New York city, to serve two years; mustered in as private, Co. A, May 17, 1898; mustered out with company, November 15, 1898, at New York city.

BURKE, THOMAS L.—Age, 29 years. Enlisted, May 2, 1898, at New York city, to serve two years; mustered in as private, Co. M, May 17, 1898; promoted corporal, August 10, 1898; sergeant, September 2, 1898; mustered out with company, November 15, 1898, at New York city.

BURKENBUSH, AUGUST.—Age, — years. Enlisted, July 5, 1898, at New York city, to serve two years; mustered in as private, Co. L, same date; deserted August 24, 1898, at Camp Thomas, Chickamauga Park, Ga.

BURKHARDT, CHARLES.—Age, 21 years. Enlisted, May 2, 1898, at New York city, to serve two years; mustered in as private, Co. A, May 17, 1898; died of typhoid fever, September 2, 1898, at New York city.

BURNETT, WILLIAM.—Age, 25 years. Enlisted, May 2, 1898, at New York city, to serve two years; mustered in as private, Co. G, May 20, 1898; mustered out with company, November 15, 1898, at New York city.

BURTON, BENJAMIN T.—Age, 29 years. Enlisted, May 2, 1898, at New York city, to serve two years; mustered in as musician, Co. F, May 21, 1898; mustered out with company, November 15, 1898, at New York city

BUTTERFIELD, WILLIAM.—Age, — years. Enlisted, June 27, 1898, at New York city, to serve two years; mustered in as private, Co. D, same date; mustered out with company, November 15, 1898, at New York city.

BUTTERWORTH, GEORGE F.—Age, 44 years. Enlisted, May 2, 1898, at New York city, to serve two years; mustered in as corporal, Co. H, May 20, 1898; mustered out with company, November 15, 1898, at New York city.

BUTZ, FREDERICK.—Age, 26 years. Enlisted, May 2, 1898, at New York city, to serve two years; mustered in as private, Co. K, May 19, 1898; mustered out with company, November 15, 1898, at New York city.

BYRNE, EMMET.—Age, — years. Enlisted, July 5, 1898, at New York city, to serve two years; mustered in as private, Co. A, same date; mustered out with company, November 15, 1898, at New York city.

BYRNE, JOHN.—Age, — years. Enlisted, June 24, 1898, at New York city, to serve two years; mustered in as private, Co. K, same date; mustered out with company, November 15, 1898, at New York city.

BYRNE JOHN J.—Age, 26 years. Enrolled, May 2, 1898, at New York city, to serve two years; mustered in as first lieutenant, Co. K, May 19, 1898; as captain, August 17, 1898; mustered out, to date, November 15, 1898; commissioned first lieutenant, May 19, 1898, with rank from same date, original; captain, August 8, 1898, with rank from same date, vice Morris, discharged.

BYRNE, JOHN J.—Age, — years. Enlisted, June 24, 1898, at New York city, to serve two years; mustered in as private Co. D, same date; mustered out with company, November 15, 1898, at New York city.

BYRNE, NICHOLAS.—Age, 27 years. Enlisted, May 2, 1898, at New York city, to serve two years; mustered in as private, Co. E, May 20, 1898; mustered out with company, November 15, 1898, at New York city.

BYRNES, GEORGE V.—Age, 22 years. Enlisted, May 2, 1898, at New York city, to serve two years; mustered in as corporal, Co. G, May 20, 1898; died of typhoid-pneumonia, October 18, 1898, at New York city.

BYRNES, PETER J.—Age, 21 years. Enlisted, May 10, 1898, at New York city, to serve two years; mustered in as private, Co. M, May 17, 1898; mustered out with company, November 15, 1898, at New York city.

CALNAN, DENNIS.—Age, — years. Enlisted, June 27, 1898, at New York city, to serve two years; mustered in as private, Co. I, same date; mustered out with company, November 15, 1898, at New York city.

CAMERON, JOHN.—Age, 18 years. Enlisted, May 2, 1898, at New York city, to serve two years; mustered in as private, Co. K, May 19, 1898; mustered out with company, November 15, 1898, at New York city.

CAMERON, JOHN W.—Age, 21 years. Enlisted, May 2, 1898, at New York city, to serve two years; mustered in as private, Co. F, May 21, 1898; mustered out with company, November 15, 1898, at New York city.

CAMPBELL, JOHN A.—Age, 20 years. Enlisted, May 2, 1898, at New York city, to serve two years; mustered in as private, Co. D, May 17, 1898; mustered out with company, November 15, 1898, at New York city.

CAMPBELL, THOMAS.—Age, — years. Enlisted, July 5, 1898, at New York city, to serve two years; mustered in as private, Co. I, same date; mustered out with company, November 15, 1898, at New York city.

CAMPBELL, WILMER W.—Age, 25 years. Enlisted, May 2, 1898, at New York city, to serve two years; mustered in as private, Co. D, May 17, 1898; discharged, September 30, 1898.

CANFIELD, MICHAEL.—Age, — years. Enlisted, July 5, 1898, at New York city, to serve two years; mustered in as private, Co. B, same date; mustered out with company, November 15, 1898, at New York city.

CAREY, JOSEPH P.—Age, 23 years. Enlisted, May 2, 1898, at New York city, to serve two years; mustered in as private, Co. A, May 17, 1898; mustered out with company, November 15, 1898, at New York city.

CARLIN, NICHOLAS P.—Age, 35 years. Enlisted, May 2, 1898, at New York city, to serve two years; mustered in as private, Co. K, May 19, 1898; mustered out with company, November 15, 1898, at New York city.

CARMODY, THOMAS.—Age, 26 years. Enlisted, May 12, 1898, at Peekskill, to serve two years; mustered in as private, Co. L, May 20, 1898; promoted corporal, July 27, 1898; sergeant, August 17, 1898; mustered out with company, November 15, 1898, at New York city.

CARPENTER, HENRY P.—Age, 28 years. Enlisted, May 2, 1898, at New York city, to serve two years; mustered in as private, Co. D, May 17, 1898; mustered out with company, November 15, 1898, at New York city.

CARRIER, GEORGE A.—Age, 24 years. Enlisted, May 2, 1898, at New York city, to serve two years; mustered in as hospital steward, May 21, 1898; discharged, October 17, 1898.

CARRIGAN, RICHARD.—Age, 24 years. Enlisted, May 2, 1898, at New York city, to serve two years; mustered in as private, Co. A, May 17, 1898; mustered out with company, November 15, 1898, at New York city.

CARTON, JOSEPH.—Age, 24 years. Enlisted, May 2, 1898, at New York city, to serve two years; mustered in as private, Co. F, May 21, 1898; mustered out with company, November 15, 1898, at New York city.

CASSIDY, JR., LUKE J.—Age, 21 years. Enlisted, May 2, 1898, at New York city, to serve two years; mustered in as private, Co. C, May 20, 1898; mustered out with company, November 15, 1898, at New York city.

CAVANAGH, JAMES.—Age, 28 years. Enlisted, May 2, 1898, at New York city, to serve two years; mustered in as principal musician, May 21, 1898; reduced to musician and transferred to Co. A, July 27, 1898; discharged, September 30, 1898, at New York city.

CAVANAUGH, JOHN.—Age, 27 years. Enlisted, May 2, 1898, at New York city, to serve two years; mustered in as private, Co. D, May 17, 1898; discharged, October 6, 1898.

CAVANAUGH, WILLIAM J.—Age, 28 years. Enlisted, May 2, 1898, at New York city, to serve two years; mustered in as private, Co. D, May 17, 1898; mustered out with company, November 15, 1898, at New York city.

CERRITA, JOHN.—Age, 20 years. Enlisted, May 2, 1898, at New York city, to serve two years; mustered in as corporal, Co. B, May 20, 1898; mustered out with company, November 15, 1898, at New York city.

CHADSEY, RALPH C.—Age, 26 years. Enlisted, May 2, 1898, at New York city, to serve two years; mustered in as sergeant, Co. M, May 17, 1898; promoted first sergeant, no date; discharged for disability, August 23, 1898, at Camp Thomas, Chickamauga Park, Ga.

CHAMBERS, GEORGE W.—Age, — years. Enlisted, June 27, 1898, at New York city, to serve two years; mustered in as private, Co. D, same date; mustered out with company, November 15, 1898, at New York city.

CHAMBERS, JAMES.—Age, — years. Enlisted, June 27, 1898, at New York city, to serve two years; mustered in as private, Co. D, same date; mustered out with company, November 15, 1898, at New York city.

CHAMBERS, WILLIAM.—Age, 26 years. Enlisted, May 2, 1898, at New York city, to serve two years; mustered in as private, Co. L, May 20, 1898; mustered out with company, November 15, 1898, at New York city.

CHASE, WILLIAM.—Age, — years. Enlisted, June 29, 1898, at New York city, to serve two years; mustered in as private, Co. B, same date; mustered out with company, November 15, 1898, at New York city.

CHIPP, JAMES W.—Age, 28 years. Enlisted, May 2, 1898, at New York city, to serve two years; mustered in as private, Co. B, May 20, 1898; promoted corporal, July 27, 1898; mustered out with company, November 15, 1898, at New York city.

CHRISTIE, WILLIAM.—Age, — years. Enlisted, May 2, 1898, at New York city, to serve two years; mustered in as private, Co. K, May 19, 1898; mustered out with company, November 15, 1898, at New York city.

CHURCHILL, WILLIAM F.—Age, — years. Enlisted, June 23, 1898, at New York city, to serve two years; mustered in as private, Co. M, same date; mustered out with company, November 15, 1898, at New York city.

CLANCY, LOUIS J.—Age, 22 years. Enlisted, May 2, 1898, at New York city, to serve two years; mustered in as private, Co. E, May 20, 1898; mustered out with company, November 15, 1898, at New York city.

CLARK, MICHAEL.—Age, — years. Enlisted, June 30, 1898, at New York city, to.serve two years; mustered in as private, Co. H, same date; mustered out with company, November 15, 1898, at New York city.

CLARK, ROBERT J.—Age, 22 years. Enlisted, May 2, 1898, at New York city, to serve two years; mustered in as private, Co. F, May 21, 1898; mustered out with company, November 15, 1898, at New York city.

CLARK, THOMAS.—Age, — years. Enlisted, June 24, 1898, at New York city, to serve two years; mustered in as private, Co. E, same date; mustered out with company, November 15, 1898, at New York city.

CLARKE, FRED B.—Age, 23 years. Enlisted, May 2, 1898, at New York city, to serve two years; mustered in as private, Co. B, May 20, 1898; mustered out with company, November 15, 1898, at New York city.

CLARKE, JOSEPH.—Age, 26 years. Enlisted, May 2, 1898, at New York city, to serve two years; mustered in as private, Co. C, May 19, 1898; mustered out with company, November 15, 1898, at New York city.

CLEARY, HARRY.—Age, — years. Enlisted, June 24, 1898, at New York city, to serve two years; mustered in as private, Co. H, same date; mustered out with company, November 15, 1898, at New York city.

CLIFFORD, FRANK J.—Age, 29 years. Enlisted, May 2, 1898, at New York city, to serve two years; mustered in as private, Co. L, May 20, 1898; mustered out with company, November 15, 1898, at New York city.

CLINCH, FREDERICK.—Age, — years. Enlisted, June 24, 1898, at New York city, to serve two years; mustered in as private, Co. K, same date; mustered out with company, November 15, 1898, at New York city.

COAN, CLARENCE ARTHUR.—Age, 30 years. Enrolled, May 2, 1898, at New York city, to serve two years; mustered in as captain, Co. L, May 20, 1898; mustered out with company, November 15, 1898, at New York city; commissioned captain, May 20, 1898, with rank from same date, original.

COFFEE, WILLIAM R.—Age, 28 years. Enlisted, May 2, 1898, at New York city, to serve two years; mustered in as private, Co. D, May 17, 1898; promoted corporal, July 28, 1898; mustered out with company, November 15, 1898, at New York city.

COFFEY, JOSEPH.—Age, — years. Enlisted, July 1, 1898, at New York city, to serve two years; mustered in as private, Co. H, same date; mustered out, to date, November 15, 1898.

COGHLAN, THOMAS F.—Age, 26 years. Enlisted, May 18, 1898, at New York city, to serve two years; mustered in as private, Co. H, May 20, 1898; mustered out with company, November 15, 1898, at New York city.

COHEN, JOHN.—Age, 21 years. Enlisted, May 2, 1898, at New York city, to serve two years; mustered in as private, Co. E, May 20, 1898; mustered out with company, November 15, 1898, at New York city.

COHEN, JOSEE.—Age, 22 years. Enlisted, May 2, 1898, at New York city, to serve two years; mustered in as private, Co. L, May 20, 1898; mustered out with company, November 15, 1898, at New York city.

COHEN, SAMUEL.—Age, — years. Enlisted, June 29, 1898, at New York city, to serve two years; mustered in as private; Co. G, same date; mustered out with company, November 15, 1898, at New York city.

COHEN, SAMUEL M.—Age, 23 years. Enlisted, May 2, 1898, at New York city, to serve three years; mustered in as private, Co. E, May 20, 1898; mustered out with company, November 15, 1898, at New York city.

COHN, ALBERT.—Age, — years. Enlisted, June 27, 1898, at New York city, to serve two years; mustered in as private, Co. C, same date; mustered out with company, November 15, 1898, at New York city.

COLBURN, GEORGE P.—Age, — years. Enlisted, June 23, 1898, at New York city, to serve two years; mustered in as private, Co. K, same date; mustered out with company, November 15, 1898, at New York city.

COLE, PARKER.—Age, — years. Enlisted, July 5, 1898, at New York city, to serve two years; mustered in as private, Co. G, same date; mustered out with company, November 15, 1898, at New York city.

COLEMAN, WILLIAM J.—Age, 21 years. Enlisted, May 2, 1898, at New York city, to serve two years; mustered in as private, Co. M, May 17, 1898; mustered out with company, November 15, 1898, at New York city.

COLLINS, STEPHEN F.—Age, 22 years. Enlisted, May 2, 1898, at New York city, to serve two years; mustered in as private, Co. C, May 19, 1898; mustered out with company, November 15, 1898, at New York city.

COLWELL, JOSEPH.—Age, 30 years. Enlisted, May 2, 1898, at New York city, to serve two years; mustered in as musician, Co. H, May 20, 1898; promoted principal musician, May 23, 1898; returned to ranks and transferred to Co. H, July 27, 1898; promoted corporal, August 7, 1898; mustered out with company, November 15, 1898, at New York city.

COMERFORD, JAMES.—Age, — years. Enlisted, June 27, 1898, at New York city, to serve two years; mustered in as private, Co. I, same date; mustered out with company, November 15, 1898, at New York city.

COMMONS, FRANK.—Age, — years. Enlisted, July 5, 1898, at New York city, to serve two years; mustered in as private, Co. F, same date; mustered out with company, November 15, 1898. at New York city.

COMTE, FRANK.—Age, 21 years. Enlisted, May 2, 1898, at New York city, to serve two years; mustered in as private, Co. B, May 20, 1898; mustered out with company, November 15, 1898 at New York cit .

COMTE, JOSEPH.—Age, 28 years. Enlisted, May 2, 1898, at New York city, to serve two years; mustered in as private, Co. B, May 20, 1898; mustered out with company, November 15, 1898, at New York city.

CONDEN, JOSEPH A.—Age, 22 years. Enlisted, May 2, 1898, at New York city, to serve two years; mustered in as private, Co. E, May 20, 1898; promoted corporal, July 27, 1898; mustered out with company, November 15, 1898, at New York city.

CONDON, RICHARD J.—Age, 23 years. Enlisted, May 2, 1898, at New York city, to serve two years; mustered in as private, Co. B, May 20, 1898; deserted, July 9, 1898, at Camp Thomas, Chickamauga Park, Ga.

CONDON, THOMAS.—Age, 25 years. Enlisted, May 2, 1898, at New York city, to serve two years; mustered in as private, Co. H, May 20, 1898; mustered out with company, November 15. 1898, at New York city.

CONLEY, WILLIAM J.—Age, 30 years. Enlisted, May 2, 1898, at New York city, to serve two years; mustered in as sergeant, Co. E, May 20, 1898; mustered out with company, November 15, 1898, at New York city.

CONLON, PATRICK.—Age, — years. Enlisted, July 1, 1898, at New York city, to serve two years; mustered in as private, Co. C, same date; mustered out with company, November 15, 1898, at New York city.

CONNELL, THOMAS F.—Age, 21 years. Enlisted, May 2, 1898, at New York city, to serve two years; mustered in as private, Co. F, May 21, 1898; died of disease, October 13, 1898, in St. Vincent's Hospital, New York city.

CONNET, ALLEN L.—Age, 44 years. Enlisted, May 2, 1898, at New York city, to serve two years; mustered in as artificer, Co. E, May 20, 1898; mustered out with company, November 15, 1898, at New York city.

CONNOLLY, DANIEL A.—Age, 21 years. Enlisted, May 2, 1898, at New York city, to serve two years; mustered in as private, Co. C, May 19, 1898; promoted corporal, July 27, 1898; mustered out with company, November 15, 1898, at New York city.

CONNOR, JOHN J.—Age, 21 years. Enlisted, May 2, 1898, at New York city, to serve two years; mustered in as private, Co. I, May 19, 1898; mustered out with company, November 15, 1898, at New York city.

CONROY, JAMES.—Age, 37 years. Enlisted, May 2, 1898, at New York city, to serve two years; mustered in as private, Co. G, May 20, 1898; mustered out with company, November 15, 1898, at New York city.

CONROY, JOSEPH F.—Age, 25 years. Enlisted, May 2, 1898, at New York city, to serve two years; mustered in as private, Co. A, May 17, 1898; mustered out with company, November 15, 1898, at New York city.

CONSIDINE, JOSEPH.—Age, 21 years. Enlisted, May 16, 1898, at New York city, to serve two years; mustered in as private, Co. E, May 20, 1898; mustered out with company, November 15, 1898, at New York city.

CONWAY, LAWRENCE H.—Age, — years. Enlisted, June 25, 1898, at New York city, to serve two years; mustered in as private, Co. B, same date; mustered out with company, November 15, 1898, at New York city.

COOGAN, HERBERT.—Age, 20 years. Enlisted, May 2, 1898, at New York city, to serve two years; mustered in as private, Co. L, May 20, 1898; discharged, November 11, 1898, to enlist in regular army.

COOK, JR., CHARLES E.—Age, — years. Enlisted, June 27, 1898, at New York city, to serve two years; mustered in as private, Co. M, same date; mustered out, to date, November 15, 1898.

COOK, WILLIAM S.—Age, 21 years. Enlisted, May 11, 1898, at New York city, to serve two years; mustered in as private, Co. L, May 20, 1898; mustered out with company, November 15, 1898, at New York city.

COONEY, CHARLES P.—Age, 18 years. Enlisted, May 2, 1898, at New York city, to serve two years; mustered in as private, Co. E, May 20, 1898; mustered out with company, November 15, 1898, at New York city.

COOPER, CHARLES E.—Age, — years. Enlisted, July 8, 1898, at New York city, to serve two years; mustered in as private, Co. I, same date; transferred to band, July 27, 1898; mustered out with regiment, November 15, 1898, at New York city.

COOPER, FRANK G.—Age, 21 years. Enlisted, May 2, 1898, at New York city, to serve two years; mustered in as private, Co. B, May 20, 1898; deserted, August 23, 1898, at Camp Thomas, Chickamauga Park, Ga.

COOPER, JOSEPH A.—Age, 21 years. Enlisted, May 2, 1898, at New York city, to serve two years; mustered in as private, Co. K, May 19, 1898; mustered out with company, November 15, 1898, at New York city.

COOPER, ROBERT L.—Age, — years. Enlisted, June 18, 1898, at Camp Thomas, Ga., to serve two years; mustered in as private, Co. E, same date; mustered out with company, November 15, 1898, at New York city.

CORDE, DAVID F.—Age, 35 years. Enlisted, May 2, 1898, at New York city, to serve two years; mustered in as private, Co. M, May 17, 1898; discharged, September 12, 1898.

CORDES, HENRY.—Age, — years. Enlisted, July 6, 1898, at New York city, to serve two years; mustered in as private, Co. F, same date; mustered out with company, November 15, 1898, at New York city.

CORR, JOHN J.—Age, 44 years. Enlisted, May 2, 1898, at New York city, to serve two years; mustered in as private, Co. A, May 17, 1898; mustered out with company, November 15, 1898, at New York city.

CORRODY, STUART.—Age, 20 years. Enlisted, May 2, 1898, at New York city, to serve two years; mustered in as private, Co. K, May 19, 1898; deserted, May 30, 1898, at Camp Thomas, Chickamauga Park, Ga.

COSGROVE, EDWARD P.—Age, — years. Enlisted, July 1, 1898, at New York city, to serve two years; mustered in as private, Co. A, same date; mustered out with company, November 15, 1898, at New York city.

COSTARD, JR., EMILE P.—Age, 26 years. Enlisted, May 2, 1898, at New York city, to serve two years; mustered in as private, Co. D, May 17, 1898; died of typhoid fever, August 1, 1898, in United States General Hospital, Fort McPherson, Ga.

COSTELLO, BARTLETT C.—Age, — years. Enlisted, July 4, 1898, at New York city, to serve two years; mustered in as private, Co. B, same date; mustered out with company, November 15, 1898, at New York city.

COSTELLO, THOMAS A.—Age, 26 years. Enlisted, May 2, 1898, at New York city, to serve two years; mustered in as private, Co. F, May 21, 1898; appointed wagoner, July 7, 1898; mustered out with company, November 15, 1898, at New York city.

COURTNEY, JAMES.—Age, 21 years. Enlisted, May 2, 1898, at New York city, to serve two years; mustered in as private, Co. H, May 20, 1898; mustered out with company, November 15, 1898, at New York city.

COX, GEORGE.—Age, — years. Enlisted, July 8, 1898, at New York city, to serve two years; mustered in as private, Co. E, same date; transferred to band, July 27, 1898; died of typhoid fever, August 26, 1898, in Sternberg Hospital, Camp Thomas, Chickamauga Park, Ga.

CRAMBLETT, BYRON J.—Age, 25 years. Enlisted, May 19, 1898, at New York city, to serve two years; mustered in as private, Co. H, May 20, 1898; mustered out, to date, November 15, 1898.

CRANE, THOMAS B.—Age, 21 years. Enlisted, May 2, 1898, at New York city, to serve two years; mustered in as private, Co. E, May 20, 1898; died of typhoid fever, October 26, 1898, in New York Hospital, New York city.

CRAVEN, CHARLES J.—Age, 22 years. Enlisted, May 16, 1898, at New York city, to serve two years; mustered in as private, Co. B, May 20, 1898; mustered out with company, November 15, 1898, at New York city.

CRAWFORD, ALEXANDER.—Age, 28 years. Enlisted, May 2, 1898, at New York city, to serve two years; mustered in as corporal, Co. K, May 19, 1898; mustered out with company, November 15, 1898, at New York city.

CRAWFORD, GUY H.—Age, 22 years. Enlisted, May 2, 1898, at New York city, to serve two years; mustered in as private, Co. M, May 17, 1898; promoted corporal, July 27, 1898; mustered out with company, November 15, 1898, at New York city.

CRISWELL, BYRON G.—Age, 23 years. Enlisted, May 2, 1898, at New York city, to serve two years; mustered in as private, Co. B, May 20, 1898; mustered out with company, November 15, 1898, at New York city.

CROFT, ULYSSES S. G.—Age, 34 years. Enlisted, May 2, 1898, at New York city, as first sergeant of Co. M, to serve two years; mustered in as second lieutenant, Co. L, May 20, 1898; as first lieutenant, August 20, 1898; mustered out with company, November 15, 1898, at New York city; commissioned second lieutenant, May 20, 1898, with rank from same date, original; first lieutenant, August 8, 1898, with rank from same date, vice Willcocks, discharged.

CROWLEY, THOMAS.—Age, 42 years. Enlisted, May 2, 1898, at New York city, to serve two years; mustered in as private, Co. K, May 19, 1898; discharged, October 14, 1898.

CRUMLEY, JOHN.—Age, 22 years. Enlisted, May 2, 1898, at New York city, to serve two years; mustered in as private, Co. C, May 19, 1898; mustered out with company, November 15, 1898, at New York city.

CULLEN, EDWARD J.—Age, 27 years. Enlisted, May 2, 1898, at New York city, to serve two years; mustered in as first sergeant, Co. A, May 17, 1898; as second lieutenant, Co. K, August 8, 1898; mustered out with company, November 15, 1898, at New York city; commissioned second lieutenant, August 8, 1898, with rank from same date, vice Lynch, promoted.

CULLINAN, WILLIAM J.—Age, 26 years. Enlisted, May 2, 1898, at New York city, to serve two years; mustered in as private, Co. G, May 21, 1898; mustered out, to date, November 15, 1898.

CUNNERN, MATTHEW J.—Age, 25 years. Enlisted, May 2, 1898, at New York city, to serve two years; mustered in as private, Co. K, May 19, 1898; mustered out with company, November 15, 1898, at New York city.

CUNNINGHAM, JAMES E.—Age, 24 years. Enlisted, May 2, 1898, at New York city, to serve two years; mustered in as private, Co. G, May 21, 1898; mustered out with company, November 15, 1898, at New York city.

CUNNINGHAM, JOHN J.—Age, 22 years. Enlisted, May 2, 1898, at New York city, to serve two years; mustered in as private, Co. H, May 20, 1898; mustered out with company, November 15, 1898, at New York city.

CUNNINGHAM, LOUIS.—Age, — years. Enlisted, July 6, 1898, at New York city, to serve two years; mustered in as private, Co. A, same date; mustered out with company, November 15, 1898, at New York city.

CUNNINGHAM, MICHAEL.—Age, 22 years. Enlisted, May 2, 1898, at New York city, to serve two years; mustered in as private, Co. K, May 19, 1898; transferred to Co. F, July 27, 1898; mustered out with company, November 15, 1898, at New York city.

CUNNINGHAM, ROBERT.—Age, — years. Enlisted, July 1, 1898, at New York city, to serve two years; mustered in as private, Co. H, same date; mustered out with company, November 15, 1898, at New York city.

CURRY, CHARLES H.—Age, — years. Enlisted, June 24, 1898, at New York city, to serve two years; mustered in as private, Co. B, same date; mustered out with company, November 15, 1898, at New York city.

CURTIS, CLAUDE F.—Age, — years. Enlisted, July 5, 1898, at New York city, to serve two years; mustered in as private, Co. L, same date; mustered out with company, November 15, 1898, at New York city.

CURTISS, IRVING C.—Age, — years. Enlisted, June 29, 1898, at New York city, to serve two years; mustered in as private, Co. E, same date; mustered out with company, November 15, 1898, at New York city.

DAHL, FREDERICK C.—Age, 19 years. Enlisted, May 2, 1898, at New York city, to serve two years; mustered in as private, Co. E, May 20, 1898; mustered out with company, November 15, 1898, at New York city.

DALY, JOHN F.—Age, 22 years. Enlisted, May 2, 1898, at New York city, to serve two years; mustered in as private, Co. F, May 21, 1898; deserted, July 10, 1898, at Camp Thomas, Chickamanga Park, Ga.

DALY, THOMAS.—Age, 41 years. Enlisted, May 2, 1898, at New York city, to serve two years; mustered in as corporal, Co. I, May 19, 1898; mustered out with company, November 15, 1898, at New York city.

DARCEY, JOHN M.—Age, 23 years. Enlisted, May 2, 1898, at New York city, to serve two years; mustered in as private, Co. K, May 19, 1898; mustered out with company, November 15, 1898, at New York city.

DARDINGKILLER, HARRY C.—Age, 19 years. Enlisted, May 2, 1898, at New York city, to serve two years; mustered in as musician, Co. C, May 19, 1898; mustered out with company, November 15, 1898, at New York city.

DARDINGKILLER, HERBERT L.—Age, 22 years. Enlisted, May 2, 1898, at New York city, to serve two years; mustered in as musician, Co. G, May 20, 1898; mustered out with company, November 15, 1898, at New York city.

DAVIDSON, JAMES W.—Age, 25 years. Enlisted, May 2, 1898, at New York city, to serve two years; mustered in as private, Co. L, May 20, 1898; mustered out with company, November 15, 1898, at New York city.

DAVIS, FREDERICK.—Age, 27 years. Enlisted, May 2, 1898, at New York city, to serve two years; mustered in as private, Co. D, May 17, 1898; mustered out with company, November 15, 1898, at New York city.

DAVIS, GEORGE H.—Age, 28 years. Enlisted, May 2, 1898, at New York city, to serve two years; mustered in as private, Co. D, May 17, 1898; mustered out with company, November 15, 1898, at New York city.

DAVIS, GEORGE M.—Age, — years. Enlisted, June 24, 1898, at New York city, to serve two years; mustered in as private, Co. L, same date; mustered out with company, November 15, 1898, at New York city.

DAVIS, ROBERT M.—Age, 22 years. Enlisted, May 2, 1898, at New York city, to serve two years; mustered in as private, Co. K, May 19, 1898; mustered out with company, November 15, 1898, at New York city.

DAVIS, THOMAS C.—Age, — years. Enlisted, July 1, 1898, at New York city, to serve two years; mustered in as private, Co. L, same date; mustered out with company, November 15, 1898, at New York city.

DAWKINS, WILLIAM A.—Age, — years. Enlisted, June 30, 1898, at New York city, to serve two years; mustered in as private, Co. M, same date; mustered out with company, November 15, 1898, at New York city.

DEAN, FRANK J.—Age, 26 years. Enlisted, May 2, 1898, at New York city, to serve two years; mustered in as private, Co. C, May 19, 1898; died of typhoid fever, August 26, 1898, in Sternberg Hospital, Chickamauga, Ga.

DEAN, JOHN J.—Age, 25 years. Enlisted, May 2, 1898, at New York city, to serve two years; mustered in as private, Co. A, May 17, 1898; promoted corporal, July 27, 1898; mustered out with company, November 15, 1898, at New York city.

DEAVEY, JOSEPH.—Age, 30 years. Enlisted, May 2, 1898, at New York city, to serve two years; mustered in as private, Co. C, May 19, 1898; mustered out with company, November 15, 1898, at New York city.

DEIDRICK, WILLIAM.—Age, — years. Enlisted, July 11, 1898, at New York city, to serve two years; mustered in as private, Co. D, same date; transferred to band, July 27, 1898; mustered out with regiment, November 15, 1898, at New York city.

DELANY, EDWARD F.—Age, 22 years. Enlisted, May 2, 1898, at New York city, to serve two years; mustered in as private, Co. I, May 19, 1898; mustered out with company, November 15, 1898, at New York city.

DEMSEAUX, EMILE.—Age, 27 years. Enlisted, May 2, 1898, at New York city, to serve two years; mustered in as quarter-master-sergeant, Co. K, May 19, 1898; mustered out with company, November 15, 1898, at New York city.

DENNISON, HERMAN.—Age, — years. Enlisted, June 30, 1898, at New York city, to serve two years; mustered in as private, Co. H, same date; mustered out with company, November 15, 1898, at New York city.

DERN, WILLIAM A.—Age, 25 years. Enlisted, May 2, 1898, at New York city, to serve two years; mustered in as private, Co. E, May 20, 1898; mustered out with company, November 15, 1898, at New York city.

DESOT, CHARLES.—Age 22 years. Enlisted, May 15, 1898, at camp near Peekskill, to serve two years; mustered in as private, Co. F, May 19, 1898; mustered out with company, November 15, 1898, at New York city.

DE VANSNEY, FRANK.—Age, — years. Enlisted, July 6, 1898, at New York city, to serve two years; mustered in as private, Co. B, same date; mustered out with company, November 15, 1898, at New York city

DEVEREUX, CHILTON.—Age, — years. Enlisted, July 6, 1898, at New York city, to serve two years; mustered in as private, Co. M, same date; mustered out with company, November 15, 1898, at New York city.

DIAMOND, EDWARD J.—Age, 21 years. Enlisted, May 2, 1898, at New York city, to serve two years; mustered in as private, Co. K, May 19, 1898; mustered out with company, November 15, 1898, at New York city.

DIAMOND, FRANCIS P.—Age, — years. Enlisted, June 23, 1898, at New York city, to serve two years; mustered in as private, Co. K, same date; mustered out with company, November 15, 1898, at New York city.

DICK, WILLETT G.—Age, 21 years. Enlisted, May 2, 1898, at New York city, to serve two years; mustered in as private, Co L, May 20, 1898; mustered out with company, November 15. 1898, at New York city.

DODD, SAMUEL A.—Age, 28 years. Enlisted, May 2, 1898, at New York city, to serve two years; mustered in as private, Co. M, May 17, 1898; died of typhoid fever, August 29, 1898, in Second Division Hospital, Chickamauga, Ga.

DOHERTY, JOHN A.—Age, 22 years. Enlisted, May 2, 1898, at New York city, to serve two years; mustered in as artificer, Co. D, May 17, 1898; mustered out with company, November 15, 1898, at New York city.

DOLAN, THOMAS J.—Age, 28 years. Enlisted, May 2, 1898, at New York city, to serve two years; mustered in as sergeant, Co. H, May 20, 1898; promoted first sergeant, August 8, 1898; mustered out with company, November 15, 1898, at New York city.

DONAHUE, MICHAEL.—Age, — years. Enlisted, June 30, 1898, at New York city, to serve two years; mustered in as private, Co. D, same date; mustered out with company, November 15, 1898, at New York city.

DONNELLY, JOHN.—Age, — years. Enlisted, June 24, 1898, at New York city, to serve two years; mustered in as private, Co. B, same date; mustered out with company November 15 1898, at New York city.

DONNELLY, JOHN.—Age, — years. Enlisted, June 24, 1898, at New York city, to serve two years; mustered in as private, Co. B, same date; mustered out with company, November 15, 1898, at New York city.

DONOHUE, EDWARD J.—Age, 23 years. Enlisted, May 2, 1898, at New York city, to serve two years; mustered in as private, Co. C, May 19, 1898; mustered out with company, November 15, 1898, at New York city.

DONOHUE, GEORGE F.—Age 25 years. Enlisted, May 2, 1898, at New York city, to serve two years; mustered in as private, Co. A May 17, 1898; mustered out with company, November 15, 1898, at New York city.

DONOHUE, JAMES E.—Age, 21 years. Enlisted, May 20, 1898, at Peekskill, to serve two years; mustered in as private, Co. H, same date; discharged, June 27, 1898.

DONOHUE, MARTIN F.—Age, 24 years. Enlisted, May 2, 1898, at New York city, to serve two years; mustered in as corporal, Co. A, May 17, 1898; promoted sergeant, August 25, 1898; returned to ranks, August 28, 1898; promoted sergeant, September 5, 1898; died of typhoid fever, October 2, 1898, at New York city.

DONOHUE ROGER J.—Age, 32 years. Enlisted, May 2, 1898, at New York city, to serve two years; mustered in as private, Co. K, May 19, 1898; dishonorably discharged, July 24, 1898.

DORAN, EDWARD F.—Age, — years. Enlisted, June 23, 1898, at New York city, to serve two years; mustered in as private, Co. K, same date; mustered out with company November 15, 1898, at New York city.

DORAN, JR., WILLIAM.—Age, — years. Enlisted, June 27, 1898, at New York city, to serve two years; mustered in as private, Co. G, same date; mustered out with company, November 15, 1898, at New York city.

DOUGHERTY, JAMES.—Age, 30 years. Enlisted, May 2, 1898, at New York city, to serve two years; mustered in as private, Co. C, May 19, 1898; mustered out with company, November 15, 1898, at New York city.

DOWD, WILLIAM.—Age, — years. Enlisted, July 7, 1898, at New York city to serve two years; mustered in as private, Co. H, same date; died of typhoid fever, October 25, 1898, in Presbyterian Hospital, New York city.

DOWDEN, JAMES H.—Age, 23 years. Enlisted, May 2, 1898, at New York city, to serve two years; mustered in as private Co. M, May 17, 1898; mustered out with company, November 15, 1898, at New York city.

DOWLING, JOHN E.—Age, — years. Enlisted, July 7, 1898, at New York city, to serve two years; mustered in as private, Co. C, same date; mustered out with company, November 15, 1898, at New York city.

DOYLE, PATRICK J.—Age, 27 years. Enlisted, May 2, 1898, at New York city, to serve two years; mustered in as sergeant, Co. A, May 17, 1898; promoted first sergeant, October 27, 1898; mustered out with company, November 15, 1898, at New York city.

DRAKE, CHARLES D.—Age, 26 years. Enlisted, May 2, 1898, at New York city, to serve two years; mustered in as corporal, Co. K, May 19, 1898; mustered out with company, November 15, 1898, at New York city.

DRAKE, CHARLES H.—Age, 27 years. Enlisted, May 2, 1898, at New York city, to serve two years; mustered in as private, Co. I, May 21, 1898; mustered out with company, November 15, 1898, at New York city.

DUFF, JOHN R.—Age, — years. Enlisted, June 24, 1898, at New York city, to serve two years; mustered in as private, Co. D, same date; mustered out with company, November 15, 1898, at New York city.

DUFFY, JOSEPH F.—Age, 30 years. Enlisted, May 2, 1898, at New York city, to serve two years; mustered in as private, Co. A, May 17, 1898; mustered out with company, November 15, 1898, at New York city.

DUGAN, EDGAR M.—Age, — years. Enlisted, June 29, 1898, at New York city, to serve two years; mustered in as private, Co. M, same date; promoted corporal, July 27, 1898; mustered out with company, November 15, 1898, at New York city.

DUGGAN, WILLIAM J.—Age, — years. Enlisted, June 27, 1898, at New York city, to serve two years; mustered in as private, Co. A, same date; mustered out with company, November 15, 1898, at New York city.

DUNN, HARRY.—Age, 26 years. Enlisted, May 2, 1898, at New York city, to serve two years; mustered in as private, Co. C, May 19, 1898; promoted corporal, July 27, 1898; mustered out with company November 15, 1898, at New York city.

DUNN, JOHN.—Age, 27 years. Enlisted, May 2, 1898, at New York city, to serve two years; mustered in as private, Co. C, May 20, 1898; mustered out with company, November 15, 1898, at New York city.

DURANT, JR., REGINALD S.—Age, 23 years. Enlisted, May 2, 1898, at New York city, to serve two years; mustered in as private, Co. F, May 21, 1898; mustered out with company, November 15, 1898, at New York city.

DURENMATT, CHARLES.—Age, 24 years. Enlisted, May 2, 1898, at New York city, to serve two years; mustered in as private, Co. H, May 20, 1898; transferred to Troop C, Third United States Cavalry, July 12, 1898.

DURYEE, HENRY W.—Age, 29 years. Enlisted, May 2, 1898, at New York city, to serve two years; mustered in as private, Co. H, May 20, 1898; promoted corporal, July 22, 1898; mustered out with company, November 15, 1898, at New York city.

DWYER, WILLIAM C.—Age, — years. Enlisted, July 5, 1898, at New York city, to serve two years; mustered in as private, Co. K, same date; mustered out with company, November 15, 1898, at New York city.

DYKE, EDWARD L.—Age, 28 years. Enlisted, May 2, 1898, at New York city, to serve two years; mustered in as private, Co. K, May 19, 1898; deserted, August 21, 1898, at Camp Thomas, Chickamauga Park, Ga.

DYKSTRA, BOUKE.—Age, — years. Enlisted, June 27, 1898, at New York city, to serve two years; mustered in as private, Co. H, same date; mustered out with company, November 15, 1898, at New York city.

EAGAN, JOSEPH J.—Age, 25 years. Enlisted, May 2, 1898, at New York city, to serve two years; mustered in as artificer, Co. H, May 20, 1898; mustered out with company, November 15, 1898, at New York city.

EAGAN, MICHAEL J.—Age, 25 years. Enlisted, May 2, 1898, at New York city, to serve two years; mustered in as private, Co. I, May 19, 1898; mustered out with company, November 15, 1898, at New York city.

EAGAN, WILLIAM F.—Age, 21 years. Enlisted, May 2, 1898, at New York city, to serve two years; mustered in as private, Co. A, May 17, 1898; mustered out with company, November 15, 1898, at New York city.

EARLE, EDWARD J.—Age, 22 years. Enlisted, May 2, 1898, at New York city, to serve two years; mustered in as private, Co. E, May 20, 1898; mustered out with company, November 15, 1898, at New York city.

ECKSTINE, ALBERT.—Age, 23 years. Enlisted, May 2, 1898, at New York city, to serve two years; mustered in as private, Co. A, May 17, 1898; died of typhoid fever, August 9, 1898, in hospital, Fort McPherson, Ga.

EDENS, JOHN H.—Age, 18 years. Enlisted, May 19, 1898, at New York city, to serve two years; mustered in as private, Co. H, May 20, 1898; mustered out, to date, November 15, 1898.

EGAN, JAMES.—Age, — years. Enlisted, June 24, 1898, at New York city, to serve two years; mustered in as private, Co. L, same date; mustered out with company, November 15, 1898, at New York city.

EGBERT, CARL.—Age, — years. Enlisted, July 11, 1898, at New York city, to serve two years; mustered in as private, Co. G, same date; transferred to band, July 27, 1898; mustered out with regiment, November 15, 1898, at New York city.

EHRMAN, WILLIAM H.—Age, 39 years. Enlisted, May 2, 1898, at New York city, to serve two years; mustered in as quarter-master-sergeant, Co. L, May 20, 1898; mustered out with company, November 15, 1898, at New York city.

EICHER, BERNARD.—Age, 25 years. Enlisted, May 2, 1898, at New York city, to serve two years; mustered in as private, Co. M, May 17, 1898; deserted, July 13, 1898, at Camp Thomas, Chickamauga Park, Ga.

EIDMAN, JOHN G.—Age, — years. Enlisted, July 1, 1898, at New York city, to serve two years; mustered in as private, Co. C, same date; mustered out with company, November 15, 1898, at New York city.

ELLER, JOSEPH N.—Age, 19 years. Enlisted, May 17, 1898, at New York city, to serve two years; mustered in as private, Co. E, May 20, 1898; mustered out with company, November 15, 1898, at New York city.

EMMONS, WILLIAM.—Age, 25 years. Enlisted, May 2, 1898, at New York city, to serve two years; mustered in as first sergeant, Co. C, May 19, 1898; mustered out with company, November 15, 1898, at New York city.

ENGLISH, WILLIAM J.—Age, 23 years. Enlisted, May 2, 1898, at New York city, to serve two years; mustered in as private, Co. C, May 19, 1898; mustered out with company, November 15, 1898, at New York city.

ENNIS, FRANCIS F.—Age, 29 years. Enlisted, May 2, 1898, at New York city, to serve two years; mustered in as private, Co. A, May 17, 1898; mustered out with company, November 15, 1898, at New York city.

ERNST, GEORGE F.—Age, 24 years. Enlisted, May 2, 1898, at New York city, to serve two years; mustered in as private, Co. H, May 20, 1898; mustered out with company, November 15, 1898, at New York city.

EUSTON, ARTHUR.—Age, — years. Enlisted, July 1, 1898, at New York city, to serve two years; mustered in as private, Co. L, same date; mustered out with company, November 15, 1898, at New York city.

EWING, EDWARD.—Age, 21 years. Enlisted, May 2, 1898, at New York city, to serve two years; mustered in as private, Co. H, May 20, 1898; mustered out with company, November 15, 1898, at New York city.

EWING, JOSEPH E.—Age, 21 years. Enlisted, May 2, 1898, at New York city, to serve two years; mustered in as private, Co. B, May 20, 1898; died of typhoid fever, September 8, 1898, in Sternberg Hospital, Chickamauga Park, Ga.

FAGAN, FELIX.—Age, 31 years. Enlisted, May 2, 1898, at New York city, to serve two years; mustered in as private, Co. B, May 20, 1898; mustered out with company, November 15, 1898, at New York city.

FAGER, WILLIAM.—Age, 22 years. Enlisted, May 2, 1898, at New York city, to serve two years; mustered in as private, Co. G, May 20, 1898; appointed cook, August 25, 1898; mustered out with company, November 15, 1898, at New York city.

FAHRENHOLTZ, BRUNO.—Age, 26 years. Enlisted, May 2, 1898, at New York city, to serve two years; mustered in as private, Co. M, May 17, 1898; appointed musician, no date; mustered out with company, November 15, 1898, at New York city.

FAIRBANKS, FREDERICK.—Age, 40 years. Enlisted, May 2, 1898, at New York city, to serve two years; mustered in as private, Co. M, May 17, 1898; mustered out with company, November 15, 1898, at New York city.

FALCONER, FRANK N.—Age, 28 years. Enlisted, May 2, 1898, at New York city, to serve two years; mustered in as private, Co. B, May 20, 1898; mustered out with company, November 15, 1898, at New York city.

FALES, CHAS. E.—Age, 34 years. Enlisted, May 2, 1898, at New York city, to serve two years; mustered in as private, Co. K, May 19, 1898; mustered out with company, November 15, 1898, at New York city.

FALIHEE, PATRICK H.—Age, 28 years. Enlisted, May 2, 1898, at New York city, to serve two years; mustered in as private, Co. H, May 20, 1898; died of typhoid fever, August 16, 1898, in Second Division Hospital, Chickamauga, Ga.

FALK, BARNEY.—Age, 30 years. Enlisted, May 2, 1898, at New York city, to serve two years; mustered in as private, Co. F, May 21, 1898; mustered out with company, November 15, 1898, at New York city.

FALL, THOMAS J.—Age, 32 years. Enlisted, May 2, 1898, at New York city, to serve two years; mustered in as private, Co. M, May 17, 1898; mustered out with company, November 15, 1898, at New York city.

FALLER, OTTO A.—Age, 22 years. Enlisted, May 2, 1898, at New York city, to serve two years; mustered in as corporal, Co. K, May 19, 1898; promoted sergeant, October 21, 1898; mustered out with company, November 15, 1898, at New York city.

FALLON, JAMES.—Age, — years. Enlisted, June 27, 1898, at New York city, to serve two years; mustered in as private, Co. C, same date; mustered out with company, November 15, 1898, at New York city.

FALTERMAN, L.—Age, 20 years. Enlisted, May 2, 1898, at New York city, to serve two years; mustered in as private, Co. D, May 17, 1898; discharged, October 13, 1898.

FARELL, PATRICK.—Age, — years. Enlisted, July 5, 1898, at New York city, to serve two years; mustered in as private, Co. I, same date; mustered out with company, November 15, 1898, at New York city.

FARQUHARSON, JAMES H.—Age, — years. Enrolled, July 23, 1898, at Chickamauga, Ga., to serve two years; mustered in as second lieutenant, Co. M, same date; mustered out with company, November 15, 1898, at New York city; commissioned second lieutenant, July 30, 1898, with rank from same date, vice Peck, promoted.

FARRELL, JAMES.—Age, — years. Enlisted, June 23, 1898, at New York city, to serve two years; mustered in as private, Co. G, same date; mustered out with company, November 15, 1898, at New York city.

FARRON, EDWARD J.—Age, 21 years. Enlisted, May 2, 1898, at New York city, to serve two years; mustered in as private, Co. F, May 21, 1898; mustered out with company, November 15, 1898, at New York city.

FAY, RICHARD.—Age, 26 years. Enlisted, May 2, 1898, at New York city, to serve two years; mustered in as private, Co. K, May 19, 1898; mustered out with company, November 15, 1898, at New York city.

FEARL, JAMES S.—Age, — years. Enlisted, July 1, 1898, at New York city, to serve two years; mustered in as private, Co. M, same date; mustered out with company, November 15, 1898, at New York city.

FEGAN, JOHN.—Age, 25 years. Enlisted, May 2, 1898, at New York city, to serve two years; mustered in as private, Co. F, May 21, 1898; mustered out with company, November 15, 1898, at New York city.

FEHNER, WILLIAM.—Age, 23 years. Enlisted, May 2, 1898, at New York city, to serve two years; mustered in as private, Co. A, May 17, 1898; mustered out with company, November 15, 1898, at New York city.

FEILBACH, JACOB.—Age, — years. Enlisted, July 1, 1898, at New York city, to serve two years; mustered in as private, Co. I, same date; appointed artificer, August 6, 1898; mustered out with company, November 15, 1898, at New York city.

FELDMAN, LOUIS.—Age, 26 years. Enlisted, May 2, 1898, at New York city, to serve two years; mustered in as private, Co. M, May 17, 1898; mustered out with company, November 15, 1898, at New York city.

FELTER, JOHN.—Age, 23 years. Enlisted, May 2, 1898, at New York city, to serve two years; mustered in as private, Co. C, May 19, 1898; promoted corporal, July 27, 1898; mustered out with company, November 15, 1898, at New York city.

FERGUSON, PATRICK.—Age, 21 years. Enlisted, May 2, 1898, at New York city, to serve two years; mustered in as private, Co. A, May 17, 1898; mustered out with company, November 15, 1898, at New York city.

FERRARI, WILLIAM R.—Age, — years. Enlisted, June 29, 1898, at New York city, to serve two years; mustered in as private, Co. E, same date; mustered out with company, November 15, 1898, at New York city.

FIELDS, WILLIAM F.—Age, — years. Enlisted, June 23, 1898, at New York city, to serve two years; mustered in as private, Co. E, same date; mustered out with company, November 15, 1898, at New York city.

FIESELER, WILLIAM.—Age, 38 years. Enlisted, May 2, 1898, at New York city, to serve two years; mustered in as private, Co. I, May 19, 1898; mustered out with company, November 15, 1898, at New York city.

FINLEY, EDWARD.—Age, — years. Enlisted, June 29, 1898, at New York city, to serve two years; mustered in as private, Co. H, same date; mustered out with company, November 15, 1898, at New York city.

FINN, JOHN.—Age, — years. Enlisted, June 23, 1898, at New York city, to serve two years; mustered in as private, Co. H, same date; mustered out with company, November 15, 1898, at New York city.

FISHER, HERMAN.—Age, — years. Enlisted, June 24, 1898, at New York city, to serve two years; mustered in as cook, Co. C, same date; mustered out with company, November 15, 1898, at New York city.

FISHER, ROBERT.—Age, — years. Enlisted, June 30, 1898, at New York city, to serve two years; mustered in as private, Co. G, same date; mustered out with company, November 15, 1898, at New York city.

FISHER, WILLIAM.—Age, — years. Enlisted, June 30, 1898, at New York city, to serve two years; mustered in as private, Co. H, same date; mustered out with company, November 15, 1898, at New York city.

FITZGERALD, EDWARD.—Age, — years. Enlisted, July 1, 1898, at New York city, to serve two years; mustered in as private, Co. I, same date; mustered out with company, November 15, 1898, at New York city.

FITZGERALD, GEORGE F.—Age, 27 years. Enlisted, May 2, 1898, at New York city, to serve two years; mustered in as private, Co. H, May 20, 1898; mustered out with company, November 15, 1898, at New York city.

FITZGERALD, JOHN.—Age, 28 years. Enlisted, May 2, 1898, at New York city, to serve two years; mustered in as private, Co. K, May 19, 1898; mustered out with company, November 15, 1898, at New York city.

FITZGERALD, MICHAEL.—Age, 21 years. Enlisted, May 2, 1898, at New York city, to serve two years; mustered in as private, Co. C, May 19, 1898; promoted corporal, June 16, 1898; mustered out with company, November 15, 1898, at New York city.

FITZMAURICE, JOHN.—Age, 28 years. Enlisted, May 2, 1898, at New York city, to serve two years; mustered in as private, Co. M, May 17, 1898; mustered out with company, November 15, 1898, at New York city.

FITZPATRICK, HAROLD L.—Age, 22 years. Enlisted, May 2, 1898, at New York city, to serve two years; mustered in as private, Co. C, May 19, 1898; promoted corporal, July 20, 1898; mustered out with company, November 15, 1898, at New York city.

FITZPATRICK, MATHEW P.—Age, 21 years. Enlisted, May 2, 1898, at New York city, to serve two years; mustered in as private, Co. A, May 17, 1898; promoted corporal, September 3, 1898; mustered out with company, November 15, 1898, at New York city.

FLANAGAN, THOMAS A.—Age, 27 years. Enlisted, May 2, 1898, at New York city, to serve two years; mustered in as private, Co. C, May 19, 1898; mustered out with company, November 15, 1898, at New York city.

FLANIGAN, MICHAEL J.—Age, — years. Enlisted, June 24, 1898, at New York city, to serve two years; mustered in as private, Co. B, same date; mustered out with company, November 15, 1898, at New York city.

FLECK, HERMAN.—Age, 26 years. Enlisted, May 2, 1898, at New York city, to serve two years; mustered in as musician, Co. H, May 20, 1898; mustered out with company, November 15, 1898, at New York city.

FLEISCHER, HENRY.—Age, 23 years. Enlisted, May 2, 1898, at New York city, to serve two years; mustered in as private, Co. A, May 17, 1898; mustered out with company, November 15, 1898, at New York city.

FLEMING, JOHN F.—Age, 18 years. Enlisted, May 2, 1898, at New York city, to serve two years; mustered in as private, Co. M, May 17, 1898; mustered out with company, November 15, 1898, at New York city.

FLOREA, MORRIS.—Age, 27 years. Enlisted, May 2, 1898, at New York city, to serve two years; mustered in as private, Co. M, May 17, 1898; mustered out with company, November 15, 1898, at New York city.

FLUCKIGER, MELBOURNE W.—Age, 22 years. Enlisted, May 2, 1898, at New York city, to serve two years; mustered in as private, Co. B, May 20, 1898; mustered out, to date, November 15, 1898.

FLUHR, EDWARD.—Age, 27 years Enlisted, May 2, 1898, at New York city, to serve two years; mustered in as private, Co. F, May 21, 1898; mustered out with company, November 15, 1898, at New York city.

FLYNN, JOHN J.—Age, 28 years. Enlisted, May 2, 1898, at New York city, to serve two years; mustered in as private, Co. A, May 17, 1898; mustered out with company, November 15, 1898, at New York city.

FLYNN, JOSEPH E.—Age, 27 years. Enlisted, May 2, 1898, at New York city, to serve two years; mustered in as private, Co. M, May 17, 1898; mustered out with company, November 15, 1898, at New York city.

FLYNN, THOMAS C.—Age, 34 years. Enlisted, May 2, 1898, at New York city, to serve two years; mustered in as private, Co. C, May 19, 1898; mustered out with company, November 15, 1898, at New York city.

FLYNN, WILLIAM C.—Age, — years. Enlisted, June 30, 1898, at New York city, to serve two years; mustered in as private, Co. F, same date; mustered out with company, November 15, 1898, at New York city.

FOCACCI, JOSEPH.—Age, — years. Enlisted, June 23, 1898, at New York city, to serve two years; mustered in as private, Co. G, same date; mustered out with company, November 15, 1898, at New York city.

FOLEY, EUGENE H.—Age, — years. Enlisted, June 27, 1898, at New York city, to serve two years; mustered in as private, Co. E, same date; mustered out with company, November 15, 1898, at New York city.

FOLEY, JOHN.—Age, — years. Enlisted, July 2, 1898, at New York city, to serve two years; mustered in as private, Co. H, same date; mustered out with Co. November 15, 1898, at New York city.

FORD, CHARLES J.—Age, 22 years. Enlisted, May 2, 1898, at New York city, to serve two years; mustered in as private, Co. L, May 20, 1898; mustered out with company, November 15, 1898, at New York city.

FORD, ELMER AINSLIE.—Age, 23 years. Enlisted, May 2, 1898, at New York city, to serve two years; mustered in as private, Co. K, May 19, 1898; mustered out, to date, November 15, 1898.

FORDEN, CHARLES.—Age, — years. Enlisted, June 23, 1898, at New York city, to serve two years; mustered in as private, Co. M, same date; mustered out with company, November 15, 1898, at New York city.

FORKIN, JOHN.—Age, 21 years. Enlisted, May 2, 1898, at New York city, to serve two years; mustered in as private, Co. F, May 21, 1898; mustered out with company, November 15, 1898, at New York city.

FORREST, BUCK.—Age, 39 years. Enlisted, May 2, 1898, at New York city, to serve two years; mustered in as quartermaster-sergeant, Co. E, May 20, 1898; mustered out with company, November 15, 1898, at New York city.

FOSTER, JOSEPH W.—Age, — years. Enlisted, July 7, 1898, at New York city, to serve two years; mustered in as private, Co. B, same date; mustered out with company, November 15, 1898, at New York city.

FOTSCH, CHARLES.—Age, 23 years. Enlisted, May 2, 1898, at New York city, to serve two years; mustered in as private, Co. E, May 20, 1898; mustered out with company, November 15, 1898, at New York city.

FRANCOIS, CAMILLE A.—Age, 44 years. Enlisted, May 2, 1898, at New York city, to serve two years; mustered in as private, Co. G, May 20, 1898; promoted corporal, July 27, 1898; mustered out with company, November 15, 1898, at New York city.

FRANK, JACOB.—Age, 23 years. Enlisted, May 2, 1898, at New York city, to serve two years; mustered in as sergeant, Co. B, May 20, 1898; killed by cars, August 23, 1898, at Chattanooga, Tenn.

FRANKS, SAMUEL.—Age, 27 years. Enlisted, May 16, 1898, at New York city, to serve two years; mustered in as private, Co. D, May 17, 1898; mustered out with company, November 15, 1898, at New York city.

FRASCAR, WILLIAM.—Age, 21 years. Enlisted, May 2, 1898, at New York city, to serve two years; mustered in as private, Co. I, May 19, 1898; mustered out with company, November 15, 1898, at New York city.

FRASER, JOHN.—Age, 21 years. Enlisted, May 2, 1898, at New York city, to serve two years; mustered in as private, Co. F, May 21, 1898; deserted, September 6, 1898, at Camp Thomas, Chickamauga Park, Ga.

FREDERICK, GEORGE E.—Age, 24 years. Enlisted, May 2, 1898, at New York city, to serve two years; mustered in as corporal, Co. C, May 19, 1898; returned to ranks, September 9, 1898; discharged, October 14, 1898.

FREISE, HENRY.—Age, 26 years. Enlisted, May 2, 1898, at New York city, to serve two years; mustered in as private, Co. H, May 20, 1898; mustered out with company, November 15, 1898, at New York city.

FREUND, WILLIAM.—Age, 21 years. Enlisted, May 2, 1898, at New York city, to serve two years; mustered in as private, Co. E, May 20, 1898; mustered out with company, November 15, 1898, at New York city.

FREY, HENRY J.—Age, 19 years. Enlisted, May 2, 1898, at New York city, to serve two years; mustered in as private, Co. L, May 20, 1898; mustered out with company, November 15, 1898, at New York city.

FREY, SAMUEL.—Age, 24 years. Enlisted, May 2, 1898, at New York city, to serve two years; mustered in as corporal, Co. C, May 19, 1898; returned to ranks, August 1, 1898; mustered out with company, November 15, 1898, at New York city.

FREYER, PATRICK F.—Age, — years. Enlisted, July 11, 1898, at New York city, to serve two years; mustered in as private, Co. L, same date; transferred to band, July 27, 1898; mustered out with regiment, November 15, 1898, at New York city.

FRIEND, ARTHUR.—Age, 27 years. Enlisted, May 18, 1898, at New York city, to serve two years; mustered in as private, Co. F, May 21, 1898; mustered out with company, November 15, 1898, at New York city.

FRIEND, BENTON G.—Age, 23 years. Enlisted, May 2, 1898, at New York city, to serve two years; mustered in as corporal, Co. E, May 20, 1898; mustered out with company, November 15, 1898, at New York city.

FRITZMIER, GEORGE J.—Age, 30 years. Enlisted, May 2, 1898, at New York city, to serve two years; mustered in as quartermaster-sergeant, Co. A, May 17, 1898; as second lieutenant, October 28, 1898; mustered out with company, November 15, 1898 at New York city; commissioned second lieutenant, October 27, 1898, with rank from same date, vice Hinckley, discharged.

FRITZSCHE, RICHARD.—Age, 28 years.   Enlisted, May 2, 1898, at New York city, to serve two years; mustered in as private, Co. C, May 19, 1898; mustered out with company, November 15, 1898, at New York city.

FUHRMANN, HENRY A.—Age, 32 years.   Enlisted, May 17, 1898, at New York city, to serve two years; mustered in as private, Co. H, May 20, 1898; mustered out with company, November 15, 1898, at New York city.

FULTON, JR., JOHN.—Age, 27 years. Enlisted, May 11, 1898, at camp near Peekskill, to serve two years; mustered in as private, Co. L, May 20, 1898; promoted corporal, August 17, 1898; mustered out with company, November 15, 1898, at New York city.

FURNIVAL, JOSEPH.—Age, — years.   Enlisted, June 23, 1898, at New York city, to serve two years; mustered in as private, Co. K, same date; mustered out with company, November 15, 1898, at New York city.

FURRY, WARDEN B.—Age, 21 years.   Enlisted, May 2, 1898, at New York city, to serve two years; mustered in as private, Co. C, May 19, 1898; mustered out with company November 15, 1898, at New York city.

GALLIGHER, JAMES.—Age, 28 years.   Enlisted, May 2, 1898, at New York city, to serve two years; mustered in as private, Co. C, May 19 1898; mustered out with company, November 15, 1898, at New York city.

GANEY, JOSEPH A.—Age, 24 years.   Enlisted, May 2, 1898, at New York city, to serve two years; mustered in as private, Co. A, May 17, 1898; mustered out with company, November 15, 1898, at New York city.

GANG, JOSEPH F.—Age, 24 years.   Enlisted, May 2, 1898, at New York city, to serve two years; mustered in as private, Co. C, May 19, 1898; mustered out with company, November 15, 1898, at New York city.

GARDNER, JAMES C.—Age, 24 years.   Enlisted, May 2, 1898, at New York city, to serve two years; mustered in as sergeant, Co. C, May 17, 1898; mustered out with company, November 15, 1898, at New York city.

GATLEY, JOHN J.—Age, 41 years. Enlisted, May 2, 1898, at New York city, to serve two years; mustered in as private, Co. D, May 17, 1898; promoted corporal, July 28, 1898; mustered out with company, November 15, 1898, at New York city.

GAULEY, JOHN.—Age, 23 years. Enlisted, May 2, 1898, at New York city, to serve two years; mustered in as private, Co. D, May 17, 1898; mustered out with company, November 15, 1898, at New York city.

GAYLOR, JOSEPH H.—Age, 21 years. Enlisted, May 2, 1898, at New York city, to serve two years; mustered in as private, Co. E, May 20, 1898; mustered out with company, November 15, 1898, at New York city.

GAYNOR, JOSEPH.—Age, — years. Enlisted, June 24, 1898, at New York city, to serve two years; mustered in as private, Co. K, same date; mustered out with company, November 15, 1898, at New York city.

GEARY, EDWIN J.—Age, 23 years. Enlisted, May 2, 1898, at New York city, to serve two years; mustered in as private, Co. A, May 17, 1898; mustered out with company, November 15, 1898, at New York city.

GEBHARD, EDWARD.—Age, 27 years. Enlisted, May 2, 1898, at New York city, to serve two years; mustered in as first sergeant, Co. K, May 19, 1898; died of typhoid fever, September 22, 1898, in New York Hospital, New York city.

GEISER, CHARLES.—Age, — years. Enlisted, June 30, 1898, at New York city, to serve two years; mustered in as private, Co. C, same date; mustered out with company, November 15, 1898, at New York city.

GERAGHTY, CHARLES J.—Age, — years. Enlisted, June 29, 1898, at New York city, to serve two years; mustered in as private, Co. L, same date; mustered out with company, November 15, 1898, at New York city.

GERARD, AMOS L.—Age, 19 years. Enlisted, May 2, 1898, at New York city, to serve two years; mustered in as private, Co. B, May 20, 1898; mustered out with company, November 15, 1898, at New York city.

GERDES, CHARLES.—Age, 19 years. Enlisted, May 2, 1898, at New York city, to serve two years; mustered in as private, Co. A, May 17, 1898; mustered out with company, November 15, 1898, at New York city.

GERSTENLANER, JR., JOHN.—Age, 23 years. Enlisted, May 19, 1898, at New York city, to serve two years; mustered in as private, Co. H, May 20, 1898; mustered out with company, November 15, 1898, at New York city.

GIBSON, WALTER A.—Age, 32 years. Enlisted, May 2, 1898, at New York city, to serve two years; mustered in as private, Co. K, May 19, 1898; mustered out with company, November 15, 1898, at New York city.

GIESEN, AUGUST.—Age, 24 years. Enlisted, May 2, 1898, at New York city, to serve two years; mustered in as private, Co. E, May 20, 1898; mustered out with company, November 15, 1898, at New York city.

GILBERTSON, WILLIAM.—Age, 25 years.   Enlisted, May 2, 1898, at New York city, to serve two years; mustered in as private, Co. G, May 21, 1898; promoted corporal, July 27, 1898; mustered out with company, November 15, 1898, at New York city.

GILLESPIE, RICHARD—.Age, — years. Enlisted, July 1, 1898, at New York city, to serve two years; mustered in as private, Co. A, same date; mustered out with company, November 15, 1898, at New York city.

GILLON, JOHN.—Age, 30 years. Enlisted, May 2, 1898, at New York city, to serve two years; mustered in as private, Co. D, May 17, 1898; mustered out with company, November 15, 1898, at New York city.

GLENDENNING, JOHN J.—Age, — years.   Enlisted, June 2, 1898, at New York city, to serve two years; mustered in as private, Co. K, same date; appointed cook, August 19, 1898; mustered out with company, November 15, 1898, at New York city.

GLUCK, HERMANN.—Age, 32 years. Enlisted, May 2, 1898, at New York city, to serve two years; mustered in as private, Co. M, May 17, 1898; mustered out with company, November 15, 1898, at New York city.

GOERZ, JOHN E.—Age, 24 years. Enlisted, May 2, 1898, at New York city, to serve two years; mustered in as private, Co. B, May 20, 1898; promoted corporal, July 27, 1898; mustered out with company, November 15, 1898, at New York city.

GOLDING, JOHN T.—Age, 27 years. Enlisted, May 2, 1898, at New York city, to serve two years; mustered in as musician, Co. B, May 20, 1898; mustered out with company, November 15, 1898, at New York city.

GOLDMAN, RUDOLPH F.—Age, 22 years. Enlisted, May 2, 1898, at New York city, to serve two years; mustered in as private, Co. H, May 20, 1898; promoted corporal, May 20, 1898; mustered out with company, November 15, 1898, at New York city.

GOLDSMITH, WILLIAM.—Age, — years. Enlisted, July 1, 1898, at New York city, to serve two years; mustered in as private, Co. C, same date; mustered out with company, November 15, 1898, at New York city.

GOLDSTEIN, HENRY.—Age, — years. Enlisted, July 6, 1898, at New York city, to serve two years; mustered in as private, Co. D, same date; mustered out with company, November 15, 1898, at New York city.

GOLDSTEIN, MAX.—Age, 20 years. Enlisted, May 2, 1898, at New York city, to serve two years; mustered in as private, Co. F, May 21, 1898; mustered out with company, November 15, 1898, at New York city.

GOLE, CAMPBELL E. N.—Age, 30 years. Enlisted, May 2, 1898, at New York city, to serve two years; mustered in as private, Co. C, May 19, 1898; mustered out with company, November 15, 1898, at New York city.

GOLL, JR., ROSTINA O.—Age, 27 years. Enlisted, May 2, 1898, at New York city, to serve two years; mustered in as private, Co. E, May 20, 1898; promoted corporal, July 27, 1898; mustered out with company, November 15, 1898, at New York city.

GOLLE, HENRY J.—Age, — years. Enlisted, June 24, 1898, at New York city, to serve two years; mustered in as private, Co. F, same date; mustered out with company, November 15, 1898, at New York city.

GOOD, JOHN J.—Age, — years. Enlisted, July 5, 1898, at New York city, to serve two years; mustered in as private, Co. B, same date; mustered out with company, November 15, 1898, at New York city.

GOODFELLOW, GEORGE H.—Age, 33 years. Enlisted, May 2, 1898, at New York city, to serve two years; mustered in as corporal, Co. E, May 20, 1898; mustered out with company, November 15, 1898, at New York city.

GORDON, EDWARD R.—Age, 21 years. Enlisted, May 2, 1898, at New York city, to serve two years; mustered in as private, Co. D, May 17, 1898; mustered out with company, November 15, 1898, at New York city.

GORDON, JOHN J.—Age, 23 years. Enlisted, May 2, 1898, at New York city, to serve two years; mustered in as private, Co. F, May 21, 1898; mustered out with company, November 15, 1898, at New York city.

GORDON, MARTIN.—Age, — years. Enlisted, July 5, 1898, at New York city, to serve two years; mustered in as private, Co. M, same date; mustered out with company, November 15, 1898, at New York city.

GORRY, THOMAS F.—Age, 25 years. Enlisted, May 2, 1898, at New York city, to serve two years; mustered in as private, Co. L, May 20, 1898; promoted corporal, July 27, 1898; mustered out with company, November 15, 1898, at New York city.

GOTTHOLD, JAMES M.—Age, 27 years. Enlisted, May 18, 1898, at New York city, to serve two years; mustered in as private, Co. A, May 20, 1898; mustered out with company, November 15, 1898, at New York city.

GOTTSCHALK, WALTER.—Age, 30 years. Enlisted, May 2, 1898, at New York city, to serve two years; mustered in as private, Co. E, May 20, 1898; mustered out with company, November 15, 1898, at New York city.

GRACE, EDWARD V.—Age, 26 years. Enlisted, May 2, 1898, at New York city, to serve two years; mustered in as private, Co. A, May 17, 1898; promoted corporal, September 3, 1898; mustered out with company, November 15, 1898, at New York city.

GRACE, JAMES.—Age, 23 years. Enlisted, May 2, 1898, at New York city, to serve two years; mustered in as private, Co. A, May 17, 1898; mustered out with company, November 15, 1898, at New York city.

GRADY, PATRICK J.—Age, 26 years. Enlisted, May 2, 1898, at New York city, to serve two years; mustered in as private, Co. H, May 20, 1898; mustered out with company, November 15, 1898, at New York city.

GRAFF, EDWIN D.—Age, 29 years. Enrolled, May 2, 1898, at New York city, to serve two years; mustered in as first lieutenant, Co. M, May 17, 1898; mustered out with company, November 15, 1898, at New York city; commissioned first lieutenant, May 17, 1898, with rank from same date, original.

GRAFF, HORACE M.—Age, 23 years. Enrolled, May 2, 1898, at New York city as second lieutenant, to serve two years; mustered in as captain, Co. E, May 21, 1898; mustered out with company, November 15, 1898, at New York city; commissioned captain, May 21, 1898, with rank from same date, original.

GRAHAM, HAMILTON.—Age, — years. Enlisted, July 8, 1898, at New York city, to serve two years; mustered in as private, Co. I, same date; transferred to band, July 27, 1898; mustered out with regiment, November 15, 1898, at New York city.

GRAHAM, THOMAS.—Age, 21 years. Enlisted, May 2, 1898, at New York city, to serve two years; mustered in as private, Co. K, May 19, 1898; mustered out with company, November 15, 1898, at New York city.

GRAHAM, WILLIAM C.—Age, 25 years. Enlisted, May 2, 1898, at New York city, to serve two years; mustered in as corporal, Co. D, May 17, 1898; discharged, October 13, 1898.

GRAHAM, WILLIAM P.—Age, 21 years. Enlisted, May 2, 1898, at New York city, to serve two years; mustered in as private, Co. B, May 20, 1898; mustered out with company, November 15, 1898, at New York city.

GRAMM, EDWARD J.—Age, 21 years. Enlisted, May 2, 1898, at New York city, to serve two years; mustered in as private, Co. G, May 20, 1898; transferred to Co. B, July 27, 1898; to Co. I, Twelfth New York Volunteer Infantry, August 19, 1898.

GRASTY, JR., ENOCH H.—Age, 20 years. Enlisted, May 2, 1898, at New York city, to serve two years; mustered in as private, Co. K, May 19, 1898; promoted corporal, July 27, 1898; mustered out with company, November 15, 1898, at New York city.

GRAY, EDWIN S.—Age, 20 years. Enlisted, May 2, 1898, at New York city, to serve two years; mustered in as private, Co. G, May 20, 1898; mustered out with company, November 15, 1898, at New York city.

GRAY, WILLIAM H.—Age, — years. Enlisted, June 27, 1898, at New York city, to serve two years; mustered in as private, Co. K, same date; mustered out with company, November 15, 1898, at New York city.

GREANAWALT, IRVING.—Age, — years. Enlisted, June 24, 1898, at New York city, to serve two years; mustered in as private, Co. L, same date; mustered out with company, November 15, 1898, at New York city.

GREBE, WILLIAM.—Age, — years. Enlisted, June 24, 1898, at New York city, to serve two years; mustered in as private, Co. D, same date; mustered out with company, November 15, 1898, at New York city.

GREEN, FRED W.—Age, 28 years. Enlisted, May 2, 1898, at New York city, to serve two years; mustered in as private, Co. G, May 20, 1898; transferred to Co. B, July 27, 1898; mustered out with company, November 15, 1898, at New York city.

GREEN, NELS.—Age, 26 years. Enlisted, May 2, 1898, at New York city, to serve two years; mustered in as private, Co. E, May 20, 1898; mustered out with company, November 15, 1898, at New York city.

GREENE, GOODMAN JAMES.—Age, 38 years. Enrolled, May 2, 1898, at New York city, to serve two years; mustered in as colonel, May 21, 1898; mustered out with regiment, November 15, 1898, at New York city; commissioned colonel, May 18, 1898, with rank from same date, original.

GREENLAW, JOSEPH J.—Age, 24 years. Enlisted, May 2, 1898, at New York city, to serve two years; mustered in as private, Co. H, May 20, 1898; mustered out with company, November 15, 1898, at New York city.

GREFE, GEORGE NICHOLS.—Age, 22 years. Enlisted, May 2, 1898, at New York city, to serve two years; mustered in as private, Co. G, May 20, 1898; mustered out with company, November 15, 1898, at New York city.

GREISLER, FRANZ.—Age, 22 years. Enlisted, May 18, 1898, at New York city, to serve two years; mustered in as private, Co. I, May 19, 1898; mustered out with company, November 15, 1898, at New York city.

GRIFFIN, EDWARD J.—Age, 24 years. Enlisted, May 2, 1898, at New York city, to serve two years; mustered in as private Co. I, May 19, 1898; mustered out with company, November 15, 1898, at New York city.

GRIFFITH, JOHN A.—Age, 25 years. Enlisted, May 2, 1898, at New York city, to serve two years; mustered in as private, Co. D, May 17, 1898; promoted corporal, July 27, 1898; discharged, October 13, 1898.

GRIGGS, JAMES G.—Age, 27 years. Enlisted, May 2, 1898, at New York city, to serve two years; mustered in as private, Co. K, May 19, 1898; mustered out with company, November 15, 1898, at New York city.

GRIMES, ROBERT.—Age, 22 years. Enlisted, May 2, 1898, at New York city, to serve two years; mustered in as private, Co. F, May 21, 1898; mustered out with company, November 15, 1898, at New York city.

GROGAN, ARTHUR R.—Age, — years. Enlisted, June 23, 1898, at New York city, to serve two years; mustered in as private, Co. A, same date; mustered out with company, November 15, 1898, at New York city.

GROSS, SAMUEL P.—Age, — years. Enlisted, July 6, 1898, at New York city, to serve two years; mustered in as private, Co. E, same date; mustered out with company, November 15, 1898, at New York city.

GRUELLE, JOSEPH.—Age, — years. Enlisted, July 8, 1898, at New York city, to serve two years; mustered in as private, Co. F, same date; transferred to band, July 27, 1898; mustered out with regiment, November 15, 1898, at New York city.

GRUNEWALD, CHARLES.—Age, 33 years. Enlisted, May 2, 1898, at New York city, to serve two years; mustered in as private, Co. K, May 19, 1898; mustered out with company, November 15, 1898, at New York city.

GUERSING, HENRY J.—Age, 21 years. Enlisted, May 2, 1898, at New York city, to serve two years; mustered in as private, Co. E, May 20, 1898; mustered out with company, November 15, 1898, at New York city.

GUILFOYLE, WILLIAM.—Age, — years. Enlisted, July 6, 1898, at New York city, to serve two years; mustered in as private, Co. F, same date; mustered out with company, November 15, 1898, at New York city.

GUNDREY, WILLIAM.—Age, 20 years. Enlisted, May 2, 1898, at New York city, to serve two years; mustered in as private, Co. G, May 20, 1898; discharged, October 12, 1898.

GUNNELL, ALBERT E.—Age, 21 years. Enlisted, May 2, 1898, at New York city, to serve two years; mustered in as private, Co. G, May 20, 1898; mustered out with company, November 15, 1898, at New York city.

HACKER, EDWARD H.—Age, 18 years. Enlisted, May 2, 1898, at New York city, to serve two years; mustered in as corporal, Co. M, May 17, 1898; mustered out with company, November 15, 1898, at New York city.

HACKETT, CHARLES J.—Age, 23 years. Enlisted, May 2, 1898, at New York city, to serve two years; mustered in as private, Co. G, May 20, 1898; mustered out with company, November 15, 1898, at New York city.

HAETNER, WILLIAM.—Age, 27 years. Enlisted, May 16, 1898, at New York city, to serve two years; mustered in as private, Co. D, May 17, 1898; discharged, October 12, 1898; also borne as William J. Haertner.

HAGAN, GUSTAV.—Age, 39 years. Enlisted, May 10, 1898, at New York city, to serve two years; mustered in as private, Co. M, May 17, 1898; transferred to United States Hospital Corps, August 22, 1898; retransferred to this regiment, October 16, 1898, and detailed as hospital steward; mustered out with regiment, November 15, 1898, at New York city.

HAGEBOOM, JOHN.—Age, 22 years. Enlisted, May 2, 1898, at New York city, to serve two years; mustered in as private, Co. L, May 20, 1898; discharged, November 11, 1898, to enlist in regular army.

HAHN, LOUIS A.—Age, 23 years. Enlisted, May 2, 1898, at New York city, to serve two years; mustered in as private, Co. F, May 21, 1898; promoted corporal, September 5, 1898; mustered out with company, November 15, 1898, at New York city.

HALE, CHARLES.—Age, — years. Enlisted, June 30, 1898, at New York city, to serve two years; mustered in as private, Co. B, same date; mustered out with company, November 15, 1898, at New York city.

HALL, WILLIAM H.—Age, 28 years. Enlisted, May 2, 1898, at New York city, to serve two years; mustered in as sergeant, Co. G, May 20, 1898; promoted first sergeant, October 22, 1898; mustered out with company, November 15, 1898, at New York city.

HALLAHAN, GEORGE.—Age, — years. Enlisted, July 9, 1898, at New York city, to serve two years; mustered in as private, Co. A, same date; transferred to band, July 27, 1898; mustered out with regiment, November 15, 1898, at New York city.

HALLEY, HERMAN R.—Age, 21 years. Enlisted, May 2, 1898, at New York city, to serve two years; mustered in as private, Co. E, May 20, 1898; mustered out with company, November 15, 1898, at New York city.

HALPIN, EDWARD V.—Age, 22 years. Enlisted, May 2, 1898, at New York city, to serve two years; mustered in as private, Co. C, May 19, 1898; mustered out with company, November 15, 1898, at New York city.

HALSEY, GEORGE B.—Age, 39 years. Enlisted, May 2, 1898, at New York city, to serve two years; mustered in as private, Co. K, May 19, 1898; mustered out with company, November 15, 1898, at New York city.

HAMILL, HARRY J.—Age, 25 years. Enlisted, May 2, 1898, at New York city, to serve two years; mustered in as private, Co. F, May 21, 1898; mustered out with company, November 15, 1898, at New York city.

HANDRICK, FREDERICK.—Age, 19 years. Enlisted, May 2, 1898, at New York city, to serve two years; mustered in as private, Co. H, May 20, 1898; promoted corporal, September 7, 1898; mustered out with company, November 15, 1898, at New York city. .

HANIFY, FREDERICK J.—Age, 21 years. Enlisted, May 2, 1898, at New York city, to serve two years; mustered in as private, Co. F, May 21, 1898; mustered out with company, November 15, 1898, at New York city.

HANLEY, JOHN J.—Age, — years. Enlisted, June 24, 1898, at New York city; to serve two years; mustered in as private, Co. F, same date; mustered out with company, November 15, 1898, at New York city.

HANLEY, JOSEPH A.—Age, 22 years. Enlisted, May 2, 1898, at New York city, to serve two years; mustered in as corporal, Co. F, May 21, 1898; promoted sergeant, June 28, 1898; mustered out with company, November 15, 1898, at New York city.

HANNA, CHARLES.—Age, — years. Enlisted, June 27, 1898, at New York city, to serve two years; mustered in as private, Co. I, same date; appointed wagoner, September 1, 1898; mustered out with company, November 15, 1898, at New York city.

HANNAWAY, JAMES J.—Age, — years. Enlisted, June 23, 1898, at New York city, to serve two years; mustered in as private, Co. K, same date; mustered out with company, November 15, 1898, at New York city.

HANNEGAN, THOMAS M. J.—Age, 21 years. Enlisted, May 2, 1898, at New York city, to serve two years; mustered in as private, Co. A, May 17, 1898; mustered out with company, November 15, 1898, at New York city.

HANNUM, HAROLD A.—Age, 38 years. Enlisted, May 2, 1898, at New York city, to serve two years; mustered in as private, Co. C, May 19, 1898; mustered out, to date, November 15, 1898.

HARDING, WILLIAM F.—Age, 23 years. Enlisted, May 2, 1898, at New York city, to serve two years; mustered in as private, Co. A, May 17, 1898; promoted corporal, July 27, 1898; regimental quartermaster-sergeant, August 26, 1898; mustered out with regiment, November 15, 1898, at New York city.

HARDY, GEORGE J.—Age, 29 years. Enrolled, May 2, 1898, at New York city, to serve two years; mustered in as regimental adjutant, May 21, 1898; assigned, June 12, 1898, to Co. I, as first lieutenant; mustered out, to date, November 15, 1898, at New York city; commissioned captain and regimental adjutant, May 21, 1898, with rank from same date, original.

HARDY, JAMES T.—Age, 27 years. Enrolled, May 2, 1898, at New York city, to serve two years; mustered in as battalion adjutant, May 21, 1898; discharged, November 25, 1898; commissioned first lieutenant and battalion adjutant, May 17, 1898, with rank from same date, original.

HARKINS, MICHAEL.—Age, — years. Enlisted, July 5, 1898, at New York city, to serve two years; mustered in as private, Co. K, same date; mustered out with company, November 15, 1898, at New York city.

HARNEY, MARTIN J.—Age, 24 years. Enlisted, May 2, 1898, at New York city to serve two years; mustered in as private, Co. E, May 20, 1898; mustered out with company, November 15, 1898, at New York city.

HARRINGTON, PATRICK.—Age, — years. Enlisted, June 29, 1898, at New York city, to serve two years; mustered in as private, Co. A, same date; discharged, October 19, 1898.

HARRINGTON, PATRICK W.—Age, 28 years. Enlisted, May 2, 1898, at New York city, to serve two years; mustered in as private, Co. D, May 17, 1898; discharged, October 14, 1898.

HARRIS, HENRY A.—Age, 41 years. Enlisted, May 2, 1898, at New York city, to serve two years; mustered in as sergeant, Co. A, May 17, 1898; mustered out with company, November 15, 1898, at New York city.

HARRIS, RICHARD V.—Age, 22 years. Enlisted, May 2, 1898, at New York city, to serve two years; mustered in as sergeant, Co. A, May 17, 1898; mustered out with company, November 15, 1898, at New York city.

HARRIS, STEPHEN J.—Age, 19 years. Enlisted, May 2, 1898, at New York city, to serve two years; mustered in as private, Co. H, May 20, 1898; mustered out with company, November 15, 1898, at New York city.

HARRISON, FREDERICK.—Age, 21 years. Enlisted, May 2, 1898, at New York city, to serve two years; mustered in as private, Co. C, May 19, 1898; mustered out with company, November 15, 1898, at New York city.

HARRISON, SAMUEL.—Age, 20 years. Enlisted, May 11, 1898, at camp, near Peekskill, to serve two years; mustered in as private, Co. L, May 20, 1898; discharged, no date.

HARRSCH, JULIUS.—Age, 35 years. Enlisted, May 16, 1898, at New York city, to serve two years; mustered in as private, Co. B, May 20, 1898; mustered out with company, November 15, 1898, at New York city.

HART, EDWARD J.—Age, 45 years. Enlisted, May 2, 1898, at New York city, to serve two years; mustered in as private, Co. M, May 17, 1898; mustered out with company, November 15, 1898, at New York city.

HART, HENRY D.—Age, 27 years. Enlisted, May 19, 1898, at New York city, to serve two years; mustered in as private, Co. H, May 20, 1898; mustered out with company, November 15, 1898, at New York city.

HARTER, FREDERICK.—Age, — years. Enlisted, July 1, 1898, at New York city, to serve two years; mustered in as private, Co. B, same date; mustered out with company, November 15, 1898, at New York city.

HARTNETT, EDWARD J.—Age, — years. Enlisted, July 8, 1898, at New York city, to serve two years; mustered in as private, Co. M, same date; mustered out with company, November 15, 1898, at New York city.

HARTNEY, PERRY.—Age, — years. Enlisted, June 30, 1898, at New York city, to serve two years; mustered in as private, Co. E, same date; mustered out with company, November 15, 1898, at New York city.

HARVEY, FREDERICK.—Age, — years. Enlisted, June 29, 1898, at New York city, to serve two years; mustered in as private, Co. B, same date; mustered out with company, November 15, 1898, at New York city.

HASSARD, FRANK.—Age, 22 years. Enlisted, May 18, 1898, at New York city, to serve two years; mustered in as private, Co. I, May 19, 1898; mustered out with company, November 15, 1898, at New York city.

HASSETT, ALBERT.—Age, 21 years. Enlisted, May 2, 1898, at New York city, to serve two years; mustered in as private, Co. K, May 19, 1898; mustered out with company, November 15, 1898, at New York city.

HAVEN, VICTOR.—Age, 19 years. Enlisted, May 2, 1898, at New York city, to serve two years; mustered in as private, Co. G, May 20, 1898; mustered out with company, November 15, 1898, at New York city.

HAY, JOHN.—Age, 35 years. Enlisted, May 2, 1898, at New York city, to serve two years; mustered in as private, Co. F, May 21, 1898; mustered out with company, November 15, 1898, at New York city.

HAYDEN, THOMAS CHARLES.—Age, 18 years. Enlisted, May 2, 1898, at New York city, to serve two years; mustered in as private, Co. G, May 20, 1898; mustered out with company, November 15, 1898, at New York city.

HAYES, EDWARD.—Age, — years. Enlisted, June 23, 1898, at New York city to serve two years; mustered in as private, Co. H, same date; mustered out with company, November 15, 1898, at New York city.

HEALY, THOMAS F.—Age, 27 years. Enlisted, May 2, 1898, at New York city, to serve two years; mustered in as corporal, Co. D, May 17, 1898; returned to ranks, no date; mustered out with company, November 15, 1898, at New York city.

HEBSCHER, WILLIAM.—Age, — years. Enlisted, June 30, 1898, at New York city, to serve two years; mustered in as private, Co. C, same date; mustered out with company, November 15, 1898, at New York city.

HECK, JAMES GEORGE.—Age, 21 years. Enlisted, May 2, 1898, at New York city, to serve two years; mustered in as musician, Co. L, May 20, 1898; mustered out with company, November 15, 1898, at New York city.

HEGARTY, JOHN C.—Age, 25 years. Enrolled, May 2, 1898, at New York city, to serve two years; mustered in as second lieutenant, Co. M, May 17, 1898; as first lieutenant, Co. B, to date, July 23, 1898; mustered out with company, November 15, 1898, at New York city; subsequent service as captain, Forty-first Regiment, United States Volunteer Infantry; commissioned second lieutenant, May 17, 1898, with rank from same date, original; first lieutenant, July 30, 1898, with rank from same date, vice Winterroth, discharged.

HEGELLMAN, JACOB.—Age, 29 years. Enlisted, May 2, 1898, at New York city, to serve two years; mustered in as private, Co. E, May 20, 1898; promoted corporal, July 27, 1898; mustered out with company, November 15, 1898, at New York city.

HEINLEIN, NICHOLAS R.—Age, 27 years. Enlisted, May 2, 1898, at New York city, to serve two years; mustered in as corporal, Co. B, May 20, 1898; returned to ranks, August 22, 1898; mustered out with company, November 15, 1898, at New York city.

HEITKAMP, EDWARD S.—Age, 24 years. Enlisted, May 2, 1898, at New York city, to serve two years; mustered in as private, Co. K, May 19, 1898; promoted corporal, July 27, 1898; mustered out with company, November 15, 1898, at New York city.

HELLERICK, WILLIAM.—Age, 23 years. Enlisted, May 2, 1898, at New York city, to serve two years; mustered in as corporal, Co. I, May 19, 1898; mustered out with company, November 15, 1898, at New York city.

HENDERSON, WILLIAM.—Age, 21 years. Enlisted, May 2, 1898, at New York city, to serve two years; mustered in as private, Co. G, May 20, 1898; mustered out with company, November 15, 1898, at New York city.

HENDRICKSON, JOHN F.—Age, 37 years. Enrolled, May 2, 1898, at New York city, as second lieutenant, to serve two years; mustered in as first lieutenant, Co. D, May 17, 1898; mustered out, to date, November 15, 1898, at New York city; commissioned first lieutenant, May 17, 1898, with rank from same date, original.

HENRY, PATRICK W.—Age, — years. Enlisted, July 1, 1898, at New York city, to serve two years; mustered in as private, Co. I, same date; mustered out with company, November 15, 1898, at New York city.

HEPPELL, WALTER A.—Age, 27 years. Enlisted, May 2, 1898, at New York city, to serve two years; mustered in as private, Co. C, May 19, 1898; mustered out with company, November 15, 1898, at New York city.

HERBERT, CHARLES.—Age, 21 years. Enlisted, May 2, 1898, at New York city, to serve two years; mustered in as private, Co. F, May 21, 1898; mustered out with company, November 15, 1898, at New York city.

HERBISON, JAMES.—Age, 34 years. Enlisted, May 2, 1898, at New York city, to serve two years; mustered in as private, Co. D, May 17, 1898; mustered out with company, November 15, 1898, at New York city.

HERDER, FREDERICK.—Age, — years. Enlisted, June 27, 1898, at New York city, to serve two years; mustered in as private, Co. I, same date; mustered out, to date, November 15, 1898, at New York city.

HERING, FRANCIS R.—Age, 21 years. Enlisted, May 2, 1898, at New York city, to serve two years; mustered in as private, Co. E, May 20, 1898; mustered out with company, November 15, 1898, at New York city.

HERMANN, HARRY.—Age, 23 years. Enlisted, May 2, 1898, at New York city, to serve two years; mustered in as musician, Co. L, May 20, 1898; mustered out with company, November 15, 1898, at New York city.

HERRON, JOHN.—Age, 32 years. Enlisted, May 2, 1898, at New York city, to serve two years; mustered in as private, Co. A, May 17, 1898; mustered out with company, November 15, 1898, at New York city.

HESS, THEODORE.—Age, 21 years. Enlisted, May 2, 1898, at New York city, to serve two years; mustered in as private, Co. H, May 20, 1898; mustered out with company, November 15, 1898, at New York city.

HESSELLS, DAVID.—Age, — years. Enlisted, June 30, 1898, at New York city, to serve two years; mustered in as private, Co. E, same date; mustered out with company, November 15, 1898, at New York city.

HEUSTON, JAMES W.—Age, — years. Enlisted, July 5, 1898,
at New York city, to serve two years; mustered in as private,
Co. F, same date; mustered out with company, November 15,
1898, at New York city.

HICKS, THOMAS B.—Age, — years. Enlisted, June 24, 1898,
at New York city, to serve two years; mustered in as private,
Co. D, same date; mustered out with company, November 15,
1898, at New York city.

HIGGINS, AUGUST.—Age, — years. Enlisted, July 5, 1898, at
New York city, to serve two years; mustered in as private, Co.
B, same date; mustered out with company, November 15, 1898,
at New York city.

HIGGINS, JAMES.—Age, 23 years. Enlisted, May 2, 1898, at
New York city, to serve two years; mustered in as private,
Co. G, May 20, 1898; mustered out with company, November
15, 1898, at New York city.

HIGGINS, WILLIAM F, J.—Age, 41 years. Enrolled, May 2,
1898, at New York city, to serve two years; mustered in as
second lieutenant, Co. I, May 19, 1898; mustered out with company, November 15, 1898, at New York city; commissioned
second lieutenant, May 19, 1898, with rank from same date,
original.

HILL, GEORGE W.—Age, 19 years. Enlisted, May 2, 1898, at
New York city, to serve two years; mustered in as private,
Co. E, same date; mustered out with company, November 15,
1898, at New York city.

HILL, WILLIS P.—Age, 24 years. Enlisted, May 2, 1898, at New
York city, to serve two years; mustered in as chief musician,
May 21, 1898; transferred to Co. M, July 27, 1898, as sergeant;
to Co. H, September 5, 1898; mustered out with company,
November 15, 1898, at New York city.

HILLOCK, ROBERT E.—Age, 25 years. Enlisted, May 2, 1898,
at New York city, to serve two years; mustered in as private,
Co. K, May 19, 1898; mustered out with company, November 15,
1898, at New York city.

HINCKLEY, CHARLES E.—Age, 41 years. Enlisted, May 2, 1898, at New York city, to serve two years; mustered in as private, Co. H, May 20, 1898; promoted corporal,* no date; mustered in as second lieutenant, Co. A, July 30, 1898; discharged, to date, October 17, 1898; commissioned second lieutenant, July 30, 1898, with rank from same date, vice Hegarty, promoted.

HINES, JOHN.—Age, — years. Enlisted, June 27, 1898, at New York city, to serve two years; mustered in as private, Co. F, same date; mustered out with company, November 15, 1898, at New York city.

HINMANN, WILLIAM M.—Age, — years. Enlisted, July 5, 1898, at New York city, to serve two years; mustered in as private, Co. G, same date; discharged, September 29, 1898.

HINZ, PAUL R.—Age, 30 years. Enlisted, May 10, 1898, at New York city, to serve two years; mustered in as private, Co. M, May 17, 1898; mustered out with company, November 15, 1898, at New York city.

HIRTZ, WILLIAM.—Age, — years. Enlisted, June 24, 1898, at New York city, to serve two years; mustered in as private, Co. G, same date; mustered out with company, November 15, 1898, at New York city.

HISCOCK, FRANK S.—Age, 21 years. Enlisted, May 2, 1898, at New York city, to serve two years; mustered in as private, Co. D, May 17, 1898; mustered out with company, November 15, 1898, at New York city.

HITZLER, GEORGE.—Age, 21 years. Enlisted, May 2, 1898, at New York city, to serve two years; mustered in as private, Co. M, May 17, 1898; mustered out with company, November 15, 1898, at New York city.

HOCKIN, H. J.—Age, — years. Enlisted, July 7, 1898, at New York city, to serve two years; mustered in as private, Co. M, same date; mustered out with company, November 15, 1898, at New York city.

HOFER, OTTO.—Age, 23 years. Enlisted, May 2, 1898, at New York city, to serve two years; mustered in as wagoner, Co. C, May 19, 1898; returned to ranks, July 13, 1898; promoted corporal, July 27, 1898; killed by lightning, August 19, 1898, at Camp Thomas, Chickamauga Park, Ga.

HOFFMANN, ALFRED CHARLES.—Age, 31 years. Enlisted, May 2, 1898, at New York city, to serve two years; mustered in as sergeant, Co. I, May 19, 1898; mustered out with company, November 15, 1898, at New York city.

HOGAN, DENNIS V.—Age, 22 years. Enlisted, May 2, 1898, at New York city, to serve two years; mustered in as private, Co. I, May 19, 1898; mustered out with company, November 15, 1898, at New York city.

HOLAHAN, THOMAS FRANCIS.—Age, 21 years. Enlisted, May 11, 1898, at camp, near Peekskill, to serve two years; mustered in as private, Co. L, May 20, 1898; mustered out with company, November 15, 1898, at New York city.

HOLM, CHRIST.—Age, 27 years. Enlisted, May 2, 1898, at New York city, to serve two years; mustered in as wagoner, Co. K, May 19, 1898; mustered out with company, November 15, 1898, at New York city.

HOLMES, ARTHUR E.—Age, 23 years. Enlisted, May 2, 1898, at New York city, to serve two years; mustered in as private, Co. F, May 21, 1898; mustered out with company, November 15, 1898, at New York city.

HOLT, THOMAS J.—Age, 24 years. Enlisted, May 2, 1898, at New York city, to serve two years; mustered in as musician, Co. D, May 17, 1898; mustered out with company, November 15, 1898, at New York city.

HORAN, JOHN H.—Age, 26 years. Enlisted, May 2, 1898, at New York city, to serve two years; mustered in as private, Co. L, May 20, 1898; mustered out with company, November 15, 1898, at New York city.

HORNBROOK, JOHN H.—Age, 24 years. Enlisted, May 2, 1898. at New York city, to serve two years; mustered in as sergeant, Co. C, May 19, 1898; promoted quartermaster-sergeant, June 9, 1898; mustered out with company, November 15, 1898, at New York city.

HORTON, ELBERT C.—Age, 20 years. Enlisted, May 2, 1898, at New York city, to serve two years; mustered in as first sergeant, Co. L, May 20, 1898; returned to ranks, September 10, 1898; discharged, October 18, 1898.

HOWARD, GEORGE.—Age, 37 years. Enlisted, May 2, 1898, at New York city, to serve two years; mustered in as private, Co. G, May 20, 1898; mustered out with company, November 15, 1898, at New York city.

HOYT, LOUIS H.—Age, 30 years. Enlisted, May 2, 1898, at New York city, to serve two years; mustered in as private, Co. A, May 17, 1898; mustered out with company, November 15, 1898, at New York city.

HUBACHER, HERMAN.—Age, — years. Enlisted, July 2, 1898, at New York city, to serve two years; mustered in as private, Co. M, same date; died of typhoid fever, October 30, 1898, in St. Francis' Hospital, New York city.

HUBBARD, SAMUEL D.—Age, 33 years. Enrolled, May 2, 1898, at New York city, to serve two years; mustered in as major and surgeon, May 21, 1898; mustered out, to date, November 15, 1898; commissioned surgeon, May 7, 1898, with rank from same date, original.

HUDSON, JAMES H.—Age, 26 years. Enlisted, May 2, 1898, at New York city, to serve two years; mustered in as private, Co. F, May 21, 1898; mustered out with company, November 15, 1898, at New York city.

HUDSON, WILLIAM.—Age, 25 years. Enlisted, May 2, 1898, at New York city, to serve two years; mustered in as private, Co. A, May 17, 1898; mustered out with company, November 15, 1898, at New York city.

HUFF, WILLIAM A.—Age, 44 years. Enlisted, May 2, 1898, at New York city, to serve two years; mustered in as private, Co. C, May 19, 1898; promoted corporal, September 2, 1898; mustered out with company, November 15, 1898, at New York city.

HUGHES, BERNARD.—Age, — years. Enlisted, June 27, 1898, at New York city, to serve two years; mustered in as private, Co. H, same date; mustered out with company, November 15, 1898, at New York city.

HUGHES, DENNIS.—Age, — years. Enlisted, June 23, 1898, at New York city, to serve two years; mustered in as private, Co. A, same date; mustered out with company, November 15, 1898, at New York city.

HUGHES, GEORGE.—Age, 18 years. Enlisted, May 2, 1898, at New York city, to serve two years; mustered in as private, Co. M. May 17, 1898; mustered out with company, November 15, 1898, at New York city.

HUGHES, HENRY M.—Age, 20 years. Enlisted, May 16, 1898, at New York city, to serve two years; mustered in as private, Co. B, May 20, 1898; mustered out with company, November 15, 1898, at New York city.

HUGHES, JAMES J.—Age, 33 years. Enlisted, May 2, 1898, at New York city, to serve two years; mustered in as corporal, Co. H, May 20, 1898; mustered out with company, November 15, 1898, at New York city.

HUGHES, JOHN.—Age, 24 years. Enlisted, May 2, 1898, at New York city, to serve two years; mustered in as first sergeant, Co. H, May 20, 1898; returned to ranks, June 6, 1898; mustered out with company, November 15, 1898, at New York city.

HUGHES, WILLIAM.—Age, 21 years. Enlisted, May 19, 1898, at New York city, to serve two years; mustered in as private, Co. H, May 20, 1898; mustered out with company, November 15, 1898, at New York city.

HULETT, PAUL.—Age, 21 years. Enlisted, May 2, 1898, at New York city, to serve two years; mustered in as private, Co. F, May 21, 1898; mustered out with company, November 15, 1898, at New York city.

HULL, ARTHUR B.—Age, 23 years. Enlisted, May 2, 1898, at New York city, to serve two years; mustered in as private, Co. G, May 20, 1898; mustered out with company, November 15, 1898, at New York city.

HUNT, ALVERN.—Age, 23 years. Enlisted, May 2, 1898, at New York city, to serve two years; mustered in as private, Co. G, May 20, 1898; mustered out with company, November 15, 1898, at New York city.

HUNTER, MALCOLM A.—Age, 21 years. Enlisted, May 2, 1898, at New York city, to serve two years; mustered in as private, Co. C, May 19, 1898; mustered out with company, November 15, 1898, at New York city.

HURLBURT, T. RICHARD.—Age, 23 years. Enlisted, May 2, 1898, at New York city, to serve two years; mustered in as private, Co. B, May 20, 1898; mustered out with company, November 15, 1898, at New York city.

HURLEY, JOSEPH F.—Age, 25 years. Enlisted, May 11, 1898, at camp, near Peekskill, to serve two years; mustered in as private, Co. L, May 20, 1898; promoted corporal, July 27, 1898; mustered out with company, November 15, 1898, at New York city.

HUSEMEYER, HENRY.—Age, 38 years. Enlisted, May 2, 1898, at New York city, to serve two years; mustered in as private, Co. A, May 17, 1898; mustered out with company, November 15, 1898, at New York city.

HUSSION, PATRICK.—Age, 20 years. Enlisted, May 2, 1898, at New York city, to serve two years; mustered in as private, Co. K, May 19, 1898; discharged, October 1, 1898.

HUSTEDT, HERMAN.—Age, 30 years. Enlisted, May 2, 1898, at New York city, to serve two years; mustered in as private, Co. C, May 20, 1898; mustered out with company, November 15, 1898, at New York city.

HUSTON, WILLIAM.—Age, —years. Enlisted, June 23, 1898, at New York city, to serve two years; mustered in as private, Co. A, same date; mustered out with company, November 15, 1898, at New York city.

HUTER, WILLIAM.—Age, 27 years. Enlisted, May 2, 1898, at camp near Peekskill, to serve two years; mustered in as private, Co. H, May 20, 1898; mustered out with company, November 15, 1898, at New York city.

HUTH, JR., AUGUST.—Age, 29 years. Enlisted, May 17, 1898, at New York city, to serve two years; mustered in as private, Co. E, May 20, 1898; mustered out with company, November 15, 1898, at New York city.

HUTTEMANN, GUSTAVE.—Age, 25 years.   Enlisted, May 2,
1898, at New York city, to serve two years; mustered in as
corporal, Co. B, May 20, 1898; mustered out with company,
November 15, 1898, at New York city.

HYNDS, JAMES.—Age, — years.   Enlisted, June 23, 1898, at
New York city, to serve two years; mustered in as private, Co.
G, same date; mustered out with company, November 15, 1898,
at New York city.

HYSON, JR., JOHN.—Age, 25 years.   Enlisted, May 21, 1898, at
New York city, to serve two years; mustered in as private, Co.
G, June 19, 1898; mustered out with company, November 15,
1898, at New York city.

IMRIE, ARTHUR E.—Age, — years.   Enlisted, June 24, 1898,
at New York city, to serve two years; mustered in as private,
Co. K, same date; mustered out with company, November 15,
1898, at New York city.

INCLORSKY, LOUIS.—Age, 21 years.   Enlisted, May 2, 1898,
at New York city, to serve two years; mustered in as private,
Co. L, May 20, 1898; mustered out with company, November 15,
1898, at New York city.

INGRAM, EDWARD W.—Age, 38 years.   Enlisted, May 2, 1898,
at New York city, to serve two years; mustered in as private,
Co. A, May 17, 1898; mustered out with company, November 15,
1898, at New York city.

JACKSON, CHARLES N.—Age, 21 years. Enlisted, May 2, 1898,
at New York city, to serve two years; mustered in as private,
Co. C, May 19, 1898; mustered out with company, November 15,
1898, at New York city.

JACOBI, EMILE J.—Age, 23 years.   Enlisted,, May 2, 1898, at
New York city, to serve two years; mustered in as private, Co.
K, May 19, 1898; mustered out with company, November 15,
1898, at New York city.

JAMES, OSCAR F.—Age, 25 years.   Enlisted, May 2, 1898, at
New York city, to serve two years; mustered in as private, Co.
B, May 20, 1898; promoted corporal, July 27, 1898; returned to
ranks, August 27, 1898; mustered out with company, November
15, 1898, at New York city.

JAMISEN, OTTO W.—Age, — years. Enlisted, June 27, 1898, at New York city, to serve two years; mustered in as private, Co. F, same date; mustered out with company, November 15, 1898, at New York city.

JARVIS, JR., ROBERT.—Age, 28 years. Enlisted, May 2, 1898, at New York city, to serve two years; mustered in as private, Co. M, May 17, 1898; mustered out with company, November 15, 1898, at New York city.

JENKINS, HAROLD L.—Age, — years. Enlisted, June 23, 1898, at New York city, to serve two years; mustered in as private, Co. C, same date; mustered out with company, November 15, 1898, at New York city.

JENKINS, JAMES.—Age, — years. Enlisted, July 1, 1898, at New York city, to serve two years; mustered in as private, Co. L, same date; mustered out with company, November 15, 1898, at New York city.

JENKINS, WILLIAM P.—Age, 20 years. Enlisted, May 2, 1898, at New York city, to serve two years; mustered in as private, Co. F, May 21, 1898; promoted corporal, June 28, 1898; mustered out with company, November 15, 1898, at New York city.

JOEL, RUTHERFORD B. H.—Age, 25 years. Enlisted, May 2, 1898, at New York city, to serve two years; mustered in as first sergeant, Co. G, May 20, 1898; reduced to sergeant, August 31, 1898; mustered out with company, November 15, 1898, at New York city.

JOHNSON, CHARLES E.—Age, 21 years. Enlisted, May 2, 1898, at New York city, to serve two years; mustered in as musician, Co. I, May 19, 1898; mustered out with company, November 15, 1898, at New York city.

JOHNSON, JAMES.—Age, 24 years. Enlisted, May 2, 1898, at New York city, to serve two years; mustered in as private, Co. L, May 20, 1898; mustered out with company, November 15, 1898, at New York city.

JOHNSON, JAMES.—Age, 28 years. Enlisted, May 2, 1898, at New York city, to serve two years; mustered in as private, Co. H, May 20, 1898; mustered out with company, November 15, 1898, at New York city.

JOHNSON, JOHN.—Age, 29 years.   Enlisted, May 2, 1898, at
New York city, to serve two years; mustered in as private, Co.
H, May 20, 1898; mustered out with company, November 15,
1898, at New York city.

JOHNSON, WILLIAM C.—Age, 25 years.   Enlisted, May 2, 1898,
at New York city, to serve two years; mustered in as private,
Co. I, May 19, 1898; promoted corporal, July 9, 1898; mustered
out with company, November 15, 1898, at New York city.

JOHNSON, WILLIAM H.—Age, 26 years.   Enlisted, May 2,
1898, at New York city, to serve two years; mustered in as quartermaster-sergeant, Co. I, May 19, 1898; mustered out with
company, November 15, 1898, at New York city.

JOHNSTON, CHARLES L.—Age, 21 years.   Enlisted, May 2,
1898, at New York city, to serve two years; mustered in as private, Co. B, May 20, 1898; mustered out with company, November 15, 1898, at New York city.

JOHNSTON, JAMES H.—Age, 41 years.   Enlisted, May 2, 1898,
at New York city, to serve two years; mustered in as private,
Co. G, May 20, 1898; promoted corporal, September 12, 1898;
mustered out with company, November 15, 1898, at New York
city.

JONES, HENRY E.—Age, — years.   Enlisted, June 29, 1898, at
New York city, to serve two years; mustered in as private, Co.
G, same date; mustered out with company, November 15, 1898,
at New York city.

JONES, JOHN M.—Age, 35 years.   Enrolled, May 21, 1898, at
camp, near Peekskill, to serve two years; mustered in as battalion adjutant, same date; mustered out, to date, November
15, 1898, at New York city; commissioned first lieutenant and
battalion adjutant, May 21, 1898, with rank from same date,
original.

JONES, WILLIAM F. H.—Age, 25 years.   Enlisted, May 2, 1898,
at New York city, to serve two years; mustered in as private,
Co. B, May 20, 1898; mustered out with company, November 15,
1898, at New York city.

JOOS, GUSTAV.—Age, 21 years. Enlisted, May 2, 1898, at New York city, to serve two years; mustered in as private, Co. H, May 20, 1898; promoted corporal, June 7, 1898; mustered out with company, November 15, 1898, at New York city.

JOSEPH, NOAH D.—Age, 20 years. Enlisted, May 2, 1898, at New York city, to serve two years; mustered in as private, Co. L, May 20, 1898; discharged, October 18, 1898.

JUDSON, CHARLES Y.—Age, 21 years. Enlisted, May 2, 1898, at New York city, to serve two years; mustered in as private, Co. E, May 20, 1898; promoted corporal, July 27, 1898; mustered in as second lieutenant, July 29, 1898; mustered out with company, November 15, 1898, at New York city; commissioned second lieutenant, July 30, 1898, with rank from same date, vice Mahoney, promoted.

KAHN, SAMUEL.—Age, 21 years. Enlisted, May 2, 1898, at New York city, to serve two years; mustered in as private, Co. C, May 19, 1898; mustered out with company, November 15, 1898, at New York city.

KAISER, HENRY.—Age, — years. Enlisted, June 24, 1898, at New York city, to serve two years; mustered in as private, Co. B, same date; promoted corporal, October 22, 1898; mustered out with company, November 15, 1898, at New York city.

KALIS, JOSEPH.—Age, 21 years. Enlisted, May 2, 1898, at New York city, to serve two years; mustered in as private, Co. I, May 19, 1898; mustered out with company, November 15, 1898, at New York city.

KALLENBERG, FRANK G.—Age, 35 years. Enlisted, May 2, 1898, at New York city, to serve two years; mustered in as private, Co. M, May 17, 1898; mustered out with company, November 15, 1898, at New York city.

KANE, JOHN.—Age, — years. Enlisted, July 6, 1898, at New York city, to serve two years; mustered in as private, Co. H, same date; mustered out with company, November 15, 1898, at New York city.

KANE, ROBERT J.—Age, 22 years. Enlisted, May 2, 1898, at New York city, to serve two years; mustered in as private, Co. M, May 17, 1898; mustered out with company, November 15, 1898, at New York city.

KANE, THOMAS.—Age, — years. Enlisted, June 30, 1898, at New York city, to serve two years; mustered in as private, Co. C, same date; mustered out with company, November 15, 1898, at New York city.

KATZENBERGER, WALTER.—Age, 20 years. Enlisted, May 16, 1898, at New York city, to serve two years; mustered in as private, Co. B, May 20, 1898; mustered out with company, November 15, 1898, at New York city.

KAUFMANN, HERMAN H.—Age, 22 years. Enlisted, May 2, 1898, at New York city, to serve two years; mustered in as private, Co. B, May 20, 1898; mustered out with company, November 15, 1898, at New York city.

KAUTZMAN, VICTOR.—Age, 24 years. Enlisted, May 2, 1898, at New York city, to serve two years; mustered in as private, Co. F, May 21, 1898; mustered out with company, November 15, 1898, at New York city.

KEEGAN, CHAUNCEY V.—Age, 25 years. Enlisted, May 2, 1898, at New York city, to serve two years; mustered in as private, Co. C, May 19, 1898; mustered out with company, November 15, 1898, at New York city.

KEEGAN, WILLIAM J.—Age, 40 years. Enlisted, May 2, 1898, at New York city, to serve two years; mustered in as musician, Co. A, May 17, 1898; mustered out with company, November 15, 1898, at New York city.

KEENAN, EDWARD J.—Age, 20 years. Enlisted, May 2, 1898, at New York city, to serve two years; mustered in as private, Co. L, May 20, 1898; mustered out with company, November 15, 1898, at New York city.

KEENEY, EDWARD.—Age, — years. Enlisted, May 2, 1898, at New York city, to serve two years; mustered in as private, Co. C, May 19, 1898; mustered out with company, November 15, 1898, at New York city.

KEHRER, ERNEST F.—Age, 24 years. Enlisted, May 2, 1898, at New York city, to serve two years; mustered in as corporal, Co. M, May 17, 1898; mustered out with company, November 15, 1898, at New York city.

KEIFER, JOSEPH F.—Age, 24 years. Enlisted, May 2, 1898, at New York city, to serve two years; mustered in as wagoner, Co. I, May 19, 1898; returned to ranks, no date; died of typhoid fever, September 4, 1898, at New York city.

KEIMMERER, WILLIAM F.—Age, 21 years. Enlisted, May 2, 1898, at New York city, to serve two years; mustered in as private, Co. G, May 20, 1898; mustered out with company, November 15, 1898, at New York city.

KELLY, DANIEL J.—Age, 24 years. Enlisted, May 2, 1898, at New York city, to serve two years; mustered in as sergeant, Co. D, May 17, 1898; mustered out with company, November 15, 1898, at New York city.

KELLY, JAMES J.—Age, — years. Enlisted, June 23, 1898, at New York city, to serve two years; mustered in as private, Co. K, same date; mustered out with company, November 15, 1898, at New York city.

KELLY, JAMES J.—Age, 19 years. Enlisted, May 2, 1898, at New York city, to serve two years; mustered in as private, Co. G, May 20, 1898; mustered out with company, November 15, 1898, at New York city.

KELLY, JOHN E.—Age, — years. Enlisted, June 30, 1898, at New York city, to serve two years; mustered in as private, Co. B, same date; mustered out with company, November 15, 1898, at New York city.

KELLY, JOHN F.—Age, 22 years. Enlisted, May 2, 1898, at New York city, to serve two years; mustered in as private, Co. D, May 17, 1898; mustered out with company, November 15, 1898, at New York city.

KELLY, JOHN J.—Age, 23 years. Enlisted, May 2, 1898, at New York city, to serve two years; mustered in as sergeant, Co. L, May 20, 1898; returned to ranks, August 17, 1898; mustered out with company, November 15, 1898, at New York city.

KELLY, MICHAEL A.—Age, 22 years. Enlisted, May 2, 1898, at New York city, to serve two years; mustered in as private, Co. B, May 20, 1898; mustered out with company, November 15, 1898, at New York city.

KELLY, THOMAS A.—Age, 24 years. Enlisted, May 2, 1898, at New York city, to serve two years; mustered in as corporal, Co. H, May 20, 1898; promoted sergeant, no date; mustered out with company, November 15, 1898, at New York city.

KEMMY, JAMES J.—Age, — years. Enlisted, June 24, 1898, at New York city, to serve two years; mustered in as private, Co. L, same date; promoted corporal, August 17, 1898; sergeant, September 10, 1898; mustered out with company, November 15, 1898, at New York city.

KENNEDY, JAMES.—Age, 36 years. Enlisted, May 2, 1898, at New York city, to serve two years; mustered in as corporal, Co. L, May 20, 1898; returned to ranks, no date; mustered out with company, November 15, 1898, at New York city.

KENNEDY, WILLIAM P.—Age, — years. Enlisted, June 27, 1898, at New York city, to serve two years; mustered in as private, Co. E, same date; mustered out with company, November 15, 1898, at New York city.

KENNELLY, DANIEL A.—Age, 21 years. Enlisted, May 2, 1898, at New York city, to serve two years; mustered in as private, Co. G, May 20, 1898; mustered out with company, November 15, 1898, at New York city.

KENNELLY, JOHN J.—Age, — years. Enlisted, July 5, 1898, at New York city, to serve two years; mustered in as private, Co. G, same date; mustered out with company, November 15, 1898, at New York city.

KENNY, THOMAS.—Age, 21 years. Enlisted, May 2, 1898, at New York city, to serve two years; mustered in as private, Co. E, May 20, 1898; transferred to Co. F, July 28, 1898; mustered out with company, November 15, 1898, at New York city.

KERNOCHAN, JAMES.—Age, — years. Enlisted, June 27, 1898, at New York city, to serve two years; mustered in as private, Co. D, same date; mustered out with company, November 15, 1898, at New York city.

KERR, JOHN.—Age, 21 years Enlisted, May 2, 1898, at New York city, to serve two years; mustered in as private, Co. C, May 19, 1898; mustered out with company, November 15, 1898, at New York city.

KERR, JOHN.—Age, 21 years. Enlisted, May 2, 1898, at New New York city, to serve two years; mustered in as corporal, Co. K, May 19, 1898; mustered out with company, November 15, 1898, at New York city.

KETCHAM, ALBERT T.—Age, 35 years. Enlisted, May 2, 1898, at New York city, to serve two years; mustered in as private, Co. K, May 19, 1898; promoted corporal, October 21, 1898; mustered out with company, November 15, 1898, at New York city.

KIELY, MAURICE.—Age, — years. Enlisted, July 6, 1898, at New York city, to serve two years; mustered in as private, Co. E, same date; mustered out, to date, November 15, 1898.

KIENAST, EDWARD.—Age, — years. Enlisted, June 23, 1898, at New York city, to serve two years; mustered in as private, Co. I, same date; mustered out with company, November 15, 1898, at New York city.

KIERSTED, LOUIS O.—Age, 21 years. Enlisted, May 2, 1898, at New York city, to serve two years; mustered in as private, Co. M, May 17, 1898; mustered out with company, November 15, 1898, at New York city.

KIESSLING, GUSTAVE.—Age, 24 years. Enlisted, May 2, 1898, at New York city, to serve two years; mustered in as corporal, Co. A, May 17, 1898; mustered out with company, November 15, 1898, at New York city.

KIMBALL, HARRY.—Age, 29 years. Enlisted, May 2, 1898, at New York city, to serve two years; mustered in as private, Co. F, May 21, 1898; discharged, July 13, 1898, at Chickamauga, Ga.

KINNEY, BENJAMIN.—Age, 24 years. Enlisted, May 16, 1898, at New York city, to serve two years; mustered in as private, Co. D, May 17, 1898; deserted, July 28, 1898, at Camp Thomas, Chickamauga Park, Ga.

KINNICUTT, WILLIAM H.—Age, 35 years. Enlisted, May 2, 1898, at New York city, to serve two years; mustered in as pripate, Co. E, May 20, 1898; mustered out with company, November 15, 1898, at New York city.

KINSLER, JOSEPH.—Age, 19 years. Enlisted, May 2, 1898, at New York city, to serve two years; mustered in as private, Co. G, May 20, 1898; promoted corporal, September 12, 1898; mustered out with company, November 15, 1898, at New York city.

KIP, HENRY S.—Age, 23 years. Enrolled, May 22, 1898, at camp near Peekskill, to serve two years; mustered in as battalion adjutant, May 24, 1898; mustered out, to date, November 15, 1898; commissioned first lieutenant and battalion adjutant, May 24, 1898, with rank from same date, original.

KIRBY, JAMES P.—Age, 26 years.   Enlisted, May 2, 1898, at New York city, to serve two years; mustered in as private, Co. B, May 20, 1898; mustered out with company, November 15, 1898, at New York city.

KIRKPATRICK, ARTHUR C.—Age, 27 years. Enlisted, May 2, 1898, at New York city, to serve two years; mustered in as private, Co. D, May 17, 1898; discharged, October 12, 1898.

KISSELL, JOHN.—Age, 23 years. Enlisted, May 2, 1898, at New York city, to serve two years; mustered in as private, Co. C, May 19, 1898; mustered out with company, November 15, 1898, at New York city.

KLEIN, MORRIS J.—Age, — years. Enlisted, June 27, 1898, at New York city, to serve two years; mustered in as private, Co. C, same date; mustered out with company, November 15, 1898, at New York city.

KNAEPPLE, FRANK.—Age, 25 years.   Enlisted, May 2, 1898, at New York city, to serve two years; mustered in as private, Co. H, May 20, 1898; appointed cook, September 5, 1898; returned to ranks, no date; mustered out with company, November 15, 1898, at New York city.

KNAEPPLE, GEORGE.—Age, 23 years.   Enlisted, May 2, 1898, at New York city, to serve two years; mustered in as private, Co. H, May 20, 1898; mustered out with company, November 15, 1898, at New York city. ·

KNAPP, WILLIAM K.—Age, 23 years.   Enlisted, May 2, 1898, at New York city, to serve two years; mustered in as musician, Co. C, May 19, 1898; mustered out with company, November 15, 1898, at New York city.

KNEISEL, WILLIAM.—Age, — years. Enlisted, June 24, 1898, at New York city, to serve two years; mustered in as private, Co. C, same date; mustered out with company, November 15, 1898, at New York city.

KNIFFIN, JOHN.—Age, — years. Enlisted, June 25, 1898, at New York city, to serve two years; mustered in as private, Co. F, same date; mustered out with company, November 15, 1898, at New York city.

KNIPSCHER, FREDERICK.—Age, — years. Enlisted, June ·30, 1898, at New York city, to serve two years; mustered in as private, Co. C, same date; mustered out with company, November 15, 1898, at New York city.

KNITTLE, WILLIAM H. P.—Age, — years. Enlisted, July 6, 1898, at New York city, to serve two years; mustered in as private, Co. A, same date; mustered out with company, November 15, 1898, at New York city.

KOCH, ANDREW.—Age, 21 years. Enlisted, May 16, 1898, at New York city, to serve two years; mustered in as private, Co. I, May 19, 1898; mustered out with company, November 15, 1898, at New York city.

KOCH, GUSTAV.—Age, — years. Enlisted, June 23, 1898, at New York city, to serve two years; mustered in as private, Co. G, same date; died of disease, November 5, 1898, at New York city.

KOCH, JOHN.—Age, 23 years. Enlisted, May 2, 1898, at New York city, to serve two years; mustered in as corporal, Co. C, May 19, 1898; returned to ranks, July 30, 1898; mustered out with company, November 15, 1898, at New York city.

KOEHL, OSCAR.—Age, — years. Enlisted, June 25, 1898, at New York city, to serve two years; mustered in as private, Co. E, same date; mustered out with company, November 15, 1898, at New York city.

KOEHN, RUDOLPH B.—Age, 26 years. Enlisted, May 2, 1898, at New York city, to serve two years; mustered in as sergeant, Co. B, May 20, 1898; mustered out with company, November 15, 1898, at New York city.

KOEHN, WILLIAM G.—Age, 21 years. Enlisted, May 2, 1898, at New York city, to serve two years; mustered in as private, Co. B, May 20, 1898; promoted corporal, July 27, 1898; sergeant, September 3, 1898; mustered out with company, November 15, 1898, at New York city.

KOENIG, VICTOR.—Age, — years. Enlisted, July 5, 1898, at New York city to serve two years; mustered in as private, Co. M, same date; mustered out with company, November 15, 1898, at New York city.

KOHLBERGER, CHARLES E.—Age, 46 years. Enrolled, May 2, 1898, at New York city, to serve two years; mustered in as captain, Co. I, May 19, 1898; mustered out, to date, November 15, 1898, at New York city; commissioned captain, May 20, 1898, with rank from same date, original.

KOHLBERGER, EDWARD A.—Age, 37 years. Enlisted, May 2, 1898, at New York city, to serve two years; mustered in as private, Co. I, May 19, 1898; mustered out with company, November 15, 1898, at New York city.

KOHMUENCH, WILLIAM.—Age, — years. Enlisted, June 27, 1898, at New York city, to serve two years; mustered in as private, Co. H, same date; mustered out with company, November 15, 1898, at New York city.

KOMAREK, LOUIS.—Age, — years. Enlisted, June 23, 1898, at New York city, to serve two years; mustered in as private, Co. I, same date; mustered out with company, November 15, 1898, at New York city.

KORTEN, HERMAN J.—Age, 24 years. Enlisted, May 2, 1898, at New York city, to serve two years; mustered in as private, Co. B, May 20, 1898; mustered out with company, November 15, 1898, at New York city.

KOTHE, HENRY.—Age, 21 years. Enlisted, May 17, 1898, at New York city, to serve two years; mustered in as private, Co. H, May 20, 1898; mustered out with company, November 15, 1898, at New York city.

KRAMER, CHARLES.—Age, 24 years. Enlisted, May 2, 1898, at New York city, to serve two years; mustered in as private, Co. L, May 20, 1898; mustered out with company, November 15, 1898, at New York city.

KRAMER, FREDERICK.—Age, 38 years. Enlisted, May 2, 1898, at New York city, to serve two years; mustered in as sergeant, Co. E, May 20, 1898; mustered out with company, November 15, 1898, at New York city.

KRAMER, JULIUS B.—Age, 21 years. Enlisted, May 2, 1898, at New York city, to serve two years; mustered in as private, Co. I, May 19, 1898; mustered out with company, November 15, 1898, at New York city.

KRANKEL, JACOB.—Age, 23 years. Enlisted, May 2, 1898, at New York city, to serve two years; mustered in as private, Co. E, May 20, 1898; mustered out with company, November 15, 1898, at New York city.

KRAUSS, LOUIS LEPOLE.—Age, 23 years. Enlisted, May 2, 1898, at New York city, to serve two years; mustered in as private, Co. G, May 20, 1898; discharged for disability, August 21, 1898, at Chickamauga, Ga.

KRONE, ALBERT.—Age, 27 years. Enlisted, May 2, 1898, at New York city, to serve two years; mustered in as private, Co. D, May 17, 1898; mustered out with company, November 15, 1898, at New York city.

KRULISH, LOUIS.—Age, — years. Enlisted, June 23, 1898, at New York city, to serve two years; mustered in as private, Co. I, same date; mustered out with company, November 15, 1898, at New York city.

KRUM, FRANK.—Age, 22 years. Enlisted, May 2, 1898, at New York city, to serve two years; mustered in as private, Co. I, May 19, 1898; mustered out with company, November 15, 1898, at New York city.

KRUSKE, CHAS. A.—Age, 22 years. Enlisted, May 2, 1898, at New York city, to serve two years; mustered in as private, Co. K, May 19, 1898; mustered out with company, November 15, 1898, at New York city.

KUGH, FRANK.—Age, 24 years. Enlisted, May 2, 1898, at New York city, to serve two years; mustered in as private, Co. D, May 17, 1898; discharged, September 30, 1898; also borne as Kusch.

KUHFAHL, HERMAN.—Age, 23 years. Enlisted, May 2, 1898, at New York city, to serve two years; mustered in as private, Co. A, May 17, 1898; mustered out with company, November 15, 1898, at New York city.

KUHFAHL, JULIUS O.—Age, 21 years. Enlisted, May 2, 1898, at New York city, to serve two years; mustered in as private, Co. A, May 17, 1898; mustered out with company, November 15, 1898, at New York city.

KUNZLE, JACOB.—Age, 23 years. Enlisted, May 16, 1898, at New York city, to serve two years; mustered in as private, Co. H, May 20, 1898; mustered out with company, November 15, 1898, at New York city.

KURTZ, ARTHUR L.—Age, 33 years. Enlisted, May 2, 1898, at New York city, to serve two years; mustered in as private. Co. M, May 17, 1898; promoted corporal, July 27, 1898; mustered out with company, November 15, 1898, at New York city.

KUSCH, FRANK, see Frank Kugh.

KUTIL, JOHN.—Age, 19 years. Enlisted, May 17, 1898, at New York city, to serve two years; mustered in as private, Co. I, May 19, 1898; mustered out with company, November 15, 1898, at New York city.

LACY, MICHAEL J.—Age, 24 years. Enlisted, May 17, 1898, at New York city, to serve two years; mustered in as private, Co. H, May 20, 1898; mustered out with company, November 15, 1898, at New York city.

LA GRASSA, PETER.—Age, 21 years. Enlisted, May 2, 1898, at New York city, to serve two years; mustered in as private, Co. I, May 19, 1898; deserted, May 24, 1898, at Jersey City, N. J.

LAMBERT, ALFRED J.—Age, 23 years. Enlisted, May 2, 1898, at New York city, to serve two years; mustered in as corporal, Co. C, May 19, 1898; returned to ranks, June 14, 1898; mustered out with company, November 15, 1898, at New York city.

LAMBERT, WILLIAM B.—Age, 19 years. Enlisted, May 2, 1898, at New York city, to serve two years; mustered in as private, Co. I, May 19, 1898; mustered out with company, November 15, 1898, at New York city.

LAMBERT, WILLIAM THOMAS.—Age, 33 years. Enlisted, May 2, 1898, at New York city, to serve two years; mustered in as private, Co. C, May 19, 1898; mustered out with company, November 15, 1898, at New York city.

LANG, JR., EDWARD F.—Age, 20 years. Enlisted, May 2, 1898, at New York city, to serve two years; mustered in as corporal, Co. E, May 20, 1898; mustered out with company, November 15, 1898, at New York city.

LANGRIDGE, GEORGE A.—Age, — years. Enlisted, June 23, 1898, at New York city, to serve two years; mustered in as private, Co. G, same date; mustered out with company, November 15, 1898, at New York city.

LANGTON, WILLIAM H.—Age, 28 years. Enlisted, May 2, 1898, at New York city, to serve two years; mustered in as private, Co. F, May 21, 1898; mustered out with company, November 15, 1898, at New York city.

LANSING, HENRY L.—Age, — years. Enlisted, July 2, 1898, at New York city, to serve two years; mustered in as private, Co. F, same date; mustered out with company, November 15, 1898, at New York city.

LAVEY, JOHN S.—Age, 27 years. Enlisted, May 2, 1898, at New York city, to serve two years; mustered in as private, Co. B, May 20, 1898; mustered out with company, November 15, 1898, at New York city.

LAVIN, SAMUEL.—Age, 21 years. Enlisted, May 2, 1898, at New York city, to serve two years; mustered in as private, Co. M, May 17, 1898; mustered out with company, November 15, 1898, at New York city; also borne as Levin.

LAWRENCE, EDWARD.—Age, — years. Enlisted, June 24, 1898, at New York city, to serve two years; mustered in as private, Co. F, same date; mustered out with company, November 15, 1898, at New York city.

LAWRENCE, WILLIAM H.—Age, 29 years. Enlisted, May 2, 1898, at New York city, to serve two years; mustered in as private, Co. G, May 20, 1898; died of typhoid fever, October 2, 1898, in New York Hospital, New York city.

LEAHY, ARTHUR F.—Age, 26 years. Enlisted, May 2, 1898, at New York city, to serve two years; mustered in as private, Co. M, May 17, 1898; appointed cook, August 19, 1898; mustered out with company, November 15, 1898, at New York city.

LEAHY, THOMAS.—Age, 34 years. Enlisted, May 16, 1898, at New York city, to serve two years; mustered in as private, Co. H, May 20, 1898; mustered out with company, November 15, 1898, at New York city.

LEBECK, CHARLES C.—Age, 22 years. Enlisted, May 11, 1898, at New York city, to serve two years; mustered in as private, Co. L, May 20, 1898; died of disease, August 2, 1898, in Division Hospital, Camp Thomas, Chickamauga Park, Ga.

LE BOURVEAN, FRANCIS E.—Age, 24 years. Enlisted, May 2, 1898, at New York city, to serve two years; mustered in as private, Co. K, May 19, 1898; deserted, August 1, 1898, at Camp Thomas, Chickamauga Park, Ga.

LE BOURVEAN, WILLIAM A.—Age, 24 years. Enlisted, May 2, 1898, at New York city, to serve two years; mustered in as private, Co. K, May 19, 1898; deserted, August 1, 1898, at Camp Thomas, Chickamauga Park, Ga.

LEE, JAMES H.—Age, 33 years. Enrolled, May 2, 1898, at camp, near Peekskill, to serve two years; mustered in as second lieutenant, Co. G, May 24, 1898; mustered out with company, November 15, 1898, at New York city; commissioned second lieutenant, May 24, 1898, with rank from same date, original.

LEEB,.JOSEPH.—Age, 22 years. Enlisted, May 2, 1898, at New York city, to serve two years; mustered in as private, Co. I, May 19, 1898; transferred to Hospital Corps, June 16, 1898.

LEHNE, GEORGE.—Age, 21 years. Enlisted, May 2, 1898, at New York city, to serve two years; mustered in as private, Co. C, May 19, 1898; discharged, July 12, 1898.

LEIBROCK, GEORGE.—Age, 30 years. Enlisted, May 2, 1898, at New York city, to serve two years; mustered in as corporal, Co. D, May 17, 1898; mustered out with company, November 15, 1898, at New York city.

LEIKAUF, JOHN.—Age, — years. Enlisted, June 24, 1898, at New York city, to serve two years; mustered in as private, Co. B, same date; mustered out with company, November 15, 1898, at New York city.

LENSKY, HARRY.—Age, — years. Enlisted, June 27, 1898, at New York city, to serve two years; mustered in as private, Co. H, same date; discharged for disability, September 5, 1898.

LEONARD, EDWARD J.—Age, 21 years. Enlisted, May 16, 1898, at New York city, to serve two years; mustered in as private, Co. H, May 20, 1898; mustered out with company, November 15, 1898, at New York city.

LEONARD, JOHN J.—Age, 25 years. Enlisted, May 18, 1898, at New York city, to serve two years; mustered in as private, Co. H, May 20, 1898; appointed wagoner, July 16, 1898; mustered out with company, November 15, 1898, at New York city.

LEONARD, RICHARD F.—Age, 21 years. Enlisted, May 18, 1898, at New York city, to serve two years; mustered in as private, Co. H, May 20, 1898; mustered out with company, November 15, 1898, at New York city.

LEONHARDI, HERMAN C.—Age, 26 years. Enrolled, May 2, 1898, at New York city, to serve two years; mustered in as first lieutenant, Co. B, May 20, 1898; discharged, to date, July 22, 1898; commissioned first lieutenant, May 20, 1898, with rank from same date, original.

LE RAY, FRANK.—Age, — years. Enlisted, June 24, 1898, at New York city, to serve two years; mustered in as private, Co. K, same date; transferred to Hospital Corps, United States Army, September 6, 1898.

LESTER, DENNIS.—Age, — years. Enlisted, June 23, 1898, at New York city, to serve two years; mustered in as private, Co. G, same date; deserted, July 6, 1898.

LEUFFER, FRANK G.—Age, — years. Enlisted, July 6, 1898, at New York city, to serve two years; mustered in as private, Co. G, same date; mustered out with company, November 15, 1898, at New York city.

LEVIN, SAMUEL, see Samuel Lavin.

L'HOMMEDIEU, JOHN B.—Age, 32 years. Enrolled, May 4, 1898, at New York city, to serve two years; mustered in as first lieutenant and assistant surgeon, May 21, 1898; discharged, September 8, 1898; commissioned first lieutenant and assistant surgeon, May 7, 1898, with rank from same date, original.

LIEBGOLD, CHARLES.—Age, — years. Enlisted, July 1, 1898, at New York city, to serve two years; mustered in as private, Co. I, same date; mustered out with company, November 15, 1898, at New York city.

LILLEY, GEORGE.—Age, 28 years. Enlisted, May 2, 1898, at New York city, to serve two years; mustered in as private, Co. B, May 20, 1898; mustered out with company, November 15, 1898, at New York city.

LIND, JOHN E.—Age, 31 years. Enlisted, May 2, 1898, at New York city to serve two years; mustered in as private, Co. A, May 17, 1898; mustered out with company, November 15, 1898, at New York city.

LINDAUER, JOSEPH.—Age, 34 years. Enlisted, May 2, 1898, at New York city, to serve two years; mustered in as private, Co. G, May 20, 1898; mustered out with company, November 15, 1898, at New York city.

LISTNER, GEORGE A.—Age, — years. Enlisted, June 29, 1898, at New York city, to serve two years; mustered in as private, Co. G, same date; mustered out with company, November 15, 1898, at New York city.

LIVINGSTON, CHARLES.—Age, — years. Enlisted, June 27, 1898, at New York city, to serve two years; mustered in as private, Co. G, same date; mustered out with company, November 15, 1898, at New York city.

LOCKWOOD, CHARLES E.—Age, 21 years. Enlisted, May 2, 1898, at New York city, to serve two years; mustered in as private, Co. I, May 19, 1898; discharged, October 1, 1898, at New York city.

LOCKWOOD, PHILIP M.—Age, 24 years. Enlisted, May 2, 1898, at New York city, to serve two years; mustered in as private, Co. E, May 20, 1898; mustered out with company, November 15, 1898, at New York city.

LOPARD, GEORGE N.—Age, — years. Enlisted, June 27, 1898, at New York city, to serve two years; mustered in as private, Co. C, same date; mustered out with company, November 15, 1898, at New York city.

LORIGAN, GEORGE T.—Age, 53 years. Enrolled, May 2, 1898, at New York city, to serve two years; mustered in as major, May 21, 1898; discharged, July 16, 1898; prior service as private, Eighth Regiment, New York State Militia, War of Rebellion; commissioned major, May 21, 1898, with rank from same date, original.

LOUGHRAN, CHARLES E.—Age, 35 years. Enlisted, May 2, 1898, at New York city, to serve two years; mustered in as private, Co. K, May 19, 1898; mustered out with company, November 15, 1898, at New York city.

LOUGHRAN, VINCENT J.—Age, 22 years. Enlisted, May 2, 1898, at New York city, to serve two years; mustered in as private, Co. C, May 19, 1898; mustered out with company, November 15, 1898, at New York city.

LOVETT, JAMES.—Age, 19 years. Enlisted, May 2, 1898, at New York city, to serve two years; mustered in as corporal, Co. F, May 21, 1898; mustered out with company, November 15, 1898, at New York city.

LOWE, CHARLES H.—Age, 22 years. Enlisted, May 2, 1898, at New York city, to serve two years; mustered in as hospital steward, May 21, 1898; mustered out with regiment, November 15, 1898, at New York city.

LUDKE, JOHN J.—Age, — years. Enlisted, June 24, 1898, at New York city, to serve two years; mustered in as private, Co. K, same date; mustered out with company, November 15, 1898, at New York city.

LUGAR, CHARLES E.—Age, 35 years. Enlisted, May 2, 1898, at New York city, to serve two years; mustered in as private, Co. D, May 17, 1898; mustered out with company, November 15, 1898, at New York city.

LUKE, JOSEPH.—Age, — years. Enlisted, July 2, 1898, at New York city, to serve two years; mustered in as private, Co. L, same date; mustered out with company, November 15, 1898, at New York city.

LUND, HENRY P. C.—Age, 28 years. Enlisted, May 2, 1898, at New York city, to serve two years; mustered in as private, Co. K, May 19, 1898; mustered out with company, November 15, 1898, at New York city.

LUNDGREN, NELSON A.—Age, 40 years. Enlisted, May 10, 1898, at New York city, to serve two years; mustered in as sergeant, Co. M, May 17, 1898; mustered out with company, November 15, 1898, at New York city.

LUTHER, GUS.—Age, 22 years. Enlisted, May 2, 1898, at New York city, to serve two years; mustered in as private, Co. E, May 20, 1898; mustered out with company, November 15, 1898, at New York city.

LYNCH, EDWARD C.—Age, — years. Enlisted, June 24, 1898, at New York city, to serve two years; mustered in as private, Co. K, same date; mustered out with company, November 15, 1898, at New York city.

LYNCH, FRANK.—Age, 21 years. Enlisted, May 2, 1898, at New York city, to serve two years; mustered in as private, Co. G, May 20, 1898; mustered out with company, November 15, 1898, at New York city.

LYNCH, JAMES.—Age, 34 years. Enrolled, May 2, 1898, at New York city, to serve two years; mustered in as second lieutenant, Co. K, May 19, 1898; as first lieutenant, August 20, 1898; mustered out, to date, November 15, 1898; commissioned second lieutenant, May 19, 1898, with rank from same date, original; first lieutenant, August 8, 1898, with rank from same date, vice Byrne, promoted.

LYNCH, JOHN J.—Age, 24 years. Enlisted, May 2, 1898, at New York city, to serve two years; mustered in as private, Co. K, May 19, 1898; mustered out with company, November 15, 1898, at New York city.

LYNCH, JOHN J.—Age, 20 years. Enlisted, May 16, 1898, at New York city, to serve two years; mustered in as private, Co. E, May 20, 1898; mustered out with company, November 15, 1898, at New York city.

LYNCH, PETER F.—Age, 28 years. Enlisted, May 2, 1898, at New York city, to serve two years; mustered in as private, Co. D, May 17, 1898; mustered out with company, November 15, 1898, at New York city.

LYNCH, RICHARD.—Age, 18 years. Enlisted, May 2, 1898, at New York city, to serve two years; mustered in as private, Co. H, May 20, 1898; mustered out with company, November 15, 1898, at New York city.

LYNCH, THOMAS E.—Age, 22 years. Enlisted, May 2, 1898, at New York city, to serve two years; mustered in as private, Co. K, May 19, 1898; died of typhoid fever, July 10, 1898, in Second Division Hospital, Camp Thomas, Chickamauga Park, Gá.

LYNCH, THOMAS L.—Age, 21 years. Enlisted, May 2, 1898, at New York city, to serve two years; mustered in as private, Co. E, May 20, 1898; mustered out with company, November 15, 1898, at New York city.

LYNT, WILLIAM S.—Age, 22 years. Enlisted, May 2, 1898, at New York city, to serve two years; mustered in as artificer, Co. I, May 19, 1898; promoted corporal, July 27, 1898; mustered out with company, November 15, 1898, at New York city.

LYONS, JAMES.—Age, 29 years. Enlisted, May 2, 1898, at New York city, to serve two years; mustered in as private, Co. D, May 17, 1898; mustered out with company, November 15, 1898, at New York city.

MAAS, EDWARD.—Age, 22 years. Enlisted, May 2, 1898, at New York city, to serve two years; mustered in as private, Co. A, May 17, 1898; mustered out with company, November 15, 1898, at New York-city.

MACKAY, CHARLES W.—Age, — years. Enlisted, June 29, 1898, at New York city, to serve two years; mustered in as private, Co. G, same date; discharged, October 19, 1898.

MACKIN, ROBERT N.—Age, 37 years. Enrolled, May 2, 1898, at New York city, to serve two years; mustered in as first lieutenant, Co. F, May 21, 1898; discharged, August 15, 1898, at Chickamauga Park, Ga.; commissioned first lieutenant, May 21, 1898, with rank from same date, original.

MADDEN, JOHN J.—Age, 28 years. Enlisted, May 18, 1898, at New York city, to serve two years; mustered in as private, Co. A, May 20, 1898; mustered out with company, November 15, 1898, at New York city.

MAHE, JOSEPH.—Age, 23 years. Enlisted, May 2, 1898, at New York city, to serve two years; mustered in as private, Co. K, May 19, 1898; mustered out with company, November 15, 1898, at New York city.

MAHER, DENNIS.—Age, 26 years. Enlisted, May 2, 1898, at New York city, to serve two years; mustered in as private, Co. K, May 19, 1898; mustered out with company, November 15, 1898, at New York city.

MAHER, JOHN A.—Age, 37 years. Enlisted, May 2, 1898, at New York city, to serve two years; mustered in as corporal, Co. L, May 20, 1898; promoted sergeant, August 17, 1898; mustered out with company, November 15, 1898, at New York city.

MAHER, WILLIAM.—Age, 23 years. Enlisted, May 2, 1898, at New York city, to serve two years; mustered in as private, Co. I, May 19, 1898; mustered out with company, November 15, 1898, at New York city.

MAHER, WILLIAM.—Age, 23 years. Enlisted, May 2, 1898, at New York city, to serve two years; mustered in as private, Co. A, May 17, 1898; mustered out with company, November 15, 1898, at New York city.

MAHON, MICHAEL F.—Age, 35 years. Enlisted, May 2, 1898, at New York city, to serve two years; mustered in as private, Co. B, May 20, 1898; mustered out, to date, November 15, 1898.

MAHONEY, EDWARD.—Age, 22 years. Enlisted, May 2, 1898, at New York city, to serve two years; mustered in as private, Co. A, May 17, 1898; mustered out with company, November 15, 1898, at New York city.

MAHONEY, JAMES F.—Age, 23 years. Enlisted, May 2, 1898, at New York city, to serve two years; mustered in as private, Co. K, May 19, 1898; mustered out, to date, November 15, 1898.

MAHONEY, MICHAEL J.—Age, 30 years. Enrolled, May 2, 1898, at New York city, to serve two years; mustered in as second lieutenant, Co. A, May 17, 1898; as first lieutenant, July 25, 1898; died of typhoid fever, October 3, 1898, at New York city; commissioned second lieutenant, May 17, 1898, with rank from same date, original; first lieutenant, July 30, 1898, with rank from same date, vice O'Donnell, promoted.

MAILLARD, GEORGE H.—Age, 33 years. Enlisted, May 2, 1898, at New York city, to serve two years; mustered in as wagoner, Co. E, May 20, 1898; discharged, September 5, 1898, at Chickamauga Park, Ga.

MAILLE, ROBERT B.—Age, 22 years. Enlisted, May 2, 1898, at New York city, to serve two years; mustered in as musician, Co. M, May 17, 1898; mustered out with company, November 15, 1898, at New York city.

MALONE, FREDERICK.—Age, 21 years. Enlisted, May 2, 1898, at New York city, to serve years; mustered in as private, Co. D, May 17, 1898; mustered out with company, November 15, 1898, at New York city.

MALONE, JOHN.—Age, 31 years. Enlisted, May 2, 1898, at New York city, to serve two years; mustered in as quartermaster-sergeant, Co. C, May 19, 1898; returned to ranks, June 9, 1898; appointed artificer, August 18, 1898; mustered out with company, November 15, 1898, at New York city.

MALONE, JOSEPH.—Age, — years. Enlisted, July 6, 1898, at New York city, to serve two years; mustered in as private, Co. E, same date; mustered out with company, November 15, 1898, at New York city.

MALONE, THOMAS.—Age, 25 years. Enlisted, May 2, 1898, at New York city, to serve two years; mustered in as private, Co. D, May 17, 1898; discharged, October 13, 1898.

MALONEY, PATRICK T.—Age, — years. Enlisted, July 9,
1898, at New York city, to serve two years; mustered in as
private, Co. G, same date; transferred to band, July 27, 1898;
discharged, September 30, 1898.

MANING, GEORGE B.—Age, — years. Enlisted, June 29, 1898,
at New York city, to serve two years; mustered in as private,
Co. F, same date; mustered out with company, November 15,
1898, at New York city.

MANOVILL, HUGO.—Age, 20 years. Enlisted, May 2, 1898, at
camp near Peekskill, to serve two years; mustered in as private,
Co. L, May 20, 1898; promoted corporal, July 27, 1898; discharged, October 18, 1898.

MANUEL, THOMAS H.—Age, 30 years. Enlisted, May 2, 1898,
at New York city, to serve two years; mustered in as corporal,
Co. D, May 17, 1898; mustered out with company, November
15, 1898, at New York city.

MARKOVITZ, LOUIS.—Age, 24 years. Enlisted, May 2, 1898,
at New York city, to serve two years; mustered in as private,
Co. I, May 19, 1898; mustered out with company, November 15,
1898, at New York city.

MARKS, ABRAHAM.—Age, — years. Enlisted, June 29, 1898,
at New York city, to serve two years; mustered in as private,
Co. I, same date; mustered out with company, November 15,
1898, at New York city.

MARKUS, CHARLES.—Age, — years. Enlisted, June 27, 1898,
at New York city, to serve two years; mustered in as private,
Co. B, same date; mustered out with company, November 15,
1898, at New York city.

MARLOW, SAMUEL.—Age, 24 years. Enlisted, May 2, 1898, at
New York city, to serve two years; mustered in as private, Co.
K, May 19, 1898; mustered out with company, November 15,
1898, at New York city.

MARNER, MATTHEW.—Age, — years. Enlisted, July 2, 1898,
at New York city, to serve two years; mustered in as private,
Co. H, same date; mustered out with company, November 15,
1898, at New York city.

MARTIN, CHARLES A.—Age, 34 years. Enlisted, May 2, 1898, at New York city, to serve two years; mustered in as wagoner, Co. M, May 17, 1898; mustered out with company, November 15, 1898, at New York city.

MARTIN, EDWARD K.—Age, 30 years. Enlisted, May 10, 1898, at New York city, to serve two years; mustered in as private, Co. M, May 17, 1898; mustered out with company, November 15, 1898, at New York city.

MARTIN, FRANK L.—Age, 21 years. Enlisted, May 17, 1898, at New York city, to serve two years; mustered in as private, Co. F, May 21 1898; mustered out with company, November 15, 1898, at New York city.

MARTIN, FREDERICK W.—Age, 22 years. Enlisted, May 2, 1898, at New York city, to serve two years; mustered in as private, Co. E, May 20, 1898; mustered out with company, November 15, 1898, at New York city.

MARTIN, LYLE T.—Age, 23 years. Enlisted, May 2, 1898, at New York city, to serve two years; mustered in as private, Co. G, May 20, 1898; mustered out with company, November 15, 1898, at New York city.

MARTINO, GEORGE.—Age, 26 years. Enlisted, May 12, 1898, at camp near Peekskill, to serve two years; mustered in as private, Co. L, May 20, 1898; mustered out with company, November 15, 1898, at New York city.

MASON, WALTER, P.—Age, 39 years. Enlisted, May 2, 1898, at New York city, to serve two years; mustered in as private, Co. G, May 20, 1898; promoted corporal, September 16, 1898; mustered out with company, November 15, 1898, at New York city.

MATTHEY, JOSEPH J.—Age, 21 years. Enlisted, May 2, 1898, at New York city, to serve two years; mustered in as private, Co. F, May 21, 1898; promoted corporal, no date; mustered out with company, November 15, 1898, at New York city.

MATZKUHN, WILLIAM.—Age, 27 years. Enlisted, May 16, 1898, at New York city, to serve two years; mustered in as private, Co. H, May 20, 1898; promoted corporal, July 22, 1898; mustered out with company, November 15, 1898, at New York city.

MAYCRINK, LOUIS A.—Age, 36 years. Enlisted, May 22, 1898, at New York city, to serve two years; mustered in as private, Co. M, May 17, 1898; mustered out with company, November 15, 1898 at New York city.

MAYER, GEORGE.—Age, 29 years. Enlisted, May 18, 1898, at New York city, to serve two years; mustered in as private, Co. H, May 20, 1898; mustered out with company, November 15, 1898, at New York city.

MAYER, GEORGE.—Age, 22 years. Enlisted, May 2, 1898, at New York city, to serve two years; mustered in as private, Co. C, May 19, 1898; mustered out with company, November 15, 1898, at New York city.

MAYFIELD, JOSEPH.—Age, 29 years. Enlisted, May 2, 1898, at New York city, to serve two years; mustered in as corporal, Co. L, May 20, 1898; mustered out with company, November 15, 1898, at New York city.

MAZZIN, ANTHONY.—Age, — years. Enlisted, June 24, 1898, at New York city, to serve two years; mustered in as private, Co. B, same date; mustered out with company, November 15, 1898, at New York city.

McBENNETT, JAMES.—Age, 21 years. Enlisted, May 2, 1898, at New York city, to serve two years; mustered in as private, Co. E, May 20, 1898; mustered out with company, November 15, 1898, at New York city.

McCAFFERY, TERENCE.—Age, 27 years. Enlisted, May 2, 1898, at New York city, to serve two years; mustered in as private, Co. K, May 19, 1898; mustered out with company, November 15, 1898, at New York city.

McCANN, WILLIAM F.—Age, 21 years. Enlisted, May 18, 1898, at New York city, to serve two years; mustered in as private, Co. H, May 20, 1898; mustered out with company, November 15, 1898, at New York city.

McCARTHY, GEORGE.—Age, 23 years. Enlisted, May 2, 1898, at New York city, to serve two years; mustered in as private, Co. C, May 19, 1898; mustered out with company, November 15, 1898, at New York city.

McCARTHY, JOHN J.—Age, 24 years. Enlisted, May 2, 1898, at New York city, to serve two years; mustered in as private, Co. I, May 19, 1898; promoted corporal, July 27, 1898; mustered out with company, November 15, 1898, at New York city.

McCARTHY, TIMOTHY.—Age, 25 years. Enlisted, May 2, 1898, at New York city, to serve two years; mustered in as private, Co. M, May 17, 1898; mustered out with company, November 15, 1898, at New York city.

McCLANE, JOHN E.—Age, 32 years. Enlisted, May 2, 1898, at New York city, to serve two years; mustered in as private, Co. F, May 21, 1898; mustered out with company, November 15, 1898, at New York city.

McCLERNAN, JOHN.—Age, 25 years. Enlisted, May 2, 1898, at New York city, to serve two years; mustered in as private, Co. B, May 20, 1898; mustered out with company, November 15, 1898, at New York city.

McCOPPIN, CHARLES.—Age, — years. Enlisted, June 25, 1898, at New York city, to serve two years; mustered in as private, Co. E, same date; mustered out with company, November 15, 1898, at New York city.

McCOURT, ROBERT J.—Age, — years. Enlisted, July 9, 1898, at New York city, to serve two years; mustered in as private, Co. C, same date; transferred to band, July 27, 1898; discharged for disability, October 17, 1898, at New York city.

McCRANN, FRANCIS J.—Age, — years. Enlisted, June 27, 1898, at New York city, to serve two years; mustered in as private, Co. C, same date; mustered out with company, November 15, 1898, at New York city.

McCULLOUGH, EDWARD P.—Age, 32 years. Enlisted, May 2, 1898, at New York city, to serve two years; mustered in as wagoner, Co. L, May 20, 1898; returned to ranks, no date; discharged for disability, August 12, 1898, at Camp Thomas, Chickamanga Park, Ga.

McCULLOUGH, JOHN J.—Age, 24 years. Enlisted, May 2, 1898, at New York city, to serve two years; mustered in as private, Co. F, May 21, 1898; mustered out with company, November 15, 1898, at New York city.

McDERMOTT, ALBERT C.—Age, 28 years. Enlisted, May 2, 1898, at New York city, to serve two years; mustered in as private, Co. D, May 17, 1898; promoted corporal, July 27, 1898; discharged, October 13, 1898.

McDONALD, JOHN.—Age, 22 years. Enlisted, May 2, 1898, at New York city, to serve two years; mustered in as private, Co. E, May 20, 1898; mustered out with company, November 15, 1898, at New York city.

McDONALD, MICHAEL J.—Age, — years. Enlisted, July 6, 1898, at New York city, to serve two years; mustered in as private, Co. A, same date; mustered out with company, November 15, 1898, at New York city.

McDONALD, WILLIAM.—Age, 26 years. Enlisted, May 2, 1898, at New York city, to serve two years; mustered in as private, Co. F, May 21, 1898; mustered out with company, November 15, 1898, at New York city.

McDONNELL, PATRICK.—Age, — years. Enlisted, July 2, 1898, at New York city, to serve two years; mustered in as private, Co. C, same date; mustered out with company, November 15, 1898, at New York city.

McDOUGALL, ADDISON.—Age, 42 years. Enrolled, May 22, 1898, at camp near Peekskill, to serve two years; mustered in as first lieutenant, Co. E, May 22, 1898; mustered out with company, November 15, 1898, at New York city; commissioned first lieutenant, May 21, 1898, with rank from same date, original.

McDOUGALL, HARRY W.—Age, 31 years. Enlisted, May 2, 1898, at New York city, to serve two years; mustered in as corporal, Co. E, May 20, 1898; mustered out with company, November 15, 1898, at New York city.

McDOWELL, SAMUEL.—Age, 21 years. Enlisted, May 2, 1898, at New York city, to serve two years; mustered in as private, Co. C, May 19, 1898; promoted corporal, July 28, 1898; mustered out with company, November 15, 1898, at New York city.

McEVOY, WALTER R.—Age, 21 years. Enlisted, May 2, 1898, at New York city, to serve two years; mustered in as private, Co. F, May 21, 1898; mustered out with company, November 15, 1898, at New York city.

McFARLAND, JAMES.—Age, 27 years. Enlisted, May 2, 1898, at New York city, to serve two years; mustered in as private, Co. M, May 17, 1898; mustered out with company, November 15, 1898, at New York city.

McGARRY, PATRICK A.—Age, 21 years. Enlisted, May 2, 1898, at New York city, to serve two years; mustered in as private, Co. D, May 17, 1898; mustered out with company, November 15, 1898, at New York city.

McGEE, WILLIAM.—Age, 21 years. Enlisted, May 2, 1898, at New York city, to serve two years; mustered in as private, Co. L, May 20, 1898; mustered out with company, November 15, 1898, at New York city.

McGILL, JR., JAMES.—Age, 26 years. Enlisted, May 2, 1898, at New York city, to serve two years; mustered in as private, Co. K, May 19, 1898; mustered out with company, November 15, 1898, at New York city.

McGOWAN, OWEN.—Age, 21 years. Enlisted, May 2, 1898, at New York city, to serve two years; mustered in as private, Co. G, May 21, 1898; mustered out with company, November 15, 1898, at New York city.

McGUFFIE, JAMES.—Age, 21 years. Enlisted, May 2, 1898, at New York city, to serve two years; mustered in as private, Co. C, May 19, 1898; mustered out with company, November 15, 1898, at New York city.

McGUIRE, HENRY.—Age, — years. Enlisted, June 25, 1898, at New York city, to serve two years; mustered in as private, Co. H, same date; mustered out with company, November 15, 1898, at New York city.

McILRAVY, SAMUEL.—Age, 37 years. Enlisted, May 2, 1898, at New York city, to serve two years; mustered in as private, Co. C, May 19, 1898; mustered out with company, November 15, 1898, at New York city.

McILVENNY, HUGH.—Age, 23 years. Enlisted, May 2, 1898, at New York city, to serve two years; mustered in as private, Co. I, May 19, 1898; mustered out with company, November 15, 1898, at New York city.

McINIRNEY, JAMES.—Age, — years. Enlisted, July 1, 1898, at New York city, to serve two years; mustered in as private, Co. H, same date; mustered out with company, November 15, 1898, at New York city.

McKENNA, JAMES.—Age, 28 years. Enlisted, May 2, 1898, at New York city, to serve two years; mustered in as private, Co. I, May 19, 1898; mustered out with company, November 15, 1898, at New York city.

McKENNA, JOSEPH D.—Age, 21 years. Enlisted, May 2, 1898, at New York city, to serve two years; mustered in as private, Co. L, May 20, 1898; mustered out with company, November 15, 1898, at New York city.

McKENNA, PATRICK.—Age, 34 years. Enlisted, May 2, 1898, at New York city, to serve two years; mustered in as private, Co. B, May 20, 1898; mustered out with company, November 15, 1898, at New York city.

McKENNA, PETER.—Age, 26 years. Enlisted, May 2, 1898, at New York city, to serve two years; mustered in as private, Co. L, May 20, 1898; promoted corporal, August 17, 1898; mustered out with company, November 15, 1898, at New York city.

McKENSEY, ARTHUR.—Age, 27 years. Enlisted, May 17, 1898, at New York city, to serve two years; mustered in as private, Co. E, May 20, 1898; mustered out with company, November 15, 1898, at New York city.

McKEON, THOMAS.—Age, 18 years. Enlisted, May 2, 1898, at New York city, to serve two years; mustered in as private, Co. L, May 20, 1898; mustered out with company, November 15, 1898, at New York city.

McLACHLAN, WILLIAM H.—Age, 23 years. Enlisted, May 2, 1898, at New York city, to serve two years; mustered in as corporal, Co. G, May 20, 1898; mustered out with company, November 15, 1898, at New York city.

McLEAN, JOHN A.—Age, 27 years. Enlisted, May 2, 1898, at New York city, to serve two years; mustered in as private, Co. G, May 20, 1898; mustered out with company, November 15, 1898, at New York city.

McLEAN, NORMAN.—Age, 26 years. Enlisted, May 2, 1898, at New York city, to serve two years; mustered in as private, Co. G, May 20, 1898; mustered out with company, November 15, 1898, at New York city.

McLELLAN, NIEL R.—Age, 24 years. Enlisted, May 2, 1898, at New York city, to serve two years; mustered in as private, Co. K, May 19, 1898; mustered out with company, November 15, 1898, at New York city.

McMAHON, JUNE.—Age, 26 years. Enlisted, May 2, 1898, at New York city, to serve two years; mustered in as private, Co. M, May 17, 1898; mustered out with company, November 15, 1898, at New York city.

McMANUS, BERNARD.—Age, 25 years. Enlisted, May 2, 1898, at New York city, to serve two years; mustered in as private, Co. C, May 19, 1898; promoted corporal, September 2, 1898; mustered out with company, November 15, 1898, at New York city.

McMANUS, DAVID.—Age, — years. Enlisted, June 27, 1898, at New York city, to serve two years; mustered in as private, Co. B, same date; mustered out with company, November 15, 1898, at New York city.

McMANUS, HUGH.—Age, — years. Enlisted, July 6, 1898, at New York city, to serve two years; mustered in as private, Co. M, same date; mustered out with company, November 15, 1898, at New York city.

McMANUS, JOHN J.—Age, 33 years. Enlisted, May 2, 1898, at New York city, to serve two years; mustered in as corporal, Co. L, May 20, 1898; mustered out with company, November 15, 1898, at New York city.

McMONIGLE, WILLIAM D.—Age, — years. Enlisted, May 2, 1898, at New York city, to serve two years; mustered in as sergeant, Co. F, May 21, 1898; promoted first sergeant, August 4, 1898; mustered out with company, November 15, 1898, at New York city.

McNALLY, BERNARD.—Age, 23 years. Enlisted, May 2, 1898, at New York city, to serve two years; mustered in as private, Co. A, May 17, 1898; mustered out with company, November 15, 1898, at New York city.

McNALLY, JOHN F.—Age, 24 years. Enlisted, May 2, 1898, at
New York city, to serve two years; mustered in as private,
Co. L, May 20, 1898; deserted, July 20, 1898.

McNAUGHTON, DAVID.—Age, — years. Enlisted, July 5, 1898,
at New York city, to serve two years; mustered in as private,
Co. F, same date; mustered out with company, November 15,
1898, at New York city.

McNIECE, THOMAS.—Age, — years. Enlisted, June 23, 1898,
at New York city, to serve two years; mustered in as private,
Co. K, same date; mustered out with company, November 15,
1898, at New York city.

McNIEL, HENRY E.—Age, 35 years. Enlisted, May 2, 1898, at
New York city, to serve two years; mustered in as private,
Co. I, May 19, 1898; mustered out with company, November
15, 1898, at New York city.

McNULTY, JOHN.—Age, — years. Enlisted, July 7, 1898, at
New York city, to serve two years; mustered in as private, Co.
D, same date; mustered out with company, November 15, 1898,
at New York city.

McQUADE, RALPH J.—Age, 21 years. Enlisted, May 2, 1898,
at New York city to serve two years; mustered in as private,
Co. L, May 20, 1898; mustered out with company, November 15,
1898, at New York city.

MEAD, EDWARD H.—Age, 25 years. Enlisted, May 2, 1898, at
New York city, to serve two years; mustered in as private, Co.
I, May 19, 1898; mustered out with company, November 15,
1898, at New York city.

MEEKIN, WILLIAM.—Age, — years. Enlisted, June 30, 1898,
at New York city, to serve two years; mustered in as private,
Co. C, same date; mustered out with company, November 15,
1898, at New York city.

MEIER, CHARLES A.—Age, 22 years. Enlisted, May 2, 1898,
at New York city, to serve two years; mustered in as private,
Co. C, May 19, 1898; mustered out with company, November 15,
1898, at New York city.

MELIA, WILLIAM.—Age, — years. Enlisted, June 25, 1898, at New York city, to serve two years; mustered in as private, Co. E, same date; mustered out with company, November 15, 1898, at New York city.

MELLICK, SAMUEL D.—Age, — years. Enlisted, July 1, 1898, at New York city, to serve two years; mustered in as private, Co. M, same date; mustered out with company, 'November 15, 1898, at New York city.

MENABER, OTTO F.—Age, — years. Enlisted, June 27, 1898, at New York city, to serve two years; mustered in as private, Co. B, same date; mustered out with company, November 15, 1898, at New York city.

MENDEL, ALBERT L.—Age, 21 years. Enlisted, May 2, 1898, at New York city, to serve two years; mustered in as corporal, Co. B, May 20, 1898; returned to ranks, October 22, 1898; mustered out with company, November 15, 1898, at New York city.

MENNECKE, HERMAN.—Age, 27 years. Enlisted, May 2, 1898, at New York city, to serve two years; mustered in as private, Co. B, May 20, 1898; mustered out with company, November 15, 1898, at New York city.

MERRICK, CHARLES M.—Age, 25 years. Enlisted, May 2, 1898, at New York city, to serve two years; mustered in as private, Co. M, May 17, 1898; died of dysentry, August 26, 1898, at New York city.

METAHL, NETEN.—Age, 31 years. Enlisted, May 2, 1898, at New York city, to serve two years; mustered in as private, Co. K, May 19, 1898; discharged, October 1, 1898.

METZ, EDWARD W.—Age, 21 years. Enlisted, May 2, 1898, at New York city, to serve two years; mustered in as private, Co. M, May 17, 1898; died of typhoid fever, September 4, 1898, in Second Division Hospital, Camp Thomas, Chickamauga Park, Ga.

METZE, ALBERT.—Age, — years. Enlisted, June 25, 1898, at New York city, to serve two years; mustered in as private, Co. E, same date; mustered out with company, November 15, 1898, at New York city.

MEYER, JR., CHARLES A.—Age, 33 years. Enrolled, May 2,
1898, at New York city, as first sergeant, to serve two years;
mustered in as first lieutenant, Co. I, May 19, 1898; transferred
to Co. B, July 27, 1898; mustered in as captain, Co. D, July 30,
1898; mustered out, to date, November 15, 1898, at New York
city; commissioned first lieutenant, May 19, 1898, with rank
from same date, original; captain, July 30, 1898, with rank from
same date, vice Walton, discharged.

MEYER, FREDERICK.—Age, 21 years. Enlisted, May 2, 1898,
at New York city, to serve two years; mustered in as private,
Co. C, May 19, 1898; mustered out with company, November 15,
1898, at New York city.

MEYER, EDWARD.—Age, 22 years. Enlisted, May 2, 1898, at
New York city, to serve two years; mustered in as private, Co.
D, May 17, 1898; mustered out with company, November 15,
1898, at New York city.

MEYER, HENRY M.—Age, 21 years. Enlisted, May 2, 1898, at
New York city, to serve two years; mustered in as private, Co.
I, May 19, 1898; mustered out with company, November 15,
1898, at New York city.

MEYER, LOUIS.—Age, — years. Enlisted, July 9, 1898, at New
York city, to serve two years; mustered in as private, Co. H,
same date; transferred to band. July 27, 1898; mustered out
with regiment, November 15, 1898, at New York city.

MEYER, RICHARD A.—Age, 22 years. Enlisted, May 16, 1898,
at New York city, to serve two years; mustered in as private,
Co. H, May 20, 1898; mustered out with company, November 15,
1898, at New York city.

MEYER, SIMON J.—Age, 21 years. Enlisted, May 2, 1898, at
New York city, to serve two years; mustered in as private, Co.
E, May 20, 1898; mustered out with company, November 15,
1898, at New York city.

MICHAEL, CHARLES F.—Age, 28 years. Enlisted, May 2, 1898,
at New York city, to serve two years; mustered in as private,
Co. K, May 19, 1898; mustered out with company, November 15,
1898, at New York city.

MICHAELS, FREDERICK A.—Age, 21 years. Enlisted, May 2, 1898, at New York city, to serve two years; mustered in as wagoner, Co. G, May 20, 1898; returned to ranks, June 27, 1898; mustered out with company, November 15, 1898, at New York city.

MIDDLETON, JOHN.—Age, — years. Enlisted, June 23, 1898, at New York city, to serve two years; mustered in as private, Co. G, same date; mustered out with company, November 15, 1898, at New York city.

MILGEN, EDWARD.—Age, — years. Enlisted, June 24, 1898, at New York city, to serve two years; mustered in as private, Co. D, same date; discharged, October 13, 1898.

MILLER, ALBERT.—Age, 29 years. Enlisted, May 2, 1898, at New York city, to serve two years; mustered in as private, Co. D, May 17, 1898; discharged, October 3, 1898.

MILLER, DAVID H.—Age, 23 years. Enrolled, May 2, 1898, at New York city, to serve two years; mustered in as second lieutenant, Co. E, May 21, 1898; as first lieutenant, Co. G, July 22, 1898; mustered out with company, November 15, 1898, at New York city; commissioned second lieutenant, May 21, 1898, with rank from same date, original; first lieutenant, July 30, 1898, with rank from same date, vice Meyer, Jr., promoted.

MIRABELLA, CARMINA.—Age, 24 years. Enlisted, May 2, 1898, at New York city, to serve two years; mustered in as private, Co. C, May 19, 1898; promoted corporal, June 16, 1898; returned to ranks, July 10, 1898; mustered out with company, November 15, 1898, at New York city.

MIXON, LESLIE S.—Age, 24 years. Enlisted, May 2, 1898, at New York city, to serve two years; mustered in as private, Co. L, May 20, 1898; promoted corporal, August 17, 1898; mustered out with company, November 15, 1898, at New York city.

MOE, ANTON C.—Age, 27 years. Enlisted, May 2, 1898, at New York city, to serve two years; mustered in as corporal, Co. D, May 17, 1898; mustered out with company, November 15, 1898, at New York city.

MOFFET, JOHN.—Age, — years. Enlisted, July 7, 1898, at New York city, to serve two years; mustered in as private, Co. I, same date; mustered out with company, November 15, 1898, at New York city.

MOLE, ARTHUR.—Age, 24 years. Enlisted, May 2, 1898, at New York city, to serve two years; mustered in as private, Co. F, May 21, 1898; promoted corporal, no date; mustered out with company, November 15, 1898, at New York city.

MOLKENBUR, HENRY.—Age, — years. Enlisted, July 1, 1898, at New York city, to serve two years; mustered in as private, Co. I, same date; mustered out with company, November 15, 1898, at New York city.

MOLLOY, PATRICK.—Age, 33 years. Enlisted, May 2, 1898, at New York city, to serve two years; mustered in as private, Co. E, May 20, 1898; mustered out with company, November 15, 1898, at New York city.

MONROE, EDWARD W.—Age, 29 years. Enlisted, May 2, 1898, at New York city, to serve two years; mustered in as sergeant, Co. L, May 20, 1898; promoted first sergeant, September 16, 1898; mustered out with company, November 15, 1898, at New York city.

MONTANI, VIRGIL.—Age, 20 years. Enlisted, May 2, 1898, at New York city, to serve two years; mustered in as private, Co. L, May 20, 1898; mustered out with company, November 15, 1898, at New York city.

MOORE, FRANK.—Age, 25 years. Enlisted, May 2, 1898, at New York city, to serve two years; mustered in as private, Co. L, May 20, 1898; promoted corporal, August 17, 1898; died of typhoid fever, September 4, 1898, at Division Hospital, Camp Thomas, Chickamauga Park, Ga.

MOORE, THOMAS W.—Age, 24 years. Enlisted, May 2, 1898, at New York city, to serve two years; mustered in as private, Co. F, May 21, 1898; appointed artificer, no date; mustered out with company, November 15, 1898, at New York city.

MOORE, WARREN J.—Age, 22 years. Enlisted, May 2, 1898, at New York city, to serve two years; mustered in as private, Co. K, May 19, 1898; died of typhoid fever, August 29, 1898, at Sternberg Hospital, Camp Thomas, Chickamauga Park, Ga.

MORAN, DENIS J.—Age, — years. Enlisted, July 8, 1898, at New York city, to serve two years; mustered in as private, Co. I, same date; transferred to Co. K, July 27, 1898; to band, same date; discharged, November 1, 1898, at New York city, to enlist in regular army.

MORAN, DENNIS.—Age, — years. Enlisted, July 6, 1898, at New York city, to serve two years; mustered in as private, Co. B, same date; mustered out with company, November 15, 1898, at New York city.

MORGAN, JAMES.—Age, 27 years. Enlisted, May 2, 1898, at New York city, to serve two years; mustered in as private, Co. D, May 17, 1898; mustered out with company, November 15, 1898, at New York city.

MORGAN, ROBERT F.—Age, 21 years. Enlisted, May 2, 1898, at New York city, to serve two years; mustered in as corporal, Co. M, May 17, 1898; promoted sergeant, August 5, 1898; mustered out with company, November 15, 1898, at New York city.

MORK, EUGENE.—Age, 22 years. Enlisted, May 2, 1898, at New York city, to serve two years; mustered in as private, Co. M, May 17, 1898; mustered out with company, November 15, 1898, at New York city.

MORRIS, EDWARD C.—Age, 21 years. Enlisted, May 2, 1898, at New York city, to serve two years; mustered in as private, Co. H, May 20, 1898; mustered out with company, November 15, 1898, at New York city.

MORRIS, JOHN F.—Age, 21 years. Enlisted, May 2, 1898, at New York city, to serve two years; mustered in as private, Co. K, May 19, 1898; mustered out with company, November 15, 1898, at New York city.

MORRIS, WILLIAM F.—Age, 44 years. Enrolled, May 2, 1898, at New York city, to serve two years; mustered in as captain, Co. K, May 19, 1898; discharged, August 3, 1898; commissioned captain, May 20, 1898, with rank from same date, original.

MORRIS, WILLIAM F.—Age, 27 years. Enlisted, May 2, 1898, at New York city, to serve two years; mustered in as private, Co. M, May 17, 1898; mustered out with company, November 15, 1898, at New York city.

MORRISON, JAMES F.—Age, 25 years. Enlisted, May 2, 1898, at New York city, to serve two years; mustered in as private, Co. D, May 17, 1898; discharged, October 6, 1898.

MORRISSON, PAUL F.—Age, 21 years. Enlisted, May 2, 1898, at New York city, to serve two years; mustered in as private, Co. M, May 17, 1898; mustered out with company, November 15, 1898, at New York city.

MOSS, THOMAS E.—Age, 21 years. Enlisted, May 2, 1898, at New York city, to serve two years; mustered in as private, Co. K, May 19, 1898; mustered out with company, November 15, 1898, at New York city.

MOST, PETER.—Age, 23 years. Enlisted, May 2, 1898, at New York city, to serve two years; mustered in as private, Co. G, May 20, 1898; mustered out with company, November 15, 1898, at New York city.

MUEGER, JOHN.—Age, 20 years. Enlisted, May 2, 1898, at New York city, to serve two years; mustered in as private, Co. A, May 17, 1898; mustered out with company, November 15, 1898, at New York city.

MUIR, WALTER S.—Age, 21 years. Enlisted, May 2, 1898, at New York city, to serve two years; mustered in as private, Co. M, May 17, 1898; mustered out with company, November 15, 1898, at New York city.

MULCAHY, MAURICE.—Age, 30 years. Enlisted, May 2, 1898, at New York city, to serve two years; mustered in as private, Co. K, May 19, 1898; promoted corporal, July 27, 1898; mustered out with company, November 15, 1898, at New York city.

MULHOLLAND, DENNIS J.—Age, 21 years. Enlisted, May 2, 1898, at New York city, to serve two years; mustered in as sergeant, Co. L, May 20, 1898; returned to ranks, August 9, 1898; promoted corporal, September 10, 1898; mustered out with company, November 15, 1898, at New York city.

MULLALY, JOHN J.—Age, 26 years. Enlisted, May 17, 1898, at New York city, to serve two years; mustered in as private, Co. E, May 20, 1898; mustered out with company, November 15, 1898, at New York city.

MULLEN, JOHN C.—Age, — years. Enlisted, June 29, 1898, at New York city, to serve two years; mustered in as private, Co. F, same date; mustered out with company, November 15, 1898, at New York city.

MULLER, CHARLES.—Age, 26 years. Enlisted, May 2, 1898, at New York city, to serve two years; mustered in as private, Co. B, May 20, 1898; promoted corporal, July 27, 1898; mustered out with company, November 15, 1898, at New York city.

MULLER, HENRY.—Age, 24 years. Enlisted, May 2, 1898, at New York city, to serve two years; mustered in as private, Co. L, May 20, 1898; mustered out with company, November 15, 1898, at New York city.

MULLER, JAMES.—Age, — years. Enlisted, June 29, 1898, at New York city, to serve two years; mustered in as private, Co. B, same date; mustered out with company, November 15, 1898, at New York city.

MULLIGAN, PETER V.—Age, 18 years. Enlisted, May 2, 1898, at New York city, to serve two years; mustered in as private, Co. E, May 20, 1898; mustered out with company, November 15, 1898, at New York city.

MULVIHILL, THOMAS J.—Age, 28 years. Enlisted, May 2, 1898, at New York city, to serve two years; mustered in as artificer, Co. A, May 17, 1898; mustered out with company, November 15, 1898, at New York city.

MUNOZ, SIMON M.—Age, — years. Enlisted, July 8, 1898, at New York city, to serve two years; mustered in as private, Co. E, same date; discharged for disability, August 24, 1898, at Chickamauga Park, Ga.

MUNSON, WYNNE P.—Age, 33 years. Enlisted, May 2, 1898, at New York city, to serve two years; mustered in as private, Co. F, May 21, 1898; promoted corporal, July 27, 1898; returned to ranks, August 16, 1898; mustered out with company, November 15, 1898, at New York city.

MURPHY, DENNIS.—Age, — years. Enlisted, June 24, 1898, at New York city, to serve two years; mustered in as private, Co. E, same date; transferred to Co. F, July 28, 1898; mustered out with company, November 15, 1898, at New York city.

MURPHY, THOMAS.—Age, — years.   Enlisted, June 29, 1898, at New York city, to serve two years; mustered in as private, Co. D, same date; discharged, October 11, 1898.

MURRAY, JAMES.—Age, 23 years.   Enlisted, May 2, 1898, at New York city, to serve two years; mustered in as private, Co. E, May 20, 1898; transferred to Troop H, Sixth United States Cavalry, July 19, 1898.

MURTHA, JOSEPH H.—Age, 23 years.   Enlisted, May 2, 1898, at New York city, to serve two years; mustered in as corporal, Co. I, May 19, 1898; returned to ranks, July 21, 1898; mustered out with company, November 15, 1898, at New York city.

MYERS, WILLIAM B.—Age, 23 years.   Enlisted, May 2, 1898, at New York city, to serve two years; mustered in as private, Co. F, May 21, 1898; promoted corporal, no date; mustered out with company, November 15, 1898, at New York city.

NASH, FRANK.—Age, 34 years.   Enlisted, May 2, 1898, at New York city, to serve two years; mustered in as private, Co. F, May 21, 1898; mustered out with company, November 15, 1898, at New York city.

NATHAN, EDWARD.—Age, — years.   Enlisted, June 23, 1898, at New York city, to serve two years; mustered in as private, Co. G, same date; discharged, October 15, 1898.

NAUHEIMER, JOHN.—Age, 22 years.   Enlisted, May 2, 1898, at New York city, to serve two years; mustered in as private, Co. A, May 17, 1898; died of typhoid fever, August 29, 1898, at Camp Thomas, Chickamauga Park, Ga.

NELLE, ROBERT E.—Age, 21 years.   Enlisted, May 2, 1898, at New York city, to serve two years; mustered in as private, Co. F, May 21, 1898; died of disease, October 17, 1898, at Lebanon Hospital, New York city.

NELSON, JAMES E.—Age, 35 years.   Enlisted, May 2, 1898, at New York city, to serve two years; mustered in as private, Co. E, May 20, 1898; mustered out with company, November 15, 1898, at New York city.

NEMETZ, FRANK.—Age, 25 years. Enlisted, May 11, 1898, at camp, near Peekskill, to serve two years; mustered in as private, Co. L, May 20, 1898; discharged, October 18, 1898.

NEUFELD, CHARLES.—Age, — years. Enlisted, June 29, 1898, at New York city, to serve two years; mustered in as private, Co. G, same date; discharged, October 15, 1898.

NEUMAN, MAX.—Age, — years. Enlisted, June 24, 1898, at New York city, to serve two years; mustered in as private, Co. C, same date; mustered out with company, November 15, 1898, at New York city.

NEWMILLER, WILLIAM.—Age, — years. Enlisted, July 6, 1898, at New York city, to serve two years; mustered in as private, Co. A, same date; mustered out with company, November 15, 1898, at New York city.

NICHOLS, ROWLAND S.—Age, — years. Enrolled, May 24, 1898, at Camp Thomas, Ga., to serve two years; mustered in as chaplain, June 3, 1898; mustered out with regiment, November 15, 1898, at New York city; subsequent service as chaplain, United States Army; commissioned chaplain, May 23, 1898, with rank from same date, original.

NICHOLSON, GEORGE.—Age, — years. Enlisted, June 29, 1898, at New York city, to serve two years; mustered in as private, Co. K, same date; mustered out with company, November 15, 1898, at New York city.

NIGRO, LEON.—Age, 18 years. Enlisted, May 2, 1898, at New York city, to serve two years; mustered in as private, Co. G, May 20, 1898; mustered out with company, November 15, 1898, at New York city.

NILL, J. ALBERT.—Age, 18 years. Enlisted, May 2, 1898, at New York city, to serve two years; mustered in as private, Co. F, May 21, 1898; mustered out with company, November 15, 1898, at New York city.

NOBLE, HARRY L.—Age, 22 years. Enlisted, May 2, 1898, at New York city, to serve two years; mustered in as private, Co. F, May 21, 1898; mustered out with company, November 15, 1898, at New York city.

NOBLE, JOHN.—Age, 34 years. Enlisted, May 2, 1898, at New York city, to serve two years; mustered in as private, Co. L, May 20, 1898; mustered out with company, November 15, 1898, at New York city.

NOBLE, WILLIAM A.—Age, 21 years. Enlisted, May 2, 1898, at New York city, to serve two years; mustered in as private, Co. F, May 21, 1898; promoted sergeant, September 5, 1898; mustered out with company, November 15, 1898, at New York city.

NOLAN, PATRICK.—Age, — years. Enlisted, July 9, 1898, at New York city, to serve two years; mustered in as private, Co. D, same date; transferred to band, July 27, 1898; mustered out with regiment, November 15, 1898, at New York city.

NOLAN, THOMAS F.—Age, 25 years. Enlisted, May 2, 1898, at New York city, to serve two years; mustered in as sergeant, Co. C, May 19, 1898; mustered out with company, November 15, 1898, at New York city.

NORMAN, EDWARD C.—Age, 23 years. Enlisted, May 2, 1898, at New York city, to serve two years; mustered in as corporal, Co. D, May 17, 1898; mustered out with company, November 15, 1898, at New York city.

NORTHRUP, WILLIAM G.—Age, 24 years. Enlisted, May 2, 1898, at New York city, to serve two years; mustered in as private, Co. G, May 20, 1898; mustered out with company, November 15, 1898, at New York city.

NORTON, WILLIAM T.—Age, 24 years. Enlisted, May 2, 1898, at New York city, to serve two years; mustered in as sergeant, Co. K, May 19, 1898; mustered out with company, November 15, 1898, at New York city.

NOVOTNY, JOSEPH.—Age, 24 years. Enlisted, May 2, 1898, at New York city, to serve two years; mustered in as private, Co. I, May 19, 1898; promoted corporal, August 25, 1898; mustered out with company, November 15, 1898, at New York city.

NUGENT, ANTHONY F.—Age, 21 years. Enlisted, May 2, 1898, at New York city, to serve two years; mustered in as private, Co. G, May 20, 1898; mustered out with company, November 15, 1898, at New York city.

NUNNS, CLARENCE C.—Age, 32 years. Enlisted, May 2, 1898, at New York city, to serve two years; mustered in as private, Co. A, May 17, 1898; transferred to Second Division Hospital Corps, June 16, 1898, at Chickamauga Park, Ga.

OAKES, JOHN D.—Age, — years. Enlisted, July 6, 1898, at New York city, to serve two years; mustered in as private, Co. A, same date; mustered out with company, November 15, 1898, at New York city.

O'BRIEN, EDWARD W.—Age, 28 years. Enlisted, May 2, 1898, at New York city, to serve two years; mustered in as private, Co. A, May 17, 1898; promoted sergeant, October 27, 1898; mustered out with company, November 15, 1898, at New York city.

O'BRIEN, GEORGE F.—Age, 22 years. Enlisted, May 2, 1898, at New York city, to serve two years; mustered in as private, Co. D, May 17, 1898; mustered out with company, November 15, 1898, at New York city.

O'BRIEN, PATRICK J.—Age, 30 years. Enlisted, May 2, 1898, at New York city, to serve two years; mustered in as private, Co. B, May 20, 1898; mustered out with company, November 15, 1898, at New York city.

O'BRIEN, PATRICK J.—Age, 25 years. Enlisted, May 2, 1898, at New York city, to serve two years; mustered in as private, Co. A, May 17, 1898; mustered out with company, November 15, 1898, at New York city.

O'BRIEN, THOMAS J.—Age, — years. Enlisted, July 6, 1898, at New York city, to serve two years; mustered in as private, Co. C, same date; mustered out with company, November 15, 1898, at New York city.

O'CONNELL, CHARLES D.—Age, 21 years. Enlisted, May 2, 1898, at New York city, to serve two years; mustered in as private, Co. A, May 17, 1898; mustered out with company, November 15, 1898, at New York city.

O'CONNELL, EDWARD.—Age, — years. Enlisted, July 1, 1898, at New York city, to serve two years; mustered in as private, Co. C, same date; mustered out with company, November 15, 1898, at New York city.

O'CONNOR, EDWARD F.—Age, — years. Enlisted, July 5, 1898, at New York city, to serve two years; mustered in as private, Co. A, same date; mustered out with company, November 15, 1898, at New York city.

O'CONNOR, JAMES.—Age, — years. Enlisted, July 5, 1898, at New York city, to serve two years; mustered in as private, Co. F, same date; mustered out with company, November 15, 1898, at New York city.

O'CONNOR, MICHAEL J.—Age, 26 years. Enlisted, May 2, 1898, at New York city, to serve two years; mustered in as private, Co. D, May 17, 1898; mustered out with company, November 15, 1898, at New York city.

O'CONNOR, SAMUEL S.—Age, 35 years. Enrolled, May 2, 1898, at New York city, to serve two years; mustered in as captain, Co. A, May 17, 1898; mustered out with company, November 15, 1898, at New York city; subsequent service as captain, Forty-sixth Regiment, United States Volunteer Infantry; commissioned captain, May 17, 1898, with rank from same date, original.

O'DELL, JAMES.—Age, 21 years. Enlisted, May 2, 1898, at New York city, to serve two years; mustered in as corporal, Co. C, May 19, 1898; promoted sergeant, June 6, 1898; discharged, October 18, 1898.

ODELL, RICHARD.—Age, 19 years. Enlisted, May 2, 1898, at New York city, to serve two years; mustered in as private, Co. I, May 19, 1898; mustered out with company, November 15, 1898, at New York city.

ODELL, ROBERT S.—Age, 24 years. Enlisted, May 2, 1898, at New York city, to serve two years; mustered in as private, Co. G, May 20, 1898; mustered out with company, November 15, 1898, at New York city.

O'DONNELL, JAMES M.—Age, 35 years. Enrolled, May 2, 1898, at New York city, to serve two years; mustered in as first lieutenant, Co. A, May 17, 1898; as captain, Co. B, July 23, 1898; mustered out with company, November 15, 1898, at New York city; commissioned first lieutenant, May 17, 1898, with rank from same date, original; captain, July 30, 1898, with rank from same date, vice Tompkins, discharged.

O'DONNELL, JOHN A.—Age, 25 years. Enlisted, May 2, 1898, at New York city, to serve two years; mustered in as private, Co. A, May 17, 1898; transferred to Co. B, August 13, 1898; promoted sergeant, August 16, 1898; first sergeant, August 24, 1898; mustered out with company, November 15, 1898, at New York city.

O'HARE, JOHN J.—Age, 28 years. Enlisted, May 2, 1898, at New York city, to serve two years; mustered in as private, Co. E, May 20, 1898; mustered out with company, November 15' 1898, at New York city.

O'KEEFE, JEREMIAH.—Age, — years. Enlisted, July 5, 1898, at New York city, to serve two years; mustered in as private, Co. D, same date; discharged, October 14, 1898.

O'KEEFE, PATRICK.—Age, — years. Enlisted, July 6, 1898, at New York city, to serve two years; mustered in as private, Co. D, same date; discharged, October 20, 1898.

O'NEIL, JOHN H.—Age, — years. Enlisted, June 24, 1898, at New York city, to serve two years; mustered in as private, Co. K, same date; mustered out with company, November 15, 1898, at New York city.

O'NEILL, THOMAS.—Age, 22 years. Enlisted, May 2, 1898, at New York city, to serve two years; mustered in as private, Co. F, May 21, 1898; mustered out with company, November 15, 1898, at New York city.

OPDYCK, WILLIAM M.—Age, 33 years. Enlisted, May 2, 1898, at New York city, to serve two years; mustered in as private, Co. G, May 20, 1898; promoted corporal, July 27, 1898; quartermaster-sergeant, October 22, 1898; mustered out with company, November 15, 1898, at New York city.

OPPELL, JUNIUS W.—Age, 32 years. Enlisted, May 2, 1898, at New York city, to serve two years; mustered in as private, Co. K, May 19, 1898; mustered out with company, November 15, 1898, at New York city.

O'ROURKE, THOMAS.—Age, — years. Enlisted, July 1, 1898, at New York city, to serve two years; mustered in as private, Co. L, same date; mustered out with company, November 15, 1898, at New York city.

OSBORN, CHARLES H.—Age, 23 years. Enlisted, May 2, 1898, at New York city, to serve two years; mustered in as private, Co. B, May 20, 1898; promoted regimental quartermaster-sergeant, July 20, 1898; returned to company as private, August 12, 1898; promoted corporal, September 3, 1898; mustered out with company, November 15, 1898, at New York city.

OSBORN, HARRY.—Age, 21 years. Enlisted, May 2, 1898, at New York city, to serve two years; mustered in as private, Co. B, May 20, 1898; mustered out with company, November 15, 1898, at New York city.

O'SHAUGHNESSY, FRANCIS J.—Age, 21 years. Enlisted, May 2, 1898, at New York city, to serve two years; mustered in as private, Co. C, May 20, 1898; died of typhoid fever, September 21, 1898, at New York city.

O'SHAUGHNESSY, WILLIAM.—Age, 22 years. Enlisted, May 2, 1898, at New York city, to serve two years; mustered in as private, Co. L, May 20, 1898; mustered out with company, November 15, 1898, at New York city.

OTT, JACOB.—Age, 24 years. Enlisted, May 2, 1898, at New York city, to serve two years; mustered in as private, Co. F, May 21, 1898; mustered out with company, November 15, 1898, at New York city.

OTTENBURG, JOSEPH.—Age, 42 years. Enlisted, May 2, 1898, at New York city, to serve two years; mustered in as private, Co. E, May 20, 1898; mustered out with company, November 15, 1898, at New York city.

OWENS, WALTER W.—Age, 21 years. Enlisted, May 20, 1898, at camp, near Peekskill, to serve two years; mustered in as private, Co. H, same date; mustered out with company, November 15, 1898, at New York city.

PALMER, FRANK.—Age, 21 years. Enlisted, May 2, 1898, at New York city, to serve two years; mustered in as sergeant, Co. M, May 17, 1898; promoted first sergeant, August 23, 1898; mustered out with company, November 15, 1898, at New York city.

PARENTINI, JOSEPH.—Age, 22 years. Enlisted, May 2, 1898, at New York city, to serve two years; mustered in as private, Co. D, May 17, 1898; discharged, October 14, 1898.

PARKER, FREDERICK.—Age, 35 years. Enlisted, May 2, 1898, at New York city, to serve two years; mustered in as private, Co. E, May 20, 1898; mustered out with company, November 15, 1898, at New York city.

PARKER, GEORGE H.—Age, 25 years. Enlisted, May 2, 1898, at New York city, to serve two years; mustered in as sergeant, Co. D, May 17, 1898; mustered out with company, November 15, 1898, at New York city.

PARKER, WALLACE S.—Age, 27 years. Enrolled, May 2, 1898, at New York city, to serve two years; mustered in as second lieutenant, Co. H, May 20, 1898; mustered out with company, November 15, 1898, at New York city; commissioned second lieutenant, May 21, 1898, with rank from same date, original.

PATH, JOSEPH J.—Age, 26 years. Enlisted, May 2, 1898, at New York city, to serve two years; mustered in as private, Co. C, May 19, 1898; mustered out with company, November 15, 1898, at New York city.

PATRICK, CLARENCE.—Age, 21 years. Enlisted, May 2, 1898, at New York city, to serve two years; mustered in as private, Co. F, May 21, 1898; mustered out with company, November 15, 1898, at New York city.

PEARSON, CHARLES G.—Age, 27 years. Enlisted, May 2, 1898, at New York city, to serve two years; mustered in as private, Co. G, May 21, 1898; promoted corporal, September 12, 1898; mustered out with company, November 15, 1898, at New York city.

PEBLOW, HENRY.—Age, 25 years. Enlisted, May 2, 1898, at New York city, to serve two years; mustered in as private, Co. F, May 21, 1898; mustered out with company, November 15, 1898, at New York city.

PECK, FRANK H.—Age, 42 years. Enrolled, May 21, 1898, at camp, near Peekskill, to serve two years; mustered in as sergeant-major, same date; returned to ranks, and transferred to Co. L, May 23, 1898; mustered in as second lieutenant, Co. F, June 3, 1898; as captain, July 22, 1898; mustered out, to date, November 15, 1898, at New York city; subsequent service as captain, Twenty-sixth Regiment, United States Volunteer Infantry; commissioned second lieutenant, May 23, 1898, with rank from same date, original; captain, July 30, 1898, with rank from same date, vice Bryde, discharged.

PERIS, EDMUND.—Age, 24 years. Enlisted, May 18, 1898, at New York city, to serve two years; mustered in as private, Co. I, May 19, 1898; mustered out with company, November 15, 1898, at New York city.

PEROCH, WILLIAM A.—Age, 36 years. Enlisted, May 2, 1898, at New York city, to serve two years; mustered in as private, Co. G, May 20, 1898; promoted corporal, September 12, 1898; mustered out with company, November 15, 1898, at New York city.

PETERS, JOHN.—Age, — years. Enlisted, July 6, 1898, at New York city, to serve two years; musterd in as private, Co. L, same date; mustered out with company, November 15, 1898, at New York city.

PETERSON, PETER G.—Age, 24 years. Enlisted, May 2, 1898, at New York city, to serve two years; mustered in as private, Co. A, May 17, 1898; promoted corporal, August 25, 1898; mustered out with company, November 15, 1898, at New York city.

PETRY, WILLIAM P.—Age, 22 years. Enlisted, May 2, 1898, at New York city, to serve two years; mustered in as private, Co. B, May 20, 1898; mustered out with company, November 15, 1898, at New York city.

PFIEFFER, CHARLES.—Age, 23 years. Enlisted, May 2, 1898, at New York city, to serve two years; mustered in as sergeant, Co. K, May 19, 1898; promoted first sergeant, October 1, 1898; mustered out with company, November 15, 1898, at New York city.

PHAROAH, HUGH.—Age, — years. Enlisted, June 29, 1898, at New York city, to serve two years; mustered in as private, Co. L, same date; mustered out with company, November 15, 1898, at New York city.

PHELPS, CHARLES O.—Age, 32 years. Enlisted, May 2, 1898, at New York city, to serve two years; mustered in as private, Co. I, May 19, 1898; discharged for disability, August 19, 1898, at Chickamauga, Ga.

PLECHNER, JOHN C.—Age, 23 years. Enlisted, May 2, 1898, at New York city, to serve two years; mustered in as private, Co. M, May 17, 1898; mustered out with company, November 15, 1898, at New York city.

PLUNKETT, RICHARD.—Age, 23 years. Enlisted, May 2, 1898, at New York city, to serve two years; mustered in as corporal, Co. K, May 19, 1898; mustered out with company, November 15, 1898, at New York city.

PLUSS, OTTO.—Age, 20 years. Enlisted, May 14, 1898, at New York city, to serve two years; mustered in as private, Co. I, May 19, 1898; mustered out with company, November 15, 1898, at New York city.

PNEUMAN, JOHN D.—Age, 32 years. Enlisted, May 2, 1898, at New York city, to serve two years; mustered in as private, Co. G, May 20, 1898; appointed wagoner, June 27, 1898; mustered out with company, November 15, 1898, at New York city.

POHL, JOSEPH J.—Age, 31 years. Enlisted, May 2, 1898, at New York city, to serve two years; mustered in as private, Co. G, May 20, 1898; mustered out with company, November 15, 1898, at New York city.

POLHILL, EDWARD J.—Age, 25 years. Enlisted, May 2, 1898, at New York city, to serve two years; mustered in as private, Co. G, May 20, 1898; promoted corporal, October 22, 1898; mustered out with company, November 15, 1898, at New York city.

POLLOCK, WILLIAM H.—Age, 41 years. Enlisted, May 2, 1898, at New York city, to serve two years; mustered in as corporal, Co. H, May 20, 1898; promoted sergeant, June 7, 1898; mustered out with company, November 15, 1898, at New York city.

PORTER, ARTHUR F.—Age, 24 years. Enlisted, May 2, 1898, at New York city, to serve two years; mustered in as private, Co. H, May 20, 1898; promoted corporal, July 27, 1898; mustered out with company, November 15, 1898, at New York city.

PORTER, WILLIAM.—Age, 25 years. Enlisted, May 17, 1898, at New York city, to serve two years; mustered in as private, Co. E, May 20, 1898; mustered out with company, November 15, 1898, at New York city.

POTTER, HARRY.—Age, — years. Enlisted, July 1, 1898, at New York city, to serve two years; mustered in as private, Co. L, same date; mustered out with company, November 15, 1898, at New York city.

POULS, ERNST.—Age, — years. Enlisted, June 29, 1898, at New York city, to serve two years; mustered in as private, Co. C, same date; mustered out with company, November 15, 1898, at New York city.

POWER, LAWRENCE H.—Age, 26 years. Enlisted, May 2, 1898, at New York city, to serve two years; mustered in as private, Co. D, May 17, 1898; mustered out with company, November 15, 1898, at New York city.

PRENTICE, WATSON.—Age, — years. Enlisted, July 5, 1898, at New York city, to serve two years; mustered in as private, Co. I, same date; mustered out with company, November 15, 1898, at New York city.

PRESCOTT, WILLIAM.—Age, 33 years. Enlisted, May 17, 1898, at New York city, to serve two years; mustered in as private, Co. H, May 20, 1898; mustered out with company, November 15, 1898, at New York city.

PRESTON, ALBERT W.—Age, 29 years. Enrolled, May 15, 1898, at New York city, to serve two years; mustered in as first lieutenant and assistant surgeon, May 21, 1898; mustered out with regiment, November 15, 1898, at New York city; commissioned first lieutenant and assistant surgeon, May 15, 1898, with rank from same date, original.

PREUSSNER, THEODORE.—Age, 23 years. Enlisted, May 2, 1898, at New York city, to serve two years; mustered in as private, Co. C, May 19, 1898; mustered out with company, November 15, 1898, at New York city.

PRIN, JAMES.—Age, 21 years. Enlisted, May 2, 1898, at New York city, to serve two years; mustered in as private, Co. A, May 17, 1898; mustered out with company, November 15, 1898, at New York city.

PROVOST, OSCAR S.—Age, 27 years. Enlisted, May 2, 1898, at New York city, to serve two years; mustered in as private, Co. L, May 20, 1898; mustered out with company, November 15, 1898, at New York city.

QUINBY, FREDERICK J.—Age, 34 years. Enrolled, May 2, 1898, at New York city, to serve two years; mustered in as captain, Co. C, May 19, 1898; mustered out with company, November 15, 1898, at New York city; commissioned captain, May 19, 1898, with rank from same date, original.

QUINN, WILLIAM B.—Age, 24 years. Enlisted, May 16, 1898, at New York city, to serve two years; mustered in as private, Co. B, May 20, 1898; mustered out with company, November 15, 1898, at New York city.

RAFFERTY, JAMES.—Age, — years. Enlisted, June 24, 1898, at New York city, to serve two years; mustered in as private, Co. D, same date; mustered out with company, November 15, 1898, at New York city.

RAFFERTY, JAMES.—Age, 28 years. Enlisted, May 2, 1898, at New York city, to serve two years; mustered in as private, Co. G, May 20, 1898; mustered out with company. November 15, 1898, at New York city.

RAFFERTY, JOHN.—Age, — years. Enlisted, June 24, 1898, at New York city, to serve two years; mustered in as private, Co. F, same date; mustered out with company, November 15 1898, at New York city.

RAFTERY, THOMAS F.—Age, 22 years. Enlisted, May 2, 1898, at New York city, to serve two years; mustered in as private, Co. H, May 20, 1898; mustered out with company, November 15, 1898, at New York city.

RALUGH, EDWARD.—Age, — years. Enlisted, July 29, 1898, at New York city, to serve two years; mustered in as private, Co. G, same date; discharged, October 12, 1898.

RAND, THOMAS B.—Age, 59 years. Enrolled, May 2, 1898, at New York city, to serve two years; mustered in as lieutenant-colonel, May 21, 1898; mustered out with regiment, November 15, 1898, at New York city; prior service as captain, Thirty-third Massachusetts Volunteer Infantry, War of Rebellion; commissioned lieutenant-colonel, May 21, 1898, with rank from same date, original.

RANDALL, EDMOND.—Age, — years. Enlisted, June 27, 1898, at New York city, to serve two years; mustered in as private, Co. A, same date; mustered out with company, November 15, 1898, at New York city.

RANKIN, JR., WALTER A.—Age, 25 years. Enlisted, May 2, 1898, at New York city, to serve two years; mustered in as corporal, Co. G, May 20, 1898; promoted sergeant, October 22, 1898; mustered out with company, November 15, 1898, at New York city.

RANLET, DANIEL M.—Age, 21 years. Enlisted, May 2, 1898, at
New York city, to serve two years; mustered in as sergeant
Co. B, May 20, 1898; mustered out with company, November
15, 1898, at New York city.

RATHBURN, BERNARD.—Age, — years. Enlisted, July 8,
1898, at New York city, to serve two years; mustered in as
private, Co. B, same date; transferred to band, July 27, 1898;
mustered out with regiment, November 15, 1898, at New York
city.

RATHERS, EDWARD J.—Age, 25 years. Enlisted, May 2, 1898,
at New York city, to serve two years; mustered in as private,
Co. C, May 19, 1898; promoted corporal, July 28, 1898; mustered out with company, November 15, 1898, at New York
city.

RAUBITSCHET, EDMUND G.—Age, 24 years.   Enlisted, May
2, 1898, at New York city, to serve two years; mustered in as
private, Co. L, May 20, 1898;   mustered out with company,
November 15, 1898, at New York city.

REARDON, GEORGE.—Age, — years.   Enlisted, June 24, 1898,
at New York city, to serve two years; mustered in as private,
Co. E, same date; died of typhoid fever, August 2, 1898, at
Chickamauga Park, Ga.

REDDING, JAMES P.—Age, — years.   Enlisted, June 24, 1898,
at New York city, to serve two years; mustered in as private,
Co. E, same date; mustered out with company, November 15,
1898, at New York city.

REDDING, MIKE.—Age, 41 years. Enlisted, May 2, 1898, at
New York city, to serve two years; mustered in as artificer,
Co. B, May 20, 1898; mustered out with company, November 15,
1898, at New York city.

REDMAN, AUGUST J.—Age, 22 years. Enlisted, May 2, 1898,
at New York city, to serve two years; mustered in as private,
Co. A, May 17, 1898; mustered out with company, November 15,
1898, at New York city.

REDMOND, JOHN J.—Age, — years. Enlisted, July 11, 1898,
at New York city, to serve two years; mustered in as private,
Co. C, same date; transferred to band, July 27, 1898; mustered
out with regiment, November 15, 1898, at New York city.

REEB, CLARENCE C.—Age, 25 years. Enlisted, May 2, 1898, at New York city, to serve two years; mustered in as private, Co. B, May 20, 1898; mustered out with company, November 15, 1898, at New York city.

REED, JOSEPH.—Age, 20 years. Enlisted, May 18, 1898, at New York city, to serve two years; mustered in as private, Co. I, May 19, 1898; mustered out with company, November 15, 1898, at New York city.

REHORN, JOSEPH.—Age, 24 years. Enlisted, May 2, 1898, at New York city, to serve two years; mustered in as private, Co. F, May 21, 1898; promoted corporal, July 27, 1898; mustered out with company, November 15, 1898, at New York city.

REIDY, JAMES J.—Age, 24 years. Enlisted, May 2, 1898, at New York city, to serve two years; mustered in as corporal, Co. F, May 21, 1898; promoted sergeant, no date; mustered out with company, November 15, 1898, at New York city.

REILLY, PATRICK.—Age, 26 years. Enlisted, May 2, 1898, at New York city, to serve two years; mustered in as private, Co. B, May 20, 1898; mustered out with company, November 15, 1898, at New York city.

REKOSIK, JULIUS.—Age, 26 years. Enlisted, May 2, 1898, at New York city, to serve two years; mustered in as private, Co. L, May 20, 1898; mustered out with company, November 15, 1898, at New York city.

REMERS, HENRY.—Age, 21 years. Enlisted, May 2, 1898, at New York city, to serve two years; mustered in as private, Co. K, May 20, 1898; died of typhoid fever, July 22, 1898, at Second Division Hospital, Camp Thomas, Chickamauga Park, Ga.

REYNOLDS, JEREMIAH A.—Age, 23 years. Enlisted, May 2, 1898, at New York city, to serve two years; mustered in as private, Co. G, May 20, 1898; mustered out with company, November 15, 1898, at New York city.

RICE, ANDREW T.—Age, 23 years. Enlisted, May 2, 1898, at New York city, to serve two years; mustered in as private, Co. H, May 20, 1898; mustered out with company, November 15, 1898, at New York city.

RICE, FREDERICK S.—Age, 44 years.   Enlisted, May 2, 1898, at New York city, to serve two years; mustered in as private, Co. G, May 20, 1898; mustered out with company, November 15, 1898, at New York city.

RICE, MARTIN.—Age, 26 years.   Enlisted, May 2, 1898, at New York city, to serve years; mustered in as sergeant, Co. M, May 17, 1898; returned to ranks, July 27, 1898; mustered out with company, November 15, 1898, at New York city.

RICE, JR., WILLIAM H.—Age, — years.   Enlisted, June 27, 1898, at New York city, to serve two years; mustered in as private, Co. M, same date; mustered out with company, November 15, 1898, at New York city.

RICHARDS, JOHN S.—Age, 22 years.   Enlisted, May 2, 1898, at New York city, to serve two years; mustered in as private, Co. F, May 21, 1898; promoted corporal, July 27, 1898; mustered out with company, November 15, 1898, at New York city.

RICHARDS, THOMAS S.—Age, 24 years.   Enlisted, May 2, 1898, at New York city, to serve two years; mustered in as sergeant, Co. L, May 20, 1898; returned to ranks, August 8, 1898; discharged, October 15, 1898.

RICKEMAN, HERMAN.—Age, 21 years.   Enlisted, May 2, 1898, at New York city, to serve two years; mustered in as private, Co. B, May 20, 1898; mustered out with company, November 15, 1898, at New York city.

RILEY, JOHN H.—Age, 19 years.   Enlisted, May 2, 1898, at New York city, to serve two years; mustered in as private, Co. D, May 17, 1898; mustered out with company, November 15, 1898, at New York city.

RILEY, PATRICK.—Age, 21 years.   Enlisted, May 16, 1898, at New York city, to serve two years; mustered in as private, Co. B, May 20, 1898; mustered out with company, November 15, 1898, at New York city.

RINCKHOFF, JULIUS A.—Age, 21 years.   Enlisted, May 2, 1898, at New York city, to serve two years; mustered in as musician, Co. M, May 17, 1898; returned to ranks, May 18, 1898; mustered out with company, November 15, 1898, at New York city.

RIORDAN, FRANK J.—Age, — years. Enlisted, June 23, 1898, at New York city, to serve two years; mustered in as private, Co. A, same date; promoted corporal, October 3, 1898; mustered out with company, November 15, 1898, at New York city.

RITZDORF, FREDERICK.—Age, — years. Enlisted, July 9, 1898, at New York city, to serve two years; mustered in as private, Co. M, same date; appointed principal musician, July 27, 1898; mustered out with regiment, November 15, 1898, at New York city.

ROACH, MARTIN.—Age, — years. Enlisted, June 27, 1898, at New York city, to serve two years; mustered in as private, Co. G, same date; discharged, October 15, 1898.

ROAN, GEORGE S.—Age, 24 years. Enlisted, May 2, 1898, at New York city, to serve two years; mustered in as sergeant, Co. I, May 19, 1898; mustered out with company, November 15, 1898, at New York city.

ROBB, JOSEPH.—Age, 26 years. Enlisted, May 2, 1898, at New York city, to serve two years; mustered in as private, Co. F, May 21, 1898; mustered out with company, November 15, 1898, at New York city.

ROBERTS, CHARLES F.—Age, 26 years. Enlisted, May 2, 1898, at New York city, to serve two years; mustered in as private, Co. K, May 19, 1898; mustered out with company, November 15, 1898, at New York city.

ROBERTSON, GEORGE W.—Age, 22 years. Enlisted, May 2, 1898, at New York city, to serve two years; mustered in as private, Co. F, May 21, 1898; mustered out with company, November 15, 1898, at New York city.

ROBERTSON, JACOB J.—Age, 24 years. Enlisted, May 2, 1898, at New York city, to serve two years; mustered in as private, Co. F, May 21, 1898; promoted corporal, September 5, 1898; mustered out with company, November 15, 1898, at New York city.

ROBERTSON, WILLIAM B.—Age, 20 years. Enlisted, May 2, 1898, at New York city, to serve two years; mustered in as private, Co. L, May 20, 1898; mustered out with company, November 15, 1898, at New York city.

ROBINSON, JOHN.—Age, 25 years. Enlisted, May 2, 1898, at New York city, to serve two years; mustered in as private, Co. K, May 19, 1898; mustered out with company, November 15, 1898, at New York city.

ROBINSON, WILLIAM.—Age, — years. Enlisted, July 5, 1898, at New York city, to serve two years; mustered in as private, Co. F, same date; mustered out with company, November 15, 1898, at New York city.

ROGAN, THOMAS.—Age, 22 years. Enlisted, May 2, 1898, at New York city, to serve two years; mustered in as private, Co. E, May 20, 1898; mustered out with company, November 15, 1898, at New York city.

ROHRBACK, OTTO.—Age, 24 years. Enlisted, May 2, 1898, at New York city, to serve two years; mustered in as private, Co. H, May 20, 1898; mustered out with company, November 15, 1898, at New York city.

ROLAND, CHARLES.—Age, — years. Enlisted, May 19, 1898, at New York city, to serve two years; mustered in as musician, Co. H, May 20, 1898; mustered out with company, November 15, 1898, at New York city.

ROLLINS, CHARLES F.—Age, — years. Enlisted, June 24, 1898, at New York city, to serve two years; mustered in as private, Co. D, same date; mustered out with company, November 15, 1898, at New York city.

ROLLINS, HARRY.—Age, — years. Enlisted, June 23, 1898, at New York city, to serve two years; mustered in as private, Co. D, same date; mustered out with company, November 15, 1898, at New York city.

ROMAINE, WILLIAM GARRETT.—Age, 30 years. Enlisted, May 2, 1898, at New York city, to serve two years; mustered in as corporal, Co. G, May 21, 1898; as second lieutenant, Co. L, August 8, 1898; mustered out with company, November 15, 1898, at New York city; commissioned second lieutenant, August 8, 1898, with rank from same date, vice Croft, promoted. 1898, with rank from same date, vice Croft, promoted.

ROONEY, FRANCIS.—Age, — years. Enlisted, June 24, 1898, at New York city, to serve two years; mustered in as private, Co. A, same date; mustered out, to date, November 15, 1898.

ROSENBERG, JACOB.—Age, — years. Enlisted, June 23, 1898, at New York city, to serve two years; mustered in as private, Co. K, same date; mustered out with company, November 15, 1898, at New York city.

ROSENBERG, JACOB.—Age, 33 years. Enlisted, May 2, 1898, at New York city, to serve two years; mustered in as private, Co. I, May 19, 1898; mustered out with company, November 15, 1898, at New York city.

ROSENGARTEN, MARK C.—Age, — years. Enlisted, June 30, 1898, at New York city, to serve two years; mustered in as private, Co. C, same date; mustered out with company, November 15, 1898, at New York city.

ROSER, CHARLES.—Age, 23 years. Enlisted, May 2, 1898, at New York city, to serve two years; mustered in as corporal, Co. H, May 20, 1898; mustered out with company, November 15, 1898, at New York city.

ROSETT, LOUIS J.—Age, 20 years. Enlisted, May 2, 1898, at New York city, to serve two years; mustered in as private, Co. M, May 17, 1898; promoted corporal, no date; mustered out with company, November 15, 1898, at New York city.

ROSS, JOHN E.—Age, — years. Enlisted, June 30, 1898, at New York city, to serve two years; mustered in as private, Co. A, same date; mustered out with company, November 15, 1898, at New York city.

ROTH, DAVID.—Age, — years. Enlisted, June 27, 1898, at New York city, to serve two years; mustered in as private, Co. D, same date; mustered out with company, November 15, 1898, at New York city.

ROTH, JOHN.—Age, — years. Enlisted, May 21, 1898, at camp, near Peekskill, to serve two years; mustered in as musician, Co. E, same date; mustered out with company, November 15, 1898, at New York city.

ROTTGARDT, GEORGE.—Age, — years. Enlisted, June 24, 1898, at New York city, to serve two years; mustered in as private, Co. I, same date; mustered out with company, November 15, 1898, at New York city.

ROWE, WILLIAM.—Age, 42 years. Enlisted, May 2, 1898, at New York city, to serve two years; mustered in as private, Co. I, May 19, 1898; mustered out with company, November 15, 1898, at New York city.

RUSSELL, ROBERT J.—Age, 25 years. Enlisted, May 2, 1898, at New York city, to serve two years; mustered in as sergeant, Co. G, May 20, 1898; promoted first sergeant, August 30, 1898; discharged, October 15, 1898.

RUSSELL, WALTER B.—Age, 32 years. Enlisted, May 2, 1898, at New York city, to serve two years; mustered in as corporal, Co. E, May 20, 1898; mustered out with company, November 15, 1898, at New York city.

RYAN, EDMUND A.—Age, 25 years. Enlisted, May 2, 1898, at New York city, to serve two years; mustered in as private, Co. B, May 20, 1898; promoted sergeant, September 3, 1898; quartermaster-sergeant, same date; mustered out with company, November 15, 1898, at New York city.

RYAN, EDWARD L.—Age, 23 years. Enlisted, May 10, 1898, at New York city, to serve two years; mustered in as private, Co. M, May 17, 1898; mustered out with company, November 15, 1898, at New York city.

RYAN, PATRICK.—Age, 21 years. Enlisted, May 2, 1898, at New York city, to serve two years; mustered in as private, Co. F, May 21, 1898; deserted, July 10, 1898, at Camp Thomas, Chickamauga Park, Ga.

RYAN, JR., PATRICK.—Age, 21 years. Enlisted, May 17, 1898, at New York city, to serve two years; mustered in as private, Co. F, May 21, 1898; mustered out with company, November 15, 1898, at New York city; also borne as Patrick S. Ryan.

RYAN, THOMAS F.—Age, 28 years. Enlisted, May 2, 1898, at New York city, to serve two years; mustered in as private, Co. H, May 20, 1898; mustered out with company, November 15, 1898, at New York city.

RYAN, WILLIAM J.—Age, — years. Enlisted, June 24, 1898, at New York city, to serve two years; mustered in as private, Co. E, same date; mustered out with company, November 15, 1898, at New York city.

RYBA, CHARLES.—Age, — years. Enlisted, July 2, 1898, at New York city, to serve two years; mustered in as private, Co. L, same date; died of uraemic coma, September 25, 1898, at Fort Thomas, Ky.

SANBORN, EUGENE B.—Age, 23 years. Enlisted, May 2, 1898, at New York city, to serve two years; mustered in as private, Co. C, May 19, 1898; promoted corporal, August 18, 1898; discharged, September 29, 1898.

SAWYER, GEORGE J.—Age, — years. Enlisted, June 29, 1898, at New York city, to serve two years; mustered in as private, Co. H, same date; mustered out with company, November 15, 1898, at New York city.

SCANLAN, JOSEPH A.—Age, 23 years. Enlisted, May 2, 1898, at New York city, to serve two years; mustered in as corporal, Co. K, May 19, 1898; mustered out with company, November 15, 1898, at New York city.

SCHEIHING, CHARLES W.—Age, 35 years. Enlisted, May 2, 1898, at New York city, to serve two years; mustered in as sergeant, Co. D, May 17, 1898; mustered out with company, November 15, 1898, at New York city.

SCHERPF, ALPHONS J.—Age, 21 years. Enlisted, May 2, 1898, at New York city, to serve two years; mustered in as private, Co. L, May 20, 1898; mustered out with company, November 15, 1898, at New York city.

SCHEUR, JACK J.—Age, 26 years. Enlisted, May 2, 1898, at New York city, to serve two years; mustered in as private, Co. E, May 20, 1898; promoted corporal, September 7, 1898; mustered out with company, November 15, 1898, at New York city.

SCHICK, GEORGE L.—Age, 21 years. Enlisted, May 2, 1898, at New York city, to serve two years; mustered in as corporal, Co. M, May 17, 1898; mustered out with company, November 15, 1898, at New York city.

SCHIPPELL, JR., AUGUST.—Age, 21 years. Enlisted, May 2, 1898, at New York city, to serve two years; mustered in as private, Co. I, May 19, 1898; mustered out with company, November 15, 1898, at New York city.

SCHLEGEL, WILLIAM.—Age, — years. Enlisted, June 24, 1898, at New York city, to serve two years; mustered in as private, Co. K, same date; mustered out with company, November 15, 1898, at New York city.

SCHNEIDER, CHARLES.—Age, 23 years. Enlisted, May 2, 1898, at New York city, to serve two years; mustered in as private, Co. D, May 17, 1898; mustered out with company, November 15, 1898, at New York city.

SCHNEIDER, JR., CHARLES.—Age, 26 years. Enlisted, May 2, 1898, at New York city, to serve two years; mustered in as private, Co. H, May 20, 1898; promoted sergeant-major, July 16, 1898; discharged, October 18, 1898.

SCHOENWEG, HERMAN.—Age, — years. Enlisted, June 30, 1898, at New York city, to serve two years; mustered in as private, Co. F, same date; mustered out with company, November 15, 1898, at New York city.

SCHRAUBE, JACOB A.—Age, 33 years. Enlisted, May 2, 1898, at New York city, to serve two years; mustered in as quartermaster-sergeant, May 21, 1898; returned to ranks and transferred to Co. K, July 20, 1898; mustered out with company, November 15, 1898, at New York city; also borne as Jacob A. Schrank.

SCHUBERT, ALBERT.—Age, 34 years. Enlisted, May 17, 1898, at New York city, to serve two years; mustered in as private, Co. M, May 19, 1898; mustered out with company, November 15, 1898, at New York city.

SCHUBERT, HENRY W.—Age, 21 years. Enlisted, May 2, 1898, at New York city, to serve two years; mustered in as private, Co. G, May 21, 1898; mustered out with company, November 15, 1898, at New York city.

SCHUETT, AUGUST.—Age, 33 years. Enlisted, May 2, 1898, at New York city, to serve two years; mustered in as private, Co. H, May 20, 1898; mustered out with company, November 15, 1898, at New York city.

SCHULTZ, WILLIAM F.—Age, 34 years. Enlisted, May 2, 1898, at New York city, to serve two years; mustered in as sergeant, Co. E, May 20, 1898; mustered out with company, November 15, 1898, at New York city.

SCHULZE, WILLIAM H.—Age, 25 years. Enlisted, May 2, 1898, at New York city, to serve two years; mustered in as private, Co. C, May 19, 1898; mustered out with company, November 15, 1898, at New York city.

SCHUMANN, WILLIAM.—Age, 27 years. Enlisted, May 2, 1898, at New York city, to serve two years; mustered in as sergeant, Co. G, May 20, 1898; mustered out with company, November 15, 1898, at New York city.

SCHWARTZ, GUSTAVE.—Age, — years. Enlisted, June 23, 1898, at New York city, to serve two years; mustered in as private, Co. K, same date; mustered out with company, November 15, 1898, at New York city.

SCHWARTZ, PETER.—Age, 21 years. Enlisted, May 11, 1898, at New York city, to serve two years; mustered in as private, Co. L, May 20, 1898; mustered out with company, November 15, 1898, at New York city.

SCHWARTZ, SAMUEL F.—Age, 22 years. Enlisted, May 2, 1898 at New York city, to serve two years; mustered in as hospital steward, May 21, 1898; mustered out with regiment, November 15, 1898, at New York city.

SCKIRA, HUGO.—Age, 23 years. Enlisted, May 2, 1898, at New York city, to serve two years; mustered in as private, Co. F, May 21, 1898; mustered out with company, November 15, 1898, at New York city.

SCOTT, FRANK L.—Age, 31 years. Enlisted, May 2, 1898, at New York city, to serve two years; mustered in as private, Co. A, May 17, 1898; mustered out with company, November 15, 1898, at New York city.

SCOTT, WALTER E.—Age, 30 years. Enlisted, May 2, 1898, at New York city, to serve two years; mustered in as private, Co. I, May 19, 1898; mustered out with company, November 15, 1898, at New York city.

SCOTTI, CHARLES.—Age, — years. Enlisted, June 24, 1898, at New York city, to serve two years; mustered in as private, Co. B, same date; mustered out with company, November 15, 1898, at New York city.

SCULLY, WILLIAM H.—Age, 29 years. Enlisted, May 2, 1898, at New York city, to serve two years; mustered in as musician, Co. F, May 21, 1898; mustered out with company, November 15, 1898, at New York city.

SEGER, JOHN.—Age, 21 years.   Enlisted, May 2, 1898, at New York city, to serve two years; mustered in as private, Co. L, May 20, 1898; discharged, November 11, 1898, to enlist in regular army.

SELIGMAN, GEORGE.—Age, — years.   Enlisted, June 29, 1898, at New York city, to serve two years; mustered in as private, Co. C, same date; mustered out with company, November 15, 1898, at New York city.

SERF, JOSEPH.—Age, 28 years.   Enlisted, May 2, 1898, at New York city, to serve two years; mustered in as private, Co. G, May 20, 1898; mustered out with company, November 15, 1898, at New York city.

SEVER, WILLIAM P.—Age, 21 years.   Enlisted, May 2, 1898, at New York city, to serve two years; mustered in as private, Co. D, May 17, 1898; discharged, October 13, 1898.

SEWARD, CHARLES W.—Age, 23 years. Enrolled, May 2, 1898, at New York city, to serve two years; mustered in as second lieutenant, Co. C, May 19, 1898; died of typhoid fever, September 16, 1898, at Montclair, N. J.; commissioned second lieutenant, May 19, 1898, with rank from same date, original.

SEWARD, JR., EMOTT.—Age, 21 years. Enrolled, May 2, 1898, at New York city, to serve two years; mustered in as first lieutenant, Co. C, May 19, 1898; died of typhoid fever, October 17, 1898, at Leiter United States Hospital, Chickamauga, Ga.; commissioned first lieutenant, May 19, 1898, with rank from same date, original.

SEXTON, MICHAEL J.—Age, 34 years.   Enlisted, May 2, 1898, at New York city, to serve two years; mustered in as private, Co. B, May 20, 1898; mustered out with company, November 15, 1898, at New York city.

SEYMOUR, THOMAS.—Age, — years. Enlisted, June 23, 1898, at New York city, to serve two years; mustered in as private, Co. A, same date; mustered out with company, November 15, 1898, at New York city.

SEYMOUR, WILLIAM.—Age, 19 years. Enlisted, May 2, 1898, at New York city, to serve two years; mustered in as private, Co. A, May 17, 1898; mustered out with company, November 15, 1898, at New York city.

SHANNON, CHARLES P.—Age, 22 years. Enlisted, May 2, 1898, at New York city, to serve two years; mustered in as private, Co. D, May 17, 1898; discharged, October 15, 1898.

SHANNON, EDWARD.—Age, — years. Enlisted, July 5, 1898, at New York city, to serve two years; mustered in as private, Co. B, same date; mustered out with company, November 15, 1898, at New York city.

SHANNON, JAMES P.—Age, — years. Enlisted, July 6, 1898, at New York city, to serve two years; mustered in as private, Co. K, same date; died of typhoid fever, September 3, 1898, at Sternberg Hospital, Camp Thomas, Chickamauga Park, Ga.

SHARP, EDWARD.—Age, 22 years. Enlisted, May 2, 1898, at New York city, to serve two years; mustered in as private, Co. M, May 17, 1898; mustered out with company, November 15, 1898, at New York city.

SHAW, LE ROY T.—Age, 28 years. Enlisted, May 2, 1898, at New York city, to serve two years; mustered in as private, Co. I, May 19, 1898; discharged for disability, August 21, 1898, at Chickamauga, Ga.

SHEALS, SAMUEL.—Age, 22 years. Enlisted, May 2, 1898, at New York city, to serve two years; mustered in as private, Co. E, May 20, 1898; transferred to Co. F, July 28, 1898; mustered out with company, November 15, 1898, at New York city.

SHEAR, GEORGE S.—Age, 30 years. Enlisted, May 2, 1898, at New York city, to serve two years; mustered in as private, Co. I, May 19, 1898; mustered out, to date, November 15, 1898.

SHEARER, WILLIAM.—Age, 29 years. Enlisted, May 2, 1898, at New York city, to serve two years; mustered in as private, Co. I, May 19, 1898; mustered out with company, November 15, 1898, at New York city.

SHEFFIELD, EVERETTE R.—Age, — years. Enlisted, May 2, 1898, at New York city, to serve two years; mustered in as private, Co. B, May 20, 1898; transferred to Co. E, July 27, 1898; mustered out with company, November 15, 1898, at New York city.

SHERIDAN, ALEXANDER P.—Age, 28 years. Enlisted, May 2, 1898, at New York city, to serve two years; mustered in as private, Co. M, May 17, 1898; mustered out with company, November 15, 1898, at New York city.

SHERIDAN, GEORGE.—Age, 22 years. Enlisted, May 2, 1898, at New York city, to serve two years; mustered in as private, Co. C, May 19, 1898; mustered out with company, November 15, 1898, at New York city.

SHERIFF, ADOLPH W.—Age, 21 years. Enlisted, May 2, 1898, at New York city, to serve two years; mustered in as private, Co. H, May 20, 1898; promoted corporal, July 22, 1898; mustered out with company, November 15, 1898, at New York city.

SHERRY, JOHN M.—Age, 25 years. Enlisted, May 2, 1898, at New York city, to serve two years; mustered in as private, Co. E, May 20, 1898; mustered out with company, November 15, 1898, at New York city.

SHEVLIN, THOMAS C.—Age, 21 years. Enlisted, May 2, 1898, at New York city, to serve two years; mustered in as private, Co. L, May 20, 1898; mustered out with company, November 15, 1898, at New York city.

SHINE, EUGENE A.—Age, 26 years. Enlisted, May 12, 1898, at camp, near Peekskill, to serve two years; mustered in as private, Co. L, May 20, 1898; mustered out with company, November 15, 1898, at New York city.

SHORTELL, JOHN W.—Age, 26 years. Enlisted, May 2, 1898, at New York city, to serve two years; mustered in as wagoner, Co. D, May 17, 1898; mustered out with company, November 15, 1898, at New York city.

SHUPPERT, HENRY.—Age, — years. Enlisted, June 24, 1898, at New York city, to serve two years; mustered in as private, Co. E, same date; mustered out with company, November 15, 1898, at New York city.

SIEBERT, ARTHUR.—Age, 19 years. Enlisted, May 2, 1898, at New York city, to serve two years; mustered in as private, Co. M, May 17, 1898; mustered out with company, November 15, 1898, at New York city.

SIEBERT, LOUIS.—Age, 27 years. Enlisted, May 2, 1898, at New York city, to serve two years; mustered in as private, Co. M, May 17, 1898; mustered out with company, November 15, 1898, at New York city.

SIEGMAN, GEORGE.—Age, — years. Enlisted, June 23, 1898, at New York city, to serve two years; mustered in as private, Co. I, same date; mustered out with company, November 15, 1898, at New York city.

SILLERY, FREDERICK W.—Age, — years. Enlisted, June 23, 1898, at New York city, to serve two years; mustered in as private, Co. G, same date; mustered out with company, November 15, 1898, at New York city.

SILVERIN, SAMUEL.—Age, — years. Enlisted, June 30, 1898, at New York city, to serve two years; mustered in as private, Co. M, same date; mustered out with company, November 15, 1898, at New York city.

SILVERMAN, LEWIS.—Age, 31 years. Enlisted, May 2, 1898, at New York city, to serve two years; mustered in as private, Co. C, May 19, 1898; promoted corporal, July 27, 1898; mustered out with company, November 15, 1898, at New York city.

SIMPSON, CHARLES E.—Age, 24 years. Enlisted, May 2, 1898, at New York city, to serve two years; mustered in as private, Co. K, May 19, 1898; mustered out with company, November 15, 1898, at New York city.

SIMPSON, GEORGE McC.—Age, — years. Enlisted, June 23, 1898, at New York city, to serve two years; mustered in as private, Co. B, same date; promoted sergeant, July 20, 1898; first sergeant, same date; returned to ranks, August 16, 1898; died of typhoid fever, August 23, 1898, at Second Division Hospital, Chickamauga Park, Ga.

SIMPSON, JEREMIAH.—Age, — years. Enlisted, June 23, 1898, at New York city, to serve two years; mustered in as private, Co. A, same date; mustered out with company, November 15, 1898, at New York city.

SIMPSON, JOSEPH F.—Age, 25 years. Enlisted, May 2, 1898, at New York city, to serve two years; mustered in as private, Co. I, May 19, 1898; transferred to Hospital Corps, July 16, 1898.

SINCLAIR, JAMES.—Age, 33 years. Enlisted, May 21, 1898, at New York city, to serve two years; mustered in as private, Co. D, same date; discharged, October 15, 1898.

SINGER, FRANK.—Age, 22 years. Enlisted, May 2, 1898, at New York city, to serve two years; mustered in as private, Co. M, May 17, 1898; mustered out with company, November 15, 1898, at New York city.

SIRON, JOHN F.—Age, 20 years. Enlisted, May 16, 1898, at New York city, to serve two years; mustered in as private, Co. D, May 17, 1898; mustered out with company, November 15, 1898, at New York city.

SMART, THOMAS G.—Age, 28 years. Enlisted, May 7, 1898, at New York city, to serve two years; mustered in as private, Co. K, May 20, 1898; dishonorably discharged, July 22, 1898, at Camp Thomas, Chickamauga Park, Ga.

SMITH, ANDREW J.—Age, 23 years. Enlisted, May 2, 1898, at New York city, to serve two years; mustered in as private, Co. F, May 21, 1898; mustered out with company, November 15, 1898, at New York city.

SMITH, EARL WRIGHT.—Age, 23 years. Enlisted, May 2, 1898, at New York city, to serve two years; mustered in as private, Co. F, May 21, 1898; promoted corporal, July 27, 1898; mustered out with company, November 15, 1898, at New York city.

SMITH, FRANK D.—Age, 21 years. Enlisted, May 2, 1898, at New York city, to serve two years; mustered in as private, Co. G, May 21, 1898; mustered out with company, November 15, 1898, at New York city.

SMITH, FRANK H.—Age, 21 years. Enlisted, May 2, 1898, at New York city, to serve two years; mustered in as private, Co. I, May 19, 1898; mustered out with company, November 15, 1898, at New York city.

SMITH, GEORGE.—Age, 28 years. Enlisted, May 2, 1898, at New York city, to serve two years; mustered in as wagoner, Co. H, May 20, 1898; mustered out with company, November 15, 1898, at New York city.

SMITH, JAMES L.—Age, 25 years. Enlisted, May 2. 1898, at New York city, to serve two years; mustered in as private, Co. I, May 19, 1898; mustered out with company, November 15, 1898, at New York city.

SMITH, LITTLETON K.—Age, 22 years. Enlisted, May 16, 1898, at New York city, to serve two years; mustered in as private, Co. E, May 20, 1898; mustered out with company. November 15, 1898, at New York city.

SMITH, MATTHEW P.—Age, 29 years. Enlisted, May 2, 1898, at New York city, to serve two years; mustered in as private, Co. M, May 17, 1898; mustered out with company, November 15, 1898, at New York city.

SMITH, THOMAS M.—Age, — years. Enlisted, June 23, 1898, at New York city, to serve two years; mustered in as private, Co. G, same date; mustered out with company, November 15, 1898, at New York city.

SMITH, WILLIAM H.—Age, 29 years. Enlisted, May 21, 1898, camp near Peekskill, to serve two years; mustered in as principal musician, May 21, 1898; transferred to Co. H, May 23, 1898; promoted first sergeant, same date; mustered in as second lieutenant, Co. F, July 23, 1898; mustered out with company, November 15, 1898, at New York city; commissioned second lieutenant, July 30, 1898, with rank from same date. vice Miller, promoted.

SMRKORSKY, LOUIS.—Age, 26 years. Enlisted, May 2, 1898, at New York city, to serve two years; mustered i   private, Co. F, May 21, 1898; mustered out with company,   mber 15, 1898, at New York city.

SNEDEN, FRANK P.—Age, 18 years. Enlisted, May 2, 1898, at New York city, to serve two years; mustered in as private, Co. F, May 21, 1898; mustered out with company, November 15, 1898, at New York city.

SNYDER, LOUIS J.—Age, 25 years. Enlisted, May 2, 1898, at New York city, to serve two years; mustered in as private, Co. E, May 20, 1898; transferred to Co. M, September 6, 1898; promoted sergeant, same date; mustered out with company, November 15, 1898, at New York city; also borne as Louis I. Snyder.

SOFSKY, ARTHUR.—Age, — years. Enlisted, June 24, 1898, at New York city, to serve two years; mustered in as private, Co. E, same date; mustered out with company, November 15, 1898, at New York city.

SOLOMON, HARRY.—Age, — years. Enlisted, June 23, 1898, at New York city, to serve two years; mustered in as private, Co. L, same date; deserted, July 20, 1898, at Camp Thomas, Chickamauga Park, Ga.

SOULE, DIME.—Age, 21 years. Enlisted, May 17, 1898, at New York city, to serve two years; mustered in as private, Co. E, May 20, 1898; mustered out with company, November 15, 1898, at New York city.

SOUSA, GEORGE J.—Age, — years. Enlisted, July 8, 1898, at New York city, to serve two years; mustered in as private, Co. L, same date; transferred to Co. M, July 27, 1898; to band, same date; mustered out with regiment, November 15, 1898, at New York city.

SPANTON, ALVIN H.—Age, — years. Enlisted, June 24, 1898, at New York city, to serve two years; mustered in as private, Co. K, same date; mustered out with company, November 15, 1898, at New York city.

SPICE, ROBERT.—Age, — years. Enlisted, June 24, 1898, at New York city, to serve two years; mustered in as private, Co. L, same date; mustered out with company, November 15, 1898, at New York city.

SPOONER, GEORGE C.—Age, 25 years. Enlisted, May 2, 1898, at New York city, to serve two years; mustered in as corporal, Co. G, May 20, 1898; returned to ranks, September 2, 1898; mustered out with company, November 15, 1898, at New York city.

STAAS, CHARLES.—Age, — years. Enlisted, June 29, 1898, at New York city, to serve two years; mustered in as private, Co. H, same date; mustered out with company, November 15, 1898, at New York city.

STAATS, FREDERICK.—Age, 29 years. Enlisted, May 2, 1898, at New York city, to serve two years; mustered in as sergeant, Co. I May 19, 1898; returned to ranks, no date; mustered out with company, November 15, 1898, at New York city.

STAFFORD, ARCHIBALD S.—Age, 21 years. Enlisted, May 2, 1898, at New York city, to serve two years; mustered in as sergeant, Co. B, May 20, 1898; mustered out with company, November 15, 1898, at New York city.

STANLEY, ROBERT A.—Age, 35 years. Enlisted, May 2, 1898, at New York city, to serve two years; mustered in as private, Co. H, May 20, 1898; mustered out with company, November 15, 1898, at New York city.

STARLIGHT, CHARLES I.—Age, 22 years. Enlisted, May 2, 1898, at New York city, to serve two years; mustered in as private, Co. B, May 20, 1898; deserted, July 9, 1898, at Camp Thomas, Chickamauga Park, Ga.

STEED, GEORGE W.—Age, 20 years. Enlisted, May 11, 1898, at camp, near Peekskill, to serve two years; mustered in as private, Co. L, May 20, 1898; promoted corporal, July 27, 1898; mustered out with company, November 15, 1898, at New York city.

STEFFENS, WILLIAM.—Age, 21 years. Enlisted, May 2, 1898, at New York city, to serve two years; mustered in as private, Co. B, May 20, 1898; mustered out with company, November 15, 1898, at New York city.

STEIN, JR., CHARLES.—Age, 28 years. Enlisted, May 2, 1898, New York city, to serve two years; mustered in as private, Co. L, May 20, 1898; mustered out with company, November 15, 1898, at New York city.

STEPHENSON, WILLIAM.—Age, 28 years. Enlisted, May 2, 1898, at New York city, to serve two years; mustered in as private, Co. C, May 19, 1898; mustered out with company, November 15, 1898, at New York city.

STERN, ARNOLD E.—Age, 21 years. Enlisted, May 2, 1898, at New York city, to serve two years; mustered in as private, Co. B, May 20, 1898; mustered out with company, November 15, 1898, at New York city.

STERNBACH, EDWARD.—Age, — years. Enlisted, June 29, 1898, at New York city, to serve two years; mustered in as private, Co. G, same date; mustered out with company, November 15, 1898, at New York city.

STEVENS, DENNIS H.—Age, — years. Enlisted, July 6, 1898, at New York city, to serve two years; mustered in as private, Co. B, same date; mustered out with company, November 15, 1898, at New York city.

STEWART, HERBERT L.—Age, 28 years. Enlisted, May 2, 1898, at New York city, to serve two years; mustered in as private, Co. D, May 17, 1898; mustered out with company, November 15, 1898, at New York city.

STEWART, JOHN.—Age, — years. Enlisted, June 27, 1898, at New York city, to serve two years; mustered in as private, Co. E, same date; mustered out with company, November 15, 1898, at New York city.

STEWART, KAE.—Age, — years. Enlisted, June 23, 1898, at New York city, to serve two years; mustered in as private, Co. L, same date; mustered out with company, November 15, 1898, at New York city.

STEWART, WILLIAM F.—Age, 28 years. Enlisted, May 2, 1898, at New York city, to serve two years; mustered in as wagoner, Co. A, May 17, 1898; returned to ranks, June 1, 1898; mustered out with company, November 15, 1898, at New York city.

STOFFERS, GEORGE H.—Age, 19 years. Enlisted, May 2, 1898, at New York city, to serve two years; mustered in as private, Co. B, May 20, 1898; promoted corporal, no date; died of heart disease, October 9, 1898, at Sternberg Hospital, Chickamauga Park, Ga.

STOFFLET, CHARLES A.—Age, — years. Enlisted, July 1, 1898, at New York city, to serve two years; mustered in as private, Co. M, same date; died of typhoid fever, September 17, 1898, at Stroudsburg, Pa.

STONE, ITTIEL.—Age, 40 years. Enlisted, May 2, 1898, at New York city, to serve two years; mustered in as first sergeant, Co. I, May 19, 1898; mustered out with company, November 15, 1898, at New York city.

STONE, NICHOLAS.—Age, 29 years. Enlisted, May 17, 1898, at New York city, to serve two years; mustered in as private, Co. E, May 20, 1898; mustered out with company, November 15, 1898, at New York city.

STONE, WILLIAM.—Age, — years. Enlisted, June 29, 1898, at New York city, to serve two years; mustered in as private, Co. B, same date; discharged for disability, September 10, 1898, at Chickamauga, Ga.

STUART, FRANCIS J.—Age, 44 years. Enlisted, May 2, 1898, at New York city, to serve two years; mustered in as quarter-master-sergeant, Co. M, May 17, 1898; reduced to sergeant, no date; died of typhoid fever, September 10, 1898, at New York Hospital, New York city

SUBURGER, PHILIP.—Age, 23 years. Enlisted, May 2, 1898, at New York city, to serve two years; mustered in as corporal, Co. I, May 19, 1898; mustered out with company, November 15, 1898, at New York city.

SULKIS, SAMUEL.—Age, 21 years. Enlisted, May 2, 1898, at New York city, to serve two years; mustered in as private, Co. A, May 17, 1898; mustered out with company, November 15, 1898, at New York city.

SULLIVAN, TIMOTHY J.—Age, 21 years. Enlisted, May 2, 1898, at New York city, to serve two years; mustered in as private, Co. B, May 20, 1898; mustered out with company, November 15, 1898, at New York city.

SUNSHINE, MAX.—Age, — years. Enlisted, July 9, 1898, at New York city, to serve two years; mustered in as private, Co. E, same date; transferred to band, July 27, 1898; mustered out with regiment, November 15, 1898, at New York city.

SUNTHEIMER, BENJAMIN.—Age, 21 years. Enlisted, May 17, 1898, at New York city, to serve two years; mustered in as private, Co. E, May 20, 1898; mustered out with company, November 15, 1898, at New York city.

SURRIDGE, ROBERT O.—Age, 21 years. Enlisted, May 2, 1898, at New York city, to serve two years; mustered in as private, Co. G, May 20, 1898; mustered out with company, November 15, 1898, at New York city.

SWAN, HENRY J.—Age, 21 years. Enlisted, May 2, 1898, at New York city, to serve two years; mustered in as private, Co. F, May 21, 1898; mustered out with company, November 15, 1898, at New York city.

SWEENEY, JAMES H.—Age, 24 years. Enlisted, May 2, 1898, at New York city, to serve two years; mustered in as private, Co. L, May 20, 1898; mustered out with company, November 15, 1898, at New York city.

SWEENEY, JOSEPH.—Age, 19 years. Enlisted, May 18, 1898, at New York city, to serve two years; mustered in as private, Co. D, same date; mustered out with company, November 15, 1898, at New York city.

TAEGER, JOHN.—Age, — years. Enlisted, June 24, 1898, at New York city, to serve two years; mustered in as private, Co. D, same date; mustered out with company, November 15, 1898, at New York city.

TAGGERT, JOSEPH.—Age, 28 years. Enlisted, May 2, 1898, at New York city, to serve two years; mustered in as private, Co. G, May 20, 1898; mustered out with company, November 15, 1898, at New York city.

TAYLOR, WALTER.—Age, 37 years. Enlisted, May 2, 1898, at New York city, to serve two years; mustered in as first sergeant, Co. E, May 20, 1898; mustered out with company, November 15, 1898, at New York city.

TEARN, THOMAS.—Age, 27 years. Enlisted, May 2, 1898, at New York city, to serve two years; mustered in as artificer, Co. L, May 20, 1898; discharged, October 12, 1898.

TEED, EDWARD G.—Age, 23 years. Enlisted, May 2, 1898, at New York city, to serve two years; mustered in as private, Co. A, May 17, 1898; mustered out with company, November 15, 1898, at New York city; also borne as Edgar Teed.

TERLUME, WILLIAM.—Age, 25 years. Enlisted, May 2, 1898, at New York city, to serve two years; mustered in as private, Co. M, May 17, 1898; mustered out with company, November 15, 1898, at New York city.

TERWILLIGER, FRANK.—Age, 29 years. Enlisted, May 2, 1898, at New York city, to serve two years; mustered in as corporal, Co. H, May 20, 1898; promoted sergeant, no date; mustered out with company, November 15, 1898, at New York city.

TEVLIN, WILLIAM M.—Age, 24 years. Enlisted, May 2, 1898, at New York city, to serve two years; mustered in as private, Co. K, May 19, 1898; promoted corporal, October 21, 1898; mustered out with company, November 15, 1898, at New York city.

THIELL, EDWARD.—Age, 30 years. Enlisted, May 2, 1898, at New York city, to serve two years; mustered in as private, Co. L, May 20, 1898; promoted corporal, August 17, 1898; mustered out with company, November 15, 1898, at New York city.

THOMAS, THOMAS.—Age, 23 years. Enlisted, May 2, 1898, at New York city, to serve two years; mustered in as corporal, Co. L, May 20, 1898; returned to ranks, August 17, 1898; mustered out with company, November 15, 1898, at New York city.

THOMPSON, FRED L.—Age, — years. Enlisted, July 1, 1898, at New York city, to serve two years; mustered in as private, Co. M, same date; mustered out with company, November 15, 1898, at New York city.

THOMPSON, ROBERT L.—Age, 33 years. Enlisted, May 2, 1898, at New York city, to serve two years; mustered in as private, Co. K, May 19, 1898; promoted corporal, July 27, 1898; mustered out with company, November 15, 1898, at New York city.

THOMPSON, WILLIAM F.—Age, 25 years. Enlisted, May 2, 1898, at New York city, to serve two years; mustered in as corporal, Co. E, May 20, 1898; mustered out with company, November 15, 1898, at New York city.

THORMAN, JESSE C.—Age, 24 years. Enlisted, May 2, 1898, at New York city, to serve two years; mustered in as private, Co. D, May 17, 1898; mustered out with company, November 15, 1898, at New York city.

THORNE, LEO B.—Age, 23 years. Enlisted, May 2, 1898, at New York city, to serve two years; mustered in as private, Co. I, May 19, 1898; mustered out with company, November 15, 1898, at New York city.

THORPE, HERBERT.—Age, 25 years. Enlisted, May 2, 1898, at New York city, to serve two years; mustered in as private, Co. I, May 19, 1898; mustered out with company, November 15, 1898, at New York city.

THURBER, JOHN A.—Age, 31 years. Enlisted, May 2, 1898, at New York city, to serve two years; mustered in as private, Co. L, May 20, 1898; mustered out with company, November 15, 1898, at New York city.

THYROLF, WILLIAM C.—Age, 23 years. Enlisted, May 2, 1898, at New York city, to serve two years; mustered in as private, Co. H, May 20, 1898; mustered out with company, November 15, 1898, at New York city.

TIENKEN, GEORGE J.—Age, 32 years. Enlisted, May 2, 1898, at New York city, to serve two years; mustered in as private, Co. F, May 21, 1898; mustered out with company, November 15, 1898, at New York city.

TIERNEY, JR., JOHN J.—Age, 24 years. Enlisted, May 16, 1898, at New York city, to serve two years; mustered in as private, Co. H, May 20, 1898; mustered out with company, November 15, 1898, at New York city.

TIGHE, THOMAS.—Age, — years. Enlisted, June 27, 1898, at New York city, to serve two years; mustered in as private, Co. A, same date; discharged, October 31, 1898, to enlist in regular army.

TIMPSON, THOMAS W.—Age, 32 years. Enrolled, May 2, 1898, at New York city, to serve two years; mustered in as captain, Co. M, May 17, 1898; mustered out with company, November 15, 1898, at New York city; commissioned captain, May 17, 1898, with rank from same date, original.

TOBEY, FRED H.—Age, 42 years. Enlisted, May 2, 1898, at New York city, to serve two years; mustered in as artificer, Co. M, May 17, 1898; mustered out with company, November 15, 1898, at New York city.

TOBIN, JAMES E.—Age, 22 years. Enlisted, May 2, 1898, at New York city, to serve two years; mustered in as sergeant, Co. C, May 19, 1898; mustered out with company, November 15, 1898, at New York city.

TOMKINS, JOHN.—Age, 24 years. Enlisted, May 2, 1898, at New York city, to serve two years; mustered in as private, Co. I, May 19, 1898; mustered out with company, November 15, 1898, at New York city.

TOMLIN, JAMES J.—Age, 29 years. Enlisted, May 17, 1898, at New York city, to serve two years; mustered in as private, Co. B, May 20, 1898; mustered out with company, November 15, 1898, at New York city.

TOMPKINS, ARTHUR M.—Age, 32 years. Enrolled, May 2, 1898, at New York city, to serve two years; mustered in as captain, Co. B, May 20, 1898; discharged for disability, to date, July 26, 1898; commissioned captain, May 20, 1898; with rank from same date, original.

TOMPKINS, FREDERICK.—Age, 26 years. Enlisted, May 2, 1898, at New York city, to serve two years; mustered in as private, Co. I, May 19, 1898; promoted corporal, July 27, 1898; mustered out with company, November 15, 1898, at New York city.

TORLICK, HENRY C.—Age, 22 years. Enlisted, May 16, 1898, at New York city, to serve two years; mustered in as private, Co. B, May 20, 1898; mustered out with company, November 15, 1898, at New York city.

TOWNSEND, WILLIAM.—Age, — years. Enlisted, June 24, 1898, at New York city, to serve two years; mustered in as private, Co. F, same date; mustered out with company, November 15, 1898, at New York city.

TRACY, JOHN.—Age, — years. Enlisted, July 8, 1898, at New York city, to serve two years; mustered in as private, Co. F, same date; transferred to band, July 27, 1898; mustered out with regiment, November 15, 1898, at New York city.

TRAINOR, JOHN.—Age, — years. Enlisted, June 27, 1898, at
New York city, to serve two years; mustered in as private,
Co. I, same date; mustered out with company, November 15,
1898, at New York city.

TRAUD, JOSEPH.—Age, 24 years. Enlisted, May 2, 1898, at
New York city, to serve two years; mustered in as private,
Co. D, May 17, 1898; mustered out with company, November
15, 1898, at New York city.

TRAVERS, FREDERICK.—Age, — years. Enlisted, July 2,
1898, at New York city, to serve two years; mustered in as
private, Co. I, same date; mustered out with company, November 15, 1898, at New York city.

TREACY, JOHN J.—Age, 24 years. Enlisted, May 2, 1898, at
New York city, to serve two years; mustered in as corporal,
Co. A, May 17, 1898; promoted sergeant, October 3, 1898; mus-
tered out with company, November 15, 1898, at New York city.

TRESHAM, JAMES H.—Age, 23 years. Enlisted, May 2, 1898,
at New York city, to serve two years; mustered in as private,
Co. M, May 17, 1898; mustered out with company, November
15, 1898, at New York city.

TURCK, CHARLES L.—Age, — years. Enlisted, June 24, 1898,
at New York city, to serve two years; mustered in as private,
Co. I, same date; mustered out with company, November 15,
1898. at New York city.

TURNER, EDSON J.—Age, 38 years. Enlisted, May 2, 1898, at
New York city, to serve two years; mustered in as private,
Co. E, May 20, 1898; appointed cook, August 19, 1898; mustered
out with company, November 15, 1898, at New York city.

ULRICH, AUGUST C. F.—Age, — years. Enlisted, July 8, 1898,
at New York city, to serve two years; mustered in as private,
Co. M, same date; appointed chief musician, July 27, 1898; mustered out with regiment, November 15, 1898, at New York city.

UNDERWOOD, ALEXANDER.—Age, — years. Enlisted, June
23, 1898, at New York city, to serve two years; mustered in as
private, Co. A, same date; appointed cook, September 1, 1898;
mustered out with company, November 15, 1898, at New York
city.

UNSHINE, EDWARD.—Age, 27 years. Enlisted, May 2, 1898, at New York city, to serve two years; mustered in as private, Co. L, May 20, 1898; mustered out with company, November 15, 1898, at New York city.

UPTON, EDWARD P.—Age, 21 years. Enlisted, May 2, 1898, at New York city, to serve two years; mustered in as private, Co. E, May 20, 1898; mustered out with company, November 15, 1898, at New York city.

URQUHART, ALBERT.—Age, — years. Enlisted, July 2, 1898, at New York city, to serve two years; mustered in as private, Co. I, same date; mustered out with company, November 15, 1898, at New York city.

VAHLE, JOSEPH.—Age, 24 years. Enlisted, May 2, 1898, at New York city, to serve two years; mustered in as private, Co. H, May 20, 1898; mustered out with company, November 15, 1898, at New York city.

VAIL, JAMES W.—Age, 38 years. Enlisted, May 2, 1898, at New York city, to serve two years; mustered in as private, Co. D, May 17, 1898; mustered out with company, November 15. 1898, at New York city.

VAN DER HARST, FRANK.—Age, 19 years. Enlisted, May 2, 1898, at New York city, to serve two years; mustered in as private, Co. I, May 19, 1898; mustered out with company, November 15, 1898, at New York city.

VATH, EDWARD.—Age, — years. Enlisted, June 25, 1898, at New York city, to serve two years; mustered in as private Co. F, same date; mustered out with company, November 15, 1898, at New York city.

VATH, GEORGE F.—Age, 27 years. Enlisted, May 2, 1898, at New York city, to serve two years; mustered in as musician, Co. I, May 19, 1898; mustered out with company, November 15, 1898, at New York city.

VERA, FREDERICK L.—Age, 22 years. Enlisted, May 2, 1898, at New York city to serve two years; mustered in as private, Co. K, May 19, 1898; mustered out with company, November 15, 1898, at New York city.

VERBECK, HUGO A.—Age, 24 years. Enlisted, May 2, 1898, at New York city, to serve two years; mustered in as corporal, Co. I, May 19, 1898; mustered out with company, November 15, 1898, at New York city.

VERNON, HARRY BOYD.—Age, — years. Enlisted, June 23, 1898, at New York city, to serve two years; mustered in as private, Co. M same date; accidentally killed October 17, 1898, at New York city.

VETTER, GEORGE.—Age, — years. Enlisted, June 29, 1898, at New York city, to serve two years; mustered in as private, Co. H, same date; mustered out with company, November 15, 1898, at New York city.

VETTER, HENRY.—Age, — years. Enlisted, June 27, 1898, at New York city, to serve two years; mustered in as private, Co. H, same date; mustered out with company, November 15, 1898, at New York city.

VICKERS, JAMES.—Age, — years. Enlisted, June 23, 1898, at New York city, to serve two years; mustered in as private, Co. A, same date; mustered out with company, November 15, 1898, at New York city.

VIVES, LAWRENCE.—Age, 25 years. Enlisted, May 12, 1898, at camp, near Peekskill, to serve two years; mustered in as private, Co. L, May 20, 1898; transferred to Hospital Corps, June 16, 1898.

VOLLMOELLER, JR., PHILIP C.—Age, 20 years. Enlisted, May 2, 1898, at New York city, to serve two years; mustered in as private, Co. G, May 21, 1898; discharged, September 24, 1898.

VON DER HOFF, ENGELBERT.—Age, 34 years. Enlisted, May 2, 1898, at New York city, to serve two years; mustered in as private, Co. F, May 21, 1898; mustered out with company, November 15, 1898, at New York city.

WADHAMS, HERBERT G.—Age, 21 years. Enlisted, May 2, 1898, at New York city, to serve two years; mustered in as private, Co. H, May 20, 1898; promoted corporal July 27, 1898; mustered out with company, November 15, 1898, at New York city.

WAHLE, WILLIAM.—Age, 29 years. Enlisted May 2, 1898, at New York city, to serve two years; mustered in as sergeant, Co. K, May 19, 1898; mustered out with company, November 15, 1898, at New York city.

WALKER, FRANKLIN D. L.—Age, 28 years. Enrolled May 2, 1898, at New York city, to serve two years; mustered in as first lieutenant, Co. H, May 20, 1898; died of typhoid fever, September 20, 1898, at Presbyterian Hospital, New York city; commissioned first lieutenant, May 20, 1898, with rank from same date, original.

WALKER, JOHN K.—Age, 23 years. Enlisted, May 2, 1898, at New York city, to serve two years; mustered in as corporal, Co. G, May 21, 1898; returned to ranks, September 2, 1898; mustered out with company, November 15, 1898, at New York city.

WALLACE, ANDREW.—Age, — years. Enlisted, July 5, 1898, at New York city, to serve two years; mustered in as private, Co. F, same date; discharged, October 12, 1898.

WALLACE, JOSEPH.—Age, — years. Enlisted, May 2, 1898, at New York city, to serve two years; mustered in as private, Co. H, May 20, 1898; promoted corporal, July 27, 1898; mustered out with company, November 15, 1898, at New York city.

WALLER, HERMAN.—Age, 29 years. Enlisted, May 17, 1898, at New York city, to serve two years; mustered in as private, Co. H, May 20, 1898; mustered out with company, November 15 1898, at New York city.

WALSH, JAMES J.—Age, 27 years. Enlisted, May 2, 1898, at New York city, to serve two years; mustered in as sergeant, Co. A, May 17, 1898; promoted first sergeant, August 27, 1898; mustered in as first lieutenant, October 28, 1898; mustered out with company, November 15, 1898, at New York city; commissioned first lieutenant October 27, 1898, with rank from same date, vice Mahoney, deceased.

WALSH, JAMES J.—Age, — years. Enlisted May 2, 1898, at New York city, to serve two years; mustered in as private, Co. L, June 19, 1898; mustered out with company, November 15, 1898 at New York city.

WALTON, JOHN D.—Age, 39 years. Enrolled, May 2, 1898, at New York city to serve two years; mustered in as captain, Co. D, May 17 1898; discharged for disability, July 14, 1898; commissioned captain, May 17, 1898, with rank from same date, original.

WARD, MAURICE PETER.—Age, 21 years. Enlisted, May 2, 1898, at New York city, to serve two years; mustered in as private, Co. B, May 20, 1898; mustered out with company, November 15, 1898, at New York city.

WARD, WILLIAM W.—Age, 27 years. Enlisted, May 2, 1898, at New York city, to serve two years; mustered in as private, Co. M, May 17, 1898; promoted corporal, October 20, 1898; mustered out with company, November 15, 1898, at New York city.

WARNKEN, GEORGE.—Age, 24 years. Enlisted, May 21, 1898, at New York city to serve two years; mustered in as private, Co. D, same date; promoted corporal, July 21, 1898; discharged, October 10, 1898.

WATKINS, EDWIN W.—Age, 50 years. Enrolled, May 2, 1898, at New York city, to serve two years; mustered in second lieutenant, Co. B, May 20, 1898; mustered out, to date, November 15, 1898, at New York city; commissioned second lieutenant, May 20, 1898, with rank from same date, original.

WATSON, JOHN W.—Age, 29 years. Enlisted, May 2, 1898, at New York city, to serve two years; mustered in as corporal, Co. M, May 17, 1898; died of typhoid fever, October 5, 1898, at New York city.

WATTERS, CLAUDE A.—Age, 27 years. Enlisted, May 2, 1898, at New York city, to serve two years; mustered in as corporal, Co. L, May 20, 1898; promoted sergeant, August 17, 1898; discharged, August 20, 1898.

WEBB, JOHN J.—Age, 21 years. Enlisted, May 2, 1898, at New York city, to serve two years; mustered in as private, Co. F, May 21, 1898; promoted corporal, September 5, 1898; quartermaster-sergeant, October 14, 1898; mustered out with company, November 15, 1898, at New York city.

WEED, OSCAR D.—Age, 36 years. Enrolled, May 2, 1898, at New York city, to serve two years; mustered in as captain, Co. G, May 20, 1898; mustered out with company, November 15, 1898, at New York city; subsequent service as first lieutenant, Twenty-seventh Regiment, United States Volunteer Infantry; commissioned captain, May 20, 1898, with rank from same date, original.

WEGMANN, JOHN W.—Age, 22 years. Enlisted. May 2, 1898, at New York city, to serve two years; mustered in as private, Co. A, May 17, 1898; mustered out with company, November 15, 1898, at New York city.

WEHRENBERG, FREDERICK C.—Age, 21 years. Enlisted, May 2, 1898, at New York city, to serve two years; mustered in as private; Co. F, May 21, 1898; mustered out with. company, November 15, 1898, at New York city.

WEINSTOCK, MAX.—Age, 34 years. Enlisted, May 10, 1898, at New York city, to serve two years; mustered in as private, Co. M, May 17, 1898; promoted corporal, July 27, 1898; mustered out with company, November 15, 1898, at New York city.

WEIS, FERDINAND A.—Age, 31 years. Enlisted, May 2, 1898, at New York city, to serve two years; mustered in as private, Co. M, May 17, 1898; mustered out with company, November 15, 1898, at New York city.

WEISBURGER, BENJAMIN.—Age, 29 years. Enlisted, May 2, 1898, at New York city, to serve two years; mustered in as private, Co. L, May 20, 1898; mustered out with company, November 15, 1898, at New York city.

WEISNER, FREDERICK C.—Age, 20 years. Enlisted, May 2, 1898, at New York city, to serve two years; mustered in as private, Co. K, May 19, 1898; promoted corporal, July 27, 1898; mustered out with company, November 15, 1898, at New York city.

WEISS, CARL.—Age, 26 years. Enlisted, May 16, 1898, at New York city, to serve two years; mustered in as private, Co. D, May 17, 1898; discharged, October 5, 1898.

WELCH, JOSEPH T.—Age, 29 years. Enlisted, May 11, 1898, at camp near Peekskill, to serve two years; mustered in as private, Co. L, May 20, 1898; mustered out with company, November 15, 1898, at New York city.

WELLS, JOHN.—Age, 35 years. Enlisted, May 2, 1898' at New York city, to serve two years; mustered in as private, Co. I, May 19, 1898; mustered out with company, November 15, 1898, at New York city.

WERNER, FRANK.—Age, 34 years. Enlisted, May 2, 1898, at New York city, to serve two years; mustered in as private, Co. D, May 17, 1898; promoted corporal, August 17, 1898; discharged, October 12, 1898.

WESCOE, MORRIS L.—Age, 28 years. Enlisted, May 2, 1898, at New York city, to serve two years; mustered in as sergeant, Co. E, May 20, 1898; mustered out with company, November 15, 1898, at New York city.

WESSOLECK, AUGUST.—Age, — years. Enlisted, May 21, 1898, at camp near Peekskill, to serve two years; mustered in as musician, Co. E, May 21, 1898; mustered out with company, November 15, 1898, at New York city.

WESTBROOK, RALPH.—Age, 24 years. Enlisted, May 2, 1898, at New York city, to serve two years; mustered in as private, Co. K, May 19, 1898; promoted corporal, no date; discharged, October 17, 1898.

WESTERVELT, LUNDY.—Age, — years. Enlisted, June 23, 1898, at New York city, to serve two years; mustered in as private, Co. B, same date; mustered out with company, November 15, 1898, at New York city.

WHALEN, GERALD.—Age, 21 years. Enlisted, May 2, 1898, at New York city, to serve two years; mustered in as private, Co. C, May 19, 1898; mustered out with company, November 15, 1898, at New York city.

WHITE, ANTHONY.—Age, — years. Enlisted, July 8, 1898, at New York city, to serve two years; mustered in as private, Co. L, same date; transferred to Co. B, July 27, 1898; appointed musician, no date; mustered out with company, November 15, 1898, at New York city.

WHITE, DAVID C.—Age, — years. Enlisted, June 27, 1898, at New York city, to serve two years; mustered in as private, Co. L, same date; mustered out with company, November 15, 1898, at New York city.

WHITE, FRANCIS.—Age, — years. Enlisted, June 29, 1898, at New York city, to serve two years; mustered in as private, Co. D, same date; mustered out with company, November 15, 1898, at New York city.

WHITE, GEORGE.—Age, 32 years. Enlisted, May 2, 1898, at New York city, to serve two years; mustered in as private, Co. M, May 17, 1898; died of typhoid fever, September 25, 1898, at Saranac Lake, N. Y.

WHITE, JOHN P.—Age, 26 years. Enlisted, May 2, 1898, at New York city, to serve two years; mustered in as private, Co. M, May 17, 1898; mustered out with company, November 15, 1898, at New York city.

WHITE, WILLIAM B.—Age, 25 years. Enlisted, May 2, 1898, at New York city, to serve two years; mustered in as private, Co. M, May 17, 1898; mustered out with company, November 15, 1898, at New York city.

WHITEHEAD, ARTHUR L.—Age, 28 years. Enlisted, May 2, 1898, at New York city, to serve two years; mustered in as private, Co. H, May 20, 1898; mustered out with company, November 15, 1898, at New York city.

WHITING, CHARLES C.—Age, — years. Enlisted, July 5, 1898, at New York city, to serve two years; mustered in as private, Co. K, same date; mustered out with company, November 15, 1898, at New York city.

WHITMEYER, JOHN H.—Age, 21 years. Enlisted, May 2, 1898, at New York city, to serve two years; mustered in as private, Co. D, May 17, 1898; mustered out with company, November 15, 1898, at New York city.

WHITMORE, CHARLES.—Age, 28 years. Enlisted, May 2, 1898, at New York city, to serve two years; mustered in as corporal, Co. M, May 17, 1898; deserted, June 13, 1898, at Camp Thomas, Chickamauga Park, Ga.

WHITTMAN, ANDREW.—Age, — years. Enlisted, June 29, 1898, at New York city, to serve two years; mustered in as private, Co. D, same date; mustered out with company, November 15, 1898, at New York city.

WHITTY, THOMAS.—Age, 27 years. Enlisted, May 18, 1898, at New York city, to serve two years; mustered in as private, Co. D, same date; mustered out with company, November 15, 1898, at New York city.

WIEDMAN, GEORGE.—Age, 20 years. Enlisted, May 2, 1898, at New York city, to serve two years; mustered in as corporal, Co. A, May 17, 1898; returned to ranks, August 28, 1898; promoted corporal, September 3, 1898; mustered out with company, November 15, 1898, at New York city.

WIEDMAN, JOHN R.—Age, — years. Enlisted, June 23, 1898, at New York city, to serve two years; mustered in as private, Co. A, same date; mustered out with company, November 15, 1898, at New York city.

WIEDMAN, WILLIAM J.—Age, 29 years. Enlisted, May 2, 1898, at New York city, to serve two years; mustered in as quartermaster-sergeant, Co. D, May 17, 1898; mustered out with company, November 15, 1898, at New York city.

WIEMANN, ADOLF.—Age, 21 years. Enlisted, May 2, 1898, at New York city, to serve two years; mustered in as private, Co. I, May 19, 1898; mustered out with company, November 15, 1898, at New York city.

WIENERS, GODFREY A. S.—Age, 31 years. Enrolled, May 2, 1898, at New York city, to serve two years; mustered in as major, May 21, 1898; mustered out, to date, November 15, 1898; commissioned major, May 17, 1898, with rank from same date, original.

WIESHOFER, JOHN.— Age, 22 years. Enlisted, May 2, 1898, at New York city, to serve two years; mustered in as private, Co. A, May 17, 1898; mustered out with company, November 15, 1898, at New York city.

WILBUR, GUY.—Age, 25 years. Enlisted, May 20, 1898, at New York city, to serve two years; mustered in as private, Co. H, same date; mustered out with company, November 15, 1898, at New York city.

WILDA, HANS J.—Age, — years. Enlisted, June 24, 1898, at New York city, to serve two years; mustered in as private, Co. L, same date; mustered out with company, November 15, 1898, at New York city.

WILHELMI, EMIL GUSTAV.—Age, 22 years. Enlisted, May 11, 1898, at camp near Peekskill, to serve two years; mustered in as private, Co. L, May 20, 1898; mustered out with company, November 15, 1898, at New York city.

WILKENSON, RICHARD.—Age, 22 years. Enlisted, May 2, 1898, at New York city, to serve two years; mustered in as private, Co. I, May 19, 1898; mustered out with company, November 15, 1898, at New York city.

WILKS, BENJAMIN.—Age, 22 years. Enlisted, May 2, 1898, at New York city, to serve two years; mustered in as private, Co. G, May 20, 1898; mustered out with company, November 15, 1898, at New York city.

WILLARD, ARTHUR C.—Age, 22 years. Enlisted, May 2, 1898, at New York city, to serve two years; mustered in as private, Co. F, May 21, 1898; promoted corporal, October 14, 1898; mustered out with company, November 15, 1898, at New York city.

WILLARD, FRANK M.—Age, 26 years. Enlisted, May 2, 1898, at New York city, to serve two years; mustered in as private, Co. F, May 21, 1898; promoted corporal, July 27, 1898; mustered out with company, November 15, 1898, at New York city.

WILLCOCKS, ABRAHAM L.—Age, 30 years. Enrolled, May 2, 1898, at New York city, to serve two years; mustered in as first lieutenant, Co. G, May 20, 1898; discharged, August 3, 1898; commissioned first lieutenant, May 20, 1898, with rank from same date, original.

WILLCOCKS, WASHINGTON.—Age, 39 years. Enrolled, May 2, 1898, at New York city, to serve two years; mustered in as major, May 21, 1898; mustered out with regiment, November 15, 1898, at New York city; commissioned major, May 21, 1898, with rank from same date, original.

WILLIAMS, FRANK L.—Age, — years. Enlisted, June 30, 1898, at New York city, to serve two years; mustered in as private, Co. A, same date; mustered out with company, November 15, 1898, at New York city.

WILLIAMS, FRANK S.—Age, 21 years. Enlisted, May 2, 1898, at New York city, to serve two years; mustered in as corporal, Co. I, May 19, 1898; returned to ranks, July 6, 1898; promoted corporal, July 27, 1898; mustered out with company, November 15, 1898, at New York city.

WILLIAMS, FREDERICK.—Age, 24 years. Enlisted, May 2, 1898, at New York city, to serve two years; mustered in as private, Co. I, May 19, 1898; promoted corporal, July 27, 1898; mustered out with company, November 15, 1898, at New York city.

WILLIAMS, THOMAS F.—Age, 22 years. Enlisted, May 2, 1898, at New York city, to serve two years; mustered in as private, Co. G, May 20, 1898; promoted corporal, October 22, 1898; mustered out with company, November 15, 1898, at New York city.

WILLIAMS, WILLIAM G.—Age, 27 years. Enlisted, May 2, 1898, at New York city, to serve two years; mustered in as private, Co. A, May 17, 1898; promoted corporal, July 27, 1898; mustered out with company, November 15, 1898, at New York city.

WILLIAMSON, DAVID J.—Age, 21 years. Enlisted, May 16, 1898, at New York city, to serve two years; mustered in as private, Co. B, May 20, 1898; mustered out with company, November 15, 1898, at New York city.

WILLIS, HENRY P.—Age, 20 years. Enlisted, May 2, 1898, at New York city, to serve two years; mustered in as wagoner, Co. B, May 20, 1898; returned to ranks, no date; mustered out with company, November 15, 1898, at New York city.

WILSON, ARTHUR.—Age, 21 years. Enlisted, May 2, 1898, at New York city, to serve two years; mustered in as private, Co. A, May 17, 1898; mustered out with company, November 15, 1898, at New York city.

WILSON, CHARLES B.—Age, 39 years. Enlisted, May 2, 1898, at New York city, to serve two years; mustered in as private, Co. G, May 20, 1898; promoted corporal, July 27, 1898; mustered out with company, November 15, 1898, at New York city.

WILSON, FREDERICK F.—Age, 21 years. Enlisted, May 2, 1898, at New York city, to serve two years; mustered in as private, Co. G, May 20, 1898; mustered out with company, November 15, 1898, at New York city.

WILSON, JOHN W.—Age, 24 years. Enlisted, May 2, 1898, at New York city, to serve two years; mustered in as corporal, Co. F, May 21, 1898; promoted sergeant, no date; mustered out with company, November 15, 1898, at New York city.

WILSON, OLIVER.—Age, 24 years. Enlisted, May 2, 1898, at New York city, to serve two years; mustered in as musician, Co. D, May 17, 1898; mustered out with company, November 15, 1898, at New York city.

WILTBANKS, JAMES.—Age, — years. Enlisted, July 1, 1898, at New York city, to serve two years; mustered in as private, Co. L, same date; discharged, October 10, 1898.

WINKELMANN, LOUIS.—Age, 21 years. Enlisted, May 2, 1898, at New York city, to serve two years; mustered in as private, Co. G, May 20, 1898; mustered out with company, November 15, 1898, at New York city.

WINSEMAN, LOUIS.—Age, 26 years. Enlisted, May 2, 1898, at New York city, to serve two years; mustered in as sergeant, Co. D, May 17, 1898; mustered out with company, November 15, 1898, at New York city.

WINTERROTH, EMIL JOHN.—Age, 34 years. Enrolled, May 2, 1898, at New York city, as second lieutenant, to serve two years; mustered in as first lieutenant, Co. L, May 20, 1898; discharged July 27, 1898; commissioned first lieutenant, May 20, 1898, with rank from same date, original.

WINTERS, JOHN E.—Age, 21 years. Enlisted, May 2, 1898, at New York city, to serve two years; mustered in as private, Co. M, May 17, 1898; mustered out with company, November 15, 1898, at New York city.

WISTRAND, HENRY.—Age, 18 years. Enlisted, May 2, 1898, at New York city, to serve two years; mustered in as private, Co. E, May 20, 1898; mustered out with company, November 15, 1898, at New York city.

WOLD, FREDERICK.—Age, 33 years. Enlisted, May 2, 1898,
at New York city, to serve two years; mustered in as private,
Co. E, May 20, 1898; died of typhoid fever, September 1, 1898,
at Sternberg Hospital, Chickamauga Park, Ga.

WOLF, HENRY C.—Age, 21 years. Enlisted, May 2, 1898, at
New York city, to serve two years; mustered in as private, Co.
B, May 20, 1898; mustered out with company, November 15,
1898, at New York city.

WOLLENBERGER, PAUL.—Age, 19 years. Enlisted, May 2,
1898, at New York city, to serve two years; mustered in as private, Co. L, May 20, 1898; mustered out with company, November 15, 1898, at New York city.

WOOD, IRVING B.—Age, 21, years. Enlisted, May 2, 1898, at
New York city, to serve two years; mustered in as private, Co.
H, May 20, 1898; appointed principal musician, July 27, 1898;
mustered out with regiment, November 15, 1898, at New York
city.

WOOLFE, DAVID W.—Age, 21 years. Enlisted, May 2, 1898,
at New York city, to serve two years; mustered in as private,
Co. H, May 20, 1898; mustered out with company, November
15, 1898, at New York city.

WORRELL, JAMES G.—Age, 21 years. Enlisted, May 2, 1898,
at New York city, to serve two years; mustered in as private,
Co. I, May 19, 1898; mustered out with company, November 15,
1898, at New York city.

WYATT, MAYNARD B.—Age, — years. Enlisted, June 29,
1898, at New York city, to serve two years; mustered in as private, Co. M, same date; mustered out with company, November
15, 1898, at New York city.

WYMAN, FREDERICK.—Age, 22 years. Enlisted, May 2, 1898,
at New York city, to serve two years; mustered in as private,
Co. I, May 19, 1898; mustered out with company, November 15,
1898, at New York city.

WYMAN, WILLIAM S.—Age, — years. Enlisted, June 24, 1898,
at New York city, to serve two years; mustered in as private,
Co. I, same date; mustered out with company, November 15,
1898, at New York city.

YOUNG, GEORGE R.—Age, 21 years. Enlisted, May 2, 1898, at New York city, to serve two years; mustered in as private, Co. D, May 17, 1898; discharged, October 14, 1898.

YOUNG, WARNER S.—Age, 31 years. Enrolled, May 2, 1898, at New York city, to serve two years; mustered in as captain, Co. H, May 21, 1898; mustered out with company, November 15, 1898, at New York city; commissioned captain, May 20, 1898, with rank from same date, original.

ZUBER, EUGENE L.—Age, — years. Enlisted, July 1, 1898, at New York city, to serve two years; mustered in as private, Co. I, same date; mustered out with company, November 15, 1898, at New York city.

TWELFTH REGIMENT, INFANTRY.

The twelfth regiment, national guard, having volunteered its services, was one of the regiments selected in general orders, No. 8, general headquarters, state of New York, dated adjutant-general's office, Albany, April 27, 1898, to enter the service of the United States as a volunteer regiment.

The regiment at that time consisted of ten companies, and at once commenced recruiting to fill its companies and to organize two additional ones. Its prior history follows:

TWELFTH REGIMENT.

(First Brigade.)

Armory, Columbus avenue and Sixty-second street, New York city.

This regiment was organized as the eleventh regiment by a general order, dated June 21, 1847, and was of eight companies, viz.: Light Guard, of one hundred and sixth regiment; Bensen Guard, of one hundred and twenty-fifth regiment; Independence Guard, of two hundred and sixty-fourth regiment; Italian Guard, of two hundred and fifty-second regiment; Monroe Blues, of two hundred and thirty-fifth regiment; Tompkins Blues, of fifty-first regiment; Independent Tompkins Blues, of two hundred and twenty-second regiment, and Lafayette Fusileers, of eighty-fifth regiment. By a general order, dated July 27, 1847, the designation of the regiment was changed to the twelfth. A new company, under command of Captain Henry Johnson, was organized and attached to the regiment, April 25, 1849. Company H of the third regiment was transferred to the twelfth regiment, April 25, 1849. Company D was consolidated with company C, June 5, 1849. A new company, under Captain Adolphus I. Johnson, was organized, April 15, 1850. Company L was transferred to the eleventh regiment, May 3, 1858. On March 16, 1859, companies A and C, B and H, and G and E were consolidated, and the consolidated companies, with company D, transferred to the tenth

regiment. On June 29, 1859, these transferred companies were
disbanded. On November 16, 1859, five companies (A, B, C, D
and G) were organized in the twenty-second regimental district.
On November 22, 1859, company E was organized and an election
ordered for field officers of the twenty-second regiment. These
companies were composed principally of former members of the
old twelfth regiment. The designation of the twenty-second regiment was changed, December 19, 1859, to twelfth regiment. Company H was organized, January 28, 1860, and company F, February 2, 1860. Company C was consolidated with company E,
March 21, 1861, and company K was organized, May 8, 1861.
Company I, twenty-third regiment, was transferred to twelfth
regiment as company I, April 2, 1861. New company C was
organized, December 31, 1861. Company K was disbanded February 12, 1862, and new company K organized, September 22, 1862.
Company C was consolidated with company H, January 12, 1876.
Co. I was consolidated with Co. G, January 12, 1876. New Co. I,
organized, February 21, 1876. Co. D was consolidated with Co. E,
March 11, 1876. New Co. D was organized, July 16, 1884, and
new Co. C was organized, June 3, 1885.

The regiment performed duty during the Astor Place riots in
1849. April 21, 1861, the regiment entered the United States service for three months; July 12th, took part in a skirmish near
Martinsburgh, Va., and July 15th, near Bunker Hill, W. Va.;
August 5, 1861, it was mustered out of service at New York
city. May 27, 1862, the regiment again entered the United
States service for three months, during which it was engaged
in the defense and was present at the surrender of Harper's
Ferry, W. Va., although its term of service expired August
27th, having volunteered to remain in service until October
15th; September 16th, the regiment was paroled; October 8th,
it was mustered out, and January 11, 1863, declared exchanged.
June 20, 1863, the regiment re-entered the service of the United
States for thirty days, serving in Pennsylvania and Maryland, and
in suppressing the draft riots at New York city; it was mustered
out by companies between July 20th and 25th, but remained in
the service of the state until September, 1863. The regiment was
on duty during the Orange riots in July, 1871; during the railroad

riots in July, 1877; during the switchmen's strike at Buffalo, in August, 1892, and at Brooklyn during the motormen's strike in January, 1895.

Special orders No. 72, A. G. O., May 1, 1898, ordered the regiment to report at the foot of Twenty-second street, North river, New York city, at noon of the 2d of May, there to embark for the Camp of Instruction, near Peekskill, and on arrival at the camp to report to Brigadier-General Peter C. Doyle, national guard, commanding the camp. The order was duly carried out.

Under the provisions of general orders, No. 11, A.G.O., Albany, May 3, 1898, the regiment was at this camp fully organized as a twelve-company regiment, and was mustered in the service of the United States, May 13, 1898, as the " twelfth regiment infantry, New York volunteers."

It left Camp Townsend (Camp of Instruction heretofore) under war department orders, dated May 16th, for Chickamauga Park, Ga., at 11 a. m., on the 17th, and arrived at Chattanooga, Tenn., May 19th, at about 6 a. m.; left Chattanooga for Rossville, Tenn., at 4 p. m., and bivouacked at that place; left for Chickamauga Park at 6.30 a. m., May 20th, and pitched camp at Alexander road in the park.

The regiment there performed the usual camp routine, drills, rifle practice and outpost duties.

August 24th, it left Camp George H. Thomas, Chickamauga Park, Ga., and moved to Lexington, Ky., establishing Camp Hamilton, near that city.

November 13th, the regiment left its camp at Lexington, Ky., and arrived on the morning of the 15th, at Americus, Ga., establishing Camp Gilman outside of the town.

December 26th, the regiment left this camp en-route for Cuba and January 1, 1899, it was stationed at Matanzas, the first battalion occupying Cardenas.

March 20, 1899, the regiment was placed en-route to New York city, where it arrived, March 27, 1899, and was mustered out of the United States service, April 20, 1899.

Commissioned Officers.

COLONEL:

Robert Woodward Leonard, May 2, 1898, to April 20, 1899.

LIEUTENANT-COLONELS:

Charles Jacob Seiter, May 2 to September 30, 1898.
James Parker, October 3, 1898, to April 20, 1899.

MAJORS:

Charles Stewart Burns, May 2, 1898, to April 20, 1899.
James Parker, May 13 to October 3, 1898.
George Rathbone Dyer, May 13, 1898, to April 20, 1899.

REGIMENTAL ADJUTANTS:

William Jay Schieffelin, May 2 to September 30, 1898.
Frederick Montgomery Vermilye, September 30, 1898, to April
    20, 1899.

BATTALION ADJUTANTS:

James Walden Schermerhorn Cleland, May 2 to November 21,
    1898.
John Herbert Claiborne, May 2 to July 23, 1898.
Robert Meade Parker, May 2 to June 7, 1898.
Winthrop Cowdin, June 7 to September 15, 1898.

QUARTERMASTERS:

Winthrop Cowdin, May 2 to June 7, 1898.
Robert Meade Parker, June 7 to August 27, 1898.
Alexander Moss White, Jr., September 6, 1898, to January 12,
    1899.
John Macauley, January 12 to April 20, 1899.

SURGEONS:

George Gray Ward, Jr., May 2 to September 8, 1898.
Thomas Clark Chalmers, November 1, 1898, to April 20, 1899.

ASSISTANT SURGEONS:

John Brannum Haden, May 2 to August 29, 1898.

Thomas Clark Chalmers, May 2 to November 1, 1898.

Jesse Smith De Muth, August 29, 1898, to April 20, 1899.

Thomas Crook McCleave, November 11, 1898, to April 20, 1899.

CHAPLAINS:

Roderick Terry, May 2 to September 17, 1898.

Albert Joseph Bader, October 3, 1898, to April 20, 1899.

COMPANY A.

CAPTAIN:

Ernest Rollin Tilton, May 2, 1898, to April 20, 1899.

FIRST LIEUTENANTS:

Frederick Montgomery Vermilye, May 2 to September 30, 1898.

Edward Ormonde Power, September 30, 1898, to April 20, 1899.

SECOND LIEUTENANTS:

Alexander Moss White, Jr., May 17 to August 27, 1898.

John Stewart Adair, August 27 to October 28, 1898.

Robert Dewey Russell, November 19, 1898, to February 1, 1899.

Edward Francis Hackett, Jr., February 21 to April 20, 1899.

COMPANY B.

CAPTAINS:

Washington Tyson Romaine, May 16 to December 7, 1898.

Theodore B. Taylor, December 23, 1898, to April 20, 1899.

FIRST LIEUTENANTS:

Francis Lauren Vinton Hoppin, May 13 to September 14, 1898.

Theodore B. Taylor, September 27 to December 23, 1898.

Robert Dewey Russell, February 1 to April 20, 1899.

SECOND LIEUTENANTS:

Francis Lauren Vincent Hoppin, May 2 to May 13, 1898.

Robert Linlithgow Livingston, May 13 to October 31, 1898.

Thomas Joseph Coloe, December 19, 1898, to April 20, 1899.

COMPANY C.

CAPTAIN:

Thomas William Huston, May 2, 1898, to April 20, 1899.

FIRST LIEUTENANTS:

Washington Tyson Romaine, May 2 to May 16, 1898.
Francis James Burke, May 17 to October 26, 1898.
Percy M. Burrill, December 8 to December 24, 1898.
Henry W. Parker, December 29, 1898, to April 20, 1899.

SECOND LIEUTENANTS:

Francis James Burke, May 2 to May 17, 1898.
Lawrence Haughton, May 22 to November 25, 1898.
Wilbur Eddy, December 21, 1898, to April 20, 1899.

COMPANY D.

CAPTAINS:

Samuel Scheiffelin Stebbins, May 2 to October 15, 1898.
Francis James Burke, October 26, 1898, to April 20, 1899.

FIRST LIEUTENANTS:

René Amedee de Russy, May 2 to July 18, 1898.
Percy M. Burrill, July 21 to December 8, 1898.
Thomas Mason Raborg, December 21 to December 24, 1898.
Richard S. Satterlee, February 16 to April 20, 1899.

SECOND LIEUTENANT:

James Francis Dowling, May 31, 1898, to April 20, 1899.

COMPANY E.

CAPTAIN:

William Francis Judson, May 2, 1898, to April 20, 1899.

FIRST LIEUTENANTS:

William Edward Downs, May 2 to October 20, 1898.
Monson Morris, November 17, 1898, to April 20, 1899.

SECOND LIEUTENANTS:

Monson Morris, May 2 to September 7, 1898.
John McDermott, September 17, 1898, to April 20, 1899.

COMPANY F.

CAPTAIN:

Thomas Charles Buck, May 2, 1898, to April 20, 1899.

FIRST LIEUTENANT:

Charles Howard Wainwright, May 2, 1898, to April 20, 1899.

SECOND LIEUTENANTS:

Percy M. Burrill, May 2 to July 21, 1898.
John Clausen, July 21, 1898, to April 20, 1899.

COMPANY G.

CAPTAINS:

George Rathbone Dyer, May 2 to May 13, 1898.
Frederick Charles Harriman, May 13 to July '23' 1898.
John Herbert Claiborne, July 23 to October 15, 1898.
John Philip Benkard, October 27, 1898, to April 20, 1899.

FIRST LIEUTENANTS:

Frederick Charles Harriman, May 2 to May 13, 1898.
John Philip Benkard, May 13 to October 27, 1898.
Walter Bryant Hotchkin, December 5 to December 23, 1898.
John Patrick Fennell, January 11 to April 20, 1899.

SECOND LIEUTENANTS:

John Philip Benkard, May 2 to May 13, 1898.
John Patrick Fennell, May 31, 1898, to January 11, 1899.
Charles Ernest Ravens, January 11 to January 12, 1899.
Frederick Brinsmaid Van Kleeck, Jr., January 12 to February
    7, 1899.
William Lush Martin, February 17 to April 20, 1899.

COMPANY H.

Captains:

Albertson Van Zo-Post, May 13 to December 22, 1898.
Osgood Smith, January 11 to April 20, 1899.

First Lieutenants:

Albertson Van Zo Post, May 2 to May 13, 1898.
Osgood Smith, May 24, 1898, to January 11, 1899.
Lawrence Vincent Meehan, January 31 to April 20, 1899.

Second Lieutenants:

Alexander Moss White, Jr., May 2 to May 17, 1898.
Lawrence Vincent Meehan, June 20, 1898, to January 31, 1899.
William Rowland Cruger, February 1 to April 20, 1899.

COMPANY I.

Captain:

Charles William Smith, May 2, 1898, to April 20, 1899.

First Lieutenants:

Nelson Beardsley Burr, May 2 to October 28, 1898.
Ernest A. Greenough, December 8, 1898, to April 20, 1899.

Second Lieutenants:

Thomas Mason Raborg, May 2 to December 21, 1898.
Thomas Hunter Williamson, January 11 to April 20, 1899.

COMPANY K.

Captains:

John Reginald Blake, May 2 to September 3, 1898.
William Murray Connell, September 7, 1898, to April 20, 1899.

First Lieutenants:

William Murray Connell, May 2 to September 7, 1898.
Monson Morris, September 7 to November 17, 1898.
Alfred A. Mitchell, November 23, 1898, to April 20, 1899.

SECOND LIEUTENANTS:

Edward Ormonde Power, May 2 to September 30, 1898.

John Herbert George Lawrance, January 11 to April 20, 1899.

COMPANY L.

CAPTAINS:

Jonathan Mayhew Wainwright, May 2 to September 7, 1898.

Frederick Goodwin Turner, October 18 to December 16, 1898.

Walter Bryant Hotchkin, January 11 to April 20, 1899.

FIRST LIEUTENANTS:

Frederick Goodwin Turner, May 2 to October 18, 1898.

Walter Bryant Hotchkin, December 23, 1898, to January 11, 1899.

Alexander Moss White, Jr., January 12 to February 10, 1899.

Calhoun Cragin, February 27 to April 20, 1899.

SECOND LIEUTENANTS:

Osgood Smith, May 2 to May 24, 1898.

Thomas K. Russell, May 24 to September 15, 1898.

Ord Myers, December 10, 1898, to April 20, 1899.

COMPANY M.

CAPTAINS:

Newbold Morris, May 2 to September 30, 1898.

William Edward Downs, October 20 to November 17, 1898.

James Walden Schermerhorn Cleland, November 21, 1898, to April 20, 1899.

FIRST LIEUTENANTS:

Peter Stuyvesant Pillot, May 2 to July 18, 1898.

Tompkins McIlvaine, July 21 to December 24, 1898.

James R. Goodale, March 17 to April 20, 1899.

SECOND LIEUTENANTS:

Tompkins McIlvaine, May 2 to July 21, 1898.

Frederick Brinsmaid Van Kleeck, Jr., July 26, 1898, to January 12, 1899.

Charles Ernest Ravens, January 12 to April 20, 1899.

OFFICERS WHO WERE COMMISSIONED, BUT DID NOT SERVE IN GRADES NAMED.

First Lieutenant, Frederick Montgomery Vermilye, as battalion adjutant, revoked.

Battalion Quartermaster, James Walden Schermerhorn Cleland, as captain, declined.

Assistant Surgeon, John Brannon Hayden, as surgeon.

Captain, Frederick J. Quinby, late 9th N. Y. Volunteers, as first lieutenant, cancelled.

RECORDS OF THE OFFICERS AND ENLISTED MEN.

ABBOTT, CLEMENT C.—Age, 23 years. Enlisted, May 2, 1898, at New York city, to serve two years; mustered in as private, Co. G, May 13, 1898; promoted corporal, March 9, 1899; mustered out with company, April 20, 1899, at New York city.

ABEL, JOHN. S.—Age, 22 years. Enlisted, May 13, 1898, at New York city, to serve two years; mustered in as private, Co. C, same date; mustered out with company, April 20, 1899, at New York city.

ACKERMAN, OLAF H.—Age, 22 years. Enlisted, May 2, 1898, at New York city, to serve two years; mustered in as private, Co. I, May 13, 1898; appointed wagoner, January 9, 1899; returned to ranks, February 7, 1899; re-appointed wagoner, February 9, 1899; mustered out with company, April 20, 1899, at New York city.

ADAIR, JOHN STEWART.—Age, 30 years. Enlisted, May 2, 1898, at New York city, to serve two years; mustered in as sergeant-major, May 13, 1898; as second lieutenant, Co. A, August 27, 1898; discharged, October 28, 1898, at New York city; commissioned second lieutenant, August 27, 1898, with rank from same date, vice White, promoted.

ADERTON, ALPHONSO.—Age, — years. Enlisted, June 21, 1898, at New York city, to serve two years; mustered in as private, Co. A, same date; transferred to Hospital Corps, December 7, 1898.

ALLEN, FRANK.—Age, 23 years. Enlisted, May 2, 1898, at New York city, to serve two years; mustered in as private, Co. E, May 13, 1898; promoted corporal, January 1, 1899; mustered out with company, April 20, 1899, at New York city.

ALLEN, GEORGE WASHINGTON.—Age, 27 years. Enlisted, May 2, 1898, at New York city, to serve two years; mustered in as sergeant, Co. E, May 13, 1898; discharged, January 24, 1899, at Fort McPherson, Ga.

ALPERT, SALLY.—Age, 21 years. Enlisted, May 13, 1898, at camp, near Peekskill, to serve two years; mustered in as private, Co. E, same date; transferred to Hospital Corps, December 7, 1898.

ANDERSON, CARL L.—Age, 19 years. Enlisted, May 10, 1898, at New York city, to serve two years; mustered in as private, Co. K, May 13, 1898; mustered out with company, April 20, 1899, at New York city.

ANDERSON, CHARLES.—Age, 23 years. Enlisted, May 2, 1898, at New York city, to serve two years; mustered in as private, Co. F, May 13, 1898; discharged for disability, January 4, 1899, at Americus, Ga.

ANDERSON, MICHAEL.—Age, 21 years. Enlisted, May 2, 1898, at New York city, to serve two years; mustered in as private, Co. I, May 13, 1898; discharged, January 25, 1899, at New York city.

ANDRADE, ALBERT E.—Age, 21 years. Enlisted, May 2, 1898, at New York city, to serve two years; mustered in as private, Co. L, May 13, 1898; promoted corporal, July 5, 1898; discharged, March 21, 1899, at Cardenas, Cuba.

ANGER, CHARLES FREDERICK HENRY.—Age, 23 years. Enlisted, May 2, 1898, at New York city, to serve two years; mustered in as private, Co. C, May 13, 1898; mustered out with company, April 20, 1899, at New York city.

ANGLUM, JAMES.—Age, 23 years. Enlisted, May 2, 1898, at New York city, to serve two years; mustered in as private, Co. L, May 13, 1898; mustered out with company, April 20, 1899, at New York city.

ANTON, JAMES.—Age, — years. Enlisted, June 23, 1898, at New York city, to serve two years; mustered in as private, Co. C, same date; mustered out with company, April 20, 1899, at New York city.

ASPROOTH, CHARLES.—Age, — years. Enlisted, November 15, 1898, at New York city, to serve two years; mustered in as private, Co. F, November 30, 1898; mustered out with company, April 20, 1899, at New York city.

ATTILIO, FASCOLO.—Age, 19 years. Enlisted, May 11, 1898, at camp, near Peekskill, to serve two years; mustered in as private, Co. K, May 13, 1898; mustered out with company, April 20, 1899, at New York city.

AUSTIN, WALDO EMERSON.—Age, 23 years. Enlisted, May 2, 1898, at New York city, to serve two years; mustered in as quartermaster-sergeant, Co. B, May 13, 1898; returned to ranks, August 16, 1898; discharged for disability no date, at Americus, Ga.

AVERY, FRANK.—Age, — years. Enlisted, June 23, 1898, at New York city, to serve two years; mustered in as private, Co. M, same date; discharged, October 25, 1898, at Lexington, Ky.

AYE, ROBERT.—Age, 21 years. Enlisted, May 2, 1898, at New York city, to serve two years; mustered in as private, Co. L, May 13, 1898; mustered out with company, April 20, 1899, at New York city.

AYLWARD, HENRY.—Age, — years. Enlisted, June 28, 1898, at New York city, to serve two years; mustered in as private, Co. B, same date; mustered out with company, April 20, 1899, at New York city.

BADER, ALBERT JOSEPH.—Enrolled, September 17, 1898, at Lexington, Ky., to serve two years; mustered in as chaplain, October 3, 1898; mustered out with regiment, April 20, 1899, at New York city; commissioned chaplain, September 13, 1898, with rank from same date, vice Terry, discharged.

BADGER, WILLIAM D.—Age, — years. Enlisted, June 20, 1898, at New York city, to serve two years; mustered in as private, Co. C, same date; mustered out with company, April 20, 1899, at New York city.

BAILEY, ARTHUR G.—Age, 21 years. Enlisted, May 2, 1898, at New York city, to serve two years; mustered in as private, Co. D, May 13, 1898; mustered out with company, April 20, 1899, at New York city.

BAILEY, LEVI.—Age, 25 years. Enlisted, May 2, 1898, at New York city, to serve two years; mustered in as private, Co. D, May 13, 1898; appointed wagoner, January 27, 1899; mustered out with company, April 20, 1899, at New York city.

BAISLEY, JOHN.—Age, 19 years. Enlisted, May 2, 1898, at New York city, to serve two years; mustered in as private, Co. L, May 13, 1898; mustered out with company, April 20, 1899, at New York city.

BAKER, FREDERICK A.—Age, — years. Enlisted, June 18, 1898, at New York city, to serve two years; mustered in as private, Co. E, same date; promoted corporal, January 1, 1899; mustered out with company, April 20, 1899, at New York city.

BAKER, JOHN J.—Age, 24 years. Enlisted, May 10, 1898, at camp, near Peekskill, to serve two years; mustered in as private, Co. M, May 13, 1898; mustered out with company, April 20, 1899, at New York city.

BAKER, JOHN J.—Age, 28 years. Enlisted, May 2, 1898, at New York city, to serve two years; mustered in as private, Co. F, May 13, 1898; mustered out with company, April 20, 1899, at New York city.

BAKER, THOMAS J.—Age, 21 years. Enlisted, May 2, 1898, at New York city, to serve two years; mustered in as private, Co. F, May 13, 1898; mustered out with company, April 20, 1899, at New York city.

BALDWIN, JOHN ELLIOTT.—Age, 21 years. Enlisted, May 2, 1898, at New York city, to serve two years; mustered in as private, Co. B, May 13, 1898; mustered out with company, April 20, 1899, at New York city.

BALMER, WALTER M.—Age, — years. Enlisted, June 25, 1898, at New York city, to serve two years; mustered in as private, Co. C, same date; appointed cook, July 1, 1898; mustered out with company, April 20, 1899, at New York city.

BALZ, JOHN.—Age, 26 years. Enlisted, May 2, 1898, at New York city, to serve two years; mustered in as private, Co. H, May 13, 1898; mustered out with company, April 20, 1899, at New York city.

BAMBERGER, RAYMOND L.—Age, 21 years. Enlisted, May 2, 1898, at New York city, to serve two years; mustered in as private, Co. L, May 13, 1898; transferred to First Army Corps Hospital, July 20, 1898.

BANCROFT, CLAUD.—Age, 25 years. Enlisted, May 13, 1898, at camp near Peekskill, to serve two years; mustered in as private, Co. L, same date; transferred to Co. E, May 20, 1898; mustered out with company, April 20, 1899, at New York city.

BANMAN, FRANK.—Age, 30 years. Enlisted, May 2, 1898, at New York city, to serve two years; mustered in as corporal, Co. D, May 13, 1898; returned to ranks, May 31, 1898; appointed artificer, September 26, 1898; returned to ranks, December 15, 1898; discharged for disability, January 4, 1899, at Camp Gilman, Ga.

BARCLAY, BYRON.—Age, 19 years. Enlisted, May 10, 1898, at New York city, to serve two years; mustered in as private, Co. F, May 13, 1898; deserted, October 24, 1898, at Camp Hamilton, Lexington, Ky.

BARKER, HARRY.—Age, — years. Enlisted, November 15, 1898, at New York city, to serve two years; mustered in as private, Co. B, November 30, 1898; mustered out with company, April 20, 1899, at New York city; prior service in Eighth New York Volunteer Infantry.

BARNES, ARCHIE H.—Age, 23 years. Enlisted, May 2, 1898, at New York city, to serve two years; mustered in as private, Co. E, May 13, 1898; mustered out with company, April 20, 1899, at New York city.

BARNES, JAMES.—Age, 20 years. Enlisted, May 11, 1898, at camp, near Peekskill, to serve two years; mustered in as private, Co. G, May 13, 1898; mustered out with company, April 20, 1899, at New York city.

BARNETT, FREDERICK.—Age, — years. Enlisted, June 20, 1898, at New York city, to serve two years; mustered in as private, Co. K, same date; mustered out with company, April 20, 1899, at New York city.

BARR, JAMES A.—Age, 21 years. Enlisted, May 2, 1898, at New York city, to serve two years; mustered in as private, Co. K, May 13, 1898; mustered out with company, April 20, 1899, at New York city.

BARRETT, EDWARD J.—Age, — years. Enlisted, June 18, 1898, at New York city, to serve two years; mustered in as private, Co. A, same date; mustered out with company, April 20, 1899, at New York city.

BARRETT, JOSEPH J.—Age, 26 years. Enlisted, May 2, 1898, at New York city, to serve two years; mustered in as private, Co. G, May 13, 1898; mustered out with company, April 20, 1899, at New York city.

BARRY, EDWARD.—Age, — years. Enlisted, June 20, 1898, at New York city, to serve two years; mustered in as private, Co. H, same date; mustered out with company, April 20, 1899, at New York city.

BARRY, GROSVENOR W.—Age, — years. Enlisted, June 25, 1898, at New York city, to serve two years; mustered in as private, Co. G, same date; deserted, December 1, 1898, at Americus, Ga.

BARRY, WILLIAM S.—Age, — years. Enlisted, June 25, 1898, at New York city, to serve two years; mustered in as private, Co. A, same date; promoted corporal, April 3, 1899; mustered out with company, April 20, 1899, at New York city.

BARTELL, ALBERT.—Age, — years. Enlisted, June 25, 1898, at New York city, to serve two years; mustered in as private, Co. I, same date; promoted corporal, August 20, 1898; mustered out with company, April 20, 1899, at New York city.

BARTLETT, CHARLES T.—Age, 29 years. Enlisted, May 13, 1898, at New York city, to serve two years; mustered in as private, Co. I, same date; promoted corporal, January 13, 1899; mustered out with company, April 20, 1899, at New York city.

BASSO, ANGELO.—Age, 28 years. Enlisted, May 13, 1898, at camp, near Peekskill, to serve two years; mustered in as private, Co. K, same date; mustered out with company, April 20, 1899, at New York city.

BATTLE, BERNARD J.—Age, 23 years. Enlisted, May 2, 1898, at New York city, to serve two years; mustered in as corporal, Co. H, May 13, 1898; mustered out with company, April 20, 1899, at New York city.

BAUER, ANTON G.—Age, 22 years. Enlisted, May 2, 1898, at New York city, to serve two years; mustered in as private, Co. H, May 13, 1898; deserted, August 22, 1898, at Camp Thomas, Chickamauga Park, Ga.

BAURY, FREDERIC F.—Age, 19 years. Enlisted, May 2, 1898, at New York city, to serve two years; mustered in as corporal, Co. G, May 13, 1898; returned to ranks, June 21, 1898; discharged, June 17, 1899, at New York city.

BEATTY, EPHRIAM S.—Age, — years. Enlisted, June 21, 1898, at New York city, to serve two years; mustered in as private, Co. B, same date; mustered out with company, April 20, 1899, at New York city.

BECHMANN, WILLIAM E.—Age, — years. Enlisted, June 28, 1898, at New York city, to serve two years; mustered in as private, Co. E, same date; mustered out with company, April 20, 1899, at New York city.

BECKER, AUGUST.—Age, 20 years. Enlisted, May 2, 1898, at New York city, to serve two years; mustered in as private, Co. L, May 13, 1898; mustered out with company, April 20, 1899, at New York city.

BECKER, WILLIAM.—Age, — years. Enlisted, June 17, 1898, at New York city, to serve two years; mustered in as private, Co. L, same date; mustered out with company, April 20, 1899, at New York city.

BECKH, ERNEST F.—Age, 22 years. Enlisted, May 2, 1898, at New York city, to serve two years; mustered in as private, Co. B, May 13, 1898; promoted corporal, August 1, 1898; mustered out with company, April 20, 1899, at New York city.

BECKHARDT, ABRAHAM LOUIS.—Age, 25 years. Enlisted, May 2, 1898, at New York city, to serve two years; mustered in as private, Co. B, May 13, 1898; promoted corporal, August 1, 1898; quartermaster-sergeant, February 14, 1899; mustered out with company, April 20, 1899, at New York city.

BEDDLE, FREDERICK B.—Age, — years. Enlisted, November 15, 1898, at New York city, to serve two years; mustered in as private, Co. M, November 30, 1898; mustered out with company, April 20, 1899, at New York city.

BEERMAN, OTTO.—Age, — years. Enlisted, June 24, 1898, at New York city, to serve two years; mustered in as private, Co. M, same date; discharged, October 25, 1898, at New York city.

BEHRENS, EDWARD C.—Age, 21 years.   Enlisted, May 2, 1898, at New York city, to serve two years; mustered in as private, Co. I, May 13, 1898; promoted corporal, December 9, 1898; mustered out with company, April 20, 1899, at New York city.

BEHRINGER, CHARLES A.—Age, 18 years. Enlisted, May 2, 1898, at New York city, to serve two years; mustered in as private, Co. B, May 13, 1898; discharged, December 17, 1898, at Americus, Ga.

BEHRINGER, JR., GEORGE F.—Age, 23 years. Enlisted, May 2, 1898, at New York city, to serve two years; mustered in as private, Co. B, May 13, 1898; discharged, October 24, 1898, at Lexington, Ky.

BEHUNE, HUGO.—Age, 24 years. Enlisted, May 2, 1898, at New York city, to serve two years; mustered in as sergeant, Co. I, May 13, 1898; returned to ranks, August 27, 1898; transferred to Signal Corps, October 26, 1898.

BELL, ALEXANDER.—Age, 23 years. Enlisted, May 2, 1898, at New York city, to serve two years; mustered in as private, Co. H, May 13, 1898; promoted corporal, August 16, 1898; returned to ranks, September 10, 1898; discharged for disability, January 4, 1899, at Camp Gilman, Ga.

BELLANDER, GOTTFRID.—Age, 31 years. Enlisted, May 10, 1898, at camp, near Peekskill, to serve two years; mustered in as private, Co. D, May 13, 1898; mustered out with company, April 20, 1899, at New York city.

BELLUSCH, PETER.—Age, — years. Enlisted, June 25, 1898, at New York city, to serve two years; mustered in as private, Co. G, same date; transferred to band, July 3, 1898; re-transferred to Co. G, September 25, 1898; appointed musician, same date; mustered out with company, April 20, 1899, at New York city.

BENDER, FREDERICK.—Age, 33 years. Enlisted, May 2, 1898, at New York city, to serve two years; mustered in as private, Co. L, May 13, 1898; mustered out with company, April 20, 1899, at New York city.

BENDER, ROBERT.—Age, 20 years. Enlisted, May 11, 1898, at New York city, to serve two years; mustered in as private, Co. I, May 13, 1898; died of typhoid fever, August 27, 1898, at Camp Thomas, Chickamauga Park, Ga.

BENKARD, JOHN PHILIP.—Age, 25 years. Enrolled, May 2, 1898, at New York city, to serve two years; mustered in as second lieutenant, Co. G, May 13, 1898; as first lieutenant, July 13, 1898, to date, May 13, 1898; as captain, October 27, 1898; mustered out with company, April 20, 1899, at New York city; commissioned second lieutenant, May 13, 1898, with rank from same date, original; first lieutenant, May 13, 1898, with rank from same date, vice Harriman, promoted; captain, October 27, 1898, with rank from same date, vice Claiborne, discharged.

BENNETT, EDWARD J.—Age, 22 years. Enlisted, May 2, 1898, at New York city, to serve two years; mustered in as private, Co. F, May 13, 1898; mustered out with company, April 20, 1899, at New York city.

BENNETT, JOHN J.—Age, 32 years. Enlisted, May 2, 1898, at New York city, to serve two years; mustered in as corporal, Co. A, May 13, 1898; returned to ranks, June 22, 1898; discharged, no date.

BENNETT, MICHAEL.—Age, 21 years. Enlisted, May 2, 1898, at New York city, to serve two years; mustered in as musician, Co. F, May 13, 1898; discharged as a minor, June 2, 1898, at Chickamauga, Ga.

BENNETT, WILLIAM G.—Age, 33 years. Enlisted, May 2, 1898, at New York city, to serve two years; mustered in as private, Co. K, May 13, 1898; mustered out with company, April 20, 1899, at New York city.

BENNI, CHARLES.—Age, 21 years. Enlisted, May 11, 1898, at camp, near Peekskill, to serve two years; mustered in as private, Co. K, May 13, 1898; transferred to Hospital Corps, United States Army, December 18, 1898.

BERG, JOHN B.—Age, 23 years. Enlisted, May 11, 1898, at camp, near Peekskill, to serve two years; mustered in as private, Co. A, May 13, 1898; mustered out with company, April 20, 1899, at New York city.

BERG, LESTER.—Age, 23 years. Enlisted, May 2, 1898, at New York city, to serve two years; mustered in as private, Co. A, May 13, 1898; mustered out with company, April 20, 1899, at New York city.

BERGER, HENRY.—Age, 21 years. Enlisted, May 2, 1898, at New York city, to serve two years; mustered in as private, Co. F, May 13, 1898; mustered out with company, April 20, 1899, at New York city.

BERGER, RICHARD.—Age, — years. Enlisted, June 29, 1898, at New York city, to serve two years; mustered in as private, Co. I, same date; mustered out with company, April 20, 1899, at New York city.

BERGMANN, PHILIP.—Age, — years. Enlisted, June 23, 1898, at New York city, to serve two years; mustered in as private, Co. E, same date; mustered out with company, April 20, 1899, at New York city.

BERNARD, ARTHUR G.—Age, 36 years. Enlisted, May 13, 1898, at camp, near Peekskill, to serve two years; mustered in as private, Co. M, same date; promoted corporal, July 5, 1898; mustered out with company, April 20, 1899, at New York city.

BETZ, CHARLES F.—Age, 22 years. Enlisted, May 2, 1898, at New York city, to serve two years; mustered in as private, Co. A, May 13, 1898; mustered out with company, April 20, 1899, at New York city,

BEYER, JOHN.—Age, 23 years. Enlisted, May 2, 1898, at New York city, to serve two years; mustered in as private, Co. E, May 14, 1898; transferred to Co. G, October 7, 1898; mustered out with company, April 20, 1899, at New York city.

BICKART, LOUIS.—Age, — years. Enlisted, June 18, 1898, at New York city, to serve two years; mustered in as private, Co. D, same date; mustered out with company, April 20, 1899, at New York city.

BILLINGHAM, HENRY.—Age, 19 years. Enlisted, May 2, 1898, at New York city, to serve two years; mustered in as private, Co. H, May 13, 1898; mustered out with company, April 20, 1899, at New York city.

BILLS, RICHARD B.—Age, — years. Enlisted, June 28, 1898, at New York city, to serve two years; mustered in as private, Co. B, same date; mustered out with company, April 20, 1899, at New York city.

BISSONETT, EUGENE F.—Age, 23 years. Enlisted, May 2, 1898, at New York city, to serve two years; mustered in as private, Co. D, May 13, 1898; mustered out with company, April 20, 1899, at New York city.

BLACKMAN, ARTHUR C.—Age, 23 years. Enlisted, May 2, 1898, at New York city, to serve two years; mustered in as private, Co. D, May 13, 1898; promoted corporal, May 31, 1898; quartermaster-sergeant, July 24, 1898; returned to ranks, November 8, 1898; promoted corporal, January 18, 1899; mustered out with company, April 20, 1899, at New York city.

BLAKE, EDWARD M.—Age, — years. Enlisted, June 30, 1898, at New York city, to serve two years; mustered in as private, Co. M, same date; promoted corporal, November 22, 1898; mustered out with company, April 20, 1899, at New York city.

BLAKE, JOHN REGINALD.—Age, 29 years. Enrolled, May 2, 1898, at New York city, to serve two years; mustered in as captain, Co. K, May 13, 1898; discharged, September 3. 1898, at Lexington, Ky.; commissioned captain, May 13, 1898, with rank from same date, original.

BLANCKE, RUDOLPH C.—Age, 23 years. Enlisted, May 2, 1898, at New York city, to serve two years; mustered in as private, Co. G, May 13, 1898; deserted, October 3, 1898, at Lexington, Ky.

BLAUVELT, ARTHUR E.—Age, 27 years. Enlisted, May 2, 1898, at New York city, to serve two years; mustered in as private, Co. H, May 13, 1898; discharged without honor, January 16, 1899, at New York city.

BLAUVELT, LOUIS L.—Age, 18 years. Enlisted, May 13, 1898, at New York city, to serve two years; mustered in as private, Co. B, same date; promoted corporal, February 19, 1899; mustered out with company, April 20, 1899, at New York city.

BLIVEN, ALBERT A.—Age, 18 years . Enlisted, May 2, 1898, at New York city, to serve two years; mustered in as private, Co. B, May 13, 1898; mustered out with company, April 20, 1899, at New York city.

BLIVEN, ROBERT A.—Age, 18 years. Enlisted, May 2, 1898, at New York city, to serve two years; mustered in as private, Co. B, May 13, 1898; mustered out with company, April 20, 1899, at New York city.

BOCK, WILLIAM C.—Age, 25 years. Enlisted, May 11, 1898, at New York city, to serve two years; mustered in as private, Co. I, May 13, 1898; dishonorably discharged, to date, September 1, 1898, at Lexington, Ky.

BOHRER, PHILIPP.—Age, 27 years. Enlisted, May 2, 1898, at New York city, to serve two years; mustered in as private, Co. C, May 13, 1898; mustered out with company, April 20, 1899, at New York city.

BOING, GEORGE J.—Age, 30 years. Enlisted, May 2, 1898, at New York city, to serve two years; mustered in as private, Co. M, May 13, 1898; promoted corporal, September 20, 1898; returned to ranks, November 12, 1898; committed suicide, November 17, 1898, at Americus, Ga.

BOLES, PATRICK C.—Age, 23 years. Enlisted, May 2, 1898, at New York city, to serve two years; mustered in as private, Co. K, May 13, 1898; discharged, to date, April 20, 1899, at New York city.

BOLLAG, HENRY V.—Age, 21 years. Enlisted, May 2, 1898, at New York city, to serve two years; mustered in as private, Co. L, May 13, 1898; mustered out with company, April 20, 1899, at New York city.

BOLMER, RAYMOND L.—Age, 21 years. Enlisted, May 13, 1898, at New York city, to serve two years; mustered in as private, Co. B, same date; mustered out with company, April 20, 1899, at New York city.

BOMAN, BENJAMIN.—Age, 25 years. Enlisted, May 2, 1898, at New York city, to serve two years; mustered in as private, Co. A, May 13, 1898; mustered out with company, April 20, 1899, at New York city.

BOMAN, WILLIAM J.—Age, 23 years. Enlisted, May 2, 1898, at New York city, to serve two years; mustered in as private, Co. L, May 13, 1898; mustered out with company, April 20, 1899, at New York city.

BONFANTI, FRANK.—Age, 22 years. Enlisted, May 13, 1898, at New York city, to serve two years; mustered in as private, Co. F, same date; mustered out with company, April 20, 1899, at New York city.

BONN, WILLIAM A.—Age, — years. Enlisted, November 15, 1898, at New York city, to serve two years; mustered in as musician in band, November 30, 1898; mustered out with regiment, April 20, 1899, at New York city.

BONNER, ALBERT.—Age, 22 years. Enlisted, May 2, 1898, at New York city, to serve two years; mustered in as private, Co. I, May 13, 1898; discharged for disability, October 28, 1898, at Lexington, Ky.

BOOKSTAVER, CHARLES.—Age, 29 years. Enlisted, May 2, 1898, at New York city, to serve two years; mustered in as corporal, Co. E, May 13, 1898; promoted sergeant, October 13, 1898; first sergeant, December 21, 1898; returned to ranks, February 13, 1899; transferred to Co. M, February 14, 1899; promoted corporal, February 23, 1899; sergeant, March 10, 1899; mustered out with company, April 20, 1899, at New York city.

BOSE, WILLIAM.—Age, 23 years. Enlisted, May 2, 1898, at New York city, to serve two years; mustered in as private, Co. H, May 13, 1898; appointed wagoner, June 5, 1898; returned to ranks, July 15, 1898; mustered out with company, April 20, 1899, at New York city.

BOTSFORD, CAMERON W.—Age, 23 years. Enlisted, May 10, 1898, at New York city, to serve two years; mustered in as private, Co. M, May 13, 1898; promoted corporal, May 22, 1898; returned to ranks, August 17, 1898; deserted, November 10, 1898, at Lexington, Ky.

BOTSFORD, JOHN F.—Age, — years. Enlisted, June 17, 1898, at New York city, to serve two years; mustered in as private, Co. M, same date; discharged, January 26, 1899, at New York city.

BOTT, MAX G.—Age, — years. Enlisted, June 29, 1898, at New York city, to serve two years; mustered in as private, Co. B, same date; appointed cook, January 1, 1899; mustered out with company, April 20, 1899, at New York city.

BOTTSFORD, RANSOM M.—Age, — years. Enlisted, June 17, 1898, at New York city, to serve two years; mustered in as private, Co. M, same date; deserted, July 30, 1898, at Chickamauga, Ga.

BOUKER, JAMES.—Age, 21 years. Enlisted, May 2, 1898, at New York city, to serve two years; mustered in as private, Co. M, May 13, 1898; mustered out with company, April 20, 1899, at New York city.

BOURKE, EDWARD J.—Age, — years. Enlisted, June 29, 1898, at New York city, to serve two years; mustered in as private, Co. H, same date; mustered out with company, April 20, 1899, at New York city.

BOURNE, WALTER C.—Age, 23 years. Enlisted, May 2, 1898, at New York city, to serve two years; mustered in as private, Co. G, May 13, 1898; discharged, October 15, 1898, at Camp Hamilton, Lexington, Ky.

BOWER, FRANK.—Age, — years. Enlisted, June 18, 1898, at New York city, to serve two years; mustered in as private, Co. H, same date; deserted, January 16, 1899, at camp, near Matanzas, Cuba.

BOYLAN, CHARLES M.—Age, — years. Enlisted, June 17, 1898, at New York city, to serve two years; mustered in as private, Co. E, same date; mustered out with company, April 20, 1899, at New York city.

BOYLE, JOHN J.—Age, 23 years. Enlisted, May 2, 1898, at New York city, to serve two years; mustered in as sergeant, Co. G, May 13, 1898; promoted quartermaster-sergeant, May 26, 1898; reduced to sergeant, January 1, 1899; mustered out with company, April 20, 1899, at New York city.

BOYLE, WILLIAM A.—Age, 37 years. Enlisted, May 2, 1898, at New York city, to serve two years; mustered in as first sergeant, Co. K, May 13, 1898; mustered out with company, April 20, 1899, at New York city; prior service Battalion of Engineers, United States Army.

BRADY, EDWARD J.—Age, 22 years. Enlisted, May 2, 1898, at New York city, to serve two years; mustered in as private, Co. F, May 13, 1898; transferred to Third Division Hospital Corps, June 13, 1898.

BRADY, PATRICK.—Age, 28 years. Enlisted, May 2, 1898, at New York city, to serve two years; mustered in as artificer, Co. L, May 13, 1898; returned to ranks, June 2, 1898; appointed wagoner, June 4, 1898; mustered out with company, April 20, 1899, at New York city.

BRADY, PHILIP.—Age, — years. Enlisted, June 28, 1898, at New York city, to serve two years; mustered in as private, Co. F, same date; transferred to Co. D, July 5, 1898; mustered out with company, April 20, 1899, at New York city.

BRAND, EDWARD.—Age, 19 years. Enlisted, May 11, 1898, at New York city, to serve two years; mustered in as private, Co. I, May 13, 1898; discharged for disability, to date, September 12, 1898, at Lexington, Ky.

BRANNIGAN, JR., HUGH.—Age, 21 years. Enlisted, May 13, 1898, at New York city, to serve two years; mustered in as private, Co. H, same date; mustered out with company, April 20, 1899, at New York city.

BRASKETT, GEORGE F.—Age, — years. Enlisted, June 23, 1898, at New York city, to serve two years; mustered in as private, Co. A, same date; mustered out with company, April 20, 1899, at New York city.

BRAUN, CHARLES.—Age, 27 years. Enlisted, May 2, 1898, at New York city, to serve two years; mustered in as private, Co. A, May 13, 1898; mustered out with company, April 20, 1899, at New York city.

BRECHT, LUDWIG.—Age, 26 years. Enlisted, May 13, 1898, at camp, near Peekskill, to serve two years; mustered in as private, Co. G, same date; discharged, February 8, 1899, at New York city.

BREINING, GEORGE F.—Age, 24 years. Enlisted, May 2, 1898, at New York city, to serve two years; mustered in as private, Co. M, May 13, 1898; discharged, October 25, 1898, at New York city.

BREMER, HARRY F.—Age, 22 years. Enlisted, May 2, 1898, at New York city, to serve two years; mustered in as private, Co. I, May 13, 1898; discharged for disability, January 4, 1899, at Americus, Ga.

BRENNAN, JOSEPH J.—Age, — years. Enlisted, June 18, 1898, at New York city, to serve two years; mustered in as private, Co. H, same date; mustered out with company, April 20, 1899, at New York city.

BRERETON, EDWARD E.—Age, 22 years. Enlisted, May 2, 1898, at New York city, to serve two years; mustered in as corporal, Co. A, May 13, 1898; promoted sergeant, December 3, 1898; mustered out with company, April 20, 1899, at New York city.

BRETON, AUGUSTIN A.—Age, 21 years. Enlisted, May 2, 1898, at New York city, to serve two years; mustered in as private, Co. I, May 13, 1898; mustered out with company, April 20, 1899, at New York city.

BRIERTY, JOHN W.—Age, 24 years. Enlisted, May 2, 1898, at New York city, to serve two years; mustered in as artificer, Co. H, May 13, 1898; returned to ranks, May 29, 1898; mustered out with company, April 20, 1899, at New York city.

BRINKMEIER, CHARLES.—Age, — years. Enlisted, June 20, 1898, at New York city, to serve two years; mustered in as private, Co. K, same date; appointed artificer, October 25, 1898; mustered out with company, April 20, 1898, at New York city.

BRINKMEIR, LOUIS.—Age, 24 years. Enlisted, May 2, 1898, at New York city, to serve two years; mustered in as private, Co. K, May 13, 1898; discharged, February 8, 1899, at New York city.

BRISSMAN, CARL E.—Age, 21 years. Enlisted, May 10, 1898, at camp, near Peekskill, to serve two years; mustered in as private, Co. G, May 13, 1898; mustered out with company, April 20, 1899, at New York city.

BRITTON, FREDERICK J.—Age, 22 years. Enlisted, May 2, 1898, at New York city, to serve two years; mustered in as private, Co. M, May 13, 1898; discharged, January 4, 1899, at Americus, Ga.

BROGAN, JOHN J.—Age, 32 years. Enlisted, May 2, 1898, at New York city, to serve two years; mustered in as private, Co. A, May 13, 1898; discharged, December 22, 1898, at Fort Columbus, New York Harbor.

BROOKS, JAMES M.—Age, 21 years. Enlisted, May 2, 1898, at New York city, to serve two years; mustered in as private, Co. H, May 13, 1898; discharged, November 27, 1898, at Camp Gilman, Ga.

BROWER, WILLIAM F.—Age, — years. Enlisted, November 15, 1898, at New York city, to serve two years; mustered in as private, Co. B, November 30, 1898; mustered out with company, April 20, 1899, at New York city; prior service in Eighth New York Volunteer Infantry.

BROWN, ABRAHAM H.—Age, 26 years. Enlisted, May 2, 1898, at New York city, to serve two years; mustered in as sergeant, Co. D, May 13, 1898; returned to ranks, November 4, 1898; promoted sergeant, November 12, 1898; mustered out with company, April 20, 1899, at New York city.

BROWN, ALEXANDER.—Age, — years. Enlisted, June 25, 1898, at New York city, to serve two years; mustered in as private, Co. M, same date; mustered out with company, April 20, 1899, at New York city.

BROWN, EDWARD J.—Age, 22 years. Enlisted, May 2, 1898, at New York city, to serve two years; mustered in as private, Co. C, May 13, 1898; mustered out with company, April 20, 1899, at New York city.

BROWN, FRANK S.—Age, 32 years. Enlisted, May 10, 1898, at New York city, to serve two years; mustered in as private, Co. B, May 13, 1898; mustered out with company, April 20, 1899, at New York city.

BROWN, FREDERICK L.—Age, 23 years. Enlisted, May 2, 1898, at New York city, to serve two years; mustered in as private, Co. A, May 13, 1898; appointed wagoner, January 27, 1899; mustered out with company, April 20, 1899, at New York city.

BROWN, JR., HARRY F.—Age, 23 years. Enlisted, May 13, 1898, at New York city, to serve two years; mustered in as private, Co. H, same date; mustered out with company, April 20, 1899, at New York city.

BROWN, WILLIAM.—Age, 26 years. Enlisted, May 2, 1898, at New York city, to serve two years; mustered in as sergeant, Co. C ,May 13, 1898; mustered out with company, April 20, 1899, at New York city.

BRUETTING, JOHN J.—Age, 22 years. Enlisted, May 2, 1898, at New York city, to serve two years; mustered in as wagoner, Co. M, May 13, 1898; mustered out with company, April 20, 1899, at New York city.

BRUSH, FRANK J.—Age, 22 years. Enlisted, May 2, 1898, at New York city, to serve two years; mustered in as private, Co. G, May 13, 1898; mustered out with company, April 20, 1899, at New York city.

BUCHANAN, WILLIAM A.—Age, 23 years. Enlisted, May 2, 1898, at New York city, to serve two years; mustered in as private, Co. I, May 13, 1898; mustered out with company, April 20, 1899, at New York city.

BUCK, JR., CHARLES.—Age, 20 years. Enlisted, May 2, 1898, at New York city, to serve two years; mustered in as sergeant, Co. I, May 13, 1898; mustered out with company, April 20, 1899, at New York city.

BUCK, THOMAS CHARLES.—Age, 25 years. Enrolled, May 2, 1898, at New York city, to serve two years; mustered in as captain, Co. F, May 13, 1898; mustered out with company, April 20, 1899, at New York city; commissioned captain, May 13, 1898, with rank from same date, original.

BUCKRIDGE, CHARLES J.—Age, 21 years. Enlisted, May 2, 1898, at New York city, to serve two years; mustered in as private, Co. E, May 13, 1898; mustered out with company, April 20, 1899, at New York city.

BUNCE, JR., GEORGE C.—Age, 25 years. Enlisted, May 2, 1898, at New York city, to serve two years; mustered in as corporal, Co. H, May 13, 1898; mustered out with company, April 20, 1899, at New York city.

BURCHELL, EDGAR B.—Age, 26 years. Enlisted, May 2, 1898, at New York city, to serve two years; mustered in as hospital steward, May 13, 1898; mustered out with regiment, April 20, 1899, at New York city.

BURGEY, JOHN M.—Age, — years. Enlisted, June 25, 1898, at New York city, to serve two years; mustered in as private, Co. L, same date; discharged, July 1, 1898.

BURKE, FRANCIS JAMES.—Age, 34 years. Enrolled, May 2, 1898, at New York city, to serve two years; mustered in as second lieutenant, Co. C, May 13, 1898; as first lieutenant, June 20, 1898, to date May 17, 1898; as captain of Co. D, October 26, 1898; mustered out with company, April 20, 1899, at New York city; commissioned second lieutenant, May 13, 1898, with rank from same date, original; first lieutenant, May 17, 1898, with rank from same date, vice Romaine, promoted; captain, October 17, 1898, with rank from same date, vice Stebbins, discharged.

BURNS, ARTHUR F.—Age, 23 years. Enlisted, May 2, 1898, at New York city, to serve two years; mustered in as private, Co. G, May 13, 1898; discharged for disability, January 4, 1899, at Americus, Ga.

BURNS, CHARLES STEWART.—Age, 56 years. Enrolled, May 2, 1898, at New York city, to serve two years; mustered in as major, May 13, 1898; mustered out with regiment, April 20, 1899, at New York city; prior service as private, Seventy-ninth New York Volunteer Infantry, and first sergeant, Seventy-sixth Pennsylvania Volunteer Infantry, War of Rebellion; subsequent service as captain, Forty-second Regiment, United States Volunteer Infantry; commissioned major, May 13, 1898, with rank from same date, original.

BURNS, PETER.—Age, 22 years. Enlisted, May 13, 1898, at New York city, to serve two years; mustered in as private, Co. E, same date; appointed cook, December 1, 1898; returned to ranks, February 1, 1899; mustered out with company, April 20, 1899, at New York city.

BURNS, THOMAS A.—Age, 37 years. Enlisted, May 2, 1898, at New York city, to serve two years; mustered in as sergeant, Co. F, May 13, 1898; discharged, January 19, 1899, at Matanzas, Cuba.

BURNS, WILLIAM.—Age, — years. Enlisted, June 28, 1898, at New York city, to serve two years; mustered in as private, Co. G, same date; mustered out with company, April 20, 1899, at New York city.

BURR, NELSON BEARDSLEY.—Age, 27 years. Enrolled, May 2, 1898, at New York city, to serve two years; mustered in as first lieutenant, Co. I, May 13, 1898; discharged, October 28, 1898, at Lexington, Ky.; commissioned first lieutenant, May 13, 1898, with rank from same date, original.

BURRILL, PERCY M.—Age, 25 years. Enrolled, May 2, 1898, at New York city, to serve two years; mustered in as second lieutenant, Co. F, May 13, 1898; as first lieutenant, Co. D, July 21, 1898; transferred to Co. C, December 8, 1898; discharged, December 24, 1898, at Americus, Ga.; commissioned second lieutenant, May 13, 1898, with rank from same date, original; first lieutenant, July 21, 1898, with rank from same date, vice de Russy, discharged.

BURTCHBY, THOMAS.—Age, — years. Enlisted, June 22, 1898, at New York city, to serve two years; mustered in as private, Co. B, same date; discharged, April 20, 1899.

BUTCH, PETER.—Age, 19 years. Enlisted, May 11, 1898, at camp, near Peekskill, to serve two years; mustered in as private, Co. L, May 13, 1898; deserted, September 15, 1898, at Lexington, Ky.

BUTLER, ANDREW A.—Age, 23 years. Enlisted, May 2, 1898, at New York city, to serve two years; mustered in as private, Co. H, May 13, 1898; mustered out with company, April 20, 1899, at New York city.

BUTLER, FREDERICK G.—Enlisted, December 3, 1898, at Americus, Ga., to serve two years; mustered in as musician in band, December 15, 1898; mustered out with regiment, April 20, 1899, at New York city.

BUTLER, LAURENCE J.—Age, 22 years. Enlisted, May 2, 1898, at New York city, to serve two years; mustered in as private, Co. H, May 13, 1898; promoted corporal, March 23, 1899; mustered out with company, April 20, 1899, at New York city.

BUTLER, RICHARD.—Age, 21 years. Enlisted, May 2, 1898, at New York city, to serve two years; mustered in as private, Co. A, May 13, 1898; mustered out with company, April 20, 1899, at New York city.

BUTLER, THOMAS J.—Enlisted, December 3, 1898, at Americus, Ga., to serve two years; mustered in as musician, band, December 15, 1898; mustered out with regiment, April 20, 1899, at New York city.

BUTLER, YORK.—Age, 18 years. Enlisted, May 2, 1898, at New York city, to serve two years; mustered in as musician, Co. L, May 13, 1898; mustered out with company, April 20, 1899, at New York city.

BUTZBACK, FREDERICK.—Age, 22 years. Enlisted, May 2, 1898, at New York city, to serve two years; mustered in as private, Co. C, May 13, 1898; discharged, April 20, 1899, at New York city.

BUYHO, ANTON.—Age, 29 years. Enlisted, May 11, 1898, at camp, near Peekskill, to serve two years; mustered in as private, Co. E, May 13, 1898; appointed artificer, September 1, 1898; discharged, October 11, 1898, at Lexington, Ky.

BYRNE, EDWARD R.—Age, 28 years. Enlisted, May 2, 1898, at New York city, to serve two years; mustered in as private, Co. M, May 13, 1898; promoted corporal, June 23, 1898; died, September 12, 1898, at New York city.

BYRNE, RICHARD.—Age, — years. Enlisted, June 24, 1898, at New York city, to serve two years; mustered in as private, Co. F, same date; mustered out with company, April 20, 1899, at New York city.

BYRNES, THOMAS J.—Age, — years. Enlisted, June 24, 1898, at New York city, to serve two years; mustered in as private, Co. D, same date; mustered out with company, April 20, 1899, at New York city.

CAHILL, JOHN C.—Age, 30 years. Enlisted, May 2, 1898, at New York city, to serve two years; mustered in as wagoner, Co. L, May 13, 1898; returned to ranks, June 4, 1899; mustered out with company, April 20, 1899, at New York city.

CAIN, JOHN H.—Age, — years. Enlisted, June 25, 1898, at New York city, to serve two years; mustered in as private, Co. D, same date; transferred to band, July 2, 1898; discharged, November 30, 1898.

CALLAGHAN, JOHN J.—Age, — years. Enlisted, May 2, 1898, at New York city, to serve two years; mustered in as private, Co. L, May 13, 1898; promoted corporal, November 26, 1898; mustered out with company, April 20, 1899, at New York city.

CAMERON, WILLIAM B.—Age, 32 years. Enlisted, May 2, 1898, at New York city, to serve two years; mustered in as private, Co. C, May 13, 1898; appointed wagoner, September 1, 1898; mustered out with company, April 20, 1899, at New York city.

CAMPBELL, CORTLAND.—Age, 20 years. Enlisted, May 13, 1898, at camp near Peekskill, to serve two years; mustered in as private, Co. A, same date; mustered out with company, April 20, 1899, at New York city.

CAMPBELL, EDWARD.—Age, 22 years. Enlisted, May 2, 1898, at New York city, to serve two years; mustered in as private, Co. M, May 13, 1898; mustered out with company, April 20, 1899, at New York city.

CAMPBELL, JACK.—Enlisted, June 17, 1898, at New York city, to serve two years; mustered in as private, Co. G, same date; discharged for disability, August 1, 1898, at Camp Thomas, Ga.

CAMPBELL, WILLIAM.—Age, 36 years. Enlisted, May 2, 1898, at New York city, to serve two years; mustered in as private, Co. D, May 13, 1898; mustered out with company, April 20, 1899, at New York city.

CAMPBELL, WILLIAM A.—Age, 21 years. Enlisted, May 2, 1898, at New York city, to serve two years; mustered in as private, Co. L, May 13, 1898; promoted corporal, December 9, 1898; mustered out with company, April 20, 1899, at New York city.

CAPPER, CHARLES J.—Age, 22 years. Enlisted, May 2, 1898, at New York city, to serve two years; mustered in as private, Co. M, May 13, 1898; discharged, April 20, 1899, at New York city.

CARLEY, JOHN J.—Age, 20 years. Enlisted, May 2, 1898, at New York city, to serve two years; mustered in as private, Co. E, May 13, 1898; mustered out with company, April 20, 1899, at New York city.

CARPENTER, CHARLES G.—Age, — years. Enlisted, June 28, 1898, at New York city, to serve two years; mustered in as private, Co. M, same date; promoted corporal, August 2, 1898; sergeant, January 24, 1899; returned to ranks, February 24, 1899; mustered out with company, April 20, 1899, at New York city.

CARROLL, WILLIAM J.—Enlisted, June 29, 1898, at New York city, to serve two years; mustered in as private, Co. H, same date; discharged, January 14, 1899, at New York city.

CASEY, JOHN J.—Age, 21 years. Enlisted, May 2, 1898, at New York city, to serve two years; mustered in as private, Co. M, May 13, 1898; promoted corporal, July 4, 1898; returned to ranks, July 14, 1898; mustered out with company, April 20, 1899, at New York city.

CASSERLY, THOMAS.—Age, 21 years. Enlisted, May 2, 1898, at New York city, to serve two years; mustered in as private, Co. F, May 13, 1898; discharged for disability, January 4, 1899, at Americus, Ga.

CASSIDY, LOUIS P.—Age, — years. Enlisted, June 19, 1898, at New York city, to serve two years; mustered in as private, Co. B, same date; mustered out with company, April 20, 1899, at New York city.

CASWELL, CHARLES S.—Age, — years. Enlisted, June 30, 1898, at New York city, to serve two years; mustered in as private, Co. L, same date; transferred to band, July 3, 1898; to Co. L, July 18, 1898; to Co. F, September 12, 1898; appointed musician, no date; deserted, November 10, 1898, at Camp Hamilton, Lexington, Ky.

CATHIE, ALBERT H.—Age, — years. Enlisted, May 2, 1898, at New York city, to serve two years; mustered in as private, Co. E, May 13, 1898; died of typhoid fever, September 2, 1898, at New York city.

CATLIN, JOSEPH H.—Age, — years. Enlisted, June 21, 1898, at New York city, to serve two years; mustered in as private, Co. C, same date; deserted, September 13, 1898, at Lexington, Ky.

CAVANAGH, HUGH P.—Age, 21 years. Enlisted, May 2, 1898, at New York city, to serve two years; mustered in as private, Co. K, May 13, 1898; mustered out with company, April 20, 1899, at New York city.

CEDERGREN, CARL.—Age, 33 years. Enlisted, May 13, 1898, at New York city, to serve two years; mustered in as private, Co. M, same date; transferred to Hospital Corps, October 25, 1898.

CEDERSTROM, JOHN.—Age, 19 years. Enlisted, May 13, 1898, at New York city, to serve two years; mustered in as private, Co. C, same date; mustered out with company, April 20, 1899, at New York city.

CERVANTES, WALTER W.—Age, 21 years. Enlisted, May 2, 1898, at New York city, to serve two years; mustered in as private, Co. D, May 13, 1898; discharged, January 7, 1899, at Fort Columbus, N. Y.

CHALMERS, THOMAS C.—Age, 30 years. Enrolled, May 2, 1898, at New York city, to serve two years; mustered in as first lieutenant and assistant surgeon, May 6, 1898; re-mustered as captain and assistant surgeon, October 7, 1898; mustered in as major and surgeon, November 1, 1898; mustered out with regiment, April 20, 1899, at New York city; subsequent service as major and surgeon, Twenty-eighth Regiment, United States Volunteer Infantry; commissioned assistant surgeon, May 6, 1898, with rank of captain from same date, original; surgeon, October 1, 1898, with rank from same date, vice Ward, discharged.

CHAPMAN, RALPH.—Enlisted, June 25, 1898, at New York city, to serve two years; mustered in as private, Co. C, same date; discharged, November 7, 1898, at Lexington, Ky.

CHARBANO, FREDERICK.—Age, 30 years. Enlisted, May 13, 1898, at camp, near Peekskill, to serve two years; mustered in as private, Co. A, same date; mustered out with company, April 20, 1899, at New York city.

CHARTERS, PATRICK J.—Age, 21 years. Enlisted, May 2, 1898, at New York city, to serve two years; mustered in as private, Co. E, May 13, 1898; mustered out with company, April 20, 1899, at New York city.

CHATTLE, WILLIAM M. K.—Age, 20 years. Enlisted, May 2, 1898, at New York city, to serve two years; mustered in as corporal, Co. A, May 13, 1898; returned to ranks, February 3, 1899; promoted corporal, February 22, 1899; mustered out with company. April 20, 1899, at New York city.

CHLEBOWSKI, HENRY.—Age, 22 years. Enlisted, May 2, 1898, at New York city, to serve two years; mustered in as private, Co. I, May 13, 1898; mustered out with company, April 20, 1899, at New York city.

CHRISTENSEN, CHRISTIAN.—Age, — years. Enlisted, November 15, 1898, at New York city, to serve two years; mustered in as private, Co. G, November 30, 1898; appointed musician, December 2, 1898; mustered out with company, April 20, 1899, at New York city.

CHRISTENSEN, HERMAN.—Age, 21 years. Enlisted, May 10, 1898, at camp, near Peekskill, to serve two years; mustered in as private, Co. M, May 13, 1898; mustered out with company, April 20, 1899, at New York city.

CHRISTIANSON, ALFRED TOBIAS.—Age, 23 years. Enlisted, May 2, 1898, at New York city, to serve two years; mustered in as corporal, Co. E, May 13, 1898; returned to ranks, January 18, 1899; discharged, March 21, 1899, at New York city.

CHRISTIE, SEBA G.—Age, 30 years. Enlisted, May 2, 1898, at New York city, to serve two years; mustered in as corporal, Co. C, May 13, 1898; returned to ranks, July 10, 1898; transferred to band, July 14, 1898; discharged, November 3, 1898.

CHRISTMAN, FELIX.—Age, 28 years. Enlisted, May 2, 1898, at New York city, to serve two years; mustered in as first sergeant, Co. H, May 13, 1898; discharged, October 22, 1898, at Camp Hamilton, Ky.

CLABBY, NICHOLAS.—Age, 21 years. Enlisted, May 2, 1898, at New York city, to serve two years; mustered in as private, Co. E, May 13, 1898; mustered out with company, April 20, 1899, at New York city.

CLAIBORNE, JOHN HERBERT.—Age, 36 years. Enrolled, May 2, 1898, at New York city, to serve two years; mustered in as first lieutenant and battalion adjutant, May 13, 1898; as captain, Co. G, July 23, 1898; discharged, October 15, 1898, at Camp Hamilton, Ky.; commissioned first lieutenant and battalion adjutant, May 13, 1898, with rank from same date, original; captain, July 23, 1898, with rank from same date, vice Harriman, discharged.

CLANCY, THOMAS F.—Age, 34 years. Enlisted, May 10, 1898, at New York city, to serve two years; mustered in as private, Co. F, May 13, 1898; transferred to Third Division Hospital Corps, July 19, 1898.

CLARE, JOHN J.—Age, 34 years. Enlisted, May 2, 1898, at New York city, to serve two years; mustered in as private, Co. I, May 13, 1898; deserted, November 19, 1898.

CLARK, FRANK.—Age, 24 years. Enlisted, May 2, 1898, at New York city, to serve two years; mustered in as sergeant, Co. M, May 13, 1898; returned to ranks, June 17, 1898; transferred to Co. G, same date; appointed artificer, no date, returned to ranks, September 1, 1898; promoted corporal, December 5, 1898; returned to ranks, January 27, 1899; mustered out with company, April 20, 1899, at New York city.

CLARK, PHILIP.—Age, 18 years. Enlisted, May 10, 1898, at New York city, to serve two years; mustered in as private, Co. F, May 13, 1898; mustered out with company, April 20, 1899, at New York city.

CLARKE, ROBERT.—Age, 25 years. Enlisted, May 2, 1898, at New York city, to serve two years; mustered in as private, Co. L, May 13, 1898; promoted corporal, July 12, 1898; mustered out with company, April 20, 1899, at New York city.

CLAUSEN, JOHN.—Age, — years. Enlisted, May 11, 1898, at New York city, to serve two years; mustered in as sergeant, Co. L, May 13, 1898; promoted first sergeant, June 2, 1898; mustered in as second lieutenant, Co. F, July 21, 1898; mustered out with company, April 20, 1899, at New York city; commissioned second lieutenant, July 21, 1898, with rank from same date, vice Burrill, promoted.

CLEAR, DAVID FRANCIS.—Age, 20 years. Enlisted, May 2,
1898, at New York city, to serve two years; mustered in as private, Co. B, May 13, 1898; mustered out with company, April
20, 1899, at New York city.

CLEARWATER, JOHN H.—Age, 23 years. Enlisted, May 2,
1898, at New York city, to serve two years; mustered in as private, Co. G, May 13, 1898; mustered out with company, April
20, 1899, at New York city.

CLELAND, JAMES WALDEN SCHERMERHORN.—Age, 31
years. Enrolled, May 2, 1898, at New York city, to serve two
years; mustered in as first lieutenant and battalion adjutant,
May 13, 1898; as captain, Co. M, November 21, 1898; mustered
out with company, April 20, 1899, at New York city; commissioned first lieutenant and battalion adjutant, May 13, 1898,
with rank from same date, original; commissioned, not mustered, declined captain, October 27, 1898, with rank from same
date, vice Claiborne, discharged; re-commissioned captain,
November 17, 1898, with rank from same date, vice Downs, discharged.

CLIFFE, JOHN W.—Age, — years. Enlisted, June 28, 1898, at
New York city, to serve two years; mustered in as private, Co.
I, same date; transferred to band, July 3, 1898; deserted, Octo-
ber 25, 1898.

CLOW, EDWARD.—Age, 24 years. Enlisted, May 2, 1898, at
New York city, to serve two years; mustered in as quartermaster sergeant, Co. D, May 13, 1898; returned to ranks, at own
request, July 24, 1898; promoted corporal, July 24, 1898; quartermaster-sergeant, November 26, 1898; mustered out with company, April 20, 1899, at New York city.

COBERG, CHARLES A.—Age, 28 years. Enlisted, May 2, 1898,
at New York city, to serve two years; mustered in as private,
Co. E, May 13, 1898; mustered out with company, April 20,
1899, at New York city.

CODNEY, WILLIAM.—Age, 25 years. Enlisted, May 2, 1898, at
New York city, to serve two years; mustered in as private, Co.
A, May 13, 1898; mustered out with company, April 20, 1899, at
New York city.

COFFEY, FRANCIS J.—Age, — years. Enlisted, June 29, 1898, at New York city, to serve two years; mustered in as private, Co. K, same date; discharged, January 20, 1899, at New York city.

COFFIN, VALENTINE.—Age, — years. Enlisted, June 22, 1898, at New York city, to serve two years; mustered in as private, Co. G, same date; mustered out with company, April 20, 1899, at New York city.

COGGESHALL, LOUIS I.—Age, 23 years. Enlisted, May 2, 1898, at New York city, to serve two years; mustered in as private, Co. B, May 13, 1898; promoted corporal, August 1, 1898; discharged, March 1, 1899, at Cardenas, Cuba.

COHEN, HARRY.—Age, 22 years. Enlisted, May 13, 1898, at New York city, to serve two years; mustered in as private, Co. G, same date; mustered out with company, April 20, 1899, at New York city.

COHEN, JACQUES.—Age, 24 years. Enlisted, May 2, 1898, at New York city, to serve two years; mustered in as private, Co. D, May 13, 1898; promoted corporal, May 31, 1898; mustered out with company, April 20, 1899, at New York city.

COLES, WILLIAM E.--Age, 21 years. Enlisted, May 2, 1898, at New York city, to serve two years; mustered in as musician, Co. K, May 13, 1898; mustered out with company, April 20, 1899, at New York city.

COLLINS, JAMES L.—Enlisted, June 25, 1898, at New York city, to serve two years; mustered in as private, Co. F, same date; mustered out with company, April 20, 1899, at New York city.

COLOE, THOMAS JOSEPH.—Age, 23 years. Enlisted, May 2, 1898, at New York city, to serve two years; mustered in as sergeant, Co. E, May 13, 1898; promoted first sergeant, September 18, 1898; mustered in as second lieutenant, Co. B, December 19, 1898; mustered out with company, April 20, 1899, at New York city; commissioned second lieutenant, December 8, 1898, with rank from same date, vice Livingston, discharged.

COLOE, WILLIAM S.—Age, 21 years. Enlisted, May 2, 1898, at New York city, to serve two years; mustered in as private, Co. E, May 13, 1898; promoted corporal, August 1, 1898; sergeant, January 25, 1899; mustered out with company, April 20, 1899, at New York city.

COMB, DAVID M.—Age, — years. Enlisted, June 22, 1898, at New York city, to serve two years; mustered in as private, Co. G, same date; appointed artificer, November 1, 1898; mustered out with company, April 20, 1899, at New York city.

COMIO, FRANK.—Age, 24 years. Enlisted, May 2, 1898, at New York city, to serve two years; mustered in as private, Co. B, May 13, 1898; mustered out with company, April 20, 1899, at New York city.

CONGER, JR., ARTHUR L.—Age, 26 years. Enlisted, May 2, 1898, at New York city, to serve two years; mustered in as corporal, Co. M, May 13, 1898; promoted sergeant, May 30, 1898; discharged, September 9, 1898, at Washington, D. C.; subsequent service as second lieutenant, Eighteenth United States Infantry.

CONKLIN, ELMER L.—Age, 25 years. Enlisted, May 2, 1898, at New York city, to serve two years; mustered in as sergeant, Co. E, May 13, 1898; discharged, January 29, 1899, at Fort Columbus, New York Harbor.

CONKLIN, JAMES G.—Age, 18 years. Enlisted, May 13, 1898, at camp, near Peekskill, to serve two years; mustered in as private, Co. E, same date; discharged, February 27, 1899, at Fort McPherson, Ga.

CONNELL, WILLIAM MURRAY.—Age, 26 years. Enrolled, May 2, 1898, at New York city, to serve two years; mustered in as first lieutenant, Co. K, May 13, 1898; as captain, November 13, 1898; mustered out with company, April 20, 1899, at New York city; subsequent service as captain, Twenty-sixth Regiment, United States Volunteer Infantry; commissioned first lieutenant, May 13, 1898, with rank from same date, original; captain, September 7, 1898, with rank from same date, vice Blake, discharged.

CONNELLY, MARTIN.—Age, 21 years. Enlisted, May 2, 1898, at New York city, to serve two years; mustered in as private, Co. B, May 13, 1898; discharged, January 13, 1899, at New York city.

CONNOLLY, CHARLES MATHEW.—Age, 34 years. Enlisted, May 2, 1898, at New York city, to serve two years; mustered in as private, Co. A, May 13, 1898; promoted quartermaster-sergeant, June 13, 1898; mustered out with company, April 20, 1899, at New York city.

CONNOLLY, LAWRENCE.—Age, 31 years. Enlisted, May 13, 1898, at New York city, to serve two years; mustered in as private, Co. C, same date; discharged for disability, April 20, 1899, at New York city.

CONNOLLY, PATRICK H.—Age, 28 years. Enlisted, May 2, 1898, at New York city, to serve two years; mustered in as private, Co. H, May 13, 1898; appointed wagoner, July 16, 1898; returned to ranks, February 17, 1899; promoted corporal, March 23, 1899; mustered out with company, April 20, 1899, at New York city.

CONNOLLY, PHILIP.—Age, — years. Enlisted, June 25, 1898, at New York city, to serve two years; mustered in as private, Co. M, same date; mustered out with company, April 20, 1899, at New York city.

CONNORS, HENRY.—Age, — years. Enlisted, June 20, 1898, at New York city, to serve two years; mustered in as private, Co. B, same date; mustered out with company, April 20, 1899, at New York city.

CONNORS, JOHN J.—Age, 23 years. Enlisted, May 11, 1898, at camp near Peekskill, to serve two years; mustered in as private, Co. D, May 13, 1898; appointed wagoner, October 18, 1898; returned to ranks, January 27, 1899; mustered out with company, April 20, 1899, at New York city.

CONRAD, REINHOLD.—Age, — years. Enlisted, November 15, 1898, at New York city, to serve two years; mustered in as private, Co. G, November 30, 1898; mustered out with company, April 20, 1899, at New York city.

CONROY, JAMES J.—Age, 20 years. Enlisted, June 20, 1898, at New York city, to serve two years; mustered in as private, Co. F, same date; promoted corporal, February 8, 1899; mustered out with company, April 20, 1899, at New York city.

CONSIDINE, NEIL J.—Age, — years. Enlisted, June 20, 1898, at New York city, to serve two years; mustered in as private, Co. G, same date; promoted corporal, September 12, 1898; returned to ranks, March 6, 1899; mustered out with company, April 20, 1899, at New York city.

CONWAY, CHARLES A.—Age, — years. Enlisted, June 20, 1898, at New York city, to serve two years; mustered in as private, Co. D, same date; discharged, March 23, 1898, at Fort Columbus, New York Harbor.

COOK, HOWARD T.—Age, 20 years. Enlisted, May 2, 1898, at New York city, to serve two years; mustered in as private, Co. G, May 13, 1898; promoted corporal, July 5, 1898; returned to ranks, September 20, 1898; discharged, October 28, 1898, at Camp Hamilton, Ky.

COOK, JAMES O.—Age, 32 years. Enlisted, May 2, 1898, at New York city, to serve two years; mustered in as private, Co. I, May 13, 1898; transferred to Hospital Corps, October 30, 1898.

COOK, WILLIAM H.—Age, 21 years. Enlisted, May 2, 1898, at New York city, to serve two years; mustered in as corporal, Co. K, May 13, 1898; died of typhoid fever, September 2, 1898, at Third Division, First Army Corps Hospital, Lexington, Ky.

COOLEY, MICHAEL.—Age, — years. Enlisted, June 20, 1898, at New York city, to serve two years; mustered in as private, Co. H, same date; mustered out with company, April 20, 1899, at New York city.

COONEY, JAMES.—Age, — years. Enlisted, June 28, 1898, at New York city, to serve two years; mustered in as private, Co. E, same date; mustered out with company, April 20, 1899, at New York city.

COOPE, JOSEPH W.—Age, 23 years. Enlisted, May 2, 1898, at New York city, to serve two years; mustered in as private, Co. L, May 13, 1898; mustered out with company, April 20, 1899, at New York city.

COOPER, WILLIAM.—Age, — years. Enlisted, November 15, 1898, at New York city, to serve two years; mustered in as private, Co. G, February 4, 1899; mustered out with company, April 20, 1899, at New York city.

COPPINGER, WILLIAM F.—Age, 20 years. Enlisted, May 2, 1898, at New York city, to serve two years; mustered in as private, Co. L, May 13, 1898; mustered out with company, April 20, 1899, at New York city.

CORRIGAN, JOHN B.—Age, 20 years. Enlisted, May 2, 1898, at New York city, to serve two years; mustered in as private, Co. A, May 13, 1898; discharged, January 22, 1899, at New York city.

CORSO, JOHN J.—Age, 18 years. Enlisted, May 2, 1898, at New York city, to serve two years; mustered in as private, Co. M, May 13, 1898; discharged, December 14, 1898, at Americus, Ga.

CORTESE, JOHN.—Age, 22 years. Enlisted, May 2, 1898, at New York city to serve two years; mustered in as private, Co. A, May 13, 1898; mustered out with company, April 20, 1899, at New York city.

COSGROVE, PATRICK.—Age, — years. Enlisted, June 27, 1898, at New York city, to serve two years; mustered in as private, Co. C, same date; mustered out with company, April 20, 1899, at New York city.

COTTE, WALTER R.—Age, 25 years. Enlisted, May 2, 1898, at New York city, to serve two years; mustered in as private, Co. C, May 13, 1898; promoted corporal, November 5, 1898; mustered out with company, April 20, 1899, at New York city.

COUGHLIN, DANIEL J.—Age, 25 years. Enlisted, May 2, 1898, at New York city, to serve two years; mustered in as private, Co. H, May 13, 1898; died of typhoid fever, August 23, 1898, at Third Division, First Army Corps Hospital, Chickamauga, Ga.

COURTNEY, JOHN.—Age, 21 years. Enlisted, May 2, 1898, at New York city, to serve two years; mustered in as private, Co. L, May 13, 1898; mustered out with company, April 20, 1899, at New York city.

COWAN, PATRICK E.—Age, 27 years. Enlisted, May 2, 1898, at New York city, to serve two years; mustered in as private, Co. B, May 13, 1898; promoted corporal, December 16, 1898; mustered out with company, April 20, 1899, at New York city.

COWDIN, WINTHROP.—Age, 36 years. Enrolled, May 2, 1898, at New York city, to serve two years; mustered in as first lieutenant and regimental quartermaster, May 13, 1898; transferred, June 10, 1898, as first lieutenant and battalion adjutant; discharged, September 15, 1898; commissioned first lieutenant and regimental quartermaster, May 13, 1898, with rank from same date, original; battalion adjutant, June 7, 1898, with same rank and date, vice Parker, assigned as regimental quartermaster.

COX, CHARLES F.—Age, — years. Enlisted, June 29, 1898, at New York city, to serve two years; mustered in as private, Co. K, same date; mustered out with company, April 20, 1899, at New York city.

COX, JOHN A.—Age, 21 years. Enlisted, May 2, 1898, at New York city, to serve two years; mustered in as private, Co. E, May 13, 1898; mustered out with company, April 20, 1899, at New York city.

COX, JOHN J.—Age, 20 years. Enlisted, May 2, 1898, at New York city, to serve two years; mustered in as private, Co. F, May 13, 1898; discharged, February 2, 1899, at New York city.

COX, JOHN J.—Age, — years. Enlisted, June 20, 1898, at New York city, to serve two years; mustered in as private, Co. G, same date; mustered out with company, April 20, 1899, at New York city.

COYLE, GEORGE J.—Age, — years. Enlisted, June 25, 1898, at New York city, to serve two years; mustered in as private, Co. F, same date; deserted, October, 24, 1898, at Camp Hamilton, Lexington, Ky.

CRAGIN, CALHOUN.—Age, 26 years. Enrolled, February 27, 1899, at New York city, to serve two years; mustered in as first lieutenant, Co. L, same date; mustered out with company, April 20, 1899, at New York city; prior service as first lieutenant and battalion adjutant, Fourteenth New York Volunteer Infantry; commissioned first lieutenant, February 24, 1899, with rank from same date, vice White, discharged.

CRAIG, EDWARD A.—Age, 22 years. Enlisted, May 2, 1898, at New York city, to serve two years; mustered in as private, Co. F, May 13, 1898; mustered out with company, April 20, 1899, at New York city.

CRAIG, JOHN W. J.—Age, 21 years. Enlisted, May 2, 1898, at New York city, to serve two years; mustered in as private, Co. M, May 13, 1898; promoted corporal, February 8, 1899; mustered out with company, April 20, 1899, at New York city.

CRANE, JOHN J.—Age, 22 years. Enlisted, May 13, 1898, at camp, near Peekskill, to serve two years; mustered in as private, Co. H, same date; mustered out with company, April 20, 1899, at New York city.

CRAWFORD, ALBERT M.—Age, 28 years. Enlisted, May 2, 1898, at New York city, to serve two years; mustered in as sergeant, Co. F, May 13, 1898; mustered out with company, April 20, 1899, at New York city.

CRAWFORD, THOMAS J.—Age, 22 years. Enlisted May 2, 1898, at New York city, to serve two years; mustered in as private, Co. M, May 13, 1898; mustered out with company, April 20, 1899, at New York city.

CROLL, ALBERT M.—Age, 22 years. Enlisted, May 2, 1898, at New York city, to serve two years; mustered in as private, Co. C, May 13, 1898; appointed musician, January 16, 1899; mustered out with company, April 20, 1899, at New York city.

CRONIN, ANDREW V.—Age, 32 years. Enlisted, May 11, 1898, at camp, near Peekskill, to serve two years; mustered in as private, Co. D, May 13, 1898; died of typhoid fever, August 13, 1898, at Camp Thomas, Chickamauga Park, Ga.

CRONIN, CORNELIUS F.—Age, — years. Enlisted, June 22, 1898, at New York city, to serve two years; mustered in as private, Co. B, same date; transferred to Co. E, June 27, 1898; discharged, December 24, 1898, at Americus, Ga.

CROSSEN, JOHN L.—Age, 39 years. Enlisted, May 2, 1898, at New York city, to serve two years; mustered in as private, Co. L, May 13, 1898; mustered out with company, April 20, 1899, at New York city.

CROTTY, JOHN P.—Age, 25 years. Enlisted, May 13, 1898, at New York city, to serve two years; mustered in as private, Co. H, same date; discharged, January 29, 1899, at Fort Mc-Pherson, Ga.

CROWE, GEORGE H.—Age, 21 years. Enlisted, May 13, 1898, at camp near Peekskill, to serve two years; mustered in as private, Co. K, same date; mustered out with company, April 20, 1899, at New York city.

CROWE, JOHN.—Age, 30 years. Enlisted, May 2, 1898, at New York city, to serve two years; mustered in as private, Co. D, May 13, 1898; mustered out with company, April 20, 1899, at New York city.

CROWLEY, JAMES W.—Age, — years. Enlisted, November 15, 1898, at New York city, to serve two years; mustered in as private, Co. K, November 30, 1898; mustered out with company, April 20, 1899, at New York city; prior service in Eighth New York Volunteer Infantry.

CROWN, JAMES.—Age, — years. Enlisted, June 17, 1898, at New York city, to serve two years; mustered in as private, Co. F, same date; discharged, January 10, 1899, at General Hospital, Fort Thomas, Ky.

CRUGER, WILLIAM ROWLAND.—Age, 34 years. Enlisted, May 2, 1898, at New York city, to serve two years; mustered in as first sergeant, Co. C, May 13, 1898; as second lieutenant, Co. H, February 1, 1899; mustered out, to date, April 20, 1899, at New York city; commissioned second lieutenant, January 12, 1899, with rank from same date, vice Meehan, promoted.

CULBERTSON, JOHN F.—Age, — years. Enlisted and mustered in as private, Co. D, date and place not stated; discharged, November 25, 1898.

CULHANE, THOMAS J.—Age, 22 years. Enlisted, May 2, 1898, at New York city, to serve two years; mustered in as private, Co. G, May 13, 1898; promoted corporal, September 20, 1898; mustered out with company, April 20, 1899, at New York city.

CULLEN, EDWARD.—Age, 19 years. Enlisted, May 2, 1898, at New York city, to serve two years; mustered in as private, Co. E, May 13, 1898; appointed artificer, July 1, 1898; mustered out with company, April 20, 1899, at New York city.

CULLEN, WALTER H.—Age, 23 years. Enlisted, May 2, 1898,
at New York city, to serve two years; mustered in as private,
Co. F, May 13, 1898; mustered out with company, April 20,
1899, at New York city.

CUNNIAM, WILLIAM J.—Age, 30 years. Enlisted, May 2, 1898,
at New York city, to serve two years; mustered in as private,
Co. K, May 13, 1898; promoted corporal, July 5, 1898; returned
to ranks, October 28, 1898; mustered out with company, April
20, 1899, at New York city.

CUNNINGHAM, EDWARD.—Age, — years. Enlisted, June 21,
1898, at New York city, to serve two years; mustered in as private, Co. B, same date; promoted corporal, August 1, 1898;
returned to ranks, September 1, 1898; discharged, March 6,
1899, at Atlanta, Ga.

CUNNINGHAM, JEREMIAH P.—Age, 29 years. Enlisted, May
11, 1898, at camp, near Peekskill, to serve two years; mustered
in as private, Co. D, May 13, 1898; discharged, January 17,
1899, at Fort Columbus, New York Harbor.

CURRIE, RUBEN O.—Age, — years. Enlisted, June 23, 1898,
at New York city, to serve two years; mustered in as private,
Co. K, same date; mustered out with company, April 20, 1899,
at New York city.

CUSACK, ANDREW J.—Age, 21 years. Enlisted, May 2, 1898,
at New York city, to serve two years; mustered in as corporal,
Co. I, May 13, 1898; promoted sergeant, January 31, 1899; mustered out with company, April 20, 1899, at New York city.

CUSACK, MICHAEL J.—Age, 23 years. Enlisted, May 2, 1898,
at New York city, to serve two years; mustered in as private,
Co. K, May 13, 1898; mustered out with company, April 20,
1899, at New York city.

DAHL, ABRAHAM.—Age, 18 years. Enlisted, May 11, 1898, at
camp near Peekskill, to serve two years; mustered in as private,
Co. A, May 13, 1898; mustered out with company, April 20,
1899, at New York city.

DAILEY, JOHN H.—Age, 23 years. Enlisted, May 2, 1898, at
New York city, to serve two years; mustered in as private, Co.
B, May 13, 1898; mustered out with company, April 20, 1899, at
New York city.

DAILEY, THOMAS F.—Age, 21 years. Enlisted, May 2, 1898, at New York city, to serve two years; mustered in as private, Co. B, May 13, 1898; promoted corporal, January 1, 1899; mustered out with company, April 20, 1899, at New York city.

DALY, ANDREW J.—Age, — years. Enlisted, June 20, 1898, at New York city, to serve two years; mustered in as private, Co. A, same date; mustered out with company, April 20, 1899, at New York city.

DALY, JR., DENNIS.—Age, 24 years. Enlisted, May 13, 1898, at New York city, to serve two years; mustered in as private, Co. C, same date; discharged, January 7, 1899, at Fort Columbus, New York Harbor.

DALY, JOHN F.—Age, — years. Enlisted, June 17, 1898, at New York city, to serve two years; mustered in as private, Co. I, same date; mustered out with company, April 20, 1899, at New York city.

DAME, CHARLES H.—Age, 40 years. Enlisted, May 2, 1898, at New York city, to serve two years; mustered in as private, Co. E, May 13, 1898; died of typhoid fever, September 22, 1898, at Division Hospital.

DAMROSCH, PETER A.—Age, 23 years. Enlisted, May 2, 1898, at New York city, to serve two years; mustered in as private, Co. I, May 13, 1898; appointed cook, January 17, 1899; promoted corporal, January 31, 1899; returned to ranks, March 6, 1899; mustered out with company, April 20, 1899, at New York city.

DANIELSEN, BENJAMIN.—Age, 29 years. Enlisted, May 10, 1898, at New York city, to serve two years; mustered in as private, Co. B, May 13, 1898; appointed wagoner, July 1, 1898; mustered out with company, April 20, 1899, at New York city.

DANNEFELSER, JACOB J.—Age, 28 years. Enlisted, May 2, 1898, at New York city, to serve two years; mustered in as private, Co. A, May 13, 1898; mustered out with company, April 20, 1899, at New York city.

DARDINGKILLER, FREDERICK.—Age, 26 years. Enlisted, May 2, 1898, at New York city, to serve two years; mustered in as principal musician, May 13, 1898; returned to ranks and transferred to Co. E, July 25, 1898; discharged, February 8, 1899, at New York city, as a musician.

DARRELL, FREDERICK.—Age, 26 years. Enlisted, May 10, 1898, at camp, near Peekskill, to serve two years; mustered in as private, Co. M, May 13, 1898; discharged, January 20, 1899, at Philadelphia, Pa.

DAUPHIN, GUSTAVE A.—Age, 21 years. Enlisted, May 2, 1898, at New York city, to serve two years; mustered in as private, Co. K, May 13, 1898; promoted corporal, January 1, 1899; mustered out with company, April 20, 1899, at New York city.

DAVIDSON, GEORGE W.—Age, 24 years. Enlisted, May 2, 1898, at New York city, to serve two years; mustered in as private, Co. B, May 13, 1898; discharged, October 24, 1898, at Lexington, Ky.

DAVIS, CHRISTOPHER.—Age, — years. Enlisted, June 28, 1898, at New York city, to serve two years; mustered in as private, Co. L, same date; mustered out with company, April 20, 1899, at New York city.

DAVIS, GEORGE F. W.—Age, 20 years. Enlisted, May 13, 1898, at camp near Peekskill, to serve two years; mustered in as private, Co. B. same date; mustered out with company, April 20, 1899, at New York city.

DAVIS JOHN J.—Age, 26 years. Enlisted, May 2, 1898, at New York city, to serve two years; mustered in as private, Co. F, May 13, 1898; promoted corporal, August 11, 1898; mustered out with company, April 20, 1899, at New York city.

DAVIS, MARTIN.—Age, — years. Enlisted, June 28, 1898, at New York city, to serve two years; mustered in as private, Co. F, same date; mustered out with company, April 20, 1899, at New York city.

DAY, JAMES H.—Age, 22 years. Enlisted, May 2, 1898, at New York city, to serve two years; mustered in as sergeant, Co. K, May 13, 1898; mustered out with company, April 20, 1899, at New York city.

DAY, JOSEPH F.—Age, 21 years. Enlisted, May 2, 1898. at New York city, to serve two years; mustered in as private, Co. H, May 13, 1898; mustered out with company, April 20, 1899, at New York city.

DAY, JOSIAH C.—Age, 21 years. Enlisted, May 2, 1898, at New York city, to serve two years; mustered in as private, Co. G, May 13, 1898; deserted, September 28, 1898, at Lexington, Ky.

DEAN, JOHN.—Age, 18 years. Enlisted, May 11, 1898, at camp, near Peekskill, to serve two years; mustered in as musician, Co. L, May 13, 1898; mustered out with company, April 20, 1899, at New York city.

DEAN, WILLIAM C.—Age, 22 years. Enlisted, May 2, 1898, at New York city, to serve two years; mustered in as private, Co. K, May 13, 1898; promoted corporal, July 5, 1898; returned to ranks, January 26, 1899; mustered out with company, April 20, 1899, at New York city.

DE GROOT, CHARLES J.—Age, — years. Enlisted, June 20, 1898, at New York city, to serve two years; mustered in as private, Co. D, same date; discharged, March 25, 1899, at Columbus Barracks, Ohio.

DELANEY, JOHN HUGH.—Age, 28 years. Enlisted, May 2, 1898, at New York city, to serve two years; mustered in as private, Co. A, May 13, 1898; mustered out with company, April 20, 1899, at New York city.

DELEHANTY, JOHN J.—Age, — years. Enlisted, June 28, 1898, at New York city, to serve two years; mustered in as private, Co. K, same date; discharged for disability, January 4, 1899, at Americus, Ga.

DELL, ANDREW J.—Age, — years. Enlisted, November 15, 1898, at New York city, to serve two years; mustered in as private, Co. G, November 30, 1898; mustered out with company, April 20, 1899, at New York city.

DELMONICO, NICHOLIS.—Age, — years. Enlisted, June 27, 1898, at New York city, to serve two years; mustered in as private, Co. D, same date; transferred to band, July 2, 1898; to Co. H, December 15, 1898; deserted, January 16, 1899, at camp, near Matanzas, Cuba.

D'ELSEAUX, OTTO.—Age, 21 years. Enlisted, May 2, 1898, at
New York city, to serve two years; mustered in as private, Co.
M, May 13, 1898; discharged, October 25, 1898, at New York
city.

DEMPSEY, JAMES A.—Age, 21 years. Enlisted, May 2, 1898,
at New York city, to serve two years; mustered in as corporal,
Co. A, May 13, 1898; mustered out with company, April 20,
1899, at New York city.

DE MUTH, JESSE SMITH.—Age, 25 years. Enlisted, May 2,
1898, at New York city, to serve two years; mustered in as private, Co. I, May 13, 1898; mustered in as first lieutenant and
assistant surgeon, August 24, 1898; mustered out with regiment, April 20, 1899, at New York city; commissioned first lieutenant and assistant surgeon, August 24, 1898, with rank from
same date, vice Haden, discharged.

DENCKER, KARL.—Age, 23 years. Enlisted, May 10, 1898, at
camp, near Peekskill, to serve two years; mustered in as private, Co. L, May 13, 1898; mustered out with company, April
20, 1899, at New York city.

DENECKE, LOUIS.—Age, 21 years. Enlisted, May 2, 1898, at
New York city, to serve two years; mustered in as private, Co.
B, May 13, 1898; mustered out with company, April 20, 1899, at
New York city.

DE RUSSY, RENÉ AMEDEE.—Age, 26 years. Enrolled, May 2,
1898, at New York city, to serve two years; mustered in as first
lieutenant, Co. D, May 13, 1898; discharged, July 18, 1898; commissioned first lieutenant, May 13, 1898, with rank from same
date, original.

DEVIN, PHILIP M.—Age, 21 years. Enlisted, May 2, 1898, at
New York city, to serve two years; mustered in as private, Co.
I, May 13, 1898; discharged, January 20, 1899, at New York
city.

DEVINE, THOMAS J.—Age, — years. Enlisted, June 20, 1898,
at New York city, to serve two years; mustered in as private,
Co. A, same date; mustered out with company, April 20, 1899,
at New York city.

DEVINS, THOMAS.—Age, — years. Enlisted, June 20, 1898, at New York city, to serve two years; mustered in as private, Co. H, same date; mustered out with company, April 20, 1899, at New York city.

DEVINS, WILLIAM J.—Age, — years. Enlisted, June 24, 1898, at New York city, to serve two years; mustered in as private, Co. I, same date; mustered out with company, April 20, 1899, at New York city.

DEWEY, WILLIAM E.— Age, 39 years. Enlisted, May 2, 1898, at New York city, to serve two years; mustered in as private, Co. K, May 13, 1898; mustered out with company, April 20, 1899, at New York city.

DICKSON, JAMES J.—Age, — years. Enlisted, June 18, 1898, at New York city, to serve two years; mustered in as private, Co. B, same date; mustered out with company, April 20, 1899, at New York city.

DIETZ, CHARLES.—Age, 23 years. Enlisted, May 2, 1898, at New York city, to serve two years; mustered in as private, Co. K, May 13, 1898; mustered out with company, April 20, 1899, at New York city.

DIETZ, CONRAD JOSEPH.—Age, 28 years. Enlisted, May 2, 1898, at New York city, to serve two years; mustered in as corporal, Co. E, May 13, 1898; discharged, November 18, 1898, at Americus, Ga.

DILLON, JOHN.—Age, 22 years. Enlisted, May 2, 1898, at New York city, to serve two years; mustered in as private, Co. M, May 13, 1898; mustered out with company, April 20, 1899, at New York city.

DINNEEN, THOMAS S.—Age, 28 years. Enlisted, May 2, 1898, at New York city, to serve two years; mustered in as private, Co. H, May 13, 1898; discharged, January 29, 1899, at Fort McPherson, Ga.

DOD, ROBERT S.—Age, 24 years. Enlisted, May 2, 1898, at New York city, to serve two years; mustered in as sergeant, Co. C, May 13, 1898; mustered out with company, April 20. 1899, at New York city.

DOHERTY, GIVEN.—Age, 33 years. Enlisted, May 2, 1898, at New York city, to serve two years; mustered in as private, Co. C, May 13, 1898; promoted corporal, July 5, 1898; died of disease, October 4, 1898, at St. Luke Hospital, South Bethlehem, Pa.

DOHERTY, JAMES.—Age, 21 years. Enlisted, May 2, 1898, at New York city, to serve two years; mustered in as private, Co. E, May 13, 1898; promoted corporal, January 31, 1899; mustered out with company, April 20, 1899, at New York city.

DOHERTY, WILLIAM F.—Age, 32 years. Enlisted, May 2, 1898, at New York city, to serve two years; mustered in as private, Co. C, May 13, 1898; promoted corporal, July 5, 1898; returned to ranks, August 20, 1898; promoted corporal, September 1, 1898; returned to ranks, February 20, 1899; died of disease, March 9, 1899, on United States Hospital Ship, "Missouri."

DOMINE, CONEILIOUS.—Age, 19 years. Enlisted, May 10, 1898, camp, near Peekskill, to serve two years; mustered in as private, Co. G, May 13, 1898; appointed cook, February 1, 1899; mustered out with company, April 20, 1899, at New York city.

DONCET, MICHAEL.—Age, 22 years. Enlisted, May 13, 1898, at New York city, to serve two years; mustered in as private, Co. I, same date; died of typhoid fever, October 8, 1898, at Camp Hamilton, Lexington, Ky.

DONNELLY, JOHN.—Age, — years. Enlisted, June 22, 1898, at New York city, to serve two years; mustered in as private, Co. H, same date; discharged, December 21, 1898, at Camp Gilman, Ga.

DONNELLY, JOHN JOSEPH.—Age, 23 years. Enlisted, May 2, 1898, at New York city, to serve two years; mustered in as private, Co. B, May 13, 1898; mustered out with company, April 20, 1899, at New York city.

DONNELLY, WILLIAM J.—Age, 21 years. Enlisted, May 2, 1898, at New York city, to serve two years; mustered in as private, Co. K, May 13, 1898; discharged for disability, October 9, 1898, at Lexington, Ky.

DONOHUE, JR., THOMAS F.—Age, 20 years. Enlisted, May 2, 1898, at New York city, to serve two years; mustered in as private, Co. F, May 13, 1898; appointed artificer, June 16, 1898; promoted corporal, February 8, 1899; mustered out with company, April 20, 1899, at New York city.

DOOLEY, MICHAEL J.—Age, 21 years. Enlisted, May 2, 1898, at New York city, to serve two years; mustered in as private, Co. B, May 13, 1898; mustered out with company, April 20, 1899, at New York city.

DOTZERT, WILLIAM.—Age, — years. Enlisted, June 28, 1898, at New York city, to serve two years; mustered in as private, Co. A, same date; mustered out with company, April 20, 1899, at New York city.

DOUGHERTY, THOMAS A.—Age, 18 years. Enlisted, May 2, 1898, at New York city, to serve two years; mustered in as private, Co. F, May 13, 1898; mustered out with company, April 20, 1899, at New York city.

DOW, RALPH H.—Age, 24 years. Enlisted, May 2, 1898, at New York city, to serve two years; mustered in as private, Co. H, May 13, 1898; died of typhoid fever, July 29, 1898, at Third Division, First Army Corps, Hospital.

DOWLING, JAMES FRANCIS.—Age, 24 years. Enlisted, May 2, 1898, at New York city, to serve two years; mustered in as first sergeant, Co. D, May 13, 1898; as second lieutenant, June 20, 1898, to date, May 31, 1898; mustered out with company, April 20, 1899, at New York city; commissioned second lieutenant, May 26, 1898, with rank from same date, original.

DOWLING, JOSEPH F.—Age, 23 years. Enlisted, May 2, 1898, at New York city, to serve two years; mustered in as private, Co. A, May 13, 1898; mustered out with company, April 20, 1899, at New York city.

DOWLING, WILLIAM J.—Age, 24 years. Enlisted, May 2, 1898, at New York city, to serve two years; mustered in as wagoner, Co. I, May 13, 1898; returned to ranks, July 12, 1898; mustered out with company, April 20, 1899, at New York city.

DOWNES, EDWARD J.—Age, 29 years. Enlisted, May 2, 1898, at New York city, to serve two years; mustered in as private, Co. K, May 13, 1898; mustered out with company, April 20, 1899, at New York city.

DOWNS, WILLIAM EDWARD.—Age, 30 years. Enrolled, May 2, 1898, at New York city, to serve two years; mustered in as first lieutenant, Co. E, May 13, 1898; as captain, Co. M, October 20, 1898; discharged, November 17, 1898; commissioned first lieutenant, May 13, 1898, with rank from same date, original; captain, October 7, 1898, with rank from same date, vice Morris, discharged.

DOYLE, DAVID.—Age, 22 years. Enlisted, May 2, 1898, at New York city, to serve two years; mustered in as private, Co. M, May 13, 1898; promoted corporal, December 10, 1898; mustered out with company, April 20, 1899, at New York city.

DOYLE, JAMES E.—Age, 24 years. Enlisted, May 2, 1898, at New York city, to serve two years; mustered in as private, Co. A, May 13, 1898; mustered out with company, April 20, 1899, at New York city.

DOYLE, JOHN.—Age, 21 years. Enlisted, May 10, 1898, at New York city, to serve two years; mustered in as private, Co. D, May 13, 1898; mustered out with company, April 20, 1899, at New York city.

DRENNAN, DANIEL JOHN JOSEPH.—Age, 27 years. Enlisted, May 2, 1898, at New York city, to serve two years; mustered in as private, Co. B, May 13, 1898; appointed artificer, July 1, 1898; returned to ranks, January 1, 1899; discharged, January 30, 1899, at Washington, D. C.

DREYER, FRANK A.—Age, — years. Enlisted, June 18, 1898, at New York city, to serve two years; mustered in as private, Co. I, same date; mustered out with company, April 20, 1899, at New York city.

DUCEY, JAMES.—Age, 23 years. Enlisted, May 11, 1898, at New York city, to serve two years; mustered in as private, Co. I, May 13, 1898; mustered out with company, April 20, 1899, at New York city.

DUFF, ROBERT.—Age, 25 years. Enlisted, May 2, 1898, at New York city to serve two years; mustered in as private, Co. F, May 13, 1898; mustered out with company, April 20, 1899, at New York city.

DUFFY, EUGENE J.—Age, 27 years. Enlisted, May 2, 1898, at New York city, to serve two years; mustered in as corporal, Co. F, May 13, 1898; mustered out with company, April 20, 1899, at New York city.

DUFFY, JOSEPH.—Age, — years. Enlisted, June 17, 1898, at New York city, to serve two years; mustered in as private, Co. C, same date; mustered out with company, April 20, 1899, at New York city.

DUFFY, MICHAEL J.—Age, 27 years. Enlisted, May 2, 1898, at New York city, to serve two years; mustered in as private, Co. K, May 13, 1898; mustered out with company, April 20, 1899, at New York city.

DUNHAM, WILLIAM.—Age, 21 years. Enlisted, May 2, 1898, at New York city, to serve two years; mustered in as private, Co. M, May 13, 1898; mustered out with company, April 20, 1899, at New York city.

DUNN, JOHN.—Age, — years. Enlisted, June 23, 1898, at New York city, to serve two years; mustered in as private, Co. H, same date; mustered out with company, April 20, 1899, at New York city.

DUNNE, MICHAEL E.—Age, 25 years. Enlisted, May 11, 1898, at New York city, to serve two years; mustered in as private, Co. I, May 13, 1898; appointed artificer, July 6, 1898; mustered out with company, April 20, 1899, at New York city.

DWYER, DANIEL A.—Age, — years. Enlisted, June 22, 1898, at New York city, to serve two years; mustered in as private, Co. H, same date; discharged for disability, January 4, 1899, at Camp Gilman, Ga.

DWYER, GEORGE.—Age, — years. Enlisted, June 25, 1898, at New York city, to serve two years; mustered in as private, Co. C, same date; mustered out with company, April 20, 1899, at New York city.

DWYER, JOHN J.—Age, 22 years. Enlisted, May 13, 1898, at
camp, near Peekskill, to serve two years; mustered in as private. Co. A, May 13, 1898; mustered out with company, April
20, 1899, at New York city.

DYER, GEORGE RATHBONE.—Age, 29 years. Enrolled, May
2, 1898, at New York city, to serve two years; mustered in as
captain, Co. G, May 13, 1898; as major, June 28, 1898, to date,
May 13, 1898; mustered out with regiment, April 20, 1899, at
New York city; commissioned captain, May 13, 1898, with rank
from same date, original; major, May 13, 1898, with rank from
same date, original.

DYSON, WILLIAM.—Age, 34 years. Enlisted, May 2, 1898, at
New York city, to serve two years; mustered in as sergeant,
Co. K, May 13, 1898; mustered out with company, April 20,
1899, at New York city.

EARNEY, CHARLES W.—Age, 23 years. Enlisted, May 2, 1898,
at New York city, to serve two years; mustered in as private,
Co. G, May 13, 1898; mustered out with company, April 20,
1899, at New York city.

EASTMAN, CHARLES.—Age, — years. Enlisted, November 15,
1898, at New York city, to serve two years; mustered in as
private, Co. G, November 30, 1898; mustered out with company,
April 20, 1899, at New York city.

EBELT, WILLIAM H.—Age, — years. Enlisted, November 15,
1898, at New York city, to serve two years; mustered in as
private, Co. G, November 30, 1898; discharged, to date, April
20, 1899, at New York city.

EDDY, WILBUR.—Age, 37 years.   Enrolled, December 21, 1898,
at Camp Gilman, Ga., to serve two years; mustered in as second lieutenant, Co. C, same date; mustered out with company, April 20, 1899, at New York city; commissioned second
lieutenant, November 27, 1898, with rank from same date, vice
Haughton, resigned.

EDEN, JOHN J.—Age, — years.   Enlisted, June 18, 1898, at
New York city, to serve two years; mustered in as private,
Co. A, same date; promoted corporal, December 3, 1898; mus-
tered out with company, April 20, 1899, at New York city.

EDWARDS, THOMAS R.—Age, 25 years. Enlisted, May 2, 1898, at New York city, to serve two years; mustered in as private, Co. H, May 13, 1898; promoted corporal, July 5, 1898; mustered out, to date, April 20, 1899, at New York city.

EHMANN, GEORGE.—Age, 23 years. Enlisted, May 11, 1898, at New York city, to serve two years; mustered in as private, Co. K, May 13, 1898; appointed artificer, June 6, 1898; returned to ranks, August 31, 1898; mustered out with company, April 20, 1899, at New York city.

EICHELE, WILLIAM.—Age, — years. Enlisted, June 24, 1898, at New York city, to serve two years; mustered in as private, Co. G, same date; mustered out with company, April 20, 1899, at New York city.

EILERSFICKEN, FRED B. C.—Age, 22 years. Enlisted, May 2, 1898, at New York city, to serve two years; mustered in as private, Co. M, May 13, 1898; transferred to Hospital Corps, October 25, 1898.

EISENBROWN, FREDERICK.—Age, 20 years. Enlisted, May 2, 1898, at New York city, to serve two years; mustered in as corporal, Co. E, May 13, 1898; promoted sergeant, September 3, 1898; first sergeant, February 14, 1899; mustered out with company, April 20, 1899, at New York city.

EISENSTEIN, LOUIS.—Age, 23 years. Enlisted, May 2, 1898, at New York city, to serve two years; mustered in as artificer, Co. K, May 13, 1898; returned to ranks, June 6, 1898; mustered out with company, April 20, 1899, at New York city.

EKBERG, JOHN A.—Age, 21 years. Enlisted, May 10, 1898, at camp, near Peekskill, to serve two years; mustered in as private, Co. D, May 13, 1898; mustered out with company, April 20, 1899, at New York city.

ELLIS, ANDREW J.—Age, 23 years. Enlisted, May 2, 1898, at New York city, to serve two years; mustered in as corporal, Co. A, May 13, 1898; returned to ranks, December 18, 1898; promoted corporal, December 23, 1898; mustered out with company, April 20, 1899, at New York city.

ELLIS, SAMUEL H.—Age, 34 years. Enlisted, May 2, 1898, at New York city, to serve two years; mustered in as private, Co. I, May 13, 1898; mustered out with company, April 20, 1899, at New York city.

ELLIS, WILLIAM L.—Age, 40 years. Enlisted, May 2, 1898, at New York city, to serve two years; mustered in as private, Co. M, May 13, 1898; promoted corporal, August 2, 1898; quartermaster-sergeant, September 20, 1898; reduced to sergeant, no date; mustered out with company, April 20, 1899, at New York city.

EMMETT, WILMER S.—Age, 23 years. Enlisted, May 2, 1898, at New York city, to serve two years; mustered in as corporal, Co. C, May 13, 1898; promoted quartermaster-sergeant, September 15, 1898; mustered out with company, April 20, 1899, at New York city.

ENNIS, EDGAR L.—Age, 22 years. Enlisted, May 2, 1898, at New York city, to serve two years; mustered in as private, Co. G, May 13, 1898; promoted corporal, February 1, 1899; mustered out with company, April 20, 1899, at New York city.

ENNIS, HENRY M.—Age, 21 years. Enlisted, May 2, 1898, at New York city, to serve two years; mustered in as sergeant, Co. G, May 13, 1898; discharged, January 17, 1899, at New York city.

ERICSSON, EDWARD.—Age, — years. Enlisted, November 15, 1898, at New York city, to serve two years; mustered in as private, Co. G, February 22, 1899; mustered out with company, April 20, 1899, at New York city.

ESTERHAZY, ALBERT.—Age, 25 years. Enlisted, May 2, 1898, at New York city, to serve two years; mustered in as private, Co. G, May 13, 1898; died of disease, January 14, 1899, at Seten Sanitarium, Spuyten Duyvil, N. Y.

EUSTACE, WILLIAM J.—Age, 36 years. Enlisted, May 2, 1898, at New York city, to serve two years; mustered in as private, Co. E, May 13, 1898; discharged, October 15, 1898, at Lexington, Ky.

EXLER, CHRISTOPHER G.—Age, 21 years. Enlisted, May 2, 1898, at New York city, to serve two years; mustered in as private, Co. G, May 13, 1898; deserted, October 3, 1898, at Lexington, Ky.

EYLWARD, PATRICK.—Age, 27 years. Enlisted, May 2, 1898, at New York city, to serve two years; mustered in as private, Co. I, May 13, 1898; mustered out with company, April 20, 1899, at New York city.

FAGAN, BERNARD J.—Age, — years. Enlisted, June 24, 1898, at New York city, to serve two years; mustered in as private, Co. A, same date; promoted corporal, July 5, 1898; sergeant, December 3, 1898; mustered out with company, April 20, 1899, at New York city.

FALDO, ALBERT.—Age, — years. Enlisted, June 20, 1898, at New York city, to serve two years; mustered in as private, Co. I, same date; mustered out with company, April 20, 1899, at New York city.

FALLON, CHARLES L.—Age, 21 years. Enlisted, May 2, 1898, at New York city, to serve two years; mustered in as private, Co. D, May 13, 1898; mustered out with company, April 20, 1899, at New York city.

FALLON, FRANK J.—Age, 22 years. Enlisted, May 2, 1898, at New York city, to serve two years; mustered in as private, Co. D, May 13, 1898; promoted corporal, July 13, 1898; mustered out with company, April 20, 1899, at New York city.

FARBER, JACOB.—Age, 29 years. Enlisted, May 2, 1898, at New York city, to serve two years; mustered in as private, Co. K, May 13, 1898; discharged, December 18, 1898, at Americus, Ga.

FARLEY, WILLIAM H.—Age, 19 years. Enlisted, May 2, 1898, at New York city, to serve two years; mustered in as private, Co. I, May 13, 1898; mustered out with company, April 20, 1899, at New York city.

FARNAM, BARGER.—Age, — years. Enlisted, June 23, 1898, at New York city, to serve two years; mustered in as private, Co. K, same date; promoted corporal, January 1, 1899; mustered out with company, April 20, 1899, at New York city.

FARRELL, EDWARD D.—Age, — years. Enlisted, November 15, 1898, at New York city, to serve two years; mustered in as private, Co. I, November 30, 1898; mustered out with company, April 20, 1899, at New York city.

FARRELL, JOHN J.—Age, 21 years. Enlisted, May 2, 1898, at New York city, to serve two years; mustered in as private, Co. D, May 13, 1898; mustered out with company, April 20, 1899, at New York city.

FARRELL, NICHOLAS.—Age, 21 years. Enlisted, May 11, 1898, at New York city, to serve two years; mustered in as private, Co. I, May 13, 1898; deserted, October 20, 1898.

FARRELL, THOMAS.—Age, 28 years. Enlisted, May 2, 1898, at New York city, to serve two years; mustered in as private, Co. M, May 13, 1898; promoted corporal, May 30, 1898; discharged, January 11, 1899, at New York city.

FAUST, JOSEPH.—Age, — years. Enlisted, November 15, 1898, at New York city, to serve two years; mustered in as private, Co. C, November 30, 1898; mustered out with company, April 20, 1899, at New York city.

FAY, PATRICK A.—Age, 20 years. Enlisted, May 2, 1898, at New York city, to serve two years; mustered in as corporal, Co. F, May 13, 1898; returned to ranks, July 19, 1898; discharged, December 1, 1898, at Americus, Ga.

FEICK, JR., GEORGE.—Age, 32 years. Enlisted, May 2, 1898, at New York city, to serve two years; mustered in as private, Co. L, May 13, 1898; mustered out with company, April 20, 1899, at New York city.

FELD, CLARENCE.—Age, 24 years. Enlisted, May 11, 1898, at camp, near Peekskill, to serve two years; mustered in as corporal, Co. L, May 13, 1898; promoted quartermaster-sergeant, July 1, 1898; reduced to sergeant, August 1, 1898; mustered out with company, April 20, 1899, at New York city.

FELTER, CLARENCE H.—Age, 33 years. Enlisted, May 13, 1898, at camp, near Peekskill, to serve two years; mustered in as private, Co. K, same date; mustered out with company, April 20, 1899, at New York city.

FENNELL, JOHN PATRICK.—Age, 23 years. Enlisted, May 2, 1898, at New York city, to serve two years; mustered in as first sergeant, Co. G, May 13 1898; as second lieutenant, June 20, 1898, to date, May 31, 1898; as first lieutenant, January 11, 1899; mustered out with company, April 20, 1899, at New York city; commissioned second lieutenant, May 26, 1898, with rank from same date, vice Berkard, promoted; first lieutenant, December 23, 1898, with rank from same date, vice Hotchkin, promoted.

FENNEN, JAMES P.—Age, 19 years. Enlisted, May 13, 1898, at New York city, to serve two years; mustered in as private, Co. H, same date; mustered out with company, April 20, 1899, at New York city.

FENTON, FREDERICK L.—Age, 18 years. Enlisted, May 13, 1898, at camp, near Peekskill, to serve two years; mustered in as private, Co. B, same date; mustered out with company, April 20, 1899, at New York city.

FESTER, ROBERT P.—Age, — years. Enlisted, June 18, 1898, at New York city, to serve two years; mustered in as private, Co. G, same date; mustered out with company, April 20, 1899, at New York city.

FIELDS, ROBERT M.—Age, 23 years. Enlisted, May 2. 1898, at New York city, to serve two years; mustered in as sergeant, Co. G, May 13, 1898; discharged, November 10, 1898, at Camp Hamilton, Ky.

FILSON, JOHN M.—Age, 20 years. Enlisted, May 2, 1898, at New York city, to serve two years; mustered in as private, Co. K, May 13, 1898; promoted corporal, July 5, 1898; mustered out with company, April 20, 1899, at New York city.

FINERTY, JOHN.—Age, — years. Enlisted, June 20, 1898, at New York city, to serve two years; mustered in as private, Co. F, same date; mustered out with company, April 20, 1899. at New York city.

FINK, GEORGE D.—Age, 19 years. Enlisted, May 2, 1898, at
New York city, to serve two years; mustered in as musician,
Co. A, May 13, 1898; mustered out with company, April 20,
1899, at New York city.

FINLEY, GEORGE.—Age, 27 years. Enlisted, May 2, 1898, at
New York city, to serve two years; mustered in as artificer,
Co. G, May 13, 1898; returned to ranks, July 23, 1898; promoted
corporal, August 7, 1898; mustered out with company, April
20, 1899, at New York city.

FINLEY, JOHN.—Age, — years. Enlisted, June 28, 1898, at
New York city, to serve two years; mustered in as private,
Co. E, same date; mustered out with company, April 20, 1899,
at New York city.

FINNERTY, MICHAEL L.—Age, 26 years. Enlisted, May 2,
1898, at New York city, to serve two years; mustered in as
private, Co. C, May 13, 1898; promoted corporal, July 5, 1898;
returned to ranks, August 30, 1898; promoted corporal, December 5, 1898; mustered out with company, April 20, 1899, at
New York city.

FINNIGAN, WILLIAM B.—Age, 21 years. Enlisted, May 2,
1898, at New York city, to serve two years; mustered in as
private, Co. D, May 13, 1898; mustered out with company, April
20, 1899, at New York city.

FISCHER, ADOLH.—Age, — years. Enlisted, June 22, 1898, at
New York city, to serve two years; mustered in as private,
Co. E, same date; mustered out with company, April 20, 1899,
at New York city.

FISCHER, CHARLES L.—Age, 28 years. Enlisted, May 2, 1898,
at New York city, to serve two years; mustered in as private,
Co. L, May 13, 1898; mustered out with company, April 20,
1899, at New York city.

FISCHER, PAUL.—Age, — years. Enlisted, November 15, 1898,
at New York city, to serve two years; mustered in as private,
Co. B, November 30, 1898; mustered out with company, April
20, 1899, at New York city.

FISCHER, WILLIAM H.—Age, — years. Enlisted, June 20, 1898, at New York city, to serve two years; mustered in as private, Co. C, same date; deserted, January 8, 1899, at Matanzas, Cuba.

FISH, ALBERT HAMILTON.—Age, 22 years. Enlisted, May 2, 1898, at New York city, to serve two years; mustered in as private, Co. E, May 13, 1898; died of typhoid fever, September 9, 1898, at Division Hospital.

FISH, HARRY W.—Age, 22 years. Enlisted, May 2, 1898. at New York city, to serve two years; mustered in as private, Co. C, May 13, 1898; promoted corporal, September 1, 1898; mustered out with company, April 20, 1899, at New York city.

FISHER, CHARLES W.—Age, 22 years. Enlisted, May 11, 1898, at camp near Peekskill, to serve two years; mustered in as private, Co. A, May 13, 1898; mustered out with company, April 20, 1899, at New York city.

FISHER, EDWIN.—Age, 38 years. Enlisted, May 2, 1898, at New York city, to serve two years; mustered in as private, Co. C, May 13, 1898; discharged, January 17, 1899, at Sullivan's Island, S. C.

FISK, ROBERT A.—Age, — years. Enlisted, June 23, 1898, at New York city, to serve two years; mustered in as private, Co. G, same date; transferred to band, July 3, 1898; deserted, October 25, 1898.

FITCH, JOHN H.—Age, 22 years. Enlisted, May 2, 1898, at New York city, to serve two years; mustered in as private, Co. D, May 13, 1898; mustered out with company, April 20, 1899, at New York city.

FITZGERALD, JAMES J.—Age, — years. Enlisted, June 21, 1898, at New York city, to serve two years; mustered in as private, Co. A, same date; mustered out with company, April 20, 1899, at New York city.

FITZGIBBONS, WILLIAM J.—Age, 22 years. Enlisted, May 2, 1898, at New York city, to serve two years; mustered in as private, Co. H, May 13, 1898; appointed artificer, May 29, 1898; died of typhoid fever, July 19, 1898, at Third Division Hospital.

FITZPATRICK, CHARLES J.—Age, 21 years. Enlisted, May 2, 1898, at New York city, to serve two years; mustered in as private, Co. D, May 13, 1898; promoted corporal, December 3, 1898; mustered out with company, April 20, 1899, at New York city.

FITZPATRICK, JOHN.—Age, 27 years. Enlisted, May 11, 1898, at New York city, to serve two years; mustered in as private, Co. G, May 13, 1898; discharged, January 20, 1899, at New York city.

FITZPATRICK, JOSEPH.—Age, 24 years. Enlisted, May 11, 1898, at New York city, to serve two years; mustered in as private, Co. K, May 13, 1898; deserted, October 26, 1898, at Lexington, Ky.

FITZPATRICK, THOMAS F.—Age, 27 years. Enlisted, May 2, 1898, at New York city, to serve two years; mustered in as private, Co. K, May 13, 1898; promoted corporal, January 1, 1899; returned to ranks, January 26, 1899; mustered out with company, April 20, 1899, at New York city.

FLANAGAN, EDWARD.—Age, — years. Enlisted, June 17, 1898, at New York city, to serve two years; mustered in as private, Co. M, same date; discharged, February 11, 1899, at Fort McPherson, Ga.

FLANAGAN, JOHN J.—Age, 21 years. Enlisted, May 2, 1898, at New York city, to serve two years; mustered in as private, Co. A, May 13, 1898; mustered out with company, April 20, 1898, at New York city.

FLANNERY, DANIEL.—Age, — years. Enlisted, June 23, 1898, at New York city, to serve two years; mustered in as private, Co. K, same date; deserted, October 26, 1898, at Lexington, Ky.

FLEER, JOHN.—Age, — years. Enlisted, June 20, 1898, at New York·city, to serve two years; mustered in as private, Co. F, same date; mustered out with company, April 20, 1899, at New York city.

FLETCHER, JOSEPH.—Age, 24 years. Enlisted, May 2, 1898, at New York city, to serve two years; mustered in as private, Co. K, May 13, 1898; discharged, to date, April 20, 1899, at New York city.

FLIGNER, MORRIS.—Age, 21 years. Enlisted, May 2, 1898, at New York city, to serve two years; mustered in as private, Co. M, May 13, 1898; transferred to Hospital Corps, October 25, 1898.

FLINCH, ROBERT.—Age, 23 years. Enlisted, May 10, 1898, at New York city, to serve two years; mustered in as private, Co. B, May 13, 1898; discharged for disability, January 4, 1899, at Americus, Ga.

FLOWERS, GEORGE.—Age, — years. Enlisted, June 29, 1898, at New York city, to serve two years; mustered in as private, Co. H, same date; mustered out with company, April 20, 1899, at New York city.

FLYNN, FRANK P.—Age, 28 years. Enlisted, May 2, 1898, at New York city, to serve two years; mustered in as sergeant, Co. D, May 13, 1898; returned to ranks, September 26, 1898; discharged, October 19, 1898.

FLYNN, RICHARD J.—Age, 22 years. Enlisted, May 10, 1898, at New York city, to serve two years; mustered in as private, Co. F, May 13, 1898; discharged, February 18, 1899, at hospital, Fort Thomas, Ky.

FOGARTY, JAMES.—Age, 23 years. Enlisted, May 11, 1898, at camp, near Peekskill, to serve two years; mustered in as private, Co. L, May 13, 1898; mustered out with company, April 20, 1899, at New York city.

FOGARTY, JAMES J.—Age, — years. Enlisted, November 15, 1898, at New York city, to serve two years; mustered in as private, Co. C, November 30, 1898; promoted corporal, March 2, 1899; mustered out with company, April 20, 1899, at New York city.

FORMER, WILLIAM H.—Age, 21 years. Enlisted, May 2, 1898, at New York city, to serve two years; mustered in as private, Co. A, May 13, 1898; mustered out with company, April 20, 1899, at New York city.

FORSTER, JOHN.—Age, 28 years. Enlisted, May 2, 1898, at New York city, to serve two years; mustered in as private, Co. G, May 13, 1898; discharged, to date, April 20, 1898, at New York city.

FOSTER, JOHN.—Age, — years. Enlisted, June 22, 1898, at
New York city, to serve two years; mustered in as private, Co.
H, same date; mustered out with company, April 20, 1899, at
New York city.

FOSTER, THOMAS.—Age, 24 years. Enlisted, May 2, 1898, at
New York.city, to serve two years; mustered in as private, Co.
H, May 13, 1898; discharged for disability, January 4, 1899, at
Camp Gilman, Ga.

FOWLER, CHARLES H.—Age, 19 years. Enlisted, May 2, 1898,
at New York city, to serve two years; mustered in as private,
Co. G, May 13, 1898; mustered out with company, April 20, 1899,
at New York city.

FOY, MARTIN.—Age, — years. Enlisted, June 18, 1898, at New
York city, to serve two years; mustered in as private, Co. E,
same date; mustered out with company, April 20, 1899, at New
York city.

FRAE, FRANK.—Age, 23 years. Enlisted, May 2, 1898, at New
York city, to serve two years; mustered in as private, Co. B,
May 13, 1898; mustered out with company, April 20, 1899, at
New York city.

FRANK, CHRISTIAN P.—Age, — years. Enlisted, June 25,
1898, at New York city, to serve two years; mustered in as private, Co. I, same date; appointed chief musician, July 1, 1898;
transferred to band, July 3, 1898; returned to ranks and transferred to Co. I, October 31, 1898; discharged, November 23,
1898, at New York city.

FRANK, SAMUEL.—Age, 36 years. Enlisted, May 2, 1898, at
New York city, to serve two years; mustered in as private, Co.
K, May 13, 1898; promoted corporal, July 5, 1898; discharged,
November 22, 1898, at Americus, Ga.

FRANKLIN, JOHN B.—Age, 26 years. Enlisted, May 2, 1898, at
New York city, to serve two years; mustered in as private, Co.
C, May 13, 1898; mustered out with company, April 20, 1899, at
New York city.

FRANKLIN, WILLIAM M.—Age, 23 years. Enlisted, May 2,
1898, at New York city, to serve two years; mustered in as
private, Co. I, May 13, 1898; deserted, July 7, 1898, at Camp
Thomas, Ga.

FRASER, ALEXANDER.—Age, 22 years. Enlisted, May 2, 1898, at New York city, to serve two years; mustered in as private, Co. D, May 13, 1898; mustered out with company, April 20, 1898, at New York city.

FREDERICKSON, ALBERT F. C.—Age, 27 years. Enlisted, May 10, 1898, at New York city, to serve two years; mustered in as private, Co. B, May 13, 1898; transferred to Hospital Corps, United States Army, February 5, 1899.

FREEMAN, PATRICK J.—Age, 23 years. Enlisted, May 11, 1898, at Camp, near Peekskill, to serve two years; mustered in as private, Co. A, May 13, 1898; mustered out with company, April 20, 1899, at New York city.

FREISE, ALBERT.—Age, 22 years. Enlisted, May 2, 1898, at New York city, to serve two years; mustered in as private, Co. H, May 13, 1898; discharged, October 9, 1898, at Camp Hamilton, Ky.

FRENCH, GEORGE W.—Age, 24 years. Enlisted, May 14, 1898, at New York city, to serve two years; mustered in as private, Co. C, same date; promoted corporal, July 5, 1898; discharged, February 19, 1899, at Matanzas, Cuba.

FRENCH, HUGH.—Age, — years. Enlisted, November 15, 1898, at New York city, to serve two years; mustered in as private, Co. B, November 30, 1898; mustered out with company, April 20, 1899, at New York city.

FRIDL, FREDERICK A.—Age, 19 years. Enlisted, May 2, 1898, at New York city, to serve two years; mustered in as private, Co. E, May 13, 1898; discharged, February 9, 1899, at New York city.

FRIDL, WILLIAM L.—Age, — years. Enlisted, June 20, 1898, at New York city, to serve two years; mustered in as private, Co. E, same date; mustered out with company, April 20, 1899, at New York city.

FRIEDLANDER, WILFORD.—Age, 25 years. Enlisted, May 2, 1898, at New York city, to serve two years; mustered in as private, Co. I, May 13, 1898; deserted, November 19, 1898, at Americus, Ga.

FROST, WARREN L.—Age, 44 years. Enlisted, May 2, 1898, at New York city, to serve two years; mustered in as corporal, Co. C, May 13, 1898; promoted sergeant, February 6, 1899; mustered out with company, April 20, 1899, at New York city.

FROTHINGHAM, GEORGE W.—Age, 39 years. Enlisted, May 2, 1898, at New York city, to serve two years; mustered in as sergeant, Co. H, May 13, 1898; mustered out with company, April 20, 1899, at New York city.

FULBROOK, CHARLES E.—Age, 25 years. Enlisted, May 2, 1898, at New York city, to serve two years; mustered in as private, Co. B, May 13, 1898; mustered out with company, April 20, 1899, at New York city.

FUNKE, FREDRICK W.—Age, 21 years. Enlisted, May 2, 1898, at New York city, to serve two years; mustered in as private, Co. H, May 13, 1898; mustered out with company, April 20, 1899, at New York city.

FURMAN, ROBERT M.—Age, 21 years. Enlisted, May 2, 1898, at New York city, to serve two years; mustered in as private, Co. D, May 13, 1898; promoted corporal, July 13, 1898; discharged for disability, November 10, 1898, at Camp Hamilton, Ky.

GAFFNEY, JAMES E.—Age, 25 years. Enlisted, May 2, 1898, at New York city, to serve two years; mustered in as private, Co. E, May 13, 1898; promoted corporal, February 26, 1899; mustered out with company, April 20, 1899, at New York city.

GAINES, JOHN.—Age, 21 years. Enlisted, May 11, 1898, at camp, near Peekskill, to serve two years; mustered in as private, Co. L, May 13, 1898; deserted, August 14, 1898, at Chickamauga, Ga.

GAINEY, JEREMIAH.—Age, 21 years. Enlisted, May 13, 1898, at New York city, to serve two years; mustered in as private, Co. C, same date; discharged, January 21, 1899, at Lewistown, Me.

GALLAGHER, ANDREW.—Age, 34 years. Enlisted, May 11, 1898, at New York city, to serve two years; mustered in as private, Co. I, May 13, 1898; appointed wagoner, August 28, 1898; returned to ranks, September 9, 1898; deserted, February 9, 1899, at Matanzas, Cuba.

GALLAGHER, EDWARD W.—Age, 25 years. Enlisted, May 2, 1898, at New York city, to serve two years; mustered in as private, Co. L, May 13, 1898; mustered out with company, April 20, 1899, at New York city.

GALLAGHER, JOHN J.—Age, 23 years. Enlisted, May 2, 1898, at New York city, to serve two years; mustered in as private, Co. K, May 13, 1898; mustered out with company, April 20, 1899, at New York city.

GALLAGHER, THOMAS J.—Age, 29 years. Enlisted, May 2, 1898, at New York city, to serve two years; mustered in as private, Co. L, May 13, 1898; mustered out with company, April 20, 1899, at New York city.

GANLEY, JOHN JOSEPH.—Age, 25 years. Enlisted, May 2, 1898, at New York city, to serve two years; mustered in as private, Co. E, May 13, 1898; mustered out with company, April 20, 1899, at New York city.

GANSS, CHARLES.—Age, 19 years. Enlisted, May 2, 1898, at New York city, to serve two years; mustered in as private, Co. I, May 13, 1898; mustered out with company, April 20, 1899, at New York city; also borne as Gousse.

GARBENZEH, JEROME.—Age, 23 years. Enlisted, May 13, 1898, at New York city, to serve two years; mustered in as private, Co. H, same date; mustered out with company, April 20, 1899, at New York city.

GARBRIGHT, WILLIAM.—Age, 22 years. Enlisted, May 2, 1898, at New York city, to serve two years; mustered in as wagoner, Co. K, May 13, 1898; returned to ranks, September 12, 1898; discharged, February 8, 1899, at Matanzas, Cuba; also borne as Garbrecht.

GAUS, FREDERICK G.—Age, 21 years. Enlisted, May 2, 1898, at New York city, to serve two years; mustered in as private, Co. D, May 13, 1898; promoted corporal, July 13, 1898; mustered out to date, April 20, 1899, at New York city.

GEARY, EUGENE J.—Age, 20 years. Enlisted, May 2, 1898, at New York city, to serve two years; mustered in as private, Co. L, May 13, 1898; discharged for disability, no date, at Americus, Ga.

GEARY, JOHN.—Age, — years. Enlisted, June 20, 1898, at New York city, to serve two years; mustered in as private, Co. F, same date; deserted, November 23, 1898, at Americus, Ga.

GEBHARDT, LOUIS.—Age, 22 years. Enlisted, May 2, 1898, at New York city, to serve two years; mustered in as private, Co. C, May 13, 1898; mustered out with company, April 20, 1899, at New York city.

GEE, FREDERICK.—Age, — years. Enlisted, June 25, 1898, at New York city, to serve two years; mustered in as private, Co. M, same date; appointed artificer, February 6, 1899; mustered out with company, April 20, 1899, at New York city.

GEER, ELMER.—Age, 29 years. Enlisted, May 13, 1898, at New York city, to serve two years; mustered in as private, Co. C, same date; mustered out with company, April 20, 1899, at New York city.

GEISSEL, PHILIP C.—Age, 33 years. Enlisted, May 2, 1898, at New York city, to serve two years; mustered in as private, Co. I, May 13, 1898; mustered out with company, April 20, 1899, at New York city.

GENTSCH, GEORGE C.—Age, 24 years. Enlisted, May 2, 1898, at New York city, to serve two years; mustered in as corporal, Co. F, May 13, 1898; promoted sergeant, February 8, 1899; mustered out with company, April 20, 1899, at New York city.

GEORGE, CHARLES.—Age, 25 years. Enlisted, May 2, 1898, at New York city, to serve two years; mustered in as private, Co. K, May 13, 1898; mustered out with company, April 20, 1899, at New York city.

GEORGE, FRANK.—Age, 29 years. Enlisted, May 2, 1898, at New York city, to serve two years; mustered in as private, Co. M, May 13, 1898; promoted corporal, March 14, 1899; mustered out with company, April 20, 1899, at New York city.

GERBER, GODFRED.—Age, — years. Enlisted, June 24, 1898, at New York city, to serve two years; mustered in as private, Co. A, same date; mustered out with company, April 20, 1899, at New York city.

GERETY, EDWARD.—Age, 27 years. Enlisted, May 2, 1898, at New York city, to serve two years; mustered in as private, Co. L, May 13, 1898; mustered out with company, April 20, 1899, at New York city.

GESNER, HARRY.—Age, 18 years. Enlisted, May 13, 1898, at camp, near Peekskill, to serve two years; mustered in as private, Co. B, same date; mustered out with company, April 20, 1899, at New York city.

GETZGER, FREDERICK J.—Age, 21 years. Enlisted, May 2, 1898, at New York city, to serve two years; mustered in as private, Co. K, May 13, 1898; mustered out with company, April 20, 1899, at New York city.

GHIGGERI, ANDREW.—Age, 21 years. Enlisted, May 10, 1898, at New York city, to serve two years; mustered in as private, Co. M, May 13, 1898; mustered out with company, April 20, 1899, at New York city.

GIBBONS, THOMAS JOSEPH.—Age, 23 years. Enlisted, May 2, 1898, at New York city, to serve two years; mustered in as quartermaster-sergeant, Co. M, May 13, 1898; relieved as quartermaster-sergeant, July 10, 1898; promoted first sergeant, December 1, 1898; mustered out with company, April 20, 1899, at New York city.

GIBNEY, FREDERICK R.—Age, 21 years. Enlisted, May 2, 1898, at New York city, to serve two years; mustered in as private, Co. D, May 13, 1898; promoted corporal, July 13, 1898; mustered out with company, April 20, 1899, at New York city.

GIBSON, JOHN.—Age, 27 years. Enlisted, May 2, 1898, at New York city, to serve two years; mustered in as wagoner, Co. D, May 13, 1898; discharged, October 11, 1898.

GILES, THOMAS J.—Age, — years. Enlisted, June 17, 1898, at New York city, to serve two years; mustered in as private, Co. L, same date; discharged, January 26, 1899, at New York city.

GILFEATHER, FELIX.—Age, 30 years. Enlisted, May 2, 1898, at New York city, to serve two years; mustered in as private, Co. L, May 13, 1898; mustered out with company, April 20, 1899, at New York city.

GILLIGAN, TIMOTHY A.—Age, — years. Enlisted, June 25, 1898, at New York city, to serve two years; mustered in as private, Co. C, same date; mustered out with company, April 20, 1899, at New York city.

GILMAN, FRANK.—Age, — years. Enlisted, June 25, 1898, at New York city, to serve two years; mustered in as private, Co. M, same date; transferred to band, July 3, 1898; mustered out with regiment, April 20, 1899, at New York city.

GILMARTIN, JOHN.—Age, 22 years. Enlisted, May 2, 1898, at New York city, to serve two years; mustered in as private, Co. M, May 13, 1898; mustered out with company, April 20, 1899, at New York city.

GILMARTIN, JR., PETER.—Age, — years. Enlisted, June 20, 1898, at New York city, to serve two years; mustered in as private, Co. F, same date; mustered out with company, April 20, 1899, at New York city.

GILMORE, PATRICK.—Age, 30 years. Enlisted, May 11, 1898, at camp, near Peekskill, to serve two years; mustered in as private, Co. L, May 13, 1898; deserted, November 16, 1898, at Lexington, Ky.

GILRONAN, JAMES P.—Age, 22 years. Enlisted, May 2, 1898, at New York city, to serve two years; mustered in as private, Co. M, May 13, 1898; discharged, October 13, 1899, at Washington, D. C.

GILSON, EDWARD.—Age, 22 years. Enlisted, May 2, 1898, at New York city, to serve two years; mustered in as private, Co. L, May 13, 1898; mustered out with company, April 20, 1899, at New York city.

GILSON, HARRY.—Age, 25 years. Enlisted, May 2, 1898, at New York city, to serve two years; mustered in as private, Co. L, May 13, 1898; mustered out with company, April 20, 1899, at New York city.

GLASER, AUGUST A.—Age, 21 years. Enlisted, May 2, 1898, at New York city, to serve two years; mustered in as corporal, Co. E, May 13, 1898; promoted sergeant, January 1, 1899; mustered out with company, April 20, 1899, at New York city.

GLASER, WILLIAM.—Age, 21 years. Enlisted, May 2, 1898, at New York city, to serve two years; mustered in as private, Co. F, May 13, 1898; mustered out with company, April 20, 1899, at New York city; also borne as Glaiser and Glaeser.

GLASS, ROBERT.—Age, 22 years. Enlisted, May 2, 1898, at New York city, to serve two years; mustered in as private, Co. L, May 13, 1898; promoted corporal, July 12, 1898; returned to ranks, January 25, 1899; mustered out with company, April 20, 1899, at New York city.

GLEAVEY, JAMES P.—Age, 22 years. Enlisted, May 2, 1898, at New York city, to serve two years; mustered in as private, Co. F, May 13, 1898; mustered out with company, April 20, 1899, at New York city.

GLEAVEY, JOHN.—Age, 26 years. Enlisted, May 2, 1898, at New York city, to serve two years; mustered in as private, Co. L, May 13, 1898; mustered out with company, April 20, 1899, at New York city.

GODET, HENRY.—Age, 20 years. Enlisted, May 1, 1898, at New York city, to serve two years; mustered in as private, Co. H, May 13, 1898; promoted corporal, August 16, 1898; mustered out with company, April 20, 1899, at New York city.

GODFREY, WILLIAM T.—Age, 26 years. Enlisted, May 2, 1898, at New York city, to serve two years; mustered in as quarter-master sergeant, Co. C, May 13, 1898; discharged, September 10, 1898, at Lexington, Ky.

GODWIN, CLAIBORNE W.—Age, 29 years. Enlisted, May 2, 1898, at New York city, to serve two years; mustered in as private, Co. D, May 13, 1898; promoted corporal, May 31, 1898; returned to ranks, June 20, 1898; promoted corporal, September 1, 1898; returned to ranks, September 19, 1898; discharged for disability, January 4, 1899, at Camp Gilman, Ga.

GOGAN, JAMES.—Age, 21 years. Enlisted, May 2, 1898, at New York city, to serve two years; mustered in as private, Co. M, May 13, 1898; mustered out with company, April 20, 1899, at New York city.

GOGGINS, WILLIAM W.—Age, 22 years. Enlisted, May 10, 1898, at Camp, near Peekskill, to serve two years; mustered in as private, Co. G, May 13, 1898; mustered out with company, April 20, 1899, at New York city.

GOLDFINGER, EMANUEL.—Age, 21 years. Enlisted, May 2, 1898, at New York city, to serve two years; mustered in as private, Co. D, May 13, 1898; mustered out with company, April 20, 1899, at New York city.

GOODALE, JAMES R.—Age, 35 years. Enrolled, March 27, 1899, at New York city, to serve two years; mustered in as first lieutenant, Co. M, same date; to date, March 17, 1899; mustered out with company, April 20, 1899, at New York city; prior service as second lieutenant in First New York Volunteer Infantry; subsequent service as first lieutenant, Twenty-sixth Regiment, United States Volunteer Infantry; commissioned first lieutenant, March 17, 1899, with rank from same date, vice McIlvaine, discharged.

GOODALE, WILLIAM D.—Age, 32 years. Enlisted, May 2, 1898, at New York city, to serve two years; mustered in as private, Co. C, May 13, 1898; transferred to United States Hospital Corps, July 19, 1898.

GOODBODY, EDWARD JOHN.—Age, 22 years. Enlisted, May 2, 1898, at New York city, to serve two years; mustered in as corporal, Co. E, May 13, 1898; returned to ranks, June 30, 1898; promoted corporal, October 31, 1898; mustered out with company, April 20, 1899, at New York city.

GOODE, MICHAEL F.—Age, 33 years. Enlisted, May 2, 1898, at New York city, to serve two years; mustered in as private, Co. H, May 13, 1898; promoted corporal, May 27, 1898; returned to ranks, January 1, 1899; mustered out with company, April 20, 1899, at New York city.

GOODE, ROBERT F.—Age, — years. Enlisted, June 17, 1898, at New York city, to serve two years; mustered in as private, Co. B, same date; mustered out with company, April 20, 1899, at New York city.

GOODWIN, THEODORE R.—Age, 21 years. Enlisted, May 2, 1898, at New York city, to serve two years; mustered in as corporal, Co. D, May 13, 1898; promoted sergeant, January 18, 1899; mustered out with company, April 20, 1899, at New York city.

GORMAN, WILLIAM JOSEPH.—Age, 22 years. Enlisted, May 14, 1898, at Camp, near Peekskill, to serve two years; mustered in as private, Co. E, same date; discharged, December 16, 1898, at Americus, Ga.

GORMLEY, HARRY L.—Age, — years. Enlisted, June 28, 1898, at New York city, to serve two years; mustered in as private, Co. C, same date; mustered out with company, April 20, 1899, at New York city.

GOTTREX, BENJAMIN.—Age, — years. Enlisted, June 28, 1898, at New York city, to serve two years; mustered in as private, Co. B, same date; mustered out with company, April 20, 1899, at New York city.

GOUDIN, HENRI.—Age, 36 years. Enlisted, May 2, 1898, at New York city, to serve two years; mustered in as quarter-master-sergeant, Co. K, May 13, 1898; mustered out with company, April 20, 1898, at New York city.

GRACE, HUGH R.—Age, 21 years. Enlisted, May 2, 1898, at New York city, to serve two years; mustered in as private, Co. M, May 13, 1898; mustered out with company, April 20, 1899, at New York city.

GRAHAM, RICHARD M.—Age, 21 years. Enlisted, May 2, 1898, at New York city, to serve two years; mustered in as private, Co. I, May 13, 1898; mustered out with company, April 20, 1899, at New York city.

GRAHAM, ROBERT S.—Age, 23 years. Enlisted, May 2, 1898, at New York city, to serve two years; mustered in as corporal, Co. I, May 13, 1898; deserted, September 19, 1898.

GRANAI, EUGENIO.—Age, 33 years. Enlisted, May 2, 1898, at New York city, to serve two years; mustered in as private, Co. C, May 13, 1898; discharged, October 9, 1898, at Lexington, Ky.

GRANMANN, BENJAMIN.—Age, 21 years. Enlisted, May 2, 1898, at New York city, to serve two years; mustered in as private, Co. F, May 13, 1898; promoted corporal, January 13, 1899; mustered out to date, April 20, 1899, at New York city; also borne as Graumann.

GRANMANN, RUDOLPH.—Age, 22 years. Enlisted, May 2, 1898, at New York city, to serve two years; mustered in as private, Co. F, May 13, 1898; appointed artificer, January 13, 1899; promoted corporal, February 8, 1899; mustered out with company, April 20, 1899, at New York city.

GRANNER, EDWARD J.—Transferred, from Co. B, Ninth New York Volunteer Infantry, to Co. I, this regiment, August 19, 1898; mustered out with company, April 20, 1899, at New York city.

GRAUER, PHILIP.—Age, 31 years. Enlisted, May 14, 1898, at New York city, to serve two years; mustered in as private, Co. C, same date; mustered out with company, April 20, 1899, at New York city.

GRAY, WALTER B.—Age, — years. Enlisted, June 28, 1898, at Camp Thomas, Ga., to serve two years; mustered in as private, Co. F, same date; discharged, February 18, 1899, at Oatewah, Tenn.

GREEN, EDWARD H.—Age, 18 years. Enlisted, May 13, 1898, at camp, near Peekskill, to serve two years; mustered in as private, Co. E, same date; mustered out with company, April 20, 1899, at New York city.

GREEN, FRANK.—Age, date, place of enlistment and muster-in as private, Co. D, not stated; discharged, November 25, 1898.

GREEN, GEORGE C.—Age, 22 years. Enlisted, May 2, 1898, at New York city, to serve two years; mustered in as private, Co. H, May 13, 1898; mustered out with company, April 20, 1899, at New York city.

GREEN, JOHN A.—Age, 34 years. Enlisted, May 11, 1898, at New York city, to serve two years; mustered in as private, Co. I, May 13, 1898; appointed wagoner, September 9, 1898; returned to ranks, no date; deserted, October 18, 1898, at Camp Hamilton, Ky.

GREENKAUS, LOUIS.—Age, — years. Enlisted, June 25, 1898, at New York city, to serve two years; mustered in as private, Co. M, same date; transferred to band, July 3, 1898; discharged, December 7, 1898, at New York city.

GREENOUGH, ERNEST A.—Age, — years. Enrolled, December 8, 1898, at Americus, Ga., to serve two years; mustered in as first lieutenant, Co. I, same date; mustered out with company, April 20, 1899, at New York city; prior service as captain, Co. I, Second New York Volunteer Infantry; subsequent service as captain, Forty-first Regiment, United States Volunteer Infantry; commissioned first lieutenant, November 28, 1898, with rank from same date, vice Burr, discharged.

GRENAN, MARK.—Age, 26 years. Enlisted, May 13, 1898, at New York city, to serve two years; mustered in as private, Co. H, same date; deserted, November 19, 1898, at Camp Gilman, Ga.

GRIFFIN, EDWARD.—Age, — years. Enlisted, June 27, 1898, at New York city, to serve two years; mustered in as private, Co. M, same date; promoted corporal, July 18, 1898; returned to ranks, August 17, 1898; promoted corporal, September 4, 1898; discharged, October 25, 1898, at New York city.

GRIFFIN, JAMES J.—Age, — years. Enlisted, June 28, 1898, at New York city, to serve two years; mustered in as private, Co. E, same date; mustered out with company, April 20, 1899, at New York city.

GRIFFITH, STOWE.—Age, 27 years. Enlisted, May 13, 1898, at New York city, to serve two years; mustered in as private, Co. C, same date; mustered out with company, April 20, 1899, at New York city.

GROELL, HENRY.—Age, 25 years. Enlisted, May 2, 1898, at New York city, to serve two years; mustered in as private, Co. M, May 13, 1898; mustered out with company, April 20, 1899, at New York city.

GRUPP, JOSEPH.—Age, 21 years. Enlisted, May 2, 1898, at New York city, to serve two years; mustered in as private, Co. A, May 13, 1898; deserted, November 24, 1898.

GUILFOYLE, WILLIAM.—Age, 21 years. Enlisted, May 2, 1898, at New York city, to serve two years; mustered in as private, Co. E, May 13, 1898; discharged, February 2, 1899, at New York city.

GUNDESHEIM, HENRY.—Age, 23 years. Enlisted, May 2, 1898, at New York city, to serve two years; mustered in as private, Co. B, May 13, 1898; discharged, October 24, 1898, at Lexington, Ky.

GUNST, JOSEPH HENRY.—Age, 22 years. Enlisted, May 2, 1898, at New York city, to serve two years; mustered in as private, Co. B, May 13, 1898; mustered out with company, April 20, 1899, at New York city.

GURR, FRED H.—Age, 24 years. Enlisted, May 2, 1898, at New York city, to serve two years; mustered in as private, Co. K, May 13, 1898; transferred to Hospital Corps, United States Army, December 3, 1898.

GUYRE, WILLIAM.—Age, 24 years. Enlisted, May 2, 1898, at New York city, to serve two years; mustered in as sergeant, Co. K, May 13, 1898; discharged, December 4, 1898, at Americus, Ga.

HAAS, FREDERICK.—Age, 23 years. Enlisted, May 2, 1898, at New York city, to serve two years; mustered in as private, Co. H, May 13, 1898; deserted, November 19, 1898, at Camp Gilman, Ga.

HACKETT, JR., EDWARD FRANCIS.—Age, 21 years. Enrolled, February 21, 1899, at New York city, to serve two years; mustered in as second lieutenant, Co. A, same date; mustered out with company, April 20, 1899, at New York city; prior service in First New York Volunteer Infantry; subsequent service as second lieutenant, Forty-second Regiment, United States Volunteer Infantry; commissioned second lieutenant, February 4, 1899, with rank from same date, vice R. D. Russell, promoted.

HACKETT, GEORGE L.—Age, — years. Enlisted, June 18, 1898, at New York city, to serve two years; mustered in as private, Co. G, same date; mustered out with company, April 20, 1899, at New York city.

HACKNEY, EDWARD.—Age, 27 years. Enlisted, May 2, 1898, at New York city, to serve two years; mustered in as private, Co. H, May 13, 1898; discharged, January 29, 1899, at Fort McPherson, Ga.

HADEN, JOHN B.—Age, 26 years. Enrolled, May 2, 1898, at New York city, to serve two years; mustered in as first lieutenant and assistant surgeon, May 6, 1898; discharged, August 29, 1898; commissioned captain and assistant surgeon, May 6, 1898, with rank from same date, original; major and surgeon, not mustered, August 24, 1898, with rank from same date, vice Ward, discharged.

HAEFFNER, CHARLES.—Age, 21 years. Enlisted, May 10, 1898, at camp, near Peekskill, to serve two years; mustered in as private, Co. L, May 13, 1898; mustered out with company, April 20, 1899, at New York city.

HAFELY, OTTO.—Age, — years. Enlisted, June 25, 1898, at New York city, to serve two years; mustered in as private, Co. M, same date; transferred to band, July 3, 1898; mustered out with regiment, April 20, 1899, at New York city.

HAHNLEIN, FREDERICK.—Age, 37 years. Enlisted, May 13, 1898, at camp, near Peekskill, to serve two years; mustered in as private, Co. L, same date; transferred to Co. E, May 20, 1898; appointed musician, January 2, 1899; mustered out with company, April 20, 1899, at New York city.

HAIGHT, RUSSELL W.—Age, 21 years. Enlisted, May 2, 1898, at New York city, to serve two years; mustered in as sergeant, Co. D, May 13 ,1898; promoted first sergeant, January 13, 1899; mustered out with company, April 20, 1899, at New York city.

HAINES, LORENZO.—Age, 20 years. Enlisted, May 13, 1898, at New York city, to serve two years; mustered in as private, Co. G, same date; discharged, to date, April 20, 1899, at New York city.

HALE, FRANK E.—Age, — years. Enlisted, June 22, 1898, at New York city, to serve two years; mustered in as private, Co. A, same date; mustered out with company, April 20, 1899, at New York city.

HALEKIOPOLOS, EVANGOLUS.—Age, 21 years. Enlisted, May 10, 1898, at New York city, to serve two years; mustered in as private, Co. F, May 13, 1898; mustered out with company, April 20, 1899, at New York city.

HALL, WILLIAM.—Age, 23 years. Enlisted, May 2, 1898, at New York city, to serve two years; mustered in as private, Co. F, May 13, 1898; mustered out with company, April 20, 1899, at New York city.

HANDY, FRANK.—Age, 22 years. Enlisted, May 2, 1898, at New York city, to serve two years; mustered in as private, Co. B, May 13, 1898; mustered out with company, April 20, 1899, at New York city.

HANSEN, ALBERT.—Age, 20 years. Enlisted, May 2, 1898, at New York city, to serve two years; mustered in as musician, Co. I, May 13, 1898; mustered out with company, April 20, 1899, at New York city.

HANSEN, HENRY.—Age, 18 years. Enlisted, May 11, 1898, at camp, near Peekskill, to serve two years; mustered in as private, Co. A, May 13, 1898; mustered out with company, April 20, 1899, at New York city.

HANSEN, PETER.—Age, — years. Enlisted, June 23, 1898, at New York city, to serve two years; mustered in as private, Co. H, same date; transferred to band, July 2, 1898; to Co. H, September 25, 1898; mustered out with company, April 20, 1899, at New York city.

HANSON, HARRY.—Age, — years. Enlisted, June 28, 1898, at New York city, to serve two years; mustered in as private, Co. L, same date; deserted, September 16, 1898, at Lexington, Ky.

HANSON, LEWIS.—Age, 27 years. Enlisted, May 10, 1898, at New York city, to serve two years; mustered in as private, Co. M, May 13, 1898; mustered out with company, April 20, 1899, at New York city.

HANZ, WILLIAM M. F.—Age, 24 years. Enlisted, May 2, 1898, at New York city, to serve two years; mustered in as private, Co. A, May 13, 1898; promoted corporal, July 3, 1898; mustered out with company, April 20, 1899, at New York city.

HARBRIDGE, EDWARD C.—Age, 23 years. Enlisted, May 2, 1898, at New York city, to serve two years; mustered in as private, Co. A, May 13, 1898; deserted, October 19, 1898.

HARDING, SANFORD.—Age, — years. Enlisted, June 25, 1898, at New York city, to serve two years; mustered in as private, Co. M, same date; deserted, November 10, 1898, at Lexington, Ky.

HARMEY, JOHN A.—Age, 22 years. Enlisted, May 2, 1898, at New York city, to serve two years; mustered in as private, Co. F, May 13, 1898; promoted corporal, January 13, 1899; mustered out with company, April 20, 1899, at New York city.

HARRIMAN, FREDERICK CHARLES.—Age, 26 years. Enrolled, May 2, 1898, at New York city, to serve two years; mustered in as first lieutenant, Co. G, May 13, 1898; as captain, June 20, 1898, to date, May 13, 1898; discharged, July 23, 1898, and discharged at Camp Thomas, Ga.; commissioned first lieutenant, May 13, 1898, with rank from same date, original; captain, May 13, 1898, with rank from same date, vice Dyer, promoted.

HARRIS, GEORGE W.—Age, 29 years. Enlisted, May 2, 1898, at New York city, to serve two years; mustered in as sergeant, Co. H, May 13, 1898; reduced to corporal, July 11, 1898; returned to ranks, October 17, 1898; discharged, November 9, 1898, at Camp Hamilton, Ky.

HARRIS, JOHN J.—Age, 22 years. Enlisted, May 10, 1898, at camp, near Peekskill, to serve two years; mustered in as private, Co. M, May 13, 1898; mustered out with company, April 20, 1899, at New York city.

HART, JOHN JOSEPH.—Age, 20 years. Enlisted, May 2, 1898, at New York city, to serve two years; mustered in as private, Co. B, May 13, 1898; mustered out with company, April 20, 1899, at New York city.

HART, MARTIN FRANCIS.—Age, 20 years. Enlisted, May 2, 1898, at New York city, to serve two years; mustered in as private, Co. B, May 13, 1898; mustered out with company, April 20, 1899, at New York city.

HART, WILLIAM.—Age, 24 years. Enlisted, May 13, 1898, at camp, near Peekskill, to serve two years; mustered in as private, Co. G, same date; appointed wagoner, November 18, 1898; mustered out with company, April 20, 1899, at New York city.

HART, WILLIAM H.—Age, 21 years. Enlisted, May 11, 1898, at camp, near Peekskill, to serve two years; mustered in as private, Co. D, May 13, 1898; mustered out with company, April 20, 1899, at New York city.

HARTLEY, JOHN.—Age, — years. Enlisted, June 17, 1898, at New York city, to serve two years; mustered in as private, Co. M, same date; mustered out with company, April 20, 1899, at New York city.

HARTMAN, HENRY J.—Age, — years. Enlisted, June 23, 1898, at New York city, to serve two years; mustered in as private, Co. B, same date; deserted, October 27, 1898.

HASSELDJIAN, LEON.—Age, 22 years. Enlisted, May 2, 1898, at New York city, to serve two years; mustered in as private, Co. B, May 13, 1898; discharged, January 28, 1899, at hospital, Atlanta, Ga.

HASSLER, ARTHUR PAUL.—Age, 39 years. Enlisted, May 2, 1898, at New York city, to serve two years; mustered in as private, Co. B, May 13, 1898; appointed musician, May 13, 1898; returned to ranks, October 12, 1898; discharged, February 8, 1899, at New York city.

HAUCK, LOUIS.—Age, — years. Enlisted, June 21, 1898, at New York city, to serve two years; mustered in as private, Co. L, same date; deserted, July 19, 1898, at Chickamauga, Ga.

HAUGHTON, LAWRENCE.—Age, 34 years. Enrolled, May 22, 1898, at Camp Thomas, Ga., to serve two years; mustered in as second lieutenant, Co. C, June 20, 1898, to date, May 22, 1898; discharged, November 25, 1898; commissioned second lieutenant, May 22, 1898, with rank from same date, vice Burke, promoted.

HAWES, JOHN D.—Age, — years. Enlisted, June 22, 1898, at New York city, to serve two years; mustered in as private, Co. L, same date; discharged, March 11, 1899, at Cardenas, Cuba.

HAYES, DANIEL T.—Age, 25 years. Enlisted, May 2, 1898, at New York city, to serve two years; mustered in as private, Co. F, May 13, 1898; mustered out with company, April 20, 1899, at New York city.

HAYES, HARRY C—Age, 24 years. Enlisted, May 2, 1898, at New York city, to serve two years; mustered in as private, Co. C, May 14, 1898; promoted corporal, November 5, 1898; mustered out with company, April 20, 1899, at New York city.

HAYES, PETER E.—Age, 22 years. Enlisted, May 2, 1898, at New York city, to serve two years; mustered in as private, Co. K, May 13, 1898; appointed wagoner, October 10, 1898; mustered out with company, April 20, 1899, at New York city.

HAYS, JOSEPH MEAD.—Age, 32 years. Enlisted, May 2, 1898, at New York city, to serve two years; mustered in as private, 1899, at New York city.

HEELY, GEORGE K.—Age, 43 years. Enlisted, May 2, 1898, at New York city, to serve two years; mustered in as wagoner, Co. G, May 13, 1898; mustered out with company, April 20, 1899, at New York city.

HEFFERMAN, THOMAS F.—Age, 21 years. Enlisted, May 2, 1898, at New York city, to serve two years; mustered in as private, Co. L, May 13, 1898; mustered out with company, April 20, 1899, at New York city.

HEFFERNAN, MICHAEL JOSEPH.—Age, 24 years. Enlisted, May 2, 1898, at New York city, to serve two years; mustered in as private, Co. B, May 13, 1898; promoted corporal, August 1, 1898; returned to ranks, December 16, 1898; mustered out with company, April 20, 1899, at New York city.

HEILMANN, ALFRED H.—Age, 29 years. Enlisted, May 13, 1898, at New York city, to serve two years; mustered in as private, Co. H, same date; discharged for disability, January 28, 1899, at United States General Hospital, Presidio, Cal.

HEINTZ, CHARLES R.—Age, 28 years. Enlisted, May 2, 1898, at New York city, to serve two years; mustered in as private, Co. F, May 13, 1898; mustered out with company, April 20, 1899, at New York city.

HEITMAN, FRANK E.—Age, 19 years. Enlisted, May 2, 1898, at New York city, to serve two years; mustered in as private, Co. G, May 13, 1898; died of disease, September 18, 1898, at New York city.

HELBIG, ADAM.—Age, 21 years. Enlisted, May 2, 1898, at New York city, to serve two years; mustered in as private, Co. K, May 13, 1898; mustered out with company, April 20, 1899, at New York city

HELBIG, MARTIN J.—Age, 24 years. Enlisted, May 2, 1898, at New York city, to serve two years; mustered in as private, Co. K, May 13, 1898; mustered out with company, April 20, 1899, at New York city.

HELLFRITCH, ALBERT.—Age, 37 years.   Enlisted, May 2, 1898, at New York city, to serve two years; mustered in as private, Co. F, May 13, 1898; appointed cook, January 15, 1899; mustered out with company, April 20, 1899, at New York city.

HELLMANN, ANTHONY P.—Age, — years. Enlisted, November 15, 1898, at New York city, to serve two years; mustered in as private, Co B, November 30, 1898; mustered out with company, April 20, 1899, at New York city.

HELLSTROM, ALBIN.—Age, 32 years. Enlisted, May 10, 1898, at camp, near Peekskill, to serve two years; mustered in as private, Co. G, May 13, 1898; mustered out with company, April 20, 1899, at New York city.

HELMS, PERRY S.—Age, 26 years. Enlisted, May 2, 1898, at New York city, to serve two years; mustered in as private, Co. A, May 13, 1898; mustered out with company, April 20, 1899, at New York city.

HENDERSON, ALBERT J.—Age, 27 years. Enlisted, May 2, 1898, at New York city, to serve two years; mustered in as quartermaster-sergeant, Co. L, May 13, 1898; reduced to corporal, July 1, 1898; returned to ranks, July 12, 1898; mustered out with company, April 20, 1899, at New York city.

HENDERSON, EDWARD.—Age, — years. Enlisted, June 27, 1898, at New York city, to serve two years; mustered in as private, Co. K, same date; mustered out with company, April 20, 1899, at New York city.

HENDERSON, WILLIAM.—Age, — years. Enlisted, June 21, 1898, at New York city, to serve two years; mustered in as private, Co. D, same date; deserted, July 18, 1898.

HENNING, RICHARD J.—Age, 23 years. Enlisted, May 2, 1898, at New York city, to serve two years; mustered in as sergeant, Co. A, May 13, 1898; mustered out with company, April 20, 1899, at New York city.

HERBERT, GEORGE H.—Age, 29 years. Enlisted, May 2, 1898, at New York city to serve two years; mustered in as corporal, Co. C, May 13, 1898; mustered out with company, April 20, 1899, at New York city.

HERDLING, GEORGE.—Age, 29 years. Enlisted, May 2, 1898, at New York city, to serve two years; mustered in as private, Co. H, May 13, 1898; discharged, November 19, 1898, at Camp Gilman, Ga.

HERON, GEORGE.—Age, — years. Enlisted, November 15, 1898, at New York city, to serve two years; mustered in as private, Co. G, November 30, 1898; mustered out with company, April 20, 1899, at New York city.

HERPEL, LOUIS.—Age, 22 years. Enlisted, May 2, 1898, at New York city, to serve two years; mustered in as private, Co. C, May 13, 1898; promoted corporal, November 25, 1898; mustered out with company, April 20, 1899, at New York city.

HERRMANN, JOHN F.—Age, 26 years. Enlisted, May 10, 1898, at New York city, to serve two years; mustered in as private, Co. B, May 13, 1898; mustered out with company, April 20, 1899, at New York city.

HERRMANN, OSWALD E.—Age, 34 years. Enlisted, May 2, 1898, at New York city, to serve two years; mustered in as private, Co. H, May 13, 1898; promoted corporal, October 17, 1898; discharged for disability, October 27, 1898, at Camp Hamilton, Ky.

HESSLER, PETER L.—Age, 36 years. Enlisted, May 13, 1898, at New York city, to serve two years; mustered in as private, Co. C, same date; promoted corporal, July 5, 1898; deserted, October 11, 1898 at Lexington, Ky.

HICKEY, JR., JOHN.—Age, 24 years. Enlisted, May 2, 1898, at New York city, to serve two years; mustered in as private. Co. C, May 13, 1898; mustered out with company, April 20, 1899, at New York city.

HICKEY, JOHN A.—Age, — years. Enlisted, November 15, 1898, at New York city, to serve two years; mustered in as private, Co. H, November 30, 1898; discharged for disability, January 4, 1899, at Camp Gilman, Ga.

HIGGINS, JOHN.—Age, 25 years. Enlisted, May 11, 1898, at New York city, to serve two years; mustered in as private. Co. I, May 13, 1898; mustered out with company, April 20, 1899, at New York city.

HIGGINS, WILLIAM I.—Age, — years. Enlisted, June 21, 1898, at New York city, to serve two years; mustered in as private, Co. G, same date; discharged for disability, October 28, 1898, at Camp Hamilton, Ky.

HILL, ALEXANDER L.—Age, 24 years. Enlisted, May 2, 1898, at New York city, to serve two years; mustered in as private, Co. C, May 13, 1898; mustered out with company, April 20, 1899, at New York city.

HISCOCK, HENRY.—Age, 22 years. Enlisted, May 2, 1898, at New York city, to serve two years; mustered in as private, Co. K, May 13, 1898; promoted corporal, June 28, 1898; returned to ranks, October 28, 1898; promoted corporal, February 9, 1899; mustered out with company, April 20, 1899, at New York city.

HOAG, EDWARD.—Age, 26 years. Enlisted, May 2, 1898, at New York city, to serve two years; mustered in as private, Co. L, May 13, 1898; discharged, October 21, 1898, at New York city.

HOAG, JOHN.—Age, 43 years. Enlisted, May 2, 1898, at New York city, to serve two years; mustered in as quartermaster-sergeant, Co. I, May 13, 1898; mustered out with company, April 20, 1899, at New York city.

HODELL, JULIUS.—Age, 21 years. Enlisted, May 10, 1898, at New York city, to serve two years; mustered in as private, Co. L, May 13, 1898; mustered out with company, April 20, 1899, at New York city.

HOEFLING, JOHN C.—Age, — years. Enlisted, June 22, 1898, at New York city, to serve two years; mustered in as private, Co. K, same date; discharged, December 8, 1898, at Americus, Ga.

HOFER, WILLIAM.—Age, 24 years. Enlisted, May 2, 1898, at New York city, to serve two years; mustered in as private, Co. A, May 13, 1898; deserted, October 18, 1898.

HOFFMAN, CHARLES.—Age, — years. Enlisted, June 28, 1898, at New York city, to serve two years; mustered in as private, Co. F, same date; promoted corporal, March 9, 1899; mustered out with company, April 20, 1899, at New York city.

HOGAN, DENNIS.—Age, — years. Enlisted, June 17, 1898, at New York city, to serve two years; mustered in as private, Co. H, same date; mustered out with company, April 20, 1899, at New York city.

HOGAN, MICHAEL J.—Age, — years. Enlisted, June 17, 1898, at New York city, to serve two years; mustered in as private, Co. M, same date; mustered out with company, April 20, 1899, at New York city.

HOLLWORTH, JOSEPH.—Age, 22 years. Enlisted, May 2, 1898, at New York city, to serve two years; mustered in as private, Co. D, May 13, 1898; transferred to Hospital Corps, First Army Corps, June 13, 1898.

HOLT, HENRY T.—Age, 21 years. Enlisted, May 2, 1898, at New York city, to serve two years; mustered in as private, Co. B, May 13, 1898; promoted corporal, February 19, 1899; mustered out with company, April 20, 1899, at New York city.

HONE, PHILIP.—Age, 26 years. Enlisted, May 2, 1898, at New York city, to serve two years; mustered in as corporal, Co. H, May 13, 1898; died of typhoid fever, August 15, 1898, at Roosevelt Hospital, New York city.

HONEBEIN, JR., HENRY.—Age, 20 years. Enlisted, May 12, 1898, at camp, near Peekskill, to serve two years; mustered in as private, Co. E, May 13, 1898; appointed artificer, October 13, 1898; promoted corporal, February 19, 1899; mustered out with company, April 20, 1899, at New York city.

HOPKINS, JOSEPH.—Age, — years. Enlisted, December 3, 1898, at Americus, Ga., to serve two years; mustered in as musician in band, December 15, 1898; mustered out with regiment, April 20, 1899, at New York city.

HOPPIN, FRANCIS LAUREN VINTON.—Age, 31 years. Enrolled, May 2, 1898, at New York city, to serve two years; mustered in as second lieutenant, Co. B, May 13, 1898; as first lieutenant, June 20, 1898, to date, May 13, 1898; discharged, September 14, 1898, at Lexington, Ky.; not commissioned second lieutenant, commissioned first lieutenant, May 13, 1898, with rank from same date, original.

HORAN, THOMAS.—Age, — years. Enlisted, June 25, 1898, at New York city, to serve two years; mustered in as private, Co. H, same date; deserted, January 16, 1899, at camp, near Matanzas, Cuba.

HORAN, WILLIAM H. W.—Age, 22 years. Enlisted, May 2, 1898, at New York city, to serve two years; mustered in as private, Co. M, May 13, 1898; mustered out with company, April 20, 1899, at New York city.

HORNBROOK, FRANK E.—Age, 19 years. Enlisted, May 2, 1898, at New York city, to serve two years; mustered in as private, Co. L, May 13, 1898; promoted corporal, July 12, 1898; returned to ranks, September 20, 1898; mustered out with company, April 20, 1899, at New York city.

HORTON, WILLIAM D.—Age, — years. Enlisted, June 18, 1898, at New York city, to serve two years; mustered in as private, Co. L, same date; promoted corporal, July 12, 1898; returned to ranks, August 1, 1898; mustered out with company, April 20, 1899, at New York city.

HOTCHKIN, WALTER BRYANT.—Enrolled, December 5, 1898, at Americus, Ga., to serve two years; mustered in as first lieutenant, Co. G, same date; transferred to Co. L, December 23, 1898; mustered in as captain, January 11, 1899; mustered out with company, April 20, 1899, at New York city; prior service as major, Twenty-second Regiment, New York Volunteer Infantry; commissioned first lieutenant, November 26, 1898, with rank from same date, vice Benkard, promoted; captain, December 22, 1898, with rank from same date, vice Turner, discharged.

HOWELL, GEORGE H.—Age, — years. Enlisted, June 25, 1898, at New York city, to serve two years; mustered in as private, Co. G, same date; promoted corporal, December 5, 1898; mustered out with company, April 20, 1899, at New York city.

HOYT, CHARLES E.—Age, — years. Enlisted, June 27, 1898, at New York city, to serve two years; mustered in as private, Co. D, same date; mustered out with company, April 20, 1899, at New York city.

HUETTNER, OSWIN C.—Age, 31 years. Enlisted, May 2, 1898, at New York city, to serve two years; mustered in as private, Co. D, May 13, 1898; mustered out with company, April 20, 1899, at New York city.

HUGHES, JAMES M.—Age, 31 years. Enlisted, May 2, 1898, at New York city, to serve two years; mustered in as private, Co. M, May 13, 1898; mustered out with company, April 20, 1899, at New York city.

HUGHES, JOHN.—Age, — years. Enlisted, June 21, 1898, at New York city, to serve two years; mustered in as private, Co. G, same date; mustered out with company, April 20, 1899, at New York city.

HUMMEL, GEORGE H.—Age, 22 years. Enlisted, May 2, 1898, at New York city, to serve two years; mustered in as hospital steward, May 13, 1898; mustered out with regiment, April 20, 1899, at New York city.

HUNT, JAMES M.—Age, 34 years. Enlisted, May 10, 1898, at New York city, to serve two years; mustered in as private, Co. M, May 13, 1898; discharged for disability, January 4, 1899, at Americus, Ga.

HUNTER, WILLIAM F.—Age, 23 years. Enlisted, May 2, 1898, at New York city, to serve two years; mustered in as private, Co. E, May 13, 1898; promoted corporal, November 18, 1898; sergeant, January 31, 1899; mustered out with company, April 20, 1899, at New York city.

HUSON, GEORGE L.—Age, 27 years. Enlisted, May 2, 1898, at New York city, to serve two years; mustered in as private, Co. F, May 13, 1898; promoted corporal, August 11, 1898; mustered out with company, April 20, 1899, at New York city.

HUSTER, OTTO K.—Age, 26 years. Enlisted, May 2, 1898, at
New York city, to serve two years; mustered in as corporal,
Co. D, May 13, 1898; promoted sergeant, May 31, 1898; returned,
to ranks, August 26, 1898; promoted sergeant, September 1,
1898; discharged, October 25, 1898.

HUSTON, THOMAS WILLIAM.—Age, 28 years. Enrolled, May
2, 1898, at New York city, to serve two years; mustered in as
captain, Co. C, May 13, 1898; mustered out with company,
April 20, 1899, at New York city; commissioned captain, May
13, 1898, with rank from same date, original.

IMHOF, JOHN C.—Age, 21 years. Enlisted, May 2, 1898, at New
York city, to serve two years; mustered in as private, Co. B,
May 13, 1898; discharged for disability, January 4, 1899, at
Americus, Ga.

INNES, BERNARD T.—Age, 26 years. Enlisted, May 2, 1898,
at New York city, to serve two years; mustered in as private,
Co. H, May 13, 1898; mustered out with company, April 20,
1899, at New York city.

INNES, JAMES S.—Age, 25 years. Enlisted, May 2, 1898, at
New York city, to serve two years; mustered in as private,
Co. D, May 13, 1898; mustered out with company, April 20,
1899, at New York city.

IRELAND, WILLIAM DE F.—Age, 22 years. Enlisted, May 2,
1898, at New York city, to serve two years; mustered in as private, Co. E, May 13, 1898; mustered out with company, April
20, 1899, at New York city.

IRVINE, STANLEY.—Age, 23 years. Enlisted, May 2, 1898, at
New York city, to serve two years; mustered in as private, Co.
A, May 13, 1898; transferred to Hospital Corps, December 7,
1898.

IRWIN, WILLIAM G.—Age, 21 years. Enlisted, May 2, 1898, at
New York city, to serve two years; mustered in as corporal, Co.
G, May 13, 1898; promoted sergeant, May 26, 1898; first sergeant, September 15, 1898; mustered out with company, April
20, 1899, at New York city.

ISAACS, HARRY.—Age, 21 years. Enlisted, May 13, 1898, at
New York city, to serve two years; mustered in as private, Co.
H, same date; mustered out with company, April 20, 1899, at
New York city.

JACOBS, HARRY JAMES.—Age, 22 years. Enlisted, May 2, 1898, at New York city, to serve two years; mustered in as private, Co. B, May 13, 1898; promoted corporal, August 1, 1898; mustered out with company, April 20, 1899, at New York city.

JACOBS, JOHN.—Age, — years. Enlisted, June 18, 1898, at New York city, to serve two years; mustered in as private, Co. E, same date; mustered out with company, April 20, 1899, at New York city.

JACOBS, SOLOMAN.—Age, 24 years. Enlisted, May 2, 1898, at New York city, to serve two years; mustered in as private, Co. C, May 13, 1898; mustered out with company, April 20, 1899, at New York city.

JACOBSON, IRVING A.—Age, 24 years. Enlisted, May 2, 1898, at New York city, to serve two years; mustered in as private, Co. I, May 13, 1898; deserted, July 1, 1898, at Camp Thomas, Chickamauga Park, Ga.

JACQUES, JOHN P.—Age, 32 years. Enlisted, May 10, 1898, at New York city, to serve two years; mustered in as private, Co. M, May 13, 1898; mustered out with company, April 20, 1899, at New York city.

JAEGER, HERMAN.—Age, — years. Enlisted, June 27, 1898, at New York city, to serve two years; mustered in as private. Co. D, same date; transferred to band, July 2, 1898; promoted principal musician, July 22, 1898; returned to ranks, October 31, 1898; promoted principal musician, February 1, 1899; mustered out with regiment, April 20, 1899, at New York city.

JAFFE, ABRAHAM.—Age, 19 years. Enlisted, May 11, 1898, at New York city, to serve two years; mustered in as private, Co. F, May 13, 1898; mustered out with company, April 20, 1899, at New York city.

JAMIESON, JOHN P.—Age, 19 years. Enlisted, May 2, 1898, at New York city, to serve two years; mustered in as private, Co. G, May 13, 1898; discharged, November 18, 1898, at Camp Gilman, Ga.

JANDREW, FRANK.—Age, 18 years. Enlisted, May 2, 1898, at New York city, to serve two years; mustered in as private, Co. L, May 13, 1898; mustered out with company, April 20, 1898, at New York city.

JANSEN, MAURITIUS.—Age, 22 years. Enlisted, May 13, 1898, at camp, near Peekskill, to serve two years; mustered in as private, Co. A, same date; mustered out with company, April 20, 1899, at New York city.

JANTZEN, CHARLES.—Age, — years. Enlisted, June 25, 1898, at New York city, to serve two years; mustered in as private, Co. E, same date; mustered out with company, April 20, 1899, at New York city.

JARVIS, HARRY.—Age, — years. Enlisted, November 15, 1898, at New York city, to serve two years; mustered in as private, Co. I, November 30, 1898; mustered out with company, April 20, 1899, at New York city.

JARVIS, JOHN J.—Age, — years. Enlisted, June 22, 1898, at New York city, to serve two years; mustered in as private, Co. L, same date; mustered out with company, April 20, 1899, at New York city.

JENKS, FRANK.—Age, — years. Enlisted, June 27, 1898, at New York city, to serve two years; mustered in as private, Co. C, same date; deserted, July 8, 1898, at Chickamauga, Ga.

JENSEN, HENRY M.—Age, 21 years. Enlisted, May 2, 1898, at New York city, to serve two years; mustered in as private, Co. G, May 13, 1898; discharged for disability, subsequent to November 1, 1898, at Fort Columbus, New York Harbor.

JENSEN, JOHANNES P.—Age, 26 years. Enlisted, May 11, 1898, at camp, near Peekskill, to serve two years; mustered in as private, Co. E, May 13, 1898; discharged for disability, October 11, 1898, at New York city.

JOHNSON, ANDREW.—Age, 21 years. Enlisted, May 10, 1898, at camp, near Peekskill, to serve two years; mustered in as private, Co. G, May 13, 1898; died of disease, October 9, 1898, at Division Hospital, Camp Hamilton, Lexington, Ky.

JOHNSON, CARL A.—Age, 23 years. Enlisted, May 10, 1898, at camp, near Peekskill, to serve two years; mustered in as private, Co. G, May 13, 1898; deserted, March 15, 1899.

JOHNSON, JR., FREDERICK J.—Age, 23 years. Enlisted, May 2, 1898, at New York city, to serve two years; mustered in as private, Co. H, May 13, 1898; discharged for disability, January 4, 1899, at Camp Gilman, Ga.

JOHNSON, JOHN W.—Age, 29 years. Enlisted, May 2, 1898, at New York city, to serve two years; mustered in as private, Co. F, May 13, 1898; mustered out with company, April 20, 1899, at New York city.

JOHNSON, VALDEMAR.—Age, 21 years. Enlisted, May 10, 1898, at camp, near Peekskill, to serve two years; mustered in as private, Co. G, May 13, 1898; transferred to Co. M, June 17, 1898; discharged, March 31, 1899, at New York city; also borne as Valdimar Jorgenson.

JOHNSTON, ALBERT L.—Age, 21 years. Enlisted, May 2, 1898, at New York city, to serve two years; mustered in as private, Co. I, May 13, 1898; promoted corporal, July 5, 1898; discharged, January 31, 1899, at New York city.

JOHNSTON, HERBERT E.—Age, 21 years. Enlisted, May 2, 1898, at New York city, to serve two years; mustered in as private, Co. I, May 13, 1898; promoted corporal, December 9, 1898; mustered out with company, April 20, 1899, at New York city.

JOHNSTON, JAMES W.—Age, 21 years. Enlisted, May 2, 1898, at New York city, to serve two years; mustered in as corporal, Co. I, May 13, 1898; discharged, January 26, 1899, at New York city.

JOHNSTON, WILLIAM.—Age, — years. Enlisted, June 29, 1898, at New York city, to serve two years; mustered in as corporal, Co. A, same date; mustered out with company, April 20, 1899, at New York city.

JOHNSTON, WILLIAM.—Age, 21 years. Enlisted, May 2, 1898, at New York city, to serve two years; mustered in as private, Co. K, May 13, 1898; mustered out with company, April 20, 1899, at New York city.

JONES, BRADFORD.—Age, 20 years. Enlisted, May 13, 1898, at camp, near Peekskill, to serve two years; mustered in as private, Co. E, same date; promoted corporal, August 1, 1898; discharged, January 30, 1899, at Matanzas, Cuba.

JONES, EDWARD S.—Age, — years. Enlisted, June 25, 1898,
at New York city, to serve two years; mustered in as private,
Co. K, same date; transferred to band, July 3, 1898; returned
to company, December 16, 1898; discharged for disability, January 4, 1899, at Americus, Ga.

JONES, ELIAS.—Age, 22 years. Enlisted, May 2, 1898, at New
York city, to serve two years; mustered in as private, Co. F,
May 13, 1898; mustered out with company, April 20, 1899, at
New York city.

JONES, JOSEPH.—Age, 20 years. Enlisted, May 11, 1898, at
camp, near Peekskill, to serve two years; mustered in as private, Co. A, May 13, 1898; mustered out with company, April
20, 1899, at New York city.

JONES, THOMAS P.—Age, — years. Enlisted, November 15,
1898, at New York city, to serve two years; mustered in as
private, Co. B, February 4, 1899; mustered out with company,
April 20, 1899, at New York city.

JONES, WILLIAM B.—Age, — years. Enlisted, June 28, 1898,
at New York city, to serve two years; mustered in as private,
Co. F, same date; discharged for disability, January 4, 1899, at
Americus, Ga.

JORDAN, WILLIAM J.—Age, 37 years. Enlisted, May 2, 1898,
at New York city, to serve two years; mustered in as private,
Co. F, May 13, 1898; discharged for disability, January 4, 1899,
at Americus, Ga.

JORGENSEN, OLUF.—Age, 26 years. Enlisted, May 10, 1898,
at New York city, to serve two years; mustered in as private,
Co. B, May 13, 1898; discharged, February 13, 1899, at New
York city.

JORGENSON, VALDIMAR, see Valdemar Johnson.

JUDSON, WILLIAM FRANCIS.—Age, 29 years. Enrolled, May
2, 1898, at New York city, to serve two years; mustered in as
captain, Co. E, May 13, 1898; detailed aide de camp to General
Wood, January 16, 1899, at Santiago, Cuba; discharged, April
20, 1899; subsequent service as captain, Twenty-seventh Regiment, United States Volunteer Infantry; commissioned captain, May 13, 1898, with rank from same date, original.

JUST, WILLIAM.—Age, — years. Enlisted, June 20, 1898, at New York city, to serve two years; mustered in as private, Co. F, same date; mustered out with company, April 20, 1899, at New York city.

KAISER, HENRY.—Age, 26 years. Enlisted, May 2, 1898, at New York city, to serve two years; mustered in as private, Co. A, May 13, 1898; transferred to Hospital Corps, United States Army, June 13, 1898.

KAISER, JOHN.—Age, 35 years. Enlisted, May 10, 1898, at camp, near Peekskill, to serve two years; mustered in as private, Co. G, May 13, 1898; mustered out with company, April 20, 1899, at New York city.

KALAB, FRANK.—Age, — years. Enlisted, November 15, 1898, at New York city, to serve two years; mustered in as private, Co. K, November 30, 1898; mustered out with company, April 20, 1899, at New York city.

KALBFLEISCH, CHRISTIAN.—Age, — years. Enlisted, June 25, 1898, at New York city, to serve two years; mustered in as private, Co. C, same date; mustered out with company, April 20, 1899, at New York city.

KALEN, MORRIS.—Age, 23 years. Enlisted, May 2, 1898, at New York city, to serve two years; mustered in as private, Co. F, May 13, 1898; discharged, February 6, 1899, at New York city; also borne as Morris Kolen.

KAMMER, MORRIS, see Morris Kanner.

KANE, JEREMIAH.—Age, — years. Enlisted, June 25, 1898, at New York city, to serve two years; mustered in as private, Co. I, same date; mustered out with company, April 20, 1899, at New York city.

KANE, MICHAEL.—Age, 28 years. Enlisted, May 2, 1898, at New York city, to serve two years; mustered in as private, Co. L, May 13, 1898; mustered out with company, April 20, 1899, at New York city.

KANNANE, THOMAS F.—Age, — years. Enlisted, June 20, 1898, at New York city, to serve two years; mustered in as private, Co. F, June 21, 1898; mustered out with company, April 20, 1899, at New York city.

KANNER, MORRIS.—Age, 22 years. Enlisted, May 10, 1898, at camp, near Peekskill, to serve two years; mustered in as private, Co. G, May 13, 1898; discharged, November 10, 1898, at Camp Hamilton, Ky.; also borne as Morris Kammer.

KARL, ANDREW.—Age, — years. Enlisted, June 20, 1898, at New York city, to serve two years; mustered in as private, Co. K, same date; discharged, January 13, 1899, at New York city.

KARLEIN, OSCAR F.—Age, 23 years. Enlisted, May 2, 1898, at New York city, to serve two years; mustered in as private, Co. E, May 13, 1898; promoted corporal, August 1, 1898; discharged, December 24, 1898, at Americus, Ga.

KARLISON, HAROLD.—Age, 21 years. Enlisted, May 10, 1898, at camp, near Peekskill, to serve two years; mustered in as private, Co. G, May 13, 1898; promoted corporal, March 9, 1899; mustered out with company, April 20, 1899, at New York city.

KEATING, FRANK D.—Age, 23 years. Enlisted, May 2, 1898, at New York city, to serve two years; mustered in as private, Co. D, May 13, 1898; promoted corporal, January 18, 1899; mustered out with company, April 20, 1899, at New York city.

KEATING, JOHN J.—Age, 30 years. Enlisted, May 2, 1898, at New York city, to serve two years; mustered in as private, Co. A, May 13, 1898; mustered out with company, April 20, 1899, at New York city.

KEEFER, EDWARD A.—Age, 24 years. Enlisted, May 2, 1898, at New York city, to serve two years; mustered in as hospital steward, May 13, 1898; mustered out with regiment, April 20, 1899, at New York city.

KEEGAN, THOMAS F.—Age, — years. Enlisted, June 25, 1898, at New York city, to serve two years; mustered in as private, Co. H, same date; transferred, to First Army Corps Hospital Corps, October 22, 1898.

KEEN, EDWARD T.—Age, 22 years. Enlisted, May 2, 1898, at New York city, to serve two years; mustered in as sergeant, Co. I, May 13, 1898; returned to ranks, June 2, 1898; mustered out with company, April 20, 1899, at New York city.

KEENAN, JR., JAMES.—Age, 18 years. Enlisted, May 2, 1898, at New York city, to serve two years; mustered in as private, Co. I, May 13, 1898; mustered out with company, April 20, 1899, at New York city.

KEENAN, JOSEPH P.—Age, 21 years. Enlisted, May 2, 1898, at New York city, to serve two years; mustered in as private, Co. K, May 13, 1898; mustered out with company, April 20, 1899, at New York city.

KEENAN, PATRICK.—Age, — years. Enlisted, June 28, 1898, at New York city, to serve two years; mustered in as private, Co. I, same date; mustered out with company, April 20, 1899, at New York city.

KEHOE, WILLIAM.—Age, 20 years. Enlisted, May 2, 1898, at New York city, to serve two years; mustered in as private, Co. L, May 13, 1898; mustered out with company, April 20, 1899, at New York city.

KELLER, FRANK P.—Age, — years. Enlisted, June 20, 1898, at New York city, to serve two years; mustered in as private, Co. B, same date; mustered out with company, April 20, 1899, at New York city.

KELLEY, JOHN.—Age, 21 years. Enlisted, May 2, 1898, at New York city, to serve two years; mustered in as private, Co. I, May 13, 1898; promoted corporal, July 5, 1898; mustered out with company, April 20, 1899, at New York city.

KELLEY, JOHN J.—Age, 31 years. Enlisted, May 13, 1898, at camp, near Peekskill, to serve two years; mustered in as private, Co. C, same date; mustered out with company, April 20, 1899, at New York city.

KELLY, DENNIS W.—Age, — years. Enlisted, June 27, 1898, at New York city, to serve two years; mustered in as private, Co. C, same date; mustered out with company, April 20, 1899, at New York city.

KELLY, FRANK.—Age, — years. Enlisted, June 27, 1898, at New York city, to serve two years; mustered in as private, Co. M, same date; mustered out with company, April 20, 1899, at New York city.

KELLY, PATRICK.—Age, 21 years. Enlisted, May 2, 1898, at New York city, to serve two years; mustered in as private, Co. G, May 13, 1898; appointed artificer, September 1, 1898; returned to ranks, November 1, 1898; mustered out with company, April 30, 1899, at New York city.

KELLY, WILLIAM J.—Age, 23 years. Enlisted, May 2, 1898, at New York city, to serve two years; mustered in as sergeant, Co. H, May 13, 1898; promoted first sergeant, November 1, 1898; mustered out with company, April 20, 1899, at New York city.

KENEHAN, RICHARD J.—Age, 21 years. Enlisted, May 2, 1898, at New York city, to serve two years; mustered in as sergeant, Co. L, May 13, 1898; returned to ranks, July 3, 1898; deserted, December 22, 1898, at Americus, Ga.

KENNEDY, JAMES A.—Age, — years. Enlisted, June 21, 1898, at New York city, to serve two years; mustered in as private, Co. G, same date; promoted corporal, December 10, 1898; mustered out with company, April 20, 1899, at New York city.

KENNEDY, PATRICK.—Age, — years. Enlisted, June 23, 1898, at New York city, to serve two years; mustered in as private, Co. H, same date; mustered out with company, April 20, 1899, at New York city.

KENNEDY, PATRICK.—Age, — years. Enlisted, November 15, 1898, at New York city, to serve two years; mustered in as private, Co. M, November 30, 1898; mustered out with company, April 20, 1899, at New York city

KENNEDY, WILLIAM.—Age, 31 years. Enlisted, May 2, 1898, at New York city, to serve two years; mustered in as sergeant, Co. M, May 13, 1898; returned to ranks, May 29, 1898; promoted corporal, May 30, 1898; returned to ranks, June 10, 1898; discharged for disability, November 19, 1898, at Lexington, Ky.

KENT, ALVAN P.—Age, — years. Enlisted, June 20, 1898, at New York city, to serve two years; mustered in as private, Co. B, same date; transferred to Hospital Corps, October 22, 1898.

KENT, EDWARD V.—Age, 22 years. Enlisted, May 2, 1898, at New York city, to serve two years; mustered in as private, Co. F, May 13, 1898; discharged, December 1, 1898, at Americus, Ga.

KERN, JOSEPH.—Age, 23 years. Enlisted, May 2, 1898, at New York city, to serve two years; mustered in as private, Co. E, May 13, 1898; discharged for disability, January 4, 1899, at Fort McPherson, Ga.

KESSLER, JOHN HENRY.—Age, 21 years. Enlisted, May 13, 1898, at New York city, to serve two years; mustered in as private, Co. B, same date; discharged, January 20, 1899, at New York city.

KETCHEALE, JOHN.—Age, 19 years. Enlisted, May 2, 1898, at New York city, to serve two years; mustered in as private, Co. K, May 13, 1898; mustered out with company, April 20, 1899, at New York city.

KIEFERDORF, FREDERICK.—Age, 19 years. Enlisted, May 2, 1898, at New York city, to serve two years; mustered in as private, Co. D, May 13, 1898; mustered out with company, April 20, 1899, at New York city.

KIERNAN, JOHN J.—Age, 29 years. Enlisted, May 2, 1898, at New York city, to serve two years; mustered in as corporal, Co. A, May 13, 1898; discharged, November 10, 1898, at New York city.

KIERNAN, PATRICK.—Age, 26 years. Enlisted, May 10, 1898, at New York city, to serve two years; mustered in as private, Co. F, May 13, 1898; mustered out with company, April 20, 1899, at New York city.

KILGALLEN, STEPHEN.—Age, — years. Enlisted, June 18, 1898, at New York city, to serve two years; mustered in as private, Co. E, same date; mustered out with company, April 20, 1899, at New York city.

KILLEEN, DANIEL T.—Age, 30 years. Enlisted, May 2, 1898, at New York city, to serve two years; mustered in as corporal, Co. F, May 13, 1898; discharged, January 11, 1899, at New York city.

KIMBARK, ALEXANDER.—Age, 35 years. Enlisted, May 2, 1898, at New York city, to serve two years; mustered in as corporal, Co. K, May 13, 1898; promoted sergeant, January 1, 1899; mustered out with company, April 20, 1899, at New York city.

KING, GEORGE B.—Age, — years. Enlisted, June 22, 1898, at New York city, to serve two years; mustered in as private, Co. L, same date; mustered out with company, April 20, 1899, at New York city.

KING, HARRY A.—Age, — years. Enlisted, November 15, 1898, at New York city, to serve two years; mustered in as private, Co. M, November 30, 1898; mustered out with company, April 20, 1899, at New York city.

KING, HENRY J.—Age, 30 years. Enlisted, May 2, 1898, at New York city, to serve two years; mustered in as private, Co. K, May 13, 1898; promoted corporal, July 5, 1898; mustered out with company, April 20, 1899, at New York city.

KING, WILLIAM S.—Age, 28 years. Enlisted, May 2, 1898, at New York city, to serve two years; mustered in as private, Co. L, May 13, 1898; promoted corporal, July 12, 1898; mustered out with company, April 20, 1899, at New York city.

KINNANE, PATRICK.—Age, — years. Enlisted, June 21, 1898, at New York city, to serve two years; mustered in as private, Co. F, same date; mustered out with company, April 20, 1899, at New York city.

KINSLEY, EDWARD J.—Age, 28 years. Enlisted, May 2, 1898, at New York city, to serve two years; mustered in as private, Co. F, May 13, 1898; mustered out with company, April 20, 1899, at New York city.

KINZLER, WILLIAM.—Age, — years. Enlisted, June 21, 1898, at New York city, to serve two years; mustered in as private, Co. E, same date; mustered out with company, April 20, 1899, at New York city.

KLEFLER, WALTER JOHN ANDREW.—Age, 22 years. Enlisted, May 2, 1898, at New York city, to serve two years; mustered in as private, Co. B, May 13, 1898; transferred to Hospital Corps, November 18, 1898.

KLEI, WILLIAM.—Age, 27 years. Enlisted, May 2, 1898, at New York city, to serve two years; mustered in as private, Co. F, May 13, 1898; mustered out with company, April 20, 1899, at New York city.

KLEINHANS, HARRY.—Age, 25 years. Enlisted, May 2, 1898, at New York city, to serve two years; mustered in as sergeant, Co. G, May 13, 1898; promoted quartermaster-sergeant May 22, 1898; first sergeant, May 26, 1898; reduced to sergeant, September 15, 1898; returned to ranks, November 10, 1898; discharged, December 9, 1898, at Camp Gilman, Americus, Ga.

KLEMMER, JOHN F.—Age, 21 years. Enlisted, May 2, 1898, at New York city, to serve two years; mustered in as private, Co. M, May 13, 1898; deserted, October 23, 1898, at Lexington, Ky.

KLOTH, ARTHUR R.—Age, — years. Enlisted, December 3, 1898, at Americus, Ga., to serve two years; mustered in as musician in band, December 13, 1898; mustered out with regiment, April 20, 1899, at New York city.

KNAPP, CHARLES W.—Age, — years. Enlisted, November 12, 1898, at Lexington, Ky., to serve two years; mustered in as musician in band, November 30, 1898; mustered out with regiment, April 20, 1899, at New York city.

KNECHT, THOMAS C.—Age, 26 years. Enlisted, May 2, 1898, at New York city, to serve two years; mustered in as private, Co. C, May 13, 1898; transferred to United States Army Hospital Corps, July 19, 1898.

KOCH, HENRY.—Age, 29 years. Enlisted, May 13, 1898, at New York city, to serve two years; mustered in as private, Co. I, same date; mustered out with company, April 20, 1899, at New York city.

KOESLING, HERMANN.—Age, 29 years. Enlisted, May 2, 1898, at New York city, to serve two years; mustered in as artificer, Co. C, May 13, 1898; returned to ranks, June 20, 1898; discharged for disability, January 28, 1899, at Fort McPherson, Ga.

KOLEN, MORRIS, see Morris Kalen.

KOLLER, EDWARD.—Age, 21 years. Enlisted, May 2, 1898, at New York city, to serve two years; mustered in as private, Co. I, May 13, 1898; appointed cook, August 2, 1898; returned to ranks, September 7, 1898; mustered out with company, April 20, 1899, at New York city.

KOSTER, AUGUST P.—Age, — years. Enlisted, June 24, 1898, at New York city, to serve two years; mustered in as private, Co. D, same date; discharged, February 6, 1899, at Fort Columbus, New York Harbor.

KRAEMER, BERNHARDT.—Age, — years. Enlisted, June 20, 1898, at New York city, to serve two years; mustered in as private, Co. I, same date; mustered out with company, April 20, 1899, at New York city.

KRAGH, JENS L.—Age, 19 years. Enlisted, May 11, 1898, at camp, near Peekskill, to serve two years; mustered in as private, Co. E, May 13, 1898; mustered out with company, April 20, 1899, at New York city.

KREMBEL, ADOLPH.—Age, 27 years. Enlisted, May 2, 1898, at New York city, to serve two years; mustered in as private, Co. C, May 13, 1898; discharged, October 26, 1898, at Lexington, Ky.

KROEDEL, JOSEPH H.—Age, 30 years. Enlisted, May 2, 1898, at New York city, to serve two years; mustered in as private, Co. M, May 13, 1898; promoted corporal, August 25, 1898; returned to ranks, December 29, 1898; discharged, to date, April 20, 1899, at New York city.

KROEGEL, FRANCIAS.—Age, 18 years. Enlisted, May 2, 1898, at camp, near Peekskill, to serve two years; mustered in as musician, Co. M, May 13, 1898; deserted, August 1, 1898, at Chickamauga, Ga.

KUHN, PETER JOSEPH.—Age, 24 years. Enlisted, May 2, 1898, at New York city, to serve two years; mustered in as wagoner, Co. C, May 13, 1898; returned to ranks, September 12, 1898; mustered out with company, April 20, 1899, at New York city.

KURZ, JOHN.—Age, — years. Enlisted, June 22, 1898, at New York city, to serve two years; mustered in as private, Co. E, same date; transferred to band, July 3, 1898; mustered out with regiment, April 20, 1899, at New York city.

KUSSEL, ADOLPH.—Age, — years. Enlisted, June 27, 1898, at New York city, to serve two years; mustered in as private, Co. L. same date; mustered out with company, April 20, 1899, at New York city.

KUTCHER, JOHN.—Age, — years. Enlisted, November 15, 1898, at New York city, to serve two years; mustered in as private, Co. K, November 30, 1898; mustered out with company, April 20, 1899, at New York city.

LA GRASS, PETER J.—Age, — years. Enlisted, June 20, 1898, at New York city, to serve two years; mustered in as private, Co. H, same date; dishonorably discharged, February 13, 1899, at camp, near Matanzas, Cuba.

LAMBERT, JOHN S.—Age, 33 years. Enlisted, May 2, 1898, at New York city, to serve two years; mustered in as private, Co. A, May 13, 1898; promoted corporal, July 3, 1898; returned to ranks, January 3, 1899; promoted corporal, February 27, 1899; mustered out with company, April 20, 1899, at New York city.

LAMBERT, WILLIAM E.—Age, 34 years. Enlisted, May 2, 1898, at New York city, to serve two years; mustered in as sergeant, Co. L, May 13, 1898; promoted first sergeant, August 1, 1898; reduced to sergeant, September 1, 1898; returned to ranks, December 20, 1898; mustered out with company, April 20, 1899, at New York city.

LANDAUER, ROBERT E. A.—Age, 25 years. Enlisted, May 11, 1898, at New York city, to serve two years; mustered in as private, Co. I, May 13, 1898; deserted, September 17, 1898.

LANE, JAMES H.—Age, — years. Enlisted, June 22, 1898, at New York city, to serve two years; mustered in as private, Co. A, same date; discharged, January 10, 1899, at New York city.

LANG, JOHN.—Age, 20 years. Enlisted, May 2, 1898, at New York city, to serve two years; mustered in as private, Co. M, May 13, 1898; promoted corporal, July 4, 1898; returned to ranks, prior to November 30, 1898; mustered out with company, April 20, 1899, at New York city.

LA PLACE, GEORGE EDWARD.—Age, — years. Enlisted, June 23, 1898, at New York city, to serve two years; mustered in as private, Co. I, same date; transferred to band, July 3, 1898; returned to ranks, December 17, 1898; deserted, January 3, 1899.

LARSEN, HANS.—Age, 31 years. Enlisted, May 11, 1898, at
camp, near Peekskill, to serve two years; mustered in as private, Co. A, May 13, 1898; mustered out with company, April
20, 1899, at New York city.

LARSEN, LAURITZ P.—Age, 33 years. Enlisted, May 10, 1898,
at New York city, to serve two years; mustered in as private,
Co. B, May 13, 1898; mustered out with company, April 20,
1899, at New York city.

LASHER, GEORGE A.—Age, 21 years. Enlisted, May 2, 1898,
at New York city, to serve two years; mustered in as private,
Co. E, May 13, 1898; promoted corporal, August 1, 1898;
returned to ranks, December 16, 1898; musterd out with company, April 20, 1899, at New York city.

LAUSEN, HERMAN.—Age, 38 years. Enlisted, May 11, 1898,
at camp, near Peekskill, to serve two years; mustered in as private, Co. A, May 13, 1898; mustered out with company, April
20, 1899, at New York city.

LAWLER, PETER A.—Age, — years. Enlisted, June 28, 1898,
at New York city, to serve two years; mustered in as private,
Co. E, same date; mustered out with company, April 20, 1899,
at New York city.

LAWRANCE, JOHN HERBERT GEORGE.—Age, 24 years.
Enlisted, May 2, 1898, at New York city, to serve two years;
mustered in as private, Co. B, May 13, 1898; as second lieutenant, Co. K, January 11, 1899; mustered out with company,
April 20, 1899, at New York city; commissioned second lieutenant, December 24, 1898, with rank from same date, vice
Power, promoted.

LAWRENCE, JAMES W.—Age, 29 years. Enlisted, May 2,
1898, at New York city, to serve two years; mustered in as
corporal, Co. H, May 13, 1898; promoted sergeant, March 24,
1899; mustered out with company, April 20, 1899, at New York
city.

LAWRENCE, JOAQUIN A.—Age, 26 years. Enlisted, May 2,
1898, at New York city, to serve two years; mustered in as
corporal, Co. H, May 13, 1898; promoted sergeant, August 1,
1898; returned to ranks, November 17, 1898; promoted corporal,
March 23, 1899; mustered out with company, April 20, 1899,
at New York city.

LAYER, WILLIAM.—Age, 29 years. Enlisted, May 2, 1898, at New York city, to serve two years; mustered in as quarter-master-sergeant, Co. F, May 13, 1898; discharged, November 21, 1898, at Americus, Ga.

LEE, HUGH C.—Age, 21 years. Enlisted, May 2, 1898, at New York city, to serve two years; mustered in as private, Co. B, May 13, 1898; promoted corporal, January 1, 1899; mustered out with company, April 20, 1899, at New York city.

LEE, JOSEPH M.—Age, — years. Enlisted, June 17, 1898, at New York city, to serve two years; mustered in as private, Co. F, same date; deserted, October 27, 1898, at Camp Hamilton, Lexington, Ky.

LEMILY, HARRY G.—Age, — years. Enlisted, June 20, 1898, at New York city, to serve two years; mustered in as private, Co. G, same date; discharged, to date, April 20, 1899, at New York city.

LENIHAN, WILLIAM J.—Age, 29 years. Enlisted, May 2, 1898, at New York city, to serve two years; mustered in as private, Co. M, May 13, 1898; promoted corporal, May 22, 1898; sergeant, June 16, 1898; quartermaster-sergeant, July 10, 1898; returned to ranks, September 2, 1898; promoted corporal, November 22, 1898; returned to ranks, January 21, 1899; mustered out with company, April 20, 1899, at New York city.

LENNON, ALFRED.—Age, 22 years. Enlisted, May 2, 1898, at New York city, to serve two years; mustered in as private, Co. K, May 13, 1898; mustered out with company, April 20, 1899, at New York city.

LENNON, PHILIP.—Age, 22 years. Enlisted, May 2, 1898, at New York city, to serve two years; mustered in as private, Co. L, May 13, 1898; deserted, December 22, 1898, at Americus, Ga.

LEON, PETER.—Age, 21 years. Enlisted, May 2, 1898, at New York city, to serve two years; mustered in as private, Co. M, May 13, 1898; mustered out with company, April 20, 1899, at New York city.

LEONARD, ROBERT WOODWARD.—Age, 35 years. Enrolled,
May 2, 1898, at New York city, to serve two years; mustered
in as colonel, May 13, 1898; mustered out with regiment, April
20, 1899, at New York city; prior service as major, One Hundred and Sixty-second New York Volunteer Infantry; brevet
lieutenant-colonel, United States Volunteers, War of Rebellion;
subsequent service as lieutenant-colonel, Twenty-eighth Regiment, United States Volunteer Infantry; commissioned colonel,
May 5, 1898, with rank from same date, original.

LEPPERT, PHILLIP.—Age, — years. Enlisted, June 20, 1898,
at New York city, to serve two years; mustered in as private,
Co. H, same date; discharged for disability, September 1, 1898,
at New York city.

LEVEY, ISADORE J.—Age, — years. Enlisted, June 21, 1898,
at New York city, to serve two years; mustered in as private,
Co. B, same date; promoted corporal, February 19, 1899; mustered out with company, April 20, 1899, at New York city.

LEVINS, JOHN.—Age, 19 years. Enlisted, May 13, 1898, at
camp, near Peekskill, to serve two years; mustered in as private, Co. E, same date; mustered out with company, April 20,
1899, at New York city.

LEVY, ABRAHAM.—Age, 19 years. Enlisted, May 2, 1898, at
New York city, to serve two years; mustered in as private,
Co. C, May 13, 1898; mustered out with company, April 20,
1899, at New York city.

LEVY, EDWARD N.—Age, 25 years. Enlisted, May 2, 1898,
at New York city, to serve two years; mustered in as sergeant,
Co. F, May 13, 1898; discharged, January 26, 1899, at New York
city.

LEWIS, JAMES.—Age, 25 years. Enlisted, May 2, 1898, at New
York city, to serve two years; mustered in as private, Co. L,
May 13, 1898; promoted corporal, February 28, 1899; mustered
out with company, April 20, 1899, at New York city.

LEWIS, NATHAN C.—Age, 23 years. Enlisted, May 2, 1898, at
New York city, to serve two years; mustered in as private,
Co. H, May 13, 1898; mustered out with company, April 20,
1899, at New York city.

LITTLEFIELD, LEMUEL.—Age, 25 years. Enlisted, May 2, 1898, at New York city, to serve two years; mustered in as private, Co. D, May 13, 1898; promoted corporal, July 13, 1898; mustered out with company, April 20, 1899, at New York city.

LIVINGSTON, ROBERT LINLITHGOW.—Age, 22 years. Enrolled, May 11, 1898, at camp, near Peekskill, to serve two years; mustered in as second lieutenant, Co. B, June 21, 1898, to date, May 13, 1898; discharged, October 31, 1898, at Lexington, Ky.; commissioned second lieutenant, May 26, 1898, with rank from same date, original.

LOCH, JR., WILLIAM.—Age, 24 years. Enlisted, May 11, 1898, at New York city, to serve two years; mustered in as private, Co. I, May 13, 1898; dishonorably discharged, subsequent to December 31, 1898, at Matanzas, Cuba.

LOGAN, JAMES.—Age, — years. Enlisted, June 25, 1898, at New York city, to serve two years; mustered in as private, Co. B, same date; transferred to Co. C, July 5, 1898; mustered out with company, April 20, 1899, at New York city.

LOOSE, WILLIAM H.—Age, 21 years. Enlisted, May 11, 1898, at camp, near Peekskill, to serve two years; mustered in as private, Co. L, May 13, 1898; dishonorably discharged, no date.

LORD, ROBERT.—Age, 22 years. Enlisted, May 2, 1898, at New York city, to serve two years; mustered in as private, Co. H, May 13, 1898; appointed wagoner, February 17, 1899; returned to ranks, March 1, 1899; mustered out with company, April 20, 1899, at New York city.

LOUGHLIN, JOHN.—Age, — years. Enlisted, June 18, 1898, at New York city, to serve two years; mustered in as private, Co. C, same date; deserted, December 7, 1898, at Americus, Ga.

LOVETT, CHARLES H.—Age, 28 years. Enlisted, May 2, 1898, at New York city, to serve two years; mustered in as private, Co. I, May 13, 1898; mustered out with company, April 20, 1899, at New York city.

LOWE, ROBERT ALLEN.—Age, 27 years. Enlisted, May 2, 1898, at New York city, to serve two years; mustered in as private, Co. A, May 13, 1898; mustered out with company, April 20, 1899, at New York city.

LUEKE, CHARLES E.—Age, 21 years. Enlisted, May 10, 1898, at New York city, to serve two years; mustered in as private, Co. B, May 13, 1898; discharged, November 5, 1898, at Lexington, Ky.

LUNDGREN, WILLIAM.—Age, 22 years. Enlisted, May 10, 1898, at camp, near Peekskill, to serve two years; mustered in as private, Co. L, May 13, 1898; mustered out with company, April 20, 1899, at New York city.

LUPTON, LOUIS A.—Age, 26 years. Enlisted, May 2, 1898, at New York city, to serve two years; mustered in as private, Co. K, May 13, 1898; promoted corporal, November 5, 1898; returned to ranks, February 22, 1899; mustered out with company, April 20, 1899, at New York city.

LUTZ, LOUIS.—Age, 21 years. Enlisted, May 2, 1898, at New York city, to serve two years; mustered in as private, Co. G, May 13, 1898; promoted corporal, August 1, 1898; discharged, November 18, 1898, at Camp Gilman, Ga.

LYNCH, FRANCIS J.—Age, 21 years. Enlisted, May 2, 1898, at New York city, to serve two years; mustered in as private, Co. E, May 13, 1898; mustered out with company, April 20, 1899, at New York city.

LYNCH, ROBERT J.—Age, — years. Enlisted, June 20, 1898, at New York city, to serve two years; mustered in as private, Co. L, same date; mustered out with company, April 20, 1899, at New York city.

LYNN, FRANCIS H.—Age, 21 years. Enlisted, May 2, 1898, at New York city, to serve two years; mustered in as private, Co. I, May 13, 1898; promoted corporal, July 5, 1898; mustered out with company, April 20, 1899, at New York city.

MACAULEY, JOHN.—Age, — years. Enlisted, June 27, 1898, at New York city, to serve two years; mustered in as private, Co. E, same date; promoted corporal, August 1, 1898; mustered in as first lieutenant and regimental quartermaster, December 22, 1898; mustered out with regiment, April 20, 1899, at New York city; commissioned first lieutenant and regimental quartermaster, Decemebr 22, 1898, with rank from same date, vice White, transferred to Co. L.

MACCOLL, ARCHIBALD.—Age, 21 years. Enlisted, May 2, 1898, at New York city, to serve two years; mustered in as private, Co. C, May 13, 1898; mustered out with company, April 20, 1899, at New York city.

MACE, JAMES HENRY.—Age, 29 years. Enlisted, May 2, 1898, at New York city, to serve two years; mustered in as private, Co E, May 13, 1898; transferred to United States Hospital Corps, November 23, 1898.

MACK, EDWARD J.—Enlisted, June 25, 1898, at New York city, to serve two years; mustered in as private, Co. I, same date; promoted corporal, September 10, 1898; mustered out with company, April 20, 1899, at New York city.

MACKEY, JOSEPH JAMES.—Age, 23 years. Enlisted, May 2, 1898, at New York city, to serve two years; mustered in as corporal, Co. B, May 13, 1898; mustered out with company, April 20, 1899, at New York city.

MAC PHERSON, ROBERT.—Enlisted, June 29, 1898, at New York city, to serve two years; mustered in as private, Co. M, same date; mustered out with company, April 20, 1899, at New York city.

MACREADY, FRANK J.—Age, 25 years. Enlisted, May 2, 1898, at New York city, to serve two years; mustered in as private, Co. D, May 13, 1898; died of heart disease, May 20, 1899, at Rossville, Tenn.

MAC VEAN, STUART.—Age, 30 years. Enlisted, May 11, 1898, at New York city, to serve two years; mustered in as private, Co. I, May 13, 1898; mustered out with company, April 20, 1899, at New York city.

MADDEN, WILLIAM F.—Age, — years. Enlisted, June 18, 1898, at New York city, to serve two years; mustered in as private, Co. C, same date; deserted, September 19, 1898, at Lexington, Ky.

MAGEE, GEORGE J.—Age, 26 years. Enlisted, May 2, 1898, at New York city, to serve two years; mustered in as private, Co. E, May 13, 1898; mustered out with company, April 20, 1899, at New York city.

MAGER, HUGO W.—Age, 22 years. Enlisted, May 2, 1898, at
New York city, to serve two years; mustered in as private, Co.
E, May 13, 1898; mustered out with company, April 20, 1899, at
New York city.

MAGNAN, ARTHUR J.—Age, 26 years. Enlisted, May 2, 1898,
at New York city, to serve two years; mustered in as corporal,
Co. M, May 13, 1898; returned to ranks, May 29, 1898; promoted
corporal, July 5, 1898; mustered out with company, April 20,
1899, at New York city.

MAGNOLIA, LOUIS F.—Age, 20 years. Enlisted, May 2, 1898,
at New York city, to serve two years; mustered in as private,
Co. G, May 13, 1898; discharged, November 23, 1898, at Camp
Gilman, Ga.

MAHER, CHRISTOPHER ARTHUR.—Age, 21 years. Enlisted,
May 2, 1898, at New York city, to serve two years; mustered in
as private, Co. E, May 13, 1898; mustered out with company,
April 20, 1899, at New York city.

MAHON, JAMES F.—Age, 23 years. Enlisted, May 2, 1898, at
New York city, to serve two years; mustered in as sergeant,
Co. H, May 13, 1898; mustered out with company, April 20,
1899, at New York city.

MAIDHOFF, GEORGE E.—Age, 19 years. Enlisted, May 2,
1898, at New York city, to serve two years; mustered in as private, Co. K, May 13, 1898; mustered out with company, April
20, 1899, at New York city.

MAIRWOOD, FREDERICK H.—Age, — years. Enlisted, June
28, 1898, at New York city, to serve two years; mustered in as
private, Co. L, same date; mustered out with company, April
20, 1899, at New York city.

MALLEY, CHARLES.—Age, 23 years. Enlisted, May 11, 1898,
at camp, near Peekskill, to serve two years; mustered in as
musician, Co. D, May 13, 1898; returned to rank, June 1, 1898;
mustered out with company, April 20, 1899, at New York city.

MALLOY, JAMES A.—Age, — years. Enlisted, June 18, 1898,
at New York city, to serve two years; mustered in as private,
Co. D, same date; mustered out with company, April 20, 1899,
at New York city.

MALLOY, JAMES JOHN.—Age, 22 years. Enlisted, May 2, 1898, at New York city, to serve two years; mustered in as private, Co. B, May 13, 1898; mustered out with company, April 20, 1899, at New York city.

MALLOY, JAMES P.—Age, 33 years. Enlisted, May 2, 1898, at New York city, to serve two years; mustered in as private, Co. K, May 13, 1898; promoted corporal, July 5, 1898; mustered out with company, April 20, 1899, at New York city.

MALONE, GEORGE.—Age, 25 years. Enlisted, May 2, 1898, at New York city, to serve two years; mustered in as artificer, Co. M, May 13, 1898; promoted corporal, February 6, 1899; mustered out with company, April 20, 1899, at New York city.

MALONE, MARTIN J.—Age, — years. Enlisted, June 28, 1898, at New York city, to serve two years; mustered in as private, Co. I, same date; mustered out with company, April 20, 1899, at New York city.

MALONEY, GEORGE W.—Age, 22 years. Enlisted, May 2, 1898, at New York city, to serve two years; mustered in as private, Co. H, May 13, 1898; deserted, November 19, 1898, at Camp Gilman, Ga.

MANN, GUSTAV.—Age, 31 years. Enlisted, May 2, 1898, at New York city, to serve two years; mustered in as private, Co. K, May 13, 1898; promoted corporal, August 1, 1898; discharged, to date, April 20, 1899, at New York city.

MANN, JOSEPH.—Age, — years. Enlisted, June 20, 1898, at New York city, to serve two years; mustered in as private, Co. I, same date; mustered out with company, April 20, 1899, at New York city.

MANOOGIAN, GARABED H.—Age, 27 years. Enlisted, May 2, 1898, at New York city, to serve two years; mustered in as private, Co. B, May 13, 1898; mustered out with company, April 20, 1899, at New York city.

MANSFIELD, WILLIAM E.—Age, 27 years. Enlisted, May 2, 1898, at New York city, to serve two years; mustered in as private, Co. L, May 13, 1898; promoted corporal, July 12, 1898; quartermaster-sergeant, September 1, 1898; mustered out with company, April 20, 1899, at New York city.

MARCLEY, WILLIAM C.—Age, — years. Enlisted, June 17, 1898, at New York city, to serve two years; mustered in as private, Co. K, same date; mustered out with company, April 20, 1899, at New York city.

MARSH, FREDERICK S.—Age, — years. Enlisted, June 21, 1898, at New York city, to serve two years; mustered in as private, Co. A, same date; mustered out with company, April 20, 1899, at New York city.

MARSH, WILLIAM JOHN.—Age, 23 years. Enlisted, May 2, 1898, at New York city, to serve two years; mustered in as private, Co. E, May 13, 1898; mustered out with company, April 20, 1899, at New York city.

MARTIN, EDWARD J.—Age, 24 years. Enlisted, May 2, 1898, at New York city, to serve two years; mustered in as private, Co. M, May 13, 1898; mustered out with company, April 20, 1899, at New York city.

MARTIN, MICHAEL T.—Age, 22 years. Enlisted, May 2, 1898, at New York city, to serve two years; mustered in as private, Co. G, May 13, 1898; mustered out with company, April 20, 1899, at New York city.

MARTIN, WILLIAM G.—Age, 23 years. Enlisted, May 10, 1898, at camp, near Peekskill, to serve two years; mustered in as private, Co. G, May 13, 1898; mustered out with company, April 20, 1899, at New York city.

MARTIN, JR., WILLIAM H.—Age, 23 years. Enlisted, May 2, 1898, at New York city, to serve two years; mustered in as private, Co. G, May 13, 1898; promoted corporal, July 5, 1898; died of disease, October 13, 1898, at New York city.

MARTIN, WILLIAM LUSH.—Age, 25 years. Enrolled, at New York city, to serve two years and mustered in as second lieutenant, Co. G, February 17, 1899; mustered out with company, April 20, 1899, at New York city; prior service as corporal in Co. A, First Regiment, New York Volunteer Infantry; commissioned second lieutenant, February 24, 1899, with rank from same date, vice Fennell, promoted.

MARTINEZ, LOUIS.—Age, 25 years. Enlisted, May 10, 1898, at New York city, to serve two years; mustered in as private, Co. F, May 13, 1898; mustered out with company, April 20, 1899, at New York city.

MATHESON, JOHN.—Age, 21 years. Enlisted, May 13, 1898, at New York city, to serve two years; mustered in as private, Co. F, same date; promoted corporal, August 11, 1898; mustered out with company, April 20, 1899, at New York city.

MATHEWS, THOMAS F.—Age, — years. Enlisted, November 15, 1898, at New York city, to serve two years; mustered in as private, Co. D, December 15, 1898; mustered out with company, April 20, 1899, at New York city.

MATHIAS, CHARLES.—Age, 26 years. Enlisted, May 2, 1898, at New York city, to serve two years; mustered in as corporal, Co. B, May 13, 1898; returned to ranks, January 25, 1899; mustered out with company, April 20, 1899, at New York city.

MAYER, CLARENCE.—Age, 23 years. Enlisted, May 2, 1898, at New York city, to serve two years; mustered in as private, Co. K, May 13, 1898; promoted corporal, December 23, 1898; mustered out with company, April 20, 1899, at New York city.

McALEER, MICHAEL S.—Age, — years. Enlisted, June 22, 1898, at New York city, to serve two years; mustered in as private, Co. L, same date; mustered out with company, April 20, 1899, at New York city.

McCAFFREY, ROBERT F.—Age, 21 years. Enlisted, May 2, 1898, at New York city, to serve two years; mustered in as private, Co. H, May 13, 1898; mustered out with company, April 20, 1899, at New York city.

McCANN, JAMES H.—Age, 22 years. Enlisted, May 2, 1898, at New York city, to serve two years; mustered in as private, Co. H, May 13, 1898; discharged, January 7, 1899, at camp, near Matanzas, Cuba.

McCARTHY, ALFRED B.—Age, 22 years. Enlisted, May 2, 1898, at New York city, to serve two years; mustered in as private, Co. G, May 13, 1898; discharged for disability, October 28, 1898, at Camp Hamilton, Ky.

McCARTHY, CHRISTOPHER JOSEPH.—Age, 21 years. Enlisted, May 2, 1898, at New York city, to serve two years; mustered in as private, Co. E, May 13, 1898; mustered out with company, April 20, 1899, at New York city.

McCARTHY, EDWARD J.—Age, — years. Enlisted, June 20, 1898, at New York city, to serve two years; mustered in as private, Co. D, same date; mustered out with company, April 20, 1899, at New York city.

McCARTHY, JOSEPH FRANCIS.—Age, 19 years. Enlisted, May 2, 1898, at New York city, to serve two years; mustered in as private, Co. E, May 13, 1898; promoted corporal, November 18, 1898; sergeant, February 19, 1899; mustered out with company, April 20, 1899, at New York city.

McCARTHY, THOMAS J.—Age, 21 years. Enlisted, May 2, 1898, at New York city, to serve two years; mustered in as private, Co. F, May 13, 1898; mustered out with company, April 20, 1899, at New York city.

McCARTHY, WILLIAM.—Age, 22 years. Enlisted, May 2, 1898, at New York city, to serve two years; mustered in as private, Co. C, May 13, 1898; mustered out with company, April 20, 1899, at New York city.

McCLEAVE, THOMAS CROOK.—Age, — years. Enrolled, November 11, 1898, at Lexington, Ky., to serve.two years; mustered in as first lieutenant and assistant surgeon, December 5, 1898; mustered out with regiment, April 20, 1899, at New York city; commissioned first lieutenant and assistant surgeon, November 11, 1898, with rank from same date, vice Chalmers, promoted.

McCLUSKY, JOHN.—Age, 22 years. Enlisted, May 11, 1898, at New York city, to serve two years; mustered in as private, Co. I, May 13, 1898; promoted corporal, December 9, 1898; returned to ranks, December 16, 1898; mustered out with company, April 20, 1899, at New York city.

McCOMB, DAVID.—Age, — years. Enlisted, June 22, 1898, at New York city, to serve two years; mustered in as private, Co. G, same date; appointed artificer, November 1, 1898; mustered out with company, April 20, 1899, at New York city.

McCORMACK, JOHN F.—Age, 25 years. Enlisted, May 2, 1898, at New York city, to serve two years; mustered in as private, Co. H, May 13, 1898; discharged for disability, October 9, 1898, at Camp Hamilton, Ky.

McCORMACK, JOHN J.—Age, 22 years. Enlisted, May 2, 1898, at New York city, to serve two years; mustered in as private, Co. B, May 13, 1898; mustered out with company, April 20, 1899, at New York city.

McCORMICK, GEORGE A.—Age, 21 years. Enlisted, May 2, 1898, at New York city, to serve two years; mustered in as private, Co. I, May 13, 1898; discharged, January 31, 1899, at New York city.

McCORMICK, JAMES J.—Age, — years. Enlisted, May 14, 1898, at New York city, to serve two years; mustered in as private, Co. C, same date; promoted corporal, March 2, 1899; mustered out with company, April 20, 1899, at New York city.

McCORMICK, THOMAS M.—Age, — years. Enlisted, June 25, 1898, at New York city, to serve two years; mustered in as private, Co. M, same date; promoted corporal, September 20, 1898; discharged, February 11, 1899, at Fort McPherson, Ga.

McCOY, ALEXANDER.—Age, 21 years. Enlisted, May 11, 1898, at camp, near Peekskill, to serve two years; mustered in as private, Co. A, May 13, 1898; deserted, October 16, 1898.

McDERMOTT, JOHN.—Age, 39 years. Enlisted, May 2, 1898, at New York city, to serve two years; mustered in as first sergeant, Co. E, May 13, 1898; as second lieutenant, September 17, 1898; mustered out with company, April 20, 1899, at New York city; commissioned second lieutenant, September 7, 1898, with rank from same date, vice Morris, promoted.

McDONALD, JOHN JAY.—Age, 27 years. Enlisted, May 13, 1898, at New York city, to serve two years; mustered in as private, Co. C, same date; mustered out with company, April 20, 1899, at New York city.

McDONOUGH, JAMES J.—Age, 21 years. Enlisted, May 2, 1898, at New York city, to serve two years; mustered in as private, Co. K, May 13, 1898; mustered out with company, April 20, 1899, at New York city.

McGIRR, JOHN.—Age, — years. Enlisted, June 21, 1898, at New York city, to serve two years; mustered in as private, Co. A, same date; mustered out with company, April 20, 1899, at New York city.

McGIVNEY, ANDREW J.—Age, 25 years. Enlisted, May 2, 1898, at New York city, to serve two years; mustered in as wagoner, Co. G, May 13, 1898; discharged, November 18, 1898, at Camp Gilman, Ga.

McGIVNEY, JAMES.—Age, — years. Enlisted, June 18, 1898, at New York city, to serve two years; mustered in as private, Co. K, same date; discharged for disability, January 4, 1899, at Americus, Ga.

McGOVERN, FRANCIS J.—Age, 26 years. Enlisted, May 2, 1898, at New York city, to serve two years; mustered in as private, Co. D, May 13, 1898; mustered out with company, April 20, 1899, at New York city.

McGOWAN, DANIEL.—Age, — years. Enlisted, June 23, 1898, at New York city, to serve two years; mustered in as private, Co. G, same date; mustered out with company, April 20, 1899, at New York city.

McGOWAN, ISADORE V.—Age, 21 years. Enlisted, May 2, 1898, at New York city, to serve two years; mustered in as private, Co. D, May 13, 1898; discharged November 3, 1898.

McGOWAN, THOMAS L.—Age, 24 years. Enlisted, May 2, 1898, at New York city, to serve two years; mustered in as private, Co. C, May 13, 1898; mustered out with company, April 20, 1899, at New York city; also borne as Thomas J. McGowan.

McGOWN, MALCOLM.—Age, 18 years. Enlisted, May 11, 1898, at New York city, to serve two years; mustered in as private, Co. I, May 13, 1898; discharged, January 26, 1899, at New York city; also borne as McGowan.

McGOWN, WILLIAM F. J.—Age, — years. Enlisted, November 15, 1898, at New York city, to serve two years; mustered in as private, Co. D, December 15, 1898; mustered out with company, April 20, 1899, at New York city.

McGRATH, JAMES.—Age, — years. Enlisted, June 21, 1898, at New York city, to serve two years; mustered in as private, Co. B, same date; transferred to Co. L, July 6, 1898; mustered out with company, April 20, 1899, at New York city.

McGREGOR, H. BRADFORD.—Age, — years. Enlisted, December 3, 1898, at Americus, Ga., to serve two years; mustered in as musician, in band, December 26, 1898; mustered out with regiment, April 20, 1899, at New York city.

McGUIRE, CHARLES.—Age, 21 years. Enlisted, May 2, 1898, at New York city, to serve two years; mustered in as private, Co. K, May 13, 1898; mustered out with company, April 20, 1899, at New York city.

McGUIRE, PHINEAS W.—Age, 21 years. Enlisted, May 2, 1898, at New York city, to serve two years; mustered in as private, Co. M, May 13, 1898; mustered out with company, April 20, 1899, at New York city.

McGUIRK, JOHN J.—Age, — years. Enlisted, June 17, 1898, at New York city, to serve two years; mustered in as private, Co. H, same date; mustered out with company, April 20, 1899, at New York city.

McGUIRK, PETER.—Age, — years. Enlisted, June 21, 1898, at New York city, to serve two years; mustered in as private, Co. A, same date; mustered out with company, April 20, 1899, at New York city.

McILVAINE, TOMPKINS.—Age, 29 years. Enrolled, May 2, 1898, at New York city, to serve two years; mustered in as second lieutenant, Co. M, May 13, 1898; as first lieutenant, July 21, 1898; discharged, December 24, 1898, at New York city; commissioned second lieutenant May 13, 1898, with rank from date, original; first lieutenant, July 21, 1898, with rank from same date, vice Pillot, discharged.

McKAY, CHARLES F.—Age, 22 years. Enlisted, May 2, 1898, at New York city, to serve two years; mustered in as private, Co. H, May 13, 1898; transferred to First Army Hospital Corps, July 19, 1898.

McKEAN, WILLIAM.—Age, — years. Enlisted, June 22, 1898, at New York city, to serve two years; mustered in as private, Co. L, same date; mustered out with company, April 20, 1899, at New York city.

McKEEVER, JOSEPH B.—Age, — years. Enlisted, June 22, 1898, at New York city, to serve two years; mustered in as private, Co. I, same date; mustered out with company, April 20, 1899, at New York city.

McKEEVER, PATRICK.—Age, — years. Enlisted, June 25, 1898, at New York city, to serve two years; mustered in as private, Co. C, same date; mustered out with company, April 20, 1899, at New York city.

McKENNA, JOHN JAMES.—Age, 28 years. Enlisted, May 2, 1898, at New York city, to serve two years; mustered in as private, Co. E, May 13, 1898; appointed wagoner, June 2, 1898; returned to ranks, no date; mustered out with company, April 20, 1899, at New York city.

McKENNA, PETER.—Age, — years. Enlisted, June 22, 1898, at New York city, to serve two years; mustered in as private, Co. K, same date; mustered out with company, April 20, 1899, at New York city.

McKEOWN, JOSEPH.—Age, 23 years. Enlisted, May 10, 1898, at New York city, to serve two years; mustered in as private, Co. F, May 13, 1898; mustered out with company, April 20, 1899, at New York city.

McLAUGHLIN, JAMES J.—Age, 23 years. Enlisted, May 11, 1898, at New York city, to serve two years; mustered in as private, Co. F, May 13, 1898; transferred to Third Division Hospital, First Army Corps, October 30, 1898.

McLOUGHLIN, DANIEL M.—Age, 18 years. Enlisted, May 10, 1898, at camp, near Peekskill, to serve two years; mustered in as private, Co. E, May 13, 1898; mustered out with company, April 20, 1899, at New York city.

McMASTER, WILLIAM C.—Age, 21 years. Enlisted, May 2, 1898, at New York city, to serve two years; mustered in as private, Co. D, May 13, 1898; mustered out with company, April 20, 1899, at New York city.

McNALLY, HENRY.—Age, 27 years. Enlisted, May 2, 1898, at New York city, to serve two years; mustered in as private, Co. M, May 13, 1898; mustered out with company, April 20, 1899, at New York city.

McNALLY, TERENCE.—Age, 21 years. Enlisted, May 2, 1898, at New York city, to serve two years; mustered in as private, Co. M, May 13, 1898; promoted corporal, June 16, 1898; returned to ranks, no date; deserted, September 19, 1898, at Lexington, Ky.

McNARY, ROBERT L.—Age, 33 years. Enlisted, May 2, 1898, at New York city, to serve two years; mustered in as corporal, Co. L, May 13, 1898; promoted sergeant, July 5, 1898; quarter-master-sergeant, August 1, 1898; first sergeant, September 1, 1898; reduced to sergeant, November 21, 1898; mustered out with company, April 20, 1899, at New York city.

McPYKE, JOHN B.—Age, 26 years. Enlisted, May 2, 1898, at New York city, to serve two years; mustered in as private, Co. L, May 13, 1898; mustered out with company, April 20, 1899, at New York city.

McQUADE, OWEN.—Age, 21 years. Enlisted, May 13, 1898, at New York city, to serve two years; mustered in as private, Co. H, same date; mustered out with company, April 20, 1899, at New York city.

McQUADE, THOMAS F.—Age, 24 years. Enlisted, May 2, 1898, at New York city, to serve two years; mustered in as private, Co. L, May 13, 1898; died of disease, September 1, 1898, at Sternberg Hospital, Chickamauga, Ga.

McQUAID, BERNARD.—Age, — years. Enlisted, June 28, 1898, at New York city, to serve two years; mustered in as private, Co. L, same date; mustered out with company, April 20, 1899, at New York city.

McRAE, JOHN A.—Age, 20 years. Enlisted, May 11, 1898, at camp, near Peekskill, to serve two years; mustered in as musician, Co. D, May 13, 1898; returned to ranks, no date; deserted, November 27, 1898, at Camp Gilman, Ga.

McSORLEY, PATRICK.—Age, 30 years. Enlisted, May 10, 1898, at camp, near Peekskill, to serve two years; mustered in as private, Co. D, May 13, 1898; discharged, February 4, 1899, at Fort Columbus, New York Harbor.

McTERNAM, JAMES J.—Age, 29 years. Enlisted, May 2, 1898, at New York city, to serve two years; mustered in as corporal, Co. K, May 13, 1898; returned to ranks, July 30, 1898; mustered out with company, April 20, 1899, at New York city.

McTIGHE, JOHN.—Age, — years. Enlisted, June 20, 1898, at New York city, to serve two years; mustered in as private, Co. D, same date; discharged for disability, January 4, 1899, at Camp Gilman, Ga.

MEEHAN, LAWRENCE VINCENT.—Age, 26 years. Enlisted, May 2, 1898, at New York city, to serve two years; mustered in as first sergeant, Co. M, May 13, 1898; transferred to Co. H, same date; mustered in as second lieutenant, Co. H, June 20, 1898, to date, May 13, 1898; as first lieutenant, January 31, 1899; mustered out with company, April 20, 1899, at New York city; commissioned second lieutenant, May 13, 1898, with rank from same date, vice White, transferred; first lieutenant, January 12, 1899, with rank from same date.

MEIER, ROBERT.—Age, 29 years. Enlisted, May 2, 1898, at New York city, to serve two years; mustered in as artificer, Co. D, May 13, 1898; promoted corporal, January 20, 1898; sergeant, November 4, 1898; mustered out with company, April 20, 1899, at New York city.

MEISSNER, GEORGE.—Enlisted, December 3, 1898, at Americus, Ga., to serve two years; mustered in as private, in band, December 15, 1898; mustered out with regiment, April 20, 1899, at New York city.

MELBOURNE, HARRY C.—Age, — years. Enlisted, November 15, 1898, at New York city, to serve two years; mustered in as private, Co. K, November 30, 1898; mustered out with company, April 20, 1899, at New York city.

MELIUS, JERRY.—Age, — years. Enlisted, June 21, 1898, at New York city, to serve two years; mustered in as private, Co. B, same date; mustered out with company, April 20, 1899, at New York city.

MELLON, WILLIAM.—Age, — years. Enlisted, June 30, 1898, at New York city, to serve two years; mustered in as private, Co. M, same date; transferred to Hospital Corps, July 21, 1898.

MENANCH, WILLIAM G.—Age, 20 years. Enlisted, May 2, 1898, at New York city, to serve two years; mustered in as private, Co. F, May 13, 1898; mustered out with company, April 20, 1899, at New York city.

MENNINGER, GUSTAVE.—Age, 24 years. Enlisted, May 2, 1898, at New York city, to serve two years; mustered in as private, Co. E, May 13, 1898; appointed artificer, June 13, 1898; returned to ranks, September 1, 1898; mustered out with company, April 20, 1899, at New York city.

MENZIES, ALEXANDER GEORGE.—Age, 40 years. Enlisted, May 2, 1898, at New York city, to serve two years; mustered in as color-sergeant, Co. B, May 13, 1898; mustered out with company, April 20, 1899, at New York city.

MENZL, ROBERT.—Age, 22 years. Enlisted, May 2, 1898, at New York city, to serve two years; mustered in as private, Co. E, May 13, 1898; mustered out with company, April 20, 1899, at New York city.

MERSEREAU, WILLIAM.—Age, — years. Enlisted, June 18, 1898, at New York city, to serve two years; mustered in as private, Co. G, same date; died of disease, March 31, 1899, at Fort Columbus Hospital, New York Harbor.

METZ, HARRY W.—Age, 22 years. Enlisted, May 2, 1898, at New York city, to serve two years; mustered in as private. Co. I, May 13, 1898; mustered out with company, April 20, 1899, at New York city.

MEYER, JOHN.—Enlisted, December 3, 1898, at New York city, to serve two years; mustered in as private, in band, December 26, 1898; mustered out with regiment, April 20, 1899, at New York city.

MEYERS, CHARLES.—Age, 26 years. Enlisted, May 2, 1898, at New York city, to serve two years; mustered in as private, Co. L, May 13, 1898; transferred to Hospital Corps, February 28, 1899; mustered out, April 18, 1899, at Matanzas, Cuba.

MICHAELS, OTTO.—Age, 23 years. Enlisted, May 2, 1898, at New York city, to serve two years; mustered in as private, Co. M, May 13, 1898; mustered out with company, April 20, 1899, at New York city.

MILLER, ALBERT F. T.—Age, 23 years. Enlisted, May 2, 1898, at New York city, to serve two years; mustered in as corporal, Co. G, May 13, 1898; mustered out with company, April 20, 1899, at New York city.

MILLER, EUGENE.—Age, 21 years. Enlisted, May 2, 1898, at New York city, to serve two years; mustered in as private, Co. K, May 13, 1898; deserted, October 27, 1898, at Lexington, Ky.

MILLER, MARTIN.—Age, 21 years. Enlisted, May 11, 1898, at New York city, to serve two years; mustered in as private, Co. I, May 13, 1898; mustered out with company, April 20, 1899, at New York city; also borne as Martin Müeller.

MILWARD, JAMES.—Age, — years. Enlisted, June 23, 1898, at New York city, to serve two years; mustered in as private, Co. M, same date; appointed cook, March 14, 1899; mustered out with company, April 20, 1899, at New York city.

MINNEMAN, WALLACE.—Age, 22 years. Enlisted, May 10, 1898, at New York city, to serve two years; mustered in as private, Co. M, May 13, 1898; mustered out with company, April 20, 1899, at New York city.

MITCHELL, ALFRED A.—Age, — years. Enrolled, November 3, 1898, at Columbus, Ga., to serve two years; mustered in as first lieutenant, Co. K, same date; mustered out with company, April 20, 1899, at New York city; prior service as captain in Eighth Regiment, New York Volunteer Infantry; commissioned first lieutenant, November 3, 1898, with rank from same date, vice Morris, transferred.

MITCHELL, FREDERICK F.—Age, 28 years. Enlisted, May 2, 1898, at New York city, to serve two years; mustered in as private, Co. L, May 13, 1898; mustered out with company, April 20, 1899, at New York city.

MITCHELL, JAMES F.—Age, 24 years. Enlisted, May 2, 1898, at New York city, to serve two years; mustered in as corporal, Co. C, May 13, 1898; discharged, October 26, 1898, at Lexington, Ky.

MITCHELL, PETER.—Age, 28 years. Enlisted, May 2, 1898, at New York city, to serve two years; mustered in as private, Co. K, May 13, 1898; mustered out with company, April 20, 1899, at New York city.

MONAHAN, JOHN J.—Age, 22 years. Enlisted, May 2, 1898, at New York city, to serve two years; mustered in as private, Co. A, May 13, 1898; deserted, December 26, 1898.

MONOGHAN, PATRICK.—Age, — years. Enlisted, June 20, 1898, at New York city, to serve two years; mustered in as private, Co. I, same date; discharged, to date, October 25, 1898, at Lexington, Ky.

MONTGOMERY, HENRY.—Age, — years. Enlisted, June 20, 1898, at New York city, to serve two years; mustered in as private, Co. F, same date; deserted, October 24, 1898, at Camp Hamilton, Lexington, Ky.

MOON, CARY H.—Age, — years. Enlisted, June 24, 1898, at New York city, to serve two years; mustered in as private, Co. K, same date; discharged, to date, April 20, 1899, at New York city.

MOORE, JOHN T.—Age, 29 years. Enlisted, May 2, 1898, at New York city, to serve two years; mustered in as private, Co. H, May 13, 1898; promoted corporal, August 22, 1898; mustered out with company, April 20, 1899, at New York city.

MORAN, EUGENE F.—Age, 26 years. Enlisted, May 2, 1898, at New York city, to serve two years; mustered in as private, Co. C, May 13, 1898; discharged, December 11, 1898, at Americus, Ga.

MORAN, JOHN J.—Age, 23 years. Enlisted, May 10, 1898, at camp, near Peekskill, to serve two years; mustered in as private, Co. D, May 13, 1898; discharged for disability, November 10, 1898.

MORAN, MARCY C.—Age, — years. Enlisted, June 28, 1898, at New York city, to serve two years; mustered in as private, Co. B, same date; transferred to Co. L, July 6, 1898; deserted, October 11, 1898, at Lexington, Ky.

MORE, WILLIAM M.—Age, 26 years. Enlisted, May 2, 1898, at New York city, to serve two years; mustered in as sergeant, Co. A, May 14, 1898; discharged, November 17, 1898, at Americus, Ga.

MORF, FRED.—Age, 22 years. Enlisted, May 13, 1898, at camp, near Peekskill, to serve two years; mustered in as private, Co. B, same date; mustered out with company, April 20, 1899, at New York city.

MORGAN, GEORGE J.—Age, 23 years. Enlisted, May 2, 1898, at New York city, to serve two years; mustered in as private, Co. M, May 13, 1898; promoted corporal, August 1, 1898; returned to ranks, no date; deserted, September 14, 1898, at Lexington, Ky.

MORLEY, STEPHEN S.—Age, 44 years. Enlisted, May 2, 1898, at New York city, to serve two years; mustered in as private, Co. A, May 13, 1898; mustered out with company, April 20, 1899, at New York city.

MORRIS, JAMES.—Age, 23 years. Enlisted, May 2, 1898, at New York city, to serve two years; mustered in as private, Co. M, May 13, 1898; promoted corporal, January 1, 1899; mustered out with company, April 20, 1899, at New York city.

MORRIS, JAMES A.—Age, 21 years. Enlisted, May 2, 1898, at New York city, to serve two years; mustered in as private, Co. L, May 13, 1898; died, September 19, 1898, in Division Hospital, Lexington, Ky.

MORRIS, MONSON.—Age, 22 years. Enrolled, May 2, 1898, at New York city, to serve two years; mustered in as second lieutenant, Co. E, May 16, 1898; as first lieutenant, Co. K, September 7, 1898; transferred to Co. E, November 17, 1898; mustered out with company, April 20, 1899, at New York city; commissioned second lieutenant, May 13, 1898, with rank from same date, original; first lieutenant, September 7, 1898, with rank from same date, vice Connell, promoted.

MORRIS, NEWBOLD.—Age, 30 years. Enrolled, May 2, 1898, at New York city, to serve two years; mustered in as captain, Co. M, May 13, 1898; discharged, September 30, 1898, at Lexington, Ky.; commissioned captain, May 13, 1898, with rank from same date, original.

MORRISON. EDWARD L.—Age, 27 years. Enlisted, May 2, 1898, at New York city, to serve two years; mustered in as private, Co. H, May 13, 1898; mustered out with company, April 20, 1899, at New York city.

MORRISON, WILLIAM B.—Age, 29 years. Enlisted, May 2, 1898, at New York city, to serve two years; mustered in as private, Co. H, May 13, 1898; promoted corporal, March 23, 1899; mustered out with company, April 20, 1899, at New York city.

MORRISSEY, JOHN J.—Age, 22 years. Enlisted, May 2, 1898, at New York city, to serve two years; mustered in as private, Co. D, May 13, 1898; discharged for disability, January 4, 1899, at Camp Gilman, Ga.

MOSER, ALBERT.—Age, — years. Enlisted, November 15, 1898, at New York city, to serve two years; mustered in as private, Co. K, November 30, 1898; mustered out with company, April 20, 1899, at New York city.

MOUNTAINE, JOHN.—Age, 28 years. Enlisted, May 2, 1898, at New York city, to serve two years; mustered in as private, Co. E, May 13, 1898; mustered out with company, April 20, 1899, at New York city.

MÜELLER, MARTIN, see Martin Miller.

MUIR, ALEXANDER G.—Age, 32 years. Enlisted, May 2, 1898, at New York city, to serve two years; mustered in as private, Co. L, May 13, 1898; mustered out with company, April 20, 1899, at New York city.

MULDOON, JOHN.—Age, — years. Enlisted, June 17, 1898, at New York city, to serve two years; mustered in as private, Co. F, same date; mustered out with company, April 20, 1899, at New York city.

MULDOON, MARTIN.—Age, — years. Enlisted, June 20, 1898, at New York city, to serve two years; mustered in as private, Co. H, same date; deserted, July 11, 1898, at Camp Thomas, Chickamauga, Park, Ga.

MULLER, PETER A.—Age, — years. Enlisted, November 15, 1898, at New York city, to serve two years; mustered in as private, Co. K, November 30, 1898; mustered out with company, April 20, 1899, at New York city; prior service in Eighth New York Volunteer Infantry.

MULVEY, WILLIAM H.—Age, — years. Enlisted, June 21, 1898, at New York city, to serve two years; mustered in as private, Co. E, same date; mustered out with company, April 20, 1899, at New York city.

MURPHY, BARTLEY.—Age, 23 years. Enlisted, May 2, 1898, at New York city, to serve two years; mustered in as musician, Co. K, May 13, 1898; transferred to band, October 14, 1898; mustered out with regiment, April 20, 1899, at New York city.

MURPHY, GEORGE J.—Age, 29 years. Enlisted, May 2, 1898, at New York city, to serve two years; mustered in as first sergeant, Co. F, May 13, 1898; mustered out with company, April 20, 1899, at New York city.

MURPHY, JOHN J.—Age, 22 years. Enlisted, May 2, 1898, at New York city, to serve two years; mustered in as private, Co. K, May 13, 1898; deserted, November 23, 1898, at Americus, Ga.

MURPHY, JOHN W.—Age, — years. Enlisted, June 20, 1898, at New York city, to serve two years; mustered in as private, Co. F, same date; mustered out with company, April 20, 1899, at New York city.

MURPHY, JOSEPH.—Age, 32 years. Enlisted, May 13, 1898, at New York city, to serve two years; mustered in as private, Co. C, same date; mustered out with company, April 20, 1899, at New York city.

MURPHY, THOMAS F.—Age, 21 years. Enlisted, May 2, 1898, at New York city, to serve two years; mustered in as private, Co. H, May 13, 1898; promoted corporal, July 5, 1898; mustered out with company, April 20, 1899, at New York city.

MURRAY, JOHN J.—Age, 33 years. Enlisted, May 2, 1898, at New York city, to serve two years; mustered in as sergeant, Co. A, May 13, 1898; discharged, November 21, 1898, at Americus, Ga.

MURTHA, WILLIAM.—Age, — years. Enlisted, June 17, 1898, at New York city, to serve two years; mustered in as private, Co. G, same date; mustered out with company, April 20, 1899, at New York city.

MYERS, ORD.—Age 27 years. Enlisted, May 2, 1898, at New York city, to serve two years; mustered in as private, Co. I, May 13, 1898; promoted corporal, July 5, 1898; sergeant, September 10, 1898; mustered in as second lieutenant, Co. L, December 10, 1898; mustered out with company, April 20, 1899, at New York city; commissioned second lieutenant, November 27, 1898, with rank from same date, vice T. K. Russell, discharged.

NACKOWITSCH, GEORGE.—Age, 33 years. Enlisted, May 10, 1898, at camp, near Peekskill, to serve two years; mustered in as private, Co. G, May 13, 1898; mustered out with company, April 20, 1899, at New York city.

NADRAMIA, JOHN.—Age, — years. Enlisted, June 18, 1898, at New York city, to serve two years; mustered in as private, Co. E, same date; mustered out with company, April 20, 1899, at New York city.

NASH, WILLIAM HUNTT.—Age, 35 years. Enlisted, May 2, 1898, at New York city, to serve two years; mustered in as private, Co. C, May 13, 1898; mustered out with company, April 20, 1899, at New York city.

NASON, JOHN.—Age, 23 years. Enlisted, May 11, 1898, at New York city, to serve two years; mustered in as private, Co. I, May 13, 1898; deserted, October 11, 1898.

NAYLOR, JOHN W.—Age, 30 years. Enlisted, May 2, 1898, at New York city, to serve two years; mustered in as wagoner, Co. A, May 13, 1898; returned to ranks, no date; deserted, November 24, 1898.

NEAR, RICHARD A.—Age, 22 years. Enlisted, May 2, 1898, at New York city, to serve two years; mustered in as corporal, Co. C, May 13, 1898; promoted sergeant, January 10, 1899; mustered out with company, April 20, 1899, at New York city.

NEFF, JR., EDWARD.—Age, 21 years. Enlisted, May 2, 1898, at New York city, to serve two years; mustered in as private, Co. M, May 13, 1898; promoted corporal, March 10, 1899; mustered out with company, April 20, 1899, at New York city.

NEISH, JOHN.—Age, — years.   Enlisted, June 24, 1898, at
New York city, to serve two years; mustered in as private,
Co. I, same date; mustered out with company, April 20, 1899,
at New York city.

NELSON, WILLIAM B.—Age, 22 years.   Enlisted, May 2, 1898,
at New York city, to serve two years; mustered in as private,
Co. D, May 13, 1898; mustered out with company, April 20,
1899, at New York city.

NELSON, WILLIAM N.—Age, 19 years.   Enlisted, May 2, 1898,
at New York city, to serve two years; mustered in as private,
Co. B, May 13, 1898; appointed artificer, January 1, 1899; mustered out with company, April 20, 1899, at New York city.

NEUMANN, LOUIS C.—Age, 26 years.   Enlisted, May 2, 1898,
at New York city, to serve two years; mustered in as private,
Co. G, May 13, 1898; discharged, October 31, 1898, at Camp
Hamilton, Lexington, Ky.

NEVILLE, MICHAEL J.—Age, 30 years.   Enlisted, May 2, 1898,
at New York city, to serve two years; mustered in as private,
Co. F, May 13, 1898; deserted, December 24, 1898, at Americus,
Ga.

NEWBERGER, BERNHARD.—Age, — years.   Enlisted, November 15, 1898, at New York city, to serve two years; mustered
in as private, Co. G, November 30, 1898; mustered out with
company, April 20, 1899, at New York city.

NEWBERTH, ALBERT L.—Age, — years.   Enlisted, June 24,
1898, at New York city, to serve two years; mustered in as
private, Co. I, same date; discharged for disability, November
21, 1898, at Americus, Ga.

NEWMAN, HENRY V.—Age, 37 years.   Enlisted, May 11, 1898,
at New York city, to serve two years; mustered in as private,
Co. I, May 13, 1898; mustered out with company, April 20,
1899, at New York city.

NEYLON, JAMES.—Age, — years.   Enlisted, November 15,
1898, at New York city, to serve two years; mustered in as
private, Co. M, November 30, 1898; mustered out with company,
April 20, 1899, at New York city.

NIELSEN, HANS CHRISTIAN.—Age, 30 years. Enlisted, May 10, 1898, at New York city, to serve two years; mustered in as private, Co. B, May 13, 1898; mustered out with company, April 20, 1899, at New York city.

NIELSEN, JOHN W.—Age, 29 years. Enlisted, May 10, 1898, at camp, near Peekskill, to serve two years; mustered in as private, Co. L, May 13, 1898; mustered out with company, April 20, 1899, at New York city.

NIELSON, WALDMAR.—Age, 18 years. Enlisted, May 11, 1898, at camp, near Peekskill, to serve two years; mustered in as private, Co. A, May 13, 1898; mustered out with company, April 20, 1899, at New York city.

NOBLE, ALBERT H.—Age, 22 years. Enlisted, May 2, 1898, at New York city, to serve two years; mustered in as private, Co. D, May 13, 1898; appointed artificer, July 1, 1898; promoted corporal, July 13, 1898; returned to ranks, October 10, 1898; mustered out with company, April 20, 1899, at New York city.

NOLAN, THOMAS.—Age,—years. Enlisted, November 15, 1898, at New York city, to serve two years; mustered in as private, Co. E, same date; mustered out with company, April 20, 1899, at New York city.

NOLAN, THOMAS F.—Age, 27 years. Enlisted, May 2, 1898, at New York city, to serve two years; mustered in as private, Co. F, May 13, 1898; mustered out with company, April 20, 1899, at New York city.

NOONAN, WILLIAM F.—Age,—years. Enlisted, June 22, 1898, at New York city, to serve two years; mustered in as private, Co. H, same date; mustered out with company, April 20, 1899, at New York city.

NORD, ANDREW.—Age, 24 years. Enlisted, May 2, 1898, at New York city, to serve two years; mustered in as corporal, Co. G, May 13, 1898; promoted sergeant, November 9, 1898; quartermaster-sergeant, January 1, 1899; mustered out with company, April 20, 1899, at New York city.

NORTON, AUGUSTUS.—Age, 28 years. Enlisted, May 11, 1898, at camp, near Peekskill, to serve two years; mustered in as private, Co. D, May 13, 1898; transferred to Hospital Corps, United States Army, December 7, 1898, at Camp Gilman, Ga.

NYE, CORNELIUS.—Age, 20 years. Enlisted, May 13, 1898, at New York city, to serve two years; mustered in as private, Co. C, same date; mustered out with company, April 20, 1899, at New York city.

NYGREN, HENRY.—Age, — years. Enlisted, June 28, 1898, at New York city, to serve two years; mustered in as private, Co. B, same date; killed by Provost Guard, October 10, 1898, at Lexington, Ky.

NYLUND, JULIUS.—Age, 23 years. Enlisted, May 10, 1898, at New York city, to serve two years; mustered in as private, Co. M, May 13, 1898; mustered out with company, April 20, 1899, at New York city.

OALSCHLAGER, BERNARD.—Age, 38 years. Enlisted, May 2, 1898, at New York city, to serve two years; mustered in as private, Co. I, May 13, 1898; appointed cook, November 1, 1898; returned to ranks, to date, December 25, 1898; mustered out with company, April 20, 1899, at New York city.

OATES, JAMES.—Age, 25 years. Enlisted, May 2, 1898, at New York city, to serve two years; mustered in as private, Co. E, May 13, 1898; discharged for disability, October 18, 1898, at Governor's Island, New York Harbor.

OBERKIRK, ERNEST.—Age, 21 years. Enlisted, May 2, 1898, at New York city, to serve two years; mustered in as private, Co. M, May 13, 1898; discharged for disability, January 5, 1899, at Americus, Ga.

O'BRIEN, DENNIS J.—Age, — years. Enlisted, June 24, 1898, at New York city, to serve two years; mustered in as private, Co. A, same date; mustered out with company, April 20, 1899, at New York city.

O'BRIEN, JAMES.—Age, — years. Enlisted, June 17, 1898, at New York city, to serve two years; mustered in as private, Co. D, same date; mustered out with company, April 20, 1899, at New York city.

O'BRIEN, JAMES J.—Age, 22 years. Enlisted, May 2, 1898, at New York city, to serve two years; mustered in as private, Co. G, May 13, 1898; discharged, February 6, 1899, at New York city.

O'BRIEN, JOHN C.—Age, — years. Enlisted, June 29, 1898, at New York city, to serve two years; mustered in as private, Co. M, same date; discharged, November 12, 1898, at Lexington, Ky.

O'BRIEN, JOHN J.—Age, 23 years. Enlisted, May 2, 1898, at New York city, to serve two years; mustered in as private, Co. A, May 13, 1898; mustered out with company, April 20, 1899, at New York city.

O'BRIEN, JOHN J.—Age, 26 years. Enlisted, May 2, 1898, at New York city, to serve two years; mustered in as private, Co. K, May 13, 1898; transferred to Hospital Corps, United States Army, June 15, 1898.

O'BRIEN, JOHN W.—Age, 22 years. Enlisted, May 2, 1898, at New York city, to serve two years; mustered in as private, Co. K, May 13, 1898; mustered out with company, April 20, 1899, at New York city.

O'BRIEN, PETER J.—Age, 22 years. Enlisted, May 2, 1898, at New York city, to serve two years; mustered in as private, Co. G, May 13, 1898; promoted corporal, September 20, 1898; mustered out with company, April 20, 1899, at New York city.

O'BRIEN, WILLIAM W.—Age, 21 years. Enlisted, May 2, 1898, at New York city, to serve two years; mustered in as private, Co. D, May 13, 1898; promoted corporal, March 17, 1899; mustered out with company, April 20, 1899, at New York city.

O'BYRNE, EDWARD J.—Age, 21 years. Enlisted, May 2, 1898, at New York city, to serve two years; mustered in as private, Co. K, May 13, 1898; mustered out with company, April 20, 1899, at New York city.

O'DONNELL, ARTHUR.—Age, — years. Enlisted, June 23, 1898, at New York city, to serve two years; mustered in as private, Co. E, same date; mustered out with company, April 20, 1899, at New York city.

O'DONNELL, MICHAEL.—Age, — years. Enlisted, June 22, 1898, at New York city, to serve two years; mustered in as private, Co. L, same date; mustered out with company, April 20, 1899, at New York city.

O'DONOHUE, JAMES.—Age, — years. Enlisted, June 21, 1898, at New York city, to serve two years; mustered in as private, Co. B, same date; promoted corporal, January 1, 1899; mustered out with company, April 20, 1899, at New York city.

O'GRADY, JOHN.—Age, — years. Enlisted, June 29, 1898, at New York city, to serve two years; mustered in as private, Co. E, same date; transferred to band, July 3, 1898; promoted principal musician, October 31, 1898; chief musician, December 26, 1898; mustered out with regiment, April 20, 1899, at New York city.

O'HARE, THOMAS J.—Age, 24 years. Enlisted, May 2, 1898, at New York city, to serve two years; mustered in as private, Co. A, May 13, 1898; mustered out with company, April 20, 1899, at New York city.

O'LEARY, TIMOTHY JAMES.—Age, 22 years. Enlisted, May 13, 1898, at camp, near Peekskill, to serve two years; mustered in as private, Co. B, same date; discharged, October 24, 1898, at Lexington, Ky.

OLIVER, EDGAR E.—Age, — years. Enlisted, June 24, 1898, at New York city, to serve two years; mustered in as private, Co. B, same date; deserted, November 12, 1898.

OLSEN, BERNHARDT.—Age, — years. Enlisted, June 24, 1898, at New York city, to serve two years; mustered in as private, Co. K, same date; transferred to band, July 3, 1898; to Co. K, December 24, 1898; discharged for disability, January 4, 1899, at Americus, Ga.

OLSEN, GEORGE E.—Age, 35 years. Enlisted, May 10, 1898, at New York city, to serve two years; mustered in as private, Co. B, May 13, 1898; mustered out with company, April 20, 1899, at New York city.

OLSEN, OLOOF.—Age, 27 years. Enlisted, May 2, 1898, at New York city, to serve two years; mustered in as sergeant, Co. K, May 13, 1898; discharged, December 23, 1898, at Americus, Ga.

O'NEIL, DANIEL J.—Age, — years. Enlisted, June 24, 1898, at New York city, to serve two years; mustered in as private, Co. I, same date; discharged, July 20, 1898, at Chickamauga Park, Ga.

O'NEIL, JOSEPH.—Age, 21 years. Enlisted, May 13, 1898, at camp, near Peekskill, to serve two years; mustered in as private, Co. L, May 13, 1898; no further record.

O'NEILL, JAMES.—Age, — years. Enlisted, June 28, 1898, at New York city, to serve two years; mustered in as private, Co. L, same date; mustered out with company, April 20, 1899, at New York city.

O'NEILL, JAMES.—Age, — years. Enlisted, June 28, 1898, at New York city, to serve two years; mustered in as private, Co. L, same date; mustered out with company, April 20, 1899, at New York city.

O'NEILL, JOHN.—Age, — years. Enlisted, June 29, 1898, at New York city, to serve two years; mustered in as private, Co. C, same date; mustered out with company, April 20, 1899, at New York city.

O'NEILL, JOHN J.—Age, 35 years. Enlisted, May 2, 1898, at New York city, to serve two years; mustered in as artificer, Co. A, May 13, 1898; mustered out with company, April 20, 1899, at New York city.

O'NEILL, JOHN J.—Age, 21 years. Enlisted, May 2, 1898, at New York city, to serve two years; mustered in as private, Co. A, May 13, 1898; mustered out with company, April 20, 1899, at New York city.

O'NEILL, JOSEPH.—Age, — years. Enlisted, May 14, 1898, at New York city, to serve two years; mustered in as private, Co. E, same date; deserted, May 22, 1898.

ORAM, BENJAMIN.—Age, — years. Enlisted, December 3, 1898, at Americus, Ga., to serve two years; mustered in as musician in band, December 15, 1898; mustered out with regiment, April 20, 1899, at New York city.

ORAM, WILLIAM W.—Age, — years. Enlisted, December 3, 1898, at Americus, Ga., to serve two years; mustered in as musician in band, December 15, 1898; mustered out with regiment, April 20, 1899, at New York city.

O'REILLY, EUGENE.—Age, 23 years. Enlisted, May 11, 1898, at New York city, to serve two years; mustered in as private, Co. I, May 13, 1898; transferred to Hospital Corps, December 19, 1898.

ORMEND, JAMES F.—Age, 23 years. Enlisted, May 2, 1898, at New York city, to serve two years; mustered in as private, Co. A, May 13, 1898; discharged for disability, January 4, 1899, at Americus, Ga.

O'ROURKE, PATRICK F.—Age, 22 years. Enlisted, May 2, 1898, at New York city, to serve two years; mustered in as private, Co. H, May 13, 1898; mustered out with company, April 20, 1899, at New York city.

OSBORN, JR., AMOS G.—Age, 27 years. Enlisted, May 2, 1898, at New York city, to serve two years; mustered in as private, Co. K, May 13, 1898; promoted corporal, August 1, 1898; mustered out with company, April 20, 1899, at New York city.

O'SULLIVAN, DANIEL J.—Age, 28 years. Enlisted, May 2, 1898, at New York city, to serve two years; mustered in as private, Co. D, May 13, 1898; mustered out with company, April 20, 1899, at New York city.

OTT, CHRISTIAN T.—Age, 28 years. Enlisted, May 2, 1898, at New York city, to serve two years; mustered in as sergeant, Co. B, May 13, 1898; discharged, no date, at Americus, Ga.

OTTOSON, FREDERICK.—Age, — years. Enlisted, June 25, 1898, at New York city, to serve two years; mustered in as private, Co. K, same date; mustered out with company, April 20, 1899, at New York city.

OWENS, JOHN T.—Age, 22 years. Enlisted, May 11, 1898, at New York city, to serve two years; mustered in as private, Co. I, May 13, 1898; mustered out with company, April 20, 1899, at New York city.

PARCELLS, FREDERICK.—Age, — years. Enlisted, June 25, 1898, at New York city, to serve two years; mustered in as private, Co. M, same date; mustered out with company, April 20, 1899, at New York city.

PARKER, GEORGE B.—Age, — years. Enlisted, June 30, 1898, at New York city, to serve two years; mustered in as private, Co. B, same date; transferred to Co. L, July 2, 1898; mustered out with company, April 20, 1899, at New York city.

PARKER, HENRY W.—Age, — years. Enrolled, December 29, 1898, at Charleston, S. C., to serve two years; mustered in as first lieutenant, Co. C, same date; mustered out with company, April 20, 1899, at New York city; subsequent service as second lieutenant, Second United States Cavalry; commissioned first lieutenant, December 24, 1898, with rank from same date, vice Smith, promoted.

PARKER, JAMES.—Captain, Second United States Cavalry. Age, 44 years. Enrolled, May 13, 1898, at camp, near Peekskill, to serve two years; mustered in as major, same date; as lieutenant-colonel, October 3, 1898; mustered out with regiment, April 20, 1899, at New York city; subsequent service as lieutenant-colonel, Forty-fifth Regiment, United States Volunteer Infantry; commissioned major, May 13, 1898, with rank from same date, original; lieutenant-colonel, September 30, 1898, with rank from same date, vice Seiter, discharged.

PARKER, ROBERT MEADE.—Age, 33 years. Enrolled, May 2, 1898, at New York city, to serve two years; mustered in as first lieutenant and battalion adjutant, May 13, 1898; appointed regimental quartermaster, June 7, 1898; discharged, August 27, 1898; commissioned first lieutenant and battalion adjutant, May 13, 1898, with rank from same date, original; captain and regimental quartermaster, not mustered, June 7, 1898, with rank from same date, vice Cowdin, relieved and assigned battalion adjutant.

PARSIKIAN, MARTIN.—Age, 23 years. Enlisted, May 2, 1898, at New York city, to serve two years; mustered in as private, Co. B, May 13, 1898; mustered out with company, April 20, 1899, at New York city.

PASCO, HARRY H. R.—Age, 20 years. Enlisted, May 2, 1898, at New York city, to serve two years; mustered in as corporal, Co. L, May 13, 1898; returned to ranks, July 4, 1898; mustered out with company, April 20, 1899, at New York city.

PAUL, GEORGE H.—Age, — years.   Enlisted, June 22, 1898, at New York city, to serve two years; mustered in as private, Co. G, same date; mustered out with company, April 20, 1899, at New York city.

PAUL, ROBERT.—Age, 32 years.   Enlisted, May 2, 1898, at New York city, to serve two years; mustered in as private, Co. D, May 13, 1898; appointed cook, July 1, 1898; returned to ranks, December 1, 1898; discharged for disability, January 4, 1899, at Camp Gilman, Ga.

PAULSAY, FREDERICK.—Age, — years.   Enlisted, June 24, 1898, at New York city, to serve two years; mustered in as private, Co. E, June 28, 1898; promoted corporal, February 19, 1899; mustered out with company, April 20, 1899, at New York city.

PEARSE, FREDERICK W.—Age, 24 years.   Enlisted, May 2, 1898, at New York city, to serve two years; mustered in as corporal, Co. D, May 13, 1898; returned to ranks, May 31, 1898; discharged, March 8, 1899, at Matanzas, Cuba.

PENNRICH, JOHN F.—Age, 31 years.   Enlisted, May 2, 1898, at New York city, to serve two years; mustered in as private, Co. A, May 13, 1898; promoted corporal, July 3, 1898; mustered out with company, April 20, 1899, at New York city.

PERKINS, PERK L.—Age, — years.   Enlisted, June 24, 1898, at New York city, to serve two years; mustered in as private, Co. D, same date; appointed musician, October 29, 1898; mustered out with company, April 20, 1899, at New York city.

PETZ, JOHN.—Age, 24 years.   Enlisted, May 13, 1898, at New York city, to serve two years; mustered in as private, Co. H, same date; mustered out with company, April 20, 1899, at New York city.

PFISTER, LOUIS A.—Age, — years.   Enlisted, June 24, 1898, at New York city, to serve two years; mustered in as private, Co. C, same date; promoted corporal, March 2, 1899; mustered out with company, April 20, 1899, at New York city.

PFORZHEIMER, HARRY.—Age, 21 years.   Enlisted, May 2, 1898, at New York city, to serve two years; mustered in as private, Co. G, May 13, 1898; promoted corporal, April 3, 1899; mustered out with com an   A ril 20 1899 at New York cit .

PHELAN, JOHN.—Age, — years. Enlisted, November 15, 1898, at New York city, to serve two years; mustered in as private, Co. B, November 30, 1898; mustered out with company, April 20, 1899, at New York city.

PHILLIPS, THOMAS H.—Age, 24 years. Enlisted, May 2, 1898, at New York city, to serve two years; mustered in as private, Co. H, May 13, 1898; discharged, no date, at New York city.

PIERSON, JOHN J.—Age, 20 years. Enlisted, May 2, 1898, at New York city, to serve two years; mustered in as private, Co. E, May 13, 1898; appointed artificer, February 18, 1899; mustered out with company, April 20, 1899, at New York city.

PILLOT, PETER STUYVESANT.—Age, 27 years. Enrolled May 2, 1898, at New York city, to serve two years; mustered in as first lieutenant, Co. M, May 13, 1898; discharged, July 18, 1898, at New York city; commissioned first lieutenant, May 13, 1898, with rank from same date, original.

PLASTOW, HENRY J.—Age, 21 years. Enlisted, May 13, 1898, at camp, near Peekskill, to serve two years; mustered in as private, Co. A, same date; mustered out with company, April 20, 1899, at New York city.

PLATNER, JR., CHARLES.—Age, — years. Enlisted, June 17, 1898, at New York city, to serve two years; mustered in as private, Co. F, same date; discharged, October 25, 1898, at Lexington, Ky.

POHLER, CHARLES H.—Age, — years. Enlisted, June 23, 1898, at New York city, to serve two years; mustered in as private, Co. K, same date; mustered out with company, April 20, 1899, at New York city.

PORTER, EDWARD B.—Age, — years. Enlisted, June 29, 1898, at New York city, to serve two years; mustered in as private, Co. D, same date; mustered out with company, April 20, 1899, at New York city.

POST, ALBERTSON VAN ZO.—Age, 31 years. Enrolled, May 2, 1898, at New York city, to serve two years; mustered in as first lieutenant, Co. H, May 13, 1898; as captain, June 20, 1898; to date, May 13, 1898; discharged, December 22, 1898, at Camp Gilman, Ga.; commissioned first lieutenant, May 13, 1898, with rank from same date, original; captain, May 13, 1898, with rank from same date, original.

POST, NATHAN E.—Age, 24 years. Enlisted, May 2, 1898, at New York city, to serve two years; mustered in as corporal, Co. K, May 13, 1898; promoted sergeant, January 1, 1899; mustered out with company, April 20, 1899, at New York city.

POTTS, WILLIAM S.—Age, 24 years. Enlisted, May 13, 1898, at New York city, to serve two years; mustered in as private, Co. H, same date; mustered out with company, April 20, 1899, at New York city.

POWELL, EDWARD J.—Age, 25 years. Enlisted, May 2, 1898, at New York city, to serve two years; mustered in as private, Co. F, May 13, 1898; promoted corporal, August 11, 1898; mustered out with company, April 20, 1899, at New York city.

POWER, EDWARD ORMONDE.—Age, 25 years. Enrolled, May 2, 1898, at New York city, to serve two years; mustered in as second lieutenant, Co. K, May 13, 1898; as first lieutenant, Co. A, September 30, 1898; mustered out, to date, April 20, 1899; subsequent service as first lieutenant, Forty-third Regiment, United States Volunteer Infantry; commissioned second lieutenant, May 13, 1898, with rank from same date, original; first lieutenant, September 30, 1898, with rank from same date, vice Vermilyea, appointed battalion adjutant.

POWERS, DAVID.—Age, — years. Enlisted, June 20, 1898, at New York city, to serve two years; mustered in as private, Co. K, same date; deserted, October 26, 1898, at Lexington, Ky.

PRATEL, ERNST.—Age, — years. Enlisted, June 25, 1898, at New York city, to serve two years; mustered in as private, Co. B, same date; discharged for disability, January 4, 1899, at Americus, Ga.

PREECE, GEORGE W.—Age, 29 years. Enlisted, May 2, 1898, at New York city, to serve two years; mustered in as first sergeant, Co. I, May 13, 1898; discharged, to date, October 25, 1898, at Lexington, Ky.

PRICE, JOSEPH.—Age, 22 years. Enlisted, May 10, 1898, at camp, near Peekskill, to serve two years; mustered in as private, Co. G, May 13, 1898; mustered out with company, April 20, 1899, at New York city.

PRICHARD, DUDLEY.—Age, 21 years. Enlisted, May 2, 1898, at New York city, to serve two years; mustered in as private, Co. G, May 13, 1898; promoted corporal, July 5, 1898; returned to ranks, no date; discharged, January 16, 1899.

PRINDLE, CHARLES H.—Age, 21 years. Enlisted, May 13, 1898, at New York city, to serve two years; mustered in as private, Co. K, same date; mustered out with company, April 20, 1899, at New York city.

PRINGLE, JOHN.—Age, 28 years. Enlisted, May 2, 1898, at New York city, to serve two years; mustered in as private, Co. A, May 13, 1898; mustered out with company, April 20, 1899, at New York city.

PROW, JOHN.—Age, 30 years. Enlisted, May 13, 1898, at New York city, to serve two years; mustered in as private, Co. H, same date; appointed cook, February 1, 1899; discharged, April 20, 1899, at New York city.

PULIS, ALLAN H.—Age, 21 years. Enlisted, May 2, 1898, at New York city, to serve two years; mustered in as private, Co. K, May 13, 1898; mustered out with company, April 20, 1899, at New York city.

PULLAR, WILLIAM.—Age, 30 years. Enlisted, May 2, 1898, at New York city, to serve two years; mustered in as first sergeant, Co. L, May 13, 1898; reduced to sergeant, June 2, 1898; returned to ranks, July 12, 1898; deserted, July 16, 1898, at Chickamauga, Ga.

PYLE, KENNETH.—Age, 21 years. Enlisted, May 2, 1898, at New York city, to serve two years; mustered in as private, Co. C, May 13, 1898; discharged, March 7, 1899, at New York city.

QUIGLEY, JAMES.—Age, 21 years. Enlisted, May 13, 1898, at New York city, to serve two years; mustered in as private, Co. H, same date; mustered out with company, April 20, 1899, at New York city.

QUINBY, FREDERICK J.—Enrolled as first lieutenant, Co. C, date and place, not stated; commissioned, not mustered, first lieutenant, October 18, 1898, with rank from same date, vice Burke, promoted.

QUINLAN, PATRICK J.—Age, 21 years. Enlisted, May 2, 1898, at New York city, to serve two years; mustered in as private, Co. I, May 13, 1898; mustered out with company, April 20, 1899, at New York city.

QUINN, CHARLES J.—Age, 21 years. Enlisted, May 2, 1898, at New York city, to serve two years; mustered in as private, Co. K, May 13, 1898; deserted, November 10, 1898, at Lexington, Ky.

QUINN, EDWARD J.—Age, — years. Enlisted, June 22, 1898, at New York city, to serve two years; mustered in as private, Co. I, same date; mustered out with company, April 20, 1899, at New York city.

RAAB, SIMON.—Age, 20 years. Enlisted, May 2, 1898, at New York city, to serve two years; mustered in as private, Co. F, May 13, 1898; mustered out with company, April 20, 1899, at New York city.

RABORG, THOMAS MASON.—Age, — years. Enrolled, May 2, 1898, at New York city, to serve two years; mustered in as second lieutenant, Co. I, June 20, 1898; to date, May 13, 1898; as first lieutenant, Co. D, December 21, 1898; discharged, December 24, 1898, at Camp Gilman, Ga.; commissioned second lieutenant, May 13, 1898, with rank from same date, original; first lieutenant, December 8, 1898, with rank from same date, vice Burrill, transferred.

RAIS, JOSEPH.—Age, — years. Enlisted, November 15, 1898, at New York city, to serve two years; mustered in as private, Co. L, November 30, 1898; mustered out with company, April 20, 1899, at New York city.

RAMSEY, JOHN P.—Age, 25 years. Enlisted, May 2, 1898, at New York city, to serve two years; mustered in as private, Co. H, May 13, 1898; discharged, November 26, 1898, at Camp Gilman, Ga.

RANGER, GEORGE.—Age, — years. Enlisted, June 21, 1898, at New York city, to serve two years; mustered in as private, Co. L, same date; mustered out with company, April 20, 1899, at New York city.

RATNER, ABRAHAM.—Age, 18 years. Enlisted, May 13, 1898, at New York city, to serve two years; mustered in as private, Co. H, same date; mustered out with company, April 20, 1899, at New York city.

RAVENS, CHARLES ERNEST.—Age, 26 years. Enlisted, May 2, 1898, at New York city, to serve two years; mustered in as sergeant, Co. C, May 13, 1898; as second lieutenant, Co. G, January 11, 1899; transferred to Co. M, January 12, 1899; mustered out with company, April 20, 1899, at New York city; commissioned second lieutenant, December 25, 1898, with rank from same date, vice Fennell, promoted.

REARDON, WILLIAM CLARENCE.—Age, 26 years. Enlisted, May 2, 1898, at New York city, to serve two years; mustered in as musician, Co. C, May 13, 1898; discharged, January 20, 1899, at New York city.

REBEL, JACOB.—Age, 23 years. Enlisted, May 2, 1898, at New York city, to serve two years; mustered in as private, Co. A, May 13, 1898; mustered out with company, April 20, 1899, at New York city.

REDDINGTON, SYLVESTER F.—Age, 22 years. Enlisted, May 2, 1898, at New York city, to serve two years; mustered in as private, Co. G, May 13, 1898; promoted corporal, July 5, 1898; sergeant, January 17, 1899; mustered out with company, April 20, 1899, at New York city.

REDMOND, THOMAS E.—Age, 24 years. Enlisted, May 2, 1898, at New York city, to serve two years; mustered in as private, Co. A, May 13, 1898; mustered out with company, April 20, 1899, at New York city.

REED, ALBERT L.—Age, — years. Enlisted, June 22, 1898, at New York city, to serve two years; mustered in as private, Co. I, same date; mustered out with company, April 20, 1899, at New York city.

REGAN, MICHAEL.—Age, — years. Enlisted, November 15, 1898, at New York city, to serve two years; mustered in as private, Co. E, same date; mustered out with company, April 20, 1899, at New York city.

REGAN, MORRIS J.—Age, 23 years. Enlisted, May 2, 1898, at New York city, to serve two years; mustered in as private, Co. L, May 13, 1898; mustered out with company, April 20, 1899, at New York city.

REGETZKI, RICHARD R. R.—Age, 22 years. Enlisted, May 2, 1898, at New York city, to serve two years; mustered in as corporal, Co. B, May 13, 1898; promoted sergeant, January 1, 1899; mustered out with company, April 20, 1899, at New York city; also borne as Rudolph Rinhold.

REHM, JOHN JOSEPH.—Age, 28 years. Enlisted, May 2, 1898, at New York city, to serve two years; mustered in as first ser-geant, Co. A, May 13, 1898; mustered out with company, April 20, 1899, at New York city.

REILLEY, THOMAS W.—Age, 27 years. Enlisted, May 13, 1898, at State Camp, Peekskill, to serve two years; mustered in as private, Co. E, same date; appointed wagoner, October 19, 1898; mustered out with company, April 20, 1899, at New York city.

REILLY, JAMES.—Age, 18 years. Enlisted, May 2, 1898, at New York city, to serve two years; mustered in as private, Co. I, May 13, 1898; mustered out with company, April 20, 1899, at New York city.

REILLY, JAMES J.—Age, 23 years. Enlisted, May 2, 1898, at New York city, to serve two years; mustered in as private, Co. A, May 13, 1898; promoted corporal, December 11, 1898; returned to ranks, January 30, 1899; mustered out with com-pany, April 20, 1899, at New York city.

REILLY, JOHN.—Age, 26 years. Enlisted, May 2, 1898, at New York city, to serve two years; mustered in as corporal, Co. F, May 13, 1898; discharged, December 17, 1898, at Americus, Ga.

REILLY, JOSEPH M.—Age, 25 years. Enlisted, May 2, 1898, at New York city, to serve two years; mustered in as private, Co. F, May 13, 1898; mustered out with company, April 20, 1899, at New York city.

REILLY, THOMAS.—Age, — years. Enlisted, November 15, 1898, at New York city, to serve two years; mustered in as pri-vate, Co. M, November 30, 1898; mustered out with company, April 30, 1899, at New York city.

REILLY, WILLIAM J.—Age, 22 years. Enlisted, May 2, 1898, at New York city, to serve two years; mustered in as private, Co. H, May 13, 1898; appointed artificer, July 20, 1898; mustered out with company, April 20, 1899, at New York city.

REINL, OTTO G.—Age, 27 years. Enlisted, May 2, 1898, at New York city, to serve two years; mustered in as private, Co. D, May 13, 1898; mustered out with company, April 20, 1899, at New York city.

REXSEN, MARTIN.—Age, 20 years. Enlisted, May 13, 1898, at camp, near Peekskill, to serve two years; mustered in as private, Co. G, same date; mustered out with company, April 20, 1899, at New York city.

REYNOLDS, WILLIAM J.—Age, 21 years. Enlisted, May 2, 1898, at New York city, to serve two years; mustered in as corporal, Co. L, May 13, 1898; promoted sergeant, September 28, 1898; mustered out with company, April 20, 1899, at New York city.

RICE, FRANK L.—Age, — years. Enlisted, June 23, 1898, at New York city, to serve two years; mustered in as private, Co. K, same date; discharged, to date, April 20, 1899, at New York city.

RICH, JOHN J.—Age, 21 years. Enlisted, May 2, 1898, at New York city, to serve two years; mustered in as private, Co. D, May 13, 1898; mustered out with company, April 20, 1899, at New York city.

RICH, PATRICK H.—Age, 22 years. Enlisted, May 2, 1898, at New York city, to serve two years; mustered in as private, Co. D, May 13, 1898; mustered out with company, April 20, 1899, at New York city.

RICHARDSON, FRED.—Age, 23 years. Enlisted, May 2, 1898, at New York city, to serve two years; mustered in as private, Co. E, May 13, 1898; promoted corporal, August 1, 1898; returned to ranks, October 24, 1898; deserted, October 24, 1898.

RICHTER, MAX.—Age, 30 years. Enlisted, May 2, 1898, at New York city, to serve two years; mustered in as private, Co. L, May 13, 1898; mustered out with company, April 20, 1899, at New York city.

RICKERT, JR., FREDERICK J.—Age, 28 years. Enlisted, May 2, 1898, at New York city, to serve two years; mustered in as artificer, Co. I, May 13, 1898; returned to ranks, July 6, 1898; appointed cook, December 26, 1898; returned to ranks, January 16, 1899; mustered out with company, April 20, 1899, at New York city.

RILEY, JOHN W.—Age, — years. Enlisted, June 24, 1898, at New York city, to serve two years; mustered in as private, Co. F, same date; mustered out with company, April 20, 1899, at New York city.

RINGWOOD, JAMES.—Age, 21 years. Enlisted, May 2, 1898, at New York city, to serve two years; mustered in as private, Co. M, May 13, 1898; mustered out with company, April 20, 1899, at New York city.

RIORDAN, JAMES.—Age, 21 years. Enlisted, May 2, 1898, at New York city, to serve two years; mustered in as private, Co. C, May 13, 1898; discharged for disability, January 5, 1899, at Americus, Ga.

RITTER, GEORGE F.—Age, 23 years. Enlisted, May 2, 1898, at New York city, to serve two years; mustered in as wagoner, Co. H, May 13, 1898; returned to ranks, June 5, 1898; discharged, January 26, 1899, at New York city.

RIVERS, FREDERICK G.—Age, 19 years. Enlisted, May 2, 1898, at New York city, to serve two years; mustered in as private, Co. I, May 13, 1898; mustered out with company, April 20, 1899, at New York city.

ROBERT, PHILLIP.—Age, 38 years. Enlisted, May 2, 1898, at New York city, to serve two years; mustered in as private, Co. D, May 13, 1898; mustered out with company, April 20, 1899, at New York city.

ROBERTS, WILLIAM W.—Age, — years. Enlisted, June 20, 1898, at New York city, to serve two years; mustered in as private, Co. D, same date; discharged, October 14, 1898.

ROBERTSON, CHARLES.—Age, — years. Enlisted, November 15, 1898, at New York city, to serve two years; mustered in as private, Co. C, November 30, 1898; mustered out with company, April 20, 1899, at New York city.

ROBINSON, MILNOR.—Age, — years. Enlisted, June 17, 1898, at New York city, to serve two years; mustered in as private, Co. A, same date; discharged, January 11, 1899, at New York city.

ROCHE, JOSEPH W.—Age, 33 years. Enlisted, May 11, 1898, at camp, near Peekskill, to serve two years; mustered in as private, Co. L, May 13, 1898; mustered out with company, April 20, 1899, at New York city.

ROGERS, CHARLES P.—Age, — years. Enlisted, June 22, 1898, at New York city, to serve two years; mustered in as private, Co. M, same date; promoted corporal, March 14, 1899; mustered out with company, April 20, 1899, at New York city.

ROGERS, JAMES C.—Age, — years. Enlisted, November 15, 1898, at New York city, to serve two years; mustered in as private, Co. B, November 30, 1898; discharged, April 20, 1899, at hospital, Fort Monroe, Va.; prior service in Eighth New York Volunteer Infantry.

ROGERS, JOSEPH W.—Age, 36 years. Enlisted, May 2, 1898, at New York city, to serve two years; mustered in as sergeant, Co. L, May 13, 1898; mustered out with company, April 20, 1899, at New York city.

ROLSON, GEORGE.—Age, 27 years. Enlisted, May 2, 1898, at New York city, to serve two years; mustered in as private, Co. F, May 13, 1898; mustered out with company, April 20, 1899, at New York city.

ROMAINE, WASHINGTON TYSON.—Age, 28 years. Enrolled, May 2, 1898, at New York city, to serve two years; mustered in as first lieutenant, Co. C, May 13, 1898; as captain, Co. B, June 20, 1898, to date, May 16, 1898; discharged, December 7, 1898, at New York city; commissioned first lieutenant, May 13, 1898, with rank from same date, original; captain, May 16, 1898, with rank from same date, original.

ROMANELLI, PICTRO.—Age, 25 years. Enlisted, May 2, 1898, at New York city, to serve two years; mustered in as private, Co. E, May 13, 1898; promoted corporal, January 31, 1899; mustered out with company, April 20, 1899, at New York city.

RONAN, JOSEPH A.—Age, 32 years. Enlisted, May 2, 1898, at New York city, to serve two years; mustered in as private, Co. K, May 13, 1898; discharged, February 6, 1899, at New York city.

RONICLE, JAMES J.—Age, — years. Enlisted, June 22, 1898, at New York city, to serve two years; mustered in as private, Co. E, same date; transferred to Co. B, June 26, 1898; mustered out, April 20, 1899, at New York city.

RONNE, PETER S. J.—Age, 30 years. Enlisted, May 2, 1898, at New York city, to serve two years; mustered in as private, Co. K, May 13, 1898; discharged for disability, January 4, 1899, at Americus, Ga.

ROONEY, ALLEN F.—Age, 19 years. Enlisted, May 2, 1898, at New York city, to serve two years; mustered in as private, Co. M, May 13, 1898; discharged for disability, January 4, 1899, at Americus, Ga.

ROONEY, JOHN.—Age, 23 years. Enlisted, May 2, 1898, at New York city, to serve two years; mustered in as private, Co D, May 13, 1898; promoted corporal, December 3, 1898; mustered out with company, April 20, 1899, at New York city.

ROONEY, WILLIAM P.—Age, 21 years. Enlisted, May 2, 1898, at New York city, to serve two years; mustered in as private, Co. G, May 13, 1898; promoted corporal, May 26, 1898; discharged, January 26, 1899, at New York city.

ROSE, CHARLES.—Age, — years. Enlisted, November 15, 1898, at New York city, to serve two years; mustered in as private, Co. K, November 30, 1898; mustered out with company, April 20, 1899, at New York city.

ROSENBERG, EDWARD.—Age, 22 years. Enlisted, May 2, 1898, at New York city, to serve two years; mustered in as private, Co. C, May 13, 1898; mustered out with company, April 30, 1899, at New York city.

ROSENTHAL, SAMUEL.—Age, 23 years. Enlisted, May 2, 1898, at New York city, to serve two years; mustered in as private, Co. G, May 13, 1898; mustered out with company, April 20, 1899, at New York city.

ROSENZWEIG, HERMAN S.—Age, — years.   Enlisted, June 25, 1898, at New York city, to serve two years; mustered in as private, Co. F, same date; appointed artificer, February 25, 1899; mustered out with company, April 20, 1899, at New York city.

ROSER, ALFRED J.—Age, 23 years.   Enlisted, May 2, 1898, at New York city, to serve two years; mustered in as private, Co. E, May 13, 1898; discharged for disability, September 13, 1898, at Americus, Ga.

ROSSMUSSEN, SOREN P.—Age, — years.   Enlisted, June 20, 1898, at New York city, to serve two years; mustered in as private, Co. D, same date; died of typhoid fever, September 26, 1898, at Camp Hamilton, Lexington, Ky.

ROSSNER, WILLIAM.—Age, 28 years.   Enlisted, May 2, 1898, at New York city, to serve two years; mustered in as private, Co. H, May 13, 1898; appointed cook, December 5, 1898; returned to ranks, February 1, 1899; mustered out with company, April 20, 1899, at New York city.

ROTTHOFF, JOHN F.—Age, — years.   Enlisted, November 15, 1898, at New York city, to serve two years; mustered in as private, Co. K, December 25, 1898; mustered out with company, April 20, 1899, at New York city; prior service in Eighth New York Volunteer Infantry.

ROWE, EDWARD.—Age, 21 years.   Enlisted, May 10, 1898, at camp, near Peekskill, to serve two years; mustered in as private, Co. M, May 13, 1898; mustered out with company, April 20, 1899, at New York city.

ROWLAND, DANIEL.—Age, 23 years.   Enlisted, May 2, 1898, at New York city, to serve two years; mustered in as private, Co. B, May 13, 1898; mustered out with company, April 20, 1898, at New York city.

ROWLEY, ROBERT.—Age, 24 years.   Enlisted, May 13, 1898, at New York city, to serve two years; mustered in as private, Co. H, same date; mustered out with company, April 20, 1899, at New York city.

RUCKERT, FERDERICK C.—Age, 20 years. Enlisted, May 2, 1898, at New York city, to serve two years; mustered in as private, Co. A, May 13, 1898; mustered out with company, April 20, 1899, at New York city.

RUDDEN, EDWARD.—Age, — years. Enlisted, June 28, 1898, at New York city, to serve two years; mustered in as private, Co. L, same date; mustered out with company, April 20, 1899, at New York city.

RUPP, CHARLES.—Age, 26 years. Enlisted, May 11, 1898, at New York city, to serve two years; mustered in as private, Co. I, May 13, 1898; promoted corporal, January 24, 1899; mustered out with company, April 20, 1899, at New York city.

RUSSELL, ROBERT C.—Age, 26 years. Enlisted, May 2, 1898, at New York city, to serve two years; mustered in as private, Co. D, May 13, 1898; discharged for disability, January 4, 1899, at Camp Gilman, Ga.

RUSSELL, ROBERT DEWEY.—Age, — years. Enrolled, November 19, 1898, at Columbus, Ga., to serve two years; mustered in as second lieutenant, Co. A, November 21, 1898; as first lieutenant, Co. B, February 1, 1899; mustered out with company, April 20, 1899, at New York city; subsequent service as second lieutenant, Twenty-eighth Regiment, United States Volunteer Infantry; commissioned second lieutenant, November 7, 1898, with rank from same date, vice Adair, discharged; first lieutenant, January 12, 1899, with rank from same date, vice Taylor, promoted.

RUSSELL, THOMAS K.—Age, 28 years. Enrolled, June 21, 1898, at New York city, to serve two years; mustered in as second lieutenant, Co. L, same date, to date, May 24, 1898; discharged, September 15, 1898; commissioned second lieutenant, June 9, 1898, with rank from same date, vice Smith, promoted.

RUSSELL, WILLIAM H.—Age, 28 years. Enlisted, May 2, 1898, at New York city, to serve two years; mustered in as private, Co. C, May 13, 1898; mustered out with company, April 20, 1899, at New York city.

RYAN, MICHAEL F.—Age, 21 years. Enlisted, May 2, 1898, at New York city, to serve two years; mustered in as private, Co. A, May 13, 1898; discharged, no date, at New York city.

RYAN, MICHAEL J.—Age, 28 years. Enlisted, May 2, 1898, at New York city, to serve two years; mustered in as sergeant, Co. F, May 13, 1898; mustered out with company, April 20, 1899, at New York city.

RYAN, THOMAS.—Age, 21 years. Enlisted, May 2, 1898, at New York city, to serve two years; mustered in as private, Co. M, May 13, 1898; deserted, October 12, 1898, at Lexington, Ky.

RYAN, THOMAS F.—Age, — years. Enlisted, June 29, 1898, at New York city, to serve two years; mustered in as private, Co. H, same date; discharged, to date, April 20, 1899, at New York city.

RYAN, WILLIAM H.—Age, 28 years. Enlisted, May 11, 1898. at camp, near Peekskill, to serve two years; mustered in as private, Co. D, May 13, 1898; transferred to Hospital Corps, September 22, 1898.

SACCO, JOSEPH.—Age, 25 years. Enlisted, May 11, 1898, at New York city, to serve two years; mustered in as private, Co. M, May 13, 1898; mustered out with company, April 20, 1899, at New York city.

SAINZ, THOMAS J.—Age, 24 years. Enlisted, May 2, 1898, at New York city, to serve two years; mustered in as private, Co. H, May 13, 1898; promoted corporal, July 5, 1898; discharged, December 7, 1898, at Camp Gilman, Ga.

SALTER, EDWIN D.—Age, 25 years. Enlisted, May 2, 1898, at New York city, to serve two years; mustered in as private, Co. I, May 13, 1898; appointed cook, March 6, 1899; mustered out, April 20, 1899, at New York city; also borne as Edwin T. Salter.

SAND, EMIL C.—Age, 42 years. Enlisted, May 11, 1898, at camp, near Peekskill, to serve two years; mustered in as private, Co. D, May 13, 1898; mustered out with company, April 20, 1898, at New York city.

SANDERS, THEOFRON.—Age, 18 years. Enlisted, May 13, 1898, at New York city, to serve two years; mustered in as private, Co. C, same date; mustered out with company, April 20, 1899, at New York city.

SANDS, JOHN L.—Age, 27 years. Enlisted, May 2, 1898, at New York city, to serve two years; mustered in as sergeant, Co. B, May 13, 1898; mustered out with company, April 20, 1899, at New York city.

SATTERLEE, RICHARD S.—Age, 38 years. Enrolled, February 16, 1899, at New York city, to serve two years; mustered in as first lieutenant, Co. D, February 21, 1899; mustered out with company, April 20, 1899, at New York city; commissioned first lieutenant, February 4, 1899, with rank from same date, vice Raborg, discharged.

SAUNDRY, HENRY.—Age, 26 years. Enlisted, May 2, 1898, at New York city, to serve two years; mustered in as sergeant, Co. I, May 13, 1898; promoted first sergeant, November 1, 1898; mustered out with company, April 20, 1899, at New York city.

SAUSE, FRANK H.—Age, 21 years. Enlisted, May 2, 1898, at New York city, to serve two years; mustered in as private, Co. H, May 13, 1898; discharged, April 20, 1899, at New York city.

SAVAGE, THOMAS.—Age, 20 years. Enlisted, May 12, 1898, at camp near Peekskill, to serve two years; mustered in as private, Co. L, May 13, 1898; mustered out with company, April 20, 1899, at New York city.

SAXTORPH, CHARLES J.—Age, 24 years. Enlisted, May 2, 1898, at New York city, to serve two years; mustered in as private, Co. G, May 13, 1898; mustered out with company, April 20, 1899, at New York city.

SAYERS, HENRY.—Age, — years. Enlisted, June 18, 1898, at New York city, to serve two years; mustered in as private, Co. C, same date; discharged, April 20, 1899, at Matanzas, Cuba.

SCHATT, WILLIAM.—Age, — years. Enlisted, June 16, 1898, at New York city, to serve two years; mustered in as private, Co. A, June 21, 1898; mustered out with company, April 20, 1899, at New York city.

SCHIEFFELIN, WILLIAM JAY.—Age, 32 years. Enrolled, May 2, 1898, at New York city, to serve two years; mustered in as first lieutenant and regimental adjutant, May 13, 1898; appointed aid-de-camp on staff of General Hain, June 25, 1898; discharged, September 8, 1898, to date, September 30, 1898; commissioned captain and regimental adjutant, May 13, 1898,

SCHMIDT, ELMER.—Age, 24 years. Enlisted, May 10, 1898, at camp, near Peekskill, to serve two years; mustered in as private, Co. D, May 13, 1898; mustered out with company, April 20, 1899, at New York city.

SCHMIDT, HERMAN H.—Age, 25 years. Enlisted, May 2, 1898, at New York city, to serve two years; mustered in as private, Co. E, May 13, 1898; mustered out with company, April 20, 1899, at New York city.

SCHMIDT, WILLIAM.—Age, — years. Enlisted, June 20, 1898, at New York city, to serve two years; mustered in as private, Co. D, same date; mustered out with company, April 20, 1899, at New York city.

SCHMOUSEES, GEORGE.—Age, 21 years. Enlisted, May 2, 1898, at camp, near Peekskill, to serve two years; mustered in as private, Co. E, May 13, 1898; transferred to Co. L, same date; mustered out with company, April 20, 1899, at New York city.

SCHNEIDER, WILLIAM.—Age, — years. Enlisted, November 15, 1898, at New York city, to serve two years; mustered in as private, Co. M, February 3, 1899; mustered out with company, April 20, 1899, at New York city.

SCHNIPPEL, HERMAN E.—Age, 24 years. Enlisted, May 2, 1898, at New York city, to serve two years; mustered in as private, Co. F, May 13, 1898; promoted corporal, August 11, 1898; sergeant, February 8, 1899; mustered out with company, April 20, 1899, at New York city.

SCHOENER, HARRY.—Age, 22 years. Enlisted, May 2, 1898 at New York city, to serve two years; mustered in as private, Co. A, May 13, 1898; mustered out with company, April 20, 1899, at New York city.

SCHOENHAUS, JOHN C.—Age, 21 years. Enlisted, May 2, 1898, at New York city, to serve two years; mustered in as private, Co. D, May 13, 1898; mustered out with company, April 20, 1899, at New York city.

SCHONDEL, IRVING.—Age, 23 years. Enlisted, May 2, 1898, at New York city, to serve two years; mustered in as private, Co. K, May 13, 1898; transferred to Hospital Corps, United States Army, August 1, 1898.

SCHONFIELD, LOUIS.—Age, 21 years. Enlisted, May 13, 1898, at New York city, to serve two years; mustered in as private, Co. F, same date; mustered out with company, April 20, 1899, at New York city.

SCHOPPE, SAMUEL.—Age, 29 years. Enlisted, May 2, 1898, at New York city, to serve two years; mustered in as private, Co. F, May 13, 1898; discharged, February 18, 1899, at New York city.

SCHOPPMYER, JOSEPH.—Age, 21 years. Enlisted, May 2, 1898, at New York city, to serve two years; mustered in as private, Co. M, May 13, 1898; discharged, January 15, 1899, at New York city.

SCHOTTLER, CHARLES.—Age, 38 years. Enlisted, May 10, 1898, at New York city, to serve two years; mustered in as private, Co. K, May 13, 1898; mustered out with company, April 20, 1899, at New York city.

SCHREDER, DAVID B.—Age, 31 years. Enlisted, May 2, 1898, at New York city, to serve two years; mustered in as private, Co. C, May 13, 1898; discharged for disability, January 5, 1899, at Americus, Ga.

SCHROEDER, CHARLES L.—Age, 21 years. Enlisted, May 2, 1898, at New York city, to serve two years; mustered in as private, Co. I, May 13, 1898; mustered out with company, April 20, 1899, at New York city.

SCHUCK, SEIBERT G.—Age, 23 years. Enlisted, May 2, 1898, at New York city, to serve two years; mustered in as private, Co. M, May 13, 1898; promoted corporal, March 14, 1899; mustered out with company, April 20, 1899, at New York city.

SCHULER, JR., JOSEPH.—Age, 19 years. Enlisted, May 2, 1898, at New York city, to serve two years; mustered in as private, Co. C, May 13, 1898; mustered out with company, April 20, 1899, at New York city.

SCHUMACHER, GEORGE H.—Age, 32 years. Enlisted, May 2, 1898, at New York city, to serve two years; mustered in as private, Co. F, May 13, 1898; deserted, November 10, 1898, at Camp Hamilton, Lexington, Ky.

SCOTT, BECHTIL.—Age, 22 years. Enlisted, May 11, 1898, at camp, near Peekskill, to serve two years; mustered in as private, Co. G, May 13, 1898; mustered out with company, April 20, 1899, at New York city.

SEITER, CHARLES JACOB.—Age, 38 years. Enrolled, May 2, 1898, at New York city, to serve two years; mustered in as lieutenant-colonel, May 13, 1898; discharged, September 30, 1898; commissioned lieutenant-colonel, May 13, 1898, with rank from same date, original.

SEITZ, CHRISTOPHER N.—Age, 20 years. Enlisted, May 2, 1898, at New York city, to serve two years; mustered in as private, Co. F, May 13, 1898; mustered out with company, April 20, 1899, at New York city.

SEMBLER, ADOLPHUS A.—Age, 21 years. Enlisted, May 10, 1898, at camp, near Peekskill, to serve two years; mustered in as private, Co. G, May 13, 1898; mustered out with company, April 20, 1899, at New York city.

SEVERANCE, WALTER A.—Age, 29 years. Enlisted, May 12, 1898, at New York city, to serve two years; mustered in as private, Co. F, May 13, 1898; discharged for disability, November 21, 1898, at Americus, Ga.

SHAW, JAMES P.—Age, 21 years. Enlisted, May 2, 1898, at New York city, to serve two years; mustered in as private, Co. D, May 13, 1898; mustered out with company, April 20, 1899, at New York city.

SHEA, EDWARD S.—Age, 24 years. Enlisted, May 10, 1898, at New York city, to serve two years; mustered in as private, Co. F, May 13, 1898; discharged, February 2, 1899, at New York city.

SHEA, JOSEPH D.—Age, — years. Enlisted, June 30, 1898, at New York city, to serve two years; mustered in as private, Co. L, same date; discharged for disability, October 15, 1898, at Lexington, Ky.

SHEARER, DAVID S.—Age, 22 years. Enlisted, May 2, 1898, at New York city, to serve two years; mustered in as sergeant, Co. E, May 13, 1898; discharged, November 29, 1898, at Americus, Ga.

SHELDON, HARRY N.—Age, — years. Enlisted, November 15, 1898, at New York city, to serve two years; mustered in as private, Co. D, December 15, 1898; mustered out with company, April 20, 1898, at New York city.

SHERIDAN, JEFFREY.—Age, 21 years. Enlisted, May 2, 1898, at New York city, to serve two years; mustered in as private, Co. A, May 13, 1898; discharged, January 26, 1899, at New York city.

SICKLES, AVERY C.—Age, 24 years. Enlisted, May 2, 1898, at New York city, to serve two years; mustered in as private, Co. C, May 13, 1898; promoted corporal, July 5, 1898; discharged, December 14, 1898, at Fort Adams, R. I.

SIMON, EDWARD.—Age, 19 years. Enlisted, May 11, 1898, at camp near Peekskill, to serve two years; mustered in as private, Co. D, May 13, 1898; discharged, June 16, 1898.

SIMONS, JOHN G.—Age, 21 years. Enlisted, May 2, 1898, at New York city, to serve two years; mustered in as private, Co. E, May 13, 1898; transferred to Co. M, February 3, 1899; promoted corporal, same date; mustered out with company, April 20, 1899, at New York city.

SIMONSON, GEORGE C.—Age, 31 years. Enlisted, May 2, 1898, at New York city, to serve two years; mustered in as private, Co. F, May 13, 1898; discharged, November 6, 1898, at Lexington, Ky.

SIMONSON, WILLIAM H.—Age, 40 years. Enlisted, May 2, 1898, at New York city, to serve two years; mustered in as private, Co. F, May 13, 1898; mustered out, to date, April 20, 1899, at New York city.

SIMONTON, HERBERT F.—Age, 24 years. Enlisted, May 2, 1898, at New York city, to serve two years; mustered in as corporal, Co. L, May 13, 1898; promoted sergeant, July 12, 1898; first sergeant, November 21, 1898; mustered out with company, April 20, 1898, at New York city.

SINJOHN, JOHN.—Age, 26 years. Enlisted, May 2, 1898, at New York city, to serve two years; mustered in as private, Co. A, May 13, 1898; promoted corporal, December 11, 1898; returned to ranks, January 30, 1899; mustered out with company, April 20, 1899, at New York city.

SKINNER, STEPHEN G.—Age, date, place of enlistment and muster-in not stated; attached to Hospital Corps; discharged, no date, at Matanzas, Cuba.

SLEVIN, DANIEL.—Age, — years. Enlisted, November 15, 1898, at New York city, to serve two years; mustered in as private, Co. E, same date; mustered out with company, April 20, 1899, at New York city.

SMITH, ALBERT H.—Age, 26 years. Enlisted, May 2, 1898, at New York city, to serve two years; mustered in as corporal, Co. K, May 13, 1898; returned to ranks, June 22, 1898; mustered out with company, April 20, 1899, at New York city.

SMITH, ANDREW J.—Age, — years. Enlisted, June 23, 1898, at New York city, to serve two years; mustered in as private, Co. A, same date; mustered out with company, April 20, 1899, at New York city.

SMITH, ANTHONY W.—Age, 20 years. Enlisted, May 2, 1898, at New York city, to serve two years; mustered in as private, Co. A, May 13, 1898; mustered out with company, April 20, 1899, at New York city.

SMITH, CHARLES A.—Age, — years. Enlisted, June 18, 1898, at New York city, to serve two years; mustered in as private, Co. C, same date; transferred to Hospital Corps, United States Army, November 12, 1898.

SMITH, CHARLES MORGAN.—Age, 28 years. Enlisted, May 2, 1898, at New York city, to serve two years; mustered in as first sergeant, Co. B, May 13, 1898; discharged, December 31, 1898, at New York city.

SMITH, CHARLES, WILLIAM.—Age, 32 years. Enrolled, May 2, 1898, at New York city, to serve two years; mustered in as captain, Co. I, May 13, 1898; mustered out with company, April 20, 1899, at New York city; commissioned captain, May 13, 1898, with rank from same date, original.

SMITH, EDWARD.—Age, — years. Enlisted, June 22, 1898, at New York city, to serve two years; mustered in as private, Co. B, same date; transferred to Hospital Corps, United States Army, October 25, 1898.

SMITH, ERNEST.—Age, 20 years. Enlisted, May 10, 1898, at New York city, to serve two years; mustered in as private, Co. I, May 13, 1898; mustered out with company, April 20, 1899, at New York city.

SMITH, EUGENE F.—Age, 21 years. Enlisted, May 2, 1898, at New York city, to serve two years; mustered in as private, Co. I, May 13, 1898; discharged for disability, no date.

SMITH, GEORGE H.—Age, — years. Enlisted, June 29, 1898, at New York city, to serve two years; mustered in as private, Co. C, same date; mustered out with company, April 20, 1899, at New York city.

SMITH, JOHN.—Age, 22 years. Enlisted, May 10, 1898, at camp near Peekskill, to serve two years; mustered in as private, Co. G, May 13, 1898; mustered out with company, April 20, 1899, at New York city.

SMITH, JOSEPH.—Age, 25 years. Enlisted, May 2, 1898, at New York city, to serve two years; mustered in as private, Co. M, May 13, 1898; transferred to Hospital Corps, June 16, 1898.

SMITH, OSGOOD.—Age, 35 years. Enrolled, May 2, 1898, at New York city, to serve two years; mustered in as second lieutenant, Co. L, May 13, 1898; as first lieutenant, Co. H, June 20, 1898, to date, May 24, 1898; as captain, January 11, 1899; discharged April 20, 1899, in Cuba; commissioned second lieutenant, May 13, 1898, with rank from same date, original; first lieutenant, May 24, 1898, with rank from same date, vice Post, promoted; captain, December 24, 1898, with rank from same date, vice Post, discharged.

SMITH, RALPH.—Age, 23 years. Enlisted, May 2, 1898, at New York city, to serve two years; mustered in as corporal, Co. F, May 13, 1898; discharged, November 6, 1898, at Lexington, Ky.

SMITH, ROBERT.—Age, 21 years. Enlisted, May 13, 1898, at New York city, to serve two years; mustered in as private, Co. H, same date; discharged, January 13, 1899, at New York city.

SMITH, THOMAS.—Age, — years. Enlisted, June 25, 1898, at New York city, to serve two years; mustered in as private, Co. A, same date; transferred to band, July 3, 1898; promoted prin-. cipal musician, December 1, 1898; returned to ranks, January 31, 1899; mustered out with regiment, April 20, 1899, at New York city.

SMITH, THOMAS J.—Age, — years. Enlisted, June 21, 1898, at New York city, to serve two years; mustered in as private, Co. B, same date; promoted corporal, August 1, 1898; returned to ranks, January 16, 1899; mustered out with company, April 20, 1899, at New York city.

SMITH, WILLIAM.—Age, 25 years. Enlisted, May 2, 1898, at New York city, to serve two years; mustered in as private, Co. H, May 13, 1898; discharged, November 6, 1898, at Camp Hamilton, Lexington, Ky.

SMITH, JR., WILLIAM H.—Age, — years. Enlisted, June 28, 1898, at New York city, to serve two years; mustered in as private, Co. D, same date; transferred to band, July 2, 1898; promoted principal musician, July 22, 1898; returned to ranks, October 31, 1898; mustered out with regiment, April 20, 1899, at New York city.

SMITHMAN, CHARLES.—Age, 29 years. Enlisted, May 11, 1898, at camp, near Peekskill, to serve two years; mustered in as private, Co. L, May 13, 1898; deserted, November 16, 1898, at Lexington, Ky.

SNYDER CLAUDE.—Age, — years. Enlisted, November 15, 1898, at New York city, to serve two years; mustered in as private, Co. K, November 30, 1898; mustered out with company, April 30, 1899, at New York city; prior service in Eighth New York Volunteer Infantry.

SOMMERFELD, FELIX.—Age, 22 years. Enlisted, May 2, 1898, at New York city, to serve two years; mustered in as private, Co. K, May 13, 1898; deserted, October 1, 1898, at Lexington, Ky.

SOMMERS, FREDERICK.—Age, 21 years. Enlisted, May 2, 1898, at New York city, to serve two years; mustered in as private, Co. M, May 13, 1898; mustered out with company, April 20, 1899, at New York city.

SOUSA, GEORGE J.—Age, — years. Enlisted, November 23, 1898, at Americus, Ga., to serve two years; mustered in as musician, band, November 30, 1898; promoted principal musician, December 26, 1898; mustered out with regiment, April 20, 1899, at New York city.

SPELLMAN, GEORGE.—Age, — years. Enlisted, June 28, 1898, at New York city, to serve two years; mustered in as private, Co. K, same date; mustered out with company, April 20, 1899, at New York city.

SPENCE, WILLIAM L.—Age, 23 years. Enlisted, May 2, 1898, at New York city, to serve two years; mustered in as private, Co. D, May 13, 1898; mustered out with company, April 20, 1899, at New York city.

SPENCER, WILLIAM J.—Age, 23 years. Enlisted, May 2, 1898, at New York city, to serve two years; mustered in as private, Co. D, May 13, 1898; appointed cook, December 20, 1898; mustered out with company, April 20, 1899, at New York city.

SQUIRE, WALTER W.—Age, 30 years. Enlisted, May 2, 1898, at New York city, to serve two years; mustered in as corporal, Co. M, May 13, 1898; promoted sergeant, May 22, 1898; first sergeant, July 28, 1898; returned to ranks, November 19, 1898; discharged, January 25, 1899, at United States General Hospital, Fort McPherson, Ga.

STACH, MAX.—Age, 21 years. Enlisted, May 13, 1898, at camp, near Peekskill, to serve two years; mustered in as private, Co. E, same date; mustered out with company, April 20, 1899, at New York city.

STADTMILLER, HENRY.—Age, 40 years. Enlisted, May 2, 1898, at New York city, to serve two years; mustered in as quartermaster-sergeant, Co. A, May 13, 1898; reduced to sergeant, June 13, 1898; mustered out with company, April 20, 1899, at New York city.

STAMBAUGH, PHILIP J.—Age, 23 years. Enlisted, May 2, 1898, at New York city, to serve two years; mustered in as corporal, Co. M, May 13, 1898; returned to ranks, June 14, 1898; mustered out with company, April 20, 1899, at New York city.

STAMM, JULIUS.—Age, 23 years. Enlisted, May 2, 1898, at camp, near Peekskill, to serve two years; mustered in as private, Co. E, May 13, 1898; transferred to Co. L, same date; mustered out with company, April 20, 1899, at New York city.

STANDACHER, BENEDICT A.—Age, — years. Enlisted, November 15, 1898, at New York city, to serve two years; mustered in as private, Co. M, November 30, 1898; mustered out with company, April 20, 1899, at New York city.

STANLEY, HENRY.—Age, 30 years. Enlisted, May 11, 1898, at camp, near Peekskill, to serve two years; mustered in as private, Co. L, May 13, 1898; appointed artificer, June 2, 1898; mustered out with company, April 20, 1899, at New York city.

STARLING, JOHN.—Age, — years. Enlisted, June 22, 1898, at New York city, to serve two years; mustered in as private, Co. B, same date; mustered out with company, April 20, 1898, at New York city.

STARR, FRANK LOUIS.—Age, 24 years. Enlisted, May 2, 1898, at New York city, to serve two years; mustered in as private, Co. C, May 13, 1898; mustered out with company, April 20, 1899, at New York city.

STEBBINS, SAMUEL SCHEIFFELIN.—Age, 26 years. Enrolled, May 2, 1898, at New York city, to serve two years; mustered in as captain, Co. D, May 13, 1898; discharged, October 15, 1898; commissioned captain, May 13, 1898, with rank from same date, original.

STEELE, JOHN.—Age, — years. Enlisted, June 29, 1898, at New York city, to serve two years; mustered in as private, Co. D, same date; mustered out with company, April 20, 1899, at New York city.

STEIN, BENJAMIN H.—Age, 25 years. Enlisted, May 2, 1898, at New York city, to serve two years; mustered in as quartermaster-sergeant, Co. E, May 13, 1898; mustered out with company, April 20, 1899, at New York city.

STEINBRECHER, CHARLES.—Age, — years. Enlisted, June 27, 1898, at New York city, to serve two years; mustered in as private, Co. L, same date; mustered out with company, April 20, 1899, at New York city.

STEINGASS, HENRY.—Age, 21 years.   Enlisted, May 2, 1898, at New York city, to serve two years; mustered in as private, Co. G, May 13, 1898; mustered out with company, April 20, 1899, at New York city.

STERNEMANN, CHARLES.—Age, — years.   Enlisted, November 15, 1898, at New York city, to serve two years; mustered in as private, Co. E, same date; mustered out with company, April 20, 1899, at New York city.

STEWART, CHARLES R.—Age, 21 years.   Enlisted, May 2, 1898, at New York city, to serve two years; mustered in as private, Co. M, May 13, 1898; mustered out with company, April 20, 1899, at New York city.

STEWART, FRANK.—Age, 24 years.   Enlisted, May 2, 1898, at New York city, to serve two years; mustered in as private, Co. A, May 13, 1898; mustered out with company, April 20, 1899, at New York city.

STEWART, WILLIAM H.—Age, — years.   Enlisted, June 20, 1898, at New York city, to serve two years; mustered in as private, Co. I, same date; mustered out with company, April 20, 1899, at New York city.

STOBBE, PAUL.—Age, — years.   Enlisted, June 18, 1898, at New York city, to serve two years; mustered in as private, Co. I, same date; mustered out with company, April 20, 1899, at New York city.

STOKES, EDWARD J.—Age, 24 years.   Enlisted, May 2, 1898, at New York city, to serve two years; mustered in as private, Co. H, May 14, 1898; promoted corporal, August 22, 1898; returned to ranks, October 16, 1898; mustered out with company, April 20, 1899, at New York city.

STONE, FREDERICK J.—Age, 22 years.   Enlisted, May 2, 1898, at New York city, to serve two years; mustered in as corporal, Co. L, May 13, 1898; mustered out with company, April 20, 1899, at New York city.

STONE, LEWIS S.—Age, 21 years.   Enlisted, May 14, 1898, at New York city, to serve two years; mustered in as private, Co. H, same date; promoted corporal, July 5, 1898; sergeant, December 21, 1898; mustered out with company, April 20, 1899, at New York city.

STOOTHOFF, ROBERT GARDNER.—Age, 22 years. Enlisted, May 13, 1898, at camp, near Peekskill, to serve two years; mustered in as private, Co. B, same date; mustered out with company, April 20, 1899, at New York city.

STRAUSS, RUDOLPH.—Age, 25 years. Enlisted, May 2, 1898, at New York city, to serve two years; mustered in as quarter-master-sergeant, Co. G, May 13, 1898; reduced to sergeant, May 22, 1898; promoted sergeant-major, September 7, 1898; mustered out with regiment, April 20, 1899, at New York city.

STRAUSS, JR., WILLIAM.—Age, 21 years. Enlisted, May 2, 1898, at New York city, to serve two years; mustered in as private, Co. G, May 13, 1898; promoted corporal, July 5, 1898; died of disease, August 6, 1898, in United States General Hospital, Fort McPherson, Ga.

STREBEL, BARTHOLD F.—Age, — years. Enlisted, June 29, 1898, at New York city, to serve two years; mustered in as private, Co. F, same date; promoted quartermaster-sergeant, November 22, 1898; mustered out with company, April 20, 1899, at New York city.

STREYFFERT, OSCAR W.—Age, 31 years. Enlisted, May 10, 1898, at camp, near Peekskill, to serve two years; mustered in as private, Co. G, May 13, 1898; mustered out with company, April 20, 1899, at New York city.

STROBEL, CHARLES.—Age, 24 years. Enlisted, May 2, 1898, at New York city, to serve two years; mustered in as private, Co. E, May 13, 1898; mustered out with company, April 20, 1899, at New York city.

STRUTHERS, DAVID C.—Age, 28 years. Enlisted, May 2, 1898, at New York city, to serve two years; mustered in as private, Co. D, May 13, 1898; appointed artificer, July 13, 1898; returned to ranks, September 26, 1898; appointed artificer, February 15, 1899; mustered out with company, April 20, 1899, at New York city.

STRUTHERS, EDWIN.—Age, — years. Enlisted, June 20, 1898, at New York city, to serve two years; mustered in as private, Co. D, same date; mustered out with company, April 20, 1899, at New York city.

STUART, WILLIAM J.—Age, 19 years. Enlisted, May 11, 1898, at New York city, to serve two years; mustered in as private, Co. F, May 13, 1898; mustered out with company, April 20, 1899, at New York city.

STURM, GEORGE.—Age, 24 years. Enlisted, May 2, 1898, at New York city, to serve two years; mustered in as private, Co. B, May 13, 1898; deserted, December 17, 1898, while at Headquarters, First Army Corps; reported killed in railroad wreck, January 2, 1899, at New Concord, Ohio.

SUDHOFF, MAX.—Age, 21 years. Enlisted, May 2, 1898, at camp, near Peekskill, to serve two years; mustered in as private, Co. E, May 13, 1898; transferred to Co. L, same date; appointed cook, February 2, 1899; mustered out with company, April 20, 1899, at New York city.

SULFSTEDE, CLEMENS A.—Enlisted, December 3, 1898, at Americus, Ga., to serve two years; mustered in as musician in band, December 15, 1898; mustered out with regiment, April 20, 1899, at New York city.

SULLIVAN, HARRY.—Age, — years. Enlisted, November 15, 1898, at New York city, to serve two years; mustered in as private, Co. M, November 30, 1898; mustered out with company, April 20, 1898, at New York city.

SULLIVAN, JAMES W.—Age, — years. Enlisted, November 15, 1898, at New York city, to serve two years; mustered in as private, Co. M, November 30, 1898; mustered out with company, April 20, 1899, at New York city.

SULLIVAN, ROBERT D.—Age, 30 years. Enlisted, May 2, 1898, at New York city, to serve two years; mustered in ; · musician, Co. B, May 13, 1898; mustered out with company, April 20, 1899, at New York city.

SULLIVAN, WILLIAM D.—Age, 24 years. Enlisted, May 2, 1898, at New York city, to serve two years; mustered in as corporal, Co. D, May 13, 1898; returned to ranks, July 30, 1898; promoted corporal, August 1, 1898; returned to ranks, no date; mustered out with company, April 20, 1899, at New York city.

SULLIVAN, WILLIAM H.—Age, 22 years. Enlisted, May 2, 1898, at New York city, to serve two years; mustered in as private, Co. F, May 13, 1898; mustered out with company, April 20, 1899, at New York city.

SUNDERMEYER, HENRY W.—Age, 23 years. Enlisted, May 2, 1898, at New York city, to serve two years; mustered in as corporal, Co. G, May 13, 1898; promoted sergeant, September 12, 1898; mustered out, to date, April 20, 1899, at New York city.

SWANSON, EDWARD.—Age, 30 years. Enlisted, May 10, 1898, at New York city, to serve two years; mustered in as private, Co. B, May 13, 1898; mustered out with company, April 20, 1899, at New York city.

SWANSON, JAMES B.—Age, 21 years. Enlisted, May 11, 1898, at New York city, to serve two years; mustered in as private, Co. I, May 13, 1898; promoted corporal, June 21, 1898; sergeant, November 25, 1898; mustered out with company, April 20, 1899, at New York. city.

SWARTHOUT, WILLIAM H.—Age, — years. Enlisted, June 24, 1898, at New York city, to serve two years; mustered in as private, Co. D, same date; appointed musician, January 1, 1899; mustered out with company, April 20, 1899, at New York city.

SWEETEN, EDWIN E.—Age, 21 years. Enlisted, May 14, 1898, at New York city, to serve two years; mustered in as private, Co. C, same date; discharged, January 20, 1899, at New York city.

TAYLOR, FRANK.—Age, 27 years. Enlisted, May 2, 1898, at New York city, to serve two years; mustered in as private, Co. D, May 13, 1898; mustered out with company, April 20, 1898, at New York city.

TAYLOR, JOHN E.—Age, 23 years. Enlisted, May 2, 1898, at New York city, to serve two years; promoted corporal, Co. D, May 13, 1898; promoted sergeant, September 1, 1898; mustered out with company, April 20, 1899, at New York city.

TAYLOR, THEODORE B.—Enrolled and mustered in as first lieutenant, Co. B, September 27, 1898; as captain, January 11, 1899, to date, December 23, 1898; mustered out with company, April 20, 1899, at New York city; prior service as first and second lieutenant in Co. A, Eighth New York Volunteer Infantry; subsequent service as captain, Thirty-seventh Regiment, United States Volunteer Infantry; commissioned first lieutenant, September 27, 1898, with rank from same date, vice Hoppin, discharged; captain, December 23, 1898, with rank from same date, vice Romaine, discharged.

TEETS, EDWARD H.—Age, 30 years. Enlisted, May 2, 1898, at New York city, to serve two years; mustered in as private, Co. E, May 13, 1898; mustered out with company, April 20, 1898, at New York city.

TERRY, RODERICK.—Age, 49 years. Enrolled, May 2, 1898, at New York city, to serve two years; mustered in as chaplain, May 13, 1898; discharged, September 17, 1898; commissioned chaplain, May 13, 1898, with rank from same date, original.

THOM, CHARLES.—Age, 28 years. Enlisted, May 13, 1898, at New York city, to serve two years; mustered in as private, Co. C, same date; mustered out with company, April 20, 1899, at New York city.

THOMPSON, ANGUS JOSEPH.—Age, 32 years. Enlisted, May 2, 1898, at New York city, to serve two years; mustered in as musician, Co. C, May 13, 1898; discharged, November 29, 1898, at Americus, Ga.

THOMPSON, JOHN.—Age, — years. Enlisted, June 21, 1898, at New York city, two serve two years; mustered in as private, Co. L, same date; deserted, September 16, 1898, at Lexington, Ky.

THOMPSON, WILLIAM.—Age, — years. Enlisted, June 21, 1898, at New York city, to serve two years; mustered in as private, Co. A, same date; mustered out with company, April 20, 1899, at New York city.

THORMAN, BENJAMIN.—Age, — years. Enlisted, June 28, 1898, at New York city, to serve two years; mustered in as private, Co. F, same date; mustered out with company, April 20, 1899, at New York city.

THROOP, THEODORE F.—Age, 22 years. Enlisted, May 2, 1898, at New York city, to serve two years; mustered in as private, Co. G, May 13, 1898; deserted, November 20, 1898.

TIERNAN, JAMES B.—Age, 22 years. Enlisted, May 13, 1898, at camp near Peekskill, to serve two years; mustered in as private, Co. A, same date; mustered out with company, April 20, 1899, at New York city.

TIETZ, THEODORE.—Age, — years. Enlisted, June 21, 1898, at New York city, to serve two years; mustered in as private, Co. A, same date; mustered out with company, April 20, 1899, at New York city.

TILTON, ERNEST ROLLIN.—Age, 31 years. Enrolled, May 2, 1898, at New York city, to serve two years; mustered in as captain, Co. A, May 13, 1898; mustered out with company, April 20, 1899, at New York city; subsequent service as captain, Forty-third Regiment, United States Volunteer Infantry; commissioned captain, May 13, 1898, with rank from same date, original.

TIMOTHY, JOHN.—Age, 21 years. Enlisted, May 2, 1898, at New York city, to serve two years; mustered in as private, Co. G, May 13, 1898; promoted corporal, June 22, 1898; sergeant, March 4, 1899; mustered out with company, April 20, 1899, at New York city.

TOEPFER, VIGGO.—Age, 20 years. Enlisted, May 11, 1898, at camp, near Peekskill, to serve two years; mustered in as private, Co. E, May 13, 1898; discharged, October 17, 1898, at Lexington, Ky.

TOMPKINS, WALTER P.—Age, — years. Enlisted, June 22, 1898, at New York city, to serve two years; mustered in as private, Co. H, June 23, 1898; mustered out with company, April 20, 1899, at New York city.

TOOMEY, MICHAEL J.—Age, 21 years. Enlisted, May 2, 1898, at New York city, to serve two years; mustered in as private, Co. F, May 13, 1898; mustered out with company, April 20, 1899, at New York city.

TORRANCE, CHARLES E.—Age, 19 years. Enlisted, May 2, 1898, at New York city, to serve two years; mustered in as private, Co. C, May 13, 1898; mustered out with company, April 20, 1899, at New York city.

TORREY, CHARLES S.—Age, 30 years. Enlisted, May 2, 1898, at New York city, to serve two years; mustered in as private, Co. C, May 13, 1898; discharged, October 25, 1898, at Lexington, Ky.

TOTTEN, CHARLES C.—Age, 32 years. Enlisted, May 2, 1898, at New York city, to serve two years; mustered in as private, Co. B, May 13, 1898; promoted corporal, August 1, 1898; discharged, October 24, 1898, at Lexington, Ky.

TRACEY, JAMES F.—Age, 23 years. Enlisted, May 2, 1898, at New York city, to serve two years; mustered in as sergeant, Co. M, May 13, 1898; promoted quartermaster-sergeant, December 29, 1898; mustered out with company, April 20, 1899, at New York city.

TRACY, JOSEPH P.—Age, 23 years. Enlisted, May 2, 1898, at New York city, to serve two years; mustered in as private, Co. H, May 13, 1898; promoted corporal, December 21, 1898; mustered out with company, April 20, 1899, at New York city.

TRANGATT, EDWARD R.—Age, 35 years. Enlisted, May 2, 1898, at New York city, to serve two years; mustered in as regimental quartermaster-sergeant, May 13, 1898; discharged for disability, January 4, 1899, at Americus, Ga.

TRANGOTT, ALEXANDER G.—Age, 30 years. Enlisted, May 2, 1898, at New York city, to serve two years; mustered in as private, Co. C, May 13, 1898; mustered out with company, April 20, 1899, at New York city.

TROMBLEY, JOSEPH.—Age, — years. Enlisted, June 28, 1898, at New York city, to serve two years; mustered in as private, Co. E, same date; appointed cook, February 1, 1899; mustered out with company, April 20, 1899, at New York city.

TUCKER, ALLEN J.—Age, — years. Enlisted, November 15, 1898, at New York city, to serve two years; mustered in as private, Co. D, December 15, 1898; mustered out with company, April 20, 1899, at New York city.

TUCKER, JAMES A.—Age, 40 years. Enlisted, May 2, 1898, at New York city, to serve two years; mustered in as private, Co. A, May 13, 1898; promoted corporal, July 3, 1898; returned to ranks, February 27, 1899; promoted corporal, March 20, 1899; mustered out with company, April 20, 1899, at New York city.

TURNER, FREDERICK GOODWIN.—Age, 26 years. Enrolled, May 2, 1898, at New York city, to serve two years; mustered in as first lieutenant, Co. L, May 13, 1898; as captain, October 18, 1898; discharged, December 16, 1898, at Americus, Ga.; subsequent service as second lieutenant, Twenty-eighth Regiment, United States Volunteer Infantry; commissioned first lieutenant, May 13, 1898, with rank from same date, original; captain, October 18, 1898, with rank from same date, vice Wainwright, discharged.

TURNVALL, GUSTAF.—Age, 23 years. Enlisted, May 10, 1898, at camp, near Peekskill, to serve two years; mustered in as private, Co. M, May 13, 1898; mustered out with company, April 20, 1899, at New York city.

TUTTLE, CLARENCE P.—Age, 21 years. Enlisted, May 2, 1898, at New York city, to serve two years; mustered in as private, Co. C, May 13, 1898; deserted, September 19, 1898, at Lexington, Ky.

TWILLMAN, WILLIAM.—Age, 23 years. Enlisted, May 12, 1898, at camp, near Peekskill, to serve two years; mustered in as private, Co. E, May 13, 1898; promoted corporal, February 26, 1899; mustered out with company, April 20, 1899, at New York city.

ULRICH, AUGUST.—Age, — years. Enlisted, June 27, 1898, at New York city, to serve two years; mustered in as private, Co. C, same date; deserted, October 12, 1898 at Lexington Ky.

ULRICH, FRANK.—Age, — years. Enlisted, June 18, 1898, at New York city, to serve two years; mustered in as private, Co. E, same date; mustered out with company, April 20, 1899, at New York city.

ULRICH, HOWARD B.—Age, 22 years. Enlisted, May 2, 1898, at New York city, to serve two years; mustered in as private, Co. E, May 13, 1898; promoted corporal, January 24, 1899; mustered out with company, April 20, 1899, at New York city.

URBANSKY, LOUIS E.—Age, — years. Enlisted, May 22, 1898, at Camp Thomas, Chickamauga, Ga., to serve two years; mustered in as private, Co. D, May 31, 1898; mustered out with company, April 20, 1899, at New York city.

VAIL, ERASTUS M.—Age, — years. Enlisted, June 22, 1898, at
New York city, to serve two years; mustered in as private, Co.
C, same date; transferred to band, July 13, 1898; mustered out
with regiment, April 20, 1899, at New York city.

VAN BILLIARD, EDGAR.—Age, — years. Enlisted, June 27,
1898, at New York city, to serve two years; mustered in as private, Co. D, same date; mustered out with company, April 20,
1899, at New York city.

VANDERHOOF, HARRY.—Age, 27 years. Enlisted, May 2,
1898, at New York city, to serve two years; mustered in as private, Co. B, May 13, 1898; discharged, February 6, 1899, at
New York city.

VAN KLEECK, JR., FREDERICK BRINSMAID.—Enlisted,
May 2, 1898, at Peekskill, to serve two years; mustered in as sergeant, Co. M, May 13, 1898; promoted first sergeant, same date;
mustered in as second lieutenant, July 26, 1898; transferred to
Co. G, January 12, 1899; discharged, February 7, 1899, at
Americus, Ga.; commissioned second lieutenant, July 21, 1898,
with rank from same date, vice McIlvaine, promoted.

VAN RENSSELAER, JR., KILIAEN.—Age, 19 years. Enlisted,
May 13, 1898, at New York city, to serve two years; mustered
in as private, Co. M, same date; promoted corporal, May 23,
1898; sergeant, August 1, 1898; mustered out with company,
April 20,1899, at New York city.

VERDON, JAMES.—Age, 21 years.   Enlisted, May 2, 1898, at
New York city, to serve two years; mustered in as private, Co.
E, May 13, 1898; mustered out with company, April 20, 1899, at
New York city.

VERMILYE, FREDERICK MONTGOMERY.—Age, 33 years.
Enrolled, May 2, 1898, at New York city, to serve two years;
mustered in as first lieutenant, Co. A, May 13, 1898; as regimental adjutant, September 30, 1898; mustered out with regiment, April 20, 1899, at New York city; commissioned first lieutenant, May 13, 1898, with rank from same date, original; battalion adjutant, not mustered, July 23, 1898, with rank from
same date, vice Claiborne, promoted; regimental adjutant, September 30, 1898, with rank from same date, vice Schieffelin,
discharged.

VERMILYEA, FRANK MERRITT.—Age, 22 years. Enlisted, May 2, 1898, at New York city, to serve two years; mustered in as private, Co. C, May 13, 1898; mustered out with company, April 20, 1899, at New York city.

VIALLS, WILLIAM G. P.—Age, 39 years. Enlisted, May 2, 1898, at New York city, to serve two years; mustered in as private, Co. C, May 13, 1898; mustered out with company, April 20, 1899, at New York city.

VICTORY, FRANCIS.—Age, 21 years. Enlisted, May 11, 1898, at New York city, to serve two years; mustered in as musician, Co. I, May 13, 1898; mustered out with company, April 20, 1899, at New York city.

VIDLER, WILLIAM.—Age, 36 years. Enlisted, May 2, 1898, at New York city, to serve two years; mustered in as private, Co. A, May 13, 1898; mustered out with company, April 20, 1899, at New York city.

VILLAR, ALBERT E.—Age, — years. Enlisted, June 21, 1898, at New York city, to serve two years; mustered in as private, Co. G, same date; deserted, September 28, 1898, at Lexington, Ky.

VINCENT, FRANK W.—Enlisted, December 3, 1898, at Americus, Ga., to serve two years; mustered in as musician, band, December 26, 1898; mustered out with regiment, April 20, 1899, at New York city.

VOLLMEYER, ERNEST W.—Age, 25 years. Enlisted, May 2, 1898, at New York city, to serve two years; mustered in as private, Co. G, May 13, 1898; transferred to Hospital Corps, July 5, 1898.

VON DAMENBERG, RICHARD.—Age, — years. Enlisted, June 25, 1898, at Camp Thomas, Ga., to serve two years; mustered in as private, Co. G, June 27, 1898; discharged, September 25, 1898, at Camp Hamilton, Ky.; also borne as R. von Dannenberg.

VOSLER, CLAUDE E.—Age, — years. Enlisted, June 23, 1898, at New York city, to serve two years; mustered in as private, Co. G, same date; mustered out with company, April 20, 1899, at New York city.

VOSSELLER, FRANK.—Age, — years. Enlisted, June 22, 1898, at New York city, to serve two years; mustered in as private, Co. A, same date; discharged, January 16, 1899, at New York city.

WAGNER, HARRY.—Age, — years Enlisted, June 18, 1898, at New York city, to serve two years; mustered in as private, Co. I, same date; mustered out with company, April 20, 1899, at New York city.

WAIDLER, HENRY L.—Age, 24 years.   Enlisted, May 2, 1898, at New York city, to serve two years; mustered in as corporal, Co. L, May 13, 1898; promoted sergeant, January 1, 1899; mustered out with company, April 20, 1899, at New York city.

WAIDLER, WILLIAM J.—Age, 26 years. Enlisted, May 2, 1898, at New York city, to serve two years; mustered in as private, Co. L, May 13, 1898; mustered out with company, April 20, 1899, at New York city.

WAINWRIGHT, CHARLES HOWARD.—Age, 28 years. Enrolled, May 2, 1898, at New York city, to serve two years; mustered in as first lieutenant, Co. F, May 13, 1898; mustered out with company, April 20, 1899, at New York city; commissioned first lieutenant, May 13, 1898, with rank from same date, original.

WAINWRIGHT, JONATHAN MAYHEW.—Age, 33 years. Enrolled, May 2, 1898, at New York city, to serve two years; mustered in as captain, Co. L, May 13, 1898; discharged, September 7, 1898, at Lexington, Ky.; commissioned captain, May 13, 1898, with rank from same date, original.

WALDHEIM, LOUIS.—Age, 21 years.   Enlisted, May 2, 1898, at New York city, to serve two years; mustered in as private, Co. D, May 13, 1898; promoted corporal, July 13, 1898; mustered out with company, April 20, 1899, at New York city.

WALLACE, GEORGE M.—Age, 20 years.   Enlisted, May 13, 1898, at New York city, to serve two years; mustered in as private, Co. H, same date; mustered out with company, April 20, 1899, at New York city.

WALSH, JOHN.—Age, 24 years. Enlisted, May 2, 1898, at New York city, to serve two years; mustered in as private, Co. A, May 13, 1898; deserted, October 3, 1898, at expiration of furlough.

WALSH, JOSEPH.—Age, — years. Enlisted, June 28, 1898, at New York city, to serve two years; mustered in as private, Co. F, same date; mustered out with company, April 20, 1899, at New York city.

WALSH, WILLIAM H.—Age, 20 years. Enlisted, May 2, 1898, at New York city, to serve two years; mustered in as private, Co. A, May 13, 1898; mustered out with company, April 20, 1899, at New York city.

WALTON, ERNEST.—Age, — years. Enlisted, June 25, 1898, at New York city, to serve two years; mustered in as private, Co. E, same date; deserted, October 25, 1898.

WARCH, EDMUND.—Age, 24 years. Enlisted, May 2, 1898, at New York city, to serve two years; mustered in as corporal, Co. G, May 13, 1898; discharged, November 8, 1898, at Camp Hamilton, Ky.; also borne as Edwin Ward.

WARD, EDWARD J.—Age, 26 years. Enlisted, May 2, 1898, at New York city, to serve two years; mustered in as corporal, Co. H, May 13, 1898; promoted quartermaster-sergeant, May 14, 1898; mustered out with company, April 20, 1899, at New York city.

WARD, JR., GEORGE G.—Age, 29 years. Enrolled, May 2, 1898, at New York city, to serve two years; mustered in as major and surgeon, May 6, 1898; discharged, September 8, 1898; commissioned major and surgeon, May 6, 1898, with rank from same date, original.

WARD, JOHN.—Age, 21 years. Enlisted, May 2, 1898, at New York city, to serve two years; mustered in as private, Co. K, May 13, 1898; mustered out with company, April 20, 1899, at New York city.

WARE, JAMES H.—Age, 22 years. Enlisted, May 2' 1898, at New York city, to serve two years; mustered in as private, Co. G, May 13, 1898; mustered out with company, April 20, 1899, at New York city.

WARNER, ANTHONY J.—Age, 32 years. Enlisted, May 10, 1898, at New York city, to serve two years; mustered in as private, Co. I, May 13, 1898; appointed wagoner, July 12, 1898; returned to ranks, no date; discharged for disability, to date, August 24, 1898, at Chickamauga Park, Ga.

WARSHAW, MORRIS.—Age, 27 years. Enlisted, May 2, 1898, at New York city, to serve two years; mustered in as private, Co. F, May 13, 1898; mustered out with company, April 20, 1899, at New York city.

WEAVER, BENJAMIN.—Age, 22 years. Enlisted, May 10, 1898, at camp near Peekskill, to serve two years; mustered in as private, Co. G, May 13, 1898; transferred to Second Brigade Hospital Corps, October 25, 1898.

WEBBER, HENRY F.—Age, 22 years. Enlisted, May 2, 1898, at New York city, to serve two years; mustered in as private, Co. K, May 13, 1898; mustered out with company, April 20, 1899, at New York city.

WEBER, BRUNO.—Age, 21 years. Enlisted, May 10, 1898, at New York city, to serve two years; mustered in as private, Co. L, May 13, 1898; transferred to Second Division Hospital Corps, October 8, 1898.

WEBER, CHARLES.—Age, — years. Enlisted, June 25, 1898, at New York city, to serve two years; mustered in as private, Co. D, same date; mustered out with company, April 20, 1899, at New York city.

WEBER, EDWARD JOHN.—Age, 23 years. Enlisted, May 2, 1898, at New York city, to serve two years; mustered in as private, Co. E, May 13, 1898; mustered out with company, April 20, 1899, at New York city.

WEBER, PHILIP.—Age, — years. Enlisted, June 21, 1898, at New York city, to serve two years; mustered in as private, Co. H, same date; mustered out with company, April 20, 1899, at New York city.

WEHRLEN, CHARLES ALBERT.—Age, 22 years. Enlisted, May 2, 1898, at New York city, to serve two years; mustered in as corporal, Co. B, May 13, 1898; promoted sergeant, February 19, 1899; mustered out with company, April 20, 1899, at New York city.

WEINBERGER, CHARLES.—Age, — years. Enlisted, June 29, 1898, at New York city, to serve two years; mustered in as private, Co. L, same date; transferred to band, July 3, 1898; mustered out with regiment, April 20, 1899, at New York city.

WEIR, JOHN JAMES.—Age, 31 years. Enlisted, May 2, 1898, at New York city, to serve two years; mustered in as private, Co. A, May 13, 1898; mustered out with company, April 20, 1899, at New York city.

WEISS, GEORGE.—Age, 24 years. Enlisted, May 2, 1898, at New York city, to serve two years; mustered in as private, Co. G, May 13, 1898; discharged, November 3, 1898, at Camp Hamilton, Ky.

WEISS, MAX H. R.—Age, 28 years. Enlisted, May 2, 1898, at New York city, to serve two years; mustered in as corporal, Co. I, May 13, 1898; mustered out with company, April 20, 1899, at New York city.

WELK, CONRAD.—Age, — years. Enlisted, June 17, 1898, at New York city, to serve two years; mustered in as private, Co. D, same date; mustered out with company, April 20, 1899, at New York city.

WELLINGHAUSEN, CHRISTIAN.—Age, — years. Enlisted, November 15, 1898, at New York city, to serve two years; mustered in as private, Co. M, November 30, 1898; mustered out with company, April 20, 1899, at New York city.

WELLS, JAMES J.—Age, 32 years. Enlisted, May 2, 1898, at New York city, to serve two years; mustered in as sergeant, Co. C, May 13, 1898; promoted first sergeant, February 1, 1899; mustered out with company, April 20, 1899, at New York city.

WELSCH, WILLIAM.—Age, 21 years. Enlisted, May 2, 1898, at camp near Peekskill, to serve two years; mustered in as private, Co. E, May 13, 1898; transferred to Co. L, May 13, 1898; mustered out with company, April 20, 1899, at New York city.

WESLEY, EDWARD.—Age, 24 years. Enlisted, May 2, 1898, at New York city, to serve two years; mustered in as corporal, Co. I, May 13, 1898; promoted sergeant, June 4, 1898; returned to ranks, November 17, 1898; deserted, November 19, 1898, at Americus, Ga.

WESTON, WILLIAM.—Age, 23 years. Enlisted, May 2, 1898, at
New York city, to serve two years; mustered in as private, Co.
F, May 13, 1898; deserted, October 28, 1898, at Camp Hamilton,
Lexington, Ky.

WEYRICH, RUDOLPH.—Age, — years. Enlisted, June 24,
1898, at New York city, to serve two years; mustered in as private, Co. D, same date; promoted corporal, January 18, 1899;
mustered out with company, April 20, 1899, at New York city.

WHEELER, FOREST C.—Age, — years. Enlisted, June 28,
1898, at New York city, to serve two years; mustered in as private, Co. B, same date; mustered out with company, April 20,
1899, at New York city.

WHITE, JR., ALEXANDER MOSS.—Age, 27 years. Enrolled,
May 2, 1898, at New York city, to serve two years; mustered in
as second lieutenant, Co. H, May 13, 1898; transferred to Co.
A, May 17, 1898; mustered in as first lieutenant and regimental
quartermaster, September 6, 1898; transferred to Co. L, January 12, 1899; discharged, February 10, 1899; commissioned
second lieutenant, May 13, 1898, with rank from same date,
original; first lieutenant and regimental quartermaster, August
27, 1898, with rank from same date, vice Parker, discharged.

WHITE, ARTHUR F.—Age, — years. Enlisted, June 20, 1898,
at New York city, to serve two years; mustered in as private,
Co. C, same date; discharged, no date.

WHITE, GEORGE E.—Age, — years. Enlisted, June 20, 1898,
at New York city, to serve two years; mustered in as private,
Co. M, same date; mustered out with company, April 20, 1899,
at New York city.

WHITHE, RUDOLPH.—Age, 41 years. Enlisted, May 2, 1898, at
New York city, to serve two years; mustered in as private, Co.
M, May 13, 1898; mustered out with company, April 20, 1899,
at New York city.

WICHERT, HERMAN.—Age, 21 years. Enlisted, May 2, 1898,
at New York city, to serve two years; mustered in as private,
Co. K, May 13, 1898; mustered out with company, April 20,
1899, at New York city.

WILLIAMS, HARRY.—Age, 18 years. Enlisted, May 2, 1898, at New York city, to serve two years; mustered in as private, Co. B, May 13, 1898; discharged, October 24, 1898, at Lexington, Ky.

WILLIAMS, WILLIAM F.—Age, — years. Enlisted, June 18, 1898, at New York city, to serve two years; mustered in as private, Co. K, same date; promoted corporal, November 5, 1898; mustered out with company, April 20, 1899, at New York city.

WILLIAMSON, BEN.—Age, — years. Enlisted, June 29, 1898, at New York city, to serve two years; mustered in as private, Co. K, same date; mustered out with company, April 20, 1899, at New York city.

WILLIAMSON, THOMAS HUNTER.—Age, 26 years. Enlisted, May 2, 1898, at New York city, to serve two years; mustered in as sergeant, Co. D, May 13, 1898; promoted first sergeant, May 31, 1898; mustered in as second lieutenant, Co. I, January 11, 1899; mustered out with company, April 20, 1899, at New York city; commissioned second lieutenant, December 23, 1898, with rank from same date; vice Raborg, promoted.

WILSON, JOHN W.—Age, 29 years. Enlisted, May 2, 1898, at New York city, to serve two years; mustered in as musician, Co. F, May 13, 1898; returned to ranks, no date; discharged, February 13, 1899, at Fort McPherson, Ga.

WILSON, WILLIAM J.—Age, 23 years. Enlisted, May 2, 1898, at New York city, to serve two years; mustered in as private, Co. D, May 13, 1898; mustered out with company, April 20, 1899, at New York city.

WINKLER, GUSTAVE.—Age, 22 years. Enlisted, May 2, 1898, at New York city, to serve two years; mustered in as sergeant, Co. B, May 13, 1898; promoted first sergeant, January 1, 1899; mustered out with company, April 20, 1899, at New York city.

WISHART, LEONARD T.—Age, 26 years. Enlisted, May 2, 1898, at New York city, to serve two years; mustered in as private, Co. E, May 13, 1898; promoted corporal, August 1, 1898; mustered out with company, April 20, 1899, at New York city.

WITKOSKI, SAMUEL.—Age, 25 years. Enlisted, May 14, 1898, at New York city, to serve two years; mustered in as private, Co. C, same date; transferred to Co. B, July 4, 1898; promoted corporal, August 6, 1898; quartermaster-sergeant, August 16, 1898; regimental quartermaster-sergeant, February 1, 1899; mustered out with regiment, April 20, 1899, at New York city.

WOBIE, GEORGE A.—Age, 18 years. Enlisted, May 13, 1898, at camp near Peekskill, to serve two years; mustered in as private, Co. B, same date; discharged, January 26, 1899, at New York city.

WOLF, ABRAHAM.—Age, 21 years. Enlisted, May 13, 1898, at New York city, to serve two years; mustered in as private, Co. C, same date; deserted, July 10, 1898, at Chickamauga, Ga.

WOLF, WILLIAM.—Age, 21 years. Enlisted, May 2, 1898, at New York city, to serve two years; mustered in as private, Co. D, May 13, 1898; mustered out with company, April 20, 1899, at New York city.

WOLFMAN, HERMAN.—Age, 23 years. Enlisted, May 2, 1898, at New York city, to serve two years; mustered in as corporal, Co. I, May 13, 1898; promoted sergeant, November 25, 1898; mustered out with company, April 20, 1899, at New York city.

WOOD, EDWIN.—Age, 18 years. Enlisted, May 2, 1898, at New York city, to serve two years; mustered in as private, Co. B, May 13, 1898; discharged, January 20, 1899, at New York city.

WOODS, PATRICK J.—Age, 28 years. Enlisted, May 2, 1898, at New York city, to serve two years; mustered in as private, Co. A, May 13, 1898; promoted corporal, July 7, 1898; mustered out with company, April 20, 1899, at New York city.

WORN, CHARLES.—Age, — years. Enlisted, June 29, 1898, at New York city, to serve two years; mustered in as private, Co. D, same date; mustered out with company, April 20, 1899, at New York city.

WREDE, ALBERT W.—Age, 21 years. Enlisted, May 2, 1898, at New York city, to serve two years; mustered in as private, Co. H, May 13, 1898; mustered out with company, April 20, 1899, at New York city.

WRIGHT, WALTER.—Age, 27 years. Enlisted, May 13, 1898, at camp near Peekskill, to serve two years; mustered in as private, Co. L, same date; transferred to Co. E, May 20, 1898; promoted corporal, February 19, 1899; mustered out with company, April 20, 1899, at New York city.

WUNDER, JOHN.—Age, 29 years. Enlisted, May 2, 1898, at New York city, to serve two years; mustered in as private, Co. F, May 13, 1898; mustered out with company, April 20, 1899, at New York city.

WURZ, OTTO.—Age, 22 years. Enlisted, May 13, 1898, at New York city, to serve two years; mustered in as private, Co. C, same date; deserted, September 19, 1898, at Lexington, Ky.

WYRE, HOWARD J.—Age, 21 years. Enlisted, May 13, 1898, at camp near Peekskill, to serve two years; mustered in as private, Co. B, same date; discharged for disability, January 4, 1899, at Americus, Ga.

ZAISSER, FREDERICK S.—Age, 29 years. Enlisted, May 2, 1898, at New York city, to serve two years; mustered in as private, Co. B, May 13, 1898; promoted corporal, February 19, 1899; mustered out with company, April 20, 1899, at New York city.

ZENTGRAF, CHARLES W.—Age, — years. Enlisted, June 23, 1898, at New York city, to serve two years; mustered in as private, Co. G, same date; discharged, October 28, 1898, at Camp Hamilton, Lexington, Ky.

ZIMMERMAN, MATTHEW C.—Age, 21 years. Enlisted, May 2, 1898, at New York city, to serve two years; mustered in as corporal. Co. D, May 13, 1898; returned to ranks, July 10, 1898; mustered out with company, April 20, 1899, at New York city.

THIRTEENTH REGIMENT, INFANTRY.

The thirteenth regiment, national guard, having volunteered its services, was one of the regiments selected in general orders, No. 8, general headquarters, state of New York, dated adjutant-general's office, Albany, April 27, 1898, to enter the service of the United States as a volunteer regiment.

The regiment, which consisted of ten companies, was in the same order required to recruit and organize as a twelve-company regiment.

In special orders, No. 72, A. G. O., May 1, 1898, the regiment was directed to report at the Flatbush avenue station of the Long Island railroad, Brooklyn, at 10 o'clock a. m., May 2d., to take train there for Camp Black, Hempstead, L. I., and on arrival at the camp to report to Major-General Charles F. Roe, commanding national guard and camp. The regiment arrived duly at Camp Black.

General orders, No. 11, general headquarters, state of New York, dated Albany, May 3, 1898, directed the regiments ordered to the camp to perfect their organization, so that each should consist of twelve companies of 81 enlisted men each. In this the regiment failed.

May 7th, it was ordered back to its home station, excepting such of its members as had meanwhile positively volunteered to enter the service of the United States. These men were organized in four companies, under the command of Major George D. Russell, and were formed into a battalion, and as such assigned, May 9th, to the twenty-second regiment, forming companies, D, F, L and M of that regiment. They were mustered out with the twenty-second regiment, November 23, 1898.

FOURTEENTH REGIMENT, INFANTRY.

The fourteenth regiment, national guard, having volunteered its services, was one of the regiments selected in general orders, No. 8, general headquarters, state of New York, dated adjutant-general's office, Albany, April 27, 1898, to enter the service of the United States as a volunteer regiment.

The regiment at the time consisted of ten companies, and at once commenced recruiting to fill its companies and to organize two additional ones. Its history to that date follows:

FOURTEENTH REGIMENT.

(Second Brigade.)

Armory, Eighth avenue and Fifteenth street, Brooklyn.

This regiment was organized in 1847. It entered the service of the United States for three years in May, June and July, 1861; June 1, 1864, those entitled to discharges were mustered out and the re-enlisted men and recruits transferred to the fifth New York volunteers. During this service it was also known as the eighty-fourth New York volunteers. The regiment was in active service during the quarantine disturbances at Fire Island, September, 1892, and the Brooklyn motormen's strike, January, 1895, and received authority to place on the lances of its colors silver rings inscribed as follows:

On the national color.—Advance into Virginia, May 24, 1861; Bull Run, Va., July 21, 1861; Ball's Cross Roads, Va., August 27, 1861; Upton's Hill, Va., October 5, 1861; Binn's Hill, Va., November 18, 1861; Falmouth, Va., April 17-18, 1862; Carmel Church, Va., July 23, 1862; Massaponax, Va., August 6, 1862; General Pope's Campaign, Va., August 16–September 3, 1862; Rappahannock River, Va., August 21, 1862; Rappahannock Station, Va., August 23, 1862; Sulphur Springs, Va., August 26, 1862; Gainesville, Va., August 28, 1862; Groveton, Va., August 29, 1862; Second Bull Run, Va., August 30, 1862; South Mountain, Md., September 14, 1862; Keedysville, Md., September 15-16, 1862; Antietam, Md., September 17, 1862; Fredericksburg, Va., December 13-15, 1862; Port Royal, Va., April 22-23, 1863; Fitzhugh's Crossing, Va., April 29–May 2, 1863; Chancellorsville, Va., May 3, 1863; Gettysburg, Pa., July 1-3, 1863; Mine Run, Va., November

28-30, 1863; Wilderness, Va., May 5-7, 1864; Spottsylvania, Va., May 8-21, 1864; Piney Branch Church, Va., May 8, 1864; Laurel Hill, Va., May 10, 1864; Spanish-American War, 1898.

On the state color.—Fire Island, September, 1892; Brooklyn, January, 1895.

Special orders, No. 72, A. G. O., May 1, 1898, ordered the regiment to report at 10 a. m., May 2d, at the Flatbush avenue station of the Long Island railroad, Brooklyn; there to take train for the camp at Hempstead, and on arrival at the latter place to report to Major-General Charles F. Roe, commanding national guard and the camp. This order was duly carried out.

Recruiting was continued to fill up and replace the men rejected by the medical officers, and the regiment was fully organized as a twelve-company regiment under the provisions of general orders, No. 11, A. G. O., Albany, May 3, 1898. It was mustered in the service of the United States as follows: Companies A, G, K and M, May 13th; the other companies, May 16th, 1898, and became thereby the "fourteenth regiment, infantry, New York volunteers."

Pursuant to telegraphic instructions, dated war department, Washington, D. C., May 15, 1898, the regiment left camp at Hempstead on May 17th, and proceeded by rail to Camp George H. Thomas, Chickamauga Park, Ga., where it arrived on May 20th, and was assigned to the first brigade, first division, third army corps. The regiment remained in this camp, undergoing equipment, instructions, etc., until September 3d.

While in camp at Chickamauga Park, Ga., recruiting officers were sent in June to Brooklyn, who returned to the regiment early in July with 302 recruits.

Pursuant to general orders, No. 41, first division, headquarters third army corps, August 31, 1898, the regiment proceeded September 3d, by rail to Camp Shipp, at Anniston, Alabama, arriving there on September 4th, where it went into camp with the remainder of the brigade and division.

September 5th, the regiment received orders to prepare for muster-out and to proceed as soon as preliminary steps could be taken to corner Eighth avenue and Fifteenth street, Brooklyn, N. Y., where the officers and men would be granted leaves of absence and furloughs for thirty days, after which they would be mustered out of the service of the United States. It left its camp at Anniston, Ala., September 14th, for Brooklyn, via Seaboard Air Line to Richmond and Washington, and via Pennsylvania railroad to Jersey City, arriving at the armory in Brooklyn, September 16th, where it was mustered out of the service of the United States, October 27, 1898.

Commissioned Officers.

COLONELS:

Frederick Dent Grant, May 2 to June 1, 1898.
Wilbur E. Wilder, June 6 to October 27, 1898.

LIEUTENANT-COLONEL:

Ardolph Loges Kline, May 2 to October 27, 1898.

MAJORS:

Bennett H. Tobey, May 2 to September 5, 1898.
Edmund Harmon Mitchell, May 2 to October 27, 1898.
Charles A. Andrews, June 13 to October 27, 1898.

REGIMENTAL ADJUTANTS:

John W. Nutt, May 2 to July 21, 1898.
Henry H. Adams, Jr., July 21 to September 11, 1898.
Lewis Hamilton Foley, September 13 to October 27, 1898.

BATTALION ADJUTANTS:

Henry B. Welsh, May 17 to June 21, 1898.
Joseph Bryan Beatty, June 18 to October 27, 1898.
Calhoun Cragin, June 18 to October 27, 1898.
Carl Wilhelm, August 1 to October 27, 1898.

REGIMENTAL QUARTERMASTER:

George Redmond Jennings, May 2 to October 27, 1898.

SURGEONS:

John Lincoln Macumber, May 2 to August 25, 1898.
Arthur H. Bogart, September 7 to November 28, 1898.

ASSISTANT SURGEONS:

Arthur H. Bogart, May 2 to September 7, 1898.
Thomas B. Spence, May 2 to November 28, 1898.

CHAPLAIN:

James Oliver Wilson, May 16 to October 27, 1898.

COMPANY A.

CAPTAIN:

William C. Noble, May 2 to October 27, 1898.

FIRST LIEUTENANT:

Philip Elsdon Wingate, May 2 to October 27, 1898.

SECOND LIEUTENANTS:

Gustave Theodore Bruckman, May 9 to June 14, 1898.
Alfred C. Rautsch, June 14 to October 27, 1898.

COMPANY B.

CAPTAIN:

John Henry Foote, May 2 to October 27, 1898.

FIRST LIEUTENANT:

Timothy Francis Donovan, May 2 to October 27, 1898.

SECOND LIEUTENANTS:

Lewis Hamilton Foley, May 7 to July 23, 1898.
Louis Bedell Grant, July 24 to October 27, 1898.

COMPANY C.

CAPTAIN:

Thomas Heape Avery, May 2 to October 27, 1898.

FIRST LIEUTENANT:

John Patrick McNamara, May 2 to October 27, 1898.

SECOND LIEUTENANTS:

Edward Denton Raymond, May 2 to June 15, 1898.
Louis Morris Greer, June 22 to August 30, 1898.
Andrew Armstrong, October 17 to October 27, 1898.

COMPANY D.

CAPTAIN:

William Lewis Garcia, May 2 to October 27, 1898.

FIRST LIEUTENANTS:

Henry H. Adams, Jr., May 2 to July 21, 1898.
John W. Nutt, July 21 to October 27, 1898.

SECOND LIEUTENANT:

Joseph T. Griffin, May 2 to October 27, 1898.

COMPANY E.

CAPTAIN:

Benjamin Franklin Cross, May 17 to October 27, 1898.

FIRST LIEUTENANT:

Patrick F. McLaughlin, May 2 to October 27, 1898.

SECOND LIEUTENANT:

William Macauley, May 2 to October 27, 1898.

COMPANY F.

CAPTAIN:

John Francis Carroll, May 2 to October 27, 1898.

FIRST LIEUTENANTS:

Harry Van Cott Bell, May 2 to July 26, 1898.
Carl Wilhelm, July 26 to October 27, 1898.

SECOND LIEUTENANT:

John W. Creighton, May 2 to October 27, 1898.

COMPANY G.

CAPTAIN:

Carl Leonard Holemberg, May 2 to October 27, 1898.

FIRST LIEUTENANT:

Charles Hamilton, May 2 to October 27, 1898.

SECOND LIEUTENANT:

George Rydberg, May 2 to October 27, 1898.

COMPANY H.

CAPTAIN:

Frank Elbridge Sweet, May 2 to October 27, 1898.

FIRST LIEUTENANTS:

Homer Cecil Croscup, May 2 to October 10, 1898.
James Otis Moore, October 10 to October 27, 1898.

SECOND LIEUTENANTS:

James Otis Moore, May 10 to October 10, 1898.
Thomas J. Brown, Jr., October 10 to October 27, 1898.

COMPANY I.

CAPTAINS:

Joseph Richard Kendrick Barlow, May 2 to September 5, 1898.
Homer Cecil Croscup, October 10 to October 27, 1898.

FIRST LIEUTENANT:

John Joseph Bergen, May 2 to September 3, 1898.

SECOND LIEUTENANT:

H. Millard Horton, May 2 to October 27, 1898.

COMPANY K.

CAPTAINS:

Charles A. Andrews, May 2 to June 13, 1898.
David Patterson Henry, June 14 to September 3, 1898.
Henry H. Adams, Jr., September 15 to October 27, 1898.

FIRST LIEUTENANT:

Charles W. Bridges, May 3 to September 3, 1898.

SECOND LIEUTENANTS:

Joseph Bryan Beatty, May 2 to June 18, 1898.
Athelstane Kendrick, June 18 to October 17, 1898.
Joseph T. Griffin, October 17 to October 27, 1898.

COMPANY L.

CAPTAINS:

Bernard Mathew Wagner, May 2 to July 14, 1898.
Van D. Macumber, July 23 to October 27, 1898.

FIRST LIEUTENANTS:

Van D. Macumber, May 2 to July 23, 1898.
Lewis Hamilton Foley, July 23 to September 13, 1898.
Ovington B. Bogart, October 10 to October 27, 1898.

SECOND LIEUTENANTS:

Calhoun Cragin, May 4 to June 18, 1898.
Adelbert S. Hart, June 18 to September 7, 1898.
Fernando H. Mickelborough, September 15 to October 27, 1898.

COMPANY M.

CAPTAINS:

Richard H. Harding, Jr., May 2 to October 27, 1898.

FIRST LIEUTENANTS:

David Patterson Henry, May 2 to June 14, 1898.
Gustave Theodore Bruckman, June 14 to October 27, 1898.

SECOND LIEUTENANTS:

Ovington B. Bogart, May 2 to October 9, 1898.
Francis A. Adams, October 14 to October 27, 1898.

RECORDS OF THE OFFICERS AND ENLISTED MEN.

AARVIG, GABRIEL.—Age, 26 years. Enlisted, May 2, 1898, at Brooklyn, to serve two years; mustered in as first sergeant, Co. G, May 13, 1898; mustered out with company, October 27, 1898, at Brooklyn, N. Y.

ADAMS, FRANCIS A.—Age, 23 years. Enlisted, May 2, 1898, at Brooklyn, to serve two years; mustered in as private, Co. M, May 13, 1898; promoted corporal, May 26, 1898; sergeant, June 5, 1898; mustered in as second lieutenant, October 14, 1898; mustered out, to date, October 27, 1898; commissioned second lieutenant, September 14, 1898, with rank from same date, vice Bogart, promoted first lieutenant.

ADAMS, JR., HENRY H.—Age, — years. Enrolled, May 2, 1898, at Brooklyn, to serve two years; mustered in first lieutenant, Co. D, May 16, 1898; appointed regimental adjutant, July 21, 1898; relieved from duty as adjutant and assigned to Co. L, September 11, 1898; mustered in as captain, Co. K, September 15, 1898; mustered out with company, October 27, 1898, at Brooklyn, N. Y.; commissioned first lieutenant, May 16, 1898, with rank from same date, original; not commissioned adjutant; commissioned captain, September 7, 1898, with rank from same date, vice Henry, discharged.

ADAMS, HERBERT J.—Age, 21 years. Enlisted, May 2, 1898, at Brooklyn, to serve two years; mustered in as private, Co. M, May 13, 1898; promoted sergeant, June 5, 1898; mustered out with company, October 27, 1898, at Brooklyn, N. Y.

ADAMS, PETER.—Age, 23 years. Enlisted, May 13, 1898, at Hempstead, to serve two years; mustered in as private, Co. E, May 16, 1898; mustered out with company, October 27, 1898, at Brooklyn, N. Y.

AHL, CHARLES V.—Age, 28 years. Enlisted, May 2, 1898, at Brooklyn, to serve two years; mustered in as private, Co. G, May 13, 1898; mustered out with company, October 27, 1898, at Brooklyn, N. Y.

AHLBERG, IVAR.—Age, 27 years. Enlisted, May 2, 1898, at Brooklyn, to serve two years; mustered in as private, Co. G, May 13, 1898; mustered out with company, October 27, 1898, at Brooklyn, N. Y.

AHLGREN, CARL F.—Age, 28 years. Enlisted, May 2, 1898, at Brooklyn, to serve two years; mustered in as private, Co. G, May 13, 1898; mustered out with company, October 27, 1898, at Brooklyn, N. Y.

AHLSTEAD, CLARENCE E.—Age, — years. Enlisted, June 18, 1898, at Brooklyn, to serve two years; mustered in as private, Co. A, same date; mustered out with company, October 27, 1898, at Brooklyn, N. Y.

AITKEN, THOMAS T.—Age, 25 years. Enlisted, May 2, 1898, at Brooklyn, to serve two years; mustered in as private, Co. K, May 13, 1898; mustered out with company, October 27, 1898, at Brooklyn, N. Y.

ALBIN, BRUNO.—Age, 23 years. Enlisted, May 11, 1898, at Camp Black, to serve two years; mustered in as private, Co. M, May 13, 1898; discharged, October 6, 1898.

ALBRIGHT, CHARLES W.—Age, 33 years. Enlisted, May 2, 1898, at Brooklyn, to serve two years; mustered in as private, Co. K, May 13, 1898; transferred to Hospital Corps, June 12, 1898; returned to company, September 13, 1898; mustered out with company, October 27, 1898, at Brooklyn, N. Y.

ALCORN, WILLIAM J.—Age, 30 years. Enlisted, May 2, 1898, at Brooklyn, to serve two years; mustered in as quartermaster-sergeant, Co. B, May 16, 1898; reduced to sergeant, May 25, 1898; mustered out with company, October 27, 1898, at Brooklyn, N. Y.

ALLEN, JOHN H.—Age, 39 years. Enlisted, May 2, 1898, at Brooklyn, to serve two years; mustered in as private, Co. C, May 16, 1898; mustered out with company, October 27, 1898, at Brooklyn, N. Y.

ALLEN, WILLIAM J.—Age, 27 years. Enlisted, May 2, 1898, at Brooklyn, to serve two years; mustered in as corporal, Co. A, May 13, 1898; mustered out with company, October 27, 1898, at Brooklyn, N. Y.

ALLER, THOMAS G.—Age, 44 years. Enlisted, May 13, 1898, at Camp Black, to serve two years; mustered in as private, Co. C, May 16, 1898; mustered out with company, October 27, 1898, at Brooklyn, N. Y.

ALMGVIST, NELS.—Age, — years. Enlisted, July 5, 1898, at
Brooklyn, to serve two years; mustered in as private, Co. G,
same date; mustered out with company, October 27, 1898, at
Brooklyn, N. Y.

ALWANG, ANDREW A.—Age, 21 years. Enlisted, May 16,
1898, at Camp Black, to serve two years; mustered in as private, Co. F, same date; mustered out with company, October 27,
1898, at Brooklyn, N. Y.

AMBACK, ERNEST.—Age, 22 years. Enlisted, May 2, 1898, at
Brooklyn, to serve two years; mustered in as private, Co. D,
May 16, 1898; mustered out with company, October 27, 1898, at
Brooklyn, N. Y.

ANDERSON, ANDREW.—Age, — years. Enlisted, June 27,
1898, at Brooklyn, to serve two years; mustered in as private,
Co. G, same date; mustered out, to date, October 27, 1898.

ANDERSON, CARL AUGUST.—Age, 29 years. Enlisted, May
2, 1898, at Brooklyn, to serve two years; mustered in as private,
Co. G, May 13, 1898; mustered out with company, October 27,
1898, at Brooklyn, N. Y.

ANDERSON, EDWARD.—Age, 21 years. Enlisted, May 2, 1898,
at Brooklyn, to serve two years; mustered in as private, Co. G,
May 13, 1898; mustered out with company, October 27, 1898, at
Brooklyn, N. Y.

ANDERSON, FRANK E.—Age, 23 years. Enlisted, May 2, 1898,
at Brooklyn, to serve two years; mustered in as corporal, Co. G,
May 13, 1898; mustered out with company, October 27, 1898, at
Brooklyn, N. Y.

ANDERSON, ROBERT.—Age, 26 years. Enlisted, May 2, 1898,
at Brooklyn, to serve two years; mustered in as private, Co. F,
May 16, 1898; deserted, July 21, 1898, at Camp Thomas, Chickamauga Park, Ga.

ANDERSON, WILLIAM.—Age, 30 years. Enlisted, May 2, 1898,
at Brooklyn, to serve two years; mustered in as private, Co. A,
May 13, 1898; promoted corporal, July 20, 1898; discharged for
disability, October 6, 1898.

ANDRES, JOHN G.—Age, 21 years. Enlisted, May 2, 1898, at Brooklyn, to serve two years; mustered in as private, Co. B, May 16, 1898; mustered out with company, October 27, 1898, at Brooklyn, N. Y.

ANDREWS, CHARLES A.—Age, 38 years. Enrolled, May 2, 1898, at Brooklyn, to serve two years; mustered in as captain, Co. K, May 13, 1898; as major, June 13, 1898; mustered out with regiment, October 27, 1898, at Brooklyn, N. Y.; commissioned captain, May 13, 1898, with rank from same date, original; major, May 28, 1898, with rank from same date, original.

ANGERER, WILLIAM F.—Age, 21 years. Enlisted, May 2, 1898, at Brooklyn, to serve two years; mustered in as private, Co. H, May 16, 1898; mustered out with company, October 27, 1898, at Brooklyn, N. Y.

ANGLUM, EDWARD.—Age, 20 years. Enlisted, May 2, 1898, at Brooklyn, to serve two years; mustered in as private, Co. A, May 13, 1898; mustered out with company, October 27, 1898, at Brooklyn, N. Y.

ARCHIMBAND, ANTHONY.—Age, 21 years. Enlisted, May 11, 1898, at Camp Black, to serve two years; mustered in as private, Co. I, May 16, 1898; mustered out with company, October 27, 1898, at Brooklyn, N. Y.

ARMSTRONG, ANDREW.—Age, 26 years. Enlisted, May 14, 1898, at Hempstead, to serve two years; mustered in as sergeant, Co. L, May 16, 1898; promoted first sergeant, June 27, 1898; mustered in as second lieutenant, Co. C, October 17, 1898; mustered out with company, October 27, 1898, at Brooklyn, N. Y.; commissioned second lieutenant, September 14, 1898, with rank from same date, vice Greer, discharged.

ARNOLD, CHARLES.—Age, 18 years. Enlisted, May 2, 1898, at Brooklyn, to serve two years; mustered in as private, Co. H, May 16, 1898; mustered out with company, October 27, 1898, at Brooklyn, N. Y.

ARNOLD, RICHARD J.—Age, — years. Enlisted, June 20, 1898, at Brooklyn, to serve two years; mustered in as private, Co. A, same date; mustered out with company, October 27, 1898, at Brooklyn, N. Y.

ASHENDEN, FRANCIS.—Age, 24 years. Enlisted, May 2, 1898, at Brooklyn, to serve two years; mustered in as private, Co. K, May 13, 1898; mustered out with company, October 27, 1898, at Brooklyn, N. Y.

ASPELIN, HJALMER.—Age, — years. Enlisted, June 20, 1898, at Brooklyn, to serve two years; mustered in as private, Co. G, same date; mustered out with company, October 27, 1898, at Brooklyn, N. Y.

ATWOOD, CHARLES M.—Age, 24 years. Enlisted, May 2, 1898, at Brooklyn, to serve two years; mustered in as private, Co. M, May 13, 1898; mustered out with company, October 27, 1898, at Brooklyn, N. Y.

AUERBACK, CLARENCE B.—Age, 18 years. Enlisted, May 2, 1898, at Hempstead, to serve two years; mustered in as private, Co. E, May 16, 1898; mustered out with company, October 27, 1898, at Brooklyn, N. Y.

AVERY, THOMAS HEAPE.—Age, — years. Enrolled, May 2, 1898, at Brooklyn, to serve two years; mustered in as captain, Co. C, May 16, 1898; mustered out with company, October 27, 1898, at Brooklyn, N. Y.; commissioned captain, May 16, 1898, with rank from same date, original.

AXTMAN, CHRISTOPHER J.—Age, 18 years. Enlisted, May 14, 1898, at Camp Black, to serve two years; mustered in as private, Co. H, May 16, 1898; mustered out with company, October 27, 1898, at Brooklyn, N. Y.

AYERS, WILLIAM B.—Age, 20 years. Enlisted, May 2, 1898, at Brooklyn, to serve two years; mustered in as private, Co. D, May 16, 1898; promoted corporal, August 1, 1898; mustered out with company, October 27, 1898, at Brooklyn, N. Y.

BAGNALL, WILLIAM A.—Age, 33 years. Enlisted, May 2, 1898, at Brooklyn, to serve two years; mustered in as private, Co. C, May 16, 1898; mustered out with company, October 27, 1898, at Brooklyn, N. Y.

BAKER, GEORGE J.—Age, 28 years. Enlisted, May 2, 1898, at Brooklyn, to serve two years; mustered in as private, Co. E, May 16, 1898; mustered out with company, October 27, 1898, at Brooklyn, N. Y.

BAKER, LOUIS W.—Age, 24 years. Enlisted, May 2, 1898, at Brooklyn, to serve two years; mustered in as corporal, Co. M, May 13, 1898; mustered out with company, October 27, 1898, at Brooklyn, N. Y.

BANNON, EDWARD.—Age, 22 years. Enlisted, May 2, 1898, at Brooklyn, to serve two years; mustered in as private, Co. L, May 16, 1898; mustered out with company, October 27, 1898, at Brooklyn, N. Y.

BANTA, WILLIAM C. J.—Age, 22 years. Enlisted, May 2, 1898, at Brooklyn, to serve two years; mustered in as private, Co. L, May 16, 1898; promoted corporal, June 28, 1898; mustered out with company, October 27, 1898, at Brooklyn, N. Y.

BARBER, EDWARD W.—Age, 25 years. Enlisted, May 2, 1898, at Brooklyn, to serve two years; mustered in as sergeant, Co. H, May 16, 1898; mustered out with company, October 27, 1898, at Brooklyn, N. Y.

BARDEN, MICHAEL.—Age, — years. Enlisted, June 27, 1898, at Brooklyn, to serve two years; mustered in as private, Co. C, same date; discharged, December 30, 1898.

BARDRAM, CARL.—Age, 21 years. Enlisted, May 2, 1898, at Brooklyn, to serve two years; mustered in as private, Co. G, May 13, 1898; mustered out with company, October 27, 1898, at Brooklyn, N. Y.

BARDRAM, OLAF.—Age, — years. Enlisted, July 1, 1898, at Brooklyn, to serve two years; mustered in as private, Co. G, same date; mustered out with company, October 27, 1898, at Brooklyn, N. Y.; also borne as Oluf P. Bardram.

BARLOW, JOSEPH RICHARD KENDRICK.—Age, 44 years. Enrolled, May 2, 1898, at Brooklyn, to serve two years; mustered in as captain, Co. I, May 16, 1898; discharged, September 5, 1898; commissioned captain, May 16, 1898, with rank from same date, original.

BARNES, JOHN J.—Age, — years. Enlisted, June 20, 1898, at Brooklyn, to serve two years; mustered in as private, Co. C, same date; discharged, October 18, 1898.

BARNES, WILLIAM P.—Age, 25 years. Enlisted, May 11, 1898, at Camp Black, to serve two years; mustered in as private, Co. M, May 15, 1898; mustered out with company, October 27, 1898, at Brooklyn, N. Y.

BARRETT, H. SIDNEY.—Age, 22 years. Enlisted, May 2, 1898, at Brooklyn, to serve two years; mustered in as private, Co. L, May 16, 1898; mustered out with company, October 27, 1898, at Brooklyn, N. Y.

BARTELS, CHARLES.—Age, 21 years. Enlisted, May 14, 1898, at Hempstead, to serve two years; mustered in as private, Co. D, May 16, 1898; mustered out with company, October 27, 1898, at Brooklyn, N. Y.

BARTH, THOMAS.—Age, 24 years. Enlisted, May 14, 1898, at Hempstead, to serve two years; mustered in as private, Co. E, May 16, 1898; mustered out with company, October 27, 1898, at Brooklyn, as Thomas J. Barth.

BARTO, CLARENCE M.—Age, 19 years. Enlisted, May 6, 1898, at Camp Black, to serve two years; mustered in as private, Co. L, May 16, 1898; mustered out with company, October 27, 1898, at Brooklyn, N. Y.

BATTERSBY, MICHAEL.—Age, 21 years. Enlisted, May 2, 1898, at Brooklyn, to serve two years; mustered in as private, Co. B, May 16, 1898; mustered out with company, October 27, 1898, at Brooklyn, N. Y.

BAYLEY, ANDREW E.—Age, 22 years. Enlisted, May 2, 1898, at Hempstead, to serve two years; mustered in as sergeant. Co. E, May 16, 1898; mustered out with company, October 27, 1898, at Brooklyn, N. Y.

BAYLIS, EDWARD E.—Age, — years. Enlisted, July 5, 1898, at Brooklyn, to serve two years; mustered in as private, Co. K, same date; mustered out with company, October 27, 1898, at Brooklyn, N. Y.

BEAL, JR., ROBERT.—Age, — years. Enlisted, June 22, 1898, at Brooklyn, to serve two years; mustered in as private, Co. E, June 23, 1898; mustered out, to date, October 27, 1898.

BEARDSLEY, EDWIN H.—Age, 34 years. Enlisted, May 2, 1898, at Brooklyn, to serve two years; mustered in as musician, Co. I, May 16, 1898; mustered out with company, October 27, 1898, at Brooklyn, N. Y.

BEATTY, FRANCIS.—Age, 28 years. Enlisted, May 11, 1898, at Camp Black, to serve two years; mustered in as private, Co. M, May 13, 1898; mustered out with company, October 27, 1898, at Brooklyn, N. Y.

BEATTY, JOSEPH BRYAN.—Age, 38 years. Enrolled, May 2, 1898, at Brooklyn, to serve two years; mustered in as second lientenant, Co. K, May 13,1898; as first lieutenant and battalion-adjutant, June 18, 1898; mustered out with regiment, October 27, 1898, at Brooklyn, N. Y.; commissioned second lieutenant, May 13, 1898, with rank from same date, original; first lieutenant and battalion-adjutant, May 28, 1898, with rank from same date, original

BECK, CONRAD C.—Age, — years. Enlisted, June 21, 1898, at Brooklyn, to serve two years; mustered in as private, Co. C, same date; mustered out with company, October 27, 1898, at Brooklyn, N. Y.

BEDNALL, ROBERT E.—Age, 24 years. Enlisted, May 2, 1898, at Brooklyn, to serve two years; mustered in as quartermaster-sergeant, Co. I, May 16, 1898; mustered out with company, October 27, 1898, at Brooklyn, N. Y.

BEER, WILLIAM.—Age, 21 years. Enlisted, May 2, 1898, at Brooklyn, to serve two years; mustered in as private, Co. A, May 13, 1898; transferred to Hospital Corps, United States Army, September 2, 1898.

BEHMAN, JOSEPH C.—Age, 19 years. Enlisted, May 2, 1898, at Brooklyn, to serve two years; mustered in as private, Co. C, May 16, 1898; mustered out with company, October 27, 1898, at Brooklyn, N. Y.

BEHMANN, FRED L.—Age, 24 years. Enlisted, May 2, 1898, at Brooklyn, to serve two years; mustered in as private, Co. L, May 16, 1898; mustered out with company, October 27, 1898, at Brooklyn, N. Y.

BEINERT, BENJAMIN.—Age, 21 years. Enlisted, May 13, 1898, at Camp Black, to serve two years; mustered in as private, Co. F, May 16, 1898; mustered out with company, October 27, 1898, at Brooklyn, N. Y.

BELFILS, EMIL C.—Age, 21 years. Enlisted, May 11, 1898, at Camp Black, to serve two years; mustered in as private, Co. M, May 13, 1898; mustered out with company, October 27, 1898, at Brooklyn, N. Y.

BELL, ERNST.—Age, 23 years. Enlisted, May 2, 1898, at Brooklyn, to serve two years; mustered in as private, Co. L, May 16, 1898; mustered out with company, October 27, 1898, at Brooklyn, N. Y.

BELL, HARRY J. P.—Age, 25 years. Enlisted, May 2, 1898, at Brooklyn, to serve two years; mustered in as regimental quartermaster-sergeant, May 16, 1898; mustered out with regiment, October 27, 1898, at Brooklyn, N. Y.

BELL, HARRY VAN COTT.—Age, 37 years. Enrolled, May 2, 1898, at Brooklyn, to serve two years; mustered in as first lieutenant, Co. F, May 16, 1898; commanding Co. L, from June 11, 1898, to July 22, 1898, when returned to Co. F; discharged, July 26, 1898; commissioned first lieutenant, May 16, 1898, with rank from same date, original.

BELL, ROBERT G.—Age, 19 years. Enlisted, May 2, 1898, at Brooklyn, to serve two years; mustered in as private, Co. B, May 16, 1898; mustered out with company, October 27, 1898, at Brooklyn, N. Y.

BENNETT, ALONZO L.—Age, — years. Enlisted, June 24, 1898, at Brooklyn, to serve two years; mustered in as private, Co. D, same date; mustered out with company, October 27, 1898, at Brooklyn, N. Y.

BENNETT, FRANK R.—Age, 22 years. Enlisted, May 2, 1898, at Brooklyn, to serve two years; mustered in as private, Co. G, May 13, 1898; mustered out with company, October 27, 1898, at Brooklyn, N. Y.

BENSON, JOHN.—Age, 27 years. Enlisted, May 2, 1898, at Brooklyn, to serve two years; mustered in as private, Co. G, May 13, 1898; mustered out with company, October 27, 1898, at Brooklyn, N. Y.

BENSON, LOUIS.—Age, — years. Enlisted, June 21, 1898, at Brooklyn, to serve two years; mustered in as private, Co. M, same date; promoted corporal, September 10, 1898; mustered out with company, October 27, 1898, at Brooklyn, N. Y., as Louis A. Benson.

BERG, ALBERT.—Age, — years. Enlisted, June 21, 1898, at Brooklyn, to serve two years; mustered in as private, Co. C, same date; mustered out with company, October 27, 1898, at Brooklyn, N. Y.

BERG, EMANUEL.—Age, 24 years. Enlisted, May 2, 1898, at Brooklyn, to serve two years; mustered in as private, Co. G, May 13, 1898; mustered out with company, October 27, 1898, at Brooklyn, N. Y.

BERGEN, DANIEL C.—Age, 23 years. Enlisted, May 2, 1898, at Brooklyn, to serve two years; mustered in as sergeant, Co. I, May 16, 1898; mustered out with company, October 27, 1898, at Brooklyn, N. Y.

BERGEN, JOHN JOSEPH.—Age, 31 years. Enrolled, May 2, 1898, at Brooklyn, to serve two years; mustered in as first lieutenant, Co. I, May 16, 1898; discharged, September 3, 1898; commissioned first lieutenant, May 16, 1898, with rank from same date, original.

BERGMAN, JOHN E.—Age, 21 years. Enlisted, May 2, 1898, at Brooklyn, to serve two years; mustered in as private, Co. G, May 13, 1898; mustered out with company, October 27, 1898, at Brooklyn, N. Y.

BERRIEN, FRANK M.—Age, 23 years. Enlisted, May 12, 1898, at Hempstead, to serve two years; mustered in as private, Co. K, May 13, 1898; mustered out with company, October 27, 1898, at Brooklyn, N.Y.

BERTHOFF, CLARENCE S.—Age, 21 years. Enlisted, May 11, 1898, at Hempstead, to serve two years; mustered in as private, Co. A, May 13, 1898; mustered out, to date, October 27, 1898.

BESTERMANN, WILLIAM J.—Age, 22 years. Enlisted, May 7, 1898, at Hempstead, to serve two years; mustered in as private, Co. A, May 13, 1898; mustered out with company, October 27, 1898, at Brooklyn, N. Y.

BEYER, OTTO L.—Age, 27 years. Enlisted, May 2, 1898, at Brooklyn, to serve two years; mustered in as musician, Co. K, May 13. 1898; promoted principal musician, May 25, 1898; mustered out with regiment, October 27, 1898, at Brooklyn, N. Y.

BIANCHI, ANGELO.—Age, 27 years. Enlisted, May 2, 1898, at Brooklyn, to serve two years; mustered in as private, Co. A, May 13, 1898; promoted corporal, July 20, 1898; mustered out with company, October 27, 1898, at Brooklyn, N. Y.

BIFFI, ALFRED.—Age, 18 years. Enlisted, May 2, 1898, at Brooklyn, to serve two years; mustered in as private, Co. B, May 16, 1898; mustered out with company, October 27, 1898, at Brooklyn, N. Y.

BIFFI, CHARLES R.—Age, 22 years. Enlisted, May 2, 1898, at Brooklyn, to serve two years; mustered in as private, Co. B, May 16, 1898; mustered out with company, October 27, 1898, at Brooklyn, N. Y.

BILLINGS, EDWARD C.—Age, 25 years. Enlisted, May 2, 1898, at Brooklyn, to serve two years; mustered in as private, Co. C, May 16, 1898; mustered out with company, October 27, 1898, at Brooklyn, N. Y.

BILLSTROM, JOHN.—Age, — years. Enlisted, June 23, 1898, at Brooklyn, to serve two years; mustered in as private, Co. G, same date; mustered out with company, October 27, 1898, at Brooklyn, N. Y.

BIRCH, FORBES L.—Age, — years. Enlisted, June 28, 1898, at Brooklyn, to serve two years; mustered in as private, Co. M, same date; mustered out with company, October 27, 1898, at Brooklyn, N. Y.

BLACKLEDGE, OLIVER B.—Age, 21 years. Enlisted, May 2, 1898, at Brooklyn, to serve two years; mustered in as private, Co. C, May 16, 1898; mustered out, to date, October 27, 1898.

BLACKWOOD, JOHN.—Age, — years. Enlisted, June 26, 1898, at Brooklyn, to serve two years; mustered in as private. Co. L, same date; mustered out with company, October 27, 1898, at Brooklyn, N. Y.

BLANCH, WILLIAM W.—Age, — years. Enlisted, June 21, 1898, at Brooklyn, to serve two years; mustered in as private, Co. C, same date; mustered out with company, October 27, 1898, at Brooklyn, N. Y.

BLASE, HENRY P.—Age, 21 years. Enlisted, May 10, 1898, at Hempstead, to serve two years; mustered in as private, Co. K, May 13, 1898; mustered out with company, October 27, 1898, at Brooklyn, N. Y.

BLIGH, THOMAS G.—Age, 18 years. Enlisted, May 2, 1898, at Brooklyn, to serve two years; mustered in as private, Co. B, May 16, 1898; mustered out with company, October 27, 1898, at Brooklyn, N. Y.

BLOMBERG, GUSTAF A.—Age, 22 years. Enlisted, May 2, 1898, at Brooklyn, to serve two years; mustered in as private, Co. G, May 13, 1898; promoted corporal, July 12, 1898; mustered out with company, October 27, 1898, at Brooklyn, N. Y.

BLOMSTEDT, OTTO.—Age, — years. Enlisted, June 20, 1898, at Brooklyn, to serve two years; mustered in as private, Co. G, same date; mustered out with company, October 27, 1898, at Brooklyn, N. Y.

BLOOM, CHARLES.—Age, 21 years. Enlisted, May 2, 1898, at Brooklyn, to serve two years; mustered in as private, Co. G, May 13, 1898; mustered out with company, October 27, 1898, at Brooklyn, N. Y.

BLOOM, THEODOR.—Age, 21 years. Enlisted, May 2, 1898, at Brooklyn, to serve two years; mustered in as private, Co. G, May 13, 1898; mustered out with company, October 27, 1898 at Brooklyn, N. Y.

BLUME, GUSTAF A.—Age, — years. Enlisted, June 29, 1898, at Brooklyn, to serve two years; mustered in as private, Co. G, same date; mustered out with company, October 27, 1898, at Brooklyn, N. Y.

BODEN, JOSEPH.—Age, 21 years. Enlisted, May 2, 1898, at Brooklyn, to serve two years; mustered in as private, Co. B, May 16, 1898; mustered out with company, October 27, 1898, at Brooklyn, N. Y.

BODEN, WILLIAM C.—Age, 22 years. Enlisted, May 13, 1898, at Hempstead, to serve two years; mustered in as private, Co. B, May 16, 1898; mustered out with company, October 27, 1898, at Brooklyn, N. Y.

BODINE, ELMER E.—Age, 26 years. Enlisted, May 2, 1898, at Hempstead, to serve two years; mustered in as private, Co. E, May 16, 1898; mustered out with company, October 27, 1898, at Brooklyn, N. Y.

BOETZEL, CHARLES F.—Age, — years. Enlisted, June 21, 1898, at Brooklyn, to serve two years; mustered in as private, Co. I, same date; mustered out with company, October 27, 1898, at Brooklyn, N. Y.

BOGART, ARTHUR H.—Age, 29 years. Enrolled, May 2, 1898, at Brooklyn, to serve two years; mustered in as assistant surgeon, May 4, 1898; as surgeon, September 7, 1898; mustered out, November 28, 1898, at New York city; commissioned captain and assistant surgeon, May 4, 1898, with rank from same date, original; major and surgeon, September 7, 1898, with rank from same date, vice Macumber, promoted brigade surgeon.

BOGART, OVINGTON B.—Age, 24 years. Enrolled, May 2, 1898, at Brooklyn, to serve two years; mustered in as second lieutenant, Co. M, May 13, 1898; as first lieutenant, Co. L. October 11, 1898; mustered out with company, October 27, 1898, at Brooklyn, N. Y.; commissioned second lieutenant, May 13, 1898, with rank from same date, original; first lieutenant, September 14, 1898, with rank from same date, vice Adams, promoted captain.

BOHN, ARTHUR T.—Age, 22 years. Enlisted, May 2, 1898, at Brooklyn, to serve two years; mustered in as sergeant, Co. H, May 16, 1898; mustered out with company, October 27, 1898, at Brooklyn, N. Y.

BOHN, WILLIAM J.—Age, 28 years. Enlisted, May 2, 1898, at Brooklyn, to serve two years; mustered in as private, Co. H, May 16, 1898; transferred to Hospital Corps, June 12, 1898.

BOLLE, HARRY W.—Age, 25 years. Enlisted, May 2, 1898, at Brooklyn, to serve two years; mustered in as private, Co. C, May 16, 1898; mustered out with company, October 27, 1898, at Brooklyn, N. Y.

BOLLING, ERIC.—Age, 28 years. Enlisted, May 2, 1898, at Brooklyn, to serve two years; mustered in as private, Co. G, May 13, 1898; mustered out with company, October 27, 1898, at Brooklyn, N. Y.

BOND, RUBEN B.—Age, 22 years. Enlisted, May 2, 1898, at Brooklyn, to serve two years; mustered in as private, Co. H, May 16, 1898; mustered out with company, October 27, 1898, at Brooklyn, N. Y.

BONING, BERNARD.—Age, 22 years. Enlisted, May 2, 1898, at Brooklyn, to serve two years; mustered in as private, Co. I, May 16, 1898; mustered out with company, October 27, 1898, at Brooklyn, N. Y.

BORSMANN, ROBERT W.—Age, 29 years. Enlisted, May 11, 1898, at Hempstead, to serve two years; mustered in as private, Co. A, May 13, 1898; mustered out with company, October 27, 1898, at Brooklyn, N. Y.

BORTOW, ALFRED.—Age, 22 years. Enlisted, May 2, 1898, at Brooklyn, to serve two years; mustered in as hospital steward, May 16, 1898; died of typhoid fever, September 18, 1898, at Anniston, Ala.

BOUTON, GEORGE L.—Age, 23 years. Enlisted, May 7, 1898, at Hempstead, to serve two years; mustered in as private, Co. A, May 13, 1898; mustered out with company, October 27, 1898, at Brooklyn, N. Y.

BOWMAN, WILLIAM C.—Age, 21 years. Enlisted, May 2, 1898, at Brooklyn, to serve two years; mustered in as corporal, Co. B, May 16, 1898; mustered out with company, October 27, 1898, at Brooklyn, N. Y.

BOWNE, HARRY.—Age, — years. Enlisted, June 27, 1898, at Brooklyn, to serve two years; mustered in as private, Co. H, same date; mustered out with company, October 27, 1898, at Brooklyn, N. Y.

BOWRA, JAMES E.—Age, 25 years. Enlisted, May 12, 1898, at Hempstead, to serve two years; mustered in as private, Co. A, May 13, 1898; mustered out with company, October 27, 1898, at Brooklyn, N. Y.

BOYCE, JOHN PETER.—Age, 20 years. Enlisted, May 2, 1898, at Brooklyn, to serve two years; mustered in as private, Co. A, May 13, 1898; mustered out with company, October 27, 1898, at Brooklyn, N. Y.

BOYER, HARRY B.—Age, — years. Enlisted, June 29, 1898, at Brooklyn, to serve two years; mustered in as private, Co. F, same date; discharged for disability, August 23, 1898.

BOYLE, JOHN.—Age, — years. Enlisted, June 23, 1898, at Brooklyn, to serve two years; mustered in as private, Co. C, same date; mustered out with company, October 27, 1898, at Brooklyn, N. Y.

BOYLE, PHILIP.—Age, — years. Enlisted, June 29, 1898, at Brooklyn, to serve two years; mustered in as private, Co. I, same date; mustered out with company, October 27, 1898, at Brooklyn, N. Y.

BOYLE, RICHARD.—Age, 21 years. Enlisted, May 2, 1898, at Camp Black, to serve two years; mustered in as private, Co. F, May 16, 1898; mustered out with company, October 27, 1898, at Brooklyn, N. Y.

BRANWHITE, CLARENCE K.—Age, — years. Enlisted, June 30, 1898, at Brooklyn, to serve two years; mustered in as private, Co. I, same date; mustered out with company, October 27, 1898, at Brooklyn, N. Y.

BRATTMULLER, HENRY.—Age, 32 years. Enlisted, May 2, 1898, at Brooklyn, to serve two years; mustered in as private, Co. B, May 16, 1898; mustered out with company, October 27, 1898, at Brooklyn, N. Y.

BREMAN, NEIL.—Age, 22 years. Enlisted, May 12, 1898, at Brooklyn, to serve two years; mustered in as private, Co. D, May 16, 1898; mustered out with company, October 27, 1898, at Brooklyn, N. Y.

BRENNAN, WILLIAM.—Age, — years. Enlisted, July 5, 1898, at Brooklyn, to serve two years; mustered in as private, Co M, same date; mustered out with company, October 27, 1898, at Brooklyn, N. Y.

BRIDGES, CHARLES W.—Age, 41 years. Enrolled, May 3, 1898, at Hempstead, to serve two years; mustered in as first lieutenant, Co. K, May 13, 1898; discharged, September 3, 1898; commissioned first lieutenant, May 13, 1898, with rank from same date, original.

BROSNAN, EDWIN D.—Age, 24 years. Enlisted, May 2, 1898, at Brooklyn, to serve two years; mustered in as corporal, Co. C, May 16, 1898; mustered out with company, October 27, 1898, at Brooklyn, N. Y.

BROWER, GEORGE F.—Age, 25 years. Enlisted, May 2, 1898, at Brooklyn, to serve two years; mustered in as private, Co. I, May 16, 1898; mustered out with company, October 27, 1898, at Brooklyn, N. Y.

BROWN, EMANUEL.—Age, 23 years. Enlisted, May 2, 1898, at Brooklyn, to serve two years; mustered in as private, Co. A, May 13, 1898; died of typhoid fever, September 28, 1898, at hospital at Anniston, Ala.

BROWN, FRED B.—Age, 20 years. Enlisted, May 2, 1898, at Brooklyn, to serve two years; mustered in as private, Co. F, May 16, 1898; promoted corporal, July 14, 1898; mustered out with company, October 27, 1898, at Brooklyn, N. Y.

BROWN, JOHN.—Age, — years. Enlisted, June 29, 1898, at Brooklyn, to serve two years; mustered in as private, Co. L, same date; mustered out with company, October 27, 1898, at Brooklyn, N. Y.

BROWN, JOSEPH F.—Age, 28 years. Enlisted, May 2, 1898, at Hempstead, to serve two years; mustered in as private, Co. K, June 13, 1898; mustered out with company, October 27, 1898, at Brooklyn, N. Y.

BROWN, JR., THOMAS J.—Age, 24 years. Enlisted, May 2, 1898, at Brooklyn, to serve two years; mustered in as sergeant, Co. D, May 16, 1898; as second lieutenant, Co. H, October 10, 1898; mustered out with company, October 27, 1898, at Brooklyn, N. Y.; commissioned second lieutenant, September 14, 1898, with rank from same date, vice Moore, promoted first lieutenant.

BROWN, WILLIAM A.—Age, — years. Enlisted, June 20, 1898, at Brooklyn, to serve two years; mustered in as private, Co. H, same date; mustered out with company, October 27, 1898, at Brooklyn, N. Y.

BROWN, WILLIAM J.—Age, 24 years. Enlisted, May 2, 1898, at Brooklyn, to serve two years; mustered in as private, Co. K, May 13, 1898; mustered out with company, October 27, 1898, at Brooklyn, N. Y.

BROWNE, VALENTINE J.—Age, 21 years. Enlisted, May 2, 1898, at Brooklyn, to serve two years; mustered in as private, Co. L, May 16, 1898; mustered out, to date, October 27, 1898.

BROWNE, VALENTINE S.—Age, 25 years. Enlisted, May 2, 1898, at Brooklyn, to serve two years; mustered in as private, Co. L, May 16, 1898; mustered out with company, October 27, 1898, at Brooklyn, N. Y.

BROWNE, WILLIAM J.—Age, 18 years. Enlisted, May 13, 1898, at Hempstead, to serve two years; mustered in as private, Co. L, May 16, 1898; transferred to Co. D, May 28, 1898; mustered out with company, October 27, 1898, at Brooklyn, N. Y.

BRUCKMAN, GUSTAVE THEODORE.—Age, 29 years. Enrolled, May 9, 1898, at Hempstead, to serve two years; mustered in as second lieutenant, Co. A, May 13, 1898; as first lieutenant, Co. M, June 14, 1898; mustered out, December 9, 1898, to date, October 27, 1898, at New York city; commissioned second lieutenant, May 13, 1898, with rank from same date, original; first lieutenant, May 28, 1898, with rank from same date, vice Henry, promoted captain.

BUCHANAN, WILLIAM H.—Age, — years. Enlisted, July 5, 1898, at Brooklyn, to serve two years; mustered in as private, Co. L, same date; mustered out with company, October 27, 1898, at Brooklyn, N. Y.

BUGGY, JOHN.—Age, 24 years. Enlisted, May 12, 1898, at Camp Black, to serve two years; mustered in as private, Co. F, May 16, 1898; mustered out with company, October 27, 1898, at Brooklyn, N. Y.

BUNDE, CHARLES L.—Age, — years.   Enlisted, July 7, 1898, at Brooklyn, to serve two years; mustered in as private, Co. E, same date; mustered out with company, October 27, 1898, at Brooklyn, N. Y.

BURCKERSRODA, LOUIS W.—Age, 32 years. Enlisted, May 2, 1898, at Brooklyn, to serve two years; mustered in as sergeant, Co. C, May 16, 1898; mustered out with company, October 27, 1898, at Brooklyn, N. Y.

BURGER, JUSTICE E. G.—Age, — years.   Enlisted, June 20, 1898, at Brooklyn, to serve two years; mustered in as private, Co. I, same date; mustered out with company, October 27, 1898, at Brooklyn, N. Y.

BURKE, FRANK M.—Age, 21 years.   Enlisted, May 13, 1898, at Hempstead, to serve two years; mustered in as private, Co. E, May 16, 1898; mustered out with company, October 27, 1898, at Brooklyn, N. Y.

BURKE, GEORGE T.—Age, — years. Enlisted, June 18, 1898, at Brooklyn, to serve two years; mustered in as private, Co. D, same date; mustered out with company, October 27, 1898, at Brooklyn, N. Y.

BURKE, PATRICK F.—Age, 28 years.   Enlisted, May 9, 1898, at Brooklyn, to serve two years; mustered in as private, Co. D, May 16, 1898; mustered out with company, October 27, 1898, at Brooklyn, N. Y.

BURKE, WALTER M.—Age, 18 years.   Enlisted, May 14, 1898, at Camp Black, to serve two years; mustered in as private, Co. H, May 16, 1898; mustered out with company, October 27, 1898, at Brooklyn, N. Y.

BURKE, JR., WILLIAM J.—Age, 23 years.   Enlisted, May 13, 1898, at Hempstead, to serve two years; mustered in as private, Co. E, May 16, 1898; mustered out with company, October 27, 1898, at Brooklyn, N. Y.

BURNS, JOHN F.—Age, 37 years. Enlisted, May 2, 1898, at Hempstead, to serve two years; mustered in as quartermaster-sergeant, Co. E, May 16, 1898; returned to ranks, June 15, 1898; mustered out with company, October 27, 1898, at Brooklyn, N. Y.

BURNS, JOHN P.—Age, 23 years. Enlisted, May 2, 1898, at
Brooklyn, to serve two years; mustered in as private, Co. K
May 13, 1898; mustered out with company, October 27, 1898,
at Brooklyn, N. Y.

BURRILL, ALBERT E.—Age, 21 years. Enlisted, May 2, 1898,
at Brooklyn, to serve two years; mustered in as private, Co. C.
May 16, 1898; promoted corporal, August 1, 1898; mustered out
with company, October 27, 1898, at Brooklyn, N. Y.

BUSHEY, WILLIAM F.—Age, — years. Enlisted, June 24,
1898, at Brooklyn, to serve two years; mustered in as private,
Co. D, same date; mustered out with company, October 27,
1898, at Brooklyn, N. Y.

BUSS, HANS.—Age, 21 years. Enlisted, May 14, 1898, at Camp
Black, to serve two years; mustered in as private, Co. H, May
16, 1898; mustered out with company, October 27' 1898, at
Brooklyn, N. Y.

BUTLER, EDMUND J.—Age, 35 years. Enlisted, May 13, 1898,
at Hempstead, to serve two years; mustered in as private, Co.
E, May 16, 1898; mustered out with company, October 27, 1898,
at Brooklyn, N. Y.

BUTLER, FREDERICK.—Age, 27 years. Enlisted, May 2, 1898,
at Brooklyn, to serve two years; mustered in as private, Co. B,
May 16, 1898; mustered out, to date, October 27, 1898.

BYE, HALMAR.—Age, 29 years. Enlisted, May 2, 1898, at
Brooklyn, to serve two years; mustered in as private, Co. G,
May 13, 1898; mustered out with company, October 27, 1898,
at Brooklyn, N. Y.

BYRNE, JAMES.—Age, 23 years. Enlisted, May 11, 1898, at
Camp Black, to serve two years; mustered in as private, Co. M,
May 13, 1898; mustered out with company, October 27, 1898,
at Brooklyn, N. Y.

BYRNE, JOHN J.—Age, 25 years. Enlisted, May 2, 1898, at
Brooklyn, to serve two years; mustered in as wagoner, Co. B,
May 16, 1898; mustered out with company, October 27, 1898,
at Brooklyn, N. Y.

BYRON, PATRICK J.—Age, — years. Enlisted, July 5, 1898, at Brooklyn, to serve two years; mustered in as private, Co. A, same date; mustered out with company, October 27, 1898, at Brooklyn, N. Y.

CAIN, JR., JOHN H.—Age, 23 years. Enlisted, May 14, 1898, at Camp Black, to serve two years; mustered in as private, Co. I, same date; mustered out with company, October 27, 1898, at Brooklyn, N. Y.

CAMPBELL, FREDERICK.—Age, — years. Enlisted, June 30, 1898, at Brooklyn, to serve two years; mustered in as private, Co. F, same date; mustered out with company, October 27, 1898, at Brooklyn, N. Y.

CAMPBELL, JOHN J.—Age, 22 years. Enlisted, May 2, 1898, at Brooklyn, to serve two years; mustered in as private, Co. A, May 13, 1898; transferred to Hospital Corps, June 14, 1898; returned to company, September 13, 1898; mustered out with company, October 27, 1898, at Brooklyn, N. Y.

CAMPBELL, WILLIAM A.—Age, — years. Enlisted, June 20, 1898, at Brooklyn, to serve two years; mustered in as private, Co. D, same date; mustered out with company, October 27, 1898, at Brooklyn, N. Y.

CANN, JR., BALDWIN.—Age, 26 years. Enlisted, May 13, 1898, at Hempstead, to serve two years; mustered in as private, Co. E, May 16, 1898; mustered out with company, October 27, 1898, at Brooklyn, N. Y.

CANN, JOHN H.—Age, 42 years. Enlisted, May 12, 1898, at Camp Black, to serve two years; mustered in as private, Co. H, May 16, 1898; appointed wagoner, May 31, 1898; mustered out with company, October 27, 1898, at Brooklyn, N. Y.

CANNER, GEORGE W.—Age, 26 years. Enlisted, May 2, 1898, at Brooklyn, to serve two years; mustered in as corporal, Co. B, May 16, 1898; mustered out with company, October 27, 1898, at Brooklyn, N. Y.

CANNING, BERNARD.—Age, 24 years. Enlisted, May 2, 1898, at Brooklyn, to serve two years; mustered in as private, Co. F, May 16, 1898; appointed wagoner, July 27, 1898; mustered out with company, October 27, 1898, at Brooklyn, N. Y.

CAPSTICKS, GEORGE T.—Age, 40 years. Enlisted, May 2, 1898, at Brooklyn, to serve two years; mustered in as quarter-master-sergeant, Co. C, May 16, 1898; mustered out with company, October 27, 1898, at Brooklyn, N. Y.

CARLETON, EDGAR A.—Age, 25 years. Enlisted, May 2, 1898, at Brooklyn, to serve two years; mustered in as private, Co. B, May 16, 1898; mustered out with company, October 27, 1898, at Brooklyn, N. Y.

CARLSON, GEORGE E.—Age, 21 years. Enlisted, May 2, 1898, at Brooklyn, to serve two years; mustered in as private, Co. G, May 13, 1898; mustered out with company, October 27, 1898, at Brooklyn, N. Y.

CARLSON, GEORGE EDWARD.—Age, 22 years. Enlisted, May 2, 1898, at Brooklyn, to serve two years; mustered in as private, Co. A, May 13, 1898; transferred to Hospital Corps, June 14, 1898; returned to company, October 17, 1898; mustered out with company, October 27, 1898, at Brooklyn, N. Y.

CARLSON, OSCAR.—Age, 21 years. Enlisted, May 2, 1898, at Brooklyn, to serve two years; mustered in as private, Co. G, May 13, 1898; mustered out with company, October 27, 1898, at Brooklyn, N. Y.

CARLSON, VICTOR.—Age, — years. Enlisted, June 30, 1898, at Brooklyn, to serve two years; mustered in as private, Co. F, same date; mustered out with company, October 27, 1898, at Brooklyn, N. Y.

CARNEY, JOHN F.—Age, 28 years. Enlisted, May 2, 1898, at Brooklyn, to serve two years; mustered in as private, Co. B, May 16, 1898; discharged, September 7, 1898.

CARPENTER, HOWARD F.—Age, 24 years. Enlisted, May 12, 1898, at Hempstead, to serve two years; mustered in as private, Co. K, May 13, 1898; mustered out with company, October 27, 1898, at Brooklyn, N. Y.

CARPENTER, THOMAS.—Age, — years. Enlisted, June 27, 1898, at Brooklyn, to serve two years; mustered in as private, Co. C, same date; mustered out with company, October 27, 1898, at Brooklyn, N. Y.

CARROLL, GEORGE A.—Age, 24 years. Enlisted, May 2, 1898, at Brooklyn, to serve two years; mustered in as private, Co. I, May 16, 1898; mustered out with company, October 27, 1898, at Brooklyn, N. Y.

CARROLL, JOHN FRANCIS.—Age, 33 years. Enrolled, May 2, 1898, at Brooklyn, to serve two years; mustered in as captain, Co. F, May 16, 1898; mustered out, December 6, 1898, to date, October 27, 1898, at New York city; commissioned captain, May 16, 1898, with rank from same date, original.

CASE, FREDERICK H.—Age, 31 years. Enlisted, May 2, 1898, at Brooklyn, to serve two years; mustered in as private, Co. B, May 16, 1898; promoted corporal, July 27, 1898; mustered out with company, October 27, 1898, at Brooklyn,·N. Y.

CASSIDY, ARTHUR H.—Age, 25 years. Enlisted, May 13, 1898, at Camp Black, to serve two years; mustered in as private, Co. F, May 16, 1898; mustered out with company, October 27, 1898, at Brooklyn, N. Y.

CASSIDY, CHARLES.—Age, — years. Enlisted, June 24, 1898, at Brooklyn, to serve two years; mustered in as private, Co. I, same date; mustered out with company, October 27, 1898, at Brooklyn, N. Y.

CASSIDY, JAMES.—Age, — years. Enlisted, June 22, 1898, at Brooklyn, to serve two years; mustered in as private, Co. I, same date; mustered out with company, October 27, 1898, at Brooklyn, N. Y.

CASSIDY, JOHN.—Age, — years. Enlisted, June 30, 1898, at Brooklyn, to serve two years; mustered in as private, Co. B, same date; mustered out with company, October 27, 1898, at Brooklyn, N. Y.

CASSIDY, WILLIAM.—Age, 25 years. Enlisted, May 2, 1898, at Brooklyn, to serve two years; mustered in as artificer, Co. I, May 16, 1898; mustered out with company, October 27, 1898, at Brooklyn, N. Y.

CASTRONI, JOSEPH M.—Age, 39 years. Enlisted, May 11, 1898, at Camp Black, to serve two years; mustered in as private, Co. M, May 13, 1898; promoted corporal, July 28, 1898; mustered out with company, October 27, 1898, at Brooklyn, N. Y.

CAVANAGH, FRANK P.—Age, — years.   Enlisted, June 23,
1898, at Brooklyn, to serve two years; mustered in as private,
Co. E, same date; mustered out with company, October 27,
1898, at Brooklyn, N. Y.

CAVANAGH, HARRY.—Age, — years.   Enlisted, June 27, 1898,
at Brooklyn, to serve two years; mustered in as private, Co.
E, same date; mustered out with company, October 27, 1898,
at Brooklyn, N. Y.

CHAPPELL, EDWARD.—Age, 26 years.   Enlisted, May 9, 1898,
at Brooklyn, to serve two years; mustered in as private, Co.
C, May 16, 1898; mustered out with company, October 27, 1898,
at Brooklyn, N. Y.

CHATTERTON, THOMAS.—Age, — years.   Enlisted, June 25,
1898, at Brooklyn, to serve two years; mustered in as private,
Co. I, same date; mustered out with company, October 27, 1898,
at Brooklyn, N. Y.

CHERBUCK, GEORGE B.—Age, — years.   Enlisted, July 6,
1898, at Brooklyn, to serve two years; mustered in as private,
Co. L, same date; promoted corporal, July 19, 1898; mustered
out with company, October 27, 1898, at Brooklyn, N. Y.

CHEVALIER, ANDREA.—Age, 34 years.   Enlisted, May 11,
1898, at Camp Black, to serve two years; mustered in as private, Co. M, May 13, 1898; appointed cook, July 29, 1898; mustered out with company, October 27, 1898, at Brooklyn, N. Y.

CHILDS, MAYNARD.—Age, 29 years.   Enlisted, May 2, 1898,
at Brooklyn, to serve two years; mustered in as private, Co.
C, May 16, 1898; mustered out with company, October 27, 1898,
at Brooklyn, N. Y.

CHRISTIE, HUGH A.—Age, 26 years.   Enlisted, May 2, 1898,
at Brooklyn, to serve two years; mustered in as private, Co.
A, May 13, 1898; mustered out with company, October 27, 1898,
at Brooklyn, N. Y.

CHRISTIE, WILLIAM O.—Age, 36 years.   Enlisted, May 11,
1898, at Camp Black, to serve two years; mustered in as private, Co. M, May 13, 1898; promoted corporal, July 20, 1898;
sergeant, September 8, 1898; mustered out with company,
October 27, 1898, at Brooklyn, N. Y.

CHRISTMANN, NICHOLAS.—Age, 22 years. Enlisted, May 2, 1898, at Brooklyn, to serve two years; mustered in as private, Co. H, May 16, 1898; appointed musician, June 19, 1898; mustered out with company, October 27, 1898, at Brooklyn, N. Y.

CLANCY, CHARLES.—Age, 21 years. Enlisted, May 2, 1898, at Brooklyn, to serve two years; mustered in as private, Co. L, May 16, 1898; mustered out with company, October 27, 1898, at Brooklyn, N.Y.

CLARENDON, GEORGE T.—Age, — years. Enlisted, June 30, 1898, at Brooklyn, to serve two years; mustered in as private, Co. I, same date; mustered out with company, October 27, 1898, at Brooklyn, N. Y.

CLARK, EDWARD P.—Age, 27 years. Enlisted, May 2, 1898, at Brooklyn, to serve two years; mustered in as private, Co. A, May 13, 1898; died of typhoid fever, July 5, 1898, in First Division Hospital, Third Army Corps, Chickamauga, Ga.

CLARK, JOHN.—Age, 24 years. Enlisted, May 13, 1898, at Camp Black, to serve two years; mustered in as private, Co. F, May 16, 1898; mustered out with company, October 27, 1898, at Brooklyn, N. Y.

CLARKE, EDWARD J.—Age, 21 years. Enlisted, May 2, 1898, at Brooklyn, to serve two years; mustered in as private, Co. M, May 13, 1898; promoted corporal, June 15, 1898; mustered out, to date, October 27, 1898.

CLAUSEN, CLAUS.—Age, 24 years. Enlisted, May 2, 1898, at Brooklyn, to serve two years; mustered in as private, Co. G, May 13, 1898; mustered out with company, October 27, 1898, at Brooklyn, N. Y.

CLEMENTS, ALBERT.—Age, 23 years. Enlisted, May 2, 1898, at Brooklyn, to serve two years; mustered in as private, Co. A, May 14, 1898; mustered out with company, October 27, 1898, at Brooklyn, N. Y.

CLEMENTS, FRANK G.—Age, 25 years. Enlisted, May 2, 1898, at Brooklyn, to serve two years; mustered in as wagoner, Co. D, May 16, 1898; mustered out with company, October 27, 1898. at Brooklyn, N. Y.

CLOSE, ARTHER.—Age, 36 years. Enlisted, May 13, 1898, at Hempstead, to serve two years; mustered in as private, Co. E, May 16, 1898; mustered out with company, October 27, 1898, at Brooklyn, N. Y.

CLOWES, SAMUEL V.—Age, 26 years. Enlisted, May 16, 1898, at Camp Black, to serve two years; mustered in as private, Co. C, same date; mustered out with company, October 27, 1898, at Brooklyn, N. Y.

COLE, GEORGE E.—Age, — years. Enlisted, June 18, 1898, at Brooklyn, to serve two years; mustered in as private, Co. A, same date; mustered out with company, October 27, 1898, at Brooklyn, N. Y.

COLEMAN, JOSEPH A.—Age, 24 years. Enlisted, May 2, 1898, at Brooklyn, to serve two years; mustered in as corporal, Co. I, May 16, 1898; returned to ranks, July 20, 1898; mustered out with company, October 27, 1898, at Brooklyn, N. Y.

COLEMAN, THOMAS A.—Age, 23 years. Enlisted, May 2, 1898, at Brooklyn, to serve two years; mustered in as private, Co. K, May 13, 1898; mustered out with company, October 27, 1898, at Brooklyn, N. Y., as Thomas Coleman.

COLEMAN, THOMAS F. J.—Age, 25 years. Enlisted, May 2, 1898, at Brooklyn, to serve two years; mustered in as private, Co. B, May 16, 1898; transferred to Hospital Corps, June 14, 1898; returned to company, no date; mustered out with company, October 27, 1898, at Brooklyn, N. Y.

COLLINS, CHARLES A.—Age, 38 years. Enlisted, May 2, 1898, at Brooklyn, to serve two years; mustered in as corporal, Co. H, May 16, 1898; mustered out with company, October 27, 1898, at Brooklyn, N. Y.

COLLINS, HERBERT E.—Age, 24 years. Enlisted, May 2, 1898, at Brooklyn, to serve two years; mustered in as private, Co. K, May 13, 1898; mustered out with company, October 27, 1898, at Brooklyn, N. Y.

COLLINS, JOHN F.—Age, 18 years. Enlisted, May 2, 1898, at Brooklyn, to serve two years; mustered in as private, Co. D, May 16, 1898; mustered out, to date, October 27, 1898.

COLLUM, THOMAS F.—Age, 26 years. Enlisted, May 11, 1898, at Camp Black, to serve two years; mustered in as private, Co. M, May 13, 1898; mustered out with company, October 27, 1898, at Brooklyn, N. Y.

CONDON, RICHARD J.—Age, — years. Enlisted, June 21, 1898, at Brooklyn, to serve two years; mustered in as private, Co. F, same date; mustered out with company, October 27, 1898, at Brooklyn, N. Y.

CONE, JOHN E.—Age, 22 years. Enlisted, May 2, 1898, at Brooklyn, to serve two years; mustered in as corporal, Co. K, May 13, 1898; returned to ranks, May 22, 1898; mustered out with company, October 27, 1898, at Brooklyn, N. Y.

CONKLIN, EGBERT H.—Age, 20 years. Enlisted, May 2, 1898, at Brooklyn, as corporal, to serve two years; mustered in as sergeant, Co. B, May 16, 1898; mustered out with company, October 27, 1898, at Brooklyn, N. Y.

CONKLIN, JOHN E.—Age, 22 years. Enlisted, May 2, 1898, at Brooklyn, to serve two years; mustered in as private, Co. B, May 16, 1898; mustered out with company, October 27, 1898, at Brooklyn, N. Y.

CONKLIN, WILLIAM P.—Age, 31 years. Enlisted, May 2, 1898, at Brooklyn, to serve two years; mustered in as private, Co. B, May 16, 1898; mustered out with company, October 27, 1898, at Brooklyn, N. Y.

CONLIN, PATRICK.—Age, 23 years. Enlisted, May 13, 1898, at Hempstead, to serve two years; mustered in as private, Co. E, May 16, 1898; mustered out with company, October 27, 1898, at Brooklyn, N. Y.

CONNAUGHTON, CHALES P.—Age, 29 years. Enlisted, May 2, 1898, at Brooklyn, to serve two years; mustered in as sergeant, Co. M, May 13, 1898; returned to ranks, June 1, 1898; mustered out with company, October 27, 1898, at Brooklyn, N. Y.

CONNELL, JAMES J.—Age, 27 years. Enlisted, May 2, 1898, at Brooklyn, to serve two years; mustered in as private, Co. K, May 13, 1898; mustered out with company, October 27, 1898, at Brooklyn, N. Y.

CONNELLY, JOHN.—Age, 23 years. Enlisted, May 13, 1898, at Hempstead, to serve two years; mustered in as private, Co. L, May 16, 1898; mustered out with company, October 27, 1898, at Brooklyn, N. Y.

CONNELLY, WILLIAM.—Age, 26 years. Enlisted, May 14, 1898, at Hempstead, to serve two years; mustered in as private, Co. F, May 16, 1898; mustered out with company, October 27, 1898, at Brooklyn, N. Y.

CONNERS, MICHAEL.—Age, 29 years. Enlisted, May 12, 1898, at Hempstead, to serve two years; mustered in as private, Co. B, May 16, 1898; mustered out with company, October 27, 1898, at Brooklyn, N. Y.

CONNOLLY, HARRY J.—Age, 23 years. Enlisted, May 2, 1898, at Brooklyn, to serve two years; mustered in as private, Co. D, May 16, 1898; mustered out with company, October 27, 1898, at Brooklyn, N. Y.

CONNOLLY, JOHN W.—Age, 22 years. Enlisted, May 12, 1898, at Brooklyn, to serve two years; mustered in as private, Co. C, May 16, 1898; mustered out with company, October 27, 1898, at Brooklyn, N. Y.

CONNOR, JAMES A.—Age, 22 years. Enlisted, May 14, 1898, at Hempstead, to serve two years; mustered in as private, Co. L, May 16, 1898; promoted corporal, July 19, 1898; mustered out with company, October 27, 1898, at Brooklyn, N. Y.

CONSTABLE, WALTER H.—Age, 29 years. Enlisted, May 2, 1898, at Brooklyn, to serve two years; mustered in as private, Co. H, May 16, 1898; promoted corporal, August 1, 1898; mustered out, to date, October 27, 1898.

CONWAY, LESTER J.—Age, 20 years. Enlisted, May 2, 1898, at Brooklyn, to serve two years; mustered in as private, Co. B, May 16, 1898; mustered out with company, October 27, 1898, at Brooklyn, N. Y.

CONZELMAN, THEOPHILE.—Age, 32 years. Enlisted, May 12, 1898, at Brooklyn, to serve two years; mustered in as private, Co. D, May 16, 1898; mustered out with company, October 27, 1898, at Brooklyn, N. Y.

COOMBS, THOMAS.—Age, 20 years. Enlisted, May 12, 1898, at Camp Black, to serve two years; mustered in as private, Co. M, May 13, 1898; promoted corporal, June 15, 1898; mustered out with company, October 27, 1898, at Brooklyn, N. Y.

COOMES, JAMES E.—Age, 32 years. Enlisted, May 12, 1898, at Brooklyn, to serve two years; mustered in as private, Co. C, May 16, 1898; mustered out with company, October 27, 1898, at Brooklyn, N. Y.

COONEY, JAMES J.—Age, 21 years. Enlisted, May 14, 1898, at Camp Black, to serve two years; mustered in as private. Co. I, May 16, 1898; died of typhoid fever, September 3, 1898, in Sternberg Hospital, Camp Thomas, Chickamauga Park, Ga.

COONEY, PATRICK M.—Age, 34 years. Enlisted, May 2, 1898, at Brooklyn, to serve two years; mustered in as private, Co. A, May 13, 1898; mustered out with company, October 27, 1898, at Brooklyn, N. Y.

COOPER, CHARLES.—Age, — years. Enlisted, June 27, 1898, at Brooklyn, to serve two years; mustered in as private, Co. C, same date; mustered out with company, October 27, 1898, at Brooklyn, N. Y.

COOPER, CHARLES A.—Age, — years. Enlisted, June 22, 1898, at Brooklyn, to serve two years; mustered in as private, Co. K, same date; mustered out with company, October 27, 1898, at Brooklyn, N. Y.

COOPER, JACOB W.—Age, 36 years. Enlisted, May 12, 1898, at Hempstead, to serve two years; mustered in as private, Co. K, May 13, 1898; mustered out with company, October 27, 1898, at Brooklyn, N. Y.

CORCORAN, JOSEPH H.—Age, 28 years. Enlisted, May 12, 1898, at Brooklyn, to serve two years; mustered in as private, Co. C, May 16, 1898; mustered out with company, October 27, 1898, at Brooklyn, N. Y.

CORCORAN, PATRICK.—Age, — years. Enlisted, June 20, 1898, at Brooklyn, to serve two years; mustered in as private, Co. F, same date; mustered out with company, October 27, 1898, at Brooklyn, N. Y.

CORCORAN, THOMAS.—Age, — years. Enlisted, June 25, 1898, at Brooklyn, to serve two years; mustered in as private, Co. H, same date; mustered out with company, October 27, 1898, at Brooklyn, N. Y.

CORNELL, FRANCIS.—Age, 32 years. Enlisted, May 2, 1898, at Brooklyn, to serve two years; mustered in as musician, Co. I, May 16, 1898; mustered out with company, October 27, 1898, at Brooklyn, N. Y.

CORSON, CORNELIUS.—Age, 27 years. Enlisted, May 2, 1898, at Brooklyn, to serve two years; mustered in as corporal, Co. K, May 13, 1898; mustered out with company, October 27, 1898, at Brooklyn, N. Y.

CORYELL, JR., GEORGE H.—Age, 21 years. Enlisted, May 13, 1898, at Hempstead, to serve two years; mustered in as private, Co. D, May 16, 1898; transferred to field hospital, June 14, 1898; returned to company, August 26, 1898; mustered out with company, October 27, 1898, at Brooklyn, N. Y.

COSGROVE, WALTER B.—Age, 28 years. Enlisted, May 2, 1898, at Brooklyn, to serve two years; mustered in as private, Co. I, May 16, 1898; mustered out with company, October 27, 1898, at Brooklyn, N. Y.

COSSEY, CHARLES M.—Age, 35 years. Enlisted, May 2, 1898, at Brooklyn, to serve two years; mustered in as private, Co. M, May 13, 1898; mustered out with company, October 27, 1898, at Brooklyn, N. Y.

COTTER, RICHARD A.—Age, 20 years. Enlisted, May 2, 1898, at Brooklyn, to serve two years; mustered in as corporal, Co. D, May 16, 1898; mustered out with company, October 27, 1898, at Brooklyn, N. Y.

.COTTOM, HENRY A.—Age, 21 years. Enlisted, May 2, 1898, at Brooklyn, to serve two years; mustered in as private, Co. D, May 16, 1898; mustered out, to date, October 27, 1898.

COUTLIS, VASILIOS N.—Age, 28 years. Enlisted, May 13, 1898, at Hempstead, to serve two years; mustered in as private, Co. D, May 16, 1898; mustered out with company, October 27, 1898, at Brooklyn, N. Y.

COX, JR., ANDREW A.—Age, 23 years. Enlisted, May 2, 1898, at Brooklyn, to serve two years; mustered in as private, Co. I, May 16, 1898; mustered out with company, October 27, 1898, at Brooklyn, N. Y.

COX, LUKE A.—Age, 22 years. Enlisted, May 2, 1898, at Brooklyn, to serve two years; mustered in as private, Co. F, May 16, 1898; mustered out with company, October 27, 1898, at Brooklyn, N. Y.

COYLE, JAMES.—Age, — years. Enlisted, July 5, 1898, at Brooklyn, to serve two years; mustered in as private, Co. B, same date; mustered out with company, October 27, 1898, at Brooklyn, N. Y.

COYSH, WILLIAM.—Age, 22 years. Enlisted, May 2, 1898, at Brooklyn, to serve two years; mustered in as corporal, Co. A, May 13, 1898; mustered out with company, October 27, 1898, at Brooklyn, N. Y.

CRAGIN, CALHOUN.—Age, 25 years. Enrolled, May 4, 1898, at Camp Black, to serve two years; mustered in as second lieutenant, Co. L, May 16, 1898; as first lieutenant and battalion-adjutant, June 18, 1898; mustered out with regiment, October 27, 1898, at Brooklyn, N. Y.; commissioned second lieutenant, May 16, 1898, with rank from same date, original; first lieutenant and battalion-adjutant, May 28, 1898, with rank from same date, original.

CRAIG, JAMES M.—Age, 25 years. Enlisted, May 2, 1898, at . Brooklyn, to serve two years; mustered in as private, Co. C, May 16, 1898; mustered out with company, October 27, 1898, at Brooklyn, N. Y.

CRAIG, JOSEPH.—Age, 24 years. Enlisted, May 2, 1898, at Brooklyn, to serve two years; mustered in as private, Co. B, May 16, 1898; mustered out with company, October 27, 1898, at Brooklyn, N. Y.

CRAWFORD, HUGH.—Age, 25 years. Enlisted, May 2, 1898, at Brooklyn, to serve two years; mustered in as private, Co. E, May 16, 1898; mustered out with company, October 27, 1898, at Brooklyn, N. Y.

CREIGHTON, JOHN W.—Age, 27 years. Enlisted, May 2, 1898, at Brooklyn, as sergeant, to serve two years; mustered in as second lieutenant, Co. F, May 16, 1898; mustered out with company, October 27, 1898, at Brooklyn, N. Y.; commissioned second lieutenant, May 16, 1898, with rank from same date, original.

CROKE, THOMAS J.—Age, 22 years. Enlisted, May 2, 1898, at Brooklyn, to serve two years; mustered in as private, Co. F, May 16, 1898; promoted corporal, June 15, 1898; returned to ranks, August 7, 1898; mustered out with company, October 27, 1898, at Brooklyn, N. Y.

CROSCUP, HOMER CECIL.—Age, 28 years. Enrolled, May 2, 1898, at Brooklyn, to serve two years; mustered in as first lieutenant, Co. H, May 16, 1898; as captain, Co. I. October 10, 1898; mustered out with company, October 27, 1898, at Brooklyn, N. Y.; commissioned first lieutenant, May 16, 1898, with rank from same date, original; captain, September 14, 1898, with rank from same date, vice Barlow, discharged

CROSS, BENJAMIN FRANKLIN.—Age, 29 years. Enrolled, May 17, 1898, at Camp Black, to serve two years; mustered in as captain, Co. E, same date; mustered out, December 6, 1898, to date, October 27, 1898, at New York city; commissioned captain, May 17, 1898, with rank from same date, original.

CUDMORE, CHRISTOPHER.—Age, 20 years. Enlisted, May 14, 1898, at Camp Black, to serve two years; mustered in as private, Co. H, May 16, 1898; mustered out with company, October 27, 1898, at Brooklyn, N. Y.

CULBERT, JAMES B.—Age, 30 years. Enlisted, May 2, 1898, at Brooklyn, to serve two years; mustered in as private, Co. C, May 16, 1898; promoted corporal, July 8, 1898; mustered out with company, October 27, 1898, at Brooklyn, N. Y.

CURLEY, ALEXANDER.—Age, 21 years. Enlisted, May 14, 1898, at Camp Black, to serve two years; mustered in as private, Co. H, May 16, 1898; mustered out with company, October 27, 1898, at Brooklyn, N. Y.

CURLEY, FRANK.—Age, 28 years. Enlisted, May 12, 1898, at Brooklyn, to serve two years; mustered in as private, Co. C, May 16, 1898; mustered out with company, October 27, 1898, at Brooklyn, N. Y.

CURRY, JOHN.—Age, — years. Enlisted, June 22, 1898, at Brooklyn, to serve two years; mustered in as private, Co. L, same date; mustered out, to date, October 27, 1898.

DAGGETT, JAMES F.—Age, 21 years. Enlisted, May 11, 1898, at Camp Black, to serve two years; mustered in as private. Co M, May 13, 1898; mustered out with company, October 27, 1898. at Brooklyn, N. Y.

DAHL, GEORGE W.—Age, 23 years. Enlisted, May 2, 1898, at Brooklyn, to serve two years; mustered in as private, Co. M, May 13, 1898; promoted corporal, May 26, 1898; sergeant, June 5, 1898; first sergeant, October 15, 1898; mustered out with company, October 27, 1898, at Brooklyn, N. Y.

DAHLEEN, ROBERT.—Age, 24 years. Enlisted, May 2, 1898, at Brooklyn, to serve two years; mustered in as sergeant, Co. G, May 13, 1898; mustered out, to date, October 27, 1898.

DALEEN, OSCAR A.—Age, 21 years. Enlisted, May 2, 1898, at Hempstead, to serve two years; mustered in as private, Co. G, May 13, 1898; mustered out with company, October 27, 1898, at Brooklyn. N. Y.

DAILEY, GEORGE E.—Age, — years. Enlisted, July 6, 1898, at Brooklyn, to serve two years; mustered in as private. Co. L, same date; mustered out with company, October 27, 1898, at Brooklyn, N. Y..

DAILEY, WILLIAM H.—Age, 21 years. Enlisted, May 2, 1898, at Brooklyn, to serve two years; mustered in as private, Co. F, May 16 1898; mustered out with company, October 27, 1898, at Brooklyn, N. Y.

DALEY, WILLIAM F.—Age. 27 years. Enlisted, May 2, 1898, at Brooklyn.to serve two years; mustered in as private, Co. A, May 13, 1898; promoted corporal, June 14, 1898; mustered out with company, October 27, 1898, at Brooklyn, N. Y.

DALY, WILLIAM H.—Age, 34 years. Enlisted, May 12, 1898, at Camp Black, to serve two years; mustered in as private, Co. F, May 16, 1898; mustered out with company, October 27, 1898, at Brooklyn, N. Y.

DAMON, GEORGE.—Age, 21 years. Enlisted, May 2, 1898, at Brooklyn ,to serve two years; mustered in as private, Co. F, May 16, 1898; mustered out with company, October 27, 1898 at Brooklyn, N. Y.

DANIELS, THEODORE.—Age, — years. Enlisted, June 20, 1898, at Brooklyn, to serve two years; mustered in as private, Co. E, same date; mustered out with company, October 27, 1898, at Brooklyn, N. Y.

DAVIES, HARRY H.—Age, 21 years. Enlisted, May 2, 1898, at Brooklyn, to serve two years; mustered in as private, Co. A, May 13, 1898; mustered out with company, October 27, 1898, at Brooklyn, N. Y.

DAVIS, SAMSON.—Age, 26 years. Enlisted, May 13, 1898, at Hempstead, to serve two years; mustered in as private, Co. L, May 16, 1898; mustered out with company, October 27, 1898, at Brooklyn, N. Y.

DAVIS, THOMAS B.—Age, — years. Enlisted, June 24, 1898, at Brooklyn, to serve two years; mustered in as private, Co. A, same date; mustered out with company, October 27, 1898, at Brooklyn, N. Y.

DEACON, JOHN E.—Age, — years. Enlisted, June 21, 1898, at Brooklyn, to serve two years; mustered in as private, Co. K, same date; mustered out with company, October 27, 1898, at Brooklyn, N. Y.

DEANE, J. PERCY.—Age, 21 years. Enlisted, May 2, 1898, at Brooklyn, to serve two years; mustered in as private, Co. C, May 16, 1898; no further record.

DEATS, EDWARD A.—Age, 25 years. Enlisted, May 2, 1898, at Brooklyn, to serve two years; mustered in as private, Co. B, May 16, 1898; mustered out with company, October 27, 1898, at Brooklyn, N. Y.

DEFFLEY, EDWARD W.—Age, 23 years. Enlisted, May 2, 1898, at Brooklyn, to serve two years; mustered in as private, Co. E, May 16, 1898; mustered out with company, October 27, 1898, at Brooklyn, N. Y.

DEGNAN, WILLIAM E.—Age, 23 years.   Enlisted, May 11, 1898, at Hempstead, to serve two years; mustered in as private, Co. B, May 16, 1898; mustered out with company, October 27, 1898, at Brooklyn, N. Y.

DE HART, JOHN.—Age, — years.   Enlisted, June 20, 1898, at Brooklyn, to serve two years; mustered in as private, Co. A, same date; mustered out with company, October 27, 1898, at Brooklyn, N. Y.

DELANEY, CHARLES B.—Age, 29 years.   Enlisted, May 2, 1898, at Brooklyn, to serve two years; mustered in as private, Co. C, May 16, 1898; mustered out with company, October 27, 1898, at Brooklyn, N. Y.

DELIN, PETER G.—Age, 21 years.   Enlisted, May 2, 1898, at Brooklyn, to serve two years; mustered in as private, Co. G, May 13, 1898; promoted corporal, May 14, 1898; mustered out with company, October 27, 1898, at Brooklyn, N. Y.

DEMANDERVILLE, CHARLES.—Age, 21 years.   Enlisted, May 11, 1898, at Camp Black, to serve two years; mustered in as private, Co. M, May 13, 1898; mustered out with company, October 27, 1898, at Brooklyn, N. Y.

DEMONDE, GEORGE A.—Age, 21 years.   Enlisted, May 2, 1898, at Brooklyn, to serve two years; mustered in as private, Co. C, May 16, 1898; mustered out with company, October 27, 1898, at Brooklyn, N. Y.

DE PAUW, EDGAR, see Edgar Pauw.

DERIVAN, WILLIAM.—Age, 24 years.   Enlisted, May 12, 1898, at Hempstead, to serve two years; mustered in as artificer, Co. B, May 16, 1898; mustered out with company, October 27, 1898, at Brooklyn, N. Y.

DERRING, DANIEL.—Age, 22 years.   Enlisted, May 2, 1898, at Brooklyn, to serve two years; mustered in as private, Co. B, May 16, 1898; discharged, no date.

DEVINE, DANIEL.—Age, — years.   Enlisted, June 23, 1898, at Brooklyn, to serve two years; mustered in as private, Co. F, same date; mustered out with company, October 27, 1898, at Brooklyn, N. Y.

DEVINE, PATRICK C.—Age, — years.   Enlisted, June 23, 1898, at Brooklyn, to serve two years; mustered in as private, Co. B, same date; mustered out with company, October 27, 1898, at Brooklyn, N. Y.

DE YOUNG, IRVING A.—Age, 22 years.   Enlisted, May 13, 1898, at Hempstead, to serve two years; mustered in as private, Co. L, May 16, 1898; mustered out with company, October 27, 1898, at Brooklyn, N. Y.

DILLMAN, ALFRED E.—Age, 24 years.   Enlisted, May 2, 1898, at Brooklyn, to serve two years; mustered in as sergeant, Co. B, May 16, 1898; mustered out with company, October 27, 1898, at Brooklyn, N. Y.

DINEEN, LAWRENCE.—Age, — years.   Enlisted, July 5, 1898, at Brooklyn, to serve two years; mustered in as private, Co. I, same date; mustered out with company, October 27, 1898, at Brooklyn, N. Y.

DIXON, JAMES A.—Age, 19 years.   Enlisted, May 2, 1898, at Brooklyn, to serve two years; mustered in as private, Co. I, May 16, 1898; mustered out with company, October 27, 1898, at Brooklyn, N. Y.

DOLAN, BERNHARD J.—Age, 21 years.   Enlisted, May 2, 1898, at Brooklyn, to serve two years; mustered in as private, Co. D, May 16, 1898; mustered out with company, October 27, 1898, at Brooklyn, N. Y.

DOLAN, EUGENE S. L.—Age, 24 years.   Enlisted, May 12, 1898, at Hempstead, to serve two years; mustered in as private, Co. E, May 16, 1898; mustered out with company, October 27, 1898, at Brooklyn, N. Y.

DONAGHY, PATRICK.—Age, 21 years.   Enlisted, May 11, 1898, at Camp Black, to serve two years; mustered in as private, Co. I, May 16, 1898; mustered out with company, October 27, 1898, at Brooklyn, N. Y.

DONAHUE, JOHN C.—Age, 23 years.   Enlisted, May 16, 1898, at Camp Black, to serve two years; mustered in as private, Co. C, same date; mustered out with company, October 27, 1898, at Brooklyn, N. Y.

DONAHUE, JOSEPH F.—Age, — years. Enlisted, July 1, 1898, at Brooklyn, to serve two years; mustered in as private, Co. L, same date; mustered out, to date, October 27, 1898.

DONLON, PETER F.—Age, 25 years. Enlisted, May 2, 1898, at Brooklyn, to serve two years; mustered in as sergeant, Co. A, May 13, 1898; mustered out with company, October 27, 1898, at Brooklyn, N. Y.

DONNELL, JOHN.—Age, 25 years. Enlisted, May 11, 1898, at Camp Black, to serve two years; mustered in as private, Co. M, May 13, 1898; mustered out with company, October 27, 1898, at Brooklyn, N. Y.

DONOHUE, MICHAEL.—Age, — years. Enlisted, July 6, 1898, at Brooklyn, to serve two years; mustered in as private, Co. K, same date; mustered out with company, October 27, 1898, at Brooklyn, N. Y.

DONOVAN, TIMOTHY FRANCIS.—Age, 25 years. Enrolled, May 2, 1898, at Brooklyn, to serve two years; mustered in as first lieutenant, Co. B, May 16, 1898; mustered out with company, October 27, 1898, at Brooklyn, N. Y.; commissioned first lieutenant, May 16, 1898, with rank from same date, original.

DOODY, GEORGE J.—Age, 21 years. Enlisted, May 14, 1898, at Camp Black, to serve two years; mustered in as private, Co. I, May 16, 1898; mustered out with company, October 27, 1898, at Brooklyn, N. Y.

DOODY, RICHARD E.—Age, 26 years. Enlisted, May 2, 1898, at Brooklyn, to serve two years; mustered in as private, Co. E, May 16, 1898; mustered out with company, October 27, 1898, at Brooklyn, N. Y.

DOUGHERTY, JOSEPH.—Age, 21 years. Enlisted, May 2, 1898, at Brooklyn, to serve two years; mustered in as private, Co. K, May 13, 1898; mustered out with company, October 27, 1898, at Brooklyn, N. Y.

DOUGHERTY, PATRICK JOSEPH.—Age, — years. Enlisted, June 20, 1898, at Brooklyn, to serve two years; mustered in as private, Co. H, same date; mustered out with company, October 27, 1898, at Brooklyn, N. Y.

DOUGLAS, RICHMOND L.—Age, — years. Enlisted, June 22, 1898, at Brooklyn, to serve two years; mustered in as private, Co. M, same date; mustered out with company, October 27, 1898, at Brooklyn, N. Y.

DOVE, EDGAR G.—Age, 25 years. Enlisted, May 13, 1898, at Camp Black, to serve two years; mustered in as private, Co. H, May 16, 1898; mustered out with company, October 27, 1898, at Brooklyn, N. Y.

DOWD, CHARLES F.—Age, 25 years. Enlisted, May 14, 1898, at Camp Black, to serve two years; mustered in as private, Co. F, May 16, 1898; mustered out with company, October 27, 1898, at Brooklyn, N. Y.

DOWER, FRANK J.—Age, 21 years. Enlisted, May 13, 1898, at Hempstead, to serve two years; mustered in as musician, Co. L, May 16, 1898; mustered out with company, October 27, 1898, at Brooklyn, N. Y.

DOWLING, THOMAS.—Age, — years. Enlisted, June 27, 1898, at Brooklyn, to serve two years; mustered in as private, Co. F, same date; discharged for disability, August 23, 1898.

DOWNES, ARTHUR P.—Age, — years. Enlisted, June 17, 1898, at Brooklyn, to serve two years; mustered in as private, Co. I, same date; mustered out with company, October 27, 1898, at Brooklyn, N. Y.

DOYLE, JAMES P.—Age, 24 years. Enlisted, May 2, 1898, at Brooklyn, to serve two years; mustered in as private, Co. A, May 13, 1898; mustered out with company, October 27, 1898, at Brooklyn, N. Y.

DRAKE, EDWARD F.—Age, 18 years. Enlisted, May 2, 1898, at Brooklyn, to serve two years; mustered in as private, Co. A, May 13, 1898; mustered out with company, October 27, 1898, at Brooklyn, N. Y.

DRANEY, JOHN F.—Age, 27 years. Enlisted, May 10, 1898, at Hempstead, to serve two years; mustered in as private, Co. D, May 16, 1898; mustered out with company, October 27, 1898, at Brooklyn, N. Y.

DRAY, JAMES M.—Age, — years. Enlisted, July 6, 1898, at Brooklyn, to serve two years; mustered in as private, Co. L, same date; discharged, August 27, 1898.

DREW, ROBERT M.—Age, — years. Enlisted, June 23, 1898, at Brooklyn, to serve two years; mustered in as private, Co. K, same date; mustered out with company, October 23, 1898, at Brooklyn, N. Y.

DRISCOLL, THOMAS J.—Age, — years. Enlisted, July 1, 1898, at Brooklyn, to serve two years; mustered in as private, Co. L, same date; mustered out with company, October 27, 1898, at Brooklyn, N. Y.

DUDLEY, HARRY J.—Age, 25 years. Enlisted, May 2, 1898, at Brooklyn, to serve two years; mustered in as private, Co. A, May 13, 1898; mustered out with company, October 27, 1898, at Brooklyn, N. Y.

DUFFY, PETER.—Age, 33 years. Enlisted, May 11, 1898, at Camp Black, to serve two years; mustered in as private. Co. I, May 16, 1898; mustered out with company, October 27, 1898, at Brooklyn, N. Y.

DUFFY, PETER A.—Age, 25 years. Enlisted, May 12, 1898, at Hempstead, to serve two years; mustered in as private, Co. K, May 13, 1898; discharged for disability, August 27, 1898.

DUNBAR, ROBERT T.—Age, 21 years. Enlisted, May 2, 1898, at Brooklyn, to serve two years; mustered in as musician, Co. M, May 13, 1898; mustered out with company, October 27, 1898, at Brooklyn, N. Y.

DUNN, ANTHONY J.—Age, 28 years. Enlisted, May 7, 1898, at Hempstead, to serve two years; mustered in as private, Co. D, May 16, 1898; mustered out with company, October 27, 1898, at Brooklyn, N. Y.

DUNN, MICHAEL J.—Age, 27 years. Enlisted, May 2, 1898, at Brooklyn, to serve two years; mustered in as private, Co. H, May 16, 1898; mustered out with company, October 27, 1898, at Brooklyn, N. Y.

DUNN, THOMAS V.—Age, 22 years. Enlisted, May 10, 1898, at Camp Black, to serve two years; mustered in as private, Co. I, May 16, 1898; appointed cook, May 20, 1898; mustered out with company, October 27, 1898, at Brooklyn, N. Y.

DUNNE, FRANK T.—Age, — years. Enlisted, June 27, 1898, at Brooklyn, to serve two years; mustered in as private, Co. B, same date; mustered out with company, October 27, 1898, at Brooklyn, N. Y.

DUNNE, JOHN.—Age, 35 years. Enlisted, May 2, 1898, at Brooklyn, to serve two years; mustered in as private, Co. K, May 13, 1898; discharged, October 3, 1898.

DUNPHY, JOHN J.—Age, 28 years. Enlisted, May 2, 1898, at Brooklyn, to serve two years; mustered in as corporal, Co. H, May 16, 1898; mustered out with company, October 27, 1898, at Brooklyn, N. Y.

DUPPEN, JAMES G.—Age, 22 years. Enlisted, May 2, 1898, at Brooklyn, to serve two years; mustered in as private, Co. D, May 16, 1898; mustered out with company, October 27, 1898, at Brooklyn, N. Y.

DURKIN, PATRICK.—Age, 18 years. Enlisted, May 2, 1898, at Brooklyn, to serve two years; mustered in as private, Co. D, May 16, 1898; mustered out with company, October 27, 1898, at Brooklyn, N. Y.

DWYER, JAMES.—Age, — years. Enlisted, June 20, 1898, at Brooklyn, to serve two years; mustered in as private, Co. F, same date; mustered out with company, October 27, 1898, at Brooklyn, N. Y.

EARLS, ARTHUR.—Age, 25 years. Enlisted, May 2, 1898, at Brooklyn, to serve two years; mustered in as corporal, Co. K, May 13, 1898; mustered out with company, October 27, 1898, at Brooklyn, N. Y.

EBER, LOUIS O.—Age, 22 years. Enlisted, May 2, 1898, at Brooklyn, to serve two years; mustered in as private, Co. H, May 16, 1898; mustered out with company, October 27, 1898, at Brooklyn, N. Y.

EDLUND, AUGUST N.—Age, 27 years. Enlisted, May 2, 1898, at Brooklyn, to serve two years; mustered in as sergeant, Co. G, May 13, 1898; mustered out with company, October 27, 1898, at Brooklyn, N. Y.

EDMINSTER, ARTHUR C.—Age, 18 years. Enlisted, May 2, 1898, at Brooklyn, to serve two years; mustered in as private, Co. E, May 16, 1898; discharged, August 3, 1898.

EDWARDS, GEORGE C.—Age, — years. Enlisted, June 21, 1898, at Brooklyn, to serve two years; mustered in as private, Co. C, same date; mustered out with company, October 27, 1898, at Brooklyn, N. Y.

EDWARDS, JOHN W.—Age, 19 years. Enlisted, May 2, 1898, at Brooklyn, to serve two years; mustered in as private, Co. C, May 16, 1898; mustered out with company, October 27, 1898, at Brooklyn, N. Y.

EICHENBURY, EDWARD.—Age, 21 years. Enlisted, May 14, 1898, at Hempstead, to serve two years; mustered in as private, Co. L, May 16, 1898; mustered out with company, October 27, 1898, at Brooklyn, N. Y.

EICKSTEDT, ANDREW.—Age, 30 years. Enlisted, May 2, 1898, at Brooklyn, to serve two years; mustered in as private, Co. G, May 13, 1898; mustered out with company, October 27, 1898, at Brooklyn, N. Y.

EKSTROM, CARL.—Age, 34 years. Enlisted, May 2, 1898, at Brooklyn, to serve two years; mustered in as private, Co. G, May 13, 1898; mustered out with company, October 27, 1898, at Brooklyn, N. Y.

ELDRIDGE, GEORGE P.—Age, 31 years. Enlisted, May 2, 1898, at Brooklyn, to serve two years; mustered in as first sergeant, Co. C, May 16, 1898; mustered out with company, October 27, 1898, at Brooklyn, N. Y.

ELLER, FREDERICK.—Age, — years. Enlisted, June 17, 1898, at Brooklyn, to serve two years; mustered in as private, Co. A, same date; mustered out with company, October 27, 1898, at Brooklyn, N. Y.

ELLIOTT, JR., JOHN.—Age, 27 years. Enlisted May 10, 1898,
at Camp Black, to serve two years; mustered in as private, Co.
I, May 16, 1898; mustered out with company, October 27, 1898,
at Brooklyn, N. Y.

ELLIOTT, WARREN J.—Age, 22 years. Enlisted, May 2, 1898,
at Brooklyn, to serve two years; mustered in as private,Co. I,
May 16, 1898; mustered out with company, October 27, 1898, at
Brooklyn, N. Y.

EMRICK, HARRY H.—Age, — years. Enlisted, June 17, 1898,
at Brooklyn, to serve two years; mustered in as private, Co. M,
same date; promoted corporal, September 10, 1898; mustered
out with company, October 27, 1898, at Brooklyn, N. Y.

ENDERMARK, EMIL.—Age, — years. Enlisted, June 22, 1898,
at Brooklyn, to serve two years; mustered in as private, Co. H,
same date; mustered out with company, October 27, 1898, at
Brooklyn, N. Y.

ENGLERT, LEWIS.—Age, 19 years. Enlisted, May 14, 1898,
at Camp Black, to serve two years; mustered in as private, Co.
H, May 16, 1898; mustered out with company, October 27, 1898,
at Brooklyn, N. Y.

ENGSTROM, ANDREW S.—Age, 25 years. Enlisted, May 2,
1898, at Brooklyn, to serve two years; mustered in as sergeant,
Co. G, May 13, 1898; mustered out with company, October 27,
1898, at Brooklyn, N. Y.

ENNIS, EUGENE L.—Age, 20 years. Enlisted, May 14, 1898, at
Hempstead, to serve two years; mustered in as private, Co. E,
May 16, 1898; promoted corporal, June 15, 1898; mustered out
with company, October 27, 1898, at Brooklyn, N. Y.

ERICKSON, EDWARD.—Age, 23 years. Enlisted, May 2, 1898,
at Brooklyn, to serve two years; mustered in as private, Co. G,
May 13, 1898; mustered out with company, October 27, 1898, at
Brooklyn, N. Y.

ERICKSON, GEORGE H.—Age, 18 years. Enlisted, May 2, 1898,
at Brooklyn, to serve two years; mustered in as private, Co. G,
May 13, 1898; mustered out with company, October 27, 1898, at
Brooklyn, N. Y., as George Ericcan.

ERLWEIN, GEORGE.—Age, 23 years. Enlisted, May 12, 1898, at Camp Black, to serve two years; mustered in as private, Co. C, May 16, 1898; no further record.

ERNST, EDWARD T.—Age, 19 years. Enlisted, May 14, 1898, at Camp Black, to serve two years; mustered in as private, Co. I, May 16, 1898; mustered out with company, October 27, 1898, at Brooklyn, N. Y.

ESKILANDER, AXEL S.—Age, — years. Enlisted, June 20, 1898, at Brooklyn, to serve two years; mustered in as private, Co. G, same date; mustered out with company, October 27, 1898, at Brooklyn, N. Y.

EVERINGHIM, JR., BENJAMIN C.—Age, 21 years. Enlisted, May 2, 1898, at Brooklyn, to serve two years; mustered in as private, Co. K, May 13, 1898; discharged, October 3, 1898.

EWALD, CHARLES.—Age, 21 years. Enlisted, May 11, 1898, at Hempstead, to serve two years; mustered in as private, Co. A, May 13, 1898; mustered out with company, October 27, 1898, at Brooklyn, N. Y.

FAGAN, PETER F.—Age, 23 years. Enlisted, May 2, 1898, at Brooklyn, to serve two years; mustered in as private, Co. D, May 16, 1898; mustered out with company, October 27, 1898, at Brooklyn, N. Y.

FALCO, GEORGE A.—Age, 23 years. Enlisted, May 13, 1898, at Hempstead, to serve two years; mustered in as private, Co. E, May 16, 1898; mustered out with company, October 27, 1898, at Brooklyn, N. Y.

FALK, ALBERT.—Age, — years. Enlisted, June 18, 1898, at Brooklyn, to serve two years; mustered in as private, Co. H, same date; mustered out with company, October 27, 1898, at Brooklyn, N. Y.

FANNON, GEORGE E.—Age, 29 years. Enlisted, May 2, 1898, at Brooklyn, to serve two years; mustered in as private, Co. F, May 16, 1898; mustered out with company, October 27, 1898, at Brooklyn, N. Y.

FARLEY, BERNARD B.—Age, — years. Enlisted, July 5, 1898,. at Brooklyn, to serve two years; mustered in as private, Co. H, same date; mustered out with company, October 27, 1898, at Brooklyn, N. Y.

FAULISI, SALVATOR.—Age, 20 years. Enlisted, May 2, 1898, at Brooklyn, to serve two years; mustered in as private, Co. A, May 13, 1898; mustered out with company, October 27, 1898, at Brooklyn, N. Y.

FAY, JOHN F.—Age, 28 years. Enlisted, May 9, 1898, at Camp Black, to serve two years; mustered in as private, Co. C, May 16, 1898; mustered out with company, October 27, 1898, at Brooklyn, N. Y.

FAY, PATRICK J. I.—Age, 39 years. Enlisted, May 2, 1898, at Brooklyn, to serve two years; mustered in as first sergeant, Co. E, May 16, 1898; relieved and appointed quartermaster-sergeant, August 19, 1898 mustered out with company, October 27, 1898, at Brooklyn, N. Y.

FEENEY, THOMAS J.—Age, — years. Enlisted, June 22, 1898, at Brooklyn, to serve two years; mustered in as private, Co. E. same date; mustered out with company, October 27, 1898, at Brooklyn, N. Y.

FEICKERT, HENRY.—Age, — years. Enlisted, July 6, 1898, at Brooklyn, to serve two years; mustered in as private, Co. H, same date; mustered out with company, October 27, 1898, at Brooklyn, N. Y.

FELTON, GEORGE J.—Age, 25 years. Enlisted, May 11, 1898,. at Brooklyn, to serve two years; mustered in as private, Co. M, May 13, 1898; mustered out ot date, October 27, 1898.

FENNELL, JOHN T.—Age, — years. Enlisted, June 30, 1898, at Brooklyn, to serve two years; mustered in as private, Co. B, same date; mustered out with company, October 27, 1898, at Brooklyn, N. Y.

FINKEL, AUGUST B.—Age, 21 years. Enlisted, May 2, 1898, at Brooklyn, to serve two years; mustered in as private, Co. K, May 13, 1898; mustered out with company, October 27, 1898, at Brooklyn, N. Y.

FISHER, ALBERT O.—Age, — years. Enlisted, June 18, 1898, at Brooklyn, to serve two years; mustered in as private, Co. D, same date; mustered out with company, October 27, 1898, at Brooklyn, N. Y.

FITZGERALD, EDWARD.—Age, 39 years. Enlisted, May 2, 1898, at Brooklyn, to serve two years; mustered in as private, Co. A, May 13, 1898; promoted wagoner, May 14, 1898; mustered out with company, October 27, 1898, at Brooklyn, N. Y.

FITZPATRICK, THOMAS H.—Age, 25 years. Enlisted, May 12, 1898, at Camp Black, to serve two years; mustered in as private, Co. F, May 16, 1898; mustered out, to date, October 27, 1898.

FITZPATRICK, THOMAS J.—Age, — years. Enlisted, June 18, 1898, at Brooklyn, to serve two years; mustered in as private, Co. L, same date; mustered out with company, October 27, 1898, at Brooklyn, N. Y.

FITZWILLIAM, JAMES T.—Age, — years. Enlisted, June 24, 1898, at Brooklyn, to serve two years; mustered in as private, Co. I, same date; mustered out with company, October 27, 1898, at Brooklyn, N. Y.

FLANAGAN, JAMES.—Age, 21 years. Enlisted, May 2, 1898, at Brooklyn, to serve two years; mustered in as private, Co. A, May 13, 1898; mustered out with company, October 27, 1898, at Brooklyn, N. Y.

FLANAGAN, WILLIAM E.—Age, 41 years. Enlisted, May 2, 1898, at Brooklyn, to serve two years; mustered in as private, Co..K, May 13, 1898; mustered out with company, October 27, 1898, at Brooklyn, N. Y.

FLANIGAN, JAMES.—Age, — years. Enlisted, June 18, 1898, at Brooklyn, to serve two years; mustered in as private, Co. F, same date; mustered out with company, October 27, 1898, at Brooklyn, N. Y.

FLANIGAN, LEWIS.—Age, 23 years. Enlisted, May 2, 1898, at Brooklyn, to serve two years; mustered in as private, Co. A, May 13, 1898; mustered out with company, October 27, 1898, at Brooklyn, N. Y.

FLOOD, HARRY.—Age, 21 years. Enlisted, May 7, 1898, at
Hempstead, to serve two years; mustered in as private, Co.
A, May 13, 1898; mustered out with company, October 27, 1898,
at Brooklyn, N. Y.

FLOOD, WILLIAM J.—Age, 21 years. Enlisted, May 2, 1898,
at Brooklyn, to serve two years; mustered in as private, Co.
A, May 13, 1898; mustered out with company, October 27, 1898,
at Brooklyn, N. Y.

FLOWER, ROBERT G.—Age, 21 years. Enlisted, May 9, 1898, at
Camp Black, to serve two years; mustered in as private, Co.
C, May 16, 1898; mustered out with company, October 27, 1898,
at Brooklyn, N. Y.

FLYNN, JOHN J.—Age, 22 years. Enlisted, May 13, 1898, at
Hempstead, to serve two years; mustered in as private, Co.
E, May 16, 1898; mustered out with company, October 27, 1898,
at Brooklyn, N. Y.

FLYNN, JOSEPH T.—Age, 21 years. Enlisted, May 2, 1898, at
Camp Black, to serve two years; mustered in as private, Co.
C, May 16, 1898; discharged, July 9, 1898, at Camp Thomas,
Chickamauga Park, Ga.; also borne as Joseph G. Flynn.

FLYNN, WILLIAM J.—Age, 34 years. Enlisted, May 2, 1898,
at Brooklyn, to serve two years; mustered in as corporal, Co.
F, May 16, 1898; mustered out with company, October 27, 1898,
at Brooklyn, N. Y.

FOLEY, DANIEL M.—Age, — years. Enlisted, July 5, 1898, at
Brooklyn, to serve two years; mustered in as private, Co. A,
same date; mustered out, to date, October 27, 1898.

FOLEY, LEWIS H.—Age, 23 years. Enrolled, May 7, 1898, at
Hempstead, to serve two years; mustered in as second lieutenant, Co. B, May 16, 1898; as first lieutenant, Co. L, July 23,
1898; as regimental adjutant, September 13, 1898; mustered out
with company, October 27, 1898, at Brooklyn, N. Y.; commissioned second lieutenant, May 16, 1898, with rank from same
date, original; first lieutenant, July 18, 1898, with rank from
same date, vice Macumber, promoted captain; adjutant, to
date, July 18, 1898, with rank from same date, vice John W.
Nutt, relieved.

FOLLETTE, FREDERICK H.—Age, 22 years. Enlisted, May 2, 1898, at Brooklyn, to serve two years; mustered in as private, Co. K, May 13, 1898; promoted corporal, July 7, 1898; mustered out with company, October 27, 1898, at Brooklyn, N. Y.

FOOTE, CHARLES D.—Age, 24 years. Enlisted, May 15, 1898, at Camp Black, to serve two years; mustered in as private, Co. C, May 16, 1898; mustered out with company, October 27, 1898, at Brooklyn, N. Y.

FOOTE, JOHN HENRY.—Age, 31 years. Enrolled, May 2, 1898, at Brooklyn, to serve two years; mustered in as captain, Co. B, May 16, 1898; mustered out, November 26, 1898, to date, October 27, 1898, at New York city; commissioned captain, May 16, 1898, with rank from same date, original.

FORBES, HARRY H.—Age, 28 years. Enlisted, May 2, 1898, at Brooklyn, to serve two years; mustered in as private, Co. E, May 16, 1898; promoted corporal, June 15, 1898; mustered out with company, October 27, 1898, at Brooklyn N. Y.

FORMAN, JOHN W.—Age, 37 years. Enlisted, May 2, 1898, at Brooklyn, to serve two years; mustered in as private, Co. F, May 16 1898; mustered out with company, October 27, 1898, at Brooklyn, N. Y.

FOSTMAR, WILHELM.—Age, 26 years. Enlisted, May 14, 1898, at Camp Black, to serve two years; mustered in as private, Co. C, May 16, 1898; discharged, September 8, 1898, at Anniston, Ala.

FOX, JAMES J.—Age, 22 years. Enlisted, May 14, 1898, at Camp Black, to serve two years; mustered in as private, Co. I, May 16, 1898; mustered out with company, October 27, 1898, at Brooklyn, N. Y.

FOX, JAMES JOSEPH.—Age, 29 years. Enlisted, May 2, 1898, at Brooklyn, to serve two years; mustered in as quartermaster-sergeant, Co. H, May 16, 1898; mustered out with company, October 27, 1898, at Brooklyn, N. Y.

FRANCISCO, PETER.—Age, 19 years. Enlisted, May 2, 1898, at Brooklyn, to serve two years; mustered in as private, Co. B, May 16, 1898; mustered out with company, October 27, 1898, at Brooklyn, N. Y.

FRANKLIN, REUTEN B.—Age, 31 years. Enlisted, May 12, 1898, at Brooklyn, to serve two years; mustered in as private, Co B, May 16, 1898; mustered out with company, October 27, 1898, at Brooklyn, N. Y.

FREDERICKS, WILLIAM.—Age, 26 years. Enlisted, May 13, 1898, at Camp Black, to serve two years; mustered in as private, Co. H, May 16, 1898; mustered out with company, October 27, 1898, at Brooklyn, N. Y.

FREITAG, WILLIAM.—Age, 23 years. Enlisted, May 13. 1898, at Hempstead, to serve two years; mustered in as private, Co. E, May 16, 1898; mustered out with company, October 27, 1898, at Brooklyn, N. Y.

FRICKE, JR., CONRAD.—Age, 31 years. Enlisted, May 2, 1898, at Brooklyn, to serve two years; mustered in as first sergeant, Co. M, May 13, 1898; returned to the ranks, no date; died of typhoid fever, October 13, 1898, at 763 Union street, Brooklyn, N. Y.

FRIEDMAN, JR., JOHN.—Age, 31 years. Enlisted, May 14, 1898, at Camp Black, to serve two years; mustered in as private, Co. I, May 16, 1898; mustered out with company, October 27, 1898, at Brooklyn, N. Y.

FRIES, JOHN.—Age, 22 years. Enlisted, May 2, 1898, at Brooklyn, to serve two years; mustered in as private, Co. L, May 16, 1898; promoted corporal, July 19, 1898; mustered out with company, October 27, 1898, at Brooklyn, N. Y.

FRITZ, RICHARD M.—Age, 25 years. Enlisted, May 2, 1898, at Brooklyn, to serve two years; mustered in as private, Co. K, May 13, 1898; mustered out with company, October 27, 1898, at Brooklyn, N. Y.

FUREY, JOHN T.—Age, — years. Enlisted, July 6, 1898, at Brooklyn, to serve two years; mustered in as private, Co. B, same date; mustered out with company, October 27, 1898, at Brooklyn, N. Y.

GAFFNEY, HARRY E.—Age, 25 years. Enlisted, May 2, 1898, at Brooklyn, to serve two years; mustered in as private, Co. F, May 16, 1898; mustered out with company, October 27, 1898, at Brooklyn, N. Y.

GAGE, JAMES P.—Age, 22 years. Enlisted, May 7, 1898, at Hempstead, to serve two years; mustered in as private, Co. A, May 13. 1898; mustered out with company, October 27, 1898, at Brooklyn, N. Y.

GALLEY, CONRAD.—Age, 26 years. Enlisted, May 10, 1898, at Hempstead, to serve two years; mustered in as private, Co. K, May 13, 1898; mustered out with company, October 27, 1898, at Brooklyn, N. Y.

GARDNER, WM. P.—Age, 21 years. Enlisted, May 14, 1898, at Camp Black, to serve two years; mustered in as private, Co. H, May 16, 1898; mustered out with company, October 27, 1898, at Brooklyn, N. Y.

GARCIA, WILLIAM LEWIS.—Age, 31 years. Enrolled, May 2, 1898, at Brooklyn, to serve two years; mustered in as captain, Co. D, May 16, 1898; mustered out, November 26, 1898, to date, October 27, 1898, at New York city; commissioned captain, May 16, 1898, with rank from same date, original.

GARNAR, GEORGE W.—Age, 21 years. Enlisted, May 5, 1898, at Camp Black, to serve two years; mustered in as private, Co. L, May 16, 1898; mustered out with company, October 27, 1898, at Brooklyn, N. Y.

GASTON, THOMAS.—Age, — years. Enlisted, July 6, 1898, at Brooklyn, to serve two years; mustered in as private, Co. K, same date; mustered out with company, October 27, 1898, at Brooklyn, N. Y.

GEDNEY, HARRY W.—Age, 20 years. Enlisted, May 2, 1898, at Brooklyn, to serve two years; mustered in as private, Co. M, May 13, 1898; mustered out with company, October 27, 1898, at Brooklyn, N. Y.

GEHRLING, FRED. G.—Age, 26 years. Enlisted, May 12, 1898, at Hempstead, to serve two years; mustered in as private, Co. A, May 13, 1898; mustered out with company, October 27, 1898, at Brooklyn, N. Y.

GELSTON, JAMES.—Age, 23 years. Enlisted, May 2, 1898, at Brooklyn, to serve two years; mustered in as private, Co. F, May 16, 1898; promoted corporal, September 13, 1898; mustered out with company, October 27, 1898, at Brooklyn, N. Y.

GERGER, DANIEL.—Age, 22 years. Enlisted, May 14, 1898, at
Brooklyn, to serve two years; mustered in as private, Co. H,
May 16, 1898; mustered out with company, October 27, 1898,
at Brooklyn, N. Y.

GESCHWIND, GEORGE.—Age, — years. Enlisted, June 27,
1898, at Brooklyn, to serve two years; mustered in as private,
Co. A, same date; transferred to Hospital Corps, United States.
Army, September 2, 1898.

GHYR, LOUIS.—Age, 26 years. Enlisted, May 2, 1898, at
Brooklyn, to serve two years; mustered in as private, Co. F,
May 16, 1898; mustered out with company, October 27, 1898, at
Brooklyn, N. Y.

GIBSON, WILLIAM.—Age, 25 years. Enlisted, May 14, 1898,
at Camp Black, to serve two years; mustered in as private,
Co. H, May 16, 1898; mustered out with company, October 27,
1898, at Brooklyn, N. Y.

GILLIGAN, PETER S.—Age, 22 years. Enlisted, May 12, 1898,
at Camp Black, to serve two years; mustered in as private,
Co. F, May 16, 1898; mustered out with company, October 27,
1898, at Brooklyn, N. Y.

GILLIN, JR., JOHN J.—Age, 18 years. Enlisted, May 2, 1898,
at Brooklyn, to serve two years; mustered in as private, Co. I,
May 16, 1898; mustered out, to date, October 27, 1898.

GILLMAN, JOSEPH G.—Age, — years. Enlisted, June 29,
1898, at Brooklyn, to serve two years; mustered in as private,
Co. K, same date; mustered out with company, October 27,
1898, at Brooklyn, N. Y.

GILMORE, WILLIAM F.—Age, 19 years. Enlisted, May 14,
1898, at Camp Black, to serve two years; mustered in as private, Co. I, May 16, 1898; mustered out with company, October
27, 1898, at Brooklyn, N. Y.

GLACEE, EDWARD.—Age, 33 years. Enlisted, May 2, 1898, at
Brooklyn, to serve two years; mustered in as private, Co. C,
May 16, 1898; mustered out with company, October 27, 1898,
at Brooklyn, N. Y.

GLACY, JUNIUS.—Age, 19 years. Enlisted, May 10, 1898, at Hempstead, to serve two years; mustered in as private, Co. D, May 16, 1898; mustered out with company, October 27, 1898, at Brooklyn, N. Y.

GODDARD, WILLIÁM.—Age, 23 years. Enlisted, May 13, 1898, at Camp Black, to serve two years; mustered in as private, Co. F, May 16, 1898; mustered out with company, October 27, 1898, at Brooklyn, N. Y.

GODSTROM, OSCAR C.—Age, 20 years. Enlisted, May 2, 1898, at Brooklyn, to serve two years; mustered in as private, Co. G, May 13, 1898; mustered out with company, October 27, 1898, at Brooklyn, N. Y.

GOLDWATER, LOUIS.—Age, 22 years. Enlisted, May 2, 1898, at Brooklyn, to serve two years; mustered in as private, Co. D, May 16, 1898; mustered out with company, October 27, 1898, at Brooklyn, N. Y.

GOOZEN, JOHN H.—Age, — years. Enlisted, June 28, 1898, at Brooklyn, to serve two years; mustered in as private, Co. L, same date; mustered out with company, October 27, 1898, at Brooklyn, N. Y.

GORMAN, JOSEPH L.—Age, 21 years. Enlisted, May 2, 1898, at Brooklyn, to serve two years; mustered in as private, Co. D, May 16, 1898; mustered out with company, October 27, 1898, at Brooklyn, N. Y.

GORMLEY, HARRY.—Age, — years. Enlisted, July 6, 1898, at Brooklyn, to serve two years; mustered in as private, Co. K, same date; mustered out, to date, October 27, 1898.

GOSS, JACOB.—Age, — years. Enlisted, July 7, 1898, at Brooklyn, to serve two years; mustered in as private, Co. C, same date; mustered out with company, October 27, 1898, at Brooklyn, N. Y.

GOULD, GEORGE.—Age, 28 years. Enlisted, May 2, 1898, at Brooklyn, to serve two years; mustered in as private, Co. A, May 13, 1898; appointed cook, August 23, 1898; mustered out with company, October 27, 1898, at Brooklyn, N. Y.

GRAEZKOWSKI, IGNATIUS M.—Age, — years. Enlisted, July 6, 1898, at Brooklyn, to serve two years; mustered in as private, Co. B, same date; mustered out with company, October 27, 1898, at Brooklyn, N. Y.

GRAFTON, HOWARD B.—Age, 37 years. Enlisted, May 2, 1898, at Brooklyn, to serve two years; mustered in as private, Co. H, May 16, 1898; mustered out with company, October 27, 1898, at Brooklyn, N. Y.

GRAHAM, MARTIN.—Age, 24 years. Enlisted, May 14, 1898, at Camp Black, to serve two years; mustered in as private, Co. F, May 16, 1898; promoted corporal, July 14, 1898; mustered out with company, October 27, 1898, at Brooklyn, N. Y.

GRANT, CHARLES S.—Age, 21 years. Enlisted, May 2, 1898, at Brooklyn, to serve two years; mustered in as private, Co. I, May 16, 1898; mustered out, to date, October 27, 1898.

GRANT, FREDERICK DENT.—Age, 47 years. Enrolled, May 2, 1898, at Brooklyn, to serve two years; mustered in as colonel, May 16, 1898; discharged, June 1, 1898; subsequent service as brigadier-general, United States Volunteers; commissioned colonel, May 10, 1898, with rank from same date, original.

GRANT, JOHN D.—Age, — years. Enlisted, June 18, 1898, at Brooklyn, to serve two years; mustered in as private, Co. D, same date; promoted corporal, September 2, 1898; mustered out with company, October 27, 1898, at Brooklyn, N. Y.

GRANT, LOUIS BEDELL.—Age, 30 years. Enlisted, May 11, 1898, at Hempstead, to serve two years; mustered in as private, Co. B, May 16, 1898; promoted corporal, no date; mustered in as second lieutenant, July 24, 1898; mustered out with company, October 27, 1898, at Brooklyn, N. Y.; commissioned second lieutenant, July 18, 1898, with rank from same date, vice Foley, promoted first lieutenant.

GRAVEN, HENRY J.—Age, 21 years. Enlisted, May 12, 1898, at Camp Black, to serve two years; mustered in as private, Co. C, May 16, 1898; mustered out with company, October 27, 1898, at Brooklyn, N. Y.

GRAVESON, JULIUS G.—Age, 21 years. Enlisted, May 2, 1898, at Brooklyn, to serve two years; mustered in as private, Co. A, May 13, 1898; mustered out with company, October 27, 1898, at Brooklyn, N. Y.

GRAY, JAMES M.—Age, — years. Enlisted, July 1, 1898, at Brooklyn, to serve two years; mustered in as private, Co. L, same date; discharged to accept commission, August 27, 1898.

GREEN, DAVID W.—Age, 32 years. Enlisted, May 2, 1898, at Brooklyn, to serve two years; mustered in as musician, Co. D, May 16, 1898; mustered out with company, October 27, 1898, at Brooklyn, N. Y.

GREEN, ETHELBERT.—Age, 21 years. Enlisted, May 14, 1898, at Camp Black, to serve two years; mustered in as sergeant, Co. H, May 16, 1898; mustered out with company, October 27, 1898, at Brooklyn, N. Y.

GREEN, JOHN A.—Age, 25 years. Enlisted, May 2, 1898, at Brooklyn, to serve two years; mustered in as private, Co. K, May 13, 1898; promoted corporal, July 7, 1898; sergeant, August 14, 1898; mustered out with company, October 27, 1898, at Brooklyn, N. Y.

GREEN, JOSEPH P.—Age, 23 years. Enlisted, May 2, 1898, at Brooklyn, to serve two years; mustered in as private, Co. K, May 13, 1898; mustered out with company, October 27, 1898, at Brooklyn, N. Y.

GREEN, SAMUEL R.—Age, — years. Enlisted, June 27, 1898, at Brooklyn, to serve two years; mustered in as private, Co. H, same date; mustered out with company, October 27, 1898, at Brooklyn, N. Y.

GREENE, WILLIAM L.—Age, 27 years. Enlisted, May 2, 1898, at Brooklyn, to serve two years; mustered in as private, Co. M, May 13, 1898; mustered out with company, October 27, 1898, at Brooklyn, N. Y.

GREER, JAMES H.—Age, 21 years. Enlisted, May 2, 1898, at Brooklyn, to serve two years; mustered in as private, Co. I, May 16, 1898; mustered out with company, October 27, 1898, at Brooklyn, N. Y.

GREER, LOUIS MORRIS.—Age, 29 years. Enrolled, June 22, 1898, at Brooklyn, to serve two years; mustered in as second lieutenant, Co. C, June 28, 1898; discharged, August 30, 1898; commissioned second lieutenant, June 22, 1898, with rank from same date, vice Raymond, discharged.

GREGERSON, GEORGE N.—Age, 23 years. Enlisted, May 2, 1898, at Brooklyn, to serve two years; mustered in as corporal, Co. A, May 13, 1898; mustered out with company, October 27, 1898, at Brooklyn, N. Y.

GRIENER, ARTHUR G.—Age, 34 years. Enlisted, May 7, 1898, at Hempstead, to serve two years; mustered in as private, Co. A, May 13, 1898; mustered out with company, October 27, 1898, at Brooklyn, N. Y.

GRIFFIN, JOHN J.—Age, 33 years. Enlisted, May 2, 1898, at Brooklyn, to serve two years; mustered in as private, Co. M, May 13, 1898; appointed artificer, May 25, 1898; mustered out with company, October 27, 1898, at Brooklyn, N. Y.

GRIFFIN, JOHN L.—Age, 26 years. Enlisted, May 2, 1898, at Brooklyn, to serve two years; mustered in as private, Co. D, May 16, 1898; mustered out with company, October 27, 1898, at Brooklyn, N. Y.

GRIFFIN, JOSEPH T.—Age, 22 years. Enrolled, May 2, 1898, at Brooklyn, to serve two years; mustered in as second lieutenant, Co. D, May 16, 1898; mustered out with company, October 27, 1898, at Brooklyn, N. Y.; commissioned second lieutenant, May 16, 1898, with rank from same date, original.

GRIFFIN, PHILIP J.—Age, — years. Enlisted, June 18, 1898, at Brooklyn, to serve two years; mustered in as private, Co. C, same date; mustered out with company, October 27, 1898, at Brooklyn, N. Y.

GRINER, CHARLES H.—Age, 31 years. Enlisted, May 2, 1898, at Brooklyn, to serve two years; mustered in as private, Co. F, May 16, 1898; mustered out with company, October 27, 1898, at Brooklyn, N. Y.

GRITZ, WILLIAM J.—Age, 23 years. Enlisted, May 2, 1898, at Brooklyn, to serve two years; mustered in as private, Co. F. May 16, 1898; mustered out with company, October 27, 1898, at Brooklyn, N. Y.

GROGAN, STEPHEN.—Age, 28 years. Enlisted, May 2, 1898, at Brooklyn, to serve two years; mustered in as corporal, Co. I, May 16, 1898; mustered out with company, October 27, 1898, at Brooklyn, N. Y.

GROSS, FRANK L.—Age, 24 years. Enlisted, May 2, 1898, at Brooklyn, to serve two years; mustered in as private, Co. B, May 16, 1898; mustered out with company, October 27, 1898, at Brooklyn, N. Y.

GROSS, JR., GEORGE.—Age, 22 years. Enlisted, May 2, 1898, at Brooklyn, to serve two years; mustered in as private, Co. B, May 16, 1898; mustered out with company, October 27, 1898, at Brooklyn, N. Y.

GROSS, HENRY W.—Age, — years. Enlisted, June 18, 1898, at Brooklyn, to serve two years; mustered in as private, Co. I, same date; mustered out with company, October 27, 1898, at Brooklyn, N. Y.

GROTH, THEODORE.—Age, 30 years. Enlisted, May 2, 1898, at Brooklyn, to serve two years; mustered in as sergeant, Co. A, May 13, 1898; mustered out with company, October 27, 1898, at Brooklyn, N. Y.

GROTYOHANN, JOHN H.—Age, 18 years. Enlisted, May 2, 1898, at Brooklyn, to serve two years; mustered in as private, Co. D, May 16, 1898; mustered out, to date, October 27, 1898.

GROWVOGLE, JOHN J.—Age, 24 years. Enlisted, May 2, 1898, at Brooklyn, to serve two years; mustered in as wagoner, Co. H, May 16, 1898; appointed artificer, May 31, 1898; mustered out with company, October 27, 1898, at Brooklyn, N. Y.

GSELL, ANTON G.—Age, 26 years. Enlisted, May 13, 1898, at Hempstead, to serve two years; mustered in as private, Co. E, May 16, 1898; discharged, September 20, 1898.

GUINSBURY, NATHAN M.—Age, 22 years. Enlisted, May 12, 1898, at Hempstead, to serve two years; mustered in as private, Co. K, May 13, 1898; mustered out with company, October 27, 1898, at Brooklyn, N. Y.

GUMALIUS, CHARLES.—Age, 34 years. Enlisted, May 2, 1898, at Brooklyn, to serve two years; mustered in as private, Co. G, May 13, 1898; promoted corporal, July 12, 1898; mustered out with company, October 27, 1898, at Brooklyn, N. Y.

GUNN, JOHN A.—Age, — years. Enlisted, June 27, 1898, at Brooklyn, to serve two years; mustered in as private, Co. M, same date; mustered out with company, October 27, 1898, at Brooklyn, N. Y.

GUNN, WILLIAM.—Age, 27 years. Enlisted, May 13, 1898, at Brooklyn, to serve two years; mustered in as private, Co. H, May 16, 1898; mustered out with company, October 27, 1898, at Brooklyn, N. Y.

GUNTHER, MAX.—Age, 21 years. Enlisted, May 11, 1898, at Camp Black, to serve two years; mustered in as private, Co. M, May 13, 1898; mustered out with company, October 27, 1898, at Brooklyn, N. Y.

GUSTAPSON, ROBERT.—Age, 23 years. Enlisted, May 2, 1898, at Brooklyn, to serve two years; mustered in as private, Co. G, May 13, 1898; mustered out with company, October 27, 1898, at Brooklyn, N. Y.

GUY, ARTHUR.—Age, 22 years. Enlisted, May 14, 1898, at Camp Black, to serve two years; mustered in as private, Co. H, May 16, 1898; mustered out with company, October 27, 1898, at Brooklyn, N. Y.

HACKER, EDWARD W.—Age, 43 years. Enlisted, May 2, 1898, at Brooklyn, to serve two years; mustered in as quartermaster-sergeant, Co. F, May 16, 1898; mustered out with company, October 27, 1898, at Brooklyn, N. Y.

HACKETT, JOHN.—Age, — years. Enlisted, June 28, 1898, at Brooklyn, to serve two years; mustered in as private, Co. L, same date; mustered out with company, October 27, 1898, at Brooklyn, N. Y.

HADLER, WILLIAM F.—Age, 23 years. Enlisted, May 11, 1898, at Camp Black, to serve two years; mustered in as private, Co. M, May 13, 1898; mustered out with company, October 27, 1898, at Brooklyn, N. Y.

HAFF, ALBERT S.—Age, 21 years. Enlisted, May 13, 1898, at Hempstead, to serve two years; mustered in as private, Co. E, May 16, 1898; mustered out, to date, October 27, 1898.

HAGGERTY, JERE R.—Age, 30 years. Enlisted, May 11, 1898, at Hempstead, to serve two years; mustered in as private, Co. B, May 16, 1898; mustered out with company, October 27, 1898, at Brooklyn, N. Y.

HAINES, PENROSE W.—Age, — years. Enlisted, July 6, 1898, at Brooklyn, to serve two years; mustered in as private, Co. K, same date; mustered out with company, October 27, 1898, at Brooklyn, N. Y.

HAKONSON, AUGUST.—Age, — years. Enlisted, June 25, 1898, at Brooklyn, to serve two years; mustered in as private, Co. G, same date; mustered out with company, October 27, 1898, at Brooklyn, N. Y.

HALL, CHARLES.—Age, — years. Enlisted, June 22, 1898, at Brooklyn, to serve two years; mustered in as private, Co. L, same date; deserted, July 28, 1898, at Camp Thomas, Chickamauga Park, Ga.

HALL, EMIL.—Age, 25 years. Enlisted, May 2, 1898, at Brooklyn, to serve two years; mustered in as private, Co. G, May 13, 1898; died of typhoid fever, October 14, 1898, in hospital, Brooklyn, N. Y.

HALL, GEORGE E.—Age, 23 years. Enlisted, May 13, 1898, at Hempstead, to serve two years; mustered in as private, Co. E, May 16, 1898; mustered out with company, October 27, 1898, at Brooklyn, N. Y.

HALLER, WILLIAM.—Age, 27 years. Enlisted, May 12, 1898, at Hempstead, to serve two years; mustered in as private, Co. B, May 16, 1898; mustered out with company, October 27, 1898, at Brooklyn, N. Y.

HALLINAN, MICHAEL.—Age, — years. Enlisted, June 24, 1898, at Brooklyn, to serve two years; mustered in as private, Co. B, same date; mustered out with company, October 27, 1898- at Brooklyn, N. Y.

HALLOWELL, WALTER C.—Age, 23 years. Enlisted, May 2, 1898, at Hempstead, as sergeant, Co. H, to serve two years; mustered in as first sergeant, Co. D, May 16, 1898; mustered out with company, October 27, 1898, at Brooklyn, N. Y.

HAMILTON, CHARLES.—Age, 41 years. Enrolled, May 2, 1898, at Brooklyn, to serve two years; mustered in as first lieutenant, Co. G, May 13, 1898; mustered out with company, October 27, 1898, at Brooklyn, N. Y.; commissioned first lieutenant, May 13, 1898, with rank from same date, original.

HAMILTON, PETER.—Age, 22 years. Enlisted, May 5, 1898, at Hempstead, to serve two years; mustered in as private, Co. B, May 16, 1898; mustered out with company, October 27, 1898, at Brooklyn, N. Y.

HAMMERSLEY, GEORGE.—Age, — years. Enlisted, June 20, 1898, at Brooklyn, to serve two years; mustered in as private, Co. C, same date; mustered out with company, October 27, 1898, at Brooklyn, N. Y.

HAND, JAMES J.—Age, 22 years. Enlisted, May 2, 1898, at Brooklyn, to serve two years; mustered in as corporal, Co. C, May 16, 1898; discharged, to date, October 27, 1898.

HANGE, DAVID.—Age, — years. Enlisted, June 18, 1898, at Brooklyn, to serve two years; mustered in as private, Co. G, same date; promoted corporal, July 12, 1898; mustered out with company, October 27, 1898, at Brooklyn, N. Y.

HANLAN, MARTIN.—Age, — years. Enlisted, June 21, 1898, at Brooklyn, to serve two years; mustered in as private, Co. K, same date; mustered out with company, October 27, 1898, at Brooklyn, N. Y.

HANLON, JOHN F.—Age, 31 years. Enlisted, May 12, 1898, at Camp Black, to serve two years; mustered in as private, Co. F, May 16, 1898; mustered out with company, October 27, 1898, at Brooklyn, N. Y.

HANRAHAN, PATRICK J.—Age, 24 years. Enlisted, May 2, 1898, at Brooklyn, to serve two years; mustered in as corporal, Co. I, May 16, 1898; mustered out with company, October 27, 1898, at Brooklyn, N. Y.

HANSEN, THOMAS E.—Age, 19 years. Enlisted, May 2, 1898, at Brooklyn, to serve two years; mustered in as private, Co. K, May 13, 1898; mustered out with company, October 27, 1898, at Brooklyn, N. Y.

HANSON, GEORGE E.—Age, 21 years. Enlisted, May 2, 1898, at Brooklyn, to serve two years; mustered in as private, Co. A, May 13, 1898; mustered out with company, October 27, 1898, at Brooklyn, N. Y.

HANSON, HANS.—Age, 24 years. Enlisted, May 11, 1898, at Camp Black, to serve two years; mustered in as private, Co. M, May 13, 1898; appointed wagoner, May 25, 1898; mustered out with company, October 27, 1898, at Brooklyn, N. Y.

HANSON, OTTO H.—Age, 21 years. Enlisted, May 2, 1898, at Brooklyn, to serve two years; mustered in as private, Co. G, May 13, 1898; mustered out, to date, October 27, 1898, at Brooklyn, N. Y.

HARDING, JR., RICHARD H.—Age, 29 years. Enrolled, May 2, 1898, at Brooklyn, to serve two years; mustered in as captain, Co. M, May 13, 1898; mustered out, December 7, 1898, to date, October 27, 1898, at New York city; commissioned captain, May 13, 1898, with rank from same date, original.

HARDY, THOMAS.—Age, — years. Enlisted, June 22, 1898, at Brooklyn, to serve two years; mustered in as private, Co. A, same date; mustered out with company, October 27, 1898, at Brooklyn, N. Y.

HARKINS, JAMES J.—Age, 23 years. Enlisted, May 2, 1898, at Brooklyn, to serve two years; mustered in as private, Co. K, May 13, 1898; mustered out with company, October 27, 1898, at Brooklyn, N. Y.

HARKINS, JOHN J.—Age, 28 years. Enlisted, May 2, 1898, at Brooklyn, to serve two years; mustered in as sergeant, Co. K, May 13, 1898; mustered out with company, October 27, 1898, at Brooklyn, N. Y.

HARKINS, THOMAS F.—Age, — years. Enlisted, June 27, 1898, at Brooklyn, to serve two years; mustered in as private, Co. A, same date; mustered out with company, October 27, 1898, at Brooklyn, N. Y.

HARLEY, JAMES J.—Age, 23 years. Enlistend, May 2, 1898, at Brooklyn, to serve two years; mustered in as corporal, Co. D, May 16, 1898; mustered out with company, October 27, 1898, at Brooklyn, N. Y.

HARMON, JOHN A.—Age, 23 years. Enlisted, May 13, 1898, at Hempstead, to serve two years; mustered in as private, Co. E, May 16, 1898; mustered out with company, October 27, 1898, at Brooklyn, N. Y.

HARNEY, WILLIAM E.—Age, 21 years. Enlisted, May 2, 1898, at Brooklyn, to serve two years; mustered in as private, Co. K, May 13, 1898; mustered out with company, October 27, 1898, at Brooklyn, N. Y.

HARPER, GEORGE M.—Age, 25 years. Enlisted, May 2, 1898, at Brooklyn, to serve two years; mustered in as private, Co. K, May 13, 1898; discharged for disability, July 17, 1898, at Camp Thomas, Chickamauga Park, Ga.

HARPER, JAMES.—Age, — years. Enlisted, July 6, 1898, at Brooklyn, to serve two years; mustered in as private, Co. B, same date; deserted, August 23, 1898, at Camp Thomas, Chicka-manga Park, Ga.

HARRINGTON, JOHN T.—Age, 24 years. Enlisted, May 2, 1898, at Brooklyn, to serve two years; mustered in as private, Co. A, May 13, 1898; discharged for disability, July 14, 1898, at Chickamauga, Ga.

HART, ADELBERT S.—Age, 29 years. Enlisted, May 2, 1898, at Brooklyn, to serve two years; mustered in as first sergeant, Co. L, May 16, 1898; as second lieutenant, June 18, 1898; discharged, September 7, 1898; commissioned second lieutenant, May 28, 1898, with rank from same date, vice Cragin, promoted first lieutenant and battalion adjutant.

HART, HIRAM N.—Age, 23 years. Enlisted, May 16, 1898, at Camp Black, to serve two years; mustered in as private, Co. C, same date; discharged, October 18, 1898.

HART, JR., JOHN J.—Age, — years. Enlisted, June 25, 1898, at Brooklyn, to serve two years; mustered in as private, Co. C, same date; mustered out with company, October 27, 1898, at Brooklyn, N. Y.

HARVEY, PATRICK B.—Age, 22 years. Enlisted, May 2, 1898, at Brooklyn, to serve two years; mustered in as private, Co. K, May 13 1898; mustered out with company, October 27, 1898, at Brooklyn, N. Y.

HAUXWELL, RICHARD J.—Age, — years. Enlisted, June 21, 1898, at Brooklyn, to serve two years; mustered in as private, Co. K, same date; mustered out with company, October 27, 1898, at Brooklyn, N. Y.

HAYES, EDWARD J.—Age, — years. Enlisted, July 5, 1898, at Brooklyn, to serve two years; mustered in as private, Co. A, same date; mustered out with company, October 27, 1898, at Brooklyn, N. Y.

HAYES, WILLIAM.—Age, — years. Enlisted, June 28, 1898, at Brooklyn, to serve two years; mustered in as private, Co. E, same date; died of disease, September 16, 1898, at Division Hospital, Anniston, Ala.

HEALY, THOMAS.—Age, 29 years. Enlisted, May 2, 1898, at Brooklyn, to serve two years; mustered in as private, Co. E, May 16, 1898; mustered out with company, October 27, 1898, at Brooklyn, N. Y.

HEALY, THOMAS F.—Age, — years. Enlisted, June 20, 1898, at Brooklyn, to serve two years; mustered in as private, Co. D, same date; mustered out with company, October 27, 1898, at Brooklyn, N. Y.

HEDBERG, JOHN P.—Age, 20 years. Enlisted, May 2, 1898, at Brooklyn, to serve two years; mustered in as private, Co. G, May 13, 1898; mustered out with company, October 27, 1898, at Brooklyn, N. Y.

HEFFERNAN, JAMES J.—Age, 24 years. Enlisted, May 2, 1898, at Brooklyn, to serve two years; mustered in as corporal, Co. K, May 13, 1898; mustered out with company, October 27, 1898, at Brooklyn, N. Y.

HEGARTY, SAMUEL J.—Age, 29 years. Enlisted, May 2, 1898, at Brooklyn, to serve two years; mustered in as private, Co. K, May 13, 1898; mustered out with company, October 27, 1898, at Brooklyn, N. Y.

HEICGHT, JOHN W.—Age, 24 years. Enlisted, May 2, 1898, at Camp Black, to serve two years; mustered in as private, Co. C, May 16, 1898; no further record.

HEMMETT, PERCY E.—Age, — years. Enlisted, June 22, 1898, at Brooklyn, to serve two years; mustered in as private, Co. B, same date; mustered out with company, October 27, 1898, at Brooklyn, N. Y.

HEMMINGS, FREDERICK A.—Age, 22 years. Enlisted, May 2, 1898, at Brooklyn, to serve two years; mustered in as private, Co. K, May 13, 1898; mustered out with company, October 27, 1898, at Brooklyn, N. Y.

HENDERSON, WILLIS S.—Age, 27 years. Enlisted, May 4, 1898, at Camp Black, to serve two years; mustered in as private, Co. L, May 16, 1898; promoted corporal, July 5, 1898; mustered out with company, October 27, 1898, at Brooklyn, N. Y.

HENDRICKSON, JOSEPH.—Age, 20 years. Enlisted, May 10, 1898, at Hempstead, to serve two years; mustered in as private, Co D, May 16, 1898; mustered out with company, October 27, 1898, at Brooklyn, N. Y.

HENLEY, WILBER S.—Age, — years. Enlisted, June 24, 1898, at Brooklyn, to serve two years; mustered in as private, Co. H, same date; mustered out with company, October 27, 1898, at Brooklyn, N. Y.

HENRICH, PHILLIP.—Age, 20 years. Enlisted, May 14, 1898, Camp Black, to serve two years; mustered in as private, Co. H, May 16, 1898; promoted corporal, August 1, 1898; mustered out with company, October 27, 1898, at Brooklyn, N. Y.

HENRY, DAVID A.—Age, — years. Enlisted, June 27, 1898, at Brooklyn, to serve two years; mustered in as private, Co. B, same date; mustered out with company, October 27, 1898, at Brooklyn, N. Y.

HENRY, DAVID PATTERSON.—Age, 37 years. Enrolled, May 2, 1898, at Brooklyn, to serve two years; mustered in as first lieutenant, Co. M, May 13, 1898; as captain, Co. K, June 14, 1898; discharged, September 3, 1898; commissioned first lieutenant, May 13, 1898, with rank from same date, original; captain, May 28, 1898, with rank from same date, vice C. A.

HENRY, SAMUEL.—Age, 21 years. Enlisted, May 12, 1898, at Camp Black, to serve two years; mustered in as private, Co. F, May 16, 1898; mustered out with company, October 27, 1898, at Brooklyn, N Y.

HENSLER, ROBERT A.—Age, 21 years. Enlisted, May 11, 1898, at Camp Black, to serve two years; mustered in as private, Co. M, May 13, 1898; mustered out with company, October 27, 1898, at Brooklyn, N. Y.

HENZE, PAUL J.—Age, 23 years. Enlisted, May 2, 1898, at Brooklyn, to serve two years; mustered in as private, Co. K, May 13, 1898; mustered out with company, October 27, 1898, at Brooklyn, N. Y.

HERNANDEZ, ROBERT.—Age, 20 years. Enlisted, May 2, 1898, at Brooklyn, to serve two years; mustered in as private, Co. D, May 16, 1898; mustered out with company, October 27, 1898, at Brooklyn, N. Y.

HERRMANN, LOUIS.—Age, 34 years. Enlisted, May 11, 1898, at Camp Black, to serve two years; mustered in as private, Co. M, May 13, 1898; mustered out with company, October 27, 1898, at Brooklyn, N. Y.

HERTER, JOHN.—Age, 18 years. Enlisted, May 2, 1898, at Brooklyn, to serve two years; mustered in as private, Co. C, May 16, 1898; mustered out with company, October 27, 1898, at Brooklyn, N. Y.

HESTER, JR., JAMES.—Age, 22 years. Enlisted, May 2, 1898, at Brooklyn to serve two years; mustered in as private, Co. B, May 16, 1898; mustered out with company, October 27, 1898, at Brooklyn, N. Y.

HEYDEN, ERIC.—Age, 24 years. Enlisted, May 2, 1898, at at Brooklyn, to serve two years; mustered in as private, Co. B, May 13, 1898; appointed wagoner, no date; died of typhoid fever, August 15, 1898, in First Division, Third Army Corps Hospital.

HIBBITS, JOHN J.—Age, 30 years. Enlisted, May 13, 1898, at Brooklyn, to serve two years; mustered in as private, Co. D, May 16, 1898; mustered out with company, October 27, 1898, at Brooklyn, N. Y.

HIGGINS, DENNIS.—Age, 25 years. Enlisted, May 13, 1898, at Camp Black, to serve two years; mustered in as private, Co. H, May 16, 1898; mustered out with company, October 27, 1898, at Brooklyn, N. Y.

HILL, CHARLES L.—Age, 31 years. Enlisted, May 2, 1898, at Brooklyn, to serve two years; mustered in as private, Co. G, May 13, 1898; promoted corporal, July 12, 1898; mustered out with company, October 27, 1898, at Brooklyn, N. Y

HILL, JOHN C.—Age, 32 years. Enlisted, May 13, 1898, at Hempstead, to serve two years; mustered in as private, Co. E, May 16, 1898; discharged, September 20, 1898.

HINES, WALTER E.—Age, 22 years. Enlisted, May 2, 1898, at Brooklyn, to serve two years; mustered in as musician, Co. H, May 16, 1898; mustered out with company, October 27, 1898, at Brooklyn, N. Y.

HIRSCHKIND, CHARLES.—Age, 21 years. Enlisted, May 13, 1898, at Hempstead, to serve two years; mustered in as private, Co. E, May 16, 1898; mustered out with company, October 27, 1898, at Brooklyn, N. Y.

HITTEL, FRANK.—Age, 27 years. Enlisted, May 14, 1898, at Hempstead, to serve two years; mustered in as private, Co. L, May 16, 1898; appointed artificer, May 27, 1898; returned to ranks, July 24, 1898; mustered out with company, October 27, 1898, at Brooklyn, N. Y.

HOAGLAND, EDWIN V.—Age, 33 years. Enlisted, May 2, 1898, at Brooklyn, to serve two years; mustered in as corporal, Co. B, May 16, 1898; mustered out with company, October 27, 1898, at Brooklyn, N. Y.

HOBBY, MAURICE L.—Age, — years. Enlisted, June 20, 1898, at Brooklyn, to serve two years; mustered in as private, Co. D, same date; mustered out with company, October 27, 1898, at Brooklyn, N. Y.

HODGE, JAMES.—Age, 21 years. Enlisted, May 2, 1898, at Brooklyn, to serve two years; mustered in as private, Co. B, May 16, 1898; mustered out with company, October 27, 1898, at Brooklyn, N. Y.

HOFF, ARTHUR J.—Age, 35 years. Enlisted, May 13, 1898, at Hempstead, to serve two years; mustered in as private, Co. D, May 16, 1898; transferred to Co. L, May 27, 1898; promoted corporal, July 19, 1898; sergeant, October 28, 1898; mustered out with company, October 27, 1898, at Brooklyn, N. Y.

HOFFMANN, JOSEPH.—Age, 32 years. Enlisted, May 14, 1898, at Hempstead, to serve two years; mustered in as private, Co. L, May 16, 1898; appointed wagoner, June 5, 1898; returned to ranks, August 9, 1898; mustered out with company, October 27, 1898, at Brooklyn, N. Y.

HOGAN, JAMES E.—Age, — years. Enlisted, June 21, 1898, at Brooklyn, to serve two years; mustered in as private, Co. K, same date; mustered out with company, October 27, 1898, at Brooklyn, N. Y.

HOHMANN, FREDERICK.—Age, 24 years. Enlisted, May 14, 1898, at Hempstead, to serve two years; mustered in as private, Co. E, May 16, 1898; mustered out with company, October 27, 1898, at Brooklyn, N. Y.

HOLDER, ERNEST.—Age, 22 years. Enlisted, May 13, 1898, at Camp Black, to serve two years; mustered in as private, Co. H, May 16, 1898; mustered out with company, October 27, 1898, at Brooklyn, N. Y.

HOLEMBERG, CARL LEONARD.—Age, 36 years. Enrolled, May 2, 1898, at Brooklyn, to serve two years; mustered in as captain, Co. G, May 13, 1898; mustered out with company, October 27, 1898, at Brooklyn, N. Y.; commissioned captain, May 13, 1898, with rank from same date, original.

HOLLIS, EDWARD G.—Age, 22 years. Enlisted, May 2, 1898, at Brooklyn, to serve two years; mustered in as private, Co. I, May 16, 1898; mustered out with company, October 27, 1898, at Brooklyn, N. Y.

HOLTZ, FREDERICK.—Age, — years. Enlisted, July 1, 1898, at Brooklyn, to serve two years; mustered in as private, Co. M, same date; mustered out with company, October 27, 1898, at Brooklyn, N. Y.

HOOPER, TIMOTHY A.—Age, 33 years. Enlisted, May 2, 1898, at Brooklyn, to serve two years; mustered in as private, Co. C, May 16, 1898; promoted corporal, July 8, 1898; mustered out with company, October 27, 1898, at Brooklyn, N. Y.

HOPPING, GEORGE W.—Age, — years. Enlisted, June 27, 1898, at Brooklyn, to serve two years; mustered in as private, Co. A, same date; mustered out with company, October 27, 1898, at Brooklyn, N. Y.

HORAN, THOMAS F.—Age, 22 years. Enlisted, May 14, 1898, at Camp Black, to serve two years; mustered in as private, Co. H, May 16, 1898; mustered out with company, October 27, 1898, at Brooklyn, N. Y.

HORTON, H. MILLARD.—Age, 23 years. Enrolled, May 2, 1898, at Brooklyn, to serve two years; mustered in as second lieutenant, Co. I, May 16, 1898; mustered out with company, October 27, 1898, at Brooklyn, N. Y.; commissioned second lieutenant, May 16, 1898, with rank from same date, original.

HOSFORD, SAMUEL J.—Age, 26 years. Enlisted, May 2, 1898, at Brooklyn, to serve two years; mustered in as private, Co. E, May 16, 1898; mustered out with company, October 27, 1898, at Brooklyn, N. Y.

HOUSE, GEORGE F.—Age, 18 years. Enlisted, May 2, 1898, at Brooklyn, to serve two years; mustered in as private, Co. D, May 16, 1898; mustered out, to date, October 27, 1898.

HOWARD, JOSEPH F.—Age, 27 years. Enlisted, May 2, 1898, at Brooklyn, to serve two years; mustered in as sergeant, Co. E, May 16, 1898; mustered out with company, October 27, 1898, at Brooklyn, N. Y.

HUDLESON, SAMUEL.—Age, 35 years. Enlisted, May 13, 1898, at Hempstead, to serve two years; mustered in as private, Co. L, May 16, 1898; mustered out with company, October 27, 1898, at Brooklyn, N. Y.

HUDNER, JAMES A.—Age, 23 years. Enlisted, May 2, 1898, at Brooklyn, to serve two years; mustered in as corporal, Co. C, May 16, 1898; returned to ranks, July 11, 1898; promoted corporal, August 5, 1898; mustered out with company, October 27, 1898, at Brooklyn, N. Y.

HUGHES, ROBERT.—Age, — years. Enlisted, June 28, 1898, at Brooklyn, to serve two years; mustered in as private, Co. L, same date; mustered out with company, October 27, 1898, at Brooklyn, N. Y.

HUNT, ARTHUR.—Age, 27 years. Enlisted, May 2, 1898, at Brooklyn, to serve two years; mustered in as wagoner, Co. I, May 16, 1898; mustered out with company, October 27, 1898, at Brooklyn, N. Y.

HUNT, BARTHOLOMEW J.—Age, — years. Enlisted, July 2, 1898, at Brooklyn, to serve two years; mustered in as private, Co. K, same date; mustered out with company, October 27, 1898, at Brooklyn, N. Y.

HUNT, EDWARD H.—Age, — years. Enlisted, June 23, 1898, at Brooklyn, to serve two years; mustered in as private, Co. E, same date; mustered out with company, October 27, 1898, at Brooklyn, N. Y.

HUNT, FRANCIS A.—Age, — years. Enlisted, June 18, 1898, at Brooklyn, to serve two years; mustered in as private, Co. M, same date; mustered out with company, October 27, 1898, at Brooklyn, N. Y.

HUNT, JOHN J.—Age, 31 years. Enlisted, May 2, 1898, at Brooklyn, to serve two years; mustered in as private, Co. M, May 13, 1898; mustered out with company, October 27, 1898, at Brooklyn, N. Y.

HUNTER, THOMAS W.—Age, — years. Enlisted, July 5, 1898, at Brooklyn, to serve two years; mustered in as private, Co. H, same date; mustered out, to date, October 27, 1898.

HUTZEN, HARRY.—Age, 21 years. Enlisted, May 2, 1898, at Brooklyn, to serve two years; mustered in as private, Co. G, May 13, 1898; mustered out with company, October 27, 1898, at Brooklyn, N. Y.

HYSLOP, JAMES F.—Age, 23 years. Enlisted, May 2, 1898, at Brooklyn, to serve two years; mustered in as first sergeant, Co. I, May 16, 1898; mustered out with company, October 27, 1898, at Brooklyn, N. Y.

IRVING, HUGH J.—Age, 24 years. Enlisted, May 12, 1898, at Camp Black, to serve two years; mustered in as private, Co. H, May 16, 1898; promoted corporal, August 1, 1898; mustered out with company, October 27, 1898, at Brooklyn, N. Y.

IRWIN, JOHN W.—Age, — years. Enlisted, June 22, 1898, at Brooklyn, to serve two years; mustered in as private, Co. A, same date; mustered out with company, October 27, 1898, at Brooklyn, N. Y.

JACKSON, JAMES E.—Age, 20 years. Enlisted, May 16, 1898, at Camp Black, to serve two years; mustered in as private, Co. I, same date; mustered out, to date, October 27, 1898.

JACOBS, NELSON K.—Age, 23 years. Enlisted, May 2, 1898, at Brooklyn, to serve two years; mustered in as corporal, Co. F, May 16, 1898; mustered out with company, October 27, 1898, at Brooklyn, N. Y.

JAMES, STEPHEN R.—Age, 27 years. Enlisted, May 2, 1898, at Brooklyn, to serve two years; mustered in as corporal, Co. H, May 16, 1898; mustered out with company, October 27, 1898, at Brooklyn, N. Y.

JANSON, OLOF.—Age, 28 years. Enlisted, May 2, 1898, at Brooklyn, to serve two years; mustered in as private, Co. G, May 27, 1898; mustered out with company, October 27, 1898, at Brooklyn, N. Y.

JASCHKE, FREDERICK C.—Age, 23 years. Enlisted, May 2, 1898, at Brooklyn, to serve two years; mustered in as corporal, Co. F, May 16, 1898; mustered out with company, October 27, 1898, at Brooklyn, N. Y.

JASCHKE, HENRY L.—Age, 31 years. Enlisted, May 2, 1898, at Brooklyn, to serve two years; mustered in as private, Co. F, May 16, 1898; appointed musician, June 16, 1898; mustered out with company, October 27, 1898, at Brooklyn, N. Y.

JASTER, CHARLES F.—Age, 18 years. Enlisted, May 2, 1898, at Brooklyn, to serve two years; mustered in as private, Co. L, May 16, 1898; mustered out, to date, October 27, 1898.

JENNINGS, GEORGE REDMOND.—Age, 33 years. Enrolled, May 2, 1898, at Camp Black, to serve two years; mustered in as first lieutenant and regimental quartermaster, May 12, 1898; mustered out, November 28, 1898, to date, October 27, 1898, at New York city; commissioned first lieutenant and quartermaster, May 12, 1898, with rank from same date, original.

JENNINGS, WILLIAM.—Age, 29 years. Enlisted, May 2, 1898, at Brooklyn, to serve two years; mustered in as sergeant, Co. D, May 16, 1898; mustered out with company, October 27, 1898, at Brooklyn, N. Y. ·

JOHNSBERG, CHARLES G.—Age, — years. Enlisted, July 5, 1898, at Brooklyn, to serve two years; mustered in as private, Co. L, same date; mustered out with company, October 27, 1898, at Brooklyn, N. Y.

JOHNSON, ALFRED.—Age, 27 years. Enlisted, May 2, 1898, at Brooklyn, to serve two years; mustered in as corporal, Co. G, May 13, 1898; mustered out with company, October 27, 1898, at Brooklyn, N. Y.

JOHNSON, ALFRED T.—Age, 21 years. Enlisted, May 2, 1898, at Brooklyn, to serve two years; mustered in as private, Co. D, May 16, 1898; discharged for disability, August 5, 1898, at Camp Thomas, Chickamauga Park, Ga.

JOHNSON, ARTHUR.—Age, — years. Enlisted, June 30, 1898, at Brooklyn, to serve two years; mustered in as private, Co. G, same date; mustered out with company, October 27, 1898, at Brooklyn, N. Y.

JOHNSON, CARL A.—Age, — years. Enlisted, June 23, 1898, at Brooklyn, to serve two years; mustered in as private, Co. G, same date; mustered out with company, October 27, 1898, at Brooklyn, N. Y.

JOHNSON, FRANK.—Age, 23 years. Enlisted, May 2, 1898, at Brooklyn, to serve two years; mustered in as private, Co. G, May 13, 1898; mustered out with company, October 27, 1898, at Brooklyn, N. Y.

JOHNSON, GOTTFRID.—Age, 24 years. Enlisted, May 2, 1898, at Brooklyn, to serve two years; mustered in as private, Co. G, May 13, 1898; mustered out with company, October 27, 1898, at Brooklyn, N. Y.

JOHNSON, JOHN.—Age, — years. Enlisted, June 23, 1898, at
Brooklyn, to serve two years; mustered in as private, Co. E,
same date; mustered out with company, October 27, 1898, at
Brooklyn, N. Y.

JOHNSON, NILS.—Age, 21 years. Enlisted, May 2, 1898, at
Brooklyn, to serve two years; mustered in as private, Co. G,
May 13, 1898; mustered out with company, October 27, 1898, at
Brooklyn, N. Y.

JOHNSTON, JR., BENJAMIN F.—Age, 23 years. Enlisted, May
2, 1898, at Brooklyn, to serve two years; mustered in as quartermaster-sergeant, Co. A, May 13, 1898; mustered out with company, October 27, 1898, at Brooklyn, N. Y.

JOHNSTON, WALTER H.—Age, — years. Enlisted, June 20,
1898, at Brooklyn, to serve two years; mustered in as private,
Co. A, same date; mustered out with company, October 27,
1898, at Brooklyn, N. Y.

JOHNSTON, WALTER S.—Age, 22 years. Enlisted, May 2,
1898, at Brooklyn, to serve two years; mustered in as private,
Co. A, May 13, 1898; mustered out with company, October 27,
1898, at Brooklyn, N. Y.

JONES, ADDISON J.—Age, 21 years. Enlisted, May 2, 1898,
at Brooklyn, to serve two years; mustered in as private, Co.
M, May 13, 1898; mustered out with company, October 27, 1898,
at Brooklyn, N. Y.

JONES, EDWARD.—Age, — years. Enlisted, June 23, 1898, at
Brooklyn, to serve two years; mustered in as private, Co. L,
same date; mustered out with company, October 27, 1898, at
Brooklyn, N. Y.

JONES, FRANK. —Age, — years. Enlisted, June 22, 1898, at
Brooklyn, to serve two years; mustered in as private, Co. F,
same date; mustered out with company, October 27, 1898, at
Brooklyn, N. Y.

JONES, FREDERICK A.—Age, 26 years. Enlisted, May 2, 1898,
at Brooklyn, to serve two years; mustered in as private, Co.
I, May 16, 1898; mustered out with company, October 27, 1898,
at Brooklyn, N. Y.

JONES, JOHN.—Age, 40 years. Enlisted, May 14, 1898, at Camp Black, to serve two years; mustered in as private, Co. H, May 16, 1898; mustered out with company, October 27, 1898, at Brooklyn, N. Y.

JORDAN, HENRY.—Age, 32 years. Enlisted, May 2, 1898, at Brooklyn, to serve two years; mustered in as private Co. L, May 16, 1898; mustered out with company, October 27, 1898, at Brooklyn, N. Y.

JOYCE, BARRINGTON.—Age, — years. Enlisted, June 18, 1898, at Brooklyn, to serve two years; mustered in as private, Co. I, same date; died of typhoid fever, August 11, 1898, in hospital, Camp Thomas, Chickamauga Park, Ga.

JOYCE, JOHN F.—Age, 21 years. Enlisted, May 2, 1898, at Brooklyn, to serve two years; mustered in as private, Co. F. May 16, 1898; mustered out with company, October 27, 1898, at Brooklyn, N. Y.

KAESSNER, BRUNO C.—Age, 20 years. Enlisted, May 2, 1898, at Brooklyn, to serve two years; mustered in as private, Co. D, May 16, 1898; promoted corporal, September 2, 1898; mustered out with company, October 27, 1898, at Brooklyn, N. Y.

KAISER, AUGUST.—Age, 35 years. Enlisted, May 2, 1898, at Brooklyn, to serve two years; mustered in as principal musician, May 16, 1898; appointed chief musician, May 25, 1898; mustered out with regiment, October 27, 1898, at Brooklyn, N. Y.

KAISER, WILLIAM.—Age, 25 years. Enlisted, May 13, 1898, at Camp Black, to serve two years; mustered in as private, Co. F, May 16, 1898; mustered out with company, October 27, 1898, at Brooklyn, N. Y.

KALEY, MICHAEL E.—Age, — years. Enlisted, June 20, 1898, at Brooklyn, to serve two years; mustered in as private, Co. H, same date; mustered out with company, October 27, 1898, at Brooklyn, N. Y.

KAMMERER, JOHN.—Age, — years. Enlisted, June 20, 1898, at Brooklyn, to serve two years; mustered in as private, Co. E, same date; mustered out with company, October 27, 1898, at Brooklyn, N. Y..

KANE, CHARLES J.—Age, 22 years. Enlisted, May 9, 1898, at Hempstead, to serve two years; mustered in as private, Co. D, May 16, 1898; mustered out with company, October 27, 1898, at Brooklyn, N. Y.

KANE, JOHN.—Age, 40 years. Enlisted, May 14, 1898, at Camp Black, to serve two years; mustered in as private, Co. F, May 16, 1898; mustered out with company, October 27, 1898, at Brooklyn, N. Y.

KANE, JOHN F.—Age, — years. Enlisted, May 2, 1898, at Brooklyn, to serve two years; mustered in as sergeant, Co. A, May 13, 1898; promoted first sergeant, June 14, 1898; mustered out with company, October 27, 1898, at Brooklyn, N. Y.

KARL, GEORGE J.—Age, 28 years. Enlisted, May 11, 1898, at Camp Black, to serve two years; mustered in as private, Co. M, May 13, 1898; mustered out with company, October 27, 1898, at Brooklyn, N. Y.

KAUFMAN, HENRY.—Age, 38 years. Enlisted, May 14, 1898, at Hempstead, to serve two years; mustered in as private, Co. L, May 16, 1898; mustered out with company, October 27, 1898, at Brooklyn, N. Y.

KAY, ARTHUR WESLEY.—Age, 21 years. Enlisted, May 2, 1898, at Brooklyn, to serve two years; mustered in as private, Co. E, May 16, 1898; mustered out with company, October 27, 1898, at Brooklyn, N. Y.

KEABLES, JR., GEORGE H.—Age, —years. Enlisted, July 6, 1898, at Brooklyn, to serve two years; mustered in as private, Co. B, same date; mustered out with company, October 27, 1898, at Brooklyn, N. Y.

KEATING, CLARENCE.—Age, 21 years. Enlisted, May 9, 1898, at Camp Black, to serve two years; mustered in as private, Co. C, May 16, 1898; mustered out, to date, October 27, 1898.

KEATING, THOMAS F.—Age, 34 years. Enlisted, May 2, 1898, at Brooklyn, to serve two years; mustered in as private, Co. D, May 16, 1898; mustered out with company, October 27, 1898, at Brooklyn, N. Y.

KEATING, WILLIAM J.—Age, 21 years. Enlisted, May 2, 1898, at Brooklyn, to serve two years; mustered in as corporal, Co. F, May 16, 1898; promoted sergeant, June 15, 1898; mustered out with company, October 27, 1898, at Brooklyn, N. Y.

KEAYES, WILLIAM.—Age, 22 years. Enlisted, May 15, 1898, at Camp Black, to serve two years; mustered in as private, Co. F, May 16, 1898; mustered out with company, October 27, 1898, at Brooklyn, N. Y.

KEEFE, MICHAEL.—Age, 27 years. Enlisted, May 14, 1898, at Camp Black, to serve two years; mustered in as private, Co. H, May 16, 1898; promoted corporal, July 29, 1898; mustered out with company, October 27, 1898, at Brooklyn, N. Y.

KEEGAN, CHARLES S.—Age, 27 years. Enlisted, May 2, 1898, at Brooklyn, to serve two years; mustered in as private, Co. M, May 13, 1898; mustered out with company, October 27, 1898, at Brooklyn, N. Y.

KEELER, HUGH.—Age, 20 years. Enlisted, May 16, 1898, at Camp Black, to serve two years; mustered in as private, Co. H, May 16, 1898; mustered out with company, October 27, 1898, at Brooklyn, N. Y.

KEEPERS, WILLIAM.—Age, — years. Enlisted, July 5, 1898, at Brooklyn, to serve two years; mustered in as private, Co. B, same date; mustered out, to date, October 27, 1898.

KEINATH, RICHARD.—Age, 35 years. Enlisted, May 2, 1898, at Brooklyn, to serve two years; mustered in as private, Co. K, May 13, 1898; mustered out with company, October 27, 1898, at Brooklyn, N. Y.

KELLEY, HARRY E.—Age, — years. Enlisted, June 18, 1898, at Brooklyn, to serve two years; mustered in as private, Co. F, same date; mustered out with company, October 27, 1898, at Brooklyn, N. Y.

KELLY, HENRY.—Age, 26 years. Enlisted, May 13, 1898, at Hempstead, to serve two years; mustered in as private, Co. A, May 13, 1898; mustered out with company, October 27, 1898, at Brooklyn, N. Y.

KELLY, JOHN F.—Age, 25 years.   Enlisted, May 7, 1898, at Camp Black, to serve two years; mustered in as private, Co. H, May 16, 1898; mustered out with company, October 27, 1898, at Brooklyn, N. Y.

KELLY, JOHN J.—Age, — years.   Enlisted, June 18, 1898, at Brooklyn, to serve two years; mustered in as private, Co. D, same date; mustered out with company, October 27, 1898, at Brooklyn, N. Y.

KELLY, WILLIAM J.—Age, — years.   Enlisted, July 6, 1898, at Brooklyn, to serve two years; mustered in as private, Co. H, same date; mustered out with company, October 27, 1898, at Brooklyn, N. Y.

KEMPE, OTTO.—Age, — years.   Enlisted, June 24, 1898, at Brooklyn, to serve two years; mustered in as private, Co. G, same date; mustered out with company, October 27, 1898, at Brooklyn, N. Y.

KENDRICK, ATHELSTANE.—Age, 22 years.   Enlisted, May 2, 1898, at Brooklyn, to serve two years; mustered in as sergeant, Co. K, May 13, 1898; second lieutenant, June 18, 1898; mustered out with company, October 27, 1898, at Brooklyn, N. Y.; commissioned second lieutenant, May 28, 1898, with rank from same date, vice Beatty, promoted first lieutenant and battalion adjutant.

KENNEDY, JAMES E.—Age, 22 years.   Enlisted, May 14, 1898, at Camp Black, to serve two years; mustered in as private, Co. H, May 16, 1898; mustered out with company, October 27, 1898, at Brooklyn, N. Y.

KENNEDY, JOHN F.—Age, 23 years.   Enlisted. May 2, 1898, at Brooklyn, to serve two years; mustered in as private, Co. D, May 16, 1898; mustered out with company, October 27, 1898, at Brooklyn, N. Y.

KENNEDY, JOSEPH F.—Age, 23 years.   Enlisted. May 2, 1898, at Brooklyn, to serve two years; mustered in as private, Co. K, May 13, 1898; mustered out with company, October 27, 1898, at Brooklyn, N. Y.

KENNEDY, THOMAS H.—Age, 21 years.   Enlisted. May 14, 1898, at Camp Black, to serve two years; mustered in as private, Co. H, May 16, 1898; mustered out with company, October 27 1898 at Brooklyn N. Y.

KENNEY, FELIX F.—Age, 18 years. Enlisted, May 2, 1898, at Brooklyn, to serve two years; mustered in as private, Co. D, May 16, 1898; mustered out with company, October 27, 1898, at Brooklyn, N. Y.

KENNEY, JOHN B.—Age, — years. Enlisted, July 5, 1898, at Brooklyn, to serve two years; mustered in as private, Co. I, same date; mustered out with company, October 25, 1898, at Brooklyn, N. Y.

KENNEY, JOHN M.—Age, 24 years. Enlisted, May 2, 1898, at Brooklyn, to serve two years; mustered in as private, Co. C, May 16, 1898; promoted corporal, July 8, 1898; mustered out with company, October 27, 1898, at Brooklyn, N. Y.

KENNEY, JOSEPH F.—Age, 26 years. Enlisted, May 2, 1898, at Brooklyn, to serve two years; mustered in as private, Co. C, May 16, 1898; mustered out with company, October 27, 1898, at Brooklyn, N. Y.

KENNISH, PAUL R.—Age, 22 years. Enlisted, May 2, 1898, at Brooklyn, to serve two years; mustered in as corporal, Co. K, May 13, 1898; mustered out with company, October 27, 1898, at Brooklyn, N. Y.

KENNY, JAMES J.—Age, — years. Enlisted, June 28, 1898, at Brooklyn, to serve two years; mustered in as private, Co. M, same date; mustered out with company, October 27, 1898, at Brooklyn, N. Y.

KERNS, WILLIAM J.—Age, — years. Enlisted, June 20, 1898, at Brooklyn, to serve two years; mustered in as private, Co. F, same date; mustered out with company, October 27, 1898, at Brooklyn, N. Y.

KETCHAM, VINCENT P.—Age, 21 years. Enlisted, May 2, 1898, at Brooklyn, to serve two years; mustered in as private, Co. C, May 16, 1898; mustered out with company, October 27, 1898, at Brooklyn, N. Y.

KEYSER, WILLIAM W.—Age, — years. Enlisted, May 13, 1898, at Camp Black, to serve two years; mustered in as private, Co. C, May 16, 1898; discharged, October 19, 1898.

KIELLANDER, CARL.—Age, 21 years. Enlisted, May 2, 1898, at Brooklyn, to serve two years; mustered in as private, Co. G, May 13, 1898; mustered out with company, October 27, 1898, at Brooklyn, N. Y.

KIELLANDER, JOHN E.—Age, 28 years. Enlisted, May 2, 1898, at Brooklyn, to serve two years; mustered in as private, Co. G, May 13, 1898; promoted corporal, July 12, 1898; mustered out with company, October 29, 1898, at Brooklyn, N. Y.

KIENLE, FREDERICK F.—Age, 29 years. Enlisted, May 2, 1898, at Brooklyn, to serve two years; mustered in as private, Co. M, May 13, 1898; mustered out with company, October 27, 1898, at Brooklyn, N. Y.

KILCOYNE, JAMES.—Age, — years. Enlisted, July 5, 1898, at Brooklyn, to serve two years; mustered in as private, Co. A, same date; mustered out with company, October 27, 1898, at Brooklyn, N. Y.

KIMBALL, CHARLES E.—Age, 27 years. Enlisted, May 5, 1898, at Camp Black, to serve two years; mustered in as private, Co. L, May 16, 1898; promoted corporal, May 28, 1898; sergeant, June 28, 1898; first sergeant, October 10, 1898; mustered out with company, October 27, 1898, at Brooklyn, N. Y.

KING, AUGUSTUS F. L.—Age, 21 years. Enlisted, May 10, 1898, at Camp Black, to serve two years; mustered in as private, Co. M, May 13, 1898; mustered out with company, October 27, 1898, at Brooklyn, N. Y.

KING, CHARLES A.—Age, 25 years. Enlisted, May 11, 1898, at Camp Black, to serve two years; mustered in as private, Co. M, May 13, 1898; mustered out with company, October 27, 1898, at Brooklyn, N. Y.

KING, HARRY.—Age, 20 years. Enlisted, May 2, 1898, at Brooklyn, to serve two years; mustered in as private, Co. B, May 16, 1898; mustered out with company, October 27, 1898, at Brooklyn, N. Y.

KING, JAMES P.—Age, 21 years. Enlisted, May 2, 1898, at Brooklyn, to serve two years; mustered in as private, Co. M, May 13, 1898; mustered out with company, October 27, 1898, at Brooklyn, N. Y.

KIRBY, WILLIAM.—Age, — years. Enlisted, June 25, 1898, at Brooklyn, to serve two years; mustered in as private, Co. M, same date; mustered out with company, October 27, 1898, at Brooklyn, N. Y.

KIRCHER, JOHN.—Age, — years. Enlisted, June 21, 1898, at Brooklyn, to serve two years; mustered in as private, Co. I, same date; mustered out with company, October 27, 1898, at Brooklyn, N. Y.

KIRK, CHARLES T.—Age, 20 years. Enlisted, May 11, 1898, at Hempstead, to serve two years; mustered in as musician, Co. B, May 16, 1898; died of typhoid fever, September 15, 1898, in Sternberg Hospital, Chickamauga, Ga.

KIRK, ROBERT J.—Age, 44 years. Enlisted, May 14, 1898, at Hempstead, to serve two years; mustered in as private, Co. E, May 16, 1898; mustered out with company, October 27, 1898, at Brooklyn, N. Y.

KIVLEN, CHARLES H.—Age, 32 years. Enlisted, May 2, 1898, at Brooklyn, to serve two years; mustered in as sergeant, Co. K, May 13, 1898; mustered out with company, October 27, 1898, at Brooklyn, N. Y.

KLEIN, MARTIN MICHAEL.—Age, 28 years. Enlisted, May 6, 1898, at Camp Black, to serve two years; mustered in as private, Co. L, May 16, 1898; mustered out with company, October 27, 1898, at Brooklyn, N. Y.

KLINE, ARDOLPH LOGES.—Age, 41 years. Enrolled, May 2, 1898, at Brooklyn, to serve two years; mustered in as lieutenant-colonel, May 16, 1898; mustered out with regiment, October 27, 1898, at Brooklyn, N. Y.; commissioned lieutenant-colonel, May 16, 1898, with rank from same date, original.

KLINE, JOHN A.—Age, 26 years. Enlisted, May 11, 1898, at Camp Black, to serve two years; mustered in as private, Co. M, May 13, 1898; mustered out with company, October 27, 1898, at Brooklyn, N. Y.

KLINGBERG, CARL C.—Age, — years. Enlisted, June 22, 1898, at Brooklyn, to serve two years; mustered in as private, Co. G, same date; mustered out with company, October 27, 1898, at Brooklyn, N. Y.

KNAPP, ANDREW.—Age, 27 years. Enlisted, May 13, 1898, at Hempstead, to serve two years; mustered in as private, Co. E, May 16, 1898; mustered out with company, October 27, 1898, at Brooklyn, N. Y.

KNIGHT, HARRY E.—Age, 21 years. Enlisted, May 7, 1898, at Hempstead, to serve two years; mustered in as private, Co. K, May 13, 1898; discharged, July 20, 1898; subsequent service as first lieutenant, Fifth United States Infantry.

KNOUSE, FREDERICK V. R.—Age, 28 years. Enlisted, May 2, 1898, at Brooklyn, to serve two years; mustered in as private, Co. A, May 13, 1898; mustered out with company, October 27, 1898, at Brooklyn, N. Y.

KOLLER, CHARLES.—Age, 21 years. Enlisted, May 14, 1898, at Hempstead, to serve two years; mustered in as private, Co. B, May 16, 1898; mustered out with company, October 27, 1898, at Brooklyn, N. Y.

KOSECK, JR., FRANK.—Age, 24 years. Enlisted, May 2, 1898, at Brooklyn, to serve two years; mustered in as sergeant, Co. H, May 16, 1898; mustered out with company, October 27, 1898, at Brooklyn, N. Y.

KRAMER, HENRY C.—Age, — years. Enlisted, June 17, 1898, at Brooklyn, to serve two years; mustered in as private, Co. A, same date; mustered out with company, October 27, 1898, at Brooklyn, N. Y.

KRENZURG, JOHN.—Age, 25 years. Enlisted, May 2, 1898, at Brooklyn, to serve two years; mustered in as sergeant, Co. D, May 16, 1898; mustered out with company, October 27, 1898, at Brooklyn, N. Y.

KRIPP, WILLIAM F.—Age, 23 years. Enlisted, May 12, 1898, at Hempstead, to serve two years; mustered in as private, Co. K, May 13, 1898; mustered out with company, October 27, 1898, at Brooklyn, N. Y.

KUNZE, HENRY W.—Age, 28 years. Enlisted, May 2, 1898, at Brooklyn, to serve two years; mustered in as private, Co. H, May 16, 1898; mustered out with company, October 27, 1898, at Brooklyn, N. Y.

KURZ, EMILE R.—Age, 18 years. Enlisted, May 2, 1898, at Brooklyn, to serve two years; mustered in as private, Co B, May 16, 1898; died of typhoid fever, September 28, 1898, in Long Island College Hospital, Brooklyn, N. Y.

LARSSON, AREL L.—Age, 21 years. Enlisted, May 2, 1898, at Brooklyn, to serve two years; mustered in as private, Co. G, May 13, 1898; mustered out, to date, October 27, 1898.

LAULESS, PETER J.—Age, — years. Enlisted, June 27, 1898, at Brooklyn, to serve two years; mustered in as private, Co. F, same date; mustered out with company, October 27, 1898, at Brooklyn, N. Y.

LAUNZINGER, HENRY.—Age, 22 years. Enlisted, May 11, 1898, at Camp Black, to serve two years; mustered in as private, Co. M, May 13, 1898; mustered out with company, October 27, 1898, at Brooklyn, N. Y.

LAVALL, AXEL.—Age, — years. Enlisted, June 23, 1898, at Brooklyn, to serve two years; mustered in as private, Co. G, same date; mustered out with company, October 27, 1898, at Brooklyn, N. Y.

LAVIN, THOMAS.—Age, — years. Enlisted, June 20, 1898, at Brooklyn, to serve two years; mustered in as private, Co. C, same date; mustered out with company, October 27, 1898, at Brooklyn, N. Y.

LAYTON, GEORGE S.—Age, 28 years. Enlisted, May 2, 1898, at Brooklyn, to serve two years; mustered in as sergeant, Co. B, May 16, 1898; promoted quartermaster-sergeant, May 25, 1898; died of typhoid fever, September 20, 1898, in Seney Hospital, Brooklyn, N. Y.

LEACH, HARVEY L. L.—Age, 21 years. Enlisted, May 14, 1898, at Brooklyn, to serve two years; mustered in as private, Co. I, May 16, 1898; discharged for disability, September 1, 1898, at Camp Thomas, Chickamauga Park, Ga.

LEARY, JOHN F.—Age, 23 years. Enlisted, May 10, 1898, at Hempstead, to serve two years; mustered in as private, Co. E, May 16, 1898; mustered out with company, October 27, 1898, at Brooklyn, N. Y.

LEARY, WILLIAM J.—Age, 29 years. Enlisted, May 2, 1898, at Brooklyn, to serve two years; mustered in as private, Co. E, May 16, 1898; mustered out with company, October 27, 1898, at Brooklyn, N. Y

LECOCQ, JULES E.—Age, 27 years. Enlisted, May 13, 1898, at Hempstead, to serve two years; mustered in as musician, Co. L, May 16, 1898; mustered out with company, October 27, 1898, at Brooklyn, N. Y.

LEDERER, KAMILL.—Age, 22 years. Enlisted, May 2, 1898, at Brooklyn, to serve two years; mustered in as private, Co. L, May 16, 1898; mustered out with company, October 27, 1898, at Brooklyn, N. Y.

LEE, PHILLIP H.—Age, 21 years. Enlisted, May 11, 1898, at Hempstead, to serve two years; mustered in as private, Co. A, May 13, 1898; mustered out with company, October 27, 1898, at Brooklyn, N. Y.

LEMPERLE, JOHN.—Age, 21 years. Enlisted, May 13, 1898, at Hempstead, to serve two years; mustered in as private, Co. E, May 16, 1898; mustered out with company, October 27, 1898, at Brooklyn, N. Y.

LENNON, PHILIP E.—Age, 22 years. Enlisted, May 2, 1898, at Brooklyn, to serve two years; mustered in as private, Co. D, May 16, 1898; mustered out with company, October 27, 1898, at Brooklyn, N Y.

LEONARD, JOSEPH.—Age, — years. Enlisted, June 23, 1898, at Brooklyn, to serve two years; mustered in as private, Co. A, same date; mustered out with company, October 27, 1898, at Brooklyn, N. Y.

LEONARD, THOMAS JOHN.—Age, 20 years. Enlisted, May 6, 1898, at Camp Black, to serve two years; mustered in as private, Co. H, May 16, 1898; mustered out with company, October 27, 1898, at Brooklyn, N. Y.

LE ROY, HUGH.—Age, 24 years. Enlisted, May 12, 1898, at Camp Black, to serve two years; mustered in as private, Co. F, May 16, 1898; mustered out, to date, October 27, 1898.

LEVY, MAXWELL.—Age, 22 years. Enlisted, May 2, 1898, at Brooklyn, to serve two years; mustered in as private, Co. E, May 16, 1898; mustered out with company, October 27, 1898, at Brooklyn, N. Y.

LEWING, WILLIAM G.—Age, 22 years. Enlisted, May 2, 1898, at Brooklyn, to serve two years; mustered in as private, Co. A, May 13, 1898; mustered out with company, October 27, 1898, at Brooklyn, N. Y.

LIBBEY, FRANK D.—Age, 42 years. Enlisted, May 14, 1898, at Hempstead, to serve two years; mustered in as private, Co. B, May 16, 1898; transferred to Hospital Corps, United States Army, September 2, 1898, at Camp Thomas, Chickamauga Park, Ga.

LICKEFELT, JULIUS.—Age, — years. Enlisted, June 30, 1898, at Brooklyn, to serve two years; mustered in as private, Co. C, same date; mustered out with company, October 27, 1898, at Brooklyn, N. Y.

LIEPOLD, GEORGE.—Age, — years. Enlisted, July 2, 1898, at Brooklyn, to serve two years; mustered in as private, Co. E, same date; mustered out with company, October 27, 1898, at Brooklyn, N. Y.

LIGNANTE, ANTONIO.—Age, 21 years. Enlisted, May 2, 1898, at Brooklyn, to serve two years; mustered in as corporal, Co. E, May 16, 1898; returned to ranks, June 15, 1898; mustered out, to date, October 27, 1898.

LIND, CHARLES E.—Age, 22 years. Enlisted, May 2, 1898, at Brooklyn, to serve two years; mustered in as private, Co. G, May 13, 1898; mustered out with company, October 27, 1898, at Brooklyn, N. Y.

LIND, VICTOR.—Age, 21 years. Enlisted, May 2, 1898, at Brooklyn, to serve two years; mustered in as private, Co. G, May 13, 1898; mustered out with company, October 27, 1898, at Brooklyn, N. Y.

LINDGIRST, BERNHARD.—Age, 24 years. Enlisted, May 2, 1898, at Brooklyn, to serve two years; mustered in as private, Co. G, May 13, 1898; mustered out with company, October 27, 1898, at Brooklyn, N. Y.

LINGVALL, CHARLES G.—Age, 25 years. Enlisted, May 2, 1898, at Brooklyn, to serve two years; mustered in as private, Co. G, May 13, 1898; mustered out with company, October 27, 1898, at Brooklyn, N. Y.

LLOYD, GILBERT.—Age, 38 years. Enlisted, May 2, 1898, at Brooklyn, to serve two years; mustered in as private, Co. E, May 16, 1898; promoted corporal, September 8, 1898; mustered out with company, October 27, 1898, at Brooklyn, N. Y.

LOESER, ROBERT C.—Age, 26 years. Enlisted, May 12, 1898, at Hempstead, to serve two years; mustered in as private, Co. D, May 16, 1898; promoted corporal, September 2, 1898; mustered out with company, October 27, 1898, at Brooklyn, N. Y.

LOESING, JOSEPH B.—Age, — years. Enlisted, June 20, 1898, at Brooklyn, to serve two years; mustered in as private, Co. M, same date; mustered out with company, October 27, 1898, at Brooklyn, N. Y.

LOGAN, EDWARD D. B.—Age, 42 years. Enlisted, May 2, 1898, at Brooklyn, to serve two years; mustered in as first sergeant, Co. H, May 16, 1898; mustered out with company, October 27, 1898, at Brooklyn, N. Y.

LOGUE, JAMES F.—Age, 36 years. Enlisted, May 2, 1898, at Brooklyn, to serve two years; mustered in as quartermaster-sergeant, Co. D, May 16, 1898; mustered out with company, October 27, 1898, at Brooklyn, N. Y.

LOHR, CONRAD.—Age, 22 years. Enlisted, May 2, 1898, at Brooklyn, to serve two years; mustered in as private, Co. A, May 13, 1898; mustered out with company, October 27, 1898, at Brooklyn, N. Y.

LONCAS, ANGELLO H.—Age, 28 years. Enlisted, May 14, 1898, at Hempstead, to serve two years; mustered in as private, Co. D, May 16, 1898; mustered out with company, October 27, 1898, at Brooklyn, N. Y.

LOTTERLE, WILLIAM.—Age, 24 years. Enlisted, May 2, 1898, at Brooklyn, to serve two years; mustered in as private, Co. L, May 16, 1898; mustered out with company, October 27, 1898, at Brooklyn, N. Y.

LUNDBERG, GUSTAF.—Age, 21 years. Enlisted, May 2, 1898, at Brooklyn, to serve two years; mustered in as private, Co. G, May 13, 1898; transferred to Hospital Corps, June 14, 1898; returned to company, September 13, 1898; mustered out with company, October 27, 1898, at Brooklyn, N. Y.

LUNDGREN, MARTIN.—Age, 21 years. Enlisted, May 2, 1898, at Brooklyn, to serve two years; mustered in as private, Co. G, May 13, 1898; mustered out with company, October 27, 1898, at Brooklyn, N. Y.

LYNCH, JAMES A.—Age, 24 years. Enlisted, May 11, 1898, at Hempstead, to serve two years; mustered in as private, Co. L, May 16, 1898; discharged, October 14, 1898, to enlist in Regular Army.

LYNCH, JAMES J.—Age, 23 years. Enlisted, May 2, 1898, at Brooklyn, to serve two years; mustered in as private, Co. I, May 16, 1898; promoted corporal, August 1, 1898; mustered out with company, October 27, 1898, at Brooklyn, N. Y.

LYNCH, JAMES T.—Age, 23 years. Enlisted, May 2, 1898, at Brooklyn, to serve two years; mustered in as private, Co. C, May 16, 1898; mustered out with company, October 27, 1898, at Brooklyn, N. Y.

LYNCH, JOHN J.—Age, 21 years. Enlisted, May 2, 1898, at Brooklyn, to serve two years; mustered in as private, Co. M, May 13, 1898; mustered out with company, October 27, 1898, at Brooklyn, N. Y.

LYNCH, LEON M.—Age, 27 years. Enlisted, May 13, 1898, at Hempstead, to serve two years; mustered in as corporal, Co. L, May 13, 1898; promoted sergeant, May 21, 1898; transferred to Hospital Corps, June 12, 1898; returned to company, September 13, 1898; returned to ranks, no date; discharged, September 28, 1898.

LYON, CHESTER.—Age, 19 years. Enlisted, May 12, 1898, at Hempstead, to serve two years; mustered in as private, Co. B, May 16, 1898; mustered out with company, October 27, 1898, at Brooklyn, N. Y.

LYONS, EDWARD J.—Age, 21 years. Enlisted, May 14, 1898, at Camp Black, to serve two years; mustered in as private, Co. H, May 16, 1898; mustered out with company, October 27, 1898, at Broklyn, N. Y.

MACAULEY, WILLIAM.—Age, 30 years.   Enrolled, May 2, 1898, at Brooklyn, to serve two years; mustered in as second lieutenant, Co. E, May 16, 1898; mustered out with company, October 27, 1898, at Brooklyn, N. Y.; commissioned second lieutenant, May 16, 1898, with rank from same date, original.

MACDONALD, JOHN A.—Age, 29 years. Enlisted, May 2, 1898, at Brooklyn, to serve two years; mustered in as private, Co. F, May 16, 1898; promoted corporal, September 28, 1898; mustered out with company, October 27, 1898, at Brooklyn, N. Y.

MACDONALD, JOHN J.—Age, 25 years. Enlisted, May 2, 1898, at Brooklyn, to serve two years; mustered in as private, Co. K, May 13, 1898; discharged, October 18, 1898, as John A. McDonald.

MACKEY, EDWARD.—Age, 25 years.   Enlisted, May 13, 1898, at Camp Black, to serve two years; mustered in as private, Co. I, May 16, 1898; mustered out with company, October 27, 1898, at Brooklyn, N. Y.

MACKEY, HERBERT E.—Age, 28 years. Enlisted, May 2, 1898, at Brooklyn, to serve two years; mustered in as private, Co. H, May 16, 1898; mustered out, to date, October 27, 1898.

MACUMBER, JOHN LINCOLN.—Age, 37 years.   Enrolled, May 2, 1898, at Brooklyn, to serve two years; mustered in as surgeon, May 4, 1898; mustered out on individual muster-out roll, August 25, 1898, at Chickamauga Park, Ga.; commissioned surgeon, May 4, 1898, with rank from same date, original.

MACUMBER, VAN D.—Age, 48 years.   Enrolled, May 2, 1898, at Brooklyn, to serve two years; mustered in as first lieutenant, Co. L, May 16, 1898; captain, July 23, 1898; mustered out, to date, October 27, 1898; commissioned first lieutenant, May 16, 1898, with rank from same date, original; captain, July 18, 1898, with rank from same date, vice Wagner, discharged.

MADDEN, JAMES J.—Age, 32 years.   Enlisted, May 11, 1898, at Brooklyn, to serve two years; mustered in as private, Co. M, May 13, 1898; mustered out with company, October 27, 1898, at Brooklyn, N. Y.

MAEDER, CHARLES L.—Age, — years.   Enlisted, June 18, 1898, at Brooklyn, to serve two years; mustered in as private, Co. H, same date; mustered out with company, October 27, 1898, at Brooklyn, N. Y.

MAGNER, WILLIAM J.—Age, — years. Enlisted, June 23, 1898, at Brooklyn, to serve two years; mustered in as private, Co. I, same date; mustered out with company, October 27, 1898, at Brooklyn, N. Y.

MAGUIRE, GEORGE P.—Age, 20 years. Enlisted, May 2, 1898, at Brooklyn, to serve two years; mustered in as private, Co. D, May 16, 1898; mustered out with company, October 27, 1898, at Brooklyn, N. Y.

MAHAN, JOHN.—Age, — years. Enlisted, June 22, 1898, at Brooklyn, to serve two years; mustered in as private, Co. E, same date; mustered out with company, October 27, 1898, at Brooklyn, N. Y., as John J. Mahan.

MAHLSTEDT, JOHN.—Age, 28 years. Enlisted, May 2, 1898, at Brooklyn, to serve two years; mustered in as private, Co. M, May 13, 1898; mustered out with company, October 27, 1898, at Brooklyn, N. Y.

MAHONEY, JOHN C.—Age, 20 years. Enlisted, May 2, 1898, at Brooklyn, to serve two years; mustered in as private, Co. F, May 16, 1898; promoted corporal, August 23, 1898; died of typhoid fever, September 21, 1898, in First Division, Third Army Corps, Hospital.

MALEHOW, CHARLES.—Age, 20 years. Enlisted, May 11, 1898, at Hempstead, to serve two years; mustered in as private, Co B, May 16, 1898; deserted, August 11, 1898, from Camp Thomas, Chickamauga Park, Ga.

MALLIE, WILLIAM.—Age, — years. Enlisted, June 20, 1898, at Brooklyn, to serve two years; mustered in as private, Co. I, same date; mustered out with company, October 27, 1898, at Brooklyn, N. Y.

MALLON, BERNARD J.—Age, 26 years. Enlisted, May 2, 1898, at Brooklyn, to serve two years; mustered in as private, Co. M, May 13, 1898; mustered out with company, October 27, 1898, at Brooklyn, N. Y.

MALLON, WILLIAM J.—Age, 21 years. Enlisted, May 14, 1898, at Hempstead, to serve two years; mustered in as private, Co. L, May 16, 1898; mustered out with company, October 27, 1898, at Brooklyn, N. Y.

MALLONE, RALPH.—Age, 23 years.   Enlisted, May 11, 1898, at Camp Black, to serve two years; mustered in as private, Co. I, May 16, 1898; mustered out with company, October 27, 1898, at Brooklyn, N. Y.

MALLOY, JOHN P.—Age, 25 years.   Enlisted, May 2, 1898, at Brooklyn, to serve two years; mustered in as private, Co. 1, May 16, 1898; mustered out with company, October 27, 1898, at Brooklyn, N. Y.

MALONE, FRANK.—Age, — years.   Enlisted, June 29, 1898, at Brooklyn, to serve two years; mustered in as private, Co. E, same date; mustered out with company, October 27, 1898, at Brooklyn, N. Y.

MALONEY, GEORGE F.—Age, 21 years.   Enlisted, May 3, 1898 at Camp Black, to serve two years; mustered in as private, Co. L, May 16, 1898; mustered out with company, October 27, 1898, at Brooklyn, N. Y.

MALONEY, STEPHEN T.—Age, — years.   Enlisted, July 5, 1898, at Brooklyn, to serve two years; mustered in as private, Co. H, same date; mustered out with company, October 27, 1898, at Brooklyn, N. Y.

MANNING, JOHN S.—Age, 21 years.   Enlisted, May 2, 1898, at Brooklyn, to serve two years; mustered in as private, Co. B, May 16, 1898; promoted corporal, July 7, 1898; mustered out with company, October 27, 1898, at Brooklyn, N. Y.

MARINUS, CHARLES R.—Age, 18 years.   Enlisted, May 2, 1898, at Brooklyn, to serve two years; mustered in as private, Co. C, May 16, 1898; mustered out with company, October 27, 1898, at Brooklyn, N. Y.

MARLE, JOSEPH H.—Age, 39 years.   Enlisted, May 12, 1898, at Hempstead, to serve two years; mustered in as private, Co. B, May 16, 1898; mustered out with company, October 27, 1898, at Brooklyn, N. Y.

MARONEY, JR., THOMAS F.—Age, — years.   Enlisted, July 1, 1898, at Brooklyn, to serve two years; mustered in as private, Co. H, same date; mustered out, to date, October 27, 1898.

MARSH, JR., GEORGE W.—Age, 21 years. Enlisted, May 2, 1898, at Brooklyn, to serve two years; mustered in as private, Co. A, May 13, 1898; mustered out with company, October 27, 1898, at Brooklyn, N. Y.

MARSH, WILLIAM D.—Age, 27 years. Enlisted, May 2, 1898, at Brooklyn, to serve two years; mustered in as quartermaster-sergeant, Co. K, May 13, 1898; discharged, October 20, 1898.

MARTIN, CONRAD.—Age, 20 years. Enlisted, May 2, 1898, at Brooklyn, to serve two years; mustered in as private, Co. D, May 16, 1898; mustered out with company, October 27, 1898, at Brooklyn, N. Y.

MARTIN, ERNEST C.—Age, — years. Enlisted, June 22, 1898, at Brooklyn, to serve two years; mustered in as private, Co. A, same date; mustered out with company, October 27, 1898, at Brooklyn, N. Y.

MARTIN, GEORGE M.—Age, 35 years. Enlisted, May 2, 1898, at Brooklyn, to serve two years; mustered in as private, Co. H, May 16, 1898; mustered out with company, October 27, 1898, at Brooklyn, N. Y.

MARTIN, HARRY L.—Age, 30 years. Enlisted, May 2, 1898, at Brooklyn, to serve two years; mustered in as private, Co. C, May 16, 1898; promoted corporal, July 8, 1898; mustered out with company, October 27, 1898, at Brooklyn, N. Y.

MARTIN, JAMES C.—Age, 21 years. Enlisted, May 12, 1898, at Hempstead, to serve two years; mustered in as private, Co. K, May 13, 1898; died of heart failure, August 11, 1898, in Division Hospital.

MATHEWS, JOHN T.—Age, 22 years. Enlisted, May 2, 1898, at Brooklyn, to serve two years; mustered in as corporal, Co. E, May 16, 1898; returned to ranks, no date; deserted, August 21, 1898.

MAXWELL, JAMES.—Age, 31 years. Enlisted, May 13, 1898, at Hempstead, to serve two years; mustered in as private, Co. L, May 16, 1898; mustered out with company, October 27, 1898, at Brooklyn, N. Y.

MAXWELL, JAMES J.—Age, — years. Enlisted, June 21, 1898, at Brooklyn, to serve two years; mustered in as private, Co. C, same date; mustered out with company, October 27, 1898, at Brooklyn, N. Y.

MAXWELL, JOHN A.—Age, 21 years. Enlisted, May 2, 1898, at Brooklyn, to serve two years; mustered in as private, Co. M, May 13, 1898; promoted corporal, July 20, 1898; sergeant, October 14, 1898; mustered out with company, October 27, 1898, at Brooklyn, N. Y.

MAXWELL, SAMUEL D.—Age, 22 years. Enlisted, May 2, 1898, at Brooklyn, to serve two years; mustered in as corporal, Co. C, May 16, 1898; mustered out with company, October 27, 1898, at Brooklyn, N. Y.

MAY, FRANK.—Age, 35 years. Enlisted, May 2, 1898, at Brooklyn, to serve two years; mustered in as private, Co. C, May 16, 1898; mustered out with company, October 27, 1898, at Brooklyn, N. Y.

MAY, JAMES.—Age, 25 years. Enlisted, May 12, 1898, at Hempstead, to serve two years; mustered in as private, Co. B, May 16, 1898; promoted corporal, July 27, 1898; mustered out with company, October 27, 1898, at Brooklyn, N. Y.

MAYER, JOSEPH.—Age, 19 years. Enlisted, May 2, 1898, at Brooklyn, to serve two years; mustered in as corporal, Co. E, May 16, 1898; mustered out with company, October 27, 1898, at Brooklyn, N. Y.

McCABE, JAMES.—Age, — years. Enlisted, June 22, 1898, at Brooklyn, to serve two years; mustered in as private, Co. E, same date; mustered out with company, October 27, 1898, at Brooklyn, N. Y.

McCABE, THOMAS J.—Age, 30 years. Enlisted, May 11, 1898, at Hempstead, to serve two years; mustered in as private, Co. D, May 16, 1898; mustered out with company, October 27, 1898, at Brooklyn, N. Y.

McCABE, WILFRED E.—Age, — years. Enlisted, June 22, 1898, at Brooklyn, to serve two years; mustered in as private, Co. E, same date; mustered out with company, October 27, 1898, at Brooklyn, N. Y.

McCADDEN, ERNEST.—Age, 21 years. Enlisted, May 12, 1898, at Hempstead, to serve two years; mustered in as private, Co. D, May 16, 1898; mustered out with company, October 27, 1898, at Brooklyn, N. Y.

McCAFFERY, JR., ARTHUR.—Age, 44 years. Enlisted, May 2, 1898, at Brooklyn, to serve two years; mustered in as private, Co. M, May 13, 1898; mustered out with company, October 27, 1898, at Brooklyn, N. Y.

McCANN, JOSEPH D.—Age, 26 years. Enlisted, May 2, 1898, at Brooklyn, to serve two years; mustered in as private, Co. H, May 16, 1898; mustered out with company, October 27, 1898, at Brooklyn, N. Y.

McCARTHY, ANTHONY.—Age, — years. Enlisted, June 27, 1898, at Brooklyn, to serve two years; mustered in as private, Co. E, same date; mustered out with company, October 27, 1898, at Brooklyn, N. Y.

McCARTHY, CAL.—Age, 20 years. Enlisted, May 2, 1898, at Brooklyn, to serve two years; mustered in as corporal, Co. D, May 16, 1898; mustered out with company, October 27, 1898, at Brooklyn, N. Y.

McCARTHY, CHARLES F.—Age, 21 years. Enlisted, May 12, 1898, at Camp Black, to serve two years; mustered in as private, Co. F, May 16, 1898; mustered out with company, October 27, 1898, at Brooklyn, N. Y.

McCARTHY, JOHN.—Age, 35 years. Enlisted, May 14, 1898, at Camp Black, to serve two years; mustered in as private, Co. H, May 16, 1898; mustered out with company, October 27, 1898, at Brooklyn, N. Y.

McCARTHY, JOHN J.—Age, 19 years. Enlisted, May 14, 1898, at Camp Black, to serve two years; mustered in as private, Co. I, May 16, 1898; mustered out with company, October 27, 1898, at Brooklyn, N. Y.

McCAULEY, EDWARD J.—Age, 24 years. Enlisted, May 2, 1898, at Brooklyn, to serve two years; mustered in as private, Co. E, May 16, 1898; discharged, August 24, 1898.

McCLOSKEY, GUSTAVE B.—Age, 35 years. Enlisted, May 11, 1898, at Camp Black, to serve two years; mustered in as private, Co. I, May 16, 1898; mustered out with company, October 27, 1898, at Brooklyn, N. Y.

McCLOSKEY, JAMES J.—Age, — years. Enlisted, July 5, 1898, at Brooklyn, to serve two years; mustered in as private, Co. H, same date; mustered out with company, October 27, 1898, at Brooklyn, N. Y.

McCLOSKEY, JAMES S.—Age, 21 years. Enlisted, May 12, 1898, at Camp Black, to serve two years; mustered in as private, Co. F, May 16, 1898; mustered out with company, October 27, 1898, at Brooklyn, N. Y.

McCOLLUM, JACOB J.—Age, 22 years. Enlisted, May 2, 1898, at Brooklyn, to serve two years; mustered in as private, Co. K, May 13, 1898; promoted corporal, July 7, 1898; mustered out with company, October 27, 1898, at Brooklyn, N. Y.

McCONNIN, JOHN J.—Age, 20 years. Enlisted, May 2, 1898, at Brooklyn, to serve two years; mustered in as private, Co. I, May 16, 1898; mustered out with company, October 27, 1898, at Brooklyn, N. Y.

McCOOL, WILLIAM.--Age, — years. Enlisted, June 28, 1898, at Brooklyn, to serve two years; mustered in as private, Co. F, same date; discharged for disability, August 23, 1898.

McCORKLE, CHARLES P.—Age, 25 years. Enlisted, May 2, 1898, at Brooklyn, to serve two years; mustered in as private, Co. B, May 16, 1898; appointed cook, August 3, 1898; mustered out with company, October 27, 1898, at Brooklyn, N. Y.

McCORMACK, CHARLES A.—Age, 30 years. Enlisted, May 2, 1898, at Brooklyn, to serve two years; mustered in as private, Co. H, May 16, 1898; mustered out with company, October 27, 1898, at Brooklyn, N. Y.

McCORMACK, FRANCIS J.—Age, 26 years. Enlisted, May 2, 1898, at Brooklyn, to serve two years; mustered in as private, Co. F, May 16, 1898; promoted corporal, July 14, 1898; mustered out, to date, October 27, 1898.

McCORMACK, HARRY J.—Age, 22 years. Enlisted, May 2, 1898, at Brooklyn, to serve two years; mustered in as private, Co. E, May 16, 1898; mustered out with company, October 27, 1898, at Brooklyn, N. Y.

McCORMICK, JOHN F.—Age, — years. Enlisted, June 21, 1898, at Brooklyn, to serve two years; mustered in as private, Co. C, same date; mustered out with company, October 27, 1898, at Brooklyn, N. Y.

McCORMICK, MICHAEL J.—Age, 22 years. Enlisted, May 14, 1898, at Camp Black, to serve two years; mustered in as private, Co. H, May 16, 1898; mustered out with company, October 27, 1898, at Brooklyn, N. Y.

McCORMICK, WILLIAM J.—Age, 26 years. Enlisted, May 13, 1898, at Camp Black, to serve two years; mustered in as private, Co. F, May 16, 1898; mustered out with company, October 27, 1898, at Brooklyn, N. Y.

McCOY, CHARLES E.—Age, 30 years. Enlisted, May 2, 1898, at Brooklyn, to serve two years; mustered in as private, Co. M, May 13, 1898; transferred to Co. I, May 26, 1898; died of disease, October 15, 1898, at his home.

McCULLEY, HARRY.—Age, — years. Enlisted, June 29, 1898, at Brooklyn, to serve two years; mustered in as private, Co. F, same date; mustered out with company, October 27, 1898, at Brooklyn, N. Y.

McCULLOUGH, CLAYTON.—Age, 20 years. Enlisted, May 14, 1898, at Camp Black, to serve two years; mustered in as private, Co. H, May 16, 1898; mustered out with company, October 27, 1898, at Brooklyn, N. Y.

McCULLOUGH, FRANK.—Age, 27 years. Enlisted, May 14, 1898, at Camp Black, to serve two years; mustered in as private, Co. I, May 16, 1898; mustered out with company, October 27, 1898, at Brooklyn, N. Y.

McDERMOTT, HARRY J.—Age, — years. Enlisted, June 27, 1898, at Brooklyn, to serve two years; mustered in as private, Co. B, same date; promoted corporal, July 27, 1898; mustered out with company, October 27, 1898, at Brooklyn, N. Y.

McDERMOTT, JOHN.—Age, — years. Enlisted, June 27, 1898, at Brooklyn, to serve two years; mustered in as private, Co. F, same date; mustered out with company, October 27, 1898, at Brooklyn, N. Y.

McDERMOTT, JOHN A.—Age, 26 years. Enlisted, May 13, 1898, at Hempstead, to serve two years; mustered in as private, Co. B, May 16, 1898; mustered out with company, October 27, 1898, at Brooklyn, N. Y.

McDONALD, EDWARD C.—Age, 27 years.   Enlisted, May 2, 1898, at Brooklyn, to serve two years; mustered in as private, Co. E, May 16, 1898; mustered out with company, October 27, 1898, at Brooklyn, N. Y.

McDONALD, THOMAS F.—Age, 29 years.   Enlisted, May 2, 1898, at Brooklyn, to serve two years; mustered in as private, Co. E, May 16, 1898; mustered out with company, October 27, 1898, at Brooklyn, N. Y.

McDONOUGH, LAWRENCE.—Age, — years.   Enlisted, June 22, 1898, at Brooklyn, to serve two years; mustered in as private, Co. K, same date; mustered out with company, October 27, 1898, at Brooklyn, N. Y.

McDONOUGH, PATRICK W.—Age, — years.   Enlisted, June 25, 1898, at Brooklyn, to serve two years; mustered in as private, Co. I, same date; mustered out with company, October 27, 1898, at Brooklyn, N. Y.

McDONOUGH, WILLIAM J.—Age, — years.   Enlisted, June 27, 1898, at Brooklyn, to serve two years; mustered in as private, Co. M, same date; died of malaria, September 20, 1898, in Brooklyn City Hospital, Brooklyn, N. Y.

McELGIN, EUGENE A.—Age, 21 years. Enlisted, May 2, 1898, at Brooklyn, to serve two years; mustered in as private, Co. M, May 13, 1898; mustered out with company, October 27, 1898, at Brooklyn, N. Y.

McELGIN, HUGH J. B.—Age, 18 years. Enlisted, May 2, 1898, at Brooklyn, to serve two years; mustered in as private, Co. H, May 16, 1898; mustered out with company, October 27, 1898, at Brooklyn, N. Y.; subsequent service as second lieutenant, Forty-sixth Regiment, United States Volunteer Infantry.

McEVOY, PATRICK.—Age, — years. Enlisted, June 20, 1898, at Brooklyn, to serve two years; mustered in as private, Co. H, same date; mustered out, to date, October 27, 1898.

McFEELEY, JOHN J.—Age, 44 years. Enlisted, May 7, 1898, at Hempstead, to serve two years; mustered in as private, Co. A, May 13, 1898; mustered out with company, October 27, 1898, at Brooklyn, N. Y.

McFEELEY, WILLIAM C.—Age, 43. years. Enlisted, May 2, 1898, at Brooklyn, to serve two years; mustered in as private, Co. A, May 13, 1898; mustered out with company, October 27, 1898, at Brooklyn, N. Y.

McGINN, JOSEPH.—Age, 22 years. Enlisted, May 14, 1898, at Hempstead, to serve two years; mustered in as private, Co. L, May 16, 1898; appointed artificer, August 1, 1898; mustered out with company, October 27, 1898, at Brooklyn, N. Y.

McGIVONEY, THOMAS.—Age, 25 years. Enlisted, May 2, 1898, at Brooklyn, to serve two years; mustered in as private, Co. C, May 16, 1898; mustered out with company, October 27, 1898, at Brooklyn, N. Y.

McGONIGAL, JAMES J.—Age, — years. Enlisted, July 5, 1898, at Brooklyn, to serve two years; mustered in as private, Co. H, same date; mustered out with company, October 27, 1898, at Brooklyn, N. Y.

McGOUGH, JOHN J.—Age, 23 years. Enlisted, May 2, 1898, at Brooklyn, to serve two years; mustered in as private, Co. B, May 16, 1898; promoted corporal, July 7, 1898; mustered out with company, October 27, 1898, at Brooklyn, N. Y.

McGOVERN, JAMES F.—Age, 22 years. Enlisted, May 3, 1898, at Hempstead, to serve two years; mustered in as private, Co. K, May 13, 1898; mustered out with company, October 27, 1898, at Brooklyn, N. Y.

McGOWAN, JOHN J.—Age, — years. Enlisted, July 5, 1898, at Brooklyn, to serve two years; mustered in as private, Co. A, same date; mustered out, to date, October 27, 1898.

McGRAIL, JOHN J.—Age, — years. Enlisted, June 27, 1898, at
Brooklyn, to serve two years; mustered in as private, Co. M,
same date; mustered out with company, October 27, 1898, at
Brooklyn, N. Y.

McGRATH, JOHN T.—Age, 34 years. Enlisted, May 2, 1898, at
Brooklyn, to serve two years; mustered in as private, Co. L,
May 16, 1898; mustered out with company, October 27, 1898, at
Brooklyn, N. Y.

McGRATH, THOMAS P.—Age, 24 years. Enlisted, May 2, 1898,
at Brooklyn, to serve two years; mustered in as private, Co. F,
May 16, 1898; mustered out with company, October 27, 1898, at
Brooklyn, N. Y.

McGRAYNE, SAMUEL.—Age, 31 years. Enlisted, May 11, 1898,
at Camp Black, to serve two years; mustered in as private, Co.
M, May 13, 1898; mustered out with company, October 27, 1898,
at Brooklyn, N. Y.

McGUIRE, JOHN.—Age, — years. Enlisted, June 28, 1898, at
Brooklyn, to serve two years; mustered in as private, Co. M,
same date; mustered out with company, October 27, 1898, at
Brooklyn, N. Y., as John Maguire.

McGUIRE, THOMAS.—Age, 24 years. Enlisted, May 13, 1898, at
Camp Black, to serve two years; mustered in as private, Co. F,
May 16, 1898; mustered out, to date, October 27, 1898.

McILVAINE, GEORGE S.—Age, 22 years. Enlisted, May 11,
1898, at Hempstead, to serve two years; mustered in as private,
Co. B, May 16, 1898; mustered out with company, October 27,
1898, at Brooklyn, N. Y.

McKAY, GEORGE T.—Age, 23 years. Enlisted, May 6, 1898, at
Camp Black, to serve two years; mustered in as private, Co. M,
May 13, 1898; mustered out with company, October 27, 1898, at
Brooklyn, N. Y.

McKEE, JAMES F.—Age, — years. Enlisted, June 25, 1898, at
Brooklyn, to serve two years; mustered in as private, Co. M,
same date; mustered out with company, October 27, 1898, at
Brooklyn, N. Y.

McKEEVER, JOSEPH.—Age, — years. Enlisted, June 27, 1898, at Brooklyn, to serve two years; mustered in as private, Co. C, same date; mustered out with company, October 27, 1898, at Brooklyn, N. Y.

McKEON, JOHN J.—Age, — years. Enlisted, June 25, 1898, at Brooklyn, to serve two years; mustered in as private, Co. M, same date; mustered out with company, October 27, 1898, at Brooklyn, N. Y.

McLAREN, DUNCAN.—Age, 24 years. Enlisted, May 2, 1898, at Brooklyn, to serve two years; mustered in as musician, Co. C, May 16, 1898; mustered out with company, October 27, 1898, at Brooklyn, N. Y.

McLAUGHLIN, EDWARD J.—Age, 28 years. Enlisted, May 13, 1898, at Hempstead, to serve two years; mustered in as corporal, Co. E, May 16, 1898; mustered out with company, October 27, 1898, at Brooklyn, N. Y.

McLAUGHLIN, JAMES F.—Age, — years. Enlisted, June 29, 1898, at Brooklyn, to serve two years; mustered in as private, Co. D, same date; mustered out with company, October 27, 1898, at Brooklyn, N. Y.

McLAUGHLIN, JOSEPH.—Age, — years. Enlisted, July 5, 1898, at Brooklyn, to serve two years; mustered in as private, Co. K, same date; mustered out with company, October 27, 1898, at Brooklyn, N. Y.

McLAUGHLIN, LOUIS K.—Age, 26 years. Enlisted, May 2, 1898, at Brooklyn, to serve two years; mustered in as sergeant, Co. E, May 16, 1898; discharged, June 12, 1898.

McLAUGHLIN, PATRICK F.—Age, 38 years. Enrolled, May 2, 1898, at Brooklyn, to serve two years; mustered in as first lieutenant, Co. E, May 16, 1898; mustered out with company, October 27, 1898, at Brooklyn, N. Y.; commissioned first lieutenant, May 16, 1898, with rank from same date, original.

McLAUGHLIN, JOHN T.—Age, 38 years. Enlisted, May 2, 1898, at Brooklyn, to serve two years; mustered in as musician, Co. B, May 16, 1898; mustered out with company, October 27, 1898, at Brooklyn, N. Y.

McLAUGHLIN, WILLIAM J.—Age, 27 years   Enlisted, May 2, 1898, at Brooklyn, to serve two years; mustered in as private, Co. E, May 16, 1898; mustered out with company, October 27, 1898, at Brooklyn, N. Y.

McLEAN, AUSTIN.—Age, 34 years.   Enlisted, May 14, 1898, at Camp Black, to serve two years; mustered in as private, Co. H, May 16, 1898; mustered out, to date, October 27, 1898.

McMANUS, JAMES W.—Age, — years.   Enlisted, June 22, 1898, at Brooklyn, to serve two years; mustered in as private, Co. C, same date; mustered out with company, October 27, 1898, at Brooklyn, N. Y.

McMANUS, WILLIAM.—Age, 21 years.   Enlisted, May 12, 1898, at Camp Black, to serve two years; mustered in as private, Co. F, May 16, 1898; mustered out with company, October 27, 1898, at Brooklyn, N Y.

McNALLY, JAMES F.—Age, 24 years.   Enlisted, May 2, 1898, at Brooklyn, to serve two years; mustered in as sergeant, Co. D, May 16, 1898; mustered out with company, October 27, 1898, at Brooklyn, N. Y.

McNAMARA, JOHN PATRICK.—Age, — years.   Enrolled, May 2, 1898, at Brooklyn, to serve two years; mustered in as first lieutenant, Co. C, May 16, 1898; mustered out with company, October 27, 1898, at Brooklyn, N. Y.; commissioned first lieutenant, May 16, 1898, with rank from same date, original.

McNAMARA, JR., THOMAS J.—Age, 27 years.   Enlisted, May 2, 1898, at Brooklyn, to serve two years; mustered in as private, Co. H, May 16, 1898; mustered out with company, October 27, 1898, at Brooklyn, N. Y.

McNAMEE, MICHAEL.—Age, 44 years.   Enlisted, May 2, 1898, at Brooklyn, to serve two years; mustered in as private, Co. E, May 16, 1898; mustered out with company, October 27, 1898, at Brooklyn, N. Y.

McNICHOLS, MARTIN.—Age, — years.   Enlisted, June 22, 1898, at Brooklyn, to serve two years; mustered in as private, Co. H, same date; mustered out with company, October 27, 1898, at Brooklyn, N. Y.

McPEAK, SAMUEL F.—Age, 22 years. Enlisted, May 14, 1898, at Camp Black, to serve two years; mustered in as private, Co. I, May 16, 1898; mustered out with company, October 27, 1898, at Brooklyn, N. Y.

McQUEEN, JOHN H.—Age, 30 years. Enlisted, May 2, 1898, at Brooklyn, to serve two years; mustered in as private. Co. F, May 16, 1898; promoted corporal, September 13, 1898; mustered out with company, October 27, 1898, at Brooklyn, N. Y.

MEAD, EDWARD A.—Age, 25 years. Enlisted, May 2, 1898, at Brooklyn, to serve two years; mustered in as private, Co. E, May 16, 1898; mustered out with company, October 27, 1898, at Brooklyn, N. Y.

MEAD, JOHN F.—Age, 22 years. Enlisted, May 2, 1898, at Brooklyn, to serve two years; mustered in as private, Co. L, May 16, 1898; promoted corporal, May 30, 1898; sergeant, June 28, 1898; mustered out with company, October 27, 1898, at Brooklyn, N. Y.

MEADE, RICHARD A.—Age, 25 years. Enlisted, May 11, 1898, at Hempstead, to serve two years; mustered in as private, Co. B, May 16, 1898; mustered out with company, October 27, 1898, at Brooklyn, N. Y.

MEANSY, MICHAEL J.—Age, — years. Enlisted, June 27, 1898, at Brooklyn, to serve two years; mustered in as private, Co. F, same date; discharged for disability, August 4, 1898.

MECARG, CHARLES W.—Age, — years. Enlisted, June 28, 1898, at Brooklyn, to serve two years; mustered in as private, Co. F, same date; mustered out with company, October 27, 1898, at Brooklyn, N. Y.

MEHRTENS, WILLIAM H.—Age, 22 years. Enlisted, May 2, 1898, at Brooklyn, to serve two years; mustered in as private, Co. I, May 16, 1898; mustered out with company, October 27, 1898, at Brooklyn, N. Y.

MELLOR, FREDERICK W.—Age, — years. Enlisted, June 27, 1898, at Brooklyn, to serve two years; mustered in as private, Co. B, same date; mustered out with company, October 27, 1898, at Brooklyn, N. Y.

MERK, ALBERT.—Age, 27 years. Enlisted, May 5, 1898, at Camp Black, to serve two years; mustered in as private, Co. M, May 13, 1898; discharged for disability, September 23, 1898, at Washington, D. C.

MERRILL, FRANCIS H.—Age, 24 years. Enlisted, May 2, 1898, at Brooklyn, to serve two years; mustered in as sergeant, Co. K, May 13, 1898; mustered out with company, October 27, 1898, at Brooklyn, N. Y.

MERRITT, DANIEL B.—Age, 19 years. Enlisted, May 13, 1898, at Camp Black, to serve two years; mustered in as private, Co. F, May 16, 1898; discharged for disability, August 4, 1898.

MERRITT, EDWIN.—Age, — years. Enlisted, June 25, 1898, at Brooklyn, to serve two years; mustered in as private, Co. K, same date; mustered out with company, October 27, 1898, at Brooklyn, N. Y.

MERRITT, THOMAS L.—Age, 39 years. Enlisted, May 12, 1898, at Hempstead, to serve two years; mustered in as private, Co. K, May 13, 1898; mustered out with company, October 27, 1898, at Brooklyn, N. Y.

MEYER, CONRAD.—Age, 31 years. Enlisted, May 11, 1898, at Camp Black, to serve two years; mustered in as private, Co. M, May 13, 1898; mustered out with company, October 27, 1898, at Brooklyn, N. Y.

MEYERHOFF, HERBERT.—Age, 21 years. Enlisted, May 5, 1898, at Camp Black, to serve two years; mustered in as private, Co. M, May 13, 1898; no further record.

MEYERHOFFER, JOHN.—Age, 22 years. Enlisted, May 14, 1898, at Hempstead, to serve two years; mustered in as private, Co. L, May 16, 1898; mustered out with company, October 27, 1898, at Brooklyn, N. Y.

MICKLEBOROUGH, FERNANDO H.—Age, 31 years. Enlisted, May 2, 1898, at Brooklyn, to serve two years; mustered in as private, Co. M, May 13, 1898; promoted corporal, May 26, 1898; sergeant, June 5, 1898; first sergeant, no date; mustered in as second lieutenant, Co. L, September 15, 1898; mustered out with company, October 27, 1898, at Brooklyn, N. Y.; commissioned second lieutenant, September 14, 1898, with rank from same date, vice Hart, discharged.

MILLER, CHARLES P.—Age, 22 years. Enlisted, May 12, 1898, at Hempstead, to serve two years; mustered in as private, Co. D, May 16, 1898; mustered out with company, October 27, 1898, at Brooklyn, N. Y.

MILLER, HENRY.—Age, — years. Enlisted, June 27, 1898, at Brooklyn, to serve two years; mustered in as private, Co. D, same date; mustered out with company, October 27, 1898, at Brooklyn, N. Y., as Henry Miller, Jr.

MILLER, HERMAN.—Age, 31 years. Enlisted, May 14, 1898, at Brooklyn, to serve two years; mustered in as private, Co. H, May 16, 1898; mustered out with company, October 27, 1898, at Brooklyn, N. Y.

MILLER, JAMES J.—Age, 21 years. Enlisted, May 12, 1898, at Camp Black, to serve two years; mustered in as private, Co. C, May 16, 1898; mustered out with company, October 27, 1898, at Brooklyn, N. Y.

MILLER, JOHN.—Age, — years. Enlisted, June 28, 1898, at Brooklyn, to serve two years; mustered in as private, Co. D, same date; mustered out, to date, October 27, 1898.

MILLER, JOSEPH.—Age, — years. Enlisted, June 28, 1898, at Brooklyn, to serve two years; mustered in as private, Co. D, same date; mustered out with company, October 27, 1898, at Brooklyn, N. Y.

MILLIKIN, FRANK B.—Age, 24 years. Enlisted, May 13, 1898, at Hempstead, to serve two years; mustered in as private, Co. L, May 16, 1898; mustered out with company, October 27, 1898, at Brooklyn, N. Y.

MILLOR, DAVID J.—Age, — years. Enlisted, July 6, 1898, at Brooklyn, to serve two years; mustered in as private, Co. B, same date; mustered out with company, October 27, 1898, at Brooklyn, N. Y., as David J. Miller.

MINER, GEORGE H.—Age, — years. Enlisted, June 29, 1898, at Brooklyn, to serve two years; mustered in as private, Co. L, same date; mustered out with company, October 27, 1898, at Brooklyn, N. Y.

MINER, WALTER H.—Age, 21 years. Enlisted, May 12, 1898,
at Hempstead, to serve two years; mustered in as private, Co.
A, May 13, 1898; mustered out with company, October 27, 1898,
at Brooklyn, N. Y.

MISCH, HENRY H.—Age, 21 years. Enlisted, May 2, 1898, at
Brooklyn, to serve two years; mustered in as private, Co. A,
May 13, 1898; mustered out with company, October 27, 1898,
at Brooklyn, N. Y.

MITCHELL, CHARLES W.—Age, 26 years. Enlisted, May 2,
1898, at Brooklyn, to serve two years; mustered in as private,
Co. K, May 13, 1898; mustered out with company, October 27,
1898, at Brooklyn, N. Y.

MITCHELL, EDMUND HARMON.—Age, 52 years. Enrolled,
May 2, 1898, at Brooklyn, to serve two years; mustered in as
major, May 16, 1898; mustered out with regiment, October 27,
1898, at Brooklyn, N. Y.; prior service as private, Fifty-first
New York Volunteer Infantry, War of the Rebellion; commissioned major, May 16, 1898, with rank from same date, original.

MITCHELL, HENRY T.—Age, 25 years. Enlisted, May 14, 1898,
at Hempstead, to serve two years; mustered in as private, Co.
E, May 16, 1898; promoted corporal, June 15, 1898; sergeant,
June 30, 1898; mustered out with company, October 27, 1898,
at Brooklyn, N. Y.; subsequent service as second lieutenant,
Forty-first Regiment, United States Volunteer Infantry.

MITCHELL, JOHN A.—Age, — years. Enlisted, July 5, 1898, at
Brooklyn, to serve two years; mustered in as private, Co. H,
same date; mustered out with company, October 27, 1898, at
Brooklyn, N. Y.

MITCHELL, LANSING T.—Age, — years. Enlisted, June 25,
1898, at Brooklyn, to serve two years; mustered in as private,
Co. C, same date; transferred to Hospital Corps, Third Army
Corps, September 19, 1898, at Anniston, Ala.

MITCHELL, THOMAS.—Age, — years. Enlisted, June 28, 1898,
at Brooklyn, to serve two years; mustered in as private, Co. H,
same date; mustered out with company, October 27, 1898, at
Brooklyn, N. Y.

MITCHELL, WILLIAM W.—Age, — years. Enlisted, June 28, 1898, at Brooklyn, to serve two years; mustered in as private, Co. D, same date; mustered out with company, October 27, 1898, at Brooklyn, N. Y.

MOFFAT, WILLIAM R.—Age, 19 years. Enlisted, May 2, 1898, at Brooklyn, to serve two years; mustered in as artificer, Co. D, May 16, 1898; returned to ranks, July 1, 1898; mustered out with company, October 27, 1898, at Brooklyn, N. Y.

MOLANDER, THEODORE.—Age, — years. Enlisted, June 17, 1898, at Brooklyn, to serve two years; mustered in as private, Co. G, same date; mustered out with company, October 27, 1898, at Brooklyn, N. Y.

MOLONEY, THOMAS.—Age, 25 years. Enlisted, May 12, 1898, at Hempstead, to serve two years; mustered in as private, Co. K. May 13, 1898; mustered out with company, October 27, 1898, at Brooklyn, N. Y.

MONAHAN, THOMAS J.—Age, 21 years. Enlisted, May 2, 1898, at Brooklyn, to serve two years; mustered in as private, Co. B, May 16, 1898; mustered out with company, October 27, 1898, at Brooklyn, N. Y.

MONROE, CLARENCE G.—Age, 21 years. Enlisted, May 2, 1898, at Brooklyn, to serve two years; mustered in as private, Co. M, May 13, 1898; mustered out with company, October 27, 1898, at Brooklyn, N. Y.

MONTGOMERY, ROBERT T.—Age, 40 years. Enlisted, May 16, 1898, at Camp Black, to serve two years; mustered in as private, Co. I, same date; mustered out with company, October 27, 1898, at Brooklyn, N. Y.

MONTROSS, WILLIAM.—Age, 21 years. Enlisted, May 2, 1898, at Brooklyn, to serve two years; mustered in as private, Co. A, May 13, 1898; mustered out with company, October 27, 1898, at Brooklyn, N. Y.

MOONEY, FRANK L.—Age, 23 years. Enlisted, May 14, 1898, at Camp Black, to serve two years; mustered in as private, Co. I, May 16, 1898; mustered out with company, October 27, 1898, at Brooklyn, N. Y.

MOONEY, PATRICK J.—Age, 20 years. Enlisted, May 14, 1898, at Camp Black, to serve two years; mustered in as private, Co. H, May 16, 1898; mustered out with company, October 27, 1898, at Brooklyn, N. Y.

MOORE, JR., ELISHA B.—Age, 21 years. Enlisted, May 13, 1898, at Hempstead, to serve two years; mustered in as private, Co. E, May 16, 1898; mustered out with company, October 27, 1898, at Brooklyn, N. Y.

MOORE, FRANCIS A.—Age, 32 years. Enlisted, May 13, 1898, at Hempstead, to serve two years; mustered in as private, Co. D, May 16, 1898; appointed artificer, July 1, 1898; mustered out with company, October 27, 1898, at Brooklyn, N. Y.

MOORE, JAMES OTIS.—Age, 25 years. Enrolled, May 10, 1898, at Camp Black, to serve two years; mustered in as second lieutenant, Co. H, May 16, 1898; first lieutenant, October 10, 1898; mustered out with company, October 27, 1898, at Brooklyn, N. Y.; commissioned second lieutenant, May 16, 1898, with rank from same date, original; first lieutenant, September 14, 1898, with rank from same date, vice Croscup, promoted captain.

MOORE, LOYALL F.—Age, 21 years. Enlisted, May 2, 1898, at Brooklyn, to serve two years; mustered in as private, Co. F, May 16, 1898; mustered out with company, October 27, 1898, at Brooklyn, N. Y.

MOORE, WILLIAM D.—Age, 28 years. Enlisted, May 13, 1898, at Camp Black, to serve two years; mustered in as corporal, Co. H, May 16, 1898; mustered out with company, October 27, 1898, at Brooklyn, N. Y.

MORAN, WILLIAM J.—Age, — years. Enlisted, July 5, 1898, at Brooklyn, to serve two years; mustered in as private, Co. M, same date; mustered out with company, October 27, 1898, at Brooklyn, N. Y.

MORGAN, ALBERT E.—Age, — years. Enlisted, June 18, 1898, at Brooklyn, to serve two years; mustered in as musician, Co. A, same date; mustered out, to date, October 27, 1898.

MORGAN, JOHN K.—Age, 44 years. Enlisted, May 2, 1898, at Brooklyn, to serve two years; mustered in as corporal, Co. C, May 16, 1898; mustered out with company, October 27, 1898, at Brooklyn, N. Y.

MORGAN, JOSEPH J.—Age, — years. Enlisted, June 25, 1898, at Brooklyn, to serve two years; mustered in as private, Co. B, same date; mustered out with company, October 27, 1898, at Brooklyn, N. Y.

MORRIS, EDWARD F.—Age, 21 years. Enlisted, May 2, 1898, at Brooklyn, to serve two years; mustered in as private, Co. D, May 16, 1898; mustered out with company, October 27, 1898, at Brooklyn, N. Y.

MORRISON, JR., ANDREW W.—Age, 24 years. Enlisted, May 2, 1898, at Brooklyn, to serve two years; mustered in as private, Co. E, May 16, 1898; mustered out with company, October 27, 1898, at Brooklyn, N. Y.

MORSE, WALTER W.—Age, — years. Enlisted, June 22, 1898, at Brooklyn, to serve two years; mustered in as private, Co. E, same date; mustered out with company, October 27, 1898, at Brooklyn, N. Y.

MOSSCROPP, JR., SAMUEL O.—Age, 23 years. Enlisted, May 2, 1898, at Brooklyn, to serve two years; mustered in as corporal, Co. D, May 16, 1898; mustered out with company, October 27, 1898, at Brooklyn, N. Y.

MULCAHY, JOSEPH M.—Age, — years. Enlisted, June 17, 1898, at Brooklyn, to serve two years; mustered in as private, Co. E, same date; mustered out, to date, October 27, 1898.

MULLEN, JOHN A.—Age, 28 years. Enlisted, May 11, 1898, at Hempstead, to serve two years; mustered in as private, Co. L, May 16, 1898; mustered out with company, October 27, 1898, at Brooklyn, N. Y.

MULLIN, FRANCIS B.—Age, — years. Enlisted, June 25, 1898, at Brooklyn, to serve two years; mustered in as private, Co. D, same date; discharged for disability, August 3, 1898, at Camp Thomas, Chickamauga Park, Va.

MULLEN, WILLIAM J.—Age, 37 years. Enrolled, May 2, 1898, at Brooklyn, to serve two years; mustered in as sergeant-major, May 16, 1898; mustered out with regiment, October 27, 1898, at Brooklyn, N. Y.

MUNSON, ALFRED C.—Age, 22 years. Enlisted, May 13, 1898, at Hempstead, to serve two years; mustered in as corporal, Co. L, May 16, 1898; promoted sergeant, June 28, 1898; mustered out with company, October 27, 1898, at Brooklyn, N. Y.

MURPHY, FRANCIS E.—Age, 22 years. Enlisted, May 2, 1898, at Brooklyn, to serve two years; mustered in as private, Co. E, May 16, 1898; mustered out with company, October 27, 1898, at Brooklyn, N. Y.

MURPHY, JAMES E.—Age, 26 years. Enlisted, May 2, 1898, at Brooklyn, to serve two years; mustered in as private, Co. E, May 16, 1898; promoted corporal, June 30, 1898; mustered out with company, October 27, 1898, at Brooklyn, N. Y.

MURPHY, JOHN A.—Age, 23 years. Enlisted, May 2, 1898, at Brooklyn, to serve two years; mustered in as musician, Co. K, May 13, 1898; discharged for disability, August 22, 1898.

MURPHY, JOHN J.—Age, 21 years. Enlisted, May 2, 1898, at Brooklyn, to serve two years; mustered in as corporal, Co. E, May 16, 1898; mustered out with company, October 27, 1898, at Brooklyn, N. Y.

MURPHY, MICHAEL J.—Age, — years. Enlisted, July 6, 1898, at Brooklyn, to serve two years; mustered in as private, Co. D, same date; mustered out with company, October 27, 1898, at Brooklyn, N. Y.

MURPHY, THOMAS F.—Age, 20 years. Enlisted, May 2, 1898, at Brooklyn, to serve two years; mustered in as private, Co. E, May 16, 1898; dishonorably discharged, August 23, 1898.

MURRAY, THOMAS.—Age, — years. Enlisted, June 23, 1898, at Brooklyn, to serve two years; mustered in as private, Co. L, same date; mustered out with company, October 27, 1898, at Brooklyn, N. Y.

MURRAY, WILLIAM.—Age, 26 years. Enlisted, May 2, 1898, at Brooklyn, to serve two years; mustered in as private, Co. A, May 13, 1898; mustered out with company, October 27, 1898, at Brooklyn, N. Y.

MURRAY, WILLIAM H.—Age, 21 years. Enlisted, May 6, 1898, at Camp Black, to serve two years; mustered in as private, Co. I, May 16, 1898; mustered out with company, October 27, 1898, at Brooklyn, N. Y.

MUSCHLER, JOHN.—Age, 23 years. Enlisted, May 12, 1898, at Camp Black, to serve two years; mustered in as private, Co. H, May 16, 1898; mustered out with company, October 27, 1898, at Brooklyn, N. Y.

MUSGRAVE, JOHN J.—Age, 22 years. Enlisted, May 2, 1898, at Brooklyn, to serve two years; mustered in as private, Co. I, May 16, 1898; mustered out with company, October 27, 1898, at Brooklyn, N. Y.

MUSGRAVE, WILLIAM S.—Age, 27 years. Enlisted, May 2, 1898, at Brooklyn, to serve two years; mustered in as private, Co. I, May 16, 1898; mustered out with company, October 27, 1898, at Brooklyn, N. Y.

MUSTAUGH, EDWARD V.—Age, 23 years. Enlisted, May 2, 1898, at Brooklyn, to serve two years; mustered in as private, Co. L, May 16, 1898; mustered out with company, October 27, 1898, at Brooklyn, N. Y.

NADEAU, ARTHUR J.—Age, 27 years. Enlisted, May 2, 1898, at Brooklyn, to serve two years; mustered in as private, Co. K, May 13, 1898; promoted corporal, May 27, 1898; mustered out with company, October 27, 1898, at Brooklyn, N. Y.

NANS, CHARLES M.—Age, 32 years. Enlisted, May 14, 1898, at Hempstead, to serve two years; mustered in as private, Co. D, May 16, 1898; mustered out with company, October 27, 1898, at Brooklyn, N. Y.

NASH, JOHN F.—Age, 21 years. Enlisted, May 2, 1898, at Brooklyn, to serve two years; mustered in as private, Co. H, May 16, 1898; mustered out with company, October 27, 1898, at Brooklyn, N. Y.

NATTER, WILLIAM H.—Age, 21 years. Enlisted, May 11, 1898, at Camp Black, to serve two years; mustered in as private, Co. M, May 13, 1898; mustered out with company, October 27, 1898, at Brooklyn, N. Y.

NEALIS, PETER.—Age, 28 years. Enlisted, May 2, 1898, at Brooklyn, to serve two years; mustered in as musician, Co. C, May 16, 1898; promoted principal musician, May 25, 1898; mustered out with regiment, October 27, 1898, at Brooklyn, N. Y.

NEARY, MICHAEL J.—Age, — years. Enlisted, June 20, 1898, at Brooklyn, to serve two years; mustered in as private, Co. I, same date; mustered out with company, October 27, 1898, at Brooklyn, N. Y.

NEIL, ARTHER.—Age, 27 years. Enlisted, May 2, 1898, at Brooklyn, to serve two years; mustered in as private, Co. K, May 13, 1898; mustered out with company, October 27, 1898, at Brooklyn, N. Y.

NELSON, CHARLES.—Age, 31 years. Enlisted, May 2, 1898, at Brooklyn, to serve two years; mustered in as musician, Co. G, May 13, 1898; returned to ranks, August 17, 1898; died of typhoid fever, September 27, 1898, in Sternburg Hospital, Lytle, Ga.

NELSON, CHARLES G.—Age, — years. Enlisted, June 23, 1898, at Brooklyn, to serve two years; mustered in as private, Co. G, same date; mustered out with company, October 27, 1898, at Brooklyn, N. Y.

NELSON, EDWARD A.—Age, 35 years. Enlisted, May 12, 1898, at Camp Black, to serve two years; mustered in as private, Co. F, May 16, 1898; mustered out with company, October 27, 1898, at Brooklyn, N. Y.

NELSON, GEORGE W.—Age, — years. Enlisted, July, 1898, at Brooklyn, to serve two years; mustered in as private, Co. M, same date; mustered out with company, October 27, 1898, at Brooklyn, N. Y.

NELSON, HARRY.—Age, 22 years. Enlisted, May 2, 1898, at Brooklyn, to serve two years; mustered in as corporal, Co. G, May 13, 1898; mustered out, to date, October 27, 1898.

NELSON, HARRY A.—Age, 20 years. Enlisted, May 2, 1898, at Brooklyn, to serve two years; mustered in as private, Co. G, May 13, 1898; mustered out with company, October 27, 1898, at Brooklyn, N. Y.

NELSON, JOHN A.—Age, — years. Enlisted, June 20, 1898, at Brooklyn, to serve two years; mustered in as private, Co. G, same date; mustered out with company, October 27, 1898, at Brooklyn, N. Y.

NESBITT, JR., WEBSTER A.—Age, 21 years. Enlisted, May 2, 1898, at Brooklyn, to serve two years; mustered in as private, Co. A, May 13, 1898; mustered out with company, October 27, 1898, at Brooklyn, N. Y.

NEVINS, VAN OLINDA.—Age, 24 years. Enlisted, May 7, 1898, at Hempstead, to serve two years; mustered in as private, Co. A, May 13, 1898; mustered out with company, October 27, 1898, at Brooklyn, N. Y.

NEWELL, JOHN H.—Age, 42 years. Enlisted, May 2, 1898, at ·Brooklyn, to serve two years; mustered in as private, Co. H, May 16, 1898; discharged, August 1, 1898.

NICHOLS, ISAAC.—Age, 26 years. Enlisted, May 2, 1898, at Brooklyn, to serve two years; mustered in as private, Co. L, May 16, 1898; mustered out, to date, October 27, 1898.

NICHOLS, RANSOM P.—Age, 24 years. Enlisted, May 2, 1898, at Brooklyn, to serve two years; mustered in as private, Co. M, May 13, 1898; promoted corporal, July 25, 1898; mustered out, to date, July 25, 1898, at Brooklyn, N. Y.

NIELSEN, ALBERT.—Age, — years. Enlisted, June 17, 1898, at Brooklyn, to serve two years; mustered in as private, Co. G, same date; discharged to date, December 15, 1898.

NIELSON, ROBERT J.—Age, — years. Enlisted, June 30, 1898, at Brooklyn, to serve two years; mustered in as private, Co. A, same date; mustered out with company, October 27, 1898, at Brooklyn, N. Y.   .

NILSSON, CARL G.—Age, 32 years. Enlisted, May 2, 1898, at Brooklyn, to serve two years; mustered in as private, Co. G, May 13, 1898; appointed cook, July 29, 1898; mustered out with company, October 27, 1898, at Brooklyn, N. Y.

NILSSON, CONRAD.—Age, 28 years. Enlisted, May 11, 1898, at Hempstead, to serve two years; mustered in as private, Co. D, May 16, 1898; mustered out with company, October 27, 1898, at Brooklyn, N. Y.·

NIVISON, EDWIN F.—Age, 20 years. Enlisted, May 14, 1898, at Camp Black, to serve two years; mustered in as private, Co. I, May 16, 1898; discharged, August 8, 1898.

NOBLE, JOHN.—Age, 27 years. Enlisted, May 2, 1898, at Brooklyn, to serve two years; mustered in as sergeant, Co. C, May 16, 1898; mustered out with company, October 27, 1898, at Brooklyn, N. Y.

NOBLE, WILLIAM C.—Age, 47 years. Enrolled, May 2, 1898, at Brooklyn, to serve two years; mustered in as captain, Co. A, May 13, 1898; mustered out on individual muster-out roll, November 29, 1898, to date, October 27, 1898, at New York city; commissioned captain, May 13, 1898, with rank from same date, original.

NOE, ROWLAND D.—Age, 18 years. Enlisted, May 2, 1898, at Brooklyn, to serve two years; mustered in as private, Co. B, May 16, 1898; mustered out with company, October 27, 1898, at Brooklyn, N. Y.

NOLAN, CORNELIUS P.—Age, 22 years. Enlisted, May 2, 1898, at Brooklyn, to serve two years; mustered in as private, Co. K, May 13, 1898; mustered out with company, October 27, 1898, at Brooklyn, N. Y.

NOLAN, JAMES J.—Age, — years. Enlisted, July 2, 1898, at Brooklyn, to serve two years; mustered in as private, Co. H, same date; mustered out with company, October 27, 1898, at Brooklyn, N. Y.

NOLAN, WILLIAM F.—Age, 26 years. Enlisted, May 2, 1898, at Brooklyn, to serve two years; mustered in as private, Co. L. May 16, 1898; mustered out with company, October 27, 1898, at Brooklyn, N. Y.

NOLANS, FREDERICK.—Age, 24 years. Enlisted, May 2, 1898, at Hempstead, to serve two years; mustered in as private, Co. E, May 16, 1898; mustered out with company, October 27, 1898, at Brooklyn, N. Y.

NOONAN, WILLIAM H.—Age, 22 years. Enlisted, May 13, 1898, at Hempstead, to serve two years; mustered in as private. Co. E, May 16, 1898; discharged, September 20, 1898.

NORDENBORG, JOSEPH.—Age, 32 years. Enlisted, May 2, 1898, at Brooklyn, to serve two years; mustered in as private, Co. G, May 13, 1898; mustered out with company, October 27, 1898, at Brooklyn, N. Y.

NOREN, CHARLES E.—Age, 23 years. Enlisted, May 2, 1898, at Brooklyn, to serve two years; mustered in as private, Co. G, May 13, 1898; mustered out with company, October 27, 1898, at Brooklyn, N. Y.

NORTON, THOMAS M.—Age, — years. Enlisted, July 2, 1898, at Brooklyn, to serve two years; mustered in as private, Co. A, same date; mustered out with company, October 27, 1898, at Brooklyn, N. Y.

NUTT, JOHN W.—Age, 41 years. Enrolled, May 2, 1898, at Brooklyn, to serve two years; mustered in as first lieutenant and regimental adjutant, May 14, 1898; relieved as adjutant and assigned to Co. D, as first lieutenant, July 21, 1898; mustered out on individual muster-out roll, November 30, 1898, to date, October 27, 1898, at New York city; commissioned captain and regimental adjutant, May 12, 1898, with rank from same date, original.

OATES, JOHN T.—Age, 28 years. Enlisted, May 13, 1898, at Camp Black, to serve two years; mustered in as private, Co. H, May 16, 1898; mustered out with company, October 27, 1898, at Brooklyn, N. Y.

OBERG, ANTON V.—Age, — years. Enlisted, June 22, 1898, at Brooklyn, to serve two years; mustered in as private, Co. G, same date; discharged, October 22, 1898.

O'BRIEN, JR., EDWIN A.—Age, 32 years. Enlisted, May 12, 1898, at Hempstead, to serve two years; mustered in as private, Co. B, May 16, 1898; mustered out with company, October 27, 1898, at Brooklyn, N. Y.

O'BRIEN, EDWARD F.—Age, 22 years. Enlisted, May 11, 1898, at Camp Black, to serve two years; mustered in as private, Co. M, May 13, 1898; promoted corporal, July 16, 1898; mustered out with company, October 27, 1898, at Brooklyn, N. Y.

O'BRIEN, JOHN.—Age, — years.   Enlisted, June 20, 1898, at
Brooklyn, to serve two years; mustered in as private, Co. H,
same date; promoted corporal, July 29, 1898; mustered out with
company, October 27, 1898, at Brooklyn, N. Y., as John P.
O'Brien.

O'BRIEN, JOHN T.—Age, 18 years.   Enlisted, May 14, 1898, at
Camp Black, to serve two years; mustered in as private, Co.
I, May 16, 1898; mustered out with company, October 27, 1898,
at Brooklyn, N. Y.

O'BRIEN, WILLIAM J.—Age, 22 years.   Enlisted, May 2, 1898,
at Brooklyn, to serve two years; mustered in as corporal, Co.
B, May 16, 1898; promoted quartermaster-sergeant, September
24, 1898; mustered out with company, October 27, 1898, at
Brooklyn, N. Y.

O'BRIEN, WILLIAM J.—Age, — years.   Enlisted, June 21,
1898, at Brooklyn, to serve two years; mustered in as private,
Co. L, same date; mustered out with company, October 27,
1898, at Brooklyn, N. Y.

O'BRIEN, WILLIAM S.—Age, 21 years.   Enlisted, May 2, 1898,
at Brooklyn, to serve two years; mustered in as private, Co. I,
May 16, 1898; mustered out with company, October 27, 1898,
at Brooklyn, N. Y.

O'CALLAHAN, MICHAEL J.—Age, 28 years.   Enlisted, May 2,
1898, at Brooklyn, as sergeant, to serve two years; mustered in
as first sergeant, Co. B, May 16, 1898; mustered out with company, October 27, 1898, at Brooklyn, N. Y.

O'CONNOR, JOHN F.—Age, 23 years.   Enlisted, May 11, 1898,
at Hempstead, to serve two years; mustered in as private, Co.
L, May 16, 1898; mustered out with company, October 27, 1898,
at Brooklyn, N. Y.

O'CONNOR, JOHN J.—Age, 21 years.   Enlisted, May 14, 1898,
at Hempstead, to serve two years; mustered in as private, Co.
E, May 16, 1898; mustered out with company, October 27, 1898,
at Brooklyn, N. Y.

O'DONNELL, JOHN.—Age, 28 years   Enlisted, May 2, 1898, at
Brooklyn, to serve two years; mustered in as private, Co. E,
May 16, 1898; mustered out with company, October 27, 1898,
at Brooklyn, N. Y.

O'DONNELL, WILLIAM.—Age, — years. Enlisted, June 29, 1898, at Brooklyn, to serve two years; mustered in as private, Co. L, same date; mustered out with company, October 27, 1898, at Brooklyn, N. Y.

O'DONOGHUE, DAVID M.—Age, — years. Enlisted, June 22, 1898, at Brooklyn, to serve two years; mustered in as private, Co. K, same date; mustered out with company, October 27, 1898, at Brooklyn, N. Y.

O'GRADY, JAMES.—Age, 23 years. Enlisted, May 4, 1898, at Brooklyn, to serve two years; mustered in as private, Co. E, May 16, 1898; mustered out with company, October 27, 1898, at Brooklyn, N. Y.

O'HARA, PATRICK.—Age, 22 years. Enlisted, May 13, 1898, at Camp Black, to serve two years; mustered in as private, Co. H, May 16, 1898; mustered out with company, October 27, 1898, at Brooklyn, N. Y.

OLIN, CHARLES G.—Age, 22 years. Enlisted, May 2, 1898, at Brooklyn, to serve two years; mustered in as private, Co. G, May 13, 1898; mustered out with company, October 27, 1898, at Brooklyn, N. Y.

OLSEN, JOHN A.—Age, — years. Enlisted, June 20, 1898, at Brooklyn, to serve two years; mustered in as private, Co. G, same date; mustered out with company, October 27, 1898, at Brooklyn, N. Y.

OLSON, OLE.—Age, 19 years. Enlisted, May 2, 1898, at Brooklyn, to serve two years; mustered in as musician, Co. G, May 13, 1898; mustered out with company, October 27, 1898, at Brooklyn, N. Y.

O'NEILL, JOHN J.—Age, 26 years. Enlisted, May 2, 1898, at Brooklyn, to serve two years; mustered in as private, Co. E, May 16, 1898; mustered out with company, October 27, 1898, at Brooklyn, N. Y.

O'NEILL, RAYMOND A.—Age, 21 years. Enlisted, May 14, 1898, at Camp Black, to serve two years; mustered in as private, Co. I, May 16, 1898; mustered out with company, October 27, 1898, at Brooklyn, N. Y.

O'NEILL, THOMAS E.—Age, 21 years. Enlisted, May 2, 1898, at Brooklyn, to serve two years; mustered in as private, Co. E, May 16, 1898; mustered out with company, October 27, 1898, at Brooklyn, N. Y.

O'NEILL, WILLIAM C.—Age, 28 years. Enlisted, May 2, 1898, at Brooklyn, to serve two years; mustered in as private, Co. F, May 16, 1898; mustered out with company, October 27, 1898, at Brooklyn, N. Y.

O'REILLY, STEPHEN W.—Age, 23 years. Enlisted, May 2, 1898, at Brooklyn, to serve two years; mustered in as private, Co. H, May 16, 1898; appointed artificer, May 21, 1898; returned to ranks, May 31, 1898; discharged for disability, July 24, 1898, at Camp Thomas, Chickamauga Park, Ga.

ORMISTON, EDWARD F.—Age, 21 years. Enlisted, May 2, 1898, at Brooklyn, to serve two years; mustered in as private, Co. L, May 16, 1898; promoted corporal, July 12, 1898; mustered out with company, October 27, 1898, at Brooklyn, N. Y.

ORMOND, JAMES R.—Age, — years. Enlisted, June 18, 1898, at Brooklyn, to serve two years; mustered in as private, Co. D, same date; promoted corporal, August 1, 1898; mustered out with company, October 27, 1898, at Brooklyn, N. Y.

ORMOND, JOHN J.—Age, 27 years. Enlisted, May 12, 1898, at Hempstead, to serve two years; mustered in as private, Co. D, May 16, 1898; appointed cook, August 1, 1898; mustered out with company, October 27, 1898, at Brooklyn, N. Y.

O'ROURKE, THOMAS.—Age, — years. Enlisted, June 29, 1898, at Brooklyn, to serve two years; mustered in as private, Co. L, same date; mustered out with company, October 27, 1898, at Brooklyn, N. Y.

OSBORNE, JOHN W.—Age, — years. Enlisted, June 27, 1898, at Brooklyn, to serve two years; mustered in as private, Co. D, same date; mustered out with company, October 27, 1898, at Brooklyn, N. Y.

PAASCH, OTTO A.—Age, 21 years. Enlisted, May 5, 1898, at Camp Black, to serve two years; mustered in as private, Co. M, May 13, 1898; mustered out with company, October 27, 1898, at Brooklyn, N. Y.

PANTHER, JR., JOSEPH.—Age, 21 years. Enlisted, May 12, 1898, at Camp Black, to serve two years; mustered in as private, Co. F, May 16, 1898; mustered out with company, October 27, 1898, at Brooklyn, N. Y.

PATTERSON, EDWARD F.—Age, 25 years. Enlisted, May 14, 1898, at Hempstead, to serve two years; mustered in as private, Co. L, May 16, 1898; discharged for disability, July 6, 1898.

PAULSON, CHARLES.—Age, 21 years. Enlisted, May 2, 1898, at Brooklyn, to serve two years; mustered in as private, Co. G, May 13, 1898; mustered out with company, October 27, 1898, at Brooklyn, N. Y.

PAUW, EDGAR.—Age, 32 years. Enlisted, May 2, 1898, at Brooklyn, to serve two years; mustered in as first sergeant, Co. K, May 13, 1898; mustered out with company, October 27, 1898, at Brooklyn, N. Y., as Edgar De Pauw.

PEARCE, JOSEPH F.—Age, 21 years. Enlisted, May 2, 1898, at Brooklyn, to serve two years; mustered in as private, Co. M, May 13, 1898; mustered out with company, October 27, 1898, at Brooklyn, N. Y.

PENISTON, JERRY B. H.—Age, 21 years. Enlisted, May 2, 1898, at Brooklyn, to serve two years; mustered in as private, Co. H, May 16, 1898; mustered out with company, October 27, 1898, at Brooklyn, N. Y.

PENNELL, JR., THOMAS E.—Age, 24 years. Enlisted, May 2, 1898, at Brooklyn, to serve two years; mustered in as private, Co. K, May 13, 1898; mustered out with company, October 27, 1898, at Brooklyn, N. Y.

PERKINS, FRED.—Age, 22 years. Enlisted, May 2, 1898, at Brooklyn, to serve two years; mustered in as private, Co. L, May 16, 1898; mustered out with company, October 27, 1898, at Brooklyn, N. Y.

PERRY, JAMES.—Age, — years. Enlisted, June 25, 1898, at Brooklyn, to serve two years; mustered in as private, Co. C, same date; discharged, October 18, 1898.

PESSINGER, GEORGE A.—Age, — years. Enlisted, June 28, 1898, at Brooklyn, to serve two years; mustered in as private, Co. H, same date; mustered out with company, October 27, 1898, at Brooklyn, N. Y.

PETERSON, ALFRED.—Age, 21 years. Enlisted, May 2, 1898, at Brooklyn, to serve two years; mustered in as private, Co. G, May 13, 1898; mustered out with company, October 27, 1898, at Brooklyn, N. Y.

PETERSON, AUGUST.—Age, 27 years. Enlisted, May 2, 1898, at Brooklyn, to serve two years; mustered in as private, Co. G, May 13, 1898; transferred to Hospital Corps, June 14, 1898; returned to company, September 13, 1898; mustered out with company, October 27, 1898, at Brooklyn, N. Y.

PETERSON, FRITHIOF.—Age, 23 years. Enlisted, May 2, 1898, at Brooklyn, to serve two years; mustered in as private, Co. G, May 13, 1898; mustered out, to date, October 27, 1898.

PETERSON, HENRY G.—Age, — years. Enlisted, June 27, 1898, at Brooklyn, to serve two years; mustered in as private, Co. C, same date; mustered out with company, October 27, 1898, at Brooklyn, N. Y.

PFAFFENZELLEN, ALBERT E.—Age, 20 years. Enlisted, May 2, 1898, at Brooklyn, to serve two years; mustered in as private, Co. L, May 16, 1898; mustered out with company, October 27, 1898, at Brooklyn, N. Y.

PFISTER, CHARLES.—Age, 21 years. Enlisted, May 2, 1898, at Brooklyn, to serve two years; mustered in as private, Co. D, May 16, 1898; mustered out, to date, October 27, 1898.

PHILCOX, GEORGE A.—Age, 28 years. Enlisted, May 2, 1898, at Brooklyn, to serve two years; mustered in as private, Co. C, May 16, 1898; mustered out with company, October 27, 1898, at Brooklyn, N. Y.

PHILLIPS, ROBERT C.—Age, 22 years. Enlisted, May 11, 1898, at Camp Black, to serve two years; mustered in as private, Co. M, May 13, 1898; promoted corporal, October 14, 1898; mustered out with company, October 27, 1898, at Brooklyn, N. Y.

PHILLIPS, SAMUEL A.—Age, 24 years. Enlisted, May 10, 1898, at Camp Black, to serve two years; mustered in as private, Co. I, May 16, 1898; mustered out with company, October 27, 1898, at Brooklyn, N. Y.

PICHARD, ALFRED L.—Age, 25 years. Enlisted, May 2, 1898, at Brooklyn, to serve two years; mustered in as private, Co. B, May 16, 1898; discharged for disability, July 14, 1898, at Camp Thomas, Chickamauga Park, Ga.

PIERQUET, JOSEPH C.—Age, 24 years. Enlisted, May 2, 1898, at Brooklyn, to serve two years; mustered in as private, Co. H, May 16, 1898; mustered out with company, October 27, 1898, at Brooklyn, N. Y.

PIERCE, DAVID M.—Age, 23 years. Enlisted, May 12, 1898, at Hempstead, to serve two years; mustered in as private, Co. K, May 13, 1898; mustered out with company, October 27, 1898, at Brooklyn, N. Y.

PIERCE, FRANK E.—Age, 23 years. Enlisted, May 2, 1898, at Brooklyn, to serve two years; mustered in as private, Co. C, May 16, 1898; discharged for disability, August 15, 1898, at Camp Thomas, Chickamauga Park, Ga.

PIGOT, JOHN I.—Age, — years. Enlisted, June 18, 1898, at Brooklyn, to serve two years; mustered in as private, Co. K, same date; discharged, July 18, 1898.

PINE, ALBERT W.—Age, 28 years. Enlisted, May 2, 1898, at Brooklyn, to serve two years; mustered in as private, Co. L, May 16, 1898; mustered out with company, October 27, 1898, at Brooklyn, N. Y.

PLATTS, WILLIAM G.—Age, 19 years. Enlisted, May 11, 1898, at Camp Black, to serve two years; mustered in as private, Co. C, May 16, 1898; died of typhoid fever, September 5, 1898, in Division Hospital, Anniston, Ala.

POHASKE, MAURICE.—Age, 30 years. Enlisted, May 4, 1898, at Hempstead, to serve two years; mustered in as private, Co. L, May 16, 1898; deserted, July 19, 1898.

POLLOCK, JR., WILLIAM L.—Age, — years. Enlisted, June 23, 1898, at Brooklyn, to serve two years; mustered in as private, Co. D, same date; mustered out with company, October 27, 1898, at Brooklyn, N. Y.

POTTS, ROBERT F.—Age, 22 years. Enlisted, May 2, 1898, at Brooklyn, to serve two years; mustered in as private, Co. B, May 16, 1898; mustered out with company, October 27, 1898, at Brooklyn, N. Y.

POUCH, ROBERT H.—Age, 21 years. Enlisted, May 2, 1898, at Brooklyn, to serve two years; mustered in as private, Co. H, May 16, 1898; promoted corporal, July 29, 1898; mustered out with company, October 27, 1898, at Brooklyn, N. Y.

PRENDERGAST, FRANK.—Age, 32 years. Enlisted, May 2, 1898, at Brooklyn, to serve two years; mustered in as corporal, Co. A, May 13, 1898; mustered out with company, October 27, 1898, at Brooklyn, N. Y.

PRENDERGAST, FREDERICK.—Age, 23 years. Enlisted, May 2, 1898, at Brooklyn, to serve two years; mustered in as musician, Co. A, May 13, 1898; mustered out with company, October 27, 1898, at Brooklyn, N. Y.

PRENDERGAST, JAMES P.—Age, 28 years. Enlisted, May 14, 1898, at Camp Black, to serve two years; mustered in as private, Co. I, May 16, 1898; promoted corporal, August 1, 1898; mustered out, to date, October 27, 1898.

PRENDERGAST, WILLIAM E.—Age, 39 years.. Enlisted, May 2, 1898, at Brooklyn, to serve two years; mustered in as corporal, Co. A, May 13, 1898; promoted sergeant, June 14, 1898; mustered out with company, October 27, 1898, at Brooklyn, N. Y.

PRESTON, OTIS J.—Age, — years. Enlisted, July 1, 1898, at Brooklyn, to serve two years; mustered in as musician, Co. L, same date; discharged, October 6, 1898.

PRICE, JOSEPH F.—Age, — years. Enlisted, June 29, 1898, at Brooklyn, to serve two years; mustered in as private, Co. F, same date; mustered out with company, October 27, 1898, at Brooklyn, N. Y.

PRINGLE, JAMES S.—Age, 30 years. Enlisted, May 2, 1898, at Brooklyn, to serve two years; mustered in as wagoner, Co. K, May 13, 1898; mustered out with company, October 27, 1898, at Brooklyn, N. Y.

PRITCHARD, RICHARD H.—Age, — years. Enlisted, June 27, 1898, at Brooklyn, to serve two years; mustered in as private, Co. M, same date; mustered out with company, October 27, 1898, at Brooklyn, N. Y.

PURDY, JR., GEORGE A.—Age, 27 years. Enlisted, May 14, 1898, at Hempstead, to serve two years; mutered in as private, Co. L, May 16, 1898; mustered out with company, October 27, 1898, at Brooklyn, N. Y.

PYATT, WILLIAM H.—Age, — years. Enlisted, June 25, 1898, at Brooklyn, to serve two years; mustered in as private, Co. M, same date; mustered out with company, October 27, 1898, at Brooklyn, N. Y.

QUARTY, FRED.—Age, 23 years. Enlisted, May 2, 1898, at Brooklyn, to serve two years; mustered in as private, Co. L, May 16, 1898; died of typhoid fever, September 14, 1898, in German Hospital, New York city.

QUENTIN, FREDERICK H.—Age, 21 years. Enlisted, May 14, 1898, at Hempstead, to serve two years; mustered in as musician, Co. D, May 16, 1898; mustered out with company, October 27, 1898, at Brooklyn, N. Y.

QUIGLEY, JAMES J.—Age, 21 years. Enlisted, May 13, 1898, at Hempstead, to serve two years; mustered in as private, Co. L, May 16, 1898; mustered out with company, October 27, 1898, at Brooklyn, N. Y.

QUINN, PATRICK H.—Age, — years. Enlisted, June 18, 1898, at Brooklyn, to serve two years; mustered in as private, Co. I, same date; mustered out with company, October 27, 1898, at Brooklyn, N. Y.

RAFFERTY, JOHN.—Age, 22 years. Enlisted, May 2, 1898, at Brooklyn, to serve two years; mustered in as private, Co. E, May 16, 1898; mustered out with company, October 27, 1898, at Brooklyn, N. Y.

RAHMN, KNUT O.—Age, — years. Enlisted, June 27, 1898, at Brooklyn, to serve two years; mustered in as private, Co. G, same date; mustered out with company, October 27, 1898, at Brooklyn, N. Y.

RALL, JOHN J.—Age, 27 years. Enlisted, May 7, 1898, at Hempstead, to serve two years; mustered in as private, Co. A, May 13, 1898; mustered out, to date, October 27, 1898.

RANEY, ANDREW.—Age, — years. Enlisted, June 29, 1898, at Brooklyn, to serve two years; mustered in as private, Co. L, same date; mustered out with company, October 27, 1898, at Brooklyn, N. Y., as Andrew Reaney.

RAU, ADOLPH A.—Age, 22 years. Enlisted, May 11, 1898, at Hempstead, to serve two years; mustered in as private, Co. K, May 13, 1898; mustered out with company, October 27, 1898, at Brooklyn, N. Y.

RAUSCH, CHARLES W.—Age, 18 years. Enlisted, May 13, 1898, at Hempstead, to serve two years; mustered in as private, Co. D, May 16, 1898; mustered out, to date, October 27, 1898.

RAUTSCH, ALFRED C.—Age, 22 years. Enlisted, May 2, 1898, at Brooklyn, to serve two years; mustered in as first sergeant, Co. A, May 13, 1898; as second lieutenant, June 14, 1898; mustered out with company, October 27, 1898, at Brooklyn, N. Y.; commissioned second lieutenant, May 28, 1898, with rank from same date, vice Bruckman, promoted first lieutenant.

RAYMOND, EDWARD DENTON.—Age, — years. Enrolled, May 2, 1898, at Brooklyn, to serve two years; mustered in as second lieutenant, Co. C, May 16, 1898; discharged, June 15, 1898; commissioned second lieutenant, May 16, 1898, with rank from same date, original.

READER, WILLIAM A.—Age, 21 years. Enlisted, May 2, 1898, at Brooklyn, to serve two years; mustered in as private, Co. I, May 16, 1898; promoted corporal, August 1, 1898; mustered out with company, October 27, 1898, at Brooklyn, N. Y.

REARDON, DENNIS.—Age, 39 years. Enlisted, May 13, 1898 at Hempstead, to serve two years; mustered in as private, Co. B, May 16, 1898; mustered out with company, October 27, 1898, at Brooklyn, N. Y.

REDDINGTON, FRANCIS A.—Age, 27 years. Enlisted, May 11, 1898, at Camp Black, to serve two years; mustered in as private, Co. I, May 16, 1898; mustered out with company, October 27, 1898, at Brooklyn, N. Y.

REDFERN, ARTHUR W.—Age, 22 years. Enlisted, May 2, 1898, at Brooklyn, to serve two years; mustered in as private, Co. K, May 13, 1898; mustered out with company, October 27, 1898, at Brooklyn, N. Y.

REED, FRANK M.—Age, — years. Enlisted, June 24, 1898, at Brooklyn, to serve two years; mustered in as private, Co. B, same date; mustered out with company, October 27, 1898, at Brooklyn, N. Y.

REED, OSCAR.—Age, 30 years. Enlisted, May 2, 1898, at Brooklyn, to serve two years; mustered in as artificer, Co. G, May 13, 1898; died of typhoid fever, September 24, 1898, in Division Hospital, at Anniston, Ala.

REED, THOMAS F.—Age, 19 years. Enlisted, May 2, 1898, at Brooklyn, to serve two years; mustered in as private, Co. D, May 16, 1898; mustered out with company, October 27, 1898, at Brooklyn, N. Y.

REEVES, FRANK.—Age, — years. Enlisted, June 22, 1898, at Brooklyn, to serve two years; mustered in as private, Co. E, same date; mustered out with company, October 27, 1898, at Brooklyn, N. Y.

REEVES, LOUIS.—Age, 30 years. Enlisted, May 2, 1898, at Brooklyn, to serve two years; mustered in as corporal, Co. B, May 16, 1898; mustered out with company, October 27, 1898, at Brooklyn, N. Y.

REGAN, JOHN.—Age, — years. Enlisted, June 30, 1898, at Brooklyn, to serve two years; mustered in as private, Co. D, same date; mustered out with company, October 27, 1898, at Brooklyn, N. Y.

REGAN, JOHN J.—Age, 23 years. Enlisted, May 12, 1898, at Hempstead, to serve two years; mustered in as private, Co. A, May 13, 1898; mustered out with company, October 27, 1898, at Brooklyn, N. Y.

REHBIEN, JOHN W.—Age, — years. Enlisted, July 5, 1898, at Brooklyn, to serve two years; mustered in as private, Co. H, same date; mustered out with company, October 27, 1898, at Brooklyn, N. Y.

REID, GEORGE F.—Age, 23 years. Enlisted, May 2, 1898, at Brooklyn, to serve two years; mustered in as private, Co. H, May 16, 1898; promoted corporal, July 29, 1898; mustered out with company, October 27, 1898, at Brooklyn, N. Y.

REID, THOMAS E.—Age, 22 years. Enlisted, May 13, 1898, at Camp Black, to serve two years; mustered in as private, Co. C, May 16, 1898; mustered out with company, October 27, 1898, at Brooklyn, N. Y.

REIHL, WILLIAM.—Age, — years. Enlisted, June 23, 1898, at Brooklyn, to serve two years; mustered in as private, Co. F, same date; mustered out with company, October 27, 1898, at Brooklyn, N. Y.

REILLY, ALBERT A.—Age, 18 years. Enlisted, May 16, 1898, at Camp Black, to serve two years; mustered in as private, Co. F, May 16, 1898; discharged, July 27, 1898.

REILLY, CHARLES J.—Age, — years. Enlisted, July 5, 1898, at Brooklyn, to serve two years; mustered in as private Co. B, same date; mustered out with company, October 27, 1898, at Brooklyn, N. Y.

REILLY, JOSEPH F.—Age, 29 years. Enlisted, May 2, 1898, at Brooklyn, to serve two years; mustered in as corporal, Co. F, May 16, 1898; returned to ranks, July 13, 1898; promoted corporal, September 13, 1898; mustered out with company, October 27, 1898, at Brooklyn, N. Y.

REINHEIMER, PAUL.—Age, — years. Enlisted, July 2, 1898, at Brooklyn, to serve two years; mustered in as private, Co. C, same date; mustered out with company, October 27, 1898, at Brooklyn, N. Y.

RELYEA, JESSE.—Age, 33 years. Enlisted, May 7, 1898, at Camp Black, to serve two years; mustered in as private, Co. C, May 16, 1898; mustered out with company, October 27, 1898, at Brooklyn, N. Y.

RENNERT, EDWARD J.—Age, — years. Enlisted, June 27, 1898, at Brooklyn, to serve two years; mustered in as private, Co. K, same date; mustered out with company, October 27, 1898, at Brooklyn, N. Y.

REYNOLDS, BERNARD P.—Age, — years. Enlisted, July 4, 1898, at Brooklyn, to serve two years; mustered in as private, Co. M, same date; mustered out with company, October 27, 1898, at Brooklyn, N. Y.

REYNOLDS, FREDERICK.—Age, — years. Enlisted, June 28, 1898, at Brooklyn, to serve two years; mustered in as private, Co. H, same date; mustered out with company, October 27, 1898, at Brooklyn, N. Y.

REYNOLDS, GEORGE.—Age, 24 years. Enlisted, May 12, 1898, at Camp Black, to serve two years; mustered in as sergeant, Co. F, May 16, 1898; mustered out with company, October 27, 1898, at Brooklyn, N. Y.

REYNOLDS, THOMAS P.—Age, 32 years. Enlisted, May 6, 1898, at Camp Black, to serve two years; mustered in as private, Co. L, May 16, 1898; mustered out with company, October 27, 1898, at Brooklyn, N. Y.

RHATIGAN, JAMES.—Age, 25 years. Enlisted, May 14, 1898, at Camp Black, to serve two years; mustered in as private, Co. F, May 16, 1898; mustered out with company, October 27, 1898, at Brooklyn, N. Y.

RHODEBECK, CHARLES R.—Age, 21 years. Enlisted, May 2, 1898, at Brooklyn, to serve two years; mustered in as private, Co. I, May 16, 1898; transferred to Co. M, May 26, 1898; appointed musician, no date; mustered out with company, October 27, 1898, at Brooklyn, N. Y.

RHODEBECK, WILLIAM M.—Age, 24 years. Enlisted, May 2, 1898, at Brooklyn, to serve two years; mustered in as sergeant, Co. I, May 16, 1898; mustered out with company, October 27, 1898, at Brooklyn, N. Y.

RICHARDSON, JOHN G.—Age, 25 years. Enlisted, May 12, 1898, at Brooklyn, to serve two years; mustered in as private, Co. D, May 16, 1898; mustered out with company, October 27, 1898, at Brooklyn, N. Y.

RICKER, ROBERT A.—Age, 21 years. Enlisted, May 2, 1898, at Brooklyn, to serve two years; mustered in as sergeant, Co. E, May 16, 1898; mustered out with company, October 27, 1898, at Brooklyn, N. Y.

RIEKERS, HENRY A.—Age, — years. Enlisted, June 27, 1898, at Brooklyn, to serve two years; mustered in as private, Co. A, same date; mustered out with company, October 27, 1898, at Brooklyn, N. Y.

RIELLY, PATRICK J.—Age, 32 years. Enlisted, May 12, 1898, at Camp Black, to serve two years; mustered in as private, Co. I, May 16, 1898; mustered out with company, October 27, 1898, at Brooklyn, N. Y.

RIKEL, CHARLES C.—Age, — years. Enlisted, June 17, 1898, at Brooklyn, to serve two years; mustered in as private, Co. K, same date; mustered out with company, October 27, 1898, at Brooklyn, N. Y.

RIKEL, WILLIAM H.—Age, 24 years. Enlisted, May 2, 1898, at Brooklyn, to serve two years; mustered in as corporal, Co. K, May 13, 1898; died of typhoid fever, September 30, 1898, in Sternberg Hospital, Camp Thomas, Chickamauga Park, Ga.

RILEY, EDWARD J.—Age, — years. Enlisted, June 20, 1898, at Brooklyn, to serve two years; mustered in as private, Co. I, same date; mustered out with company, October 27, 1898, at Brooklyn, N. Y.

RILEY, WILLIAM H.—Age, 24 years. Enlisted, May 11, 1898, at Camp Black, to serve two years; mustered in as private, Co. M, May 13, 1898; detailed to Sternberg United States Field Hospital, Camp Thomas, Chickamauga Park, Ga., no date; mustered out, to date, October 27, 1898.

ROACH, JAMES H.—Age, 22 years. Enlisted, May 2, 1898, at Brooklyn, to serve two years; mustered in as private, Co. M, May 13, 1898; mustered out with company, October 27, 1898, at Brooklyn, N. Y.

ROARTY, JAMES.—Age, — years. Enlisted, June 18, 1898, at Brooklyn, to serve two years; mustered in as private, Co. L, same date; mustered out with company, October 27, 1898, at Brooklyn, N. Y.

ROBERTS, CHARLES W.—Age, 21 years. Enlisted, May 15, 1898, at Camp Black, to serve two years; mustered in as private, Co. C, May 16, 1898; mustered out with company, October 27, 1898, at Brooklyn, N. Y.

ROBERTS, THOMAS.—Age, 22 years. Enlisted, May 2, 1898, at Brooklyn, to serve two years; mustered in as private, Co. L, May 16, 1898; mustered out with company, October 27, 1898, at Brooklyn, N. Y.

ROBINSON, JESSE C.—Age, 24 years. Enlisted, May 14, 1898, at Camp Black, to serve two years; mustered in as private, Co. C, May 16, 1898; mustered out with company, October 27, 1898, at Brooklyn, N. Y.

ROBINSON, SAMUEL A.—Age, 19 years. Enlisted, May 12, 1898, at Hempstead, to serve two years; mustered in as private, Co. D, May 16, 1898; mustered out with company, October 27, 1898, at Brooklyn, N. Y.

ROGERS, FRANK B.—Age, 21 years. Enlisted, May 2, 1898, at Brooklyn, to serve two years; mustered in as private, Co. A, May 13, 1898; discharged for disability, July 12, 1898, at Chickamauga, Ga.

ROGERS, JOHN F.—Age, 26 years. Enlisted, May 2, 1898, at Brooklyn, to serve two years; mustered in as first sergeant, Co. F, May 16, 1898; mustered out with company, October 27, 1898, at Brooklyn, N. Y.

ROGERS, WILLIAM J.—Age, 24 years. Enlisted, May 2, 1898, at Brooklyn, to serve two years; mustered in as private, Co. F, May 16, 1898; appointed artificer, July 27, 1898; mustered out with company, October 27, 1898, at Brooklyn, N. Y.

ROLAND, LEROY W.—Age, — years. Enlisted, July 6, 1898, at Brooklyn, to serve two years; mustered in as private, Co. B, same date; mustered out with company, October 27, 1898, at Brooklyn, N. Y.

ROLFF, JACOB.—Age, 23 years. Enlisted, May 2, 1898, at Brooklyn, to serve two years; mustered in as private, Co. L, May 16, 1898; mustered out with company, October 27, 1898, at Brooklyn, N. Y.

ROMANO, GATANS.—Age, 25 years. Enlisted, May 2, 1898, at Brooklyn, to serve two years; mustered in as private, Co. F, May 16, 1898; mustered out with company, October 27, 1898, at Brooklyn, N. Y.

ROME, THOMAS.—Age, 20 years. Enlisted, May 2, 1898, at Brooklyn, to serve two years; mustered in as sergeant, Co. I, May 16, 1898; mustered out with company, October 27, 1898, at Brooklyn, N. Y.

ROONEY, WILLIAM J.—Age, 26 years. Enlisted, May 2, 1898, at Brooklyn, to serve two years; mustered in as private, Co. C, May 16, 1898; mustered out with company, October 27, 1898, at Brooklyn, N. Y.

ROSE, FRANK G.—Age, — years. Enlisted, June 18, 1898, at Brooklyn, to serve two years; mustered in as private, Co. E, same date; promoted corporal, June 30, 1898; first sergeant, August 19, 1898; mustered out with company, October 27, 1898, at Brooklyn, N. Y.

ROSE, WILLIAM J.—Age, — years. Enlisted, June 22, 1898, at Brooklyn, to serve two years; mustered in as private, Co. M, same date; mustered out with company, October 27, 1898, at Brooklyn, N. Y.

ROSENBERG, DANIEL.—Age, — years. Enlisted, June 27, 1898, at Brooklyn, to serve two years; mustered in as private, Co. B, same date; transferred to United States Hospital Corps, August 11, 1898.

ROSHCHILD, JR., FREDERICK.—Age, 25 years. Enlisted, May 2, 1898, at Brooklyn, to serve two years; mustered in as private, Co. H, May 16, 1898; mustered out with company, October 27, 1898, at Brooklyn, N. Y.

ROSQUIST, GEORGE A.—Age, 21 years. Enlisted, May 2, 1898, at Brooklyn, to serve two years; mustered in as private, Co. I, May 16, 1898; promoted corporal, August 4, 1898; mustered out with company, October 27, 1898, at Brooklyn, N. Y.

ROSS, JOHN R.—Age, 28 years. Enlisted, May 2, 1898, at Hempstead, to serve two years; mustered in as private, Co. E, May 16, 1898; mustered out with company, October 27, 1898, at Brooklyn, N. Y.

ROSSBACK, ALBERT.—Age, 21 years. Enlisted, May 14, 1898, at Hempstead, to serve two years; mustered in as private, Co. B, May 16, 1898; mustered out with company, October 27, 1898, at Brooklyn, N. Y.

ROSSELL, OSCAR B.—Age, — years. Enlisted, June 23, 1898, at Brooklyn, to serve two years; mustered in as private, Co. G, same date; mustered out with company, October 27, 1898, at Brooklyn, N. Y.

ROSSELL, WILLIAM L.—Age, — years. Enlisted, June 28, 1898, at Brooklyn, to serve two years; mustered in as private, Co. F, same date; mustered out with company, October 27, 1898, at Brooklyn, N. Y.

ROSSIS, ADOLPHUS R.—Age, 25 years. Enlisted, May 2, 1898, at Brooklyn, to serve two years; mustered in as private, Co. D, May 16, 1898; mustered out with company, October 27, 1898, at Brooklyn, N. Y.

ROTHERMEL, GEORGE.—Age, — years. Enlisted, June 18, 1898, at Brooklyn, to serve two years; mustered in as private, Co. K, same date; mustered out with company, October 27, 1898, at Brooklyn, N. Y.

ROWAN, GEORGE W.—Age, 20 years. Enlisted, May 2, 1898, . at Brooklyn, to serve two years; mustered in as private, Co. L, May 16, 1898; mustered out, to date, October 27, 1898.

ROWAN, THOMAS F.—Age, 22 years. Enlisted, May 2, 1898, at Brooklyn, to serve two years; mustered in as private, Co. F, May 16, 1898; mustered out, to date, October 27, 1898.

ROYILE, THOMAS.—Age, — years. Enlisted July 1, 1898, at Brooklyn, to serve two years; mustered in as private, Co. B, same date; mustered out with company, October 27, 1898, at Brooklyn, N. Y.

RUSH, WILLIAM S.—Age, — years. Enlisted, June 30, 1898, at Brooklyn, to serve two years; mustered in as private, Co. D, same date; mustered out with company, October 27, 1898, at Brooklyn, N. Y.

RUSSELL, JOHN W.—Age, 24 years   Enlisted, May 2, 1898, at Brooklyn, to serve two years; mustered in as private, Co. K, May 13, 1898; mustered out with company, October 27, 1898, at Brooklyn, N. Y.

RUSSELL, WILLIAM G.—Age, 26 years.   Enlisted, May 2, 1898, at Brooklyn, to serve two years; mustered in as sergeant, Co. C, May 16, 1898; discharged, July 31, 1898, at camp, Chickamauga, Ga.

RYAN, EDWARD F.—Age, 21 years.   Enlisted, May 2, 1898, at Brooklyn, to serve two years; mustered in as private, Co. A, May 13, 1898; promoted corporal, July 20, 1898; mustered out with company, October 27, 1898, at Brooklyn, N. Y.

RYAN, EDMOND.—Age, 28 years.   Enlisted, May 2, 1898, at Brooklyn, to serve two years; mustered in as private, Co. B, May 16, 1898; mustered out, to date, October 27, 1898.

RYAN, HENRY.—Age, 30 years.   Enlisted, May 2, 1898, at Brooklyn, to serve two years; mustered in as private, Co. L, May 16, 1898; mustered out, to date, October 27, 1898.

RYAN, JOSEPH A.—Age, 21 years.   Enlisted, May 7, 1898, at Camp Black, to serve two years; mustered in as private, Co. M, May 13, 1898; promoted corporal, July 15, 1898; mustered out with company, October 27, 1898, at Brooklyn, N. Y.

RYAN, PATRICK.—Age, 25 years.   Enlisted, May 13, 1898, at Camp Black, to serve two years; mustered in as private, Co. F, May 16, 1898; died of typhoid fever, September 3, 1898, at Brooklyn, N. Y.

RYAN, ROBERT H.—Age, 29 years.   Enlisted, May 11, 1898, at Camp Black, to serve two years; mustered in as private, Co. M, May 13, 1898; mustered out with company, October 27, 1898, at Brooklyn, N. Y.

RYDBERG, GEORGE.—Age, 32 years.   Enrolled, May 2, 1898, at Brooklyn, to serve two years; mustered in as second lieutenant, Co. G, May 13, 1898; mustered out with company, October 27, 1898, at Brooklyn, N. Y.; commissioned second lieutenant, May 13, 1898, with rank from same date, original.

RYDER, EDWARD A.—Age, 20 years. Enlisted, May 12, 1898, at Camp Black, to serve two years; mustered in as private, Co. M, May 13, 1898; mustered out with company, October 27, 1898, at Brooklyn, N. Y.

RYLANDER, CARL.—Age, — years. Enlisted, June 23, 1898, at Brooklyn, to serve two years; mustered in as private, Co. G, same date; mustered out with company, October 27, 1898, at Brooklyn, N. Y.

RYSTROM, KARL.—Age, 38 years. Enlisted, May 2, 1898, at Brooklyn, to serve two years; mustered in as private, Co. G, May 13, 1898; mustered out with company, October 27, 1898, at Brooklyn, N. Y.

SABIN, GEORGE E.—Age, — years. Enlisted, June 18, 1898, at Brooklyn, to serve two years; mustered in as private, Co. K, same date; mustered out with company, October 27, 1898, at Brooklyn, N. Y.

SADLIER, GEORGE H.—Age, 21 years. Enlisted, May 5, 1898, at Camp Black, to serve two years; mustered in as private, Co. L, May 16, 1898; discharged for disability, August 18, 1898.

SALLFORS, GATTFRIED O.—Age, 28 years. Enlisted, May 2, 1898, at Brooklyn, to serve two years; mustered in as private, Co. G, May 13, 1898; mustered out with company, October 27, 1898, at Brooklyn, N. Y.

SAUTIMIRE, CHARLES.—Age, — years. Enlisted, June 27, 1898, at Brooklyn, to serve two years; mustered in as private, Co. M, same date; mustered out with company, October 27, 1898, at Brooklyn, N Y.

SAVAGE, JOHN J.—Age, — years. Enlisted, June 27, 1898, at Brooklyn, to serve two years; mustered in as private, Co. M, same date; mustered out, to date, October 27, 1898.

SCHAFER, GEORGE C.—Age, 31 years. Enlisted, May 2, 1898, at Brooklyn, to serve two years; mustered in as private, Co. F, May 16, 1898; mustered out with company, October 27, 1898, at Brooklyn, N. Y.

SCHALLER, AUGUST.—Age, 22 years. Enlisted, May 13, 1898, at Hempstead, to serve two years; mustered in as private, Co. L, May 16, 1898; mustered out with company, October 27, 1898, at Brooklyn, N. Y.

SCHELINSKY, CHARLES.—Age, 21 years. Enlisted, May 2, 1898, at Brooklyn, to serve two years; mustered in as private, Co. M, May 13, 1898; mustered out with company, October 27, 1898, at Brooklyn, N. Y.

SCHENCK, JOHN.—Age, 32 years. Enlisted, May 2, 1898, at Brooklyn, to serve two years; mustered in as private, Co. L, May 16, 1898; mustered out with company, October 27, 1898, at Brooklyn, N. Y.

SCHEURER, ERNEST.—Age, — years. Enlisted, July 5, 1898, at Brooklyn, to serve two years; mustered in as private, Co. B, same date; mustered out with company, October 27, 1898, at Brooklyn, N. Y.

SCHIFF, FREDERICK.—Age, 20 years. Enlisted, May 2, 1898, at Brooklyn, to serve two years; mustered in as private, Co. D, May 16, 1898; mustered out with company, October 27, 1898, at Brooklyn, N. Y.

SCHLAPP, ANDREW.—Age, — years. Enlisted, June 20, 1898, at Brooklyn, to serve two years; mustered in as private, Co. K, same date; mustered out with company, October 27, 1898, at Brooklyn, N. Y.

SCHLENKER, ALBERT.—Age, 32 years. Enlisted, May 14, 1898, at Hempstead, to serve two years; mustered in as private, Co. L, May 16, 1898; mustered out with company, October 27, 1898, at Brooklyn, N. Y.

SCHMID, FREDERICK.—Age, — years. Enlisted, June 27, 1898, at Brooklyn, to serve two years; mustered in as private, Co. D, same date; mustered out with company, October 27, 1898, at Brooklyn, N. Y.

SCHMIDT, CHRISTIAN.—Age, — years. Enlisted, June 23, 1898, at Brooklyn, to serve two years; mustered in as private, Co. E, same date; mustered out, to date, October 27, 1898.

SCHMIDT, WOLFGANG.—Age, 30 years. Enlisted, May 2, 1898, at Brooklyn, to serve two years; mustered in as private, Co. K, May 13, 1898; mustered out with company, October 27, 1898, at Brooklyn, N. Y.

SCHMUTZ, ALFRED.—Age, 20 years. Enlisted, May 2, 1898, at Brooklyn, to serve two years; mustered in as private, Co. I, May 16, 1898; mustered out with company, October 27, 1898, at Brooklyn, N. Y.

SCHOLL, KLAUS.—Age, 30 years. Enlisted, May 14, 1898, at Camp Black, to serve two years; mustered in as private, Co. G, same date; mustered out with company, October 27, 1898, at Brooklyn, N. Y.

SCHORR, JOHN T.—Age, 21 years. Enlisted, May 10, 1898, at Hempstead, to serve two years; mustered in as private, Co. D, May 16, 1898; mustered out with company, October 27, 1898, at Brooklyn, N. Y.

SCHRANTZ, JOHN.—Age, 22 years. Enlisted, May 3, 1898, at Hempstead, to serve two years; mustered in as private, Co. B, May 16, 1898; mustered out with company, October 27, 1898, at Brooklyn, N. Y.

SCHRIBER, JOHN.—Age, — years. Enlisted, July 17, 1898, at Brooklyn, to serve two years; mustered in as private, Co. L, same date; mustered out with company, October 27, 1898, at Brooklyn, N. Y.

SCHRODER, WILLIAM C.—Age, 23 years. Enlisted, May 2, 1898, at Brooklyn, to serve two years; mustered in as private, Co. B, May 16, 1898; mustered out with company, October 27, 1898, at Brooklyn, N. Y.

SCHROEDER, HENRY.—Age, 24 years. Enlisted, May 10, 1898, at Camp Black, to serve two years; mustered in as private, Co. I, May 16, 1898; mustered out, to date, October 27, 1898.

SCHUH, CHARLES.—Age, 22 years. Enlisted, May 9, 1898, at Hempstead, to serve two years; mustered in as private, Co. K, May 13, 1898; discharged, August 18, 1898.

SCHULTZ, AXEL B.—Age, 38 years. Enlisted, May 2, 1898, at Brooklyn, to serve two years; mustered in as private, Co. G, May 13, 1898; mustered out with company, October 27, 1898, at Brooklyn, N. Y.

SCHUMELL, MATTHEW.—Age, — years. Enlisted, June 22, 1898, at Brooklyn, to serve two years; mustered in as private, Co. F, same date; mustered out with company, October 27, 1898, at Brooklyn, N. Y.

SCHWANER, FRANK R.—Age, — years. Enlisted, June 27, 1898, at Brooklyn, to serve two years; mustered in as private, Co. I, same date; mustered out with company, October 27, 1898, at Brooklyn, N. Y.

SCHWARTZ, WILLIAM L.—Age, 38 years. Enlisted, May 2, 1898, at Brooklyn, to serve two years; mustered in as artificer, Co. A, May 13, 1898; mustered out with company, October 27, 1898, at Brooklyn, N. Y.

SCHWENSEN, LOUIS.—Age, 23 years. Enlisted, May 2, 1898, at Brooklyn, to serve two years; mustered in as quartermaster-sergeant, Co. G, May 13, 1898; mustered out with company, October 27, 1898, at Brooklyn, N. Y.

SCNEAR, CHARLES.—Age, 21 years. Enlisted, May 12, 1898, at Camp Black, to serve two years; mustered in as private, Co. I, May 16, 1898; discharged for disability, October 27, 1898.

SCRIVEN, FRANK J.—Age, 24 years. Enlisted, May 2, 1898, at Brooklyn, to serve two years; mustered in as private, Co. L, May 16, 1898; mustered out with company, October 27, 1898, at Brooklyn, N. Y.

SCRIVEN, FREDERICK.—Age, — years. Enlisted, June 30, 1898, at Brooklyn, to serve two years; mustered in as private, Co. L, same date; died of typhoid fever, September 6, 1898, in Sternberg Hospital, Chickamauga, Ga.

SEIFERD, EDWARD E.—Age, 25 years. Enlisted, May 14, 1898, at Camp Black, to serve two years; mustered in as private, Co. I, May 16, 1898; mustered out with company, October 27, 1898, at Brooklyn, N. Y.

SENGER, CONRAD.—Age, 32 years. Enlisted, May 14, 1898, at Hempstead, to serve two years; mustered in as private, Co. D, May 16, 1898; mustered out with company, October 27, 1898, at Brooklyn, N. Y.

SENHOLZI, THEODORE.—Age, 21 years. Enlisted, May 12, 1898, at Camp Black, to serve two years; mustered in as private, Co. C, May 16, 1898; mustered out with company, October 27, 1898, at Brooklyn, N. Y.

SERENE, HARRY N.—Age, 21 years. Enlisted, May 2, 1898, at Brooklyn, to serve two years; mustered in as private, Co. C, May 16 1898; discharged for disability, July 12, 1898, at Camp Thomas, Chickamauga Park, Ga.

SEYMOUR, EDWARD H.—Age, — years. Enlisted, June 25, 1898, at Brooklyn, to serve two years; mustered in as private, Co. A, same date; mustered out with company, October 27, 1898, at Brooklyn, N. Y.

SEYMOUR, JOHN J.—Age, — years. Enlisted, June 27, 1898, at Brooklyn, to serve two years; mustered in as private, Co. A, same date; mustered out with company, October 27, 1898, at Brooklyn, N. Y.

SEYMOUR, MICHAEL F.—Age, — years. Enlisted, June 27, 1898, at Brooklyn, to serve two years; mustered in as private, Co. A, same date; mustered out with company, October 27, 1898, at Brooklyn, N. Y.

SHANNON, JAMES A.—Age, 44 years. Enlisted, May 2, 1898, at Brooklyn, to serve two years; mustered in as private, Co. E, May 16, 1898; mustered out with company, October 27, 1898, at Brooklyn, N. Y.

SHAW, THOMAS S.—Age, 29 years. Enlisted, May 2, 1898, at Brooklyn, to serve two years; mustered in as private, Co. C, May 16, 1898; promoted corporal, July 8, 1898; mustered out with company, October 27, 1898, at Brooklyn, N. Y.

SHEARMAN, HARRY.—Age, 21 years. Enlisted, May 2, 1898, at Brooklyn, to serve two years; mustered in as private, Co. C, May 16, 1898; mustered out with company, October 27, 1898, at Brooklyn, N. Y.

SHEPPARD, ABRAHAM L.—Age, 25 years. Enlisted, May 3, 1898, at Hempstead, to serve two years; mustered in as private, Co. K, May 13, 1898; mustered out with company, October 27, 1898, at Brooklyn, N. Y.

SHERIDEN, FRED H.—Age, 28 years. Enlisted, May 12, 1898, at Hempstead, to serve two years; mustered in as private, Co. L, May 16, 1898; mustered out with company, October 27, 1898, at Brooklyn, N. Y.

SHIELDS, JOHN J.—Age, — years. Enlisted, June 17, 1898, at Brooklyn, to serve two years; mustered in as private, Co. K, same date; mustered out with company, October 27, 1898, at Brooklyn, N. Y.

SHINNER, FRANK K.—Age, 28 years. Enlisted, May 2, 1898, at Brooklyn, to serve two years; mustered in as private, Co. E, May 16, 1898; mustered out, to date, October 27, 1898.

SHOULER, GEORGE E.—Age, 23 years. Enlisted, May 2, 1898, at Brooklyn, to serve two years; mustered in as corporal, Co. I, May 16, 1898; mustered out with company, October 27, 1898, at Brooklyn, N. Y.

SHUTTLETON, JOHN.—Age, 21 years. Enlisted, May 10, 1898, at Hempstead, to serve two years; mustered in as private, Co. K, May 13, 1898; mustered out with company, October 27, 1898, at Brooklyn, N. Y.

SIMPSON, DAVID G.—Age, 21 years. Enlisted, May 14, 1898, at Camp Black, to serve two years; mustered in as private, Co. H, May 16, 1898; mustered out, to date, October 27, 1898.

SINNING, GEORGE.—Age, 29 years. Enlisted, May 13, 1898, at Hempstead, to serve two years; mustered in as private, Co. E, May 16, 1898; mustered out, to date, October 27, 1898.

SITTER, THEODORE.—Age, — years. Enlisted, June 21, 1898, at Brooklyn, to serve two years; mustered in as private, Co. I, same date; mustered out, to date, October 27, 1898.

SKELLY, JOSEPH P.—Age, 21 years. Enlisted, May 9, 1898, at Camp Black, to serve two years; mustered in as private, Co. C, May 16, 1898; mustered out with company, October 27, 1898, at Brooklyn, N. Y.

SKELLY, PATRICK J.—Age, — years. Enlisted, June 14, 1898, at Camp Thomas, to serve two years; mustered in as private, Co. D, same date; mustered out with company, October 27, 1898, at Brooklyn, N. Y.

SKOOG, WILLIAM.—Age, 24 years. Enlisted, May 2, 1898, at Brooklyn, to serve two years; mustered in as corporal, Co. G, May 13, 1898; mustered out with company, October 27, 1898, at Brooklyn, N. Y.

SLADE, JAMES.—Age, 21 years. Enlisted, May 2, 1898, at Brooklyn, to serve two years; mustered in as private, Co. L, May 16, 1898; no further record.

SLADE, GEORGE.—Age, — years. Enlisted, May 2, 1898, at Brooklyn, to serve two years; mustered in as private, Co. L, May 16, 1898; mustered out with company, October 27, 1898, at Brooklyn, N. Y.; also borne as James Slade.

SLAIN, FREDERICK F.—Age, 30 years. Enlisted, May 2, 1898, at Brooklyn, to serve two years; mustered in as corporal, Co. C, May 16, 1898; promoted sergeant, August 1, 1898; mustered out with company, October 27, 1898, at Brooklyn, N. Y.

SMITH, ALBERT J.—Age, 24 years. Enlisted, May 2, 1898, at Brooklyn, to serve two years; mustered in as private, Co. C, May 16, 1898; mustered out with company, October 27, 1898, at Brooklyn, N. Y.

SMITH, ANDREW.—Age, — years. Enlisted, June 27, 1898, at Brooklyn, to serve two years; mustered in as private, Co. D, same date; mustered out, to date, October 27, 1898.

SMITH, DOUGLAS B.—Age, 32 years. Enlisted, May 13, 1898, at Brooklyn, to serve two years; mustered in as private, Co. E, May 16, 1898; promoted quartermaster-sergeant, June 15, 1898; returned to ranks, August 19, 1898; mustered out with company, October 27, 1898, at Brooklyn, N. Y.

SMITH, EDWARD J.—Age, 26 years. Enlisted, May 2, 1898, at Brooklyn, to serve two years; mustered in as artificer, Co. C, May 16, 1898; mustered out with company, October 27, 1898, at Brooklyn, N. Y.

SMITH, FREDERICK F.—Age, 20 years. Enlisted, May 14, 1898, at Camp Black, to serve two years; mustered in as private, Co. I, May 16, 1898; mustered out with company, October 27, 1898, at Brooklyn, N. Y.

SMITH, GEORGE W.—Age, 21 years. Enlisted, May 2, 1898, at Brooklyn, to serve two years; mustered in as corporal, Co. D, May 16, 1898; mustered out with company, October 27, 1898, at Brooklyn, N. Y.

SMITH, JAMES J. R.—-Age, 22 years. Enlisted, May 2, 1898, at Brooklyn, to serve two years; mustered in as private, Co. B, May 16, 1898; mustered out with company, October 27, 1898, at Brooklyn, N. Y.

SMITH, JOSEPH.—Age, 24 years. Enlisted, May 13, 1898, at Camp Black, to serve two years; mustered in as private, Co. F, May 16, 1898; mustered out with company, October 27, 1898, at Brooklyn, N. Y.

SMITH, JOSEPH H.—Age, 21 years. Enlisted, May 11, 1898, at Camp Black, to serve two years; mustered in as private, Co. M, May 13, 1898; mustered out with company, October 27, 1898, at Brooklyn, N. Y.

SMITH, JOSEPH H.—Age, — years. Enlisted, June 21, 1898, at Brooklyn, to serve two years; mustered in as private, Co. C, same date; mustered out with company, October 27, 1898, at Brooklyn, N. Y.

SMITH, PETER.—Age, — years. Enlisted, June 29, 1898, at Brooklyn, to serve two years; mustered in as private, Co. L, same date; mustered out with company, October 27, 1898, at Brooklyn, N. Y.

SMITH, STANLEY A.—Age, 23 years. Enlisted, May 2, 1898, at Brooklyn, to serve two years; mustered in as private, Co. K, May 13, 1898; promoted corporal, July 29, 1898; died of typhoid fever, September 22, 1898, at Division Hospital, Anniston, Ala.

SNYDER, HARRY.—Age, 21 years. Enlisted, May 11, 1898, at Hempstead, to serve two years; mustered in as private, Co. B, May 16, 1898; mustered out with company, October 27, 1898, at Brooklyn, N. Y.

SODERSTROM, CARL O.—Age, — years. Enlisted, June 22, 1898, at Brooklyn, to serve two years; mustered in as private, Co. G, same date; mustered out with company, October 27, 1898, at Brooklyn, N. Y.

SOULS, GEORGE F.—Age, 29 years. Enlisted, May 2, 1898, at Brooklyn, to serve two years; mustered in as private, Co. L, May 16, 1898; promoted corporal, June 11, 1898; mustered out with company, October 27, 1898, at Brooklyn, N. Y.

SPANN, GEORGE C.—Age, — years. Enlisted, June 17, 1898, at Brooklyn, to serve two years; mustered in as private, Co. C, same date; discharged, October 7, 1898.

SPECK, HENRY J.—Age, 34 years. Enlisted, May 14, 1898, at Camp Black, to serve two years; mustered in as private, Co. H, May 16, 1898; mustered out with company, October 27, 1898, at Brooklyn, N. Y.

SPELLMAN, WILLIAM.—Age, — years. Enlisted, July 5, 1898, at Brooklyn, to serve two years; mustered in as private, Co. B, same date; mustered out with company, October 27, 1898, at Brooklyn, N. Y.

SPENCE, THOMAS B.—Age, 30 years. Enrolled, May 2, 1898, at Brooklyn, to serve two years; mustered in as assistant-surgeon, May 4, 1898; mustered out on detachment muster-out roll, November 28, 1898, at New York city; commissioned captain and assistant surgeon, May 4, 1898, with rank from same date, original.

SPINDLER, BENJAMIN.—Age, 33 years. Enlisted, May 13, 1898, at Camp Black, to serve two years; mustered in as private, Co. C, May 16, 1898; mustered out with company, October 27, 1898, at Brooklyn, N. Y.

SPITZ, RICHARD.—Age, 27 years. Enlisted, May 2, 1898, at Brooklyn, to serve two years; mustered in as private, Co. A, May 13, 1898; promoted corporal, July 20, 1898; mustered out, to date, October 27, 1898.

SQUIRES, CHARLES C.—Age, 21 years. Enlisted, May 12, 1898, at Hempstead, to serve two years; mustered in as private, Co. B, May 16, 1898; mustered out with company, October 27, 1898, at Brooklyn, N. Y.

STAPLES, HENRY G.—Age, 24 years. Enlisted, May 12, 1898, at Hempstead, to serve two years; mustered in as private, Co. B, May 16, 1898; mustered out with company, October 27, 1898, at Brooklyn, N. Y.

STARRATT, HARRY C.—Age, 20 years. Enlisted, May 16, 1898, at Camp Black, to serve two years; mustered in as private, Co. C, same date; mustered out with company, October 27, 1898, at Brooklyn, N. Y.

ST. CLAIR, JOHN.—Age, 21 years. Enlisted, May 21, 1898, at Brooklyn, to serve two years; mustered in as private, Co. A, May 13, 1898; mustered out with company, October 27, 1898, at Brooklyn, N. Y.

STEEN, OLAF.—Age, — years. Enlisted, June 27, 1898, at Brooklyn, to serve two years; mustered in as private, Co. G, same date; appointed musician, August 17, 1898; mustered out with company, October 27, 1898, at Brooklyn, N. Y.

STEENBERG, HANS H.—Age, 21 years. Enlisted, May 16, 1898, at Camp Black, to serve two years; mustered in as private, Co. I, same date; mustered out with company, October 27, 1898, at Brooklyn, N. Y.

STEFFENS, EMILE.—Age, 28 years. Enlisted, May 2, 1898, at Brooklyn, to serve two years; mustered in as private, Co. E, May 16, 1898; mustered out with company, October 27, 1898, at Brooklyn, N. Y.

STEHLIK, EMIL.—Age, 21 years. Enlisted, May 14, 1898, at Camp Black, to serve two years; mustered in as private, Co. I, May 16, 1898; mustered out, to date, October 27, 1898.

STEIN, MORTON.—Age, 23 years. Enlisted, May 2, 1898, at Brooklyn, to serve two years; mustered in as private, Co. B, May 16, 1898; discharged, September 12, 1898.

STENBERG, GEORGE F.—Age, 34 years. Enlisted, May 2, 1898, at Brooklyn, to serve two years; mustered in as private, Co. G, May 13, 1898; promoted corporal, July 12, 1898; mustered out with company, October 27, 1898, at Brooklyn, N. Y.

STEPHENSON, PERCY O.—Age, — years. Enlisted, June 30, 1898, at Brooklyn, to serve two years; mustered in as private, Co. C, same date; mustered out with company, October 27, 1898, at Brooklyn, N. Y.

STEUCK, HENRY.—Age, 23 years. Enlisted, May 2, 1898, at Brooklyn, to serve two years; mustered in as private, Co. A, May 13, 1898; mustered out with company, October 27, 1898, at Brooklyn, N. Y.

STEVENS, CHARLES.—Age, — years. Enlisted, June 20, 1898, at Brooklyn, to serve two years; mustered in as private, Co. K, same date; mustered out with company, October 27, 1898, at Brooklyn, N. Y.

STEVENS, CHARLES V.—Age, 22 years. Enlisted, May 11, 1898, at Camp Black, to serve two years; mustered in as private, Co. M, May 13, 1898; mustered out with company, October 27, 1898, at Brooklyn, N. Y.

STEVENS, CHARLES W.—Age, — years. Enlisted, June 21, 1898, at Brooklyn, to serve two years; mustered in as private, Co. B, same date; mustered out with company, October 27, 1898, at Brooklyn, N. Y.

STILLWELL, ROSCOE.—Age, 21 years. Enlisted, May 13, 1898, at Camp Black, to serve two years; mustered in as private, Co. H, May 16, 1898; mustered out with company, October 27, 1898, at Brooklyn, N. Y.

STIVERS, ISAAC.—Age, — years. Enlisted, June 18, 1898, at Brooklyn to serve two years; mustered in as private, Co. K, same date; mustered out with company, October 27, 1898, at Brooklyn, N. Y.

STONE, FRANK.—Age, 31 years. Enlisted, May 12, 1898, at Camp Black, to serve two years; mustered in as private, Co. C, May 16, 1898; mustered out with company, October 27, 1898, at Brooklyn, N. Y.

STONE, MITCHELL.—Age, 24 years. Enlisted, May 2, 1898, at Brooklyn, to serve two years; mustered in as private, Co. D, May 16, 1898; mustered out with company, October 27, 1898, at Brooklyn, N. Y.

STRACK, ALEXANDER G.—Age, 21 years. Enlisted, May 2, 1898, at Brooklyn, to serve two years; mustered in as private, Co. B, May 16, 1898; promoted corporal, July 7, 1898; mustered out with company, October 27, 1898, at Brooklyn, N. Y.

STRAMBERG, CHARLES W.—Age, — years. Enlisted, July 6, 1898, at Brooklyn, to serve two years; mustered in as private, Co. B, same date; mustered out with company, October 27, 1898, at Brooklyn, N. Y.

STRINGHAM, GEORGE W.—Age, — years. Enlisted, June 29, 1898, at Brooklyn, to serve two years; mustered in as private, Co. I, same date; promoted corporal, August 1, 1898; mustered out with company, October 27, 1898, at Brooklyn, N. Y.

STROM, CARL A.—Age, — years. Enlisted, June 24, 1898, at Brooklyn, to serve two years; mustered in as private, Co. G, same date; mustered out with company, October 27, 1898, at Brooklyn, N. Y.

STUART, DAVID P.—Age, 39 years. Enlisted, May 2, 1898, at Brooklyn; to serve two years; mustered in as corporal, Co. B, May 16, 1898; discharged for disability, July 14, 1898, at Camp Thomas, Chickamauga Park, Ga.

STYLES, HARRY S.—Age, 29 years. Enlisted, May 2, 1898, at Brooklyn, to serve two years; mustered in as private, Co. M, May 13, 1898; mustered out with company, October 27, 1898, at Brooklyn, N. Y.

SULLIVAN, CHARLES S.—Age, — years. Enlisted, June 17, 1898, at Brooklyn, to serve two years; mustered in as private, Co. E, same date; mustered out, to date, October 27, 1898.

SULLIVAN, EDWARD V.—Age, 19 years. Enlisted, May 2, 1898, at Brooklyn, to serve two years; mustered in as sergeant, Co. A, May 13, 1898; mustered out with company, October 27, 1898, at Brooklyn, N. Y.

SULLIVAN, JAMES P.—Age, 25 years. Enlisted, May 14, 1898, at Camp Black, to serve two years; mustered in as private, Co. H, May 16, 1898; mustered out with company, October 27, 1898, at Brooklyn, N. Y.

SULLIVAN, WILLIAM J.—Age, 21 years. Enlisted, May 16, 1898, at Camp Black, to serve two years; mustered in as private, Co. I, same date; mustered out with company, October 27, 1898, at Brooklyn, N. Y.

SUTHERLAND, CHARLES D.—Age, 20 years. Enlisted, May 2, 1898, at Brooklyn to serve two years; mustered in as private, Co. D, May 16, 1898; promoted corporal, May 17, 1898; mustered out with company, October 27, 1898, at Brooklyn, N. Y.

SWEENEY, MILES.—Age, — years. Enlisted, July 2, 1898, at Brooklyn, to serve two years; mustered in as private, Co. L, same date; mustered out with company, October 27, 1898, at Brooklyn, N. Y.

SWEET, FRANK ELBRIDGE.—Age, 40 years. Enrolled, May 2, 1898, at Brooklyn, to serve two years; mustered in as captain, Co. H, May 16, 1898; mustered out on individual muster-out roll, November 28, 1898, to date, October 27, 1898, at New York city; commissioned captain, May 16, 1898, with rank from same date, original.

SWENSON, CARL OSKAR.—Age, 21 years. Enlisted, May 2, 1898, at Brooklyn, to serve two years; mustered in as private, Co. G, May 13, 1898; mustered out with company, October 27, 1898, at Brooklyn, N. Y.

SWENSON, CHARLES W.—Age, 20 years. Enlisted, May 2, 1898, at Brooklyn, to serve two years; mustered in as private, Co. G, May 13, 1898; mustered out with company, October 27, 1898, at Brooklyn, N. Y.

SWIFT, RICHARD B.—Age, 25 years. Enlisted, May 2, 1898, at Brooklyn, to serve two years; mustered in as private, Co. F, May 16, 1898; mustered out with company, October 27, 1898, at Brooklyn, N. Y.

SYRON, JOHN.—Age, — years. Enlisted, June 20, 1898, at Brooklyn, to serve two years; mustered in as private, Co. E, same date; mustered out with company, October 27, 1898, at Brooklyn, N. Y.

TAGER, CHARLES A.—Age, — years. Enlisted, June 29, 1898, at Brooklyn, to serve two years; mustered in as private, Co. C, same date; mustered out with company, October 27, 1898, at Brooklyn, N. Y.

TAIT, WILLIAM D.—Age, 22 years.   Enlisted, May 2, 1898, at Brooklyn, to serve two years; mustered in as private, Co. D, May 16, 1898; mustered out with company, October 27, 1898, at Brooklyn, N. Y.

TATE, GEORGE C.—Age, — years.   Enlisted, June 22, 1898, at Brooklyn, to serve two years; mustered in as private, Co. L, same date; mustered out with company, October 27, 1898, at Brooklyn, N. Y.

TAYLOR, JOHN.—Age, 27 years.   Enlisted, May 2, 1898, at Brooklyn, to serve two years; mustered in as private, Co. K, May 13, 1898; appointed artificer, May 13, 1898; mustered out with company, October 27, 1898, at Brooklyn, N. Y.

TENNANT, GEORGE A.—Age, 27 years.   Enlisted, May 16, 1898, at Camp Black, to serve two years; mustered in as private, Co. I, May 16, 1898; promoted corporal, August 1, 1898; mustered out with company, October 27, 1898, at Brooklyn, N. Y.

TETAMORE, CLARENCE.—Age, 19 years.   Enlisted, May 2, 1898, at Brooklyn, to serve two years; mustered in as private, Co. M, May 13, 1898; promoted corporal, June 15, 1898; mustered out with company, October 27, 1898, at Brooklyn, N. Y.

TETAMORE, WALTER D.—Age, 24 years.   Enlisted, May 2, 1898, at Brooklyn, to serve two years; mustered in as private, Co. F, May 16, 1898; mustered out with company, October 27, 1898, at Brooklyn, N. Y.

TETLEY, LEVI H.—Age, — years.   Enlisted, June 30, 1898, at Brooklyn, to serve two years; mustered in as private, Co. I, same date; mustered out with company, October 27, 1898, at Brooklyn, N. Y.

THATCHER, SAMUEL M.—Age, 21 years.   Enlisted, May 5, 1898, at Camp Black, to serve two years; mustered in as private, Co. M, May 13, 1898; mustered out with company, October 27, 1898, at Brooklyn, N. Y.

THOLLEN, THURE.—Age, 24 years.   Enlisted, May 2, 1898, at Brooklyn, to serve two years; mustered in as sergeant, Co. G, May 13, 1898; mustered out with company, October 27, 1898, at Brooklyn, N. Y.

THOMAS, ARTHUR J.—Age, 27 years   Enlisted, May 2, 1898, at Brooklyn, to serve two years; mustered in as private, Co. K, May 13, 1898; mustered out with company, October 27, 1898, at Brooklyn, N. Y.

THOMAS, GEORGE A.—Age, 22 years.   Enlisted, May 2, 1898, at Brooklyn, to serve two years; mustered in as corporal, Co. I, May 16, 1898; mustered out with company, October 27, 1898, at Brooklyn, N. Y.

THOMPSON, WILLIAM L.—Age, 26 years.   Enlisted, May 8, 1898, at Camp Black, to serve two years; mustered in as private, Co. H, May 16, 1898; mustered out with company, October 27, 1898, at Brooklyn, N. Y.

THONET, JOSEPH.—Age, 19 years.   Enlisted, May 2, 1898, at Brooklyn, to serve two years; mustered in as private, Co. F, May 16, 1898; mustered out with company, October 27, 1898, at Brooklyn, N. Y.

THORNE, DAVID C.—Age, 28 years.   Enlisted, May 2, 1898, at Brooklyn, to serve two years; mustered in as sergeant, Co. C, May 16, 1898; mustered out with company, October 27, 1898, at Brooklyn, N. Y.

THORNE, JAMES.—Age, 28 years.   Enlisted, May 2, 1898, at Brooklyn, to serve two years; mustered in as private, Co. C, May 16, 1898; appointed wagoner, no date; mustered out with company, October 27, 1898, at Brooklyn, N. Y.

TICHENOR, WALTER A.—Age, 23 years.   Enlisted, May 2, 1898, at Brooklyn, to serve two years; mustered in as hospital steward, May 16, 1898; mustered out with regiment, October 27, 1898, at Brooklyn, N. Y.

TIERNAN, JOHN J.—Age, 23 years.   Enlisted, May 2, 1898, at Brooklyn, to serve two years; mustered in as private, Co. F, May 16, 1898; promoted corporal, June 15, 1898; sergeant, August 23, 1898; mustered out with company, October 27, 1898, at Brooklyn, N. Y.

TIERNEY, DENNIS A.—Age, — years.   Enlisted, July 1, 1898, at Brooklyn, to serve two years; mustered in as private, Co. M, same date; mustered out with company, October 27, 1898, at Brooklyn, N. Y.

TIERNEY, JOHN W.—Age, 19 years.   Enlisted, May 2, 1898, at
Brooklyn, to serve two years; mustered in as private, Co. A,
May 13, 1898; mustered out with company, October 27, 1898,
at Brooklyn, N. Y.

TOBEY, BENNETT H.—Age, — years.   Enrolled, May 2, 1898,
at Brooklyn, to serve two years; mustered in as major, May
14, 1898; discharged, September 5, 1898; commissioned major,
May 14, 1898, with rank from same date, original.

TODD, CHARLES S.—Age, 22 years.   Enlisted, May 2, 1898, at
Brooklyn, to serve two years; mustered in as private, Co. M,
May 13, 1898; promoted corporal, October 14, 1898; mustered
out with company, October 27, 1898, at Brooklyn, N. Y.

TOMPKINS, FREDERICK C.—Age, 21 years.   Enlisted, May 2,
1898, at Brooklyn, to serve two years; mustered in as private,
Co. D, May 16, 1898; mustered out with company, October 27,
1898, at Brooklyn, N. Y.

TOOHIG, JAMES H.—Age, 24 years.   Enlisted, May 2, 1898, at
Brooklyn, to serve two years; mustered in as private, Co. F,
May 16, 1898; appointed musician, June 16, 1898; mustered out,
to date, October 27, 1898.

TOWNSEND, GEORGE.—Age, 22 years.   Enlisted, May 2, 1898,
at Brooklyn, to serve two years; mustered in as private, Co. F,
May 16, 1898; promoted corporal, July 14, 1898; mustered out
with company, October 27, 1898, at Brooklyn, N. Y.

TRAUB, SAMUEL.—Age, 24 years.   Enlisted, May 11, 1898, at
Hempstead, to serve two years; mustered in as private, Co. L,
May 16, 1898; mustered out with company, October 27, 1898, at
Brooklyn, N. Y.

TRAUERTS, CHRISTOPHER L.—Age, 22 years.   Enlisted, May
13, 1898, at Camp Black, to serve two years; mustered in as private, Co. H, May 16, 1898; mustered out with company, October
27, 1898, at Brooklyn, N. Y.

TRAUTMAN, JACOB.—Age, — years.   Enlisted, July 5, 1898, at
Brooklyn, to serve two years; mustered in as private, Co. D,
same date; mustered out with company, October 27, 1898, at
Brooklyn, N. Y.

TRAVERS, JOSEPH.—Age, — years. Enlisted, June 27, 1898, at Brooklyn, to serve two years; mustered in as private, Co. F, same date; mustered out, to date, October 27, 1898.

TRIGGS, HERBERT R.—Age, 20 years. Enlisted, May 2, 1898, at Brooklyn, to serve two years; mustered in as private, Co. D, May 16, 1898; mustered out with company, October 27, 1898, at Brooklyn, N. Y.

TRIMMER, DANIEL M.—Age, 21 years. Enlisted, May 2, 1898, at Brooklyn, to serve two years; mustered in as private, Co. I, May 16, 1898; promoted corporal, August 1, 1898; mustered out with company, October 27, 1898, at Brooklyn, N. Y.

TRUMAN, ALBERT E.—Age, 22 years. Enlisted, May 2, 1898, at Brooklyn, to serve two years; mustered in as private, Co. L, May 16, 1898; mustered out with company, October 27, 1898, at Brooklyn, N. Y.

TRYGG, PER. G.—Age, — years. Enlisted, June 27, 1898, at Brooklyn, to serve two years; mustered in as private, Co. G, same date; mustered out with company, October 27, 1898, at Brooklyn, N. Y.

TUCKER, GEORGE M.—Age, 22 years. Enlisted, May 11, 1898, at Camp Black, to serve two years; mustered in as private, Co. C, May 16, 1898; discharged, October 8, 1898.

TUCKER, JOHN.—Age, — years. Enlisted, June 22, 1898, at Brooklyn, to serve two years; mustered in as private, Co. I, same date; mustered out, to date, October 27, 1898, at Brooklyn, N. Y.

TULLY, DAVID A.—Age, 21 years. Enlisted, May 2, 1898, at Brooklyn, to serve two years; mustered in as private, Co. C, May 16, 1898; no further record.

TURNER, JAMES C.—Age, 25 years. Enlisted, May 2, 1898, at Brooklyn, to serve two years; mustered in as private, Co. A, May 15, 1898; mustered out with company, October 27, 1898, at Brookyln, N. Y.

TURNER, JAMES B.—Age, 21 years. Enlisted, May 2, 1898, at Brooklyn, to serve two years; mustered in as private, Co. K, May 13, 1898; mustered out with company, October 27, 1898, at Brooklyn, N. Y.

TURPIE, JR., JAMES J.—Age, 25 years. Enlisted, May 2, 1898, at Brooklyn, to serve two years; mustered in as private, Co. H, May 16, 1898; mustered out with company, October 27, 1898, at Brooklyn, N. Y.

TUTTLE, STERLING B.—Age, 37 years. Enlisted, May 2, 1898, at Brooklyn, to serve two years; mustered in as private, Co. A, May 13, 1898; mustered out with company, October 27, 1898, at Brooklyn, N. Y.

UHRE, HARRY A.—Age, 24 years. Enlisted, May 2, 1898, at Brooklyn, to serve two years; mustered in as private, Co. L, May 16, 1898; mustered out with company, October 27, 1898, at Brooklyn, N. Y.

UNDERMARK, DANIEL.—Age, — years. Enlisted, June 29, 1898, at Brooklyn, to serve two years; mustered in as private, Co. D, same date; promoted corporal, September 2, 1898; mustered out with company, October 27, 1898, at Brooklyn, N. Y.

VAISTER, CHRISTIAN.—Age, 25 years. Enlisted, May 2, 1898, at Brooklyn, to serve two years; mustered in as private, Co. G, May 13, 1898; mustered out with company, October 27, 1898, at Brooklyn, N. Y.

VAN DUYNE, NEWTON R.—Age, — years. Enlisted, July 1, 1898, at Brooklyn, to serve two years; mustered in as private, Co. A, same date; mustered out with company, October 27, 1898, at Brooklyn, N. Y.

VAN INGEN, JOSEPH H.—Age, 22 years. Enlisted, May 4, 1898, at Hempstead, to serve two years; mustered in as private, Co. K, May 13, 1898; mustered out with company, October 27, 1898, at Brooklyn, N. Y.

VAN KIRK, CHARLES W.—Age, 23 years. Enlisted, May 2, 1898, at Brooklyn, to serve two years; mustered in as corporal, Co. H. May 16, 1898; mustered out with company, October 27, 1898, at Brooklyn, N. Y.

VAN TASSEL, IRA D.—Age, 25 years. Enlisted, May 2, 1898. at Brooklyn, to serve two years; mustered in as private, Co. A, May 13, 1898; mustered out with company, October 27, 1898, at Brooklyn, N. Y.

VAN VLACK, CHESTER C.—Age, 24 years. Enlisted, May 2, 1898, at Brooklyn, to serve two years; mustered in as private, Co. L, May 16, 1898; promoted corporal, August 19, 1898; mustered out with company, October 27, 1898, at Brooklyn, N. Y.

VAN WICKLEN, ALBERT C.—Age, 31 years. Enlisted, May 2, 1898, at Brooklyn, to serve two years; mustered in as private, Co. C, May 16, 1898; mustered out with company, October 27, 1898, at Brooklyn, N. Y.

VESSEY, JOHN F.—Age, 32 years. Enlisted, May 2, 1898, at Brooklyn, to serve two years; mustered in as private, Co. A, May 13, 1898; mustered out with company, October 27, 1898, at Brooklyn, N. Y.

VOGAL, CHARLES.—Age, — years. Enlisted, June 18, 1898, at Brooklyn, to serve two years; mustered in as private, Co. L, same date; discharged, October 15, 1898, to enlist in regular army.

VOLKERS, ALFRED.—Age, 21 years. Enlisted, May 2, 1898, at Brooklyn, to serve two years; mustered in as corporal, Co. I, May 16, 1898; mustered out with company, October 27, 1898, at Brooklyn, N. Y.

VONUSCH, GUSTAF WALFRIED.—Age, 22 years. Enlisted, May 2, 1898, at Brooklyn, to serve two years; mustered in as private, Co. G, May 13, 1898; mustered out with company, October 27, 1898, at Brooklyn, N. Y.

VON WENING, EUGENE.—Age, 27 years. Enlisted, May 11, 1898, at Camp Black, to serve two years; mustered in as private, Co. M, May 13, 1898; promoted corporal, July 20, 1898; sergeant, October 14, 1898; mustered out with company, October 27, 1898, at Brooklyn, N. Y.

WAGNER, BERNARD MATHEW.—Age, 29 years. Enrolled, May 2, 1898, at Brooklyn, to serve two years; mustered in as captain, Co. L, May 16, 1898; discharged for disability, July 14, 1898, at Camp Thomas, Chickamauga Park, Ga.; commissioned captain, May 16, 1898, with rank from same date, original.

WAGNER, PER R.—Age, 26 years. Enlisted, May 2, 1898, at Brooklyn, to serve two years; mustered in as corporal, Co. G, May 13, 1898; returned to ranks, May 14, 1898; mustered out with company, October 27, 1898, at Brooklyn, N. Y.

WALKER, WILLIAM A.—Age, 34 years. Enlisted, May 11, 1898, at Camp Black, to serve two years; mustered in as private, Co. M, May 13, 1898; mustered out with company, October 27, 1898, at Brooklyn, N. Y.

WALLBERG, FRANK O.—Age, 21 years. Enlisted, May 2, 1898, at Brooklyn, to serve two years; mustered in as corporal, Co. G, May 13, 1898; mustered out with company, October 27, 1898, at Brooklyn, N. Y.

WALSCH, WILLIAM J.—Age, 19 years. Enlisted, May 12, 1898, at Hempstead, to serve two years; mustered in as private, Co. D, May 16, 1898; mustered out with company, October 27, 1898, at Brooklyn, N. Y.

WALSH, BENJAMIN F.—Age, 26 years. Enlisted, May 2, 1898, at Brooklyn, to serve two years: mustered in as private, Co. L, May 16, 1898; promoted corporal, June 9, 1898; sergeant, July 2, 1898; mustered out with company, October 27, 1898, at Brooklyn, N. Y.

WALSH, MARTIN.—Age, — years. Enlisted, June 20, 1898, at Brooklyn, to serve two years; mustered in as private, Co. L, same date; mustered out with company, October 27, 1898, at Brooklyn, N. Y.

WALSH, OWEN.—Age, 21 years. Enlisted, May 10, 1898, at Hempstead, to serve two years; mustered in as private, Co. K, May 13, 1898; mustered out with company, October 27, 1898, at Brooklyn, N. Y.

WALSH, PATRICK F.—Age, — years. Enlisted, June 17, 1898, at Brooklyn, to serve two years; mustered in as private, Co. F, same date; appointed cook, September 13, 1898; mustered out with company, October 27, 1898, at Brooklyn, N. Y.

WALSH, THOMAS.—Age, 33 years. Enlisted, May 10, 1898, at Camp Black, to serve two years; mustered in as private, Co. I, May 16, 1898; mustered out with company, October 27, 1898, at Brooklyn, N. Y.

WALSH, WILLIAM.—Age, 22 years. Enlisted, May 11, 1898, at Hempstead, to serve two years; mustered in as private, Co. A, May 13, 1898; mustered out with company, October 27, 1898, at Brooklyn, N. Y.

WALSTEDT, JULIUS.—Age, 31 years. Enlisted, May 2, 1898, at Brooklyn, to serve two years; mustered in as private, Co. G, May 13, 1898; mustered out with company, October 27, 1898, at Brooklyn, N. Y.

WALTON, JOSEPH.—Age, — years. Enlisted, May 2, 1898, at Brooklyn, to serve two years; mustered in as private, Co. A, May 13, 1898; mustered out with company, October 27, 1898, at Brooklyn, N. Y.

WANMAKER, GEORGE H.—Age, 22 years. Enlisted, May 11, 1898, at Hempstead, to serve two years; musterer in as private, Co. B, May 16, 1898; deserted, May 31, 1898, at Camp Thomas, Chickamauga Park, Ga.

WANSER, LOUIS.—Age, 21 years. Enlisted, May 2, 1898, at Brooklyn, to serve two years; mustered in as private, Co. B, May 16, 1898; mustered out with company, October 27, 1898, at Brooklyn, N. Y.

WARD, DANIEL.—Age, 28 years. Enlisted, May 2, 1898, at Brooklyn, to serve two years; mustered in as private, Co. E, May 16, 1898; mustered out with company, October 27, 1898, at Brooklyn, N. Y.

WARD, DANIEL C.—Age, 23 years. Enlisted, May 2, 1898, at Brooklyn, to serve two years; mustered in as private, Co. F, May 16, 1898; mustered out with company, October 27, 1898, at Brooklyn, N. Y.

WARTMANN, JACOB.—Age, 22 years. Enlisted, May 14, 1898, at Hempstead, to serve two years; mustered in as private, Co. L, May 16, 1898; mustered out with company, October 27, 1898, at Brooklyn, N. Y.

WASILEISKI, THEODORE.—Age, 23 years. Enlisted, May 14, 1898, at Hempstead, to serve two years; mustered in as private, Co. L, May 16, 1898; mustered out with company, October 27, 1898, at Brooklyn, N. Y.

WASSIOLLER, JOHN.—Age, 21 years. Enlisted, May 14, 1898, at Hempstead, to serve two years; mustered in as private, Co. L, May 16, 1898; mustered out with company, October 27, 1898, at Brooklyn, N. Y.

WATERHOUSE, REINHARDT.—Age, 20 years. Enlisted, May 2, 1898, at Brooklyn, to serve two years; mustered in as private, Co. L, May 16, 1898; mustered out with company, October 27, 1898, at Brooklyn, N. Y.

WATSON, ANGELO.—Age, 24 years. Enlisted, May 2, 1898, at Brooklyn, to serve two years; mustered in as private, Co. C, May 16, 1898; mustered out with company, October 27, 1898, at Brooklyn, N. Y.

WATSON, JAMES J.—Age, 26 years. Enlisted, May 2, 1898, at Brooklyn, to serve two years; mustered in as corporal, Co. E, May 16, 1898; returned to ranks, June 15, 1898; mustered out with company, October 27, 1898, at Brooklyn, N. Y.

WATTS, ROBERT W.—Age, — years. Enlisted, June 20, 1898, at Brooklyn, to serve two years; mustered in as private, Co. D, same date; mustered out with company, October 27, 1898, at Brooklyn, N. Y.

WEBBER, LAWRENCE.—Age, — years. Enlisted, June 20, 1898, at Brooklyn, to serve two years; mustered in as private, Co. K, same date; mustered out with company, October 27, 1898, at Brooklyn, N. Y., as Laurence Weber.

WEBSTER, HENRY.—Age, 21 years. Enlisted, May 12, 1898, at Hempstead, to serve two years; mustered in as private, Co. A, May 13, 1898; mustered out with company, October 27, 1898, at Brooklyn, N. Y.

WEDDERBURN, RICHARD.—Age, 23 years. Enlisted, May 13, 1898, at Hempstead, to serve two years; mustered in as private, Co. D, May 16, 1898; mustered out with company, October 27, 1898, at Brooklyn, N. Y.

WEEDA, HARRY.—Age, 28 years. Enlisted, May 2, 1898, at Brooklyn, to serve two years; mustered in as private, Co. M, May 13, 1898; discharged for disability, July 12, 1898, at Camp Thomas, Chickamauga Park, Ga.

WEIKEL, FRED A.—Age, 26 years. Enlisted, May 2, 1898, at Brooklyn, to serve two years; mustered in as sergeant, Co. F, May 16, 1898; mustered out with company, October 27, 1898, at Brooklyn, N. Y.

WEINPHAL, JUSTUS C.—Age, 21 years.   Enlisted, May 14, 1898, at Camp Black, to serve two years; mustered in as private, Co. C, May 16, 1898; mustered out with company, October 27, 1898, at Brooklyn, N. Y.

WEISMANTEL, JOSEPH.—Age, 21 years.   Enlisted, May 13, 1898, at Camp Black, to serve two years; mustered in as private, Co. C, May 16, 1898; died of typhoid fever, September 27, 1898, in Division Hospital, Anniston, Ala.

WELIN, ERIC.—Age, — years.   Enlisted, June 22, 1898, at Brooklyn, to serve two years; mustered in as private, Co. G, same date; mustered out with company, October 27, 1898, at Brooklyn, N. Y.

WELSH, HENRY B.—Age, 30 years.   Enrolled, May 17, 1898, at Camp Black, to serve two years; mustered in as first lieutenant and battalion adjutant, same date; discharged on surgeon's certificate of disability, June 21, 1898; commissioned first lieutenant and battalion adjutant, May 17, 1898, with rank from same date, original.

WENDT, CHARLES S.—Age, 22 years.   Enlisted, May 12, 1898, at Camp Black, to serve two years; mustered in as private, Co. F, May 16, 1898; mustered out with company, October 27, 1898, at Brooklyn, N. Y.

WERNER, GEORGE P.—Age, — years.   Enlisted, June 23, 1898, at Brooklyn, to serve two years; mustered in as private, Co. K, same date; mustered out with company, October 27, 1898, at Brooklyn, N. Y.

WESTON, CHARLES.—Age, 23 years.   Enlisted, May 11, 1898, at Camp Black, to serve two years; mustered in as private, Co. C, May 16, 1898; mustered out with company, October 27, 1898, at Brooklyn, N. Y.

WESTON, JR., HENRY G.—Age, 29 years.   Enlisted, May 2, 1898, at Brooklyn, to serve two years; mustered in as sergeant, Co. M, May 13, 1898; promoted quartermaster-sergeant, June 5, 1898; mustered out with company, October 27, 1898, at Brooklyn, N. Y.

WESCHLER, CHARLES H.—Age, — years.   Enlisted, June 23, 1898, at Brooklyn, to serve two years; mustered in as private, Co. F, same date; mustered out, to date, October 27, 1898.

WESSELBRAND, HENRY.—Age, — years.   Enlisted, July 5, 1898, at Brooklyn, to serve two years; mustered in as private, Co. A, same date; mustered out with company, October 27, 1898, at Brooklyn, N. Y.

WHALEN, MICHAEL.—Age, — years.   Enlisted, July 1, 1898, at Brooklyn, to serve two years; mustered in as private, Co. F, same date; mustered out with company, October 27, 1898, at Brooklyn, N. Y.

WHEEDEN, JAMES M.—Age, 30 years.   Enlisted, May 13, 1898, at Camp Black, to serve two years; mustered in as private, Co. C, May 16, 1898; promoted corporal, July 8, 1898; discharged, October 18, 1898.

WHEELER, LEONARD G.—Age, — years.   Enlisted, June 17, 1898, at Brooklyn, to serve two years; mustered in as private, Co. D, same date; mustered out with company, October 27, 1898, at Brooklyn, N. Y.

WHITE, JOHN.—Age, 27 years.   Enlisted, May 2, 1898, at Brooklyn, to serve two years; mustered in as private, Co. E, May 16, 1898; mustered out with company, October 27, 1898, at Brooklyn, N. Y.

WHITE, OWEN J.—Age, — years.   Enlisted, July 5, 1898, at Brooklyn, to serve two years; mustered in as private, Co. A, same date; mustered out with company, October 27, 1898, at Brooklyn, N. Y.

WHITE, RANDOLPH.—Age, 32 years.   Enlisted, May 2, 1898, at Brooklyn, to serve two years; mustered in as sergeant, Co. B, May 16, 1898; mustered out with company, October 27, 1898, at Brooklyn, N. Y.

WIESE, ADOLPH.—Age, 40 years.   Enlisted, May 12, 1898, at Camp Black, to serve two years; mustered in as private, Co. F, May 16, 1898; mustered out with company, October 27, 1898, at Brooklyn, N. Y.

WIGGINS, JR., JAMES B.—Age, 23 years.   Enlisted, May 2, 1898, at Brooklyn, to serve two years; mustered in as private, Co. K, May 13, 1898; mustered out with company, October 27, 1898, at Brooklyn, N. Y.

WILDER, BENJAMIN F.—Age, 24 years. Enlisted, May 2, 1898, at Brooklyn, to serve two years; mustered in as sergeant, Co. I, May 16, 1898; mustered out with company, October 27, 1898, at Brooklyn, N. Y.

WILDER, JAMES J.—Age, 24 years. Enlisted, May 2, 1898, at Brooklyn, to serve two years; mustered in as private, Co. F, May 16, 1898; mustered out with company, October 27, 1898, at Brooklyn, N. Y.

WILDER, WILBER E.—Captain, Fourth United States Cavalry. Age, 42 years. Enrolled, June 6, 1898, at Washington, D. C., to serve two years; mustered in as colonel, same date; mustered out with regiment, October 27, 1898, at Brooklyn, N. Y.; subsequent service as lieutenant-colonel, Forty-third Regiment, United States Volunteer Infantry; commissioned colonel, June 4, 1898, with rank from same date, vice Grant, promoted brigadier-general of volunteers.

WILDMAN, NATHAN.—Age, 18 years. Enlisted, May 2, 1898, at Brooklyn, to serve two years; mustered in as private, Co. D, May 16, 1898; mustered out with company, October 27, 1898, at Brooklyn, N. Y.

WILHELM, CARL.—Age, 34 years. Enlisted, May 2, 1898, at Brooklyn, to serve two years; mustered in as private, Co. D, May 16, 1898; promoted corporal, July 4, 1898; mustered in as first lieutenant, Co. F, July 24, 1898; assigned to duty as battalion adjutant, August 1, 1898; mustered out with Co. F, October 27, 1898, at Brooklyn, N. Y.; commissioned first lieutenant, July 16, 1898, with rank from same date, vice Welch, discharged.

WILKINS, FRANK L.—Age, 18 years. Enlisted, May 2, 1898, at Hempstead, to serve two years; mustered in as private, Co. K, May 13, 1898; mustered out with company, October 27, 1898, at Brooklyn, N. Y.

WILKINSON, HERBERT H.—Age, 31 years. Enlisted, May 2, 1898, at Brooklyn, to serve two years; mustered in as private, Co. A, May 13, 1898; promoted corporal, same date; mustered out with company, October 27, 1898, at Brooklyn, N. Y.

WILLIAMS, ADRIAN D.—Age, 23 years. Enlisted, May 2, 1898, at Brooklyn, to serve two years; mustered in as hospital steward, May 16, 1898; mustered out with regiment, October 27, 1898, at Brooklyn, N. Y.

WILLIAMS, ARTHUR S.—Age, 21 years. Enlisted, May 3, 1898, at Hempstead, to serve two years; mustered in as private, Co. K, May 13, 1898; mustered out with company, October 27, 1898, at Brooklyn, N. Y.

WILLIAMSON, GEORGE B.—Age, 20 years. Enlisted, May 2, 1898, at Brooklyn, to serve two years; mustered in as private, Co. F, May 16, 1898; mustered out with company, October 27, 1898, at Brooklyn, N. Y.

WILSIE, HALSTEAD.—Age, 19 years. Enlisted, May 10, 1898, at Camp Black, to serve two years; mustered in as private, Co. I, May 16, 1898; discharged for disability, July 17, 1898.

WILSON, CHARLES C.—Age, 21 years. Enlisted, May 4, 1898, at Brooklyn, to serve two years; mustered in as private, Co. M, May 13, 1898; mustered out with company, October 27, 1898, at Brooklyn, N. Y.

WILSON, EDWARD A.—Age, 25 years. Enlisted, May 2, 1898, at Hempstead, to serve two years; mustered in as private, Co. E, May 16, 1898; mustered out with company, October 27, 1898, at Brooklyn, N. Y.

WILSON, JAMES OLIVER.—Age, 49 years. Enrolled, May 16, 1898, at Camp Black, to serve two years; mustered in as chaplain, August 3, 1898; mustered out with regiment, October 27, 1898, at Brooklyn, N. Y.; commissioned chaplain, May 16, 1898, with rank from same date, original.

WILSON, JAMES W.—Age, — years. Enlisted, June 27, 1898, at Brooklyn, to serve two years; mustered in as private, Co. E, same date; mustered out with company, October 27, 1898, at Brooklyn, N. Y.

WILSON, MATHEW J. A.—Age, 21 years. Enlisted, May 2, 1898, at Brooklyn, to serve two years; mustered in as private, Co. I, May 16, 1898; mustered out with company, October 27 1898, at Brooklyn, N. Y.

WILSON, WILLIAM J.—Age, 22 years. Enlisted, May 2, 1898, at Brooklyn, to serve two years; mustered in as private, Co. L, May 16, 1898; promoted corporal, June 9, 1898; mustered out with company, October 27, 1898, at Brooklyn, N. Y.

WINANS, CLARENCE.—Age, — years. Enlisted, June 21, 1898, at Brooklyn, to serve two years; mustered in as private, Co. E, same date; mustered out with company, October 27, 1898, at Brooklyn, N. Y.

WINANS, WILLIAM E.—Age, 32 years. Enlisted, May 13, 1898, at Hempstead, to serve two years; mustered in as private, Co. E, May 16, 1898; mustered out with company, October 27, 1898, at Brooklyn, N. Y.

WINGATE, BENJAMIN F.—Age, 21 years. Enlisted, May 2, 1898, at Brooklyn, to serve two years; mustered in as private, Co. M, May 13, 1898; mustered out, to date, October 27, 1898.

WINGATE, PHILIP ELSDON.—Age, 28 years. Enrolled, May 2, 1898, at Brooklyn, to serve two years; mustered in as first lieutenant, Co. A, May 13, 1898; mustered out with company, October 27, 1898, at Brooklyn, N. Y.; commissioned first lieutenant, May 13, 1898, with rank from same date, original.

WINTERS, LOUIS.—Age, — years. Enlisted, June 20, 1898, at Brooklyn, to serve two years; mustered in as private, Co. K, same date; mustered out with company, October 27, 1898, at Brooklyn, N. Y.

WISCTED, WILLIAM.—Age, — years. Enlisted, June 16, 1898, at Camp Thomas, Ga., to serve two years; mustered in as private, Co. C, same date; mustered out with company, October 27, 1898, at Brooklyn, N. Y.

WITZ, JR., ANTON.—Age, 25 years. Enlisted, May 11, 1898, at Camp Black, to serve two years; mustered in as private, Co. I, May 16, 1898; died, no date, in Sternberg Hospital, Chickamanga, Ga.

WOODHAMS, DOUGLAS.—Age, 28 years. Enlisted, May 13, 1898, at Camp Black, to serve two years; mustered in as quartermaster-sergeant, Co. L, May 16, 1898; mustered out, to date, October 27, 1898.

WOODS, FRANK.—Age, — years. Enlisted, June 24, 1898, at
Brooklyn, to serve two years; mustered in as private, Co. B,
same date; deserted, August 11, 1898, at Camp Thomas, Chickamauga Park, Ga.

WOODS, JOHN F.—Age, — years. Enlisted, June 30, 1898, at
Brooklyn, to serve two years; mustered in as private, Co. M,
same date; discharged, August 8, 1898.

WOODS, RICHARD.—Age, — years. Enlisted, June 27, 1898,
at Brooklyn, to serve two years; mustered in as private, Co.
F, same date; mustered out with company, October 27, 1898,
at Brooklyn, N. Y.

WOODS, WILLIAM H.—Age, — years. Enlisted, June 27, 1898,
at Brooklyn, to serve two years; mustered in as private, Co. K,
same date; mustered out with company, October 27, 1898, at
Brooklyn, N. Y.

WREN, CHARLES.—Age, — years. Enlisted, July 1, 1898, at
Brooklyn, to serve two years; mustered in as private, Co. B,
same date; mustered out with company, October 27, 1898, at
Brooklyn, N. Y.

WRENCH, WILLIAM A.—Age, 22 years. Enlisted, May 2, 1898,
at Brooklyn, to serve two years; mustered in as private, Co. A,
May 13, 1898; mustered out, to date, October 27, 1898.

WRIGHT, WILLIAM C.—Age, 29 years. Enlisted, May 12, 1898,
at Camp Black, to serve two years; mustered in as private, Co.
F, May 16, 1898; promoted corporal, August 23, 1898; mustered out with company, October 27, 1898, at Brooklyn, N. Y.

WRY, JAMES J.—Age, — years. Enlisted, June 27, 1898, at
Brooklyn, to serve two years; mustered in as private, Co. E,
same date; promoted corporal, September 8, 1898; mustered
out with company, October 27, 1898, at Brooklyn, N. Y.

WYNN, PETER.—Age, — years. Enlisted, June 24, 1898, at
Brooklyn, to serve two years; mustered in as private, Co. I,
same date; mustered out with company, October 27, 1898, at
Brooklyn, N. Y.

WYNN, WILLIAM J.—Age, 21 years. Enlisted, May 2, 1898, at Brooklyn, to serve two years; mustered in as private, Co. K, May 13, 1898; mustered out with company, October 27, 1898, at Brooklyn, N. Y.

YORK, JOSEPH J.—Age, — years. Enlisted, June 24, 1898, at Brooklyn, to serve two years; mustered in as private, Co. H, same date; mustered out with company, October 27, 1898, at Brooklyn, N. Y.

YOUNG, DAVID L.—Age, 19 years. Enlisted, May 13, 1898, at Hempstead, to serve two years; mustered in as private, Co. D, May 16, 1898; mustered out with company, October 27, 1898, at Brooklyn, N. Y.

ZAZZALI, EMILO.—Age, 23 years. Enlisted, May 11, 1898, at Hempstead, to serve two years; mustered in as private, Co. B, May 16, 1898; mustered out with company, October 27, 1898, at Brooklyn, N. Y.

ZIMMON, WILLIAM.—Age, 21 years. Enlisted, May 11, 1898, at Camp Black, to serve two years; mustered in as private, Co. M, May 13, 1898; mustered out with company, October 27, 1898, at Brooklyn, N. Y.

ZUNDT, LOUIS.—Age, — years. Enlisted, June 26, 1898, at Brooklyn, to serve two years; mustered in as private, Co. E, same date; mustered out with company, October 27, 1898, at Brooklyn, N. Y.

ZWETZIG, WILLIAM.—Age, 22 years. Enlisted, May 2, 1898, at Brooklyn, to serve two years; mustered in as private, Co. F, May 16, 1898; mustered out with company, October 27, 1898, at Brooklyn, N. Y.

TWENTY-SECOND REGIMENT, INFANTRY.

The twenty-second regiment, national guard, having volunteered its services, was May 7, 1898, in special orders, No. 81, A. G. O., ordered to be organized into eight companies; to proceed from New York city to Camp Black, and there receive the battalion of the thirteenth regiment, four companies, as part of its organization into a twelve-company regiment.

The regiment arrived at the camp, May 9th, and the above orders were carried out and recruiting continued to replace the men rejected by the medical officers. Its prior history follows:

TWENTY-SECOND REGIMENT.

(First Brigade.)

Armory, Broadway and Sixty-seventh street, New York city.

This regiment was organized in April, 1861. It entered the United States service, May 28, 1862, for three months, and was mustered out, September 5, 1862, having been stationed at Washington, D. C., and later forming part of the garrison at Harper's Ferry, Va. June 18, 1863, it was again mustered in the service of the United States for thirty days, and was mustered out, July 24, 1863, having, during the service, taken part in the Gettysburg campaign. In 1867 the regiment took up rifle practice as part of its drill, and in 1871 it established for itself a rifle range and system of practice, which was in 1873, adopted by the National Rifle Association. Company G was disbanded, March 22, 1878, and new company G organized, April 30, 1879. Company F was disbanded, October 10, 1890, and new company F organized, January 8, 1891. Company I was disbanded, October 10, 1890, and new company I organized, October 6, 1862.

The regiment received authority to place silver rings on the lances of its colors, engraved as follows:

On the national color.—Harper's Ferry, 1862; Gettysburg campaign, 1863; Sporting Hill, Pa., June 30, 1863; Carlisle, Pa., July 1, 1863.

On the state color.—Draft riots, 1863; Orange riot, 1871; Buf.
falo, 1892; Brooklyn, 1895.

The regiment was mustered in the service of the United States
as the " twenty-second regiment, infantry, New York volunteers,"
May 24, 1898, and remained at Camp Black until June 10, 1898.

In compliance with special orders, No. 122, department of the
east, of June 6, 1898, the regiment left Camp Black at noon, June
10th, and proceeded by way of the Long Island railroad to Long
Island City. From that place the steamer " John G. Carlisle "
transported companies D, F, L and M, under the command of
Major Russell, and company G, commanded by Captain Dayton,
assigned to duty at the Engineer Depot, to their new station,
Willet's Point, where they arrived at 7 p. m., and companies A,
C, H and K, under command of Major Hotchkin, to their new
station at Fort Schuyler, where they arrived at 10 p. m. Regi
mental headquarters and companies B, E and I went by steamer
" General Meigs," to their station, Fort Slocum, arriving there
about 10 p. m.

The regiment was mustered out of the United States service,
November 23, 1898, and returned to its home station, New York
city, the same day.

Commissioned Officers.

COLONEL:

Franklin Bartlett. May 9 to November 23, 1898.

LIEUTENANT-COLONEL:

Nathaniel Blunt Thurston, May 1 to November 23, 1898.

MAJORS:

Stephen Fowler Hart, May 2 to November 23, 1898.
George D. Russell, May 2 to November 23, 1898.
Walter Bryant Hotchkins, May 9 to November 23, 1898.

REGIMENTAL ADJUTANT:

Harry Hayden Treadwell. May 9 to November 23. 1898.

BATTALION ADJUTANTS:

Robert Joseph Daly, May 9 to November 23, 1898.
Frederick Charles Ringer, May 9 to November 23, 1898.
Clement Frederick Kross, May 9 to November 23, 1898.

REGIMENTAL QUARTERMASTERS:

William Francis Carey, May 9 to October 12, 1898.
Henry Sherman Sternberger, October 14 to November 23, 1898.

SURGEON:

John Smith Wilson, May 2 to November 23, 1898.

ASSISTANT SURGEONS:

Arthur R. Jarrett, May 2 to November 23, 1898.
William Cameron Johnson, May 19, to November 23, 1898.

CHAPLAIN:

Richard Cobden, August 16 to November 23, 1898.

COMPANY A.

CAPTAIN:

Daniel J. Murphy, May 9 to November 23, 1898.

FIRST LIEUTENANT:

Arthur W. Rider, May 9 to November 23, 1898.

SECOND LIEUTENANT:

Walter B. Porter, May 9 to November 23, 1898.

COMPANY B.

CAPTAINS:

Rudolph O. Haubold, May 9 to October 21, 1898.
Charles E. Asten, November 1 to November 23, 1898.

FIRST LIEUTENANTS:

Charles E. Asten, May 9 to November 1, 1898.
Louis A. Hamilton, November 1 to November 23, 1898.

SECOND LIEUTENANTS:

Louis A. Hamilton, May 9 to November 1, 1898.
Edward P. Serrell, November 1 to November 23, 1898.

COMPANY C.

CAPTAIN:

John G. R. Lilliendahl, May 9 to November 23, 1898.

FIRST LIEUTENANT:

William S. Conrow, May 9 to November 23, 1898.

SECOND LIEUTENANT:

Harvey Garrison, May 9 to November 23, 1898.

COMPANY D.

CAPTAIN:

Samuel F. Fahnestock, May 2 to November 23, 1898.

FIRST LIEUTENANTS:

Avery McDougall, May 6 to November 1, 1898.
James F. Cooper, November 1 to November 23, 1898.

SECOND LIEUTENANTS:

James F. Cooper, May 2 to November 1, 1898.
Edward J. Rice, November 4 to November 23, 1898.

COMPANY E.

CAPTAIN:

Matthew M. Miles, May 9 to November 23, 1898.

FIRST LIEUTENANT:

Bloomfield Usher, May 9 to November 23, 1898.

SECOND LIEUTENANT:

William A. Kenny, May 9 to November 23, 1898.

COMPANY F.

CAPTAIN:

George H. Kemp, May 2 to November 23, 1898.

FIRST LIEUTENANT:

Charles O. Davis, May 2 to November 23, 1898.

SECOND LIEUTENANT:

Allan S. Farwell, May 3 to November 23, 1898.

COMPANY G.

CAPTAIN:

Edwin W. Dayton, May 9 to November 23, 1898.

FIRST LIEUTENANT:

Louis F. Buck, May 9 to November 23, 1898.

SECOND LIEUTENANTS:

Nestell B. Doubleday, May 9 to August 16, 1898.
Edwin J. Parks, August 24 to November 23, 1898.

COMPANY H.

CAPTAIN:

Frank Isherwood, May 9 to November 23, 1898.

FIRST LIEUTENANTS:

Henry G. Romaine, May 9 to August 27, 1898.
David Lowenbein, September 1 to September 27, 1898.
George H. Clarke, October 2 to November 23, 1898.

SECOND LIEUTENANTS:

David Lowenbein, May 9 to September 1, 1898.
George H. Clarke, September 1 to October 2, 1898.
Vincent Price, October 4 to November 23, 1898.

COMPANY I.

CAPTAIN:

Frank I. Stott, May 9 to November 23, 1898.

FIRST LIEUTENANT:

Albert H. Dyett, May 9 to November 23, 1898.

SECOND LIEUTENANTS:

Charles G. Moses, May 9 to October 12, 1898.
Edward F. MacGrotty, October 14 to November 23, 1898.

COMPANY K.

CAPTAIN:

Benjamin S. Hart, May 9 to November 23, 1898.

FIRST LIEUTENANTS:

Wilbur F. Barber, May 9 to September 13, 1898.
Henry S. Sternberger, September 25 to October 14, 1898.
Avery McDougall, November 1 to November 23, 1898.

SECOND LIEUTENANTS:

Henry S. Sternberger, May 9 to September 25, 1898.
Joseph B. Graham, September 27 to November 23, 1898.

COMPANY L.

CAPTAIN:

Frank C. Murphy, May 2 to November 23, 1898.

FIRST LIEUTENANT:

Clarence W. Smith, May 2 to November 23, 1898.

SECOND LIEUTENANT:

Thomas R. Fleming, May 2 to November 23, 1898.

COMPANY M.

CAPTAIN:

William A. Turpin, May 2 to November 23, 1898.

FIRST LIEUTENANT:

James Lynch, Jr., May 2 to November 23, 1898.

SECOND LIEUTENANT:

John T. Jennings, May 2 to November 23, 1898.

.

RECORDS OF THE OFFICERS AND ENLISTED MEN.

ACKERMANN, ADOLPH.—Age, 18 years. Enlisted, May 9, 1898, at New York city, to serve two years; mustered in as private, Co. G, May 24, 1898; mustered out with company, November 23, 1898, at Fort Slocum, New York Harbor.

ADRIANCE, ADRIAN D.—Age, 21 years. Enlisted, May 2, 1898, at Brooklyn, to serve two years; mustered in as private, Co. F, May 24, 1898; mustered out with company, November 23, 1898, at Fort Slocum, New York Harbor.

ADRIANCE, HARRY.—Age, 19 years. Enlisted, May 21, 1898, at Camp Black, to serve two years; mustered in as private, Co. A, May 24, 1898; mustered out with company, November 23, 1898, at Fort Slocum, New York Harbor.

AESCHIMANN, CHARLES A.—Age, 35 years. Enlisted, May 9, 1898, at New York city, to serve two years; mustered in as sergeant, Co. B, May 24, 1898; mustered out with company, November 23, 1898, at Fort Slocum, New York Harbor.

ALLEN, HERBERT C.—Age, 22 years. Enlisted, May 9, 1898, at New York city, to serve two years; mustered in as private, Co. G, May 24, 1898; mustered out with company, November 23, 1898, at Fort Slocum, New York Harbor.

ALLEN, JOHN M.—Age, 33 years. Enlisted, July 5, 1898, at Brooklyn, to serve two years; mustered in as private, Co. D, same date; mustered out with company, November 23, 1898, at Fort Slocum, New York Harbor.

ALLEN, WILLIAM P.—Age, 31 years. Enlisted, May 23, 1898, at Camp Black, to serve two years; mustered in as private, Co. L, May 24, 1898; mustered out with company, November 23, 1898, at Fort Slocum, New York Harbor.

ALTON, JR., HENRY.—Age, 29 years. Enlisted, May 9, 1898, at New York city, to serve two years; mustered in as sergeant, Co. H, May 24, 1898; mustered out with company, November 23, 1898, at Fort Slocum, New York Harbor.

ANGELL, PERCY R.—Age, 26 years. Enlisted, May 16, 1898, at Camp Black, to serve two years; mustered in as private, Co. I, May 24, 1898; mustered out with company, November 23, 1898, at Fort Slocum, New York Harbor.

ANGELL, WILLIAM H.—Age, 21 years. Enlisted, May 2, 1898, at Brooklyn, to serve two years; mustered in as private, Co. M, May 24, 1898; mustered out with company, November 23, 1898, at Fort Slocum, New York Harbor.

ARMSTRONG, ALFRED.—Age, 27 years. Enlisted, May 9, 1898, at New York city, to serve two years; mustered in as corporal, Co. E, May 24, 1898; promoted sergeant, October 7, 1898; mustered out with company, November 23, 1898, at Fort Slocum, New York Harbor.

ASTEN, CHARLES E.—Age, 32 years. Enrolled, May 9, 1898, at New York city, to serve two years; mustered in as first lieutenant, Co. B, May 24, 1898; mustered out with company, November 23, 1898, at Fort Slocum, New York Harbor; commissioned first lieutenant, May 24, 1898, with rank from same date, original; captain, but not mustered, November 1, 1898, with rank from same date, vice Haubold, discharged.

AUGUSTINE, HERMAN.—Age, 31 years. Enlisted, July 2, 1898, at New York city, to serve two years; mustered in as private, Co. A, same date; mustered out with company, November 23, 1898, at Fort Slocum, New York Harbor.

AUSTIN, DAVID S.—Age, 21 years. Enlisted, May 2, 1898, at Brooklyn, to serve two years; mustered in as private, Co. L, May 24, 1898; mustered out with company, November 23, 1898, at Fort Slocum, New York Harbor.

BAISLEY, CHARLES F.—Age, 33 years. Enlisted, May 21, 1898, at Brooklyn, to serve two years; mustered in as private, Co. D, May 24, 1898; promoted corporal, July 1, 1898; mustered out with company, November 23, 1898, at Fort Slocum, New York Harbor.

BAKER, ADELBERT S.—Age, 21 years. Enlisted, May 9, 1898, at New York city, to serve two years; mustered in as private, Co. H, May 24, 1898; mustered out with company, November 23, 1898, at Fort Slocum, New York Harbor.

BAKER, LLOYD.—Age, 21 years. Enlisted, May 9, 1898, at New York city, to serve two years; mustered in as private, Co. G, May 24, 1898; discharged for disability, October 18, 1898, at Fort Slocum, New York Harbor.

BAKER, WILLIAM.—Age, 21 years. Enlisted, July 5, 1898, at Brooklyn, to serve two years; mustered in as private, Co. F, same date; mustered out with company, November 23, 1898, at Fort Slocum, New York Harbor.

BALDWIN, WILLIAM C.—Age, 19 years. Enlisted, May 9, 1898, at New York city, to serve two years; mustered in as private, Co. C, May 24, 1898; mustered out with company, November 23, 1898, at Fort Slocum, New York Harbor.

BANZHAFF, ALBERT H.—Age, 19 years. Enlisted, May 19, 1898, at Camp Black, to serve two years; mustered in as private, Co. D, May 24, 1898; mustered out, November 23, 1898, at Fort Slocum, New York Harbor; also borne as Banzhof.

BARBER, WILBUR F.—Age, 35 years. Enrolled, May 9, 1898, at New York city, to serve two years; mustered in as first lieutenant, Co. K, May 24, 1898; discharged, September 13, 1898; commissioned first lieutenant, May 24, 1898, with rank from same date, original.

BARCALOW, GEORGE.—Age, 25 years. Enlisted, May 9, 1898, at New York city, to serve two years; mustered in as private, Co. E, May 24, 1898; mustered out with company, November 23, 1898, at Fort Slocum, New York Harbor.

BARCLAY, CECIL D.—Age, 20 years. Enlisted, May 9, 1898, at New York city, to serve two years; mustered in as private, Co. E, May 24, 1898; mustered out with company, November 23, 1898, at Fort Slocum, New York Harbor.

BARNASKEY, LATHROP W.—Age, 29 years. Enlisted, May 9, 1898, at New York city, to serve two years; mustered in as private, Co. I, May 24, 1898; appointed cook, July 21, 1898; mustered out with company, November 23, 1898, at Fort Slocum, New York Harbor; also borne as Barneskey.

BARNES, FRANK J.—Age, 36 years. Enlisted, June 22, 1898, at Brooklyn, to serve two years; mustered in as private, Co. F, same date; mustered out with company, November 23, 1898, at Fort Slocum, New York Harbor.

BARNES, JR., LAWRENCE K.—Age, 23 years. Enlisted, May 25, 1898, at Camp Black, to serve two years; mustered in as private, Co. D, June 7, 1898; mustered out, November 23, 1898, at Fort Slocum, New York Harbor.

BARRETT, RICHARD E.—Age, 24 years. Enlisted, May 2, 1898, at Brooklyn, to serve two years; mustered in as private, Co. M, May 24, 1898; mustered out with company, November 23, 1898, at Fort Slocum, New York Harbor.

BARRETT, WILLIAM A.—Age, 20 years. Enlisted, May 9, 1898, at New York city, to serve two years; mustered in as private, Co. A, May 24, 1898; mustered out with company, November 23, 1898, at Fort Slocum, New York Harbor.

BARRY, LUKE.—Age, 20 years. Enlisted, June 28, 1898, at New York city, to serve two years; mustered in as private, Co. G, same date; mustered out with company, November 23, 1898, at Fort Slocum, New York Harbor.

BARTER, JOHN FRANK.—Age, 24 years. Enlisted, June 29, 1898, at New York city, to serve two years; mustered in as private, Co. A, same date; mustered out with company, November 23, 1898, at Fort Slocum, New York Harbor.

BARTLETT, FRANKLIN.—Age, 50 years. Enrolled, May 9, 1898, at New York city, to serve two years; mustered in as colonel, May 24, 1898; mustered out with regiment, November 23, 1898, at Fort Slocum, New York Harbor; commissioned colonel, May 4, 1898, with rank from same date, original.

BAUER, HENRY.—Age, 21 years. Enlisted, May 12, 1898, at Camp Black, to serve two years; mustered in as private, Co. F, May 24, 1898; mustered out with company, November 23, 1898, at Fort Slocum, New York Harbor.

BAUMAN, EDWARD H.—Age, 30 years. Enlisted, June 21, 1898, at Brooklyn, to serve two years; mustered in as private, Co. F, same date; deserted, July 27, 1898, at Willet's Point, N. Y.; also borne as Bowman.

BAXTER, ORVILLE.—Age, 27 years. Enlisted, May 9, 1898, at New York city, to serve two years; mustered in as corporal, Co. K, May 24, 1898; mustered out with company, November 23, 1898, at Fort Slocum, New York Harbor.

BAYON, CHARLES C.—Age, 21 years. Enlisted, May 9, 1898, at New York city, to serve two years; mustered in as private, Co. B, May 24, 1898; mustered out with company, November 23, 1898, at Fort Slocum, New York Harbor.

BEADLE, MAXWELL A.—Age, 20 years. Enlisted, May 9, 1898, at New York city, to serve two years; mustered in as private, Co. C, May 24, 1898; discharged for disability, October 3, 1898, at Fort Slocum, New York Harbor.

BECKER, CHARLES.—Age, 21 years. Enlisted, June 28, 1898, at New York city, to serve two years; mustered in as private, Co. G, same date; mustered out with company, November 23, 1898, at Fort Slocum, New York Harbor.

BECKMAN, BERTHOLD.—Age, 23 years. Enlisted, May 18, 1898, at Camp Black, to serve two years; mustered in as private, Co. F, May 24, 1898; mustered out with company, November 23, 1898, at Fort Slocum, New York Harbor.

BEDELL, CLARENCE W.—Age, 24 years. Enlisted, May 9, 1898, at New York city, to serve two years; mustered in as private, Co. C, May 24, 1898; mustered out with company, November 23, 1898, at Fort Slocum, New York Harbor.

BEDELLE, SAMUEL M.—Age, 20 years. Enlisted, June 20, 1898, at Brooklyn, to serve two years; mustered in as private, Co. L, same date; discharged without honor, July 30, 1898, at Willet's Point, N. Y.

BEECHER, WILLIAM P.—Age, 19 years. Enlisted, May 2, 1898, at Brooklyn, to serve two years; mustered in as private, Co. L, May 24, 1898; promoted corporal, October 1, 1898; mustered out with company, November 23, 1898, at Fort Slocum, New York Harbor.

BEERS, WALTER S.—Age, 21 years. Enlisted, May 9, 1898, at New York city, to serve two years; mustered in as private, Co. G, May 24, 1898; mustered out with company, November 23, 1898, at Fort Slocum, New York Harbor.

BELL, DANIEL H. V.—Age, 24 years. Enlisted, May 2, 1898, at Brooklyn, to serve two years; mustered in as corporal, Co. F, May 24, 1898; returned to ranks, August 1, 1898; mustered out with company, November 23, 1898, at Fort Slocum, New York Harbor.

BELL, ROBERT V.—Age, 19 years. Enlisted, June 28, 1898, at Brooklyn, to serve two years; mustered in as private, Co. F, same date; mustered out with company, November 23, 1898, at Fort Slocum, New York Harbor.

BELL, ROWLAND H.—Age, 22 years. Enlisted, May 9, 1898, at New York city, to serve two years; mustered in as private, Co. G, May 24, 1898; mustered out with company, November 23, 1898, at Fort Slocum, New York Harbor.

BELLOWS, ELBERT E.—Age, 23 years. Enlisted, June 17, 1898, at New York city, to serve two years; mustered in as private, Co. B, same date; mustered out with company, November 23, 1898, at Fort Slocum, New York Harbor.

BENEDICT, CLARENCE E.—Age, 31 years. Enlisted, May 20, 1898, at Camp Black, to serve two years; mustered in as private, Co. K, May 24, 1898; mustered out with company, November 23, 1898, at Fort Slocum, New York Harbor.

BENNETT, ALFRED H.—Age, 28 years. Enlisted, May 2, 1898, at Brooklyn, to serve two years; mustered in as private, Co. M, May 24, 1898; mustered out with company, November 23, 1898, at Fort Slocum, New York Harbor.

BENSON, GEORGE R.—Age, 25 years. Enlisted, May 2, 1898, at Brooklyn, to serve two years; mustered in as private, Co. D, May 24, 1898; mustered out with company, November 23, 1898, at Fort Slocum, New York Harbor.

BERESFORD, FREDERICK.—Age, 22 years. Enlisted, May 22, 1898, at Camp Black, to serve two years; mustered in as private, Co. B, May 24, 1898; mustered out with company, November 23, 1898, at Fort Slocum, New York Harbor.

BERNARD, ALPHONSO G.—Age, 28 years. Enlisted, May 21, 1898, at New York city, to serve two years; mustered in as private, Co. B, May 24, 1898; promoted corporal, June 30, 1898; quartermaster-sergeant, July 15, 1898; mustered out with company, November 23, 1898, at Fort Slocum, New York Harbor.

BERNHEIMER, SIDNEY G.—Age, 23 years. Enlisted, May 9, 1898, at New York city, to serve two years; mustered in as private, Co. K, May 24, 1898; promoted corporal, July 29, 1898; discharged, October 15, 1898, at Fort Slocum, New York Harbor.

BERWICK, EDWIN A.—Age, 23 years. Enlisted, May 9, 1898, at New York city, to serve two years; mustered in as corporal, Co. H, May 24, 1898; returned to ranks, October 25, 1898; mustered out with company, November 23, 1898, at Fort Slocum, New York Harbor.

BETHEL, EDGAR A.—Age, 21 years. Enlisted, May 9, 1898, at New York city, to serve two years; mustered in as musician, Co. A, May 24, 1898; mustered out with company, November 23, 1898, at Fort Slocum, New York Harbor.

BETTS, RITCHIE G.—Age, 29 years. Enlisted, May 18, 1898, at Camp Black, to serve two years; mustered in as private, Co. B, May 24, 1898; discharged, October 27, 1898, at Fort Slocum, New York Harbor.

BETTS, WILLIAM W.—Age, 32 years. Enlisted, May 23, 1898, at Camp Black, to serve two years; mustered in as private, Co. I, May 24, 1898; mustered out with company, November 23, 1898, at Fort Slocum, New York Harbor.

BEYER, LEOPOLD.—Age, 19 years. Enlisted, May 9, 1898, at New York city, to serve two years; mustered in as private, Co. B, May 24, 1898; mustered out with company, November 23, 1898, at Fort Slocum, New York Harbor.

BIDDLE, WALTER.—Age, 21 years. Enlisted, May 12, 1898, at Camp Black, to serve two years; mustered in as private, Co. F, May 24, 1898; mustered out with company, November 23, 1898, at Fort Slocum, New York Harbor.

BIJUR, NATHAN I.—Age, 22 years. Enlisted, May 9, 1898, at New York city, to serve two years; mustered in as private, Co. K, May 24, 1898; promoted corporal, October 4, 1898; discharged, October 19, 1898, at Fort Slocum, New York Harbor.

BISCHOFF, JOHN HENRY.—Age, 28 years. Enlisted, June 24, 1898, at New York city, to serve two years; mustered in as private, Co. B, same date; mustered out with company, November 23, 1898, at Fort Slocum, New York Harbor.

BISHOP, JOHN T.—Age, 22 years. Enlisted, May 2, 1898, at Brooklyn, to serve two years; mustered in as private, Co. M, May 24, 1898; mustered out with company, November 23, 1898, at Fort Slocum, New York Harbor.

BISHOP, OSCAR E.—Age, 21 years. Enlisted, May 24, 1898, at Camp Black, to serve two years; mustered in as private, Co. B, same date; mustered out with company, November 23, 1898, at Fort Slocum, New York Harbor; also borne as Bischoff.

BLAKE, JOHN K.—Age, 23 years. Enlisted, May 2, 1898, at Brooklyn, to serve two years; mustered in as private, Co. M, May 24, 1898; promoted corporal, July 1, 1898; mustered out with company, November 23, 1898, at Fort Slocum, New York Harbor.

BLAURET, CHARLES W.—Age, 23 years. Enlisted, June 18, 1898, at New York city, to serve two years; mustered in as private, Co. E, same date; mustered out with company, November 23, 1898, at Fort Slocum, New York Harbor.

BLAUVELT, WILLIAM E.—Age, 28 years. Enlisted, May 2, 1898, at Brooklyn, to serve two years; mustered in as corporal, Co. L, May 24, 1898; returned to ranks, September 13, 1898; mustered out with company, November 23, 1898, at Fort Slocum, New York Harbor.

BLISS, ABRAM A.—Age, 42 years. Enlisted, June 20, 1898, at Brooklyn, to serve two years; mustered in as private, Co. F, same date; mustered out with company, November 23, 1898, at Fort Slocum, New York Harbor; also borne as Abraham A. Bliss.

BLUMENTHAL, WILLIAM.—Age, 25 years. Enlisted, May 18, 1898, at Camp Black, to serve two years; mustered in as private, Co. D, May 24, 1898; mustered out with company, November 23, 1898, at Fort Slocum, New York Harbor.

BOBB, CLARENCE H.—Age, — years. Enlisted, September 20, 1898, at Fort Schuyler, to serve two years; mustered in as private, Co. C, same date; mustered out with company, November 23, 1898, at Fort Slocum, New York Harbor.

BOCKELMAN, TRISTAN C.—Age, 21 years. Enlisted, May 9, 1898, at New York city, to serve two years; mustered in as private, Co. G, May 24, 1898; discharged, September 17, 1898, at Willet's Point, N. Y.

BOHLMAN, JOHN D.—Age, 19 years. Enlisted, May 2, 1898, at Brooklyn, to serve two years; mustered in as private, Co. D, May 24, 1898; mustered out with company, November 23, 1898, at Fort Slocum, New York Harbor.

BOLAN, JAMES.—Age, 22 years.   Enlisted, May 2, 1898, at Brooklyn, to serve two years; mustered in as private, Co. D, May 24, 1898; mustered out with company, November 23, 1898, at Fort Slocum, New York Harbor, as James L. Bolan.

BOLGIANI, ALBERT.—Age, 18 years. Enlisted, May 9, 1898, at New York city, to serve two years; mustered in as private, Co. H, May 24, 1898; mustered out with company, November 23, 1898, at Fort Slocum, New York Harbor.

BOND, OLIVER W.—Age, 20 years. Enlisted, June 30, 1898, at Brooklyn, to serve two years; mustered in as private, Co. L, same date; mustered out with company, November 23, 1898, at Fort Slocum, New York Harbor.

BOOTHE, FRANK M.—Age, 40 years. Enlisted, June 18, 1898, at New York city, to serve two years; mustered in as private, Co. E, same date; mustered out with company, November 23, 1898, at Fort Slocum, New York Harbor.

BOSWORTH, RUTHERFORD H.—Age, 20 years.   Enlisted, June 28, 1898, at Brooklyn, to serve two years; mustered in as private, Co. F, same date; mustered out with company, November 23, 1898, at Fort Slocum, New York Harbor.

BOULAG, GEORGE.—Age, 26 years. Enlisted, June 30, 1898, at New York city, to serve two years; mustered in as private, Co. H, same date; deserted, August 11, 1898, at Fort Schuyler, New York Harbor.

BOWES, WILLIAM J.—Age, 21 years. Enlisted, May 9, 1898, at New York city, to serve two years; mustered in as private, Co. B, May 24, 1898; mustered out with company, November 23, 1898, at Fort Slocum, New York Harbor.

BOWMAN, EDWARD H., see Edward H. Bauman.

BOYCE, ROBERT.—Age, 19 years. Enlisted, May 17, 1898, at Camp Black, to serve two years; mustered in as private, Co. E, May 24, 1898; mustered out with company, November 23, 1898, at Fort Slocum, New York Harbor.

BOYD, ARTHUR J.—Age, 21 years. Enlisted, May 5, 1898, at Camp Black, to serve two years; mustered in as private, Co. F, May 24, 1898; mustered out with company, November 23, 1898, at Fort Slocum, New York Harbor.

BOYLE, JOSEPH P.—Age, 31 years. Enlisted, May 9, 1898, at New York city, to serve two years; mustered in as private, Co. C, May 24, 1898; discharged, September 18, 1898, at Fort Schuyler, New York Harbor.

BRACKEN, JAMES H.—Age, 21 years. Enlisted, June 20, 1898, at New York city, to serve two years; mustered in as private, Co. B, same date; mustered out with company, November 23, 1898, at Fort Slocum, New York Harbor.

BRAMM, ROBERT F.—Age, 33 years. Enlisted, May 2, 1898, at Brooklyn, to serve two years; mustered in as private, Co. D, May 24, 1898; mustered out with company, November 23, 1898, at Fort Slocum, New York Harbor.

BRENNAN, JOHN.—Age, 23 years. Enlisted, May 21, 1898, at Camp Black, to serve two years; mustered in as private, Co. B, May 24, 1898; mustered out with company, November 23, 1898, at Fort Slocum, New York Harbor.

BRESLER, ARTHUR L.—Age, 25 years. Enlisted, May 9, 1898, at New York city, to serve two years; mustered in as wagoner, Co. E, May 24, 1898; promoted corporal, July 1, 1898; mustered out with company, November 23, 1898, at Fort Slocum, New York Harbor.

BRIGGS, ROBERT T.—Age, 24 years. Enlisted, May 13, 1898, at Brooklyn, to serve two years; mustered in as private, Co. M, May 24, 1898; promoted hospital steward, September 25, 1898; mustered out with regiment, November 23, 1898, at Fort Slocum, New York Harbor.

BRISTOL, GEORGE W.—Age, 33 years. Enlisted, May 24, 1898, at Camp Black, to serve two years; mustered in as private, Co. F, same date; mustered out with company, November 23, 1898, at Fort Slocum, New York Harbor.

BROAS, GEORGE W.—Age, 22 years. Enlisted, May 2, 1898, at Brooklyn, to serve two years; mustered in as private, Co. L, May 24, 1898; mustered out with company, November 23, 1898, at Fort Slocum, New York Harbor.

BROAS, WILLIAM H.—Age, 28 years. Enlisted, May 2, 1898, at Brooklyn, to serve two years; mustered in as private, Co. L, May 24, 1898; mustered out with company, November 23, 1898, at Fort Slocum, New York Harbor.

BRODERICK, ARTHUR C.—Age, 20 years. Enlisted, May 9, 1898, at New York city, to serve two years; mustered in as private, Co. A, May 24, 1898; discharged, October 7, 1898, at Fort Slocum, New York Harbor.

BROOKS, ALBERT.—Age, 22 years. Enlisted, May 9, 1898, at New York city, to serve two years; mustered in as private, Co. A, May 24, 1898; mustered out with company, November 23, 1898, at Fort Slocum, New York Harbor.

BROOKS, WILLIAM E.—Age, 23 years. Enlisted, June 4, 1898, at Hempstead, to serve two years; mustered in as private, Co. M, June 7, 1898; promoted corporal, July 1, 1898; mustered out with company, November 23, 1898, at Fort Slocum, New York Harbor.

BROOMFIELD, GEORGE W.—Age, 32 years. Enlisted, May 4, 1898, at Camp Black, to serve two years; mustered in as private, Co. F, May 24, 1898; mustered out with company, November 23, 1898, at Fort Slocum, New York Harbor.

BROPHY, MICHAEL F.—Age, 23 years. Enlisted, May 12, 1898, at Camp Black, to serve two years; mustered in as private, Co. F, May 24, 1898; transferred to Co. B, June 10, 1898; promoted corporal, October 25, 1898; mustered out with company, November 23, 1898, at Fort Slocum, New York Harbor.

BROPHY, WILLIAM A.—Age, — years. Enlisted, August 11, 1898, at Fort Schuyler, to serve two years; mustered in as private, Co. C, same date; mustered out with company, November 23, 1898, at Fort Slocum, New York Harbor.

BROSS, FREDERICK A.—Age, 21 years. Enlisted, May 2, 1898, at Brooklyn, to serve two years; mustered in as private, Co. L, May 24, 1898; mustered out with company, November 23, 1898, at Fort Slocum, New York Harbor.

BROWN, ALFRED THOMAS.—Age, 21 years. Enlisted, July 5, 1898, at New York city, to serve two years; mustered in as private, Co A, same date; mustered out with company, November 23, 1898, at Fort Slocum, New York Harbor

BROWN, JR., DAVID.—Age, 24 years. Enlisted, May 4, 1898, at Brooklyn, to serve two years; mustered in as private, Co. M, May 24, 1898; mustered out with company, November 23, 1898, at Fort Slocum, New York Harbor.

BROWN, GEORGE.—Age, 21 years. Enlisted, May 20, 1898, at Camp Black, to serve two years; mustered in as private, Co. A, May 24, 1898; mustered out with company, November 23, 1898, at Fort Slocum, New York Harbor.

BROWN, JOHN.—Age, 21 years. Enlisted, July 5, 1898, at New York city, to serve two years; mustered in as private, Co. A, same date; mustered out with company, November 23, 1898, at Fort Slocum, New York Harbor.

BROWN, ORVILLE.—Age, 22 years. Enlisted, June 20, 1898, at Brooklyn, to serve two years; mustered in as private, Co. D, June 30, 1898; mustered out with company, November 23, 1898, at Fort Slocum, New York Harbor.

BROWN, SAMUEL H.—Age, 21 years. Enlisted, May 8, 1898, at Camp Black, to serve two years; mustered in as private, Co. F, May 24, 1898; mustered out with company, November 23, .1898, at Fort Slocum, New York Harbor.

BROWNELL, BERTRAM.—Age, 21 years. Enlisted, May 19, 1898, at Camp Black, to serve two years; mustered in as private, Co. E, May 24, 1898; mustered out with company, November 23, 1898, at Fort Slocum, New York Harbor.

BRUGGEMANN, ALBERT.—Age, 21 years. Enlisted, May 9, 1898, at New York city, to serve two years; mustered in as private, Co. K, May 24, 1898; mustered out with company, November 23, 1898, at Fort Slocum, New York Harbor.

BRUSH, WILLIAM H.—Age, 24 years. Enlisted, June 20, 1898, at New York city, to serve two years; mustered in as private, Co. E, same date; mustered out with company, November 23, 1898, at Fort Slocum, New York Harbor.

BRUSSEL, HERBERT S.—Age, 22 years. Enlisted, May 9, 1898, at New York city, to serve two years; mustered in as private, Co. K, May 24, 1898; promoted corporal, September 21, 1898; discharged, September 28, 1898, at Fort Slocum, New York Harbor.

BRYAN, HENRY L.—Age, 28 years. Enlisted, July 5, 1898, at Brooklyn, to serve two years; mustered in as private, Co. L, same date; mustered out with company, November 23, 1898, at Fort Slocum, New York Harbor.

BUCHANAN, KING D. N.—Age, 19 years. Enlisted, May 9, 1898, at New York city, to serve two years; mustered in as private, Co. G, May 24, 1898; mustered out with company, November 23, 1898, at Fort Slocum, New York Harbor.

BUCK, LOUIS F.—Age, 33 years. Enrolled, May 9, 1898, at New York city, to serve two years; mustered in as first lieutenant, Co. G, May 24, 1898; mustered out with company, November 23, 1898, at Fort Slocum, New York Harbor; commissioned first lieutenant, May 24, 1898, with rank from same date, original.

BUCKHOLZ, GEORGE.—Age, 26 years. Enlisted, May 2, 1898, at Brooklyn, to serve two years; mustered in as wagoner, Co. D, May 24, 1898; returned to ranks, June 5, 1898; discharged, September 30, 1898, at Fort Slocum, New York Harbor, as George L. Buckholz.

BUCKLEY, JOHN.—Age, 24 years. Enlisted, June 22, 1898, at New York city, to serve two years; mustered in as private, Co. I, same date; mustered out with company, November 23, 1898, at Fort Slocum, New York Harbor.

BUCKLEY, MICHAEL P.—Age, 21 years. Enlisted, May 9, 1898, at New York city, to serve two years; mustered in as private, Co. C, May 24, 1898; mustered out with company, November 23, 1898, at Fort Slocum, New York Harbor.

BULL, WILLIAM E.—Age, 28 years. Enlisted, May 11, 1898, at Camp Black, to serve two years; mustered in as musician, Co, F, May 24, 1898; mustered out with company, November 23, 1898, at Fort Slocum, New York Harbor.

BULLOCK, PRESCOTT F.—Age, 27 years. Enlisted, May 9, 1898, at New York city, to serve two years; mustered in as private, Co. C, May 24, 1898; mustered out with company, November 23, 1898, at Fort Slocum, New York Harbor.

BULMER, FREDERICK T.—Age, 37 years. Enlisted, May 9, 1898, at New York city, to serve two years; mustered in as private, Co. G, May 24, 1898; discharged, October 20, 1898, at Fort Slocum, New York Harbor.

BULTMAN, CLARENCE J.—Age, 24 years. Enlisted, May 9, 1898, at New York city, to serve two years; mustered in as private, Co. E, May 24, 1898; mustered out with company, November 23, 1898, at Fort Slocum, New York Harbor.

BURKE, JAMES F.—Age, 21 years. Enlisted, May 20, 1898, at Camp Black, to serve two years; mustered in as private, Co. I, May 24, 1898; mustered out with company, November 23, 1898, at Fort Slocum, New York Harbor.

BURKLE, GEORGE L.—Age, 22 years. Enlisted, May 9, 1898, at New York city, to serve two years; mustered in as private, Co. H, May 24, 1898; mustered out with company, November 23, 1898, at Fort Slocum, New York Harbor.

BURKMASTER, JOSEPH.—Age, 24 years. Enlisted, May 8, 1898, at Camp Black, to serve two years; mustered in as corporal, Co. F, May 24, 1898; mustered out with company, November 23, 1898, at Fort Slocum, New York Harbor.

BURNS, PETER F.—Age, 28 years. Enlisted, May 9, 1898, at New York city, to serve two years; mustered in as sergeant, Co. G, May 24, 1898; promoted first sergeant, August 27, 1898; mustered out with company, November 23, 1898, at Fort Slocum, New York Harbor.

BURROWS, HERBERT V.—Age, 27 years. Enlisted, May 9, 1898, at New York city, to serve two years; mustered in as corporal, Co. B, May 24, 1898; mustered out with company, November 23, 1898, at Fort Slocum, New York Harbor.

BUSH, ARTHUR H.—Age, 21 years. Enlisted, May 2, 1898, at Brooklyn, to serve two years; mustered in as private, Co. D, May 24, 1898; appointed artificer, November 1, 1898; mustered out with company, November 23, 1898, at Fort Slocum, New York Harbor.

BUTLER, EDWARD F.—Age, 23 years. Enlisted, May 24, 1898, at Camp Black, to serve two years; mustered in as private, Co. B, same date; mustered out with company, November 23, 1898, at Fort Slocum, New York Harbor.

BUTLER, JOSEPH F.—Age, 19 years. Enlisted, May 9, 1898, at New York city, to serve two years; mustered in as private, Co. B, May 24, 1898; mustered out with company, November 23, 1898, at Fort Slocum, New York Harbor.

BUTTLE, STEPHEN D.—Age, 26 years. Enlisted, May 4, 1898, at Camp Black, to serve two years; mustered in as private, Co. F, May 24, 1898; discharged, October 4, 1898, at Fort Slocum, New York Harbor.

BYRNE, FRANK.—Age, 24 years. Enlisted, May 9, 1898, at New York city, to serve two years; mustered in as private, Co. H. May 24, 1898; promoted corporal, July 29, 1898; mustered out with company, November 23, 1898, at Fort Slocum, New York Harbor.

BYRNES, CORNELIUS JOHN.—Age, 22 years. Enlisted, July 7, 1898, at New York city, to serve two years; mustered in as private, Co. H, same date; mustered out with company, November 23, 1898, at Fort Slocum, New York Harbor; also borne as Byrne.

CALHOUN, HENRY S.—Age, 21 years. Enlisted, May 9, 1898, at New York city, to serve two years; mustered in as private, Co. G, May 24, 1898; mustered out with company, November 23, 1898, at Fort Slocum, New York Harbor.

CALLAGHAN, CHARLES J.—Age, 24 years. Enlisted, May 9, 1898, at New York city, to serve two years; mustered in as private, Co. C, May 24, 1898; mustered out with company, November 23, 1898, at Fort Slocum, New York Harbor.

CALLAGHAN, WILLIAM A.—Age, 31 years. Enlisted, May 9, 1898, at New York city, to serve two years; mustered in as principal musician, May 24, 1898; promoted regimental quarter-master-sergeant, October 19, 1898; mustered out with regiment, November 23, 1898, at Fort Slocum, New York Harbor.

CALLAHAN, WALTER C.—Age, 19 years. Enlisted, May 9, 1898, at New York city, to serve two years; mustered in as private, Co. K, May 24, 1898; appointed wagoner, October 12, 1898; mustered out with company, November 23, 1898, at Fort Slocum, New York Harbor.

CALLENDER, WILLIAM D.—Age, 27 years. Enlisted, May 18, 1898, at Camp Black, to serve two years; mustered in as private, Co. B, May 24, 1898; mustered out with company, November 23, 1898, at Fort Slocum, New York Harbor.

CAMERON, ARTHUR.—Age, 23 years. Enlisted, May 2, 1898, at Brooklyn, to serve two years; mustered in as private, Co. F, May 24, 1898; mustered out with company, November 23, 1898, at Fort Slocum, New York Harbor, as Arthur St. John Cameron.

CAMERON, DAVID F.—Age, 25 years. Enlisted, May 2, 1898, at Brooklyn, to serve two years; mustered in as private, Co. F, May 24, 1898; mustered out with company, November 23, 1898, at Fort Slocum, New York Harbor.

CAMERON, WILLIAM L.—Age, 21 years. Enlisted, May 9, 1898, at New York city, to serve two years; mustered in as private, Co. A, May 24, 1898; mustered out with company, November 23, 1898, at Fort Slocum, New York Harbor.

CAMPBELL, EDWARD M.—Age, 21 years. Enlisted, May 9, 1898, at New York city, to serve two years; mustered in as musician, Co. E, May 24, 1898; mustered out with company, November 23, 1898, at Fort Slocum, New York Harbor.

CAMPBELL, FRANK.—Age, 21 years. Enlisted, June 3, 1898, at Camp Black, to serve two years; mustered in as private, Co. B, same date; mustered out with company, November 23, 1898, at Fort Slocum, New York Harbor.

CAMPBELL, THOMAS S.—Age, 25 years. Enlisted, May 9, 1898, at New York city, to serve two years; mustered in as private, Co. E, May 24, 1898; promoted corporal, May 31, 1898; mustered out with company, November 23, 1898, at Fort Slocum, New York Harbor.

CAMPION, JAMES G.—Age, 22 years. Enlisted, May 9, 1898, at New York city, to serve two years; mustered in as quarter-master-sergeant, Co. H, May 24, 1898; returned to ranks, October 27, 1898; mustered out with company, November 23, 1898, at Fort Slocum, New York Harbor.

CARBONELL, EMIL.—Age, 22 years. Enlisted, May 9, 1898, at New York city, to serve two years; mustered in as private, Co. B, May 24, 1898; mustered out with company, November 23, 1898, at Fort Slocum, New York Harbor.

CAREY, FRANK.—Age, 31 years. Enlisted, July 1, 1898, at New York city, to serve two years; mustered in as private, Co. C, same date; mustered out with company, November 23, 1898, at Fort Slocum, New York Harbor.

CAREY, WILLIAM F.—Age, 40 years. Enrolled, May 9, 1898, at New York city, to serve two years; mustered in as first lieutenant and quartermaster, May 24, 1898; discharged, October 12, 1898; commissioned captain and regimental quartermaster, May 24, 1898, with rank from same date, original.

CARMICHAEL, ALPHONSO.—Age, 28 years. Enlisted, May 9, 1898, at New York city, to serve two years; mustered in as musician, Co. E, May 24, 1898; promoted corporal, October 7, 1898; mustered out with company, November 23, 1898, at Fort Slocum, New York Harbor.

CARNEY, JOHN P.—Age, 19 years. Enlisted, May 2, 1898, at Brooklyn, to serve two years; mustered in as private, Co. L, May 24, 1898; mustered out with company, November 23, 1898, at Fort Slocum, New York Harbor.

CARPENTER, JAMES A. S.—Age, 22 years. Enlisted, May 2, 1898, at Brooklyn, to serve two years; mustered in as private, Co. D, May 24, 1898; mustered out with company, November 23, 1898, at Fort Slocum, New York Harbor.

CARR, EDWARD J.—Age, 19 years. Enlisted, May 2, 1898, at Brooklyn, to serve two years; mustered in as private, Co. M, May 24, 1898; mustered out with company, November 23, 1898, at Fort Slocum, New York Harbor.

CARR, THOMAS.—Age, 28 years. Enlisted, May 9, 1898, at New York city, to serve two years; mustered in as corporal, Co. B. May 24, 1898; promoted sergeant, September 9, 1898; mustered out with company, November 23, 1898, at Fort Slocum, New York Harbor.

CARROLL, EDWARD A.—Age, 19 years. Enlisted, May 22. 1898, at Camp Black, to serve two years; mustered in as private, Co. A, May 24, 1898; mustered out with company, November 23, 1898, at Fort Slocum, New York Harbor.

CARROLL, JAMES C.—Age, — years. Enlisted, August 11, 1898, at Fort Schuyler, to serve two years; mustered in as private, Co. C, same date; mustered out with company, November 23, 1898, at Fort Slocum, New York Harbor.

CARROLL, JOSEPH JOHN.—Age, 26 years. Enlisted, June 23, 1898, at New York city, to serve two years; mustered in as private, Co. B, same date; mustered out with company, November 23, 1898, at Fort Slocum, New York Harbor.

CARSON, WILLIAM.—Age, 21 years. Enlisted, May 2, 1898, at Brooklyn, to serve two years; mustered in as private, Co. D, May 24, 1898; mustered out with company, November 23, 1898, at Fort Slocum, New York Harbor.

CARTER, ENOS.—Age, 26 years. Enlisted, May 9, 1898, at New York city, to serve two years; mustered in as musician, Co. C, May 24, 1898; mustered out with company, November 23, 1898, at Fort Slocum, New York Harbor.

CASEY, DANIEL J.—Age, 22 years. Enlisted, May 19, 1898, at Camp Black, to serve two years; mustered in as private, Co. D, May 24, 1898; mustered out with company, November 23, 1898, at Fort Slocum, New York Harbor.

CASH, JACOB.—Age, 27 years. Enlisted, May 9, 1898, at New York city, to serve two years; mustered in as private, Co. G, May 24, 1898; mustered out with company, November 23, 1898, at Fort Slocum, New York Harbor.

CASSIDY, JAMES F.—Age, 26 years. Enlisted, May 17, 1898, at Camp Black, to serve two years; mustered in as private, Co. D, May 24, 1898; mustered out with company, November 23, 1898, at Fort Slocum, New York Harbor.

CASSIDY, MATTHEW P.—Age, 32 years. Enlisted, May 9, 1898, at New York city, to serve two years; mustered in as private, Co. C, May 24, 1898; discharged, October 29, 1898, at Fort Slocum, New York Harbor.

CASSIDY, THOMAS E.—Age, 23 years. Enlisted, May 9, 1898, at New York city, to serve two years; mustered in as private, Co. H, May 24, 1898; mustered out with company, November 23, 1898, at Fort Slocum, New York Harbor.

CASSIDY, WILLIAM J.—Age, 22 years. Enlisted, May 21, 1898, at Camp Black, to serve two years; mustered in as private, Co. E, May 24, 1898; mustered out with company, November 23, 1898, at Fort Slocum, New York Harbor.

CASTLES, GEORGE C.—Age, 23 years. Enlisted, May 9, 1898, at New York city, to serve two years; mustered in as private, Co. E, May 24, 1898; mustered out with company, November 23, 1898, at Fort Slocum, New York Harbor.

CAVANAGH, JOHN JOSEPH.—Age, 22 years. Enlisted, June 23, 1898, at New York city, to serve two years; mustered in as private, Co. I, same date; mustered out with company, November 23, 1898, at Fort Slocum, New York Harbor.

CHAMBERS, ROBERT J.—Age, 19 years. Enlisted, May 2, 1898, at Brooklyn, to serve two years; mustered in as private, Co. F, May 24, 1898; mustered out with company, November 23, 1898, at Fort Slocum, New York Harbor.

CHANDLER, LOUIS B.—Age, 28 years. Enlisted, May 9, 1898, at New York city, to serve two years; mustered in as private, Co. K, May 24, 1898; promoted corporal, September 21, 1898; mustered out with company, November 23, 1898, at Fort Slocum, New York Harbor.

CHAVES, MANUEL L.—Age, 25 years. Enlisted, May 9, 1898, at New York city, to serve two years; mustered in as private, Co. K, May 24, 1898; mustered out with company, November 23, 1898, at Fort Slocum, New York Harbor.

CHAVES, ROBERT L.—Age, 26 years. Enlisted, May 9, 1898, at New York city, to serve two years; mustered in as private, Co. K, May 24, 1898; mustered out with company, November 23, 1898, at Fort Slocum, New York Harbor.

CHILVERS, WILLIAM WHITE.—Age, 21 years. Enlisted, July 1, 1898, at New York city, to serve two years; mustered in as private, Co. K, same date; mustered out with company, November 23, 1898, at Fort Slocum, New York Harbor; also born as Chilvier.

CHIZZOLA, MAURICE.—Age, 25 years. Enlisted, May 9, 1898, at New York city, to serve two years; mustered in as private, Co. B, May 24, 1898; mustered out with company, November 23, 1898, at Fort Slocum, New York Harbor.

CHURCH, GEORGE I.—Age, 21 years. Enlisted, May 20, 1898, at Camp Black, to serve two years; mustered in as private, Co. I, May 24, 1898; mustered out with company, November 23, 1898, at Fort Slocum, New York Harbor.

CHURCH, JOHN K.—Age, 21 years. Enlisted, May 9, 1898, at New York city, to serve two years; mustered in as private, Co. I, May 24, 1898; mustered out with company, November 23, 1898, at Fort Slocum, New York Harbor.

CITRON, JOSEPH.—Age, 24 years. Enlisted, June 20, 1898, at New York city, to serve two years; mustered in as private, Co. B, same date; mustered out with company, November 23, 1898, at Fort Slocum, New York Harbor.

CLAPP, JASON E.—Age, 28 years. Enlisted, May 2, 1898, at Brooklyn, to serve two years; mustered in as private, Co. M, May 24, 1898; mustered out with company, November 23, 1898, at Fort Slocum, New York Harbor.

CLARE, JOHN E. J.—Age, 27 years. Enlisted, May 9, 1898, at New York city, to serve two years; mustered in as private, Co. C, May 24, 1898; promoted corporal, July 29, 1898; discharged, October 27, 1898, at Fort Slocum, New York Harbor.

CLARK, EDGAR A.—Age, 21 years. Enlisted, May 21, 1898, at Camp Black, to serve two years; mustered in as private, Co. B, May 24, 1898; promoted corporal, June 30, 1898; mustered out with company, November 23, 1898, at Fort Slocum, New York Harbor.

CLARK, THEODORE D.—Age, 32 years. Enlisted, May 9, 1898,
at New York city, to serve two years; mustered in as private,
Co. A, May 24, 1898; mustered out with company, November
23, 1898, at Fort Slocum, New York Harbor.

CLARKE, FRANK J.—Age, 21 years. Enlisted, May 17, 1898,
at Camp Black, to serve two years; mustered in as private,
Co. D, May 24, 1898; mustered out, November 23, 1898, at Fort
Slocum, New York Harbor.

CLARKE, GEORGE HERBERT.—Age, 24 years. Enlisted, May
9, 1898, at New York city, to serve two years; mustered in as
first sergeant, Co. I, May 24, 1898; as second lieutenant, Co. H,
September 1, 1898; as first lieutenant, October 2, 1898; mustered out with company, November 23, 1898, at Fort Slocum,
New York Harbor; commissioned second lieutenant, September
1, 1898, with rank from same date, vice Lowenbein, promoted;
first lieutenant, October 2. 1898, with rank from same date.
vice Lowenbein, discharged.

CLARKE, JOHN F.—Age, 29 years. Enlisted, May 9, 1898, at
New York city, to serve two years; mustered in as private,
Co. E, May 24, 1898; mustered out with company, November
23, 1898, at Fort Slocum, New York Harbor.

CLARKIN, JAMES JOSEPH.—Age, 22 years. Enlisted, July
6, 1898, at New York city, to serve two years; mustered in as
private, Co. H, same date; mustered out with company, November 23, 1898, at Fort Slocum, New York Harbor.

CLEARWATER, CHARLES J.—Age, 26 years. Enlisted, June
25, 1898, at Brooklyn, to serve two years; mustered in as private, Co. M, same date; mustered out with company, November
23, 1898, at Fort Slocum, New York Harbor.

CLEARY, CHARLES E.—Age, 30 years.   Enlisted, June 17,
1898, at New York city, to serve two years; mustered in as
private, Co. A, same date; mustered out with company, November 23, 1898, at Fort Slocum, New York Harbor.

CLELAND, FRANK D.—Age, 26 years. Enlisted, May 20, 1898,
at Camp Black, to serve two years; mustered in as private,
Co. I, May 24, 1898; mustered out with company, November
23, 1898, at Fort Slocum, New York Harbor.

CLELAND, HARRY E.—Age, 23 years. Enlisted, May 9, 1898, at New York city, to serve two years; mustered in as private, Co. I, May 24, 1898; promoted corporal, June 30, 1898; mustered out with company, November 23, 1898, at Fort Slocum, New York Harbor.

CLIFFORD, DANIEL F.—Age, 25 years. Enlisted, May 9, 1898, at New York city, to serve two years; mustered in as private, Co. H, May 24, 1898; mustered out with company, November 23, 1898, at Fort Slocum, New York Harbor.

CLINTON, HUGH E.—Age, 18 years. Enlisted, May 9, 1898, at New York city, to serve two years; mustered in as musician, Co. G, May 24, 1898; mustered out with company, November 23, 1898, at Fort Slocum, New York Harbor.

COBB, WILLIAM D.—Age, 22 years. Enlisted, May 9, 1898, at New York city, to serve two years; mustered in as private, Co. C, May 24, 1898; mustered out with company, November 23, 1898, at Fort Slocum, New York Harbor.

COBDEN, RICHARD.—Age, 33 years. Enrolled, August 16, 1898, at Fort Slocum, to serve two years; mustered in as chaplain, same date; mustered out, November 23, 1898; commissioned chaplain, August 16, 1898, with rank from same date, original.

COCHRAN, JAMES W.—Age, 26 years. Enlisted, May 2, 1898, at Brooklyn, to serve two years; mustered in as private, Co. L, May 24, 1898; transferred to Fourth United States Volunteer Infantry, September 28, 1898.

CODY, JR., EDWARD T.—Age, 20 years. Enlisted, May 9, 1898, at New York city, to serve two years; mustered in as private, Co. I, May 24, 1898; discharged, October 28, 1898, at Fort Slocum, New York Harbor; also borne as Edward F. Cody, Jr.

COE, EDWARD B.—Age, 32 years. Enlisted, May 2, 1898, at Brooklyn, to serve two years; mustered in as sergeant, Co. F, May 24, 1898; mustered out with company, November 23, 1898, at Fort Slocum, New York Harbor.

COFFEY, JOSEPH FRANCIS.—Age, 22 years. Enlisted, June 28, 1898, at New York city, to serve two years; mustered in as private, Co. G, same date; mustered out with company, November 23, 1898, at Fort Slocum, New York Harbor.

COGER, HENRY M.—Age, 22 years. Enlisted, May 2, 1898, at Brooklyn, to serve two years; mustered in as private, Co. M, May 24, 1898; mustered out with company, November 23, 1898, at Fort Slocum, New York Harbor.

COGGER, CHARLES S.—Age, 24 years. Enlisted, May 2, 1898, at Brooklyn, to serve two years; mustered in as sergeant, Co. F, May 24, 1898; mustered out with company, November 23, 1898, at Fort Slocum, New York Harbor.

COGSWELL, LOUIS C.—Age, 23 years. Enlisted, June 22, 1898, at Brooklyn, to serve two years; mustered in as private, Co. M, same date; mustered out with company, November 23, 1898, at Fort Slocum, New York Harbor.

COHN, SIDNEY B.—Age, 25 years. Enlisted, May 9, 1898, at New York city, to serve two years; mustered in as corporal, Co. H, May 24, 1898; mustered out with company, November 23, 1898, at Fort Slocum, New York Harbor.

COLEMAN, EDWARD J.—Age, 26 years. Enlisted, May 9, 1898, at New York city, to serve two years; mustered in as private, Co. G, May 24, 1898; mustered out with company, November 23, 1898, at Fort Slocum, New York Harbor.

COLES, JOHN B.—Age, 22 years. Enlisted, May 9, 1898, at New York city, to serve two years; mustered in as private, Co. I, May 24, 1898; promoted corporal, June 30, 1898; mustered out with company, November 23, 1898, at Fort Slocum, New York Harbor.

COLGAN, JAMES J.—Age, — years. Enlisted, August 5, 1898, at Willet's Point, to serve two years; mustered in as private, Co. G, same date; mustered out, November 23, 1898, at Fort Slocum, New York Harbor.

COLLETON, JOHN J.—Age, 23 years. . Enlisted, May 9, 1898, at New York city, to serve two years; mustered in as private, Co. A, May 24, 1898; discharged, September 25, 1898, at Fort Slocum, New York Harbor.

COLLYER, ERNEST.—Age, 29 years. Enlisted, May 9, 1898, at New York city, to serve two years; mustered in as private, Co. H, May 24, 1898; mustered out with company, November 23, 1898, at Fort Slocum, New York Harbor.

COMAN, JOHN H.—Age, 25 years. Enlisted, May 9, 1898, at New York city, to serve two years; mustered in as corporal, Co. K, May 24, 1898; promoted sergeant, October 7, 1898; mustered out, November 23, 1898.

COMSTOCK, GEORGE S.—Age, 22 years.   Enlisted, May 23, 1898, at Camp Black, to serve two years; mustered in as private, Co. D, May 24, 1898; mustered out with company, November 23, 1898, at Fort Slocum, New York Harbor.

CONDON, THOMAS P.—Age, 21 years. Enlisted, May 20, 1898, at Camp Black, to serve two years; mustered in as private, Co. I, May 24, 1898; mustered out with company, November 23, 1898, at Fort Slocum, New York Harbor.

CONKLIN, JR., CHARLES D.—Age, 23 years. Enlisted, May 2, 1898, at Brooklyn, to serve two years; mustered in as private, Co. L, May 24, 1898; mustered out with company, November 23, 1898, at Fort Slocum, New York Harbor.

CONKLIN, HENRY L.—Age, 28 years. Enlisted, May 9, 1898, at New York city, to serve two years; mustered in as sergeant, Co. A, May 24, 1898; mustered out with company, November 23, 1898, at Fort Slocum, New York Harbor.

CONNOR, CHARLES H.—Age, 21 years. Enlisted, May 9, 1898, at New York city, to serve two years; mustered in as private, Co. A, May 24, 1898; promoted corporal, August 24, 1898; quartermaster-sergeant, November 11, 1898; mustered out with company, November 23, 1898, at Fort Slocum, New York Harbor.

CONNOR, CHARLES HUBBARD.—Age, 24 years. Enlisted, July 5, 1898, at New York city, to serve two years; mustered in as private, Co. K, same date; mustered out with company, November 23, 1898, at Fort Slocum, New York Harbor.

CONNOR, FRANCIS A.—Age, 19 years. Enlisted, May 2, 1898, at Brooklyn, to serve two years; mustered in as private, Co. L, May 24, 1898; mustered out with company, November 23, 1898, at Fort Slocum, New York Harbor.

CONROW, WILLIAM S.—Age, 35 years. Enrolled, May 9, 1898, at New York city, to serve two years; mustered in as first lieutenant, Co. C, May 24, 1898; mustered out with company, November 23, 1898, at Fort Slocum, New York Harbor; subsequent service as first lieutenant, Forty-third Regiment, United States Volunteer Infantry; commissioned first lieutenant, May 24, 1898, with rank from same date, original.

COOK, HENRY T.—Age, 24 years. Enlisted, May 9, 1898, at New York city, to serve two years; mustered in as private, Co. I, May 24, 1898; promoted corporal, May 31, 1898; mustered out with company, November 23, 1898, at Fort Slocum, New York Harbor.

COOK, JOHN W.—Age, 24 years. Enlisted, May 2, 1898, at Brooklyn, to serve two years; mustered in as private, Co. M, May 24, 1898; mustered out with company, November 23, 1898, at Fort Slocum, New York Harbor.

COOK, WILLIAM T.—Age, 21 years. Enlisted, May 9, 1898, at New York city, to serve two years; mustered in as private, Co. H, May 24, 1898; promoted corporal, November 5, 1898; mustered out with company, November 23, 1898, at Fort Slocum, New York Harbor.

COOPER, JAMES F.—Age, 37 years. Enrolled, May 2, 1898, at Brooklyn, to serve two years; mustered in as second lieutenant, Co. D, May 24, 1898; as first lieutenant, November 1, 1898; mustered out with company, November 23, 1898, at Fort Slocum, New York Harbor; commissioned second lieutenant, May 24, 1898, with rank from same date, original; first lieutenant, November 1, 1898, with rank from same date, vice McDougall, transferred.

CORCORAN, JEREMIAH J.—Age, 27 years. Enlisted, May 9, 1898, at New York city, to serve two years; mustered in as corporal, Co. C, May 24, 1898; promoted sergeant, November 3, 1898; mustered out with company, November 23, 1898, at Fort Slocum, New York Harbor.

CORCORAN, PATRICK J.—Age, 23 years. Enlisted, May 9, 1898, at New York city, to serve two years; mustered in as corporal, Co. C, May 24, 1898; mustered out with company, November 23, 1898, at Fort Slocum, New York Harbor.

CORDELL, WILLIAM E.—Age, 22 years. Enlisted, May 9, 1898, at New York city, to serve two years; mustered in as private, Co. C, May 24, 1898; mustered out with company, November 23, 1898, at Fort Slocum, New York Harbor.

CORWIN, STACY M.—Age, 26 years. Enlisted, May 9, 1898, at New York city, to serve two years; mustered in as private, Co. K, May 24, 1898; promoted corporal, November 5, 1898; mustered out with company, November 23, 1898, at Fort Slocum, New York Harbor.

COSGRAVE, AUSTIN B.—Age, 21 years. Enlisted, May 9, 1898, at New York city, to serve two years; mustered in as private, Co. I, May 24, 1898; mustered out with company, November 23, 1898, at Fort Slocum, New York Harbor.

COSGROVE, JAMES PETER.—Age, 37 years. Enlisted, June 28, 1898, at New York city, to serve two years; mustered in as private, Co. G, same date; mustered out with company, November 23, 1898, at Fort Slocum, New York Harbor.

COTCHETT, JOHN P.—Age, 22 years. Enlisted, May 2, 1898, at Brooklyn, to serve two years; mustered in as corporal, Co. M, May 24, 1898; mustered out with company, November 23, 1898, at Fort Slocum, New York Harbor.

COURSER, ARTHUR L.—Age, 22 years. Enlisted, May 9, 1898, at New York city, to serve two years; mustered in as private, Co. G, May 24, 1898; mustered out with company, November 23, 1898, at Fort Slocum, New York Harbor.

COURT, JAMES F.—Age, 37 years. Enlisted, May 9, 1898, at New York city, to serve two years; mustered in as sergeant, Co. A, May 24, 1898; discharged, November 10, 1898, at Fort Slocum, New York Harbor.

COUSINS, RAYMOND.—Age, 29 years. Enlisted, June 23, 1898, at Brooklyn, to serve two years; mustered in as private, Co. L, same date; mustered out with company, November 23, 1898, at Fort Slocum, New York Harbor.

COVEY, SAMUEL.—Age, 32 years. Enlisted, May 9, 1898, at New York city, to serve two years; mustered in as corporal, Co. H, May 24, 1898; mustered out with company, November 23, 1898, at Fort Slocum, New York Harbor.

COX, ALBERT S.—Age, 33 years. Enlisted, May 9, 1898, at New York city, to serve two years; mustered in as private, Co. G, May 24, 1898; mustered out with company, November 23, 1898, at Fort Slocum, New York Harbor.

COX, CHARLES G.—Age, 19 years. Enlisted, May 2, 1898, at Brooklyn, to serve two years; mustered in as private, Co. M, May 24, 1898; mustered out with company, November 23, 1898, at Fort Slocum, New York Harbor.

COX, GEORGE K.—Age, 21 years. Enlisted, May 14, 1898, at Camp Black, to serve two years; mustered in as private, Co. D, May 24, 1898; mustered out with company, November 23, 1898, at Fort Slocum, New York Harbor.

COX, JR., HARRY A.—Age, 22 years. Enlisted, May 2, 1898, at Brooklyn, to serve two years; mustered in as private, Co. D, May 24, 1898; promoted corporal, September 1, 1898; mustered out with company, November 23, 1898, at Fort Slocum, New York Harbor.

COYNE, JOHN J.—Age, 22 years. Enlisted, June 28, 1898, at Brooklyn, to serve two years; mustered in as private, Co. L, same date; mustered out with company, November 23, 1898, at Fort Slocum, New York Harbor, as James J. Coyne.

CRAFTON, DANIEL A.—Age, 34 years. Enlisted, May 9, 1898, at New York city, to serve two years; mustered in as private, Co. C, May 24, 1898; mustered out with company, November 23, 1898, at Fort Slocum, New York Harbor.

CRANE, CHARLES W.—Age, 18 years. Enlisted, June 24, 1898, at Brooklyn, to serve two years; mustered in as private, Co. D, same date; mustered out with company, November 23, 1898, at Fort Slocum, New York Harbor.

CRANE, JAMES P.—Age, 22 years. Enlisted, May 23, 1898, at Camp Black, to serve two years; mustered in as private, Co. A, May 24, 1898; mustered out with company, November 23, 1898, at Fort Slocum, New York Harbor.

CRAWFORD, HARRY A.—Age, 23 years. Enlisted, July 5, 1898, at Brooklyn, to serve two years; mustered in as private, Co. L, same date; mustered out with company, November 23, 1898, at Fort Slocum, New York Harbor.

CREEDEN, JOSEPH.—Age, 26 years. Enlisted, May 9, 1898, at New York city, to serve two years; mustered in as private, Co. A, May 24, 1898; discharged, September 30, 1898, at Fort Slocum, New York Harbor.

CREWE, WILLIAM S.—Age, 32 years. Enlisted, May 11, 1898, at New York city, to serve two years; mustered in as private, Co. B, May 24, 1898; appointed company cook, July 29, 1898; mustered out with company, November 23, 1898, at Fort Slocum, New York Harbor.

CROOKE, GEORGE W.—Age, 20 years. Enlisted, May 2, 1898, at Brooklyn, to serve two years; mustered in as private, Co. F, May 24, 1898; appointed wagoner, July 1, 1898; mustered out with company, November 23, 1898, at Fort Slocum, New York Harbor.

CROSBY, ALBERT U. H.—Age, 36 years. Enlisted, May 2, 1898, at Brooklyn, to serve two years; mustered in as private, Co. M, May 24, 1898; promoted corporal, July 1, 1898; mustered out with company, November 23, 1898, at Fort Slocum, New York Harbor.

CROSSETT, THOMAS H.—Age, 21 years. Enlisted, July 6, 1898, at Brooklyn, to serve two years; mustered in as private, Co. D, same date; mustered out with company, November 23, 1898, at Fort Slocum, New York Harbor.

CROSSLEY, ARTHUR.—Age, 24 years. Enlisted, May 9, 1898, at New York city, to serve two years; mustered in as private, Co. C, May 24, 1898; promoted corporal, November 1, 1898; mustered out with company, November 23, 1898, at Fort Slocum, New York Harbor.

CROUTER, HARRY N.—Age, 23 years. Enlisted, May 9, 1898, at New York city, to serve two years; mustered in as private, Co. B, May 24, 1898; mustered out with company, November 23, 1898, at Fort Slocum, New York Harbor.

CROWLEY, JOHN FRANCIS.—Age, 24 years. Enlisted, June 28, 1898, at New York city, to serve two years; mustered in as private, Co. G, same date; mustered out with company, November 23, 1898, at Fort Slocum, New York Harbor.

CULLITON, FRANCIS J.—Age, 22 years. Enlisted, May 9, 1898, at New York city, to serve two years; mustered in as wagoner, Co. I, May 24, 1898; mustered out with company, November 23, 1898, at Fort Slocum, New York Harbor; also borne as Callitan.

CULLOM, WILLIAM FRANCIS.—Age, 21 years. Enlisted, June 28, 1898, at New York city, to serve two years; mustered in as private, Co. G, same date; mustered out with company, November 23, 1898, at Fort Slocum, New York Harbor.

CUMMINGS, THOMAS P.—Age, 19 years. Enlisted, May 9, 1898, at New York city, to serve two years; mustered in as private, Co. C, May 24, 1898; mustered out with company, November 23, 1898, at Fort Slocum, New York Harbor.

CUNNEEN, THOMAS JOSEPH.—Age, 22 years. Enlisted, July 1, 1898, at New York city, to serve two years; mustered in as private, Co. A, same date; mustered out with company, November 23, 1898, at Fort Slocum, New York Harbor.

CUNNINGHAM, THOMAS JOSEPH.—Age, 24 years. Enlisted, July 2, 1898, at New York city, to serve two years; mustered in as private, Co. H, same date; mustered out with company, November 23, 1898, at Fort Slocum, New York Harbor.

CURRY, JAMES H.—Age, 32 years. Enlisted, May 2, 1898, at Brooklyn, to serve two years; mustered in as private, Co. M, May 24, 1898; mustered out with company, November 23, 1898, at Fort Slocum, New York Harbor.

CURTIN, JOHN.—Age, 22 years. Enlisted, May 2, 1898, at Brooklyn, to serve two years; mustered in as sergeant, Co. F, May 24, 1898; mustered out with company, November 23, 1898, at Fort Slocum, New York Harbor.

CURTIS, MARION.—Age, 21 years. Enlisted, May 20, 1898, at Camp Black, to serve two years; mustered in as private, Co. D, May 24, 1898; discharged, September 22, 1898, at Willet's Point, N. Y.

CUTLER, ALBERT T.—Age, 22 years. Enlisted, May 20, 1898, at Camp Black, to serve two years; mustered in as private, Co. I, May 24, 1898; mustered out with company, November 23, 1898, at Fort Slocum, New York Harbor.

CUTLER, LLOYD A.—Age, 24 years. Enlisted, May 9, 1898, at New York city, to serve two years; mustered in as private, Co. I, May 24, 1898; promoted corporal, May 31, 1898; mustered out with company, November 23, 1898, at Fort Slocum, New York Harbor.

CUTTINGHAM, CHRISTOPHER.—Age, 21 years. Enlisted, May 9, 1898, at New York city, to serve two years; mustered in as private, Co. H, May 24, 1898; appointed artificer, July 1, 1898; mustered out with company, November 23, 1898, at Fort Slocum, New York Harbor.

DAFLY, JAMES.—Age, 35 years. Enlisted, June 28, 1898, at New York city, to serve two years; mustered in as private, Co. C, same date; mustered out with company, November 23, 1898, at Fort Slocum, New York Harbor; also borne as Dafley.

DAILEY, GEORGE W.—Age, 23 years. Enlisted, July 1, 1898, at Brooklyn, to serve two years; mustered in as private, Co. L, same date; mustered out with company, November 23, 1898, at Fort Slocum, New York Harbor.

DALEY, DANIEL M.—Age, 22 years. Enlisted, May 9, 1898, at New York city, to serve two years; mustered in as private, Co. H, May 24, 1898; mustered out with company, November 23, 1898, at Fort Slocum, New York Harbor.

DALY, ROBERT J.—Age, 42 years. Enrolled, May 9, 1898, at New York city, to serve two years; mustered in as battalion adjutant, May 24, 1898; mustered out with regiment, November 23, 1898, at Fort Slocum, New York Harbor; commissioned battalion adjutant, May 24, 1898, with rank from same date, original.

DALY, WILLIAM.—Age, 32 years. Enlisted, May 21, 1898, at Camp Black, to serve two years; mustered in as private, Co. E, May 24, 1898; mustered out with company, November 23, 1898, at Fort Slocum, New York Harbor.

DAMM, WILLIAM.—Age, 25 years. Enlisted, May 9, 1898, at New York city, to serve two years; mustered in as private, Co. C, May 24, 1898; discharged for disability, September 16, 1898, at Fort Schuyler, New York Harbor.

DANZIG, ALFRED.—Age, 22 years. Enlisted, May 9, 1898, at New York city, to serve two years; mustered in as corporal, Co. K, May 24, 1898; promoted quartermaster-sergeant, November 5, 1898; mustered out with company, November 23, 1898, at Fort Slocum, New York Harbor.

d'APÉRY, TELLO J.—Age, 21 years. Enlisted, May 10, 1898, at New York city, to serve two years; mustered in as private, Co. I, May 24, 1898; mustered out with company, November 23, 1898, at Fort Slocum, New York Harbor.

DARNLEY, EDWARD J.—Age, 21 years. Enlisted, May 12, 1898, at Camp Black, to serve two years; mustered in as private, Co. F, May 24, 1898; mustered out with company, November 23, 1898, at Fort Slocum, New York Harbor.

DAVIS, ALBERT H.—Age, 22 years. Enlisted, May 2, 1898, at Brooklyn, to serve two years; mustered in as private, Co. D, May 24, 1898; mustered out with company, November 23, 1898, at Fort Slocum, New York Harbor.

DAVIS, CHARLES O.—Age, 40 years. Enrolled, May 2, 1898, at Brooklyn, to serve two years; mustered in as first lieutenant, Co. F, May 24, 1898; mustered out with company, November 23, 1898, at Fort Slocum, New York Harbor; commissioned first lieutenant, May 24, 1898, with rank from same date, original.

DAVIS, RICHARD N.—Age, 32 years. Enlisted, May 9, 1898, at New York city, to serve two years; mustered in as sergeant, Co. C, May 24, 1898; mustered out with company, November 23, 1898, at Fort Slocum, New York Harbor.

DAVIS, SAMUEL.—Age, 31 years. Enlisted, May 9, 1898, at New York city, to serve two years; mustered in as private, Co. K, May 24, 1898; mustered out with company, November 23, 1898, at Fort Slocum, New York Harbor.

DAYTON, EDWIN W.—Age, 32 years. Enrolled, May 9, 1898, at New York city, to serve two years; mustered in as captain, Co. G, May 24, 1898; mustered out with company, November 23, 1898, at Fort Slocum, New York Harbor; commissioned captain, May 24, 1898, with rank from same date, original.

DEAN, JOHN J.—Age, 22 years. Enlisted, May 9, 1898, at New York city, to serve two years; mustered in as private, Co. H, May 24, 1898; mustered out with company, November 23, 1898, at Fort Slocum, New York Harbor.

DEERY, JAMES C.—Age, 24 years. Enlisted, May 2, 1898, at Brooklyn, to serve two years; mustered in as private, Co. D, May 24, 1898; mustered out with company, November 23, 1898, at Fort Slocum, New York Harbor.

DE FOREST ALFRED A.—Age, 18 years. Enlisted, May 2, 1898, at Brooklyn, to serve two years mustered in as private, Co. L, May 24, 1898; mustered out with company, November 23, 1898, at Fort Slocum, New York Harbor.

DE FOREST, FRANCIS EDGAR.—Age, 39 years. Enlisted, July 1, 1898, at New York city, to serve two years; mustered in as private, Co. A, same date; mustered out with company, November 23, 1898, at Fort Slocum, New York Harbor.

DE HAMEL, JR., ENRIQUE B.—Age, 21 years. Enlisted, May 2, 1898, at Brooklyn, to serve two years; mustered in as private, Co. L, May 24, 1898; promoted corporal, October 1, 1898; mustered out with company, November 23, 1898, at Fort Slocum, New York Harbor.

DELAVAN, FREDERICK M.—Age, 19 years. Enlisted, May 2, 1898, at Brooklyn, to serve two years; mustered in as private, Co. L, May 24, 1898; mustered out with company, November 23, 1898, at Fort Slocum, New York Harbor.

DE LEON, GEORGE.—Age, 21 years. Enlisted, May 20, 1898. at Camp Black, to serve two years; mustered in as private, Co. E, May 24, 1898; mustered out with company, November 23, 1898, at Fort Slocum, New York Harbor.

DE LUCE, FRANCIS E.—Age. 22 years. Enlisted, May 9, 1898, at New York city, to serve two years; mustered in as private. Co. G, May 24, 1898; mustered out with company, November 23, 1898, at Fort Slocum, New York Harbor.

DENHAM, THOMAS A.—Age, 33 years. Enlisted, May 9, 1898. at New York city, to serve two years; mustered in as corporal, Co. H, May 24, 1898; promoted quartermaster-sergeant, October 28, 1898; mustered out with company, November 23, 1898, at Fort Slocum, New York Harbor.

DENNISON, GEORGE HENRIQUES.—Age, 18 years. Enlisted, June 28, 1898, at New York city, to serve two years; mustered in as private, Co. K, same date; mustered out with company, November 23, 1898, at Fort Slocum, New York Harbor.

DE ROSSETT, GRAHAM D.—Age, 21 years. Enlisted, May 9, 1898, at New York city, to serve two years; mustered in as private, Co. H, May 24, 1898; mustered out with company, November 23, 1898, at Fort Slocum, New York Harbor.

DE VETT, SAMUEL S.—Age, 21 years. Enlisted, May 2, 1898, at Brooklyn, to serve two years; mustered in as private, Co. M, May 24, 1898; mustered out with company, November 23, 1898, at Fort Slocum, New York Harbor.

DEVEZE, HENRY.—Age, 22 years. Enlisted, May 18, 1898, at Camp Black, to serve two years; mustered in as private, Co. B, May 24, 1898; mustered out with company, November 23, 1898, at Fort Slocum, New York Harbor.

DE WINTER, JOSEPH A.—Age, 21 years. Enlisted, July 1, 1898, at Brooklyn, to serve two years; mustered in as private, Co. D, July 7, 1898; mustered out with company, November 23, 1898, at Fort Slocum, New York Harbor.

DICK, JOHN F.—Age, 19 years. Enlisted, May 2, 1898, at Brooklyn, to serve two years; mustered in as private, Co. L, May 24, 1898; mustered out with company, November 23, 1898, at Fort Slocum, New York Harbor.

DIETERICH, CHARLES E.—Age, 21 years. Enlisted, May 20, 1898, at Camp Black, to serve two years; mustered in as private, Co. I, May 24, 1898; mustered out with company, November 23, 1898, at Fort Slocum, New York Harbor.

DILLMAN, FRANK P.—Age, 21 years. Enlisted, May 23, 1898, at Camp Black, to serve two years; mustered in as private, Co. A, May 24, 1898; mustered out with company, November 23, 1898, at Fort Slocum, New York Harbor.

DILLON, JAMES W.—Age, 26 years. Enlisted, May 9, 1898, at New York city, to serve two years; mustered in as private, Co. E, May 24, 1898; promoted corporal, May 31, 1898; mustered out with company, November 23, 1898, at Fort Slocum, New York Harbor.

DILLON, JOHN.—Age, 21 years. Enlisted, May 9, 1898, at New York city, to serve two years; mustered in as private, Co. C, May 24, 1898; discharged for disability, October 18, 1898, at Fort Slocum, New York Harbor.

DILLON, WILLIAM C.—Age, 20 years. Enlisted, May 9, 1898, at New York city, to serve two years; mustered in as private, Co. A, May 24, 1898; mustered out with company, November 23, 1898, at Fort Slocum, New York Harbor.

DITMAS, THEODORE.—Age, 21 years. Enlisted, July 1, 1898, at New York city, to serve two years; mustered in as private, Co. K, same date; mustered out with company, November 23, 1898, at Fort Slocum, New York Harbor.

DOANE, HARVEY F.—Age, 22 years. Enlisted, May 2, 1898, at Brooklyn, to serve two years; mustered in as private, Co. F, May 24, 1898; mustered out with company, November 23, 1898, at Fort Slocum, New York Harbor.

DODD, WALTER W.—Age, 21 years. Enlisted, May 2, 1898, at Brooklyn, to serve two years; mustered in as private, Co. M, May 24, 1898; mustered out with company, November 23, 1898, at Fort Slocum, New York Harbor.

DOEHRMAN, GEORGE J.—Age, 21 years. Enlisted, May 2, 1898, at Brooklyn, to serve two years; mustered in as private. Co. D, May 24, 1898; mustered out with company, November 23, 1898, at Fort Slocum, New York Harbor.

DOHERTY, CHARLES P.—Age, 19 years. Enlisted, May 12, 1898, at Brooklyn, to serve two years; mustered in as private, Co. M, May 24, 1898; mustered out with company, November 23, 1898, at Fort Slocum, New York Harbor.

DOHERTY, JOHN.—Age, 21 years. Enlisted, May 16, 1898, at Brooklyn, to serve two years; mustered in as private, Co. M, May 24, 1898; mustered out with company, November 23, 1898, at Fort Slocum, New York Harbor.

DONNELLY, ALEXANDER.—Age, 19 years. Enlisted, June 27, 1898, at Brooklyn, to serve two years; mustered in as private, Co. D, same date; mustered out with company, November 23, 1898, at Fort Slocum, New York Harbor.

DONNELLY, MICHAEL J.—Age, 18 years. Enlisted, May 2, 1898, at Brooklyn, to serve two years; mustered in as private, Co. D, May 24, 1898; mustered out with company, November 23, 1898, at Fort Slocum, New York Harbor.

DONOVAN, JOHN R.—Age, 24 years. Enlisted, May 2, 1898, at Brooklyn, to serve two years; mustered in as sergeant, Co. L, May 24, 1898; mustered out with company, November 23, 1898, at Fort Slocum, New York Harbor.

DORIAN, FRANCIS X.—Age, 26 years. Enlisted, May 9, 1898, at New York city, to serve two years; mustered in as private, Co. G, May 24, 1898; appointed musician, July 1, 1898; mustered out with company, November 23, 1898, at Fort Slocum, New York Harbor.

DORNEY, ARTHUR F.—Age, 28 years. Enlisted, May 2, 1898, at Brooklyn, to serve two years; mustered in as sergeant, Co. M, May 24, 1898; mustered out with company, November 23, 1898, at Fort Slocum, New York Harbor.

DORSEY, THOMAS F.—Age, 20 years. Enlisted, May 9, 1898, at New York city, to serve two years; mustered in private, Co. A, May 24, 1898; mustered out with company, November 23, 1898, at Fort Slocum, New York Harbor.

DOUBLEDAY, NESTELL B.—Age, 32 years. Enrolled, May 9, 1898, at New York city, to serve two years; mustered in as second lieutenant, Co. G, May 24, 1898; discharged, August 16, 1898; commissioned second lieutenant, May 24, 1898, with rank from same date, original.

DOUGHERTY, FREDERICK H.—Age, 32 years. Enlisted, May 9, 1898, at New York city, to serve two years; mustered in as private, Co. G, May 24, 1898; discharged, October 30, 1898, at Fort Slocum, New York Harbor.

DOWLING, WILLIAM G.—Age, 22 years. Enlisted, May 2, 1898, at Brooklyn, to serve two years; mustered in as sergeant, Co. L, May 24, 1898; mustered out with company, November 23, 1898, at Fort Slocum, New York Harbor.

DOWNEY, JOHN.—Age, 25 years. Enlisted, June 29, 1898, at New York city, to serve two years; mustered in as private, Co. G, same date; mustered out with company, November 23, 1898, at Fort Slocum, New York Harbor.

DOWNEY, THOMAS JOSEPH.—Age, 22 years. Enlisted, July 5, 1898, at New York city, to serve two years; mustered in as private, Co. H, same date; mustered out with company, November 23, 1898, at Fort Slocum, New York Harbor.

DOWNWARD, HERBERT J.—Age, 19 years. Enlisted, July 1, 1898, at Brooklyn, to serve two years; mustered in as private, Co. F, same date; mustered out with company, November 23, 1898, at Fort Slocum, New York Harbor.

DOYLE, THOMAS SYLVESTER.—Age, 26 years. Enlisted, June 30, 1898, at New York city, to serve two years; mustered in as private, Co. H, same date; mustered out with company, November 23, 1898, at Fort Slocum, New York Harbor.

DRANT, GEORGE.—Age, 24 years. Enlisted, May 2, 1898, at Brooklyn, to serve two years; mustered in as musician, Co. D, May 24, 1898; mustered out with company, November 23, 1898, at Fort Slocum, New York Harbor.

DREDGER, HENRY E.—Age, 21 years. Enlisted, July 5, 1898, at Brooklyn, to serve two years; mustered in as private, Co. L, same date; mustered out with company, November 23, 1898, at Fort Slocum, New York Harbor.

DREHER, BENJAMIN.—Age 19 years. Enlisted, June 24, 1898, at Brooklyn, to serve two years; mustered in as private, Co. D, same date; mustered out with company, November 23, 1898, at Fort Slocum, New York Harbor.

DRISCALL, JOSEPH A.—Age, 19 years. Enlisted, June 30, 1898, at Brooklyn, to serve two years; mustered in as private, Co. D, same date; mustered out with company, November 23, 1898, at Fort Slocum, New York Harbor.

DRUMMON, JR., JOSEPH E.—Age, 22 years. Enlisted, May 9, 1898, at New York city, to serve two years; mustered in as private, Co. H, May 24, 1898; promoted corporal, November 5, 1898; mustered out with company, November 23, 1898, at Fort Slocum, New York Harbor.

DUCH, WILLIAM F.—Age, 26 years. Enlisted, May 9, 1898, at New York city, to serve two years; mustered in as private, Co. K, May 24, 1898; appointed artificer, no date; mustered out with company, November 23, 1898, at Fort Slocum, New York Harbor.

DUCHEMIRE, JAMES B.—Age, 24 years. Enlisted, May 19, 1898, at Camp Black, to serve two years; mustered in as private, Co. E, May 24, 1898; mustered out with company, November 23, 1898, at Fort Slocum, New York Harbor.

DUFFY, JOHN MARTIN.—Age, 27 years. Enlisted, July 6, 1898, at New York city, to serve two years; mustered in as private, Co. A, same date; mustered out with company, November 23, 1898, at Fort Slocum, New York Harbor.

DUNBAR, FORREST S.—Age, 21 years. Enlisted, May 2, 1898, at Brooklyn, to serve two years; mustered in as private, Co. F, May 24, 1898; mustered out with company, November 23, 1898, at Fort Slocum, New York Harbor.

DUNCAN, FRED N.—Age, 26 years. Enlisted, May 20, 1898, at Camp Black, to serve two years; mustered in as private, Co. D, May 24, 1898; promoted corporal, July 1, 1898; mustered out, November 23, 1898, at Fort Slocum, New York Harbor.

DUNHAM, ROBERT MARSHALL.—Age, 23 years. Enlisted, June 17, 1898, at New York city, to serve two years; mustered in as private, Co. I, same date; mustered out with company, November 23, 1898, at Fort Slocum, New York Harbor.

DUNLAP, JOHN M.—Age, 28 years. Enlisted, May 20, 1898, at Camp Black, to serve two years; mustered in as private, Co. I, May 24, 1898; mustered out with company, November 23, 1898, at Fort Slocum, New York Harbor.

DUNN, GEORGE.—Age, 21 years. Enlisted, July 1, 1898, at Brooklyn, to serve two years; mustered in as private, Co. L, same date; mustered out with company, November 23, 1898, at Fort Slocum, New York Harbor.

DUNN, JOHN J.—Age, 34 years. Enlisted, May 9, 1898, at New York city, to serve two years; mustered in as regimental quar-termaster-sergeant, May 24, 1898; discharged, October 19, 1898.

DUNTZE, JOHN A. R.—Age, 20 years. Enlisted, May 9, 1898, at New York city, to serve two years; mustered in as private, Co. A, May 24, 1898; mustered out with company, November 23, 1898, at Fort Slocum, New York Harbor.

DURLAND, GARRETT.—Age, 30 years. Enlisted, May 9, 1898, at New York city, to serve two years; mustered in as sergeant, Co. E, May 24, 1898; mustered out with company, November 23, 1898, at Fort Slocum, New York Harbor.

DYETT, ALBERT H.—Age, 31 years. Enrolled, May 9, 1898, at New York city, to serve two years; mustered in as first lieutenant, Co. I, May 24, 1898; mustered out with company, November 23, 1898, at Fort Slocum, New York Harbor; commissioned first lieutenant, May 24, 1898, with rank from same date, original.

EBBETS, HARRY H.—Age, 23 years. Enlisted, May 2, 1898, at Brooklyn, to serve two years; mustered in as private, Co. M, May 24, 1898; promoted corporal, July 1, 1898; mustered out with company, November 23, 1898, at Fort Slocum, New York Harbor.

ECHTESBRELSER, CHARLES F.—Age, 21 years. Enlisted, July 1, 1898, at New York city, to serve two years; mustered in as private, Co. C, same date; mustered out with company, November 23, 1898, at Fort Slocum, New York Harbor; also borne as Echterbecker.

ECKERT, WILLIAM.—Age, 22 years. Enlisted, June 28, 1898, at New York city, to serve two years; mustered in as private, Co. G, same date; mustered out with company, November 23, 1898, at Fort Slocum, New York Harbor.

ECKHART, STANLEY, Age, 24 years. Enlisted, May 20, 1898, at Camp Black, to serve two years; mustered in as private, Co. I, May 24, 1898; mustered out with company, November 23, 1898, at Fort Slocum, New York Harbor.

EDDY, RUFUS T.—Age, 32 years. Enlisted, May 2, 1898, at Brooklyn, to serve two years; mustered in as private, Co. D, May 24, 1898; mustered out with company, November 23, 1898, at Fort Slocum, New York Harbor.

EDGAR, FRANK W.—Age, 25 years. Enlisted, May 2, 1898, at Brooklyn, to serve two years; mustered in as musician, Co. M, May 24, 1898; discharged, October 29, 1898, at Fort Slocum, New York Harbor.

EGAN, NORMAN.—Age, 21 years. Enlisted, May 16, 1898, at Brooklyn, to serve two years; mustered in as private, Co. M, May 24, 1898; mustered out with company, November 23, 1898, at Fort Slocum, New York Harbor.

EISEMAN, CHARLES.—Age, 23 years. Enlisted, May 2, 1898, at Brooklyn, to serve two years; mustered in as private, Co. L, May 24, 1898; promoted corporal, July 1, 1898; mustered out with company, November 23, 1898, at Fort Slocum, New York Harbor.

EISEMAN, JOHN S.—Age, 23 years. Enlisted, May 2, 1898, at Brooklyn, to serve two years; mustered in as sergeant, Co. D, May 24, 1898; mustered out with company, November 23, 1898, at Fort Slocum, New York Harbor.

ELLIS, WILLIARD S.—Age, 22 years. Enlisted, June 23, 1898, at Brooklyn, to serve two years; mustered in as private, Co. D, same date; discharged, October 21, 1898, at Fort Slocum, New York Harbor.

ENGLAND, HERBERT F.—Age, 24 years. Enlisted, May 2, 1898, at Brooklyn, to serve two years; mustered in as private, Co. F, May 24, 1898; mustered out with company, November 23, 1898, at Fort Slocum, New York Harbor.

ENRIGHT, JOHN EDWARD.—Age, 22 years. Enlisted, June 28, 1898, at New York city, to serve two years; mustered in as private, Co. H, same date; mustered out with company, November 23, 1898, at Fort Slocum, New York Harbor.

ESCHBACH, GEORGE F.—Age, 25 years. Enlisted, May 9, 1898, at New York city, to serve two years; mustered in as private, Co. H, May 24, 1898; promoted corporal, July 29, 1898; mustered out with company, November 23, 1898, at Fort Slocum, New York Harbor.

ESCHBACH, HARRY F.—Age, 26 years. Enlisted, May 9, 1898, at New York city, to serve two years; mustered in as private, Co. H, May 24, 1898; mustered out with company, November 23, 1898, at Fort Slocum, New York Harbor.

ESTERHAZY, ARTHUR.—Age, 21 years. Enlisted, June 21, 1898, at New York city, to serve two years; mustered in as private, Co. E, same date; mustered out with company, November 23, 1898, at Fort Slocum, New York Harbor.

EVANS, ARCHIBALD M.—Age, 40 years. Enlisted, May 9, 1898, at New York city, to serve two years; mustered in as artificer, Co. I. May 24, 1898; promoted corporal, October 26, 1898; mustered out with company, November 23, 1898, at Fort Slocum, New York Harbor.

FAHNESTOCK, SAMUEL F.—Age, 33 years. Enrolled, May 2, 1898, as first lieutenant, at Brooklyn, to serve two years; mustered in as captain; Co. D, May 24, 1898; mustered out with company, November 23, 1898, at Fort Slocum, New York Harbor; commissioned captain, May 24, 1898, with rank from same date, original.

FAIGEL, LEWIS C.—Age, 21 years. Enlisted, May 9, 1898, at New York city, to serve two years; mustered in as private, Co. H, May 24, 1898; mustered out with company, November 23, 1898, at Fort Slocum, New York Harbor.

FAIRLAMB, ARTHUR.—Age, 24 years. Enlisted, May 9, 1898, at New York city, to serve two years; mustered in as private, Co. A, May 24, 1898; promoted corporal, July 29, 1898; mustered out with company, November 23, 1898, at Fort Slocum, New York Harbor.

FALLEN, STEPHEN J.—Age, 25 years. Enlisted, May 18, 1898, at New York city, to serve two years; mustered in as private, Co. B, May 24, 1898; mustered out with company, November 23, 1898, at Fort Slocum, New York Harbor.

FANTOM, SHAKESPEARE.—Age, 23 years. Enlisted, May 12, 1898, at Camp Black, to serve two years; mustered in as private, Co. F, May 24, 1898; mustered out with company, November 23, 1898, at Fort Slocum, New York Harbor.

FANTRY, THOMAS FRANCIS.—Age, 21 years. Enlisted, July 2, 1898, at New York city, to serve two years; mustered in as private, Co. H, same date; mustered out with company, November 23, 1898, at Fort Slocum, New York Harbor; also borne as Fautry.

FARR, GEORGE L.—Age, 23 years. Enlisted, May 2, 1898, at Brooklyn, to serve two years; mustered in as private, Co. M, May 24, 1898; mustered out with company, November 23, 1898, at Fort Slocum, New York Harbor.

FARRELL, MICHAEL J.—Age, 24 years. Enlisted, May 20, 1898, at Camp Black, to serve two years; mustered in as private, Co. K, May 24, 1898; deserted, October 28, 1898.

FARWELL, ALLAN S.—Age, 31 years. Enrolled, May 3, 1898, at Camp Black, to serve two years; mustered in as second lieutenant, Co. F, May 24, 1898; mustered out with company, November 23, 1898, at Fort Slocum, New York Harbor; commissioned second lieutenant, May 24, 1898, with rank from same date, original.

FAUTRY, THOMAS FRANCIS, see Thomas Francis Fantry.

FAY, WILLIAM S.—Age, 32 years. Enlisted, May 9, 1898, at New York city, to serve two years; mustered in as private, Co. H, May 24, 1898; promoted corporal, July 29, 1898; mustered out with company, November 23, 1898, at Fort Slocum, New York Harbor.

FEELY, JOHN J.—Age, 21 years. Enlisted, May 9, 1898, at New York city, to serve two years; mustered in as private, Co. C, May 24, 1898; mustered out with company, November 23, 1898, at Fort Slocum, New York Harbor.

FEKETO, RUDOLF.—Age, 18 years. Enlisted, May 20, 1898, at Camp Black, to serve two years; mustered in as private, Co. I, May 24, 1898; mustered out with company, November 23, 1898, at Fort Slocum, New York Harbor; also borne as Fekete.

FELLOWS, HENRY G.—Age, 22 years. Enlisted, May 9, 1898, at New York city, to serve two years; mustered in as private, Co. I, May 24, 1898; promoted corporal, September 10, 1898; mustered out with company, November 23, 1898, at Fort Slocum, New York Harbor.

FERNANDEZ, GEORGE W.—Age, 24 years. Enlisted, May 2, 1898, at Brooklyn, to serve two years; mustered in as private, Co. L, May 24, 1898; mustered out with company, November 23, 1898, at Fort Slocum, New York Harbor.

FETZER, LOUIS F.—Age, 44 years. Enlisted, May 9, 1898, at New York city, to serve two years; mustered in as private, Co. G, May 24, 1898; mustered out with company, November 23, 1898, at Fort Slocum, New York Harbor.

FIELD, CHARLES L.—Age, 20 years. Enlisted, May 9, 1898, at New York city, to serve two years; mustered in as private, Co. G, May 24, 1898; mustered out with company, November 23, 1898, at Fort Slocum, New York Harbor.

FIELD, FRANCIS PROCTOR.—Age, 21 years. Enlisted, May 9, 1898, at New York city, to serve two years; mustered in as private, Co. H, May 24, 1898; discharged, September 15, 1898, at Fort Schuyler, New York Harbor.

FINK, FRANK.—Age, 21 years. Enlisted, May 20, 1898, at Camp Black, to serve two years; mustered in as private, Co. K, May 24, 1898; mustered out with company, November 23, 1898, at Fort Slocum, New York Harbor.

FINK, HAMILTON K.—Age, 30 years. Enlisted, May 21, 1898, at Camp Black, to serve two years; mustered in as private, Co. B, May 24, 1898; mustered out with company, November 23, 1898, at Fort Slocum, New York Harbor.

FINKELSTONE, HYMAN.—Age, 29 years. Enlisted, May 9, 1898, at New York city, to serve two years; mustered in as hospital steward, May 24, 1898; discharged, September 19, 1898; also borne as Finkelstene.

FINLEY, JOHN F.—Age, 18 years. Enlisted, May 9, 1898, at New York city, to serve two years; mustered in as private, Co. G, May 24, 1898; mustered out with company, November 23, 1898, at Fort Slocum, New York Harbor.

FINNERAN, JOHN JAMES.—Age, 27 years. Enlisted, June 24, 1898, at New York city, to serve two years; mustered in as private, Co. I, same date; mustered out with company, November 23, 1898, at Fort Slocum, New York Harbor.

FINNERTY, DANIEL J.—Age, 24 years. Enlisted, May 9, 1898, at New York city, to serve two years; mustered in as private, Co. A, May 24, 1898; mustered out with company, November 23, 1898, at Fort Slocum, New York Harbor.

FINNIGAN, FRANK E.—Age, 25 years. Enlisted, May 2, 1898, at Brooklyn, to serve two years; mustered in as sergeant, Co. M, May 24, 1898; discharged, October 31, 1898, at Fort Slocum, New York Harbor.

FISCHER, FREDERICK.—Age, 21 years. Enlisted, May 23, 1898, at Camp Black, to serve two years; mustered in as private, Co. F, May 24, 1898; mustered out with company, November 23, 1898, at Fort Slocum, New York Harbor.

FISHER, CONSTANTINE.—Age, 22 years. Enlisted, May 12, 1898, at Camp Black, to serve two years; mustered in as private, Co. F, May 24, 1898; mustered out with company, November 23, 1898, at Fort Slocum, New York Harbor.

FITZGERALD, JOHN J.—Age, 25 years.   Enlisted, May 2, 1898, at Brooklyn, to serve two years; mustered in as private, Co. F, May 24, 1898; mustered out with company, November 23, 1898, at Fort Slocum, New York Harbor.

FITZPATRICK, EDWARD C.—Age, 21 years. Enlisted, May 2, 1898, at Brooklyn, to serve two years; mustered in as private, Co. D, May 24, 1898; mustered out with company, November 23, 1898, at Fort Slocum, New York Harbor.

FITZPATRICK, JOHN.—Age, 21 years. Enlisted, May 2, 1898, at Brooklyn, to serve two years; mustered in as private, Co. L, May 24, 1898; mustered out with company, November 23, 1898, at Fort Slocum, New York Harbor.

FITZSIMMONS, EMMETT.—Age, 23 years. Enlisted, May 24, 1898, at Camp Black, to serve two years; mustered in as private, Co. B, same date; mustered out with company, November 23, 1898, at Fort Slocum, New York Harbor.

FIZELL, GEORGE B.—Age, 22 years. Enlisted, May 9, 1898, at New York city, to serve two years; mustered in as private, Co. I, May 24, 1898; promoted corporal, May 31, 1898; mustered out with company, November 23, 1898, at Fort Slocum, New York Harbor; also borne as Fizzell.

FLANAGAN, JAMES ALFRED.—Age, 23 years. Enlisted, June 28, 1898, at New York city, to serve two years; mustered in as private, Co. G, same date; mustered out with company, November 23, 1898, at Fort Slocum, New York Harbor.

FLEMING, ARCHIBALD.—Age, 23 years. Enlisted, May 22, 1898, at Camp Black, to serve two years; mustered in as private, Co. A, May 24, 1898; mustered out with company, November 23, 1898, at Fort Slocum, New York Harbor.

FLEMING, THOMAS R.—Age, 26 years. Enrolled, May 2, 1898, at Brooklyn, to serve two years; mustered in as second lieutenant, Co. L, May 24, 1898; mustered out with company, November 23, 1898, at Fort Slocum, New York Harbor; commissioned second lieutenant, May 24, 1898, with rank from same date, original.

FLIEGE, JR., JOHN AUGUST.—Age, 26 years. Enlisted, May 9, 1898, at New York city, to serve two years; mustered in as private, Co. G, May 24, 1898; promoted corporal, July 1, 1898; mustered out with company, November 23, 1898, at Fort Slocum, New York Harbor.

FLILLER, EDWARD J.—Age, 24 years. Enlisted, May 2, 1898, at Brooklyn, to serve two years; mustered in as first sergeant, Co. M, May 24, 1898; mustered out with company, November 23, 1898, at Fort Slocum, New York Harbor.

FLOOD, BERNARD A.—Age, 21 years. Enlisted, May 9, 1898, at New York city, to serve two years; mustered in as private, Co. E, May 24, 1898; mustered out with company, November 23, 1898, at Fort Slocum, New York Harbor.

FLOOD, EDWARD.—Age, 27 years. Enlisted, May 21, 1898, at Camp Black, to serve two years; mustered in as private, Co. B, May 24, 1898; mustered out with company, November 23, 1898, at Fort Slocum, New York Harbor.

FLYNN, CHARLES L.—Age, 21 years. Enlisted, May 24, 1898, at Camp Black, to serve two years; mustered in as private, Co. I, same date; mustered out with company, November 23, 1898, at Fort Slocum. New York Harbor.

FLYNN, HENRY S. J.—Age, 24 years. Enlisted, May 10, 1898, at New York city, to serve two years; mustered in as private, Co. B, May 24, 1898; promoted corporal, June 30, 1898; mustered out with company, November 23, 1898, at Fort Slocum, New York Harbor.

FLYNN, THOMAS.—Age, 35 years. Enlisted, July 5, 1898, at New York city, to serve two years; mustered in as private, Co. A, same date; mustered out with company, November 23, 1898, at Fort Slocum, New York Harbor.

FOGARTY, WILLIAM J.—Age, 27 years. Enlisted, May 9, 1898, at New York city, to serve two years; mustered in as corporal, Co. G, May 24, 1898; promoted sergeant, May 31, 1898; mustered out with company, November 23, 1898, at Fort Slocum, New York Harbor.

FOLEY, JOHN H.—Age, 27 years. Enlisted, May 9, 1898, at New York city, to serve two years; mustered in as private, Co. C, May 24, 1898; mustered out with company, November 23, 1898, at Fort Slocum, New York Harbor.

FORD, JOHN J.—Age, 24 years. Enlisted, May 9, 1898, at New York city, to serve two years; mustered in as private, Co. B, May 24, 1898; mustered out with company, November 23, 1898, at Fort Slocum, New York Harbor.

FORD, ROBERT EDWIN.—Age, 23 years. Enlisted, June 20, 1898, at New York city, to serve two years; mustered in as private, Co. I, same date; discharged, October 15, 1898, at Fort Slocum, New York Harbor.

FORD, VALENTINE H.—Age, 21 years. Enlisted, May 6, 1898, at Camp Black, to serve two years; mustered in as private, Co. F, May 24, 1898; promoted corporal, July 1, 1898; mustered out with company, November 23, 1898, at Fort Slocum, New York Harbor.

FORNES, EUGENE A.—Age, 20 years. Enlisted, May 9, 1898, at New York city, to serve two years; mustered in as private, Co. H, May 24, 1898; mustered out with company, November 23, 1898, at Fort Slocum, New York Harbor.

FOSTER, WILLIAM A.—Age, 33 years. Enlisted, May 9, 1898, at New York city, to serve two years; mustered in as corporal, Co. H, May 24, 1898; mustered out with company, November 23, 1898, at Fort Slocum, New York Harbor.

FOX, EMORY E.—Age, 22 years. Enlisted, May 9, 1898, at New York city, to serve two years; mustered in as private, Co. C, May 24, 1898; mustered out with company, November 23, 1898, at Fort Slocum, New York Harbor.

FOX, FRANK F.—Age, 22 years. Enlisted, June 20, 1898, at New York city, to serve two years; mustered in as private, Co. E, same date; mustered out with company, November 23, 1898, at Fort Slocum, New York Harbor.

FOX, GEORGE C.—Age, 21 years. Enlisted, June 17, 1898, at New York city, to serve two years; mustered in as private, Co. A, same date; mustered out with company, November 23, 1898, at Fort Slocum, New York Harbor.

FRANK, JOSEPH.—Age, 28 years. Enlisted, June 24, 1898, at New York city, to serve two years; mustered in as private, Co. B, same date; mustered out with company, November 23, 1898, at Fort Slocum, New York Harbor; also borne as Frank Joseph.

FRAZEE, HARRY C.—Age, 23 years. Enlisted, June 20, 1898, at Brooklyn, to serve two years; mustered in as private, Co. M, same date; mustered out with company, November 23, 1898, at Fort Slocum, New York Harbor.

FRAZEE, JOHN.—Age, 21 years. Enlisted, June 30, 1898, at New York city, to serve two years; mustered in as private, Co. K, same date; mustered out with company, November 23, 1898, at Fort Slocum, New York Harbor.

FREIDENBERG, JOSEPH G.—Age, 29 years. Enlisted, May 9, 1898, at New York city, to serve two years; mustered in as private, Co. K, May 24, 1898; promoted corporal, July 29, 1898; discharged, September 19, 1898.

FREIMAN, HENRY.—Age, 21 years. Enlisted, May 9, 1898, at New York city, to serve two years; mustered in as private, Co. C, May 24, 1898; mustered out with company, November 23, 1898, at Fort Slocum, New York Harbor.

FRERICHS, WALTER A.—Age, 22 years. Enlisted, May 9, 1898, at New York city, to serve two years; mustered in as private, Co. E, May 24, 1898; promoted corporal, July 1, 1898; mustered out with company, November 23, 1898, at Fort Slocum, New York Harbor.

FREUND, CHARLES.—Age, 22 years. Enlisted, May 9, 1898, at New York city, to serve two years; mustered in as private, Co. C, May 24, 1898; discharged for disability, September 2, 1898, at Fort Schuyler, New York Harbor; also borne as Charles C. Freund.

FRIEDLANDER, EDWIN M.—Age, 21 years. Enlisted, May 18, 1898, at Camp Black, to serve two years; mustered in as private, Co. B, May 24, 1898; mustered out with company, November 23, 1898, at Fort Slocum, New York Harbor.

FRITH, JOHN J.—Age, 23 years. Enlisted, June 29, 1898, at
New York city, to serve two years; mustered in as private, Co.
C, same date; mustered out with company, November 23, 1898,
at Fort Slocum, New York Harbor.

FROSIS, THOMAS.—Age, 30 years. Enlisted, June 24, 1898, at
New York city, to serve two years; mustered in as private, Co.
I, same date; mustered out with company, November 23, 1898,
at Fort Slocum, New York Harbor.

FROTHINGHAM, EDWARD.—Age, 29 years. Enlisted, May 9,
1898, at New York city, to serve two years; mustered in as
private, Co. K, May 24, 1898; mustered out with company,
November 23, 1898, at Fort Slocum, New York Harbor.

FULLER, CHARLES H.—Age, 22 years. Enlisted, May 2, 1898,
at Brooklyn, to serve two years; mustered in as private, Co.
D, May 24, 1898; mustered out with company, November 23,
1898, at Fort Slocum, New York Harbor.

FULLER, FRANCIS A.—Age, 18 years. Enlisted, June 25, 1898,
at Brooklyn, to serve two years; mustered in as private, Co.
L, same date; mustered out with company, November 23, 1898,
at Fort Slocum, New York Harbor.

FUSSELL, NORRIS.—Age, 19 years. Enlisted, June 28, 1898,
at Brooklyn, to serve two years; mustered in as private, Co.
M, same date; mustered out with company, November 23, 1898,
at Fort Slocum, New York Harbor.

GABRIEL, THEODORE G.—Age, 18 years. Enlisted, May 6,
1898, at Brooklyn, to serve two years; mustered in as private,
Co. F, May 24, 1898; mustered out with company, November
23, 1898, at Fort Slocum, New York Harbor.

GAFFNEY, JOHN V.—Age, 21 years. Enlisted, May 9, 1898,
at New York city, to serve two years; mustered in as private,
Co. H, May 24, 1898; mustered out with company, November
23, 1898, at Fort Slocum, New York Harbor.

GAFFNEY, PATRICK.—Age, 22 years. Enlisted, May 19, 1898,
at Camp Black, to serve two years; mustered in as private,
Co. I, May 24, 1898; mustered out with company, November
23, 1898, at Fort Slocum, New York Harbor; also borne as
Gebbney.

GALLAGHER, EUGENE B.—Age, 28 years. Enlisted, June 27, 1898, at Brooklyn, to serve two years; mustered in as private, Co. M, same date; mustered out with company, November 23, 1898, at Fort Slocum, New York Harbor.

GALLOWAY, GEORGE J.—Age, 21 years. Enlisted, May 18, 1898, at Camp Black, to serve two years; mustered in as private, Co. B, May 24, 1898; mustered out with company, November 23, 1898, at Fort Slocum, New York Harbor.

GAMBLE, JOHN.—Age, — years. Enlisted, August 21, 1898, at Fort Schuyler, to serve two years; mustered in as private, Co. A, same date; mustered out with company, November 23, 1898, at Fort Slocum, New York Harbor.

GANGHREN, MATTHEW THOMAS.—Age, 29 years. Enlisted, July 6, 1898, at New York city, to serve two years; mustered in as private, Co. H, same date; mustered out with company, November 23, 1898, at Fort Slocum, New York Harbor.

GARDNER, LAUSON M.—Age, 27 years. Enlisted, May 2, 1898, at Brooklyn, to serve two years; mustered in as private, Co. M, May 24, 1898; promoted corporal, August 17, 1898; mustered out with company, November 23, 1898, at Fort Slocum, New York Harbor.

GARLAND, THOMAS.—Age, 33 years. Enlisted, June 28, 1898, at New York city, to serve two years; mustered in as private, Co. G, same date; mustered out with company, November 23, 1898, at Fort Slocum, New York Harbor.

GARRAHY, PATRICK.—Age, 24 years. Enlisted, May 2, 1898, at Brooklyn, to serve two years; mustered in as private, Co. L, May 24, 1898; mustered out with company, November 23, 1898, at Fort Slocum, New York Harbor.

GARRISON, FRANK.—Age, 22 years. Enlisted, May 9, 1898, at New York city, to serve two years; mustered in as private, Co. H, May 24, 1898; mustered out with company, November 23, 1898, at Fort Slocum, New York Harbor.

GARRISON, HARVEY.—Age, 38 years. Enrolled, May 9, 1898, at New York city, to serve two years; mustered in as second lieutenant, Co. C, May 24, 1898; mustered out with company, November 23, 1898, at Fort Slocum, New York Harbor; prior service, five years in United States Cavalry; subsequent service as first lieutenant, Forty-seventh Regiment, United States Volunteer Infantry; commissioned second lieutenant, May 24, 1898, with rank from same date, original.

GAYLORD, HERBERT ALVA.—Age, 19 years. Enlisted, June 28, 1898, at New York city, to serve two years; mustered in as private, Co. K, same date; mustered out with company, November 23, 1898, at Fort Slocum, New York Harbor.

GAYLORD, WILLIAM B.—Age, 40 years.   Enlisted, May 2, 1898, at Brooklyn, to serve two years; mustered in as private, Co. D, May 24, 1898; mustered out with company, November 23, 1898, at Fort Slocum, New York Harbor.

GEBBNEY, PATRICK, see Patrick Gaffney.

GEBHARDT, MAX.—Age, 25 years. Enlisted, June 20, 1898, at New York city, to serve two years; mustered in as private, Co. K, same date; mustered out with company, November 23, 1898, at Fort Slocum, New York Harbor.

GEHRINGER, VALENTINE JACOB.—Age, 22 years. Enlisted, June 30, 1898, at New York city, to serve two years; mustered in as private, Co. H, same date; mustered out with company, November 23, 1898, at Fort Slocum, New York Harbor.

GELDNER, MARTIN G.—Age, 21 years.   Enlisted, June 27, 1898, at Brooklyn, to serve two years; mustered in as private, Co. D, same date; mustered out with company, November 23, 1898, at Fort Slocum, New York Harbor.

GERMAN, SCOTT.—Age, 23 years. Enlisted, May 2, 1898, at Brooklyn, to serve two years; mustered in as private, Co. F, May 24, 1898; mustered out with company, November 23, 1898, at Fort Slocum, New York Harbor.

GERMOND, ROBINSON.—Age, 26 years. Enlisted, May 2, 1898, at Brooklyn, to serve two years; mustered in as private, Co. L, May 24, 1898; mustered out with company, November 23, 1898, at Fort Slocum, New York Harbor.

GERNON, JOHN J.—Age, 21 years. Enlisted, May 9, 1898, at at Camp Black, to serve two years; mustered in as private, Co. B, May 24, 1898; discharged, October 30, 1898, at Fort Slocum, New York Harbor; also borne as Gernan.

GERWIN, HENRY M.—Age, 21 years. Enlisted, June 21, 1898, at New York city, to serve two years; mustered in as private, Co. E, same date; deserted, October 3, 1898, at Fort Slocum, New York Harbor.

GEYER, GEORGE.—Age, 21 years. Enlisted, June 21, 1898, at Brooklyn, to serve two years; mustered in as private, Co. L, same date; mustered out with company, November 23, 1898, at Fort Slocum, New York Harbor.

GIBBONS, THEODORE M.—Age, 20 years. Enlisted, May 9, 1898, at New York city, to serve two years; mustered in as private, Co. A, May 24, 1898; promoted corporal, July 29, 1898; mustered out with company, November 23, 1898, at Fort Slocum, New York Harbor.

GILES, MAX MILLEN.—Age, 29 years. Enlisted, May 19, 1898, at Camp Black, to serve two years; mustered in as private, Co. K, May 24, 1898; mustered out with company, November 23, 1898, at Fort Slocum, New York Harbor.

GILLESPIE, DAVID B.—Age, 19 years. Enlisted, May 9, 1898, at New York city, to serve two years; mustered in as private, Co. I, May 24, 1898; mustered out with company, November 23, 1898, at Fort Slocum, New York Harbor.

GILLESPIE, EDWARD C.—Age, 18 years. Enlisted, June 21, 1898, at Brooklyn, to serve two years; mustered in as private, Co. M, same date; mustered out with company, November 23, 1898, at Fort Slocum, New York Harbor.

GILROY, BERNARD.—Age, 23 years. Enlisted, July 1, 1898, at New York city, to serve two years; mustered in as private, Co. C, same date; mustered out with company, November 23, 1898, at Fort Slocum, New York Harbor.

GLEASON, CHARLES B.—Age, 22 years. Enlisted, June 20, 1898, at New York city, to serve two years; mustered in as private, Co. E, same date; mustered out with company, November 23, 1898, at Fort Slocum, New York Harbor.

GLEASON, JOHN F.—Age, 25 years. Enlisted, May 9, 1898, at New York city, to serve two years; mustered in as private, Co. H, May 24, 1898; mustered out with company, November 23, 1898, at Fort Slocum, New York Harbor.

GLIER, GEORGE H.—Age, 21 years. Enlisted, June 22, 1898, at Brooklyn, to serve two years; mustered in as private, Co. M, same date; mustered out with company, November 23, 1898, at Fort Slocum, New York Harbor.

GLYNN, JOHN J.—Age, 31 years. Enlisted, May 20, 1898, at Camp Black, to serve two years; mustered in as private, Co. K, May 24, 1898; mustered out with company, November 23, 1898, at Fort Slocum, New York Harbor.

GODLEY, VOORHEES I.—Age, 32 years. Enlisted, June 8, 1898, at Camp Black, to serve two years; mustered in as private, Co. L, same date; mustered out with company, November 23, 1898, at Fort Slocum, New York Harbor.

GOEBBELS, HENRY N.—Age, — years. Enlisted, August 10, 1898, at Fort Schuyler, to serve two years; mustered in as private, Co. K, same date; mustered out with company, November 23, 1898, at Fort Slocum, New York Harbor.

GOESS, THEODORE ADOLPH.—Age, 22 years. Enlisted, June 28, 1898, at New York city, to serve two years; mustered in as private, Co. G, same date; discharged, October 26, 1898, at Fort Slocum, New York Harbor.

GOESSLING, HUGO HENRY.—Age, 21 years. Enlisted, June 28, 1898, at New York city, to serve two years; mustered in as private, Co. G, same date; mustered out with company, November 23, 1898, at Fort Slocum, New York Harbor.

GOGERTY, JOHN J.—Age, 19 years. Enlisted, May 4, 1898, at Camp Black, to serve two years; mustered in as private, Co. F, May 24, 1898; mustered out with company, November 23, 1898, at Fort Slocum, New York Harbor.

GOLDSTEIN, JOSEPH.—Age, 22 years. Enlisted, May 9, 1898, at New York city, to serve two years; mustered in as private, Co. K, May 24, 1898; mustered out with company, November 23, 1898, at Fort Slocum, New York Harbor.

GOLDWATER, ISIDOR C.—Age, 22 years. Enlisted, May 19, 1898, at Camp Black, to serve two years; mustered in as private, Co. I, May 24, 1898; mustered out with company, November 23, 1898, at Fort Slocum, New York Harbor.

GOODALE, WILBER C.—Age, 22 years. Enlisted. May 9, 1898, at New York city, to serve two years; mustered in as corporal, Co. A, May 24, 1898; promoted sergeant, October 4, 1898; mustered out with company, November 23, 1898, at Fort Slocum, New York Harbor.

GOODMAN, JACOB.—Age, 21 years. Enlisted, May 9, 1898, at New York city, to serve two years; mustered in as private, Co. G, May 24, 1898; discharged, October 19, 1898, at Fort Slocum, New York Harbor; also borne as Jacob A. Goodman.

GOODMAN, OSCAR S.—Age, 27 years. Enlisted, May 9, 1898, at New York city, to serve two years; mustered in as private, Co. H, May 24, 1898; mustered out with company, November 23, 1898, at Fort Slocum, New York Harbor.

GOODWIN, EDWARD THOMAS.—Age, 23 years. Enlisted, May 9, 1898, at New York city, to serve two years; mustered in as private, Co. K, May 24, 1898; discharged for disability, September 20, 1898, at Fort Schuyler, New York Harbor; also borne as Edward F. Goodwin.

GOODWIN, WILLIAM.—Age, 27 years. Enlisted, June 21, 1898, at Brooklyn, to serve two years; mustered in as private, Co. M, same date; mustered out with company, November 23, 1898, at Fort Slocum, New York Harbor.

GORDON, VICTOR D.—Age, 19 years. Enlisted, July 5, 1898, at Brooklyn, to serve two years; mustered in as private, Co. D, same date; mustered out with company, November 23, 1898, at Fort Slocum, New York Harbor.

GORHAM, FULLER R.—Age, 24 years. Enlisted, May 9, 1898, at New York city, to serve two years; mustered in as private, Co. G, May 24, 1898; mustered out with company, November 23, 1898, at Fort Slocum, New York Harbor.

GRADY, JOSEPH E.—Age, 30 years. Enlisted, May 9, 1898, at New York city, to serve two years; mustered in as private, Co. H, May 24, 1898; mustered out with company, November 23, 1898, at Fort Slocum, New York Harbor.

GRAETER, LEWIS T.—Age, 21 years. Enlisted, May 17, 1898, at Hempstead, to serve two years; mustered in as private, Co. M, May 24, 1898; mustered out with company, November 23, 1898, at Fort Slocum, New York Harbor; also borne as Lewis S. Greater.

GRAHAM, CLIFFORD T.—Age, 23 years. Enlisted, May 2, 1898, at Brooklyn, to serve two years; mustered in as corporal, Co. M, May 24, 1898; mustered out with company, November 23, 1898, at Fort Slocum, New York Harbor.

GRAHAM, EDWARD VINCENT.—Age, 30 years. Enlisted, June 28, 1898, at New York city, to serve two years; mustered in as private, Co. C, same date; mustered out with company, November 23, 1898, at Fort Slocum, New York Harbor.

GRAHAM, JOSEPH B.—Age, 27 years. Enlisted, May 9, 1898, at New York city, to serve two years; mustered in as sergeant, Co. K, May 24, 1898; promoted first sergeant, September 14, 1898; mustered in as second lieutenant, October 3, 1898; mustered out with company, November 23, 1898, at Fort Slocum, New York Harbor; commissioned second lieutenant, September 27, 1898, with rank from same date, vice Sternberger, promoted; also borne as John P. Graham.

GRANT, JOHN.—Age, 30 years. Enlisted, May 9, 1898, at New York city, to serve two years; mustered in as private, Co. E, May 24, 1898; promoted corporal, May 31, 1898; mustered out with company, November 23, 1898, at Fort Slocum, New York Harbor.

GRAPEL, ARTHUR A.—Age, 26 years. Enlisted, May 2, 1898, at Brooklyn, to serve two years; mustered in as corporal, Co. D, May 24, 1898; returned to ranks, August 4, 1898; promoted corporal, October 26, 1898; mustered out with company, November 23, 1898, at Fort Slocum, New York Harbor.

GREATER, LEWIS S., see Lewis T. Graeter.

GREEN, GEORGE H.—Age, 30 years. Enlisted, May 9, 1898, at New York city, to serve two years; mustered in as private, Co. C, May 24, 1898; promoted corporal, July 29, 1898; mustered out with company, November 23, 1898, at Fort Slocum, New York Harbor.

GREEN, GEORGE SCOTT.—Age, 39 years. Enlisted, June 28, 1898, at New York city, to serve two years; mustered in as private, Co. C, same date; mustered out with company, November 23, 1898, at Fort Slocum, New York Harbor.

GREEN, JOHN J.—Age, 20 years. Enlisted, May 9, 1898, at New York city, to serve two years; mustered in as private, Co. H, May 24, 1898; discharged, October 26, 1898, at Fort Slocum, New York Harbor; also borne as Greene.

GREENHOOD, BERNARD A.—Age, 22 years. Enlisted, May 24, 1898, at Camp Black, to serve two years; mustered in as private, Co. B, same date; discharged without honor, September 27, 1898, at Fort Slocum, New York Harbor.

GREENWOOD, WILLIAM EDMUND.—Age, 25 years. Enlisted, July 6, 1898, at New York city, to serve two years; mustered in as private, Co. A, same date; mustered out with company, November 23, 1898, at Fort Slocum, New York Harbor.

GREER, ANDREW E.—Age, 20 years. Enlisted, June 24, 1898, at Brooklyn, to serve two years; mustered in as private, Co. M, same date; mustered out with company, November 23, 1898, at Fort Slocum, New York Harbor.

GREGORY, CHARLES H.—Age, 26 years. Enlisted, May 2, 1898, at Brooklyn, to serve two years; mustered in as quarter-master-sergeant, Co. D, May 24, 1898; mustered out with company, November 23, 1898, at Fort Slocum, New York Harbor.

GREIF, LOUIS H.—Age, 23 years. Enlisted, May 9, 1898, at New York city, to serve two years; mustered in as sergeant, Co. K, May 24, 1898; mustered out with company, November 23, 1898, at Fort Slocum, New York Harbor.

GREVILLE, JOSEPH J.—Age, 26 years. Enlisted, May 9, 1898, at New York city, to serve two years; mustered in as quarter-master-sergeant, Co. G, May 24, 1898; mustered out with company, November 23, 1898, at Fort Slocum, New York Harbor.

GRIFFIN, MICHAEL.—Age, 26 years. Enlisted, May 20, 1898, at Camp Black, to serve two years; mustered in as private, Co. K, May 24, 1898; promoted corporal, July 29, 1898; deserted, October 1, 1898; also borne as Michael J. Griffin.

GRINSEL, ROBERT A.—Age, 21 years. Enlisted, June 3, 1898, at Camp Black, to serve two years; mustered in as private, Co. B, same date; mustered out with company, November 23, 1898, at Fort Slocum, New York Harbor.

GROSHON, WILLIAM A.—Age, 26 years. Enlisted, May 9, 1898, at New York city, to serve two years; mustered in as private, Co. G, May 24, 1898; discharged, September 21, 1898, at Willet's Point, N. Y.

GROSS, CHARLES.—Age, 24 years. Enlisted, May 20, 1898, at Camp Black, to serve two years; mustered in as private, Co. I, May 24, 1898; mustered out with company, November 23, 1898, at Fort Slocum, New York Harbor.

GRUN, EMIL.—Age, 26 years. Enlisted, July 5, 1898, at New York city, to serve two years; mustered in as private, Co. K, same date; mustered out with company, November 23, 1898, at Fort Slocum, New York Harbor.

GUISE, ALEXANDER J.—Age, 18 years. Enlisted, June 30, 1898, at Brooklyn, to serve two years; mustered in as private, Co. D, July 1, 1898; deserted, October 18, 1898, at Fort Slocum, New York Harbor.

GUNN, JOHN.—Age, 27 years. Enlisted, May 2, 1898, at Brooklyn, to serve two years; mustered in as private, Co. F, May 24, 1898; mustered out with company, November 23, 1898, at Fort Slocum, New York Harbor.

HAAS, CHARLES J.—Age, 20 years. Enlisted, May 9, 1898, at New York city, to serve two years; mustered in as private, Co. A, May 24, 1898; mustered out with company, November 23, 1898, at Fort Slocum, New York Harbor.

HALL, JOHN.—Age, 25 years. Enlisted, May 9, 1898, at New York city, to serve two years; mustered in as private, Co. H, May 24, 1898; mustered out with company, November 23, 1898, at Fort Slocum, New York Harbor.

HALL, OLIVER C.—Age, 28 years. Enlisted, May 2, 1898, at Brooklyn, to serve two years; mustered in as private, Co. L, May 24, 1898; mustered out with company, November 23, 1898, at Fort Slocum, New York Harbor.

HALLE, LOUIS L.—Age, 23 years. Enlisted, May 9, 1898, at New York city, to serve two years; mustered in as corporal, Co. K, May 24, 1898; mustered out with company, November 23, 1898, at Fort Slocum, New York Harbor.

HALLMAN, HERMAN.—Age, 21 years. Enlisted, July 2, 1898, at New York city, to serve two years; mustered in as private, Co. A, same date; mustered out with company, November 23, 1898, at Fort Slocum, New York Harbor, as Hollman.

HALLOCK, LESTER A.—Age, 19 years. Enlisted, June 30, 1898, at Brooklyn, to serve two years; mustered in as private, Co. F, same date; mustered out with company, November 23, 1898, at Fort Slocum, New York Harbor.

HALSTEAD, JR., EDWARD R.—Age, 21 years. Enlisted, May 18, 1898, at Camp Black, to serve two years; mustered in as private, Co. D, May 24, 1898; mustered out with company, November 23, 1898, at Fort Slocum, New York Harbor.

HAMILTON, LOUIS A.—Age, 30 years. Enrolled, May 9, 1898, at New York city, to serve two years; mustered in as second lieutenant, Co. B, May 24, 1898; mustered out with company, November 23, 1898, at Fort Slocum, New York Harbor; commissioned second lieutenant, May 24, 1898, with rank from same date, original; first lieutenant, but not mustered, November 1, 1898, with rank from same date, vice Asten, promoted.

HAMILTON, RICHARD.—Age, 21 years. Enlisted, June 7, 1898, at Camp Black, to serve two years; mustered in as private, Co. G, same date; transferred to Co. B, June 7, 1898; mustered out with company, November 23, 1898, at Fort Slocum, New York Harbor.

HAMMERLY, RICHARD.—Age, 37 years. Enlisted, June 17, 1898, at New York city, to serve two years; mustered in as private, Co. A, same date; appointed artificer, July 1, 1898; mustered out with company, November 23, 1898, at Fort Slocum, New York Harbor.

HAMMERSTEIN, HARRY.—Age, 28 years. Enlisted, May 9, 1898, at New York city, to serve two years; mustered in as quartermaster-sergeant, Co. K, May 24, 1898; discharged, November 3, 1898, at Fort Slocum, New York Harbor.

HANDS, WILLIAM H.—Age, 21 years. Enlisted, May 9, 1898, at New York city, to serve two years; mustered in as private, Co. E, May 24, 1898; mustered out with company, November 23, 1898, at Fort Slocum, New York Harbor.

HANDY, SAMUEL H.—Age, 27 years. Enlisted, May 2, 1898, at Brooklyn, to serve two years; mustered in as private, Co. M, May 24, 1898; mustered out with company, November 23, 1898, at Fort Slocum, New York Harbor.

HANLEIN, CHARLES J.—Age, 23 years. Enlisted, May 9, 1898, at New York city, to serve two years; mustered in as private, Co. A, May 24, 1898; mustered out with company, November 23, 1898, at Fort Slocum, New York Harbor; also borne as Hanlün.

HANLEY, THOMAS B.—Age, 28 years. Enlisted, May 9, 1898, at New York city, to serve two years; mustered in as private, Co. G, May 24, 1898; mustered out with company, November 23, 1898, at Fort Slocum, New York Harbor.

HANLON, JAMES J.—Age, 25 years. Enlisted, May 9, 1898, at New York city, to serve two years; mustered in as private, Co. K, May 24, 1898; promoted corporal, July 29, 1898; mustered out with company, November 23, 1898, at Fort Slocum, New York Harbor.

HANNAF, CASPAR JOSEPH.—Age, 21 years. Enlisted, June 21, 1898, at New York city, to serve two years; mustered in as private, Co. I, same date; mustered out with company, November 23, 1898, at Fort Slocum, New York Harbor.

HANNIGAN, WILLIAM J.—Age, 25 years. Enlisted, May 9, 1898, at New York city, to serve two years; mustered in as private, Co. E, May 24, 1898; mustered out with company, November 23, 1898, at Fort Slocum, New York Harbor.

HANO, ERNEST N.—Age, 21 years. Enlisted, June 20, 1898, at New York city, to serve two years; mustered in as private, Co. E, same date; mustered out with company, November 23, 1898, at Fort Slocum, New York Harbor.

HANSEN, FERDINAND.—Age, 33 years. Enlisted, May 20, 1898, at Camp Black, to serve two years; mustered in as private, Co. K, May 24, 1898; appointed cook, August 13, 1898; mustered out with company, November 23, 1898, at Fort Slocum, New York Harbor.

HARBESON, JR., MATTHEW L.—Age, 28 years. Enlisted, May 9, 1898, at New York city, to serve two years; mustered in as private, Co. C, May 24, 1898; mustered out with company, November 23, 1898, at Fort Slocum, New York Harbor.

HARDING, FRED C.—Age, 26 years. Enlisted, May 9, 1898, at New York city, to serve two years; mustered in as private, Co. K, May 24, 1898; appointed musician, no date; mustered out with company, November 23, 1898, at Fort Slocum, New York Harbor.

HARGAN, ALFRED J.—Age, 26 years. Enlisted, May 9, 1898, at New York city, to serve two years; mustered in as private, Co. E, May 24, 1898; discharged for disability, November 10, 1898, at Fort Slocum, New York Harbor.

HARRAL, FREDERICK R.—Age, 21 years. Enlisted, May 2, 1898, at Brooklyn, to serve two years; mustered in as private, Co. L, May 24, 1898; mustered out with company, November 23, 1898, at Fort Slocum, New York Harbor.

HART, BENJAMIN S.—Age, 31 years. Enrolled, May 9, 1898, at New York city, to serve two years; mustered in as captain, Co. K, May 24, 1898; mustered out with company, November 23, 1898, at Fort Slocum, New York Harbor; commissioned captain, May 24, 1898, with rank from same date, original.

HART, EDWARD P.—Age, 21 years. Enlisted, June 21, 1898, at New York city, to serve two years; mustered in as private, Co. E, same date; mustered out, November 23, 1898, at Fort Slocum, New York Harbor.

HART, HARRY H.—Age, 20 years. Enlisted, May 9, 1898, at New York city, to serve two years; mustered in as private, Co. I, May 24, 1898; mustered out with company, November 23, 1898, at Fort Slocum, New York Harbor.

HART, STEPHEN F.—Age, 37 years. Enrolled, May 2, 1898, at New York city, to serve two years; mustered in as major, May 24, 1898; mustered out with regiment, November 23, 1898, at Fort Slocum, New York Harbor; commissioned major, May 24, 1898, with rank from same date, original.

HARTIGAN, PAUL.—Age, 26 years. Enlisted, May 9, 1898, at New York city, to serve two years; mustered in as private, Co. K, May 24, 1898; promoted corporal, October 12, 1898; mustered out with company, November 23, 1898, at Fort Slocum, New York Harbor.

HARTLEY, JR., EDWARD F.—Age, 21 years. Enlisted, May 9, 1898, at New York city, to serve two years; mustered in as private, Co. G, May 24, 1898; mustered out with company, November 23, 1898, at Fort Slocum, New York Harbor.

HARTMAN, HERMAN FRANK.—Age, 22 years. Enlisted, June 29, 1898, at New York city, to serve two years; mustered in as private, Co. K, same date; mustered out with company, November 23, 1898, at Fort Slocum, New York Harbor.

HASKELL, RUEBEN L.—Age, 19 years. Enlisted, July 5, 1898, at Brooklyn, to serve two years; mustered in as private, Co. M, same date; discharged, October 24, 1898, at Fort Slocum, New York Harbor.

HASLAN, CROMWELL.—Age, 22 years. Enlisted, May 2, 1898, at Brooklyn, to serve two years; mustered in as private, Co. M, May 24, 1898; discharged without honor, September 22, 1898, at Willet's Point, N. Y.; also borne as Haslam.

HASLETT, WILLIAM P.—Age, 27 years. Enlisted, May 9, 1898, at New York city, to serve two years; mustered in as private, Co. C, May 24, 1898; mustered out with company, November 23, 1898, at Fort Slocum, New York Harbor.

HASTIE, JAMES H.—Age, 22 years. Enlisted, May 20, 1898, at Camp Black, to serve two years; mustered in as private, Co. I, May 24, 1898; mustered out with company, November 23, 1898, at Fort Slocum, New York Harbor.

HATCH, PERCIVAL S.—Age, 25 years. Enlisted, May 9, 1898, at New York city, to serve two years; mustered in as private, Co. C, May 24, 1898; discharged, October 11, 1898, at Fort Slocum, New York Harbor.

HAUBOLD, RUDOLPH O.—Age, 28 years. Enrolled, May 9, 1898, at New York city, to serve two years; mustered in as captain, Co. B, May 24, 1898; discharged, October 21, 1898; commissioned captain, May 24, 1898, with rank from same date, original.

HAUPTNAM, WILLIAM.—Age, 26 years. Enlisted, May 20, 1898, at Camp Black, to serve two years; mustered in as private, Co. E, May 24, 1898; mustered out with company, November 23, 1898, at Fort Slocum, New York Harbor; also borne as Hauptmann.

HAUSCHEER, HENRY O.—Age, 24 years. Enlisted, May 9, 1898, at New York city, to serve two years; mustered in as private, Co. I, May 24, 1898; mustered out with company, November 23, 1898, at Fort Slocum, New York Harbor; also borne as Hausheer and Hausher.

HAVENS, WILLIAM E.—Age, 21 years. Enlisted, May 9, 1898, at New York city, to serve two years; mustered in as private, Co. C, May 24, 1898; discharged, October 15, 1898, at Fort Slocum, New York Harbor.

HAWES, RALPH E.—Age, 22 years. Enlisted, May 9, 1898, at New York city, to serve two years; mustered in as private, Co. A, May 24, 1898; promoted corporal, July 29, 1898; mustered out with company, November 23, 1898, at Fort Slocum, New York Harbor.

HAWKES, WALTER DAVID.—Age, 20 years. Enlisted, June 21, 1898, at New York city, to serve two years; mustered in as private, Co. B, same date; mustered out with company, November 23, 1898, at Fort Slocum, New York Harbor; also borne as William D.

HAWKINS, JERRY D.—Age, 21 years. Enlisted, June 28, 1898, at Brooklyn, to serve two years; mustered in as private, Co. L, same date; mustered out with company, November 23, 1898, at Fort Slocum, New York Harbor.

HAYES, ALFRED D.—Age, 22 years. Enlisted, June 25, 1898, at Brooklyn, to serve two years; mustered in as private, Co. M, same date; mustered out with company, November 23, 1898, at Fort Slocum, New York Harbor.

HAYWARD, STERLING PAINE.—Age, 25 years. Enlisted, June 28, 1898, at New York city, to serve two years; mustered in as private, Co. G, same date; discharged, October 8, 1898, at Fort Slocum, New York Harbor.

HEAD, JAMES J.—Age, 21 years. Enlisted, May 17, 1898, at Camp Black, to serve two years; mustered in as private, Co. D, May 24, 1898; mustered out with company, November 23, 1898, at Fort Slocum, New York Harbor.

HEALY, FRANCIS J.—Age, 21 years. Enlisted, May 21, 1898, at Camp Black, to serve two years; mustered in as private, Co. B, May 24, 1898; mustered out with company, November 23, 1898, at Fort Slocum, New York Harbor.

HEARN, WILLIAM H.—Age, 22 years. Enlisted, May 21, 1898, at Camp Black, to serve two years; mustered in as private, Co. B, May 24, 1898; mustered out with company, November 23, 1898, at Fort Slocum, New York Harbor.

HEARNE, FREDERICK W.—Age, 21 years. Enlisted, May 9, 1898, at New York city, to serve two years; mustered in as musician, Co. C, May 24, 1898; returned to ranks, June 1, 1898; mustered out with company, November 23, 1898, at Fort Slocum, New York Harbor.

HEARNE, JOHN F.—Age, 28 years. Enlisted, May 9, 1898, at New York city, to serve two years; mustered in as first sergeant, Co. C, May 24, 1898; mustered out with company, November 23, 1898, at Fort Slocum, New York Harbor.

HEGEMAN, PERCY S.—Age, 21 years. Enlisted, June 25, 1898, at Brooklyn, to serve two years; mustered in as private, Co. F, same date; mustered out with company, November 23, 1898, at Fort Slocum, New York Harbor.

HELLAND, OLE.—Age, 19 years. Enlisted, May 2, 1898, at Brooklyn, to serve two years; mustered in as private, Co. L, May 24, 1898; mustered out with company, November 23, 1898, at Fort Slocum, New York Harbor.

HENCE, ERNEST.—Age, 21 years. Enlisted, May 9, 1898, at New York city, to serve two years; mustered in as private, Co. I, May 24, 1898; mustered out with company, November 23, 1898, at Fort Slocum, New York Harbor.

HENRIQUES, CHARLES R.—Age, 34 years. Enlisted, May 9, 1898, at New York city, to serve two years; mustered in as corporal, Co. K, May 24, 1898; promoted sergeant, September 17, 1898; mustered out with company, November 23, 1898, at Fort Slocum, New York Harbor.

HENRIQUES, HARRY P.—Age, 29 years.   Enlisted, May 9, 1898, at New York city, to serve two years; mustered in as sergeant, Co. K, May 24, 1898; promoted first sergeant, October 3, 1898; mustered out with company, November 23, 1898, at Fort Slocum, New York Harbor.

HENRIQUES, PERCY.—Age, 23 years.   Enlisted, May 9, 1898, at New York city, to serve two years; mustered in as private, Co. K, May 24, 1898; promoted corporal, July 29, 1898; mustered out with company, November 23, 1898, at Fort Slocum, New York Harbor.

HERBST, GUSTAVE.—Age, 22 years.   Enlisted, May 9, 1898, at New York city, to serve two years; mustered in as private, Co. B, May 24, 1898; mustered out with company, November 23, 1898, at Fort Slocum, New York Harbor.

HERON, THOMAS JOHN.—Age, 19 years.   Enlisted, June 24, 1898, at New York city, to serve two years; mustered in as private, Co. I, same date; mustered out with company, November 23, 1898, at Fort Slocum, New York Harbor.

HERVEY, JR., WILLIAM C.—Age, 21 years.   Enlisted, May 2, 1898, at Brooklyn, to serve two years; mustered in as private, Co. L, May 24, 1898; discharged, October 15, 1898, at Fort Slocum, New York Harbor.

HERZIG, GEORGE W.—Age, 22 years.   Enlisted, May 9, 1898, at New York city, to serve two years; mustered in as private, Co. E, May 24, 1898; promoted corporal, May 31, 1898, mustered out with company, November 23, 1898, at Fort Slocum, New York Harbor.

HERZOG, NATHAN.—Age, 29 years.   Enlisted, May 20, 1898, at Camp Black, to serve two years; mustered in as private, Co. K, May 24, 1898; mustered out with company, November 23, 1898, at Fort Slocum, New York Harbor.

HETTINGER, ALBERT JOHN.—Age, 25 years.   Enlisted, June 21, 1898, at New York city, to serve two years; mustered in as private, Co. B, same date; appointed musician, October 1, 1898; mustered out with company, November 23, 1898, at Fort Slocum, New York. Harbor.

HICKS, LOCKWOOD.—Age, 19 years. Enlisted, May 9, 1898, at New York city, to serve two years; mustered in as private, Co. C, May 24, 1898; discharged, July 12, 1898, at Fort Schuyler, New York Harbor.

HINDS, UDOLPHO W.—Age, 31 years. Enlisted, May 9, 1898, at New York city, to serve two years; mustered in as corporal, Co. B, May 24, 1898; mustered out with company, November 23, 1898, at Fort Slocum, New York Harbor.

HINEY, MARTIN J.—Age, 32 years. Enlisted, June 30, 1898, at New York city, to serve two years; mustered in as private, Co. C, same date; mustered out with company, November 23, 1898, at Fort Slocum, New York Harbor.

HIRSCH, EDWARD.—Age, 22 years. Enlisted, May 9, 1898, at New York city, to serve two years; mustered in as private, Co. B, May 24, 1898; mustered out with company, November 23, 1898, at Fort Slocum, New York Harbor.

HIRSCHBERG, MAX.—Age, 21 years. Enlisted, June 28, 1898, at New York city, to serve two years; mustered in as private, Co. K, same date; mustered out with company, November 23, 1898, at Fort Slocum, New York Harbor.

HOBBY, PERCY A.—Age, 22 years. Enlisted, May 2, 1898, at Brooklyn, to serve two years; mustered in as private, Co. D, May 24, 1898; appointed wagoner, June 11, 1898; mustered out with company, November 23, 1898, at Fort Slocum, New York Harbor.

HOEY, JOHN J.—Age, 20 years. Enlisted, May 9, 1898, at New York city, to serve two years; mustered in as private, Co. G, May 24, 1898; mustered out with company, November 23, 1898, at Fort Slocum, New York Harbor.

HOFF, FRANK JOHN.—Age, 21 years. Enlisted, June 28, 1898, at New York city, to serve two years; mustered in as private, Co. H, same date; mustered out with company, November 23, 1898, at Fort Slocum, New York Harbor.

HOFFMAN, JACOB A.—Age, 29 years. Enlisted, May 9, 1898, at New York city, to serve two years; mustered in as sergeant, Co. C, May 24, 1898; mustered out with company, November 23, 1898, at Fort Slocum, New York Harbor.

HOFFMANN, PETER L.—Age, 25 years. Enlisted, May 2, 1898, at Brooklyn, to serve two years; mustered in as corporal, Co. D, May 24, 1898; returned to ranks, July 26, 1898; mustered out with company, November 23, 1898, at Fort Slocum, New York Harbor.

HOFHEIMER, ARTHUR.—Age, 22 years. Enlisted, May 9, 1898, at New York city, to serve two years; mustered in as private, Co. H, May 24, 1898; promoted corporal, July 29, 1898; discharged, October 8, 1898, at Fort Slocum, New York Harbor.

HOLDEN, GEORGE O.—Age, 31 years. Enlisted, May 2, 1898, at Brooklyn, to serve two years; mustered in as private, Co. M, May 24, 1898; mustered out with company, November 23, 1898, at Fort Slocum, New York Harbor.

HOLLAND, JOSEPH.—Age, 30 years. Enlisted, May 9, 1898, at New York city, to serve two years; mustered in as corporal, Co. E, May 24, 1898; promoted sergeant, May 31, 1898; first sergeant, October 6, 1898; mustered out with company, November 23, 1898, at Fort Slocum, New York Harbor.

HOLLANDER, GABRIEL G.—Age, 24 years. Enlisted, May 9, 1898, at New York city, to serve two years; mustered in as corporal, Co. E, May 24, 1898; discharged, October 16, 1898, at Fort Slocum, New York Harbor.

HOLLMAN, HERMAN, see Herman Hallman.

HOLMBERG, CHARLES M.—Age, 21 years. Enlisted, May 2, 1898, at Brooklyn, to serve two years; mustered in as private, Co. L, May 24, 1898; mustered out with company, November 23, at Fort Slocum, New York Harbor.

HOLMBERG, FRANK.—Age, 25 years. Enlisted, May 2, 1898, at Brooklyn, to serve two years; mustered in as private, Co. F, May 24, 1898; mustered out with company, November 23, 1898, at Fort Slocum, New York Harbor.

HOLSTE, ANDREW J. C.—Age, 23 years. Enlisted, May 9, 1898, at New York city, to serve two years; mustered in as private, Co. E, May 24, 1898; mustered out with company, November 23, 1898, at Fort Slocum, New York Harbor.

HOPKINS, CHARLES M.—Age, 21 years.   Enlisted, May 9,
1898, at New York city, to serve two years; mustered in as
private, Co. E, May 24, 1898; promoted corporal, July 1, 1898;
mustered out with company, November 23, 1898, at Fort Slocum, New York Harbor.

HOPKINS, ERNEST L.—Age, 25 years.   Enlisted, May 9, 1898,
at New York city, to serve two years; mustered in as private,
Co. H, May 24, 1898; promoted corporal, November 5, 1898;
mustered out with company, November 23, 1898, at Fort Slocum, New York Harbor.

HORGAN, PATRICK S.—Age, 24 years. Enlisted, June 22, 1898,
at Brooklyn, to serve two years; mustered in as private, Co.
F, same date; mustered out with company, November 23, 1898,
at Fort Slocum, New York Harbor.

HORTON, JR., THOMAS H.—Age, 24 years.   Enlisted, May 9,
1898, at New York city, to serve two years; mustered in as
private, Co. G, May 24, 1898; promoted corporal, no date; discharged, October 7, 1898, at Fort Slocum, New York Harbor.

HOTCHKIN, WALTER B.—Age, 32 years.   Enrolled, May 9,
1898, at New York city, to serve two years; mustered in as
major, May 24, 1898; mustered out with regiment, November
23, 1898, at Fort Slocum, New York Harbor; commissioned
major, May 24, 1898, with rank from same date, original.

HOUGH, DANIEL.—Age, 22 years. Enlisted, May 17, 1898, at
Camp Black, to serve two years; mustered in as private, Co.
F, May 24, 1898; mustered out with company, November 23,
1898, at Fort Slocum, New York Harbor.

HOWARD, JR., ANDREW.—Age, 18 years. Enlisted, June 1,
1898, at Hempstead, to serve two years; mustered in as private,
Co. C, June 3, 1898; appointed musician, October 12, 1898; mustered out with company, November 23, 1898, at Fort Slocum,
New York Harbor.

HOWARD, CLIFFORD I.—Age, 22 years.   Enlisted, May 9,
1898, at New York city, to serve two years; mustered in as private, Co. G, May 24, 1898; mustered out with company, November 23, 1898, at Fort Slocum, New York Harbor.

HOWARD, JOSEPH P.—Age, 23 years. Enlisted, May 9, 1898, at New York city, to serve two years; mustered in as private, Co. C, May 24, 1898; mustered out with company, November 23, 1898, at Fort Slocum, New York Harbor.

HOWELL, ALONZO.—Age, 23 years. Enlisted, May 9, 1898, at New York city, to serve two years; mustered in as private, Co. B, May 24, 1898; mustered out with company, November 23, 1898, at Fort Slocum, New York Harbor.

HUBBELL, CLIFFORD W.—Age, 18 years. Enlisted, June 28, 1898, at Brooklyn, to serve two years; mustered in as private, Co. L, same date; mustered out with company, November 23, 1898, at Fort Slocum, New York Harbor.

HUBBS, FRANKLIN.—Age, 23 years. Enlisted, May 12, 1898, at Camp Black, to serve two years; mustered in as private, Co. F, May 24, 1898; mustered out with company, November 23, 1898, at Fort Slocum, New York Harbor.

HUBBS, HENRY.—Age, 24 years. Enlisted, May 12, 1898, at Camp Black, to serve two years; mustered in as corporal, Co. F, May 24, 1898; mustered out with company, November 23, 1898, at Fort Slocum, New York Harbor.

HUDSON, JOSEPH.—Age, 21 years. Enlisted, May 24, 1898, at at Camp Black, to serve two years; mustered in as private, Co. B, same date; mustered out with company, November 23, 1898, at Fort Slocum, New York Harbor.

HUFF, JAMES.—Age, 27 years. Enlisted, May 2, 1898, at Brooklyn, to serve two years; mustered in as private, Co. D, May 24, 1898; mustered out with company, November 23, 1898, at Fort Slocum, New York Harbor.

HUGHES, BENJAMIN J.—Age, 30 years. Enlisted, May 20, 1898, at Camp Black, to serve two years; mustered in as private, Co. I, May 24, 1898; mustered out with company, November 23, 1898, at Fort Slocum, New York Harbor.

HUGHES, BERNARD L.—Age, 25 years. Enlisted, May 9, 1898, at New York city, to serve two years; mustered in as private, Co. I, May 24, 1898; promoted corporal, June 30, 1898; discharged, October 28, 1898, at Fort Slocum, New York Harbor.

HUGHES, JOSEPH B.—Age, 31 years. Enlisted, May 12, 1898, at Camp Black, to serve two years; mustered in as private, Co. F, May 24, 1898; promoted corporal, July 1, 1898; mustered out with company, November 23, 1898, at Fort Slocum, New York Harbor.

HUGHES, WILLIAM E.—Age, 23 years.   Enlisted, June 27, 1898, at Brooklyn, to serve two years; mustered in as private, Co. F, same date; mustered out with company, November 23, 1898, at Fort Slocum, New York Harbor.

HÜHN, WILHELM.—Age, 32 years. Enlisted, June 24, 1898, at New York city, to serve two years; mustered in as private, Co. I, same date; mustered out with company, November 23, 1898, at Fort Slocum, New York Harbor; also borne as William Hühn.

HUNTER, CHARLES H.—Age, 20 years. Enlisted, May 2, 1898, at Brooklyn, to serve two years; mustered in as private, Co. L, May 24, 1898; mustered out with company, November 23, 1898, at Fort Slocum, New York Harbor.

HUNTER, CHARLES H.—Age, 32 years.   Enlisted, June 27, 1898; mustered in as private, same date; assigned to Co. F, July 8, 1898; mustered out with company, November 23, 1898, at Fort Slocum, New York Harbor.

HUNTER, SAMUEL J.—Age, 21 years. Enlisted, May 21, 1898, at Camp Black, to serve two years; mustered in as private, Co. E, May 24, 1898; mustered out with company, November 23, 1898, at Fort Slocum, New York Harbor.

HUNTLEY, IRVING W.—Age, 19 years. Enlisted, June 22, 1898, at Brooklyn, to serve two years; mustered in as private, Co. M, same date; mustered out with company, November 23, 1898, at Fort Slocum, New York Harbor.

HURST, CHARLES L.—Age, 26 years. Enlisted, May 2, 1898, at Brooklyn, to serve two years; mustered in as private, Co. M, May 24, 1898; mustered out with company, November 23, 1898, at Fort Slocum, New York Harbor.

HUTCHINSON, JOHN D.—Age, 29 years. Enlisted, May 2, 1898, at Brooklyn, to serve two years; mustered in as private, Co. M, May 24, 1898; transferred to Co. D, July 13, 1898; deserted, October 25, 1898, at Fort Slocum, New York Harbor.

HUTCHINSON, WILLIAM F.—Age, 21 years. Enlisted, May 9, 1898, at New York city, to serve two years; mustered in as private, Co. H, May 24, 1898; mustered out with company, November 23, 1898, at Fort Slocum, New York Harbor.

HUTCHISON, WILLIAM J.—Age, 32 years. Enlisted, May 21, 1898, at Camp Black, to serve two years; mustered in as private, Co. B, May 24, 1898; promoted corporal, July 15, 1898; mustered out with company, November 23, 1898, at Fort Slocum, New York Harbor.

HUTHWAITE, LOUIS G.—Age, 24 years. Enlisted, May 2, 1898, at Brooklyn, to serve two years; mustered in as private, Co. M, May 24, 1898; mustered out with company, November 23, 1898, at Fort Slocum, New York Harbor.

HUYLER, GEORGE S.—Age, 21 years. Enlisted, May 9, 1898, at New York city, to serve two years; mustered in as private, Co. H, May 24, 1898; appointed musician, September 11, 1898; mustered out with company, November 23, 1898, at Fort Slocum, New York Harbor.

INGRAM, ROBERT J.—Age, 24 years. Enlisted, May 9, 1898, at New York city, to serve two years; mustered in as private, Co. E, May 24, 1898; promoted corporal, October 24, 1898; mustered out with company, November 23, 1898, at Fort Slocum, New York Harbor.

INNES, ALFRED R.—Age, 25 years. Enlisted, May 2, 1898, at Brooklyn, to serve two years; mustered in as private, Co. L, May 24, 1898; mustered out with company, November 23, 1898, at Fort Slocum, New York Harbor; also borne as Innis.

ISHERWOOD, FRANK.—Age, 32 years. Enrolled, May 9, 1898, at New York city, to serve two years; mustered in as captain, Co. H, May 24, 1898; mustered out with company, November 23, 1898, at Fort Slocum, New York Harbor; commissioned captain, May 24, 1898, with rank from same date, original.

IVES, WALTER.—Age, 18 years. Enlisted, May 9, 1898, at New York city, to serve two years; mustered in as private, Co. C, May 24, 1898; mustered out with company, November 23, 1898, at Fort Slocum, New York Harbor.

JANTZEN, JEAN B.—Age, 22 years. Enlisted, May 9, 1898, at New York city, to serve two years; mustered in as private, Co. A, May 24, 1898; mustered out with company, November 23, 1898, at Fort Slocum, New York Harbor.

JARDINE, EDWARD DUNCAN.—Age, 26 years. Enlisted, June 28, 1898, at New York city, to serve two years; mustered in as private, Co. G, same date; promoted corporal, July 1, 1898; sergeant, August 27, 1898; mustered out with company, November 23, 1898, at Fort Slocum, New York Harbor.

JARRETT, ARTHUR R.—Age, 40 years. Enrolled, May 2, 1898, at Brooklyn, to serve two years; mustered in as first lieutenant and assistant surgeon, May 17, 1898; as captain and assistant surgeon, same date; mustered out with regiment, November 23, 1898, at Fort Slocum, New York Harbor; commissioned captain and assistant surgeon, May 17, 1898, with rank form same date, original.

JARRETT, AUGUSTUS T.—Age, 20 years. Enlisted, May 2, 1898, at Brooklyn, to serve two years; mustered in as private, Co. L, May 24, 1898; mustered out with company, November 23, 1898, at Fort Slocum, New York Harbor.

JEFFERSON, WILLIAM H.—Age, 24 years. Enlisted, May 2, 1898, at Brooklyn, to serve two years; mustered in as corporal, Co. D, May 24, 1898; promoted sergeant, November 4, 1898; mustered out with company, November 23, 1898, at Fort Slocum, New York Harbor.

JENNINGS, CHARLES C.—Age, 38 years. Enlisted, May 20, 1898, at Camp Black, to serve two years; mustered in as private, Co. K, May 24, 1898; mustered out with company, November 23, 1898, at Fort Slocum, New York Harbor.

JENNINGS, EPHRAIM J.—Age, 44 years. Enlisted, May 12, 1898, at Camp Black, to serve two years; mustered in as corporal, Co. F, May 24, 1898; mustered out with company, November 23, 1898, at Fort Slocum, New York Harbor.

JENNINGS, JOHN D.—Age, 23 years. Enlisted, May 12, 1898, at Camp Black, to serve two years; mustered in as sergeant, Co. F, May 24, 1898; mustered out with company, November 23, 1898, at Fort Slocum, New York Harbor.

JENNINGS, JOHN T.—Age, 46 years. Enrolled, May 2, 1898, at Brooklyn, to serve two years; mustered in as second lieutenant, Co. M, May 24, 1898; mustered out with company, November 23, 1898, at Fort Slocum, New York Harbor; commissioned second lieutenant, May 24, 1898, with rank from same date, original.

JENNINGS, PERCY G.—Age, 22 years. Enlisted, May 2, 1898, at Brooklyn, to serve two years; mustered in as private, Co. D, May 24, 1898; mustered out with company, November 23, 1898, at Fort Slocum, New York Harbor.

JENSEN, MARTIN H.—Age, 27 years. Enlisted, May 2, 1898, at Brooklyn, to serve two years; mustered in as private, Co. D, May 24, 1898; mustered out with company, November 23, 1898, at Fort Slocum, New York Harbor.

JESSOP, GEORGE.—Age, 21 years. Enlisted, May 9, 1898, at New York city, to serve two years; mustered in as private, Co. C, May 24, 1898; mustered out with company, November 23, 1898, at Fort Slocum, New York Harbor.

JIMENEZ, OTTO.—Age, 27 years. Enlisted, May 9, 1898, at New York city, to serve two years; mustered in as private, Co. G, May 24, 1898; mustered out with company, November 23, 1898, at Fort Slocum, New York Harbor.

JOBELMAN, HERMAN F.—Age, 21 years. Enlisted, June 29, 1898, at Brooklyn, to serve two years; mustered in as private, Co. L, same date; mustered out with company, November 23, 1898, at Fort Slocum, New York Harbor; also borne as Jubelman.

JOCELYN, CHARLES D.—Age, 26 years. Enlisted, May 2, 1898, at Brooklyn, to serve two years; mustered in as private, Co. D, May 24, 1898; appointed artificer, June 5, 1898; returned to ranks, no date; transferred to Co. M, October 17, 1898; mustered out with company, November 23, 1898, at Fort Slocum, New York Harbor.

JOCHUM, BERTRAND A.—Age, 20 years. Enlisted, May 9, 1898, at New York city, to serve two years; mustered in as private, Co. A, May 24, 1898; mustered out with company, November 23, 1898, at Fort Slocum, New York Harbor.

JOHNSON, ALBERT S.—Age, 23 years. Enlisted, May 2, 1898, at Brooklyn, to serve two years; mustered in as corporal, Co. F, May 24, 1898; mustered out with company, November 23, 1898, at Fort Slocum, New York Harbor.

JOHNSON, D. FRED.—Age, 25 years. Enlisted, May 2, 1898, at Brooklyn, to serve two years; mustered in as private, Co. F, May 24, 1898; mustered out with company, November 23, 1898, at Fort Slocum, New York Harbor.

JOHNSON, GEORGE H.—Age, 26 years. Enlisted, May 9, 1898, at New York city, to serve two years; mustered in as private, Co. H, May 24, 1898; mustered out with company, November 23, 1898, at Fort Slocum, New York Harbor.

JOHNSON, HENRY.—Age, 22 years. Enlisted, May 2, 1898, at Brooklyn, to serve two years; mustered in as private, Co. L, May 24, 1898; mustered out with company, November 23, 1898, at Fort Slocum, New York Harbor.

JOHNSON, JAMES EDWARD.—Age, 31 years. Enlisted, July 6, 1898, at New York city, to serve two years; mustered in as private, Co. A, same date; mustered out with company, November 23, 1898, at Fort Slocum, New York Harbor.

JOHNSON, JR., RICHARD E.—Age, 21 years. Enlisted, May 9, 1898, at New York city, to serve two years; mustered in as private, Co. H, May 24, 1898; mustered out with company, November 23, 1898, at Fort Slocum, New York Harbor.

JOHNSON, WALTER S.—Age, 22 years. Enlisted, June 20, 1898, at Brooklyn, to serve two years; mustered in as private, Co. M, same date; mustered out with company, November 23, 1898, at Fort Slocum, New York Harbor.

JOHNSTON, WILLIAM C.—Age, 25 years. Enrolled, May 19, 1898, at Camp Black, to serve two years; mustered in as first lieutenant and assistant surgeon, May 19, 1898; captain and assistant surgeon, same date; mustered out with regiment, November 23, 1898, at Fort Slocum, New York Harbor; commissioned captain and assistant surgeon, May 19, 1898, with rank from same date, original.

JOHNSTON, WILLIAM H.—Age, 21 years. Enlisted, June 23, 1898, at Brooklyn, to serve two years; mustered in as private, Co. D, same date; mustered out with company, Novemebr 23, 1898, at Fort Slocum, New York Harbor.

JONES, HERBERT.—Age, 23 years. Enlisted, May 2, 1898, at Brooklyn, to serve two years; mustered in as private, Co. F, May 24, 1898; mustered out with company, November 23, 1898, at Fort Slocum, New York Harbor, as Herbert L. Jones.

JONES, HOWARD E.—Age, 25 years. Enlisted, May 9, 1898, at New York city, to serve two years; mustered in as private, Co. E. May 24. 1898; mustered out with company, November 23, 1898, at Fort Slocum, New York Harbor.

JOSEPH, FRANK, see Joseph Frank.

JOYCE, CLARENCE W.—Age, 23 years. Enlisted, May 2, 1898, at Brooklyn, to serve two years; mustered in as private, Co. L, May 24, 1898; promoted corporal, July 1, 1898; returned to ranks, September 19, 1898; deserted, October 24, 1898, at Fort Slocum, New York Harbor.

JUBELMAN, HERMAN F., see Herman F. Jobelman.

JUDAH, WALTER LUIS.—Age, 23 years. Enlisted, June 25, 1898, at New York city, to serve two years; mustered in as private, Co. I, same date; discharged, October 19, 1898, at Fort Slocum, New York Harbor.

JUDSON, FRANK S.—Age, 28 years. Enlisted, May 9, 1898, at New York city, to serve two years; mustered in as sergeant, Co. H, May 24, 1898; mustered out with company, November 23, 1898, at Fort Slocum, New York Harbor.

JUKES, GEORGE W.—Age, 18 years. Enlisted, May 2, 1898, at Brooklyn, to serve two years; mustered in as private, Co. L, May 24, 1898; mustered out with company, November 23, 1898, at Fort Slocum, New York Harbor.

JUNGKIND, ADOLPH.—Age, 22 years. Enlisted, May 9, 1898, at New York city, to serve two years; mustered in as private, Co. E, May 24, 1898; promoted corporal, October 19, 1898; mustered out with company, November 23, 1898, at Fort Slocum, New York Harbor.

JUNGREEN, JOHN A.—Age, 18 years. Enlisted, June 22, 1898, at Brooklyn, to serve two years; mustered in as private, Co. L, same date; mustered out with company, November 23, 1898, at Fort Slocum, New York Harbor; also borne as Jungren.

KAHN, JOSEPH.—Age, 31 years. Enlisted, May 9, 1898, at New York city, to serve two years; mustered in as private, Co. G, May 24, 1898; discharged, October 23, 1898, at Fort Slocum, New York Harbor.

KALEY, FRANK.—Age, 25 years. Enlisted, May 9, 1898, at New York city, to serve two years; mustered in as private, Co. A, May 24, 1898; mustered out with company, November 23, 1898, at Fort Slocum, New York Harbor.

KANE, MARTIN JOSEPH.—Age, 26 years. Enlisted, June 21, 1898, at New York city, to serve two years; mustered in as private, Co. I, same date; mustered out with company, November 23, 1898, at Fort Slocum, New York Harbor.

KARNS, WILLIAM ARTHUR.—Age, 23 years. Enlisted, May 9, 1898, at New York city, to serve two years; mustered in as sergeant, Co. H, May 24, 1898; mustered out with company, November 23, 1898, at Fort Slocum, New York Harbor.

KATZENBERG, JOSEPH.—Age, 21 years. Enlisted, May 2, 1898, at Brooklyn, to serve two years; mustered in as private, Co. M, May 24, 1898; mustered out with company, November 23, 1898, at Fort Slocum, New York Harbor.

KEEGAN, FRANCIS H.—Age, 22 years. Enlisted, May 12, 1898, at Camp Black, to serve two years; mustered in as private, Co. F, May 24, 1898; mustered out with company, November 23, 1898, at Fort Slocum, New York Harbor.

KEEGAN, FREDERICK J.—Age, 21 years. Enlisted, May 9, 1898, at New York city, to serve two years; mustered in as corporal, Co. A, May 24, 1898; returned to ranks, August 24, 1898; promoted corporal, November 11, 1898; mustered out with company, November 23, 1898, at Fort Slocum, New York Harbor.

KEELER, BERNARD J.—Age, 23 years. Enlisted, May 9, 1898, at New York city, to serve two years; mustered in as private, Co. E, May 24, 1898; appointed wagoner, July 1, 1898; mustered out with company, November 23, 1898, at Fort Slocum, New York Harbor.

KEELER, FREDERICK.—Age, 23 years. Enlisted, May 22, 1898. at Camp Black, to serve two years; mustered in as private, Co. H, May 24, 1898; promoted corporal, November 5, 1898; mustered out with company, November 23, 1898, at Fort Slocum. New York Harbor.

KEELER, WILLIAM H.—Age, 27 years. Enlisted, May 21, 1898, at Camp Black, to serve two years; mustered in as private, Co. A, May 24, 1898; drowned, August 10, 1898, at Fort Schuyler, New York Harbor.

KEELING, JAMES J.—Age, 27 years. Enlisted, May 9, 1898, at New York city, to serve two years; mustered in as private, Co. G, May 24, 1898; mustered out with company, November 23, 1898, at Fort Slocum, New York Harbor.

KELLY, HENRY.—Age, 21 years. Enlisted, May 10, 1898, at New York city. to serve two years; mustered in as private, Co. E, May 24, 1898; mustered out with company, November 23, 1898, at Fort Slocum, New York Harbor.

KELLY, JAMES E.—Age, 22 years. Enlisted, June 8, 1898, at Camp Black, to serve two years; mustered in as private, Co. L, same date; transferred to Co. B, June 9, 1898; mustered out with company, November 23, 1898, at Fort Slocum, New York Harbor.

KELLY, JAMES W.—Age, 26 years. Enlisted, May 9, 1898, at New York city, to serve two years; mustered in as private, Co. B, May 24, 1898; mustered out with company, November 23, 1898, at Fort Slocum, New York Harbor.

KEMP, EDWARD J.—Age, 24 years. Enlisted, May 2, 1898, at Brooklyn, to serve two years; mustered in as quartermaster-sergeant, Co. F, May 24,.1898; mustered out with company, November 23. 1898, at Fort Slocum, New York Harbor.

KEMP, GEORGE H.—Age, 32 years. Enrolled, May 2, 1898, at Brooklyn, to serve two years; mustered in as captain. Co. F, May 24, 1898; mustered out with company, November 23, 1898, at Fort Slocum, New York Harbor; commissioned captain, May 24, 1898, with rank from same date, original.

KENNEDY, ALFRED J.—Age, 22 years. Enlisted, May 2, 1898, at Brooklyn, to serve two years; mustered in as private, Co. F, May 24, 1898; promoted corporal, July 1, 1898; mustered out with company, November 23, 1898, at Fort Slocum, New York Harbor.

KENNEDY, ARTHUR.—Age, 29 years. Enlisted, May 9, 1898, at New York city, to serve two years; mustered in as private, Co. C, May 24, 1898; mustered out with company, November 23, 1898, at Fort Slocum, New York Harbor.

KENNEDY, JOHN JOSEPH.—Age, 22 years. Enlisted, June 22, 1898, at New York city, to serve two years; mustered in as private, Co. I, same date; mustered out with company, November 23, 1898, at Fort Slocum, New York Harbor.

KENNEDY, JOHN W.—Age, 28 years. Enlisted, May 9, 1898, at New York city, to serve two years; mustered in as private, Co. K, May 24, 1898; discharged, October 15, 1898, at Fort Slocum, New York Harbor; also borne as John H. Kennedy.

KENNEDY, JOHN W.—Age, 21 years. Enlisted, May 20, 1898, at Camp Black, to serve two years; mustered in as private, Co. E, May 24, 1898; mustered out with company, November 23, 1892, at Fort Slocum, New York Harbor.

KENNEDY, WALTER T.—Age, 18 years. Enlisted, July 5, at Brooklyn, to serve two years; mustered in as private, Co. D, same date; mustered out with company, November 23, 1898, at Fort Slocum, New York Harbor.

KENNEDY, WILLIAM H.—Age, 19 years. Enlisted, May 9, 1898, at New York city, to serve two years; mustered in as private, Co. C, May 24, 1898; mustered out with company, November 23, 1898, at Fort Slocum, New York Harbor.

KENNISH, JR., THOMAS P.—Age, 21 years. Enlisted, May 20, 1898, at Camp Black, to serve two years; mustered in as private, Co. D, May 24, 1898; mustered out with company, November 23, 1898, at Fort Slocum, New York Harbor.

KENNY, JOHN T. H.—Age, 25 years. Enlisted, May 9, 1898, at New York city, to serve two years; mustered in as private, Co. E, May 24, 1898; discharged for disability, August 9, 1898, at Fort Slocum, New York Harbor.

KENNY, WILLIAM A.—Age, 35 years. Enrolled, May 9, 1898, at New York city, to serve two years; mustered in as second lieutenant, Co. E, May 24, 1898; mustered out with company, November 23, 1898, at Fort Slocum, New York Harbor; commissioned second lieutenant, May 24, 1898, with rank from same date, original; also borne as Kenney.

KENT, HARRY CHARLES.—Age, 20 years. Enlisted, June 29, 1898, at New York city, to serve two years; mustered in as private, Co. H, same date; mustered out with company, November 23, 1898, at Fort Slocum, New York Harbor.

KENWORTHY, JOHN.—Age, 28 years. Enlisted, May 9, 1898, at New York city, to serve two years; mustered in as quartermaster-sergeant, Co. E, May 24, 1898; mustered out with company, November 23, 1898, at Fort Slocum, New York Harbor.

KENYON, HAROLD E.—Age, 20 years. Enlisted, May 9, 1898, at New York city, to serve two years; mustered in as private, Co. E, May 24, 1898; promoted corporal, July 1, 1898; mustered out with company, November 23, 1898, at Fort Slocum, New York Harbor.

KEOUGH, PATRICK.—Age, 21 years. Enlisted, May 14, 1898, at Camp Black, to serve two years; mustered in as private, Co. D, May 24, 1898; mustered out with company, November 23, 1898, at Fort Slocum, New York Harbor.

KEOWN, JOHN J.—Age, 26 years. Enlisted, May 9, 1898, at New York city, to serve two years; mustered in as corporal, Co. C, May 24, 1898; mustered out with company, November 23, 1898, at Fort Slocum, New York Harbor.

KERN, FRANK ADAM.—Age, 21 years. Enlisted, May 9, 1898, at New York city, to serve two years; mustered in as private, Co. G, May 24, 1898; mustered out with company, November 23, 1898, at Fort Slocum, New York Harbor.

KERRIGAN, FRANK M.—Age, 22 years.   Enlisted, June 20,
1898, at New York city, to serve two years; mustered in as
private, Co. E, same date; mustered out with company, November 23, 1898, at Fort Slocum, New York Harbor.

KERSTEN, ANTHONY J.—Age, 28 years.   Enlisted, May 20,
1898, at Camp Black, to serve two years; mustered in as private, Co. I, May 24, 1898; mustered out with company, November 24, 1898, at Fort Slocum, New York Harbor.

KEYMER, CLIFFORD.—Age, 23 years.   Enlisted, May 23, 1898,
at Camp Black, to serve two years; mustered in as private,
Co. F, May 24, 1898; mustered out with company, November
23, 1898, at Fort Slocum, New York Harbor.

KEYS, FURMAN B.—Age, 21 years.   Enlisted, May 9, 1898, at
New York city, to serve two years; mustered in as private, Co.
I, May 24, 1898; promoted corporal, June 30, 1898; mustered
out with company, November 23, 1898, at Fort Slocum, New
York Harbor.

KIERNAN, PETER H.—Age, 20 years.   Enlisted, May 9, 1898,
at New York city, to serve two years; mustered in as private,
Co. G, May 24, 1898; mustered out with company, November
23, 1898, at Fort Slocum, New York Harbor.

KING, CHARLES C.—Age, 23 years.   Enlisted, May 2, 1898, at
Brooklyn, to serve two years; mustered in as private, Co. D,
May 24, 1898; mustered out with company, November 23, 1898,
at Fort Slocum, New York Harbor.

KING, GEORGE B.—Age, 21 years.   Enlisted, May 2, 1898, at
Brooklyn, to serve two years; mustered in as private, Co. M,
May 24, 1898; mustered out with company, November 23, 1898,
at Fort Slocum, New York Harbor.

KING, WILLIAM W.—Age, 29 years.   Enlisted, May 9, 1898, at
New York city, to serve two years; mustered in as private, Co.
E, May 24, 1898; mustered out with company, November 23,
1898, at Fort Slocum, New York Harbor.

KINGSBURY, WALTER E.—Age, 22 years.   Enlisted, May 2,
1898, at Brooklyn, to serve two years; mustered in as private,
Co. D, May 24, 1898; promoted corporal, November 1, 1898;
mustered out with company, November 23, 1898, at Fort Slocum, New York Harbor.

KINGSLAND, NELSON.—Age, 23 years.   Enlisted, May 12, 1898, at Brooklyn, to serve two years; mustered in as private, Co. M, May 24, 1898; promoted corporal, July 1, 1898; returned to ranks, August 17, 1898; mustered out with company, November 23, 1898, at Fort Slocum, New York Harbor.

KINGSTON, WILLIAM A.—Age, 23 years.   Enlisted, June 18, 1898, at New York city, to serve two years; mustered in as private, Co. B, same date; mustered out with company, November 23, 1898, at Fort Slocum, New York Harbor.

KINZIE, WILLIAM H.—Age, 20 years.   Enlisted, June 20, 1898, at Brooklyn, to serve two years; mustered in as private, Co. M, same date; mustered out with company, November 23, 1898, at Fort Slocum, New York Harbor; also borne as Kinsey.

KIRBY, JOSEPH.—Age, 26 years.   Enlisted, May 20, 1898, at Camp Black, to serve two years; mustered in as private, Co. K, May 24, 1898; mustered out with company, November 23, 1898, at Fort Slocum, New York Harbor.

KIRCHER, EDWARD.—Age, 38 years.   Enlisted, May 2, 1898, at Brooklyn, to serve two years; mustered in as wagoner, Co. M, May 24, 1898; mustered out with company, November 23, 1898, at Fort Slocum, New York Harbor.

KIRCHNER, WILLIAM.—Age, 19 years.   Enlisted, May 20, 1898, at Camp Black, to serve two years; mustered in as private, Co. K, May 24, 1898; mustered out with company, November 23, 1898, at Fort Slocum, New York Harbor.

KIRK, JOHN.—Age, 21 years.   Enlisted, May 20, 1898, at Camp Black, to serve two years; mustered in as private, Co. I, May 24, 1898; mustered out with company, November 23, 1898, at Fort Slocum, New York Harbor; also borne as John B. and John G. Kirk.

KIRKLAND, GEORGE WALTER.—Age, 30 years.   Enlisted, June 28, 1898, at New York city, to serve two years; mustered in as private, Co. H, same date; mustered out with company, November 23, 1898, at Fort Slocum, New York Harbor.

KIRKLAND, JR., THOMAS.—Age, 24 years. Enlisted, May 9, 1898, at New York city, to serve two years; mustered in as private, Co. G, May 24, 1898; promoted corporal, July 1, 1898; mustered out with company, November 23, 1898, at Fort Slocum, New York Harbor.

KIRKPATRICK, DANIEL C.—Age, 24 years. Enlisted, May 9, 1898, at New York city, to serve two years; mustered in as private, Co. K, May 24, 1898; mustered out with company, November 23, 1898, at Fort Slocum, New York Harbor.

KIRWAN, JOHN.—Age, 23 years. Enlisted, May 22, 1898, at Camp Black, to serve two years; mustered in as private, Co. A, May 24, 1898; mustered out with company, November 23, 1898, at Fort Slocum, New York Harbor; also borne as Kirwin.

KITCHEN, CHARLES H.—Age, 24 years. Enlisted, May 9, 1898, at New York city, to serve two years; mustered in as private, Co. A, May 24, 1898; mustered out with company, November 23, 1898, at Fort Slocum, New York Harbor.

KITCHEN, FRANK M.—Age, 22 years. Enlisted, June 22, 1898, at Brooklyn, to serve two years; mustered in as private, Co. F, same date; mustered out with company, November 23, 1898, at Fort Slocum, New York Harbor.

KITTS, WILLIAM P.—Age, 22 years. Enlisted, May 2, 1898, at Brooklyn, to serve two years; mustered in as private, Co. D, May 24, 1898; promoted corporal, July 1, 1898; mustered out with company, November 23, 1898, at Fort Slocum, New York Harbor; subsequent service as second lieutenant, Forty-second Regiment, United States Volunteer Infantry.

KLETCHKA, HENRY.—Age, 20 years. Enlisted, May 9, 1898, at New York city, to serve two years; mustered in as private, Co. K, May 24, 1898; promoted corporal, October 12, 1898; mustered out with company, November 23, 1898, at Fort Slocum, New York Harbor; also borne as Henry L. Kletchka.

KLINE, DAVID.—Age, 24 years. Enlisted, May 9, 1898, at New York city, to serve two years; mustered in as private, Co. I, May 24, 1898; promoted corporal, May 31, 1898; mustered out with company, November 23, 1898, at Fort Slocum, New York Harbor.

KNOBLOCK, FRED.—Age, 24 years. Enlisted, June 3, 1898, at Camp Black, to serve two years; mustered in as private, Co. I, same date; mustered out with company, November 23, 1898, at Fort Slocum, New York Harbor.

KNOX, ROBERT J.—Age, 40 years. Enlisted, May 14, 1898, at Hempstead, to serve two years; mustered in as corporal, Co. M, May 24, 1898; mustered out with company, November 23, 1898, at Fort Slocum, New York Harbor.

KOCH, WILLIAM F.—Age, 21 years. Enlisted, May 9, 1898, at New York city, to serve two years; mustered in as private, Co. A, May 24, 1898; promoted corporal, October 4, 1898; mustered out with company, November 23, 1898, at Fort Slocum, New York Harbor.

KOLB, JR., JOHN D.—Age, 22 years. Enlisted, May 9, 1898, at New York city, to serve two years; mustered in as private, Co. G, May 24, 1898; promoted corporal, July 29, 1898; mustered out with company, November 23, 1898, at Fort Slocum, New York Harbor.

KRAMER, CHARLES.—Age, 20 years. Enlisted, June 4, 1898, at Hempstead, to serve two years; mustered in as private, Co. M, June 7, 1898; mustered out with company, November 23, 1898, at Fort Slocum, New York Harbor.

KRAMER, GEORGE P.—Age, 21 years. Enlisted, July 1, 1898, at Brooklyn, to serve two years; mustered in as private, Co. F, same date; mustered out with company, November 23, 1898, at Fort Slocum, New York Harbor.

KRODER, GEORGE.—Age, 21 years. Enlisted, May 9, 1898, at New York city, to serve two years; mustered in as private, Co. A, May 24, 1898; mustered out with company, November 23, 1898, at Fort Slocum, New York Harbor.

KROEGEL, FRED M.—Age, 27 years. Enlisted, May 9, 1898, at New York city, to serve two years; mustered in as private, Co. C, May 24, 1898; appointed wagoner, June 9, 1898; discharged for disability, September 27, 1898, at Fort Slocum, New York Harbor.

KRONENBERGER, FERDINAND.—Age, 23 years. Enlisted, July 1, 1898, at New York city, to serve two years; mustered in as private, Co. K, same date; mustered out with company, November 23, 1898, at Fort Slocum, New York Harbor.

KROSS, CLEMENT F.—Age, 38 years. Enrolled, May 9, 1898, at New York city, to serve two years; mustered in as first lieutenant and battalion-adjutant, May 24, 1898; mustered out with regiment, November 23, 1898, at Fort Slocum, New York Harbor; commissioned battalion-adjutant, May 24, 1898, with rank from same date, original.

KRUG, CHRISTIAN W.—Age, 22 years. Enlisted, May 2, 1898, at Brooklyn, to serve two years; mustered in as private, Co. M, May 24, 1898; mustered out with company, November 23, 1898, at Fort Slocum, New York Harbor.

KUCK, HENRY B.—Age, 22 years. Enlisted, May 2, 1898, at Brooklyn, to serve two years; mustered in as private, Co. L, May 24, 1898; mustered out with company, November 23, 1898, at Fort Slocum, New York Harbor.

KUHLMAN, RICHARD.—Age, 21 years. Enlisted, May 9, 1898, at New York city, to serve two years; mustered in as private, Co. E, May 24, 1898; mustered out with company, November 23, 1898, at Fort Slocum, New York Harbor.

KURKA, CHARLES R.—Age, 21 years. Enlisted, May 2, 1898, at Brooklyn, to serve two years; mustered in as private, Co. F, May 24, 1898; mustered out with company, November 23, 1898, at Fort Slocum, New York Harbor.

KURKA, RUDOLPH.—Age, 19 years. Enlisted, May 16, 1898, at Camp Black, to serve two years; mustered in as private, Co. F, May 24, 1898; mustered out with company, November 23, 1898, at Fort Slocum, New York Harbor.

LA BAIE, JOHN J.—Age, 22 years. Enlisted, June 22, 1898, at Brooklyn, to serve two years; mustered in as private, Co. L, same date; mustered out with company, November 23, 1898, at Fort Slocum, New York Harbor; also borne as La Bair.

LA FORGE, LEONARD.—Age, 20 years. Enlisted, June 20, 1898, at Brooklyn, to serve two years; mustered in as private, Co. M, same date; mustered out with company, November 23, 1898, at Fort Slocum, New York Harbor; also borne as Leonard D. La Forge.

LAMB, FRANCIS P. S.—Age, 38 years. Enlisted, May 24, 1898, at Camp Black, to serve two years; mustered in as private, Co. B, same date; mustered out with company, November 23, 1898, at Fort Slocum, New York Harbor.

LAMPE, EDWARD C.—Age, 21 years. Enlisted, June 20, 1898, at New York city, to serve two years; mustered in as private, Co. E, same date; mustered out with company, November 23, 1898, at Fort Slocum, New York Harbor; also borne as Lempe.

LANDAN, SAMUEL.—Age, 23 years. Enlisted, May 9, 1898, at New York city, to serve two years; mustered in as private, Co. B, May 24, 1898; mustered out with company, November 23, 1898, at Fort Slocum, New York Harbor.

LANDON, SAMUEL W.—Age, 27 years. Enlisted, May 2, 1898, at Brooklyn, to serve two years; mustered in as private, Co. L, May 24, 1898; appointed cook, September 21, 1898; returned to ranks, October 7, 1898; mustered out with company, November 23, 1898, at Fort Slocum, New York Harbor.

LANE, CHARLES F.—Age, 21 years. Enlisted, May 9, 1898, at New York city, to serve two years; mustered in as private, Co. E, May 24, 1898; mustered out with company, November 23, 1898, at Fort Slocum, New York Harbor.

LANGWORTHY, DAVID J. C.—Age, 19 years. Enlisted, May 9, 1898, at New York city, to serve two years; mustered in as private, Co. B, May 24, 1898; transferred to Co. F, June 9, 1898; discharged for disability, August 16, 1898, at Willet's Point, N. Y.; also borne as Langorthy.

LARKIN, FRANCIS JOHN.—Age, 22 years. Enlisted, July 5, 1898, at New York city, to serve two years; mustered in as private, Co. H, same date; mustered out with company, November 23, 1898, at Fort Slocum, New York Harbor.

LARSON, JOHN G.—Age, 28 years. Enlisted, May 9, 1898, at New York city, to serve two years; mustered in as private, Co. A, May 24, 1898; mustered out with company, November 23, 1898, at Fort Slocum, New York Harbor.

LASHWAY, ALBERT W.—Age, 25 years. Enlisted, May 9, 1898, at New York city, to serve two years; mustered in as private, Co. E, May 24, 1898; mustered out with company, November 23, 1898, at Fort Slocum, New York Harbor; also borne as Laschway.

LATTA, HIRAM H.—Age, 27 years. Enlisted, May 20, 1898, at Camp Black, to serve two years; mustered in as private, Co. I, May 24, 1898; mustered out with company, November 23, 1898, at Fort Slocum, New York Harbor.

LAUGHLIN, CHARLES H.—Age, 20 years. Enlisted, May 9, 1898, at New York city, to serve two years; mustered in as private, Co. A, May 24, 1898; discharged, November 4, 1898, at Fort Slocum, New York Harbor.

LAUVAUX, ALLEN CHARLES.—Age, 19 years. Enlisted, June 24, 1898, at New York city, to serve two years; mustered in as private, Co. I, same date; mustered out with company, November 23, 1898, at Fort Slocum, New York Harbor; also borne as Lauveaux.

LAWLER, FRANK.—Age, 24 years. Enlisted, May 12, 1898, at Camp Black, to serve two years; mustered in as private, Co. D, May 24, 1898; mustered out with company, November 23, 1898, at Fort Slocum, New York Harbor.

LAWLESS, PETTIT J.—Age, 19 years. Enlisted, May 2, 1898, at Brooklyn, to serve two years; mustered in as private, Co. L, May 24, 1898; mustered out with company, November 23, 1898, at Fort Slocum, New York Harbor.

LAWLESS, REUBEN R.—Age, 20 years. Enlisted, May 2, 1898, at Brooklyn, to serve two years; mustered in as private, Co. L, May 24, 1898; mustered out with company, November 23, 1898, at Fort Slocum, New York Harbor.

LAWLOR, WILLIAM V.—Age, 21 years. Enlisted, May 20, 1898, at Camp Black, to serve two years; mustered in as private, Co. I, May 24, 1898; mustered out with company, November 23, 1898, at Fort Slocum, New York Harbor; also borne as Wm. B. Lawler.

LAWRENCE, CHARLES A.—Age, 24 years. Enlisted, May 9, 1898, at New York city, to serve two years; mustered in as private, Co. G, May 24, 1898; mustered out with company, November 23, 1898, at Fort Slocum, New York Harbor.

LAWRENCE, CHARLES G.—Age, 26 years. Enlisted, June 17, 1898, at New York city, to serve two years; mustered in as private, Co. E, same date; mustered out with company, November 23, 1898, at Fort Slocum, New York Harbor.

LAWRENCE, LEONARD.—Age, 21 years. Enlisted, May 2, 1898, at Brooklyn, to serve two years; mustered in as private, Co. M, May 24, 1898; mustered out with company, November 23, 1898, at Fort Slocum, New York Harbor.

LAWRENCE, REGINALD A.—Age, 32 years. Enlisted, May 24, 1898, at Camp Black, to serve two years; mustered in as private, Co. I, same date; mustered out with company, November 23, 1898, at Fort Slocum, New York Harbor.

LAWSON, JOHN.—Age, 21 years. Enlisted, May 20, 1898, at Camp Black, to serve two years; mustered in as private, Co. K, May 24, 1898; mustered out with company, November 23, 1898, at Fort Slocum, New York Harbor.

LE BOURVEAU, ELMER J.—Age, 21 years. Enlisted, May 9, 1898, at New York city, to serve two years; mustered in as private, Co. H, May 24, 1898; discharged, October 29, 1898, at Fort Slocum, New York Harbor; also borne as Leborveau.

LEE, JR., HENRY L.—Age, 23 years. Enlisted, June 24, 1898, at Brooklyn, to serve two years; mustered in as private, Co. L, same date; mustered out with company, November 23, 1898, at Fort Slocum, New York Harbor.

LEE, WILLIAM JAMES.—Age, 27 years. Enlisted, June 21, 1898, at New York city, to serve two years; mustered in as private, Co. B, same date; mustered out with company, November 23, 1898, at Fort Slocum, New York Harbor.

LEMPE, EDWARD C., see Edward C. Lampe.

LENT, WILLIAM H.—Age, 27 years. Enlisted, May 11, 1898, at Hempstead, to serve two years; mustered in as private, Co. M, May 24, 1898; mustered out with company, November 23, 1898, at Fort Slocum, New York Harbor.

LEONARD, MICHAEL J.—Age, 22 years. Enlisted, May 20, 1898, at Camp Black, to serve two years; mustered in as private, Co. K, May 24, 1898; mustered out with company, November 23, 1898, at Fort Slocum, New York Harbor.

LEONARD, WILLIAM AUGUSTUS.—Age, 22 years. Enlisted, June 30, 1898, at New York city, to serve two years; mustered in as private, Co. K, same date; mustered out with company, November 30, 1898, at Fort Slocum, New York Harbor.

LE ROY, FRANK A.—Age, 25 years. Enlisted, May 9, 1898, at New York city, to serve two years; mustered in as hospital steward, May 24, 1898; mustered out with regiment, November 23, 1898, at Fort Slocum, New York Harbor.

LESLIE, WILFORD.—Age, 22 years. Enlisted, May 9, 1898, at New York city, to serve two years; mustered in as private, Co. K, May 24, 1898; mustered out with company, November 23, 1898, at Fort Slocum, New York Harbor.

LEUPER, WILLIAM F.—Age, 24 years. Enlisted, May 11, 1898, at Camp Black, to serve two years; mustered in as private, Co. H, May 24, 1898; mustered out with company, November 23, 1898, at Fort Slocum, New York Harbor.

LEVIEN, ALEXANDER D.—Age, 21 years. Enlisted, May 9, 1898, at New York city, to serve two years; mustered in as private, Co. G, May 24, 1898; mustered out with company, November 23, 1898, at Fort Slocum, New York Harbor.

LEVIEN, CHRISTOPHER L.—Age, 31 years. Enlisted, May 9, 1898, at New York city, to serve two years; mustered in as private, Co. G, May 24, 1898; promoted corporal, no date; discharged, November 6, 1898, at Fort Slocum, New York Harbor.

LEVY, LOUIS.—Age, 23 years. Enlisted, May 9, 1898, at New York city, to serve two years; mustered in as private, Co. K, May 24, 1898; mustered out with company, November 23, 1898, at Fort Slocum, New York Harbor.

LEWIS, HUGH.—Age, 29 years. Enlisted, May 2, 1898, at Brooklyn, to serve two years; mustered in as sergeant, Co. D, May 24, 1898; discharged, November 2, 1898, at Fort Slocum, New York Harbor; also borne as Hugh S. Lewis.

LEZINSKI, EUGENE L.—Age, 30 years. Enlisted, May 9, 1898, at New York city, to serve two years; mustered in as private, Co. K, May 24, 1898; discharged, October 31, 1898, at Fort Slocum, New York Harbor; also borne as Lezinsky.

LIEBER, CHARLES P.—Age, 28 years. Enlisted, June 2, 1898, at Camp Black, to serve two years; mustered in as private, Co. D, June 7, 1898; transferred to Co. B, June 8, 1898; mustered out with company, November 23, 1898, at Fort Slocum, New York Harbor.

LILLIENDAHL, JOHN G. R.—Age, 39 years. Enrolled, May 9, 1898, at New York city, to serve two years; mustered in as captain, Co. C, May 24, 1898; mustered out with company, November 23, 1898, at Fort Slocum, New York Harbor; commissioned captain, May 24, 1898, with rank from same date, original.

LIPP, GEORGE J.—Age, 34 years. Enlisted, June 30, 1898, at New York city, to serve two years; mustered in as private, Co. C, same date; mustered out with company, November 23, 1898, at Fort Slocum, New York Harbor.

LLOYD, HERBERT J.—Age, 27 years. Enlisted, May 9, 1898, at New York city, to serve two years; mustered in as private, Co. H, May 24, 1898; mustered out with company, November 23, 1898, at Fort Slocum, New York Harbor.

LOCHMAN, FREDERICK W.—Age, 31 years. Enlisted, May 9, 1898, at New York city, to serve two years; mustered in as private, Co. E, May 24, 1898; mustered out with company, November 23, 1898, at Fort Slocum, New York Harbor.

LOEW, JR., WILLIAM.—Age, 20 years. Enlisted, May 9, 1898, at New York city, to serve two years; mustered in as private, Co. K, May 24, 1898; mustered out with company, November 23, 1898, at Fort Slocum, New York Harbor.

LOEWI, JOSEPH.—Age, 31 years. Enlisted, May 9, 1898, at New York city, to serve two years; mustered in as private, Co. K, May 24, 1898; promoted corporal, October 4, 1898; discharged, October 8, 1898, at Fort Slocum, New York Harbor.

LOMAX, CHARLES H.—Age, 36 years. Enlisted, May 9, 1898, at New York city, to serve two years; mustered in as private, Co. E, May 24, 1898; mustered out with company, November 23, 1898, at Fort Slocum, New York Harbor.

LOONIE, JAMES GEORGE.—Age, 22 years. Enlisted, June 29, 1898, at New York city, to serve two years; mustered in as private, Co. H, same date; mustered out with company, November 23, 1898, at Fort Slocum, New York Harbor.

LORING, WILLIAM THOMAS.—Age, 25 years. Enlisted, June 21, 1898, at New York city, to serve two years; mustered in as private, Co. B, same date; mustered out with company, November 23, 1898, at Fort Slocum, New York Harbor.

LOSEE, EUGENE E.—Age, 19 years. Enlisted, May 2, 1898, at Brooklyn, to serve two years; mustered in as private, Co. L, May 24, 1898; mustered out with company, November 23, 1898, at Fort Slocum, New York Harbor.

LOUNSBERY, JUDSON L.—Age, 18 years. Enlisted, May 12, 1898, at Camp Black, to serve two years; mustered in as private, Co. D, May 24, 1898; mustered out with company, November 23, 1898, at Fort Slocum, New York Harbor; also borne as Loundsbury and Lounsbury.

LOWENBEIN, DAVID.—Age, 44 years. Enrolled, May 9, 1898, at New York city, to serve two years; mustered in as second lieutenant, Co. H, May 24, 1898; as first lieutenant, September 1, 1898; discharged, September 27, 1898; commissioned second lieutenant, May 24, 1898, with rank from same date, original; first lietuenant, September 1, 1898, with rank from same date, vice Romaine, discharged; also borne as Lowenbien.

LUHRS, AUGUST L.—Age, 22 years. Enlisted, May 9, 1898, at New York city, to serve two years; mustered in as private, Co. I, May 24, 1898; mustered out with company, November 23, 1898, at Fort Slocum, New York Harbor.

LUSK, ROBERT J.—Age, 35 years. Enlisted, May 9, 1898, at New York city, to serve two years; mustered in as private, Co. A, May 24, 1898; discharged, Septemebr 17, 1898, at Fort Schuyler, New York Harbor.

LYMAN, EDWARD A.—Age, 21 years. Enlisted, May 9, 1898, at New York city, to serve two years; mustered in as private, Co. H, May 24, 1898; promoted corporal, July 29, 1898; mustered out with company, November 23, 1898, at Fort Slocum, New York Harbor.

LYNCH, JR., JAMES.—Age, 24 years. Enrolled, May 2, 1898, at Brooklyn, to serve two years; mustered in as first lieutenant, Co. M, May 24, 1898; mustered out with company, November 23, 1898, at Fort Slocum, New York Harbor; commissioned first lieutenant, May 24, 1898, with rank from same date, original.

LYNN, JOHN T.—Age, 28 years. Enlisted, May 9, 1898, at New York city, to serve two years; mustered in as private, Co. G, May 24, 1898; mustered out with company, November 23, 1898, at Fort Slocum, New York Harbor.

MACAULEY, GEORGE A.—Age, 28 years. Enlisted, May 15, 1898, at Camp Black, to serve two years; mustered in as private, Co. I, May 24, 1898; mustered out with company, November 23, 1898, at Fort Slocum, New York Harbor.

MACFARLAND, FREDERICK W.—Age, 32 years. Enlisted, May 9, 1898, at New York city, to serve two years; mustered in as private, Co. C, May 24, 1898; promoted corporal, October 1, 1898; mustered out with company, November 23, 1898, at Fort Slocum, New York Harbor.

MACGROTTY, EDWARD F.—Age, 25 years. Enlisted, May 9, 1898, at New York city, to serve two years; mustered in as sergeant, Co. I, May 24, 1898; promoted first sergeant, September 10, 1898; mustered in as second lieutenant, October 25, 1898; mustered out with company, November 23, 1898, at Fort Slocum, New York Harbor; commissioned second lieutenant, October 14, 1898, with rank from same date, vice Moses, discharged; also borne as McGrotty.

MACILRAVY, HENRY B.—Age, 23 years. Enlisted, June 20, 1898, at Brooklyn, to serve two years; mustered in as private, Co. L, same date; mustered out with company, November 23, 1898, at Fort Slocum, New York Harbor.

MACK, CHRISTIAN N.—Age, 18 years. Enlisted, June 29, 1898, at Brooklyn, to serve two years; mustered in as private, Co. F, same date; mustered out with company, November 23, 1898, at Fort Slocum, New York Harbor.

MACK, JAMES F.—Age, 28 years. Enlisted, May 15, 1898, at Camp Black, to serve two years; mustered in as private, Co. K, May 24, 1898; transferred to Co. A, August 15, 1898; discharged, September 11, 1898, at Fort Schuyler, New York Harbor.

MACKAY, CHARLES D.—Age, 36 years. Enlisted, May 2, 1898, at Brooklyn, to serve two years; mustered in as private, Co. M, May 24, 1898; mustered out with company, November 23, 1898, at Fort Slocum, New York Harbor.

MACKENNA, JR., JOHN.—Age, 26 years. Enlisted, May 9, 1898, at New York city, to serve two years; mustered in as private, Co. H, May 24, 1898; mustered out with company, November 23, 1898, at Fort Slocum, New York Harbor.

MACKENZIE, CHARLES A.—Age, 25 years. Enlisted, May 9, 1898, at New York city, to serve two years; mustered in as artificer, Co. C, May 24, 1898; mustered out with company, November 23, 1898, at Fort Slocum, New York Harbor.

MACKENZIE, GEORGE B.—Age, 24 years. Enlisted, May 12, 1898, at Camp Black, to serve two years; mustered in as private, Co. F, May 24, 1898; mustered out with company, November 23, 1898, at Fort Slocum, New York Harbor.

MACKIN, JOHN E.—Age, 21 years. Enlisted, May 9, 1898, at New York city, to serve two years; mustered in as private, Co. H, May 24, 1898; mustered out with company, November 23, 1898, at Fort Slocum, New York Harbor.

MADDEN, EDWARD M.—Age, 19 years. Enlisted, May 9, 1898, at New York city, to serve two years; mustered in as private, Co. A, May 24, 1898; mustered out with company, November 23, 1898, at Fort Slocum, New York Harbor.

MADIGAN, JAMES E.—Age, 24 years. Enlisted, May 9, 1898, at New York city, to serve two years; mustered in as private, Co. B, May 24, 1898; mustered out with company, November 23, 1898, at Fort Slocum, New York Harbor.

MADOCKS, CHARLES S.—Age, 21 years. Enlisted, May 9, 1898, at New York city, to serve two years; mustered in as private, Co. C, May 24, 1898; mustered out with company, November 23, 1898, at Fort Slocum, New York Harbor.

MAGEE, JOSEPH C.—Age, 25 years. Enlisted, May 9, 1898, at New York city, to serve two years; mustered in as private, Co. K, May 24, 1898; discharged, October 15, 1898, at Fort Slocum, New York Harbor.

MAHER, EDWARD J.—Age, 24 years. Enlisted, May 20, 1898, at Camp Black, to serve two years; mustered in as private, Co. I, May 24, 1898; mustered out with company, November 23, 1898, at Fort Slocum, New York Harbor.

MAHER, JOSEPH H.—Age, — years. Enlisted, September 15, 1898, at Fort Schuyler, to serve two years; mustered in as private, Co. C, same date; mustered out with company, November 23, 1898, at Fort Slocum, New York Harbor.

MAHON, GEORGE F.—Age, 22 years. Enlisted, May 9, 1898, at New York city, to serve two years; mustered in as corporal, Co. C, May 24, 1898; promoted sergeant, May 31, 1898; mustered out with company, November 23, 1898, at Fort Slocum, New York Harbor.

MALLOY, JAMES.—Age, 24 years. Enlisted, July 2, 1898, at New York city, to serve two years; mustered in as private, Co. H, same date; mustered out with company, November 23, 1898, at Fort Slocum, New York Harbor.

MANEE, FRED IRVING.—Age, 29 years. Enlisted, June 21, 1898, at New York city, to serve two years; mustered in as private, Co. I, same date; mustered out with company, November 23, 1898, at Fort Slocum, New York Harbor.

MANGE, PAUL.—Age, 23 years. Enlisted, May 9, 1898, at New York city, to serve two years; mustered in as private, Co. B, May 24, 1898; mustered out with company, November 23, 1898, at Fort Slocum, New York Harbor.

MANLEY, JAMES E.—Age, 26 years. Enlisted, June 20, 1898, at New York city, to serve two years; mustered in as private, Co. E, same date; mustered out with company, November 23, 1898, at Fort Slocum, New York Harbor.

MANNECK, CHARLES H.— Age, 36 years. Enlisted, May 2, 1898, at Brooklyn, to serve two years; mustered in as corporal, Co. D, May 24, 1898; mustered out with company, November 23, 1898, at Fort Slocum, New York Harbor.

MANNHEIMER, EDWARD.—Age, 22 years. Enlisted, May 2, 1898, at Brooklyn, to serve two years; mustered in as private, Co. L, May 24, 1898; mustered out with company, November 23, 1898, at Fort Slocum, New York Harbor.

MANSFIELD, JOHN C.—Age, 22 years. Enlisted, May 9, 1898, at New York city, to serve two years; mustered in as private, Co. A, May 24, 1898; mustered out with company, November 23, 1898, at Fort Slocum, New York Harbor.

MANUS, THOMAS R.—Age, 19 years. Enlisted, May 9, 1898, at New York city, to serve two years; mustered in as private, Co. B, May 24, 1898; mustered out with company, November 23, 1898, at Fort Slocum, New York Harbor.

MARKLE, THOMAS M.—Age, 30 years. Enlisted, June 29, 1898, at Brooklyn, to serve two years; mustered in as private, Co. M, same date; mustered out with company, November 23, 1898, at Fort Slocum, New York Harbor.

MARKS, CHAPMAN D.—Age, 21 years. Enlisted, May 9, 1898, at New York city, to serve two years; mustered in as private, Co. K, May 24, 1898; discharged, September 15, 1898, at Fort Schuyler, New York Harbor.

MARTIN, ALEXANDER F.—Age, 21 years. Enlisted, May 9, 1898, at New York city, to serve two years; mustered in as quartermaster-sergeant, Co. B, May 24, 1898; returned to ranks, July 15, 1898; transferred to Co. I, same date; mustered out with company, November 23, 1898, at Fort Slocum, New York Harbor.

MARTIN, PETER J.—Age, 21 years. Enlisted, May 10, 1898, at Camp Black, to serve two years; mustered in as private, Co. A, May 24, 1898; mustered out with company, November 23, 1898, at Fort Slocum, New York Harbor.

MARTIN, THOMAS L.—Age, 21 years. Enlisted, May 9, 1898, at New York city, to serve two years; mustered in as private, Co. E, May 24, 1898; mustered out with company, November 23, 1898, at Fort Slocum, New York Harbor.

MASE, CLARENCE W.—Age, 31 years. Enlisted, May 9, 1898, at New York city, to serve two years; mustered in as quartermaster-sergeant, Co. C, May 24, 1898; discharged, September 21, 1898, at Fort Schuyler, New York Harbor; also borne as Muse.

MASON, FRANK FREDERICK.—Age, 29 years. Enlisted, June 28, 1898, at New York city, to serve two years; mustered in as private, Co. A, same date; mustered out with company, November 23, 1898, at Fort Slocum, New York Harbor.

MASON, KENNETH.—Age, 21 years. Enlisted, May 9, 1898, at New York city, to serve two years; mustered in as private, Co. G, May 24, 1898; discharged, October 13, 1898, at Fort Slocum, New York Harbor.

MASTERSON, WARREN.—Age, 18 years. Enlisted, May 9, 1898, at New York city, to serve two years; mustered in as private, Co. C, May 24, 1898; mustered out with company, November 23, 1898, at Fort Slocum, New York Harbor. as John W. Masterson.

MATHEWS, JOSEPH H.—Age, 24 years. Enlisted, May 18, 1898, at Camp Black, to serve two years; mustered in as private, Co. D, May 24, 1898; mustered out with company, November 23, 1898, at Fort Slocum, New York Harbor.

MATHEWS, SAMUEL J.—Age, 23 years. Enlisted, May 18, 1898, at Camp Black, to serve two years; mustered in as private, Co. K, May 24, 1898; mustered out with company, November 23, 1898, at Fort Slocum, New York Harbor.

MATTESON, WALTER B.—Age, 22 years. Enlisted, June 17, 1898, at New York city, to serve two years; mustered in as private, Co. E, same date; mustered out with company, November 23, 1898, at Fort Slocum, New York Harbor; also borne as Walker B. Matteson.

MATTHIAS, JR., FREDERICK W.—Age, 24 years. Enlisted, May 9, 1898, at New York city, to serve two years; mustered in as corporal, Co. E, May 24, 1898; promoted sergeant, May 31, 1898; mustered out with company, November 23, 1898, at Fort Slocum, New York Harbor.

MAXWELL, GEORGE H.—Age, 37 years. Enlisted, May 20,
1898, at Camp Black, to serve two years; mustered in as private, Co. F, May 24, 1898; appointed cook, August 1, 1898; mustered out with company, November 23, 1898, at Fort Slocum,
New York Harbor.

MAY, LOUIS B.—Age, 34 years. Enlisted, May 9, 1898, at New
York city, to serve two years; mustered in as private, Co. G,
May 24, 1898; mustered out with company, November 23, 1898,
at Fort Slocum, New York Harbor.

MAY, WILLIAM J.—Age, 25 years. Enlisted, May 9, 1898, at
New York city, to serve two years; mustered in as private, Co.
D, May 24, 1898; transferred to Co. D, June 1, 1898; mustered
out with company, November 23, 1898, at Fort Slocum, New
York Harbor.

MAYO, JOHN G.—Age, 22 years. Enlisted, May 24, 1898, at
Camp Black, to serve two years; mustered in as private, Co. F,
same date; mustered out with company, November 23, 1898, at
Fort Slocum, New York Harbor; also borne as John J. Mayo.

McAFFE, JR., KNOX.—Age, 24 years. Enlisted, May 9, 1898, at
New York city, to serve two years; mustered in as corporal,
Co. B, May 24, 1898; mustered out with company, November 23,
1898, at Fort Slocum, New York Harbor.

McALLISTER, JR., JAMES.—Age, 27 years. Enlisted, May 9,
1898, at New York city, to serve two years; mustered in as sergeant-major, May 24, 1898; mustered out with regiment, November 23, 1898, at Fort Slocum, New York Harbor.

McARDLE, GEORGE.—Age, 25 years. Enlisted, May 9, 1898,
at New York city, to serve two years; mustered in as wagoner,
Co. C, May 24, 1898; returned to ranks, June 9, 1898; mustered
out with company, November 23, 1898, at Fort Slocum, New
York Harbor.

McBRIDE, THOMAS J.—Age, 29 years. Enlisted, May 9, 1898,
at New York city, to serve two years; mustered in as corporal,
Co. C, May 24, 1898; promoted quartermaster-sergeant, September 27, 1898; mustered out with company, November 23, 1898,
at Fort Slocum, New York Harbor.

McCALL, THOMAS F.—Age, 22 years. Enlisted, June 20, 1898, at New York city, to serve two years; mustered in as private, Co. E, same date; mustered out with company, November 23, 1898, at Fort Slocum, New York Harbor.

McCALLUM, FRANCIS WALLACE.—Age, 28 years. Enlisted, May 9, 1898, at New York city, to serve two years; mustered in as private, Co. B, May 24, 1898; transferred to Co. L, June 9, 1898; mustered out with company, November 23, 1898, at Fort Slocum, New York Harbor.

McCANN, CHARLES A.—Age, 24 years. Enlisted, May 9, 1898, at New York city, to serve two years; mustered in as private, Co. I, May 24, 1898; mustered out with company, November 23, 1898, at Fort Slocum, New York Harbor.

McCANN, WILLIAM E.—Age, 22 years. Enlisted, May 9, 1898, at New York city, to serve years; mustered in as corporal, Co. I, May 24, 1898; promoted sergeant, October 26, 1898; mustered out with company, November 23, 1898, at Fort Slocum, New York Harbor.

McCARTHY, FRED.—Age, 25 years. Enlisted, May 21, 1898, at Camp Black, to serve two years; mustered in as private, Co. B, May 24, 1898; mustered out with company, November 23, 1898, at Fort Slocum, New York Harbor.

McCARTHY, JOSEPH THOMAS.—Age, 22 years. Enlisted, June 28, 1898, at New York city, to serve two years; mustered in as private, Co. H, same date; mustered out with company, November 23, 1898, at Fort Slocum, New York Harbor.

McCLARY, JAMES.—Age, 28 years. Enlisted, June 28, 1898, at New York city, to serve two years; mustered in as private, Co. G, same date; mustered out with company, November 23, 1898, at Fort Slocum, New York Harbor.

McCOLLUM, WILLIAM.—Age, 21 years. Enlisted, July 6, 1898, at New York city, to serve two years; mustered in as private, Co. H, same date; mustered out with company, November 23, 1898, at Fort Slocum, New York Harbor.

McCORMICK, WILLIAM D.—Age, 22 years. Enlisted, May 2, 1898, at Brooklyn, to serve two years; mustered in as corporal, Co. L, May 24, 1898; mustered out with company, November 23, 1898, at Fort Slocum, New York Harbor; also borne as Mc-Cormack.

McCOURT, JAMES.—Age, 33 years. Enlisted, June 28, 1898, at New York city, to serve two years; mustered in as private, Co. G, same date; discharged for disability, July 28, 1898, at Willet's Point, N..Y.

McCOY, SAMUEL J.—Age, 25 years. Enlisted, May 19, 1898, at Camp Black, to serve two years; mustered in as private, Co. E, May 24, 1898; promoted corporal, July 21, 1898; returned to ranks, October 17, 1898; mustered out with company, November 23, 1898, at Fort Slocum, New York Harbor.

McCROSSEN, ARTHUR.—Age, 27 years. Enlisted, May 22, 1898, at Camp Black, to serve two years; mustered in as private, Co. A, May 24, 1898; mustered out with company, November 23, 1898, at Fort Slocum, New York Harbor.

McCURDY, WILLIAM W.—Age, 28 years. Enlisted, May 2, 1898, at Brooklyn, to serve two years; mustered in as private, Co. M, May 24, 1898; mustered out with company, November 23, 1898, at Fort Slocum, New York Harbor.

McDONNELL, FRANCIS X.—Age, 23 years. Enlisted, May 23, 1898, at Camp Black, to serve two years; mustered in as musician, Co. I, May 24, 1898; mustered out with company, November 23, 1898, at Fort Slocum, New York Harbor.

McDOUGALL, AVERY.—Age, 35 years. Enrolled, May 6, 1898, at Camp Black, to serve two years; mustered in as first lieutenant, Co. D, May 24, 1898; transferred to Co. K, November 1, 1898; mustered out with company, November 23, 1898, at Fort Slocum, New York Harbor; commissioned first lieutenant, May 24, 1898, with rank from same date, original.

McDOUGALL, LEWIS S.—Age, 21 years. Enlisted, May 12, 1898, at Hempstead, to serve two years; mustered in as corporal, Co. M, May 24, 1898; returned to ranks, September 14, 1898; mustered out with company, November 23, 1898, at Fort Slocum, New York Harbor.

McELROY, W. DAVID H.—Age, 22 years.   Enlisted, May 2, 1898, at Brooklyn, to serve two years; mustered in as private, Co. M, May 24, 1898; mustered out with company, November 23, 1898, at Fort Slocum, New York Harbor.

McFARLAND, WILLIAM J.—Age, 25 years.   Enlisted, June 28, 1898, at Brooklyn, to serve two years; mustered in as private, Co. D, same date; mustered out, November 23, 1898, at Fort Slocum, New York Harbor.

McGIRR, THEODORE G.—Age, 21 years.   Enlisted, May 9, 1898, at New York city, to serve two years; mustered in as private, Co. H, May 24, 1898; mustered out with company, November 23, 1898, at Fort Slocum, New York Harbor.

McGOWAN, WILLIAM.—Age, 27 years.   Enlisted, May 9, 1898, at New York city, to serve two years; mustered in as private, Co. E, May 24, 1898; promoted corporal, July 1, 1898; mustered out with company, November 23, 1898, at Fort Slocum, New York Harbor.

McGRATH, THOMAS J.—Age, 25 years.   Enlisted, June 17, 1898, at New York city, to serve two years; mustered in as private, Co. E, same date; mustered out with company, November 23, 1898, at Fort Slocum, New York Harbor.

McGUIRE, FRANK.—Age, 23 years.   Enlisted, May 20, 1898, at Camp Black, to serve two years; mustered in as private, Co. K, May 24, 1898; mustered out with company, November 23, 1898, at Fort Slocum, New York Harbor.

McKENZIE, FRANK J.—Age, 21 years.   Enlisted, May 2, 1898, at Brooklyn, to serve two years; mustered in as private. Co. M, May 24, 1898; promoted corporal, July 1, 1898; mustered out with company, November 23, 1898, at Fort Slocum, New York Harbor.

McKEWEN, JOHN WALTON.—Age, 25 years.   Enlisted, June 30, 1898, at New York city, to serve two years; mustered in as private, Co. A, same date; mustered out with company, November 23, 1898, at Fort Slocum, New York Harbor.

McKINNY, FRANCIS A.—Age, 27 years. Enlisted, May 2, 1898, at Brooklyn, to serve two years; mustered in as private, Co. F, May 24, 1898; promoted corporal, July 1, 1898; mustered out with company, November 23, 1898, at Fort Slocum, New York Harbor; also borne as McKinney.

McLAUGHLIN, EDWARD A.—Age, 24 years. Enlisted, May 9, 1898, at New York city, to serve two years; mustered in as private, Co. C, May 24, 1898; mustered out with company, November 23, 1898, at Fort Slocum, New York Harbor.

McLAUGHLIN, WILLIAM F.—Age, 21 years. Enlisted, May 9, 1898, at New York city, to serve two years; mustered in as musician, Co. I, May 24, 1898; mustered out with company, November 23, 1898, at Fort Slocum, New York Harbor.

McLAUGHLIN, WILLIAM J.—Age, 27 years. Enlisted, May 20, 1898, at Camp Black, to serve two years; mustered in as private, Co. K, May 24, 1898; mustered out with company, November 23, 1898, at Fort Slocum, New York Harbor.

McLEAN, JAMES.—Age, 21 years. Enlisted, June 22, 1898, at Brooklyn, to serve two years; mustered in as private, Co. D, same date; mustered out with company, November 23, 1898, at Fort Slocum, New York Harbor.

McMAHON, GEORGE J.—Age, 22 years. Enlisted, May 9, 1898, at New York city, to serve two years; mustered in as private, Co. C. May 24, 1898; mustered out with company, November 23, 1898, at Fort Slocum, New York Harbor.

McMANUS, CHARLES.—Age, 25 years. Enlisted, May 9, 1898, at New York city, to serve two years; mustered in as private, Co. G, May 24, 1898; mustered out with company, November 23, 1898, at Fort Slocum, New York Harbor.

McMANUS, WILLIAM F.—Age, 28 years. Enlisted, May 9, 1898, at New York city, to serve two years; mustered in as private, Co. G, May 24, 1898; appointed cook, October 7, 1898; mustered out with company, November 23, 1898, at Fort Slocum New York Harbor.

McNAMARA, HENRY.—Age, 26 years. Enlisted, May 19, 1898, at Camp Black, to serve two years; mustered in as private, Co. I, May 24, 1898; mustered out with company, November 23, 1898, at Fort Slocum, New York Harbor; also borne as Mac-Namara.

McNEILL, JOHN T.—Age, 27 years. Enlisted, May 9, 1898, at New York city, to serve two years; mustered in as private, Co. G, May 24, 1898; discharged, September 17, 1898, at Willet's Point, N. Y.

McQUADE, WILLIAM JOSEPH.—Age, 21 years. Enlisted, June 28, 1898, at New York city, to serve two years; mustered in as private, Co. G, same date; mustered out with company, November 23, 1898, at Fort Slocum, New York Harbor.

McQUAID, JR., FRANK.—Age, 22 years. Enlisted, June 25, 1898, at Brooklyn, to serve two years; mustered in as private, Co. F, same date; mustered out with company, November 23, 1898, at Fort Slocum, New York Harbor.

McREYNOLDS, WILLIAM E.—Age, 26 years. Enlisted, May 9, 1898, at New York city, to serve two years; mustered in as private, Co. A, May 24, 1898; discharged, September 22, 1898, at Fort Schuyler, New York Harbor.

McVADY, PATRICK F.—Age, 32 years. Enlisted, June 28, 1898, at New York city, to serve two years; mustered in as private, Co. C, same date; mustered out with company, November 23, 1898, at Fort Slocum, New York Harbor.

MEEK, FREDERICK.—Age, 33 years. Enlisted, May 9, 1898, at New York city, to serve two years; mustered in as private, Co. H, May 24, 1898; discharged, October 13, 1898, at Fort Slocum, New York Harbor; also borne as Meeks.

MEEKS, EDWARD D.—Age, 23 years. Enlisted, June 21, 1898, at Brooklyn, to serve two years; mustered in as private, Co. M, same date; mustered out with company, November 23, 1898, at Fort Slocum, New York Harbor.

MEHRHOFF, HERMANN.—Age, 24 years. Enlisted, May 2, 1898, at Brooklyn, to serve two years; mustered in as private, Co. L, May 24, 1898; promoted quartermaster-sergeant, May 31, 1898; mustered out with company, November 23, 1898, at Fort Slocum, New York Harbor.

MEIER, ANDREW W.—Age, 19 years. Enlisted, May 2, 1898, at Brooklyn, to serve two years; mustered in as private, Co. F, May 24, 1898; mustered out with company, November 23, 1898, at Fort Slocum, New York Harbor.

MELVIN, HENRY J.—Age, 37 years. Enlisted, June 27, 1898, at Brooklyn, to serve two years; mustered in as private, Co. D, same date; mustered out with company, November 23, 1898, at Fort Slocum, New York Harbor.

MENCKE, JOHN H.—Age, 19 years. Enlisted, May 9, 1898, at New York city, to serve two years; mustered in as private, Co. C, May 24, 1898; mustered out with company, November 23, 1898, at Fort Slocum, New York Harbor.

MENKE, CHARLES H.—Age, 21 years. Enlisted, July 1, 1898, at Brooklyn, to serve two years; mustered in as private, Co. L, same date; mustered out with company, November 23, 1898, at Fort Slocum, New York Harbor.

MERRITT, JR., CHARLES.—Age, 28 years. Enlisted, May 9, 1898, at New York city, to serve two years; mustered in as sergeant, Co. K, May 24, 1898; mustered out with company, November 23, 1898, at Fort Slocum, New York Harbor.

MERRITT, GEORGE L.—Age, 27 years. Enlisted, May 9, 1898, at New York city, to serve two years; mustered in as sergeant, Co. I, May 24, 1898; mustered out with company, November 23, 1898, at Fort Slocum, New York Harbor; also borne as George H. Merritt.

MEYER, EINAR F.—Age, 23 years. Enlisted, May 2, 1898, at Brooklyn, to serve two years; mustered in as corporal, Co. L, May 24, 1898; returned to ranks, May 31, 1898; promoted corporal, July 1, 1898; returned to ranks, August 4, 1898; mustered out with company, November 23, 1898, at Fort Slocum, New York Harbor.

MEYER, JOSEPH L.—Age, 23 years. Enlisted, May 9, 1898, at New York city, to serve two years; mustered in as private, Co. I, May 24, 1898; mustered out with company, November 23, 1898, at Fort Slocum, New York Harbor.

MEYERS, AUGUST H.—Age, 23 years. Enlisted, May 2, 1898, at Brooklyn, to serve two years; mustered in as private, Co. M, May 24, 1898; promoted corporal, October 1, 1898; mustered out with company, November 23, 1898, at Fort Slocum, New York Harbor.

MICHEL, GEORGE.—Age, 24 years. Enlisted, May 2, 1898, at Brooklyn, to serve two years; mustered in as sergeant, Co. L, May 24, 1898; mustered out with company, November 23, 1898, at Fort Slocum, New York Harbor.

MIDDLEMAS, ROBERT S.—Age, 28 years. Enlisted, May 9, 1898, at New York city, to serve two years; mustered in as private, Co. C, May 24, 1898; promoted corporal, November 1, 1898; mustered out with company, November 23, 1898, at Fort Slocum. New York Harbor.

MIDDLETON, LAWRENCE.—Age, 26 years. Enlisted, May 9, 1898, at New York city, to serve two years; mustered in as private, Co. A, May 24, 1898; promoted corporal, July 29, 1898; mustered out with company, November 23, 1898, at Fort Slocum, New York Harbor.

MIGGINS, THOMAS J.—Age, 32 years. Enlisted, May 9, 1898, at New York city, to serve two years; mustered in as private, Co. A, May 24, 1898; appointed wagoner, same date; mustered out with company, November 23, 1898, at Fort Slocum, New York Harbor.

MILES, MATTHEW M.—Age, 33 years. Enrolled, May 9, 1898, at New York city, to serve two years; mustered in as captain, Co. E, May 24, 1898; mustered out with company, November 23, 1898, at Fort Slocum, New York Harbor; commissioned captain. May 24, 1898, with rank from same date, original.

MILES, PERCY B.—Age, 21 years. Enlisted, May 9, 1898, at New York city, to serve two years; mustered in as private, Co. E, May 24, 1898; mustered out with company, November 23. 1898, at Fort Slocum, New York Harbor.

MILLER, CHARLES E.—Age, 26 years. Enlisted, June 29, 1898, at New York city, to serve two years; mustered in as private, Co. C, same date; mustered out with company, November 23, 1898, at Fort Slocum, New York Harbor.

MILLER, EDWARD F.—Age, 22 years. Enlisted, May 2, 1898, at Brooklyn, to serve two years; mustered in as corporal, Co. D, May 24, 1898; returned to ranks, July 23, 1898; mustered out with company, November 23, 1898, at Fort Slocum, New York Harbor; also borne as Edwin F. Miller.

MILLER, JR., FRED.—Age, 24 years. Enlisted, June 22, 1898, at Brooklyn, to serve two years; mustered in as private, Co. F, same date; mustered out with company, November 23, 1898, at Fort Slocum, New York Harbor.

MILLER, FREDERICK R.—Age, 27 years. Enlisted, May 9, 1898, at New York city, to serve two years; mustered in as corporal, Co. C, May 24, 1898; discharged, October 18, 1898, at Fort Slocum, New York Harbor.

MILLER, GEORGE R.—Age, 21 years. Enlisted, July 1, 1898, at Brooklyn, to serve two years; mustered in as private, Co. L, same date; mustered out with company, November 23, 1898, at Fort Slocum, New York Harbor.

MILLER, LEONARD F.—Age, 19 years. Enlisted, May 6, 1898, at Camp Black, to serve two years; mustered in as private, Co. F, May 24, 1898; mustered out with company, November 23, 1898, at Fort Slocum, New York Harbor.

MILLER, PAUL E.—Age, 21 years. Enlisted, May 9, 1898, at New York city, to serve two years; mustered in as private, Co. H, May 24, 1898; mustered out with company, November 23, 1898, at Fort Slocum, New York Harbor.

MILLER, WILLIAM.—Age, 22 years. Enlisted, May 20, 1898, at Camp Black, to serve two years; mustered in as private, Co. E, May 24, 1898; mustered out with company, November 23, 1898, at Fort Slocum, New York Harbor.

MILLHAGEN, JOHANNES LUDWIG AUGUST.—Age, 22 years. Enlisted, June 24, 1898, at New York city, to serve two years; mustered in as private, Co. I, same date; mustered out with company, November 23, 1898, at Fort Slocum, New York Harbor.

MINSHULL, PIERREPONT V.—Age, 22 years. Enlisted, June 25, 1898, at Brooklyn, to serve two years; mustered in as private, Co. M, June 26, 1898; mustered out with company, November 23, 1898, at Fort Slocum, New York Harbor; also borne as Minshell and Munshall.

MINTZ, JOSEPH MICHAEL.—Age, 20 years. Enlisted, July 5, 1898, at New York city, to serve two years; mustered in as private, Co. K, same date; mustered out with company, November 23, 1898, at Fort Slocum, New York Harbor; also borne as Joseph N. Mintz.

MITTENZWEI, JR., HENRY C.—Age, 21 years. Enlisted, June 29, 1898, at New York city, to serve two years; mustered in as private, Co. C, same date; appointed cook, October 1, 1898; mustered out with company, November 23, 1898, at Fort Slocum, New York Harbor.

MOCKLER, FRANK D.—Age, 29 years. Enlisted, May 17, 1898, at Camp Black, to serve two years; mustered in as private, Co. E, May 24, 1898; mustered out with company, November 23, 1898, at Fort Slocum, New York Harbor.

MOE, PIERRE W.—Age, 25 years. Enlisted, May 9, 1898, at New York city, to serve two years; mustered in as sergeant, Co. B, May 24, 1898; mustered out with company, November 23, 1898, at Fort Slocum, New York Harbor.

MOELLER, HENRY J.—Age, 24 years. Enlisted, May 2, 1898, at Brooklyn, to serve two years; mustered in as private, Co. L, May 24, 1898; appointed wagoner, July 1, 1898; mustered out with company, November 23, 1898, at Fort Slocum, New York Harbor.

MOLLER, CHRISTEN.—Age, 20 years. Enlisted, June 23, 1898, at Brooklyn, to serve two years; mustered in as private, Co. L, same date; mustered out with company, November 23, 1898, at Fort Slocum, New York Harbor.

MONARQUE, WILLIAM A.—Age, 24 years. Enlisted, May 18, 1898, at Camp Black, to serve two years; mustered in as private, Co. I, May 24, 1898; mustered out, November 23, 1898, at Fort Slocum, New York Harbor.

MONTAGUE, HARRY K.—Age, 23 years. Enlisted, May 9, 1898, at New York city, to serve two years; mustered in as private, Co. H, May 24, 1898; discharged, August 11, 1898, at Fort Schuyler, New York Harbor.

MONTGOMERY, WALTER.—Age, 21 years. Enlisted, June 20, 1898, at Brooklyn, to serve two years; mustered in as private, Co. M, same date; mustered out with company, November 23, 1898, at Fort Slocum, New York Harbor.

MONTGOMERY, WILLIAM R.—Age, 27 years. Enlisted, May 9, 1898, at New York city, to serve two years; mustered in as private, Co. C, May 24, 1898; promoted corporal, July 29, 1898; mustered out with company, November 23, 1898, at Fort Slocum, New York Harbor.

MOODY, ARTHUR E.—Age, 19 years. Enlisted, May 9, 1898, at New York city, to serve two years; mustered in as private, Co. C, May 24, 1898; mustered out with company, November 23, 1898, at Fort Slocum, New York Harbor.

MOORE, HARRY C.—Age, 19 years. Enlisted, May 2, 1898, at Brooklyn, to serve two years; mustered in as private, Co. M, May 24, 1898; mustered out with company, November 23, 1898, at Fort Slocum, New York Harbor.

MOORE, THOMAS.—Age, 22 years. Enlisted, June 28, 1898, at New York city, to serve two years; mustered in as private, Co. C, same date; mustered out with company, November 23, 1898, at Fort Slocum, New York Harbor.

MOORE, WALTER L.—Age, 21 years. Enlisted, May 9, 1898, at New York city, to serve two years; mustered in as private, Co. E, May 24, 1898; mustered out with company, November 23, 1898, at Fort Slocum, New York Harbor.

MOORE, WILLIAM J.—Age, 34 years. Enlisted, June 20, 1898, at New York city, to serve two years; mustered in as private, Co. E, same date; mustered out with company, November 23, 1898, at Fort Slocum, New York Harbor.

MOQUIN, CHRISTOPHER C.—Age, 25 years. Enlisted, May 2, 1898, at Brooklyn, to serve two years; mustered in as private, Co. M, May 24, 1898; mustered out with company, November 23, 1898, at Fort Slocum, New York Harbor.

MORGAN, EDWARD.—Age, 22 years. Enlisted, May 2, 1898, at Brooklyn, to serve two years; mustered in as private, Co. D, May 24, 1898; mustered out with company, November 23, 1898, at Fort Slocum, New York Harbor; also borne as Edward P. H. Morgan.

MORISON, CHARLES A.—Age, 35 years. Enlisted, May 9, 1898, at New York city, to serve two years; mustered in as private, Co. G, May 24, 1898; discharged, October 15, 1898, at Fort Slocum, New York Harbor.

MORRIS, HENRY.—Age, 29 years. Enlisted, June 3, 1898, at Camp Black, to serve two years; mustered in as private, Co. B, same date; mustered out with company, November 23, 1898, at Fort Slocum, New York Harbor, as Henry A. Morris.

MORRISON, GEORGE.—Age, 18 years. Enlisted, May 20, 1898, at Hempstead, to serve two years; mustered in as private, Co. M, May 24, 1898; discharged, September 22, 1898, at Willet's Point, N. Y.

MORRISSEY, JOHN J.—Age, 28 years. Enlisted, May 21, 1898, at Camp Black, to serve two years; mustered in as private, Co. B, May 24, 1898; mustered out with company, November 23, 1898, at Fort Slocum, New York Harbor.

MORSE, HERBERT F.—Age, 21 years. Enlisted, May 20, 1898, at Camp Black, to serve two years; mustered in as private, Co. I, May 24, 1898; mustered out with company, November 23, 1898, at Fort Slocum, New York Harbor.

MOSES, CHARLES G.—Age, 26 years. Enrolled, May 9, 1898, at New York city, to serve two years; mustered in as second lieutenant, Co. I, May 24, 1898; discharged, October 12, 1898; commissioned second lieutenant, May 24, 1898, with rank from same date, original.

MULBY, JAMES R.—Age, 28 years. Enlisted, June 29, 1898, at New York city; mustered in as private, Co. C, same date; deserted, July 8, 1898, at Fort Schuyler, New York Harbor; also borne as James Rufus Mulby.

MULDOON, JOHN.—Age, 22 years. Enlisted, May 22, 1898, at Camp Black, to serve two years; mustered in as private, Co. I, May 24, 1898; mustered out with company, November 23, 1898, at Fort Slocum, New York Harbor.

MULGREW, JR., FELIX A.—Age, 29 years. Enlisted, May 9, 1898, at New York city, to serve two years; mustered in as private, Co. G, May 24, 1898; promoted corporal, same date; mustered out with company, November 23, 1898, at Fort Slocum, New York Harbor.

MULLEN, GEORGE.—Age, 24 years. Enlisted, May 2, 1898, at Brooklyn, to serve two years; mustered in as private, Co. M, May 24, 1898; mustered out with company, November 23, 1898, at Fort Slocum, New York Harbor.

MULLER, BERNHARD.—Age, 20 years. Enlisted, June 24, 1898, at New York city, to serve two years; mustered in as private, Co. I, same date; mustered out with company, November 23, 1898, at Fort Slocum, New York Harbor.

MULLER, JOHN CHRISTIAN.—Age, 25 years. Enlisted, July 2, 1898, at New York city, to serve two years; mustered in as private, Co. H, same date; mustered out with company, November 23, 1898, at Fort Slocum, New York Harbor.

MULLER, LOUIS B.—Age, 24 years. Enlisted, May 2, 1898, at Brooklyn, to serve two years; mustered in as private, Co. L, May 24, 1898; mustered out with company, November 23, 1898, at Fort Slocum, New York Harbor.

MUNDELL, WILLIAM A.—Age, 22 years. Enlisted, May 12, 1898, at Camp Black, to serve two years; mustered in as private, Co. F, May 24, 1898; promoted corporal, July 1, 1898; mustered out with company, November 23, 1898, at Fort Slocum, New York Harbor.

MUNDHENK, ALBERT.—Age, 44 years. Enlisted, June 23, 1898, at New York city, to serve two years; mustered in as private, Co. I, same date; mustered out with company, November 23, 1898, at Fort Slocum, New York Harbor; also borne as Mundhenk.

MUNRO, SAMUEL J.—Age, 24 years. Enlisted, May 9, 1898, at New York city, to serve two years; mustered in as first sergeant, Co. H, May 24, 1898; mustered out with company, November 23, 1898, at Fort Slocum, New York Harbor.

MUNSHALL, PIERREPONT V., see Pierrepont V. Minshull.

MURPHY, DANIEL J.—Age, 38 years. Enrolled, May 9, 1898, at New York city, to serve two years; mustered in as captain, Co. A, May 24, 1898; mustered out with company, November 23, 1898, at Fort Slocum, New York Harbor; commissioned captain, May 24, 1898, with rank from same date, original.

MURPHY, EDWARD F.—Age, 25 years. Enlisted, May 9, 1898, at New York city, to serve two years; mustered in as private, Co. H, May 24, 1898; mustered out with company, November 23, 1898, at Fort Slocum, New York Harbor, as Edmund F. Murphy.

MURPHY, FRANK C.—Age, 32 years. Enrolled, May 2, 1898, at Brooklyn, to serve two years; mustered in as captain, Co. L, May 24, 1898; mustered out with company, November 23, 1898, at Fort Slocum, New York Harbor; commissioned captain, May 24, 1898, with rank from same date, original.

MURPHY, FRANK L.—Age, 31 years. Enlisted, May 9, 1898, at New York city, to serve two years; mustered in as private, Co. B, May 24, 1898; promoted corporal, June 30, 1898; mustered out with company, November 23, 1898, at Fort Slocum, New York Harbor.

MURPHY, JOHN G.—Age, 25 years. Enlisted, May 9, 1898, at New York city, to serve two years; mustered in as private, Co. H, May 24, 1898; promoted corporal, July 29, 1898; mustered out with company, November 23, 1898, at Fort Slocum, New York Harbor.

MURPHY, MARTIN JOSEPH.—Age, 19 years. Enlisted, May 20, 1898, at Camp Black, to serve two years; mustered in as private, Co. E, May 24, 1898; mustered out with company, November 23, 1898, at Fort Slocum, New York Harbor.

MURPHY, PATRICK.—Age, 21 years. Enlisted, June 29, 1898, at Brooklyn, to serve two years; mustered in as private, Co. M, same date; mustered out with company, November 23, 1898, at Fort Slocum, New York Harbor.

MURPHY, PETER A.—Age, 27 years. Enlisted, May 18, 1898, at Camp Black, to serve two years; mustered in as private, Co. B, May 24, 1898; appointed artificer, same date; returned to ranks, November 1, 1898; mustered out with company, November 23, 1898, at Fort Slocum, New York Harbor.

MURPHY, RALPH O.—Age, 19 years. Enlisted, May 2, 1898,
at Brooklyn, to serve two years; mustered in as private, Co.
L, May 24, 1898; promoted corporal, July 1, 1898; mustered out
with company, November 23, 1898, at Fort Slocum, New York
Harbor.

MURRAY, BENJAMIN B.—Age, 29 years. Enlisted, May 20,
1898, at Camp Black, to serve two years; mustered in as private, Co. I, May 24, 1898; mustered out with company, November 23, 1898, at Fort Slocum, New York Harbor.

MURRAY, MICHAEL JOHN.—Age, 21 years. Enlisted, July 5,
1898, at New York city, to serve two years; mustered in as
private, Co. K, same date; mustered out with company, November 23, 1898, at Fort Slocum, New York Harbor.

MUSE, CLARENCE W., see Clarence W. Mase.

NAGEL, LOUIS E.—Age, 21 years. Enlisted, May 20, 1898, at
Camp Black, to serve two years; mustered in as private, Co. E,
May 24, 1898; mustered out with company, November 23, 1898,
at Fort Slocum, New York Harbor.

NEAL, CHARLES.—Age, 23 years. Enlisted, June 30, 1898, at
New York city, to serve two years; mustered in as private, Co.
K, same date; mustered out with company, November 23, 1898,
at Fort Slocum, New York Harbor.

NEIMAN, HARRY.—Age, 21 years. Enlisted, May 9, 1898, at
New York city, to serve two years; mustered in as private, Co.
K, May 24, 1898; discharged, November 3, 1898, at Fort Slocum,
New York Harbor.

NEWILL, GEORGE F.—Age, 21 years. Enlisted, May 9, 1898,
at New York city, to serve two years; mustered in as private,
Co. G, May 24, 1898; mustered out with company November 23,
1898, at Fort Slocum, New York Harbor.

NEWMAN, ABRAHAM.—Age, 22 years. Enlisted, May 2, 1898,
at Brooklyn, to serve two years; mustered in as private, Co. D,
May 24, 1898; mustered out with company, November 23, 1898,
at Fort Slocum, New York Harbor.

NEWMAN, NATHAN.—Age, 27 years. Enlisted, May 20, 1898, at Camp Black, to serve two years; mustered in as private, Co. K, May 24, 1898; mustered out with company, November 23, 1898, at Fort Slocum, New York Harbor.

NICHOLSON, FRANK D.—Age, 23 years. Enlisted, May 9, 1898, at New York city, to serve two years; mustered in as private, Co. G, May 24, 1898; mustered out with company, November 23, 1898, at Fort Slocum, New York Harbor.

NIKELEWICZ, MANLEY B.—Age, 25 years. Enlisted, May 2, 1898, at Brooklyn, to serve two years; mustered in as private, Co. D, May 24, 1898; mustered out with company, November 23, 1898, at Fort Slocum, New York Harbor.

NOETZLI, EDWARD H.—Age, 25 years. Enlisted, May 23, 1898, at Camp Black, to serve two years; mustered in as private, Co. I, May 24, 1898; discharged, October 13, 1898, at Fort Slocum, New York Harbor.

NOONAN, PATRICK J.—Age, 24 years. Enlisted, June 29, 1898, at New York city, to serve two years; mustered in as private, Co. C, same date; mustered out with company, November 23, 1898, at Fort Slocum, New York Harbor.

NORTON, SIDNEY E.—Age, 24 years. Enlisted, May 2, 1898, at Brooklyn, to serve two years; mustered in as private, Co. L, May 24, 1898; promoted corporal, July 1, 1898; mustered out with company, November 23, 1898, at Fort Slocum, New York Harbor.

NORTON, WILLIAM.—Age, 24 years. Enlisted, May 20, 1898, at Camp Black, to serve two years; mustered in as private, Co. I, May 24, 1898; mustered out with company, November 23, 1898, at Fort Slocum, New York Harbor.

NOWKA, CHARLES J.—Age, 23 years. Enlisted, May 9, 1898, at New York city, to serve two years; mustered in as private, Co. H, May 24, 1898; promoted corporal, August 1, 1898; mustered out with company, November 23, 1898, at Fort Slocum, New York Harbor.

NOWKA, F. W. GUSTAVE.—Age, 28 years.   Enlisted, May 9, 1898, at New York city, to serve two years; mustered in as private, Co. H, May 24, 1898; mustered out with company, November 23, 1898, at Fort Slocum, New York Harbor.

O'BRIEN, JOHN F.—Age, 24 years.   Enlisted, May 9, 1898, at New York city, to serve two years; mustered in as private, Co. A, May 24, 1898; mustered out with company, November 23, 1898, at Fort Slocum, New York Harbor.

O'BRIEN, JOHN J.—Age, 23 years.   Enlisted, May 24, 1898, at Camp Black, to serve two years; mustered in as private, Co. I, same date; mustered out with company, November 23, 1898, at Fort Slocum, New York Harbor.

O'BRIEN, JOSEPH J.—Age, 22 years.   Enlisted, May 2, 1898, at Brooklyn, to serve two years; mustered in as private, Co. L, May 24, 1898; mustered out with company, November 23, 1898, at Fort Slocum, New York Harbor.

O'CONNELL, WILLIAM A.—Age, 21 years.   Enlisted, May 2, 1898, at Brooklyn, to serve two years; mustered in as private, Co. L, May 24, 1898; promoted corporal, August 20, 1898; mustered out with company, November 23, 1898, at Fort Slocum, New York Harbor.

O'CONNER, EDWARD J.—Age, 24 years.   Enlisted, May 9, 1898, at New York city, to serve two years; mustered in as private, Co. H, May 24, 1898; mustered out with company, November 23, 1898, at Fort Slocum, New York Harbor, as O'Connor.

O'CONNOR, JERRY FRANCIS.—Age, 34 years.   Enlisted, July 7, 1898, at New York city, to serve two years; mustered in as private, Co. A, same date; mustered out with company, November 23, 1898, at Fort Slocum, New York Harbor.

O'CONNOR, WILLIAM.—Age, 37 years.   Enlisted, July 5, 1898, at Brooklyn, to serve two years; mustered in as private, Co. M, same date; mustered out with company, November 23, 1898, at Fort Slocum, New York Harbor.

O'DONNELL, JOSEPH T.—Age, 22 years.   Enlisted, May 9, 1898, at New York city, to serve two years; mustered in as private, Co. A, May 24, 1898; discharged, November 6, 1898, at Fort Slocum, New York Harbor.

O'HARA, CHARLES.—Age, 28 years. Enlisted, May 2, 1898, at Brooklyn, to serve two years; mustered in as artificer, Co. D, May 24, 1898; reduced to ranks, June 5, 1898; mustered out with company, November 23, 1898, at Fort Slocum, New York Harbor.

O'KEEFE, JAMES.—Age, 25 years. Enlisted, May 9, 1898, at New York city, to serve two years; mustered in as sergeant, Co. H, May 24, 1898; mustered out with company, November 23, 1898, at Fort Slocum, New York Harbor.

O'KEEFE, JOSEPH.—Age, — years. Enlisted, August 13, 1898, at Fort Schuyler, to serve two years; mustered in as private, Co. K, same date; discharged for disability, September 20, 1898, at Fort Schuyler, New York Harbor.

O'LEARY, CHARLES.—Age, 27 years. Enlisted, May 9, 1898, at New York city, to serve two years; mustered in as private, Co. E, May 24, 1898; mustered out with company, November 23, 1898, at Fort Slocum, New York Harbor.

O'MEARA, WILLIAM J.—Age, 25 years. Enlisted, May 9, 1898, at New York city, to serve two years; mustered in as private, Co. G, May 24, 1898; discharged, October 30, 1898, at Fort Slocum, New York Harbor.

O'NEILL, JAMES V.—Age, 18 years. Enlisted, June 29, 1898, at New York city, to serve two years; mustered in as private, Co. C, same date; mustered out with company, November 23, 1898, at Fort Slocum, New York Harbor.

O'NEILL, JOHN J.—Age, 22 years. Enlisted, May 9, 1898, at New York city, to serve two years; mustered in as private, Co. H, May 24, 1898; mustered out with company, November 23, 1898, at Fort Slocum, New York Harbor.

OPFERKUCH, WILLIAM PHILIP.—Age, 25 years. Enlisted, June 21, 1898, at New York city, to serve two years; mustered in as private, Co. B, same date; mustered out with company, November 23, 1898, at Fort Slocum, New York Harbor.

OPPENHEIMER, PAUL H.—Age, 26 years. Enlisted, May 9, 1898, at New York city, to serve two years; mustered in as private, Co. K, May 24, 1898; promoted corporal, July 29, 1898; mustered out with company, November 23, 1898, at Fort Slocum, New York Harbor.

OPPERMANN, ALBERT J.—Age, 21 years. Enlisted, May 17,
1898, at Camp Black, to serve two years; mustered in as private,
Co. E, May 24, 1898; mustered out with company, November
23, 1898, at Fort Slocum, New York Harbor.

ORSWELL, GEORGE M.—Age, 22 years. Enlisted, May 9, 1898,
at New York city, to serve two years; mustered in as private,
Co. B, May 24, 1898; appointed musician, August 10, 1898;
returned to ranks, no date; mustered out with company, November 23, 1898, at Fort Slocum, New York Harbor.

O'SHEA, HUGH.—Age, 23 years. Enlisted, May 13, 1898, at
Hempstead, to serve two years; mustered in as private, Co.
M, May 24, 1898; mustered out with company, November 23,
1898, at Fort Slocum, New York Harbor.

O'SHEA, JR., TIMOTHY.—Age, 27 years. Enlisted, May 2,
1898, at Brooklyn, to serve two years; mustered in as corporal,
Co. M, May 24, 1898; mustered out with company, November
23, 1898, at Fort Slocum, New York Harbor.

OTT, GEORGE W.—Age, 21 years. Enlisted, May 9, 1898, at
New York city, to serve two years; mustered in as private, Co.
H, May 24, 1898; mustered out with company, November 23,
1898, at Fort Slocum, New York Harbor.

OUTWATER, MORRIS.—Age, 26 years. Enlisted, May 9, 1898,
at New York city, to serve two years; mustered in as private,
Co. G, May 24, 1898; mustered out with company, November 23,
1898, at Fort Slocum, New York Harbor.

OVERBAUGH, JAMES H.—Age, 25 years. Enlisted, May 2,
1898, at Brooklyn, to serve two years; mustered in as private,
Co. L, May 24, 1898; mustered out with company, November 23,
1898, at Fort Slocum, New York Harbor.

OVERTON, WILLIAM W.—Age, 18 years. Enlisted, June 24,
1898, at Brooklyn, to serve two years; mustered in as private,
Co. L, same date; discharged, November 2, 1898, at Fort Slocum,
New York Harbor.

OWENS, EDWARD C.—Age, 38 years. Enlisted, July 1, 1898,
at New York city, to serve two years; mustered in as private,
Co. C, same date; mustered out with company, November 23,
1898, at Fort Slocum, New York Harbor.

OWENS, WASHINGTON.—Age, 24 years.   Enlisted, May 9, 1898, at New York city, to serve two years; mustered in as private, Co. I, May 24, 1898; mustered out with company, November 23, 1898, at Fort Slocum, New York Harbor; also borne as Owen.

OXLEY, ROBERT.—Age, 20 years. Enlisted, May 2, 1898, at Brooklyn, to serve two years; mustered in as private, Co. L, May 24, 1898; appointed musician, no date; mustered out with company, November 23, 1898, at Fort Slocum, New York Harbor.

PAINTER, WILLIAM.—Age, 21 years.   Enlisted, June 20, 1898, at Brooklyn, to serve two years; mustered in as private, Co. D, same date; mustered out with company, November 23, 1898, at Fort Slocum, New York Harbor; also borne as Paynter.

PALMER, HOWARD S.—Age, 23 years.   Enlisted, May 2, 1898, at Brooklyn, to serve two years; mustered in as corporal, Co. L, May 2, 1898; returned to ranks, November 13, 1898; promoted corporal, no date; mustered out with company, November 23, 1898, at Fort Slocum, New York Harbor.

PALMER, SYDNEY H.—Age, 22 years.   Enlisted, May 2, 1898, at Brooklyn, to serve two years; mustered in as private, Co. D, May 24. 1898; mustered out with company, November 23, 1898, at Fort Slocum, New York Harbor.

PARKER, ARCHIBALD.—Age, 21 years.   Enlisted, May 20, 1898, at Camp Black, to serve two years; mustered in as private, Co. K, May 24, 1898; mustered out with company, November 23, 1898, at Fort Slocum, New York Harbor.

PARKS, EDWIN J.—Age, 26 years.   Enlisted, May 9, 1898, at New York city, to serve two years; mustered in as first sergeant, Co. G, May 24, 1898; as second lieutenant, September 26, 1898; mustered out with company, November 23, 1898, at Fort Slocum, New York Harbor; also borne as Edwin J. Parker; commissioned second lieutenant, August 24, 1898, with rank from same date, vice Doubleday, discharged.

PARSHALL, GEORGE F.—Age, 20 years.   Enlisted, May 2, 1898, at Brooklyn, to serve two years; mustered in as sergeant, Co. D, May 24, 1898; mustered out with company, November 23, 1898, at Fort Slocum, New York Harbor.

PATTERSON, JR., JAMES.—Age, 19 years. Enlisted, May 24, 1898, at Camp Black, to serve two years; mustered in as private, Co. B, same date; mustered out with company, November 23, 1898, at Fort Slocum, New York Harbor.

PATTERSON, SPENCER.—Age, 21 years. Enlisted, May 2, 1898, at Brooklyn, to serve two years; mustered in as private, Co. D, May 24, 1898; mustered out with company, November 23, 1898, at Fort Slocum, New York Harbor.

PATTERSON, THOMAS C.—Age, 34 years. Enlisted, May 11, 1898, at Camp Black, to serve two years; mustered in as corporal, Co. F, May 24, 1898; mustered out with company, November 23, 1898, at Fort Slocum, New York Harbor.

PATTERSON, WALTER B.—Age, 35 years. Enlisted, May 2, 1898, at Brooklyn, to serve two years; mustered in as corporal, Co. L, May 24, 1898; returned to ranks, August 12, 1898; promoted corporal, September 13, 1898; mustered out with company, November 23, 1898, at Fort Slocum, New York Harbor.

PATTINSON, STANLY.—Age, 21 years. Enlisted, May 2, 1898, at Brooklyn, to serve two years; mustered in as private, Co. D, May 24, 1898; promoted corporal, July 1, 1898; mustered out with company, November 23, 1898, at Fort Slocum, New York Harbor.

PAYNTER, WILLIAM, see William Painter.

PEARSALL, CLIFFORD G.—Age, 20 years. Enlisted, May 2, 1898, at Brooklyn, to serve two years; mustered in as private, Co. L, May 24, 1898; promoted corporal, October 1, 1898; mustered out with company, November 23, 1898, at Fort Slocum, New York Harbor.

PEARSON, CHARLES H.—Age, 19 years. Enlisted, May 9, 1898, at New York city, to serve two years; mustered in as musician, Co. A, May 24, 1898; mustered out with company, November 23, 1898, at Fort Slocum, New York Harbor.

PEARSON, OLIVER W.—Age, 25 years. Enlisted, May 2, 1898, at Brooklyn, to serve two years; mustered in as private, Co. L, May 24, 1898; mustered out with company, November 23, 1898, at Fort Slocum, New York Harbor.

PELTON, GILBERT BRACE.—Age, 34 years. Enlisted, June 20, 1898, at New York city, to serve two years; mustered in as private, Co. I, same date; mustered out with company, November 23, 1898, at Fort Slocum, New York Harbor.

PENNYER, WILLIAM A.—Age, 44 years. Enlisted, June 17, 1898, at New York city, to serve two years; mustered in as private, Co. E, same date; mustered out with company, November 23, 1898, at Fort Slocum, New York Harbor; also borne as Pennoyer.

PERKINS, EDWIN S.—Age, 21 years. Enlisted, May 9, 1898, at New York city, to serve two years; mustered in as private, Co. A, May 24, 1898; mustered out with company, November 23, 1898, at Fort Slocum, New York Harbor.

PERRY, FRANK J.—Age, 23 years. Enlisted, May 12, 1898, at Camp Black, to serve two years; mustered in as private, Co. F, May 24, 1898; mustered out with company, November 23, 1898, at Fort Slocum, New York Harbor.

PERRY, T. WALTER.—Age, 21 years. Enlisted, May 2, 1898, at Brooklyn, to serve two years; mustered in as private, Co. F, May 24, 1898; mustered out with company, November 23, 1898, at Fort Slocum, New York Harbor.

PESSELS, EDWARD H.—Age, 24 years. Enlisted, May 9, 1898, at New York city, to serve two years; mustered in as corporal, Co. A, May 24, 1898; mustered out with company, November 23, 1898, at Fort Slocum, New York Harbor.

PETHERBRIDGE, ALFRED COX.—Age, 34 years. Enlisted, June 30, 1898, at New York city, to serve two years; mustered in as private, Co. A, same date; mustered out with company, November 23, 1898, at Fort Slocum, New York Harbor.

PETRY, JOHN A.—Age, 20 years. Enlisted, June 3, 1898, at Camp Black, to serve two years; mustered in as private, Co. A, same date; mustered out with company, November 23, 1898, at Fort Slocum, New York Harbor.

PEYSER, OSCAR.—Age, 28 years. Enlisted, May 9, 1898, at New York city, to serve two years; mustered in as private, Co. H, May 24, 1898; mustered out with company, November 23, 1898, at Fort Slocum, New York Harbor.

PFAHLER, CHARLES ALBERT.—Age, 30 years. Enlisted, June 30, 1898, at New York city, to serve two years; mustered in as private, Co. A, same date; mustered out with company, November 23, 1898, at Fort Slocum, New York Harbor.

PHILLIPS, LEWIS.—Age, 22 years. Enlisted, May 9, 1898, at New York city, to serve two years; mustered in as private, Co. H, May 24, 1898; discharged, September 20, 1898, at Fort Schuyler, New York Harbor.

PIERCE, JEROME.—Age, 21 years. Enlisted, May 2, 1898, at Brooklyn, to serve two years; mustered in as private, Co. L, May 24, 1898; mustered out with company, November 23, 1898, at Fort Slocum, New York Harbor.

PINKERTON, TEENAN W.—Age, 26 years. Enlisted, May 2, 1898, at Brooklyn, to serve two years; mustered in as private, Co. D, May 24, 1898; mustered out with company, November 23, 1898, at Fort Slocum, New York Harbor.

PLACET, GUSTAVE J.—Age, 23 years. Enlisted, May 9, 1898, at New York city, to serve two years; mustered in as private, Co. B, May 24, 1898; transferred to Co. G, June 24, 1898; mustered out with company, November 23, 1898, at Fort Slocum, New York Harbor.

PLUMLEY, CHARLES.—Age, 31 years. Enlisted, May 2, 1898, at Brooklyn, to serve two years; mustered in as private, Co. D, May 24, 1898; mustered out with company, November 23, 1898, at Fort Slocum, New York Harbor.

POLLOCK, GEORGE HENRY.—Age, 34 years. Enlisted, June 28, 1898, at New York City, to serve two years; mustered in as private, Co. A, same date; mustered out with company, November 23, 1898, at Fort Slocum, New York Harbor.

PORTER, GEORGE.—Age, 21 years. Enlisted, May 20, 1898, at Camp Black, to serve two years; mustered in as private, Co. I, May 24, 1898; mustered out with company, November 23, 1898, at Fort Slocum, New York Harbor.

PORTER, WALTER B.—Age, 26 years. Enrolled, May 9, 1898, at New York city, to serve two years; mustered in as second lieutenant, Co. A, May 24, 1898; mustered out with company, November 23, 1898, at Fort Slocum, New York Harbor; commissioned second lieutenant, May 24, 1898, with rank from same date original.

POULSON, WILLIAM G.—Age, 26 years. Enlisted, May 9, 1898, to serve two years; mustered in as private, Co. G, May 24, 1898; discharged, October 30, 1898, at Fort Slocum, New York Harbor.

POWER, CHARLES E. V.—Age, 24 years. Enlisted, May 9, 1898, at New York city, to serve two years; mustered in as private, Co. H, May 24, 1898; mustered out with company, November 23, 1898, at Fort Slocum, New York Harbor.

PRAY, ARTHUR P.—Age, 22 years. Enlisted, May 9, 1898, at New York city, to serve two years; mustered in as private, Co. B, May 24, 1898; mustered out with company, November 23, 1898, at Fort Slocum, New York Harbor.

PRESCOTT, DANIEL.—Age, 29 years. Enlisted, June 28, 1898, at New York city, to serve two years; mustered in as private, Co. G, same date; mustered out with company, November 23, 1898, at Fort Slocum, New York Harbor.

PRICE, JR., THOMAS FRANCIS.—Age, 20 years. Enlisted, June 24, 1898, at New York city, to serve two years; mustered in as private, Co. B, same date; appointed wagoner, October 1, 1898; mustered out with company, November 23, 1898, at Fort Slocum, New York Harbor.

PRICE, VINCENT.—Age, 30 years. Enlisted, May 9, 1898, at New York city, to serve two years; mustered in as first sergeant, Co. E, May 24, 1898; second lieutenant, Co. H, October 6, 1898; mustered out with company, November 23, 1898, at Fort Slocum, New York Harbor; commissioned second lieutenant, October 4, 1898, with rank from same date, vice Clarke, promoted.

PRINGLE, HENRY.—Age, 24 years. Enlisted, May 9, 1898, at New York city, to serve two years; mustered in as private, Co. E, May 24, 1898; mustered out with company, November 23, 1898, at Fort Slocum, New York Harbor.

PRONICK, SYLVAIN B.—Age, 27 years. Enlisted, May 16, 1898, at Camp Black, to serve two years; mustered in as private, Co. K, May 24, 1898; discharged, October 20, 1898, at Fort Slocum, New York Harbor.

PUGH, THOMAS.—Age, 30 years. Enlisted, May 20, 1898, at Camp Black, to serve two years; mustered in as private, Co. K, May 24, 1898; mustered out with company, November 23, 1898, at Fort Slocum, New York Harbor.

PURCUPILE, CHARLES W.—Age, 20 years. Enlisted, May 2, 1898, at Brooklyn, to serve two years; mustered in as private, Co. M, May 24, 1898; mustered out with company, November 23, 1898, at Fort Slocum, New York Harbor.

QUACKENBUSH, ROBERT C.—Age, 34 years. Enlisted, May 9, 1898, at New York city, to serve two years; mustered in as sergeant, Co. B, May 24, 1898; mustered out with company, November 23, 1898, at Fort Slocum, New York Harbor.

QUALMAN, GEORGE.—Age, 27 years. Enlisted, May 4, 1898, at Camp Black, to serve two years; mustered in as first sergeant, Co. F, May 24, 1898; mustered out with company, November 23, 1898, at Fort Slocum, New York Harbor.

QUIMBY, FREDERICK M.—Age, 22 years. Enlisted, May 9, 1898, at New York city, to serve two years; mustered in as private, Co. H, May 24, 1898; appointed wagoner, July 1, 1898; mustered out with company, November 23, 1898, at Fort Slocum, New York Harbor.

RADLEY, FRANCIS H. J.—Age, 20 years. Enlisted, May 9, 1898, at New York city, to serve two years; mustered in as private Co. H, May 24, 1898; mustered out with company, November 23, 1898, at Fort Slocum, New York Harbor.

RANKIN, WILLIAM J.—Age, 22 years. Enlisted, May 17, 1898, at Camp Black, to serve two years; mustered in as private, Co. E, May 24, 1898; mustered out with company, November 23, 1898, at Fort Slocum, New York Harbor.

RAPHAEL, SIDNEY.—Age, 24 years. Enlisted, May 2, 1898, at Brooklyn, to serve two years; mustered in as private, Co. M, May 24, 1898; mustered out with company, November 23, 1898, at Fort Slocum, New York Harbor.

RATZ, CHARLES B.—Age, 21 years. Enlisted, May 9, 1898, at New York city, to serve two years; mustered in as private, Co. E, May 24, 1898; mustered out with company, November 23, 1898, at Fort Slocum, New York Harbor.

RAYMOND, JAMES G.—Age, 29 years. Enlisted, May 20, 1898, at Camp Black, to serve two years; mustered in as private, Co. E, May 24, 1898; mustered out with company, November 23, 1898, at Fort Slocum, New York Harbor.

REAVELY, WALTER S.—Age, — years. Enlisted, August 1, 1898, at Fort Schuyler, to serve two years; mustered in as private, Co. C, same date; mustered out with company, November 23, 1898, at Fort Slocum, New York Harbor.

REAY, JOSEPH.—Age, 20 years. Enlisted, June 29, 1898, at Brooklyn, to serve two years; mustered in as private, Co. L, same date; mustered out with company, November 23, 1898, at Fort Slocum, New York Harbor.

REDICKER, WILLIAM H.—Age, 27 years. Enlisted, May 9, 1898, at New York city, to serve two years; mustered in as private, Co. G, May 24, 1898; mustered out with company, November 23, 1898, at Fort Slocum, New York Harbor.

REDMOND, WILLIAM L.—Age, 34 years. Enlisted, May 9, 1898, at New York city, to serve two years; mustered in as private, Co. A, May 24, 1898; promoted corporal, same date; discharged, October 26, 1898, at Fort Slocum, New York Harbor.

REED, LEO J.—Age, 21 years. Enlisted, May 2, 1898, at Camp Black, to serve two years; mustered in as private, Co. D, May 24, 1898; deserted, October 27, 1898, at Fort Slocum, New York Harbor.

REICKHOFF, EDWARD, see Edward Rieckhoff.

REID, CHARLES M.—Age, 25 years. Enlisted, May 2, 1898, at Brooklyn, to serve two years; mustered in as first sergeant, Co. D, May 24, 1898; mustered out with company, November 23, 1898, at Fort Slocum, New York Harbor.

REID, FREDERICK.—Age, 31 years. Enlisted, May 2, 1898, at Brooklyn, to serve two years; mustered in as private, Co. L, May 24, 1898; promoted corporal, July 1, 1898; returned to ranks, August 4, 1898; appointed cook, October 7, 1898; mustered out with company, November 23, 1898, at Fort Slocum, New York Harbor.

REILLEY, GEORGE WALTON.—Age, 23 years. Enlisted, June 23, 1898, at New York city, to serve two years; mustered in as private, Co. I, same date; mustered out with company, November 23, 1898, at Fort Slocum, New York Harbor; also borne as Reilly.

REILLY, JOHN J.—Age, 24 years. Enlisted, June 3, 1898, at Camp Black, to serve two years; mustered in as private, Co. E, same date; mustered out with company, November 23, 1898, at Fort Slocum, New York Harbor.

REILLY, THOMAS J.—Age, 27 years. Enlisted, May 19, 1898, at Camp Black, to serve two years; mustered in as private, Co. E, May 24, 1898; mustered out with company, November 23, 1898, at Fort Slocum, New York Harbor.

REIMER, EDWARD C.—Age, 23 years. Enlisted, May 2, 1898, at Brooklyn, to serve two years; mustered in as private, Co. F, May 24, 1898; mustered out with company, November 23, 1898, at Fort Slocum, New York Harbor.

RENO, JOHN J.—Age, 21 years. Enlisted, May 2, 1898, at Brooklyn, to serve two years; mustered in as private, Co. L, May 24, 1898; mustered out with company, November 23, 1898, at Fort Slocum, New York Harbor.

REYNOLDS, ROBERT W.—Age, 30 years. Enlisted, May 9, 1898, at New York city, to serve two years; mustered in as private, Co. G, May 24, 1898; promoted corporal, November 6, 1898; mustered out with company, November 23, 1898, at Fort Slocum, New York Harbor.

REYNOLDS, WALTER S.—Age, 18 years. Enlisted, June 4, 1898, at Hempstead, to serve two years; mustered in as private, Co. M, June 7, 1898; mustered out with company, November 23, 1898, at Fort Slocum, New York Harbor.

RHODES, BERT L.—Age, 23 years. Enlisted, May 2, 1898, at Brooklyn, to serve two years; mustered in as private, Co. D, May 24, 1898; promoted corporal, September 17, 1898; discharged, October 19, 1898, at Fort Slocum, New York Harbor.

RIBLET, WILLIAM H.—Age, 21 years. Enlisted, May 9, 1898, at New York city, to serve two years; mustered in as private, Co. A, May 24, 1898; mustered out with company, November 23, 1898, at Fort Slocum, New York Harbor.

RICE, CHARLES.—Age, 21 years. Enlisted, May 20, 1898, at Camp Black, to serve two years; mustered in as private, Co. K, May 24, 1898; mustered out with company, November 23, 1898, at Fort Slocum, New York Harbor.

RICE, EDWARD J.—Age, 35 years. Enlisted, May 9, 1898, at New York city, to serve two years; mustered in as principal musician, May 24, 1898; as second lieutenant, Co. D, November 6, 1898; mustered out with company, November 23, 1898, at Fort Slocum, New York Harbor; commissioned second lieutenant, November 4, 1898, with rank from same date, vice Cooper, promoted.

RICHARD, EUGENE B.—Age, 21 years. Enlisted, June 24, 1898, at Brooklyn, to serve two years; mustered in as private, Co. F, same date; mustered out with company, November 23, 1898, at Fort Slocum, New York Harbor.

RICHARDSON, ROBERT K.—Age, 18 years. Enlisted, May 9, 1898, at New York city, to serve two years; mustered in as private, Co. G, May 24, 1898; mustered out with company, November 23, 1898, at Fort Slocum, New York Harbor.

RICHTER, JR., FRED W.—Age, 21 years. Enlisted, May 21, 1898, at Camp Black, to serve two years; mustered in as private, Co. B, May 24, 1898; mustered out with company, November 23, 1898, at Fort Slocum, New York Harbor, as Frederick W. Richter.

RIDER, ARTHUR W.—Age, 30 years. Enrolled, May 9, 1898, at New York city, to serve two years; mustered in as first lieutenant, Co. A, May 24, 1898; mustered out with company, November 23, 1898, at Fort Slocum, New York Harbor; commissioned first lieutenant, May 24, 1898, with rank from same date, original.

RIDLEY, EUGENE M.—Age, 25 years. Enlisted, May 2, 1898, at Brooklyn, to serve two years; mustered in as corporal, Co. M, May 24, 1898; mustered out with company, November 23, 1898, at Fort Slocum, New York Harbor.

RIECKHOFF, EDWARD.—Age, 21 years. Enlisted, July 1, 1898, at Brooklyn, to serve two years; mustered in as private, Co. F, same date; mustered out with company, November 23, 1898, at Fort Slocum, New York Harbor; also borne as Reickhoff.

RIGGS, JOHN JOSEPH.—Age, 19 years. Enlisted, June 28, 1898, at New York city, to serve two years; mustered in as private, Co. G, same date; mustered out with company, November 23, 1898, at Fort Slocum, New York Harbor.

RILEY, GEORGE H.—Age, 28 years. Enlisted, May 9, 1898, at New York city, to serve two years; mustered in as sergeant, Co. I, May 24, 1898; promoted first sergeant, October 25, 1898; mustered out with company, November 23, 1898, at Fort Slocum, New York Harbor.

RILEY, JAMES GORDON.—Age, 21 years. Enlisted, June 28, 1898, at New York city, to serve two years; mustered in as private, Co. K, same date; mustered out with company, November 23, 1898, at Fort Slocum, New York Harbor.

RINGER, FREDERICK C.—Age, 38 years. Enrolled, May 9, 1898, at New York city, to serve two years; mustered in as first lieutenant and battalion adjutant, May 24, 1898; mustered out with regiment, November 23, 1898, at Fort Slocum, New York Harbor; commissioned battalion adjutant, May 24, 1898, with rank from same date, original.

ROACH, RICHARD E.—Age, 22 years. Enlisted, May 9, 1898, at New York city, to serve two years; mustered in as private, Co. K, May 24, 1898; drowned, August 4, 1898, at Fort Schuyler, New York Harbor.

ROBBINS, JOHN H.—Age, 22 years. Enlisted, June 20, 1898, at New York city, to serve two years; mustered in as private, Co. E, same date; mustered out with company, November 23, 1898, at Fort Slocum, New York Harbor.

ROBERTON, WILLIAM JAMES.—Age, 23 years. Enlisted, June 27, 1898, at New York city, to serve two years; mustered in as private, Co. I, same date; mustered out with company, November 23, 1898, at Fort Slocum, New York Harbor.

ROBERTS, FRANK G.—Age, 32 years. Enlisted, May 9, 1898, at New York city, to serve two years; mustered in as private, Co. I, May 24, 1898; mustered out with company, November 23, 1898, at Fort Slocum, New York Harbor.

ROBERTS, HOWARD B.—Age, 21 years. Enlisted, May 2, 1898, at Brooklyn, to serve two years; mustered in as private, Co. M, May 24, 1898; mustered out with company, November 23, 1898, at Fort Slocum, New York Harbor.

ROBERTS, JR., THOMAS.—Age, 22 years. Enlisted, May 23, 1898, at Camp Black, to serve two years; mustered in as private, Co. I, May 24, 1898; mustered out with company, November 23, 1898, at Fort Slocum, New York Harbor.

ROBERTS, WILLIAM.—Age, 29 years. Enlisted, May 11, 1898, at New York city, to serve two years; mustered in as first sergeant, Co. B, May 24, 1898; returned to ranks, September 8, 1898; mustered out with company, November 23, 1898, at Fort Slocum, New York Harbor.

ROBINS, DAVID WILLIAM.—Age, 23 years. Enlisted, June 30, 1898, at New York city, to serve two years; mustered in as private, Co. K, same date; mustered out with company, November 23, 1898, at Fort Slocum, New York Harbor.

ROBINSON, WILLIAM H.—Age, 20 years. Enlisted, May 2, 1898, at Brooklyn, to serve two years; mustered in as private, Co. D, May 24, 1898; mustered out with company, November 23, 1898, at Fort Slocum, New York Harbor.

ROCHE, JOHN P.—Age, 35 years. Enlisted, June 28, 1898, at New York city, to serve two years; mustered in as private, Co. C, same date; mustered-out with company, November 23, 1898, at Fort Slocum, New York Harbor.

ROCK, EDWARD A.—Age, 22 years. Enlisted, July 5, 1898, at Brooklyn, to serve two years; mustered in as private, Co. D, same date; mustered out with company, November 23, 1898, at Fort Slocum, New York Harbor.

RODGERS, ARTHUR G.—Age, 26 years. Enlisted, May 2, 1898, at Brooklyn, to serve two years; mustered in as private, Co. L, May 24, 1898; mustered out with company, November 23, 1898, at Fort Slocum, New York Harbor.

ROEDER, FREDERICK A.—Age, 19 years. Enlisted, May 21, 1898, at Camp Black, to serve two years; mustered in as private, Co. F, May 24, 1898; mustered out with company, November 23, 1898, at Fort Slocum, New York Harbor.

ROEHSLER, JOHN L.—Age, 22 years. Enlisted, May 2, 1898, at Brooklyn, to serve two years; mustered in as private, Co. L, May 24, 1898; mustered out with company, November 23, 1898, at Fort Slocum, New York Harbor.

ROESE, WILLIAM E.—Age, 25 years. Enlisted, June 20, 1898, at Brooklyn, to serve two years; mustered in as private, Co. M, same date; mustered out with company, November 23, 1898, at Fort Slocum, New York Harbor.

ROGERS, CHARLES E.—Age, 22 years. Enlisted, June 27, 1898, at Brooklyn, to serve two years; mustered in as private, Co. D, same date; discharged without honor, November 19, 1898, at Fort Slocum, New York Harbor.

ROGERS, CHARLES P.—Age, 40 years. Enlisted, May 23, 1898, at Camp Black, to serve two years; mustered in as private, Co. A, May 24, 1898; mustered out with company, November 23, 1898, at Fort Slocum, New York Harbor.

ROGERS, HARRY G.—Age, 21 years. Enlisted, May 9, 1898, at New York city, to serve two years; mustered in as private, Co. K, May 24, 1898; mustered out with company, November 23, 1898, at Fort Slocum, New York Harbor.

ROGERS, IRA F.—Age, 24 years. Enlisted, May 9, 1898, at New York city, to serve two years; mustered in as private, Co. A, May 24, 1898; mustered out with company, November 23, 1898, at Fort Slocum, New York Harbor; also borne as Ira P. Rogers.

ROMAINE, HENRY G.—Age, 37 years. Enrolled, May 9, 1898, at New York city, to serve two years; mustered in as first lieutenant, Co. H, May 24, 1898; discharged, August 27, 1898; commissioned first lieutenant, May 24, 1898, with rank from same date, original.

ROSE, JOHN A.—Age, 25 years. Enlisted, May 9, 1898, at New York city, to serve two years; mustered in as private, Co. E, May 24, 1898; mustered out with company, November 23, 1898, at Fort Slocum, New York Harbor.

ROSE, WILHELM.—Age, 35 years. Enlisted, May 23, 1898, at Camp Black, to serve two years; mustered in as private, Co. K, May 24, 1898; mustered out with company, November 23, 1898, at Fort Slocum, New York Harbor.

ROSS, CHARLES MILLER.—Age, 21 years. Enlisted, May 2, 1898, at Brooklyn, to serve two years; mustered in as private, Co. F, May 24, 1898; mustered out with company, November 23, 1898, at Fort Slocum, New York Harbor.

ROSS, WALTER GRANT.—Age, 23 years. Enlisted, May 13, 1898, at Camp Black, to serve two years; mustered in as private, Co. F, May 24, 1898; promoted corporal, August 1, 1898; mustered out with company, November 23, 1898, at Fort Slocum, New York Harbor.

ROSS, WILLIAM A.—Age, 20 years. Enlisted, May 20, 1898, at Camp Black, to serve two years; mustered in as private, Co. H, May 24, 1898; mustered out with company, November 23, 1898, at Fort Slocum, New York Harbor.

ROSSI, RALPH T.—Age, — years. Enlisted, August 12, 1898, at Willet's Point, to serve two years; mustered in as private, Co. F, same date; mustered out with company, November 23, 1898, at Fort Slocum, New York Harbor.

ROSSTON, CHARLES A.—Age, 22 years. Enlisted, May 9, 1898, at New York city, to serve two years; mustered in as private, Co. A, May 24, 1898; mustered out with company, November 23, 1898, at Fort Slocum, New York Harbor.

ROTHWELL, THOMAS A.—Age, 22 years. Enlisted, May 9, 1898, at New York city, to serve two years; mustered in as hospital steward, May 24, 1898; mustered out with regiment, November 23, 1898, at Fort Slocum, New York Harbor.

ROUCHER, FREDERICK A.—Age, 28 years. Enlisted, May 9, 1898, at New York city, to serve two years; mustered in as private, Co. B, May 24, 1898; mustered out with company, November 23, 1898, at Fort Slocum, New York Harbor.

ROWLEY, HENRY EDWARD.—Age, 28 years. Enlisted, June 23, 1898, at New York city, to serve two years; mustered in as private, Co. B, same date; mustered out with company, November 23, 1898, at Fort Slocum, New York Harbor.

RUGER, JR., JULIAN.—Age, 24 years. Enlisted, June 27, 1898, at Brooklyn, to serve two years; mustered in as private, Co. F, same date; mustered out with company, November 23, 1898, at Fort Slocum, New York Harbor; also borne as Julius Ruger, Jr.

RUNDLE, EDWARD A.—Age, 25 years.   Enlisted, May 2, 1898, at Brooklyn, to serve two years; mustered in as private, Co. D, May 24, 1898; mustered out with company, November 23, 1898, at Fort Slocum, New York Harbor.

RUSSELL, FRANK L.—Age, 32 years.   Enlisted, June 20, 1898, at Brooklyn, to serve two years; mustered in as private, Co. D, same date; mustered out with company, November 23, 1898, at Fort Slocum, New York Harbor.

RUSSELL, GEORGE D.—Age, 49 years.   Enrolled, May 2, 1898, at Brooklyn, to serve two years; mustered in as major, May 24, 1898; mustered out with regiment, November 23, 1898, at Fort Slocum, New York Harbor; commissioned major, May 24, 1898, with rank from same date, original.

RUTHERFORD, ROBERT E.—Age, 19 years.   Enlisted, May 2, 1898, at Brooklyn, to serve two years; mustered in as private, Co. M, May 24, 1898; mustered out with company, November 23, 1898, at Fort Slocum, New York Harbor.

RYAN, CORNELIUS JOHN JOSEPH.—Age, 39 years.   Enlisted, June 29, 1898, at New York city, to serve two years; mustered in as private, Co. G, same date; mustered out with company, November 23, 1898, at Fort Slocum, New York Harbor.

RYAN, JOHN J.—Age, 22 years.   Enlisted, May 17, 1898, at Camp Black, to serve two years; mustered in as private, Co. E, May 24, 1898; mustered out with company, November 23, 1898, at Fort Slocum, New York Harbor.

RYAN, LAWRENCE F.—Age, 31 years.   Enlisted, July 5, 1898, at Brooklyn, to serve two years; mustered in as private, Co. D, same date; transferred to Co. M, July 15, 1898; mustered out with company, November 23, 1898, at Fort Slocum, New York Harbor.

RYAN, JR., PATRICK HENRY.—Age, 21 years.   Enlisted, June 20, 1898, at New York city, to serve two years; mustered in as private, Co. B, same date; mustered out with company, November 23, 1898, at Fort Slocum, New York Harbor.

SAHRING, GUSTAVE ADOLPH.—Age, 19 years.   Enlisted, June 23, 1898, at New York city, to serve two years; mustered in as private, Co. B, same date; mustered out with company, November 23, 1898, at Fort Slocum, New York Harbor.

SALCH, GEORGE J.—Age, 24 years. Enlisted, May 21, 1898, at Camp Black, to serve two years; mustered in as private, Co. E, May 24, 1898;-mustered out with company, November 23, 1898, at Fort Slocum, New York Harbor.

SALTER, WILLIAM H.—Age, 23 years. Enlisted, May 17, 1898, at Camp Black, to serve two years; mustered in as private, Co. E, May 24, 1898; mustered out with company, November 23, 1898, at Fort Slocum, New York Harbor; also borne as Saulter.

SAMMIS, CHARLES C.—Age, 25 years. Enlisted, May 2, 1898, at Brooklyn, to serve two years; mustered in as private, Co. D, May 24, 1898; mustered out with company, November 24, 1898, at Fort Slocum, New York Harbor.

SAMSEL, AUGUST T.—Age, 22 years. Enlisted, June 29, 1898, at New York city, to serve two years; mustered in as private, Co. C, same date; mustered out with company, November 23, 1898, at Fort Slocum, New York Harbor.

SANDERSON, EDGAR.—Age, 37 years. Enlisted, June 29, 1898, at New York city, to serve two years; mustered in as private, Co. K, same date; mustered out with company, November 23, 1898, at Fort Slocum, New York Harbor.

SASS, ALFRED.—Age, 18 years. Enlisted, May 2, 1898, at Brooklyn, to serve two years; mustered in as private, Co. L, May 24, 1898; mustered out with company, November 23, 1898, at Fort Slocum, New York Harbor.

SAYERS, FRED.—Age, 23 years. Enlisted, May 23, 1898, at Camp Black, to serve two years; mustered in as private, Co. K, May 24, 1898; discharged, October 15, 1898, at Fort Slocum, New York Harbor.

SAYLES, JULIUS A.—Age, 22 years. Enlisted, May 9, 1898, at New York city, to serve two years; mustered in as corporal, Co. G, May 24, 1898; promoted sergeant, May 31. 1898; mustered out with company, November 23, 1898, at Fort Slocum, New York Harbor.

SCHAADT, LOUIS M.—Age, 26 years. Enlisted, May 20, 1898, at Camp Black, to serve two years; mustered in as private, Co. I, May 24, 1898; mustered out with company, November 23, 1898, at Fort Slocum, New York Harbor; also borne as Schaddt.

SCHAEFER, FREDERICK.—Age, 21 years. Enlisted, May 9, 1898, at New York city, to serve two years; mustered in as private, Co. C, May 24, 1898; mustered out with company, November 23, 1898, at Fort Slocum, New York Harbor.

SCHAEFER, HENRY.—Age, 28 years. Enlisted, May 9, 1898, at New York city, to serve two years; mustered in as sergeant, Co. G, May 24, 1898; mustered out with company, November 23, 1898, at Fort Slocum, New York Harbor.

SCHAEFER, JOSEPH.—Age, 19 years. Enlisted, May 14, 1898, at Hempstead, to serve two years; mustered in as private, Co. M, May 24, 1898; mustered out with company, November 23, 1898, at Fort Slocum, New York Harbor.

SCHAN, GEORGE W.—Age, 19 years. Enlisted, May 9, 1898, at New York city, to serve two years; mustered in as private, Co. A, May 24, 1898; discharged October 3, 1898, at Fort Slocum, New York Harbor.

SCHAUER, EDWARD R.—Age, 19 years. Enlisted, May 2, 1898, at Brooklyn, to serve two years; mustered in as private, Co. D, May 24, 1898; mustered out with company, November 23, 1898, at Fort Slocum, New York Harbor.

SCHEIDECKER, EDWARD J.—Age, 21 years. Enlisted, May 2, 1898, at Brooklyn, to serve two years; mustered in as private, Co. M, May 24, 1898; mustered out with company, November 23, 1898, at Fort Slocum, New York Harbor.

SCHENCK, REGINALD H.—Age, 21 years. Enlisted, May 9, 1898, at New York city, to serve two years; mustered in as private, Co. C, May 24, 1898; discharged, October 25, 1898, at Fort Slocum, New York Harbor.

SCHENCK, TRUMAN T.—Age, 21 years. Enlisted, May 8, 1898, at Camp Black, to serve two years; mustered in as musician, Co. F, May 24, 1898; mustered out with company, November 23, 1898, at Fort Slocum, New York Harbor.

SCHENNEHEN, PAUL.—Age, 35 years. Enlisted, May 22, 1898, at Camp Black, to serve two years; mustered in as private, Co. B, May 24, 1898; mustered out with company, November 23, 1898, at Fort Slocum, New York Harbor.

SCHEPP, WILLIAM E.—Age, 21 years. Enlisted, May 2, 1898, at Brooklyn, to serve two years; mustered in as private, Co. L, May 24, 1898; mustered out with company, November 23, 1898, at Fort Slocum, New York Harbor.

SCHERRER, JR., CONRAD.—Age, 27 years. Enlisted, May 20, 1898, at Camp Black, to serve two years; mustered in as private, Co. I, May 24, 1898; mustered out with company, November 23, 1898, at Fort Slocum, New York Harbor.

SCHEURER, JOHN H.—Age, 32 years. Enlisted, May 9, 1898, at New York city, to serve two years; mustered in as private, Co. H, May 24, 1898; mustered out with company, November 23, 1898, at Fort Slocum, New York Harbor.

SCHLECHT, EDWIN CHARLES.—Age, 24 years. Enlisted, May 9, 1898, at New York city, to serve two years; mustered in as corporal, Co. K, May 24, 1898; mustered out with company, November 23, 1898, at Fort Slocum, New York Harbor.

SCHLEY, GEORGE B.—Age, 21 years. Enlisted, May 9, 1898, at New York city, to serve two years; mustered in as corporal, Co. B, May 24, 1898; mustered out with company, November 23, 1898, at Fort Slocum, New York Harbor.

SCHMIDT, JOHN.—Age, 32 years. Enlisted, May 15, 1898, at Camp Black, to serve two years; mustered in as private, Co. I, May 24, 1898; appointed artificer, October 26, 1898; mustered out with company, November 23, 1898, at Fort Slocum, New York Harbor.

SCHNAARS, HERMAN G.—Age, 24 years. Enlisted, May 12, 1898, at Camp Black, to serve two years; mustered in as private, Co. F, May 24, 1898; deserted, September 17, 1898, at Willet's Point, N. Y.; also borne as Schneers.

SCHNARR, JOHN.—Age, 25 years. Enlisted, May 17, 1898, at Camp Black, to serve two years; mustered in as private, Co. K, May 24, 1898; mustered out with company, November 23, 1898, at Fort Slocum, New York Harbor.

SCHNEIDER, JOHN.—Age, 21 years. Enlisted, May 20, 1898, at Camp Black, to serve two years; mustered in as private, Co. K, May 24, 1898; appointed musician, no date; mustered out with company, November 23, 1898, at Fort Slocum, New York Harbor.

SCHRAMM, WILLIAM.—Age, 23 years. Enlisted, May 9, 1898, at New York city, to serve two years; mustered in as private, Co. G, May 24, 1898; promoted corporal, May 31, 1898; mustered out with company, November 23, 1898, at Fort Slocum, New York Harbor.

SCHREIBER, CHARLES A.—Age, 22 years. Enlisted, June 17, 1898, at New York city, to serve two years; mustered in as private, Co. E, same date; mustered out with company, November 23, 1898, at Fort Slocum, New York Harbor.

SCHUBERT, FREDERICK B.—Age, 25 years. Enlisted, June 1, 1898, at Hempstead, to serve two years; mustered in as private, Co. C, June 3, 1898; discharged, October 30, 1898, at Fort Slocum, New York Harbor.

SCHUESSLER, ROBERT W.—Age, 20 years. Enlisted, May 9, 1898, at New York city, to serve two years; mustered in as sergeant, Co. A, May 24, 1898; promoted quartermaster-sergeant, August 5, 1898; reduced to sergeant, November 11, 1898; mustered out with company, November 23, 1898, at Fort Slocum, New York Harbor.

SCHUHMANN, SAMUEL.—Age, 27 years.   Enlisted, May 9, 1898, at New York city, to serve two years; mustered in as private, Co. G, May 24, 1898; promoted corporal, May 31, 1898; mustered out with company, November 23, 1898, at Fort Slocum, New York Harbor.

SCHULEIN, HENRY J.—Age, 23 years. Enlisted, July 1, 1898, at New York city, to serve two years; mustered in as private, Co. C, same date; mustered out with company, November 23, 1898, at Fort Slocum, New York Harbor.

SCHWAB, FREDERICK.—Age, 18 years.   Enlisted, June 24, 1898, at New York city, to serve two years; mustered in as private, Co. I, same date; mustered out with company, November 23, 1898, at Fort Slocum, New York Harbor.

SCHWARTE, JURGEN H.—Age, 25 years.   Enlisted, May 9, 1898, at New York city, to serve two years; mustered in as private, Co. C, May 24, 1898; promoted corporal, July 29, 1898; mustered out with company, November 23, 1898, at Fort Slocum, New York Harbor.

SCHWARTZ, HENRY.—Age, 23 years.   Enlisted, June 28, 1898, at New York city, to serve two years; mustered in as private, Co. K, same date; mustered out with company, November 23, 1898, at Fort Slocum, New York Harbor.

SCOFIELD, EDWARD S.—Age, 34 years.   Enlisted, May 18, 1898, at Camp Black, to serve two years; mustered in as private, Co. B, May 24, 1898; promoted corporal, June 30, 1898; returned to ranks, August 4, 1898; mustered out with company, November 23, 1898, at Fort Slocum, New York Harbor.

SCOTT, JOHN DOUGLASS.—Age, 22 years.   Enlisted, June 21, 1898, at New York city, to serve two years; mustered in as private, Co. I, same date; mustered out with company, November 23, 1898, at Fort Slocum, New York Harbor.

SCULLY, JOHN T.—Age, 19 years.   Enlisted, May 9, 1898, at New York city, to serve two years; mustered in as private, Co. C, May 24, 1898; mustered out with company, November 23, 1898, at Fort Slocum, New York Harbor.

SEEBACK, THEODORE.—Age, 33 years.   Enlisted, June 29, 1898, at New York city, to serve two years; mustered in as private, Co. G, same date; discharged for disability, June 22, 1898, at Willet's Point, N. Y.

SEEGER, CHARLES A.—Age, 22 years.   Enlisted, May 2, 1898, at Brooklyn, to serve two years; mustered in as musician, Co. D, May 24, 1898; mustered out with company, November 23, 1898, at Fort Slocum, New York Harbor.

SEIGEL, JOSEPH A.—Age, 19 years.   Enlisted, May 9, 1898, at New York city, to serve two years; mustered in as private, Co. K, May 24, 1898; mustered out with company, November 23, 1898, at Fort Slocum, New York Harbor; also borne as Siegel.

SELIG, MORRIS.—Age, 21 years.   Enlisted, May 20, 1898, at Camp Black, to serve two years; mustered in as private, Co. K, May 24, 1898; deserted, October 28, 1898, at Fort Slocum, New York Harbor.

SENN, CHARLES.—Age, 24 years.   Enlisted, June 21, 1898, at New York city, to serve two years; mustered in as private, Co. B, same date; mustered out with company, November 23, 1898, at Fort Slocum, New York Harbor.

SERR, DANIEL F.—Age, 23 years. Enlisted, May 2, 1898, at Brooklyn, to serve two years; mustered in as private, Co. L, May 24, 1898; mustered out with company, November 23, 1898, at Fort Slocum, New York Harbor.

SERRELL, EDWARD PAUL.—Age, 25 years. Enlisted, May 9, 1898, at New York city, as corporal, to serve two years; mustered in as sergeant, Co. B, May 24, 1898; promoted first sergeant, September 9, 1898; mustered in as second lieutenant, November 22, 1898; mustered out with company, November 23, 1898, at Fort Slocum, New York Harbor; commissioned second lieutenant, November 1, 1898, with rank from same date, vice Hamilton, promoted.

SÈVIGNÉ, JOHN A.—Age, 22 years. Enlisted, May 9, 1898, at New York city, to serve two years; mustered in as private, Co. I, May 24, 1898; mustered out with company, November 23, 1898, at Fort Slocum, New York Harbor.

SEXTON, JOHN.—Age, 20 years. Enlisted, May 9, 1898, at New York city, to serve two years; mustered in as private, Co. H, May 24, 1898; mustered out with company, November 23, 1898, at Fort Slocum, New York Harbor.

SHAFER, MORGAN R.—Age, 22 years. Enlisted, May 9, 1898, at New York city, to serve two years; mustered in as private, Co. E, May 24, 1898; discharged, September 17, 1898.

SHEFFIELD, WILLIAM A.—Age, 22 years. Enlisted, June 27, 1898, at Brooklyn, to serve two years; mustered in as private, Co. D, same date; mustered out with company, November 23, 1898, at Fort Slocum, New York Harbor.

SHEPARD, JR., WILLIAM E.—Age, 25 years. Enlisted, May 9, 1898, at New York city, to serve two years; mustered in as private, Co. G, May 24, 1898; mustered out with company, November 23, 1898, at Fort Slocum, New York Harbor.

SHERIDAN, EDWARD J.—Age, 31 years. Enlisted, May 9, 1898, at New York city, to serve two years; mustered in as first sergeant, Co. A, May 24, 1898; reduced to sergeant, August 4, 1898; mustered out with company, November 23, 1898, at Fort Slocum, New York Harbor.

SHERIDAN, JOHN J.—Age, 21 years. Enlisted, May 12, 1898, at Camp Black, to serve two years; mustered in as private, Co. F, May 24, 1898; mustered out with company, November 23, 1898, at Fort Slocum, New York Harbor.

SHERLOCK, JAMES A.—Age, 39 years. Enlisted, June 18, 1898, at New York city, to serve two years; mustered in as private, Co. B, same date; mustered out with company, November 23, 1898, at Fort Slocum, New York Harbor.

SHINN, CHARLES P.—Age, 28 years. Enlisted, May 2, 1898, at Brooklyn, to serve two years; mustered in as first sergeant, Co. L, May 24, 1898; mustered out with company, November 23, 1898, at Fort Slocum, New York Harbor.

SHORT, WILLIAM H.—Age, 19 years. Enlisted, May 2, 1898, at Brooklyn, to serve two years; mustered in as private, Co. M, May 24, 1898; mustered out with company, November 23, 1898, at Fort Slocum, New York Harbor.

SHUTTLEWORTH, WALTER E.—Age, 21 years. Enlisted, May 9, 1898, at New York city, to serve two years; mustered in as private, Co. K, May 24, 1898; promoted corporal, November 5, 1898; mustered out with company, November 23, 1898, at Fort Slocum, New York Harbor.

SIEGEL, JOSEPH A., see Joseph A. Seigel.

SIMPSON, CHARLES E.—Age, 29 years. Enlisted, July 5, 1898, at Brooklyn, to serve two years mustered in as private, Co. M, same date; mustered out with company, November 23, 1898, at Fort Slocum, New York Harbor.

SINCLAIR, HUGH S. M.—Age, 28 years. Enlisted, May 9, 1898, at New York city, to serve two years; mustered in as private, Co. C, May 24, 1898; discharged, October 15, 1898, at Fort Slocum, New York Harbor.

SKELLY, JOHN A.—Age, 20 years. Enlisted, May 2, 1898, at Brooklyn, to serve two years; mustered in as private, Co. M, May 24, 1898; mustered out with company, November 23, 1898, at Fort Slocum, New York Harbor.

SKELLY, THOMAS A.—Age, 23 years. Enlisted, May 9, 1898, at New York city, to serve two years; mustered in as private, Co. G, May 24, 1898; mustered out with company, November 23, 1898, at Fort Slocum, New York Harbor.

SKELTON, WILLIAM H.—Age, 28 years. Enlisted, May 2, 1898, at Brooklyn, to serve two years; mustered in as sergeant, Co. M, May 24, 1898; mustered out with company, November 23, 1898, at Fort Slocum, New York Harbor.

SLATER, WALTER L.—Age, 21 years. Enlisted, May 12, 1898, at Camp Black, to serve two years; mustered in as private, Co. D, May 24, 1898; mustered out with company, November 23, 1898, at Fort Slocum, New York Harbor.

SLATTERY, MATTHEW FRANCIS.—Age, 24 years. Enlisted, June 24, 1898, at New York city, to serve two years; mustered in as private, Co. B. same date; mustered out with company, November 23, 1898, at Fort Slocum, New York Harbor.

SLAYTON, FRANK N.—Age, 25 years. Enlisted, May 9, 1898, at New York city, to serve two years; mustered in as private, Co. K, May 24, 1898; discharged, to date, November 16, 1898.

SLAZENGER-MOSS, MARCUS.—Age, 44 years. Enlisted, May 9, 1898, at New York city, to serve two years; mustered in as sergeant, Co. I, May 24, 1898; mustered out with company, November 23, 1898, at Fort Slocum, New York Harbor.

SLY, CHARLES S.—Age, — years. Enlisted, November 1, 1898, at Fort Slocum, to serve two years; mustered in as cook, Co. G, same date; returned to ranks, November 6, 1898; mustered out with company, November 23, 1898, at Fort Slocum, New York Harbor.

SMART, MELVIN.—Age, 28 years. Enlisted, May 11, 1898, at Camp Black, to serve two years; mustered in as private, Co. A, May 24, 1898; mustered out with company, November 23, 1898, at Fort Slocum, New York Harbor.

SMELTZER, HOMER E.—Age, 30 years. Enlisted, May 2, 1898, at Brooklyn, to serve two years; mustered in as private, Co. D, May 24, 1898; mustered out with company, November 23, 1898, at Fort Slocum, New York Harbor.

SMILEY, WILLIAM B.—Age, 24 years. Enlisted, May 9, 1898, at New York city, to serve two years; mustered in as private, Co. C, May 24, 1898; promoted corporal, July 29, 1898; mustered out with company, November 23, 1898, at Fort Slocum, New York Harbor.

SMITH, BYRON B.—Age, 21 years. Enlisted, June 4, 1898, at Hempstead, to serve two years; mustered in as private, Co. M, June 7, 1898; mustered out with company, November 23, 1898, at Fort Slocum, New York Harbor.

SMITH, CHARLES H.—Age, 25 years. Enlisted, May 9, 1898, at New York city, to serve two years; mustered in as quartermaster sergeant, Co. I, May 24, 1898; mustered out with company, November 23, 1898, at Fort Slocum, New York Harbor.

SMITH, CHARLES O.—Age, 26 years. Enlisted, June 22, 1898, at Brooklyn, to serve two years; mustered in as private, Co. L, same date; mustered out with company, November 23, 1898, at Fort Slocum, New York Harbor.

SMITH, CLARENCE W.—Age, 34 years. Enrolled, May 2, 1898, at Brooklyn, to serve two years; mustered in as first lieutenant, Co. L, May 24, 1898; mustered out with company, November 23, 1898, at Fort Slocum, New York Harbor; commissioned first lieutenant, May 24, 1898, with rank from same date, original.

SMITH, CYRUS E.—Age, 21 years. Enlisted, May 2, 1898, at Brooklyn, to serve two years; mustered in as private, Co. L, May 24, 1898; mustered out with company, November 23, 1898, at Fort Slocum, New York Harbor.

SMITH, GEORGE Z.—Age, 21 years. Enlisted, May 2, 1898, at Brooklyn, to serve two years; mustered in as private, Co. L, May 24, 1898; mustered out with company, November 23, 1898, at Fort Slocum, New York Harbor.

SMITH, HARRY, FRANK.—Age, 26 years. Enlisted, June 30, 1898, at New York city, to serve two years; mustered in as private, Co. K, same date; mustered out with company, November 23, 1898, at Fort Slocum, New York Harbor.

SMITH, JR., HORATIO D.—Age, 21 years. Enlisted, July 6, 1898, at Brooklyn, to serve two years; mustered in as private, Co. D, same date; mustered out with company, November 23, 1898, at Fort Slocum, New York Harbor.

SMITH, JOHN.—Age, 38 years. Enlisted, June 29, 1898, at New York city, to serve two years; mustered in as private, Co. G, same date; mustered out with company, November 23, 1898, at Fort Slocum, New York Harbor.

SMITH, JOHN J.—Age, 21 years. Enlisted, June 21, 1898, at New York city, to serve two years; mustered in as private, Co. E, same date; mustered out with company, November 23, 1898, at Fort Slocum, New York Harbor.

SMITH, JOHN J.—Age, 23 years. Enlisted, June 29, 1898, at New York city, to serve two years; mustered in as private, Co. C, same date; deserted, July 28, 1898, at Fort Schuyler, New York Harbor.

SMITH, JOHN THOMAS.—Age, 24 years. Enlisted, June 28, 1898, at New York city, to serve two years; mustered in as private, Co. G, same date; mustered out with company, November 23, 1898, at Fort Slocum, New York Harbor.

SMITH, THOMAS L.—Age, 25 years. Enlisted, June 28, 1898, at Brooklyn, to serve two years; mustered in as private, Co. F, same date; deserted, June 28, 1898, at Brooklyn, N. Y.

SMOCK, ABNER W.—Age, 21 years. Enlisted, May 9, 1898, at New York city, to serve two years; mustered in as private, Co. A, May 24, 1898; mustered out with company, November 23, 1898, at Fort Slocum, New York Harbor.

SNOWBER, JOHN L.—Age, 23 years. Enlisted, May 9, 1898, at New York city, to serve two years; mustered in as private, Co. H, May 24, 1898; mustered out with company, November 23, 1898, at Fort Slocum, New York Harbor.

SNYDER, GUSTAVE A.—Age, 22 years. Enlisted, May 9, 1898, at New York city, to serve two years; mustered in as private, Co. A, May 24, 1898; promoted corporal, July 29, 1898; mustered out with company, November 23, 1898, at Fort Slocum, New York Harbor.

SNYDER, WILLIAM CHARLES.—Age, 21 years. Enlisted, June 23, 1898, at New York city, to serve two years; mustered in as private, Co. B, same date; mustered out with company, November 23, 1898, at Fort Slocum, New York Harbor.

SOMMERVILLE, JOHN.—Age, 25 years. Enlisted, May 9, 1898, at New York city, to serve two years; mustered in as corporal, Co. B, May 24, 1898; discharged, October 15, 1898, at Fort Slocum, New York Harbor.

SPAHR, HENRY.—Age, 19 years. Enlisted, May 20, 1898, at Camp Black, to serve two years; mustered in as private, Co. E, May 24, 1898; mustered out with company, November 23, 1898, at Fort Slocum, New York Harbor.

SPATER, HENRY H.—Age, 21 years. Enlisted, May 9, 1898, at New York city, to serve two years; mustered in as private, Co. K, May 24, 1898; mustered out with company, November 23, 1898, at Fort Slocum, New York Harbor.

SPATH, GEORGE J.—Age, 28 years. Enlisted, May 9, 1898, at New York city, to serve two years; mustered in as private, Co. B, May 24, 1898; appointed artificer, November 1, 1898; mustered out with company, November 23, 1898, at Fort Slocum, New York Harbor.

SPATZ, LOUIS.—Age, 23 years. Enlisted, May 9, 1898, at New York city, to serve two years; mustered in as private, Co. G, May 24, 1898; mustered out with company, November 23, 1898, at Fort Slocum, New York Harbor.

SPAULDING, HORACE W.—Age, 22 years. Enlisted, May 9, 1898, at New York city, to serve two years; mustered in as private, Co. B, May 24, 1898; transferred to Co. G, June 24, 1898; mustered out with company, November 23, 1898, at Fort Slocum, New York Harbor.

SPAULDING, JOHN C.—Age, 27 years. Enlisted, May 9, 1898, at New York city, to serve two years; mustered in as private, Co. C, May 24, 1898; discharged, October 29, 1898, at Fort Slocum, New York Harbor.

SPEAKMAN, WALTER.—Age, 21 years. Enlisted, May 2, 1898, at Brooklyn, to serve two years; mustered in as private, Co. F, May 24, 1898; mustered out with company, November 23, 1898, at Fort Slocum, New York Harbor.

SPECKMAN, CHARLES A.—Age, 23 years. Enlisted, June 21, 1898, at New York city, to serve two years; mustered in as private, Co. E, same date; mustered out with company, November 23, 1898, at Fort Slocum, New York Harbor.

SPELMAN, GEORGE F.—Age, 25 years. Enlisted, May 9, 1898,
at New York city, to serve two years; mustered in as private,
Co. A, May 24, 1898; promoted corporal, July 29, 1898; mustered out with company, November 23, 1898, at Fort Slocum,
New York Harbor.

SPELMAN, WILLIAM.—Age, 30 years. Enlisted, May 9, 1898,
at New York city, to serve two years; mustered in as private,
Co. A, May 24, 1898; mustered out with company, November 23,
1898, at Fort Slocum, New York Harbor.

SPROUL, CHARLES L.—Age, 24 years. Enlisted, May 21, 1898,
at Camp Black, to serve two years; mustered in as private, Co.
D, May 24, 1898; promoted corporal, July 1, 1898; mustered out
with company, November 23, 1898, at Fort Slocum, New York
Harbor.

STACY, ALBERT E.—Age, 21 years. Enlisted, May 2, 1898, at
Brooklyn, to serve two years; mustered in as private, Co. D,
May 24, 1898; discharged, October 26, 1898, at Fort Slocum,
New York Harbor.

STAPLETON, JOHN J.—Age, 21 years. Enlisted, May 9, 1898,
at New York city, to serve two years; mustered in as private,
Co. C, May 24, 1898; mustered out with company, November 23,
1898, at Fort Slocum, New York Harbor.

STAUFFER, ALBERT H.—Age, 18 years. Enlisted, June 27,
1898, at Brooklyn, to serve two years; mustered in as private,
Co. M, same date; mustered out with company, November 23,
1898, at Fort Slocum, New York Harbor.

ST. DENNIS, WALDEMAR.—Age, 21 years. Enlisted, May 9,
1898, at New York city, to serve two years; mustered in as private, Co. G, May 24, 1898; mustered out with company, November 23, 1898, at Fort Slocum, New York Harbor.

STEAD, WILLIAM A.—Age, 21 years. Enlisted, June 20, 1898,
at New York city, to serve two years; mustered in as private,
Co. E, same date; mustered out with company, November 23,
1898, at Fort Slocum, New York Harbor.

STEARNS, FREDERICK HUGO.—Age, 29 years. Enlisted,
May 9, 1898, at New York city, to serve two years; mustered in
as private, Co. E, May 24, 1898; discharged, October 15, 1898.

STEEN, JAMES.—Age, 22 years. Enlisted, May 9, 1898, at New York city, to serve two years; mustered in as private, Co. E, May 24, 1898; mustered out with company, November 23, 1898, at Fort Slocum, New York Harbor.

STEEN, THOMAS J.—Age, 23 years. Enlisted, May 9, 1898, at New York city, to serve two years; mustered in as private, Co. E, May 24, 1898; mustered out with company, November 23, 1898, at Fort Slocum, New York Harbor.

STEGMAIR, FRANK.—Age, 29 years. Enlisted, June 24, 1898, at New York city, to serve two years; mustered in as private, Co. B, June 25, 1898; mustered out with company, November 23, 1898, at Fort Slocum, New York Harbor.

STELBEN, JOHN P.—Age, 24 years. Enlisted, June 30, 1898, at New York city, to serve two years; mustered in as private, Co. C, same date; mustered out with company, November 23, 1898, at Fort Slocum, New York Harbor.

STERLING, WARNER S.—Age, 19 years. Enlisted, May 9, 1898, at New York city, to serve two years; mustered in as private, Co. E, May 24, 1898; mustered out with company, November 23, 1898, at Fort Slocum, New York Harbor.

STERNBERGER, HENRY S.—Age, 33 years. Enrolled, May 9, 1898, at New York city, to serve two years; mustered in as second lieutenant, Co. K, May 24, 1898; transferred to Co. B, June 22, 1898; mustered in as first lieutenant, Co. K, September 25, 1898; as quartermaster, October 14, 1898; mustered out with regiment, November 23, 1898, at Fort Slocum, New York Harbor; commissioned second lieutenant, May 24, 1898, with rank from same date, original; first lieutenant, September 25, 1898, with rank from same date, vice Barber, discharged; quartermaster, October 14, 1898, with rank from same date, vice Carey, discharged.

STEVENS, WILLIAM.—Age, 21 years. Enlisted, July 1, 1898, at New York city, to serve two years; mustered in as private, Co. A, same date; mustered out with company, November 23, 1898, at Fort Slocum, New York Harbor.

STEVENSON, GEORGE A.—Age, 19 years. Enlisted, May 9, 1898, at New York city, to serve two years; mustered in as private, Co. A, May 24, 1898; mustered out with company, November 23, 1898, at Fort Slocum, New York Harbor.

STEWART, REGINALD.—Age, 22 years. Enlisted, May 9, 1898, at New York city, to serve two years; mustered in as private, Co. C, May 24, 1898; deserted, June 28, 1898, at Fort Schuyler, New York Harbor.

STIGER, AUGUSTUS K.—Age, 34 years. Enlisted, May 9, 1898, at New York city, to serve two years; mustered in as sergeant, Co. A, May 24, 1898; promoted first sergeant, August 4, 1898; mustered out with company, November 23, 1898, at Fort Slocum, New York Harbor.

STILL, GARRISON WALL.—Age, 37 years. Enlisted, June 28, 1898, at New York city, to serve two years; mustered in as private, Co. G, same date; deserted, November 21, 1898.

STINER, MUNROE.—Age, 22 years. Enlisted, May 2, 1898, at Brooklyn, to serve two years; mustered in as private, Co. D, May 24, 1898; promoted corporal, September 1, 1898; mustered out with company, November 23, 1898, at Fort Slocum, New York Harbor.

STOKER, GEORGE H.—Age, 29 years. Enlisted, May 2, 1898, at Brooklyn, to serve two years; mustered in as private, Co. M, May 24, 1898; mustered out with company, November 23, 1898, at Fort Slocum, New York Harbor.

STOLPE, WILLIAM.—Age, 29 years. Enlisted, May 24, 1898, at Camp Black, to serve two years; mustered in as private, Co. K, same date; deserted, October 28, 1898.

STONEHOUSE, THOMAS A.—Age, 19 years. Enlisted, May 2, 1898, at Brooklyn, to serve two years; mustered in as private, Co. M, May 24, 1898; mustered out with company, November 23, 1898, at Fort Slocum, New York Harbor.

STORM, HERBERT EDGAR.—Age, 21 years. Enlisted, July 5, 1898, at New York city, to serve two years; mustered in as private, Co. K, same date; mustered out with company, November 23, 1898, at Fort Slocum, New York Harbor.

STOTT, FRANK I.—Age, 32 years. Enrolled, May 9, 1898, at New York city, to serve two years; mustered in as captain, Co. I, May 24, 1898; mustered out with company, November 23, 1898, at Fort Slocum, New York Harbor; commissioned captain, May 24, 1898, with rank from same date, original.

STROUSE, CLARENCE A.—Age, 26 years. Enlisted, May 9, 1898, at New York city, to serve two years; mustered in as first sergeant, Co. K, May 24, 1898; discharged, September 10, 1898, at Fort Schuyler, New York Harbor.

STUART. GEORGE B.—Age, 23 years. Enlisted, May 9, 1898, at New York city, to serve two years; mustered in as private, Co. A, May 24, 1898; promoted corporal, same date; mustered out with company, November 23, 1898, at Fort Slocum, New York Harbor.

STUART, JOHN HOLMES.—Age, 31 years. Enlisted, June 30, 1898, at New York city, to serve two years; mustered in as private, Co. H, same date; mustered out with company, November 23, 1898, at Fort Slocum, New York Harbor.

STUART, MONTROSE.—Age, 22 years. Enlisted, May 9, 1898, at New York city, to serve two years; mustered in as corporal, Co. I, May 24, 1898; promoted sergeant, September 10, 1898; mustered out with company, November 23, 1898, at Fort Slocum, New York Harbor.

STUBBE, FREDERICK H.—Age, 39 years. Enlisted, May 9, 1898, at New York city, to serve two years; mustered in as sergeant, Co. C, May 24, 1898; discharged, November 3, 1898, at Fort Slocum, New York Harbor.

STUHR, FRED C.—Age, 20 years. Enlisted, May 9, 1898, at New York city, to serve two years; mustered in as private, Co. K, May 24, 1898; discharged for disability, September 6, 1898, at Fort Schuyler, New York Harbor.

SUCKOW, WALDO.—Age, 34 years. Enlisted, May 18, 1898, at Camp Black, to serve two years; mustered in as private, Co. K, May 24, 1898; mustered out with company, November 23, 1898, at Fort Slocum, New York Harbor.

SUESS, JR., PHILIP.—Age, 21 years. Enlisted, May 20, 1898, at Camp Black, to serve two years; mustered in as private, Co. I, May 24, 1898; mustered out with company, November 23, 1898, at Fort Slocum, New York Harbor.

SUGARMAN, SOLOMON C.—Age, 21 years. Enlisted, May 9, 1898, at New York city, to serve two years; mustered in as private, Co. H, May 24, 1898; mustered out with company, November 23, 1898, at Fort Slocum, New York Harbor.

SULLIVAN, FRANK EDWARD.—Age, 25 years. Enlisted, June 28, 1898, at New York city, to serve two years; mustered in as private, Co. G, same date; mustered out with company, November 23, 1898, at Fort Slocum, New York Harbor.

SULLIVAN, JOHN THOMAS.—Age, 31 years. Enlisted, June 17, 1898, at New York city, to receive two years; mustered in as private, Co. B, same date; deserted, September 1, 1898.

SULLIVAN, PHILIP V.—Age, 27 years. Enlisted, May 9, 1898, at New York city, to serve two years; mustered in as private, Co. E, May 24, 1898; promoted corporal, July 1, 1898; returned to ranks, October 24, 1898; mustered out with company, November 23, 1898, at Fort Slocum, New York Harbor.

SWAINSKI, ALBERT.—Age, 34 years. Enlisted, May 9, 1898, at New York city, to serve two years; mustered in as private, Co. G, May 24, 1898; promoted corporal, July 1, 1898; mustered out with company, November 23, 1898, at Fort Slocum, New York Harbor, as Swainske.

SWAYZE, THEODORE.—Age, 19 years. Enlisted, May 9, 1898, at New York city, to serve two years; mustered in as private, Co. I, May 24, 1898; promoted corporal, June 30, 1898; mustered out with company, November 23, 1898, at Fort Slocum, New York Harbor.

SWEENEY, CHARLES EDWIN.—Age, 21 years. Enlisted, June 22, 1898, at New York city, to serve two years; mustered in as private, Co. I, same date; mustered out with company, November 23, 1898, at Fort Slocum, New York Harbor.

TACKNEY, JOSEPH.—Age, 27 years. Enlisted, July 5, 1898, at New York city, to serve two years; mustered in as private, Co. H, same date; mustered out with company, November 23, 1898, at Fort Slocum, New York Harbor.

TAMSEN, RUDOLPH M. F.—Age, 35 years. Enlisted, May 2, 1898, at Brooklyn, to serve two years; mustered in as private, Co. F, May 24, 1898; mustered out with company, November 23, 1898, at Fort Slocum, New York Harbor.

TANSEY, FRANK D.—Age, 23 years. Enlisted, May 9, 1898, at New York city, to serve two years; mustered in as private, Co. C, May 24, 1898; mustered out with company, November 23, 1898, at Fort Slocum, New York Harbor.

TAYLOR, EDWARD S.—Age, 21 years. Enlisted, May 9, 1898, at New York city, to serve two years; mustered in as private, Co. G, May 24, 1898; mustered out with company, November 23, 1898, at Fort Slocum, New York Harbor.

TAYLOR, HARRY C.—Age, — years. Enlisted, August 5, 1898, at Willet's Point, to serve two years; mustered in as private, Co. G, same date; mustered out with company, November 23, 1898, at Fort Slocum, New York Harbor.

TAYLOR, MATTHEW DAVENPORT.—Age, 21 years. Enlisted, June 29, 1898, at New York city, to serve two years; mustered in as private, Co. H, same date; mustered out with company, November 23, 1898, at Fort Slocum, New York Harbor.

TEEL, PERCIVAL C.—Age, 22 years. Enlisted, June 18, 1898, at New York city, to serve two years; mustered in as private, Co. E, same date; mustered out with company, November 23, 1898, at Fort Slocum, New York Harbor.

TEETSEL, HARRY B.—Age, 18 years. Enlisted, May 13, 1898, at Camp Black, to serve two years; mustered in as private, Co. D, May 24, 1898; transferred to Co. M, October 17, 1898; mustered out with company, November 23, 1898, at Fort Slocum, New York Harbor.

TEN EYCK, LEONARD.—Age, 21 years. Enlisted, May 9, 1898, at New York city, to serve two years; mustered in as private, Co. A, May 24, 1898; mustered out with company, November 23, 1898, at Fort Slocum, New York Harbor.

TENNEY, MAYNARD A.—Age, 33 years. Enlisted, May 2, 1898, at Brooklyn, to serve two years; mustered in as private, Co. L, May 24, 1898; promoted corporal, August 20, 1898; discharged, September 24, 1898, at Fort Slocum, New York Harbor.

TENNEY, WILLIS R.—Age, 32 years. Enlisted, May 2, 1898, at Brooklyn, to serve two years; mustered in as private, Co. L, May 24, 1898; promoted corporal, August 20, 1898; discharged, September 24, 1898, at Fort Slocum, New York Harbor.

THOMAS, GEORGE F.—Age, 25 years. Enlisted, May 23, 1898, at Camp Black, to serve two years; mustered in as private, Co. F, May 24, 1898; mustered out with company, November 23, 1898, at Fort Slocum, New York Harbor.

THOMPSON, JOSEPH P.—Age, 25 years. Enlisted, May 20, 1898, at Camp Black, to serve two years; mustered in as private, Co. K, May 24, 1898; promoted corporal, November 9, 1898; mustered out with company, November 23, 1898, at Fort Slocum, New York Harbor.

THOMPSON, WILLIAM M.—Age, 24 years. Enlisted, May 2, 1898, at Brooklyn, to serve two years; mustered in as musician, Co. L, May 24, 1898; mustered out with company, November 23, 1898, at Fort Slocum, New York Harbor.

THOMPSON, WINFIELD.—Age, 42 years. Enlisted, June 7, 1898, at New York city, to serve two years; mustered in as private, Co. G, same date; transferred to Co. B, same date; mustered out with company, November 23, 1898, at Fort Slocum, New York Harbor.

THOMSON, JAMES R.—Age, 27 years. Enlisted, May 2, 1898, at Brooklyn, to serve two years; mustered in as private, Co. M, May 24, 1898; mustered out with company, November 23, 1898, at Fort Slocum, New York Harbor.

THORN, FREDERICK L.—Age, 21 years. Enlisted, May 9, 1898, at New York city, to serve two years; mustered in as private, Co. C, May 24, 1898; mustered out with company, November 23, 1898, at Fort Slocum, New York Harbor.

THURBER, CHARLES A.—Age, 28 years. Enlisted, May 2, 1898, at Brooklyn, to serve two years; mustered in as private, Co. F, May 24, 1898; appointed wagoner, same date; promoted corporal, July 1, 1898; mustered out with company, November 23, 1898, at Fort Slocum, New York Harbor.

THURSTON, CHARLES D.—Age, 24 years. Enlisted, May 9, 1898, at New York city, to serve two years; mustered in as sergeant, Co. E, May 24, 1898; mustered out with company, November 23, 1898, at Fort Slocum, New York Harbor.

THURSTON, NATHANIEL B.—Age, 42 years. Enrolled, May 1, 1898, at New York city, to serve two years; mustered in as lieutenant-colonel, May 24, 1898; mustered out with regiment, November 23, 1898, at Fort Slocum, New York Harbor; commissioned lieutenant-colonel, May 24, 1898, with rank from same date, original.

TIERNEY, BENJAMIN P.—Age, 21 years. Enlisted, June 21, 1898, at New York city, to serve two years; mustered in as private, Co. E, same date; mustered out with company, November 23, 1898, at Fort Slocum, New York Harbor.

TIGHE, GEORGE F.—Age, 27 years. Enlisted, May 9, 1898, at New York city, to serve two years; mustered in as quarter-master-sergeant, Co. A, May 24, 1898; reduced to sergeant, August 5, 1898; returned to ranks, October 1, 1898; mustered out with company, November 23, 1898, at Fort Slocum, New York Harbor.

TIGHE, MARTIN E. J.—Age, 19 years. Enlisted, June 18, 1898, at New York city, to serve two years; mustered in as private, Co. I, same date; transferred to Co. B, July 15, 1898; appointed musician, no date; mustered out with company, November 23, 1898, at Fort Slocum, New York Harbor.

TIGHE, THOMAS F.—Age, 35 years. Enlisted, May 9, 1898, at New York city, to serve two years; mustered in as private, Co. A, May 24, 1898; appointed cook, September 1, 1898; mustered out with company, November 23, 1898, at Fort Slocum, New York Harbor.

TILDEN, WALTER S. N.—Age, 26 years. Enlisted, June 17, 1898, at New York city, to serve two years; mustered in as private, Co. I, same date; mustered out with company, November 23, 1898, at Fort Slocum, New York Harbor.

TILTON, ALBERT N.—Age, 23 years. Enlisted, May 2, 1898, at Brooklyn, to serve two years; mustered in as private, Co. L, May 24, 1898; mustered out with company, November 23, 1898, at Fort Slocum, New York Harbor; also borne as Alfred Tilton.

TITUS, EDMUND D.—Age, 29 years. Enlisted, May 2, 1898, at Brooklyn, to serve two years; mustered in as sergeant, Co. D, May 24, 1898; mustered out with company, November 23, 1898, at Fort Slocum, New York Harbor.

TOBIN, WILLIAM J.—Age, 23 years. Enlisted, May 9, 1898, at New York city, to serve two years; mustered in as private, Co. A, May 24, 1898; mustered out with company, November 23, 1898, at Fort Slocum, New York Harbor.

TOBOLA, JOSEPH.—Age, 24 years.   Enlisted, June 30, 1898, at New York city, to serve two years; mustered in as private, Co. H, same date; mustered out with company, November 23, 1898, at Fort Slocum, New York Harbor.

TODD, GEORGE F.—Age, 28 years.   Enlisted, May 2, 1898, at Brooklyn, to serve two years; mustered in as sergeant, Co. M, May 24, 1898; mustered out with company, November 23, 1898, at Fort Slocum, New York Harbor.

TODT, FREDERICK.—Age, 27 years.   Enlisted, May 17, 1898, at Camp Black, to serve two years; mustered in as artificer, Co. E, May 24, 1898; mustered out with company, November 23, 1898, at Fort Slocum, New York Harbor.

TOMLINSON, CHARLES H.—Age, 23 years.   Enlisted, May 9, 1898, at New York city to serve two years; mustered in as private, Co. H, May 24, 1898; mustered out with company, November 23, 1898, at Fort Slocum, New York Harbor.

TOOMEY, THOMAS H.—Age, 24 years.   Enlisted, May 9, 1898, at New York city, to serve two years; mustered in as private, Co. C, May 24, 1898; discharged, October 18, 1898, at Fort Slocum, New York Harbor.

TRAVERS, CHARLES E.—Age, 21 years.   Enlisted, May 2, 1898, at Brooklyn, to serve two years; mustered in as private, Co. L, May 24, 1898; mustered out with company, November 23, 1898, at Fort Slocum, New York Harbor.

TREADWELL, HARRY H.—Age, 42 years.   Enrolled, May 9, 1898, at New York city, to serve two years; mustered in as first lieutenant and regimental adjutant, May 24, 1898; mustered out with regiment, as captain and adjutant, November 23, 1898, at Fort Slocum, New York Harbor; commissioned captain and regimental adjutant, May 24, 1898, with rank from same date, original.

TREADWELL, JR., WILLIAM B.—Age, 18 years.   Enlisted, May 21, 1898, at Camp Black, to serve two years; mustered in as private, Co. B, May 24, 1898; mustered out with company, November 23, 1898, at Fort Slocum, New York Harbor.

TRIER, ROBERT.—Age, 20 years. Enlisted, May 9, 1898, at New York city, to serve two years; mustered in as private, Co. C, May 24, 1898; mustered out with company, November 23, 1898, at Fort Slocum, New York Harbor.

TRIMINGHAM, GEORGE G.—Age, 31 years. Enlisted, May 9, 1898, at Camp Black, to serve two years; mustered in as private, Co. I, May 24, 1898; transferred to Co. B, June 18, 1898; mustered out with company, November 23, 1898, at Fort Slocum, New York Harbor; also borne as George E. and as Primingham.

TRIMM, FORREST E.—Age, 22 years. Enlisted, May 2, 1898, at Brooklyn, to serve two years; mustered in as wagoner, Co. L, May 24, 1898; returned to ranks, June 30, 1898; mustered out with company, November 23, 1898, at Fort Slocum, New York Harbor.

TRUMM, CONRAD.—Age, 24 years. Enlisted, May 9, 1898, at New York city, to serve two years; mustered in as private, Co. H, May 24, 1898; mustered out with company, November 23, 1898, at Fort Slocum, New York Harbor.

TRUMP, WILLIAM H.—Age, 24 years. Enlisted, May 23, 1898, at Camp Black, to serve two years; mustered in as private, Co. A, May 24, 1898; mustered out with company, November 23, 1898, at Fort Slocum, New York Harbor.

TURNER, MALCOLM C.—Age, 42 years. Enlisted, May 9, 1898, at New York city, to serve two years; mustered in as private, Co. C, May 24, 1898; discharged for disability, September 7, 1898, at Fort Schuyler, New York Harbor.

TURPIN, WILLIAM A.—Age, 32 years. Enrolled, May 2, 1898, at Brooklyn, to serve two years; mustered in as captain, Co. M, May 24, 1898; mustered out with company, November 23, 1898, at Fort Slocum, New York Harbor; commissioned captain, May 24, 1898, with rank from same date, original.

ULLRICH, FRANK.—Age, 26 years. Enlisted, June 30, 1898, at New York city, to serve two years; mustered in as private, Co. K, same date; mustered out with company, November 23, 1898, at Fort Slocum, New York Harbor.

UNTERMEYER, LEONARD.—Age, 23 years. Enlisted, May 9, 1898, at New York city, to serve two years; mustered in as private, Co. H, May 24, 1898; discharged, October 7, 1898, at Fort Slocum, New York Harbor.

URLAUB, JOHN M.—Age, 19 years. Enlisted, June 29, 1898, at Brooklyn, to serve two years; mustered in as private, Co. M, same date; mustered out with company, November 23, 1898, at Fort Slocum, New York Harbor.

USHER, BLOOMFIELD.—Age, 33 years. Enrolled, May 9, 1898, at New York city, to serve two years; mustered in as first lieutenant, Co. E, May 24, 1898; mustered out with company, November 23, 1898, at Fort Slocum, New York Harbor; commissioned first lieutenant, May 24, 1898, with rank from same date, original.

UTEMARK, FREDERICK.—Age, 22 years. Enlisted, June 29, 1898, at New York city, to serve two years; mustered in as private, Co. A, same date; mustered out with company, November 23, 1898, at Fort Slocum, New York Harbor.

UTTAL, HARRY.—Age, 20 years. Enlisted, June 20, 1898, at Brooklyn, to serve two years; mustered in as private, Co. L, same date; mustered out with company, November 23, 1898, at Fort Slocum, New York Harbor; also borne as Henry Uttal.

VALENTINE, JOHN W.—Age, 21 years. Enlisted, May 9, 1898, at New York city, to serve two years; mustered in as private, Co. B, May 24, 1898; discharged, October 28, 1898, at Fort Slocum, New York Harbor.

VALENTINE, WILLIAM H.—Age, 23 years. Enlisted, May 2, 1898, at Brooklyn, to serve two years; mustered in as private, Co. D, May 24, 1898; promoted corporal, September 1, 1898; mustered out with company, November 23, 1898, at Fort Slocum, New York Harbor.

VAN AKEN, HARRY LELAND.—Age, 25 years. Enlisted, July 1, 1898, at New York city, to serve two years; mustered in as private, Co. K, same date; mustered out with company, November 23, 1898, at Fort Slocum, New York Harbor.

VAN AUKEN, HARRY V.—Age, 21 years. Enlisted, May 2, 1898, at Brooklyn, to serve two years; mustered in as sergeant, Co. L, May 24, 1898; mustered out with company, November 23, 1898, at Fort Slocum, New York Harbor.

VAN BARTHELD, FERDINAND.—Age, — years. Enlisted, August 13, 1898, at Fort Schuyler, to serve two years; mustered in as private, Co. K, same date; mustered out with company, November 23, 1898, at Fort Slocum, New York Harbor.

VAN BUREN, WILLIAM H.—Age, 22 years. Enlisted, May 21, 1898, at Camp Black, to serve two years; mustered in as private, Co. A, May 24, 1898; mustered out with company, November 23, 1898, at Fort Slocum, New York Harbor.

VAN DAGGE, JAMES E., see James E. Von Dagge.

VANDERBECK, VICTOR.—Age, 22 years. Enlisted, July 5, 1898, at New York city, to serve two years; mustered in as private, Co. K, same date; mustered out with company, November 23, 1898, at Fort Slocum, New York Harbor.

VANDER WEYDE, VINCENT W.—Age, 18 years. Enlisted, May 9, 1898, at New York city, to serve two years; mustered in as private, Co. H, May 24, 1898; mustered out with company, November 23, 1898, at Fort Slocum, New York Harbor.

VAN DYKE, CHARLES W.—Age, 21 years. Enlisted, May 2, 1898, at Brooklyn, to serve two years; mustered in as private, Co. F, May 24, 1898; mustered out with company, November 23, 1898, at Fort Slocum, New York Harbor.

VAN FLEET, CLAIR C.—Age, 24 years. Enlisted, May 9, 1898, at New York city, to serve two years; mustered in as private, Co. I, May 24, 1898; mustered out with company, November 23, 1898, at Fort Slocum, New York Harbor.

VAN HOESEN, WILLIAM E.—Age, 22 years. Enlisted, June 29, 1898, at Brooklyn, to serve two years; mustered in as private, Co. F, same date; mustered out with company, November 23, 1898, at Fort Slocum, New York Harbor.

VAN PELT, GARRETT.—Age, 21 years. Enlisted, May 9, 1898, at New York city, to serve two years; mustered in as private, Co. B, May 24, 1898; mustered out with company, November 23, 1898, at Fort Slocum, New York Harbor.

VAN ROOYEN, WILLIAM.—Age, 21 years. Enlisted, May 2, 1898, at Brooklyn, to serve two years; mustered in as private, Co. M, May 24, 1898; mustered out with company, November 23, 1898, at Fort Slocum, New York Harbor.

VAN ZEE, CLARENCE O., see George B. Van Zee.

VAN ZEE, GEORGE B.—Age, 21 years. Enlisted, May 9, 1898, at New York city, to serve two years; mustered in as private, Co. B, May 24, 1898; transferred to Co. G, June 24, 1898; mustered out with company, November 23, 1898, at Fort Slocum, New York Harbor; also borne as Clarence O. Van Zee.

VARIAN, JOHN T.—Age, 21 years. Enlisted, May 22, 1898, at Camp Black, to serve two years; mustered in as private, Co. I, May 24, 1898; mustered out with company, November 23, 1898, at Fort Slocum, New York Harbor.

VEITH, AUGUST G.—Age, 30 years. Enlisted, May 2, 1898, at Brooklyn, to serve two years; mustered in as private, Co. L, May 24, 1898; appointed artificer, May 25, 1898; mustered out with company, November 23, 1898, at Fort Slocum, New York Harbor.

VELA, FRANK L.—Age, 33 years. Enlisted, May 9, 1898, at New York city, to serve two years; mustered in as private, Co. G, May 24, 1898; mustered out with company, November 23, 1898, at Fort Slocum, New York Harbor.

VICTORY, JOSEPH J.—Age, 25 years. Enlisted, July 1, 1898, at New York city, to serve two years; mustered in as private, Co. C, same date; deserted, September 1, 1898, at Fort Schuyler, New York Harbor.

VINCENT, THOMAS J.—Age, 21 years. Enlisted, July 1, 1898, at Brooklyn, to serve two years; mustered in as private, Co. F, same date; mustered out with company, November 23, 1898, at Fort Slocum, New York Harbor.

VOLLMER, REINHOLD.—Age, 21 years. Enlisted, May 21, 1898, at Camp Black, to serve two years; mustered in as private, Co. B, May 24, 1898; discharged, October 15, 1898, at Fort Slocum, New York Harbor.

VON DAGGE, JAMES E.—Age, 28 years. Enlisted, June 20, 1898, at New York city, to serve two years; mustered in as private, Co. I, same date; mustered out with company, November 23, 1898, at Fort Slocum, New York Harbor; also borne as Van Dagge.

VOSE, CLIFTON.—Age, 27 years. Enlisted, May 2, 1898, at Brooklyn, to serve two years; mustered in as private, Co. L, May 24, 1898; mustered out with company, November 23, 1898, at Fort Slocum, New York Harbor.

WAGNER, CHARLES.—Age, 19 years. Enlisted, May 17, 1898, at Hempstead, to serve two years; mustered in as private, Co. M, May 24, 1898; mustered out with company, November 23, 1898, at Fort Slocum, New York Harbor.

WALDRON, CLARENCE O.—Age, 26 years. Enlisted, May 9, 1898, at New York city, to serve two years; mustered in as private, Co. G, May 24, 1898; mustered out with company, November 23, 1898, at Fort Slocum, New York Harbor.

WALKER, JOHN.—Age, 25 years. Enlisted, June 28, 1898, at New York city, to serve two years; mustered in as private, Co. C, same date; mustered out with company, November 23, 1898, at Fort Slocum, New York Harbor.

WALL, THOMAS B.—Age, 25 years. Enlisted, May 9, 1898, at New York city, to serve two years; mustered in as private, Co. C, May 24, 1898; mustered out with company, November 23, 1898, at Fort Slocum, New York Harbor.

WALLACE, JOHN W.—Age, 23 years. Enlisted, May 9, 1898, at New York city, to serve two years; mustered in as private, Co. H, May 24, 1898; promoted corporal, June 4, 1898; returned to ranks, August 3, 1898; mustered out with company, November 23, 1898, at Fort Slocum, New York Harbor.

WALLACE, MANLEY B.—Age, 19 years. Enlisted, May 9, 1898, at New York city, to serve two years; mustered in as private, Co. C, May 24, 1898; mustered out with company, November 23, 1898, at Fort Slocum, New York Harbor.

WALLIS, JR., EDWIN A.—Age, 18 years. Enlisted, May 21, 1898, at Camp Black, to serve two years; mustered in as private, Co. A, May 24, 1898; mustered out with company, November 23, 1898, at Fort Slocum, New York Harbor.

WALSH, JOHN J.—Age, 25 years. Enlisted, May 9, 1898, at New York city, to serve two years; mustered in as private, Co. G, May 24, 1898; promoted corporal, August 27, 1898; mustered out with company, November 23, 1898, at Fort Slocum, New York Harbor.

WALTON, ARTHUR.—Age 20 years. Enlisted, May 9, 1898, at New York city, to serve two years; mustered in as private, Co. H, May 24, 1898; mustered out with company, November 23, 1898, at Fort Slocum, New York Harbor.

WANDLING, CHARLES S.—Age, 23 years. Enlisted, May 9, 1898, at New York city, to serve two years; mustered in as private, Co. G, May 24, 1898; discharged, October 7, 1898, at Fort Slocum, New York Harbor.

WARD, CHARLES SEAMAN.—Age, 26 years. Enlisted, July 1, 1898, at New York city, to serve two years; mustered in as private, Co. A, same date; deserted, July 6, 1898, at Fort Schuyler, New York Harbor.

WARRINER, EDWARD S.—Age, 32 years. Enlisted, May 18, 1898, at Hempstead, to serve two years; mustered in as quarter-master-sergeant, Co. M, May 24, 1898; mustered out with company, November 23, 1898, at Fort Slocum, New York Harbor.

WATSON, JOHN.—Age, 28 years. Enlisted, July 5, 1898, at New York city, to serve two years; mustered in as private, Co. A, same date; mustered out with company, November 23, 1898, at Fort Slocum, New York Harbor.

WATSON, RICHARD.—Age, 29 years. Enlisted, May 2, 1898, at Brooklyn, to serve two years; mustered in as private, Co. F, May 24, 1898; mustered out with company, November 23, 1898, at Fort Slocum, New York Harbor.

WEBB, CHARLES H.—Age, 29 years. Enlisted, June 28, 1898, at Brooklyn, to serve two years; mustered in as private, Co. F, same date; mustered out with company, November 23, 1898, at Fort Slocum, New York Harbor.

WEBB, EDWARD F.—Age, 21 years. Enlisted, May 9, 1898, at New York city, to serve two years; mustered in as private, Co. G, May 24, 1898; promoted corporal, July 1, 1898; mustered out with company, November 23, 1898, at Fort Slocum, New York Harbor.

WEBER, HENRY.—Age, 22 years. Enlisted, May 9, 1898, at New York city, to serve two years; mustered in as private, Co. B, May 24, 1898; mustered out with company, November 23, 1898, at Fort Slocum, New York Harbor.

WEBER, HENRY.—Age, 22 years. Enlisted, May 9, 1898, at New York city, to serve two years; mustered in as private, Co. C, May 24, 1898; no further record.

WEEKS, WALTER H.—Age, 22 years. Enlisted, May 9, 1898, at New York city, to serve two years; mustered in as private, Co. A, May 24, 1898; mustered out with company, November 23, 1898, at Fort Slocum, New York Harbor.

WEEKS, WILLIAM H.—Age, 26 years. Enlisted, May 9, 1898, at New York city, to serve two years; mustered in as private, Co. G, May 24, 1898; mustered out with company, November 23, 1898, at Fort Slocum, New York Harbor.

WEIL, LEO.—Age, 22 years. Enlisted, May 9, 1898, at New York city, to serve two years; mustered in as private, Co. H, May 24, 1898; mustered out with company, November 23, 1898, at Fort Slocum, New York Harbor.

WEINBERGER, EDWARD.—Age, 28 years. Enlisted, July 2, 1898, at New York city, to serve two years; mustered in as private, Co. H, same date; deserted, September 20, 1898, at Fort Schuyler, New York Harbor.

WELLS, VAN VORST.—Age, 27 years. Enlisted, May 9, 1898, at New York city, to serve two years; mustered in as private, Co. G, May 24, 1898; promoted corporal, May 31, 1898; returned to ranks, no date; promoted corporal, November 6, 1898; mustered out with company, November 23, 1898, at Fort Slocum, New York Harbor.

WELNER, CHRISTOPHER N.—Age, 24 years. Enlisted, May 9, 1898, at New York city, to serve two years; mustered in as private, Co. G, May 24, 1898; mustered out with company, November 23, 1898, at Fort Slocum, New York Harbor.

WEMYSS, WALTER W.—Age, 35 years. Enlisted, May 2, 1898, at Brooklyn, to serve two years; mustered in as artificer, Co. M, May 24, 1898; mustered out with company, November 23, 1898, at Fort Slocum, New York Harbor.

WENCK, FREDERICK A.—Age, 19 years. Enlisted, May 9, 1898, at New York city, to serve two years; mustered in as private, Co. E, May 24, 1898; mustered out with company, November 23, 1898, at Fort Slocum, New York Harbor; also borne as Weuck.

WERNER, RUPERT.—Age, 25 years. Enlisted, May 2, 1898, at Brooklyn, to serve two years; mustered in as musician, Co. M, May 24, 1898; mustered out with company, November 23, 1898, at Fort Slocum, New York Harbor.

WEST, JAMES W.—Age, 23 years. Enlisted, May 12, 1898, at Camp Black, to serve two years; mustered in as private, Co. F, May 24, 1898; mustered out with company, November 23, 1898, at Fort Slocum, New York Harbor.

WEST, WILLIAM G.—Age, 23 years. Enlisted, May 9, 1898, at New York city, to serve two years; mustered in as private, Co. I, May 24, 1898; mustered out with company, November 23, 1898, at Fort Slocum, New York Harbor.

WESTAKE, CLIFTON.—Age, 18 years. Enlisted, June 29, 1898, at Brooklyn, to serve two years; mustered in as private, Co. F, same date; mustered out with company, November 23, 1898, at Fort Slocum, New York Harbor, as Westlake.

WESTBAY, ALBERT.—Age, 23 years. Enlisted, May 2, 1898, at Brooklyn, to serve two years; mustered in as private, Co. F, May 24, 1898; mustered out with company, November 23, 1898, at Fort Slocum, New York Harbor; also borne as Walter Westboy.

WESTBOY, WALTER, see Albert Westhay.

WESTERN, A. CAMPBELL, see A. Campbell Weston.

WESTERVELT, FRED.—Age, 21 years. Enlisted, May 19, 1898, at Camp Black, to serve two years; mustered in as private, Co. B, May 24, 1898; mustered out with company, November 23, 1898, at Fort Slocum, New York Harbor.

WESTLAKE, CLIFTON H., see Clifton H. Westake.

WESTON, A. CAMPBELL.—Age, 21 years. Enlisted, May 17, 1898, at Camp Black, to serve two years; mustered in as private, Co. F, May 24, 1898; mustered out with company, November 23, 1898, at Fort Slocum, New York Harbor, as A. Campbell Western.

WESTON, ALBERT W.—Age, 24 years. Enlisted, May 9, 1898, at New York city, to serve two years; mustered in as private, Co. I, May 24, 1898; promoted corporal, June 30, 1898; mustered out with company, November 23, 1898, at Fort Slocum, New York Harbor.

WEUCK, FREDERICK A., see Frederick A. Werrck.

WHEATCROFT, ALBERT E.—Age, 26 years. Enlisted, May. 2, 1898, at Brooklyn, to serve two years; mustered in as private, Co. L, May 24, 1898; mustered out with company, November 23, 1898, at Fort Slocum, New York Harbor.

WHEELER, MELVILLE J.—Age, 22 years. Enlisted, May 9, 1898, at New York city, to serve two years; mustered in as private, Co. A, May 24, 1898; promoted corporal, November 1, 1898; mustered out with company, November 23, 1898, at Fort Slocum, New York Harbor.

WHITE, GEORGE E.—Age, 23 years. Enlisted, June 17, 1898, at New York city, to serve two years; mustered in as private, Co. B, June 24, 1898; mustered out with company, November 23, 1898, at Fort Slocum, New York Harbor.

WICKWIRE, EDWARD F.—Age, 22 years. Enlisted, May 9, 1898, at New York city, to serve two years; mustered in as private, Co. A, May 24, 1898; transferred to Co. B, June 29, 1898; discharged, October 13, 1898, at Fort Slocum, New York Harbor.

WIEMANN, JOHN A.—Age, 25 years. Enlisted, May 2, 1898, at Brooklyn, to serve two years; mustered in as private, Co. F, May 24, 1898; mustered out with company, November 23, 1898, at Fort Slocum, New York Harbor; also borne as Weimann.

WIGHT, WILLIAM A.—Age, 26 years. Enlisted, May 9, 1898, at New York city, to serve two years; mustered in as private, Co. C, May 24, 1898; mustered out with company, November 23, 1898, at Fort Slocum, New York Harbor.

WILCOX, HARRY.—Age, 38 years. Enlisted, May 9, 1898, at New York city, to serve two years; mustered in as sergeant, chief musician, May 24, 1898; mustered out with regiment, November 23, 1898, at Fort Slocum, New York Harbor.

WILDING, FREDERICK J.—Age, 21 years. Enlisted, May 2, 1898, at Brooklyn, to serve two years; mustered in as private, Co. D, May 24, 1898; discharged, October 27, 1898, at Fort Slocum, New York Harbor; also borne as Frederick L. Wilding.

WILFORD, EDGAR M.—Age, 25 years. Enlisted, May 9, 1898, at New York city, to serve two years; mustered in as private, Co. G, May 24, 1898; promoted corporal, same date; mustered out with company, November 23, 1898, at Fort Slocum, New York Harbor.

WILKENS, CHARLES.—Age, 28 years. Enlisted, June 20, 1898, at New York city, to serve two years; mustered in as private, Co. C, same date; mustered out with company, November 23, 1898, at Fort Slocum, New York Harbor.

WILKINS, JOHN J.—Age, 21 years. Enlisted, May 9, 1898, at New York city, to serve two years; mustered in as private, Co. E, May 24, 1898; mustered out with company, November 23, 1898, at Fort Slocum, New York Harbor.

WILLIAMS, FRANK E.—Age, 25 years. Enlisted, June 1, 1898, at Hempstead, to serve two years; mustered in as private, Co. C, June 3, 1898; appointed cook, August 1, 1898; returned to ranks, October 1, 1898; mustered out with company, November 23, 1898, at Fort Slocum, New York Harbor.

WILLON, JOSEPH.—Age, 21 years. Enlisted, May 9, 1898, at New York city, to serve two years; mustered in as private, Co. B, May 24, 1898; mustered out with company, November 23, 1898, at Fort Slocum, New York Harbor.

WILSON, JAMES M.—Age, 22 years. Enlisted, May 9, 1898, at New York city, to serve two years; mustered in as private, Co. C, May 24, 1898; promoted corporal, May 31, 1898; mustered out with company, November 23, 1898, at Fort Slocum, New York Harbor.

WILSON, JOHN S.—Age, 33 years.   Enrolled, May 2, 1898, at Camp Black, to serve two years; mustered in as major and surgeon, May 24, 1898; mustered out with regiment, November 23, 1898, at Fort Slocum, New York Harbor; commissioned surgeon, May 24, 1898, with rank from same date, original.

WILSON, WILLIAM H.—Age, 20 years.   Enlisted, May 9, 1898, at New York city, to serve two years; mustered in as private, Co. C, May 24, 1898; promoted corporal, July 29, 1898; mustered out with company, November 23, 1898, at Fort Slocum, New York Harbor; subsequent service as second lieutenant, Forty-third Regiment, United States Volunteer Infantry.

WINTER, CHARLES F.—Age, 20 years.   Enlisted, May 9, 1898, at New York city, to serve two years; mustered in as private, Co. E, May 24, 1898; mustered out with company, November 23, 1898, at Fort Slocum, New York Harbor.

WINTER, WILLIAM H.—Age, 27 years.   Enlisted, May 2, 1898, at Brooklyn, to serve two years; mustered in as private, Co. L, May 24, 1898; mustered out with company, November 23, 1898, at Fort Slocum, New York Harbor.

WOLFF, DANIEL.—Age, 32 years.   Enlisted, May 9, 1898, at New York city, to serve two years; mustered in as private, Co. B, May 24, 1898; promoted corporal, June 30, 1898; mustered out with company, November 23, 1898, at Fort Slocum, New York Harbor.

WOLFF, PAUL.—Age, 21 years.   Enlisted, May 9, 1898, at Camp Black, to serve two years; mustered in as private, Co. F, May 24, 1898; mustered out with company, November 23, 1898, at Fort Slocum, New York Harbor.

WOOD, CHARLES D.—Age, 35 years.   Enlisted, May 9, 1898, at New York city, to serve two years; mustered in as private, Co. H, May 24, 1898; appointed musician, May 25, 1898; discharged for disability, November 1, 1898, at Fort Slocum, New York Harbor.

WOOD, EDWARD FRANCIS.—Age, 21 years.   Enlisted, June 28, 1898, at New York city, to serve two years; mustered in as private, Co. K, same date; mustered out with company, November 23, 1898, at Fort Slocum, New York Harbor.

WOOD, JR., ISAAC.—Age, 18 years. Enlisted, May 24, 1898, at Camp Black, to serve two years; mustered in as private, Co. B, same date; mustered out with company, November 23, 1898, at Fort Slocum, New York Harbor.

WOOD, MALCOLM W.—Age, 22 years. Enlisted, May 2, 1898, at Brooklyn, to serve two years; mustered in as private, Co. L, May 24, 1898; promoted corporal, July 1, 1898; mustered out with company, November 23, 1898, at Fort Slocum, New York Harbor.

WOODCOCK, JR., THOMAS S.—Age, 22 years. Enlisted, May 12, 1898, at Camp Black, to serve two years; mustered in as private, Co F, May 24, 1898; mustered out with company, November 23, 1898, at Fort Slocum, New York Harbor.

WOODS, CHARLES.—Age, 22 years. Enlisted, May 9, 1898, at New York city, to serve two years; mustered in as corporal, Co. A, May 24, 1898; mustered out with company, November 23, 1898, at Fort Slocum, New York Harbor.

WOOLSEY, GEORGE.—Age, 23 years. Enlisted, May 12, 1898, at Camp Black, to serve two years; mustered in as private, Co. F, May 24, 1898; appointed artificer, August 10, 1898; mustered out with company, November 23, 1898, at Fort Slocum, New York Harbor.

WORK, JOHN L.—Age, 25 years. Enlisted, May 9, 1898, at New York city, to serve two years; mustered in as private, Co. C, May 24, 1898; mustered out with company, November 23, 1898, at Fort Slocum, New York Harbor.

WORLEY, HENRY W.—Age, 21 years. Enlisted, May 9, 1898, at New York city, to serve two years; mustered in as private, Co. H, May 24, 1898; mustered out with company, November 23, 1898, at Fort Slocum, New York Harbor.

WORRALL, BENJAMIN ALLEN.—Age, 21 years. Enlisted, July 2, 1898, at New York city, to serve two years; mustered in as private, Co. A, same date; mustered out with company, November 23, 1898, at Fort Slocum, New York Harbor.

WORTH, JR., HENRY.—Age, 21 years. Enlisted, June 23, 1898, at Brooklyn, to serve two years; mustered in as private, Co. D, same date; mustered out with company, November 23, 1898, at Fort Slocum, New York Harbor.

WRAGGE, HERMAN.—Age, 21 years. Enlisted, May 9, 1898, at New York city to serve two years; mustered in as private, Co. A, May 24, 1898; mustered out with company, November 23, 1898, at Fort Slocum, New York Harbor.

WRIGHT, JR., FREDERICK A.—Age, 21 years. Enlisted, May 9, 1898, at New York city, to serve two years; mustered in as private, Co. H, May 24, 1898; mustered out with company, November 23, 1898, at Fort Slocum, New York Harbor.

WRIGHT, JR., FREDERICK B.—Age, 21 years. Enlisted, June 17, 1898, at New York city, to serve two years; mustered in as private, Co. A, same date; mustered out with company, November 23, 1898, at Fort Slocum, New York Harbor.

WRIGHT, HAROLD B.—Age, 21 years.   Enlisted, May 2, 1898 at Brooklyn, to serve two years; mustered in as private, Co. M May 24, 1898; mustered out with company, November 23, 1898, at Fort Slocum, New York Harbor.

WRIGHTINGTON, JOHN JOSEPH.—Age, 22 years.   Enlisted, June 28, 1898, at New York city, to serve two years; mustered in as private, Co. K, same date; mustered out with company, November 23, 1898, at Fort Slocum, New York Harbor.

WUMCHELL, LOUIS P.—Age, 23 years.   Enlisted, May 2, 1898, at Brooklyn, to serve two years; mustered in as corporal, Co. D, May 24, 1898; mustered out with company, November 23, 1898, at Fort Slocum, New York Harbor; also borne as Wünschel and Wunschil.

WYNN, CHARLES J.—Age, 21 years.   Enlisted, May 9, 1898, at New York city, to serve two years; mustered in as private, Co. C, May 24, 1898; mustered out with company, November 23, 1898, at Fort Slocum, New York Harbor.

YOUNG, GEORGE C.—Age, 25 years.   Enlisted, May 2, 1898, at Brooklyn, to serve two years; mustered in as private, Co. F, May 24, 1898; mustered out with company, November 23, 1898, at Fort Slocum, New York Harbor.

YOUNIE, GEORGE S.—Age, 20 years.   Enlisted, May 2, 1898, at Brooklyn, to serve two years; mustered in as private, Co. L, May 24, 1898; promoted corporal, October 1, 1898; mustered out with company, November 23, 1898, at Fort Slocum, New York Harbor.

ZABRISKIE, FRANCIS N.—Age, 24 years.   Enlisted, June 3,
1898, at Camp Black, to serve two years; mustered in as private,
Co. A, same date; mustered out with company, November 23,
1898, at Fort Slocum, New York Harbor.

ZAHN, FRANCIS J.—Age, 21 years.   Enlisted, May 2, 1898, at
Brooklyn, to serve two years; mustered in as private, Co. M,
May 24, 1898; mustered out with company, November 23, 1898,
at Fort Slocum, New York Harbor.

ZAHN, PETER.— Age, 22 years.   Enlisted, May 20, 1898, at
Camp Black, to serve two years; mustered in as private, Co. K,
May 24, 1898; mustered out with company, November 23, 1898,
at Fort Slocum, New York Harbor.

ZENDER, AUSTIN R.—Age, 19 years.   Enlisted, May 2, 1898,
at Brooklyn, to serve two years; mustered in as private, Co. M,
May 24, 1898; mustered out with company, November 23, 1898,
at Fort Slocum, New York Harbor.

FORTY-SEVENTH REGIMENT, INFANTRY.

The forty-seventh regiment, national guard, having volunteered its services, was selected in general orders, No. 8, A. G. O., S. N. Y., to enter the service of the United States as a volunteer regiment.

The regiment at that time consisted of eight companies, and at once commenced to fill up its companies and organize four additional ones.

Its history to that date follows:

FORTY-SEVENTH REGIMENT.

(Second Brigade.)

State Armory, Marcy avenue and Heyward street, Brooklyn.

Companies A, B, C, D, E, F, G, H and I were organized in 1862, and company K in 1872. Company C was disbanded in 1878, and companies G and H in 1863. A new company G was organized in 1864, and a new company H in 1878; the latter was disbanded in 1885. The regiment entered the United States service for three months, May 27, 1862, and was mustered out, September 1, 1862. It was re-mustered into service, June 17, 1863, and mustered out, July 23, 1863, by reason of expiration of term of service. It served the state during the draft riots, July, 1863; railroad riots, July, 1877; the quarantine disturbances at Fire Island, September, 1892, and the motormen's strike, January, 1895.

The regiment received authority to place silver rings on the lances of its colors, engraved as follows:

On the national color.—Fort McHenry, Md., 1862; Washington, D. C., 1863.

On the state color.—Draft riots, 1863; Railroad strike, 1877; Fire Island, 1892; Brooklyn, 1895.

In compliance with special orders, No. 73, A. G. O., May 1, 1898, the regiment reported at the Flatbush avenue station of the Long

Island railroad, Brooklyn, at 10 a. m., May 3d, and embarked for Camp Black, near Hempstead, L. I., reporting on arrival to Major-General Charles F. Roe, commanding the national guard.

The four additional companies, having completed their organization, reported at Camp Black, May 11th. Recruiting was continued to fill up and replace the men rejected by the medical officers, and the regiment was fully organized with twelve companies, under the provision of general orders, No. 11, A. G. O., May 3, 1898.

It was mustered into the service of the United States as the " forty-seventh infantry, New York volunteers," May 24, 1898.

Pursuant to special orders, No. 122, department of the east, dated June 6, 1898, Lieutenant-Colonel Hubbell and Major Barthman, with companies A, B, D, E, F, G, I and K, left Camp Black, June 9th, at 9.45 a. m., via Long Island railroad and Stonington line; arrived at Newport, R. I., June 10th.

Lieutenant-Colonel Hubbell and Major Barthman, with companies B, D, F, G, I and K, proceeded to Fort Adams, R. I., and companies A and E, under command of Captain D. C. Sullivan, to Fort Greble, R. I. They arrived at their respective stations about 10 a. m., the same day.

That part of special orders, No. 122, relating to headquarters and companies C, H, L and M reporting at Quanset, R. I., was countermanded.

Special orders, No. 127, department of the east, dated June 11, 1898, directed Colonel Hubbell and Majors Quick and Lyon, with companies C, H, L and M, to report at Fort Adams, R. I., where they arrived on the morning of June 15th.

Companies A and E were by special orders No. 158, department of the east, transferred from Fort Greble to Fort Adams, R. I., where they arrived, July 21st.

The regiment remained in camp at Fort Adams until October 9th, when, pursuant to special orders, No. 159, headquarters of the army, Washington, D. C., it embarked on transport " Manitoba " and sailed the next day at 4 p. m., for Porto Rico. The vessel arrived in the harbor of Ponce, October 15th, and the regiment disembarked, October 18th, proceeding to camp, four and a half miles north of Ponce. The regiment remained there until the afternoon of October 22d, when by order of Brigadier-General Guy V. Henry it broke camp and marched to Ponce, where it embarked on the transport " Chester " and sailed October 23d, for San Juan, leaving on the route detachments at the several assigned stations and relieving at the same time detachments of the fourth infantry, Ohio volunteers.

Arroyo was reached, October 24th, where companies E and K disembarked, to march to Guayama. October 25th, company A was left at Humaco; October 26th, company D at the Isla de Vieques, and October 27th, company F at Fajardo, where it was to take station.

The rest of the regiment then proceeded to San Juan, arriving in the afternoon of the same day. Companies B and G immediately disembarked and proceeded by railroad to the stations assigned them; company B to Rio Piedras and company G to Carolina. The other companies, C, H, I, L and M, disembarked October 28th, and went into camp in front of Fort San Cristobal.

The regiment broke camp, October 29th, and marched to Caguas, twenty-four miles, arriving on October 30th, where companies C, L and M took station. After resting over night, companies H and I took up the march, the former to Cayey, forty-two miles, arriving November 1st, and the latter to Aibonito, fifty-four miles, arriving November 2d. Headquarters were established at Caguas.

It was necessary while at these stations to send out patrols through the surrounding country. The condition of the roads and the distances to be patrolled were such that they were obliged to go out mounted. Native horses were principally used for this purpose. Details were also made of two or more men to remain on plantations where they were well treated by the owners.

The duties performed were of both a military and civil character. The officers earned the highest commendation from both the department and district commanders, as shown by letters of which the following are copies:

HEADQUARTERS DEPARTMENT OF PORTO RICO,

SAN JUAN, *March* 3, 1899.

The Commanding Officer, Forty-Seventh New York Volunteers.

Sir:—I am directed by the major-general commanding the department of Porto Rico to communicate to you, and through you to your regiment, his appreciation of your work while on duty in this department. The orders subordinating the military to the civil authorities were carried out faithfully, although at times the state of affairs was trying and required the exercise of judicious self-control.

The only unfortunate incident that occurred was the murder of a soldier by a civilian at Caguas, which was merely a personal affair, and one that should not reflect upon the regiment, as it was the fault of the citizen that committed the crime.

Very respectfully,

(Signed)   PETER E. TRANT,

First Lieut., First Cav., A. D. C.

HEADQUARTERS DISTRICT OF SAN JUAN,

SAN JUAN, P. R., *March* 1, 1899.

MY DEAR COLONEL HUBBELL:

As I am about to start to attend to some military duties, which takes me to the western part of the island of Porto Rico, it is not probable that I shall see you again before you and your regiment embark on the "Manitoba" to return to the United States, I therefore write to express to you my great appreciation of the faithful and efficient services of the officers and men of the forty-seventh New York infantry volunteers, which they have performed while under my command in the district of San Juan.

You and your regiment have not had the interesting excitement of an active campaign against an armed enemy, but you have sustained all the hardships and dangers of one.

The officers and enlisted men of the forty-seventh New York volunteers have performed their duties finely, while in the island of Porto Rico, and in returning to the United States they deserve the commendations and thanks of all their countrymen. They certainly have my sincere thanks, and I have greatly enjoyed having them associated with me here.

With warmest regards for yourself and all the officers of your regiment, believe me, my dear Colonel Hubbell,

Sincerely yours,
(Signed.)   F. D. GRANT,
Brig.-Gen'l Comd'g.

On January 27, 1899, the following telegram was received at headquarters at Caguas.

COMMANDING OFFICER:

Sir:—The brigadier-general commanding the military district of San Juan directs me to inform you that information has been received from the war department that transportation will be here between the 5th and 15th of February to take your regiment to the United States. He directs that you have your command in readiness to move.

Very respectfully,
(Signed.)   C. W. FENTON,
Assistant Adjt.-Gen'l.

Orders were issued to comply with this order without delay when the following telegram was received:

February 17.

COLONEL HUBBELL:

Cable just received from quartermaster-general, Washington, D. C., indicates "Manitoba" will not be here for two weeks yet to take your regiment north.

(Signed.)   COL. PULLMAN.

February 21st, company D was transferred from Isla de Vieques to San Juan and quartered there at the eleventh United States infantry barracks.

The transport "Manitoba" arrived February 27th, and the regiment, except companies E, H, I and K, was ordered to report at San Juan, March 3d.

March 2d, headquarters with companies C, L, M and H left on the march from Cagnas at 3.30 p. m., for Rio Piedras, where they arrived at 10 p. m., and remained at the railroad station until the following morning when they took train for San Juan, as did also company B, from Rio Piedras, and company G, from Carolina.

Companies B, C, D, G, L and M embarked, March 3d, on transport which then cast off and anchored in midstream to await the arrival of the steamer " Vaseo," conveying company F, from Fajardo, and company A, from Humacoa. At 5 p. m., the transport sailed for Arroyo to take up the remaining four companies, company I having marched from Aibonito to Guayama, and company H from Cayey, where they joined companies E and K, and under the command of Major Sullivan marched to Arroyo, where they arrived about 10 a. m., March 4th. The troops having all embarked, the transport sailed for New York at 6 p. m.

The dock at the foot of Pacific street, Brooklyn, was reached March 10th, at 9 a. m., and the regiment disembarked at 1 p. m., and marched to the armory of the forty-seventh regiment, national guard. A royal reception was given the regiment by the citizens during the march through the city, the escort being furnished by the fourth battalion of the forty-seventh regiment, national guard, troop C, and the grand army posts.

During the service the health of the regiment was very good. This can be accounted for by the fact that the officers took proper care of their men, and the medical officers looked well after the sanitary conditions.

The regiment assembled, March 31, 1899, and was mustered out of the United States service.

Commissioned Officers.

COLONELS:

John G. Eddy, May 3 to December 2, 1898.
William H. Hubbell, December 3, 1898, to March 31, 1899.

LIEUTENANT-COLONELS:

William H. Hubbell, May 3 to December 3, 1898.
Hewlings H. Quick, December 3, 1898, to March 31, 1899.

Majors:

Henry C. Barthman, May 3, 1898, to March 31, 1899.
Hewlings H. Quick, May 3 to December 3, 1898.
Hervey C. Lyon, May 3 to October 1, 1898.
Daniel C. Sullivan, October 3, 1898, to March 31, 1899.
John S. Strouse, December 3, 1898, to March 31, 1899.

Regimental Adjutant:

Henry D. McCutcheon, May 3, 1898, to March 31, 1899.

Battalion Adjutants:

Levi B. Case, May 3, 1898, to March 31, 1899.
Harry H. Walker, May 3, 1898, to March 31, 1899.
Timothy J. Hooley, June 6, 1898, to March 31, 1899.

Quartermaster:

Charles A. Chase, May 3, 1898, to March 31, 1899.

Surgeons:

Henry Wallace, May 3, to September 13, 1898.
John T. Gibbons, September 14, 1898, to March 31, 1899.

Assistant Surgeons:

Edward N. Bowen, May 3, 1898, to March 31, 1899.
John T. Gibbons, May 3, to September 14, 1898.
Edward Hodges, October 5, 1898, to March 31, 1899.

COMPANY A.

Captains:

Ernest E. Jannicky, May 2 to December 14, 1898.
William H. Doremus, December 20, 1898, to March 31, 1899.

First Lieutenant:

J. Arthur Meyer, May 2, 1898, to March 31, 1899.

Second Lieutenant:

Schuyler Schieffelin, June 2, 1898, to March 31, 1899.

COMPANY B.

CAPTAINS:.

Edward J. Olden, May 2 to November 11, 1898.
William T. Johnston, November 11, 1898, to March 31, 1899.

FIRST LIEUTENANTS:

William T. Johnston, May 2 to November 11, 1898.
James Erwin Lavens, November 11, 1898, to March 31, 1899.

SECOND LIEUTENANTS:

James Erwin Lavens, May 2 to November 11, 1898.
Julius J. McKay, February 3 to March 31, 1899.

COMPANY C.

CAPTAINS:

William L. Fish, May 2 to September 17, 1898.
Henry A. F. Young, November 16, 1898, to March 31, 1899.

FIRST LIEUTENANTS:

William S. Burrell, May 2 to September 19, 1898.
Frank Techter, September 26, 1898, to February 28, 1899.
William E. White, March 16 to March 31, 1899.

SECOND LIEUTENANTS:

Frank Techter, May 2 to September 26, 1898.
William E. White, September 26, 1898, to March 16, 1899.
John T. Prankard, March 16 to March 31, 1899.

COMPANY D.

CAPTAIN:

John S. Strouse, May 2 to December 3, 1898.

FIRST LIEUTENANT:

George L. Bennett, May 2, 1898, to March 31, 1899.

COMPANY E.

CAPTAINS:

Daniel C. Sullivan, May 2 to October 3, 1898.
Albert R. Bridger, October 3, 1898, to March 31, 1899.

FIRST LIEUTENANTS:

Albert R. Bridger, May 2 to October 3, 1898.
Frank B. Mezick, October 3, 1898, to March 31, 1899.

SECOND LIEUTENANTS:

Frank B. Mezick, May 2 to October 3, 1898.
Thomas A. McWhinney, November 2, 1898, to March 31, 1899.

COMPANY F.

CAPTAIN:

George C. Butcher, May 2, 1898, to March 31, 1899.

FIRST LIEUTENANTS:

Martin B. Andelfinger, May 2 to September 30, 1898.
George W. Trenchard, Jr., December 17, 1898, to March 31, 1899.

SECOND LIEUTENANTS:

George W. Trenchard, Jr., May 2 to December 17, 1898.
John N. Moncrieff, February 3 to March 31, 1899.

COMPANY G.

CAPTAINS:

Thomas E. Jackson, May 2 to September 13, 1898.
Robert A. Marshall, September 23, 1898, to March 31, 1899.

FIRST LIEUTENANTS:

Robert A. Marshall, May 2 to September 23, 1898.
Joseph L. Gillman, October 3, 1898, to March 31, 1899.

SECOND LIEUTENANTS:

Charles E. Maxfield, May 2 to September 10, 1898.
Edward J. Lamb, October 3, 1898, to March 31, 1899.

COMPANY H.

CAPTAIN:

John Mortimer Bronk, May 2, 1898, to March 31, 1899.

FIRST LIEUTENANTS:

George B. Serenbetz, May 2 to November 9, 1898.
Eugene R. Gonzalez, January 18 to March 31, 1899.

SECOND LIEUTENANTS:

Eugene R. Gonzalez, May 2, 1898, to January 18, 1899.
Amett F. Perry, January 18 to March 31, 1899.

COMPANY I.

CAPTAIN:

John A. Doremus, May 2, 1898, to March 31, 1899.

FIRST LIEUTENANTS:

William H. Doremus, May 2 to December 20, 1898.
William C. Ritter, February 3 to March 31, 1899.

SECOND LIEUTENANTS:

William C. Ritter, May 2, 1898, to February 3, 1899.
William T. Kirkham, February 3 to March 31, 1899.

COMPANY K.

CAPTAINS:

Frank Maier, June 22 to September 13, 1898.
Marchisi T. Hardy, September 21, 1898, to March 31, 1899.

FIRST LIEUTENANTS:

Marchisi T. Hardy, May 2 to September 21, 1898.
Daniel J Brinsley, October 3, 1898, to March 31, 1899.

SECOND LIEUTENANTS:

Frank Maier, May 2 to June 22, 1898.
Daniel J. Brinsley, June 29 to October 3, 1898.
William W. Baird, Jr., October 7, 1898, to March 31, 1899.

COMPANY L.

CAPTAINS:

George E. Libbey, May 2 to December 14, 1898.
S. Reynolds White, January 1 to March 31, 1899.

FIRST LIEUTENANTS:

Charles L. Gerould, May 2 to September 22, 1898.
S. Reynolds White, September 29, 1898, to January 1, 1899.

SECOND LIEUTENANTS:

S. Reynolds White, May 2 to September 29, 1898.
Leonard J. Mygatt, September 29, 1898, to March 31, 1899.
Ernest S. G. Borthwick, November 11, 1898, to March 31, 1899.

COMPANY M.

CAPTAINS:

Edward W. Rockafellow, May 2 to September 15, 1898.
Charles G. Stevenson, November 2, 1898, to March 31, 1899.

FIRST LIEUTENANTS:

Charles G. Stevenson, May 2 to November 2, 1898.
Matthew G. Addison, November 2, 1898, to March 31, 1899.

SECOND LIEUTENANTS:

Henry A. F. Young, May 2 to November 16, 1898.
Charles N. Leach, November 16, 1898, to March 31, 1899.

OFFICERS WHO WERE COMMISSIONED, BUT DID NOT
SERVE IN THE GRADES NAMED.

Second Lieutenant Leonard J. Mygatt, as first lieutenant.

Sergeant-Major Anthony C. Szkallay, as second lieutenant.

William Washington Baird, as second lieutenant.

RECORDS OF THE OFFICERS AND ENLISTED MEN.

ACKER, JOHN D.—Age, 21 years. Enlisted, May 2, 1898, at
Brooklyn, to serve two years; mustered in as private, Co. M,
May 24, 1898; mustered out with company, March 31, 1899, at
Brooklyn, N. Y.

ACKERMAN, GEORGE P.—Age, 35 years. Enlisted, May 22,
1898, at Brooklyn, to serve two years; mustered in as musician,
Co. E, May 24, 1898; mustered out with company, March 31,
1899, at Brooklyn, N. Y.

ADDISON, MATTHEW G.—Age, 28 years. Enlisted, May 2,
1898, at Brooklyn, to serve two years; mustered in as sergeant,
Co. L, May 24, 1898; promoted first sergeant, no date; mus-
tered· in as first lieutenant, Co. M, November 21, 1898; mustered out with company, March 31, 1899, at Brooklyn, N. Y.;
commissioned first lieutenant, November 2, 1898, with rank
from same date, vice Stevenson, promoted.

AHERN, JOHN J.—Age, 22 years. Enlisted, May 2, 1898, at
Brooklyn, to serve two years; mustered in as private, Co. G,
May 24, 1898; promoted corporal, August 20, 1898; mustered
out with company, March 31, 1899, at Brooklyn, N. Y.

AHERNE, DANIEL.—Age, 21 years. Enlisted, May 2, 1898, at
Brooklyn, to serve two years; mustered in as private, Co. L,
may 24, 1898; promoted corporal, February 9, 1899; mustered
out with company, March 31, 1899, at Brooklyn, N. Y.

ALBRIGHT, WILLIAM H.—Age, — years. Enlisted, August 4,
1898, at Brooklyn, to serve two years; mustered in as private,
Co. A, same date; mustered out with company, March 31, 1899,
at Brooklyn, N. Y.

ALLEN, BERTRAND W.—Age, 25 years. Enlisted, May 2, 1898,
at Brooklyn, to serve two years; mustered in as private, Co. L,

ALLEN, W ALTER F.—Age, 20 years. Enlisted, May 2, 1898, at Brooklyn, to serve two years; mustered in as private, Co. K, May 24, 1898; mustered out with company, March 31, 1899, at Brooklyn, N. Y.

ANDELFIN GER, MARTIN B.—Age, 26 years. Enrolled, May 2, 1898, at Brooklyn, to serve two years; mustered in as first lieutenant, Co. F, May 24, 1898; discharged, September 30, 1898, at Fort Adams, R. I.; commissioned first lieutenant, May 24, 1898, with rank from same date, original.

ANDERSON, ANDREW S.—Age, 23 years. Enlisted, May 2, 1898, at Brooklyn, to serve two years; mustered in as corporal, Co. L, May 24, 1898; promoted sergeant, November 2, 1898; mustered out with company, March 31, 1899, at Brooklyn, N. Y.

ANDERSON, CHARLES W.—Age, 24 years. Enlisted, May 2, 1898, at Brooklyn, to serve two years; mustered in as private, Co. A, May 24, 1898; mustered out with company, March 31, 1899, at Brooklyn, N. Y.

ANDERSON, EDWARD J.—Age, 20 years. Enlisted, May 2, 1898, at Brooklyn, to serve two years; mustered in as private, Co. F, May 24, 1898; mustered out with company, March 31, 1899, at Brooklyn, N. Y.

ANDERSON, FREDERICK.—Age, 25 years. Enlisted, May 2, 1898, at Brooklyn, to serve two years; mustered in as private, Co. A, May 24, 1898; mustered out with company, March 31, 1899, at Brooklyn, N. Y.

ANDERSON, JOHN H.—Age, 29 years. Enlisted, May 2, 1898, at Brooklyn, to serve two years; mustered in as private, Co. G, May 24, 1898; appointed cook, August 12, 1898; mustered out with company, March 31, 1899, at Brooklyn, N. Y.

ANDERSON, THOMAS E.—Age, — years. Enlisted, July 26, 1898, at Brooklyn, to serve two years; mustered in as private, Co. C, same date; mustered out with company, March 31, 1899, at Brooklyn, N. Y.

ANDREWS, CHARLES.—Age, 26 years. Enlisted, May 2, 1898, at Brooklyn, to serve two years; mustered in as private, Co. L, May 24, 1898; mustered out with company, March 31, 1899, at Brooklyn, N. Y.

ANDRUS, GROVE A.—Age, 25 years. Enlisted, May 20, 1898, at Camp Black, to serve two years; mustered in as private, Co. A, May 24, 1898; promoted corporal, August 15, 1898; mustered out with company, March 31, 1899, at Brooklyn, N. Y.

ANGEVINE, JR., FRANK.—Age, 30 years. Enlisted, May 2, 1898, at Brooklyn, to serve two years; mustered in as sergeant, Co. E, May 24, 1898; promoted first sergeant, May 24, 1898; died of bright's disease, March 6, 1899, on board United States Transport " Manitoba."

APGAR, JOSEPH D.—Age, — years. Enlisted, July 28, 1898, at Brooklyn, to serve two years; mustered in as private, Co. C, same date; promoted corporal, November 1, 1898; sergeant, January 1, 1899; mustered out with company, March 31, 1899, at Brooklyn, N. Y.

APMANN, PETER J.—Age, 22 years. Enlisted, May 2, 1898, at Brooklyn, to serve two years; mustered in as private, Co. M, May 24, 1898; mustered out with company, March 31, 1899, at Brooklyn, N. Y.

ARMSTRONG, WILLIAM G.—Age, 21 years. Enlisted, May 2, 1898, at Brooklyn, to serve two years; mustered in as private, Co. A, May 24, 1898; promoted lance corporal, March 4, 1899; mustered out with company, March 31, 1899, at Brooklyn, N. Y.

ARNOLD, CLINTON S.—Age, 34 years. Enlisted, May 2, 1898, at Brooklyn, to serve two years; mustered in as private, Co. K, May 24, 1898; mustered out with company, March 31, 1899, at Brooklyn, N. Y.

ARNOLD, OTTO.—Age, — years. Enlisted, July 26, 1898, at Brooklyn, to serve two years; mustered in as private, Co. C, same date; mustered out with company, March 31, 1899, at Brooklyn, N. Y.

ARNOULD, FELIX J.—Age, 21 years. Enlisted, May 2, 1898, at Brooklyn, to serve two years; mustered in as private, Co. M, May 24, 1898; mustered out with company, March 31, 1899, at Brooklyn, N. Y.

ASCHENBACH, FRED.—Age, — years. Enlisted, August 5, 1898, at Brooklyn, to serve two years; mustered in as private, Co. D, same date; mustered out with company, March 31, 1899, at Brooklyn, N. Y.

ASCHENBACH, PHILIP.—Age, — years. Enlisted, August 4, 1898, at Brooklyn, to serve two years; mustered in as private, Co. D, same date; mustered out with company, March 31, 1899, at Brooklyn, N. Y.

ASHLEY, JOSEPH.—Age, 21 years. Enlisted, May 2, 1898, at Brooklyn, to serve two years; mustered in as private, Co. F, May 24, 1898; mustered out with company, March 31, 1899, at Brooklyn, N. Y.

ASHWICK, HERBERT M.—Age, 22 years. Enlisted, May 2, 1898, at Brooklyn, to serve two years; mustered in as private, Co. I, May 24, 1898; mustered out with company, March 31, 1899, at Brooklyn, N. Y.

ASKINS, JOHN D.—Age, 21 years. Enlisted, May 2, 1898, at Brooklyn, to serve two years; mustered in as private, Co. I, May 24, 1898; mustered out with company, March 31, 1899, at Brooklyn, N. Y.

BACKMAN, WILLIAM F.—Age, 22 years. Enlisted, May 2, 1898, at Brooklyn, to serve two years; mustered in as private, Co. F, May 24, 1898; mustered out with company, March 31, 1899, at Brooklyn, N. Y.

BADER, AUGUST.—Age, — years. Enlisted, July 28, 1898, at Brooklyn, to serve two years; mustered in as private, Co. E, same date; mustered out with company, March 31, 1899, at Brooklyn, N. Y.

BAGLEY, JOHN.—Age, 34 years. Enlisted, May 2, 1898, at Brooklyn, to serve two years; mustered in as private, Co. B, May 24, 1898; appointed cook, August 1, 1898; mustered out with company, March 31, 1899, at Brooklyn, N. Y.

BAGLEY, WILLIAM.—Age, 34 years. Enlisted, May 2, 1898, at Brooklyn, to serve two years; mustered in as private, Co. G, May 24, 1898; discharged, October 14, 1898, at Fort Adams, R. I.

BAILEY, WILLIAM.—Age, 27 years. Enlisted, May 2, 1898, at
Brooklyn, to serve two years; mustered in as private, Co. B,
May 24, 1898; mustered out with company, March 31, 1899, at
Brooklyn, N. Y.

BAIRD, IRA.—Age, 22 years. Enlisted, May 2, 1898, at Brooklyn, to serve two years; mustered in as corporal, Co. H, May 24,
1898; returned to ranks, July 1, 1898; mustered out with company, March 31, 1899, at Brooklyn, N. Y.

BAIRD, JAMES.—Age, 22 years. Enlisted, May 2, 1898, at
Brooklyn, to serve two years; mustered in as private, Co. B,
May 24, 1898; mustered out with company, March 31, 1899, at
Brooklyn, N. Y.

BAIRD, WILLIAM WASHINGTON.—Second lieutenant; commissioned, not mustered, October 7, 1898, with rank from same
date, vice Gillman, promoted.

BAIRD, JR., WILLIAM W.—Age, — years. Enrolled, October
7, 1898, at Fort Adams, R. I, to serve two years; mustered in as
second lieutenant, Co. K, December 14, 1898; mustered out with
company, March 31, 1899, at Brooklyn, N. Y.; commissioned
second lieutenant, October 7, 1898, with rank from same date,
vice Brinsley, promoted.

BAISLEY, JAMES.—Age, 20 years. Enlisted, May 2, 1898, at
Brooklyn, to serve two years; mustered in as private, Co. M,
May 24, 1898; died of entretis, February 13, 1899, at Caguas,
P. R.

BAKER, JOSEPH W.—Age, 28 years. Enlisted, May 2, 1898,
at Brooklyn, to serve two years; mustered in as private, Co.
B, June 7, 1898; mustered out with company, March 31, 1899,
at Brooklyn, N. Y.

BALDWIN, CHARLES A.—Age, — years. Enlisted, August 4,
1898, at Fort Adams, R. I., to serve two years; mustered in as
artificer, Co. B, same date; mustered out with company, March
31, 1899, at Brooklyn, N. Y.

BALF, EDWARD.—Age, 21 years.   Enlisted, May 2, 1898, at Brooklyn, to serve two years; mustered in as private, Co. C, May 24, 1898; mustered out with company, March 31, 1899, at Brooklyn, N. Y.

BALLOU, LEVI S.—Age, 35 years.   Enlisted, May 2, 1898, at Brooklyn, to serve two years; mustered in as quartermaster-sergeant, Co. I, May 24, 1898; returned to ranks, July 23, 1898; mustered out with company, March 31, 1899, at Brooklyn, N. Y.

BANTA, HARRY.—Age, — years.   Enlisted, July 25, 1898, at Brooklyn, to serve two years; mustered in as private, Co. G, same date; mustered out with company, March 31, 1899, at Brooklyn, N. Y.

BARNES, HERBERT A.—Age, 27 years.   Enlisted, May 2, 1898, at Brooklyn, to serve two years; mustered in as sergeant, Co. H, May 24, 1898; promoted quartermaster-sergeant, February 1, 1899; mustered out with company, March 31, 1899, at Brooklyn, N. Y.

BARRETT, JAMES S.—Age, 22 years.   Enlisted, May 2, 1898, at Brooklyn, to serve two years; mustered in as private, Co. M, May 24, 1898; promoted corporal, February 16, 1899; mustered out with company, March 31, 1899, at Brooklyn, N. Y.

BARRETT, WALTER S.—Age, 32 years.   Enlisted, May 2, 1898, at Brooklyn, to serve two years; mustered in as sergeant, Co. M, May 24, 1898; discharged, December 15, 1898, at Caguas, P. R.

BARTHMAN, HENRY C.—Age, 30 years.   Enrolled, May 3, 1898, at Brooklyn, to serve two years; mustered in as major, May 24, 1898; mustered out with regiment, March 31, 1899, at Brooklyn, N. Y.; commissioned major, May 24, 1898, with rank from same date, original.

BASCH, HERMAN.—Age, 29 years.   Enlisted, May 2, 1898, at Brooklyn, to serve two years; mustered in as musician, Co. E, May 24, 1898; mustered out with company, March 31, 1899, at Brooklyn, N. Y.

BATES, JOHN.—Age, — years.   Enlisted, July 25, 1898, at Brooklyn, to serve two years; mustered in as private, Co. L, same date; appointed wagoner, October 19, 1898; mustered out with company, March 31, 1899, at Brooklyn, N. Y.

BATHE, PETER.—Age, 28 years. Enlisted, May 2, 1898, at
Brooklyn, to serve two years; mustered in as private, Co. L,
May 24, 1898; mustered out with company, March 31, 1899, at
Brooklyn, N. Y.

BAUER, GUSTAVE.—Age, 21 years. Enlisted, May 2, 1898, at
Brooklyn, to serve two years; mustered in as private, Co. L,
May 24, 1898; promoted corporal, September 1, 1898; mustered
out with company, March 31, 1899, at Brooklyn, N. Y.

BAYER, WILLIAM.—Age, 21 years. Enlisted, May 2, 1898, at
Brooklyn, to serve two years; mustered in as private, Co. C,
May 24, 1898; mustered out with company, March 31, 1899, at
Brooklyn, N. Y.

BEALLER, JOHN E.—Age, 21 years. Enlisted, May 2, 1898, at
Brooklyn, to serve two years; mustered in as private, Co. L,
May 24, 1898; promoted lance corporal, February 14, 1899; mus-
tered out with company, March 31, 1899, at Brooklyn, N. Y.

BECKER, GEORGE.—Age, — years. Enlisted, July 27, 1898, at
Brooklyn, to serve two years; mustered in as private, Co. C,
same date; mustered out with company, March 31, 1899, at
Brooklyn, N. Y.

BEERS, LOVETT.—Age, 29 years. Enlisted, May 2, 1898, at
Brooklyn, to serve two years; mustered in as private, Co. G,
May 24, 1898; promoted corporal, December 9, 1898; mustered
out with company, March 31, 1899, at Brooklyn, N. Y.

BEHRENS, GEORGE A.—Age, 23 years. Enlisted, May 2, 1898,
at Brooklyn, as private, to serve two years; mustered in as
quartermaster-sergeant, Co. F, May 24, 1898; mustered out with
company, March 31, 1899, at Brooklyn, N. Y.

BEHRINGER, FRED F.—Age, 21 years. Enlisted, May 2, 1898,
at Brooklyn, to serve two years; mustered in as private, Co. D,
May 24, 1898; discharged, October 12, 1898, at Fort Columbus,
New York Harbor.

BEILMAN, JOHN.—Age, 21 years. Enlisted, May 2, 1898, at
Brooklyn, to serve two years; mustered in as private, Co. M,
May 24, 1898; promoted corporal, February 15, 1899; mustered
out with company, March 31, 1899, at Brooklyn, N. Y.

BENJAMIN, SAMUEL J.—Age, 21 years. Enlisted, May 2, 1898, at Brooklyn, to serve two years; mustered in as private, Co. C, May 24, 1898; mustered out with company, March 31, 1899, at Brooklyn, N. Y.

BENNET, JOHN W.—Age, 21 years. Enlisted, May 2, 1898, at Brooklyn, to serve two years; mustered in as musician, Co. D, May 24, 1898; returned to ranks, October 1, 1898; mustered out with company, March 31, 1899, at Brooklyn, N. Y.

BENNETT, JR., DAVID.—Age, 26 years. Enlisted, May 2, 1898, at Brooklyn, to serve two years; mustered in as private, Co. H, May 24, 1898; mustered out with company, March 31, 1899, at Brooklyn, N. Y.

BENNETT, GEORGE H.—Age, 21 years. Enlisted, May 2, 1898, at Brooklyn, to serve two years; mustered in as private, Co. D, May 24, 1898; promoted corporal, August 27, 1898; mustered out with company, March 31, 1899, at Brooklyn, N. Y.

BENNETT, GEORGE L.—Age, 27 years. Enrolled, May 2, 1898, at Brooklyn, to serve two years; mustered in as first lieutenant, Co. D, May 24, 1898; mustered out with company, March 31, 1899, at Brooklyn, N. Y.; commissioned first lieutenant, May 24, 1898, with rank from same date, original.

BERNARD, JOSEPH H.—Age, 27 years. Enlisted, May 2, 1898, at Brooklyn, to serve two years; mustered in as private, Co. D, May 24, 1898; mustered out with company, March 31, 1899, at Brooklyn, N. Y.

BERNHARDT, EMIL M.—Age, — years. Enlisted, July 28, 1898, at Fort Adams, R. I., to serve two years; mustered in as private, Co. M, same date; mustered out with company, March 31, 1899, at Brooklyn, N. Y.

BERSEBACH, WILLIAM.—Age, — years. Enlisted, August 4, 1898, at Brooklyn, to serve two years; mustered in as private, Co. I, same date; mustered out with company, March 31, 1899, at Brooklyn, N. Y.

BETTS, FRANK D.—Age, 25 years. Enlisted, May 2, 1898, at Brooklyn, to serve two years; mustered in as private, Co. I, same date; promoted corporal, August 26, 1898; mustered out with company, March 31, 1899, at Brooklyn, N. Y.

BIDDULPH, JOHN V.—Age, 24 years. Enlisted, May 2, 1898, at Brooklyn, to serve two years; mustered in as private, Co. D, May 24, 1898; mustered out with company, March 31, 1899, at Brooklyn, N. Y.

BIERMANN, JOHN.—Age, 24 years. Enlisted, May 2, 1898, at Brooklyn, to serve two years; mustered in as private, Co. C, May 24, 1898; mustered out with company, March 31, 1899, at Brooklyn, N. Y.

BILMS, HENRY F.—Age, 32 years. Enlisted, May 2, 1898, at Brooklyn, to serve two years; mustered in as private, Co. G, May 24, 1898; mustered out with company, March 31, 1899, at Brooklyn, N. Y.

BINDRIM, MICHAEL.—Age, — years. Enlisted, July 26, 1898, at Brooklyn, to serve two years; mustered in as private, Co. K, same date; mustered out with company, March 31, 1899, at Brooklyn, N. Y.

BINDRIM, NICHOLAS.—Age, — years. Enlisted, August 4, 1898, at Brooklyn, to serve two years; mustered in as private, Co. G, same date; mustered out with company, March 31, 1899, at Brooklyn, N. Y.

BIRD, JOHN E.—Age, 22 years. Enlisted, May 2, 1898, at Brooklyn, to serve two years; mustered in as private, Co. A, May 24, 1898; mustered out with company, March 31, 1899, at Brooklyn, N. Y.

BISCHOFF, WILLIAM F.—Age, 22 years. Enlisted, May 2, 1898, at Brooklyn, to serve two years; mustered in as private, Co. L, May 24, 1898; promoted corporal, June 13, 1898; sergeant, February 14, 1899; mustered out with company, March 31, 1899, at Brooklyn, N. Y.

BITTNER, GEORGE.—Age, — years. Enlisted, August 4, 1898, at Brooklyn, to serve two years; mustered in as private, Co. D, same date; mustered out with company, March 31, 1899, at Brooklyn, N. Y.

BLASSE, THOMAS.—Age, 21 years. Enlisted, May 2, 1898, at Brooklyn, to serve two years; mustered in as private, Co. F, May 24, 1898; promoted corporal, February 8, 1899; mustered out with company, March 31, 1899, at Brooklyn, N. Y.

BLEND, LOUIS F.—Age, 25 years.   Enlisted, May 2, 1898, at Brooklyn, to serve two years; mustered in as private, Co. D, May 24, 1898; discharged, November 14, 1898, at Fort Columbus, New York Harbor.

BLOCH, ERNEST.—Age, 21 years.   Enlisted, May 18, 1898, at Brooklyn, to serve two years; mustered in as private, Co. E, May 24, 1898; mustered out with company, March 31, 1899, at Brooklyn, N. Y.

BLOHM, FRANK L.—Age, 29 years.   Enlisted, May 2, 1898, at Brooklyn, to serve two years; mustered in as private, Co. A, May 24, 1898; mustered out with company, March 31, 1899, at Brooklyn, N. Y.

BODE, HARRY W.—Age, 23 years.   Enlisted, May 2, 1898, at Brooklyn, to serve two years; mustered in as private, Co. H, May 24, 1898; mustered out with company, March 31, 1899, at Brooklyn, N. Y.

BOERCKEL, JOHN W.—Age, 40 years.   Enlisted, May 2, 1898, at Brooklyn, to serve two years; mustered in as sergeant, Co. E, May 24, 1898; discharged, October 14, 1898, at Fort Adams, R. I.

BOHAN, CORNELIUS J.—Age, 31 years.   Enlisted, May 2. 1898, at Brooklyn, to serve two years; mustered in as private, Co. D, May 24, 1898; mustered out with company, March 31, 1899, at Brooklyn, N. Y.

BOLDMANN, TONY A.—Age, 22 years.   Enlisted, May 2, 1898, at Brooklyn, to serve two years; mustered in as private, Co. H, May 24, 1898; mustered out with company, March 31, 1899, at Brooklyn, N. Y.

BOUDEN, WILLIAM A.—Age, 21 years.   Enlisted, May 2, 1898, at Brooklyn, to serve two years; mustered in as private, Co. C, May 24, 1898; discharged, October 12, 1898, at Fort Adams, R. I.

BOROWINSKI, CESLANS.—Age, — years.   Enlisted, July 26, 1898, at Brooklyn, to serve two years; mustered in as private, Co. K, same date; mustered out with company, March 31, 1899, at Brooklyn, N. Y.

BORTHWICK, ERNEST S. G.—Age, 28 years. Enlisted, May 2,
1898, at Brooklyn, to serve two years; mustered in as sergeant,
Co. L, May 24, 1898; promoted sergeant-major, June 10, 1898;
mustered in as second lieutenant, November 11, 1898; mustered
out with company, March 31, 1899, at Brooklyn, N. Y.; commissioned second lieutenant, November 11, 1898, with rank from
same date, vice Lavens, promoted.

BOSCH, JOHN.—Age, 22 years. Enlisted, May 2, 1898, at Brooklyn, to serve two years; mustered in as private, Co. I, May 24,
1898; mustered out with company, March 31, 1899, at Brooklyn,
N. Y.

BOSCHEN, FREDERICK W.—Age, 22 years. Enlisted, May 2,
1898, at Brooklyn, to serve two years; mustered in as private,
Co. K, May 24, 1898; transferred to Hospital Corps, August 21,
1898.

BOWEN, EDWARD N.—Age, 23 years. Enrolled, May 3, 1898,
at Brooklyn, to serve two years; mustered in as first lieutenant
and assistant surgeon, May 6, 1898; mustered out with regiment,
March 31, 1899, as captain and assistant surgeon, at Brooklyn,
N. Y.; commissioned assistant surgeon, May 6, 1898, with rank
from same date, original.

BOWMAN, FREDERICK C.—Age, 30 years. Enlisted, May 2,
1898, at Brooklyn, to serve two years; mustered in as private,
Co. G, May 24, 1898; mustered out with company, March 31,
1899, at Brooklyn, N. Y.

BOX, WILLIAM H.—Age, 18 years. Enlisted, May 2, 1898, at
Brooklyn, to serve two years; mustered in as private, Co. I,
May 24, 1898; mustered out with company, March 31, 1899, at
Brooklyn, N. Y.

BOYD, JR., CHARLES.—Age, 24 years. Enlisted, May 2, 1898,
at Brooklyn, to serve two years; mustered in as private, Co. M,
May 24, 1898; mustered out with company, March 31, 1899, at
Brooklyn, N. Y.

BOYD, EDWARD H.—Age, 26 years. Enlisted, May 2, 1898, at
Brooklyn, to serve two years; mustered in as private, Co. D,
May 24, 1898; deserted, September 24, 1898, at Fort Adams,
R. I.

BOYD, FREDERICK H.—Age, — years. Enlisted, July 26, 1898, at Brooklyn, to serve two years; mustered in as private, Co. B, same date; mustered out with company, March 31, 1899, at Brooklyn, N. Y.

BOYD, JAMES A.—Age, 21 years. Enlisted, May 19, 1898, at Camp Black, to serve two years; mustered in as private, Co. A, May 24, 1898; mustered out with company, March 31, 1899, at Brooklyn, N. Y.

BOYD, WILLIAM H.—Age, — years. Enlisted, August 8, 1898, at Brooklyn, to serve two years; mustered in as private, Co. B, same date; mustered out with company, March 31, 1899, at Brooklyn, N. Y.

BOYER, ISADOR.—Age, 20 years. Enlisted, May 2, 1898, at Brooklyn, to serve two years; mustered in as private, Co. E, May 24, 1898; appointed wagoner, July 11, 1898; discharged, October 20, 1898, at Fort Adams, R. I.

BRADY, CLARENCE.—Age, 21 years. Enlisted, May 2, 1898, at Brooklyn, to serve two years; mustered in as private, Co. M, May 24, 1898; mustered out with company, March 31, 1899, at Brooklyn, N. Y.

BRADY, DANIEL A.—Age, 21 years. Enlisted, May 2, 1898, at Brooklyn, to serve two years; mustered in as private, Co. G, May 24, 1898; mustered out with company, March 31, 1899, at Brooklyn, N. Y.

BRANDTBERG, ROBERT E.—Age, 21 years. Enlisted, May 2, 1898, at Brooklyn, to serve two years: mustered in as private, Co. E, May 24, 1898; mustered out with company, March 31, 1899, at Brooklyn, N. Y.

BRAZILL, ARTHUR L.—Age, 24 years. Enlisted, May 2, 1898, at Brooklyn, to serve two years; mustered in as private, Co. I, May 24, 1898; promoted corporal, June 10, 1898; returned to ranks, September 12, 1898; mustered out with company, March 31, 1899, at Brooklyn, N. Y.

BREHM, JOHN M.—Age, 22 years. Enlisted, May 2, 1898, at Brooklyn, to serve two years; mustered in as private, Co. G, May 24, 1898; mustered out with company, March 31, 1899, at Brooklyn, N. Y.

BREIT, JOSEPH.—Age, — years. Enlisted, August 5, 1898, at Brooklyn, to serve two years; mustered in as private, Co. E, same date; mustered out with company, March 31, 1899, at Brooklyn, N. Y.

BRENNAN, JAMES J.—Age, — years. Enlisted, July 29, 1898, at Brooklyn, to serve two years; mustered in as private, Co. E, same date; mustered out with company, March 31, 1899, at Brooklyn, N. Y.

BRENNAN, PETER J.—Age, 25 years. Enlisted, May 2, 1898, at Brooklyn, to serve two years; mustered in as private, Co. H, May 24, 1898; mustered out with company, March 31, 1899, at Brooklyn, N. Y.

BRIDGER, ALBERT R.—Age, 28 years. Enrolled, May 2, 1898, at Brooklyn, to serve two years; mustered in as first lieutenant, Co. E, May 24, 1898; as captain, October 3, 1898; mustered out with company, March 31, 1899, at Brooklyn, N. Y.; commissioned first lieutenant, May 24, 1898, with rank from same date, original; captain, October 3, 1898, with rank from same date, vice Sullivan, promoted.

BRIDGER, FRANK.—Age, 22 years. Enlisted, May 2, 1898, at Brooklyn, to serve two years; mustered in as private, Co. L, May 24, 1898; mustered out with company, March 31, 1899, at Brooklyn, N. Y.

BRIGGS, JAMES.—Age, — years. Enlisted, July 25, 1898, at Brooklyn, to serve two years; mustered in as private, Co. G, same date; discharged, November 18, 1898, at Governor's Island, New York Harbor.

BRINSLEY, DANIEL J.—Age, 44 years. Enlisted, May 3, 1898, at Brooklyn, to serve two years; mustered in as chief musician, May, 24, 1898; as second lieutenant. Co. K, June 29, 1898; as first lieutenant, October 3, 1898; mustered out with company, March 31, 1899, at Brooklyn, N. Y.; commissioned second lieutenant, June 29, 1898, with rank from same date, vice Maier, promoted; first lieutenant, October 3, 1898, with rank from same date, vice Hardy, promoted.

BRITT, JOSEPH P.—Age, — years. Enlisted, July 26, 1898, at Brooklyn, to serve two years; mustered in as private, Co. K, same date; mustered out with company, March 31, 1899, at Brooklyn, N. Y.

BRITTON, WILLIAM J.—Age, 21 years. Enlisted, May 2, 1898, at Brooklyn, to serve two years; mustered in as private, Co. H, May 24, 1898; appointed artificer, December 1, 1898; mustered out with company, March 31, 1899, at Brooklyn, N. Y.

BROCKHOFE, ANDREW J.—Age, 26 years. Enlisted, May 2, 1898, at Brooklyn, to serve two years; mustered in as private, Co. I, May 24, 1898; mustered out with company, March 31, 1899, at Brooklyn, N. Y.

BROCKMAN, JR., HENRY F.—Age, 20 years. Enlisted, May 2, 1898, at Brooklyn, to serve two years; mustered in as private, Co. K, May 24, 1898; discharged, December 2, 1899, at Guayama, P. R., as Henry F. Brockman.

BRONK, JOHN MORTIMER.—Age, 38 years. Enrolled, May 2, 1898, at Brooklyn, to serve two years; mustered in as captain, Co. H, May 24, 1898; mustered out with company, March 31, 1899, at Brooklyn, N. Y.; commissioned captain, May 24, 1898, with rank from same date, original.

BROWER JOHN D.—Age, 27 years. Enlisted, May 2, 1898, at Brooklyn, to serve two years; mustered in as private, Co. I, May 24, 1898; mustered out with company, March 31, 1899, at Brooklyn, N. Y.

BROWN, ARTHUR.—Age, 31 years. Enlisted, May 2, 1898, at Brooklyn, to serve two years; mustered in as private, Co. B, May 24, 1898; mustered out with company, March 31, 1899, at Brooklyn, N. Y.

BROWN, BENJ.—Age, 21 years. Enlisted, May 2, 1898, at Brooklyn, to serve two years; mustered in as private, Co. M, May 24, 1898; promoted corporal, July 29, 1898; sergeant, January 31, 1899; mustered out with company, March 31, 1899, at Brooklyn, N. Y.

BROWN, CHARLES F.—Age, — years. Enlisted, July 29, 1898, at Brooklyn, to serve two years; mustered in as private, Co. B, same date; transferred to Co. H, October 9, 1898; mustered out with company, March 31, 1899, at Brooklyn, N. Y.

BROWN, CHARLES T.—Age, 22 years. Enlisted, May 2, 1898, at Brooklyn, to serve two years; mustered in as private, Co. L, May 24, 1898; transferred to United States Signal Corps, March 3, 1899.

BROWN, FREDERICK G.—Age, 25 years.   Enlisted, May 2, 1898, at Brooklyn, to serve two years; mustered in as private, Co. F, May 24, 1898; mustered out with company, March 31, 1899, at Brooklyn, N. Y.

BROWN, JOHN E.—Age, — years.   Enlisted, August 5, 1898, at Brooklyn, to serve two years; mustered in as private, Co. B, same date; mustered out with company, March 31, 1899, at Brooklyn, N. Y.

BRUCH, HENRY.—Age, — years.   Enlisted, August 5, 1898, at Brooklyn, to serve two years; mustered in as private, Co. F, same date; mustered out with company, March 31, 1899, at Brooklyn, N. Y.

BRUMAGHIM, JESSE E.—Age, 23 years.   Enlisted, May 2, 1898, at Brooklyn, to serve two years; mustered in as private, Co. B, May 24, 1898; promoted corporal, August 15, 1898; discharged, October 9, 1898, at Fort Adams, R. I.

BRUSH, ARTHUR P.—Age, 21 years.   Enlisted, May 2, 1898, at Brooklyn, to serve two years; mustered in as corporal, Co. D, May 24, 1898; promoted sergeant, June 1, 1898; mustered out with company, March 31, 1899, at Brooklyn, N. Y.

BRUSH, ELBERT H.—Age, 26 years.   Enlisted, May 2, 1898, at Brooklyn, to serve two years; mustered in as private, Co. I, May 24, 1898; promoted sergeant, May 24, 1898; first sergeant, January 12, 1899; mustered out with company, March 31, 1899, at Brooklyn, N. Y.

BUCHAN, THOMAS.—Age, 24 years.   Enlisted, May 2, 1898, at Brooklyn, to serve two years; mustered in as private, Co. K, May 24, 1898; mustered out with company, March 31, 1899, at Brooklyn, N. Y.

BUCKBEE. WILLIAM H.—Age, 25 years.   Enlisted, May 2, 1898, at Brooklyn, to serve two years; mustered in as private. Co. I, May 24, 1898; mustered out with company, March 31, 1899, at Brooklyn, N. Y.

BUCKLEY, JOHN J.—Age, 26 years.   Enlisted, May 2, 1898, at Brooklyn, to serve two years; mustered in as private, Co. M, May 24, 1898; mustered out with company, March 31, 1899, at Brooklyn, N. Y.

BUCKLEY, WILLIAM.—Age, 25 years. Enlisted, May 2, 1898, at Brooklyn, to serve two years; mustered in as private, Co. M, May 24, 1898; mustered out with company, March 31, 1899, at Brooklyn, N. Y.

BUCKNALL, HARRY.—Age, 25 years. Enlisted, May 2, 1898, at Brooklyn, to serve two years; mustered in as private, Co. K, May 24, 1898; deserted, August 21,.1898.

BUITLES, ROBERT W.—Age, — years. Enlisted, August 5, 1898, at Brooklyn, to serve two years; ·mustered in as private, Co. H, same date; accidently killed, October 25, 1898, on board United States transport "Chester," en-route from Ponce, P. R., to San Juan, P. R.

BURGER, RUDOLPH G.—Age, 23 years. Enlisted, May 2, 1898, at Brooklyn, to serve two years; mustered in as private, Co. C, May 24, 1898; promoted corporal, November 1, 1898; mustered out with company, March 31, 1899, at Brooklyn, N. Y.

BURGLAND, FRITZ.—Age, 21 years. Enlisted, May 2, 1898, at Brooklyn, to serve two years; mustered in as wagoner, Co. K, May 24, 1898; mustered out with company, March 31, 1899, at Brooklyn, N. Y.

BURKE, JAMES.—Age, 24 years. Enlisted, May 2, 1898, at Brooklyn, to serve two years; mustered in as private, Co. D, May 24, 1898; mustered out with company, March 31, 1899, at Brooklyn, N. Y.

BURKE, JOHN.—Age, — years. Enlisted, July 28, 1898, ' at Brooklyn, to serve two years; mustered in as private, Co. C, same date; murdered, February 24, 1899, by a native, at Caguas, P. R.

BURKE, JOHN J.—Age, 26 years. Enlisted, May 2, 1898, at Brooklyn, to serve two years; mustered in as private, Co. D, May 24, 1898; mustered out with company, March 31, 1899, at Brooklyn, N. Y.

BURKE, JOHN T.—Age, — years. Enlisted, August 9, 1898, at Brooklyn, to serve two years; mustered in as private. Co. E, same date; mustered out with company, March 31, 1899, at Brooklyn, N. Y.

BURKE, MICHAEL A.—Age, — years. Enlisted, August 9, 1898, at Brooklyn, to serve two years; mustered in as private, Co. G, same date; discharged, February 14, 1899, at San Juan, P. R.

BURNETT, JOHN.—Age, 28 years. Enlisted, May 2, 1898, at Brooklyn, to serve two years; mustered in as private, Co. F, May 24, 1898; mustered out with company, March 31, 1899, at Brooklyn, N. Y.

BURNIT, CARLTON T.—Age, 24 years. Enlisted, May 2, 1898, at Brooklyn, to serve two years; mustered in as sergeant, Co. C, May 24, 1898; discharged, October 9, 1898, at Fort Adams, R. I.

BURNS, THOMAS F. A.—Age, 24 years. Enlisted, May 2, 1898, at Brooklyn, to serve two years; mustered in as sergeant, Co. K, May 24, 1898; promoted quartermaster-sergeant, October 21, 1898; mustered out with company, March 31, 1899, at Brooklyn, N. Y.

BURRELL, WILLIAM S.—Age, 28 years. Enrolled, May 2, 1898, at Brooklyn, to serve two years; mustered in as first lieutenant, Co. C, May 24, 1898; discharged, September 19, 1898, at Fort Adams, R. I.; commissioned first lieutenant, May 24, 1898, with rank from same date, original.

BURTON, JAMES H.—Age, 21 years. Enlisted, May 20, 1898, at Camp Black, to serve two years; mustered in as private, Co. A, May 24, 1898; mustered out with company, March 31, 1899, at Brooklyn, N. Y.

BUSING, JR., H. W.—Age, 23 years. Enlisted, May 2, 1898, at Brooklyn, to serve two years; mustered in as private, Co. H, May 24, 1898; mustered out with company, March 31, 1899, at Brooklyn, N. Y., as Henry W. Bussing, Jr.

BUSSE, AUGUST M.—Age, 21 years. Enlisted, May 2, 1898, at Brooklyn, to serve two years; mustered in as private, Co. L, May 24, 1898; mustered out with company, March 31, 1899, at Brooklyn, N. Y.

BUTCHER, GEORGE C.—Age, 33 years. Enrolled, May 2, 1898, at Brooklyn, to serve two years; mustered in as captain, Co. F, May 24, 1898; mustered out with company, March 31, 1899, at Brooklyn, N. Y.; commissioned captain, May 24, 1898, with rank from same date, original.

BUTLER, EDWARD G.—Age, 18 years. Enlisted, May 2, 1898, at Brooklyn, to serve two years; mustered in as private, Co. F, May 24, 1898; dishonorably discharged, August 9, 1898, at Fort Adams, R. I.

BUTLER, GEORGE W.—Age, 19 years. Enlisted, May 23, 1898, at Brooklyn, to serve two years; mustered in as private, Co. E, May 24, 1898; discharged without honor, July 10, 1898, at Fort Greble, R. I.

BYRNE, MICHAEL A.—Age, — years.   Enlisted, August 8, 1898, at Brooklyn, to serve two years; mustered in as private, Co. B, same date; mustered out with company, March 31, 1899, at Brooklyn, N. Y.

BYRNES, JOHN J.—Age, 24 years. Enlisted, May 2, 1898, at Brooklyn, to serve two years; mustered in as private, Co. A, May 24, 1898; promoted corporal, December 24, 1898; returned to ranks, March 23, 1899; mustered out with company, March 31, 1899, at Brooklyn, N. Y.

BYRON, THOMAS F.—Age, 22 years. Enlisted, May 2, 1898, at Brooklyn, to serve two years; mustered in as private, Co. B, May 24, 1898; mustered out with company, March 31, 1899, at Brooklyn, N. Y.

CACCIA, RICHARD.—Age, 22 years. Enlisted, May 2, 1898, at Brooklyn, to serve two years; mustered in as private, Co. H, May 24, 1898; mustered out with company, March 31, 1899, at Brooklyn, N. Y.

CAFFE, THEOPHILUS.—Age, 33 years. Enlisted, May 2, 1898, at Brooklyn, to serve two years; mustered in as private, Co. C, May 24, 1898; discharged, February 14, 1899, at San Juan, P. R.

CAHILL, JOHN.—Age, 26 years.   Enlisted, May 2, 1898, at Brooklyn, to serve two years; mustered in as private, Co. M, May 24, 1898; appointed wagoner, September 1, 1898; mustered out with company, March 31, 1899, at Brooklyn, N. Y.

CAIN, SARGE.—Age, 23 years. Enlisted, May 2, 1898, at Brooklyn, to serve two years; mustered in as private, Co. M, May 24, 1898; promoted corporal, August 26, 1898; mustered out with company, March 31, 1899, at Brooklyn, N. Y.

CALLAHAN, JOHN J.—Age, 28 years. Enlisted, May 2, 1898, at Brooklyn, to serve two years; mustered in as private, Co. B, May 24, 1898; mustered out with company, March 31, 1899, at Brooklyn, N. Y.

CALLAHAN, JOSEPH L.—Age, — years. Enlisted, August 3, 1898, at Brooklyn, to serve two years; mustered in as private, Co. C, same date; mustered out with company, March 31, 1899, at Brooklyn, N. Y.

CAMPBELL, CHAS.—Age, 21 years. Enlisted, May 2, 1898, at Brooklyn, to serve two years; mustered in as corporal, Co. H, May 24, 1898; mustered out with company, March 31, 1899, at Brooklyn, N. Y., as Charles L. Campbell.

CAMPBELL, CHARLES B.—Age, 21 years. Enlisted, May 2, 1898, at Brooklyn, to serve two years; mustered in as private, Co. D, May 24, 1898; discharged, December 31, 1898, at Viequas, P. R.

CAMPBELL, WILLIAM.—Age, — years. Enlisted, August 8, 1898, at Brooklyn, to serve two years; mustered in as private, Co. H, same date; mustered out with company, March 31, 1899, at Brooklyn, N. Y.

CANNING, EDWARD L.—Age, — years. Enlisted, August 9, 1898, at Brooklyn, to serve two years; mustered in as private, Co. E, same date; mustered out with company, March 31, 1899, at Brooklyn, N. Y.

CANTEL, THOMAS A.—Age, — years. Enlisted, August 9, 1898, at Brooklyn, to serve two years; mustered in as private, Co. E, same date; discharged, October 7, 1898, at Fort Adams, R. I.

CAREY, HARRY G.—Age, — years. Enlisted, July 29, 1898, at Brooklyn, to serve two years; mustered in as private, Co. M, same date; promoted corporal, November 27, 1899; mustered out with company, March 31, 1899, at Brooklyn, N. Y.

CARL, HORACE.—Age, 28 years. Enlisted, May 2, 1898, at Brooklyn, to serve two years; mustered in as private, Co. A, May 24, 1898; mustered out with company, March 31, 1899, at Brooklyn, N. Y.

CARLOS, HARRY W.—Age, 21 years. Enlisted, May 2, 1898, at Brooklyn, to serve two years; mustered in as private, Co. I, May 24, 1898; mustered out with company, March 31, 1899, at Brooklyn, N. Y., as Harvey W. Carlos.

CARMINE, GEORGE S.—Age, 20 years. Enlisted, May 2, 1898, at Brooklyn, to serve two years; mustered in as private, Co. F, May 24, 1898; mustered out with company, March 31, 1899, at Brooklyn, N. Y.

CARROLL, WILLIAM.—Age, 35 years. Enlisted, May 2, 1898, at Brooklyn, to serve two years; mustered in as private, Co. K, May 24, 1898; mustered out with company, March 31, 1899, at Brooklyn, N. Y.

CASE, FREDERICK S.—Age, 36 years. Enlisted, May 2, 1898, at Brooklyn, to serve two years; mustered in as sergeant, Co. K, May 24, 1898; mustered out with company, March 31, 1899, at Brooklyn, N. Y.

CASE, LEVI B.—Age, 35 years.   Enrolled, May 3, 1898, at Brooklyn, to serve two years; mustered in as first lieutenant and battalion adjutant, May 24, 1898; mustered out with regiment, March 31, 1899, at Brooklyn, N. Y.; commissioned battalion adjutant, May 24, 1898, with rank from same date, original.

CASEY, THOS. F.—Age, 25 years. Enlisted, May 2, 1898, at Brooklyn, to serve two years; mustered in as private, Co. E, May 24, 1898; discharged, November 14, 1898, at Fort Columbus, New York Harbor.

CASEY, WILLIAM H.—Age, 21 years. Enlisted, May 2, 1898, at Brooklyn, to serve two years; mustered in as private, Co. I, May 24, 1898; mustered out with company, March 31, 1899, at Brooklyn, N. Y.

CASEY, WILLIAM J.—Age, 28 years. Enlisted, May 2, 1898, at Brooklyn, to serve two years; mustered in as sergeant, Co. M, May 24, 1898; mustered out with company, March 31, 1899, at Brooklyn, N. Y.

CASSELS, THOMAS.—Age, 31 years. Enlisted, May 23, 1898, at Camp Black, to serve two years; mustered in as private, Co. A, May 24, 1898; mustered out with company, March 31, 1899, at Brooklyn, N. Y.

CASSIDY, JAMES L.—Age, — years. Enlisted, August 1, 1898, at Brooklyn, to serve two years; mustered in as private, Co. M, same date; mustered out with company, March 31, 1899, at Brooklyn, N. Y.

CATTICART, WILLIAM F.—Age, 28 years. Enlisted, May 2, 1898, at Brooklyn, to serve two years; mustered in as wagoner, Co. L, May 24, 1898; deserted, October 10, 1898.

CAVANAGH, JAMES.—Age, — years. Enlisted, July 30, 1898, at Brooklyn to serve two years; mustered in as private, Co. A, same date; mustered out with company, March 31, 1899, at Brooklyn, N. Y.

CAVANAGH, RICHARD J.—Age, 25 years. Enlisted, May 2, 1898, at Brooklyn, to serve two years; mustered in as private, Co. B, May 24, 1898; mustered out with company, March 31, 1899, at Brooklyn, N. Y.

CAVANAUGH, MARTIN.—Age, — years. Enlisted, August 1, 1898, at Brooklyn, to serve two years; mustered in as private, Co. K, same date; mustered out with company, March 31, 1899, at Brooklyn, N. Y.

CHASE, CHARLES A.—Age, 34 years. Enrolled, May 3, 1898, at Brooklyn, to serve two years; mustered in as regimental quartermaster, May 24, 1898; mustered out with regiment, March 31, 1899, as captain and regimental quartermaster, at Brooklyn, N. Y.; commissioned captain and regimental quartermaster, May 24, 1898, with rank from same date, original.

CHASE, GEORGE S.—Age, 25 years. Enlisted, May 2, 1898, at Brooklyn, to serve two years; mustered in as private, Co. B, May 24, 1898; transferred to Hospital Corps, United States Army, September 4, 1898.

CHASSELL, GEORGE.—Age, 18 years. Enlisted, May 2, 1898, at Brooklyn, to serve two years; mustered in as private, Co. K, May 24, 1898; promoted corporal, October 21, 1898; returned to ranks, March 21, 1899; mustered out with company, March 31, 1899, at Brooklyn, N. Y.

CHICHESTER, THOMAS K.—Age, 19 years. Enlisted, May 2, 1898, at Brooklyn, to serve two years; mustered in as private, Co. C, May 24, 1898; mustered out with company, March 31,

CLARK, ARTHUR J.—Age, 22 years. Enlisted, May 2, 1898, at Brooklyn, to serve two years; mustered in as private, Co. M, May 24, 1898; mustered out with company, March 31, 1899, at Brooklyn, N. Y.

CLARK, JOHN A.—Age, 23 years. Enlisted, May 2, 1898, at Brooklyn, to serve two years; mustered in as private, Co. B, May 24, 1898; mustered out with company, March 31, 1899, at Brooklyn, N. Y.

CLARK, JOHN C.—Age, — years. Enlisted, July 26, 1898, at Brooklyn, to serve two years; mustered in as private, Co. M, same date; mustered out with company, March 31, 1899, at Brooklyn, N. Y.

CLARK, ROBERT J.—Age, — years. Enlisted, August 9, 1898, at Brooklyn, to serve two years; mustered in as private, Co. D, same date; mustered out with company, March 31, 1899, at Brooklyn, N. Y.

CLAUS, HARRY V.—Age, 22 years. Enlisted, May 2, 1898, at Brooklyn, to serve two years; mustered in as private, Co. D, May 24, 1898; mustered out with company, March 31, 1899, at Brooklyn, N. Y.

CLAY, FRANK.—Age, — years. Enlisted, July 27, 1898, at Brooklyn, to serve two years; mustered in as private, Co. A, same date; mustered out with company, March 31, 1899, at Brooklyn, N. Y.

CLEARY, EDWARD C.—Age, 19 years. Enlisted, May 2, 1898, at Brooklyn, to serve two years; mustered in as private, Co. G, May 24, 1898; mustered out with company, March 31, 1899, at Brooklyn, N. Y.

CLEMENTS, JR., ROBERT.—Age, 21 years. Enlisted, May 2, 1898, at Brooklyn, to serve two years; mustered in as private, Co. I, May 24, 1898; mustered out with company, March 31, 1899, at Brooklyn, N. Y.

CLEMETT, FRED E.—Age, 20 years. Enlisted, May 2, 1898, at Brooklyn, to serve two years; mustered in as private, Co. K, May 24, 1898; promoted corporal, August 8, 1898; returned to ranks, October 22, 1898; mustered out, to date, March 31, 1899.

CLEMETT, SIDNEY W.—Age, 27 years. Enlisted, May 2, 1898, at Brooklyn, to serve two years; mustered in as first sergeant, Co. K, May 24, 1898; mustered out with company, March 31, 1899, at Brooklyn, N. Y.

CLIFFORD, JAMES S.—Age, 25 years. Enlisted, May 2, 1898, at Brooklyn, to serve two years; mustered in as private, Co. B, May 24, 1898; mustered out with company, March 31, 1899, at Brooklyn, N. Y.

CLINE, FRANK J.—Age, 23 years. Enlisted, May 2, 1898, at Brooklyn, to serve two years; mustered in as private, Co. A, May 24, 1898; mustered out with company, March 31, 1899, at Brooklyn, N. Y.

COHEN, GUS.—Age, 22 years. Enlisted, May 2, 1898, at Brooklyn, to serve two years; mustered in as private, Co. D, May 24, 1898; promoted corporal, August 27, 1898; mustered out with company, March 31, 1899, at Brooklyn, N. Y.

COHEN, JACOB.—Age, — years. Enlisted, July 26, 1898, at Brooklyn, to serve two years; mustered in as private, Co. E, same date; mustered out with company, March 31, 1899, at Brooklyn, N. Y.

COLBERG, EDWARD H.—Age, — years. Enlisted, July 25, 1898, at Brooklyn, to serve two years; mustered in as private, Co. I, same date; mustered out with company, March 31, 1899, at Brooklyn, N. Y

COLGAN, JOHN J.—Age, 33 years. Enlisted, May 2, 1898, at Brooklyn, to serve two years; mustered in as private, Co. B, May 24, 1898; mustered out with company, March 31, 1899, at Brooklyn, N. Y.

COLLIER, WILLIAM P.—Age, — years. Enlisted, August 4, 1898, at Brooklyn, to serve two years; mustered in as private, Co. B, same date; mustered out with company, March 31, 1899, at Brooklyn, N. Y.

COLLINS, ABE.—Age, — years. Enlisted, August 11, 1898, at Brooklyn, to serve two years; mustered in as private, Co. H, same date; mustered out with company, March 31, 1899, at Brooklyn, N. Y.

COLLINS, EDWARD J.—Age, 21 years. Enlisted, May 2, 1898, at Brooklyn, to serve two years; mustered in as private, Co. L, May 24, 1898; mustered out with company, March 31, 1899, at Brooklyn, N. Y.

COLLINS, WILLIAM R.—Age, 43 years. Enlisted, May 2, 1898, at Brooklyn, to serve two years; mustered in as quartermaster-sergeant, Co. G, May 24, 1898; mustered out with company, March 31, 1899, at Brooklyn, N. Y.

COLWELL, JOHN J.—Age, 37 years. Enlisted, May 2, 1898, at Brooklyn, to serve two years; mustered in as private, Co. C, May 24, 1898; mustered out with company, March 31, 1899, at Brooklyn, N. Y.

COMERFORD, JAMES S.—Age, 31 years.   Enlisted, May 2, 1898, at Brooklyn, to serve two years; mustered in as private, Co. H, May 24, 1898; promoted corporal, January 16, 1899; mustered out with company, March 31, 1899, at Brooklyn, N. Y.

CONCANNON, GEORGE.—Age, 25 years.   Enlisted, May 2, 1898, at Brooklyn, to serve two years; mustered in as private, Co. F, May 24, 1898; mustered out with company, March 31, 1899, at Brooklyn, N. Y.

CONNEALLY, STEPHEN D.—Age 21 years.   Enlisted, May 2, 1898, at Brooklyn, to serve two years; mustered in as private, Co. E, May 24, 1898; promoted corporal, October 21, 1898; mustered out with company, March 31, 1899, at Brooklyn, N. Y.

CONNELL, WILLIAM.—Age, 20 years. Enlisted, May 23, 1898, at Brooklyn, to serve two years; mustered in as private, Co. E, May 24, 1898; mustered out with company, March 31, 1899, at Brooklyn, N. Y.

CONNORS, JOHN J.—Age, — years. Enlisted, August 4, 1898, at Brooklyn, to serve two years; mustered in as private, Co. F, same date; mustered out with company, March 31, 1899, at Brooklyn, N. Y.

CONRAD, JOSEPH.—Age, — years. Enlisted, August 6, 1898, at Brooklyn, to serve two years; mustered in as private, Co. E, same date; mustered out with company, March 31, 1899, at Brooklyn, N. Y.

CONROY, WILLIAM H.—Age, 21 years. Enlisted, May 2, 1898, at Brooklyn, to serve two years; mustered in as private, Co. C, May 24, 1898; promoted corporal, August 5, 1898; discharged, February 14, 1899, at San Juan, P. R.

CONSIDINE, CORNELIUS.—Age, 28 years. Enlisted, May 2, 1898, at Brooklyn, to serve two years; mustered in as private, Co. I, May 24, 1898; promoted corporal, November 1, 1898; mustered out with company, March 31, 1899, at Brooklyn, N. Y.

CONSTANTINE, EDWIN B.—Age, 18 years. Enlisted, June 6, 1898, at Camp Black, to serve two years; mustered in as private, Co. F, June 7, 1898; appointed artificer, September 20, 1898; promoted corporal, October 22, 1898; mustered out with company, March 31, 1899, at Brooklyn, N. Y.

COOKE, EDWARD.—Age, 22 years. Enlisted, May 2, 1898, at Brooklyn, to serve two years; mustered in as private, Co. G, May 24, 1898; promoted corporal, December 9, 1898; mustered out with company, March 31, 1899, at Brooklyn, N. Y.

COOMBS, J. B.—Age, 28 years. Enlisted, May 2, 1898, at Brooklyn, to serve two years; mustered in as private, Co M, May 24, 1898; mustered out with company, March 31, 1899, at Brooklyn, N. Y.

COOPER, SIMEON J.—Age, 21 years. Enlisted, May 2, 1898, at Brooklyn, to serve two years; mustered in as private, Co. C, May 24, 1898; promoted corporal, June 17, 1898; sergeant, November 1, 1898; discharged, February 4, 1899, at Caguas, P. R.

COPP, RUSSELL B.—Age, 26 years. Enlisted, May 2, 1898, at Brooklyn, to serve two years; mustered in as private, Co. I, May 24, 1898; promoted corporal, August 26, 1898; mustered out with company, March 31, 1899, at Brooklyn, N. Y.

CORDES, J. H.—Age, 25 years. Enlisted, May 2, 1898, at Brooklyn, to serve two years; mustered in as private, Co. G, May 24, 1898; promoted corporal, January 1, 1899; mustered out with company, March 31, 1899, at Brooklyn, N. Y.

CORDTS, FRANK.—Age, 21 years. Enlisted, May 2, 1898, at Brooklyn, to serve two years; mustered in as private, Co. K, May 24, 1898; mustered out with company, March 31, 1899, at Brooklyn, N. Y.

CORNWELL, JAMES L.—Age, 23 years. Enlisted, May 2, 1898, at Brooklyn, to serve two years; mustered in as private, Co. G, May 24, 1898; discharged, October 14, 1898, at Fort Adams, R. I.

COSTELLO, THOMAS J.—Age, 19 years Enlisted, May 2, 1898, at Brooklyn, to serve two years; mustered in as private, Co. D, May 24, 1898; promoted corporal, December 13, 1899; mustered out with company, March 31, 1899, at Brooklyn, N. Y.

COSTER, JOHN H.—Age, — years. Enlisted, July 26, 1898, at Brooklyn, to serve two years; mustered in as private, Co. F, same date; mustered out with company, March 31, 1899, at Brooklyn, N. Y.

COVERT, C. PERCIVAL.—Age, 21 years. Enlisted, May 2, 1898, at Brooklyn, to serve two years; mustered in as private, Co. G, May 24, 1898; mustered out with company, March 31, 1899, at Brooklyn, N. Y.

COWEN, JOHN.—Age, — years. Enlisted, July 25, 1898, at Brooklyn, to serve two years; mustered in as private, Co. D, same date; promoted corporal, November 28, 1898; mustered out with company, March 31, 1899, at Brooklyn, N. Y.

COYSH, CHARLES H.—Age, 21 years. Enlisted, May 2, 1898, at Brooklyn, to serve two years; mustered in as private, Co. I, May 24, 1898; promoted corporal, August 10, 1898; mustered out with company, March 31, 1899, at Brooklyn, N. Y.

CRANE, JOHN.—Age, 22 years. Enlisted, May 2, 1898, at Brooklyn, to serve two years; mustered in as private, Co. F, May 24, 1898; mustered out with company, March 31, 1899, at Brooklyn, N. Y.

CRESTMANN, CHARLES.—Age, 23 years. Enlisted, May 2, 1898, at Brooklyn, to serve two years; mustered in as private, Co. H, May 24, 1898; deserted, October 6, 1898, at Fort Adams, R. I.

CROCHETIERE, ORVILE J.—Age, — years. Enlisted, July 26, 1898, at Brooklyn, to serve two years; mustered in as private, Co. D, same date; mustered out with company, March 31, 1899, at Brooklyn, N. Y.

CRONK, GEORGE B.—Age, 32 years. Enlisted, May 2, 1898, at
Brooklyn, to serve two years; mustered in as private, Co. B,
May 24, 1898; deserted, September 22, 1898.

CROOK, GEORGE.—Age, — years. Enlisted, August 4, 1898, at
Brooklyn, to serve two years; mustered in as private, Co. H,
same date; promoted corporal, August 16, 1898; sergeant,
December 17, 1898; first sergeant, February 1, 1899; mustered
out with company, March 31, 1899, at Brooklyn, N. Y.

CROSIER, JOSEPH T.—Age, 24 years. Enlisted, May 2, 1898,
at Brooklyn, to serve two years; mustered in as private, Co. C
May 24, 1898; promoted corporal, June 17, 1898; sergeant,
November 1, 1898; first sergeant, same date; mustered out with
company, March 31, 1899, at Brooklyn, N. Y.

CROZIER, JOHN D.—Age, 21 years. Enlisted, May 2, 1898, at
Brooklyn, to serve two years; mustered in as private, Co. K,
May 24, 1898; mustered out with company, March 31, 1899, at
Brooklyn, N. Y.

CRUGER, FREDERICK G.—Age, 18 years. Enlisted, May 2,
1898, at Brooklyn, to serve two years; mustered in as private,
Co. B, May 24, 1898; mustered out with company, March 31,
1899, at Brooklyn, N. Y.

CUMMINGS, ROBERT.—Age, 38 years. Enlisted, May 2, 1898,
at Brooklyn, to serve two years; mustered in as private, Co.
L, May 24, 1898; mustered out with company, March 31, 1899,
at Brooklyn, N. Y.

CUNNINGHAM, WILLIAM.—Age, — years. Enlisted, August 2,
1898, at Brooklyn, to serve two years; mustered in as private,
Co. D, same date; mustered out with company, March 31, 1899,
at Brooklyn, N. Y.

CURLEY, JOSEPH.—Age, 21 years. Enlisted, May 2, 1898, at
Brooklyn, to serve two years; mustered in as private, Co. M,
May 24, 1898; mustered out with company, March 31, 1899, at
Brooklyn, N. Y.

CURRY, HARRY E.—Age, 22 years. Enlisted, May 2, 1898, at
Brooklyn, to serve two years; mustered in as private, Co. D,
May 24, 1898; discharged, October 12, 1898, at Fort Columbus,
New York Harbor.

CURTIN, JAMES J.—Age, 28 years. Enlisted, May 2, 1898, at Brooklyn, to serve two years; mustered in as sergeant, Co. G, May 24, 1898; returned to ranks, June 1, 1898; promoted corporal, August 20, 1898; sergeant, November 1, 1898; mustered out with company, March 31, 1899, at Brooklyn, N. Y.

CURTIN, JOHN J.—Age, 20 years. Enlisted, May 2, 1898, at Brooklyn, to serve two years; mustered in as private, Co. G, May 24, 1898; mustered out with company, March 31, 1899, at Brooklyn, N. Y.

CURTIS, HARRY.—Age, 27 years. Enlisted, May 2, 1898, at Brooklyn, to serve two years; mustered in as private, Co. H, May 24, 1898; appointed musician, no date; mustered out with company, March 31, 1899, at Brooklyn, N. Y.

CURTISS, SUMMERFIELD S.—Age, 27 years. Enlisted, May 2, 1898, at Brooklyn, to serve two years; mustered in as sergeant, Co. K, May 24, 1898; mustered out with company, March 31, 1899, at Brooklyn, N. Y.

CUSHING, THOMAS F.—Age, 20 years. Enlisted, May 2, 1898, at Brooklyn, to serve two years; mustered in as sergeant, Co. A, May 24, 1898; discharged, October 12, 1898.

DAHLBENDER, FRANK.—Age, 22 years. Enlisted, May 2, 1898, at Brooklyn, to serve two years; mustered in as private, Co. C, May 24, 1898; promoted corporal, August 6, 1898; returned to ranks, December 5, 1898; mustered out with company, March 31, 1899, at Brooklyn, N. Y.

DAISER, LOUIS A.—Age, — years. Enlisted, July 26, 1898, at Brooklyn, to serve two years; mustered in as private, Co. K, same date; mustered out with company, March 31, 1899, at Brooklyn, N. Y.

DALY, JOSEPH A.—Age, — years. Enlisted, July 29, 1898, at Brooklyn, to serve two years; mustered in as private, Co. L, same date; mustered out with company, March 31, 1899, at Brooklyn, N. Y.

DALY, PETER J.—Age, 21 years. Enlisted, May 2, 1898, at Brooklyn, to serve two years; mustered in as private, Co. C, May 24, 1898; died from self-inflicted pistol wounds, October 7, 1898, at Fort Adams, R. I.

DARBY, JOSEPH H.—Age, 21 years. Enlisted, May 2, 1898, at Brooklyn, to serve two years; mustered in as private, Co. H, May 24, 1898; mustered out with company, March 31, 1899, at Brooklyn, N. Y.

DARDIS, JAMES L.—Age, — years. Enlisted, July 26, 1898, at Brooklyn, to serve two years; mustered in as private, Co. I, same date; mustered out with company, March 31, 1899, at Brooklyn, N. Y.

DARSONVILLE, EMILE J.—Age, 22 years. Enlisted, May 2, 1898, at Brooklyn, to serve two years; mustered in as private, Co. F, May 24, 1898; discharged for disability, February 2, 1899, at Fajaedo, P. R.

DAVIS, CHARLES M.—Age, 28 years. Enlisted, May 2, 1898, at Brooklyn, to serve two years; mustered in as quartermaster-sergeant, Co. D, May 24, 1898; mustered out with company, March 31, 1899, at Brooklyn, N. Y.

DAVIS, FRANK.—Age, — years. Enlisted, July 30, 1898, at Brooklyn, to serve two years; mustered in as private, Co. D, same date; mustered out with company, March 31, 1899, at Brooklyn, N. Y.

DAVIS, HERBERT F.—Age, 19 years. Enlisted, May 2, 1898, at Brooklyn, to serve two years; mustered in as private, Co. C, May 24, 1898; promoted corporal, November 1, 1898; mustered out with company, March 31, 1899, at Brooklyn, N. Y.

DAVIS, JEREMIAH T.—Age, 26 years. Enlisted, May 2, 1898, at Brooklyn, to serve two years; mustered in as private, Co. I, May 24, 1898; mustered out with company, March 31, 1899, at Brooklyn, N. Y.

DAWKINS, THOS. F.—Age, 20 years. Enlisted, May 2, 1898, at Brooklyn, to serve two years; mustered in as private, Co. E, May 24, 1898; mustered out with company, March 31, 1899, at Brooklyn, N. Y.

DAWKINS, WILLIAM J.—Age, 44 years. Enlisted, May 2, 1898, at Brooklyn, to serve two years; mustered in as private, Co. K, May 24, 1898; promoted corporal, August 1, 1898; discharged, January 28, 1899, at Guayama, P. R.

DAWSON, ISAAC.—Age, 25 years. Enlisted, May 2, 1898, at Brooklyn, to serve two years; mustered in as private, Co. H, May 24, 1898; mustered out with company, March 31, 1899, at Brooklyn, N. Y.

DAY, JOSEPH R.—Age, 31 years. Enlisted, May 2, 1898, at Brooklyn, to serve two years; mustered in as private, Co. I, May 24, 1898; mustered out with company, March 31, 1899, at Brooklyn, N. Y.

DEARDON, HARRY R.—Age, — years. Enlisted, July 30, 1898, at Brooklyn, to serve two years; mustered in as private, Co. B, same date; mustered out with company, March 31, 1899, at Brooklyn, N. Y.

DE CASTRO, HENRY A.—Age, 28 years. Enlisted, May 23, 1898, at Camp Black, to serve two years; mustered in as musician, Co. A, May 24, 1898; mustered out with company, March 31, 1899, at Brooklyn, N. Y.

DE CASTRO, THEODORE E.—Age, 20 years. Enlisted, May 2, 1898, at Brooklyn, to serve two years; mustered in as private, Co. D, May 24, 1898; mustered out with company, March 31, 1899, at Brooklyn, N. Y.

DEERY, JAMES.—Age, — years. Enlisted, July 28, 1898, at Brooklyn, to serve two years; mustered in as private, Co. C, same date; appointed lance corporal, January 3, 1899; promoted corporal, January 20, 1899; mustered out with company, March 31, 1899, at Brooklyn, N. Y.

DEMPSEY, JOHN J.—Age, 21 years. Enlisted, May 2, 1898, at Brooklyn, to serve two years; mustered in as private, Co. M, May 24, 1898; mustered out with company, March 31, 1899, at Brooklyn, N. Y.

DENNEN, HENRY J.—Age, 21 years. Enlisted, May 2, 1898, at Brooklyn, to serve two years; mustered in as private, Co. L, May 24, 1898; mustered out with company, March 31, 1899, at Brooklyn, N. Y.

DENVER, JAMES J.—Age, 24 years. Enlisted, May 2, 1898, at Brooklyn, to serve two years; mustered in as private, Co. C, May 24, 1898; mustered out with company, March 31, 1899, at Brooklyn, N. Y.

DESCH, JOSEPH.—Age, 23 years.   Enlisted, May 2, 1898, at
Brooklyn, to serve two years; mustered in as private, Co. I,
May 24, 1898; promoted sergeant, same date; mustered out with
company, March 31, 1899, at Brooklyn, N. Y.

DEVINE, BENEDICT T.—Age, 35 years.   Enlisted, May 2, 1898,
at Brooklyn, to serve two years; mustered in as private, Co. B,
May 24, 1898; discharged for disability, October 11, 1898, at
Fort Adams, R. I.

DEVINE, WILLIAM H.—Age, — years.   Enlisted, August 6,
1898, at Brooklyn, to serve two years; mustered in as private,
Co. K, same date; mustered out with company, March 31, 1899,
at Brooklyn, N. Y.

DICKINSON, JOHN B.—Age, 32 years.   Enlisted, May 2, 1898,
at Brooklyn, to serve two years; mustered in as private, Co. M,
May 24, 1898; discharged, October 14, 1898, at Fort Adams,
R. I.

DILLON, GEORGE.—Age, 21 years.   Enlisted, May 2, 1898, at
Brooklyn, to serve two years; mustered in as private, Co. F,
May 24, 1898; mustered out with company, March 31, 1899, at
Brooklyn, N. Y.

DIXON, MILTON S.—Age, — years.   Enlisted, August 11, 1898,
at Brooklyn, to serve two years; mustered in as private, Co. L,
August 24, 1898; discharged, October 12, 1898, at Fort Adams,
R. I.

DONAHO, STEPHEN A.—Age, 30 years.   Enlisted, May 2, 1898,
at Brooklyn, to serve two years; mustered in as private, Co. L,
May 24, 1898; mustered out with company, March 31, 1899, at
Brooklyn, N. Y.

DONAHUE, JAMES.—Age, 24 years.   Enlisted, May 2, 1898, at
Brooklyn, to serve two years; mustered in as private, Co. G,
May 24, 1898; mustered out with company, March 31, 1899, at
Brooklyn, N. Y.

DONAHUE, THOMAS.—Age, — years.   Enlisted, August 8,
1898, at Brooklyn, to serve two years; mustered in as private,
Co. M, same date; discharged, January 15, 1898, at New York
city.

DONALDSON, WILLIAM.—Age, — years. Enlisted, July 29, 1898, at Brooklyn, to serve two years; mustered in as private, Co. C, same date; mustered out with company, March 31, 1899, at Brooklyn, N. Y.

DONLON, JOHN J.—Age, 19 years. Enlisted, May 2, 1898, at Brooklyn, to serve two years; mustered in as private, Co. F, May 24, 1898; mustered out with company, March 31, 1899, at Brooklyn, N. Y.

DONNELLY, CHARLES S.—Age, 31 years. Enlisted, May 2, 1898, at Brooklyn, to serve two years; mustered in as private, Co. E, May 24, 1898; promoted corporal, same date; discharged, October 14, 1898, at Fort Adams, R. I.

DONNELLY, STEPHEN R.—Age, — years. Enlisted, July 30, 1898, at Brooklyn, to serve two years; mustered in as private, Co. H, same date; mustered out with company, March 31, 1899, at Brooklyn, N. Y.

DONNER, FRANCIS.—Age, 24 years. Enlisted, May 18, 1898, at Brooklyn, to serve two years; mustered in as private, Co. E, May 24, 1898; promoted corporal, October 21, 1898; mustered out with company, March 31, 1899, at Brooklyn, N. Y.

DONNER, THOMAS P.—Age, 28 years. Enlisted, May 18, 1898, at Brooklyn, to serve two years; mustered in as private, Co. E, May 24, 1898; mustered out with company, March 31, 1899, at Brooklyn, N. Y.

DOODY, MICHAEL J.—Age, 34 years. Enlisted, May 2, 1898, at Brooklyn, to serve two years; mustered in as private, Co. F, May 24, 1898; mustered out with company, March 31, 1899, at Brooklyn, N. Y.

DOOLEY, JOSEPH J.—Age, 30 years. Enlisted, May 2, 1898, at Brooklyn, to serve two years; mustered in as private, Co. B, May 24, 1898; mustered out with company, March 31, 1899, at Brooklyn, N. Y.

DOREMUS, DAVID T.—Age, 39 years. Enlisted, May 2, 1898, at Brooklyn, to serve two years; mustered in as private, Co. K, May 24, 1898; promoted corporal, October 21, 1898; mustered out with company, March 31, 1899, at Brooklyn, N. Y.

DOREMUS, JOHN A.—Age, 26 years. Enrolled, May 2, 1898, at Brooklyn, to serve two years; mustered in as captain, Co. I, May 24, 1898; mustered out with company, March 31, 1899, at Brooklyn, N. Y.; commissioned captain, May 24, 1898, with rank from same date, original.

DOREMUS, WILLIAM H.—Age, 23 years. Enrolled, May 2, 1898, at Brooklyn, to serve two years; mustered in as first lieutenant, Co. I, May 24, 1898; as captain, Co. A, December 20, 1898; mustered out with company, March 31, 1899, at Brooklyn, N. Y.; commissioned first lieutenant, May 24, 1898, with rank from same date, original; captain, December 17, 1898, with rank from same date, vice Jannickey, discharged.

DORMAN, SAMUEL.—Age, — years. Enlisted, July 26, 1898, at Brooklyn, to serve two years; mustered in as private, Co. G, same date; mustered out with company, March 31, 1899, at Brooklyn, N. Y.

DORRIAN, GEORGE M.—Age, 23 years. Enlisted, May 22, 1898, at Brooklyn, to serve two years; mustered in as private, Co. E, May 24, 1898; mustered out with company, March 31, 1899, at Brooklyn, N. Y.

DORSEY, JOHN J.—Age, 31 years. Enlisted, May 2, 1898, at Brooklyn, to serve two years; mustered in as private, Co. B, May 24, 1898; promoted corporal, August 15, 1898; mustered out with company, March 31, 1899, at Brooklyn, N. Y.

DOTY, GEORGE B.—Age, — years. Enlisted, August 2, 1898, at Brooklyn, to serve two years; mustered in as private, Co. I, same date; mustered out with company, March 31, 1899, at Brooklyn, N. Y.

DOUGHERTY, PETER J.—Age, 28 years. Enlisted, May 2, 1898, at Brooklyn, to serve two years; mustered in as private, Co. D, May 24, 1898; mustered out with company, March 31, 1899, at Brooklyn, N. Y.

DOUGLASS, JAMES S.—Age, 24 years. Enlisted, May 2, 1898, at Brooklyn, to serve two years; mustered in as corporal, Co. F, May 24, 1898; promoted sergeant, July 23, 1898; discharged, October 12, 1898, at Fort Adams, R. I.

DOWLING, JAMES A.—Age, 32 years. Enlisted, May 20, 1898, at Camp Black, to serve two years; mustered in as private, Co. A, May 24, 1898; mustered out with company, March 31, 1899, at Brooklyn, N. Y.

DOWLING, JOHN J.—Age, 29 years. Enlisted, May 2, 1898, at Brooklyn, to serve two years; mustered in as private, Co. L, May 24, 1898; mustered out with company, March 31, 1899, at Brooklyn, N. Y.

DOYLE, JOHN F.—Age, 24 years. Enlisted, May 2, 1898, at Brooklyn, to serve two years; mustered in as private, Co. B, May 24, 1898; mustered out, to date, March 31, 1899.

DOYLE, JOHN F.—Age, 24 years. Enlisted, May 2, 1898, at Brooklyn, to serve two years; mustered in as private, Co. K, May 24, 1898; mustered out with company, March 31, 1899, at Brooklyn, N. Y.

DOYLE, JOHN J.—Age, — years. Enlisted, July 27, 1898, at Brooklyn, to serve two years; mustered in as private, Co. M, same date; mustered out with company, March 31, 1899, at Brooklyn, N. Y.

DOYLE, JOSEPH P.—Age, — years. Enlisted, July 27, 1898, at Brooklyn, to serve two years; mustered in as private, Co. M, same date; mustered out with company, March 31, 1899, at Brooklyn, N. Y.

DRUMMOND, JOHN M.—Age, 21 years. Enlisted, May 2, 1898, at Brooklyn, to serve two years; mustered in as private, Co. E, May 24, 1898; discharged, October 14, 1898, at Fort Adams, R. I.

DRYDEN, EDWARD.—Age, 23 years. Enlisted, May 2, 1898, at Brooklyn, to serve two years; mustered in as private, Co. A, May 24, 1898; appointed wagoner, July 12, 1898; mustered out with company, March 31, 1899, at Brooklyn, N. Y.

DUCKWORTH, DORIE.—Age, 24 years. Enlisted, May 23, 1898, at Brooklyn, to serve two years; mustered in as private, Co. E, May 24, 1898; mustered out with company, March 31, 1899, at Brooklyn, N. Y.

DUCOAL, MARIM.—Age, — years. Enlisted, August 8, 1898, at Brooklyn, to serve two years; mustered in as private, Co. D, same date; discharged, December 31, 1898, at Vieques, P. R., as Marion Ducont.

DUFFY, GEORGE E.—Age, 27 years. Enlisted, May 2, 1898, at Brooklyn, to serve two years; mustered in as wagoner, Co. B, May 24, 1898; promoted corporal, June 1, 1898; sergeant, November 14, 1898; mustered out with company, March 31, 1899, at Brooklyn, N. Y.

DUFFY, JOHN.—Age, 23 years. Enlisted, May 2, 1898, at Brooklyn, to serve two years; mustered in as private, Co. K, May 24, 1898; mustered out with company, March 31, 1899, at Brooklyn, N. Y.

DUNN, PETER F.—Age, — years. Enlisted, July 28, 1898, at Brooklyn, to serve two years; mustered in as private, Co. K, same date; mustered out with company, March 31, 1899, at Brooklyn, N. Y.

DUNN, WILLIAM.—Age, 21 years. Enlisted, May 2, 1898, at Brooklyn, to serve two years; mustered in as private, Co. M, May 24, 1898; mustered out, to date, March 31, 1899.

DURLAND, ALBERT S.—Age, 32 years. Enlisted, May 2, 1898, at Brooklyn, to serve two years; mustered in as private, Co. I, May 24, 1898; mustered out with company, March 31, 1899, at Brooklyn, N. Y.

DWYER, JOHN G.—Age, 28 years. Enlisted, May 20, 1898, at Camp Black, to serve two years; mustered in as private, Co. A, May 24, 1898; mustered out with company, March 31, 1899, at Brooklyn, N. Y.

DWYER, JOHN P.—Age, 22 years. Enlisted, May 2, 1898, at Brooklyn, to serve two years; mustered in as private, Co. I, May 24, 1898; mustered out with company, March 31, 1899, at Brooklyn, N. Y.

EAGLE, CLIFFORD H.—Age, 19 years. Enlisted, May 2, 1898, at Brooklyn, to serve two years; mustered in as private, Co. C, May 24, 1898; promoted corporal, August 6, 1898; discharged, February 4, 1899, at Caguas, P. R.

ECKE, ALBERT F.—Age, 21 years. Enlisted, May 2, 1898, at Brooklyn, to serve two years; mustered in as private, Co. L, May 24, 1898; transferred to Co. H, August 22, 1898; promoted corporal, September 1, 1898; mustered out with company, March 31, 1899, at Brooklyn, N. Y.

EDER, PHILIP.—Age, — years. Enlisted, July 25, 1898, at Brooklyn, to serve two years; mustered in as private, Co. L, same date; mustered out with company, March 31, 1899, at Brooklyn, N. Y.

EDER, JR., VALENTINE.—Age, — years. Enlisted, July 26, 1898, at Brooklyn, to serve two years; mustered in as private, Co. L, same date; mustered out with company, March 31, 1899, at Brooklyn, N. Y.

EDDY, JOHN G.—Age, 45 years. Enrolled, May 3, 1898, at Brooklyn, to serve two years; mustered in as colonel, May 24, 1898; discharged, December 2, 1898; commissioned colonel, May 1, 1898, with rank from same date, original.

EDMONDSON, ARTHUR.—Age, — years. Enlisted, August 11, 1898, at Brooklyn, to serve two years; mustered in as private, Co. H, same date; deserted, October 1, 1898, at Fort Adams, R. I.

EHLENBERGER, HENRY.—Age, 29 years. Enlisted, May 2, 1898, at Brooklyn, to serve two years; mustered in as private, Co. A, May 24, 1898; mustered out with company, March 31, 1899, at Brooklyn, N. Y.

ELFORD, HUGH.—Age, — years. Enlisted, August 6, 1898, at Brooklyn, to serve two years; mustered in as private, Co. M, same date; promoted corporal, February 15, 1899; mustered out with company, March 31, 1899, at Brooklyn, N. Y.

ELIAS, JOSEPH.—Age, — years. Enlisted, July 25, 1898, at Brooklyn, to serve two years; mustered in as private, Co. E, same date; mustered out with company, March 31, 1899, at Brooklyn, N. Y.

ELLIOTT, JAMES E.—Age, 23 years. Enlisted, May 2, 1898, at Brooklyn, to serve two years; mustered in as corporal, Co. B, May 24, 1898; promoted sergeant, June 1, 1898; mustered out with company, March 31, 1899, at Brooklyn, N. Y.

ELLMERS, ISAAC J.—Age, 40 years. Enlisted, May 2, 1898, at Brooklyn, to serve two years; mustered in as corporal, Co. L, May 24, 1898; promoted sergeant, October 20, 1898; mustered out with company, March 31, 1899, at Brooklyn, N. Y.

ENCERSON, EDWARD A.—Age, 36 years. Enlisted, May 20, 1898, at Brooklyn, to serve two years; mustered in as private, Co. E, May 24, 1898; appointed artificer, July 11, 1898; promoted corporal, August 16, 1898; sergeant, October 21, 1898; mustered out with company, March 31, 1899, at Brooklyn, N. Y.

ENGLEBRIGHT, WILLIAM.—Age, — years. Enlisted, August 11, 1898, at Brooklyn, to serve two years; mustered in as private, Co. H, same date; mustered out with company, March 31, 1899, at Brooklyn, N. Y.

ENSLEY, CHARLES L.—Age, 21 years. Enlisted, May 2, 1898, at Brooklyn, to serve two years; mustered in as private, Co. B, May 24, 1898; mustered out with company, March 31, 1899, at Brooklyn, N. Y.

ERICKSON, JAMES E.—Age, 22 years. Enlisted, May 2, 1898, at Brooklyn, to serve two years; mustered in as private, Co. F, May 24, 1898; mustered out with company, March 31, 1899, at Brooklyn, N. Y.

ESCHE, ARTHUR.—Age, — years. Enlisted, August 10, 1898, at Brooklyn, to serve two years; mustered in as private, Co. A, same date; mustered out with company, March 31, 1899, at Brooklyn, N. Y.

ESSER, ARTHUR.—Age, 22 years. Enlisted, May 2, 1898, at Brooklyn, to serve two years; mustered in as private, Co. H, May 24, 1898; mustered out with company, March 31, 1899, at Brooklyn, N. Y.

ETTER, WILLIAM.—Age, — years. Enlisted, July 28, 1898, at Brooklyn, to serve two years; mustered in as private, Co. C, same date; mustered out with company, March 31, 1899, at Brooklyn, N. Y.

EUBANK, JOHN.—Age, 19 years. Enlisted, May 22, 1898, at Brooklyn, to serve two years; mustered in as private, Co. E, May 24, 1898; mustered out with company, March 31, 1899, at Brooklyn, N. Y.

EVERS, BERNARD F.—Age, 25 years. Enlisted, May 2, 1898, at Brooklyn, to serve two years; mustered in as private, Co. D, May 24, 1898; mustered out with company, March 31, 1899, at Brooklyn, N. Y.

FABER, JACOB.—Age, 22 years. Enlisted, May 2, 1898, at Brooklyn, to serve two years; mustered in as private, Co. I, May 24, 1898; mustered out with company, March 31, 1899, at Brooklyn, N. Y.

FAGAN, CHARLES.—Age, — years. Enlisted, August 9, 1898, at Brooklyn, to serve two years; mustered in as private, Co. D, same date; mustered out with company, March 31, 1899, at Brooklyn, N. Y.

FAGEN, CHARLES.—Age, 22 years. Enlisted, May 2, 1898, at Brooklyn, to serve two years; mustered in as private, Co. F, May 24, 1898; mustered out with company, March 31, 1899, at Brooklyn, N. Y.

FAHEY, JOHN.—Age, 23 years. Enlisted, May 2, 1898, at Brooklyn, to serve two years; mustered in as private, Co. G, May 24, 1898; mustered out with company, March 31, 1899, at Brooklyn, N. Y.

FALDERMEYER, JOHN.—Age, — years. Enlisted, August 5, 1898, at Brooklyn, to serve two years; mustered in as private, Co. E, same date; mustered out with company, March 31, 1899, at Brooklyn, N. Y.

FANCHER, GEORGE.—Age, 29 years. Enlisted, May 2, 1898, at Brooklyn, to serve two years; mustered in as private, Co. I, May 24, 1898; promoted corporal, June 10, 1898; returned to ranks, August 5, 1898; mustered out with company, March 31, 1899, at Brooklyn, N. Y.

FARMER, FELIX.—Age, — years. Enlisted, July 30, 1898, at Brooklyn, to serve two years; mustered in as private, Co. H, same date; discharged for disability, October —, 1898, at Fort Adams, R. I.

FARRAGHAR, JOHN.—Age, — years. Enlisted, July 25, 1898, at Brooklyn, to serve two years; mustered in as private, Co. M, same date; mustered out, to date, March 31, 1899.

FARRELL, JAMES J.—Age, 22 years. Enlisted, May 2, 1898, at
Brooklyn, to serve two years; mustered in as private, Co. A,
May 24, 1898; promoted corporal, October 21, 1898; mustered
out with company, March 31, 1899, at Brooklyn, N. Y.

FARRELL, JOHN.—Age, — years. Enlisted, July 25, 1898, at
Brooklyn, to serve two years; mustered in as private, Co. L,
same date; mustered out with company, March 31, 1899, at
Brooklyn, N. Y.

FARRELL, MICHAEL.—Age, — years.   Enlisted, August 1,
1898, at Brooklyn, to serve two years; mustered in as private,
Co. D, same date; mustered out with company, March 31, 1899,
at Brooklyn, N. Y.

FARRELL, PATRICK.—Age, 27 years. Enlisted, May 2, 1898,
at Brooklyn, to serve two years; mustered in as private, Co. M,
May 24, 1898; mustered out with company, March 31, 1899, at
Brooklyn, N. Y.

FAY, WILLIAM F.—Age, — years. Enlisted, July 29, 1898, at
Brooklyn, to serve two years; mustered in as private, Co. D,
same date; mustered out with company, March 31, 1899, at
Brooklyn, N. Y.

FEATHERSON, WILLIAM A.—Age, 26 years. Enlisted, May 2,
1898, at Brooklyn, to serve two years; mustered in as musician,
Co. I, May 24, 1898; returned to ranks, no date; discharged,
November 14, 1898.

FENETY, WILLIAM F.—Age, 22 years. Enlisted, May 2, 1898,
at Brooklyn, to serve two years; mustered in as private, Co. F,
May 24, 1898; mustered out with company, March 31, 1899, at
Brooklyn, N. Y.

FENLON, WILLIAM H.—Age, — years.   Enlisted, August 3,
1898, at Brooklyn, to serve two years; mustered in as private,
Co. K, same date; mustered out with company, March 31, 1899,
at Brooklyn, N. Y.

FICKETT, THOMAS B.—Age, 21 years. Enlisted, May 2, 1898,
at Brooklyn, to serve two years; mustered in as private, Co. B,
May 24, 1898; mustered out with company, March 31, 1898, at
Brooklyn, N. Y.

FINDLAY, ANDREW.—Age, 43 years. Enlisted, May 2, 1898, at Brooklyn, to serve two years; mustered in as private, Co. H, · May 24, 1898; appointed wagoner, October 1, 1898; mustered out with company, March 31, 1899, at Brooklyn, N. Y.

FINGER, JR., JOHN.—Age, 20 years. Enlisted, May 2, 1898, at Brooklyn, to serve two years; mustered in as private, Co. F, May 24, 1898; mustered out with company, March 31, 1899, at Brooklyn, N. Y.

FINK, HENRY J.—Age, — years. Enlisted, July 23, 1898, at Brooklyn, to serve two years; mustered in as private, Co. L, same date; mustered out with company, March 31, 1899, at Brooklyn, N. Y.

FISCHER, HERMAN.—Age, 22 years. Enlisted, May 2, 1898, at Brooklyn, to serve two years; mustered in as private, Co. I, May 24, 1898; deserted, September 15, 1898.

FISH, WILLIAM L.—Age, 32 years. Enrolled, May 2, 1898, at Brooklyn, to serve two years; mustered in as captain, Co. C, May 24, 1898; discharged, September 17, 1898, at Fort Adams, R. I.; commissioned captain, May 24, 1898, with rank from same date, original.

FISHER, ALANSON S.—Age, 26 years. Enlisted, May 2, 1898, at Brooklyn, to serve two years; mustered in as private, Co. C, May 24, 1898; mustered out with company, March 31, 1899, at Brooklyn, N. Y.

FISHER, CARMAN N.—Age, — years. Enlisted, August 12, 1898, at Brooklyn, to serve two years; mustered in as private, Co. L, same date; mustered out with company, March 31, 1899, at Brooklyn, N. Y.

FISHER, JOHN C.—Age, 23 years. Enlisted, May 2, 1898, at Brooklyn, to serve two years; mustered in as private, Co. A, May 24, 1898; mustered out with company, March 31, 1899, at Brooklyn, N. Y.

FITZ, CHARLES M.—Age, 21 years. Enlisted, May 20, 1898, at Brooklyn, to serve two years; mustered in as private, Co. E, May 24, 1898; mustered out with company, March 31, 1899, at Brooklyn, N. Y.

FITZGERALD, EDWARD.—Age, — years. Enlisted, August 3, 1898, at Brooklyn, to serve two years; mustered in as private, Co. G, same date; mustered out with company, March 31, 1899, at Brooklyn, N. Y.

FITZGERALD, JOHN.—Age, 21 years. Enlisted, May 2, 1898, at Brooklyn, to serve two years; mustered in as private, Co. L, May 24, 1898; mustered out with company, March 31, 1899, at Brooklyn, N. Y.

FITZGERALD, JOHN G.—Age, 23 years. Enlisted, May 2, 1898, at Brooklyn, to serve two years; mustered in as private, Co. I, May 24, 1898; mustered out with company, March 31, 1899, at Brooklyn, N. Y.

FITZGERALD, JOSEPH S.—Age, 21 years. Enlisted, May 2, 1898, at Brooklyn, to serve two years; mustered in as private, Co. C, May 24, 1898; promoted corporal, December 6, 1898; sergeant, February 8, 1899; mustered out with company, March 31, 1899, at Brooklyn, N. Y.

FITZPATRICK, ROBERT L.—Age, — years. Enlisted, July 30, 1898, at Brooklyn, to serve two years; mustered in as private, Co. G, same date; mustered out with company, March 31, 1899, at Brooklyn, N. Y.

FITZSIMMONS, JR., GEORGE.—Age, — years. Enlisted, July 28, 1898, at Brooklyn, to serve two years; mustered in as private, Co. C, same date; mustered out with company, March 31, 1899, at Brooklyn, N. Y.

FLEMING, MATTHEW A.—Age, 20 years. Enlisted, May 2, 1898, at Brooklyn, to serve two years; mustered in as private, Co. A, May 24, 1898; mustered out with company, March 31, 1899, at Brooklyn, N. Y.

FLETCHER, GEORGE.—Age, 25 years. Enlisted, May 2, 1898, at Brooklyn, to serve two years; mustered in as private, Co. A, May 24, 1898; deserted, July 17, 1898, from Fort Greble, R. I.

FLUOR, JOHN.—Age, — years. Enlisted, August 8, 1898, at Brooklyn, to serve two years; mustered in as private, Co. D, same date; mustered out with company, March 31, 1899, at Brooklyn, N. Y.

FLYNN, JOHN.—Age, 21 years.   Enlisted, May 2, 1898, at
Brooklyn, to serve two years; mustered in as private, Co. L,
May 24, 1898; mustered out with company, March 31, 1899, at
Brooklyn, N. Y.

FOALE, CHARLES L.—Age, — years. Enlisted, August 4, 1898,
at Brooklyn, to serve two years; mustered in as private, Co. G,
same date; mustered out with company, March 31, 1899, at
Brooklyn, N. Y.

FORD, EDWARD.—Age, — years.   Enlisted, August 4, 1898,
at Brooklyn, to serve two years; mustered in as private, Co. K,
same date; mustered out with company, March 31, 1899, at
Brooklyn, N. Y.

FORSTER, CARL.—Age, 18 years.   Enlisted, May 2, 1898, at
Brooklyn, to serve two years; mustered in as private, Co. K.
May 24, 1898; mustered out with company, March 31, 1899, at
Brooklyn, N. Y.

FORSTER, OTTO L.—Age, 25 years.   Enlisted, May 2, 1898, at
Brooklyn, to serve two years; mustered in as corporal, Co. K,
May 24, 1898; discharged, October 14, 1898, at Fort Adams.
R. I.

FOSTER, EDGAR S.—Age, 21 years.   Enlisted, May 2, 1898, at
Brooklyn, to serve two years; mustered in as private, Co. I.
May 24, 1898; mustered out with company, March 31, 1899, at
Brooklyn, N. Y.

FOULON, FRANK L.—Age, 26 years.   Enlisted, May 2, 1898, at
Brooklyn, to serve two years; mustered in as private, Co. C.
May 24, 1898; promoted corporal, June 1, 1898; mustered out
with company, March 31, 1899, at Brooklyn, N. Y.

FOUNTAIN, PAUL U.—Age, 25 years.   Enlisted, May 2, 1898,
at Brooklyn, to serve two years; mustered in as private, Co. L,
May 24, 1898; promoted corporal, no date; discharged, February 16, 1899, at Fortress Monroe, Va.

FOWLER, OSCAR S.—Age, 27 years.   Enlisted, May 2, 1898, at
Brooklyn, to serve two years; mustered in as private, Co. I,
May 24, 1898; mustered out with company, March 31, 1899, at
Brooklyn, N. Y.

FOWLER, JR., GEORGE S.—Age, 22 years. Enlisted, May 2, 1898, at Brooklyn, to serve two years; mustered in as private, Co. B, May 24, 1898; promoted corporal, June 1, 1898; discharged, November 12, 1898, at Rio Piedras, P. R.

FOX, EUGENE V.—Age, 20 years. Enlisted, May 2, 1898, at Brooklyn, to serve two years; mustered in as private, Co. E, May 24, 1898; promoted corporal, August 18, 1898; discharged, October 14, 1898, at Fort Adams, R. I.

FRANCK, CHARLES L.—Age, 26 years. Enlisted, May 2, 1898, at Brooklyn, to serve two years; mustered in as private, Co. D, May 24, 1898; appointed wagoner, November 14, 1898; mustered out with company, March 31, 1899, at Brooklyn, N. Y.

FRANK, HENRY C.—Age, 20 years. Enlisted, May 2, 1898, at Brooklyn, to serve two years; mustered in as private, Co. D, May 24, 1898; appointed cook, December 20, 1898; mustered out with company, March 31, 1899, at Brooklyn, N. Y.

FRANK, JR., MATHIAS.—Age, — years. Enlisted, July 25, 1898, at Brooklyn, to serve two years; mustered in as private, Co. A, same date; mustered out with company, March 31, 1899, at Brooklyn, N. Y.

FRANSEN, CORNELIUS.—Age, — years. Enlisted, August 4, 1898, at Brooklyn, to serve two years; mustered in as private, Co. F, same date; mustered out with company, March 31, 1899, at Brooklyn, N. Y.

FREDERICKS, OTTO C.—Age, 26 years. Enlisted, May 2, 1898, at Brooklyn, to serve two years; mustered in as private, Co. K, May 24, 1898; promoted corporal, August 1, 1898; mustered out with company, March 31, 1899, at Brooklyn, N. Y.

FRENDE, NATHAN H.—Age, — years. Enlisted, August 2, 1898, at Brooklyn, to serve two years; mustered in as private, Co. F, same date; mustered out with company, March 31, 1899, at Brooklyn, N. Y.

FREY, HENRY C.—Age, 25 years. Enlisted, May 2, 1898, at Brooklyn, to serve two years; mustered in as private, Co. C, May 24, 1898; discharged, October 12, 1898, at Fort Adams, R. I.

FRIEDMAN, FREDERICK.—Age, 23 years. Enlisted, May 2, 1898, at Brooklyn, to serve two years; mustered in as private, Co. B, May 24, 1898; mustered out with company, March 31, 1899, at Brooklyn, N. Y.

FRIEDMAN, SAMUEL.—Age, 22 years. Enlisted, May 2, 1898, at Brooklyn, to serve two years; mustered in as private, Co. C, May 24, 1898; promoted corporal, November 1, 1898; discharged, February 14, 1899, at San Juan, P. R.

FRIEDRICK, JOHN H.—Age, 21 years. Enlisted, May 2, 1898, at Brooklyn, to serve two years; mustered in as private, Co. C, May 24, 1898; appointed cook, December 15, 1898; mustered out with company, March 31, 1899, at Brooklyn, N. Y.

FRIEL, THOMAS F.—Age, 37 years. Enlisted, May 2, 1898, at Brooklyn, to serve two years; mustered in as private, Co. G, May 24, 1898; mustered out with company, March 31, 1899, at Brooklyn, N. Y.

FRITZ, CHARLES.—Age, 23 years. Enlisted, May 2, 1898, at Brooklyn, to serve two years; mustered in as private, Co. D, May 24, 1898; mustered out with company, March 31, 1899, at Brooklyn, N. Y.

FROST, JOHN J.—Age, 31 years. Enlisted, May 2, 1898, at Brooklyn, to serve two years; mustered in as private, Co. D, May 24, 1898; mustered out with company, March 31, 1899, at Brooklyn, N. Y.

FUCHS, JOHN.—Age, 24 years. Enlisted, May 2, 1898, at Brooklyn, to serve two years; mustered in as private, Co. C, May 24, 1898; mustered out with company, March 31, 1899, at Brooklyn, N. Y.

FUCHS, REINHARDT.—Age, 26 years. Enlisted, May 2, 1898, at Brooklyn, to serve two years; mustered in as musician, Co. C, May 24, 1898; mustered out with company, March 31, 1899, at Brooklyn, N. Y.

FUDINSKI, CHARLES.—Age, 21 years. Enlisted, May 2, 1898, at Brooklyn, to serve two years; mustered in as private, Co. L, May 24, 1898; mustered out with company, March 31, 1899, at Brooklyn, N. Y.

GAFFNEY, JOHN C.—Age, 34 years. Enlisted, June 6, 1898, at
Camp Black, to serve two years; mustered in as private, Co. F,
same date; mustered out with company, March 31, 1899, at
Brooklyn, N. Y.

GALBRAITH, JOSEPH E.—Age, 24 years. Enlisted, May 2,
1898, at Brooklyn, to serve two years; mustered in as private,
Co. I, May 24, 1898; mustered out with company, March 31,
1899, at Brooklyn, N. Y.

GALBRAITH, WILLIAM G.—Age, 23 years. Enlisted, May 19,
1898, at Brooklyn, to serve two years; mustered in as private,
Co. E, May 24, 1898; mustered out with company, March 31,
1899, at Brooklyn, N. Y.

GALLAGHER, HUGH C.—Age, 28 years. Enlisted, May 2, 1898,
at Brooklyn, to serve two years; mustered in as sergeant, Co.
H, May 24, 1898; deserted, August 24, 1898, at Fort Adams,
R. I.

GALLAGHER, JOHN A.—Age, 28 years. Enlisted, May 2, 1898,
at Brooklyn, to serve two years; mustered in as private, Co. G,
May 24, 1898; mustered out with company, March 31, 1899, at
Brooklyn, N. Y.

GALLUP, HARRY S.—Age, 18 years. Enlisted, May 2, 1898, at
Brooklyn, to serve two years; mustered in as private, Co. M,
. May 24, 1898; promoted corporal, August 26, 1898; mustered
out with company, March 31, 1899, at Brooklyn, N. Y.

GAMSEY, ABE.—Age, — years. Enlisted, August 9, 1898, at
Brooklyn, to serve two years; mustered in as private, Co. M,
same date; discharged for disability, October 28, 1898, at Fort
Adams, R. I.

GANDNE, WILLIAM L.—Age, 40 years. Enlisted, May 2, 1898,
at Brooklyn, to serve two years; mustered in as sergeant, Co.
G, May 24, 1898; mustered out with company, March 31, 1899,
Brooklyn, N. Y.

GANNON, JOHN R.—Age, 25 years. Enlisted, May 2, 1898, at
Brooklyn, to serve two years; mustered in as private, Co. E,
May 24, 1898; promoted sergeant, same date; first sergeant,
March 8, 1899; mustered out with company, March 31, 1899, at
Brooklyn, N. Y.

GARDNER, CHARLES F.—Age, 21 years. Enlisted, May 2, 1898, at Brooklyn, to serve two years; mustered in as private, Co. M, May 24, 1898; mustered out with company, March 31, 1899, at Brooklyn, N. Y .

GARDNER, LEO R.—Age, 21 years. Enlisted, May 2, 1898, at Brooklyn, to serve two years; mustered in as private, Co. I, May 24, 1898; mustered out with company, March 31, 1899, at Brooklyn, N. Y.

GARDNER, LOUIS.—Age, 19 years. Enlisted, May 2, 1898, at Brooklyn, to serve two years; mustered in as private, Co. D, May 24, 1898; discharged for disability, February 7, 1899, at Fort Adams, R. I.

GARDNER, MORRIS.—Age, 21 years. Enlisted, May 2, 1898, at Brooklyn, to serve two years; mustered in as corporal, Co. H, May 24, 1898; returned to ranks, June 29, 1898; mustered out with company, March 31, 1899, at Brooklyn, N. Y.

GARLICK, JACOB.—Age, 21 years. Enlisted, May 2, 1898, at Brooklyn, to serve two years; mustered in as private, Co. H, May 24, 1898; mustered out with company, March 31, 1899, at Brooklyn, N. Y.

GARRAWAY, GEORGE C.—Age, 21 years. Enlisted, May 2, 1898, at Brooklyn, to serve two years; mustered in as corporal, Co. M, May 24, 1898; promoted sergeant, November 17, 1898; mustered out with company, March 31, 1899, at Brooklyn, N. Y.

GARVEN, PATRICK.—Age, — years. Enlisted, July 1, 1898, at Brooklyn, to serve two years; mustered in as private, Co. F, same date; mustered out with company, March 31, 1899, at Brooklyn, N. Y.

GAUTCHE, AGUSTUS.—Age, 27 years. Enlisted, May 2, 1898, at Brooklyn, to serve two years; mustered in as private, Co. H, May 24, 1898; mustered out with company, March 31, 1899, at Brooklyn, N. Y.

GEBHARDT, GEORGE J.—Age, 21 years. Enlisted, May 2, 1898, at Brooklyn, to serve two years; mustered in as private, Co. H, May 24, 1898; mustered out with company, March 31, 1899, at Brooklyn, N. Y.

GEEZER, EDWARD W.—Age, 23 years. Enlisted, May 2, 1898, at Brooklyn, to serve two years; mustered in as sergeant, Co. C, May 24, 1898; promoted quartermaster-sergeant, September 29, 1898; returned to ranks, November 15, 1898; promoted corporal, December 1, 1898; returned to ranks, January 2, 1899; mustered out with company, March 31, 1899, at Brooklyn, N. Y.

GEHLMEYER, CHRIST A.—Age, 21 years. Enlisted, May 2, 1898, at Brooklyn, to serve two years; mustered in as private, Co. M, May 24, 1898; mustered out with company, March 31, 1899, at Brooklyn, N. Y.

GEROULD, CHARLES L.—Age, 38 years. Enrolled, May 2, 1898, at Brooklyn, to serve two years; mustered in as first lieutenant, Co. L, May 24, 1898; discharged, September 22, 1898, at Fort Adams, R. I.; commissioned first lieutenant, May 24, 1898, with rank from same date, original.

GIBB, CHARLES W.—Age, 24 years. Enlisted, May 2, 1898, at Brooklyn, to serve two years; mustered in as private, Co. M, May 24, 1898; promoted corporal, November 1, 1898; mustered out with company, March 31, 1899, at Brooklyn, N. Y.

GIBBONS, JOHN T.—Age, 34 years. Enrolled, May 3, 1898, at Brooklyn, to serve two years; mustered in as first lieutenant and assistant surgeon, May 6, 1898; as major and surgeon, September 14, 1898; mustered out with regiment, March 31, 1899, at Brooklyn, N. Y.; commissioned first lieutenant and assistant surgeon, May 6, 1898, with rank from same date, original; major and surgeon, September 14, 1898, with rank from same date, vice Wallace, discharged.

GIESSELMANN, PETER A.—Age, 21 years. Enlisted, May 2, 1898, at Brooklyn, to serve two years; mustered in as private, Co. C, May 24, 1898; mustered out with company, March 31, 1899, at Brooklyn, N. Y.

GILL, JOHN S.—Age, — years. Enlisted, August 10, 1898, at Brooklyn, to serve two years; mustered in as private, Co. A, same date; mustered out with company, March 31, 1899, at Brooklyn, N. Y.

GILL, WILLIAM F.—Age, 37 years. Enlisted, May 2, 1898, at Brooklyn, to serve two years; mustered in as private, Co. C, May 24, 1898; mustered out with company, March 31, 1899, at Brooklyn, N. Y.

GILLEN, JAMES B.—Age, — years. Enlisted, August 11, 1898, at Brooklyn, to serve two years; mustered in as private, Co. I, same date; discharged, October 12, 1898.

GILLMAN, JOSEPH L.—Age, 26 years. Enrolled, May 2, 1898, at Brooklyn, to serve two years; mustered in as second lieutenant, Co. D, May 24, 1898; as first lieutenant, Co. G, October 3, 1898; mustered out with company, March 31, 1899, at Brooklyn, N. Y.; commissioned second lieutenant, May 24, 1898, with rank from same date, original; first lieutenant, October 3, 1898, with rank from same date, vice Marshall, promoted.

GIUNNESS, ALBERT E.—Age, 22 years. Enlisted, May 2, 1898, at Brooklyn, to serve two years; mustered in as sergeant, Co. F, May 24, 1898; returned to ranks, June 28, 1898; promoted corporal, August 19, 1898; sergeant, October 22, 1898; mustered out with company, March 31, 1899, at Brooklyn, N. Y.

GJOBYE, THOMAS N.—Age, 21 years. Enlisted, May 2, 1898, at Brooklyn, to serve two years; mustered in as private, Co. D, May 24, 1898; promoted corporal, August 27, 1898;. mustered out with company, March 31, 1899, at Brooklyn, N. Y.

GLANNER, BERT.—Age, 21 years. Enlisted, May 2, 1898, at Brooklyn, to serve two years; mustered in as private, Co. K, May 24, 1898; transferred to Co. E, August 17, 1898; mustered out with company, March 31, 1899, at Brooklyn, N. Y.

GLEISTEN, GEORGE H.—Age, 27 years. Enlisted, May 2, 1898, at Brooklyn, to serve two years; mustered in as private, Co. H, May 24, 1898; promoted corporal, January 16, 1899; mustered out with company, March 31, 1899, at Brooklyn, N. Y.

GLODE, JOHN A.—Age, 21 years. Enlisted, May 2, 1898, at Brooklyn, to serve two years; mustered in as private, Co. C, May 24, 1898; mustered out with company, March 31, 1899, at Brooklyn, N. Y.

GOEBEL, CHARLES F.—Age, 21 years. Enlisted, May 2, 1898, at Brooklyn, to serve two years; mustered in as private, Co. F, May 24, 1898; mustered out with company, March 31, 1899, at Brooklyn, N. Y.

GOETZ, ALBERT.—Age, 21 years. Enlisted, May 2, 1898, at Brooklyn, to serve two years; mustered in as private, Co. K, May 24, 1898; mustered out with company, March 31, 1899, at Brooklyn, N. Y.

GOETZ, WILLIAM.—Age, 19 years. Enlisted, May 2, 1898, at Brooklyn, to serve two years; mustered in as private, Co. G, May 24, 1898; mustered out with company, March 31, 1899, at Brooklyn, N. Y.

GOLDEN, MICHAEL J.—Age, — years. Enlisted, July 25, 1898, at Brooklyn, to serve two years; mustered in as private, Co. L, same date; mustered out with company, March 31, 1899, at Brooklyn, N. Y.

GOLDING, BENNIE.—Age, 22 years. Enlisted, May 2, 1898, at Brooklyn, to serve two years; mustered in as private, Co. K, May 24, 1898; mustered out with company, March 31, 1899, at Brooklyn, N. Y.

GONZALEZ, EUGENE R.—Age, 23 years. Enrolled, May 2, 1898, at Brooklyn, to serve two years; mustered in as second lieutenant, Co. H, May 24, 1898; as first lieutenant, January 18, 1899; mustered out, to date, March 31, 1899; commissioned second lieutenant, May 24, 1898, with rank from same date, original; first lieutenant, January 18, 1899, with rank from same date, vice Serenbitz, discharged.

GOOLEY, DENNIS E.—Age, 21 years. Enlisted, May 2, 1898, at Brooklyn, to serve two years; mustered in as private, Co. C, May 24, 1898; mustered out with company, March 31, 1899, at Brooklyn, N. Y.

GORDON, CHARLES J.—Age, 25 years. Enlisted, May 2, 1898, at Brooklyn, to serve two years; mustered in as private, Co. F, May 24, 1898; mustered out with company, March 31, 1899, at Brooklyn, N. Y.

GORMAN, DANIEL M.—Age, 21 years. Enlisted, May 2, 1898, at Brooklyn, to serve two years; mustered in as private, Co. H, May 24, 1898; deserted, June 27, 1898, at Fort Adams, R. I.

GORMAN, HENRY.—Age, — years. Enlisted, August 4, 1898, at Brooklyn, to serve two years; mustered in as private, Co. D, same date; mustered out with company, March 31, 1899, at Brooklyn, N. Y.

GORMAN, PETER J.—Age, 32 years. Enlisted, May 2, 1898, at Brooklyn, to serve two years; mustered in as private, Co. D, May 24, 1898; committed suicide, August 29, 1898, at Fort Adams, R. I.

GOULD, JAY B.—Age, 26 years. Enlisted, May 19, 1898, at Camp Black, to serve two years; mustered in as private, Co. A, May 24, 1898; mustered out with company, March 31, 1899, at Brooklyn, N. Y.

GRAHM, FREDERICK.—Age, 19 years. Enlisted, May 2, 1898, at Brooklyn, to serve two years; mustered in as private, Co. I, May 24, 1898; mustered out with company, March 31, 1899, at Brooklyn, N. Y.

GRAHM, WILLIAM.—Age, 21 years. Enlisted, May 2, 1898, at Brooklyn, to serve two years; mustered in as private, Co. I, May 24, 1898; mustered out with company, March 31, 1899, at Brooklyn, N. Y.

GRANT, AARON.—Age, 22 years. Enlisted, May 2, 1898, at Brooklyn, to serve two years; mustered in as private, Co. D, May 24, 1898; mustered out with company, March 31, 1899, at Brooklyn, N. Y.

GRAVER, JOSEPH.—Age, — years. Enlisted, July 26, 1898, at Brooklyn, to serve two years; mustered in as private, Co. H, same date; mustered out with company, March 31, 1899, at Brooklyn, N. Y.

GRAVES, CHARLES R.—Age, 27 years. Enlisted, May 2, 1898, at Brooklyn, to serve two years; mustered in as private, Co. I, May 24, 1898; promoted corporal, same date; sergeant, no date; mustered out with company, March 31, 1899, at Brooklyn, N. Y.

GRAY, EDWARD.—Age, — years. Enlisted, July 25, 1898, at Brooklyn, to serve two years; mustered in as private, Co. C, same date; mustered out with company, March 31, 1899, at Brooklyn, N. Y.

GRAY, HOWARD B.—Age, 26 years. Enlisted, May 2, 1898, at Brooklyn, to serve two years; mustered in as private, Co. D, May 24, 1898; mustered out with company, March 31, 1899, at Brooklyn, N. Y.

GREEN, PETER J. H.—Age, 22 years. Enlisted, May 2, 1898, at
Brooklyn, to serve two years; mustered in as private, Co. C,
May 24, 1898; mustered out with company, March 31, 1899, at
Brooklyn, N. Y.

GREEN, WILLIAM J.—Age, 25 years. Enlisted, May 2, 1898, at
Brooklyn, to serve two years; mustered in as private, Co. L,
May 24, 1898; mustered out with company, March 31, 1899, at
Brooklyn, N. Y.

GREENBURG, HARRY H.—Age, 21 years.   Enlisted, May 2,
1898, at Brooklyn, to serve two years; mustered in as corporal,
Co. A, May 24, 1898; discharged, October 12, 1898.

GREENE, RODERICK E.—Age, 22 years. Enlisted, May 2, 1898,
at Brooklyn, to serve two years; mustered in as private, Co. F,
May 24, 1898; mustered out with company, March 31, 1899, at
Brooklyn, N. Y.

GREGORY, JAMES G.—Age, 21 years. Enlisted, May 23, 1898,
at Camp Black, to serve two years; mustered in as private, Co.
A, May 24, 1898; mustered out with company, March 31, 1899, at
Brooklyn, N. Y.

GREGORY, WILLIAM J.—Age, 25 years. Enlisted, May 2, 1898,
at Brooklyn, to serve two years; mustered in as private, Co.
B, May 24, 1898; promoted corporal, June 1, 1898; mustered
out with company, March 31, 1899, at Brooklyn, N. Y.

GREINER, HERMAN.—Age, 30 years. Enlisted, May 2, 1898,
at Brooklyn, to serve two years; mustered in as private, Co. G,
May 24, 1898; mustered out, to date, March 31, 1899.

GRELL, HERMANN.—Age, 21 years. Enlisted, May 2, 1898, at
Brooklyn, to serve two years; mustered in as private, Co. B,
May 24, 1898; mustered out with company, March 31, 1899, at
Brooklyn, N. Y.

GRENING, LOUIS B.—Age, 21 years. Enlisted, May 2, 1898, at
Brooklyn, to serve two years; mustered in as private, Co. B,
May 24, 1898; mustered out with company, March 31, 1899, at
Brooklyn, N. Y.

GRIFFIN, CHARLES H.—Age, 22 years. Enlisted, May 2, 1898, at Brooklyn, to serve two years; mustered in as private, Co. A, May 24, 1898; mustered out with company, March 31, 1899, at Brooklyn, N. Y.

GRODZKI, THEODORE.—Age, 29 years. Enlisted, May 2, 1898, at Brooklyn, to serve two years; mustered in as private, Co. I, May 24, 1898; mustered out with company, March 31, 1899, at Brooklyn, N. Y.

GROH, FREDERICK E.—Age, — years. Enlisted, August 1, 1898, at Brooklyn, to serve two years; mustered in as private, Co. K, same date; mustered out with company, March 31, 1899, at Brooklyn, N. Y.

GUNN, WILLIAM H.—Age, — years. Enlisted, July 27, 1898, at Brooklyn, to serve two years; mustered in as private, Co. E, same date; mustered out with company, March 31, 1899, at Brooklyn, N. Y.

GUNTHER, FREDERICK W.—Age, 22 years. Enlisted, May 2, 1898, at Brooklyn, to serve two years; mustered in as private, Co. K, May 24, 1898; mustered out with company, March 31, 1899, at Brooklyn, N. Y.

GUNTHNER, GUS.—Age, 21 years. Enlisted, May 2, 1898, at Brooklyn, to serve two years; mustered in as private, Co. D, May 24, 1898; mustered out with company, March 31, 1899, at Brooklyn, N. Y.

GUTBERLET, ERNEST.—Age, 20 years. Enlisted, May 2, 1898, at Brooklyn, to serve two years; mustered in as private, Co. B, May 24, 1898; mustered out with company, March 31, 1899, at Brooklyn, N. Y.

HAAS, JOSEPH M.—Age, 21 years. Enlisted, May 2, 1898, at Brooklyn, to serve two years; mustered in as private, Co. M, May 24, 1898; mustered out with company, March 31, 1899, at Brooklyn, N. Y.

HABER, HENRY.—Age, — years. Enlisted, July 21, 1898, at Brooklyn, to serve two years; mustered in as private, Co. F, same date; mustered out with company, March 31, 1899, at Brooklyn, N. Y.

HAERTNER, EDWARD.—Age, — years. Enlisted, August 11, 1898, at Brooklyn, to serve two years; mustered in as private, Co. H, same date; mustered out with company, March 31, 1899, at Brooklyn, N. Y.

HAERTNER, HENRY.—Age, 25 years. Enlisted, May 3, 1898, at Brooklyn, to serve two years; mustered in as principal musician, May 24, 1898; discharged, February 15, 1899.

HAEUSSLER, FRANK J.—Age, 21 years. Enlisted, May 18, 1898, at Camp Black, to serve two years; mustered in as private, Co. A, May 24, 1898; mustered out with company, March 31, 1899, at Brooklyn, N. Y.

HAFNER, WILLIAM.—Age, 24 years. Enlisted, May 2, 1898, at Brooklyn, to serve two years; mustered in as private, Co. C, May 24, 1898; mustered out with company, March 31, 1899, at Brooklyn, N. Y.

HAGAN, JOHN.—Age, — years. Enlisted, July 25, 1898, at Brooklyn, to serve two years; mustered in as private, Co. D, same date; mustered out with company, March 31, 1899, at Brooklyn, N. Y.

HAGAN, JOSEPH V.—Age, — years. Enlisted, July 27, 1898, at Brooklyn, to serve two years; mustered in as private, Co. C, same date; transferred to Co. F, August 16, 1898; deserted, October 8, 1898, at Fort Adams, R. I.

HAGAN, OTTO F.—Age, 24 years. Enlisted, May 2, 1898, at Brooklyn, to serve two years; mustered in as private, Co. B, June 7, 1898; promoted sergeant, same date; discharged, October 14, 1898, at Fort Adams, R. I.

HAIGHT, DANIEL A.—Age, 22 years. Enlisted, May 2, 1898, at Brooklyn, to serve two years; mustered in as private, Co. I, May 24, 1898; mustered out with company, March 31, 1899, at Brooklyn, N. Y.

HAIGHT, GEORGE W.—Age, 30 years. Enlisted, May 2, 1898, at Brooklyn, to serve two years; mustered in as private, Co. I, May 24, 1898; mustered out with company, March 31, 1899, at Brooklyn, N. Y.

HALE, ALONZO.—Age, — years. Enlisted, August 9, 1898, at Brooklyn, to serve two years; mustered in as private, Co. A, same date; mustered out with company, March 31, 1899, at Brooklyn, N. Y.

HALE, THEODORE J. G.—Age, 34 years. Enlisted, May 2, 1898, at Brooklyn, to serve two years; mustered in as first sergeant, Co. G, May 24, 1898; mustered out with company, March 31, 1899, at Brooklyn, N. Y.

HALL, CHARLES S.—Age, 31 years. Enlisted, May 2, 1898, at Brooklyn, to serve two years; mustered in as quartermaster-sergeant, Co. H, May 24, 1898; discharged for disability, October 12, 1898.

HALL, THOMAS E.—Age, 27 years. Enlisted, May 2, 1898, at Brooklyn, to serve two years; mustered in as private, Co. B, May 2., 1898; mustered out with company, March 31, 1899, at Brooklyn, N. Y.

HALLENBECK, EDWARD S.—Age, 34 years. Enlisted, May 2, 1898, at Brooklyn, to serve two years; mustered in as corporal, Co. H, May 24, 1898; promoted sergeant, September 1, 1898; returned to ranks, January 16, 1899; mustered out with company, March 31, 1899, at Brooklyn, N. Y.

HALLIDAY, GEORGE.—Age, 28 years. Enlisted, May 2, 1898, at Brooklyn, to serve two years; mustered in as private, Co. M, May 24, 1898; promoted corporal, June 11, 1898; sergeant, December 13, 1898; mustered out with company, March 31, 1899, at Brooklyn, N. Y.

HALLORAN, JOHN F.—Age, 22 years. Enlisted, May 2, 1898, at Brooklyn, to serve two years; mustered in as private, Co. L, May 24, 1898; mustered out with company, March 31, 1899, at Brooklyn, N. Y.

HALLORAN, STEPHEN W.—Age, 21 years. Enlisted, May 2, 1898, at Brooklyn, to serve two years; mustered in as corporal. Co. D, May 24, 1898; promoted sergeant, June 1, 1898; mustered out with company, March 31, 1899, at Brooklyn, N. Y.

HAMILTON, CLINTON P.—Age, 21 years. Enlisted, May 2, 1898, at Brooklyn, to serve two years; mustered in as corporal, Co. E, May 24, 1898; promoted sergeant, October 21, 1898; mustered out with company, March 31, 1899, at Brooklyn, N. Y.

HAMILTON, GUSTAV.—Age, 30 years. Enlisted, May 2, 1898, at Brooklyn, to serve two years; mustered in as private, Co. M, May 24, 1898; promoted corporal, June 11, 1898; returned to ranks, August 25, 1898; mustered out with company, March 31, 1899, at Brooklyn, N. Y.

HAMMILL, JOHN.—Age, 21 years. Enlisted, May 2, 1898, at Brooklyn, to serve two years; mustered in as private, Co. F, May 24, 1898; mustered out with company, March 31, 1899, at Brooklyn, N. Y.

HAMPE, CHARLES.—Age, 27 years. Enlisted, May 2, 1898, at Brooklyn, to serve two years; mustered in as private, Co. D, May 24, 1898; mustered out with company, March 31, 1899, at Brooklyn, N. Y.

HANAN, JAMES T.—Age, 21 years. Enlisted, May 20, 1898, at Brooklyn, to serve two years; mustered in as private, Co. E, May 24, 1898; promoted corporal, February 8, 1899; mustered out with company, March 31, 1899, at Brooklyn, N. Y.

HAND, AUGUSTUS.—Age, 20 years. Enlisted, May 23, 1898, at Brooklyn, to serve two years; mustered in as private, Co. E, May 24, 1898; deserted, October 10, 1898, at Fort Adams, R. I.

HANNA, EDWARD.—Age, — years. Enlisted, August 3, 1898, at Brooklyn, to serve two years; mustered in as private, Co. K, same date; mustered out with company, March 31, 1899, at Brooklyn, N. Y.

HANNAN, JOHN.—Age, 24 years. Enlisted, May 2, 1898, at Brooklyn, to serve two years; mustered in as first sergeant, Co. A, May 24, 1898; mustered out with company, March 31, 1899, at Brooklyn, N. Y.

HANOLD, JOHN A.—Age, 21 years. Enlisted, May 2, 1898, at Brooklyn, to serve two years; mustered in as private, Co. H, May 24, 1898; promoted corporal, September 1, 1898; returned to ranks, January 16, 1899; mustered out with company, March 31, 1899, at Brooklyn, N. Y.

HANSMANN, HENRY S.—Age, 22 years. Enlisted, May 2, 1898, at Brooklyn, to serve two years; mustered in as private, Co. E, May 24, 1898; mustered out with company, March 31, 1899, at Brooklyn, N. Y.

HAPPEL, GEORGE.—Age, 26 years. Enlisted, May 2, 1898, at Brooklyn, to serve two years; mustered in as private, Co. F, May 24, 1898; mustered out with company, March 31, 1899, at Brooklyn, N. Y.

HARDY, HENRY J.—Age, 22 years. Enlisted May 2, 1898, at Brooklyn, to serve two years; mustered in as private, Co. F, May 24, 1898; promoted corporal, June 23, 1898; returned to ranks, December 17, 1898; mustered out with company, March 31, 1899, at Brooklyn, N. Y.

HARDY, MARCHISI T.—Age, 34 years. Enrolled, May 2, 1898, at Brooklyn, to serve two years; mustered in as first lieutenant, Co. K, May 24, 1898; as captain, September 21, 1898; mustered out with company, March 31, 1899, at Brooklyn, N. Y.; commissioned first lieutenant, May 24, 1898, with rank from same date, original; captain, September 14, 1898, with rank from same date, vice Maier, discharged.

HARMON, THOMAS M.—Age, — years. Enlisted, August 8, 1898, at Brooklyn, to serve two years; mustered in as private, Co. A, same date; mustered out with company, March 31, 1899, at Brooklyn, N. Y.

HARRIS, MARK S.—Age, 19 years. Enlisted, May 2, 1898, at Brooklyn, to serve two years; mustered in as private, Co. E, May 24, 1898; mustered out with company, March 31, 1899, at Brooklyn, N. Y.

HART, CHARLES R.—Age, 30 years. Enlisted, May 2, 1898, at Brooklyn, to serve two years; mustered in as private, Co. K, May 24, 1898; mustered out with company, March 31, 1899, at Brooklyn, N. Y.

HARTE, PETER J.—Age, 21 years. Enlisted, May 2, 1898, at Brooklyn, to serve two years; mustered in as private, Co. L, May 24, 1898; appointed lance corporal, February 9, 1899; promoted corporal, February 14, 1899; mustered out with company, March 31, 1899, at Brooklyn, N. Y.

HARTJEN, HERMAN.—Age, 24 years. Enlisted, May 2, 1898, at Brooklyn, to serve two years; mustered in as private, Co. L, May 24, 1898; appointed lance corporal, November 28, 1898; returned to ranks, February 5, 1899; mustered out with company, March 31, 1899, at Brooklyn, N. Y.

HARTLEY, ASCHER.—Age, 21 years. Enlisted, May 2, 1898, at Brooklyn, to serve two years; mustered in as private, Co. M, May 24, 1898; mustered out with company, March 31, 1899, at Brooklyn, N. Y.

HARTLING, WILLIAM.—Age, 21 years. Enlisted, May 2, 1898, at Brooklyn, to serve two years; mustered in as private, Co. H, May 24, 1898; mustered out with company, March 31, 1899, at Brooklyn, N. Y.

HARTUNG, MAX.—Age, 25 years.   Enlisted, May 2, 1898, at Brooklyn, to serve two years;   mustered in as private, Co. H, May 24, 1898; mustered out, to date, March 31, 1899.

HARTWIG, CHARLES.—Age, 21 years. Enlisted, May 2, 1898, at Brooklyn, to serve two years; mustered in as private, Co. I, May 24, 1898; mustered out with company, March 31, 1899, at Brooklyn, N. Y.

HASLETT, CHARLES O.—Age, — years.   Enlisted, August 8, 1898, at Brooklyn, to serve two years; mustered in as private, Co. F, same date; mustered out with company, March 31, 1899, at Brooklyn, N. Y.

HASSE, ANTHONY F.—Age, 21 years. Enlisted, May 2, 1898, at Brooklyn, to serve two years; mustered in as private, Co. L, May 24, 1898; deserted, September 22, 1898.

HAWKES, WILLIAM.—Age, — years.   Enlisted, August 5, 1898, at Brooklyn, to serve two years; mustered in as private, Co. F, same date; appointed cook, August 12, 1898; mustered out with company, March 31, 1899, at Brooklyn, N. Y.

HAWKINS, CORNELIUS F.—Age, — years. Enlisted, July 25, 1898, at Brooklyn, to serve two years; mustered in as private, Co. C, same date; mustered out with company, March 31, 1899, at Brooklyn, N. Y.

HAWORTH, HENRY B.—Age, 27 years. Enlisted, May 2, 1898, at Brooklyn, to serve two years; mustered in as private, Co. I, May 24, 1898; promoted corporal, November 1, 1898; mustered out with company, March 31, 1899, at Brooklyn, N. Y.

HAYDEN, FRANK A.—Age, — years.   Enlisted, August 6, 1898, at Brooklyn, to serve two years; mustered in as private, Co. E, same date; mustered out with company, March 31, 1899, at Brooklyn, N. Y.

HAYES, FRANK S.—Age, 19 years.   Enlisted, May 2, 1898, at Brooklyn, to serve two years; mustered in as private, Co. E, May 24, 1898; mustered out with company, March 31, 1899, at Brooklyn, N. Y.

HAYES, HARRY D.—Age, 21 years.   Enlisted, May 2, 1898, at Brooklyn, to serve two years; mustered in as private, Co. E, May 24, 1898; mustered out with company, March 31, 1899, at Brooklyn, N. Y.

HAYNES, ARTHUR.—Age, — years.   Enlisted, August 4, 1898, at Brooklyn, to serve two years; mustered in as private, Co. F, same date; mustered out with company, March 31, 1899, at Brooklyn, N. Y.

HEARN, CHARLES W.—Age, 25 years.   Enlisted, May 2, 1898, at Brooklyn, to serve two years; mustered in as private, Co. D, May 24, 1898; mustered out with company, March 31, 1899, at Brooklyn, N. Y.

HEATHER, FREDERICK.—Age, 24 years   Enlisted, May 2, 1898, at Brooklyn, to serve two years; mustered in as private, Co. G, May 24, 1898; mustered out with company, March 31, 1899, at Brooklyn, N. Y.

HEATTI, CHARLES A.—Age, 24 years.   Enlisted, May 2, 1898, at Brooklyn, to serve two years; mustered in as corporal, Co. A, May 24, 1898; promoted sergeant, December 24, 1898; mustered out with company, March 31, 1899, at Brooklyn, N. Y.

HEBEL, OTTO L.—Age, 21 years.   Enlisted, May 2, 1898, at Brooklyn, to serve two years; mustered in as private, Co. H, May 24, 1898; mustered out with company, March 31, 1899, at Brooklyn, N. Y.

HEINEMAN, JOHN.—Age, — years.   Enlisted, August 5, 1898, at Brooklyn, to serve two years; mustered in as private, Co. G, same date; mustered out with company, March 31, 1899, at Brooklyn, N. Y.

HEINEMANN, HENRY W.—Age, — years. Enlisted, August 3, 1898, at Brooklyn, to serve two years; mustered in as private, Co. G, same date; mustered out with company, March 31, 1899, at Brooklyn, N. Y.

HEINER, DAVID.—Age, 23 years Enlisted, May 2, 1898, at Brooklyn, to serve two years; mustered in as private, Co L, May 24, 1898; mustered out with company, March 31, 1899, at Brooklyn, N. Y.

HEISER, JACOB.—Age, 21 years.   Enlisted, May 2, 1898, at Brooklyn, to serve two years; mustered in as private, Co. E, May 24, 1898; promoted corporal, February 8, 1899; mustered out with company, March 31, 1899, at Brooklyn, N. Y.

HEISS, GEORGE.—Age, 21 years.   Enlisted, May 2, 1898, at Brooklyn, to serve two years; mustered in as private, Co. C, May 24, 1898; mustered out with company, March 31, 1899, at Brooklyn, N. Y.

HEITKAMP, ERNEST L.—Age, — years.   Enlisted, August 5, 1898, at Brooklyn, to serve two years; mustered in as private, Co. L, same date; appointed lance corporal, October 20, 1898; promoted corporal, November 2, 1898; mustered out with company, March 31, 1899, at Brooklyn, N. Y.

HELITAS, OTTO.—Age, — years.   Enlisted, August 8, 1898, at Brooklyn, to serve two years; mustered in as private, Co. M, same date; mustered out with company, March 31, 1899, at Brooklyn, N. Y.

HEMENDINGER, CHARLES C.—Age, 21 years. Enlisted, May 2, 1898, at Brooklyn, to serve two years; mustered in as private, Co. K, May 24, 1898; mustered out with company, March 31, 1899, at Brooklyn, N. Y.

HEMMINGS, WALTER G.—Age, 19 years.   Enlisted, May 2, 1898, at Brooklyn, to serve two years; mustered in as private, Co. D, May 24, 1898; mustered out, to date, March 31, 1899.

HENN, ADAM.—Age, 25 years.   Enlisted, May 2, 1898, at Brooklyn, to serve two years; mustered in as private, Co. D, May 24, 1898; deserted, August 18, 1898, at Fort Adams, R. I.

HENRY, JOHN J.—Age, 42 years. Enlisted, May 2, 1898, at Brooklyn, to serve two years; mustered in as private, Co. D, May 24, 1898; mustered out with company, March 31, 1898, at Brooklyn, N. Y.

HERRON, THOMAS.—Age, 19 years. Enlisted, May 2, 1898, at Brooklyn, to serve two years; mustered in as private, Co. D, May 24, 1898; mustered out with company, March 31, 1899, at Brooklyn, N. Y.

HERSON, THOMAS P.—Age, 21 years. Enlisted, May 2, 1898, at Brooklyn, to serve two years; mustered in as private, Co. B, May 24, 1898; promoted corporal, August 15, 1898; mustered out with company, March 31, 1899, at Brooklyn, N. Y.

HERZOG, FREDERICK C.—Age, 21 years. Enlisted, May 2, 1898, at Brooklyn, to serve two years; mustered in as private, Co. H, May 24, 1898; promoted corporal, March 8, 1899; mustered out with company, March 31, 1899, at Brooklyn, N. Y.

HERZOG, WILLIAM.—Age, 22 years. Enlisted, May 2, 1898, at Brooklyn, to serve two years; mustered in as private, Co. H, May 24, 1898; mustered out with company, March 31, 1899, at Brooklyn, N. Y.

HESS, LEANDER G.—Age, 33 years. Enlisted, May 2, 1898, at Brooklyn, to serve two years; mustered in as private, Co. D, May 24, 1898; transferred to Hospital Corps, February 8, 1899, at Viquers, P. R.

HETHERINGTON, JOSEPH P.—Age, — years. Enlisted, August 10, 1898, at Brooklyn, to serve two years; mustered in as private, Co. A, same date; mustered out with company, March 31, 1899, at Brooklyn, N. Y.

HEYDEL, HENRY.—Age, 18 years. Enlisted, May 2, 1898, at Brooklyn, to serve two years; mustered in as private, Co. G, May 24, 1898; mustered out with company, March 31, 1899, at Brooklyn, N. Y.

HEYDTMAN, HERMAN.—Age, 26 years. Enlisted, May 2, 1898, at Brooklyn, to serve two years; mustered in as private, Co. F, May 24, 1898; discharged, October 12, 1898, at Fort Adams, R. I.

HICKEY, MICHAEL.—Age, 26 years. Enlisted, May 2, 1898, at Brooklyn, to serve two years; mustered in as private, Co. M, May 24, 1898; mustered out with company, March 31, 1899, at Brooklyn, N. Y.

HICKMAN, CHARLES.—Age, 33 years. Enlisted, May 2, 1898, at Brooklyn, to serve two years; mustered in as private, Co. M, May 24, 1898; mustered out with company, March 31, 1899, at Brooklyn, N. Y.

HIGGINS, THOMAS F.—Age, — years. Enlisted, July 27, 1898, at Brooklyn, to serve two years; mustered in as private, Co. K, same date; mustered out with company, March 31, 1899, at Brooklyn, N. Y.

HILL, CHARLES A.—Age, 27 years. Enlisted, May 2, 1898, at Brooklyn, to serve two years; mustered in as private, Co. H, May 24, 1898; promoted corporal, September 1, 1898; mustered out with company, March 31, 1899, at Brooklyn, N. Y.

HILL, DAVID B.—Age, — years. Enlisted, August 9, 1898, at Brooklyn, to serve two years; mustered in as private, Co. I, same date; mustered out with company, March 31, 1899, at Brooklyn, N. Y.

HILLS, THEODORE.—Age, — years. Enlisted, August 9, 1898, at Brooklyn, to serve two years; mustered in as private, Co. A, same date; mustered out with company, March 31, 1899, at Brooklyn, N. Y.

HIRSCHFIELD, FRANK.—Age, 21 years. Enlisted, May 2, 1898, at Brooklyn, to serve two years; mustered in as private, Co. M, May 24, 1898; mustered out with company, March 31, 1899, at Brooklyn, N. Y.

HOCHSCHROEDER, FRANK.—Age, 23 years. Enlisted, May 2, 1898, at Brooklyn, to serve two years; mustered in as private, Co. A, May 24, 1898; appointed cook, July 7, 1898; mustered out with company, March 31, 1899, at Brooklyn, N. Y.

HODGES, EDWARD.—Age, — years. Enrolled, October 5, 1898, at Fort Adams, R. I., to serve two years; mustered in as captain and assistant surgeon, December 10, 1898; mustered out with regiment, March 31, 1899, at Brooklyn, N. Y.; commissioned captain and assistant surgeon, October 6, 1898, with rank from same date, vice Gibbons, promoted.

HOELL, CHARLES.—Age, 20 years. Enlisted, May 2, 1898, at Brooklyn, to serve two years; mustered in as private, Co. F, May 24, 1898; mustered out with company, March 31, 1899, at Brooklyn, N. Y.

HOFFMANN, ALBERT G.—Age, 21 years. Enlisted, May 2, 1898, at Brooklyn, to serve two years; mustered in as private, Co. G, May 24, 1898; mustered out with company, March 31, 1899, at Brooklyn, N. Y.

HOFFMANN, CHARLES.—Age, 21 years. Enlisted, May 2, 1898, at Brooklyn, to serve two years; mustered in as private, Co. H, May 24, 1898; mustered out with company, March 31, 1899, at Brooklyn, N. Y.

HOFFMANN, JOSEPH.—Age, 19 years. Enlisted, May 2, 1898, at Brooklyn, to serve two years; mustered in as private, Co. H, May 24, 1898; mustered out with company, March 31, 1899, at Brooklyn, N. Y.

HOGEBOOM, HARRY J.—Age, 38 years. Enlisted, May 2, 1898, at Brooklyn, to serve two years; mustered in as sergeant, Co. A, May 24, 1898; mustered out with company, March 31, 1899, at Brooklyn, N. Y.

HOHENSTEIN, WILLIAM.—Age, 21 years. Enlisted, May 2, 1898, at Brooklyn, to serve two years; mustered in as private, Co. K, May 24, 1898; appointed cook, October 21, 1898; mustered out with company, March 31, 1899, at Brooklyn, N. Y.

HOHNER, LOUIS.—Age, 22 years. Enlisted, May 2, 1898, at Brookyn, to serve two years; mustered in as private, Co. F, May 24, 1898; mustered out with company, March 31, 1899, at Brookyn, N. Y.

HOLCK, GEORGE C.—Age, 20 years. Enlisted, May 2, 1898, at Brookyn, to serve two years; mustered in as private, Co. K, May 24, 1898; mustered out with company, March 31, 1899, at Brookyn, N. Y.

HOLDREIED, CHARLES A.—Age, 24 years. Enlisted, May 2, 1898, at Brookyn, to serve two years; mustered in as sergeant, Co. A, May 24, 1898; mustered out with company, March 31, 1899, at Brooklyn, N. Y.

HOLLAND, PATRICK.—Age, — years.   Enlisted, August 3,
1898, at Brooklyn, to serve two years; mustered in as private,
Co. B, same date; mustered out with company, March 31, 1899,
at Brooklyn, N. Y.

HOLT, JAMES.—Age, — years. Enlisted, August 10, 1898, at
Brooklyn, to serve two years; mustered in as private, Co. E,
same date; mustered out with company, March 31, 1899, at
Brooklyn, N. Y.

HOMMEL, JR., JOSEPH.—Age, — years.   Enlisted, July 29,
1898, at Brooklyn, to serve two years; mustered in as private,
Co. E, same date; transferred to Co. L, August 5, 1898; mustered out, to date, March 31, 1899, at Brooklyn, N. Y.

HOOLEY, TIMOTHY J.—Age, 40 years. Enrolled, June 6, 1898,
at Camp Black, to serve two years; mustered in as first lieutenant and battalion adjutant, same date; mustered out with regiment, March 31, 1899, at Brooklyn, N. Y.; commissioned battalion adjutant, June 1, 1898, with rank from same date,
original.

HORAN, EUGENE.—Age, 21 years. Enlisted, May 2, 1898, at
Brooklyn, to serve two years; mustered in as private, Co. M,
May 24, 1898; promoted corporal, November 17, 1898; mustered
out with company, March 31, 1899, at Brooklyn, N. Y.

HORAN, PETER S.—Age, 22 years. Enlisted, May 2, 1898, at
Brooklyn, to serve two years; mustered in as private, Co. I,
May 24, 1898; promoted corporal, June 10, 1898; sergeant, Jan-
uary 23, 1899; mustered out with company, March 31, 1899, at
Brooklyn, N. Y.

HORNER, ISAAC.—Age, 26 years. Enlisted, May 2, 1898, at
Brooklyn, to serve two years; mustered in as private, Co. K,
May 24, 1898; promoted corporal, March 21, 1899; mustered
out with company, March 31, 1899, at Brooklyn, N. Y.

HOWARD, DENNIS.—Age, 23 years. Enlisted, May 2, 1898, at
Brooklyn, to serve two years; mustered in as private, Co. M,
May 24, 1898; mustered out with company, March 31, 1899, at
Brooklyn, N. Y.

HOWARD, GEORGE F.—Age, 27 years. Enlisted, May 2, 1898, at Brooklyn, to serve two years; mustered in as private, Co. B, May 24, 1898; mustered out with company, March 31, 1899, at Brooklyn, N. Y.

HOWELL, HENRY T.—Age, 34 years. Enlisted, May 2, 1898, at Brooklyn, to serve two years; mustered in as private, Co. H, May 24, 1898; promoted sergeant, no date; returned to ranks, December 17, 1898; mustered out with company, March 31, 1899, at Brooklyn, N. Y.

HUBBARD, FRANK H.—Age, 22 years. Enlisted, May 2, 1898, at Brooklyn, to serve two years; mustered in as private, Co. K, May 24, 1898; mustered out with company, March 31, 1899, at Brooklyn, N. Y.

HUBBELL, WILLIAM H.—Age, 49 years. Enrolled, May 3, 1898, at Brooklyn, to serve two years; mustered in as lieutenant-colonel, May 24, 1898; as colonel, December 3, 1898; mustered out with regiment, March 31, 1899, at Brooklyn, N. Y.; commissioned lieutenant-colonel, May 24, 1898, with rank from same date, original; colonel, December 3, 1898, with rank from same date, vice Eddy, discharged.

HUDTWALKER, GEORGE W. H.—Age, 18 years. Enlisted, May 2, 1898, at Brooklyn, to serve two years; mustered in as private, Co. K, May 24, 1898; mustered out with company, March 31, 1899, at Brooklyn, N. Y.

HUETHER, CHRISTIAN J.—Age, 21 years. Enlisted, May 2, 1898, at Brooklyn, to serve two years; mustered in as private, Co. F, May 24, 1898; mustered out with company, March 31, 1899, at Brooklyn, N. Y.

HUGHES, PETER L.—Age, 19 years. Enlisted, May 2, 1898, at Brooklyn, to serve two years; mustered in as private, Co. F, May 24, 1898; promoted corporal, September 24, 1898; mustered out with company, March 31, 1899, at Brooklyn, N. Y.

HUGHS, PETER.—Age, 32 years. Enlisted, May 2, 1898, at Brooklyn, to serve two years; mustered in as private, Co. I, May 24, 1898; mustered out with company, March 31, 1899, at Brooklyn, N. Y.

HULL, STEWART H.—Age, 21 years. Enlisted, May 2, 1898, at Brooklyn, to serve two years; mustered in as private, Co. I, May 24, 1898; appointed wagoner, December 1, 1898; mustered out with company, March 31, 1899, at Brooklyn, N. Y.

HUND, HENRY.—Age, 23 years. Enlisted, May 2, 1898, at Brooklyn, to serve two years; mustered in as private, Co. C, May 24, 1898; mustered out with company, March 31, 1899, at Brooklyn, N. Y.

HUSTON, HENRY D.—Age, 28 years. Enlisted, May 2, 1898, at Brooklyn, to serve two years; mustered in as artificer, Co. K, May 24, 1898; mustered out with company, March 31, 1899, at Brooklyn, N. Y.

HUSTON, JOHN.—Age, 31 years. Enlisted, May 2, 1898, at Brooklyn, to serve two years; mustered in as quartermaster-sergeant, Co. K, May 24, 1898; returned to ranks, June 25, 1898; promoted corporal, August 1, 1898; mustered out with company, March 31, 1899, at Brooklyn, N. Y.

HUTTON, WASHINGTON.—Age, — years. Enlisted, August 9, 1898, at Brooklyn, to serve two years; mustered in as private, Co. A, same date; mustered out with company, March 31, 1899, at Brooklyn, N. Y.

IHRIG, WILLIAM G.—Age, 18 years. Enlisted, May 2, 1898, at Brooklyn, to serve two years; mustered in as private, Co. F, May 24, 1898; mustered out with company, March 31, 1899, at Brooklyn, N. Y.

IRVINE, CHARLES W.—Age, 23 years. Enlisted, May 2, 1898, at Brooklyn, to serve two years; mustered in as private, Co. I, May 24, 1898; mustered out with company, March 31, 1899, at Brooklyn, N. Y.

IRVING, HARRY B.—Age, 21 years. Enlisted, May 2, 1898, at Brooklyn, to serve two years; mustered in as private, Co. E, May 24, 1898; deserted, July 17, 1898.

IRVING, WILLIAM J.—Age, 29 years. Enlisted, May 2, 1898, at Brooklyn, to serve two years; mustered in as quartermaster-sergeant, Co. C, May 24, 1898; discharged, October 12, 1898, at Fort Adams, R. I.

IVERS, CHARLES J.—Age, 28 years. Enlisted, May 22, 1898, at Brooklyn, to serve two years; mustered in as private, Co. E, May 24, 1898; mustered out with company, March 31, 1899, at Brooklyn, N. Y.

IVERS, CHARLES J.—Age, 28 years. Enlisted, May 22, 1898, at Brooklyn, to serve two years; mustered in as private, Co. L, May 24, 1898; mustered out with company, March 31, 1899, at Brooklyn, N. Y.

IVERS, JOSEPH P.—Age, 30 years. Enlisted, May 22, 1898, at Brooklyn, to serve two years; mustered in as private, Co. E, May 24, 1898; mustered out with company, March 31, 1899, at Brooklyn, N. Y.

JACKEL, ALBERT.—Age, 21 years. Enlisted, May 19, 1898, at Camp Black, to serve two years; mustered in as private, Co. A, May 24, 1898; mustered out with company, March 31, 1899, at Brooklyn, N. Y.

JACKSON, HARRY M.—Age, 24 years. Enlisted, May 2, 1898, at Brooklyn, to serve two years; mustered in as private, Co. L, May 24, 1898; promoted corporal, October 20, 1898; mustered out with company, March 31, 1899, at Brooklyn, N. Y.

JACKSON, HERBERT A.—Age, 21 years. Enlisted, May 18, 1898, at Camp Black, to serve two years; mustered in as private, Co. A, May 24, 1898; discharged, October 12, 1898.

JACKSON, ROBERT G.—Age, 24 years. Enlisted, May 2, 1898, at Brooklyn, as corporal, to serve two years; mustered in as quartermaster-sergeant, Co. A, May 24, 1898; mustered out with company, March 31, 1899, at Brooklyn, N. Y.

JACKSON, JR., THOMAS.—Age, — years. Enlisted, July 25, 1898, at Brooklyn, to serve two years; mustered in as private, Co. L, same date; mustered out with company, March 31, 1899, at Brooklyn, N. Y.

JACKSON, THOMAS E.—Age, 32 years. Enrolled, May 2, 1898, at Brooklyn, to serve two years; mustered in as captain, Co. G, May 24, 1898; discharged, September 13, 1898, at Fort Adams, R. I.; commissioned captain, May 24, 1898, with rank from same date, original.

JACOB, GEORGE M.—Age, 26 years.   Enlisted, May 16, 1898,
at Brooklyn, to serve two years; mustered in as private, Co. A,
May 24, 1898; promoted corporal, August 15, 1898; mustered
out with company, March 31, 1899, at Brooklyn, N. Y.

JANNICKY, ERNEST E.—Age, 26 years. Enrolled, May 2, 1898,
at Brooklyn, to serve two years; mustered in as captain, Co. A,
May 24, 1898; discharged, December 14, 1898; commissioned
captain, May 24, 1898, with rank from same date, original.   .

JARMAIN, HOWARD P.—Age, 19 years. Enlisted, May 2, 1898,
at Brooklyn, to serve two years; mustered in as private, Co. B,
May 24, 1898; promoted corporal, August 15, 1898; mustered
out with company, March 31, 1899, at Brooklyn, N. Y.

JAUGER, JR., JOHN.—Age, — years. Enlisted, July 25, 1898,
at Brooklyn, to serve two years; mustered in as private, Co. L,
same date; mustered out with company, March 31, 1899, at
Brooklyn, N. Y.

JENKS, FRANK.—Age, — years.   Enlisted, July 28, 1898, at
Brooklyn, to serve two years; mustered in as private, Co. F,
same date; deserted, October 10, 1898, at Fort Adams, R. I.

JOHANN, WILLIAM.—Age, 20 years.   Enlisted, May 23, 1898,
at Brooklyn, to serve two years; mustered in as private, Co. A,
May 24, 1898; mustered out with company, March 31, 1899, at
Brooklyn, N. Y.

JOHNSTON, GEORGE W.—Age, 25 years.   Enlisted, May 2,
1898, at Brooklyn, to serve two years; mustered in as musician,
Co. M, May 24, 1898; discharged, November 1, 1898, at Caguas,
P. R.

JOHNSTON, WILLIAM T.—Age, 31 years.   Enrolled, May 2,
1898, at Brooklyn, to serve two years; mustered in as first lieutenant, Co. B, May 24, 1898; as captain, November 11, 1898;
mustered out with company, March 31, 1899, at Brooklyn,
N. Y.; commissioned first lieutenant, May 24, 1898, with rank
from same date, original; captain, November 11, 1898, with
rank from same date, vice Olden, discharged.

JONES, JR., CHARLES W.—Age, 25 years.   Enlisted, May 2,
1898, at Brooklyn, to serve two years; mustered in as musician,
Co. G, May 24, 1898; mustered out with company, March 31,
1899, at Brooklyn, N. Y.

JONES, LEWIS A.—Age, 20 years.   Enlisted, May 2, 1898, at Brooklyn, to serve two years; mustered in as private, Co. D, May 24, 1898; mustered out with company, March 31, 1899, at Brooklyn, N. Y.

JONES, SAMUEL M.—Age, — years.   Enlisted, August 1, 1898, at Brooklyn, to serve two years; mustered in as private, Co. F, same date; mustered out with company, March 31, 1899, at Brooklyn, N. Y.

KAHN, HERMAN.—Age, 21 years.   Enlisted, May 2, 1898, at Brooklyn, to serve two years; mustered in as private, Co. C, May 24, 1898; mustered out with company, March 31, 1899, at Brooklyn, N. Y.

KAISER, CHARLES.—Age, 27 years.   Enlisted, May 2, 1898, at Brooklyn, to serve two years; mustered in as private, Co. C, May 24, 1898; promoted corporal, August 5, 1898; sergeant, January 20, 1899; quartermaster-sergeant, same date; mustered out with company, March 31, 1899, at Brooklyn, N. Y.

KAISER, JOSEPH.—Age, — years.   Enlisted, July 26, 1898, at Brooklyn, to serve two years; mustered in as private, Co. D, same date; appointed artificer, November 28, 1898; mustered out with company, March 31, 1899, at Brooklyn, N. Y.

KAISER, LOUIS.—Age, — years.   Enlisted, August 8, 1898, at Brooklyn, to serve two years; mustered in as private, Co. E, same date; mustered out with company, March 31, 1899, at Brooklyn, N. Y.

KANE, JOHN.—Age, 25 years.   Enlisted, May 2, 1898, at Brooklyn, to serve two years; mustered in as private, Co. B, May 24, 1898; mustered out with company, March 31, 1899, at Brooklyn, N. Y.

KANE, WALTER.—Age, 21 years.   Enlisted, May 2, 1898, at Brooklyn, to serve two years; mustered in as private, Co. G, May 24, 1898; mustered out with company, March 31, 1899, at Brooklyn, N. Y.

KARA, FRANK R.—Age, 23 years.   Enlisted, May 2, 1898, at Brooklyn, to serve two years; mustered in as musician, Co. F, May 24, 1898; mustered out with company, March 31, 1899, at Brooklyn, N. Y.

KAVANAGH, THOMAS H.—Age, 26 years. Enlisted, May 2, 1898, at Brooklyn, to serve two years; mustered in as private, Co. M, May 24, 1898; promoted corporal, July 29, 1898; returned to ranks, October 4, 1898; discharged, November 1, 1898, at Caguas, P. R.

KEARNS, JOSEPH E.—Age, 21 years. Enlisted, May 2, 1898, at Brooklyn, to serve two years; mustered in as private, Co. F, May 24, 1898; discharged, October 12, 1898, at Fort Adams, R. I.

KEATING, JOHN A.—Age, — years. Enlisted, July 29, 1898, at Brooklyn, to serve two years; mustered in as private, Co. L, same date; mustered out with company, March 31, 1899, at Brooklyn, N. Y.

KEENAN, CLINTON.—Age, 18 years. Enlisted, May 2, 1898, at Brooklyn, to serve two years; mustered in as private, Co. D, May 24, 1898; mustered out with company, March 31, 1899, at Brooklyn, N. Y.

KEENAN, THOMAS.—Age, 22 years. Enlisted, May 2, 1898, at Brooklyn, to serve two years; mustered in as private, Co. M, May 24, 1898; mustered out with company, March 31, 1899, at Brooklyn, N. Y.

KELLY, JOHN.—Age, 25 years. Enlisted, May 2, 1898, at Brooklyn, to serve two years; mustered in as private, Co. H, May 24, 1898; deserted June 27, 1898, at Fort Adams, R. I.

KELLY, JOHN.—Age, 44 years. Enlisted, May 2, 1898, at Brooklyn, to serve two years; mustered in as sergeant, Co. G, May 24, 1898; discharged, October 14, 1898, at Fort Adams, R. I.

KELLY, JOHN H.—Age, 30 years. Enlisted, May 2, 1898, at Brooklyn, to serve two years; mustered in as private, Co. G, May 24, 1898; promoted corporal, June 1, 1898; mustered out with company, March 31, 1899, at Brooklyn, N. Y.

KELLY, RICHARD F.—Age, 29 years. Enlisted, May 2, 1898, at Brooklyn to serve two years; mustered in as private, Co. B, May 24, 1898; promoted corporal, August 15, 1898; mustered out with company, March 31, 1899, at Brooklyn, N. Y.

KELLY, THOMAS.—Age, 21 years. Enlisted, May 2, 1898, at Brooklyn, to serve two years; mustered in as private, Co. G, May 24, 1898; discharged for disability, October 11, 1898, at Fort Adams, R. I.

KELLY, WILLIAM B.—Age, 22 years. Enlisted, May 2, 1898, at Brooklyn, to serve two years; mustered in as corporal, Co. G, May 24, 1898; discharged, October 14, 1898, at Fort Adams, R. I.

KEMP, HERBERT F.—Age, 20 years. Enlisted, May 2, 1898, at Brooklyn, to serve two years; mustered in as private, Co. K, May 24, 1898; mustered out with company, March 31, 1899, at Brooklyn, N. Y.

KENNEDY, CHARLES G.—Age, 25 years. Enlisted, May 2, 1898, at Brooklyn, to serve two years; mustered in as private, Co. E, May 24, 1898; mustered out with company, March 31, 1899, at Brooklyn, N. Y.

KENNEDY, GEORGE F.—Age, 45 years. Enlisted, May 2, 1898, at Brooklyn, to serve two years; mustered in as musician, Co. K, May 24, 1898; promoted principal musician, July 7, 1898; mustered out with regiment, March 31, 1899, at Brooklyn, N. Y.

KENNEDY, JOHN J.—Age, 20 years. Enlisted, May 2, 1898, at Brooklyn, to serve two years; mustered in as private, Co. H, May 24, 1898; mustered out with company, March 31, 1899, at Brooklyn, N. Y.

KENNEY, JAMES H.—Age, 34 years. Enlisted, May 2, 1898, at Brooklyn, to serve two years; mustered in as private, Co. G, May 24, 1898; discharged, October 14, 1898, at Fort Adams, R. I.

KENNEY, JAMES J.—Age, 27 years. Enlisted, May 2, 1898, at Brooklyn, to serve two years; mustered in as private, Co. D, May 24, 1898; mustered out with company, March 31, 1899, at Brooklyn, N. Y.

KENNEY, JOHN T.—Age, 36 years. Enlisted, May 2, 1898, at Brooklyn, to serve two years; mustered in as private, Co. G, May 24, 1898; discharged, October 14, 1898, at Fort Adams, **R. I.**

KERN, ALBERT.—Age, 31 years. Enlisted, May 2, 1898, at
Brooklyn, to serve two years; mustered in as musician, Co. C,
May 24, 1898; mustered out with company, March 31, 1899, at
Brooklyn, N. Y.

KERN, JOSEPH.—Age, 26 years. Enlisted, May 2, 1898, at
Brooklyn, to serve two years; mustered in as private, Co. M,
May 24, 1898; promoted corporal, June 28, 1898; returned to
ranks, July 28, 1898; mustered out with company, March 31,
1899, at Brooklyn, N. Y.

KESSELRING, JOHN.—Age, — years. Enlisted, July 26, 1898,
at Brooklyn, to serve two years; mustered in as private, Co.
B, same date; mustered out with company, March 31, 1899, at
Brooklyn, N. Y.

KETCHAM, RICHARD H.—Age, 35 years. Enlisted, May 2,
1898, at Brooklyn, to serve two years; mustered in as private,
Co. I, May 24, 1898; promoted sergeant, no date; discharged,
October 12, 1898.

KIERNAN, DANIEL.—Age, — years. Enlisted, July 27, 1898,
at Brooklyn, to serve two years; mustered in as private, Co.
D, same date; mustered out with company, March 31, 1899, at
Brooklyn, N. Y.

KIERST, JOHN L.—Age, 22 years. Enlisted, May 2, 1898, at
Brooklyn, to serve two years; mustered in as private, Co. L,
May 24, 1898; deserted, September 10, 1898.

KILKEY, WILLIAM F.—Age, — years. Enlisted, August 4,
1898, at Brooklyn, to serve two years; mustered in as private,
Co. G, same date; mustered out with company, March 31, 1899,
at Brooklyn, N. Y.

KIMBALL, HARRY B.—Age, 28 years. Enlisted, May 2, 1898,
at Brooklyn, to serve two years; mustered in as musician,
Co. L, May 24, 1898; mustered out with company, March 31,
1899, at Brooklyn, N. Y.

KING, HARRY O.—Age, 31 years. Enlisted, May 2, 1898, at
Brooklyn, to serve two years; mustered in as corporal, Co. L,
May 24, 1898; returned to ranks, July 22, 1898; mustered out
with company, March 31, 1899, at Brooklyn, N. Y.

KING, THOMAS W.—Age, — years. Enlisted, August 3, 1898, at Brooklyn, to serve two years; mustered in as private, Co. B, same date; mustered out with company, March 31, 1899, at Brooklyn, N. Y.

KINKEL, ALBERT.—Age, — years. Enlisted, August 8, 1898, at Brooklyn, to serve two years; mustered in as private, Co. H, same date; mustered out with company, March 31, 1899, at Brooklyn, N. Y.

KINNEY, GEORGE W.—Age, 34 years. Enlisted, May 2, 1898, at Brooklyn, to serve two years; mustered in as private, Co. E, May 24, 1898; promoted corporal, same date; sergeant, October 21, 1898; returned to ranks, January 5, 1899; mustered out with company, March 31, 1899, at Brooklyn, N. Y.

KIRKLAND, WILLIAM.—Age, 21 years. Enlisted, May 2, 1898, at Brooklyn, to serve two years; mustered in as private, Co. A, May 24, 1898; mustered out with company, March 31, 1899, at Brooklyn, N. Y.

KIRKMAN, WILLIAM T.—Age, 29 years.   Enlisted, May 2, 1898, at Brooklyn, to serve two years; mustered in as private, Co. I, May 24, 1898; promoted first sergeant, to date, May 24, 1898; mustered in as second lieutenant, January 1, 1899; mustered out with company, March 31, 1899, at Brooklyn, N. Y.; commissioned second lieutenant, January 1, 1899, with rank from same date, vice Ritter, promoted.

KISSAM, CHARLES H.—Age, — years. Enlisted, July 26, 1898, at Brooklyn, to serve two years; mustered in as private, Co. I, same date; mustered out with company, March 31, 1899, at Brooklyn, N. Y.

KITINGER, JOHN A.—Age, 29 years. Enlisted, May 2, 1898, at Brooklyn, to serve two years; mustered in as private, Co. D, May 24, 1898; mustered out with company, March 31, 1899, at Brooklyn, N. Y.

KLINCK, FRANK.—Age, — years. Enlisted, August 6, 1898, at Brooklyn, to serve two years; mustered in as private, Co. E, same date; mustered out with company, March 31, 1899, at Brooklyn, N. Y.

KNAPP, FRANCIS J.—Age, 20 years. Enlisted, May 2, 1898, at
Brooklyn, to serve two years; mustered in as private, Co. E,
May 24, 1898; discharged, October 14, 1898, at Fort Adams,
R. I.

KOCH, GEORGE.—Age, 21 years. Enlisted, May 2, 1898, at
Brooklyn, to serve two years; mustered in as private, Co. M,
May 24, 1898; mustered out with company, March 31, 1899, at
Brooklyn, N. Y.

KOEHLER, HARRY.—Age, — years. Enlisted, August 9, 1898,
at Brooklyn, to serve two years; mustered in as private, Co.
F, same date; mustered out with company, March 31, 1899,
at Brooklyn, N. Y.

KOERNER, FRANK.—Age, — years. Enlisted, July 27, 1898, at
Brooklyn, to serve two years; mustered in as private, Co. M,
same date; mustered out with company, March 31, 1899, at
Brooklyn, N. Y.

KOPITSCH, WILLIAM J.—Age, 27 years. Enlisted, May 2,
1898, at Brooklyn, to serve two years; mustered in as private,
Co. A, May 24, 1898; appointed artificer, August 25, 1898; mustered out with company, March 31, 1899, at Brooklyn, N. Y.

KRAFT, HANS.—Age, 21 years. Enlisted, May 2, 1898, at Brooklyn, to serve two years; mustered in as private, Co. L, May 24.,
1898; mustered out with company, March 31, 1899, at Brooklyn,
N. Y.

KRAMER, JOHN G.—Age, 26 years. Enlisted, May 2, 1898, at
Brooklyn, to serve two years; mustered in as private, Co. I,
May 24, 1898; deserted, September 22, 1898.

KRAUL, WILLIAM.—Age, 21 years. Enlisted, May 2, 1898, at
Brooklyn, to serve two years; mustered in as private, Co. L,
May 24, 1898; mustered out with company, March 31, 1899, at
Brooklyn, N. Y.

KREIS, FRED.—Age, 33 years. Enlisted, May 2, 1898, at Brooklyn, to serve two years; mustered in as corporal, Co. D, May
24, 1898; mustered out with company, March 31, 1899, at Brooklyn, N. Y.

KREISER, ALBERT S.—Age, 20 years. Enlisted, May 2, 1898, at Brooklyn, to serve two years; mustered in as private, Co. K, May 24, 1898; mustered out with company, March 31, 1899, at Brooklyn, N. Y.

KROMER, WILLIAM.—Age, — years. Enlisted, August 8, 1898, at Brooklyn, to serve two years; mustered in as private, Co. M, same date; mustered out with company, March 31, 1899, at Brooklyn, N. Y.

KRUMM, CHARLES G.—Age, 24 years. Enlisted, May 2, 1898, at Brooklyn, to serve two years; mustered in as private, Co. C, May 24, 1898; mustered out with company, March 31, 1899, at Brooklyn, N. Y.

KUMMER, WILLIAM.—Age, 37 years. Enlisted, May 2, 1898, at Brooklyn, to serve two years; mustered in as sergeant, Co. B, May 24, 1898; discharged, October 9, 1898, at Fort Adams, R. I.

KUSTER, CHARLES R.—Age, 24 years. Enlisted, May 2, 1898, at Brooklyn, to serve two years; mustered in as private, Co. H, May 24, 1898; mustered out with company, March 31, 1899, at Brooklyn, N. Y.

LACKAS, GEORGE.—Age, 23 years. Enlistled, May 23, 1898, at Brooklyn, to serve two years; mustered in as private, Co. H, May 24, 1898; mustered out, to date, March 31, 1899.

LALLY, WILLIAM.—Age, 29 years. Enlisted, May 2, 1898, at Brooklyn, to serve two years; mustered in as private, Co. E, May 24, 1898; promoted corporal, August 18, 1898; mustered out with company, March 31, 1899, at Brooklyn, N. Y.

LAMB, EDWARD J.—Age, 25 years. Enlisted, May 2, 1898, at Brooklyn, to serve two years; mustered in as corporal, Co. G, May 24, 1898; promoted sergeant, June 1, 1898; mustered in as second lieutenant, October 3, 1898; mustered out with company, March 31, 1899, at Brooklyn, N. Y.; commissioned second lieutenant, October 3, 1898, with rank from same date, vice Maxfield, discharged.

LAMB, MICHAEL J.—Age, — years. Enlisted, August 9, 1898, at Brooklyn, to serve two years; mustered in as private, Co. A, same date; mustered out with company, March 31, 1899, at Brooklyn, N. Y.

LAMBY, PETER J.—Age, 40 years. Enlisted, May 2, 1898, at Brooklyn, to serve two years; mustered in as corporal, Co. A, May 24, 1898; mustered out with company, March 31, 1899, at Brooklyn, N. Y.

LAMOUREUX, LUCIEN.—Age, 20 years. Enlisted, May 20, 1898, at Brooklyn, to serve two years; mustered in as private, Co. M, May 24, 1898; mustered out with company, March 31, 1899, at Brooklyn, N. Y.

LANE, DANIEL.—Age, 21 years. Enlisted, May 2, 1898, at Brooklyn, to serve two years; mustered in as private, Co. E, May 24, 1898; mustered out with company, March 31, 1899, at Brooklyn, N. Y.

LANE, JAMES P.—Age, 22 years. Enlisted, May 19, 1898, at Camp Black, to serve two years; mustered in as private, Co. A, May 24, 1898; mustered out with company, March 31, 1899, at Brooklyn, N. Y.

LANG, HENRY.—Age, 24 years. Enlisted, May 2, 1898, at Brooklyn, to serve two years; mustered in as private, Co. F, May 24, 1898; mustered out with company, March 31, 1899, at Brooklyn, N. Y.

LANGE, WILLIAM F.—Age, — years. Enlisted, July 29, 1898, at Brooklyn, to serve two years; mustered in as private, Co. D, same date; mustered out with company, March 31, 1899, at Brooklyn, N. Y.

LANNAN, JOHN T.—Age, — years. Enlisted, August 5, 1898, at Brooklyn, to serve two years; mustered in as private, Co. K, same date; mustered out with company, March 31, 1899, at Brooklyn, N. Y.

LARAMEE, WILLIAM.—Age, — years. Enlisted, July 25, 1898, at Brooklyn, to serve two years; mustered in as private, Co. L, same date; mustered out with company, March 31, 1899, at Brooklyn, N. Y.

LA ROSA, WILLIAM.—Age, 19 years. Enlisted, May 2, 1898, at Brooklyn, to serve two years; mustered in as private, Co. L, May 24, 1898; mustered out with company, March 31, 1899, at Brooklyn, N. Y.

LAURENT, AMIE L.—Age, 21 years. Enlisted, May 2, 1898, at Brooklyn, to serve two years; mustered in as private, Co. I, May 24, 1898; mustered out with company, March 31, 1899, at Brooklyn, N. Y.

LAURENT, JOHN B.—Age, 22 years. Enlisted, May 2, 1898. at Brooklyn, to serve two years; mustered in as private, Co. I, May 24, 1898; mustered out with company, March 31, 1899, at Brooklyn, N. Y.

LAVENS, JAMES ERWIN.—Age, 30 years. Enrolled, May 2, 1898, at Brooklyn, to serve two years; mustered in as second lieutenant, Co. B, May 24, 1898; as first lieutenant, November 11, 1898; mustered out with company, March 31, 1899, at Brooklyn, N. Y.; commissioned second lieutenant, May 24. 1898, with rank from same date, original; first lieutenant, November 11, 1898, with rank from same date, vice Johnston, promoted.

LAVERY, JOHN Y.—Age, 27 years. Enlisted, May 2, 1898, at Brooklyn, to serve two years; mustered in as private, Co. K, May 24, 1898; promoted corporal, August 8, 1898; mustered out with company, March 31, 1899, at Brooklyn, N. Y.

LAWRENCE, JOHN.—Age, — years. Enlisted, July 25, 1898, at Brooklyn, to serve two years; mustered in as private, Co. M, same date; mustered out with company, March 31, 1899, at Brooklyn, N. Y.

LAWSON, ALBERT V.—Age, — years. Enlisted, July 30, 1898, at Brooklyn, to serve two years; mustered in as private, Co. G, same date; mustered out with company, March 31, 1899, at Brooklyn, N. Y.

LAYTON, JOHN E.—Age, 24 years. Enlisted, May 2, 1898, at Brooklyn, to serve two years; mustered in as corporal, Co. D, May 24, 1898; promoted sergeant, October 22, 1898; mustered out with company, March 31, 1899, at Brooklyn, N. Y.

LEACH, ADDISON C.—Age, 29 years. Enlisted, May 2, 1898, at Brooklyn, to serve two years; mustered in as first sergeant, Co. F, May 24, 1898; mustered out with company, March 31, 1899, at Brooklyn, N. Y.

LEACH, CHARLES N.—Age, 33 years. Enlisted, May 2, 1898, at Brooklyn, to serve two years; mustered in as sergeant, Co. L, May 24, 1898; as second lieutenant, Co. M, November 2, 1898; mustered out with company, March 31, 1899, at Brooklyn, N. Y.; commissioned second lieutenant, November 2, 1898, with rank from same date, vice Young, promoted.

LECKIE, THOMAS.—Age, 22 years. Enlisted, May 19, 1898, at Brooklyn, to serve two years; mustered in as private, Co. E, May 24, 1898; mustered out with company, March 31, 1899, at Brooklyn, N. Y.

LE COUNT, CHARLES M.—Age, 21 years. Enlisted, May 2, 1898, at Brooklyn, to serve two years; mustered in as private, Co. L, same date; mustered out, to date, March 31, 1899.

LEHMAN, OSCAR C.—Age, — years. Enlisted, July 26, 1898, at Brooklyn, to serve two years; mustered in as private, Co. E, same date; appointed cook, November 1, 1898; returned to ranks, February 14, 1899; mustered out with company, March 31, 1899, at Brooklyn, N. Y.

LENHARD, CHARLES G.—Age, 19 years. Enlisted, May 2, 1898, at Brooklyn, to serve two years; mustered in as private, Co. F, May 24, 1898; mustered out with company, March 31, 1899, at Brooklyn, N. Y.

LENKTIS, ANDREW.—Age, — years. Enlisted, August 2, 1898, at Brooklyn, to serve two years; mustered in as private, Co. G, same date; mustered out with company, March 31, 1899, at Brooklyn, N. Y.

LENOIR, JOHN C.—Age, — years. Enlisted, July 28, 1898, at Brooklyn, to serve two years; mustered in as private, Co. K, same date; mustered out with company, March 31, 1899, at Brooklyn, N. Y.

LEONARD, MICHAEL J.—Age, — years. Enlisted, August 11, 1898, at Brooklyn, to serve two years; mustered in as private, Co. K, same date; mustered out with company, March 31, 1899, at Brooklyn, N. Y.

LESSEY, GEORGE A.—Age, 24 years. Enlisted, May 3, 1898, at Brooklyn, to serve two years; mustered in as hospital steward, May 24, 1898; mustered out with regiment, March 31, 1899, at Brooklyn, N. Y.

LEVITT, JOSEPH.—Age, 20 years. Enlisted, May 2, 1898, at Brooklyn, to serve two years; mustered in as private, Co. G, May 24, 1898; discharged, February 14, 1899, at San Juan, P. R.

LEWIS, GEORGE.—Age, — years. Enlisted, July 27, 1898, at Brooklyn, to serve two years; mustered in as private, Co. C, same date; mustered out with company, March 31, 1899, at Brooklyn, N. Y.

LEWIS, OTTO.—Age, — years. Enlisted, August 8, 1898, at Brooklyn, to serve two years; mustered in as private, Co. B, same date; mustered out with company, March 31, 1899, at Brooklyn, N. Y.

LIBBEY, GEORGE E.—Age, 43 years. Enrolled, May 2, 1898, at Brooklyn, to serve two years; mustered in as captain, Co. L, May 24, 1898; discharged, December 14, 1898; commissioned captain, May 24, 1898, with rank from same date, original.

LICHTENHELD, EDWARD.—Age, 21 years. Enlisted, May 2, 1898, at Brooklyn, to serve two years; mustered in as private, Co. F, May 24, 1898; promoted corporal, June 23, 1898; mustered out with company, March 31, 1899, at Brooklyn, N. Y.

LIDDELL, ALEXANDER.—Age, 23 years. Enlisted, May 2, 1898, at Brooklyn, to serve two years; mustered in as private, Co. I, May 24, 1898; mustered out with company, March 31, 1899, at Brooklyn, N. Y.

LIEBLER, PAUL H.—Age, 31 years. Enlisted, May 2, 1898, at Brooklyn, to serve two years; mustered in as corporal, Co. L, May 24, 1898; promoted sergeant, June 13, 1898; first sergeant, January 18, 1899; mustered out with company, March 31, 1899, at Brooklyn, N. Y.

LIEBOLD, THOMAS P.—Age, — years. Enlisted, August 3, 1898, at Brooklyn, to serve two years; mustered in as private, Co. F, same date; mustered out with company, March 31, 1899, at Brooklyn, N. Y.

LINDEMANN, THEODORE.—Age, — years. Enlisted, August 10, 1898, at Brooklyn, to serve two years; mustered in as private, Co. A, same date; mustered out with company, March 31, 1899, at Brooklyn, N. Y.

LINDER, GEORGE.—Age, 19 years. Enlisted, May 2, 1898, at Brooklyn, to serve two years; mustered in as private, Co. F, May 24, 1898; transferred to Hospital Corps, United States Army, August 16, 1898.

LIPKOW, FREDERICK W.—Age, 25 years. Enlisted, May 20, 1898, at Brooklyn, to serve two years; mustered in as private, Co. E, May 24, 1898; mustered out with company, March 31, 1899, at Brooklyn, N. Y.

LIPSCOMBE, REUBEN F.—Age, 25 years. Enlisted, May 2, 1898, at Brooklyn, to serve two years; mustered in as private, Co. E, May 24, 1898; transferred to Hospital Corps, August 16, 1898.

LIPTON, THOMAS J.—Age, — years. Enlisted, July 28, 1898, at Brooklyn, to serve two years; mustered in as private, Co. K, same date; mustered out with company, March 31, 1899, at Brooklyn, N. Y.

LITTMANN, CHARLES.—Age, 27 years. Enlisted, May 2, 1898, at Brooklyn, to serve two years; mustered in as private, Co. C, May 24, 1898; promoted corporal, August 26, 1898; sergeant, November 1, 1898; quartermaster-sergeant, December 29, 1898; reduced to sergeant, January 20, 1899; mustered out with company, March 31, 1899, at Brooklyn, N. Y.

LITTMANN, WILLIAM.—Age, 21 years. Enlisted, May 2, 1898, at Brooklyn, to serve two years; mustered in as private, Co. L, May 24, 1898; mustered out with company, March 21, 1899, at Brooklyn, N. Y.

LOCH, JOHN.—Age, — years. Enlisted, July 28, 1898, at Brooklyn, to serve two years; mustered in as private, Co. M, same date; mustered out with company, March 31, 1899, at Brooklyn, N. Y.

LOCKE, EDWARD D.—Age, 22 years. Enlisted, May 16, 1898, at Camp Black, to serve two years; mustered in as private, Co. A, May 24, 1898; mustered out with company, March 31, 1899, at Brooklyn, N. Y.

LOCKE, OLIVER L.—Age, 34 years. Enlisted, May 2, 1898, at Brooklyn, to serve two years; mustered in as private, Co. C, May 24, 1898; discharged, October 12, 1898, at Fort Adams, R. I.

LOCKWOOD, JR., CHARLES H.—Age, 19 years. Enlisted, May 2, 1898, at Brooklyn, to serve two years; mustered in as corporal, Co. K, May 24, 1898; mustered out with company, March 31, 1899, at Brooklyn, N. Y.

LOMAS, HENRY.—Age, 39 years. Enlisted, May 2, 1898, at Brooklyn, to serve two years; mustered in as private, Co. E, May 24, 1898; died of pneumonia, March 12, 1899, in Long Island College Hospital, Brooklyn, N. Y.

LONERGAN, DAVID M.—Age, 23 years. Enlisted, May 2, 1898, at Brooklyn, to serve two years; mustered in as private, Co. L, May 24, 1898; mustered out with company, March 31, 1899, at Brooklyn, N. Y.

LORD, JOSEPH.—Age, 21 years. Enlisted, May 2, 1898, at Brooklyn, to serve two years; mustered in as private, Co. M, same date; transferred to Hospital Corps, United States Army, August 19, 1898.

LOTT, AUGUSTUS S.—Age, 24 years. Enlisted, May 2, 1898, at Brooklyn, to serve two years; mustered in as private, Co. C, May 24, 1898; mustered out with company, March 31, 1899, at Brooklyn, N. Y.

LOTT, JOHN.—Age, — years. Enlisted, August 5, 1898, at Brooklyn, to serve two years; mustered in as private, Co. M, same date; deserted, October 8, 1898, from Fort Adams, R. I.

LOTZ, FRANK S.—Age, — years. Enlisted, August 10, 1898, at Brooklyn, to serve two years; mustered in as private, Co. I, same date; mustered out with company, March 31, 1899, at Brooklyn, N. Y.

LOVINGHAM, PHILIP.—Age, 21 years. Enlisted, May 2, 1898, at Brooklyn, to serve two years; mustered in as private, Co. A, May 24, 1898; mustered out with company, March 31, 1899, at Brooklyn, N. Y.

LOWE, EDWARD H.—Age, — years. Enlisted, July 30, 1898, at Brooklyn, to serve two years; mustered in as private, Co. F, same date; mustered out with company, March 31, 1899, at Brooklyn, N. Y.

LOWERY, MICHAEL.—Age, 24 years. Enlisted, May 2, 1898, at Brooklyn, to serve two years; mustered in as private, Co. D, May 24, 1898; mustered out with company, March 31, 1899, at Brooklyn, N. Y.

LUDWIG, HENRY A.—Age, 21 years. Enlisted, May 2, 1898, at Brooklyn, to serve two years; mustered in as private, Co. E, May 24, 1898; mustered out with company, March 31, 1899, at Brooklyn, N. Y.

LUTZ, FRED.—Age, 26 years. Enlisted, May 2, 1898, at Brooklyn, to serve two years; mustered in as private, Co. M, May 24, 1898; appointed cook, August 1, 1898; mustered out with company, March 31, 1899, at Brooklyn, N. Y.

LYNCH, JOSEPH A.—Age, — years. Enlisted, August 10, 1898, at Brooklyn, to serve two years; mustered in as private, Co. A, same date; mustered out with company, March 31, 1899, at Brooklyn, N. Y.

LYNCH, WILLIAM H.—Age, 25 years. Enlisted, May 2, 1898, at Brooklyn, to serve two years; mustered in as private, Co. L, May 24, 1898; discharged, February 17, 1899, at Caguas, Porto Rico.

LYON, CHARLES F.—Age, 19 years. Enlisted, May 2, 1898, at Brooklyn, to serve two years; mustered in as private, Co. D, May 24, 1898; mustered out with company, March 31, 1899, at Brooklyn, N. Y.

LYON, CLARENCE W.—Age, — years. Enlisted, August 2, 1898, at Brooklyn, to serve two years; mustered in as private, Co. F, same date; mustered out with company, March 31, 1899, at Brooklyn, N. Y.

LYON, HERVEY C.—Age, 32 years. Enrolled, May 3, 1898, at Brooklyn, to serve two years; mustered in as major, May 24, 1898; discharged, October 1, 1898; commissioned major, May 24, 1898, with rank from same date, original; commissioned as Henry Calkin Lyon.

LYONS, JOHN J.—Age, 20 years. Enlisted, May 2, 1898, at Brooklyn, to serve two years; mustered in as private, Co. G, May 24, 1898; mustered out with company, March 31, 1899, at Brooklyn, N. Y.

MACBETH, GODFREY R.—Age, 23 years. Enlisted, May 2, 1898, at Brooklyn, to serve two years; mustered in as private, Co. C, May 24, 1898; appointed lance corporal, June 2, 1898; promoted corporal, to date, June 1, 1898; returned to ranks, July 23, 1898; mustered out with company, March 31, 1899, at Brooklyn, N. Y.

MACE, FRANK J.—Age, 33 years. Enlisted, May 2, 1898, at Brooklyn, to serve two years; mustered in as private, Co. I, May 24, 1898; appointed wagoner, June 1, 1898; returned to ranks, December 1, 1898; mustered out with company, March 31, 1899, at Brooklyn, N. Y.

MACK, CHARLES.—Age, 25 years. Enlisted, May 2, 1898, at Brooklyn, to serve two years; mustered in as private, Co. F, May 24, 1898; deserted, July 16, 1898, at Fort Adams, R. I.

MACKIN, CHARLES E. J.—Age, — years. Enlisted, August 9, 1898, at Brooklyn, to serve two years; mustered in as private, Co. A, same date; mustered out with company, March 31, 1899, at Brooklyn, N. Y.

MADDOCK, EDMUND.—Age, 20 years. Enlisted, May 2, 1898, at Brooklyn, to serve two years; mustered in as private, Co. H, May 24, 1898; promoted corporal, September 1, 1898; returned to ranks, January 16, 1899; mustered out with company, March 31, 1899, at Brooklyn, N. Y.

MADIGAN, JOHN.—Age, — years. Enlisted, July 26, 1898, at Brooklyn, to serve two years; mustered in as private, Co. L, same date; mustered out, to date, March 31, 1899.

MADIGAN, MATTHEW D.—Age, 26 years. Enlisted, May 2, 1898, at Brooklyn, to serve two years; mustered in as private, Co. B, same date; mustered out with company, March 31, 1899, at Brooklyn, N. Y.

MADIGAN, MICHAEL.—Age, 37 years. Enlisted, May 2, 1898, at Brooklyn, to serve two years; mustered in as quartermaster-sergeant, Co. B, May 24, 1898; mustered out with company, March 31, 1899, at Brooklyn, N. Y.

MAEURER, FRED J.—Age, 21 years. Enlisted, May 2, 1898, at Brooklyn, to serve two years; mustered in as private, Co. G, May 24, 1898; mustered out with company, March 31, 1899, at Brooklyn, N. Y.

MAHER, JOSEPH W.—Age, 25 years. Enlisted, May 2, 1898, at Brooklyn, to serve two years; mustered in as private, Co. M, May 24, 1898; promoted corporal, July 29, 1898; mustered out with company, March 31, 1899, at Brooklyn, N. Y.

MAHONEY, NICHOLAS W.—Age, 28 years. Enlisted, May 2, 1898, at Brooklyn, to serve two years; mustered in as private, Co. I, May 24, 1898; promoted corporal, August 26, 1898; mustered out with company, March 31, 1899, at Brooklyn, N. Y.

MAIER, CHARLES D.—Age, 22 years. Enlisted, May 22, 1898, at Brooklyn, to serve two years; mustered in as private, Co. E, May 24, 1898; deserted, October 1, 1898, at Fort Adams, R. I.

MAIER, FRANK.—Age, 37 years. Enrolled, May 2, 1898, at Brooklyn, to serve two years; mustered in as second lieutenant, Co. K, May 24, 1898; as captain, June 22, 1898; discharged, September 13, 1898; commissioned second lieutenant, May 24, 1898, with rank from same date, original; captain, June 22, 1898, with rank from same date, original.

MAIER, FREDERICK C.—Age, 21 years. Enlisted, May 2, 1898, at Brooklyn, to serve two years; mustered in as private, Co. F, May 24, 1898; mustered out with company, March 31, 1899, at Brooklyn, N. Y.

MAILAND, HENRY.—Age, 21 years. Enlisted, May 23, 1898, at Brooklyn, to serve two years; mustered in as private, Co. E, May 24, 1898; appointed cook, February 14, 1899; mustered out with company, March 31, 1899, at Brooklyn, N. Y.

MAJOR, CHARLES.—Age, 26 years. Enlisted, May 2, 1898, at Brooklyn, to serve two years; mustered in as private, Co. E, May 24, 1898; promoted corporal, October 21, 1898; mustered out with company, March 31, 1899, at Brooklyn, N. Y.

MALLON, EDWARD A.—Age, — years. Enlisted, August 10, 1898, at Brooklyn, to serve two years; mustered in as private, Co. I, same date; mustered out with company, March 31, 1899, at Brooklyn, N. Y.

MALONE, JOHN P.—Age, 26 years. Enlisted, May 2, 1898, at Brooklyn, to serve two years; mustered in as private, Co. H, May 24, 1898; mustered out with company, March 31, 1899, at Brooklyn, N. Y.

MANGOLD, ALFRED C.—Age, 21 years. Enlisted, May 2, 1898, at Brooklyn, to serve two years; mustered in as private, Co. L, May 24, 1898; transferred, August 20, 1898, to United States Army Medical Department, Washington, D. C.

MANNING, HARRY J.—Age, 21 years. Enlisted, May 2, 1898, at Brooklyn, to serve two years; mustered in as private, Co. K, May 24, 1898; mustered out with company, March 31, 1899, at Brooklyn, N. Y.

MANNING, PERCY B.—Age, — years. Enlisted, August 11, 1898, at Brooklyn, to serve two years; mustered in as private, Co. A, same date; mustered out with company, March 31, 1899, at Brooklyn, N. Y.

MARCO, JOHN.—Age, 24 years. Enlisted, May 2, 1898, at Brooklyn, to serve two years; mustered in as private, Co. B, May 24, 1898; discharged, February 14, 1899, at San Juan, P. R.

MARINGER, JACOB.—Age, 21 years. Enlisted, May 2, 1898, at Brooklyn, to serve two years; mustered in as private, Co. I, May 24, 1898; mustered out with company, March 31, 1899, at Brooklyn, N. Y.

MARLOW, WILLIAM J.—Age, 21 years. Enlisted, May 2, 1898, at Brooklyn, to serve two years; mustered in as private, Co. M, May 24, 1898; mustered out with company, March 31, 1899, at Brooklyn, N. Y.

MARRION, THOMAS.—Age, 21 years. Enlisted, May 2, 1898, at Brooklyn, to serve two years; mustered in as private, Co. D, May 24, 1898; mustered out with company, March 31, 1899, at Brooklyn, N. Y.

MARSELLY, PETER J.—Age, 20 years. Enlisted, May 2, 1898, at Brooklyn, to serve two years; mustered in as private, Co. C, May 24, 1898; promoted corporal, February 8, 1899; mustered out with company, March 31, 1899, at Brooklyn, N. Y.

MARSHALL, ROBERT A.—Age, 28 years. Enrolled, May 2, 1898, at Brooklyn, to serve two years; mustered in as first lieutenant, Co. G, May 24, 1898; as captain, September 23, 1898; mustered out with company, March 31, 1899, at Brooklyn, N.Y.; commissioned first lieutenant, May 24, 1898, with rank from same date, original; captain, September 23, 1898, with rank from same date, vice Jackson, discharged.

MARTIN, EDWARD L.—Age, 22 years. Enlisted, May 2, 1898,
at Brooklyn, to serve two years; mustered in as sergeant, Co.
G, May 24, 1898; discharged November 21, 1898, at Carolina,
P. R.

MARTIN, FRANK A.—Age, 23 years. Enlisted, May 2, 1898, at
Brooklyn, to serve two years; mustered in as private, Co. F,
May 24, 1898; promoted corporal, December 21, 1898; mustered
out with company, March 31, 1899, at Brooklyn, N. Y.

MARTIN, WILLIAM.—Age, 24 years.   Enlisted, May 2, 1898,
at Brooklyn, to serve two years; mustered in as private, Co.
H, May 24, 1898; promoted corporal, September 1, 1898; mustered out with company, March 31, 1899, at Brooklyn, N. Y.

MARTIN, WILLIAM C.—Age, 25 years.   Enlisted, May 2, 1898,
at Brooklyn, to serve two years; mustered in as private, Co. D,
May 24, 1898; promoted corporal, September 6, 1898; returned
to ranks, September 28, 1898; mustered out with company,
March 31, 1899, at Brooklyn, N. Y.

MASON, GEORGE W.—Age, — years.   Enlisted, July 26, 1898,
at Brooklyn, to serve two years; mustered in as private, Co.
G, same date; promoted corporal, August 11, 1898; mustered
out with company, March 31, 1899, at Brooklyn, N. Y.

MATTHEWS, WILLIAM H.—Age, 21 years.   Enlisted, May 2,
1898, at Brooklyn, to serve two years; mustered in as private,
Co. M, May 24, 1898; deserted, October 8, 1898, from Fort
Adams, R. I.

MATZDORF, AUGUST.—Age, — years.   Enlisted, August 10,
1898, at Brooklyn, to serve two years; mustered in as private,
Co. B, same date; mustered out with company, March 31, 1899,
at Brooklyn, N. Y.

MAULE, ALBERT.—Age, — years.   Enlisted, July 26, 1898, at
Brooklyn, to serve two years; mustered in as private, Co. L,
same date; discharged, October 12, 1898, at Caguas, P. R.

MAURER, WILLIAM.—Age, 29 years.   Enlisted, May 2, 1898,
at Brooklyn, to serve two years; mustered in as private, Co.
H, May 24, 1898; mustered out with company, March 31, 1899,
at Brooklyn, N. Y.

MAUSER, ALBERT A.—Age, 21 years. Enlisted, May 2, 1898, at Brooklyn, to serve two years; mustered in as private, Co. M, May 24, 1898; mustered out with company, March 31, 1899, at Brooklyn, N. Y.

MAUTHEY, FREDERICK W.—Age, — years. Enlisted, July 27, 1898, at Brooklyn, to serve two years; mustered in as private, Co. L, same date; mustered out with company, March 31, 1899, at Brooklyn, N. Y.

MAXFIELD, CHARLES E.—Age, 34 years. Enrolled, May 2, 1898, at Brooklyn, to serve two years; mustered in as second lieutenant, Co. G, May 24, 1898; discharged, September 10, 1898, at Fort Adams, R. I.; commissioned second lieutenant, May 24, 1898, with rank from same date, original.

McALEER, MICHAEL F.—Age, 22 years. Enlisted, May 2, 1898, at Brooklyn, to serve two years; mustered in as private, Co. E, May 24, 1898; promoted corporal, December 1, 1898; mustered out with company, March 31, 1899, at Brooklyn, N. Y.

McANDREWS, CHARLES M. J.—Age, 21 years. Enlisted, May 2, 1898, at Brooklyn, to serve two years; mustered in as corporal, Co. K, May 24, 1898; promoted sergeant, October 21, 1898; mustered out with company, March 31, 1899, at Brooklyn, N. Y.

McANEENY, WILLIAM J.—Age, 25 years. Enlisted, May 2, 1898, at Brooklyn, to serve two years; mustered in as private, Co. B, May 24, 1898; promoted corporal, August 15, 1898; sergeant, January 23, 1899; mustered out with company, March 31, 1899, at Brooklyn, N. Y.

McATEER, JOSEPH P.—Age, — years. Enlisted, July 25, 1898, at Brooklyn, to serve two years; mustered in as private, Co. E, same date; mustered out with company, March 31, 1899, at Brooklyn, N. Y.

McAVOY, ANDREW J.—Age, 28 years. Enlisted, May 2, 1898, at Brooklyn, to serve two years; mustered in as private, Co. A, May 24, 1898; mustered out with company, March 31, 1899, at Brooklyn, N. Y.

McBARRON, JR., JOHN J.—Age, 29 years. Enlisted, May 2, 1898, at Brooklyn, to serve two years; mustered in as private, Co. L, May 24, 1898; mustered out with company, March 31, 1899, at Brooklyn, N. Y.

McBRIDE, JAMES P.—Age, 24 years. Enlisted, May 16, 1898, at Brooklyn, to serve two years; mustered in as private, Co. E, May 24, 1898; dishonorably discharged, November 18, 1898, at Fort Adams, R. I.

McBRIDE, ROBERT J.—Age, 22 years Enlisted, May 2, 1898, at Brooklyn, to serve two-years; mustered in as private, Co. H, May 24, 1898; promoted corporal, no date; discharged, December 10, 1898.

McCAFFERY, HUGH F.—Age, — years. Enlisted, August 2, 1898, at Brooklyn, to serve two years; mustered in as private, Co. C, same date; mustered out with company, March 31, 1899, at Brooklyn, N. Y.

McCAFFERY, JAMES.—Age, 26 years. Enlisted, May 2, 1898, at Brooklyn, to serve two years; mustered in as private, Co. M, May 24, 1898; mustered out with company, March 31, 1899, at Brooklyn, N. Y.

McCAFFERY, MICHAEL F.—Age, — years. Enlisted, August 11, 1898, at Brooklyn, to serve two years; mustered in as private, Co. B, same date; mustered out with company, March 31, 1899, at Brooklyn, N. Y.

McCAFFERY, THOMAS L.—Age, 24 years. Enlisted, May 2, 1898. at Brooklyn, to serve two years; mustered in as private, Co. I, same date; mustered out with company, March 31, 1899, at Brooklyn, N. Y.

McCARTHY, DANIEL F.—Age, 28 years. Enlisted, May 2, 1898, at Brooklyn, to serve two years; mustered in as private, Co. C, May 24. 1898; mustered out with company, March 31, 1899, at Brooklyn, N. Y.

McCARTHY, EDWARD O.—Age, 22 years. Enlisted, May 2, 1898, at Brooklyn, to serve two years; mustered in as private, Co. B, May 24, 1898; mustered out with company, March 31, 1899, at Brooklyn, N. Y.

McCARTHY, JAMES J.—Age, — years.   Enlisted, August 1, 1898, at Brooklyn, to serve two years; mustered in as private, Co. L, same date; mustered out with company, March 31, 1899, at Brooklyn, N. Y.

McCARTHY, THOMAS M.—Age, 38 years.   Enlisted, May 2, 1898, at Brooklyn, to serve two years; mustered in as private, Co. B, May 24, 1898; discharged, October 14, 1898, at Fort Adams, R. I.

McCLEERY, CHARLES W.—Age, 24 years.   Enlisted, May 2, 1898, at Brooklyn, to serve two years; mustered in as private, Co. D, May 24, 1898; mustered out with company, March 31, 1899, at Brooklyn, N. Y.

McCOLE, CHARLES A.—Age, — years.   Enlisted, July 27, 1898, at Brooklyn, to serve two years; mustered in as private, Co. E, same date; mustered out with company, March 31, 1899, at Brooklyn, N. Y.

McCOMB, CHARLES A.—Age, 21 years.   Enlisted, May 2, 1898, at Brooklyn, to serve two years; mustered in as private, Co. F, May 24, 1898; deserted, September 21, 1898, at Fort Adams, R. I.

McCONNIN, JOHN F.—Age, 29 years.   Enlisted, May 2, 1898, at Brooklyn, to serve two years; mustered in as private, Co. I, May 24, 1898; mustered out with company, March 31, 1899, at Brooklyn, N. Y.

McCORMACK, EDWARD J.—Age, 28 years.   Enlisted, May 2, 1898, at Brooklyn, to serve two years; mustered in as private, Co. D, May 24, 1898; mustered out with company, March 31, 1899, at Brooklyn, N. Y.

McCORMICK, JAMES H.—Age, 21 years.   Enlisted, May 2, 1898, at Brooklyn, to serve two years; mustered in as private, Co. H, May 24, 1898; mustered out with company, March 31, 1899, at Brooklyn, N. Y.

McCREA, GEORGE.—Age, 20 years.   Enlisted, May 2, 1898, at Brooklyn, to serve two years; mustered in as private, Co. M, May 24, 1898; mustered out with company, March 31, 1899, at Brooklyn, N. Y.

McCULLOUGH, JOHN C.—Age, — years.   Enlisted, August 9,
1898, at Brooklyn, to serve two years; mustered in as private,
Co. M, same date; mustered out with company, March 31, 1899,
at Brooklyn, N. Y.

McCUTCHAN, DAVID B.—Age, 28 years.   Enlisted, May 2,
1898, at Brooklyn, to serve two years; mustered in as private,
Co. G, May 24, 1898; mustered out with company, March 31,
1899, at Brooklyn, N. Y.

McCUTCHEON, HENRY D.—Age, 38 years.   Enrolled, May 3,
1898, at Brooklyn, to serve two years; mustered in as first lieutenant and regimental adjutant, May 24, 1898; mustered out
with regiment, March 31, 1899, as captain and regimental adjutant, at Brooklyn, N. Y.; commissioned captain and regimental
adjutant, May 24, 1898, with rank from same date, original.

McDERMOTT, PETER P.—Age, 21 years.   Enlisted, May 2, 1898,
at Brooklyn, to serve two years; mustered in as private, Co. M,
May 24, 1898; promoted corporal, November 27, 1898; mustered out with company, March 31, 1899, at Brooklyn, N. Y.

McDONALD, PATRICK.—Age, — years.   Enlisted, August 1,
1898, at Brooklyn, to serve two years; mustered in as private,
Co. K, same date; died of pernicious malaria, December 7, 1898,
at Guayama. P. R.

McDONALD, WALTER L.—Age, 21 years.   Enlisted, May 2,
1898, at Brooklyn, to serve two years; mustered in as private,
Co. F, May 24, 1898; promoted corporal, June 23, 1898; mustered out with company, March 31, 1899, at Brooklyn, N. Y.

McENANEY, STEPHEN B.—Age, 22 years.   Enlisted, May 2,
1898, at Brooklyn, to serve two years; mustered in as private,
Co. M, May 24, 1898; mustered out with company, March 31,
1899, at Brooklyn, N. Y.

McENEANY, JAMES.—Age, 35 years.   Enlisted, May 2, 1898, at
Brooklyn, to serve two years; mustered in as private, Co. B,
May 24, 1898; mustered out with company, March 31, 1899, at
Brooklyn, N. Y.

McENTEE, JAMES.—Age, — years.   Enlisted, August 8, 1898,
at Brooklyn, to serve two years; mustered in as private, Co. F,
same date; mustered out with company, March 31, 1899, at
Brooklyn, N. Y.

McENTEE, WILLIAM H.—Age, 25 years. Enlisted, May 2, 1898, at Brooklyn, to serve two years; mustered in as private, Co. D, May 24, 1898; mustered out with company, March 31, 1899, at Brooklyn, N. Y.

McGEHIN, RICHARD J.—Age, 19 years. Enlisted, May 2, 1898, at Brooklyn, to serve two years; mustered in as private, Co. G, May 24, 1898; mustered out with company, March 31, 1899, at Brooklyn, N. Y.

McGOWAN, PETER.—Age, 23 years. Enlisted, May 2, 1898, at Brooklyn, to serve two years; mustered in as private, Co. D, May 24, 1898; mustered out with company, March 31, 1899, at Brooklyn, N. Y.

McGROVER, HENRY.—Age, — years. Enlisted, August 1, 1898, at Brooklyn, to serve two years; mustered in as private, Co. D, same date; mustered out with company, March 31, 1899, at Brooklyn, N. Y.

McGUIRE, ALEXANDER S.—Age, — years. Enlisted, July 26, 1898, at Brooklyn, to serve two years; mustered in as private, Co. A, same date; mustered out with company, March 31, 1899, at Brooklyn, N. Y.

McGUIRE, BENJAMIN F.—Age, — years. Enlisted, July 27, 1898, at Brooklyn, to serve two years; mustered in as private, Co. I, same date; mustered out with company, March 31, 1899, at Brooklyn, N. Y.

McGUIRE, CORNELIUS.—Age, 20 years. Enlisted, May 2, 1898, at Brooklyn, to serve two years; mustered in as private, Co. M, May 24, 1898; mustered out with company, March 31, 1899, at Brooklyn, N. Y.

McGUIRE, JAMES.—Age, 23 years. Enlisted, May 2, 1898, at Brooklyn, to serve two years; mustered in as private, Co. H, May 24, 1898; mustered out with company, March 31, 1899, at Brooklyn, N. Y.

McGUIRE, JOHN.—Age, — years. Enlisted, July 25, 1898, at Brooklyn, to serve two years; mustered in as private, Co. M, same date; mustered out with company, March 31, 1899, at Brooklyn, N. Y.

McHENRY, NORVAL E.—Age, — years. Enlisted, August 9, 1898, at Brooklyn, to serve two years; mustered in as private, Co. B, same date; deserted, September 21, 1898.

McKAY, JULIUS J.—Age, 32 years. Enlisted, May 2, 1898, at Brooklyn, as sergeant, to serve two years; mustered in as first sergeant, Co. B, May 24, 1898; as second lieutenant, February 3, 1899; mustered out with company, March 31, 1899, at Brooklyn, N. Y.; commissioned second lieutenant, January 1, 1899, with rank from same date, vice Borthwick, assigned to Co. D.

McKEEVER, CHARLES B.—Age, 25 years. Enlisted, May 2, 1898, at Brooklyn, to serve two years; mustered in as private, Co. G, May 24, 1898; mustered out with company, March 31, 1899, at Brooklyn, N. Y.

McKEEVER, EDWIN.—Age, — years. Enlisted, July 26, 1898, at Brooklyn, to serve two years; mustered in as private, Co. L, same date; mustered out with company, March 31, 1899, at Brooklyn, N. Y.

McKENNA, CHARLES E.—Age, 25 years. Enlisted, May 2, 1898, at Brooklyn, to serve two years; mustered in as private, Co. L, May 24, 1898; mustered out with company, March 31, 1899, at Brooklyn, N. Y.

McKENNA, CHARLES F.—Age, 22 years. Enlisted, May 2, 1898, at Brooklyn, to serve two years; mustered in as private, Co. H, May 24, 1898; deserted, July 25, 1898, at Fort Adams, R. I.

McKENNA, EDWARD.—Age, 21 years. Enlisted, May 2, 1898, at Brooklyn, to serve two years; mustered in as private, Co. M, May 24, 1898; mustered out with company, March 31, 1899, at Brooklyn, N. Y.

McKENNA, JAMES J.—Age, — years. Enlisted, August 3, 1898, at Brooklyn, to serve two years; mustered in as private, Co. F, same date; mustered out with company, March 31, 1899, at Brooklyn, N. Y.

McKENNA, JOHN J.—Age, 22 years. Enlisted, May 2, 1898, at Brooklyn, to serve two years; mustered in as private, Co. F, May 24, 1898; mustered out with company, March 31, 1899, at Brooklyn, N. Y.

McKINLEY, THOMAS J.—Age, 22 years. Enlisted, May 2, 1898, at Brooklyn, to serve two years; mustered in as private, Co. A, May 24, 1898; mustered out with company, March 31, 1899, at Brooklyn, N. Y.

McKINNON, JOHN.—Age, — years. Enlisted, July 25, 1898, at Brooklyn, to serve two years; mustered in as private, Co. A, same date; mustered out with company, March 31, 1899, at Brooklyn, N. Y.

McKNIGHT, WALTER.—Age, — years. Enlisted, July 27, 1898, at Brooklyn, to serve two years; mustered in as private, Co. G, same date; mustered out with company, March 31, 1899, at Brooklyn, N. Y.

McLAUGHLIN, GEORGE.—Age, — years. Enlisted, August 9, 1898, at Brooklyn, to serve two years; mustered in as private, Co. H, same date; mustered out with company, March 31, 1899, at Brooklyn, N. Y.

McLAUGHLIN, JAMES.—Age, 20 years. Enlisted, May 2, 1898, at Brooklyn, to serve two years; mustered in as private, Co. I, May 24, 1898; promoted corporal, August 26, 1898; mustered out with company, March 31, 1899, at Brooklyn, N. Y.

McLEAN, GEORGE.—Age, 22 years. Enlisted, May 2, 1898, at Brooklyn to serve two years; mustered in as private Co. M, May 24, 1898; mustered out with company, March 31, 1899, at Brooklyn, N. Y.

McMAHON, JOHN J.—Age, 25 years. Enlisted, May 2, 1898, at Brooklyn, to serve two years; mustered in as private, Co. B, May 24, 1898; mustered out with company, March 31, 1899, at Brooklyn, N. Y.

McMAHON, JOHN J.—Age, — years. Enlisted, July 26, 1898, at Brooklyn, to serve two years; mustered in as private, Co. L, same date; mustered out with company, March 31, 1899, at Brooklyn, N. Y.

McMAHON, MARTIN.—Age, 22 years. Enlisted, May 2, 1898, at Brooklyn, to serve two years; mustered in as private, Co. G, May 24, 1898; mustered out with company, March 31, 1899, at Brooklyn, N. Y.

McMAHON, WILLIAM P. H.—Age, 22 years. Enlisted, May 2, 1898, at Brooklyn, to serve two years; mustered in as musician, Co. A, May 24, 1898; mustered out with company, March 31, 1899, at Brooklyn, N. Y.

McMILLAN, JOSEPH.—Age, — years. Enlisted, August 11, 1898, at Brooklyn, to serve two years; mustered in as private, Co. M, same date; mustered out with company, March 31, 1899, at Brooklyn, N. Y.

McMILLAN, ROBERT.—Age, 28 years. Enlisted, May 2, 1898, at Brooklyn, to serve two years; mustered in as musician, Co. G, May 24, 1898; discharged, November 18, 1898, at Governor's Island, New York Harbor.

McMILLAN, THOMAS J.—Age, — years. Enlisted, August 8, 1898, at Brooklyn, to serve two years; mustered in as private, Co. F, same date; mustered out with company, March 31, 1899, at Brooklyn, N. Y.

McNALLY, JAMES.—Age, 21 years. Enlisted, May 2, 1898, at Brooklyn, to serve two years; mustered in as private, Co. F, May 24, 1898; mustered out with company, March 31, 1899, at Brooklyn, N. Y.

McNULTY, JAMES F.—Age, — years. Enlisted, August 10, 1898, at Brooklyn, to serve two years; mustered in as private, Co. I, same date; mustered out with company, March 31, 1899, at Brooklyn, N. Y.

McQUADE, NICHOLAS.—Age, 24 years. Enlisted, May 2, 1898, at Brooklyn, to serve two years; mustered in as private, Co. I, May 24, 1898; mustered out with company, March 31, 1899, at Brooklyn, N. Y.

McWHINNEY, THOMAS A.—Age, 34 years. Enlisted, May 2, 1898, at Brooklyn, to serve two years; mustered in as quarter- master-sergeant, Co. E, May 24, 1898; as second lieutenant, November 2, 1898; mustered out with company, March 31, 1899, at Brooklyn, N. Y.; commissioned second lieutenant, November 2, 1898, with rank from same date, vice Mezick, promoted.

MEAD, WILLIAM.—Age, 23 years. Enlisted, May 2, 1898, at Brooklyn, to serve two years; mustered in as private, Co. F, May 24, 1898; promoted corporal, August 7, 1898; returned to ranks, December 17, 1898; mustered out with company, March 31, 1899, at Brooklyn, N. Y.

MEAGHER, THOMAS F.—Age, 30 years. Enlisted, May 16, 1898, at Brooklyn, to serve two years; mustered in as private, Co. E, May 24, 1898; appointed artificer, October 21, 1898; mustered out with company, March 31, 1899, at Brooklyn, N. Y.

MEHRMANN, CHRISTOPHER.—Age, 21 years. Enlisted, May 2, 1898, at Brooklyn, to serve two years; mustered in as private, Co. K, May 24, 1898; mustered out with company, March 31, 1899, at Brooklyn, N. Y.

MEIER, HERMAN F., see Hermann Meyer.

MENAHAN, EDWARD J.—Age, 35 years. Enlisted, May 2, 1898, at Brooklyn, to serve two years; mustered in as private, Co. L, May 24, 1898; mustered out with company, March 31, 1899, at Brooklyn, N. Y.

MENDES, JOSEPH.—Age, — years. Enlisted, July 26, 1898, at Brooklyn, to serve two years; mustered in as private, Co. I, same date; mustered out with company, March 31, 1899, at Brooklyn, N. Y.

MENY, EMIL.—Age, 21 years. Enlisted, May 2, 1898, at Brooklyn, to serve two years; mustered in as private, Co. K, May 24, 1898; deserted, September 20, 1898.

MESLOH, GEORGE F.—Age, 22 years. Enlisted, May 2, 1898, at Brooklyn, to serve two years; mustered in as private, Co. G, May 24, 1898; mustered out with company, March 31, 1899, at Brooklyn, N. Y.

METH, WILLIAM.—Age, 23 years. Enlisted, May 2, 1898, at Brooklyn, to serve two years; mustered in as private, Co. E, May 24, 1898; discharged for disability, December 30, 1898, at Fort Columbus, New York Harbor.

MEYER, ERWIN W.—Age, — years. Enlisted, August 10, 1898, at Brooklyn, to serve two years; mustered in as private, Co. I, same date; mustered out with company, March 31, 1899, at Brooklyn, N. Y.

MEYER, FRED.—Age, 21 years.   Enlisted, May 2, 1898, at Brooklyn, to serve two years; mustered in as private, Co. K, May 24, 1898; promoted corporal, February 1, 1899; mustered out with company, March 31, 1899, at Brooklyn, N. Y.

MEYER, FRED K.—Age, 22 years.   Enlisted, May 2, 1898, at Brooklyn, to serve two years; mustered in as private, Co. C, May 24, 1898; appointed artificer, June 18, 1898; mustered out with company, March 31, 1899, at Brooklyn, N. Y., as Fred'k J. Meyer.

MEYER, GEORGE W.—Age, 24 years. Enlisted, May 2, 1898, at Brooklyn, to serve two years; mustered in as private, Co. L, May 24, 1898; mustered out with company, March 31, 1899, at Brooklyn, N. Y.

MEYER, HERMANN.—Age, 21 years. Enlisted, May 2, 1898, at Brooklyn, to serve two years; mustered in as private, Co. M, May 24, 1898; mustered out with company, March 31, 1899, at Brooklyn, N. Y., as Herman F. Meier.

MEYER, J. ARTHUR.—Age, 26 years. Enrolled, May 2, 1898, at Brooklyn, to serve two years; mustered in as first lieutenant, Co. A, May 24, 1898; mustered out with company, March 31, 1899, at Brooklyn, N. Y.; commissioned first lieutenant, May 24, 1898, with rank from same date, original.

MEYER, WILLIAM.—Age, 21 years. Enlisted, May 2, 1898, at Brooklyn, to serve two years; mustered in as private, Co. A, May 24, 1898; mustered out with company, March 31, 1899, at Brooklyn, N. Y.

MEZICK, FRANK B.—Age, 41 years. Enlisted, May 2, 1898, at Brooklyn, to serve two years; mustered in as second lieutenant, Co. E, May 24, 1898; as first lieutenant, October 3, 1898; mustered out with company, March 31, 1899, at Brooklyn, N. Y.; commissioned second lieutenant, May 24, 1898, with rank from same date, original; first lieutenant, October 3, 1898, with rank from same date, vice Bridger, promoted.

MIERS, CHARLES W.—Age, 23 years. Enlisted, May 2, 1898, at Brooklyn, to serve two years; mustered in as private, Co. M, May 24, 1898; discharged October 14, 1898, at Fort Adams, R. I.

MILES, THOMAS S.—Age, 25 years. Enlisted, May 2, 1898, at Brooklyn, to serve two years; mustered in as private, Co. D, May 24, 1898; mustered out with company, March 31, 1899, at Brooklyn, N. Y.

MILLARD, EDWARD J.—Age, 28 years. Enlisted, May 2, 1898, at Brooklyn, to serve two years; mustered in as private, Co. I, May 24, 1898; mustered out with company, March 31, 1899, at Brooklyn, N. Y.

MILLER, ALBERT.—Age, 24 years. Enlisted, May 2, 1898, at Brooklyn, to serve two years; mustered in as artificer, Co. A, May 24, 1898; promoted corporal, August 15, 1898; mustered out with company, March 31, 1899, at Brooklyn, N. Y.

MILLER, EDWARD W.—Age, — years. Enlisted, July 28, 1898, at Brooklyn, to serve two years; mustered in as private, Co. H, same date; mustered out with company, March 31, 1899, at Brooklyn, N. Y.

MILLER, FRED G.—Age, 21 years. Enlisted, May 2, 1898, at Brooklyn, to serve two years; mustered in as private, Co. L, May 24, 1898; mustered out with company, March 31, 1899, at Brooklyn, N. Y.

MILLER, FREDERICK W.—Age, 26 years. Enlisted, May 2, 1898, at Brooklyn, to serve two years; mustered in as private, Co. K, May 24, 1898; mustered out with company, March 31, 1899, at Brooklyn, N. Y.

MILLER, HENRY C.—Age, — years. Enlisted, August 1, 1898, at Brooklyn, to serve two years; mustered in as private, Co. I, same date; mustered out with company, March 31, 1899, at Brooklyn, N. Y.

MILLER, JOSEPH.—Age, — years. Enlisted, August 1, 1898, at Brooklyn, to serve two years; mustered in as private, Co. G, same date; mustered out with company, March 31, 1899, at Brooklyn, N. Y.

MILLER, JOSEPH A.—Age, 27 years. Enlisted, May 2, 1898, at Brooklyn, to serve two years; mustered in as private, Co. K, May 24, 1898; mustered out with company, March 31, 1899, at Brooklyn, N. Y.

MILLER, JOSEPH F.—Age, 21 years. Enlisted, May 2, 1898, at Brooklyn, to serve two years; mustered in as private, Co. K, May 24, 1898; mustered out with company, March 31, 1899, at Brooklyn, N. Y.

MILLER, PHILIP A.—Age, 21 years. Enlisted, May 2, 1898, at Brooklyn, to serve two years; mustered in as private, Co. H, May 24, 1898; mustered out with company, March 31, 1899, at Brooklyn, N. Y.

MILLER, ROBERT R.—Age, 23 years. Enlisted, May 2, 1898, at Brooklyn, to serve two years; mustered in as corporal, Co. F, May 24, 1898; returned to ranks, June 18, 1898; promoted corporal, September 24, 1898; mustered out with company, March 31, 1899, at Brooklyn, N. Y.

MILLER, WILLIAM L.—Age, —years. Enlisted, July 28, 1898, at Brooklyn, to serve two years; mustered in as private, Co. H, same date; mustered out with company, March 31, 1899, at Brooklyn, N. Y.

MILLHAVEN, JOHN.—Age, 21 years. Enlisted, May 2, 1898, at Brooklyn, to serve two years; mustered in as private, Co. H, May 24, 1898; promoted corporal, August 16, 1898; mustered out with company, March 31, 1899, at Brooklyn, N. Y.

MILLS, FRANK J.—Age, 24 years. Enlisted, May 2, 1898, at Brooklyn, to serve two years; mustered in as private, Co. E, May 24, 1898; promoted corporal, June 27, 1898; discharged, November 14, 1898, at Fort Columbus, New York Harbor.

MILLS, JOHN N.—Age, 21 years. Enlisted, May 2, 1898, at Brooklyn, to serve two years; mustered in as private, Co. E, May 24, 1898; discharged, October 14, 1898, at Fort Adams, R. I.

MILLS, WILLIAM J. J.—Age, 22 years. Enlisted, May 2, 1898, at Brooklyn, to serve two years; mustered in as corporal, Co. F, May 24, 1898; returned to ranks, July 8, 1898; promoted corporal, July 28, 1898; mustered out with company, March 31, 1899, at Brooklyn, N. Y.

MINGE, JOHN.—Age, 28 years. Enlisted, May 2, 1898, at Brooklyn, to serve two years; mustered in as private, Co. I, May 24, 1898; promoted sergeant, June 10, 1898; mustered out with company, March 31, 1899, at Brooklyn, N. Y.

MITCHELL, ROBERT O.—Age, 28 years. Enlisted, May 2, 1898, at Brooklyn, to serve two years; mustered in as private, Co. D, May 24, 1898; mustered out with company, March 31, 1899, at Brooklyn, N. Y.

MITCHELL, WALTER.—Age, 26 years. Enlisted, May 2, 1898, at Brooklyn, to serve two years; mustered in as private, Co. C, May 24, 1898; promoted corporal, March 9, 1899; mustered out with company, March 31, 1899, at Brooklyn, N. Y.

MOAKLEY, EDWARD.—Age, 25 years. Enlisted, May 2, 1898, at Brooklyn, to serve two years; mustered in as private, Co. K, May 24, 1898; mustered out with company, March 31, 1899, at Brooklyn, N. Y.

MOELLER, ALBERT.—Age, — years. Enlisted, August 9, 1898, at Brooklyn, to serve two years; mustered in as private, Co. G, same date; mustered out with company, March 31, 1899, at Brooklyn, N. Y.

MOHAN, WILLIAM.—Age, 23 years. Enlisted, May 2, 1898, at Brooklyn, to serve two years; mustered in as private, Co. M, May 24, 1898; mustered out with company, March 31, 1899, at Brooklyn, N. Y.

MONAHAN, EDWARD.—Age, — years. Enlisted, July 27, 1898, at Brooklyn, to serve two years; mustered in as private, Co. B, same date; deserted, September 19, 1898.

MONCRIEFF, JOHN N.—Age, 28 years. Enlisted, May 2, 1898, at Brooklyn, to serve two years; mustered in as quartermaster-sergeant, Co. L, May 24, 1898; as second lieutenant, Co. F, February 3, 1899; mustered out with company, March 31, 1899, at Brooklyn, N. Y.; commissioned second lieutenant, January 1, 1899, with rank from same date, vice Trenchard, promoted.

MONK, WILLIAM H.—Age, 27 years. Enlisted, May 2, 1898, at Brooklyn, to serve two years; mustered in as private, Co. A, May 24, 1898; mustered out with company, March 31, 1899, at Brooklyn, N. Y.

MONTELIN, CARL.—Age, 21 years. Enlisted, May 23, 1898, at Brooklyn, to serve two years; mustered in as private, Co. H, May 24, 1898; mustered out with company, March 31, 1899, at Brooklyn, N. Y.

MOORE, JOHN V.—Age, 22 years. Enlisted, May 2, 1898, at Brooklyn, to serve two years; mustered in as private, Co. A, May 24, 1898; mustered out with company, March 31, 1899, at Brooklyn, N. Y.

MOORE, SILAS H.—Age, 28 years. Enlisted, May 2, 1898, at Brooklyn, to serve two years; mustered in as sergeant, Co. K, May 24, 1898; promoted quartermaster-sergeant, June 28, 1898; discharged, October 14, 1898, at Fort Adams, R. I.

MOORE, WILLIAM H.—Age, 23 years. Enlisted, May 2, 1898, at Brooklyn, to serve two years; mustered in as private, Co. I, May 24, 1898; appointed cook, September 1, 1898; returned to ranks, February 8, 1899; mustered out with company, March 31, 1899, at Brooklyn, N. Y.

MORAN, JOHN J.—Age, — years. Enlisted, July 27, 1898, at Brooklyn, to serve two years; mustered in as private, Co. M, same date; mustered out with company, March 31, 1899, at Brooklyn, N. Y.

MORGAN, WILLIAM F.—Age, 23 years. Enlisted, May 2, 1898, at Brooklyn, to serve two years; mustered in as hospital steward, May 24, 1898; mustered out with regiment, March 31, 1899, at Brooklyn, N. Y.

MORSE, HERBERT E.—Age, 28 years. Enlisted, May 2, 1898, at Brooklyn, to serve two years; mustered in as private, Co. B, May 24, 1898; promoted corporal, November 14, 1898; mustered out with company, March 31, 1899, at Brooklyn, N. Y.

MOSS, DAVID R.—Age, 27 years. Enlisted, May 2, 1898, at Brooklyn, to serve two years; mustered in as private, Co. E, May 24, 1898; mustered out with company, March 31, 1899, at Brooklyn, N. Y.

MULLER, ANTHONY C.—Age, 21 years. Enlisted, May 2, 1898, at Brooklyn, to serve two years; mustered in as sergeant, Co. F, May 24, 1898; mustered out with company, March 31, 1899, at Brooklyn, N. Y.

MULLER, ARCHER E.—Age, — years. Enlisted, August 11, 1898, at Brooklyn, to serve two years; mustered in as private, Co. K, same date; mustered out with company, March 31, 1899, at Brooklyn, N. Y.

MUNDY, ABRAM A.—Age, 34 years. Enlisted, May 2, 1898, at Brooklyn, to serve two years; mustered in as private, Co. F, May 24, 1898; mustered out with company, March 31, 1899, at Brooklyn, N. Y.

MURPHY, FRED J.—Age, 19 years. Enlisted, May 2, 1898, at Brooklyn, to serve two years; mustered in as private, Co. D, May 24, 1898; promoted corporal, June 1, 1898; mustered out with company, March 31, 1899, at Brooklyn, N. Y.

MURPHY, HENRY.—Age, — years. Enlisted, August 4, 1898, at Brooklyn, to serve two years; mustered in as private, Co. K, same date; deserted, September 21, 1898.

MURPHY, JAMES.—Age, 26 years. Enlisted, May 2, 1898, at Brooklyn, to serve two years; mustered in as private, Co. C, May 24, 1898; mustered out with company, March 31, 1899, at Brooklyn, N. Y.

MURPHY, JAMES JOSEPH.—Age, 23 years. Enlisted, May 2, 1898, at Brooklyn, to serve two years; mustered in as private, Co. G, May 24, 1898; promoted corporal, September 19, 1898; mustered out with company, March 31, 1899, at Brooklyn, N. Y.

MURPHY, JOHN L.—Age, 27 years. Enlisted, May 2, 1898, at Brooklyn, to serve two years; mustered in as private, Co. M, May 24, 1898; deserted, June 14, 1898, at Long Island City, N. Y.

MURPHY, JOHN W.—Age, 21 years. Enlisted, May 2, 1898, at Brooklyn, to serve two years; mustered in as private, Co. K, May 24, 1898; mustered out with company, March 31, 1899, at Brooklyn, N. Y.

MURPHY, THOMAS.—Age, — years. Enlisted, August 11, 1898, at Brooklyn, to serve two years; mustered in as private, Co. K, same date; mustered out with company, March 31, 1899, at Brooklyn, N. Y.

MURRAY, JAMES L.—Age, 26 years. Enlisted, May 2, 1898, at
Brooklyn, to serve two years; mustered in as private, Co. L,
May 24, 1898; discharged, October 12, 1898, at Fort Adams,
R. I.

MURRAY, THOMAS.—Age, 24 years. Enlisted, May 2, 1898, at
Brooklyn, to serve two years; mustered in as private, Co. L,
May 24, 1898; mustered out with company, March 31, 1899, at
Brooklyn, N. Y.

MURRAY, THOMAS H.—Age, 23 years. Enlisted, May 2, 1898,
at Brooklyn, to serve two years; mustered in as private, Co. F,
May 24, 1898; mustered out with company, March 31, 1899, at
Brooklyn, N. Y.

MYERS, CHARLES W.—Age, 24 years. Enlisted, May 2, 1898,
at Brooklyn, to serve two years; mustered in as private, Co. E,
May 24, 1898; deserted, October 10, 1898, at Fort Adams, R. I.

MYERS, FREDERICK J.—Age, — years. Enlisted, August 14,
1898, at Brooklyn, to serve two years; mustered in as private,
Co. K, same date; mustered out with company, March 31, 1899,
at Brooklyn, N. Y.

MYERS, WILLIAM.—Age, 22 years. Enlisted, May 2, 1898, at
Brooklyn, to serve two years; mustered in as corporal, Co. H,
May 24, 1898; returned to ranks, September 1, 1898; mustered
out with company, March 31, 1899, at Brooklyn, N. Y.

MYGATT, LEONARD J.—Age, 25 years. Enlisted, May 2, 1898,
at Brooklyn, to serve two years; mustered in as first sergeant,
Co. L, May 24, 1898; as second lieutenant, September 26, 1898;
mustered out with company, March 31, 1899, at Brooklyn, N.
Y.; commissioned second lieutenant, September 26, 1898, with
rank from same date, vice White, promoted; first lieutenant,
not mustered, March 25, 1898, with rank from same date, vice
Techter, discharged.

NAGEL, JACOB C.—Age, 19 years. Enlisted, May 2, 1898, at
Brooklyn, to serve two years; mustered in as private, Co. G,
May 24, 1898; mustered out with company, March 31, 1899, at
Brooklyn, N. Y.

NAU, EDWARD.—Age, 19 years. Enlisted, May 2, 1898, at Brooklyn, to serve two years; mustered in as private, Co. E, May 24, 1898; discharged, October 14, 1898, at Fort Adams, R. I.

NECKER, JOHN.—Age, 19 years. Enlisted, May 2, 1898, at Brooklyn, to serve two years; mustered in as private, Co. K, May 24, 1898; mustered out with company, March 31, 1899, at Brooklyn, N. Y.

NEIDLINGER, GEORGE.—Age, — years. Enlisted, August 9, 1898, at Brooklyn, to serve two years; mustered in as private, Co. E, same date; mustered out with company, March 31, 1899, at Brooklyn, N. Y.

NEIDNAGLE, EMIL H.—Age, 20 years. Enlisted, May 2, 1898, at Brooklyn, to serve two years; mustered in as private, Co. D, May 24, 1898; promoted corporal, July 4, 1898; mustered out with company, March 31, 1899, at Brooklyn, N. Y.

NELSON, FREDERICK.—Age, 23 years. Enlisted, May 2, 1898, at Brooklyn, to serve two years; mustered in as corporal, Co. I, May 24, 1898; returned to ranks, June 10, 1898; promoted corporal, August 1, 1898; mustered out with company, March 31, 1899, at Brooklyn, N. Y.

NELSON, JOSEPH.—Age, 22 years. Enlisted, May 2, 1898, at Brooklyn, to serve two years; mustered in as private, Co. B, May 24, 1898; mustered out with company, March 31, 1899, at Brooklyn, N. Y.

NEUBERT, FREDERICK.— Age, 19 years. Enlisted, May 2, 1898, at Brooklyn, to serve two years; mustered in as musician, Co. L, May 24, 1898; mustered out with company, March 31, 1899, at Brooklyn, N. Y.

NEWMAN, FREDERICK.—Age, 26 years. Enlisted, May 2, 1898, at Brooklyn, to serve two years; mustered in as sergeant, Co. C, May 24, 1898; discharged, October 12, 1898, at Fort Adams, R. I.

NEWMAN, MICHAEL.—Age, 21 years. Enlisted, May 2, 1898, at Brooklyn, to serve two years; mustered in as private, Co. L, May 24, 1898; mustered out with company, March 31, 1899, at Brooklyn, N. Y.

NEWNHAM, WILLIAM E.—Age, 20 years.   Enlisted, May 2, 1898, at Brooklyn, to serve two years; mustered in as private, Co. D, May 24, 1898; musttered out with company, March 31, 1899, at Brooklyn, N. Y.

NEYER, GEORGE.—Age, 24 years.   Enlisted, May 2, 1898, at Brooklyn, to serve two years; mustered in as private, Co. A, May 24, 1898; promoted corporal, June 27, 1898; discharged, October 12, 1898.

NICHOLS, ROBERT J.—Age, 37 years.   Enlisted, May 2, 1898, at Brooklyn, to serve two years; mustered in as musician, Co. I, May 24, 1898; mustered out with company, March 31, 1899, at Brooklyn, N. Y.

NICHOLSON, PETER.—Age, — years.   Enlisted, August 5, 1898, at Brooklyn, to serve two years; mustered in as private, Co. L, same date; deserted, January 7, 1899.

NIELSEN, VIGGO A. F.—Age, 28 years.   Enlisted, May 2, 1898; at Brooklyn, to serve two years; mustered in as corporal, Co. E, May 24, 1898; promoted sergeant, same date; discharged, November 14, 1898, at Fort Columbus, New York Harbor.

NIGGER, MATHEW F.—Age, 25 years.   Enlisted, May 2, 1898, at Brooklyn, to serve two years; mustered in as sergeant, Co. H, May 24, 1898; returned to ranks, August 19, 1898; promoted corporal, January 16, 1899; sergeant, March 8, 1899; mustered out with company, March 31, 1899, at Brooklyn, N. Y.

NODINE, HENRY J.—Age, 23 years.   Enlisted, May, 2 1898, at Brooklyn, to serve two years; mustered in as private, Co. H, May 24, 1898; deserted, August 20, 1898, at Fort Adams, R. I.

NOE, WILLIAM H.—Age, — years.   Enlisted, August 11, 1898, at Brooklyn, to serve two years; mustered in as private, Co. M, same date; mustered out with company, March 31, 1899, at Brooklyn, N. Y.

NOLAN, JOHN.—Age, — years.   Enlisted, August 3, 1898, at Brooklyn, to serve two years; mustered in as private, Co. D, same date; mustered out with company, March 31, 1899, at Brooklyn, N. Y.

NOLAN, JOHN.—Age, 38 years. Enlisted, May 2, 1898, at Brooklyn, to serve two years; mustered in as private, Co. C, May 24, 1898; mustered out with company, March 31, 1899, at Brooklyn, N. Y.

NOLAN, WILLIAM.—Age, 21 years. Enlisted, May 2, 1898, at Brooklyn, to serve two years; mustered in as private, Co. I, May 24, 1898; mustered out with company, March 31, 1899, at Brooklyn, N. Y.

NORIARTY, DENNIS.—Age, 23 years. Enlisted, May 22, 1898, at Brooklyn, to serve two years; mustered in as private, Co. E, May 24, 1898; mustered out with company, March 31, 1899, at Brooklyn, N. Y.

NORRIS, JOHN F.—Age, — years. Enlisted, August 9, 1898, at Brooklyn, to serve two years; mustered in as private, Co. A, same date; mustered out with company, March 31, 1899, at Brooklyn, N. Y.

NORTON, EUGENE.—Age, — years. Enlisted, August 11, 1898, at Brooklyn, to serve two years; mustered in as private, Co. G, same date; mustered out with company, March 31, 1899, at Brooklyn, N. Y.

NORTON, HAYWOOD F.— Age, 19 years. Enlisted, May 17, 1898, at Camp Black, to serve two years; mustered in as private, Co. A, May 24, 1898; discharged, October 12, 1898.

NUGENT, JAMES E.—Age, 24 years. Enlisted, May 2, 1898, at Brooklyn, to serve two years; mustered in as private, Co. G, May 24, 1898; promoted corporal, August 11, 1898; mustered out with company, March 31, 1899, at Brooklyn, N. Y.

O'BRIEN, DENNIS A.—Age, — years. Enlisted, July 29, 1898, at Brooklyn, to serve two years; mustered in as private, Co. F, same date; mustered out with company, March 31, 1899, at Brooklyn, N. Y.

O'BRIEN, JOHN.—Age, — years. Enlisted, August 1, 1898, at Brooklyn, to serve two years; mustered in as private, Co. A, same date; mustered out with company, March 31, 1899, at Brooklyn, N. Y.

O'BRIEN, JOHN R.—Age, — years. Enlisted, August 4, 1898, at Brooklyn, to serve two years; mustered in as private, Co. B, same date; discharged for disability, January 16, 1899, at San Piedras, P. R.

O'BRIEN, JOSEPH.—Age, — years. Enlisted, August 10, 1898, at Brooklyn, to serve two years; mustered in as private, Co. I, same date; mustered out with company, March 31, 1899, at Brooklyn, N. Y.

O'BRIEN, WILLIAM.—Age — years. Enlisted, July 26, 1898, at Brooklyn, to serve two years; mustered in as private, Co. D, same date; mustered out with company, March 31, 1899, at Brooklyn, N. Y.

O'CONNELL, WILLIAM J.—Age, 21 years. Enlisted, May 2, 1898, at Brooklyn, to serve two years; mustered in as private, Co. B, May 24, 1898; mustered out with company, March 31, 1899, at Brooklyn, N. Y.

O'CONNOR, JOSEPH.—Age, — years. Enlisted, August 11, 1898, at Brooklyn, to serve two years; mustered in as private, Co. A, same date; mustered out with company, March 31, 1899, at Brooklyn, N. Y.

O'CONNOR, MICHAEL J.—Age, 23 years. Enlisted, May 24, 1898, at Camp Black, to serve two years; mustered in as private, Co. E, same date; promoted corporal, August 18, 1898; sergeant, January 19, 1899; mustered out with company, March 31, 1899, at Brooklyn, N. Y.

O'CONNOR, TIMOTHY.—Age, — years. Enlisted, August 9, 1898, at Brooklyn, to serve two years; mustered in as private, Co. B, same date; appointed wagoner, December 1, 1898; mustered out with company, March 31, 1899, at Brooklyn, N. Y.

O'DONNELL, FRANK.—Age, — years. Enlisted, August 3, 1898, at Brooklyn, to serve two years; mustered in as private, Co. G, same date; mustered out with company, March 31, 1899, at Brooklyn, N. Y.

O'DONNELL, JOHN.—Age, — years. Enlisted, August 10, 1898, at Brooklyn, to serve two years; mustered in as private, Co. I, same date; mustered out with company, March 31, 1899, at Brooklyn, N. Y.

O'DONNELL, JOHN E.—Age, 24 years.   Enlisted, May 2, 1898, at Brooklyn, to serve two years; mustered in as private, Co. M, May 24, 1898; mustered out with company, March 31, 1899, at Brooklyn, N. Y.

O'DONNELL, JOHN J.—Age, 23 years.   Enlisted, May 2, 1898, at Brooklyn, to serve two years; mustered in as private, Co. G, May 24, 1898; mustered out with company, March 31, 1899, at Brooklyn, N. Y.

OECHLER, HENRY F.—Age, 22 years.   Enlisted, May 2, 1898, at Brooklyn, to serve two years; mustered in as corporal, Co. K, May 24, 1898; mustered out with company, March 31, 1899, at Brooklyn, N. Y.

OECHLER, WILLIAM B.—Age, 22 years.   Enlisted, May 2, 1898, at Brooklyn, to serve two years; mustered in as private, Co. K, May 24, 1898; mustered out with company, March 31, 1899, at Brooklyn, N. Y.

OFFERDING, GEORGE.—Age, 21 years.   Enlisted, May 2, 1898, at Brooklyn, to serve two years; mustered in as private, Co. H, May 24, 1898; mustered out with company, March 31, 1899, at Brooklyn, N. Y.

O'HARA, JOSEPH O.—Age, 20 years.   Enlisted, May 2, 1898, at Brooklyn, to serve two years; mustered in as private, Co. B, May 24, 1898; mustered out with company, March 31, 1899, at Brooklyn, N. Y.

OLDEN, EDWARD J.—Age, 31 years.   Enrolled, May 2, 1898, at Brooklyn, to serve two years; mustered in as captain, Co. B, May 24, 1898; discharged, November 11, 1898, at Rio Piedras, P. R.; commissioned captain,. May 24, 1898, with rank from same date, original.

OLIVER, AUGUST F.—Age, 30 years   Enlisted, May 23, 1898, at Brooklyn, to serve two years; mustered in as private, Co. E, May 24, 1898; mustered out with company, March 31, 1899, at Brooklyn, N Y.

·OLMSTEAD, ARTHUR J.—Age, — years.   Enlisted, July 26, 1898, at Brooklyn, to serve two years; mustered in as private, Co. H, same date; mustered out with company, March 31, 1899, at Brooklyn, N. Y.

O'MALLEY, WILLIAM J.—Age, 27 years.   Enlisted, May 2, 1898, at Brooklyn, to serve two years; mustered in as private, Co. L, June 6, 1898; appointed cook, August 1, 1898; returned to ranks, December 5, 1898; mustered out with company, March 31, 1899, at Brooklyn, N. Y.

O'NEIL, MAURICE.—Age, 21 years.   Enlisted, May 2, 1898, at Brooklyn, to serve two years; mustered in as private, Co. G, May 24, 1898; mustered out with company, March 31, 1899, at Brooklyn, N. Y.

O'NEILL, DANIEL.—Age, 20 years.   Enlisted, May 2, 1898, at Brooklyn, to serve two years; mustered in as private, Co. K, May 24, 1898; mustered out with company, March 31, 1899, at Brooklyn, N. Y.

O'NEILL, JAMES M.—Age, 34 years.   Enlisted, May 2, 1898, at Brooklyn, to serve two years; mustered in as private, Co. H, May 24, 1898; promoted corporal, same date; returned to ranks, August 19, 1898; promoted corporal, January 16, 1899; sergeant, February 1, 1899; mustered out with company, March 31, 1899, at Brooklyn, N. Y.

O'NEILL, WILLIAM J.—Age, 22 years.   Enlisted, May 2, 1898, at Brooklyn, to serve two years; mustered in as private, Co. K, May 24, 1898; promoted corporal, October 21, 1898; returned to ranks, November 1, 1898; mustered out with company, March 31, 1899, at Brooklyn, N. Y.

O'ROURKE, MICHAEL F.—Age, 29 years.   Enlisted, May 2, 1898, at Brooklyn, to serve two years; mustered in as corporal, Co. F, May 24, 1898; returned to ranks, June 15, 1898; promoted corporal, July 28, 1898; returned to ranks, February 7, 1899; mustered out with company, March 31, 1899, at Brooklyn, N. Y.

OSBORNE, BURTIS S.—Age, 23 years.   Enlisted, May 2, 1898, at Brooklyn, to serve two years; mustered in as private, Co. A, May 24, 1898; discharged, October 12, 1898.

OSCHMANN, JOHN.—Age, — years.   Enlisted, August 9, 1898, at Brooklyn, to serve two years; mustered in as private, Co. H, same date; mustered out with company, March 31, 1899, at Brooklyn, N. Y.

O'SHEA, THOMAS D.—Age, 24 years.   Enlisted, May 2. 1898, at Brooklyn, to serve two years; mustered in as private, Co. L, May 24, 1898; mustered out with company, March 31, 1899, at Brooklyn, N. Y.

OSTROM, DAVID.—Age, 22 years.   Enlisted, May 2, 1898, at Brooklyn, to serve two years; mustered in as private, Co. F, May 24, 1898; appointed artificer, December 7, 1898; mustered out with company, March 31, 1899, at Brooklyn, N. Y.

OTT, ANDREW.—Age, 30 years.   Enlisted, May 2, 1898, at Brooklyn, to serve two years; mustered in as private, Co. C, May 24, 1898; promoted corporal, August 6, 1898; returned to ranks, no date; mustered out with company, March 31, 1899, at Brooklyn, N. Y.

OTTMAN, TONY.—Age, 23 years.   Enlisted, May 2, 1898, at Brooklyn, to serve two years; mustered in as corporal, Co. A, May 24, 1898; mustered out with company, March 31, 1899, at Brooklyn, N. Y.

OUGHELTREE, GEORGE W.—Age, 21 years.   Enlisted, May 2, 1898, at Brooklyn, to serve two years; mustered in as private, Co. K, May 24, 1898; promoted corporal, July 1, 1898; mustered out with company, March 31, 1899, at Brooklyn, N. Y.

OUTTEN, FRED'K N.—Age, 22 years.   Enlisted, May 20, 1898, at Brooklyn, to serve two years; mustered in as private, Co. E, May 24, 1898; discharged, October 14, 1898, at Fort Adams, R. I.

OWENS, PETER F.—Age, — years.   Enlisted, August 8, 1898, at Brooklyn, to serve two years; mustered in as private, Co. A, same date; mustered out with company, March 31, 1899, at Brooklyn, N. Y.

PACKER, ELDRIDGE H.—Age, 21 years.   Enlisted, May 2, 1898, at Brooklyn, to serve two years; mustered in as corporal, Co. F, May 24, 1898; returned to ranks, June 19, 1898; mustered out with company, March 31, 1899, at Brooklyn, N. Y.

PALMER, EDWARD.—Age, 19 years.   Enlisted, May 2, 1898, at Brooklyn, to serve two years; mustered in as private, Co. G, May 24, 1898; mustered out with company, March 31, 1899, at Brooklyn, N. Y.

PALMER, MICHAEL.—Age, 21 years. Enlisted, May 2, 1898, at
Brooklyn, to serve two years; mustered in as private, Co. C,
May 24, 1898; promoted corporal, February 8, 1899; mustered
out with company, March 31, 1899, at Brooklyn, N. Y.

PALSGRAF, ANDREW.—Age, 20 years. Enlisted, May 2, 1898,
at Brooklyn, to serve two years; mustered in as private, Co. D,
May 24, 1898; mustered out with company, March 31, 1899, at
Brooklyn, N. Y.

PAPE, EMIL.—Age, 21 years. Enlisted, May 2, 1898, at Brooklyn, to serve two years; mustered in as private, Co. L, May 24,
1898; appointed cook, January 12 1898; mustered out with company, March 31, 1899, at Brooklyn, N. Y.

PARINE, CHARLES A.—Age, — years. Enlisted, August 10,
1898, at Brooklyn, to serve two years; mustered in as private,
Co. I, same date; mustered out with company, March 31, 1899,
at Brooklyn, N. Y.

PARRETT, JR., JOHN W.—Age, 22 years.   Enlisted, May 2,
1898, at Brooklyn, to serve two years; mustered in as private,
Co. K, May 24, 1898; mustered out with company, March 31,
1899, at Brooklyn, N. Y.

PASCO, AUGUSTUS R.—Age, 34 years. Enlisted, May 2, 1898,
at Brooklyn, to serve two years; mustered in as private, Co. B,
May 24, 1898; mustered out with company, March 31, 1899, at
Brooklyn, N. Y.

PAWSON, FREDERICK.—Age, 21 years. Enlisted, May 2, 1898,
at Brooklyn, to serve two years; mustered in as private, Co. L,
May 24, 1898; promoted corporal, November 2, 1898; mustered
out with company, March 31, 1899, at Brooklyn, N. Y.

PECKA, JOSEPH.—Age, — years. Enlisted, August 11, 1898,
at Brooklyn, to serve two years; mustered in as private, Co. G,
same date; mustered out with company, March 31, 1899, at
Brooklyn, N. Y.

PEHL, CHARLES.—Age, — years. Enlisted, August 9, 1898,
at Brooklyn, to serve two years; mustered in as private, Co. A,
same date; transferred to Hospital Corps, December 22, 1898.

PEISER, MARK.—Age, 30 years. Enlisted, May 2, 1898, at Brooklyn, to serve two years; mustered in as sergeant, Co. F, May 24, 1898; returned to ranks, June 16, 1898; transferred to Co. M, July 26, 1898; promoted corporal, August 26, 1898; discharged, November 18, 1898 at Fort Columbus, New York Harbor.

PELL, DAVID.—Age, 21 years. Enlisted, May 2, 1898, at Brooklyn, to serve two years; mustered in as private, Co. K, May 24, 1898; discharged, October 14, 1898, at Fort Adams, R. I.

PENNY, GEORGE W.—Age, 23 years. Enlisted, May 2, 1898, at Brooklyn, to serve two years; mustered in as private, Co. B, May 24, 1898; promoted corporal, November 14, 1898; mustered out with company, March 31, 1899, at Brooklyn, N. Y.

PERRY, ARNETT F.—Age, 24 years. Enlisted, May 2, 1898, at Brooklyn, to serve two years; mustered in as first sergeant, Co. H, May 24, 1898; as second lieutenant, January 18, 1899; mustered out with company, March 31, 1899, at Brooklyn, N. Y.; commissioned second lieutenant, January 18, 1899, with rank from same date, vice Gonzales, promoted.

PERRY, WILLIAM.—Age, — years. Enlisted, July 26, 1898, at Brooklyn, to serve two years; mustered in as private, Co. L, same date; mustered out with company, March 31, 1899, at Brooklyn, N. Y.

PERTGEN, HENRY.—Age, 18 years. Enlisted, May 2, 1898, at Brooklyn, to serve two years; mustered in as private, Co. C, May 24, 1898; mustered out with company, March 31, 1899, at Brooklyn, N. Y.

PETEREIT, GUSTAVE.—Age, 21 years. Enlisted, May 2, 1898, at Brooklyn, to serve two years; mustered in as private, Co. D, May 24, 1898; mustered out with company, March 31, 1899, at Brooklyn, N. Y.

PETERMAN, JOSEPH N.—Age, 24 years. Enlisted, May 2, 1898, at Brooklyn, to serve two years; mustered in as private, Co. C, May 24, 1898; appointed wagoner, February 14, 1899; mustered out with company, March 31, 1899, at Brooklyn, N. Y.

PETERSON, GUS F.—Age, 23 years. Enlisted, May 2, 1898, at Brooklyn, to serve two years; mustered in as private, Co. F, May 24, 1898; mustered out with company, March 31, 1899, at Brooklyn, N. Y.

PETERSON, JOHN.—Age, — years. Enlisted, August 5, 1898, at Brooklyn, to serve two years; mustered in as private, Co. I, same date; mustered out with company, March 31, 1899, at Brooklyn, N. Y.

PFEIFER, WILLIAM.—Age, 23 years. Enlisted, May 2, 1898, at Brooklyn, to serve two years; mustered in as private, Co. F, May 24, 1898; discharged, October 12, 1898, at Fort Adams, R. I.

PFEIFFER, JACOB P.—Age, 24 years. Enlisted, May 2, 1898, at Brooklyn, to serve two years; mustered in as private, Co. C, May 24, 1898; promoted corporal, February 2, 1899; mustered out with company, March 31, 1899, at Brooklyn, N. Y.

PHALEN, JOSEPH.—Age, — years. Enlisted, July 26, 1898, at Brooklyn, to serve two years; mustered in as private, Co. L, same date; mustered out with company, March 31, 1899, at Brooklyn, N. Y.

PHILLIPS, LOUIS A.—Age, 23 years. Enlisted, May 2, 1898, at Brooklyn, to serve two years; mustered in as private, Co. B, May 24, 1898; mustered out with company, March 31, 1899, at Brooklyn, N. Y.

PHIPPS, WILLIAM.—Age, 44 years. Enlisted, May 2, 1898, at Brooklyn, to serve two years; mustered in as wagoner, Co. G, May 24, 1898; returned to ranks, October 10, 1898; discharged, October 14, 1898, at Fort Adams, R. I.

PIELSTICKER, HENRY F.—Age, — years. Enlisted, August 2, 1898, at Brooklyn, to serve two years; mustered in as private, Co. L, same date; mustered out with company, March 31, 1899, at Brooklyn, N. Y.

PILGER, WILLIAM.—Age, 22 years. Enlisted, May 2, 1898, at Brooklyn, to serve two years; mustered in as private, Co. H, May 24, 1898; promoted corporal, September 1, 1898; mustered out with company, March 31, 1899, at Brooklyn, N. Y.

PINCKNEY, THOMAS.—Age, 24 years. Enlisted, May 2, 1898, at Brooklyn, to serve two years; mustered in as private, Co. H, May 24, 1898; mustered out with company, March 31, 1899, at Brooklyn, N. Y.

PLACE, ISAAC H.—Age, 27 years. Enlisted, May 2, 1898, at Brooklyn, to serve two years; mustered in as private, Co. G, May 24, 1898; mustered out with company, March 31, 1899, at Brooklyn, N. Y.

PLACE, JOSEPH F.—Age, 30 years. Enlisted, May 2, 1898, at Brooklyn, to serve two years; mustered in as sergeant, Co. E, May 24, 1898; discharged, October 14, 1898, at Fort Adams, R. I.

POMMERENCKY, CHARLES.—Age, — years. Enlisted, August 9, 1898, at Brooklyn, to serve two years; mustered in as private, Co. B, same date; mustered out with company, March 31, 1899, at Brooklyn, N. Y.

POSIK, WILLIAM.—Age, 30 years. Enlisted, May 2, 1898, at Brooklyn, to serve two years; mustered in as private, Co. H, May 24, 1898; mustered out with company, March 31, 1899, at Brooklyn, N. Y.

POTTER, EDWARD D.—Age, — years. Enlisted, July 27, 1898, at Brooklyn, to serve two years; mustered in as private, Co. C, same date; mustered out with company, March 31, 1899, at Brooklyn, N. Y.

POWELL, ELI L.—Age, — years. Enlisted, August 11, 1898, at Brooklyn, to serve two years; mustered in as private, Co. M, same date; promoted corporal, November 1, 1898; discharged, February 14, 1899, at San Juan, P. R.

POWELL, HARRY J.—Age, — years. Enlisted, July 26, 1898, at Brooklyn, to serve two years; mustered in as private, Co. C, same date; promoted corporal, February 8, 1899; mustered out with company, March 31, 1899, at Brooklyn, N. Y.

POWLES, WALTER.—Age, — years. Enlisted, July 30, 1898, at Brooklyn, to serve two years; mustered in as private, Co. C, same date; mustered out with company, March 31, 1899, at Brooklyn, N. Y.

PRACHT, ADAM J.—Age, 22 years. Enlisted, May 2, 1898, at Brooklyn, to serve two years; mustered in as private, Co. A, May 24, 1898; promoted corporal, December 24, 1898; mustered out with company, March 31, 1899, at Brooklyn, N. Y.

PRANKARD, JOHN F.—Age, 28 years.   Enlisted, May 2, 1898, at Brooklyn, to serve two years; mustered in as sergeant, Co. L, May 24, 1898; promoted first sergeant, to date, November 2, 1898; mustered in as second lieutenant, Co. C, January 18, 1899; mustered out with company, March 31, 1899, at Brooklyn, N. Y.; commissioned second lieutenant, January 18, 1899, with rank from same date, vice White, promoted.

PREECE, WILLIAM S.—Age, 19 years.   Enlisted, May 2, 1898, at Brooklyn, to serve two years; mustered in as private, Co. G, May 24, 1898; mustered out with company, March 31, 1899, at Brooklyn, N. Y.

PRICHARD, HENRY J.—Age, — years.   Enlisted, July 28, 1898, at Brooklyn, to serve two years; mustered in as private, Co. G, same date; mustered out with company, March 31, 1899, at Brooklyn, N. Y.

PRINGLE, ALEXANDER.—Age, 25 years.   Enlisted, May 2, 1898, at Brooklyn, to serve two years; mustered in as private, Co. B, May 24, 1898; promoted corporal, June 1, 1898; sergeant, November 14, 1898; mustered out with company, March 31, 1899, at Brooklyn, N. Y.

PROBECK, WILLIAM.—Age, 22 years.   Enlisted, May 2, 1898, at Brooklyn, to serve two years; mustered in as private, Co. H, May 24, 1898; promoted corporal, August 16, 1898; returned to ranks, September 30, 1898; promoted corporal, January 16, 1899; mustered out with company, March 31, 1899, at Brooklyn, N. Y.

PURBS, JULIUS.—Age, 25 years.   Enlisted, May 2, 1898, at Brooklyn, to serve two years; mustered in as private, Co. F, May 24, 1898; mustered out with company, March 31, 1899, at Brooklyn, N. Y.

QUEREAU, IRVING W.—Age, 28 years.   Enlisted, May 2, 1898, at Brooklyn, to serve two years; mustered in as private, Co. L, May 24, 1898; promoted corporal, July 20, 1898; sergeant, February 1, 1899; mustered out with company, March 31, 1899, at Brooklyn, N. Y.

QUICK, HEWLINGS H.—Age, 42 years. Enrolled, May 3, 1898, at Brooklyn, to serve two years; mustered in as major, May 24, 1898; as lieutenant-colonel, December 3, 1898; mustered out with regiment, March 31, 1899, at Brooklyn, N. Y.; commissioned major, May 24, 1898, with rank from same date, original; lieutenant-colonel, December 3, 1898, with rank from same date, vice Hubbell, promoted.

QUIGLEY, WILLIAM F.—Age, 22 years. Enlisted, May 2, 1898, at Brooklyn, to serve two years; mustered in as private, Co. K, May 24, 1898; deserted, September 20, 1898.

QUINN, FRANK A.—Age, 24 years. Enlisted, May 19, 1898, at Brooklyn, to serve two years; mustered in as private, Co. E, May 24, 1898; mustered out with company, March 31, 1899, at Brooklyn, N. Y.

QUINN, JOHN J.—Age, 21 years. Enlisted, May 20, 1898, at Brooklyn, to serve two years; mustered in as private, Co. E, May 24, 1898; mustered out with company, March 31, 1899, at Brooklyn, N. Y.

QUINN, PATRICK L.—Age, 22 years. Enlisted, May 2, 1898, at Brooklyn, to serve two years; mustered in as private, Co. F, May 24, 1898; mustered out with company, March 31, 1899, at Brooklyn, N. Y.

RABBIT, JOHN E.—Age, — years. Enlisted, August 8, 1898, at Brooklyn, to serve two years; mustered in as private, Co. E, same date; mustered out with company, March 31, 1899, at Brooklyn, N. Y.

RABEY, DAVID H.—Age, 21 years. Enlisted, May 2, 1898, at Brooklyn, to serve two years; mustered in as private, Co. E, May 24, 1898; promoted corporal, January 19, 1899; mustered out with company, March 31, 1899, at Brooklyn, N. Y.

RAFFERTY, TERRENCE F.—Age, — years. Enlisted, July 28, 1898, at Brooklyn, to serve two years; mustered in as private, Co. G, same date; mustered out with company, March 31, 1899, at Brooklyn, N. Y.

RAMSEY, ROBERT J.—Age, — years. Enlisted, July 30, 1898, at Brooklyn, to serve two years; mustered in as private, Co. C, same date; mustered out with company, March 31, 1899, at Brooklyn, N. Y.

RATIGAN, EDWARD L.—Age, 21 years. Enlisted, May 2, 1898, at Brooklyn, to serve two years; mustered in as private, Co. I, May 24, 1898; mustered out with company, March 31, 1899, at Brooklyn, N. Y.

REAGAN, DANIEL.—Age, 23 years. Enlisted, May 2, 1898, at Brooklyn, to serve two years; mustered in as private, Co. D, May 24, 1898; mustered out with company, March 31, 1899, at Brooklyn, N. Y.

REED, CHARLES F.—Age, 20 years. Enlisted, May 2, 1898, at Brooklyn, to serve two years; mustered in as private, Co. A, May 24, 1898; mustered out with company, March 31, 1899, at Brooklyn, N. Y.

REETH, ADAM.—Age, 28 years. Enlisted, May 2, 1898, at Brooklyn, to serve two years; mustered in as private, Co. B, May 24, 1898; mustered out with company, March 31, 1899, at Brooklyn, N. Y.

REGAN, THOMAS A.—Age, — years. Enlisted, August 3, 1898, at Brooklyn, to serve two years; mustered in as private, Co. C, same date; mustered out with company, March 31, 1899, at Brooklyn, N. Y.

REIBER, GEORGE W.—Age, — years. Enlisted, July 26, 1898, at Brooklyn, to serve two years; mustered in as private, Co. L, same date; mustered out with company, March 31, 1899, at Brooklyn, N. Y.

REILLY, CHARLES B.—Age, 30 years. Enlisted, May 2, 1898, at Brooklyn, to serve two years; mustered in as private, Co. E, May 24, 1898; promoted corporal, August 18, 1898; quarter-master-sergeant, November 2, 1898; mustered out with company, March 31, 1899, at Brooklyn, N. Y.

REINHARD, JR., FRANK H.—Age, 21 years. Enlisted, May 2, 1898, at Brooklyn, to serve two years; mustered in as corporal, Co. B, May 24, 1898; promoted sergeant, June 1, 1898; first sergeant, January 23, 1899; mustered out with company, March 31, 1899, at Brooklyn, N. Y.

REISS, BENJAMIN.—Age, — years. Enlisted, July 25, 1898, at Brooklyn, to serve two years; mustered in as private, Co. D, same date; mustered out with company, March 31, 1899, at Brooklyn, N. Y.

REMMULLER, GEORGE H.—Age, 22 years. Enlisted, May 2,
1898, at Brooklyn, to serve two years; mustered in as private,
Co. C, May 24, 1898; mustered out with company, March 31,
1899, at Brooklyn, N. Y.

RENTALL, JOSEPH.—Age, 25 years. Enlisted, May 2, 1898, at
Brooklyn, to serve two years; mustered in as private, Co. L,
May 24, 1898; promoted corporal, August 22, 1898; mustered
out with company, March 31, 1899, at Brooklyn, N. Y.

RHEIN, JOSEPH W.—-Age, — years. Enlisted, August 11, 1898,
at Brooklyn, to serve two years; mustered in as private, Co. H,
same date; mustered out with company, March 31, 1899, at
Brooklyn, N. Y.

RICHARDS, RICHARD R.—Age, 27 years. Enlisted, May 2,
1898, at Brooklyn, to serve two years; mustered in as private,
Co. H, May 24, 1898; mustered out with company, March 31,
1899, at Brooklyn, N. Y.

RICHARDS, WALTER C.—Age, 20 years. Enlisted, May 2, 1898,
at Brooklyn, to serve two years; mustered in as private, Co. B,
May 24, 1898; mustered out with company, March 31, 1899, at
Brooklyn, N. Y.

RICHMAN, ERNEST M.—Age, 35 years. Enlisted, May 2, 1898,
at Brooklyn, to serve two years; mustered in as corporal, Co. L,
May 24, 1898; returned to ranks, June 24, 1898; appointed
artificer, August 27, 1898; mustered out with company, March
31, 1899, at Brooklyn, N. Y.

RICKERT, EDDIE E.—Age, 19 years. Enlisted, May 2, 1898, at
Brooklyn, to serve two years; mustered in as private, Co. H,
May 24, 1898; mustered out with company, March 31, 1899, at
Brooklyn, N. Y.

RICKERT, GUSTAVE JOHN.—Age, 22 years. Enlisted, May
2, 1898, at Brooklyn, to serve two years; mustered in as private,
Co. A, May 24, 1898; mustered out with company, March 31,
1899, at Brooklyn, N. Y.

RIEBLING, HENRY.—Age, 21 years. Enlisted, May 2, 1898, at
Brooklyn, to serve two years; mustered in as private, Co. G,
May 24, 1898; mustered out with company, March 31, 1899, at
Brooklyn, N. Y.

RIEHL, CHARLES.—Age, — years. Enlisted, July 24, 1898, at Brooklyn, to serve two years; mustered in as private, Co. C, same date; mustered out with company, March 31, 1899, at Brooklyn, N. Y.

RILEY, BERNARD.—Age, 19 years. Enlisted, May 2, 1898, at Brooklyn, to serve two years; mustered in as private, Co. L, May 24, 1898; mustered out with company, March 31, 1899, at Brooklyn, N. Y.

RILEY, FRANK.—Age, 29 years. Enlisted, May 2, 1898, at Brooklyn, to serve two years; mustered in as private, Co. L, May 24, 1898; promoted corporal, August 22, 1898; mustered out with company, March 31, 1899, at Brooklyn, N. Y.

RILEY, JAMES W.—Age, 36 years. Enlisted, May 2, 1898, at Brooklyn, to serve two years; mustered in as private, Co. C, May 24, 1898; discharged, October 12, 1898, at Fort Adams, R. I.

RILEY, JOSEPH.—Age, 26 years. Enlisted, May 2, 1898, at Brooklyn, to serve two years; mustered in as private, Co. K, May 24, 1898; mustered out with company, March 31, 1899, at Brooklyn, N. Y.

RINGEN, CHARLES.—Age, — years. Enlisted, August 8, 1898, at Brooklyn, to serve two years; mustered in as private, Co. E, same date; mustered out with company, March 31, 1899, at Brooklyn, N. Y.

RIPP, JOHN.—Age, 22 years. Enlisted, May 2, 1898, at Brooklyn, to serve two years; mustered in as private, Co. B, May 24, 1898; mustered out with company, March 31, 1899, at Brooklyn, N. Y.

RITTER, HARRY W.—Age, 26 years. Enlisted, May 2, 1898, at Brooklyn, to serve two years; mustered in as private Co. A, May 24 1898; transferred to Hospital Corps, August 21, 1898.

RITTER, WILLIAM C.—Age, 30 years. Enrolled, May 2, 1898, at Brooklyn, to serve two years; mustered in as second lieutenant, Co. I, May 24, 1898; as first lieutenant, February 3, 1899; mustered out with company March 31 1899 at Brooklyn, N. Y.; commissioned second lieutenant, May 24, 1898, with rank from same date, original; first lieutenant, January 1, 1899, with rank from same date, vice W. H. Doremus, promoted.

ROBBINS, MILTON.—Age, 23 years. Enlisted, May 2, 1898, at Brooklyn, to serve two years; mustered out with company, March 31, 1899, at Brooklyn, N. Y.

ROBERTS, ROBERT A.—Age, 28 years. Enlisted, May 2, 1898, at Brooklyn, to serve two years; mustered in as corporal, Co. L, May 24, 1898; returned to ranks, July 22, 1898; mustered out with company, March 31, 1899, at Brooklyn, N. Y.

ROBINSON, WILLIAM A.—Age, — years. Enlisted, August 4, 1898, at Brooklyn, to serve two years; mustered in as private, Co. C, same date; mustered out with company, March 31, 1899, at Brooklyn, N. Y.

ROCKAFELLOW, EDWARD W.—Age, 27 years. Enrolled, May 2, 1898, at Brooklyn, to serve two years; mustered in as captain, Co. M, May 24, 1898; discharged, September 15, 1898, at Fort Adams, R. I.; commissioned captain, May 24, 1898, with rank from same date, original.

RODENBURG, WALTER J.—Age, 23 years. Enlisted, May 2, 1898, at Brooklyn, to serve two years; mustered in as private, Co. D, May 24, 1898; promoted corporal, June 1, 1898; mustered out with company, March 31, 1899, at Brooklyn, N. Y.

ROGERS, ALFRED.—Age, 41 years. Enlisted, May 3, 1898, at Brooklyn, to serve two years; mustered in as principal musician, May 24, 1898; promoted chief musician, July 7, 1898; transferred to Co. M, as musician, December 28, 1898; mustered out with company, March 31, 1899, at Brooklyn, N. Y.

ROGERS, ARTHUR W.—Age, 22 years. Enlisted, May 2, 1898, at Brooklyn, to serve two years; mustered in as private, Co. A, May 24, 1898; mustered out with company, March 31, 1899, at Brooklyn, N. Y.

ROLOF, HENRY H.—Age, 21 years. Enlisted, May 2, 1898, at Brooklyn, to serve two years; mustered in as private, Co. B, May 24, 1898; mustered out with company, March 31, 1899, at Brooklyn, N. Y.

ROSE, WILLIAM H.—Age, 21 years. Enlisted, May 2, 1898, at Brooklyn, to serve two years; mustered in as private, Co. L, May 24, 1898; mustered out with company, March 31, 1899, at Brooklyn, N. Y.

ROSENBLATH, WILLIAM J.—Age, 23 years. Enlisted, May 2, 1898, at Brooklyn, to serve two years; mustered in as private, Co. B, May 24, 1898; mustered out with company, March 31, 1899, at Brooklyn, N. Y.

ROSENFELD, SAMUEL S.—Age, 26 years. Enlisted, May 2, 1898, at Brooklyn, to serve two years; mustered in as private, Co. B, May 24, 1898; mustered out with company, March 31, 1899, at Brooklyn, N. Y.

ROSS, FREDERICK P.—Age, 26 years. Enlisted, May 2, 1898, at Brooklyn, to serve two years; mustered in as private, Co. H, May 24, 1898; mustered out with company, March 31, 1899, at Brooklyn, N. Y.

ROTH, FREDERICK L.—Age, 21 years. Enlisted, May 2, 1898, at Brooklyn, to serve two years; mustered in as private. Co. M, May 24, 1898; mustered out with company, March 31, 1899, at Brooklyn, N. Y.

ROTHCHILD, LOUIS.—Age, — years. Enlisted, July 27, 1898, at Brooklyn, to serve two years; mustered in as private, Co. E, same date; transferred to Co. K, as musician, August 17, 1898; mustered out with company, March 31, 1899, at Brooklyn, N. Y.

ROTZMAN, GEORGE.—Age, 25 years. Enlisted, May 2, 1898, at Brooklyn, to serve two years; mustered in as private, Co. K, May 24, 1898; promoted corporal, August 8, 1898; mustered out with company, March 31, 1899, at Brooklyn, N. Y.

ROWEL, WILLIAM.—Age, 22 years. Enlisted, May 2, 1898, at Brooklyn, to serve two years; mustered in as private, Co. H, May 24, 1898; deserted, October 3, 1898, at Fort Adams, R. I.

ROWLEY, JAMES.—Age, 22 years. Enlisted, May 2, 1898, at Brooklyn, to serve two years; mustered in as private, Co. F, May 24, 1898; mustered out with company, March 31, 1899, at Brooklyn, N. Y.

RUETHER, CHRISTOPHER W.—Age, 22 years. Enlisted, May 2, 1898, at Brooklyn, to serve two years; mustered in as private, Co. F, May 24, 1898; mustered out with company, March 31, 1899, at Brooklyn, N. Y.

RUHL, FRANK.—Age, 25 years. Enlisted, May 2, 1898, at Brooklyn, to serve two years; mustered in as private, Co. M, May 24, 1898; promoted corporal, June 11, 1898; mustered out with company, March 31, 1899, at Brooklyn, N. Y., as John Ruhl.

RUSSELL, JOHN W.—Age, 28 years. Enlisted, May 2, 1898, at Brooklyn, to serve two years; mustered in as private, Co. B, May 24, 1898; died of consumption, December 14, 1898, at San Juan, P. R.

RUSSELL, WALTER.—Age, 21 years. Enlisted, May 2, 1898, at Brooklyn, to serve two years; mustered in as private, Co. K, May 24, 1898; mustered out with company, March 31, 1899, at Brooklyn, N. Y.

RUST, GEORGE F.—Age, — years. Enlisted, July 30, 1898, at Brooklyn, to serve two years; mustered in as private, Co. F, same date; mustered out with company, March 31, 1899, at Brooklyn, N. Y.

RYAN, ANDREW H.—Age, 43 years. Enlisted, May 2, 1898, at Brooklyn, to serve two years; mustered in as private Co. G, May 24, 1898; mustered out with company, March 31, 1899, at Brooklyn, N. Y.

RYAN, JAMES G.—Age, 29 years. Enlisted, May 2, 1898, at Brooklyn, to serve two years; mustered in as private, Co. G, May 24, 1898; mustered out with company, March 31, 1899, at Brooklyn, N. Y.

RYAN, JAMES J.—Age, 21 years. Enlisted, May 2, 1898, at Brooklyn, to serve two years; mustered in as private, Co. I, May 24, 1898; appointed cook, January 23, 1898; mustered out with company, March 31, 1899, at Brooklyn, N. Y.

RYAN, THOMAS.—Age, 29 years. Enlisted, May 2, 1898, at Brooklyn, to serve two years; mustered in as private, Co. G, May 24, 1898; mustered out with company, March 31, 1899, at Brooklyn, N. Y.

RYDER JOHN J.—Age, 23 years. Enlisted, May 2, 1898, at Brooklyn, to serve two years; mustered in as private, Co. K, May 24, 1898; mustered out with company, March 31, 1899, at Brooklyn, N. Y.

SAGER, JOHN.—Age, 24 years. Enlisted, May 2, 1898, at Brooklyn, to serve two years; mustered in as private, Co. C, May 24, 1898; mustered out with company, March 31, 1899, at Brooklyn, N. Y.

SAGER, JOHN.—Age, — years. Enlisted, August 2, 1898, at Brooklyn, to serve two years; mustered in as private, Co. B, same date; mustered out with company, March 31, 1899, at Brooklyn, N. Y.

SALEM, JOHN J.—Age, 21 years. Enlisted, May 2, 1898, at Brooklyn, to serve two years; mustered in as private, Co. L, May 24, 1898; mustered out with company, March 31, 1899, at Brooklyn, N. Y.

SANDERS, FRANK J.—Age, 19 years. Enlisted, May 2, 1898, at Brooklyn, to serve two years; mustered in as private, Co. K, May 24, 1898; mustered out with company, March 31, 1899, at Brooklyn, N. Y.

SANFORD, HARRY.—Age, 39 years. Enlisted, May 2, 1898, at Brooklyn, to serve two years; mustered in as private, Co. I, May 24, 1898; promoted corporal. June 10, 1898; mustered out with company, March 31, 1899, at Brooklyn N. Y.

SANTANNA, JAMES J.—Age, 21 years. Enlisted, May 2, 1898, at Brooklyn, to serve two years; mustered in as private, Co. K, May 24, 1898; mustered out with company, March 31, 1899, at Brooklyn, N. Y.

SAWTELL, FRANK W.—Age, 22 years. Enlisted, May 2, 1898, at Brooklyn, to serve two years; mustered in as private, Co. D, May 24, 1898; appointed wagoner, June 1, 1898; promoted corporal, December 1, 1898; mustered out with company, March 31, 1899, at Brooklyn, N. Y.

SAWTELLE, HORACE C.—Age, 24 years. Enlisted, May 2, 1898, at Brooklyn, to serve two years; mustered in as private, Co. G, May 24, 1898; promoted corporal, December 14, 1898; mustered out with company, March 31, 1899, at Brooklyn, N. Y.

SAYER, ALBERT V.—Age, — years. Enlisted, July 25, 1898, at Brooklyn, to serve two years; mustered in as private, Co. D, same date; mustered out with company, March 31, 1899, at Brooklyn, N. Y.

SAYER, ARCHIE B.—Age, — years.   Enlisted, July 27, 1898, at Brooklyn, to serve two years; mustered in as private, Co. I, same date; mustered out with company, March 31, 1899, at Brooklyn, N. Y.

SAYER, BERT.—Age, 21 years.   Enlisted, May 2, 1898, at Brooklyn, to serve two years; mustered in as private, Co. I, May 24, 1898; mustered out with company, March 31, 1899, at Brooklyn, N. Y.

SCALLEY, JOHN.—Age, 26 years.   Enlisted, May 2, 1898, at Brooklyn, to serve two years; mustered in as private, Co. M, May 24, 1898; died of consumption, February 14, 1899, in Josiah Simpson Hospital, Fort Monroe, Va.

SCHAEFER, AUGUST H.— Age, 21 years.   Enlisted, May 2, 1898, at Brooklyn, to serve two years; mustered in as private, Co. C, May 24, 1898; mustered out with company, March 31, 1899, at Brooklyn, N. Y.

SCHAEFER, JOHN.—Age, 22 years.   Enlisted, May 2, 1898, at Brooklyn, to serve two years; mustered in as private, Co. M, May 24, 1898; mustered out with company, March 31, 1899, at Brooklyn, N. Y.

SCHAEFFER, GEORGE.—Age, — years.   Enlisted, August 9, 1898, at Brooklyn, to serve two years; mustered in as private, Co. F, same date; mustered out with company, March 31, 1899, at Brooklyn, N. Y.

SCHAFFER, HENRY.—Age, 22 years.   Enlisted, May 2, 1898, at Brooklyn, to serve two years; mustered in as private, Co. K, May 24, 1898; mustered out with company, March 31, 1899, at Brooklyn, N. Y.

SCHAFFHAUSER, ANDREAS.—Age, 39 years.   Enlisted, May 2, 1898, at Brooklyn, to serve two years; mustered in as private, Co. A, May 24, 1898; mustered out with company, March 31, 1899, at Brooklyn, N. Y.

SCHANTZ, JOHN.—Age, 21 years.   Enlisted, May 2, 1898, at Brooklyn, to serve two years; mustered in as private, Co. E, May 24, 1898; mustered out with company, March 31, 1899, at Brooklyn, N. Y.

SCHARRINGHAUSEN, HENRY P.—Age, 32 years. Enlisted, May 3, 1898, at Brooklyn, to serve two years; mustered in as hospital steward, May 24, 1898; mustered out with regiment, March 31, 1899, at Brooklyn, N. Y.

SCHER, SAMUEL.—Age, — years. Enlisted, August 11, 1898, at Brooklyn, to serve two years; mustered in as private, Co. H, same date; mustered out with company, March 31, 1899, at Brooklyn, N. Y.

SCHERER, JOHN.—Age, 21 years. Enlisted, May 2, 1898, at Brooklyn, to serve two years; mustered in as private, Co. C, May 24, 1898; mustered out with company, March 31, 1899, at Brooklyn, N. Y.

SCHIBLE, JOHN T.—Age, — years. Enlisted, August 2, 1898, at Brooklyn, to serve two years; mustered in as private, Co. I, same date; discharged, November 14, 1898.

SCHIEFFELIN, SCHUYLER.—Age, 31 years. Enrolled, June 2, 1898, at Camp Black, to serve two years; mustered in as second lieutenant, Co. A, June 4, 1898; mustered out with company, March 31, 1899, at Brooklyn, N. Y.; commissioned second lieutenant, June 4, 1898, with rank from same date, original.

SCHILL, CHARLES L.—Age, — years. Enlisted, July 27, 1898, at Brooklyn, to serve two years; mustered in as private, Co. E, same date; appointed cook, October 27, 1898; returned to ranks, October 30, 1898; mustered out with company, March 31, 1899, at Brooklyn, N. Y.

SCHILLING, JOSEPH.—Age, 22 years. Enlisted, May 2, 1898, at Brooklyn, to serve two years; mustered in as private, Co. I, May 24, 1898; mustered out with company, March 31, 1899, at Brooklyn, N. Y.

SCHLECHT, JOHN.—Age, 22 years. Enlisted, May 2, 1898, at Brooklyn, to serve two years; mustered in as corporal, Co. K, May 24, 1898; mustered out with company, March 31, 1899, at Brooklyn, N. Y.

SCHLING, FRANK A.—Age, 21 years. Enlisted, May 2, 1898, at Brooklyn, to serve two years; mustered in as private, Co. H, May 24, 1898; mustered out with company, March 31, 1899, at Brooklyn, N. Y.

SCHLOTT, JOHN.—Age, 21 years. Enlisted, May 2, 1898, at Brooklyn, to serve two years; mustered in as private, Co. L, May 24, 1898; mustered out with company, March 31, 1899, at Brooklyn, N. Y.

SCHMELTER, JOHN.—Age, — years. Enlisted, July 28, 1898, at Brooklyn, to serve two years; mustered in as private, Co. H, same date; mustered out with company, March 31, 1899, at Brooklyn, N. Y.

SCHMELTZ, JOHN.—Age, 20 years. Enlisted, May 22, 1898, at Brooklyn, to serve two years; mustered in as private, Co. E, May 24, 1898; mustered out with company, March 31, 1899, at Brooklyn, N. Y.

SCHMIDT, SAMUEL.—Age, 23 years. Enlisted, May 2, 1898, at Brooklyn, to serve two years; mustered in as private, Co. M, May 24, 1898; discharged, October 14, 1898, at Fort Adams, R. I.

SCHMITT, FRED M.—Age, 21 years. Enlisted, May 2, 1898, at Brooklyn, to serve two years; mustered in as private, Co. M, May 24, 1898; mustered out with company, March 31, 1899, at Brooklyn, N. Y.

SCHMOLDT, OTTO G.—Age, 28 years. Enlisted, May 2, 1898, at Brooklyn, to serve two years; mustered in as private, Co. M, May 24, 1898; appointed artificer, June 1, 1898; mustered out with company, March 31, 1899, at Brooklyn, N. Y.

SCHNEE, FREDERICK.—Age, — years. Enlisted, July 29, 1898, at Brooklyn, to serve two years; mustered in as private, Co. I, same date; mustered out with company, March 31, 1899, at Brooklyn, N. Y.

SCHNEE, OTTO.—Age, 19 years. Enlisted, May 2, 1898, at Brooklyn, to serve two years; mustered in as private, Co. I, May 24, 1898; mustered out with company, March 31, 1899, at Brooklyn, N. Y.

SCHNEE, WILLIAM.—Age, 23 years. Enlisted, May 2, 1898, at Brooklyn, to serve two years; mustered in as private, Co. I, May 24, 1898; promoted, corporal, November 1, 1898; mustered out with company, March 31, 1899, at Brooklyn, N. Y.

SCHNEIDER, FERDINAND J.—Age, 23 years. Enlisted, May 2, 1898, at Brooklyn, to serve two years; mustered in as private, Co. L, May 24, 1898; promoted corporal, August 22, 1898; mustered out with company, March 31, 1899, at Brooklyn, N. Y.

SCHNEIDER, LOUIS S.—Age, 21 years. Enlisted, May 19, 1898, at Camp Black, to serve two years; mustered in as private, Co. A, May 24, 1898; mustered out with company, March 31, 1899, at Brooklyn, N. Y.

SCHNIBBEN, HENRY.—Age, 21 years. Enlisted, May 2, 1898, at Brooklyn, to serve two years; mustered in as private, Co. B, May 24, 1898; mustered out with company, March 31, 1899, at Brooklyn, N. Y.

SCHOEN, CURT.—Age, 24 years. Enlisted, May 2, 1898, at Brooklyn, to serve two years; mustered in as private, Co. K, May 24, 1898; discharged, October 5, 1898, at Washington, D. C.

SCHOLER, CHARLES E.—Age, 21 years. Enlisted, May 2, 1898, at Brooklyn, to serve two years; mustered in as private, Co. M, May 24, 1898; deserted, September 10, 1898, at Fort Adams, R. I.

SCHRAG, HERMAN.—Age, 25 years. Enlisted, May 2, 1898, at Brooklyn, to serve two years; mustered in as private, Co. M, May 24, 1898; mustered out with company, March 31, 1899, at Brooklyn, N. Y.

SCHRAGE, HENRY W.—Age, 23 years. Enlisted, May 2, 1898, at Brooklyn, to serve two years; mustered in as private, Co. H, May 24, 1898; mustered out with company, March 31, 1899, at Brooklyn, N. Y.

SCHRANK, WILLIAM H.—Age, 29 years. Enlisted, May 2, 1898, at Brooklyn, to serve two years; mustered in as private, Co. G, May 24, 1898; mustered out with company, March 31, 1899, at Brooklyn, N. Y.

SCHROEDER, CHARLES R.—Age, 21 years. Enlisted, May 2, 1898, at Brooklyn, to serve two years; mustered in as private, Co. B, May 24, 1898; mustered out with company, March 31, 1899, at Brooklyn, N. Y.

SCHULTZ, ALBERT.—Age, 25 years. Enlisted, May 2, 1898, at Brooklyn, to serve two years; mustered in as private, Co. H, May 24, 1898; mustered out with company, March 31, 1899, at Brooklyn, N. Y.

SCHULTZ, CHARLES A.—Age, 33 years. Enlisted, May 2, 1898, at Brooklyn, to serve two years; mustered in as private, Co. B, May 24, 1898; mustered out with company, March 31, 1899, at Brooklyn, N. Y.

SCHUMANN, CHARLES.—Age, 23 years. Enlisted, May 2, 1898, at Brooklyn, to serve two years; mustered in as private, Co. A, May 24, 1898; mustered out with company, March 31, 1899, at Brooklyn N. Y.

SCHUTTE, HERBERT B.—Age, — years. Enlisted, June 8, 1898, at Fort Adams, to serve two years; mustered in as private, Co. D, same date; mustered out with company, March 31, 1899, at Brooklyn, N. Y.

SCHWARTZ, ALBERT.—Age, 20 years. Enlisted, May 2, 1898, at Brooklyn, to serve two years; mustered in as private, Co. M, May 24, 1898; mustered out with company, March 31, 1899, at Brooklyn, N. Y.

SEARS, EDGAR F.—Age, 28 years. Enlisted, June 6, 1898, at Camp Black, to serve two years; mustered in as private, Co. F, June 7, 1898; promoted sergeant, June 23, 1898; mustered out with company, March 31, 1899, at Brooklyn, N. Y.

SECOR, FRANK A.—Age, 27 years. Enlisted, May 2, 1898, at Brooklyn, to serve two years; mustered in as private, Co. A, May 24, 1898; promoted corporal, August 15, 1898; mustered out with company, March 31, 1899, at Brooklyn, N. Y.

SEGUIN, FELIX C.—Age, — years. Enlisted, August 8, 1898, at Brooklyn, to serve two years; mustered in as private, Co. E, same date; mustered out with company, March 31, 1899, at Brooklyn, N. Y.

SEIFERT, GEORGE J.—Age, 25 years. Enlisted, May 2, 1898, at Brooklyn, to serve two years; mustered in as private, Co. G, May 24, 1898; mustered out with company, March 31, 1899, at Brooklyn, N. Y.

SELSMAN, HARRY.—Age, 21 years. Enlisted, May 2, 1898, at Brooklyn, to serve two years; mustered in as private, Co. G, May 24, 1898; mustered out with company, March 31, 1899, at Brooklyn, N. Y.

SERENBETZ, GEO. B.—Age, 23 years. Enrolled, May 2, 1898, at Brooklyn, to serve two years; mustered in as first lieutenant, Co. H, May 24, 1898; discharged, November 9, 1898; commissioned first lieutenant, May 24, 1898, with rank from same date, original.

SEYFFRET, HENRY F.—Age, 25 years. Enlisted, May 2, 1898, at Brooklyn, to serve two years; mustered in as private, Co. D, May 24, 1898; mustered out with company, March 31, 1899, at Brooklyn, N. Y.

SHANE, ROBERT G.—Age, 23 years. Enlisted, May 2, 1898, at Brooklyn, to serve two years; mustered in as private, Co. A, May 24, 1898; mustered out with company, March 31, 1899, at Brooklyn, N. Y.

SHAW, RICHARD H.—Age, — years. Enlisted, August 9, 1898, at Brooklyn, to serve two years; mustered in as private, Co. G, same date; mustered out with company, March 31, 1899, at Brooklyn, N. Y.

SHAY, WALTER E.—Age, 31 years. Enlisted, May 2, 1898, at Brooklyn, to serve two years; mustered in as private, Co. C, May 24, 1898; mustered out with company, March 31, 1899, at Brooklyn, N. Y.

SHEA JOHN.—Age, — years. Enlisted, August 11, 1898, at Brooklyn, to serve two years; mustered in as private, Co. B, same date; mustered out with company, March 31, 1899, at Brooklyn, N. Y.

SHEEHAN, PATRICK.—Age, 27 years. Enlisted, May 2, 1898, at Brooklyn, to serve two years; mustered in as private, Co. G, May 24, 1898; mustered out with company, March 31, 1899, at Brooklyn, N. Y.

SHEERAN, PETER J.—Age, — years. Enlisted, July 29, 1898, at Brooklyn, to serve two years; mustered in as private, Co. C, same date; mustered out with company, March 31, 1899, at Brooklyn, N. Y.

SHEFFER, CHARLES W.—Age, — years. Enlisted, August 10, 1898, at Brooklyn, to serve two years; mustered in as private, Co. A, same date; mustered out with company, March 31, 1899, at Brooklyn, N. Y.

SHEPARD, NOAH.—Age, 22 years. Enlisted, May 2, 1898, at Brooklyn, to serve two years; mustered in as private, Co. E, May 24, 1898; promoted corporal, December 1, 1898; discharged, February 28, 1899, at San Juan, P. R.

SHERMAN, WILLAM T.—Age, 26 years. Enlisted, May 2, 1898, at Brooklyn, to serve two years; mustered in as quarter-master-sergeant, Co. M, May 24, 1898; mustered out with company, March 31, 1899, at Brooklyn, N. Y.

SHERRY, JOHN B.—Age, 20 years. Enlisted, May 2, 1898, at Brooklyn, to serve two years; mustered in as private, Co. M, May 24, 1898; mustered out with company, March 31, 1899, at Brooklyn, N. Y.

SHINE, WILLIAM D.—Age, 21 years. Enlisted, May 2, 1898, at Brooklyn, to serve two years; mustered in as private, Co. C, May 24, 1898; mustered out with company, March 31, 1899, at Brooklyn, N. Y.

SHOEMAKER, HERMAN.—Age, 23 years. Enlisted, May 20, 1898, at Camp Black, to serve two years; mustered in as private, Co. A, May 24, 1898; mustered out with company, March 31, 1899, at Brooklyn, N. Y.

SHULTZ, WILLIAM J.—Age, 25 years. Enlisted, May 2, 1898, at Brooklyn, to serve two years; mustered in as musician, Co. M, May 24, 1898; mustered out with company, March 31, 1899, at Brooklyn, N. Y.

SIEGFRIED, WILLIAM.—Age, — years. Enlisted, August 5, 1898, at Brooklyn, to serve two years; mustered in as private, Co. F, same date; mustered out with company, March 31, 1899, at Brooklyn, N. Y.

SIMONS, SAMUEL.—Age, 24 years. Enlisted, May 2, 1898, at Brooklyn, to serve two years; mustered in as private, Co. C, May 24, 1898; mustered out with company, March 31, 1899, at Brooklyn, N. Y.

SIMONS, WILLIAM A.—Age, — years. Enlisted, July 27, 1898, at Brooklyn, to serve two years; mustered in as private, Co. D, same date; mustered out with company, March 31, 1899, at Brooklyn, N. Y.

SINRAM, FREDERICK.—Age, 21 years.   Enlisted, May 2, 1898, at Brooklyn, to serve two years; mustered in as private, Co. B, May 24, 1898; mustered out with company, March 31, 1899, at Brooklyn, N. Y.

SINZENICK, GEORGE S.—Age, 28 years. Enlisted, May 2, 1898, at Brooklyn, to serve two years; mustered in as private, Co. H, May 24, 1898; appointed cook, August 1, 1898; mustered out with company, March 31, 1899, at Brooklyn, N. Y. ·

SITTERLY, LAROSS E.—Age, 21 years. Enlisted, May 2, 1898, at Brooklyn, to serve two years; mustered in as private, Co. A, May 24, 1898; mustered out with company, March 31, 1899, at Brooklyn, N. Y.

SKEA, WILLIAM.—Age, 28 years. Enlisted, May 2, 1898, at Brooklyn, to serve two years; mustered in as private, Co. H, May 24, 1898; mustered out with company, March 31, 1899, at Brooklyn, N. Y.

SLINGERLAND, CHARLES C.—Age, — years.   Enlisted, August 8, 1898, at Brooklyn, to serve two years; mustered in as private, Co. F, same date; mustered out with company, March 31, 1899, at Brooklyn, N. Y.

SMITH, ARTHUR B.—Age, 21 years. Enlisted, May 2, 1898, at Brooklyn, to serve two years; mustered in as private, Co. B, May 24, 1898; mustered out with company, March 31, 1899, at Brooklyn, N. Y.

SMITH, BERNARD F.—Age, 32 years. Enlisted, May 2, 1898, at Brooklyn, to serve two years; mustered in as private, Co. G, May 24, 1898; promoted regimental quartermaster-sergeant, May 27, 1898; mustered out with regiment, March 31, 1899, at Brooklyn, N. Y.

SMITH, CHARLES H.—Age, 26 years. Enlisted, May 2, 1898, at Brooklyn, to serve two years; mustered in as private, Co. B, May 24, 1898; mustered out with company, March 31, 1899, at Brooklyn, N. Y.

SMITH, EDWARD A.—Age, — years. Enlisted, July 29, 1898, at Brooklyn, to serve two years; mustered in as private, Co. C, same date; mustered out with company, March 31, 1899, at Brooklyn, N. Y.

SMITH, EDWARD H.—Age, 26 years. Enlisted, May 2, 1898, at Brooklyn, to serve two years; mustered in as private, Co. B, May 24, 1898; promoted corporal, June 1, 1898; mustered out with company, March 31, 1899, at Brooklyn, N. Y.

SMITH, FRANK.—Age, 21 years. Enlisted, May 22, 1898, at Brooklyn, to serve two years; mustered in as private, Co. E, May 24, 1898; appointed wagoner, October 21, 1898; mustered out with company, March 31, 1899, at Brooklyn, N. Y.

SMITH, GEORGE.—Age, — years. Enlisted, July 28, 1898, at Brooklyn, to serve two years; mustered in as private, Co. K, same date; mustered out with company, March 31, 1899, at Brooklyn, N. Y.

SMITH, GEORGE ED.—Age, 23 years. Enlisted, May 2, 1898, at Brooklyn, to serve two years; mustered in as private, Co. L, May 24, 1898; promoted corporal, no date; discharged, October 12, 1898, at Fort Adams, R. I.

SMITH, GUSTAVE A.—Age, 22 years. Enlisted, May 2, 1898, at Brooklyn, to serve two years; mustered in as private, Co. F, May 24, 1898; mustered out with company, March 31, 1899, at Brooklyn, N. Y.

SMITH, JOHN.—Age, — years. Enlisted, July 25, 1898, at Brooklyn, to serve two years; mustered in as private, Co. D, same date; mustered out with company, March 31, 1899, at Brooklyn, N. Y.

SMITH, JOHN B.—Age, — years. Enlisted, July 26, 1898, at Brooklyn, to serve two years; mustered in as private, Co. H, same date; mustered out with company, March 31, 1899, at Brooklyn, N. Y.

SMITH, JOHN P.—Age, 21 years. Enlisted, May 2, 1898, at Brooklyn, to serve two years; mustered in as private, Co. F, May 24, 1898; mustered out with company, March 31, 1899, at Brooklyn, N. Y.

SMITH, WALTER T.—Age, 21 years. Enlisted, May 12, 1898, at Camp Black, to serve two years; mustered in as private, Co. A, May 24, 1898; mustered out with company, March 31, 1899, at Brooklyn, N. Y.

SMITH, WILLIAM F.—Age, 18 years. Enlisted, May 2, 1898, at Brooklyn, to serve two years; mustered in as private, Co. F, May 24, 1898; mustered out with company, March 31, 1899, at Brooklyn, N. Y.

SNOW, GEORGE W.—Age, 24 years. Enlisted, May 2, 1898, at Brooklyn, to serve two years; mustered in as private, Co. I, May 24, 1898; promoted corporal, August 26, 1898; mustered out with company, March 31, 1899, at Brooklyn, N. Y.

SNYDER, CHARLES.—Age, — years. Enlisted, August 6, 1898, at Brooklyn, to serve two years; mustered in as private, Co. G, same date; mustered out with company, March 31, 1899, at Brooklyn, N. Y.

SNYDER, JOHN L.—Age, 22 years. Enlisted, May 2, 1898, at Brooklyn, to serve two years; mustered in as private, Co. K, May 24, 1898; mustered out with company, March 31, 1899, at Brooklyn, N. Y.

SOHMER, HUGO.—Age, 25 years. Enlisted, May 2, 1898, at Brooklyn, to serve two years; mustered in as corporal, Co. A, May 24, 1898; discharged, October 12, 1898.

SOHN, CHARLES.—Age, 22 years. Enlisted, May 2, 1898, at Brooklyn, to serve two years; mustered in as private, Co. M, May 24, 1898; mustered out with company, March 31, 1899, at Brooklyn, N. Y.

SOHN, HARRY J.—Age, 23 years. Enlisted, May 2, 1898, at Brooklyn, to serve two years; mustered in as private, Co. H, May 24, 1898; mustered out with company, March 31, 1899, at Brooklyn, N. Y.

SOMERINDYKE, JOHN.—Age, 38 years. Enlisted, May 2, 1898, at Brooklyn, to serve two years; mustered in as private, Co. C, May 24, 1898; discharged, October 12, 1898, at Fort Adams, R. I.

SONDERMANN, HUBERT.—Age, 22 years.   Enlisted, May 2, 1898, at Brooklyn, to serve two years; mustered in as private, Co. K, May 24, 1898; mustered out with company, March 31, 1899, at Brooklyn, N. Y.

SONNER, WILLIAM L.—Age, 21 years.   Enlisted, May 2, 1898, at Brooklyn, to serve two years; mustered in as private, Co. B, May 24, 1898; mustered out with company, March 31, 1899, at Brooklyn, N. Y.

SOUTHARD, JULIUS S.—Age, — years.   Enlisted, August 9, 1898, at Brooklyn, to serve two years; mustered in as private, Co. E, same date; promoted corporal, January 19, 1899; mustered out with company, March 31, 1899, at Brooklyn, N. Y.

SOUTHWICK, ALBERT.—Age, 24 years.   Enlisted, May 2, 1898, at Brooklyn, to serve two years; mustered in as private, Co. C, May 24, 1898; mustered out with company, March 31, 1899, at Brooklyn, N. Y.

SPEAR, WILLIAM H.—Age, 30 years.   Enlisted, May 2, 1898, at Brooklyn, to serve two years; mustered in as private, Co. F, May 24, 1898; mustered out with company, March 31, 1899, at Brooklyn, N. Y.

SPIESMAN, ALFRED W.—Age, 19 years.   Enlisted, May 2, 1898, at Brooklyn, to serve two years; mustered in as private, Co. G, May 24, 1898; mustered out with company, March 31, 1899, at Brooklyn, N. Y.

SPRINGSTEEN, EGBERT W.—Age, — years.   Enlisted, July 25, 1898, at Brooklyn, to serve two years; mustered in as corporal, Co. L, July 25, 1898; transferred to Co. G, August 3, 1898; discharged, October 14, 1898, at Fort Adams, R. I.

SPRINGSTEEN, OSCAR H.—Age, 25 years.   Enlisted, May 2, 1898, at Brooklyn, to serve two years; mustered in as corporal, Co. B, May 24, 1898; discharged, November 18, 1898, at Fort Columbus, New York Harbor.

STAGER, ALBERT.—Age, 20 years.   Enlisted, May 2, 1898, at Brooklyn, to serve two years; mustered in as private, Co. C, May 24, 1898; promoted corporal, November 1, 1898; mustered out with company, March 31, 1899, at Brooklyn, N. Y.

STAGG, JOHN F.—Age, 26 years. Enlisted, May 2, 1898, at Brooklyn, to serve two years; mustered in as private, Co. D, May 24, 1898; promoted corporal, September 26, 1898; mustered out with company, March 31, 1899, at Brooklyn, N. Y.

STANDERMANN, PHILIP.—Age, 21 years. Enlisted, May 2, 1898, at Brooklyn, to serve two years; mustered in as corporal, Co. K, May 24, 1898; promoted sergeant, July 1, 1898; mustered out with company, March 31, 1899, at Brooklyn, N. Y.

STANLEY, WILLIAM.—Age, — years. Enlisted, July 12, 1898, at Fort Adams, R. I., to serve two years; mustered in as private, Co. F, same date; promoted corporal, August 11, 1898; mustered out with company, March 31, 1899, at Brooklyn, N. Y.

STANWISE, LAWRENCE F.—Age, 21 years. Enlisted, May 2, 1898, at Brooklyn, to serve two years; mustered in as private, Co. G, May 24, 1898; mustered out with company, March 31, 1899, at Brooklyn, N. Y.

STARK, JOHN.—Age, — years. Enlisted, July 27, 1898, at Brooklyn, to serve two years; mustered in as private, Co. M, same date; mustered out with company, March 31, 1899, at Brooklyn, N. Y.

STEIN, JOHN C.—Age, 22 years. Enlisted, May 2, 1898, at Brooklyn, to serve two years; mustered in as corporal, Co. G, May 24, 1898; promoted sergeant, November 21, 1898; mustered out with company, March 31, 1899, at Brooklyn, N. Y.

STELLJES, GEORGE H.—Age, 21 years. Enlisted, May 2, 1898, at Brooklyn, to serve two years; mustered in as private, Co. G, May 24, 1898; appointed artificer, November 3, 1898; mustered out with company, March 31, 1899, at Brooklyn, N. Y.

STEVENSON, CHARLES G.—Age, 30 years. Enrolled, May 2, 1898, at Brooklyn, to serve two years; mustered in as first lieutenant, Co. M, May 24, 1898; as captain, November 2, 1898; mustered out with company, March 31, 1899, at Brooklyn, N. Y.; commissioned first lieutenant, May 24, 1898, with rank from same date, original; captain, November 2, 1898, with rank from same date, vice Rockafellow, discharged.

STEVENSON, ROBERT.—Age, 28 years. Enlisted, May 2, 1898, at Brooklyn, to serve two years; mustered in as first sergeant, Co. M, May 24, 1898; reduced to sergeant, June 30, 1898; returned to ranks, August 25, 1898; promoted sergeant, October 9, 1898, returned to ranks, December 13, 1898; mustered out with company, March 31, 1899, at Brooklyn, N. Y.

STEWART, EDWARD J.—Age, — years. Enlisted, August 2, 1898, at Brooklyn, to serve two years; mustered in as private, Co. I, same date; mustered out with company, March 31, 1899, at Brooklyn, N. Y.

STEWART, IRA C.—Age, 20 years. Enlisted, May 2, 1898, at Brooklyn, to serve two years; mustered in as private, Co. A, May 24, 1898; promoted corporal, August 15, 1898; mustered out with company, March 31, 1899, at Brooklyn, N. Y.

STORCH, CHARLES.—Age, 21 years. Enlisted, May 2, 1898, at Brooklyn, to serve two years; mustered in as private, Co. K, May 24, 1898; mustered out with company, March 31, 1899, at Brooklyn, N. Y.

STOSSEL, JOHN.—Age, — years. Enlisted, August 11, 1898, at Brooklyn, to serve two years; mustered in as private, Co. H, same date; mustered out with company, March 31, 1899, at Brooklyn, N. Y.

STRAUSS, PETER J.—Age, 28 years. Enlisted, May 2, 1898, at Brooklyn, to serve two years; mustered in as private, Co. K, May 24, 1898; promoted corporal, February 8, 1899; mustered out with company, March 31, 1899, at Brooklyn, N. Y.

STREVER, HOWARD F.—Age, 37 years. Enlisted, May 2, 1898, at Brooklyn, to serve two years; mustered in as artificer, Co. L, May 24, 1898; promoted corporal, September 1, 1898; sergeant, November 2, 1898; quartermaster-sergeant, January 28, 1899; mustered out with company, March 31, 1899, at Brooklyn, N. Y.

STRICKLAND, JOSEPH.—Age, — years. Enlisted, August 8, 1898, at Brooklyn, to serve two years; mustered in as private, Co. M, same date; mustered out with company, March 31, 1899, at Brooklyn, N. Y.

STROUSE, JOHN S.—Age, 29 years. Enrolled, May 2, 1898, at Brooklyn, to serve two years; mustered in as captain, Co. D, May 24, 1898; as major, December 3, 1898; mustered out with regiment, March 31, 1899, at Brooklyn, N. Y.; commissioned captain, May 24, 1898, with rank from same date, original; major, December 3, 1898, with rank from same date, vice Quick, promoted.

STRUCK, JOHN.—Age, 23 years. Enlisted, May 2, 1898, at Brooklyn, to serve two years; mustered in as private, Co. B, May 24, 1898; mustered out with company, March 31, 1899, at Brooklyn, N. Y.

STUART, FRANK.—Age, — years. Enlisted, August 2, 1898, at Brooklyn, to serve two years; mustered in as private, Co. I, same date; mustered out with company, March 31, 1899, at Brooklyn, N. Y.

STUCKEY, ARTHUR.—Age, 21 years. Enlisted, May 20, 1898, at Brooklyn, to serve two years; mustered in as private, Co. E, May 24, 1898; died of typhoid fever, November 19, 1898, in United States Hospital, Ponce, P. R.

STUCKLER, ERNEST M.—Age, 21 years. Enlisted, May 2, 1898, at Brooklyn, to serve two years; mustered in as private, Co. G, May 24, 1898; mustered out with company, March 31, 1899, at Brooklyn, N. Y.

SULLIVAN, DANIEL C.—Age, 46 years. Enrolled, May 2, 1898, at Brooklyn, to serve two years; mustered in as captain, Co. E, May 24, 1898; as major, October 3, 1898; mustered out with regiment, March 31, 1899, at Brooklyn, N. Y.; commissioned captain, May 24, 1898, with rank from same date, original; major, October 3, 1898, with rank from same date, vice Lyon, discharged.

SULLIVAN, EDWARD D.—Age, 21 years. Enlisted, May 2, 1898, at Brooklyn, to serve two years; mustered in as private, Co. K, May 24, 1898; mustered out with company, March 31, 1899, at Brooklyn, N. Y.

SULLIVAN, GEORGE W.—Age, 23 years. Enlisted, May 2, 1898, at Brooklyn, to serve two years; mustered in as private, Co. B, May 24, 1898; promoted corporal, November 14, 1898; mustered out with company, March 31, 1899, at Brooklyn, N. Y.

SULLIVAN, HUGH H.—Age, 26 years. Enlisted, May 2, 1898, at Brooklyn, to serve two years; mustered in as private, Co. C, May 24, 1898; discharged, January 19, 1899, at Caguas, P. R.

SULLIVAN, JAMES G.—Age, — years. Enlisted, August 11, 1898, at Brooklyn, to serve two years; mustered in as private, Co. K, same date; mustered out with company, March 31, 1899, at Brooklyn, N. Y.

SULLIVAN, JOHN.—Age, — years. Enlisted, August 9, 1898, at Brooklyn, to serve two years; mustered in as private, Co. E, August 24, 1898; deserted, September 19, 1898.

SULLIVAN, JR., MICHAEL J.—Age, 27 years. Enlisted, May 2, 1898, at Brooklyn, to serve two years; mustered in as private, Co. B, May 24, 1898; mustered out with company, March 31, 1899, at Brooklyn, N. Y.

SULLIVAN, PATRICK.—Age, — years. Enlisted, August 11, 1898, at Brooklyn, to serve two years; mustered in as private, Co. B, same date; mustered out with company, March 31, 1899, at Brooklyn, N. Y.

SUNTZENICH, WILLIAM.—Age, 22 years. Enlisted, May 2, 1898, at Brooklyn, to serve two years; mustered in as private, Co. H, May 24, 1898; appointed artificer, August 1, 1898; returned to ranks, November 30, 1898; mustered out with company, March 31, 1899, at Brooklyn, N. Y.

SVOBODA, JACOB.—Age, 28 years. Enlisted, May 2, 1898, at Brooklyn, to serve two years; mustered in as private, Co. C, May 24, 1898; promoted corporal, November 25, 1898; mustered out with company, March 31, 1899, at Brooklyn, N. Y.

SWAIN, SPENCER F.—Age, 21 years. Enlisted, May 2, 1898, at Brooklyn, to serve two years; mustered in as private, Co. L, May 24, 1898; mustered out with company, March 31, 1899, at Brooklyn, N. Y.

SWANSON, THOMAS J.—Age, 28 years. Enlisted, May 2, 1898, at Brooklyn, to serve two years; mustered in as private, Co. G, May 24, 1898; promoted corporal, August 20, 1898; mustered out with company, March 31, 1899, at Brooklyn, N. Y.

SWART, ABRAHAM F.—Age, 21 years. Enlisted, May 2, 1898, at Brooklyn, to serve two years; mustered in as private, Co. G, May 24, 1898; mustered out with company, March 31, 1899, at Brooklyn, N. Y.

SWEENEY, CHARLES.—Age, 27 years. Enlisted, May 2, 1898, at Brooklyn, to serve two years; mustered in as private, Co. F, May 24, 1898; mustered out with company, March 31, 1899, at Brooklyn, N. Y.

SWEENEY, PETER.—Age, — years. Enlisted, August 9, 1898, at Brooklyn, to serve two years; mustered in as private, Co. H, same date; mustered out with company, March 31, 1899, at Brooklyn, N. Y.

SWIFT, SILAS.—Age, 24 years. Enlisted, May 2, 1898, at Brooklyn, to serve two years; mustered in as private, Co. F, May 24, 1898; mustered out with company, March 31, 1899, at Brooklyn, N. Y.

SWINSON, GEORGE C.—Age, 21 years. Enlisted, May 2, 1898, at Brooklyn, to serve two years; mustered in as private, Co. I, May 24, 1898; mustered out with company, March 31, 1899, at Brooklyn, N. Y.

SZKALLA, ANTHONY C.—Age, 37 years. Enlisted, May 2, 1898, at Brooklyn, to serve two years; mustered in as corporal, Co. M, May 24, 1898; promoted sergeant, June 11, 1898; transferred to Co. C, November 15, 1898; promoted sergeant-major, December 20, 1898; mustered out with regiment, March 31, 1899, at Brooklyn, N. Y.; commissioned second lieutenant, not mustered, March 25, 1898, with rank from same date, vice Mygalt, promoted.

TARRANT, SAMUEL P.—Age, — years. Enlisted, August 11, 1898, at Brooklyn, to serve two years; mustered in as private, Co. B, same date; mustered out with company, March 31, 1899, at Brooklyn, N. Y.

TAYLOR, ARTHUR M.—Age, 22 years. Enlisted, May 2, 1898, at Brooklyn, to serve two years; mustered in as private, Co. E, May 24, 1898; promoted corporal, August 18, 1898; sergeant, March 8, 1899; mustered out with company, March 31, 1899, at Brooklyn, N. Y.

TECHTER, FRANK.—Age, 32 years. Enrolled, May 2, 1898, at Brooklyn, to serve two years; mustered in as second lieutenant, May 24, 1898; as first lieutenant, September 26, 1898; discharged, February 28, 1899, at San Juan, P. R.; commissioned second lieutenant, May 24, 1898, with rank from same date, original; first lieutenant, September 23, 1898, with rank from same date, vice Burrell, discharged.

TEHNER, FRED.—Age, 28 years.   Enlisted, May 2, 1898, at Brooklyn, to serve two years; mustered in as private, Co. D, May 24, 1898; mustered out with company, March 31, 1899, at Brooklyn, N. Y.

TERHUNE, HARRY.—Age, — years.   Enlisted, August 9, 1898, at Brooklyn, to serve two years; mustered in as private, Co. H, same date; mustered out with company, March 31, 1899, at Brooklyn, N. Y.

THILL, JOHN J.—Age, 34 years. Enlisted, May 2, 1898, at Brooklyn, to serve two years; mustered in as wagoner, Co. C, May 24, 1898; returned to ranks, February 14, 1899; mustered out with company, March 31, 1899, at Brooklyn, N. Y.

THOMAS, HARRY D.—Age, 21 years.   Enlisted, May 2, 1898, at Brooklyn, to serve two years; mustered in as corporal, Co. D, May 24, 1898; promoted sergeant, June 1, 1898; mustered out with company, March 31, 1899, at Brooklyn, N. Y.

THOMPSON, HENRY.—Age, 24 years.   Enlisted, May 2, 1898, at Brooklyn, to serve two years; mustered in as in private, Co. L, May 24, 1898; discharged, November 2, 1898, at Caguas, P. R.

THOMPSON, JAY W.—Age, 27 years.   Enlisted, May 2, 1898, at Brooklyn, to serve two years; mustered in as private, Co. D, May 24, 1898; mustered out with company, March 31, 1899, at Brooklyn, N. Y.

THOMPSON, WALTER.—Age, 24 years. Enlisted, May 2, 1898, at Brooklyn, to serve two years; mustered in as private, Co. C, May 24, 1898; promoted corporal, January 1, 1899; mustered out with company, March 31, 1899, at Brooklyn, N. Y.

THRALL, EDWARD T.—Age, 23 years. Enlisted, May 2, 1898, at Brooklyn, to serve two years; mustered in as private, Co. F, May 24, 1898; promoted corporal, September 27, 1898; mustered out with company, March 31, 1899, at Brooklyn, N. Y.

TIERNEY, FRANCIS P.—Age, 23 years. Enlisted, May 2, 1898, at Brooklyn, to serve two years; mustered in as private, Co. L, May 24, 1898; mustered out, to date, March 31, 1899.

TIMMES, PETER E.—Age, 23 years. Enlisted, May 2, 1898, at Brooklyn, to serve two years; mustered in as private, Co. H, May 24, 1898; promoted corporal, July 9, 1898; returned to ranks, September 1, 1898; mustered out with company, March 31, 1899, at Brooklyn, N. Y.

TONER, FRANCIS W.—Age, — years. Enlisted, May 24, 1898, at Camp Black, to serve two years; mustered in as private, Co. A, same date; mustered out with company, March 31, 1899, at Brooklyn, N. Y.

TONER, PETER.—Age, 33 years. Enlisted, May 2, 1898, at Brooklyn, to serve two years; mustered in as private, Co. M, May 24, 1898; mustered out with company, March 31, 1899, at Brooklyn, N. Y.

TOOMEY, JOHN J.—Age, — years. Enlisted, July 28, 1898, at Brooklyn, to serve two years; mustered in as private, Co. I, same date; discharged, October 12, 1898.

TOPPAN, CHARLES H.—Age, 30 years. Enlisted, May 16, 1898, at Brooklyn, to serve two years; mustered in as private, Co. E, May 24, 1898; mustered out with company, March 31, 1899, at Brooklyn, N. Y., as Toppam.

TRAVIS, MORTIMER A.—Age, 18 years. Enlisted, May 2, 1898, at Brooklyn, to serve two years; mustered in as private, Co. H, May 24, 1898; promoted corporal, September 1, 1898; mustered out with company, March 31, 1899, at Brooklyn, N. Y.

TRENCHARD, JR., GEORGE W.—Age, 25 years. Enrolled, May 2, 1898, at Brooklyn, to serve two years; mustered in as second lieutenant, Co. F, May 24, 1898; as first lieutenant, December 17, 1898; mustered out with company, March 31, 1899, at Brooklyn, N. Y.; commissioned second lieutenant, May 24, 1898, with rank from same date, original; first lieutenant, December 17, 1898, with rank from same date, vice Andelfinger, discharged.

TRENNER, GEORGE L.—Age, 21 years. Enlisted, May 2, 1898, at Brooklyn, to serve two years; mustered in as private, Co. A, May 24, 1898; mustered out with company, March 31, 1899, at Brooklyn, N. Y.

TURNER, HENRY P.—Age, 21 years. Enlisted, May 2, 1898, at Brooklyn, to serve two years; mustered in as private, Co. F, May 24, 1898; mustered out with company, March 31, 1899, at Brooklyn, N. Y.

TURNER, JAMES J.—Age, — years. Enlisted, August 3, 1898, at Brooklyn, to serve two years; mustered in as private, Co. C, same date; mustered out with company, March 31, 1899, at Brooklyn, N. Y.

TURNER, JOSEPH J.—Age, 20 years. Enlisted, May 2, 1898, at Brooklyn, to serve two years; mustered in as private, Co. F, May 24, 1898; mustered out with company, March 31, 1899, at Brooklyn, N. Y.

TYNE, EDWARD.—Age, 24 years. Enlisted, May 2, 1898, at Brooklyn, to serve two years; mustered in as private, Co. E, May 24, 1898; mustered out with company, March 31, 1899, at Brooklyn, N. Y.

UDE, FREDERICK.—Age, 20 years. Enlisted, May 2, 1898, at Brooklyn, to serve two years; mustered in as private, Co. D, May 24, 1898; mustered out with company, March 31, 1899, at Brooklyn, N. Y.

ULLRICH, JOHN.—Age, 23 years. Enlisted, May 2, 1898, at Brooklyn, to serve two years; mustered in as private, Co. D, May 24, 1898; mustered out with company, March 31, 1899, at Brooklyn, N. Y.

VALENTINE, FRANK F.—Age, 28 years. Enlisted, May 2, 1898, at Brooklyn, to serve two years; mustered in as private, Co. I, May 24, 1898; promoted corporal, August 26, 1898; returned to ranks, December 1, 1898; mustered out with company, March 31, 1899, at Brooklyn, N. Y.

VALENTINE, JOHN.—Age, 22 years. Enlisted, May 2, 1898, at Brooklyn, to serve two years; mustered in as private, Co. A, May 24, 1898; promoted corporal, October 21, 1898; mustered out with company, March 31, 1899, at Brooklyn, N. Y.

VALENTINE, WILLIAM C.—Age, 21 years. Enlisted, May 2, 1898, at Brooklyn, to serve two years; mustered in as private, Co. H, May 24, 1898; deserted, August 20, 1898, at Fort Adams, R. I.

VALIANT, WILLIAM H.—Age, — years. Enlisted, August 2, 1898, at Brooklyn, to serve two years; mustered in as private, Co. I, same date; mustered out with company, March 31, 1899, at Brooklyn, N. Y.

VAMOSEY, MICHAEL.—Age, — years. Enlisted, August 11, 1898, at Brooklyn, to serve two years; mustered in as private, Co. A, same date; mustered out with company, March 31, 1899, at Brooklyn, N. Y.

VAN AUKEN FRANK E.—Age, 37 years. Enlisted, May 2, 1898, at Brooklyn, to serve two years; mustered in as private, Co. I, May 24, 1898; discharged, October 12, 1898; also borne as Frank Van Anken.

VANDERBECK, WILLIAM.—Age, 21 years. Enlisted, May 2, 1898, at Brooklyn, to serve two years; mustered in as private, Co. A, May 24, 1898; mustered out with company, March 31, 1899, at Brooklyn, N. Y.

VANDERHOFF, HARRY.—Age, — years. Enlisted, August 10, 1898, at Brooklyn. to serve two years; mustered in as private, Co. H, same date; promoted corporal, September 1, 1898; sergeant, December 17, 1898; mustered out with company, March 31, 1899, at Brooklyn, N. Y.

VAN DORMOLEN, PETER H.—Age, 21 years. Enlisted, May 2, 1898, at Brooklyn, to serve two years; mustered in as private, Co. H, May 24, 1898; appointed musician, no date; mustered out with company, March 31, 1899, at Brooklyn, N. Y.

VAN HORN, HARRY.—Age, — years. Enlisted. July 28, 1898, at Brooklyn, to serve two years; mustered in as private, Co. G, same date; mustered out with company, March 31, 1899, at Brooklyn, N. Y.

VAN RIPER, RICHARD.—Age, — years. Enlisted, July 28, . 1898, at Brooklyn, to serve two years; mustered in as private, Co. K, same date; mustered out with company, March 31, 1899, at Brooklyn, N. Y.

VASSAR, JOSEPH A.—Age, 22 years.   Enlisted, May 2, 1898, at Brooklyn, to serve two years; mustered in as musician, Co. K, May 24, 1898; mustered out with company, March 31, 1899, at Brooklyn, N. Y.

VOGES, FERDINAND.—Age, 40 years.   Enlisted, May 2, at Brooklyn, to serve two years; mustered in as private, Co. G, May 24, 1898; appointed artificer, September 1, 1898; returned to ranks, October 10, 1898; discharged, October 14, 1898, at Fort Adams, R. I.

VOLHARD, RUDOLPH.—Age, — years.   Enlisted, August 4, 1898, at Brooklyn, to serve two years; mustered in as private, Co. H, same date; mustered out with company, March 31, 1899, at Brooklyn, N. Y.

VOLKENS, FREDERICK L.—Age, — years.   Enlisted, July 26, 1898, at Brooklyn, to serve two years; mustered in as private, Co. M, same date; mustered out with company, March 31, 1899, at Brooklyn, N. Y.

VON BORSTEL, GEORGE J.—Age, 25 years.   Enlisted, May 2, 1898, at Brooklyn, to serve two years; mustered in as private, Co. B, May 24, 1898; promoted corporal, November 14, 1898; mustered out with company, March 31, 1899, at Brooklyn, N. Y.

VON OEHSEN, HERMAN.—Age, 21 years.   Enlisted, May 2, 1898, at Brooklyn, to serve two years; mustered in as private, Co. D, May 24, 1898; promoted corporal, June 1, 1898; returned to ranks, December 13, 1898; mustered out with company, March 31, 1899, at Brooklyn, N. Y.

VON WALSKBEN, CHARLES.—Age, 22 years.   Enlisted, May 2, 1898, at Brooklyn, to serve two years; mustered in as private, Co. M, May 24, 1898; mustered out with company, March 31, 1899, at Brooklyn, N. Y.

VOSE, PHILIP M.—Age, 30 years.   Enlisted, May 2 1898, at Brooklyn, to serve two years; mustered in as private, Co. C, May 24, 1898; promoted corporal, July 24, 1898; sergeant, November 26, 1898; discharged, January 19, 1899, at Caguas, P. R.

VOSS, GEORGE W.—Age, 24 years. Enlisted, May 2, 1898, at Brooklyn, to serve two years; mustered in as private, Co. D, May 24, 1898; appointed musician, December 1, 1898; returned to ranks, February 28, 1899; mustered out with company, March 31, 1899, at Brooklyn, N. Y.

VOSS, HENRY J.—Age, 22 years. Enlisted, May 2, 1898, at Brooklyn, to serve two years; mustered in as private, Co. D, May 24, 1898; appointed artificer, June 1, 1898; cook, September 30, 1898; returned to ranks, December 20, 1898; mustered out with company, March 31, 1899, at Brooklyn, N. Y.

WACHTER, PHILIP.—Age, 21 years. Enlisted, May 2, 1898, at Brooklyn, to serve two years; mustered in as private, Co. G, May 24, 1898; mustered out with company, March 31, 1899, at Brooklyn, N. Y., as Waechter.

WADDY, PETER A.—Age, 21 years. Enlisted, May 2, 1898, at Brooklyn, to serve two years; mustered in as private, Co. C, May 24, 1898; promoted sergeant, June 1, 1898; quartermaster-sergeant, June 27, 1898; reduced to sergeant, September 23, 1898; mustered out with company, March 31, 1899, at Brooklyn, N. Y.

WALKER, EDWARD T.—Age, 28 years. Enlisted, May 2, 1898, at Brooklyn, to serve two years; mustered in as private, Co. B, May 24, 1898; promoted corporal, January 23, 1898; mustered out with company, March 31, 1899, at Brooklyn, N. Y.

WALKER, HARRY H.—Age, 31 years. Enrolled, May 3, 1898, at Brooklyn, to serve two years; mustered in as first lieutenant and battalion adjutant, May 24, 1898; mustered out with regiment, March 31, 1899, at Brooklyn, N. Y.; commissioned first lieutenant and battalion adjutant, May 24, 1898, with rank from same date, original.

WALLACE, HENRY.—Age, 29 years. Enrolled, May 3, 1898, at Brooklyn, to serve two years; mustered in as major and surgeon, May 6, 1898; discharged, September 13, 1898; commissioned major and surgeon, May 6, 1898, with rank from same date, original.

WALLACE, MICHAEL.—Age, 27 years. Enlisted, May 22, 1898, at Brooklyn, to serve two years; mustered in as private, Co. E, May 24, 1898; mustered out with company, March 31, 1899, at Brooklyn, N. Y.

WALLACE, THOMAS J.—Age, 24 years.   Enlisted, May 2, 1898, at Brooklyn, to serve two years; mustered in as private, Co. H, May 24, 1898; mustered out with company, March 31, 1899, at Brooklyn, N. Y.

WALLACE, WILLIAM G.—Age, 29 years.   Enlisted, May 2, 1898, at Brooklyn, to serve two years; mustered in as private, Co. G, May 24, 1898; mustered out with company, March 31, 1899, at Brooklyn, N. Y.

WALSH, JOHN E.—Age, 19 years.   Enlisted, May 2, 1898, at Brooklyn, to serve two years; mustered in as private, Co. K, May 24, 1898; mustered out with company, March 31, 1899, at Brooklyn, N. Y.

WALSH, JOHN J.—Age, — years.   Enlisted, July 27, 1898, at Brooklyn, to serve two years; mustered in as private, Co. G, same date; mustered out with company, March 31, 1899, at Brooklyn, N. Y.

WALSH, PATRICK J.—Age, 24 years.   Enlisted, May 2, 1898, at Brooklyn, to serve two years; mustered in as corporal, Co. G, May 24, 1898; returned to ranks, September 12, 1898; discharged, October 14, 1898, at Fort Adams, R. I.

WALSH, RICHARD.—Age, 21 years.   Enlisted, May 2, 1898, at Brooklyn, to serve two years; mustered in as private, Co. K, May 24, 1898; mustered out with company, March 31, 1899, at Brooklyn, N. Y.

WALSH, THOMAS F.—Age, 27 years.   Enlisted, May 2, 1898, at Brooklyn, to serve two years; mustered in as first sergeant, Co. D, May 24, 1898; mustered out with company, March 31, 1899, at Brooklyn, N. Y.

WALSLEBEN, CHARLES, see Charles Von Walskben.

WANGLER, GEORGE C.—Age, 21 years.   Enlisted, May 2, 1898, at Brooklyn, to serve two years; mustered in as private, Co. F, May 24, 1898; mustered out with company, March 31, 1899, at Brooklyn, N. Y.

WANSOR, JOSEPH.—Age, 27 years.   Enlisted May 2, 1898, at Brooklyn, to serve two years; mustered in as private, Co. I, May 24, 1898; mustered out with company, March 31, 1899, at Brooklyn, N. Y.

WARD, CORNELIUS.—Age, 32 years. Enlisted, May 2, 1898, at Brooklyn, to serve two years; mustered in as private, Co. D, May 24, 1898; mustered out with company, March 31, 1899, at Brooklyn, N. Y.

WARD, HENRY.—Age, 28 years. Enlisted May 2, 1898, at Brooklyn, to serve two years; mustered in as private, Co. C, May 24, 1898; mustered out with company, March 31, 1899, at Brooklyn, N. Y.

WARNER, ROBERT L. L.—Age, 18 years. Enlisted, May 2, 1898, at Brooklyn, to serve two years; mustered in as private, Co. A, May 24, 1898; discharged for disability, January 28, 1899.

WARREN, WILLIAM J.—Age, 22 years. Enlisted, May 2, 1898, at Brooklyn, to serve two years; mustered in as private,. Co. H, May 24, 1898; transferred to Hospital Corps, August 16, 1898.

WARWICK, GEORGE H.—Age, 21 years. Enlisted, May 2, 1898, at Brooklyn, to serve two years; mustered in as private, Co. L, May 24, 1898; promoted corporal, August 22, 1898; mustered out with company, March 31, 1899, at Brooklyn, N. Y.

WATSON, OTTO.—Age, 22 years. Enlisted, May 19, 1898, at Camp Black, to serve two years; mustered in as private, Co. A, May 24, 1898; mustered out with company, March 31, 1899, at Brooklyn, N. Y.

WAY, REUBEN K.—Age, 26 years. Enlisted, May 2, 1898, at Brooklyn, to serve two years; mustered in as private, Co. C, May 24, 1898; promoted corporal, June 1, 1898; discharged, October 12, 1898, at Fort Adams, R. I.

WEBBER, GEORGE F.—Age, 20 years. Enlisted, May 2, 1898, at Brooklyn, to serve two years; mustered in as private, Co. D, May 24, 1898; promoted corporal, August 27, 1898; mustered out with company, March 31, 1899, at Brooklyn, N. Y.

WEBER, LEWIS W.—Age, — years. Enlisted, July 26, 1898, at Brooklyn, to serve two years; mustered in as private, Co. F, same date; promoted corporal, December 1, 1898; mustered out with company, March 31, 1899, at Brooklyn, N. Y.

WEBSTER, CHARLES E.—Age, 22 years. Enlisted, May 2, 1898, at Brooklyn, to serve two years; mustered in as private, Co. B, May 24, 1898; deserted, September 23, 1898.

WEIMANN, CHRISTOPHER.—Age, 19 years. Enlisted, May 2, 1898, at Brooklyn, to serve two years; mustered in as private, Co. F, May 24, 1898; promoted corporal, September 30, 1898; mustered out with company, March 31, 1899, at Brooklyn, N. Y.

WELLINGTON, HARRY A.—Age, 25 years. Enlisted, May 2, 1898, at Brooklyn, to serve two years; mustered in as corporal, Co. F, May 24, 1898; promoted sergeant, July 2, 1898; mustered out with company, March 31, 1899, at Brooklyn, N. Y.

WELSH, GUSTAVUS.—Age, 29 years. Enlisted, May 20, 1898, at Brooklyn, to serve two years; mustered in as private, Co. E, May 24, 1898; promoted corporal, October 21, 1898; mustered out with company, March 31, 1899, at Brooklyn, N. Y.

WENTZLER, CHRISTIAN W. J.—Age, 21 years. Enlisted, May 2, 1898, at Brooklyn, to serve two years; mustered in as private, Co. A, May 24, 1898; promoted corporal, August 15, 1898; mustered out with company, March 31, 1899, at Brooklyn, N. Y.

WENZ, ALBERT.—Age, 27 years. Enlisted, May 2, 1898, at Brooklyn, to serve two years; mustered in as musician, Co. D, May 24, 1898; discharged, October 12, 1898, at Fort Columbus, New York Harbor.

WENZ, CHARLES H.—Age, 21 years. Enlisted, May 2, 1898, at Brooklyn, to serve two years; mustered in as private, Co. K, May 24, 1898; mustered out with company, March 31, 1899, at Brooklyn, N. Y.

WESTHEIMER, ADOLF.—Age, — years. Enlisted, August 8, 1898, at Brooklyn, to serve two years; mustered in as private, Co. I, same date; mustered out with company, March 31, 1899, at Brooklyn, N. Y.

WHALEN, EUGENE J.—Age, 34 years. Enlisted, May 24, 1898, at Brooklyn, to serve two years; mustered in as private, Co. G, May 24, 1898; appointed wagoner, December 9, 1898; mustered out with company, March 31, 1899, at Brooklyn, N. Y.

WHALEN, GEORGE.—Age, — years. Enlisted, August 9, 1898, at Brooklyn, to serve two years; mustered in as private, Co. H, same date; mustered out with company, March 31, 1899, at Brooklyn, N. Y.

WHALEN, JAMES.—Age, 22 years. Enlisted, May 2, 1898, at Brooklyn, to serve two years; mustered in as private, Co. H, May 24, 1898; promoted corporal, March 8, 1899; mustered out with company, March 31, 1899, at Brooklyn, N. Y.

WHEARTY, JAMES H.—Age, 26 years. Enlisted, May 2, 1898, at Brooklyn, to serve two years; mustered in as private, Co. G, May 24, 1898; promoted corporal, December 9, 1898; mustered out with company, March 31, 1899, at Brooklyn, N. Y.

WHEELER, WILLIAM.—Age, 35 years. Enlisted, May 2, 1898, at Brooklyn, to serve two years; mustered in as private, Co. I, May 24, 1898; promoted corporal, same date; returned to ranks, July 1, 1898; promoted corporal, January 23, 1898; mustered out with company, March 31, 1899, at Brooklyn, N. Y.

WHELAN, THOMAS J.—Age, 25 years. Enlisted, May 19, 1898, at Brooklyn, to serve two years; mustered in as private, Co. A, May 24, 1898; mustered out with company, March 31, 1899, at Brooklyn, N. Y.

WHELAN, WILLIAM J.—Age, 27 years. Enlisted, May 2, 1898, at Brooklyn, to serve two years; mustered in as private, Co. F, May 24, 1898; appointed wagoner, August 1, 1898; mustered out with company, March 31, 1899, at Brooklyn, N. Y.

WHIAND, WILLIAM A.—Age, 28 years. Enlisted, May 2, 1898, at Brooklyn, to serve two years; mustered in as private, Co. I, May 24, 1898; appointed artificer, same date; mustered out with company, March 31, 1899, at Brooklyn, N. Y.

WHITCOMB, FREDERICK W.—Age, — years. Enlisted, August 4, 1898, at Brooklyn, to serve two years; mustered in as private, Co. B, same date; mustered out with company, March 31, 1899, at Brooklyn, N. Y.

WHITE, CHARLES P.—Age, 22 years. Enlisted, May 2, 1898, at Brooklyn, to serve two years; mustered in as private, Co. G, May 24, 1898; mustered out with company, March 31, 1899, at Brooklyn, N. Y.

WHITE, EDWARD E.—Age, 26 years. Enlisted, May 2, 1898, at Brooklyn, to serve two years; mustered in as private, Co. D, May 24, 1898; mustered out with company, March 31, 1899, at Brooklyn, N. Y.

WHITE, JAMES J.—Age, — years. Enlisted, July 26, 1898, at Brooklyn, to serve two years; mustered in as private, Co. L, same date; mustered out with company, March 31, 1899, at Brooklyn, N. Y.

WHITE, JOHN H.—Age, — years. Enlisted, August 11, 1898, at Brooklyn, to serve two years; mustered in as private, Co. H, same date; promoted corporal, September 1, 1898; quarter-master-sergeant, January 16, 1899; returned to ranks, February 1, 1899; mustered out with company, March 31, 1898, at Brooklyn, N. Y.

WHITE, RICHARD.—Age, 21 years. Enlisted, May 2, 1898, at Brooklyn, to serve two years; mustered in as private, Co. C, May 24, 1898; mustered out with company, March 31, 1899, at Brooklyn, N. Y.

WHITE, S. REYNOLDS.—Age, 29 years. Enrolled, May 2, 1898, at Brooklyn, to serve two years; mustered in as second lieuten-ant, Co. L, May 24, 1898; as first lieutenant, September 29, 1898; as captain, to date, January 1, 1899; mustered out with com-pany, March 31, 1899, at Brooklyn, N. Y.; commissioned second lieutenant, May 24, 1898, with rank from same date, original; first lieutenant, September 26, 1898, with rank from same date, vice Gerourd, discharged; captain, January 1, 1899, with rank from same date, vice Libbey, discharged.

WHITE, WILLIAM.—Age, — years. Enlisted, August 5, 1898, at Brooklyn, to serve two years; mustered in as private, Co. F, same date; mustered out with company, March 31, 1899, at Brooklyn, N. Y.

WHITE, WILLIAM E.—Age, 28 years. Enlisted, May 2, 1898, at Brooklyn, to serve two years; mustered in as first sergeant, Co. C, May 24, 1898; as second lieutenant, September 26, 1898; as first lieutenant, January 18, 1899; mustered out with com-pany, March 31, 1899, at Brooklyn, N. Y.; commissioned second lieutenant, September 26, 1898, with rank from same date, vice Techter, promoted; first lieutenant, January 18, 1899, with rank from same date, vice D. R. White, promoted.

WHITMAN, JOSEPH L.—Age, — years. Enlisted, August 9, 1898, at Brooklyn, to serve two years; mustered in as private, Co. B, same date; discharged for disability, October 28, 1898, at Fort Adams, R. I.

WHYTAL, CHARLES H.—Age, 19 years. Enlisted, May 2, 1898, at Brooklyn, to serve two years; mustered in as private, Co. G, May 24, 1898; promoted corporal, August 20, 1898; mustered out with company, March 31, 1899, at Brooklyn, N. Y.

WIEBE, ALBERT C.—Age, — years. Enlisted, July 27, 1898, at Brooklyn, to serve two years; mustered in as private, Co. M, same date; mustered out with company, March 31, 1899, at Brooklyn, N. Y.

WIEBE, FRED.—Age, 21 years. Enlisted, May 2, 1898, at Brooklyn, to serve two years; mustered in as private, Co. M, May 24, 1898; promoted corporal, August 26, 1898; returned to ranks, no date; mustered out with company, March 31, 1899, at Brooklyn, N. Y.

WIESNER, JOSEPH.—Age, 24 years. Enlisted, May 2, 1898, at Brooklyn, to serve two years; mustered in as artificer, Co. C, May 24, 1898; promoted corporal, June 1, 1898; discharged, November 10, 1898, at Caguas, P. R.

WILCOX, IRVING C.—Age, — years. Enlisted, August 11, 1898, at Brooklyn, to serve two years; mustered in as private, Co. B, same date; mustered out with company, March 31, 1899, at Brooklyn, N. Y.

WILDANGER, JACOB J.—Age, 23 years. Enlisted, May 2, 1898, at Brooklyn, to serve two years; mustered in as private, Co. L, May 24, 1898; mustered out with company, March 31, 1899, at Brooklyn, N. Y.

WILKINSON, HARRY P.—Age, 24 years. Enlisted, May 2, 1898, at Brooklyn, to serve two years; mustered in as corporal, Co. G, May 24, 1898; promoted sergeant, November 21, 1898; mustered out with company, March 31, 1899, at Brooklyn, N. Y.

WILLIAMS, DANIEL.—Age, — years. Enlisted, August 10, 1898, at Brooklyn, to serve two years; mustered in as private, Co. A, same date; mustered out with company, March 31, 1899, at Brooklyn, N. Y.

WILLIAMS, FREDERICK G.—Age, 25 years. Enlisted, May 2, 1898, at Brooklyn, to serve two years; mustered in as sergeant, Co. M, May 24, 1898; promoted first sergeant, July 1, 1898; mustered out with company, March 31, 1899, at Brooklyn, N. Y.

WILLIAMS, HUDSON.—Age, 26 years. Enlisted, May 2, 1898, at Brooklyn, to serve two years; mustered in as private, Co. I, May 24, 1898; deserted, September 21, 1898.

WILLIAMS, JOHN M.—Age, 21 years. Enlisted, May 2, 1898, at Brooklyn, to serve two years; mustered in as private, Co. K, May 24, 1898; mustered out with company, March 31, 1899, at Brooklyn, N. Y.

WILLIAMS, JOSEPH J.—Age, 23 years. Enlisted, May 2, 1898, at Brooklyn, to serve two years; mustered in as private, Co. A, May 24, 1898; deserted, October 7, 1898, at Fort Adams, R. I.

WILLIAMS, MILTON I.—Age, 21 years. Enlisted, May 2, 1898, at Brooklyn, to serve two years; mustered in as private, Co. A, May 24, 1898; discharged, October 12, 1898.

WILLIAMS, PERCY C.—Age, 23 years. Enlisted, May 2, 1898, at Brooklyn, to serve two years; mustered in as musician, Co. F, May 24, 1898; mustered out with company, March 31, 1899, at Brooklyn, N. Y.

WILLIAMS, VINCENT.—Age, — years. Enlisted, July 25, 1898, at Brooklyn, to serve two years; mustered in as private, Co. H, same date; mustered out with company, March 31, 1899, at Brooklyn, N. Y.

WILSON, ALEXANDER.—Age, — years. Enlisted, August 2, 1898, at Brooklyn, to serve two years; mustered in as private, Co. F, same date; mustered out with company, March 31, 1899, at Brooklyn, N. Y.

WILSON, JAMES S.—Age, 21 years. Enlisted, May 2, 1898, at Brooklyn, to serve two years; mustered in as private, Co. D, May 24, 1898; discharged, December 31, 1898, at Vieques, P. R.

WILSON, JOHN.—Age, 19 years. Enlisted, May 2, 1898, at Brooklyn, to serve two years; mustered in as private, Co. I, May 24, 1898; mustered out with company, March 31, 1899, at Brooklyn, N. Y.

WILSON, JOHN R.—Age, 32 years. Enlisted, May 2, 1898, at Brooklyn, to serve two years; mustered in as private, Co. E, May 24, 1898; discharged, December 31, 1898, at Vieques, P. R.

WISEMAN, GASPER C.—Age, 20 years. Enlisted, May 2, 1898, at Brooklyn, to serve two years; mustered in as private, Co. D, May 24, 1898; promoted corporal, June 1, 1898; discharged, October 12, 1898, at Fort Columbus, New York Harbor.

WOLF. GEORGE.—Age, 21 years. Enlisted, May 2, 1898, at Brooklyn, to serve two years; mustered in as private, Co. D, May 24, 1898; mustered out with company, March 31, 1899, at Brooklyn, N. Y.

WOLFE, FREDERICK.—Age, 21 years. Enlisted, May 2, 1898, at Brooklyn, to serve two years; mustered in as private, Co. F, May 24, 1898; mustered out with company, March 31, 1899, at Brooklyn, N. Y.

WOLFF, AUGUSTUS.—Age, 21 years. Enlisted, May 2, 1898, at Brooklyn, to serve two years; mustered in as private, Co. L, May 24, 1898; mustered out with company, March 31, 1899, at Brooklyn, N. Y.

WOOD, GUY A.—Age, 21 years. Enlisted, May 2, 1898, at Brooklyn, to serve two years; mustered in as private, Co. B, May 24, 1898; promoted corporal, November 14, 1898; mustered out with company, March 31, 1899, at Brooklyn, N. Y.

WOOD, JOHN.—Age, 32 years. Enlisted, May 2, 1898, at Brooklyn, to serve two years; mustered in as private, Co. C, May 24, 1898; discharged for disability, August 2, 1898, at Fort Adams, R. I.

WOOD, JOHN.—Age, 33 years. Enlisted, May 22, 1898, at Brooklyn, to serve two years; mustered in as private, Co. E, May 24, 1898; mustered out with company, March 31, 1899, at Brooklyn, N. Y.

WOOD, WILLIAM W.—Age, 28 years. Enlisted, May 2, 1898, at Brooklyn, to serve two years; mustered in as private, Co. I, May 24, 1898; mustered out with company, March 31, 1899, at Brooklyn, N. Y.

WOOLLEY, WILLIAM C.—Age, 24 years. Enlisted, May 2, 1898, at Brooklyn, to serve two years; mustered in as private, Co. L, May 24, 1898; promoted corporal, August 22, 1898; mustered out with company, March 31, 1899, at Brooklyn, N. Y.

WORDEN, HENRY J.—Age, — years. Enlisted, August 9, 1898, at Brooklyn, to serve two years; mustered in as private, Co. E, same date; mustered out with company, March 31, 1899, at Brooklyn, N. Y.

WORTHLEY, JEREMIAH H.—Age, — years. Enlisted, June 9, 1898, at Brooklyn, to serve two years; mustered in as private, Co. E, same date; appointed cook, August 1, 1898; returned to ranks, October 22, 1898; mustered out with company, March 31, 1899, at Brooklyn, N. Y.

WRANGLE, ERNEST.—Age, 30 years. Enlisted, May 2, 1898, at Brooklyn, to serve two years; mustered in as private, Co. M, May 24, 1898; promoted corporal, July 20, 1898; mustered out with company, March 31, 1899, at Brooklyn, N. Y.

WRIGHT, JAMES H.—Age, 25 years. Enlisted, May 2, 1898, at Brooklyn, to serve two years; mustered in as corporal, Co. H, May 24, 1898; promoted sergeant, September 1, 1898; mustered out with company, March 31, 1899, at Brooklyn, N. Y.

WYNN, WALTER T.—Age, 23 years. Enlisted, May 2, 1898, at Brooklyn, to serve two years; mustered in as private, Co. I, May 24, 1898; mustered out with company, March 31, 1899, at Brooklyn, N. Y.

YACKEL, HERMAN.—Age, 26 years. Enlisted, May 2, 1898, at Brooklyn, to serve two years; mustered in as private, Co. E, May 24, 1898; promoted corporal, to date, May 24, 1898; returned to ranks, August 2, 1898; discharged, October 14, 1898, at Fort Adams, R. I.

YEAMAN, WILLIAM.—Age, — years. Enlisted, August 10, 1898, at Brooklyn, to serve two years; mustered in as private, Co. K, same date; mustered out with company, March 31, 1899, at Brooklyn, N. Y.

YONGE, CHARLES A.—Age, 32 years. Enlisted, May 2, 1898, at Brooklyn, to serve two years; mustered in as private, Co. I, May 24, 1898; promoted quartermaster-sergeant, July 30, 1898; mustered out with company, March 31, 1899, at Brooklyn, N. Y.

YOUNG, HENRY A. F.—Age, 27 years. Enrolled, May 2, 1898, at Brooklyn, to serve two years; mustered in as second lieutenant, Co. M, May 24, 1898; as captain, Co. C, November 16, 1898; mustered out with company, March 31, 1899, at Brooklyn, N. Y.; commissioned second lieutenant, May 24, 1898, with rank from same date, original; captain, November 2, 1898, with rank from same date, vice Fish, discharged.

YOUNG, JOHN E.—Age, 29 years. Enlisted, May 2, 1898, at Brooklyn, to serve two years; mustered in as private, Co. C, May 24, 1898; discharged, November 10, 1898, at Caguas, P. R.

YOUNG, WILLIAM J.—Age, 23 years. Enlisted, May 2, 1898, at Brooklyn, to serve two years; mustered in as sergeant, Co. A, May 24, 1898; mustered out with company, March 31, 1899, at Brooklyn, N. Y.

ZAZALI, CONSTANTINE.—Age, — years. Enlisted, August 8, 1898, at Brooklyn, to serve two years; mustered in as private, Co. K, same date; mustered out with company, March 31, 1899, at Brooklyn, N. Y.

ZIEGLER, OTTO.—Age, 21 years. Enlisted, May 2, 1898, at Brooklyn, to serve two years; mustered in as private, Co. C, May 24, 1898; mustered out with company, March 31, 1899, at Brooklyn, N. Y.

ZUNDT, WALTER J.—Age, 21 years. Enlisted, May 2, 1898, at Brooklyn, to serve two years; mustered in as private, Co. H, May 24, 1898; deserted, June 27, 1898, at Fort Adams, R. I.

SIXTY-FIFTH REGIMENT, INFANTRY.

The sixty-fifth regiment, national guard, having volunteered its services, was one of the regiments selected and designated in general orders, No. 8, general headquarters, state of New York, dated adjutant-general's office, Albany, N. Y., April 27, 1898, to enter the service of the United States as a volunteer regiment.

The regiment then consisted of eight companies, which were immediately recruited to the required numbers; three new companies, K, L and M, were organized, and the thirteenth separate company of Jamestown was attached by special orders, No. 65, A. G. O., dated April 29, 1898, and designated as company E.

The prior history of the regiment and that of the thirteenth separate company follows:

SIXTY-FIFTH REGIMENT.

(Fourth Brigade.)

Armory, State Arsenal, Broadway, Buffalo.

The regiment was organized in 1848. Companies K and I were disbanded, the latter in 1875. A new company, designated I, was organized in 1879, and company E was consolidated with company H the same year. In 1880 company D was consolidated with company A, and troop L, cavalry, eighth division, was re-organized as a company of infantry and attached to the regiment as company E. In 1881 companies D and E were disbanded. New companies, designated B and D, were organized in 1885. It performed duty for the state in 1849, in quelling a riot; in 1863, during the draft riots; in 1877, during the railroad riots; in 1892, during the switchmen's strike at Buffalo, and at Tonawanda in 1893. It entered the service of the United States, June 19, 1863, and was mustered out, July 30, 1863. In October, 1864, practically the whole regiment, as part of the 187th regiment, N. Y. Vols., was again mustered in the United States service for one year and mustered out, July 1, 1865.

The regiment received authority to place silver rings on the lances of its colors, engraved as follows:

On the national color.—Gettysburg campaign, 1863; before Petersburg, Va., October 20, 1864, to April 2, 1865; Hatcher's Run, Va., October 27–28, 1864; Hicksford Raid, Va., December 6–11, 1864; Hatcher's Run, Va., February 5–7, 1865; Appomattox Campaign, Va., March 28 to April 9, 1864; White Oak Ridge, Va., March 29–31, 1865; Five Forks, Va., April 1, 1865; Fall of Petersburg, Va., April 2, 1865; Appomattox Court House, Va., April 9, 1865.

On the state color.—Canal riot, Buffalo, 1849; Draft riots, New York, 1863; Railroad strike, Buffalo, 1877; Railroad strike, Buffalo, 1892; Lumbermen's strike, Tonawanda, 1893.

THIRTEENTH SEPARATE COMPANY.

(Fourth Brigade.)

State Armory, South Main street and Fenton place, Jamestown.

The thirteenth separate company was organized, August 23, 1875, as the first separate company, thirty-first brigade. Designation changed to fourth separate company, December 8, 1877, and to thirteenth separate company, September 4, 1882. It was in the state service at Buffalo, during switchmen's strike in August, 1892.

In accordance with special orders, No. 72, A. G. O., May 1, 1898, the thirteenth separate company left Jamestown at 3 p. m., and the sixty-fifth regiment, Buffalo, at 5 p. m., May 1st, en-route to the camp established at Hempstead Plains, L. I., where the regiment arrived on May 2d, and reported to Major-General Charles F. Roe, commanding national guard and the camp.

Companies K, L and M ordered to remain at Buffalo, pending their completion, were later directed to leave Buffalo on May 10th, and joined the regiment at Camp Black at 4 o'clock p. m., the next day.

Recruiting was continued to replace men rejected by the medical officers, and the regiment was mustered into the service of the United States, May 17, 1898, as the " sixty-fifth regiment, infantry,

New York volunteers." Fifty officers and nine hundred and eighty enlisted men, the full number required, were present at muster.

Under orders of the war department, the regiment moved from Camp Black at one o'clock p. m., May 19th, with camp equipage and ten days' field rations, en-route for camp near Falls Church, Virginia, afterwards designated as "Camp Russell A. Alger," leaving Camp Black station, via Long Island railroad on two trains at 1.40 and 1.50 p. m., respectively. The regiment detrained at Long Island City, and took ferry for Pennsylvania railroad station, Jersey City, arriving at 6 o'clock p. m., and departing in three sections at 7.30, 7.40 and 7.50 p. m. The first section arrived at St. Asaph, Virginia, at 3.15 a. m., and second and third sections arrived at Washington at 3.00 and 3.15 a. m.

The several sections reached Dunn Loring station, Virginia, May 20th, where regiment detrained, as follows: First, 9.30; second 10, and third, 10.20 a. m. All companies, except G and I, marched to camp under the command of Lieutenant-Colonel Chapin. No corps, division or brigade headquarters had been established. There was no officer present to report to, or to assign location of camp. Through the courtesy of Major M. C. Martin, depot quartermaster at Dunn Loring, a location was secured about three and one-half miles from the station into which the command moved at 3 o'clock p. m. The commanding officer remained at Dunn Loring with Major Babcock and companies G and I to arrange for the transportation of baggage to camp. The provided transportation being entirely inadequate, the work was not finished until 5.30 p. m., May 21st, at which hour the detachment left Dunn Loring, arriving at camp at 6.45 p. m.

May 24th, the regiment was by general orders, No. 2, headquarters second army corps, attached to the first brigade, first division, second army corps. The regiments composing the brigade were the first, New Jersey; seventh, Ohio, and sixty-fifth, New York. The brigade was commanded by Colonel E. A. Campbell, first New Jersey, until July 16th, on which day Brigadier-General

Joseph W. Plume assumed command, and continued until disbandment of the brigade.

June 6th, a recruiting party of three officers and twelve enlisted men was sent to Buffalo. This party recruited 333 men for the regiment and returned in detachments, the last arriving in camp, July 8th. During the month twenty-six members of the regiment were transferred to the hospital corps of the army.

June 7th, the location of the camp was moved about three-quarters of a mile to ground formerly occupied by the fourth regiment, Missouri volunteer infantry. The command remained on this ground until August 8th, when camp was moved about two miles to the Chittenden farm. During its stay at Camp Alger the regiment participated in four reviews and performed the usual camp duties; drills and schools were held daily, except Saturday and Sunday.

September 4th, pursuant to orders from headquarters, first division, second army corps, the regiment marched from Camp Alger at 10.30 a. m., en-route for Buffalo. The regiment left Dunn Loring station via Southern railway in four sections, the first starting at 11.40 a. m., followed by the others at intervals of about twenty minutes; proceeded to Buffalo via Pennsylvania, Northern-Central and New York Central railroads, arriving in Buffalo at 10 a. m., September 5th. The regiment paraded through the principal streets, preceded by a military and civic escort, arriving at the armory of the sixty-fifth regiment, N. G. N. Y., at 1 p. m. Orders were issued constituting the armory a military post and naming it " Camp Joseph W. Plume," in honor of the commanding general, first brigade, first division, second army corps. An order was issued granting all officers leaves of absence and all enlisted men furloughs for thirty days.

October 6th, the regiment assembled upon expiration of leaves and furloughs; preparations for muster-out were begun and continued until November 19, 1898, on which date the regiment was mustered out of the United States service.

SIXTY–FIFTH REGIMENT, INFANTRY.

Commissioned Officers.

COLONEL:

Samuel M. Welch, Jr., May 1 to November 19, 1898.

LIEUTENANT-COLONEL:

William Henry Chapin, May 1 to November 19, 1898.

MAJORS:

John David Howland, May 1 to November 1. 1898.
Charles E. P. Babcock, May 1 to November 19, 1898.
Eugene Alfred Smith, May 1 to November 19, 1898.

REGIMENTAL ADJUTANT:

Walter Fairfax Nurzey, May 1 to November 19, 1898.

REGIMENTAL QUARTERMASTER:

Guilford Reed Wilson, May 1 to November 19, 1898.

BATTALION ADJUTANTS:

Ambrose Stark Bixby, May 1 to November 19, 1898.
Frank Melville Chapin, May 1 to November 19, 1898.
James Ward Scribner, May 1 to November 19, 1898.

SURGEON:

Albert H. Briggs, May 1 to November 19, 1898.

ASSISTANT SURGEONS:

Harry Meade, May 1 to November 19, 1898.
Ernest Lewis Ruffner, May 2 to November 19, 1898.

CHAPLAIN:

Harvey Sheafe Fisher, May 3 to November 19, 1898.

COMPANY A.

CAPTAIN:

Henry Adsit Bull, May 1 to November 19, 1898.

FIRST LIEUTENANT:

Gains Barrett Rich, Jr., May 6 to November 19, 1898.

SECOND LIEUTENANT:

James Francis Nuno, May 1 to November 19, 1898.

COMPANY B.

CAPTAIN:

George Alfred Milsom, May 1 to November 19, 1898.

FIRST LIEUTENANT:

John Simpson Doorty, May 1 to November 19, 1898.

SECOND LIEUTENANT:

Harry J. Smith, May 1 to November 19, 1898.

COMPANY C.

CAPTAIN:

Jesse Hatch Behrends, May 1 to August 24, 1898.

FIRST LIEUTENANT:

John M. Hancock, May 2 to August 24, 1898.

SECOND LIEUTENANT:

John Gust Anderson, May 1 to November 19, 1898.

COMPANY D.

CAPTAIN:

Jacob Dorst, May 17 to November 19, 1898.

FIRST LIEUTENANT:

Fred J. Philcox, May 1 to November 19, 1898.

SECOND LIEUTENANTS:

Jacob Dorst, May 1 to May 16, 1898.
Gustav A. R. Ziemann, May 17 to November 19, 1898.

COMPANY E.

CAPTAINS:

Albert Gilbert, Jr., May 1 to July 5, 1898.
Frank Abirt Johnson, July 16 to November 19, 1898.

FIRST LIEUTENANTS:

Frank Abirt Johnson, May 1 to July 16, 1898.
Fred H. Wilson, July 16 to November 19, 1898.

SECOND LIEUTENANTS:

Fred H. Wilson, May 1 to July 16, 1898.
Samuel Miller Porter, July 20 to September 14, 1898.

COMPANY F.

CAPTAIN:

George Harvey Norton, May 1 to November 19, 1898.

FIRST LIEUTENANT:

Louis A. Fenton, May 1 to November 19, 1898.

SECOND LIEUTENANT:

Emery F. Southworth, May 1 to November 19, 1898.

COMPANY G.

CAPTAIN:

Arthur Bryant Christey, May 1 to November 19, 1898.

FIRST LIEUTENANT:

James Porter Fowler, May 1 to November 19, 1898.

SECOND LIEUTENANT:

Walter Cushing Barker, May 1 to November 19, 1898.

COMPANY H.

CAPTAIN:

George T. Bowman, May 1 to November 19, 1898.

FIRST LIEUTENANT:

James B. Webb, May 1 to November 19, 1898.

SECOND LIEUTENANT:

John M. O'Gorman, May 1 to November 19, 1898.

COMPANY I.

CAPTAIN:

Henry William Brendel, May 1 to November 19, 1898.

FIRST LIEUTENANT:

Walter Edgar Pagan, May 1 to November 19, 1898.

SECOND LIEUTENANT:

Nelson True Barrett, May 1 to November 19, 1898.

COMPANY K.

CAPTAIN:

Louis Locke Babcock, May 1 to November 19, 1898.

FIRST LIEUTENANT:

Ariel H. Ide, May 1 to November 19, 1898.

SECOND LIEUTENANT:

Danton P. Hughes, May 1 to November 19, 1898.

COMPANY L.

CAPTAIN:

Alfred John Erickson, May 1 to November 19, 1898.

FIRST LIEUTENANT:

Albert M. Briggs, May 1 to November 19, 1898.

SECOND LIEUTENANT:

Gerrit V. S. Quackenbush, May 1 to November 19, 1898.

COMPANY M.

CAPTAIN:

Louis Henry Eller, May 1 to November 19, 1898.

FIRST LIEUTENANT:

Seymour P. White, May 1 to November 19, 1898.

SECOND LIEUTENANT:

William S. Jackson, May 1 to November 19, 1898.

RECORDS OF THE OFFICERS AND ENLISTED MEN.

ABBOTT, CHARLES R.—Age, 21 years. Enlisted, May 1, 1898, at Buffalo, to serve two years; mustered in as sergeant, Co. M, May 17, 1898; mustered out with company, November 19, 1898, at Buffalo, N. Y.

ABLE, JOHN C.—Age, 36 years. Enlisted, May 1, 1898, at Buffalo, to serve two years; mustered in as private, Co. B, May 17, 1898; promoted corporal, June 23, 1898; mustered out with company, November 19, 1898, at Buffalo, N. Y.

ACKENDORP, JOHN G.—Age, 23 years. Enlisted, May 1, 1898, at Buffalo, to serve two years; mustered in as private, Co. F, May 17, 1898; mustered out with company, November 19, 1898, at Buffalo, N. Y.

ACKERMAN, CHARLES F.—Age, — years. Enlisted, June 24, 1898, at Buffalo, to serve two years; mustered in as private, Co. F, same date; transferred to band, June 29, 1898; mustered out with band, November 19, 1898, at Buffalo, N. Y.

AHRENS, FRANK.—Age, 22 years. Enlisted, May 1, 1898, at Buffalo, to serve two years; mustered in as private, Co. L, May 17, 1898; mustered out with company, November 19, 1898, at Buffalo, N. Y.

AHRENS, LOUIS.—Age, 21 years. Enlisted, May 1, 1898, at Buffalo, to serve two years; mustered in as private, Co. D, May 17, 1898; mustered out with company, November 19, 1898, at Buffalo, N. Y.

ALLEN, CHARLES.—Age, — years. Enlisted, June 15, 1898, at Buffalo, to serve two years; mustered in as private, Co. G, same date; mustered out with company, November 19, 1898, at Buffalo, N. Y.

ALLEN, LUCIUS C.—Age, 21 years. Enlisted, May 1, 1898, at Buffalo, to serve two years; mustered in as private, Co. E, May 17, 1898; mustered out with company, November 19, 1898, at Buffalo, N. Y.

ALLEN, THOMAS.—Age, 27 years. Enlisted, May 12, 1898, at Buffalo, to serve two years; mustered in as private, Co. A, May 17, 1898; mustered out with company, November 19, 1898, at Buffalo, N. Y.

ALPERT, JOSEPH W.—Age, 22 years. Enlisted, May 1, 1898, at Buffalo, to serve two years; mustered in as first sergeant, Co. L, May 17, 1898; mustered out with company, November 19, 1898, at Buffalo, N. Y.

ALTMAN, GUSTAVE F.—Age, — years. Enlisted, June 17, 1898, at Buffalo, to serve two years; mustered in as private, Co. F, same date; mustered out with company, November 19, 1898, at Buffalo, N. Y.

ALWINE, GEORGE M.—Age, 21 years. Enlisted, May 11, 1898, at Buffalo, to serve two years; mustered in as private, Co. A, May 17, 1898; mustered out with company, November 19, 1898, at Buffalo, N. Y.

AMBELLAM, ALBERT F.—Age, — years. Enlisted, July 2, 1898, at Buffalo, to serve two years; mustered in as private, Co. M, same date; mustered out with company, November 19, 1898, at Buffalo, N. Y.

AMBERG, JOHN.—Age, 23 years. Enlisted, May 1, 1898, at Buffalo, to serve two years; mustered in as private, Co. D, May 17, 1898; mustered out with company, November 19, 1898, at Buffalo, N. Y.

ANDERSON, CARL.—Age, — years. Enlisted, June 13, 1898, at Buffalo, to serve two years; mustered in as private, Co. M, same date; mustered out with company, November 19, 1898, at Buffalo, N. Y.

ANDERSON, ERNEST M.—Age, 24 years. Enlisted, May 1, 1898, at Buffalo, to serve two years; mustered in as sergeant, Co. C, May 17, 1898; mustered out with company, November 19, 1898, at Buffalo, N. Y.

ANDERSON, JOHN A.—Age, — years. Enlisted, June 15, 1898, at Buffalo, to serve two years; mustered in as private, Co. E, same date; mustered out with company, November 19, 1898, at Buffalo, N. Y.

ANDERSON, JOHN G.—Age, 39 years. Enrolled, May 1, 1898, at Buffalo, to serve two years; mustered in as second lieutenant, Co. C, May 17, 1898; mustered out with company, November 19, 1898, at Buffalo, N. Y.; commissioned second lieutenant, May 17, 1898, with rank from same date, original.

ANDERSON, OSCAR A.—Age, –- years. Enlisted, June 21, 1898, at Buffalo, to serve two years; mustered in as private, Co. E, same date; mustered out with company, November 19, 1898, at Buffalo, N. Y.

ANDREWS, JOHN.—Age, 25 years. Enlisted, May 13, 1898, at Camp Black, to serve two years; mustered in as private, Co. L, May 17, 1898; mustered out with company, November 19, 1898, at Buffalo, N. Y.

ANHEIER, EDWARD J.—Age, — years. Enlisted, June 22, 1898, at Buffalo, to serve two years; mustered in as private, Co. D, same date; mustered out with company, November 19, 1898, at Buffalo, N. Y.

ANNA, DANIEL C.—Age, 20 years. Enlisted, May 1, 1898, at Buffalo, to serve two years; mustered in as private, Co. M, May 17, 1898; mustered out with company, November 19, 1898, at Buffalo, N. Y.

ANNA, HENRY.—Age, 21 years. Enlisted, May 1, 1898, at Buffalo, to serve two years; mustered in as private, Co. K, May 17, 1898; mustered out with company, November 19, 1898, at Buffalo, N. Y.

ARBOGAST, JOSEPH C.—Age, 21 years. Enlisted, May 1, 1898, at Buffalo, to serve two years; mustered in as private, Co. L, May 17, 1898; transferred to Hospital Corps, United States Army, June 28, 1898; to Co. D, September 2, 1898; mustered out with company, November 19, 1898, at Buffalo, N. Y.

ARENDT, JAMES.—Age, 21 years. Enlisted, May 1, 1898, at Buffalo, to serve two years; mustered in as private, Co. F, May 17, 1898; mustered out with company, November 19, 1898, at Buffalo, N. Y.

ARMOUR, HENRY M.—Age, — years. Enlisted, June 22, 1898, at Buffalo, to serve two years; mustered in as private, Co. K, same date; mustered out with company, November 19, 1898, at Buffalo, N. Y.

ARNET, JOHN.—Age, — years. Enlisted, June 13, 1898, at Buffalo, to serve two years; mustered in as private, Co. C, same date; mustered out with company, November 19, 1898, at Buffalo, N. Y.

AST, EDWARD G.—Age, 23 years. Enlisted, May 1, 1898, at Buffalo, to serve two years; mustered in as private, Co. F, May 17, 1898; mustered out with company, November 19, 1898, at Buffalo, N. Y.

ATKINS, ROBERT J.—Age, 35 years. Enlisted, May 1, 1898, at Buffalo, to serve two years; mustered in as private, Co. D, May 17, 1898; promoted corporal, July 7, 1898; mustered out with company, November 19, 1898, at Buffalo, N. Y.

AUSTIN, LEWIS D.—Age, — years. Enlisted, June 13, 1898, at Buffalo, to serve two years; mustered in as private, Co. B, same date; mustered out with company, November 19, 1898, at Buffalo, N. Y.

AUSTIN, PERCY J.—Age, 21 years. Enlisted, May 1, 1898, at Buffalo, to serve two years; mustered in as private, Co. L, May 17, 1898; discharged for disability, July 20, 1898, at Camp Alger, near Dunn Loring, Va.

BABCOCK, CHESTER D.—Age, 23 years. Enlisted, May 1, 1898, at Jamestown, to serve two years; mustered in as private, Co. E, May 17, 1898; mustered out with company, November 19, 1898, at Buffalo, N. Y.

BABCOCK, LOUIS L.—Age, 29 years. Enrolled, May 1, 1898, at Buffalo, to serve two years; mustered in as captain, Co. K, May 17, 1898; mustered out with company, November 19, 1898, at Buffalo, N. Y.; commissioned captain, May 17, 1898, with rank from same date, original.

BAIGENT, JOHN.—Age, 41 years. Enlisted, May 1, 1898, at Buffalo, to serve two years; mustered in as private, Co. I, May 17, 1898; promoted corporal, July 12, 1898; mustered out with company, November 19, 1898, at Buffalo, N. Y.

BAILEY, ALVIN H.—Age, 22 years. Enlisted, May 1, 1898, at Buffalo, to serve two years; mustered in as private, Co. I, May 17, 1898; mustered out with company, November 19, 1898, at Buffalo, N. Y.

BAILEY, HARRY L.—Age, 21 years. Enlisted, May 1, 1898, at Buffalo, to serve two years; mustered in as corporal, Co. D, May 17, 1898; mustered out with company, November 19, 1898, at Buffalo, N. Y.

BAKER, HENRY I.—Age, — years. Enlisted, June 22, 1898, at Buffalo, to serve two years; mustered in as private, Co. K, same date; mustered out with company, November 19, 1898, at Buffalo, N. Y.

BALL, RICHARD L.—Age, 27 years. Enlisted, May 1, 1898, at Buffalo, to serve two years; mustered in as private, Co. C, May 17, 1898; promoted corporal, June 1, 1898; mustered out with company, November 19, 1898, at Buffalo, N. Y.

BALLIETT, ALBERT W.—Age, 21 years. Enlisted, May 1, 1898, at Buffalo, to serve two years; mustered in as sergeant, Co. I, May 17, 1898; mustered out with company, November 19, 1898, at Buffalo, N. Y.

BAMBERGER, LOUIS F.—Age, 21 years. Enlisted, May 1, 1898, at Buffalo, to serve two years; mustered in as private, Co. B, May 17, 1898; mustered out with company, November 19, 1898, at Buffalo, N. Y.

BANKS, GEORGE B.—Age, 30 years. Enlisted, May 1, 1898, at Buffalo, to serve two years; mustered in as private, Co. C, May 17, 1898; mustered out with company, November 19, 1898, at Buffalo, N. Y.

BARKER, CHARLES.—Age, 23 years. Enlisted, May 1, 1898, at Buffalo, to serve two years; mustered in as private, Co. I, May 17, 1898; mustered out with company, November 19, 1898, at Buffalo, N. Y.

BARKER, HARRY W.—Age, 21 years. Enlisted, May 1, 1898, at Buffalo, to serve two years; mustered in as private, Co. E, May 17, 1898; mustered out with company, November 19, 1898, at Buffalo, N. Y.

BARKER, WALTER C.—Age, 31 years. Enrolled, May 1, 1898, at Buffalo, to serve two years; mustered in as second lieutenant, Co. G, May 17, 1898; mustered out with company, November 19, 1898, at Buffalo, N. Y.; commissioned second lieutenant, May 17, 1898, with rank from same date, original.

BARONCINI, JOHN.—Age, 21 years. Enlisted, May 1, 1898, at Buffalo, to serve two years; mustered in as private, Co. B, May 17, 1898; mustered out with company, November 19, 1898, at Buffalo, N. Y.

BARRETT, JOHN J.—Age, — years. Enlisted, June 27, 1898, at Buffalo, to serve two years; mustered in as private, Co. H, same date; mustered out with company, November 19, 1898, at Buffalo, N. Y.

BARRETT, NELSON T.—Age, 29 years. Enrolled, May 1, 1898, at Buffalo, to serve two years; mustered in as second lieutenant, Co. I, May 17, 1898; mustered out with company, November 19, 1898, at Buffalo, N. Y.; commissioned second lieutenant, May 17, 1898, with rank from same date, original.

BARROWS, RANSOM J.—Age, — years. Enlisted, June 15, 1898, at Buffalo, to serve two years; mustered in as private, Co. E, same date; mustered out with company, November 19, 1898, at Buffalo, N. Y.

BARTZ, ALBERT H.—Age, 21 years. Enlisted, May 1, 1898, at Buffalo, to serve two years; mustered in as private, Co. I, May 17, 1898; mustered out with company, November 19, 1898 at Buffalo N. Y.

BATTAGLIS, ANTONIO.—Age, — years. Enlisted, June 24, 1898, at Buffalo, to serve two years; mustered in as private, Co. C, same date; transferred to band, June 29, 1898; mustered out with band, November 19, 1898, at Buffalo, N. Y.

BATY, DELBERT.—Age, 25 years. Enlisted, May 1, 1898, at Buffalo, to serve two years; mustered in as private, Co. I, May 17, 1898; mustered out with company, November 19, 1898, at Buffalo, N. Y.

BAUER, LOUIS.—Age, 21 years. Enlisted, May 1, 1898, at Buffalo, to serve two years; mustered in as private, Co. F, May 17, 1898; discharged for disability, June 28, 1898.

BAUMGARTNER, CHARLES L.—Age, — years. Enlisted, June 22, 1898, at Buffalo, to serve two years; mustered in as private, Co. L, same date; mustered out with company, November 19, 1898, at Buffalo, N. Y.

BAUSS, ANTON.—Age, 28 years. Enlisted, May 1, 1898, at Buffalo, to serve two years; mustered in as corporal, Co. D, May 17, 1898; mustered out with company, November 19, 1898, at Buffalo, N. Y.

BEACH, LEO.—Age, — years. Enlisted, June 15, 1898, at Buffalo, to serve two years; mustered in as private, Co. E, same date; mustered out with company, November 19, 1898, at Buffalo, N. Y.

BEALS, EDWARD.—Age, — years. Enlisted, June 21, 1898, at Buffalo, to serve two years; mustered in as private, Co. A, same date; deserted, October 6, 1898.

BECK, ROBERT J. M.—Age, 28 years. Enlisted, May 1, 1898, at Buffalo, to serve two years; mustered in as private, Co. I, May 17, 1898; mustered out with company, November 19, 1898, at Buffalo, N. Y.

BECKER, JACOB.—Age, — years. Enlisted, June 14, 1898, at Buffalo, to serve two years; mustered in as private, Co. H, same date; mustered out with company, November 19, 1898, at Buffalo, N. Y.

BECKERT, JOSEPH.—Age, — years. Enlisted, June 14, 1898, at Buffalo, to serve two years; mustered in as private, Co. I, same date; mustered out with company, November 19, 1898, at Buffalo, N. Y.

BECKETT, HARRY.—Age, — years. Enlisted, June 14, 1898, at Buffalo, to serve two years; mustered in as private, Co. L, same date; mustered out with company, November 19, 1898, at Buffalo, N. Y.

BEHRENDS, JESSE H.—Age, 31 years. Enrolled, May 1, 1898, at Buffalo, to serve two years; mustered in as captain, Co. C, May 17, 1898; discharged, August 24, 1898; commissioned captain, May 17, 1898, with rank from same date, original.

BEHRENDS, JESSE M.—Age, — years. Enlisted, June 15, 1898, at Buffalo, to serve two years; mustered in as private, Co. F, same date; mustered out with company, November 19, 1898, at Buffalo, N. Y.

BEILMAN, CHARLES S.—Age, 22 years. Enlisted, May 1, 1898, at Buffalo, to serve two years; mustered in as corporal, Co. C, May 17, 1898; promoted sergeant, June 1, 1898; mustered out with company, November 19, 1898, at Buffalo, N. Y.

BEIRNFIELD, JOHN.—Age, 22 years. Enlisted, May 1, 1898, at Buffalo, to serve two years; mustered in as private, Co. G, May 17, 1898; mustered out with company, November 19, 1898, at Buffalo, N. Y.

BENDER, HERMAN.—Age, 23 years. Enlisted, May 1, 1898, at Buffalo, to serve two years; mustered in as private, Co. D, May 17, 1898; promoted corporal, July 7, 1898; mustered out with company, November 19, 1898, at Buffalo, N. Y.

BENDUS, JULIUS V.—Age, — years. Enlisted, June 16, 1898, at Buffalo, to serve two years; mustered in as private, Co. F, same date; mustered out with company, November 19, 1898, at Buffalo, N. Y.

BENEDICT, CHARLES E.—Age, 21 years. Enlisted, May 1, 1898, at Buffalo, to serve two years; mustered in as private, Co. F, May 17, 1898; mustered out with company, November 19, 1898, at Buffalo, N. Y.

BENNETT, JOHN W.—Age, 31 years.   Enlisted, May 1, 1898, at Buffalo, to serve two years; mustered in as private, Co. I, May 17, 1898; mustered out with company, November 19, 1898, at Buffalo, N. Y.

BENNETT, JOSEPH J.—Age, 22 years.   Enlisted, May 1, 1898, at Buffalo, to serve two years; mustered in as private, Co. K, May 17, 1898; discharged for disability, August 29, 1898, at Camp Alger, near Dunn Loring, Va.

BENTLEY, WILLIAM.—Age, 22 years.   Enlisted, May 1, 1898, at Buffalo, to serve two years; mustered in as private, Co. G, May 17, 1898; mustered out with company, November 19, 1898, at Buffalo, N. Y.

BENZINO, JULIUS.—Age, 20 years.   Enlisted, May 1, 1898, at Buffalo, to serve two years; mustered in as private, Co. M, May 17, 1898; mustered out with company, November 19, 1898, at Buffalo, N. Y.

BERESNIEWICZ, JOHN.—Age, 21 years.   Enlisted, May 1, 1898, at Buffalo, to serve two years; mustered in as private, Co. B, May 17, 1898; mustered out with company, November 19, 1898, at Buffalo, N. Y.

BERG, GUST F.—Age, 21 years.   Enlisted, May 1, 1898, at Jamestown, to serve two years; mustered in as private, Co. E, May 17, 1898; mustered out with company, November 19, 1898, at Buffalo, N. Y.

BERGLAND, WALDEMAR.—Age, 32 years.   Enlisted, May 1, 1898, at Buffalo, to serve two years; mustered in as private, Co. K, May 17, 1898; mustered out with company, November 19, 1898, at Buffalo, N. Y.

BERK, SAMUEL J.—Age 29 years.   Enlisted, May 1, 1898, at Buffalo, to serve two years; mustered in as private, Co. L, May 17, 1898; mustered out with company, November 19, 1898, at Buffalo, N. Y.

BERNHARD, JOSEPH F.—Age, — years.   Enlisted, June 14, 1898, at Buffalo, to serve two years; mustered in as private, Co. C, same date; mustered out with company, November 19, 1898, at Buffalo, N. Y.

BERST, JOHN.—Age, 19 years. Enlisted, May 1, 1898, at Buffalo, to serve two years; mustered in as private, Co. A, May 17, 1898; mustered out with company, November 19, 1898, at Buffalo, N. Y.

BEYER, HENRY E.—Age, 19 years. Enlisted, May 1, 1898, at Buffalo, to serve two years; mustered in as private, Co. G, May 17, 1898; mustered out with company, November 19, 1898, at Buffalo, N. Y.

BEYER, HERMAN.—Age, 22 years. Enlisted, May 1, 1898, at Buffalo, to serve two years; mustered in as private, Co. B, May 17, 1898; mustered out with company, November 19, 1898, at Buffalo, N. Y.

BEYER, JOSEPH.—Age, 23 years. Enlisted, May 11, 1898, at Buffalo, to serve two years; mustered in as private, Co. A, May 17, 1898; mustered out with company, November 19, 1898, at Buffalo, N. Y.

BEYER, WALTER O.—Age, 20 years. Enlisted, May 1, 1898, at Buffalo, to serve two years; mustered in as corporal, Co. G, May 17, 1898; mustered out with company, November 19, 1898, at Buffalo, N. Y.

BIDWELL, HARRY.—Age, 25 years. Enlisted, May 11, 1898, at Buffalo, to serve two years; mustered in as private, Co. A, May 17, 1898; mustered out with company, November 19, 1898, at Buffalo, N. Y.

BIGGS, HENRY.—Age, — years. Enlisted, June 24, 1898, at Buffalo, to serve two years; mustered in as private, Co. B, same date; transferred to band, June 29, 1898; mustered out with band, November 19, 1898, at Buffalo, N. Y.

BIGOSS, JOHN.—Age, 21 years. Enlisted, May 1, 1898, at Buffalo, to serve two years; mustered in as private, Co. L, May 17, 1898; mustered out with company, November 19, 1898, at Buffalo, N. Y.

BILESKI, FRANK H.—Age, — years. Enlisted, June 13, 1898, at Buffalo, to serve two years; mustered in as private, Co. L, same date; mustered out with company, November 19, 1898, at Buffalo, N. Y.

BILLINGS, ALLEN E.—Age, 27 years. Enlisted, May 1, 1898, at Jamestown, to serve two years; mustered in as private, Co. E, May 17, 1898; mustered out with company, November 19, 1898, at Buffalo, N. Y.

BILLINGS, ARTHER CONVERSE.—Age, 19 years. Enlisted, May 1, 1898, at Buffalo, to serve two years; mustered in as private, Co. I, May 17, 1898; mustered out with company, November 19, 1898, at Buffalo, N. Y.

BILLINGS, JR., HENRY E.—Age, 29 years. Enlisted, May 1, 1898, at Buffalo, to serve two years; mustered in as corporal, Co. M, May 17, 1898; mustered out with company, November 19, 1898, at Buffalo, N. Y.

BILLINGS, PHILO D.—Age, — years. Enlisted, June 13, 1898, at Buffalo, to serve two years; mustered in as private, Co. I, same date; mustered out with company, November 19, 1898, at Buffalo, N. Y.

BINGEMANN, CHARLES W.—Age, 17 years. Enlisted, May 1, 1898, at Buffalo, to serve two years; mustered in as musician, Co. G, May 17, 1898; mustered out with company, November 19, 1898, at Buffalo, N. Y.

BINGERMAN, GEORGE.—Age, 23 years. Enlisted, May 1, 1898, at Buffalo, to serve two years; mustered in as private, Co. K, May 17, 1898; mustered out with company, November 19, 1898, at Buffalo, N. Y.

BISSELL, JAY CLARK.—Age, 26 years. Enlisted, May 1, 1898, at Buffalo, to serve two years; mustered in as private, Co. F, May 17, 1898; promoted corporal, September 3, 1898; transferred to the Two Hundred and Second Regiment, New York Volunteer Infantry, November 9, 1898.

BITTNER, MICHAEL.—Age, 22 years. Enlisted, May 1, 1898, at Buffalo, to serve two years; mustered in as private, Co. L, May 17, 1898; discharged for disability, July 3, 1898, at Camp Alger, near Dunn Loring, Va.

BIXBY, AMBROSE S.—Age, 42 years. Enrolled, May 1, 1898, at Buffalo, to serve two years; mustered in as first lieutenant and battalion adjutant, May 17, 1898; mustered out with regiment, November 19, 1898, at Buffalo, N. Y.; commissioned first lieutenant and battalion adjutant, May 17, 1898, with rank from same date, original.

BLACK, LEROY C.—Age, 29 years. Enlisted, May 1, 1898, at Buffalo, to serve two years; mustered in as private, Co. A, May 17, 1898; mustered out with company, November 19, 1898, at Buffalo, N. Y.

BLACKBURN, THOMAS.—Age, 21 years. Enlisted, May 1, 1898, at Buffalo, to serve two years; mustered in as private, Co. M, May 17, 1898; mustered out with company, November 19, 1898, at Buffalo, N. Y.

BLAIR, WILLIAM J.—Age, 29 years. Enlisted, May 1, 1898, at Buffalo, to serve two years; mustered in as first sergeant, Co. D, May 17, 1898; mustered out with company, November 19, 1898, at Buffalo, N. Y.

BLAKE, EDWARD.—Age, 32 years. Enlisted, May 1, 1898, at Buffalo, to serve two years; mustered in as private, Co. H, May 17, 1898; mustered out with company, November 19, 1898, at Buffalo, N. Y.

BLARR, GEORGE.—Age, 23 years. Enlisted, May 1, 1898, at Buffalo, to serve two years; mustered in as private, Co. H, May 17, 1898; promoted corporal, July 25, 1898; mustered out with company, November 19, 1898, at Buffalo, N. Y.

BLESS, AUGUST J.—Age, 24 years. Enlisted, May 1, 1898, at Buffalo, to serve two years; mustered in as sergeant, Co. D, May 17, 1898; mustered out with company, November 19, 1898, at Buffalo, N. Y.

BLIGHTON, WILLIAM L.—Age, 26 years. Enlisted, May 1, 1898, at Buffalo, to serve two years; mustered in as private, Co. H, May 17, 1898; transferred to Hospital Corps, United States Army, June 28, 1898; to Co. C, September 2, 1898; mustered out with company, November 19, 1898, at Buffalo, N. Y.

BLISS, DANIEL R.—Age, — years. Enlisted, June 24, 1898, at Buffalo, to serve two years; mustered in as private, Co. D, same date; transferred to band, June 29, 1898; mustered out with band, November 19, 1898, at Buffalo, N. Y.

BLISS, MERLIN E.—Age, 25 years. Enlisted, May 1, 1898, at Jamestown, to serve two years; mustered in as private, Co. E, May 17, 1898; mustered out with company, November 19, 1898, at Buffalo, N. Y.

BOHN, JOSEPH F.—Age, 19 years. Enlisted, May 1, 1898, at Buffalo, to serve two years; mustered in as private, Co. K, May 17, 1898; mustered out with company, November 19, 1898, at Buffalo, N. Y.

BOLL, CHARLES J.—Age, 26 years. Enlisted, May 1, 1898, at Buffalo, to serve two years; mustered in as private, Co. C, May 17, 1898; mustered out with company, November 19, 1898, at Buffalo, N. Y.

BOLLER, JOHN M.—Age, 36 years. Enlisted, May 11, 1898, at Buffalo, to serve two years; mustered in as private, Co. A, May 17, 1898; mustered out with company, November 19, 1898, at Buffalo, N. Y.

BORDEN, GEORGE W.—Age, 29 years. Enlisted, May 1, 1898, at Buffalo, to serve two years; mustered in as private, Co. K, May 17, 1898; mustered out with company, November 19, 1898, at Buffalo, N. Y.

BORK, CHARLES.—Age, 21 years. Enlisted, May 1, 1898, at Buffalo, to serve two years; mustered in as private, Co. C, May 17, 1898; mustered out with company, November 19, 1898, at Buffalo, N. Y.

BORK, JOHN.—Age, 23 years. Enlisted, May 1, 1898, at Buffalo, to serve two years; mustered in as private, Co. B, May 17, 1898; mustered out with company, November 19, 1898, at Buffalo, N. Y.

BOSH, CHARLES.—Age, — years. Enlisted, June 22, 1898, at Buffalo, to serve two years; mustered in as private, Co. K, same date; mustered out with company, November 19, 1898, at Buffalo, N. Y.

BOUPREY, HUBERT.—Age, 24 years. Enlisted, May 1, 1898, at Buffalo, to serve two years; mustered in as private, Co. A, May 17, 1898; mustered out with company, November 19, 1898, at Buffalo, N. Y.

BOWMAN, GEORGE T.—Age, 28 years. Enrolled, May 1, 1898, at Buffalo, to serve two years; mustered in as captain, Co. H, May 17, 1898; mustered out with company, November 19, 1898, at Buffalo, N. Y.; subsequent service as first lieutenant, Thirty-sixth Regiment, United States Volunteer Infantry; commissioned captain, May 17, 1898, with rank from same date, original.

BOXALL, GEORGE H.—Age, 36 years.   Enlisted, May 1, 1898, at Buffalo, to serve two years; mustered in as first sergeant, Co. F, May 17, 1898; mustered out with company, November 19, 1898, at Buffalo, N. Y.

BOY, CHARLES W.—Age, 21 years.   Enlisted, May 1, 1898, at Buffalo, to serve two years; mustered in as private, Co.· I, May 17, 1898; mustered out with company, November 19, 1898, at Buffalo, N. Y.

BOYD, GEORGE E.—Age, — years.   Enlisted, June 17, 1898, at Buffalo, to serve two years; mustered in as private, Co. D, same date; mustered out with company, November 19, 1898, at Buffalo, N. Y.

BOYD, JAMES A.—Age, 24 years.   Enlisted, May 1, 1898, at Buffalo, to serve two years; mustered in as private, Co. D, May 17, 1898; mustered out with company, November 19, 1898, at Buffalo, N. Y.

BOYD, JAMES F.—Age, 31 years.   Enlisted, May 1, 1898, at Buffalo, to serve two years; mustered in as private, Co. B, May 17, 1898; promoted corporal, June 23, 1898; mustered out with company, November 19, 1898, at Buffalo, N. Y.

BOYLE, EDWARD G.—Age, 29 years.   Enlisted, May 1, 1898, at Buffalo, to serve two years; mustered in as private, Co. G, May 17, 1898; mustered out with company, November 19, 1898, at Buffalo, N. Y.

BOYLE, GEORGE.—Age, — years.   Enlisted, June 13, 1898, at Buffalo, to serve two years; mustered in as private, Co. F, same date; mustered out with company, November 19, 1898, at Buffalo, N. Y.

BOYLE, JAMES L.—Age, 28 years.   Enlisted, May 1, 1898, at Buffalo, to serve two years; mustered in as private, Co. M, May 17, 1898; mustered out with company, November 19, 1898, at Buffalo, N. Y.

BOYLE, JOHN D.—Age, — years.   Enlisted, June 21, 1898, at Camp Alger, near Dunn Loring, Va., to serve two years; mustered in as private, Co. G, same date; mustered out with company, November 19, 1898, at Buffalo, N. Y.

BRADFORD, CHARLES EDWARD.—Age, — years. Enlisted, July 19, 1898, at Camp Alger, near Dunn Loring, Va., to serve two years; mustered in as private, Co. K, same date; transferred to band, July 19, 1898; to Two Hundred and First New York Volunteer Infantry, November 7, 1898.

BRAIN, WILLIAM R.—Age, 23 years. Enlisted, May 11, 1898, at Buffalo, to serve two years; mustered in as private, Co. A, May 17, 1898; mustered out with company, November 19, 1898, at Buffalo, N. Y.

BRATH, EDWARD.—Age, 19 years. Enlisted, May 1, 1898, at Buffalo, to serve two years; mustered in as private, Co. M, May 17, 1898; mustered out with company, November 19, 1898, at Buffalo, N. Y.

BRAUERLISH, WILLIAM J.—Age, 32 years. Enlisted, May 1, 1898, at Buffalo, to serve two years; mustered in as private, Co. L, May 17, 1898; mustered out with company, November 19, 1898, at Buffalo, N. Y.

BRAUN, CHARLES V.—Age, — years. Enlisted, June 22, 1898, at Buffalo, to serve two years; mustered in as private, Co. D, same date; mustered out with company, November 19, 1898, at Buffalo, N. Y.

BRAUN, JOSEPH.—Age, 21 years. Enlisted, May 12, 1898, at Camp Black, to serve two years; mustered in as private, Co. H, May 17, 1898; mustered out with company, November 19, 1898, at Buffalo, N. Y.

BREEDEN, WALDO.—Age, 21 years. Enlisted, May 1, 1898, at Jamestown, to serve two years; mustered in as private, Co. E, May 17, 1898; mustered out with company, November 19, 1898, at Buffalo, N. Y.

BREITUNG, FRANK.—Age, 21 years. Enlisted, May 1, 1898, at Buffalo, to serve two years; mustered in as private, Co. L, May 17, 1898; mustered out with company, November 19, 1898, at Buffalo, N. Y.

BRENDEL, HENRY W.—Age, 40 years. Enrolled, May 1, 1898, at Buffalo, to serve two years; mustered in as captain, Co. I, May 17, 1898; mustered out, to date, November 19, 1898, at Buffalo, N. Y.; commissioned captain, May 17, 1898, with rank from same date, original.

BRETHAUER, CHARLES.—Age, — years.   Enlisted, July 1, 1898, at Buffalo, to serve two years; mustered in as private, Co. F, same date; mustered out with company, November 19, 1898, at Buffalo, N. Y.

BRICK, CHARLES G.—Age, 27 years.   Enlisted, May 1, 1898, at Buffalo, to serve two years; mustered in as private, Co. I, May 17, 1898; mustered out with company, November 19, 1898, at Buffalo, N. Y.

BRIGGS, ALBERT H.—Age, 55 years.   Enrolled, May 1, 1898, at Buffalo, to serve two years; mustered in as major and surgeon, May 6, 1898; mustered out with regiment, November 19, 1898, at Buffalo, N. Y.; commissioned major and surgeon, May 6, 1898, with rank from same date, original.

BRIGGS, ALBERT M.—Age, 24 years.   Enrolled, May 1, 1898, at Buffalo, to serve two years; mustered in as first lieutenant, Co. L, May 17, 1898; mustered out with company, November 19, 1898, at Buffalo, N. Y.; commissioned first lieutenant, May 17, 1898, with rank from same date, original.

BRIGGS, ASA J.—Age, — years.   Enlisted, June 16, 1898, at Buffalo, to serve two years; mustered in as private, Co. G, same date; mustered out with company, November 19, 1898, at Buffalo, N. Y.

BRILMAN, WILLIAM E.—Age, 19 years.   Enlisted, May 1, 1898, at Buffalo, to serve two years; mustered in as private, Co. C, May 17, 1898; mustered out with company, November 19, 1898, at Buffalo, N. Y.

BRINK, HENRY.—Age, 28 years.   Enlisted, May 1, 1898, at Buffalo, to serve two years; mustered in as private, Co. M, May 17, 1898; mustered out with company, November 19, 1898, at Buffalo, N. Y.

BROMBACHER, ALBERT J.—Age, 19 years.   Enlisted, May 1, 1898, at Buffalo, to serve two years; mustered in as private, Co. I, May 17, 1898; mustered out with company, November 19, 1898, at Buffalo, N. Y.

BROOKS, GEORGE W.—Age, 23 years.   Enlisted, May 1, 1898, at Buffalo, to serve two years; mustered in as private, Co. B,

BROST, JACOB.—Age, — years. Enlisted, June 14, 1898, at Buffalo, to serve two years; mustered in as private, Co. I, same date; mustered out with company, November 19, 1898, at Buffalo, N. Y.

BROTHERS, THOMAS P.—Age, — years. Enlisted, June 20, 1898, at Buffalo, to serve two years; mustered in as private, Co. D, same date; mustered out with company, November 19, 1898, at Buffalo, N. Y.

BROWN, ARTHUR C.—Age, 27 years. Enlisted, May 1, 1898, at Buffalo, to serve two years; mustered in as private, Co. B, May 17, 1898; mustered out with company, November 19, 1898, at Buffalo, N. Y.

BROWN, DONALD S.—Age, 43 years. Enlisted, May 1, 1898, at Jamestown, to serve two years; mustered in as corporal, Co. E, May 17, 1898; mustered out with company, November 19, 1898, at Buffalo, N. Y.

BROWN, HERBERT W.—Age, 20 years. Enlisted, May 1, 1898, at Jamestown, to serve two years; mustered in as private, Co. E, May 17, 1898; mustered out with company, November 19, 1898, at Buffalo, N. Y.

BROWN, PATRICK.—Age, 28 years. Enlisted, May 1, 1898, at Buffalo, to serve two years; mustered in as private, Co. K, May 17, 1898; mustered out with company, November 19, 1898, at Buffalo, N. Y.

BRUNNER, JOHN J.—Age, 24 years. Enlisted, May 1, 1898, at Buffalo, to serve two years; mustered in as private, Co. C, May 17, 1898; mustered out with company, November 19, 1898, at Buffalo, N. Y.

BRUNSKILL, JOHN.—Age, 21 years. Enlisted, May 1, 1898, at Buffalo, to serve two years; mustered in as corporal, Co. G, May 17, 1898; mustered out with company, November 19, 1898, at Buffalo, N. Y.

BRYANT, CHARLES W.—Age, 22 years. Enlisted, May 1, 1898, at Buffalo, to serve two years; mustered in as private, Co. B, May 17, 1898; mustered out with company, November 19, 1898, at Buffalo, N. Y.

BUCHHOLZ, AUGUST F.—Age, 19 years. Enlisted, May 1, 1898, at Buffalo, to serve two years; mustered in as private, Co. A, May 17, 1898; mustered out with company, November 19, 1898, at Buffalo, N. Y.

BUCHRINGER, JOHN M.—Age, 29 years. Enlisted, May 1, 1898, at Buffalo, to serve two years; mustered in as sergeant, Co. F, May 17, 1898; mustered out with company, November 19, 1898, at Buffalo, N. Y.

BUCKLEY, JOHN.—Age, 21 years. Enlisted, May 1, 1898, at Buffalo, to serve two years; mustered in as private, Co. L, May 17, 1898; mustered out with company, November 19, 1898, at Buffalo, N. Y.

BUDDENBORG, JOSEPH.—Age, — years. Enlisted, June 14, 1898, at Buffalo, to serve two years; mustered in as private, Co. B, same date; mustered out with company, November 19, 1898, at Buffalo, N. Y.

BUGMANN, JOHN J.—Age, 21 years. Enlisted, May 1, 1898, at Buffalo, to serve two years; mustered in as private, Co. B, May 17, 1898; mustered out with company, November 19, 1898, at Buffalo, N. Y.

BULL, CHARLES A.—Age, 21 years. Enlisted, May 1, 1898, at Buffalo, to serve two years; mustered in as private, Co. G, May 17, 1898; mustered out with company, November 19, 1898, at Buffalo, N. Y.

BULL, HENRY A.—Age, 24 years. Enrolled, May 1, 1898, at Buffalo, to serve two years; mustered in as captain, Co. A, May 17, 1898; mustered out with company, November 19, 1898, at Buffalo, N. Y.; commissioned capta'n, May 17, 1898, with rank from same date, original.

BUNZ, EDWARD.—Age, 21 years. Enlisted, May 1, 1898, at Buffalo, to serve two years; mustered in as sergeant, Co. A, May 17, 1898; mustered out with company, November 19, 1898, at Buffalo, N. Y.

BURGHEN, WILLIAM J.—Age, 35 years. Enlisted, May 1, 1898, at Buffalo, to serve two years; mustered in as private, Co. C, May 17, 1898; mustered out with company, November 19, 1898, at Buffalo, N. Y.

BURK, CHARLES.—Age, — years. Enlisted, June 13, 1898, at Buffalo, to serve two years; mustered in as private, Co. C, June 17, 1898; mustered out with company, November 19, 1898, at Buffalo, N. Y.

BURKHARD, CHARLES H.—Age, 22 years. Enlisted, May 1, 1898, at Buffalo, to serve two years; mustered in as private, Co. L, May 17, 1898; mustered out with company, November 19, 1898, at Buffalo, N. Y.

BURNS, JOHN H.—Age, — years. Enlisted, June 13, 1898, at Buffalo, to serve two years; mustered in as private, Co. H, same date; promoted corporal, July 25, 1898; mustered out with company, November 19, 1898, at Buffalo, N. Y.

BURNS, WILLIAM.—Age, 21 years. Enlisted, May 1, 1898, at Buffalo, to serve two years; mustered in as corporal, Co. L, May 17, 1898; mustered out with company, November 19, 1898, at Buffalo, N. Y.

BURRETT, DEXTER C.—Age, 26 years. Enlisted, May 1, 1898, at Buffalo, to serve two years; mustered in as private, Co. C, May 17, 1898; mustered out with company, November 19, 1898, at Buffalo, N. Y.

BUSH, LYMAN M.—Age, 22 years. Enlisted, May 15, 1898, at Jamestown, to serve two years; mustered in as private, Co. E, May 17, 1898; mustered out with company, November 19, 1898, at Buffalo, N. Y.

BUSH, MARK P.—Age, 23 years. Enlisted, May 1, 1898, at Buffalo, to serve two years; mustered in as private, Co. L, May 17, 1898; promoted corporal, July 9, 1898; mustered out with company, November 19, 1898, at Buffalo, N. Y.

BUSHEY, LEVI.—Age, — years. Enlisted, June 13, 1898, at Buffalo, to serve two years; mustered in as private, Co. B, same date; mustered out with company, November 19, 1898, at Buffalo, N. Y.

BUSHMAN, EDGAR C.—Age, — years. Enlisted, June 15, 1898, at Buffalo, to serve two years; mustered in as private, Co. A, same date; mustered out with company, November 19, 1898, at Buffalo, N. Y.

BUTLER, BENJAMIN.—Age, 25 years. Enlisted, May 1, 1898, at Buffalo, to serve two years; mustered in as private, Co. I, May 17, 1898; mustered out with company, November 19, 1898, at Buffalo, N. Y.

BUTTS, GEORGE R.—Age, 40 years. Enlisted, May 1, 1898, at Jamestown, to serve two years; mustered in as private, Co. E, May 17, 1898; promoted corporal, July 17, 1898; mustered out with company, November 19, 1898, at Buffalo, N. Y.

BUTTS, PERL A.—Age, 32 years. Enlisted, May 1, 1898, at Jamestown, to serve two years; mustered in as quartermaster-sergeant, Co. E, May 17, 1898; promoted first sergeant, July 21, 1898; mustered out with company, November 19, 1898, at Buffalo, N. Y.

BUXTON, CLARENCE B.—Age, 21 years. Enlisted, May 1, 1898, at Jamestown, to serve two years; mustered in as private, Co. E, May 17, 1898; mustered out with company, November 19, 1898, at Buffalo, N. Y.

BUZE, THEODORE R.—Age, 19 years. Enlisted, May 1, 1898, at Buffalo, to serve two years; mustered in as private, Co. M, May 17, 1898; mustered out with company, November 19, 1898, at Buffalo, N. Y.

CALLAHAN, JOHN J.—Age, — years. Enlisted, June 17, 1898, at Buffalo, to serve two years; mustered in as private, Co. G, same date; mustered out with company, November 19, 1898, at Buffalo, N. Y.

CALLAHAN, JR., JOHN.—Age, — years. Enlisted, June 25, 1898, at Buffalo, to serve two years; mustered in as private, Co. M, same date; mustered out with company, November 19, 1898, at Buffalo, N. Y.

CAMP, EDWARD.—Age, 43 years. Enlisted, May 1, 1898, at Buffalo, to serve two years; mustered in as corporal, Co. H, May 17, 1898; mustered out with company, November 19, 1898, at Buffalo, N. Y.

CANTLIN, JOHN A.—Age, — years. Enlisted, June 17, 1898, at Buffalo, to serve two years; mustered in as private, Co. A, same date; died of typhoid fever, September 17, 1898, at Buffalo, N. Y.

CAPLICK, HENRY F.—Age, 25 years. Enlisted, May 1, 1898, at Buffalo, to serve two years; mustered in as sergeant, Co. C, May 17, 1898; mustered out with company, November 19, 1898, at Buffalo, N. Y.

CAREY, JOSEPH P.—Age, 34 years. Enlisted, May 1, 1898, at Buffalo, to serve two years; mustered in as private, Co. I, May 17, 1898; promoted corporal, July 1, 1898; mustered out with company, November 19, 1898, at Buffalo, N. Y.

CARGILLE, FRED G.—Age, 22 years. Enlisted, May 1, 1898, at Buffalo, to serve two years; mustered in as private, Co. A, May 17, 1898; mustered out with company, November 19, 1898, at Buffalo, N. Y.

CARL, JOHN J.—Age, 18 years. Enlisted, May 1, 1898, at Buffalo, to serve two years; mustered in as private, Co. D, May 17, 1898; mustered out with company, November 19, 1898, at Buffalo, N. Y.

CARLIN, EDWARD.—Age, 23 years. Enlisted, May 1, 1898, at Buffalo, to serve two years; mustered in as private, Co. C, May 17, 1898; mustered out with company, November 19, 1898, at Buffalo, N. Y.

CARLSON, ANTON.—Age, 25 years. Enlisted, May 1, 1898, at Buffalo, to serve two years; mustered in as private, Co. K, May 17, 1898; mustered out with company, November 19, 1898, at Buffalo, N. Y.

CARNEY, THOMAS J.—Age, — years. Enlisted, June 13, 1898, at Buffalo, to serve two years; mustered in as private, Co. A, same date; discharged for disability, September 1, 1898, at Buffalo, N. Y.

CARSCADDIN, WILLIAM J.—Age, 24 years. Enlisted, May 1, 1898, at Buffalo, to serve two years; mustered in as private, Co. I, May 17, 1898; mustered out with company, November 19, 1898, at Buffalo, N. Y.

CARTER, EARL.—Age, 21 years. Enlisted, May 1, 1898, at Buffalo, to serve two years; mustered in as private, Co. B, May 17, 1898; died of typhoid fever, August 14, 1898, in First Division, Second Army Corps Hospital, Camp Alger, near Dunn Loring, Va.

CARTER, HERMAN.—Age, — years. Enlisted, June 20, 1898, at Buffalo, to serve two years; mustered in as private, Co. A, same date; mustered out with company, November 19, 1898, at Buffalo, N. Y.

CARY, ARTHUR.—Age, — years. Enlisted, June 25, 1898, at Buffalo, to serve two years; mustered in as private, Co. L, same date; mustered out with company, November 19, 1898, at Buffalo, N. Y.

CASANDIER, LOUIS H.—Age, 30 years. Enlisted, May 1, 1898, at Buffalo, to serve two years; mustered in as sergeant, Co. F, May 17, 1898; mustered out with company, November 19, 1898, at Buffalo, N. Y.

CASPER, EDMOND J.—Age, 22 years. Enlisted, May 1, 1898, at Buffalo, to serve two years; mustered in as private, Co. A, May 17, 1898; mustered out with company, November 19, 1898, at Buffalo, N. Y.

CASS, RAY.—Age, — years. Enlisted, June 21, 1898, at Buffalo, to serve two years; mustered in as private, Co. C, same date; mustered out with company, November 19, 1898, at Buffalo, N. Y.

CASSETY, LEMUEL H.—Age, 21 years. Enlisted, May 1, 1898, at Buffalo, to serve two years; mustered in as private, Co. C, May 17, 1898; mustered out with company, November 19, 1898, at Buffalo, N. Y.

CASTELLO, PATRICK.—Age, — years. Enlisted, July 1, 1898, at Buffalo, to serve two years; mustered in as private, Co. M, same date; mustered out with company, November 19, 1898, at Buffalo, N. Y.

CHAMPLIN, CALVIN E.—Age, 22 years. Enlisted, May 1, 1898, at Buffalo, to serve two years; mustered in as private, Co. K, May 17, 1898; mustered out with company, November 19, 1898, at Buffalo, N. Y.

CHAPIN, FRANK M.—Age, 31 years. Enrolled, May 1, 1898, at Buffalo, to serve two years; mustered in as first lieutenant and battalion adjutant, May 17, 1898; mustered out with regiment, November 19, 1898, at Buffalo, N. Y.; commissioned first lieutenant and battalion adjutant, May 17, 1898, with rank from same date, original. ·

CHAPIN, WILLIAM HENRY.—Age, 42 years. Enrolled, May 1, 1898, at Buffalo, to serve two years; mustered in as lieutenant-colonel, May 17, 1898; mustered out with regiment, November 19, 1898, at Buffalo, N. Y.; commissioned lieutenant-colonel, May 17, 1898, with rank from same date, original.

CHASE, PERRY P.—Age, 25 years. Enlisted, May 1, 1898, at Buffalo, to serve two years; mustered in as private, Co. G, May 17, 1898; promoted corporal, August 19, 1898; mustered out with company, November 19, 1898, at Buffalo, N. Y.

CHENEY, HEMAN G.—Age, 24 years. Enlisted, May 1, 1898, at Buffalo, to serve two years; mustered in as private, Co. C, May 17, 1898; mustered out with company, November 19, 1898, at Buffalo, N. Y.

CHESLEY, GEORGE Y.—Age, — years. Enlisted, June 13, 1898, at Buffalo, to serve two years; mustered in as private, Co. H, same date; mustered out with company, November 19, 1898, at Buffalo, N. Y.

CHRISTEY, ARTHUR B.—Age, 30 years. Enrolled, May 1, 1898, at Buffalo, to serve two years; mustered in as captain, Co. G, May 17, 1898; mustered out with company, November 19, 1898, at Buffalo, N. Y.; subsequent service as first lieutenant, Forty-first Regiment, United States Volunteer Infantry; commissioned captain, May 17, 1898, with rank from same date, original.

CHRISTOPP, OTTO.—Age, 24 years. Enlisted, May 1, 1898, at Buffalo, to serve two years; mustered in as private, Co. G, May 17, 1898; mustered out with company, November 19, 1898, at Buffalo, N. Y.

CHURCHILL, HENRY L.—Age, 32 years. Enlisted, May 12, 1898, at Camp Black, to serve two years; mustered in as private, Co. E, May 17, 1898; mustered out with company, November 19, 1898, at Buffalo, N. Y.

CIRA, JAMES.—Age, 23 years. Enlisted, May 1, 1898, at Buffalo, to serve two years; mustered in as corporal, Co. B, May
17, 1898; returned to ranks, no date; mustered out with company, November 19, 1898, at Buffalo, N. Y.

CITAMAN, CHARLES K.—Age, 22 years. Enlisted, May 11,
1898, at Camp Black, to serve two years; mustered in as private,
Co. E, May 17, 1898; mustered out with company, November 19,
1898, at Buffalo, N. Y.

CLARK, GEORGE D.—Age, 24 years. Enlisted, May 1, 1898, at
Buffalo, to serve two years; mustered in as sergeant, Co. G,
May 17, 1898; mustered out with company, November 19, 1898,
at Buffalo, N. Y.

CLARK, JAMES F.—Age, — years. Enlisted, June 14, 1898, at
Buffalo, to serve two years; mustered in as private, Co. B, same
date; mustered out with company, November 19, 1898, at Buffalo, N. Y.

CLARK, WILL M.—Age, 25 years. Enlisted, May 1, 1898, at
Buffalo, to serve two years; mustered in as private, Co. D, May
17, 1898; mustered out with company, November 19, 1898, at
Buffalo, N. Y.

CLARKE, ALFRED O.—Age, 22 years. Enlisted, May 1, 1898,
at Buffalo, to serve two years; mustered in as private, Co. C,
May 17, 1898; transferred to Hospital Corps, United States
Army, June 22, 1898; to Co. C, September 2, 1898; mustered
out with company, November 19, 1898, at Buffalo, N. Y.

CLARKE, FRANK A.—Age, 23 years. Enlisted, May 1, 1898, at
Buffalo, to serve two years; mustered in as private, Co. L, May
17, 1898; mustered out with company, November 19, 1898, at
Buffalo, N. Y.

CLARKE, WILLIAM.—Age, — years. Enlisted, June 14, 1898,
at Buffalo, to serve two years; mustered in as private, Co. F,
same date; mustered out with company, November 19, 1898, at
Buffalo, N. Y.

CLAUESEN, CHRIST.—Age, 21 years. Enlisted, May 1, 1898,
at Buffalo, to serve two years; mustered in as private, Co. L,
May 17, 1898; mustered out with company, November 19, 1898,
at Buffalo, N. Y.

CLAYTON, JAMES.—Age, 18 years. Enlisted, May 1, 1898, at Buffalo, to serve two years; mustered in as private, Co. M, May 17, 1898; mustered out with company, November 19, 1898, at Buffalo, N. Y.

CLEARY, PATRICK J.—Age, — years. Enlisted, June 13, 1898, at Buffalo, to serve two years; mustered in as private, Co. B, same date; mustered out with company, November 19, 1898, at Buffalo, N. Y.

CLEMENT, HAROLD L.—Age, 21 years. Enlisted, May 1, 1898, at Buffalo, to serve two years; mustered in as private, Co. K, May 17, 1898; mustered out with company, November 19, 1898, at Buffalo, N. Y.

CLENDENING, DAVID H.—Age, 29 years. Enlisted, May 1, 1898, at Buffalo, to serve two years; mustered in as private, Co. B, May 17, 1898; promoted corporal, June 23, 1898; mustered out with company, November 19, 1898, at Buffalo, N. Y.

CLUTE, JOHN D.—Age, 23 years. Enlisted, May 1, 1898, at Buffalo, to serve two years; mustered in as private, Co. A, May 17, 1898; promoted corporal, June 22, 1898; mustered out with company, November 19, 1898, at Buffalo, N. Y.

CODY, GEORGE W.—Age, — years. Enlisted, June 17, 1898, at Buffalo, to serve two years; mustered in as private, Co. A, same date; dishonorably discharged, August 15, 1898, at Camp Alger, near Dunn Loring, Va.

COLE, FRANK F.—Age, 22 years. Enlisted, May 1, 1898, at Buffalo, to serve two years; mustered in as private, Co. D, May 17, 1898; mustered out with company, November 19, 1898, at Buffalo, N. Y.

COLUMBUS, GEORGE.—Age, — years. Enlisted, June 13, 1898, at Buffalo, to serve two years; mustered in as private, Co. I, same date; mustered out with company, November 19, 1898, at Buffalo, N. Y.

COMPTON, CHARLES J.—Age, 21 years. Enlisted, May 1, 1898, at Buffalo, to serve two years; mustered in as private, Co. K, May 17, 1898; mustered out with company, November 19, 1898, at Buffalo, N. Y.

CONKLIN, FRANK B.—Age, 22 years. Enlisted, May 1, 1898, at Buffalo, to serve two years; mustered in as private, Co. D, May 17, 1898; mustered out with company, November 19, 1898, at Buffalo, N. Y.

CONNELL, EDWARD.—Age, 23 years. Enlisted, May 1, 1898, at Buffalo, to serve two years; mustered in as private, Co. C, May 17, 1898; mustered out with company, November 19, 1898, at Buffalo, N. Y.

CONNOLLY, PETER F.—Age, 22 years. Enlisted, May 1, 1898, at Buffalo, to serve two years; mustered in as private, Co. I, May 17, 1898; mustered out with company, November 19, 1898, at Buffalo, N. Y.

CONZENS, THOMAS A.—Age, 20 years. Enlisted, May 1, 1898, at Buffalo, to serve two years; mustered in as first sergeant, Co. A, May 17, 1898; reduced to sergeant, October 19, 1898; mustered out with company, November 19, 1898, at Buffalo, N. Y.

COOK, DANIEL G.—Age, 21 years. Enlisted, May 11, 1898, at Buffalo, to serve two years; mustered in as private, Co. A, May 17, 1898; mustered out with company, November 19, 1898, at Buffalo, N. Y.

COOK, ERNEST H.—Age, 39 years. Enlisted, May 1, 1898, at Jamestown, to serve two years; mustered in as corporal, Co. E, May 17, 1898; mustered out with company, November 19, 1898, at Buffalo, N. Y.

COOK, FRED J.—Age, 21 years. Enlisted, May 11, 1898, at Buffalo, to serve two years; mustered in as private, Co. A, May 17, 1898; mustered out with company, November 19, 1898, at Buffalo, N. Y.

COOK, ISAAC G.—Age, — years. Enlisted, June 22, 1898, at Buffalo, to serve two years; mustered in as private, Co. K, same date; mustered out with company, November 19, 1898, at Buffalo, N. Y.

COOMBS, SAMUEL S.—Age, 33 years. Enlisted, May 1, 1898, at Buffalo, to serve two years; mustered in as private, Co. K, May 17, 1898; mustered out with company, November 19, 1898, at Buffalo, N. Y.

COON, WILLIAM R.—Age, — years. Enlisted, June 25, 1898, at
Buffalo, to serve two years; mustered in as private, Co. L, same
date; transferred to band, June 29, 1898; mustered out with
band, November 19, 1898, at Buffalo, N. Y.

COOPER, JOHN.—Age, 28 years. Enlisted, May 1, 1898, at
Buffalo, to serve two years; mustered in as private, Co. D, May
17, 1898; mustered out with company, November 19, 1898,
at Buffalo, N. Y.

CORCILLIUS, ALEX.—Age, 24 years. Enlisted, May 1, 1898,
at Jamestown, to serve two years; mustered in as private, Co.
E, May 17, 1898; mustered out with company, November 19,
1898, at Buffalo, N. Y.

COREY, WILLIAM C.—Age, — years. Enlisted, June 20, 1898,
at Buffalo, to serve two years; mustered in as private, Co. A,
same date; deserted, October 6, 1898.

CORMICK, JOHN L.—Age, 36 years. Enlisted, May 1, 1898, at
Buffalo, to serve two years; mustered in as private, Co. H, May
17, 1898; mustered out with company, November 19, 1898, at
Buffalo, N. Y.

COSTELLO, EDWARD.—Age, 22 years. Enlisted, May 1, 1898,
at Buffalo, to serve two years; mustered in as corporal, Co. H,
May 17, 1898; mustered out with company, November 19, 1898,
at Buffalo, N. Y.

COSTELLO, THOMAS J.—Age, 25 years. Enlisted, May 1, 1898,
at Buffalo, to serve two years; mustered in as private, Co. G,
May 17, 1898; mustered out with company, November 19, 1898,
at Buffalo, N. Y.

COTRELL, JOSEPH J.—Age, 29 years. Enlisted, May 1, 1898,
at Buffalo, to serve two years; mustered in as private, Co. G,
May 17, 1898; mustered out with company, November 19, 1898,
at Buffalo, N. Y.

COTT, OSCAR.—Age, — years. Enlisted, June 14, 1898, at Buffalo, to serve two years; mustered in as principal musician,
same date; mustered out with regiment, November 19, 1898,
at Buffalo, N. Y.

COTTON, ROBERT L.—Age, — years. Enlisted, June 13, 1898, at Buffalo, to serve two years; mustered in as private, Co. G, same date; mustered out with company, November 19, 1898, at Buffalo, N. Y.

COUGHRAN, WILLIAM H.—Age, — years. Enlisted, June 17, 1898, at Buffalo, to serve two years; mustered in as private, Co. H, same date; mustered out with company, November 19, 1898, at Buffalo, N. Y.

COURSEN, WINFIELD P.—Age, — years. Enlisted, June 14, 1898, at Buffalo, to serve two years; mustered in as private, Co. H, same date; mustered out with company, November 19, 1898, at Buffalo, N. Y.

CRAMER, HERBERT G. P.—Age, 21 years. Enlisted, May 1, 1898, at Buffalo, to serve two years; mustered in as private, Co. B, May 17, 1898; mustered out with company, November 19, 1898, at Buffalo, N. Y.

CRANTZ, ELOE G.—Age, — years. Enlisted, June 13, 1898, at Buffalo, to serve two years; mustered in as private, Co. K, same date; mustered out with company, November 19, 1898, at Buffalo, N. Y.

CRONAN, SAMUEL M.—Age, 21 years. Enlisted, May 1, 1898, at Buffalo, to serve two years; mustered in as private, Co. A, May 17, 1898; mustered out with company, November 19, 1898, at Buffalo, N. Y.

CRONBERG, JOHN.—Age, 24 years. Enlisted, May 1, 1898, at Buffalo, to serve two years; mustered in as artificer, Co. C, May 17, 1898; mustered out with company, November 19, 1898, at Buffalo, N. Y.

CRONNAN, EDWARD.—Age, 27 years. Enlisted, May 1, 1898, at Buffalo, to serve two years; mustered in as private, Co. L, May 17, 1898; mustered out with company, November 19, 1898, at Buffalo, N. Y.

CROSSMAN, HERMAN.—Age, 33 years. Enlisted, May 1, 1898, at Buffalo, to serve two years; mustered in as private, Co. I, May 17, 1898; mustered out with company, November 19, 1898, at Buffalo, N. Y.

CRUDOL, JOHN.—Age, — years. Enlisted, June 29, 1898, at Buffalo, to serve two years; mustered in as private, Co. H, same date; discharged, October 10, 1898, at Buffalo, N. Y., to enlist in Thirteenth United States Infantry.

CULLEN, JOHN W.—Age, 20 years. Enlisted, May 1, 1898, at Buffalo, to serve two years; mustered in as private, Co. H, May 17, 1898; mustered out with company, November 19, 1898, at Buffalo, N. Y.

CUMMINGS, GEORGE F.—Age, 20 years. Enlisted, May 1, 1898, at Buffalo, to serve two years; mustered in as private, Co. D, May 17, 1898; mustered out with company, November 19, 1898, at Buffalo, N. Y.

CUNAN, LOUIS V.—Age, 23 years. Enlisted, May 1, 1898, at Buffalo, to serve two years; mustered in as corporal, Co. I, May 17, 1898; mustered out with company, November 19, 1898, at Buffalo, N. Y.

CURTIS, FRANK.—Age, 22 years. Enlisted, May 1, 1898, at Buffalo, to serve two years; mustered in as private, Co. B, May 17, 1898; mustered out with company, November 19, 1898, at Buffalo, N. Y.

CURTIS, ROLLIN W.—Age, 33 years. Enlisted, May 1, 1898, at Buffalo, to serve two years; mustered in as private, Co. K, May 17, 1898; promoted corporal, August 3, 1898; mustered out with company, November 19, 1898, at Buffalo, N. Y.

CUTTING, GEORGE H.—Age, 19 years. Enlisted, May 1, 1898, at Buffalo, to serve two years; mustered in as corporal, Co. K, May 17, 1898; mustered out with company, November 19, 1898, at Buffalo, N. Y.

CZOSCK, CHARLES.—Age, 25 years. Enlisted, May 12, 1898, at Buffalo, to serve two years; mustered in as private, Co. H, May 17, 1898; mustered out with company, November 19, 1898, at Buffalo, N. Y.

DAEGE, CHARLES F.—Age, 23 years. Enlisted, May 1, 1898, at Buffalo, to serve two years; mustered in as private, Co. F, May 17, 1898; mustered out with company, November 19, 1898, at Buffalo, N. Y.

DAHLEN, CONRAD F.—Age, 28 years. Enlisted, May 1, 1898, at Buffalo, to serve two years; mustered in as private, Co. I, May 17, 1898; promoted corporal, July 1, 1898; mustered out with company, November 19, 1898, at Buffalo, N. Y.

DANENHOWER, HARRIS L.—Age, — years. Enlisted, June 13, 1898, at Buffalo, to serve two years; mustered in as private, Co. C, same date; mustered out with company, November 19, 1898, at Buffalo, N. Y.

DANFORD, FAY W.—Age, 21 years. Enlisted, May 1, 1898, at Buffalo, to serve two years; mustered in as corporal, Co. L, May 17, 1898; mustered out with company, November 19, 1898, at Buffalo, N. Y.

DARBY, WILLIAM J.—Age, 18 years. Enlisted, May 1, 1898, at Buffalo, to serve two years; mustered in as private, Co. F, May 17, 1898; mustered out with company, November 19, 1898, at Buffalo, N. Y.

DAUM, CHRIST.—Age, 24 years. Enlisted, May 1, 1898, at Buffalo, to serve two years; mustered in as private, Co. F, May 17, 1898; mustered out with company, November 19, 1898, at Buffalo, N. Y.

DAVID, WILLIAM.—Age, 19 years. Enlisted, May 1, 1898, at Buffalo, to serve two years; mustered in as private, Co. H, May 17, 1898; mustered out with company, November 19, 1898, at Buffalo, N. Y.

DAVIS, FRANK G.—Age, 21 years. Enlisted, May 1, 1898, at Buffalo, to serve two years; mustered in as private, Co. H, May 17, 1898; mustered out with company, November 19, 1898, at Buffalo, N. Y.

DAVIS, FRANK L.—Age, 33 years. Enlisted, May 1, 1898, at Buffalo, to serve two years; mustered in as first sergeant, Co. M, May 17, 1898; mustered out with company, November 19, 1898, at Buffalo, N. Y.

DAVIS, HENRY.—Age, 27 years. Enlisted, May 1, 1898, at Buffalo, to serve two years; mustered in as private, Co. L, May 17, 1898; deserted, August 17, 1898.

DAVIS, JOHN.—Age, 19 years. Enlisted, May 1, 1898, at Buffalo, to serve two years; mustered in as private, Co. M, May 17, 1898; discharged for disability, July 16, 1898, at Camp Alger, near Dunn Loring, Va.

DAVIS, JOHN C.—Age, 21 years. Enlisted, May 1, 1898, at Buffalo, to serve two years; mustered in as private, Co. K, May 17, 1898; mustered out with company, November 19, 1898, at Buffalo, N. Y.

DAVIS, PERLEY M.—Age, — years. Enlisted, June 14, 1898, at Buffalo, to serve two years; mustered in as private, Co. M, same date; mustered out with company, November 19, 1898, at Buffalo, N. Y.

DAVIS, THOMAS H.—Age, 22 years. Enlisted, May 1, 1898, at Buffalo, to serve two years; mustered in as private, Co. K, May 17, 1898; promoted corporal, June 29, 1898; mustered out with company, November 19, 1898, at Buffalo, N. Y.

DAVIS, WILLIAM H.—Age, 25 years. Enlisted, May 1, 1898, at Buffalo, to serve two years; mustered in as private, Co. K, May 17, 1898; mustered out with company, November 19, 1898, at Buffalo, N. Y.

DAVIS, WILLIAM S.—Age, 22 years. Enlisted, May 1, 1898, at Jamestown, to serve two years; mustered in as private, Co. E, May 17, 1898; mustered out with company, November 19, 1898, at Buffalo, N. Y.

DAWSON, BENJAMIN.—Age, 21 years. Enlisted, May 1, 1898, at Jamestown, to serve two years; mustered in as private, Co. E, May 17, 1898; mustered out with company, November 19, 1898, at Buffalo, N. Y.

DAY, LEE.—Age, — years. Enlisted, June 23, 1898, at Buffalo, to serve two years; mustered in as private, Co. E, same date; mustered out with company, November 19, 1898, at Buffalo, N. Y.

DAYTON, FRANK H.—Age, 38 years. Enlisted, May 14, 1898, at Camp Black, to serve two years; mustered in as private, Co. A, May 17, 1898; mustered out with company, November 19, 1898, at Buffalo, N. Y.

DEAN, FRED W.—Age, 23 years. Enlisted, May 1, 1898, at Buffalo, to serve two years; mustered in as private, Co. B, May 17, 1898; mustered out with company, November 19, 1898, at Buffalo, N. Y.

DECHEND, WILLIAM.—Age, 20 years. Enlisted, May 1, 1898, at Buffalo, to serve two years; mustered in as musician, Co. I, May 17, 1898; mustered out with company, November 19, 1898, at Buffalo, N. Y.

DECKER, BENJAMIN H.—Age, — years. Enlisted, June 21, 1898, at Buffalo, to serve two years; mustered in as private, Co. H, same date; mustered out with company, November 19, 1898, at Buffalo, N. Y.

DEDLOFF, WILLIAM C.—Age, — years. Enlisted, June 20, 1898, at Buffalo, to serve two years; mustered in as private, Co. H, same date; mustered out with company, November 19, 1898, at Buffalo, N. Y.

DE FOREST, EDWARD S.—Age, 35 years. Enlisted, May 1, 1898, at Buffalo, to serve two years; mustered in as quartermaster-sergeant, Co. A, May 17, 1898; returned to ranks, at own request, September 1, 1898; mustered out with company, November 19, 1898, at Buffalo, N. Y.

DELEHANT, FRANK A.—Age, 22 years. Enlisted, May 14, 1898, at Camp Black, to serve two years; mustered in as private, Co. A, May 17, 1898; mustered out with company, November 19, 1898, at Buffalo, N. Y.

DELLER, ALFRED.—Age, 24 years. Enlisted, May 1, 1898, at Buffalo. to serve two years; mustered in as private, Co. L, May 17, 1898; mustered out with company, November 19, 1898, at Buffalo, N. Y.

DENEKE, JOHN.—Age, 21 years. Enlisted, May 1, 1898, at Buffalo, to serve two years; mustered in as private, Co. B, May 17, 1898; mustered out with company, November 19, 1898, at Buffalo, N. Y.

DENNIS, EDWARD J.—Age, — years. Enlisted, June 13, 1898, at Buffalo, to serve two years; mustered in as private, Co. L, same date; transferred to Hospital Corps, United States Army, June 28, 1898; transferred to Co. D, September 2, 1898; reported deserted, to date, August 29, 1898.

DETMAN, WILLIAM G.—Age, 24 years. Enlisted, May 1, 1898, at Buffalo, to serve two years; mustered in as private, Co. A, May 17, 1898; mustered out with company, November 19, 1898, at Buffalo, N. Y.

DEWALD, ROBERT.—Age, 27 years. Enlisted, May 1, 1898, at Buffalo, to serve two years; mustered in as private, Co. F, May 17, 1898; mustered out with company, November 19, 1898, at Buffalo, N. Y.

DICK, EDWARD M. P.—Age, 22 years. Enlisted, May 1, 1898, at Buffalo, to serve two years; mustered in as private, Co. B, May 17, 1898; mustered out with company, November 19, 1898, at Buffalo, N. Y.

DIEBOLD, HENRY W.—Age, 22 years. Enlisted, May 1, 1898, at Buffalo, to serve two years; mustered in as wagoner, Co. C, May 17, 1898; mustered out with company, November 19, 1898, at Buffalo, N. Y.

DIEFENBACH, AUGUST E.—Age, 23 years. Enlisted, May 1, 1898, at Buffalo, to serve two years; mustered in as corporal, Co. C, May 17, 1898; returned to ranks, May 22, 1898; mustered out with company, November 19, 1898, at Buffalo, N. Y.

DIEHL, PETER F.—Age, 23 years. Enlisted, May 12, 1898, at Buffalo, to serve two years; mustered in as private, Co. H, May 17, 1898; mustered out with company, November 19, 1898. at Buffalo, N. Y.   .

DIETRICH, JOHN.—Age, 21 years. Enlisted, May 1, 1898, at Buffalo, to serve two years; mustered in as private, Co. D, May 17, 1898; mustered out with company, November 19, 1898. at Buffalo, N. Y.

DINGLEY, HARVEY E.—Age, 23 years. Enlisted, May 1, 1898, at Buffalo, to serve two years; mustered in as private, Co. M, May 17, 1898; died of pneumonia, October 27, 1898, at General Hospital, Buffalo, N. Y.

DIPPOLD, FRANK.—Age, 21 years. Enlisted, May 1, 1898, at Buffalo, to serve two years; mustered in as private, Co. F, May 17, 1898; mustered out with company, November 19, 1898. at Buffalo, N. Y.

DIRNBERGER, ANTHONY J.—Age, 35 years. Enlisted, May 1, 1898, at Buffalo, to serve two years; mustered in as private, Co. M, May 17, 1898; mustered out with company, November 19, 1898, at Buffalo, N. Y.

·DISHER, GEORGE W.—Age, 25 years. Enlisted, May 1, 1898, at Buffalo, to serve two years; mustered in as private, Co. C, May 17, 1898; mustered out with company, November 19, 1898, at Buffalo, N. Y.

DITZEL, ROBERT.—Age, — years. Enlisted, June 14, 1898, at Buffalo, to serve two years; mustered in as private, Co. A, same date; mustered out with company, November 19, 1898, at Buffalo, N. Y.

DIXON, FRANK H.—Age, 25 years. Enlisted, May 1, 1898, at Buffalo, to serve two years; mustered in as sergeant, Co. F, May 17, 1898; mustered out with company, November 19, 1898, at Buffalo, N. Y.

DIXON, JOSEPH B.—Age, 22 years. Enlisted, May 1, 1898, at Buffalo, to serve two years; mustered in as private, Co. B, May 17, 1898; mustered out, to date, November 19, 1898, at Buffalo, N. Y.

DODGE, EDWARD J.—Age, 29 years. Enlisted, May 1, 1898, at Buffalo, to serve two years; mustered in as private, Co. B, May 17, 1898; appointed wagoner, June 28, 1898; mustered out with company, November 19, 1898, at Buffalo, N. Y.

DOHERTY, JAMES W.—Age, 28 years. Enlisted, May 1, 1898, at Buffalo, to serve two years; mustered in as private, Co. A, May 17, 1898; mustered out with company, November 19, 1898, at Buffalo, N. Y.

DOLAN, DANIEL.—Age, 34 years. Enlisted, May 1, 1898, at Buffalo, to serve two years; mustered in as corporal, Co. M, May 17, 1898; mustered out with company, November 19, 1898, at Buffalo, N. Y.

DONSBACH, PETER.—Age, 36 years. Enlisted, May 1, 1898, at Buffalo, to serve two years; mustered in as private, Co. H, May 17, 1898; mustered out with company, November 19, 1898, at Buffalo, N. Y.

DOORTY, JOHN S.—Age, 28 years. Enrolled, May 1, 1898, at Buffalo, to serve two years; mustered in as first lieutenant, Co. B, May 17, 1898; mustered out with company, November 19, 1898, at Buffalo, N. Y.; commissioned first lieutenant, May 17, 1898, with rank from same date, original.

DORAN, JOHN.—Age, 43 years. Enlisted, May 1, 1898, at Buffalo, to serve two years; mustered in as private, Co. F, May 17, 1898; promoted corporal, June 28, 1898; mustered out with company, November 19, 1898, at Buffalo, N. Y.

DORING, CHARLES H.—Age, — years. Enlisted, June 14, 1898, at Buffalo, to serve two years; mustered in as private, Co. H, same date; mustered out with company, November 19, 1898, at Buffalo, N. Y.

DORN, FRANK.—Age, 21 years. Enlisted, May 1, 1898, at Buffalo, to serve two years; mustered in as private, Co. B, May 17, 1898; mustered out with company, November 19, 1898, at Buffalo, N. Y.

DORN, LEO.—Age, 21 years. Enlisted, May 1, 1898, at Buffalo, to serve two years; mustered in as private, Co. B, May 17, 1898; mustered out with company, November 19, 1898, at Buffalo, N. Y.

DORNTGE, JOSEPH.—Age, 22 years. Enlisted, May 1, 1898, at Buffalo, to serve two years; mustered in as private, Co. I, May 17, 1898; promoted corporal, July 12, 1898; mustered out with company, November 19, 1898, at Buffalo, N. Y.

DORST, JACOB.—Age, 34 years. Enrolled, May 1, 1898, at Buffalo, as second lieutenant, to serve two years; mustered in as captain, Co. D, May 17, 1898; mustered out with company, November 19, 1898, at Buffalo, N. Y.; not commissioned second lieutenant; commissioned captain, May 17, 1898, with rank from same date, original.

DOSSENBACH, ALBERT.—Age, 30 years. Enlisted, May 1, 1898' at Buffalo, to serve two years; mustered in as private, Co. G, May 17, 1898; discharged, October 25, 1898.

DOUGLAS, CHARLES CARROLL.—Age, — years. Enlisted, June 15, 1898, at Buffalo, to serve two years; mustered in as private, Co. E, same date; mustered out with company, November 19, 1898, at Buffalo, N. Y.

DOWLER, ARTHUR K.—Age, 23 years. Enlisted, May 1, 1898, at Jamestown, to serve two years; mustered in as private, Co. E, May 17, 1898; mustered out with company, November 19, 1898, at Buffalo, N. Y.

DOYLE, JOHN.—Age, 37 years. Enlisted, May 1, 1898, at Buffalo, to serve two years; mustered in as private, Co. K, May 17, 1898; mustered out with company, November 19, 1898, at Buffalo, N. Y.

DRAPER, CHARLES R.—Age, 33 years. Enlisted, May 1, 1898, at Buffalo, to serve two years; mustered in as private, Co. B, May 17, 1898; mustered out with company, November 19, 1898, at Buffalo, N. Y.

DRUSENDAHL, WILLIAM.—Age, — years. Enlisted, June 14, 1898, at Buffalo, to serve two years; mustered in as private, Co. B, same date; mustered out with company, November 19, 1898, at Buffalo, N. Y.

DUERR, EDWARD W.—Age, 28 years. Enlisted, May 1, 1898, at Buffalo, to serve two years; mustered in as sergeant, Co. F, May 17, 1898; mustered out with company, November 19, 1898, at Buffalo, N. Y.

DUFFY, THOMAS F.—Age, 21 years. Enlisted, May 11, 1898, at Buffalo, to serve two years; mustered in as private, Co. A, May 17, 1898; mustered out with company, November 19, 1898, at Buffalo, N. Y.

DUMKE, FRED T.—Age, — years. Enlisted, June 15, 1898, at Buffalo, to serve two years; mustered in as private, Co. B, same date; mustered out with company, November 19, 1898, at Buffalo, N. Y.

DUNCAN, GEORGE.—Age, — years. Enlisted, June 13, 1898, at Buffalo, to serve two years; mustered in as private, Co. H, same date; died of typhoid fever, September 2, 1898, at Buffalo, N. Y.

DUNN, DANIEL J.—Age, 23 years. Enlisted, May 1, 1898, at Buffalo, to serve two years; mustered in as private, Co. K, May 17, 1898; mustered out with company, November 19, 1898, at Buffalo, N. Y.

DUSCHAK, HERMAN C.—Age, 20 years. Enlisted, May 1, 1898, at Buffalo, to serve two years; mustered in as private, Co. M, May 17, 1898; mustered out with company, November 19, 1898, at Buffalo, N. Y.

DUTCH, SAMUEL C.—Age, 19 years. Enlisted, May 1, 1898, at Buffalo, to serve two years; mustered in as private, Co. H, May 17, 1898; transferred to Hospital Corps, United States Army, June 28, 1898; to Co. D, September 12, 1898; mustered out with company, November 19, 1898, at Buffalo, N. Y.

DUTHIE, GEORGE A.—Age, — years. Enlisted, June 17, 1898, at Buffalo, to serve two years; mustered in as private, Co. C, same date; promoted corporal, July 23, 1898; mustered out with company, November 19, 1898, at Buffalo, N. Y.

EAGAN, FRANK F.—Age, 30 years. Enlisted, May 1, 1898, at Buffalo, to serve two years; mustered in as private, Co. L, May 17, 1898; mustered out with company, November 19, 1898, at Buffalo, N. Y.

EBERHART, JR., RUDOLPH.—Age, 20 years. Enlisted, May 1, 1898, at Buffalo, to serve two years; mustered in as private, Co. D, May 17, 1898; mustered out with company, November 19, 1898, at Buffalo, N. Y.

ECKAM, FRANK.—Age, — years. Enlisted, June 21, 1898, at Buffalo, to serve two years; mustered in as private, Co. C, same date; mustered out with company, November 19, 1898, at Buffalo, N. Y.

ECKERT, BERTIE M.—Age, 24 years. Enlisted, May 1, 1898, at Buffalo, to serve two years; mustered in as private, Co. B, May 17, 1898; deserted, August 18, 1898.

ECKERT, FRANK.—Age, — years. Enlisted, June 13, 1898, at Buffalo, to serve two years; mustered in as private, Co. A, same date; mustered out with company, November 19, 1898, at Buffalo, N. Y.

ECKERT, JOHN C.—Age, 25 years. Enlisted, May 1, 1898, at Buffalo, to serve two years; mustered in as sergeant, Co. D, May 17, 1898; mustered out with company, November 19, 1898, at Buffalo, N. Y.

ECKHART, HENRY C.—Age, — years. Enlisted, June 14, 1898, at Buffalo, to serve two years; mustered in as private, Co. L, same date; mustered out with company, November 19, 1898, at Buffalo, N. Y.

ECKMAN, GUST W.—Age, 25 years. Enlisted, May 1, 1898, at Jamestown, to serve two years; mustered in as private, Co. E, May 17, 1898; promoted corporal, July 17, 1898; mustered out with company, November 19 1898, at Buffalo, N. Y.

EGLING, JOHN B.—Age, — years. Enlisted, June 14, 1898, at Buffalo, to serve two years; mustered in as private, Co. I, same date; mustered out with company, November 19, 1898, at Buffalo, N. Y.

EINSPARM, JOHN B.—Age, — years. Enlisted, June 17, 1898, at Buffalo, to serve two years; mustered in as private, Co. B, same date; mustered out with company, November 19, 1898, at Buffalo, N. Y.

EKE, OSCAR C.—Age, — years. Enlisted, June 13, 1898, at Buffalo, to serve two years; mustered in as private, Co. F, same date; transferred to Co. E, June 29, 1898; mustered out with company, November 19, 1898, at Buffalo, N. Y.

ELBERS, FRED.—Age, 26 years. Enlisted, May 1, 1898, at Buffalo, to serve two years; mustered in as private, Co. C, May 17, 1898; mustered out with company, November 19, 1898, at Buffalo, N. Y.

ELLER, LOUIS H.—Age, 29 years. Enrolled, May 1, 1898, at Buffalo, to serve two years; mustered in as captain, Co. M, May 17, 1898; mustered out with company, November 19, 1898, at Buffalo, N. Y.; commissioned captain, May 17, 1898, with rank from same date, original.

ELLIOTT, JAMES.—Age, 26 years. Enlisted, May 1, 1898, at Buffalo, to serve two years; mustered in as private, Co. M, May 17, 1898; mustered out with company, November 19, 1898, at Buffalo, N. Y.

ELSAESSER, ALBERT.—Age, 20 years. Enlisted, May 1, 1898, at Buffalo, to serve two years; mustered in as principal musieian, May 17, 1898; mustered out with regiment, November 19, 1898, at Buffalo, N. Y.

ELSAESSER, LOUIS H.—Age, 26 years. Enlisted, May 1, 1898, at Buffalo, to serve two years; mustered in as musician, Co. M, May 17, 1898; mustered out with company, November 19, 1898, at Buffalo, N. Y.

ELSAESSER, ROBERT.—Age, 22 years. Enlisted, May 1, 1898, at Buffalo, to serve two years; mustered in as musician, Co. A, May 17, 1898; mustered out with company, November 19, 1898, at Buffalo, N. Y.

ELVERFELD, HERMAN A.—Age, 21 years. Enlisted, May 1, 1898, at Buffalo, to serve two years; mustered in as private, Co. G, May 17, 1898; mustered out with company, November 19, 1898, at Buffalo, N. Y.

ELVERFELD, WILLIAM.—Age, 24 years. Enlisted, May 1, 1898, at Buffalo, to serve two years; mustered in as private, Co. C, May 17, 1898; died of typhoid fever, September 18, 1898, at Buffalo, N. Y.

ENDE, JOHN.—Age, 27 years. Enlisted, May 1, 1898, at Buffalo, to serve two years; mustered in as private, Co. K, May 17, 1898; mustered out with company, November 19, 1898, at Buffalo, N. Y.

ENDERS, GEORGE M.—Age, 22 years. Enlisted, May 1, 1898, at Buffalo, to serve two years; mustered in as private, Co. M, May 17, 1898; mustered out with company, November 19, 1898, at Buffalo, N. Y.

ENGLISH, JOHN C.—Age, 23 years. Enlisted, May 1, 1898, at Buffalo, to serve two years; mustered in as first sergeant, Co. B, May 17, 1898; mustered out with company, November 19, 1898, at Buffalo, N. Y.

ERICKSON, ALFRED J.—Age, 32 years. Enrolled, May 1, 1898, at Buffalo, to serve two years; mustered in as captain, Co. L, May 17, 1898; mustered out with company, November 19, 1898, at Buffalo, N. Y.; commissioned captain, May 17, 1898, with rank from same date, original.

ERNST, GEORGE.—Age, 27 years. Enlisted, May 1, 1898, at Buffalo, to serve two years; mustered in as private, Co. D, May 17, 1898; mustered out with company, November 19, 1898, at Buffalo, N. Y.

ERNST, HENRY.—Age, 28 years. Enlisted, May 1, 1898, at Buffalo, to serve two years; mustered in as private, Co. L, May 17, 1898; mustered out with company, November 19, 1898, at Buffalo, N. Y.

ERNST, LOUIS.—Age, 36 years. Enlisted, May 1, 1898, at Buffalo, to serve two years; mustered in as private, Co. D, May 17, 1898; died of typhoid fever, September 17, 1898, at Buffalo, N. Y.

FALCONER, CLINTON B.—Age, 21 years. Enlisted, May 1, 1898, at Jamestown, to serve two years; mustered in as private, Co. E, May 17, 1898; mustered out with company, November 19, 1898, at Buffalo, N. Y.

FARNHAM, EDWARD O.—Age, 22 years. Enlisted, May 1, 1898, at Buffalo, to serve two years; mustered in as private, Co. L, May 17, 1898; promoted corporal, July 9, 1898; mustered out with company, November 19, 1898, at Buffalo, N. Y.

FARR, HARRISON C.—Age, 20 years. Enlisted, May 1, 1898, at Buffalo, to serve two years; mustered in as private, Co. F, May 17, 1898; mustered out with company, November 19, 1898, at Buffalo, N. Y.

FARRELL, JOSEPH W.—Age, — years. Enlisted, June 18, 1898, at Buffalo, to serve two years; mustered in as private, Co. A, same date; mustered out with company, November 19, 1898, at Buffalo, N. Y.

FARRELL, WILLIAM M.—Age, 19 years. Enlisted, May 1, 1898, at Buffalo, to serve two years; mustered in as private, Co. H, May 17, 1898; mustered out with company, November 19, 1898, at Buffalo, N. Y.

FAXLANGER, GEORGE A.—Age, 21 years. Enlisted, May 1, 1898, at Buffalo, to serve two years; mustered in as private, Co. H, May 17, 1898; transferred to Hospital Corps, United States Army, June 21, 1898; to Co. D, September 2, 1898; mustered out with company, November 19, 1898, at Buffalo, N. Y.

FEENEY, CHARLES W.—Age, 21 years. Enlisted, May 1, 1898, at Buffalo, to serve two years; mustered in as private, Co. K, May 17, 1898; mustered out with company, November 19, 1898, at Buffalo, N. Y.

FEHRINGER, JOHN J.—Age, — years. Enlisted, June 16, 1898, at Buffalo, to serve two years; mustered in as private, Co. C, same date; mustered out with company, November 19, 1898, at Buffalo, N. Y.

FEIGEL, J. EDWARD.—Age, — years. Enlisted, June 17, 1898, at Buffalo, to serve two years; mustered in as private, Co. G, same date; mustered out with company, November 19, 1898, at Buffalo, N. Y.

FELGER, WILLIAM C.—Age, 22 years. Enlisted, May 1, 1898, at Buffalo, to serve two years; mustered in as private, Co. L, May 17, 1898; mustered out with company, November 19, 1898, at Buffalo, N. Y.

FELLOWS, DAVID.—Age, 38 years. Enlisted, May 1, 1898, at Buffalo, to serve two years; mustered in as private, Co. I, May 17, 1898; mustered out with company, November 19, 1898, at Buffalo, N. Y.

FENTON, LOUIS A.—Age, 31 years. Enrolled, May 1, 1898, at Buffalo, to serve two years; mustered in as first lieutenant, Co. F, May 17, 1898; mustered out with company, November 19, 1898, at Buffalo, N. Y.; commissioned first lieutenant, May 17, 1898, with rank from same date, original.

FENZL, GEORGE.—Age, 19 years. Enlisted, May 1, 1898, at Buffalo, to serve two years; mustered in as private, Co. D, May 17, 1898; mustered out with company, November 19, 1898, at Buffalo, N. Y.

FENZL, LORENZO.—Age, 18 years. Enlisted, May 1, 1898, at Buffalo, to serve two years; mustered in as private, Co. D, May 17, 1898; mustered out with company, November 19, 1898, at Buffalo, N. Y.

FERGUSON, COLIN E.—Age, 32 years. Enlisted, May 1, 1898, at Buffalo, to serve two years; mustered in as private, Co. A, May 17, 1898; mustered out with company, November 19, 1898, at Buffalo, N. Y.

FERGUSON, HARRY E.—Age, 22 years. Enlisted, May 12, 1898, at Camp Black, to serve two years; mustered in as private, Co. C, May 17, 1898; deserted, June 9, 1898, at First Division, Second Army Corps Hospital, Camp Alger, near Dunn Loring, Va.

FERRY, DANIEL S.—Age, 22 years. Enlisted, May 1, 1898, at
Buffalo, to serve two years; mustered in as corporal, Co. B, May
17, 1898; promoted sergeant, June 1, 1898; mustered out, to date
November 19, 1898, at Buffalo, N. Y.

FETZNER, FRED C.—Age, — years. Enlisted, June 13, 1898,
at Buffalo, to serve two years; mustered in as private, Co. F,
same date; mustered out with company, November 19, 1898, at
Buffalo, N. Y.

FIELDS, FRED R.—Age, 25 years. Enlisted, May 1, 1898, at
Buffalo, to serve two years; mustered in as sergeant, Co. M,
May 17, 1898; mustered out with company, November 19, 1898,
at Buffalo, N. Y.

FINE, JULIUS.—Age, 27 years. Enlisted, May 1, 1898, at
Buffalo, to serve two years; mustered in as private, Co. I, May
17, 1898; mustered out with company, November 19, 1898, at
Buffalo, N. Y.

FINN, JEROME C.—Age, — years. Enlisted, June 13, 1898, at
Buffalo, to serve two years; mustered in as private, Co. F, same
date; transferred to Co. E, June 23, 1898; mustered out with
company, November 19, 1898, at Buffalo, N. Y.

FINNIGAN, EDWARD J.—Age, 38 years. Enlisted, May 12,
1898, at Camp Black, to serve two years; mustered in as private,
Co. E, May 17, 1898; mustered out with company, November 19,
1898, at Buffalo, N. Y.

FINSTESWELD, HENRY.—Age, 29 years. Enlisted, May 1,
1898, at Buffalo, to serve two years; mustered in as private, Co.
L, May 17, 1898; mustered out with company, November 19,
1898, at Buffalo, N. Y.

FISCHER, FERDINAND.—Age, — years. Enlisted, June 16,
1898, at Buffalo, to serve two years; mustered in as private, Co.
G, same date; mustered out with company, November 19, 1898,
at Buffalo, N. Y.

FISHER, ANDREW.—Age, 25 years. Enlisted, May 1, 1898, at
Buffalo, to serve two years; mustered in as private, Co. F, May
17, 1898; transferred to Hospital Corps, United States Army,
June 28, 1898; to Co. F, September 2, 1898; mustered out with
company, November 19, 1898, at Buffalo, N. Y.

FISHER, FRANCIS Z.—Age, 21 years. Enlisted, May 1, 1898, at Jamestown, to serve two years; mustered in as private, Co. E, May 17, 1898; mustered out with company, November 19, 1898, at Buffalo, N. Y.

FISHER, HARVEY SHEAFE.—Age, 32 years. Enrolled, May 3, 1898, at Buffalo, to serve two years; mustered in as chaplain, May 17, 1898; mustered out with regiment, November 19, 1898, at Buffalo, N. Y.; commissioned chaplain, May 17, 1898, with rank from same date, original.

FISHER, JR., JOSEPH.—Age, 22 years. Enlisted, May 1, 1898, at Buffalo, to serve two years; mustered in as private, Co. M, May 17, 1898; mustered out with company, November 19, 1898, at Buffalo, N. Y.

FISHER, WILLIAM J.—Age, 27 years. Enlisted, May 1, 1898, at Buffalo, to serve two years; mustered in as quartermaster-sergeant, Co. M, May 17, 1898; mustered out with company, November 19, 1898, at Buffalo, N. Y.

FLANDERS, SAMUEL.—Age, 22 years. Enlisted, May 1, 1898, at Buffalo, to serve two years; mustered in as private, Co. M, May 17, 1898; transferred to Hospital Corps, United States Army, June 28, 1898; to Co. M, September 2, 1898; mustered out with company, November 19, 1898, at Buffalo, N. Y.

FLORE, ALFRED A.—Age, 21 years. Enlisted, May 1, 1898, at Buffalo, to serve two years; mustered in as private, Co. L, May 17, 1898; mustered out with company, November 19, 1898, at Buffalo, N. Y.

FORD, FRANK C.—Age, 21 years. Enlisted, May 1, 1898, at Buffalo, to serve two years; mustered in as private, Co. B, May 17, 1898; mustered out with company, November 19, 1898, at Buffalo, N. Y.

FORNES, FREDERICK C.—Age, 24 years. Enlisted, May 1, 1898, at Buffalo, to serve two years; mustered in as sergeant, Co. H, May 17, 1898; mustered out with company, November 19, 1898, at Buffalo, N. Y.

FORREST, SYLVESTER J.—Age, — years. Enlisted, June 17, 1898, at Buffalo, to serve two years; mustered in as private, Co. M, same date; mustered out with company, November 19, 1898, at Buffalo, N. Y.

FOSTER, GEORGE.—Age, 21 years. Enlisted, May 1, 1898, at Buffalo, to serve two years; mustered in as private, Co. L, May 17, 1898; mustered out with company, November 19, 1898, at Buffalo, N. Y.

FOTCH, GEORGE W.—Age, — years. Enlisted, June 21, 1898, at Buffalo, to serve two years; mustered in as private, Co. M, same date; mustered out with company, November 19, 1898, at Buffalo, N. Y.

FOWKES, SAMUEL A.—Age, — years. Enlisted, June 29, 1898, at Buffalo, to serve two years; mustered in as private, Co. K, same date; mustered out with company, November 19, 1898, at Buffalo, N. Y.

FOWLER, JAMES P.—Age, 25 years. Enrolled, May 1, 1898, at Buffalo, to serve two years; mustered in as first lieutenant, Co. G, May 17, 1898; mustered out with company, November 19, 1898, at Buffalo, N. Y.; commissioned first lieutenant, May 17, 1898, with rank from same date, original.

FOX, EUGENE J.—Age, 20 years. Enlisted, May 1, 1898, at Buffalo, to serve two years; mustered in as corporal, Co. A, May 17, 1898; promoted sergeant, September 1, 1898; quarter-master-sergeant, October 19, 1898; mustered out with company, November 19, 1898, at Buffalo, N. Y.

FOX OLIVER E.—Age, — years. Enlisted, June 17, 1898, at Buffalo, to serve two years; mustered in as private, Co. A, same date; mustered out with company, November 19, 1898, at Buffalo, N. Y.

FRANCZ, JOSEPH.—Age, 28 years. Enlisted, May 1, 1898, at Buffalo, to serve two years; mustered in as private, Co. K, May 17, 1898; mustered out with company, November 19, 1898, at Buffalo, N. Y.

FRANK, WILLIAM.—Age, 20 years. Enlisted, May 1, 1898, at Buffalo, to serve two years; mustered in as private, Co. B, May 17, 1898; discharged, October 29, 1898.

FRAUTZEN, CARL E.—Age, — years. Enlisted, June 13, 1898, at Buffalo, to serve two years; mustered in as private, Co. M, same date; mustered out with company, November 19, 1898, at Buffalo, N. Y.

FREIHEIT, FRED C.—Age, 22 years. Enlisted, May 1, 1898, at Buffalo, to serve two years; mustered in as private, Co. I, May 17, 1898; promoted corporal, July 21, 1898; mustered out with company, November 19, 1898, at Buffalo, N. Y.

FREMONT, LAWRENCE.—Age, 21 years. Enlisted, May 1, 1898, at Buffalo, to serve two years; mustered in as private, Co. F, May 17, 1898; mustered out with company, November 19, 1898, at Buffalo, N. Y.

FRETTS, GAYLORD G.—Age, 23 years. Enlisted, May 1, 1898, at Jamestown, to serve two years; mustered in as private, Co. E, May 17, 1898; mustered out with company, November 19, 1898, at Buffalo, N. Y.

FREY, CHARLES J. M.—Age, 29 years. Enlisted, May 1, 1898, at Buffalo, to serve two years; mustered in as private, Co. C, May 17, 1898; appointed cook, August 13, 1898; mustered out with company, November 19, 1898, at Buffalo, N. Y.

FRICHBUTTER, GUSTAVE A. W.—Age, 21 years. Enlisted, May 1, 1898, at Buffalo, to serve two years; mustered in as private, Co. G, May 17, 1898; promoted corporal, June 29, 1898; mustered out with company, November 19, 1898, at Buffalo, N. Y.

FROLTE, JOHN.—Age, 28 years. Enlisted, May 1, 1898, at Buffalo, to serve two years; mustered in as private, Co. B, May 17, 1898; transferred to Hospital Corps, United States Army, June 28, 1898; to Co. B, September 4, 1898; mustered out with company, November 19, 1898, at Buffalo, N. Y.

FROOD, JOHN.—Age, 26 years. Enlisted, May 1, 1898, at Buffalo, to serve two years; mustered in as private, Co. A, May 17, 1898; mustered out with company, November 19, 1898, at Buffalo, N. Y.

FUCHS. HENRY.—Age, 24 years. Enlisted, May 1, 1898, at Buffalo, to serve two years; mustered in as private, Co. B, May 17, 1898; mustered out with company, November 19, 1898, at Buffalo, N. Y.

FULLER. GEORGE H.—Age, 26 years. Enlisted, May 1, 1898, at Buffalo. to serve two years; mustered in as private, Co. G, May 17, 1898; mustered out with company, November 19, 1898, at Buffalo, N. Y.

FULLINGTON, FRANK H.—Age, 23 years. Enlisted, May 11, 1898, at Buffalo, to serve two years; mustered in as private, Co. K, May 17, 1898; mustered out with company, November 19, 1898, at Buffalo, N. Y.

FUNK, CHRIST H.—Age, 21 years. Enlisted, May 1, 1898, at Buffalo, to serve two years; mustered in as private, Co. M, May 17, 1898; mustered out with company, November 19, 1898, at Buffalo, N. Y.

FURMAN, FLOYD A.—Age, 22 years. Enlisted, May 1, 1898, at Buffalo, to serve two years; mustered in as private, Co. L, May 17, 1898; promoted corporal, July 13, 1898; mustered out with company, November 19, 1898, at Buffalo, N. Y.

FUSS, FREDERICK.—Age, — years. Enlisted, June 24, 1898, at Buffalo, to serve two years; mustered in as private, Co. K, same date; transferred to band, June 29, 1898; mustered out, to date, November 19, 1898, at Buffalo, N. Y.

GADY, FRANK.—Age, — years. Enlisted, June 14, 1898, at Buffalo, to serve two years; mustered in as private, Co. L, same date; discharged, August 20, 1898, at Buffalo, N. Y.

GALEN, JOHN.—Age, 26 years. Enlisted, May 1, 1898, at Buffalo, to serve two years; mustered in as private, Co. F, May 17, 1898; mustered out with company, November 19, 1898, at Buffalo, N. Y.

GALVIN, HARRY C.—Age, 21 years. Enlisted, May 12, 1898, at Camp Black, to serve two years; mustered in as private, Co. C, May 17, 1898; mustered out with company, November 19, 1898, at Buffalo, N. Y.

GARLEY, THOMAS.—Age, 26 years. Enlisted, May 13, 1898, at Camp Black, to serve two years; mustered in as private, Co. F, May 17, 1898; mustered out with company, November 19, 1898, at Buffalo, N. Y.

GARMAN, JOHN B.—Age, 37 years. Enlisted, May 1, 1898, at Buffalo, to serve two years; mustered in as private, Co. D, May 17, 1898; mustered out with company, November 19, 1898, at Buffalo, N. Y.

GAUMER, CHARLES C.—Age, — years. Enlisted, June 16, 1898, at Buffalo, to serve two years; mustered in as private, Co. K, same date; mustered out with company, November 19, 1898, at Buffalo, N. Y.

GAY, FLOYD W.—Age, — years. Enlisted, June 20, 1898, at Buffalo, to serve two years; mustered in as private, Co. F, same date; dishonorably discharged, August 30, 1898.

GAYLORD, GILES A.—Age, 20 years. Enlisted, May 1, 1898, at Buffalo, to serve two years; mustered in as private, Co. A, May 17, 1898; mustered out with·company, November 19, 1898, at Buffalo, N. Y.

GEBHARD, LOUIS.—Age, 32 years. Enlisted, May 1, 1898, at Buffalo, to serve two years; mustered in as private, Co. G, May 17, 1898; mustered out with company, November 19, 1898, at Buffalo, N. Y.

GEIGER, EDWARD J.—Age, 24 years. Enlisted, May 1, 1898, at Buffalo, to serve two years; mustered in as private, Co. A, May 17, 1898; mustered out with company, November 19, 1898, at Buffalo, N. Y.

GEISELER, RICHARD A.—Age, — years. Enlisted, July 2, 1898, at Buffalo, to serve two years; mustered in as private, Co. M, same date; mustered out with company, November 19, 1898, at Buffalo, N. Y.

GENTNER, GEORGE P.—Age, 25 years. Enlisted, May 1, 1898, at Buffalo, to serve two years; mustered in as sergeant, Co. M, May 17, 1898; mustered out with company, November 19, 1898, at Buffalo, N. Y.

GEORGE, WILLIAM.—Age, 27 years. Enlisted, May 1, 1898, at Buffalo, to serve two years; mustered in as private, Co. L, May 17, 1898; mustered out with company, November 19, 1898, at Buffalo, N. Y.

GERBRACHT, AUGUST.—Age, 21 years. Enlisted, May 1, 1898, at Buffalo, to serve two years; mustered in as corporal, Co. D, May 17, 1898; mustered out with company, November 19, 1898, at Buffalo, N. Y.

GERDES, ARMIN A.—Age, 21 years. Enlisted, May 1, 1898, at Buffalo, to serve two years; mustered in as private, Co. G, May 17, 1898; mustered out with company, November 19, 1898, at Buffalo, N. Y.

GERLACH, JOHN J.—Age, — years. Enlisted, June 21, 1898, at Buffalo, to serve two years; mustered in as private, Co. M, same date; mustered out with company, November 19, 1898, at Buffalo, N. Y.

GERMAIN, ARTHUR L.—Age, 25 years. Enlisted, May 1, 1898, at Buffalo, to serve two years; mustered in as private, Co. B, May 17, 1898; mustered out with company, November 19, 1898, at Buffalo, N. Y.

GERNER, WILLIAM.—Age, 39 years. Enlisted, May 1, 1898, at Buffalo, to serve two years; mustered in as private, Co. L, May 17, 1898; mustered out with company, November 19, 1898, at Buffalo, N. Y.

GERTZ, JR., WILLIAM C.—Age, 23 years. Enlisted, May 1, 1898, at Buffalo, to serve two years; mustered in as private, Co. G, May 17, 1898; mustered out with company, November 19, 1898, at Buffalo, N. Y.

GETSINGER, ELIAS.—Age, 23 years. Enlisted, May 1, 1898, at Buffalo, to serve two years; mustered in as private, Co. 1, May 17, 1898; mustered out with company, November 19, 1898, at Buffalo, N. Y.

GIBLIN, WILLIAM P.—Age, 21 years. Enlisted, May 1, 1898, at Buffalo, to serve two years; mustered in as private, Co. L, May 17, 1898; mustered out with company, November 19, 1898, at Buffalo, N. Y.

GIESSER, EDWARD.—Age, 28 years. Enlisted, May 1, 1898, at Buffalo, to serve two years; mustered in as quartermaster-sergeant, Co. F, May 17, 1898; mustered out with company, November 19, 1898, at Buffalo, N. Y.

GILBERT, JR., ALBERT.—Age, 44 years. Enrolled, May 1, 1898, at Jamestown, to serve two years; mustered in as captain, Co. E, May 17, 1898; discharged, July·5, 1898; subsequent service as captain and assistant quartermaster, United States Volunteers; commissioned captain, May 17, 1898, with rank from same date, original.

GILBERT, LAWRENCE J.—Age, 19 years. Enlisted, May 1, 1898, at Buffalo, to serve two years; mustered in as private, Co. F, May 17, 1898; mustered out with company, November 19, 1898, at Buffalo, N. Y.

GILFILLAN, ANDREW B.—Age, 24 years. Enlisted, May 1, 1898, at Buffalo, to serve two years; mustered in as private, Co. I, May 17, 1898; promoted corporal, July 21, 1898; mustered out with company, November 19, 1898, at Buffalo, N. Y.

GILL, EDWARD H.—Age, 23 years. Enlisted, May 1, 1898, at Buffalo to serve two years; mustered in as private, Co. L, May 17, 1898; appointed artificer, same date; mustered out with company, November 19, 1898, at Buffalo, N. Y.

GILLISPIE, DONALD.—Age, — years. Enlisted, June 13, 1898, at Buffalo, to serve two years; mustered in as private, Co. B, same date; mustered out with company, November 19, 1898, at Buffalo, N. Y.

GILMORE, ALBERT.—Age, 19 years. Enlisted, May 1, 1898, at Buffalo, to serve two years; mustered in as private, Co. M, May 17, 1898; mustered out with company, November 19, 1898, at Buffalo, N. Y.

GIRARDIN, FRANCIS J.—Age, 23 years. Enlisted, May 1, 1898, at Buffalo, to serve two years; mustered in as private, Co. B, May 17, 1898; mustered out with company, November 19, 1898, at Buffalo, N. Y.

GLENOWZKI, FRANK.—Age, — years. Enlisted, June 13, 1898, at Buffalo, to serve two years; mustered in as private, Co. G, same date; mustered out with company, November 19, 1898, at Buffalo, N. Y.

GOLDBERG, JACOB A.—Age, 21 years. Enlisted, May 1, 1898, at Buffalo, to serve two years; mustered in as private, Co. M, May 17, 1898; mustered out with company, November 19, 1898, at Buffalo, N. Y.

GOOD, MATT. L.—Age, 22 years. Enlisted, May 1, 1898, at
Buffalo, to serve two years; mustered in as private, Co. I, May
17, 1898; mustered out with company, November 19, 1898, at
Buffalo, N. Y.

GOODENOUGH, JR., GEORGE H.—Age, — years. Enlisted,
June 13, 1898, at Buffalo, to serve two years; mustered in as
private, Co. G, same date; mustered out with company, November 19, 1898, at Buffalo, N. Y.

GORDON, EDWARD J.—Age, 21 years. Enlisted, May 12, 1898,
at Camp Black, to serve two years; mustered in as private, Co.
G, May 17, 1898; mustered out with company, November 19,
1898, at Buffalo, N. Y.

GORGES, EDWARD B.—Age, 21 years. Enlisted, May 1, 1898,
at Buffalo, to serve two years; mustered in as private, Co. A,
May 17, 1898; mustered out with company, November 19, 1898,
at Buffalo, N. Y.

GORTZIG, HENRY.—Age, — years. Enlisted, June 29, 1898, at
Buffalo, to serve two years; mustered in as private, Co. H, same
date; mustered out with company, November 19, 1898, at Buffalo, N. Y.

GRABER, ALVIN N.—Age, 19 years. Enlisted, May 1, 1898, at
Buffalo, to serve two years; mustered in as private, Co. F, May
17, 1898; mustered out with company, November 19, 1898, at
Buffalo, N. Y.

GRACE, CHARLES S.—Age, — years. Enlisted, June 15, 1898,
at Buffalo, to serve two years; mustered in as private, Co. E,
same date; mustered out with company, November 19, 1898, at
Buffalo, N. Y.

GRAHAM, GEORGE.—Age, 33 years. Enlisted, May 1, 1898, at
Buffalo, to serve two years; mustered in as private, Co. C, May
17, 1898; mustered out with company, November 19, 1898, at
Buffalo, N. Y.

GRAHAM, JOHN W. S.—Age, 26 years. Enlisted, May 1, 1898,
at Buffalo, to serve two years; mustered in as private, Co. G,
May 17, 1898; discharged for disability, October 10, 1898, at
Buffalo, N. Y.

GRAINER, WILLIAM B.—Age, — years. Enlisted, June 16 ., 1898, at Buffalo, to serve two years; mustered in as private, Co. I, same date; mustered out company, November 19, 1898, at Buffalo, N. Y., as William H. Grainer.

GRAM, GEORGE.—Age, 22 years. Enlisted, May 1, 1898, at Buffalo, to serve two years; mustered in as private, Co. F, May 17, 1898; mustered out with company, November 19, 1898, at Buffalo, N. Y.

GRASSELL, JR., EDWARD C.—Age, 19 years. Enlisted, May 1, 1898, at Buffalo, to serve two years; mustered in as private, Co. G, May 17, 1898; mustered out with company, November 19, 1898, at Buffalo, N. Y.

GRATHLEIN, JOHN.—Age, 28 years. Enlisted, May 1, 1898, at Buffalo, to serve two years; mustered in as quartermaster-sergeant, Co. I, May 17, 1898; mustered out with company, November 19, 1898, at Buffalo, N. Y.

GRAVES, CHARLES B.—Age, 31 years. Enlisted, May 1, 1898, at Buffalo, to serve two years; mustered in as corporal, Co. F, May 17, 1898; mustered out with company, November 19, 1898, at Buffalo, N. Y.

GRAVES, GEORGE E.—Age, 22 years. Enlisted, May 1, 1898, at Buffalo, to serve two years; mustered in as private, Co. F, May 17, 1898; transferred to Hospital Corps, June, 1898; to Co. F, September 2, 1898; mustered out with company, November 19, 1898, at Buffalo, N. Y.

GRAVES, JOHN H.—Age, 22 years. Enlisted, May 1, 1898, at Buffalo, to serve two years; mustered in as corporal, Co. M, May 17, 1898; mustered out with company, November 19, 1898, at Buffalo, N. Y.

GRAY, JAMES.—Age, 28 years. Enlisted, May 1, 1898, at Buffalo, to serve two years; mustered in as private, Co. K, May 17, 1898; deserted, July 4, 1898, at Camp Alger, near Dunn Loring, Va.

GRAY, THOMAS A.—Age, 28 years. Enlisted, May 12, 1898, at Buffalo, to serve two years; mustered in as private, Co. M, May 17, 1898; mustered out with company, November 19, 1898, at Buffalo, N. Y.

GREEN, JR., FRANK J.—Age, 21 years. Enlisted, May 1, 1898, at Buffalo, to serve two years; mustered in as private, Co. D, May 17, 1898; mustered out with company, November 19, 1898, at Buffalo, N. Y.

GREENBACKER, PHILLIP.—Age, 27 years. Enlisted, May 1, 1898, at Buffalo, to serve two years; mustered in as artificer, Co. I, May 17, 1898; mustered out with company, November 19, 1898, at Buffalo, N. Y.

GREENE, ALBERT W.—Age, — years. Enlisted, June 15, 1898, at Buffalo, to serve two years; mustered in as private, Co. C, same date; mustered out with company, November 19, 1898, at Buffalo, N. Y.

GREENE, OLIVER E.—Age, — years. Enlisted, June 15, 1898, at Buffalo, to serve two years; mustered in as private, Co. I, same date; mustered out with company, November 19, 1898, at Buffalo, N. Y.

GRIFFIN, HUGH J.—Age, 26 years. Enlisted, May 1, 1898, at Buffalo, to serve two years; mustered in as private, Co. L, May 17, 1898; mustered out with company, November 19, 1898, at Buffalo, N. Y.

GRINDAL, ROBERT.—Age, — years. Enlisted, June 13, 1898, at Buffalo, to serve two years; mustered in as private, Co. L, same date; mustered out with company, November 19, 1898, at Buffalo, N. Y.

GRISWOLD, BERT.—Age, — years. Enlisted, June 13, 1898, at Buffalo, to serve two years; mustered in as private, Co. B, same date; mustered out with company, November 19, 1898, at Buffalo, N. Y.

GROH, JOHN A.—Age, — years. Enlisted, June 27, 1898, at Buffalo, to serve two years; mustered in as private, Co. L, same date; mustered out with company, November 19, 1898, at Buffalo, N. Y.

GROSSKOPF, ALBERT A.—Age, 21 years. Enlisted, May 1, 1898, at Buffalo, to serve two years; mustered in as private, Co. A, May 17, 1898; promoted corporal, July 25, 1898; mustered out with company, November 19, 1898, at Buffalo, N. Y.

GROVE, ALFRED A.—Age, — years. Enlisted, June 27, 1898, at Buffalo, to serve two years; mustered in as private, Co. L, same date; mustered out with company, November 19, 1898, at Buffalo, N. Y.

GRUBER, FRED.—Age, 22 years. Enlisted, May 1, 1898, at Buffalo, to serve two years; mustered in as private, Co. H, May 17, 1898; mustered out with company, November 19, 1898, at Buffalo, N. Y.

GRUSZKA, LEO.—Age, 22 years. Enlisted, May 14, 1898, at Camp Black, to serve two years; mustered in as private, Co. G, May 17, 1898; mustered out with company, November 19, 1898, at Buffalo, N. Y.

GUBKOWSKI, JOSEPH.—Age, — years. Enlisted, June 14, 1898, at Buffalo, to serve two years; mustered in as private, Co. F, same date; mustered out with company, November 19, 1898, at Buffalo, N. Y.

GUCKELBERGER, JACOB.—Age, 21 years. Enlisted, May 1, 1898, at Buffalo, to serve two years; mustered in as private, Co. M, May 17, 1898; mustered out with company, November 19, 1898, at Buffalo, N. Y.

GUERTIN, JR., CASIMIRE W.—Age, 29 years. Enlisted, May 1, 1898, at Buffalo, to serve two years; mustered in as private, Co. G, May 17, 1898; mustered out with company, November 19, 1898, at Buffalo, N. Y.

GUNTHER, AUGUST.—Age, 36 years. Enlisted, May 1, 1898, at Buffalo, to serve two years; mustered in as private, Co. G, May 17, 1898; mustered out with company, November 19, 1898, at Buffalo, N. Y.

GUTA, JOHN.—Age, 25 years. Enlisted, May 12, 1898, at Buffalo, to serve two years; mustered in as private, Co. M, May 17, 1898; mustered out with company, November 19, 1898, at Buffalo, N. Y.

HAAS, CHARLES C.—Age, 23 years. Enlisted, May 1, 1898, at Jamestown, to serve two years; mustered in as private, Co. E, May 17, 1898; mustered out with company, November 19, 1898, at Buffalo, N. Y.

HACK, FRED V.—Age, — years. Enlisted, June 13, 1898, at Buffalo, to serve two years; mustered in as private, Co. H, same date; died of typhoid fever, August 18, 1898, in First Division, Second Army Corps Hospital at Camp Alger, near Dunn Loring, Va.

HACKETT, THOMAS S.—Age, 22 years. Enlisted, May 1, 1898, at Buffalo, to serve two years; mustered in as private, Co. H, May 17, 1898; mustered out with company, November 19, 1898, at Buffalo, N. Y.

HAFFA, GEORGE J.—Age, 27 years. Enlisted, May 1, 1898, at Buffalo, to serve two years; mustered in as private, Co. L. May 17, 1898; mustered out with company, November 19, 1898, at Buffalo, N. Y.

HAFFA, OSCAR J.—Age, 28 years. Enlisted, May 1, 1898, at Buffalo, to serve two years; mustered in as musician, Co. A, May 17, 1898; mustered out with company, November 19, 1898, at Buffalo, N. Y.

HAGNECH, MAX H.—Age, 26 years. Enlisted, May 1, 1898, at Buffalo, to serve two years; mustered in as corporal, Co. K, May 17, 1898; mustered out with company, November 19, 1898, at Buffalo, N. Y.

HAHN, ERNEST J.—Age, — years. Enlisted, June 14, 1898, at Buffalo, to serve two years; mustered in as private, Co. G, same date; mustered out with company, November 19, 1898, at Buffalo, N. Y.

HAIGEN, AUGUST.—Age, 20 years. Enlisted, May 1, 1898, at Buffalo, to serve two years; mustered in as private, Co. I, May 17, 1898; mustered out with company, November 19, 1898, at Buffalo, N. Y.

HALBLAUB, MICHAEL W.—Age, 34 years. Enlisted, May 1, 1898, at Buffalo, to serve two years; mustered in as private, Co. A, May 17, 1898; promoted corporal, August 3, 1898; mustered out with company, November 19, 1898, at Buffalo, N. Y.

HALE, ALFRED E.—Age, 40 years. Enlisted, May 1, 1898, at Jamestown, to serve two years; mustered in as sergeant, Co. E, May 17, 1898; mustered out with company, November 19, 1898, at Buffalo, N. Y.

HALE, GEORGE F.—Age, 35 years. Enlisted, May 1, 1898, at Jamestown, to serve two years; mustered in as sergeant, Co. E, May 17, 1898; mustered out with company, November 19, 1898, at Buffalo, N. Y.

HALEY, WILLIAM A.—Age, 25 years. Enlisted, May 1, 1898, at Buffalo, to serve two years; mustered in as private, Co. M, May 17, 1898; dishonorably discharged, July 30, 1898.

HALL, GORDON.—Age, 19 years. Enlisted, May 1, 1898, at Buffalo, to serve two years; mustered in as private, Co. H, May 17, 1898; mustered out with company, November 19, 1898, at Buffalo, N. Y.

HALL, HARRY.—Age, 26 years. Enlisted, May 1, 1898, at Jamestown, to serve two years; mustered in as private, Co. E, May 17, 1898; transferred to Signal Corps, June 25, 1898.

HALLER, JOHN.—Age, 21 years. Enlisted, May 1, 1898, at Buffalo, to serve two years; mustered in as private, Co. K, May 17, 1898; mustered out with company, November 19, 1898, at Buffalo, N. Y.

HALT, JOHN.—Age, — years. Enlisted, June 29, 1898, at Buffalo, to serve two years; mustered in as private, Co. L, same date; mustered out with company, November 19, 1898, at Buffalo, N. Y.

HALVERSON, BERNHARD.—Age, 25 years. Enlisted, May 1, 1898, at Buffalo, to serve two years; mustered in as private, Co. L, May 17, 1898; mustered out with company, November 19, 1898, at Buffalo, N. Y.

HAMILTON, BERTRAM.—Age, — years. Enlisted, June 13, 1898, at Buffalo, to serve two years; mustered in as private, Co. D, same date; mustered out with company, November 19, 1898, at Buffalo, N. Y.

HAMILTON, JR., CHARLES.—Age, 19 years. Enlisted, May 1, 1898, at Buffalo, to serve two years; mustered in as private, Co. I, May 17, 1898; mustered out with company, November 19, 1898, at Buffalo, N. Y.

HAMILTON, CLARENCE A.—Age, 21 years. Enlisted, May 1, 1898, at Buffalo, to serve two years; mustered in as private, Co. L, May 17, 1898; mustered out with company, November 19, 1898, at Buffalo, N. Y.

HAMM, CHARLES J.—Age, 21 years. Enlisted, May 1, 1898, at Buffalo, to serve two years; mustered in as musician, Co. M, May 17, 1898; mustered out with company, November 19, 1898, at Buffalo, N. Y.

HAMPP, LOUIS.—Age, — years. Enlisted, June 13, 1898, at Buffalo, to serve two years; mustered in as private, Co. B, same date; mustered out with company, November 19, 1898, at Buffalo, N. Y.

HANAUER, JOSEPH H.—Age, — years. Enlisted, June 16, 1898, at Buffalo, to serve two years; mustered in as private, Co. I, same date; mustered out with company, November 19, 1898, at Buffalo, N. Y.

HANCOCK, JOHN M.—Age, 37 years. Enrolled, May 2, 1898, at Buffalo, to serve two years; mustered in as first lieutenant, Co. C, May 17, 1898; discharged, August 24, 1898; commissioned first lieutenant, May 17, 1898, with rank from same date, original.

HANES, GEORGE L.—Age, 22 years. Enlisted, May 1, 1898, at Buffalo, to serve two years; mustered in as private, Co. B, May 17, 1898; mustered out with company, November 19, 1898, at Buffalo, N. Y.

HANES, WALTER W.—Age, 22 years. Enlisted, May 1, 1898, at Buffalo, to serve two years; mustered in as private, Co. B, May 17, 1898; mustered out with company, November 19, 1898, at Buffalo, N. Y.

HANGEN, JOHN G.—Age, 24 years. Enlisted, May 1, 1898, at Buffalo, to serve two years; mustered in as sergeant, Co. B, May 17, 1898; mustered out with company, November 19, 1898, at Buffalo, N. Y.

HANNEL, ALFRED O.—Age, — years. Enlisted, June 16, 1898, at Buffalo, to serve two years; mustered in as private, Co. D, same date; mustered out with company, November 19, 1898, at Buffalo, N. Y.

HANSEN, MARTIN.—Age, 23 years. Enlisted, May 1, 1898, at Buffalo, to serve two years; mustered in as private, Co. F, May 17, 1898; mustered out with company, November 19, 1898, at Buffalo, N. Y.

HANSON, CLINTON.—Age, 19 years. Enlisted, May 12, 1898, at Camp Black, to serve two years; mustered in as private, Co. B, May 17, 1898; mustered out with company, November 19, 1898, at Buffalo, N. Y.

HANSON, JONATHAN.—Age, 27 years. Enlisted, May 1, 1898, at Jamestown, to serve two years; mustered in as private, Co. E, May 17, 1898; promoted corporal, August 2, 1898; mustered out with company, November 19, 1898, at Buffalo, N. Y.

HARMON, VALENTINE P.—Age, 26 years. Enlisted, May 1, 1898, at Buffalo, to serve two years; mustered in as private, Co. K, May 17, 1898; mustered out with company, November 19, 1898, at Buffalo, N. Y.

HARRINGTON, JOHN F.—Age, 26 years. Enlisted, May 1, 1898, at Buffalo, to serve two years; mustered in as private, Co. H, May 17, 1898; mustered out with company, November 19, 1898, at Buffalo, N. Y.

HARRINGTON, JOHN N.—Age, — years. Enlisted, June 13, 1898, at Buffalo, to serve two years; mustered in as private, Co. L, same date; mustered out with company, November 19, 1898, at Buffalo, N. Y.

HARRIS, CHARLES A.—Age, 35 years. Enlisted, May 1, 1898, at Buffalo, to serve two years; mustered in as private, Co. G, May 17, 1898; mustered out with company, November 19, 1898, at Buffalo, N. Y.

HARRISON, ALBERT A.—Age, 24 years. Enlisted, May 1, 1898, at Jamestown, to serve two years; mustered in as private, Co. E, May 17, 1898; mustered out with company, November 19, 1898, at Buffalo, N. Y.

HARRISON, GEORGE C.—Age, 22 years. Enlisted, May 1, 1898, at Jamestown, to serve two years; mustered in as private, Co. E, May 17, 1898; promoted corporal, July 17, 1898; mustered out with company, November 19, 1898, at Buffalo, N. Y.

HARRISON, JR., WILLIAM H.—Age, 27 years. Enlisted, May 1, 1898, at Jamestown, to serve two years; mustered in as private, Co. E, May 17, 1898; promoted sergeant, no date; mustered out with company, November 19, 1898, at Buffalo, N. Y.

HARTL, CHRISTOPHER.—Age, 32 years. Enlisted, May 1, 1898, at Buffalo, to serve two years; mustered in as private, Co. G, May 17, 1898; mustered out with company, November 19, 1898, at Buffalo, N. Y.

HARTMANN, FRANK.—Age, 22 years. Enlisted, May 1, 1898, at Buffalo, to serve two years; mustered in as private, Co. H, May 17, 1898; mustered out with company, November 19, 1898, at Buffalo, N. Y.

HARTWELL, ALFRED C.—Age, 28 years. Enlisted, May 1, 1898, at Buffalo, to serve two years; mustered in as private, Co. C, May 17, 1898; mustered out with company, November 19, 1898, at Buffalo, N. Y.

HARTZBERG, WILLIAM J.—Age, 21 years. Enlisted, May 1, 1898, at Buffalo, to serve two years; mustered in as private, Co. D, May 17, 1898; mustered out with company, November 19, 1898, at Buffalo, N. Y.

HASSELBECK, JACOB.—Age, 22 years. Enlisted, May 1, 1898, at Buffalo, to serve two years; mustered in as private, Co. L, May 17, 1898; mustered out with company, November 19, 1898, at Buffalo, N. Y.

HAVENS, ROBERT.—Age, 21 years. Enlisted, May 1, 1898, at Buffalo, to servce two years; mustered in as corporal, Co. L, May 17, 1898; mustered out with company, November 19, 1898, at Buffalo, N. Y.

HAWS, JAMES S.—Age, 22 years. Enlisted, May 1, 1898, at Buffalo, to serve two years; mustered in as private, Co. C, May 17, 1898; mustered out with company, November 19, 1898, at Buffalo, N. Y.

HAZEL, RICHARD W.—Age, 32 years. Enlisted, May 1, 1898, at Buffalo, to serve two years; mustered in as private, Co. M, May 17, 1898; mustered out with company, November 19, 1898, at Buffalo, N. Y.

HECK, ALBERT.—Age, 21 years. Enlisted, May 1, 1898, at Buffalo, to serve two years; mustered in as private, Co. F, May 17, 1898: mustered out with company, November 19, 1898, at Buffalo, N. Y.

HEFNER, STEPHEN V.—Age, 32 years. Enlisted, May 1, 1898, at Buffalo, to serve two years; mustered in as private, Co. K, May 17, 1898; died of typhoid pneumonia, October 2, 1898, at home, Buffalo, N. Y.

HEHR, HENRY G.—Age, — years. Enlisted, June 25, 1898, at Buffalo, to serve two years; mustered in as private, Co. M, same date; mustered out with company, November 19, 1898, at Buffalo, N. Y.

HEID, PHILIP.—Age, 26 years. Enlisted, May 1, 1898, at Buffalo, to serve two years; mustered in as corporal, Co. D, May 17, 1898; mustered out with company, November 19, 1898, at Buffalo, N. Y.

HEIGHLING, WILLIAM.—Age, 23 years. Enlisted, May 1, 1898, at Buffalo, to serve two years; mustered in as sergeant, Co. A, May 17, 1898; mustered out with company, November 19, 1898, at Buffalo, N. Y.

HEIM, JOSEPH.—Age, 29 years. Enlisted, May 1, 1898, at Buffalo, to serve two years; mustered in as private, Co. G, May 17, 1898; mustered out with company, November 19, 1898, at Buffalo, N. Y.

HEINZ, JACOB.—Age, — years. Enlisted, June 14. 1898, at Buffalo, to serve two years; mustered in as private, Co. M, same date; mustered out with company, November 19, 1898, at Buffalo, N. Y.

HEINZENBERGER, ANDREW L.—Age, — years. Enlisted, June 15, 1898, at Buffalo, to serve two years; mustered in as private, Co. A, same date; mustered out with company, November 19, 1898, at Buffalo, N. Y.

HEINZENBERGER, JOHN.—Age, 21 years. Enlisted, May 12, 1898, at Buffalo, to serve two years; mustered in as private, Co. A, May 17, 1898; mustered out with company, November 19, 1898, at Buffalo, N. Y.

HELD, GUSTAVE.—Age, 27 years. Enlisted, May 1, 1898, at Buffalo, to serve two years; mustered in as private, Co. L, May 17, 1898; discharged for disability, June 29, 1898, at Camp Alger, near Dunn Loring, Va.

HELLRIEGEL, WILLIAM.—Age, 24 years. Enlisted, May 1, 1898, at Buffalo, to serve two years; mustered in as private, Co. H, May 17, 1898; appointed wagoner, August 4, 1898; mustered out with company, November 19, 1898, at Buffalo, N. Y.

HEMERLE JOHN C.—Age, 20 years. Enlisted, May 1, 1898, at Buffalo, to serve two years; mustered in as private, Co. F, May 17, 1898; mustered out with company, November 19, 1898, at Buffalo, N. Y.

HENNELL, ARTHUR.—Age, 18 years. Enlisted, May 1, 1898, at Buffalo, to serve two years; mustered in as musician, Co. L, May 17, 1898; mustered out with company, November 19, 1898, at Buffalo, N. Y.

HENNESEN, HENRY L.—Age, 23 years. Enlisted, May 1, 1898, at Buffalo, to serve two years; mustered in as private, Co. M, May 17, 1898; mustered out with company, November 19, 1898, at Buffalo, N. Y.

HENNING, FRED J.—Age, 23 years. Enlisted, May 1, 1898, at Buffalo, to serve two years; mustered in as private, Co. K, May 17, 1898; mustered out with company, November 19, 1898, at Buffalo, N. Y.

HENSCHEL, GEORGE H.—Age, 21 years. Enlisted, May 1, 1898, at Buffalo, to serve two years; mustered in as private, Co. G, May 17, 1898; mustered out with company, November 19, 1898, at Buffalo, N. Y.

HENSHAW, BURT.—Age, — years. Enlisted, June 13, 1898, at Buffalo, to serve two years; mustered in as private, Co. C, same date; mustered out with company, November 19, 1898, at Buffalo, N. Y.

HERB, WILLIAM.—Age, 25 years. Enlisted, May 1, 1898, at Buffalo, to serve two years; mustered in as private, Co. F, May 17, 1898; mustered out with company, November 19, 1898, at Buffalo, N. Y.

HERBOLD, WILLIAM J.—Age, — years. Enlisted, June 14, 1898, at Buffalo, to serve two years; mustered in as private, Co. C, same date; mustered out with company, November 19, 1898, at Buffalo, N. Y.

HERMAN, JACOB C.—Age, — years. Enlisted, June 13, 1898, at Buffalo, to serve two years; mustered in as private, Co. D. same date; mustered out with company, November 19, 1898, at Buffalo, N. Y.

HERMAN, JOHN J.—Age, — years. Enlisted, June 25, 1898, at Buffalo, to serve two years; mustered in as private, Co. C, same date; mustered out with company, November 19, 1898, at Buffalo, N. Y.

HERPST, GEORGE H.—Age, 20 years. Enlisted, May 1, 1898, at Jamestown. to serve two years; mustered in as private, Co. E, May 17, 1898: mustered out with company, November 19, 1898, at Buffalo, N. Y.

HERRMANN, JR., LOUIS.—Age, — years. Enlisted, June 22, 1898, at Buffalo, to serve two years; mustered in as private, Co. H, same date; mustered out with company, November 19, 1898, at Buffalo, N. Y.

HERROD, CHARLES W.—Age, — years. Enlisted, June 13, 1898, at Buffalo, to serve two years; mustered in as private, Co. L, same date; mustered out with company, November 19, 1898, at Buffalo, N. Y.

HESS, CHARLES.—Age, 20 years. Enlisted, May 1, 1898, at Buffalo, to serve two years; mustered in as private, Co. A, May 17, 1898; mustered out with company, November 19, 1898, at Buffalo, N. Y.

HESSON, JAMES.—Age, 24 years. Enlisted, May 11, 1898, at Buffalo, to serve two years; mustered in as private, Co. F, May 17, 1898; appointed cook, July 27, 1898; mustered out with company, November 19, 1898, at Buffalo, N. Y.

HETZEL, JOHN.—Age, — years. Enlisted, June 20, 1898, at Buffalo, to serve two years; mustered in as private, Co. I, same date; mustered out with company, November 19, 1898, at Buffalo, N. Y.

HICKS, HOWARD O.—Age, 31 years. Enlisted, May 1, 1898, at Buffalo, to serve two years; mustered in as private, Co. F, May 17, 1898; transferred to Hospital Corps, United States Army, June 28, 1898; to Co. F, September 2, 1898; mustered out with company, November 19, 1898, at Buffalo, N. Y.

HIESTAND, PETER.—Age, 19 years. Enlisted, May 1, 1898, at Buffalo, to serve two years; mustered in as private, Co. F, May 17, 1898; discharged, November 9, 1898.

HILBERT, EDWARD.—Age, 21 years. Enlisted, May 1, 1898, at Buffalo, to serve two years; mustered in as private, Co. D, May 17, 1898; mustered out with company, November 19, 1898, at Buffalo, N. Y.

HILBERT, FRANK W.—Age, — years. Enlisted, June 18, 1898, at Buffalo, to serve two years; mustered in as private, Co. D, same date; transferred to Co. F, June 29, 1898; mustered out with company, November 19, 1898, at Buffalo, N. Y.

HILL, HENRY T.—Age, — years. Enlisted, June 13, 1898, at Buffalo, to serve two years; mustered in as private, Co. A, same date; mustered out with company, November 19, 1898, at Buffalo, N. Y.

HILTON, CHARLES E.—Age, 23 years. Enlisted, May 1, 1898, at Buffalo, to serve two years; mustered in as quartermaster-sergeant, Co. G, May 17, 1898; mustered out with company, November 19, 1898, at Buffalo, N. Y.

HINES, WILLIAM J.—Age, 38 years. Enlisted, May 1, 1898, at Buffalo, to serve two years; mustered in as private, Co. B, May 17, 1898; discharged for disability, July 23, 1898.

HINKLEY, GUY P.—Age, — years. Enlisted, June 16, 1898, at Buffalo, to serve two years; mustered in as private, Co. I, same date; mustered out with company, November 19, 1898, at Buffalo, N. Y.

HINKLEY, WILLIAM.—Age, 27 years. Enlisted, May 1, 1898, at Buffalo, to serve two years; mustered in as private, Co. H, May 17, 1898; mustered out with company, November 19, 1898, at Buffalo, N. Y.

HITCHCOCK, MELVIN D.—Age, 22 years. Enlisted, May 13, 1898, at Camp Black, to serve two years; mustered in as private, Co. E, May 17, 1898; mustered out with company, November 19, 1898, at Buffalo, N. Y.

HOCHWARTH, MAXWELL O.—Age, — years. Enlisted, June 22, 1898, at Buffalo, to serve two years; mustered in as private, Co. M, same date; mustered out with company, November 19, 1898, at Buffalo, N. Y.

HOCK, PETER.—Age, 29 years. Enlisted, May 1, 1898, at Buffalo, to serve two years; mustered in as musician, Co. I, May 17, 1898; discharged, June 22, 1898.

HODGE, FRANK E.—Age, 19 years. Enlisted, May 1, 1898, at Buffalo, to serve two years; mustered in as corporal, Co. M, May 17, 1898; transferred to Hospital Corps, United States Army, June 28, 1898; to Co. A, September 2, 1898: returned to ranks, no date; mustered out with company, November 19, 1898, at Buffalo, N. Y.

HODGSON, HERBERT.—Age, 22 years. Enlisted, May 1, 1898, at Buffalo, to serve two years; mustered in as private, Co. I, May 17, 1898; killed by the cars, June 12, 1898, near Jackson City, Va.

HOEFLEIH, JOHN.—Age, 24 years. Enlisted, May 1, 1898, at Buffalo, to serve two years; mustered in as private, Co. L, May 17, 1898; mustered out with company, November 19, 1898, at Buffalo, N. Y.

HOERNER, LOUIS F.—Age, 21 years. Enlisted, May 1, 1898, at Buffalo, to serve two years; mustered in as private, Co. F, May 17, 1898; mustered out with company, November 19, 1898, at Buffalo, N. Y.

HOESTERMANN, FRED.—Age, 21 years. Enlisted, May 1, 1898, at Buffalo, to serve two years; mustered in as private, Co. D, May 17, 1898; mustered out with company, November 19, 1898, at Buffalo, N. Y.

HOFFMAN, CHARLES S.—Age, 23 years. Enlisted, May 11, 1898, at Camp Black, to serve two years; mustered in as private, Co. D, May 17, 1898; mustered out with company, November 19, 1898, at Buffalo, N. Y.

HOFFMAN, GEORGE.—Age, 19 years. Enlisted, May 1, 1898,
at Buffalo, to serve two years; mustered in as private, Co. H,
May 17, 1898; mustered out with company, November 19, 1898,
at Buffalo, N. Y.

HOFFMANN, CONRAD.—Age, 19 years. Enlisted, May 1, 1898,
at Buffalo, to serve two years; mustered in as private, Co. M,
May 17, 1898; mustered out with company, November 19, 1898,.
at Buffalo, N. Y.

HOFFMANN, JOHN L.—Age, 22 years. Enlisted, May 1, 1898, at
Buffalo, to serve two years; mustered in as private, Co. D, May
17, 1898; mustered out with company, November 19, 1898, at
Buffalo, N. Y.

HOFFSTETTER, HENRY.—Age, 24 years. Enlisted, May 1,.
1898, at Buffalo, to serve two years; mustered in as private, Co_
D, May 17, 1898; mustered out with company, November 19,.
1898, at Buffalo, N. Y.

HOHN, CHARLES.—Age, 26 years. Enlisted, May 1, 1898, at
Buffalo, to serve two years; mustered in as corporal, Co. C,.
May 17, 1898; promoted sergeant, same date; first sergeant,
June 1, 1898; mustered out with company, November 19, 1898,.
at Buffalo, N. Y.

HOHNGREN, RICHARD—Age, 22 years. Enlisted, May 1, 1898,.
at Buffalo, to serve two years; mustered in as private, Co. G,
May 17, 1898; mustered out with company, November 19, 1898,.
at Buffalo, N. Y.

HOLDEN, EDWARD E.—Age, — years. Enlisted, June 15,.
1898, at Camp Alger, near Dunn Loring, Va., to serve two
years; mustered in as private, Co. G, same date; mustered out
with company, November 19, 1898, at Buffalo, N. Y.

HOLDEN, FRANK S.—Age, 39 years. Enlisted, May 1, 1898, at
Buffalo, to serve two years; mustered in as private, Co. A, May
17, 1898; mustered out with company, November 19, 1898, at
Buffalo, N. Y.

HOLDEN, JOHN M.—Age, — years. Enlisted, June 21, 1898, at
Buffalo, to serve two years; mustered in as private, Co. M, same
date; mustered out with company, November 19, 1898, at
Buffalo, N. Y.

HOLTZ, FRED C.—Age, 22 years Enlisted, May 1, 1898, at. Buffalo, to serve two years; mustered in as private, Co. L, May 17, 1898; mustered out with company, November 19, 1898, at Buffalo, N. Y.

HOOPES, CHARLES L.—Age, 29 years. Enlisted, May 1, 1898, at Buffalo, to serve two years; mustered in as private, Co. C, May 17, 1898; promoted corporal, July 1, 1898; mustered out with company, November 19, 1898, at Buffalo, N. Y.

HORLOCK, HENRY.—Age, 18 years. Enlisted, May 1, 1898, at Buffalo, to serve two years; mustered in as private, Co. B, May 17, 1898; mustered out with company, November 19, 1898, at Buffalo, N. Y.

HORNER, JR., JACOB.—Age, — years. Enlisted, June 14, 1898, at Buffalo, to serve two years; mustered in as private, Co. H, same date; mustered out with company, November 19, 1898, at Buffalo, N. Y.

HOWARD, BENJAMIN F.—Age, 23 years. Enlisted, May 1, 1898, at Buffalo, to serve two years; mustered in as private, Co. C, May 17, 1898; mustered out with company, November 19, 1898, at Buffalo, N. Y.

HOWARD, HARRY O.—Age, — years. Enlisted, June 15, 1898, at Buffalo, to serve two years; mustered in as private, Co. G, same date; mustered out with company, November 19, 1898, at Buffalo, N. Y.

HOWARD, JAMES G.—Age, 22 years. Enlisted, May 1, 1898, at Buffalo, to serve two years; mustered in as private, Co. F, May 17, 1898; mustered out with company, November 19, 1898, at Buffalo, N. Y.

HOWLAND, JOHN DAVID.—Age, 33 years. Enrolled, May 1, 1898, at Buffalo, to serve two years; mustered in as major, May 17, 1898; discharged, November 1, 1898; subsequent service as first lieutenant and regimental adjutant, Two Hundred and Second Regiment, New York Volunteer Infantry; commissioned major, May 17, 1898, with rank from same date, original.

HUBER, LORENZ.—Age, 22 years. Enlisted, May 1, 1898, at Buffalo, to serve two years; mustered in as private, Co. F, May 17, 1898; mustered out with company, November 19, 1898, at Buffalo, N. Y.

HUFF, BERTH.—Age, 29 years. Enlisted, May 1, 1898, at Buffalo, to serve two years; mustered in as private, Co. F, May 17,
1898; mustered out with company, November 19, 1898, at Buffalo, N. Y.

HUFFMAN, HARLEN.—Age, 29 years. Enlisted, May 1, 1898,
at Buffalo, to serve two years; mustered in as private, Co. L,
May 17, 1898; mustered out with company, November 19, 1898,
at Buffalo, N. Y.

HUGHES, DANTON P.—Age, 23 years. Enrolled, May 1, 1898,
at Buffalo, to serve two years; mustered in as second lieutenant, Co. K, May 17, 1898; mustered out with company, November 19, 1898, at Buffalo, N. Y.; commissioned second lieutenant,
May 17, 1898, with rank from same date, original.

HUGHES, THOMAS.—Age, — years. Enlisted, June 13, 1898,
at Buffalo, to serve two years; mustered in as private, Co. A,
same date; mustered out with company, November 19, 1898, at
Buffalo, N. Y.

HURLEY, JOHN E.—Age, 23 years. Enlisted, May 1, 1898, at
Buffalo, to serve two years; mustered in as private, Co. D, May
17, 1898; died of typhoid fever, August 18, 1898, in Division
Hospital, Camp Alger, near Dunn Loring, Va.

HURN, CHARLES A.—Age, 35 years. Enlisted, May 1, 1898, at
Buffalo, to serve two years; mustered in as private, Co. K, May
17, 1898; dishonorably discharged, October 28, 1898.

HUSS, JR., LOUIS.—Age, 19 years. Enlisted, May 1, 1898, at
Buffalo, to serve two years; mustered in as private, Co. F, May
17, 1898; mustered out with company, November 19, 1898, at
Buffalo, N. Y.

HUSSONG, RODGERS L.—Age, 19 years. Enlisted, May 1,
1898, at Buffalo, to serve two years; mustered in as private, Co.
A, May 17, 1898; mustered out with company, November 19,
1898, at Buffalo, N. Y.

HUTZLER, GEORGE.—Age, 32 years. Enlisted, May 1, 1898,
at Buffalo, to serve two years; mustered in as private, Co. K,
May 17, 1898; mustered out with company, November 19, 1898,
at Buffalo, N. Y.

HYER, WILLIAM C.—Age, 21 years. Enlisted, May 1, 1898, at ·
Buffalo, to serve two years; mustered in as corporal, Co. L, May
17, 1898; mustered out with company, November 19, 1898, at
Buffalo, N. Y.

HYMAN, CHARLES.—Age, 18 years. Enlisted, May 1, 1898, at
Buffalo, to serve two years; mustered in as private, Co. I, May
17, 1898; mustered out with company, November 19, 1898, at
Buffalo, N. Y.

IDE, ARIEL H.—Age, 26 years. Enrolled, May 1, 1898, at Buffalo, to serve two years; mustered in as first lieutenant, Co. K,
May 17, 1898; mustered out with company, November 19, 1898,
at Buffalo, N. Y.; commissioned first lieutenant, May 17, 1898,
with rank from same date, original.

IRISH, MICHAEL J.—Age, 23 years. Enlisted, May 1, 1898, at
Buffalo, to serve two years; mustered in as private, Co. I, May
17, 1898; mustered out with company, November 19, 1898, at
Buffalo, N. Y.

IRWIN, THOMAS J.—Age, 23 years. Enlisted, May 1, 1898, at
Buffalo, to serve two years; mustered in as private, Co. G, May
17, 1898; mustered out with company, November 19, 1898, at
Buffalo, N. Y.

ISAACSON, WILLIAM O.—Age, 22 years. Enlisted, May 1,
1898, at Jamestown, to serve two years; mustered in as private,
Co. E, May 17, 1898; mustered out with company, November 19,
1898, at Buffalo, N. Y.

ISCH, HARRY.—Age, 21 years. Enlisted, May 1, 1898, at Buffalo, to serve two years; mustered in as private, Co. M, May
17, 1898; mustered out with company, November 19, 1898, at
Buffalo, N. Y.

ISCH, WILLIAM.—Age, 20 years. Enlisted, May 1, 1898, at
Buffalo, to serve two years; mustered in as private, Co. I, May
17, 1898; mustered out with company, November 19, 1898, at
Buffalo, N. Y.

JABLOWINZ, JULIUS.—Age, 21 years. Enlisted, May 1, 1898,
at Buffalo, to serve two years; mustered in as private, Co. H,
May 17, 1898; mustered out with company, November 19, 1898,
at Buffalo, N. Y.

JACKSON, CHARLES.—Age, — years.   Enlisted, June 13, 1898, at Buffalo, to serve two years; mustered in as private, Co. A, same date; mustered out with company, November 19, 1898, at Buffalo, N. Y.

JACKSON, JAMES F.—Age, 21 years.   Enlisted, May 1, 1898, at Buffalo, to serve two years; mustered in as private, Co. B, May 17, 1898; discharged, October 29, 1898.

JACKSON, JAMES S.—Age, 19 years.   Enlisted, May 1, 1898, at Buffalo, to serve two years; mustered in as private, Co. A, May 17, 1898; mustered out with company, November 19, 1898, at Buffalo, N. Y.

JACKSON, WILLIAM B.—Age, — years.   Enlisted, June 14, 1898, at Buffalo, to serve two years; mustered in as private, Co. B, same date; mustered out with company, November 19, 1898, at Buffalo, N. Y.

JACKSON, WILLIAM S.—Age, 29 years.   Enrolled, May 1, 1898, at Buffalo, to serve two years; mustered in as second lieutenant, Co. M, May 17, 1898; mustered out with company, November 19, 1898, at Buffalo, N. Y.; commissioned second lieutenant, May 17, 1898, with rank from same date, original.

JAEGER, DAVID.—Age, 27 years.   Enlisted, May 1, 1898, at Buffalo, to serve two years; mustered in as private, Co. L, May 17, 1898; mustered out with company, November 19, 1898, at Buffalo, N. Y.

JAEGER, OTTO W.—Age, 27 years.   Enlisted, May 1, 1898, at Buffalo, to serve two years; mustered in as private, Co. C, May 17, 1898; mustered out with company, November 19, 1898, at Buffalo, N. Y.

JAHRANS, ALBERT J.—Age, 23 years.   Enlisted, May 1, 1898, at Buffalo, to serve two years; mustered in as corporal, Co. G, May 17, 1898; mustered out with company, November 19, 1898, at Buffalo, N. Y.

JAMES, ARTHUR.—Age, 26 years.   Enlisted, May 1, 1898, at Buffalo, to serve two years; mustered in as private, Co. M, May 17, 1898; promoted corporal, to date, July 1, 1898; mustered out with company, November 19, 1898, at Buffalo, N. Y.

JAMESON, ARTHUR H.—Age, 21 years. Enlisted, May 1, 1898, at Buffalo, to serve two years; mustered in as private, Co. C, May 17, 1898; transferred to Hospital Corps, United States Army, June 22, 1898; to Co. K, September 2, 1898; mustered out with company, November 19, 1898, at Buffalo, N. Y.

JARVIS, RICHARD.—Age, 32 years. Enlisted, May 1, 1898, at Buffalo, to serve two years; mustered in as private, Co. G, May 17, 1898; mustered out with company, November 19, 1898, at Buffalo, N. Y.

JENKINS, FRED D.—Age, 18 years. Enlisted, May 1, 1898, at Buffalo, to serve two years; mustered in as private, Co. K, May 17, 1898; mustered out with company, November 19, 1898, at Buffalo, N. Y.

JERGE, EDWARD J.—Age, 18 years. Enlisted, May 1, 1898, at Buffalo, to serve two years; mustered in as private, Co. M, May 17, 1898; mustered out with company, November 19, 1898, at Buffalo, N. Y.

JERGE, EUGENE.—Age, — years. Enlisted, June 24, 1898, at Buffalo, to serve two years; mustered in as private, Co. G, same date; transferred to band, June 29, 1898; mustered out with band, November 19, 1898, at Buffalo, N. Y.

JERGE, GEORGE.—Age, 20 years. Enlisted, May 1, 1898, at Buffalo, to serve two years; mustered in as private, Co. C, May 17, 1898; mustered out with company, November 19, 1898, at Buffalo, N. Y.

JERGE, JR., JOSEPH.—Age, 29 years. Enlisted, May 1, 1898, at Buffalo, to serve two years; mustered in as musician, Co. H, May 17, 1898; mustered out with company, November 19, 1898, at Buffalo, N. Y.

JEWELL, ARTHUR C.—Age, 21 years. Enlisted, May 1, 1898, at Buffalo, to serve two years; mustered in as sergeant, Co. I, May 17, 1898: returned to ranks, May 18, 1898; promoted corporal, no date; mustered out with company, November 19, 1898, at Buffalo, N. Y.

JEWELL, JOHN W.—Age, 27 years. Enlisted, May 1, 1898, at Buffalo, to serve two years; mustered in as private, Co. G, May 17, 1898; mustered out with company, November 19, 1898, at Buffalo, N. Y.

JOHNSON, CHARLES A.—Age, 20 years. Enlisted, May 1, 1898, at Buffalo, to serve two years; mustered in as private, Co. G, May 17, 1898; promoted corporal, June 29, 1898; mustered out with company, November 19, 1898, at Buffalo, N. Y.

JOHNSON, CHARLES J.—Age, 27 years. Enlisted, May 1, 1898, at Jamestown, to serve two years; mustered in as private, Co. E, May 17, 1898; mustered out with company, November 19, 1898, at Buffalo, N. Y.

JOHNSON, EDWARD.—Age, 22 years. Enlisted, May 1, 1898, at Buffalo, to serve two years; mustered in as private, Co. K, May 17, 1898; mustered out with company, November 19, 1898, at Buffalo, N. Y.

JOHNSON, FRANK A.—Age, 39 years. Enrolled, May 1, 1898, at Jamestown, to serve two years; mustered in as first lieutenant, Co. E, May 7, 1898; as captain, July 16, 1898; mustered out with company, November 19, 1898, at Buffalo, N. Y.; commissioned first lieutenant, May 17, 1898, with rank from same date, original; captain, July 8, 1898, with rank from same date, vice Gilbert, promoted captain and assistant quartermaster, United States Volunteers.

JOHNSON, HENRY.—Age, — years. Enlisted, June 13, 1898, at Buffalo, to serve two years; mustered in as private, Co. C, same date; mustered out with company, November 19, 1898, at Buffalo, N. Y.

JOHNSON, HENRY F.—Age, 31 years. Enlisted, May 1, 1898, at Buffalo, to serve two years; mustered in as private, Co. L, May 17, 1898; mustered out with company, November 19, 1898, at Buffalo, N. Y.

JOHNSON, JERRY.—Age, 24 years. Enlisted, May 1, 1898, at Buffalo, to serve two years; mustered in as private, Co. C, May 17, 1898; mustered out with company, November 19, 1898, at Buffalo, N. Y.

JOHNSON, JOHN J.—Age, — years. Enlisted, June 15, 1898, at Buffalo, to serve two years; mustered in as private, Co. E, same date; mustered out with company, November 19, 1898, at Buffalo, N. Y.

JOHNSON, OSCAR A.—Age, 28 years. Enlisted, May 1, 1898, at Jamestown, to serve two years; mustered in as private, Co. E, May 17, 1898; mustered out with company, November 19, 1898, at Buffalo, N. Y.

JOHNSON, ROBERT F.—Age, 26 years. Enlisted, May 1, 1898, at Buffalo, to serve two years; mustered in as private, Co. B, May 17, 1898; mustered out with company, November 19, 1898, at Buffalo, N. Y.

JOHNSON, WILLIAM E.—Age, 22 years. Enlisted, May 1, 1898, at Buffalo, to serve two years; mustered in as sergeant, Co. L, May 17, 1898; mustered out with company, November 19, 1898, at Buffalo, N. Y.

JOLLIE, EDWARD F.—Age, 30 years. Enlisted, May 1, 1898, at Jamestown, to serve two years; mustered in as private, Co. E, May 17, 1898; appointed wagoner, same date; mustered out with company, November 19, 1898, at Buffalo, N. Y.

JONES, JOHN F.—Age, 33 years. Enlisted, May 1, 1898, at Buffalo, to serve two years; mustered in as sergeant, Co. E, May 17, 1898; mustered out with company, November 19, 1898, at at Buffalo, N. Y.

JONES, JOSEPH M.—Age, 26 years. Enlisted, May 1, 1898, at Buffalo, to serve two years; mustered in as musician, Co. F, May 17, 1898; returned to ranks, August 18, 1898; mustered out with company, November 19, 1898, at Buffalo, N. Y.

JOSETT, AUGUST J.—Age, — years. Enlisted, June 27, 1898, at Buffalo, to serve two years; mustered in as private, Co. M, same date; mustered out with company, November 19, 1898, at Buffalo, N. Y.

JUDD, JR., WILLIAM J.—Age, — years. Enlisted, June 17, 1898, at Buffalo, to serve two years; mustered in as private, Co. H, same date; mustered out with company, November 19, 1898, at Buffalo, N. Y.

KAHN, WILLIAM.—Age, 22 years. Enlisted, May 1, 1898, at Buffalo, to serve two years; mustered in as private, Co. F, May 17, 1898; mustered out with company, November 19, 1898, at Buffalo, N. Y.

KALAK, ANDREW.—Age, 22 years. Enlisted, May 1, 1898, at Buffalo, to serve two years; mustered in as private, Co. L, May 17, 1898; mustered out with company, November 19, 1898, at Buffalo, N. Y., as Andrew Kaklak.

KANE, HARRY G.—Age, — years. Enlisted, June 13, 1898, at Buffalo, to serve two years; mustered in as private, Co. I, same date; mustered out with company, November 19, 1898, at Buffalo, N. Y.

KANE, ROBERT.—Age, 24 years. Enlisted, May 13, 1898, at Buffalo, to serve two years; mustered in as private, Co. H, May 17, 1898; mustered out with company, November 19, 1898, at Buffalo, N. Y.

KARN, JR., JACOB.—Age, 18 years. Enlisted, May 1, 1898, at Buffalo, to serve two years; mustered in as private, Co. F, May 17, 1898; mustered out with company, November 19, 1898, at Buffalo, N. Y.

KARN, VALENTINE.—Age, 20 years. Enlisted, May 1, 1898, at Buffalo, to serve two years; mustered in as private, Co. F, May 17, 1898; mustered out with company, November 19, 1898, at Buffalo, N. Y.

KAZNOWSKI, FRANK.—Age, 24 years. Enlisted, May 1, 1898, at Buffalo, to serve two years; mustered in as private, Co. I, May 17, 1898; promoted corporal, July 1, 1898; died of typhoid fever, September 2, 1898, at Buffalo, N. Y.

KAZNOWSKI, MICHAEL.—Age, 24 years. Enlisted, May 1, 1898, at Buffalo, to serve two years; mustered in as private, Co. I, May 17, 1898; mustered out with company, November 19, 1898, at Buffalo, N. Y.

KEARNES, CARSON.—Age, 25 years. Enlisted, May 1, 1898, at Buffalo, to serve two years; mustered in as private, Co. H, May 17, 1898; dishonorably discharged, October 28, 1898, at Buffalo, N. Y.

KEHOE, EDWARD L.—Age, — years. Enlisted, June 13, 1898, at Buffalo, to serve two years; mustered in as private, Co. M, same date; mustered out with company, November 19, 1898, at Buffalo, N. Y.

KELLEHER, MATHEW.—Age, 26 years. Enlisted, May 1, 1898, at Buffalo, to serve two years; mustered in as private, Co. I, May 17, 1898; mustered out with company, November 19, 1898, at Buffalo, N. Y.

KELLER, GEORGE F.—Age, 23 years. Enlisted, May 1, 1898, at Buffalo, to serve two years; mustered in as corporal, Co. C, May 17, 1898; returned to ranks, July 18, 1898; mustered out with company, November 19, 1898, at Buffalo, N. Y.

KELLEY, WILLIAM A.—Age, — years. Enlisted, June 29, 1898, at Buffalo, to serve two years; mustered in as private, Co. L, same date; mustered out with company, November 19, 1898, at Buffalo, N. Y.

KELLOGG, HENDERSON.—Age, 20 years. Enlisted, May 1, 1898, at Buffalo, to serve two years; mustered in as quarter-master-sergeant, Co. L, May 17, 1898; mustered out with company, November 19, 1898, at Buffalo, N. Y.

KELLY, EDWARD J.—Age, 19 years. Enlisted, May 1, 1898, at Buffalo, to serve two years; mustered in as private, Co. A, May 17, 1898; mustered out with company, November 19, 1898, at Buffalo, N. Y.

KELLY, EDWARD L.—Age, 24 years. Enlisted, May 14, 1898 at Camp Black, to serve two years; mustered in as private, Co. A, May 17, 1898; mustered out with company, November 19, 1898, at Buffalo, N. Y.

KELSEY, FRANK E.—Age, 37 years. Enlisted, May 1, 1898, at Buffalo, to serve two years; mustered in as private, Co. K, May 17, 1898; mustered out with company, November 19, 1898, at Buffalo, N. Y.

KENNEY, FRANK H.—Age, — years. Enlisted. June 13, 1898, at Buffalo, to serve two years; mustered in as private, Co. C, same date; mustered out with company, November 19, 1898, at Buffalo, N. Y.

KENT, LOUIS.—Age, 22 years. Enlisted, May 1, 1898, at Buffalo, to serve two years; mustered in as private, Co. L, May 17, 1898; mustered out with company, November 19, 1898, at Buffalo, N. Y.

KERING, SAMUEL.—Age, 42 years. Enlisted, May 1, 1898, at
Buffalo, to serve two years; mustered in as private, Co. H,
May 17, 1898; mustered out with company, November 19, 1898,
at Buffalo, N. Y.

KERR, ROBERT A.—Age, 22 years. Enlisted, May 1, 1898, at
Buffalo, to serve two years; mustered in as private, Co. C, May
17, 1898; mustered out with company, November 19, 1898, at
Buffalo, N. Y.

KERSLAKE, GEORGE.—Age, 25 years. Enlisted, May 1, 1898,
at Buffalo, to serve two years; mustered in as musician. Co. H,
May 17, 1898; mustered out with company, November 19, 1898,
at Buffalo, N. Y.

KERWIN, MARK.—Age, 25 years. Enlisted, May 1, 1898, at
Buffalo, to serve two years; mustered in as private, Co. M, May
17, 1898; mustered out with company, November 19, 1898, at
Buffalo, N. Y.

KESSEL, LEO J.—Age, 21 years. Enlisted, May 1, 1898, at Buffalo, to serve two years; mustered in as private, Co. H, May
17, 1898; mustered out with company, November 19, 1898, at
Buffalo, N. Y.

KETCHUM, JESSE.—Age, 22 years. Enlisted, May 1, 1898, at
Buffalo, to serve two years; mustered in as private, Co. C, May
17, 1898; mustered out with company, November 19, 1898, at
Buffalo, N. Y.

KETCHUM, RAYMOND B.—Age, 23 years. Enlisted, May 1,
1898, at Buffalo, to serve two years; mustered in as private, Co.
C, May 17, 1898; promoted corporal, August 10, 1898; mustered
out with company, November 19, 1898, at Buffalo, N. Y.

KETCHUM, ROY F.—Age, 21 years. Enlisted, May 1, 1898, at
Buffalo, to serve two years; mustered in as private, Co. C, May
17, 1898; mustered out with company, November 19, 1898, at
Buffalo, N. Y.

KIELLY, ARCHIBALD E.—Age, 23 years. Enlisted, May 1,
1898, at Buffalo, to serve two years; mustered in as private, Co.
H, May 17, 1898; promoted corporal, no date; mustered out with
company, July 25, 1898, at Buffalo, N. Y.

KILLIAN, BENEDICT.—Age, 35 years. Enlisted, May 1, 1898, at Buffalo, to serve two years; mustered in as private, Co. L, May 17, 1898; mustered out with company, November 19, 1898, at Buffalo, N. Y.

KIMBERLE, JOHN J.—Age, 23 years. Enlisted, May 1, 1898, at Buffalo, to serve two years; mustered in as private, Co. K, May 17, 1898; mustered out with company, November 19, 1898, at Buffalo, N. Y.

KIMMAL, CHARLES H.—Age, — years. Enlisted, June 20, 1898, at Buffalo, to serve two years; mustered in as private, Co. L, same date; mustered out with company, November 19, 1898, at Buffalo, N. Y.

KING, JOHN L.—Age, — years. Enlisted, June 20, 1898, at Buffalo, to serve two years; mustered in as private, Co. B, same date; mustered out with company, November 19, 1898, at Buffalo, N. Y.

KINSKEY, CHARLES E.—Age, 25 years. Enlisted, May 1, 1898, at Buffalo, to serve two years; mustered in as private, Co. C, May 17, 1898; promoted corporal, May 22, 1898; mustered out with company, November 19, 1898, at Buffalo, N. Y.

KINZIE, LEO.—Age, 21 years. Enlisted, May 1, 1898, at Buffalo, to serve two years; mustered in as private, Co. M, May 17, 1898; mustered out with company, November 19, 1898, at Buffalo, N. Y.

KIPLER, HENRY H. F.—Age, 22 years. Enlisted, May 1, 1898, at Buffalo, to serve two years; mustered in as private, Co. C, May 17, 1898; discharged for disability, August 15, 1898.

KIRBY, HARRY O.—Age, 30 years. Enlisted, May 1, 1898, at Buffalo, to serve two years; mustered in as corporal, Co. K, May 17, 1898; mustered out with company, November 19, 1898, at Buffalo, N. Y.

KLEEBER, LEWIS F.—Age, 21 years. Enlisted, May 12, 1898, at Buffalo, to serve two years; mustered in as private, Co. M, May 17, 1898; mustered out with company, November 19, 1898, at Buffalo, N. Y.

KLEIN, ALBERT.—Age, 31 years. Enlisted, May 1, 1898, at Buffalo, to serve two years; mustered in as private, Co. K, May 17, 1898; mustered out with company, November 19, 1898, at Buffalo, N. Y.

KLEIN, JR., GEORGE H.—Age, 25 years. Enlisted, May 1, 1898, at Buffalo, to serve two years; mustered in as private, Co. D, May 17, 1898; discharged for disability, July 19, 1898, at Camp Alger, near Dunn Loring, Va.

KLEIN, HERMAN.—Age, 21 years. Enlisted, May 1. 1898, at Buffalo, to serve two years; mustered in as private, Co. I, May 17, 1898; mustered out with company, November 19. 1898, at Buffalo, N. Y.

KLEIN, WILLIAM.—Age, 28 years. Enlisted, May 1, 1898, at Buffalo, to serve two years; mustered in as private, Co. D, May 17, 1898; mustered out with company, November 19. 1898, at Buffalo, N. Y.

KLEMP, CHARLES.—Age, 22 years. Enlisted, May 1, 1898, at Buffalo, to serve two years; mustered in as private, Co. I, May 17, 1898; mustered out with company, November 19, 1898, at Buffalo, N. Y.

KLIPFEL, ANDREW C.—Age, 21 years. Enlisted, May 1, 1898, at Buffalo, to serve two years; mustered in as private, Co. L, May 17, 1898; transferred to United States Hospital Corps, June 28, 1898, at Camp Alger, Va.; to Co. B, September 3, 1898; mustered out with company, November 19, 1898, at Buffalo, N. Y.

KLOSE, JOSEPH.—Age, 24 years. Enlisted, May 1, 1898, at Buffalo, to serve two years; mustered in as private, Co. D, May 17, 1898; mustered out with company, November 19, 1898, at Buffalo, N. Y.

KNOX, JAMES H.—Age, 27 years. Enlisted, May 1, 1898, at Buffalo, to serve two years; mustered in as private, Co. M, May 17, 1898; mustered out with company, November 19, 1898, at Buffalo, N. Y.

KOCH, ALBERT H.—Age, 22 years. Enlisted, May 1, 1898, at Buffalo, to serve two years; mustered in as private, Co. C, May 17, 1898; mustered out with company, November 19, 1898, at Buffalo, N. Y.

KOEHN, CHARLES F.—Age, — years. Enlisted, June 16, 1898,. at Buffalo, to serve two years; mustered in as private, Co. D, same date; mustered out with company, November 19, 1898, at Buffalo, N. Y.

KOLB, GEORGE.—Age, — years. Enlisted, June 23, 1898, at Buffalo, to serve two years; mustered in as private, Co. K, same date; mustered out with company, November 19, 1898, at Buffalo, N. Y.

KOLB, JOHN B.—Age, 20 years. Enlisted, May 1, 1898, at Buffalo, to serve two years; mustered in as private, Co. A, May 17, 1898; promoted corporal, August 3, 1898; mustered out with company, November 19, 1898, at Buffalo, N. Y.

KOLLER, WILLIAM I.—Age, 30 years. Enlisted, May 1, 1898, at Buffalo, to serve two years; mustered in as private, Co. C, May 17, 1898; mustered out with company, November 19, 1898, at Buffalo, N. Y.

KOLLMEYER, MICHAEL.—Age, 39 years. Enlisted, May 1, 1898, at Buffalo, to serve two years; mustered in as private, Co. D, May 17, 1898; appointed cook, July 27, 1898; mustered out with company, November 19, 1898, at Buffalo, N. Y.

KOLTEN, HERMAN N.—Age, — years. Enlisted, June 13, 1898, at Buffalo, to serve two years; mustered in as private, Co. G, same date; mustered out with company, November 19, 1898, at Buffalo, N. Y.

KOPKIA, CHRIST.—Age, — years. Enlisted, June 24, 1898, at Buffalo, to serve two years; mustered in as private, Co. G, same date; transferred to band, June 29, 1898; mustered out with band, November 19, 1898, at Buffalo, N. Y.

KORHUMMEL, JOSEPH.—Age, 22 years. Enlisted, May 1, 1898, at Buffalo, to serve two years; mustered in as private, Co. H, May 17, 1898; discharged, October 26, 1898, at Buffalo, N. Y.

KOSTER, PAUL.—Age, 21 years. Enlisted, May 1, 1898, at Buffalo, to serve two years; mustered in as private, Co. D, May 17, 1898; mustered out with company, November 19, 1898, at Buffalo, N. Y.

KRAMPOWSKY, AUGUST J.—Age, 19 years. Enlisted, May 1, 1898, at Buffalo, to serve two years; mustered in as private, Co. H, May 17, 1898; mustered out with company, November 19, 1898, at Buffalo, N. Y.

KRETZMAN, CHARLES.—Age, 32 years. Enlisted, May 1, 1898, at Buffalo, to serve two years; mustered in as private, Co. K, May 17, 1898; mustered out with company, November 19, 1898, at Buffalo, N. Y.

KRIER, PAUL.—Age, 23 years. Enlisted, May 1, 1898, at Buffalo, to serve two years; mustered in as private, Co. I, May 17, 1898; mustered out with company, November 19, 1898, at Buffalo, N. Y.

KROPP, JOHN.—Age, 20 years. Enlisted, May 1, 1898, at Buffalo, to serve two years; mustered in as corporal, Co. F, May 17, 1898; mustered out with company, November 19, 1898, at Buffalo, N. Y.

KRUGER, FRANK J.—Age, 21 years. Enlisted, May 1, 1898, at Jamestown, to serve two years; mustered in as private, Co. E, May 17, 1898; mustered out with company, November 19, 1898, at Buffalo, N. Y.

KRUGER, FRED E. C.—Age, — years. Enlisted, June 14, 1898, at Buffalo, to serve two years; mustered in as private, Co. D, same date; mustered out with company, November 19, 1898, at Buffalo, N. Y.

KRULL, JOHN.—Age, 21 years. Enlisted, May 1, 1898, at Buffalo, to serve two years; mustered in as private, Co. I, May 17, 1898; mustered out with company, November 19, 1898, at Buffalo, N. Y.

KUDER, AUGUST.—Age, 22 years. Enlisted, May 1, 1898, at Buffalo, to serve two years; mustered in as private, Co. F, May 17, 1898; mustered out with company, November 19, 1898, at Buffalo, N. Y.

KUNG, AUGUST W.—Age, — years. Enlisted, June 13, 1898, at Buffalo, to serve two years; mustered in as private, Co. F, same date; mustered out with company, November 19, 1898, at Buffalo, N. Y.

KUNG, CHARLES.—Age, 21 years. Enlisted, May 1, 1898, at Buffalo, to serve two years; mustered in as private, Co. D, May 17, 1898; mustered out with company, November 19, 1898, at Buffalo, N. Y.

KUSTER, ADAM.—Age, 21 years. Enlisted, May 1, 1898, at Buffalo, to serve two years; mustered in as private, Co. M, May 17, 1898; mustered out with company, November 19, 1898, at Buffalo, N. Y.

KUSTRE, AUGUST.—Age, — years. Enlisted, June 18, 1898, at Buffalo, to serve two years; mustered in as private, Co. K, same date; mustered out with company, November 19, 1898, at Buffalo, N. Y.

LA BAHAN, CHARLES.—Age, — years. Enlisted, June 13, 1898, at Buffalo, to serve two years; mustered in as private, Co. K, same date; mustered out with company, November 19, 1898, at Buffalo, N. Y.

LAMMERT, FRED W.—Age, — years. Enlisted, June 20, 1898, at Buffalo, to serve two years; mustered in as private, Co. D, same date; transferred to Co. F, June 29, 1898; mustered out with company, November 19, 1898, at Buffalo, N. Y.

LAMPARSKI, PAUL.—Age, 21 years. Enlisted, May 1, 1898, at Buffalo, to serve two years; mustered in as private, Co. B, May 17, 1898; mustered out with company, November 19, 1898, at Buffalo, N. Y.

LAMPARTER, HARRY C.—Age, 27 years. Enlisted, May 1, 1898, at Buffalo, to serve two years; mustered in as private, Co. K, May 17, 1898; mustered out with company, November 19, 1898, at Buffalo, N. Y.

LAMPHIER, EDWARD.—Age, 20 years. Enlisted, May 1, 1898, at Buffalo, to serve two years; mustered in as private, Co. I, May 17, 1898; mustered out with company, November 19, 1898, at Buffalo, N. Y.

LANE, GEORGE W.—Age, 24 years. Enlisted, May 1, 1898, at Buffalo, to serve two years; mustered in as private, Co. M, May 17, 1898; mustered out with company, November 19, 1898, at Buffalo, N. Y.

LANE, JOHN M.—Age, — years. Enlisted, July 1, 1898, at Buffalo, to serve two years; mustered in as private, Co. H, same date; transferred to band July 6, 1898; mustered out with band, November 19, 1898, at Buffalo, N. Y.

LANG, CHRIST.—Age, 24 years. Enlisted, May 1, 1898, at Buffalo, to serve two years; mustered in as private, Co. C, May 17, 1898; mustered out with company, November 19, 1898, at Buffalo, N. Y.

LANG, HERMAN.—Age, 23 years. Enlisted, May 1, 1898, at Buffalo, to serve two years; mustered in as private, Co. A, May 17, 1898; mustered out with company, November 19, 1898, at Buffalo, N. Y.

LANG, JOHN.—Age, — years. Enlisted, June 14, 1898, at Buffalo, to serve two years; mustered in as private, Co. H, same date; mustered out with company, November 19, 1898, at Buffalo, N. Y.

LANGE, CHARLES.—Age, 24 years. Enlisted, May 1, 1898, at Buffalo, to serve two years; mustered in as private, Co. A, May 17, 1898; mustered out with company, November 19, 1898, at Buffalo, N. Y.

LANGE, HENRY.—Age, 22 years. Enlisted, May 1, 1898, at Buffalo, to serve two years; mustered in as private, Co. D, May 17, 1898; promoted corporal, September 3, 1898; mustered out with company, November 19, 1898, at Buffalo, N. Y.

LANTZ, CARL JOHN.—Age, 23 years. Enlisted, May 1, 1898, at Buffalo, to serve two years; mustered in as private, Co. F, May 17, 1898; promoted corporal, September 3, 1898; mustered out with company, November 19, 1898, at Buffalo, N. Y.

LAPP, EUGENE L.—Age, 21 years. Enlisted, May 1, 1898, at Buffalo, to serve two years; mustered in as private, Co. D, May 17, 1898; mustered out with company, November 19, 1898, at Buffalo, N. Y.

LA PRESS, HENRY L.—Age, 25 years. Enlisted, May 12, 1898, at Camp Black, to serve two years; mustered in as private, Co. C, May 17, 1898; mustered out with company, November 19, 1898, at Buffalo, N. Y.

LAU, ALBERT.—Age, — years. Enlisted, June 14, 1898, at Buffalo, to serve two years; mustered in as private, Co. D, same date; transferred to Co. F, June 29, 1898; mustered out with company, November 19, 1898, at Buffalo, N. Y.

LAU, RICHARD.—Age, 20 years. Enlisted, May 1, 1898, at Buffalo, to serve two years; mustered in as private, Co. D, May 17, 1898; mustered out with company, November 19, 1898, at Buffalo, N. Y.

LAUER, HENRY D.—Age, 24 years. Enlisted, May 1, 1898, at Buffalo, to serve two years; mustered in as private, Co. I, May 17, 1898; mustered out with company, November 19, 1898, at Buffalo, N. Y.

LAUX, FRANK X.—Age, 24 years. Enlisted, May 1, 1898, at Buffalo, to serve two years; mustered in as private, Co. L, May 17, 1898; mustered out with company, November 19, 1898, at Buffalo, N. Y.

LAWRENCE, GEORGE W.—Age, — years. Enlisted, June 17, 1898, at Buffalo, to serve two years; mustered in as private, Co. E, same date; mustered out with company, November 19, 1898, at Buffalo, N. Y.

LAWSON, FRED S.—Age, — years. Enlisted, June 13, 1898, at Buffalo, to serve two years; mustered in as private, Co. F, same date; transferred to Co. E, June 23, 1898; mustered out with company, November 19, 1898, at Buffalo, N. Y.

LEAHY, JOHN A.—Age, 23 years. Enlisted, May 11, 1898, at Buffalo, to serve two years; mustered in as private, Co. H, May 17, 1898; promoted corporal, July 28, 1898; mustered out with company, November 19, 1898, at Buffalo, N. Y.

LEARY, EDWARD E.—Age, — years. Enlisted, June 21, 1898, at Buffalo, to serve two years; mustered in as private, Co. H, same date; mustered out with company, November 19, 1898, at Buffalo, N. Y.

LE BELLE, JACK.—Age, 25 years. Enlisted, May 1, 1898, at Buffalo, to serve two years; mustered in as private, Co. D, May 17, 1898; deserted, July 10, 1898, at Camp Alger, near Dunn Loring, Va.

LEE, JOHN H.—Age, 29 years. Enlisted, May 1, 1898, at Buffalo, to serve two years; mustered in as sergeant, Co. B, May 17, 1898; mustered out with company, November 19, 1898, at Buffalo, N. Y.

LEE, WILLIAM P.—Age, 27 years. Enlisted, May 1, 1898, at Buffalo, to serve two years; mustered in as private, Co. A, May 17, 1898; promoted corporal, October 6, 1898; mustered out with company, November 19, 1898, at Buffalo, N. Y.

LEEMAN, FRED.—Age, 32 years. Enlisted, May 1, 1898, at Buffalo, to serve two years; mustered in as corporal, Co. H, May 17, 1898; mustered out with company, November 19, 1898, at Buffalo, N. Y.

LEHMANN, ROBERT C.—Age, 29 years. Enlisted, May 1, 1898, at Buffalo, to serve two years; mustered in as corporal, Co. B, May 17, 1898; returned to ranks, June 26, 1898; mustered out with company, November 19, 1898, at Buffalo, N. Y.

LEITER, FRED H.—Age, — years. Enlisted, June 15, 1898, at Buffalo, to serve two years; mustered in as private, Co. E, same date; mustered out with company, November 19, 1898, at Buffalo, N. Y.

LEITTEN, BENJAMIN J.—Age, 23 years. Enlisted, May 1, 1898, at Buffalo, to serve two years; mustered in as corporal, Co. A, May 17, 1898; mustered out with company, November 19, 1898, at Buffalo, N. Y.

LEITTEN, CHARLES C.—Age, 21 years. Enlisted, May 1, 1898, at Buffalo, to serve two years: mustered in as corporal, Co. A, May 17, 1898; mustered out with company, November 19, 1898, at Buffalo, N. Y.

LEMON, CHARLES.—Age, 39 years. Enlisted, May 1, 1898, at Buffalo, to serve two years; mustered in as private, Co. I, May 17, 1898; mustered out with company, November 19, 1898, at Buffalo, N. Y.

LENNON, WILLIAM H.—Age, 30 years. Enlisted, May 1, 1898, at Buffalo, to serve two years; mustered in as private, Co. M, May 17, 1898; promoted corporal, to date, July 1, 1898; mustered out with company, November 19, 1898, at Buffalo, N. Y.

LENZ, CHRIST.—Age, 21 years. Enlisted, May 1, 1898, at
Buffalo, to serve two years; mustered in as private, Co. D, May
17, 1898; mustered out with company, November 19, 1898, at
Buffalo, N. Y.

LEONARD, FRANK A.—Age, — years. Enlisted, May 1, 1898,
at Buffalo, to serve two years; mustered in as principal musician, May 17, 1898; returned to ranks, and transferred to Co. I,
as musician, June 28, 1898; mustered out with company, November 19, 1898, at Buffalo, N. Y.

LEONARD, GEORGE F.—Age, 20 years. Enlisted, May 1, 1898,
at Buffalo, to serve two years; mustered in as musician, Co. D,
May 17, 1898; mustered out with company, November 19, 1898,
at Buffalo, N. Y.

LESTER, ROBERT W.—Age, — years. Enlisted, June 20, 1898,
at Buffalo, to serve two years; mustered in as private, Co. M,
same date; mustered out with company, November 19, 1898, at
Buffalo, N. Y.

LEVINE, FRED C.—Age, 22 years. Enlisted, May 1, 1898, at
Buffalo, to serve two years; mustered in as private, Co. D, May
17, 1898; promoted corporal, July 7, 1898; mustered out with
company, November 19, 1898, at Buffalo, N. Y.

LEWENICHT, HENRY.—Age, — years. Enlisted, June 24,
1898, at Buffalo, to serve two years; mustered in as private,
Co. L, same date; transferred to band, June 29, 1898; mustered
out with band, November 19, 1898, at Buffalo, N. Y.

LEWIS, JEROME.—Age, 24 years. Enlisted, May 1, 1898, at
Buffalo, to serve two years; mustered in as private, Co. I, May
17, 1898; mustered out with company, November 19, 1898, at
Buffalo, N. Y.

LEYMAN, CHARLES.—Age, — years. Enlisted, June 13, 1898,
at Buffalo, to serve two years; mustered in as private, Co. I,
same date; mustered out with company, November 19, 1898,
at Buffalo, N. Y.

LICKWICK, WILLIAM.—Age, 20 years. Enlisted, May 1, 1898,
at Buffalo, to serve two years; mustered in as private, Co. M,
May 17, 1898; mustered out with company, November 19, 1898,
at Buffalo, N. Y.

LIED, GEORGE J.—Age, 21 years. Enlisted, May 1, 1898, at
Buffalo, to serve two years; mustered in as private, Co. I, May
17, 1898; mustered out with company, November 19, 1898, at
Buffalo, N. Y.

LINDHOLM, WILBEIT A.—Age, — years. Enlisted, June 15,
1898, at Buffalo, to serve two years; mustered in as private, Co.
E, same date; mustered out with company, November 19, 1898,
at Buffalo, N. Y.

LINDSAY, ROBERT J.—Age, — years. Enlisted, June 18, 1898,
at Buffalo, to serve two years; mustered in as private, Co. D,
same date; mustered out with company, November 19, 1898, at
Buffalo, N. Y.

LINDSTROM, CARL.—Age, 34 years. Enlisted, May 1, 1898, at
Camp Black, to serve two years; mustered in as private, Co. D,
May 17, 1898; mustered out with company, November 19, 1898,
at Buffalo, N. Y.

LINK, THOMAS J.—Age, — years. Enlisted, June 13, 1898, at
Buffalo, to serve two years; mustered in as private, Co. I, same
date; mustered out with company, November 19, 1898, at
Buffalo, N. Y.

LIPINSKI, FRANK.—Age, 23 years. Enlisted, May 1, 1898, at
Buffalo, to serve two years; mustered in as private, Co. D, May
17, 1898; mustered out with company, November 19, 1898, at
Buffalo, N. Y.

LOCKWOOD, A. VERDE.—Age, 21 years. Enlisted, May 1,
1898, at Jamestown, to serve two years; mustered in as private,
Co. E, May 17, 1898; promoted corporal, July 17, 1898; mustered out with company, November 19, 1898, at Buffalo, N. Y.

LOCKWOOD, GEORGE G.—Age, 24 years. Enlisted, May 1,
1898, at Buffalo, to serve two years; mustered in as private, Co.
A, May 17, 1898; discharged for disability, October 7, 1898.

LOHOUSE, ARTHUR F.—Age, 40 years. Enlisted, May 1, 1898,
at Buffalo, to serve two years; mustered in as private, Co. G,
May 17, 1898; mustered out with company, November 19, 1898,
at Buffalo, N. Y.

LOURIDGE, EUGENE L.—Age, — years. Enlisted, July 19, 1898, at Camp Alger, near Dunn Loring, Va., to serve two years; mustered in as private, Co. F, same date; mustered out with company, November 19, 1898, at Buffalo, N. Y.

LOVE, NILES G.—Age, 21 years. Enlisted, May 1, 1898, at Buffalo, to serve two years; mustered in as corporal, Co. M, May 17, 1898; mustered out with company, November 19, 1898, at Buffalo, N. Y.

LUDAESCHER, JOHN A.—Age, 18 years. Enlisted, May 1, 1898, at Buffalo, to serve two years; mustered in as private, Co. A, May 17, 1898; mustered out with company, November 19, 1898, at Buffalo, N. Y.

LUDWIG, HENRY.—Age, 26 years. Enlisted, May 11, 1898, at Buffalo, to serve two years; mustered in as private, Co. H, May 17, 1898; mustered out with company, November 19, 1898, at Buffalo, N. Y.

LUND, RALPH C.—Age, 21 years. Enlisted, May 1, 1898, at Buffalo, to serve two years; mustered in as private, Co. F, May 17, 1898; promoted corporal, July 27, 1898; mustered out with company, November 19, 1898, at Buffalo, N. Y.

LUPKE, CHARLES G.—Age, — years. Enlisted, June 14, 1898, at Buffalo, to serve two years; mustered in as private, Co. K, same date; mustered out with company, November 19, 1898, at Buffalo, N. Y.

LUSCHER, HOMER.—Age, — years. Enlisted, June 18, 1898, at Buffalo, to serve two years; mustered in as private, Co. F, same date; mustered out with company, November 19, 1898, at Buffalo, N. Y.

LUTZ, WILLIAM E.—Age, 19 years. Enlisted, May 1, 1898, at Buffalo, to serve two years; mustered in as private, Co. C, May 17, 1898; mustered out with company, November 19, 1898, at Buffalo, N. Y.

LYKE, JAMES H.—Age, 27 years. Enlisted, May 12, 1898, at Buffalo, to serve two years; mustered in as private, Co. H, May 17, 1898; promoted corporal, July 25, 1898; mustered out with company, November 19, 1898, at Buffalo, N. Y.

LYNCH, RICHARD D.—Age, 23 years. Enlisted, May 1, 1898, at Buffalo, to serve two years; mustered in as private, Co. A, May 17, 1898; mustered out with company, November 19, 1898, at Buffalo, N. Y.

LYNDSLEY, DELBERT.—Age, 24 years. Enlisted, May 1, 1898, at Buffalo, to serve two years; mustered in as private, Co. L, May 17, 1898; promoted corporal, July 9, 1898; mustered out with company, November 19, 1898, at Buffalo, N. Y.

LYON, MERTON J.—Age, 26 years. Enlisted, May 1, 1898, at Jamestown, to serve two years; mustered in as private, Co. E, May 17, 1898; mustered out with company, November 19, 1898, at Buffalo, N. Y.

MABLEY, THOMAS H.—Age, 32 years. Enlisted, May 1, 1898, at Buffalo, to serve two years; mustered in as corporal, Co. I, May 17, 1898; mustered out with company, November 19, 1898, at Buffalo, N. Y.

MAC DONALD, DONALD A.—Age, — years. Enlisted, June 14, 1898, at Buffalo, to serve two years; mustered in as private, Co. F, same date; mustered out with company, November 19, 1898, at Buffalo, N. Y.

MACDONALD, JOHN L.—Age, 30 years. Enlisted, May 1, 1898, at Buffalo, to serve two years; mustered in as quartermaster-sergeant, Co. K, May 17, 1898; mustered out with company, November 19, 1898, at Buffalo, N. Y.

MACHWIRTH, EDWARD.—Age, — years. Enlisted, June 27, 1898, at Buffalo, to serve two years; mustered in as private, Co. M, same date; mustered out with company, November 19, 1898, at Buffalo, N. Y.

MACK, JAMES.—Age, 32 years. Enlisted, May 1, 1898, at Buffalo, to serve two years; mustered in as private, Co. G, May 17, 1898; mustered out with company, November 19, 1898, at Buffalo, N. Y.

MAC PHERSON, COLIE.—Age, 22 years. Enlisted, May 1, 1898, at Buffalo, to serve two years; mustered in as private, Co. A, May 17, 1898; mustered out with company, November 19, 1898, at Buffalo, N. Y.

MADIGAN, JAMES P.—Age, 21 years. Enlisted, May 1, 1898, at Buffalo, to serve two years; mustered in as private, Co. K, May 17, 1898; mustered out with company, November 19, 1898, at Buffalo, N. Y.

MAHEUX, VICTOR.—Age, — years. Enlisted, June 13, 1898, at Buffalo, to serve two years; mustered in as private, Co. C, same date; mustered out with company, November 19, 1898, at Buffalo, N. Y.

MAHON, THOMAS P.—Age, 29 years. Enlisted, May 12, 1898, at Buffalo, to serve two years; mustered in as private, Co. M, May 17, 1898; mustered out with company, November 19, 1898, at Buffalo, N. Y.

MAHONEY, JR., THOMAS.—Age, 23 years. Enlisted, May 1, 1898, at Jamestown, to serve two years; mustered in as private, Co. E, May 17, 1898; mustered out with company, November 19, 1898, at Buffalo, N. Y.

MALONEY, FLORENCE A.—Age, — years. Enlisted, June 13, 1898, at Buffalo, to serve two years; mustered in as private, Co. B, same date; mustered out with company, November 19, 1898, at Buffalo, N. Y.

MALONEY, FRANK M.—Age, 22 years. Enlisted, May 13, 1898, at Camp Black, to serve two years; mustered in as private, Co. E, May 17, 1898; mustered out with company, November 19, 1898, at Buffalo, N. Y.

MALONEY, JAMES.—Age, — years. Enlisted, July 7, 1898, at Buffalo, to serve two years; mustered in as private, Co. F, same date; transferred, as musician, to Co. I, July 10, 1898; to band, July 14, 1898; mustered out with band, November 19, 1898, at Buffalo, N. Y.

MANGER, MARTIN.—Age, 23 years. Enlisted, May 1, 1898, at Buffalo, to serve two years; mustered in as hospital steward, May 17, 1898; mustered out with regiment, November 19, 1898, at Buffalo, N. Y.

MARR, LAWRENCE.—Age, 18 years. Enlisted, May 1, 1898, at Buffalo, to serve two years; mustered in as private, Co. G, May 17, 1898; mustered out with company, November 19, 1898, at Buffalo, N. Y.

MARRICAL, ERNST S.—Age, 24 years. Enlisted, May 1, 1898, at Buffalo, to serve two years; mustered in as private, Co. M, May 17, 1898; mustered out with company, November 19, 1898, at Buffalo, N. Y.

MARTIN, JOHN S.—Age, 29 years. Enlisted, May 1, 1898, at Buffalo, to serve two years; mustered in as private, Co. G, May 17, 1898; mustered out with company, November 19, 1898, at Buffalo, N. Y.

MARTIN, LOUIS M.—Age, — years. Enlisted, June 16, 1898, at Buffalo, to serve two years; mustered in as private, Co. B, same date; mustered out with company, November 19, 1898, at Buffalo, N. Y.

MARTIN, THOMAS.—Age, 28 years. Enlisted, May 1, 1898, at Buffalo, to serve two years; mustered in as private, Co. K, May 17, 1898; promoted corporal, June 29, 1898; mustered out with company, November 19, 1898, at Buffalo, N. Y.

MASON, WALTER C.—Age, 38 years. Enlisted, May 1, 1898, at Buffalo, to serve two years; mustered in as regimental quarter-master-sergeant, May 17, 1898; mustered out with regiment, November 19, 1898, at Buffalo, N. Y.

MATH, GEORGE A.—Age, — years. Enlisted, June 20, 1898, at Buffalo, to serve two years; mustered in as private, Co. C, same date; mustered out with company, November 19, 1898, at Buffalo, N. Y.

MATHER, JOHN J.—Age, 32 years. Enlisted, May 1, 1898, at Buffalo, to serve two years; mustered in as artificer, Co. K, May 17, 1898; mustered out with company, November 19, 1898, at Buffalo, N. Y.

MATHER, SAMUEL.—Age, 37 years. Enlisted, May 1, 1898, at Jamestown, to serve two years; mustered in as private, Co. E, May 17, 1898; appointed artificer, same date; mustered out with company, November 19, 1898, at Buffalo, N. Y.

MATHEWS, JOHN.—Age, 37 years. Enlisted, May 1, 1898, at Buffalo, to serve two years; mustered in as private, Co. I, May 17, 1898; mustered out with company, November 19, 1898, at Buffalo, N. Y.

MATHIAS, FREDERICK J.—Age, 20 years. Enlisted, May 1, 1898, at Buffalo, to serve two years; mustered in as private, Co. M, May 17, 1898; mustered out with company, November 19, 1898, at Buffalo, N. Y.

MATTICE, FRANK.—Age, 21 years. Enlisted, May 1, 1898, at Buffalo, to serve two years; mustered in as private, Co. A, May 17, 1898; deserted, July 9, 1898, at Camp Alger, near Dunn Loring, Va.

MAX, HARRY H.—Age, 21 years. Enlisted, May 1, 1898, at Buffalo, to serve two years; mustered in as private, Co. B, May 17, 1898; mustered out with company, November 19, 1898, at Buffalo, N. Y.

MAXWELL, ARTHUR J.—Age, 21 years. Enlisted, May 1, 1898, at Buffalo, to serve two years; mustered in as corporal, Co. I, May 17, 1898; promoted sergeant, July 1, 1898; mustered out with company, November 19, 1898, at Buffalo, N. Y.

MAXWELL, CHARLES W.—Age, 27 years. Enlisted, May 1, 1898, at Buffalo, to serve two years; mustered in as sergeant, Co. I, May 17, 1898; returned to ranks, June 7, 1898; promoted corporal, October 11, 1898; mustered out with company, November 19, 1898, at Buffalo, N. Y.

MAXWELL, FRANK A.—Age, 19 years. Enlisted, May 1, 1898, at Buffalo, to serve two years; mustered in as private, Co. I, May 17, 1898; mustered out with compány, November 19, 1898, at Buffalo, N. Y.

MAXWELL, JOHN.—Age, 44 years. Enlisted, May 1, 1898, at Buffalo, to serve two years; mustered in as first sergeant, Co. I, May 17, 1898; mustered out with company, November 19, 1898, at Buffalo, N. Y.

MAXWELL, RICHARD G.—Age, 20 years. Enlisted, May 1, 1898, at Buffalo, to serve two years; mustered in as private, Co. D, May 17, 1898; mustered out with company, November 19, 1898, at Buffalo, N. Y.

McABEE, LEROY.—Age, 21 years. Enlisted, May 1, 1898, at Buffalo, to serve two years; mustered in as private, Co. D, May 17, 1898; mustered out with company, November 19, 1898, at Buffalo, N. Y.

McADIR, ALEXANDER M.—Age, 20 years. Enlisted, May 1, 1898, at Buffalo, to serve two years; mustered in as private, Co. C. May 17, 1898; mustered out with company, November 19, 1898, at Buffalo, N. Y.

McALLISTER, JAMES.—Age, 33 years. Enlisted, May 1, 1898, at Buffalo, to serve two years; mustered in as private, Co. G, May 17, 1898; mustered out with company, November 19, 1898, at Buffalo, N. Y.

McBRIDE, WILLIAM H.—Age, — years. Enlisted, June 22, 1898, at Buffalo, to serve two years; mustered in as private, Co. K, same date; mustered out with company, November 19, 1898, at Buffalo, N. Y.

McCARTHY, JAMES F.—Age, 27 years. Enlisted, May 1, 1898, at Buffalo, to serve two years; mustered in as private, Co. G, May 17, 1898; promoted corporal, August 23, 1898; mustered out with company, November 19, 1898, at Buffalo, N. Y.

McCLINTOCK, HARRIE C.—Age, 22 years. Enlisted, May 1, 1898, at Buffalo, to serve two years; mustered in as private, Co. K, May 17, 1898; mustered out with company, November 19, 1898, at Buffalo, N. Y.

McCUTCHEON, CHAS. A.—Age, 20 years. Enlisted, May 1, 1898, at Jamestown, to serve two years; mustered in as private, Co. E, May 17, 1898; mustered out with company, November 19, 1898, at Buffalo, N. Y.

McDONOUGH, SEYMOUR.—Age, 29 years. Enlisted, May 1, 1898, at Buffalo, to serve two years; mustered in as private, Co. H, May 17, 1898; mustered out with company, November 19, 1898, at Buffalo, N. Y.

McDUFF, GEORGE.—Age, — years. Enlisted, June 29, 1898, at Buffalo, to serve two years; mustered in as private, Co. H, same date; mustered out with company, November 19, 1898, at Buffalo, N. Y.

McGEAN, JAMES W.—Age, 20 years. Enlisted, May 1, 1898, at Buffalo, to serve two years; mustered in as private, Co. I, May 17. 1898; mustered out with company, November 19, 1898, at Buffalo, N. Y.

McGOWAN, PATRICK.—Age, 23 years. Enlisted, May 1, 1898, at Buffalo, to serve two years; mustered in as private, Co. K, May 17, 1898; mustered out with company, November 19, 1898, at Buffalo, N. Y.

McGUIRE, FRANK I.—Age, — years. Enlisted, July 1, 1898, at Buffalo, to serve two years; mustered in as private, Co. K, same date; mustered out with company, November 19, 1898, at Buffalo, N. Y.

McGUIRE, MARTIN J.—Age, 23 years. Enlisted, May 1, 1898, at Buffalo, to serve two years; mustered in as private, Co. H, May 17, 1898; mustered out with company, November 19, 1898, at Buffalo, N. Y.

McGUIRK, EDWARD P.—Age, — years. Enlisted, June 17, 1898, at Buffalo, to serve two years; mustered in as private, Co. M, same date; mustered out with company, November 19, 1898, at Buffalo, N. Y.

McHARDY, WILLIAM.—Age, 30 years. Enlisted, May 1, 1898, at Buffalo, to serve two years; mustered in as private, Co. G, May 17, 1898; mustered out with company, November 19, 1898, at Buffalo, N. Y.

McINTYRE, JOSEPH J.—Age, 38 years. Enlisted, May 1, 1898, at Buffalo, to serve two years; mustered in as private, Co. I, May 17, 1898; mustered out with company, November 19, 1898, at Buffalo, N. Y.

McLAUGHLIN, ANDREW.—Age, 26 years. Enlisted, May 1, 1898, at Buffalo, to serve two years; mustered in as private, Co. M, May 17, 1898; promoted corporal, July 1, 1898; mustered out with company, November 19, 1898, at Buffalo, N. Y.

McLEOD, WILLIAM J.—Age, — years. Enlisted, June 20, 1898, at Buffalo, to serve two years; mustered in as private, Co. C, same date; died of typhoid fever, September 13, 1898, at Buffalo, N. Y.

McMILLAN, WILLIAM.—Age, 26 years. Enlisted, May 1, 1898, at Buffalo, to serve two years; mustered in as private, Co. I, May 17, 1898; mustered out with company, November 19, 1898, at Buffalo, N. Y.

McNALLY, JOHN.—Age, 27 years. Enlisted, May 1, 1898, at Buffalo, to serve two years; mustered in as private, Co. M, May 17, 1898; mustered out with company, November 19, 1898, at Buffalo, N. Y.

McNAMEE, ALBERT E.—Age, 18 years. Enlisted, May 1, 1898, at Buffalo, to serve two years; mustered in as musician, Co. F, May 17, 1898; mustered out with company, November 19, 1898, at Buffalo, N. Y.

McNAMEE, HARRY.—Age, 19 years. Enlisted, May 1, 1898, at Buffalo, to serve two years; mustered in as private, Co. D, May 17, 1898; mustered out with company, November 19, 1898, at Buffalo, N. Y.

McPARTLIN, JAMES.—Age, 21 years. Enlisted, May 1, 1898, at Buffalo, to serve two years; mustered in as private, Co. B, May 17, 1898; mustered out with company, November 19, 1898, at Buffalo, N. Y.

McQUILLEN, ANDREW V.—Age, 20 years. Enlisted, May 1, 1898, at Buffalo, to serve two years; mustered in as private, Co. F, May 17, 1898; mustered out with company, November 19, 1898, at Buffalo, N. Y.

McWHORTER, IRVING.—Age, 27 years. Enlisted, May 1, 1898, at Buffalo, to serve two years; mustered in as private, Co. L, May 17, 1898; transferred to Hospital Corps, United States Army, June 28, 1898; to Co. L, September 2, 1898; to Hospital Corps, United States Army, September 12, 1898, at Buffalo, N. Y.

MEAD, FRANK R.—Age, — years. Enlisted, June 23, 1898, at Buffalo, to serve two years; mustered in as private, Co. M, same date; mustered out with company, November 19, 1898, at Buffalo, N. Y

MEADE, HARRY.—Age, 28 years. Enrolled, May 1, 1898, at Buffalo, to serve two years; mustered in as first lieutenant and assistant surgeon, May 6, 1898; mustered out with regiment, November 19, 1898, at Buffalo, N. Y.; commissioned captain and assistant surgeon, May 6, 1898, with rank of captain from same date, original.

MEADER, CHARLES A.—Age, 21 years. Enlisted, May 13, 1898, at Camp Black, to serve two years; mustered in as private, Co. E, May 17, 1898; mustered out with company, November 19, 1898, at Buffalo, N. Y.

MEISNER, FRANK B.—Age, 33 years. Enlisted, May 12, 1898, at Buffalo, to serve two years; mustered in as private, Co. M, May 17, 1898; transferred to Co. B, May 18, 1898; mustered out with company, November 19, 1898, at Buffalo, N. Y.

MERCER, WALTER.—Age, 21 years. Enlisted, May 1, 1898, at Buffalo, to serve two years; mustered in as private, Co. I, May 17, 1898; mustered out with company, November 19, 1898, at Buffalo, N. Y.

MERZ, WILLIAM F.—Age, — years. Enlisted, June 15, 1898, at Buffalo, to serve two years; mustered in as private, Co. B, same date; mustered out with company, November 19, 1898, at Buffalo, N. Y.

MESMER, GEORGE W.—Age, — years. Enlisted, June 18, 1898, at Buffalo, to serve two years; mustered in as private, Co. D, same date; mustered out with company, November 19, 1898, at Buffalo, N. Y.

METZ, JR., JACOB.—Age, 24 years. Enlisted, May 12, 1898, at Buffalo, to serve two years; mustered in as private, Co. H, May 17, 1898; mustered out with company, November 19, 1898, at Buffalo, N. Y.

METZGER, CHARLES H.—Age, — years. Enlisted, June 22, 1898, at Buffalo, to serve two years; mustered in as private, Co. H, same date; mustered out with company, November 19, 1898, at Buffalo, N. Y.

METZLER, CHARLES A.—Age, 25 years. Enlisted, May 1, 1898, at Buffalo, to serve two years; mustered in as sergeant, Co. C, May 17, 1898; mustered out with company, November 19, 1898, at Buffalo, N. Y.

MEYER, AUGUST.—Age, 22 years. Enlisted, May 1, 1898, at Buffalo, to serve two years; mustered in as private, Co. F, May 17, 1898; mustered out with company, November 19, 1898, at Buffalo, N. Y.

MEYERS, FRANK J.—Age, 25 years. Enlisted, May 1, 1898, at
Buffalo, to serve two years; mustered in as corporal, Co. H, May
17, 1898; promoted sergeant, July 25, 1898; mustered out with
company, November 19, 1898, at Buffalo, N. Y.

MEYERS, JOHN H.—Age, 21 years. Enlisted, May 13, 1898, at
Camp Black, to serve two years; mustered in as private, Co. E,
May 17, 1898; discharged for disability, August 20, 1898.

MEZYDTO, ZEFHRYN EDWARD.—Age, 20 years. Enlisted,
May 1, 1898, at Buffalo, to serve two years; mustered in as private, Co. F, May 17, 1898; discharged, October 28, 1898.

MIEDENBANER, JOHN G.—Age, 24 years. Enlisted, May 1,
1898, at Buffalo, to serve two years; mustered in as private, Co.
F, May 17, 1898; mustered out with company, November 19,
1898, at Buffalo, N. Y.

MIGHT, GEORGE N.—Age, — years. Enlisted, June 22, 1898,
at Buffalo, to serve two years; mustered in as private, Co. K,
same date; mustered out with company, November 19, 1898, at
Buffalo, N. Y.

MILLER, ALBERT A.—Age, 25 years. Enlisted, May 12, 1898,
at Buffalo, to serve two years; mustered in as private, Co. H,
May 17, 1898; mustered out with company, November 19, 1898,
at Buffalo, N. Y.

MILLER, ANTHONY.—Age, 21 years. Enlisted, May 1, 1898, at
Buffalo, to serve two years; mustered in as private, Co. F, May
17, 1898; mustered out with company, November 19, 1898, at
Buffalo, N. Y.

MILLER, AUGUST W.—Age, — years. Enlisted, June 20, 1898,
at Buffalo, to serve two years; mustered in as private, Co. A,
same date; mustered out with company, November 19, 1898,
at Buffalo, N. Y.   •

MILLER, CHARLES C.—Age, 24 years. Enlisted, May 1, 1898,
at Buffalo, to serve two years; mustered in as sergeant, Co.
G, May 17, 1898; mustered out with company, November 19,
1898, at Buffalo, N. Y.

MILLER, CHARLES F.—Age, —years. Enlisted, June 13, 1898, at Buffalo, to serve two years; mustered in as private, Co. I, same date; mustered out with company, November 19, 1898, at Buffalo, N. Y.

MILLER, CHARLES H.—Age, 23 years. Enlisted, May 1, 1898, at Buffalo, to serve two years; mustered in as sergeant, Co. A, May 17, 1898; mustered out with company, November 19, 1898, at Buffalo, N. Y.

MILLER, GEORGE J.—Age, 22 years. Enlisted, May 1, 1898, at Buffalo, to serve two years; mustered in as private, Co. G, May 17, 1898; mustered out with company, November 19, 1898, at Buffalo, N. Y.

MILLER, JOHN G.—Age, 20 years. Enlisted, May 1, 1898, at Buffalo, to serve two years; mustered in as private, Co. A, May 17, 1898; mustered out with company, November 19, 1898, at Buffalo, N. Y.

MILLER, MICHAEL.—Age, 22 years. Enlisted, May 1, 1898, at Buffalo, to serve two years; mustered in as private, Co. K, May 17, 1898; mustered out with company, November 19, 1898, at Buffalo, N. Y.

MILLS, IVON S.—Age, 19 years. Enlisted, May 1, 1898, at Buffalo, to serve two years; mustered in as private, Co. C, May 17, 1898; mustered out with company, November 19, 1898, at Buffalo, N. Y.

MILLS, THOMAS.—Age, 22 years. Enlisted, May 1, 1898, at Buffalo, to serve two years; mustered in as corporal, Co. I, May 17, 1898; returned to ranks, June 7, 1898; mustered out with company, November 19, 1898, at Buffalo, N. Y.

MILSOM, GEORGE A.—Age, 36 years. Enrolled, May 1, 1898, at Buffalo, to serve two years; mustered in as captain, Co. B, May 17, 1898; mustered out with company, November 19, 1898, at Buffalo, N. Y.; commissioned captain, May 17, 1898, with rank from same date, original.

MITCHEK, FRANK J.—Age, — years. Enlisted, June 14, 1898, at Buffalo, to serve two years; mustered in as private, Co. A, June 17, 1898; discharged, October 7, 1898.

MOEST, JR., JOHN.—Age, 38 years. Enlisted, May 1, 1898, at
Buffalo, to serve two years; mustereu in as sergeant, Co. K,
May 17, 1898; mustered out with company, November 19, 1898,
at Buffalo, N. Y.

MOHR, JOHN.—Age, 21 years. Enlisted, May 1, 1898, at Buffalo,
to serve two years; mustered in as private, Co. I May 17, 1898;
mustered out with company, November 19, 1898, at Buffalo,
N. Y.

MOHR, MARTIN J.—Age, — years. Enlisted, June 14, 1898,
at Buffalo to serve two years; mustered in as private, Co. I,
same date; mustered out with company, November 19, 1898, at
Buffalo, N. Y.

MONROE, FRANK.—Age, — years. Enlisted, June 21, 1898, at
Buffalo, to serve two years; mustered in as private, Co. L, same
date; mustered out with company, November 19, 1898, at Buffalo, N. Y.

MONTGOMERY, JOHN F.—Age, 26 years. Enlisted, May 1,
1898, at Buffalo, to serve two years; mustered in as sergeant,
Co. B, May 17, 1898; mustered out with company, November 19,
1898, at Buffalo, N. Y.

MOORE, WALTER D. C.—Age, 24 years. Enlisted, May 1, 1898,
at Buffalo, to serve two years; mustered in as sergeant, Co. D,
May 17, 1898; discharged, August 29, 1898.

MORAHAM, EUGENE H.—Age, 28 years. Enlisted, May 1,
1898, at Buffalo, to serve two years; mustered in as private, Co.
G, May 17, 1898; mustered out with company, November 19,
1898, at Buffalo, N. Y.

MORGAN, JACOB A.—Age, 28 years. Enlisted, May 1, 1898; at
Buffalo, to serve two years; mustered in as private, Co. D, May
17, 1898; mustered out with company, November 19, 1898, at
Buffalo, N. Y.

MORGAT, ELMER C.—Age, 24 years. Enlisted, May 1, 1898, at
Buffalo, to serve two years; mustered in as quartermaster-
sergeant, Co. D, May 17, 1898; mustered out with company,
November 19, 1898, at Buffalo, N. Y.

MORRIS, JOSEPH A.—Age, — years. Enlisted, June 27, 1898, at Buffalo, to serve two years; mustered in as private, Co. M, same date; transferred to band, June 29, 1898; mustered out ,with band, November 19, 1898, at Buffalo, N. Y.

MORRIS, SAMUEL.—Age, 33 years. Enlisted, May 1, 1898, at Buffalo, to serve two years; mustered in as private, Co. C, May 17, 1898; mustered out with company, November 19, 1898, at Buffalo, N. Y.

MORTIMER, EDWARD J.—Age, 28 years. Enlisted, May 1, 1898, at Buffalo, to serve two years; mustered in as private, Co. B, May 17, 1898; mustered out with company, November 19, 1898, at Buffalo, N. Y.

MOSGELLER, CHRISTOPHER.—Age, 22 years. Enlisted, May 1, 1898, at Buffalo, to serve two years; mustered in as private, Co. K, May 17, 1898; mustered out with company, November 19, 1898, at Buffalo, N. Y.

MOSHIER, EMIL.—Age, 21 years. Enlisted, May 11, 1898, at Buffalo, to serve two years; mustered in as private, Co. H, May 17, 1898; mustered out with company, November 19, 1898, at Buffalo, N. Y.

MOYNIHAN, FRANK F.—Age, 23 years. Enlisted, May 1, 1898, at Jamestown, to serve two years; mustered in as private, Co. E, May 17, 1898; mustered out with company, November 19, 1898, at Buffalo, N. Y.

MUELLER, CHARLES.—Age, 21 years. Enlisted, May 12, 1898, at Buffalo, to serve two years; mustered in as private, Co. H, May 17, 1898; mustered out with company, November 19, 1898, at Buffalo, N. Y.

MUELLER, CHRIST.—Age, 25 years. Enlisted, May 1, 1898, at Buffalo, to serve two years; mustered in as private, Co. H, May 17, 1898; mustered out with company, November 19, 1898, at Buffalo, N. Y.

MUENCH, CHRIST.—Age, 25 years. Enlisted, May 1, 1898, at Buffalo, to serve two years; mustered in as private, Co. H, May 17, 1898; mustered out with company, November 19, 1898, at Buffalo, N. Y., as Christian Muersch.

MUENCH, GEORGE J.—Age, 19 years. Enlisted, May 1, 1898, at Buffalo, to serve two years; mustered in as musician, Co. L, May 17, 1898; returned to ranks, no date; mustered out with company, November 19, 1898, at Buffalo, N. Y.

MUENCH, KARL G.—Age, 21 years. Enlisted, May 1, 1898, at Buffalo, to serve two years; mustered in as private, Co. I, May 17, 1898; mustered out with company, November 19, 1898, at Buffalo, N. Y.

MULCAHY, WILLIAM H.—Age, — years. Enlisted, June 16, 1898, at Buffalo, to serve two years; mustered in as private, Co. C, same date; mustered out with company, November 19, 1898, at Buffalo, N. Y.

MULLER, NICHOLAS W.—Age, 21 years. Enlisted, May 1, 1898, at Buffalo, to serve two years; mustered in as corporal, Co. K, May 17, 1898; mustered out with company, November 19, 1898, at Buffalo, N. Y.

MULLETT, WALTER P.—Age, 21 years. Enlisted, May 1, 1898, at Buffalo, to serve two years; mustered in as private, Co. B, May 17, 1898; mustered out with company, November 19, 1898, at Buffalo, N. Y.

MULLIKEN, JOHN C.—Age, 40 years. Enlisted, May 1, 1898, at Buffalo, to serve two years; mustered in as private, Co. C, May 17, 1898; promoted corporal, July 1, 1898; mustered out with company, November 19, 1898, at Buffalo, N. Y.

MUNZERT, ALBERT W.—Age, — years. Enlisted, June 22, 1898, at Buffalo, to serve two years; mustered in as private, Co. K, same date; mustered out with company, November 19, 1898, at Buffalo, N. Y.

MUNZERT, ALONZO T.—Age, — years. Enlisted, June 25, 1898, at Buffalo, to serve two years; mustered in as private, Co. M, same date; mustered out with company, November 19, 1898, at Buffalo, N. Y.

MURPHY, FRANK.—Age, 21 years. Enlisted, May 1, 1898, at Buffalo, to serve two years; mustered in as private, Co. A, May 17, 1898; mustered out with company, November 19, 1898, at Buffalo, N. Y.

MURPHY, JETHRO N.—Age, — years. Enlisted, June 14, 1898, at Buffalo, to serve two years; mustered in as private, Co. C, same date; mustered out with company, November 19, 1898. at Buffalo, N. Y.

MURPHY, VERNON J.—Age, 21 years. Enlisted, May 1, 1898, at Buffalo, to serve two years; mustered in as private, Co. F, May 17, 1898; mustered out with company, November 19, 1898, at Buffalo, N. Y.

MURPHY, WILLIAM C.—Age, — years. Enlisted, June 25, 1898, at Buffalo, to serve two years; mustered in as private, Co. C, same date; mustered out with company, November 19, 1898, at Buffalo, N. Y.

MURRAY, EDWARD J.—Age, — years. Enlisted, June 15, 1898, at Buffalo, to serve two years; mustered in as private, Co. C, same date; mustered out with company, November 19, 1898, at Buffalo, N. Y.

MURTHA, JAMES A.—Age, 22 years. Enlisted, May 1, 1898, at Buffalo, to serve two years; mustered in as private, Co. K, May 17, 1898; mustered out with company, November 19, 1898, at Buffalo, N. Y.

MYER, GEORGE F.—Age, — years. Enlisted, June 16, 1898, at Buffalo, to serve two years; mustered in as private, Co. B, same date; mustered out with company, November 19, 1898, at Buffalo, N. Y.

MYER, HERMAN C.—Age, 25 years. Enlisted, May 1, 1898, at Buffalo, to serve two years; mustered in as private, Co. C, May 17, 1898; mustered out with company, November 19, 1898, at Buffalo, N. Y.

NAGOWSKI, ANTONY.—Age, 23 years. Enlisted, May 1, 1898, at Buffalo, to serve two years; mustered in as private, Co. B, May 17, 1898; mustered out with company, November 19, 1898. at Buffalo, N. Y.

NELSON, ELMER M.—Age, 21 years. Enlisted, May 1, 1898, at Buffalo, to serve two years; mustered in as private, Co. C, May 17, 1898; mustered out with company, November 19, 1898, at Buffalo, N. Y.

NELSON, FRED.—Age, 25 years. Enlisted, May 1, 1898, at Buffalo, to serve two years; mustered in as private, Co. K, May 17, 1898; mustered out with company, November 19, 1898, at Buffalo, N. Y.

NELSON, FRED A.—Age, 23 years. Enlisted, May 1, 1898, at Jamestown, to serve two years; mustered in as private, Co. E, May 17, 1898; mustered out with company, November 19, 1898, at Buffalo, N. Y.

NELSON, LOUIS.—Age, — years. Fnlisted, June 13, 1898, at Buffalo, to serve two years; mustered in as private, Co. M, same date; mustered out with company, November 19, 1898, at Buffalo, N. Y.

NESBITT, GREELY.—Age, 27 years. Enlisted, May 1, 1898, at Buffalo, to serve two years; mustered in as private, Co. I, May 17, 1898; mustered out with company, November 19, 1898, at Buffalo, N. Y.

NESTELL, PLIN A.—Age, — years. Enlisted, June 21, 1898, at Buffalo, to serve two years; mustered in as private, Co. H, same date; mustered out with company, November 19, 1898, at Buffalo, N. Y.

NEUNDER, WILLIAM C.—Age, 29 years.   Enlisted, May 1, 1898, at Buffalo, to serve two years; mustered in as private, Co. K, May 17, 1898; appointed cook, August 3, 1898; mustered out with company, November 19, 1898, at Buffalo, N. Y.

NEWMAN, CHARLES F.—Age, 21 years. Enlisted, May 1, 1898, at Buffalo, to serve two years; mustered in as private, Co. B, May 17, 1898; mustered out with company, November 19, 1898, at Buffalo, N. Y.

NEWMAN, EMANUEL.—Age, 21 years. Enlisted, May 1, 1898, at Buffalo, to serve two years; mustered in as private, Co. B, May 17, 1898; mustered out with company, November 19, 1898, at Buffalo, N. Y.

NOELLER, WILLIAM F.—Age, 25 years. Enlisted, May 1, 1898, at Buffalo, to serve two years; mustered in as hospital steward, May 17, 1898; mustered out with regiment, November 19, 1898, at Buffalo, N. Y.

NOLAN, THOMAS.—Age, 29 years. Enlisted, May 1, 1898, at at Buffalo, to serve two years; mustered in as private, Co. G, May 17, 1898; mustered out with company, November 19, 1898, at Buffalo, N. Y.

NORTON, GEORGE H.—Age, 35 years. Enrolled, May 1, 1898, at Buffalo, to serve two years; mustered in as captain, Co. F, May 17, 1898; mustered out with company, November 19, 1898, at Buffalo, N. Y.; commissioned captain, May 17, 1898, with rank from same date, original.

NOTT, JOHN E.—Age, 23 years. Enlisted, May 1, 1898, at Buffalo, to serve two years; mustered in as private, Co. G, May 17, 1898; mustered out with company, November 19, 1898, at Buffalo, N. Y.

NUNO, JAMES F.—Age, 24 years. Enrolled, May 1, 1898, at Buffalo, to serve two years; mustered in as second lieutenant, Co. A, May 17, 1898; mustered out with company, November 19, 1898, at Buffalo, N. Y.; commissioned second lieutenant, May 17, 1898, with rank from same date, original.

NURZEY, WALTER FAIRFAX.—Age, 42 years. Enrolled, May 1, 1898, at Buffalo, to serve two years; mustered in as first lieutenant and regimental-adjutant, May 17, 1898; mustered out with regiment, November 19, 1898, at Buffalo, N. Y.; commissioned captain and regimental-adjutant, May 17, 1898, with rank from same date, original.

NUSSBAUM, GEORGE.—Age, 27 years. Enlisted, May 1, 1898, at Buffalo, to serve two years; mustered in as private, Co. L, May 17, 1898; mustered out with company, November 19, 1898, at Buffalo, N. Y.

OAKES, ROBERT E.—Age, 35 years. Enlisted, May 1, 1898, at Buffalo, to serve two years; mustered in as corporal, Co. B, May 17, 1898; mustered out with company, November 19, 1898, at Buffalo, N. Y.

OBENAUER, JR., JACOB.—Age, 21 years. Enlisted, May 1, 1898, at Buffalo, to serve two years; mustered in as private, Co. H, May 17, 1898; mustered out with company, November 19, 1898, at Buffalo, N. Y.

O'BRIEN, EDWARD.—Age, — years. Enlisted, June 13, 1898, at Buffalo, to serve two years; mustered in as private, Co. K, same date; transferred to First Division Hospital Corps, Second Army Corps, June 28, 1898; returned to company, September 3, 1898; transferred to Hospital Corps, United States Army, September 12, 1898.

O'BRIEN, FRANK H.—Age, — years. Enlisted, July 11, 1898, at Buffalo, to serve two years; mustered in as private, Co. K, same date; mustered out with company, November 19, 1898, at Buffalo, N. Y.

O'CONNELL, RICHARD H.—Age, 24 years. Enlisted, May 1, 1898, at Buffalo, to serve two years; mustered in as private, Co. M, May 17, 1898; mustered out with company, November 19, 1898, at Buffalo, N. Y.

O'CONNOR, MICHAEL.—Age, 30 years. Enlisted, May 1, 1898, at Buffalo, to serve two years; mustered in as private, Co. F, May 17, 1898; mustered out with company, November 19, 1898, at Buffalo, N. Y.

O'DONOGHUE, ROGER.—Age, 36 years. Enlisted, May 1, 1898, at Buffalo, to serve two years; mustered in as private, Co. M, May 17, 1898; mustered out with company, November 19, 1898, at Buffalo, N. Y.

OELZ, CHARLES.—Age, 24 years. Enlisted, May 1, 1898, at Buffalo, to serve two years; mustered in as private, Co. F, May 17, 1898; died of peritonitis, September 8, 1898, at German Deaconess Hospital, Buffalo, N. Y.

OGILVIE, GEORGE F.—Age, 23 years. Enlisted, May 1, 1898, at Buffalo, to serve two years; mustered in as corporal, Co. M, May 17, 1898; mustered out with company, November 19, 1898, at Buffalo, N. Y.

O'GORMAN, JOHN M.—Age, 24 years. Enrolled, May 1, 1898, at Buffalo, to serve two years; mustered in as second lieutenant, Co. H, May 17, 1898; mustered out with company, November 19, 1898, at Buffalo, N. Y.; commissioned second lieutenant, May 17, 1898, with rank from same date, original.

O'GORMAN, STEPHEN V.—Age, 22 years. Enlisted, May 1, 1898, at Buffalo, to serve two years; mustered in as private, Co. H, May 17, 1898; promoted corporal, July 25, 1898; mustered out with company, November 19, 1898, at Buffalo, N. Y.

OLIVER, ROBERT B.—Age, 21 years. Enlisted, May 1, 1898, at Buffalo, to serve two years; mustered in as musician, Co. B, May 17, 1898; mustered out with company, November 19, 1898, at Buffalo, N. Y.

OLIVER, WILLIAM.—Age, 19 years. Enlisted, May 1, 1898, at Buffalo, to serve two years; mustered in as musician, Co. C, May 17, 1898; mustered out with company, November 19, 1898, at Buffalo, N. Y.

OLSON, GEORGE S.—Age, 19 years. Enlisted, May 1, 1898, at Buffalo, to serve two years; mustered in as private, Co. L, May 17, 1898; mustered out with company, November 19, 1898, at Buffalo, N. Y.

OLSON, LEONARD R.—Age, — years. Enlisted, June 15, 1898, at Buffalo, to serve two years; mustered in as private, Co. E, same date; mustered out with company, November 19, 1898, at Buffalo, N. Y.

OLSON, ROBERT A.—Age, — years. Enlisted, June 15, 1898, at Buffalo, to serve two years; mustered in as private, Co. E, same date; mustered out with company, November 19, 1898, at Buffalo, N. Y.

O'MALLEY, FRANK.—Age, — years. Enlisted, June 14, 1898, at Buffalo, to serve two years; mustered in as private, Co. D, same date; mustered out with company, November 19, 1898, at Buffalo, N. Y.

O'NEILL, JAMES.—Age, 18 years. Enlisted, May 1, 1898, at Buffalo, to serve two years; mustered in as private, Co. D, May 17, 1898; mustered out with company, November 19, 1898, at Buffalo, N. Y.

ORLOWSKI, STANISLAUS.—Age, — years. Enlisted, June 21, 1898, at Buffalo, to serve two years; mustered in as private, Co. M, same date; mustered out with company, November 19, 1898, at Buffalo, N. Y.

ORMSBY, JOHN S.—Age, 29 years. Enlisted, May 1, 1898, at Buffalo, to serve two years; mustered in as private, Co. G, May 17, 1898; promoted corporal, June 29, 1898; discharged, October 29, 1898.

OSWALD, MATHEW.—Age, 21 years. Enlisted, May 1, 1898, at Buffalo, to serve two years; mustered in as private, Co. D, May 17, 1898; mustered out with company, November 19, 1898, at Buffalo, N. Y.

OTT, JR., GEORGE V.—Age, 23 years. Enlisted, May 1, 1898, at Buffalo, to serve two years; mustered in as private, Co. D, May 17, 1898; mustered out with company, November 19, 1898, at Buffalo, N. Y.

OWENS, REUBEN G.—Age, 23 years. Enlisted, May 1, 1898, at Jamestown, to serve two years; mustered in as private, Co. E, May 17, 1898; mustered out with company, November 19, 1898, at Buffalo, N. Y.

PAGAN, WALTER E.—Age, 30 years. Enrolled, May 1, 1898, at Buffalo, to serve two years; mustered in as first lieutenant, Co. I, May 17, 1898; mustered out with company, November 19, 1898, at Buffalo, N. Y.; commissioned first lieutenant, May 17, 1898, with rank from same date, original.

PAGE, FREDERICK C.—Age, — years. Enlisted, June 15, 1898, at Buffalo, to serve two years; mustered in as private, Co. C, same date; mustered out with company, November 19, 1898, at Buffalo, N. Y.

PALMATIER, PETER V.—Age, — years. Enlisted, June 23, 1898, at Buffalo, to serve two years; mustered in as private, Co. L, same date; mustered out with company, November 19, 1898, at Buffalo, N. Y.

PALMER, RALPH H.—Age, 39 years. Enlisted, May 1, 1898, at Buffalo, to serve two years; mustered in as private, Co. F, May 17, 1898; mustered out with company, November 19, 1898, at Buffalo, N. Y.

PANGBURN, HARRY.—Age, 23 years. Enlisted, May 1, 1898, at Buffalo, to serve two years; mustered in as private, Co. F, May 17, 1898; promoted corporal, same date; discharged for disability, July 8, 1898.

PAPENBERG, HENRY G.—Age, 24 years. Enlisted, May 1, 1898, at Buffalo, to serve two years; mustered in as private, Co. D, May 17, 1898; mustered out with company, November 19, 1898, at Buffalo, N. Y.

PASCIAK, STANILAUS.—Age, 23 years. Enlisted, May 1, 1898, at Buffalo, to serve two years; mustered in as private, Co. I, May 17, 1898; mustered out with company, November 19, 1898, at Buffalo, N. Y.

PATRIDGE, MILTIN E.—Age, — years. Enlisted, June 13, 1898, at Buffalo, to serve two years; mustered in as private, Co. G, same date; transferred to Hospital Corps, United States Army, June 29, 1898.

PATTON, JAMES.—Age, 41 years. Enlisted, May 1, 1898, at Buffalo, to serve two years; mustered in as corporal, Co. A, May 17, 1898; mustered out with company, November 19, 1898, at Buffalo, N. Y.

PEACOCK, FREDERICK W.—Age, 21 years. Enlisted, May 1, 1898, at Buffalo, to serve two years; mustered in as private, Co. A, May 17, 1898; mustered out with company, November 19, 1898, at Buffalo, N. Y.

PEARL, JAMES.—Age, 25 years. Enlisted, May 1, 1898, at Buffalo, to serve two years; mustered in as private, Co. A, May 17, 1898; mustered out with company, November 19, 1898, at Buffalo, N. Y.

PECK, JOHN D.—Age, 37 years. Enlisted, May 1, 1898, at Buffalo, to serve two years; mustered in as private, Co. G, May 17, 1898; mustered out with company, November 19, 1898, at Buffalo, N. Y.

PEGGS, GEORGE.—Age, — years. Enlisted, May 1, 1898, at Buffalo, to serve two years; mustered in as private, Co. B, May 17, 1898; mustered out with company, November 19, 1898, at Buffalo, N. Y.

PENNEY, WALTER H.—Age, 25 years. Enlisted, May 1, 1898, at Buffalo, to serve two years; mustered in as private, Co. E, May 17, 1898; promoted corporal, July 17, 1898; mustered out with company, November 19, 1898, at Buffalo, N. Y.

PERREN, CHARLES G.—Age, 36 years. Enlisted, May 1, 1898, at Buffalo, to serve two years; mustered in as private, Co. K, May 17, 1898; mustered out with company, November 19, 1898, at Buffalo, N. Y.

PETERS. GEORGE.—Age, 19 years. Enlisted, May 1, 1898, at Buffalo, to serve two years; mustered in as private, Co. B, May 17, 1898; mustered out with company, November 19, 1898, at Buffalo, N. Y.

PETERSON, ALFRED.—Age, — years. Enlisted, May 1, 1898, at Buffalo, to serve two years; mustered in as private, Co. M, May 17, 1898; mustered out with company, November 19, 1898, at Buffalo, N. Y.

PETERSON, CLARENCE O.—Age, — years Enlisted, June 20, 1898, at Buffalo, to serve two years; mustered in as private, Co. E, same date; mustered out with company, November 19, 1898, at Buffalo, N. Y.

PETERSON, JOHN· T.—Age, 21 years. Enlisted, May 1, 1898, at Jamestown, to serve two years; mustered in as private, Co. E, May 17, 1898; mustered out with company, November 19, 1898, at Buffalo, N. Y.

PETRY, LOUIS M.—Age, — years. Enlisted, June 22, 1898, at Buffalo, to serve two years; mustered in as private, Co. E, same date; transferred to band, June 29, 1898; mustered out with band, November 19, 1898, at Buffalo, N. Y.

PFEIFFER, JOHN G.—Age, 22 years. Enlisted, May 1, 1898, at Buffalo, to serve two years; mustered in as private, Co. A, May 17, 1898; discharged, October 10, 1898.

PFLUM, JOHN.—Age, — years. Enlisted, June 13, 1898, at Buffalo, to serve two years; mustered in as private, Co. I, same date; mustered out with company, November 19, 1898, at Buffalo, N. Y.

PHELPS, GARRET P.—Age, 40 years. Enlisted, May 13, 1898, at Camp Black, to serve two years; mustered in as private, Co. E, May 17, 1898; mustered out with company, November 19, 1898, at Buffalo, N. Y.

PHELPS, GEORGE H.—Age, 30 years. Enlisted, May 1, 1898, at Buffalo, to serve two years; mustered in as private, Co. C, May 17, 1898; mustered out with company, November 19, 1898, at Buffalo, N. Y.

PHILCOX, FREDERICK T.—Age, — years. Enrolled, May 1, 1898, at Buffalo, to serve two years; mustered in as first lieutenant, Co. D, May 17, 1898; mustered out with company, November 19, 1898, at Buffalo, N. Y.; commissioned first lieutenant, May 17, 1898, with rank from same date, original.

PHILLIPEE, SAMUEL.—Age, 21 years. Enlisted, May 1, 1898, at Buffalo, to serve two years; mustered in as private, Co. D, May 17, 1898; mustered out with company, November 19, 1898, at Buffalo, N. Y.

PHILLIPS, BURLAND J.—Age, 21 years. Enlisted, May 1, 1898, at Buffalo, to serve two years; mustered in as private, Co. F, May 17, 1898; transferred to Hospital Corps, United States Army, June 28, 1898; to Co. F, September 2, 1898; mustered out with company, November 19, 1898, at Buffalo, N. Y.

PHILLIPS, THOMAS.—Age, — years. Enlisted, June 13, 1898, at Buffalo, to serve two years; mustered in as private, Co. L, same date; mustered out with company, November 19, 1898, at Buffalo, N. Y.

PICKELMAN, CHARLES H.—Age, — years. Enlisted, June 18, 1898, at Buffalo, to serve two years; mustered in as private, Co. D, same date; mustered out with company, November 19, 1898, at Buffalo, N. Y.

PIERCE, HARRY.—Age, — years. Enlisted, June 14, 1898, at Buffalo, to serve two years; mustered in as private, Co. B, same date; mustered out with company, November 19, 1898, at Buffalo, N. Y.

PIERCE, HUGH E.—Age, — years. Enlisted, June 14, 1898, at Buffalo, to serve two years; mustered in as private, Co. I, same date; mustered out with company, November 19, 1898, at Buffalo, N. Y.

PIERSON, THOMAS.—Age, — years. Enlisted, June 21, 1898, at Buffalo, to serve two years; mustered in as private, Co. F, same date; discharged for disability, July 14, 1898.

PILKEY, ADDISON P.—Age, 22 years. Enlisted, May 1, 1898, at Buffalo, to serve two years; mustered in as private, Co. G, May 17, 1898; mustered out with company, November 19, 1898, at Buffalo, N. Y.

PILKEY, THOMAS L.—Age, 24 years. Enlisted, May 1, 1898, at Buffalo, to serve two years; mustered in as first sergeant, Co. G, May 17, 1898; mustered out with company, November 19, 1898, at Buffalo, N. Y.

POLAK, ESAAK.—Age, 28 years. Enlisted, May 1, 1898, at Buffalo, to serve two years; mustered in as wagoner, Co. M, May 17, 1898; mustered out with company, November 19, 1898, at Buffalo, N. Y.

POLL, LOUIS.—Age, 37 years. Enlisted, May 1, 1898, at Buffalo, to serve two years; mustered in as sergeant, Co. B, May 17, 1898; returned to ranks, at own request, June 21, 1898; appointed cook, July 25, 1898; mustered out with company, November 19, 1898, at Buffalo, N. Y.

POLLY, CLAYTON L.—Age, — years. Enlisted, June 15, 1898, at Buffalo, to serve two years; mustered in as private, Co. E, same date; mustered out with company, November 19, 1898, at Buffalo, N. Y.

POND, CHARLES H.—Age, 22 years. Enlisted, May 1, 1898, at Buffalo, to serve two years; mustered in as sergeant, Co. G, May 17, 1898; mustered out with company, November 19, 1898, at Buffalo, N. Y.

PORTER, SAMUEL M.—Age, 31 years. Enlisted, May 1, 1898, at Jamestown, to serve two years; mustered in as first sergeant, Co. E, May 17, 1898; as second lieutenant, July 20, 1898; died of fever, September 14, 1898, at home, Jamestown, N. Y.; commissioned second lieutenant, July 8, 1898, with rank from same date, vice Wilson, promoted first lieutenant.

POWELL, JOHN.—Age, 39 years. Enlisted, May 1, 1898, at Buffalo, to serve two years; mustered in as chief musician, May 17, 1898; mustered out with regiment, November 19, 1898, at Buffalo, N. Y.

POWERS, JAMES J.—Age, 26 years. Enlisted, May 1, 1898, at Buffalo, to serve two years; mustered in as private, Co. B, May 17, 1898; mustered out with company, November 19, 1898, at Buffalo, N. Y.

PREISER, JOHN.—Age, 20 years. Enlisted, May 1, 1898, at Buffalo, to serve two years; mustered in as private, Co. H, May 17, 1898; mustered out with company, November 19, 1898, at Buffalo, N. Y.

PRENATT, GEORGE.—Age, 20 years. Enlisted, May 1, 1898, at Buffalo, to serve two years; mustered in as private, Co. H, May 17, 1898; mustered out with company, November 19, 1898, at Buffalo, N. Y.

PRICE, FRANK X.—Age, — years. Enlisted, June 21, 1898, at at Buffalo, to serve two years; mustered in as private, Co. L, same date; mustered out with company, November 19, 1898, at Buffalo, N. Y.

PRICE, HARRY W.—Age, 22 years. Enlisted, May 1, 1898, at Jamestown, to serve two years; mustered in as private, Co. E, May 17, 1898; mustered out with company, November 19, 1898, at Buffalo, N. Y.

PRINY, ALBERT.—Age, 21 years. Enlisted, May 1, 1898, at Buffalo, to serve two years; mustered in as private, Co. H, May 17, 1898; mustered out with company, November 19, 1898, at Buffalo, N. Y.

PROEPSTER, EDWARD M.—Age, 24 years. Enlisted, May 1, 1898, at Buffalo, to serve two years; mustered in as private, Co. A, May 17, 1898; promoted corporal, June 22, 1898; mustered out with company, November 19, 1898, at Buffalo, N. Y.

PROPSTER, WILLIAM J.—Age, — years. Enlisted, June 20, 1898, at Buffalo, to serve two years; mustered in as private, Co. F, same date; mustered out with company, November 19, 1898, at Buffalo, N. Y.

PRUDDEN, HARRY J.—Age, 23 years. Enlisted, May 1, 1898, at Jamestown, to serve two years; mustered in as private, Co. E, May 17, 1898; mustered out with company, November 19, 1898, at Buffalo, N. Y.

PURACKER, GEORGE.—Age, 26 years. Enlisted, May 1, 1898, at Buffalo, to serve two years; mustered in as private, Co. F, May 17, 1898; died of typhoid fever, August 25, 1898, in Division Hospital, Camp Alger, near Dunn Loring, Va.

PURSELL, FRED C.—Age, 21 years. Enlisted, May 1, 1898, at Buffalo, to serve two years; mustered in as private, Co. L, May 17, 1898; mustered out with company, November 19, 1898, at Buffalo, N. Y.

QUACKENBUSH, GERRIT V. S.—Age, 27 years. Enrolled, May 1, 1898, at Buffalo, to serve two years; mustered in as second lieutenant, Co. L, May 17, 1898; mustered out with company, November 19, 1898, at Buffalo, N. Y.; commissioned second lieutenant, May 17, 1898, with rank from same date, original.

QUIGLEY, WILLIAM.—Age, — years. Enlisted, June 18, 1898 at Buffalo, to serve two years; mustered in as private, Co. H, same date; mustered out with company, November 19, 1898, at Buffalo, N. Y.

QUILL, GEORGE J.—Age, 24 years. Enlisted, May 1, 1898, at Buffalo, to serve two years; mustered in as private, Co. M, May 17, 1898; mustered out with company, November 19, 1898, at Buffalo, N. Y.

RABBES, HENRY.—Age, 25 years. Enlisted, May 1, 1898, at Buffalo, to serve two years; mustered in as first sergeant, Co. K, May 17, 1898; mustered out with company, November 19, 1898, at Buffalo, N. Y.

RAIGEN, THOMAS.—Age, — years. Enlisted, June 13, 1898, at Buffalo, to serve two years; mustered in as private, Co. L, same date; transferred to Hospital Corps, United States Army, June 28, 1898, at Camp Alger, Va.; to Co. D, September 2, 1898; to Hospital Corps, September 12, 1898, at Fort Columbus, New York Harbor.

RAIHL, NICHOLAS R.—Age, — years. Enlisted, June 16, 1898, at Buffalo, to serve two years; mustered in as private, Co. A, same date; died of typhoid fever, October 5, 1898, at Buffalo, N. Y.

RANDALL, CLATE M.—Age, — years. Enlisted, June 21, 1898, at Buffalo, to serve two years; mustered in as private, Co. E, same date; mustered out with company, November 19, 1898, at Buffalo, N. Y.

RANDOLPH, ARTHUR E.—Age, 20 years. Enlisted, May 1, 1898, at Buffalo, to serve two years; mustered in as private, Co. A, May 17, 1898; mustered out with company, November 19, 1898, at Buffalo, N. Y.

RANDORF, CHARLES A.—Age, 22 years. Enlisted, May 1, 1898, at Buffalo, to serve two years; mustered in as private, Co. G, May 17, 1898; mustered out with company, November 19, 1898, at Buffalo, N. Y.

RANSOM, ARTHUR J.—Age, 32 years. Enlisted, May 1, 1898, at Buffalo, to serve two years; mustered in as private, Co. M, May 17, 1898; promoted corporal, July 6, 1898; mustered out with company, November 19, 1898, at Buffalo, N. Y.

RAPP, JACOB J.—Age, 19 years. Enlisted, May 1, 1898, at Buffalo, to serve two years; mustered in as private, Co. H, May 17, 1898; mustered out with company, November 19, 1898, at Buffalo, N. Y.

RAPP, MANLEY.—Age, 24 years. Enlisted, May 1, 1898, at Jamestown, to serve two years; mustered in as private, Co. E, May 17, 1898; mustered out with company, November 19, 1898, at Buffalo, N. Y.

RAPP, OTTO.—Age, 25 years. Enlisted, May 11, 1898, at Buffalo, to serve two years; mustered in as private, Co. H, May 17, 1898; mustered out with company, November 19, 1898, at Buffalo, N. Y.

RATKE, FREDERICK.—Age, 29 years. Enlisted, May 1, 1898, at Buffalo, to serve two years; mustered in as sergeant, Co. I, May 17, 1898; mustered out with company, November 19, 1898, at Buffalo, N. Y.

RAU, FRANK G.—Age, 23 years. Enlisted, May 1, 1898, at Buffalo, to serve two years; mustered in as corporal, Co. C, May 17, 1898; mustered out with company, November 19, 1898, at Buffalo, N. Y.

RAU, WILLIAM.—Age, — years. Enlisted, June 18, 1898, at Buffalo, to serve two years; mustered in as private, Co. B, same date; mustered out with company, November 19, 1898, at Buffalo, N. Y.

RAUSCHER, FREDERICK.—Age, — years. Enlisted, June 14, 1898, at Buffalo, to serve two years; mustered in as private, Co. I, same date; discharged, October 26, 1898.

RAUSCHER, GEORGE.—Age, 22 years. Enlisted, May 1, 1898, at Buffalo, to serve two years; mustered in as corporal, Co. H, May 17, 1898; mustered out with company, November 19, 1898, at Buffalo, N. Y.

RAYMOND, WILLIAM A.—Age, — years. Enlisted, June 25, 1898, at Buffalo, to serve two years; mustered in as private, Co. C, same date; mustered out with company, November 19, 1898, at Buffalo, N. Y.

REBADOW, EUGENE B.—Age, — years. Enlisted, June 14, 1898, at Buffalo, to serve two years; mustered in as private, Co. L, same date; mustered out with company, November 19, 1898, at Buffalo, N. Y.

RECHIN, JACOB.—Age, 22 years. Enlisted, May 1, 1898, at Buffalo, to serve two years; mustered in as private, Co. M, May 17, 1898; mustered out with company, November 19, 1898, at Buffalo, N. Y.

RECHIN, JOHN.—Age, — years. Enlisted, June 22, 1898, at Buffalo, to serve two years; mustered in as private, Co. M, same date; discharged for disability, July 16, 1898, at Camp Alger, near Dunn Loring, Va.

REEB, FRANK.—Age, — years. Enlisted, June 13, 1898, at Buffalo, to serve two years; mustered in as private, Co. D, same date; transferred to Co. F, June 28, 1898; mustered out with company, November 19, 1898, at Buffalo, N. Y

REESER, EDWARD B.—Age, 20 years. Enlisted, May 1, 1898, at Buffalo, to serve two years; mustered in as private, Co. G, May 17, 1898; transferred to Hospital Corps, United States Army, June 21, 1898; to Co. D, September 2, 1898; mustered out with company, November 19, 1898, at Buffalo, N. Y.

REICHERT, LOUIS J.—Age, 20 years. Enlisted, May 1, 1898, at Buffalo, to serve two years; mustered in as private, Co. A, May 17, 1898; mustered out with company, November 19, 1898, at Buffalo, N. Y.

REICHOLD, JOHN J.—Age, — years. Enlisted, June 20, 1898, at Buffalo, to serve two years; mustered in as private, Co. H, same date; mustered out with company, November 19, 1898, at Buffalo, N. Y.

REINHARD, JOHN H.—Age, 26 years. Enlisted, May 1, 1898, at Buffalo, to serve two years; mustered in as private, Co. I, May 17, 1898; mustered out with company, November 19, 1898, at Buffalo, N. Y.

REINLANDER, VALENTINE.—Age, 24 years. Enlisted, May 1, 1898, at Buffalo, to serve two years; mustered in as private, Co. G, May 17, 1898; mustered out with company, November 19, 1898, at Buffalo, N. Y.

RIBBEL, FRANK E.—Age, 34 years. Enlisted, May 1, 1898, at Buffalo, to serve two years; mustered in as private, Co. K, May 17, 1898; mustered out with company, November 19, 1898, at Buffalo, N. Y.

RICE, EDWARD H.—Age, 29 years. Enlisted, May 1, 1898, at Jamestown, to serve two years; mustered in as corporal, Co. E, May 17, 1898; mustered out with company, November 19, 1898, at Buffalo, N. Y.

RICH, JR., GAINS B.—Age, 23 years. Enrolled, May 6, 1898, at Camp Black, to serve two years; mustered in as first lieutenant, Co. A, May 17, 1898; mustered out with company, November 19, 1898, at Buffalo, N. Y.; commissioned first lieutenant, May 17, 1898, with rank from same date, original.

RICHARDS, CHARLES W.—Age, 22 years. Enlisted, May 1, 1898, at Buffalo, to serve two years; mustered in as private, Co. H, May 17, 1898; mustered out with company, November 19, 1898, at Buffalo, N. Y.

RICHARDSON, GEORGE F.—Age, 24 years. Enlisted, May 1, 1898, at Buffalo, to serve two years; mustered in as private, Co. C, May 17, 1898; mustered out with company, November 19, 1898, at Buffalo, N. Y.

RICHARDSON, HERBERT O.—Age, — years. Enlisted, June 13, 1898, at Buffalo, to serve two years; mustered in as private, Co. K, same date; mustered out with company, November 19, 1898, at Buffalo, N. Y., as Herbert A. Richardson.

RICHTER, FRED.—Age, 21 years. Enlisted, May 1, 1898, at Buffalo, to serve two years; mustered in as wagoner, Co. H, May 17, 1898; discharged for disability, July 2, 1898, at Camp Alger, near Dunn Loring, Va.

RICK, FRANK.—Age, 26 years. Enlisted, May 1, 1898, at Buffalo, to serve two years; mustered in as private, Co. L, May 17, 1898; mustered out with company, November 19, 1898, at Buffalo, N. Y.

RIEBOLD, ALEXANDER.—Age, — years. Enlisted, June 14, 1898, at Buffalo, to serve two years; mustered in as private, Co. I, same date; mustered out with company, November 19, 1898, at Buffalo, N. Y.

RIEGEL, FRANK.—Age, 24 years. Enlisted, May 1, 1898, at Buffalo, to serve two years; mustered in as private, Co. F, May 17, 1898; mustered out with company, November 19, 1898, at Buffalo, N. Y.

RIELLY, JAMES J.—Age, — years. Enlisted, June 16, 1898, at Buffalo, to serve two years; mustered in as private, Co. I, same date; discharged, October 20, 1898.

RIFE, FRED.—Age, 25 years. Enlisted, May 1, 1898, at Buffalo, to serve two years; mustered in as private, Co. G, May 17, 1898; mustered out with company, November 19, 1898, at Buffalo, N. Y.

RIKER, EDWARD C.—Age, 23 years. Enlisted, May 1, 1898, at Buffalo, to serve two years; mustered in as private, Co. G, May 17, 1898; mustered out with company, November 19, 1898, at Buffalo, N. Y.

RITER, WILLIAM F.—Age, 21 years. Enlisted, May 1, 1898, at Buffalo, to serve two years; mustered in as private, Co. D, May 17, 1898; promoted corporal, July 7, 1898; mustered out with company, November 19, 1898, at Buffalo, N. Y.

ROACH, JOHN E.—Age, — years. Enlisted, June 15, 1898, at Buffalo, to serve two years; mustered in as private, Co. K, same date; mustered out with company, November 19, 1898, at Buffalo, N. Y.

ROBINS, CHARLES.—Age, 22 years. Enlisted, May 1, 1898, at Buffalo, to serve two years; mustered in as private, Co. B, May 17, 1898; mustered out with company, November 19, 1898, at Buffalo, N. Y.

ROCKEFELLER, LEONARD L.—Age, 24 years. Enlisted, May 1, 1898, at Buffalo, to serve two years; mustered in as corporal, Co. B, May 17, 1898; mustered out with company, November 19, 1898, at Buffalo, N. Y.

ROCKWOOD, JR., WILLIAM H.—Age, — years. Enlisted, June 13, 1898, at Buffalo, to serve two years; mustered in as private, Co. F, same date; transferred to Co. E, June 29, 1898; mustered out with company, November 19, 1898, at Buffalo, N. Y.

RODERICK, WILLIAM C.—Age, 25 years. Enlisted, May 1, 1898, at Buffalo, to serve two years; mustered in as quarter-master-sergeant, Co. C, May 17, 1898; mustered out with company, November 19, 1898, at Buffalo, N. Y.

RODNEY, CHARLES H.—Age, 25 years. Enlisted, May 1, 1898, at Buffalo, to serve two years; mustered in as private, Co. B, May 17, 1898; promoted corporal, June 23, 1898; mustered out with company, November 19, 1898, at Buffalo, N. Y.

ROEMHILD, JOSEPH.—Age, — years. Enlisted, June 14, 1898, at Buffalo, to serve two years; mustered in as private, Co. F, same date; mustered out with company, November 19, 1898, at Buffalo, N. Y.

ROGERS, FREDERICK.—Age, — years. Enlisted, June 21, 1898, at Buffalo, to serve two years; mustered in as private, Co. L, same date; mustered out with company, November 19, 1898, at Buffalo, N. Y.

ROMANS, JOHN D.—Age, 23 years. Enlisted, May 1, 1898, at Jamestown, to serve two years; mustered in as private, Co. E, May 17, 1898; promoted corporal, no date; mustered out with company, November 19, 1898, at Buffalo, N. Y.

ROOT, FRANCIS S.—Age, 28 years. Enlisted, May 1, 1898, at Buffalo, to serve two years; mustered in as private, Co. M, May 17, 1898; promoted corporal, July 1, 1898; mustered out with company, November 19, 1898, at Buffalo, N. Y.

ROOT, JOSEPH H.—Age, — years. Enlisted, June 13, 1898, at Buffalo, to serve two years; mustered in as private, Co. M, same date; discharged, August 22, 1898.

ROSAR, GEORGE J.—Age, 22 years. Enlisted, May 1, 1898, at Buffalo, to serve two years; mustered in as private, Co. A, May 17, 1898; mustered out with company, November 19, 1898, at Buffalo, N. Y.

ROSE, ADOLF G.—Age, 25 years. Enlisted, May 1, 1898, at Buffalo, to serve two years; mustered in as private, Co. I, May 17, 1898; mustered out with company, November 19, 1898, at Buffalo, N. Y.

ROSSENBACK, CHARLES F.—Age, — years. Enlisted, June 13, 1898, at Buffalo, to serve two years; mustered in as private, Co. D, same date; mustered out with company, November 19, 1898, at Buffalo, N. Y.

ROUN, DAVID E.—Age, 25 years. Enlisted, May 1, 1898, at Buffalo, to serve two years; mustered in as private, Co. L, May 17, 1898; mustered out with company, November 19, 1898, at Buffalo, N. Y.

ROWLEY, AMOS B.—Age, 28 years. Enlisted, May 1, 1898, at Buffalo, to serve two years; mustered in as private, Co. B, May 17, 1898; appointed artificer, May 29, 1898; mustered out with company, November 19, 1898, at Buffalo, N. Y.

ROY, JOHN B.—Age, 26 years. Enlisted, May 1, 1898, at Buffalo, to serve two years; mustered in as private, Co. D, May 17, 1898; mustered out with company, November 19, 1898, at Buffalo, N. Y.

RUCH, GEORGE.—Age, 29 years. Enlisted, May 1, 1898, at Buffalo, to serve two years; mustered in as private, Co. G, May 17, 1898; appointed cook, August 3, 1898; mustered out with company, November 19, 1898, at Buffalo, N. Y.

RUCH, WILLIAM W.—Age, — years. Enlisted, June 13, 1898, at Buffalo, to serve two years; mustered in as private, Co. G, same date; mustered out with company, November 19, 1898, at Buffalo, N. Y.

RUDDY, ROBERT H.—Age, 22 years. Enlisted, May 1, 1898, at Buffalo, to serve two years; mustered in as private, Co. A, May 17, 1898; mustered out with company, November 19, 1898, at Buffalo, N. Y.

RUFF, JR., CONRAD.—Age, 23 years. Enlisted, May 1, 1898, at Buffalo, to serve two years; mustered in as private, Co. K, May 17, 1898; mustered out with company, November 19, 1898, at Buffalo, N. Y.

RUFENER, ERNEST L.—Age, 29 years. Enrolled, May 2, 1898, at Camp Black, to serve two years; mustered in as first lieutenant and assistant surgeon, May 6, 1898; mustered out with regiment, November 19, 1898, at Buffalo, N. Y.; commissioned captain and assistant surgeon, May 6, 1898, with rank of captain, from same date, original.

RUGENSTEIN, FRED L.—Age, 25 years. Enlisted, May 1, 1898, at Buffalo, to serve two years; mustered in as private, Co. B, May 17, 1898; promoted corporal, July 9, 1898; mustered out with company, November 19, 1898, at Buffalo, N. Y.

RUNG, HENRY F.—Age, — years. Enlisted, June 20, 1898, at Buffalo, to serve two years; mustered in as private, Co. I, same date; mustered out with company, November 19, 1898, at Buffalo, N. Y.

RUNYON, WILLIAM.—Age, 19 years. Enlisted, May 1, 1898, at Buffalo, to serve two years; mustered in as private, Co. F, May 17, 1898; mustered out with company, November 19, 1898, at Buffalo, N. Y.

RUSERT, WILLIAM H.—Age, 22 years. Enlisted, May 12, 1898, at Camp Black, Hempstead Plains, to serve two years; mustered in as private, Co. C, May 17, 1898; mustered out with company, November 19, 1898, at Buffalo, N. Y.

RUSHWORTH, LEROY A.—Age, 22 years. Enlisted, May 1, 1898, at Jamestown, to serve two years; mustered in as private, Co. E, May 17, 1898; mustered out with company, November 19, 1898, at Buffalo, N. Y.

RUSK, JOHN.—Age, — years. Enlisted, June 14, 1898, at Buffalo, to serve two years; mustered in as private, Co. I, same date; mustered out with company, November 19, 1898, at Buffalo, N. Y.

RUSS, CHARLES.—Age, — years. Enlisted, June 20, 1898, at Buffalo, to serve two years; mustered in as private, Co. C, same date; mustered out with company, November 19, 1898, at Buffalo, N. Y.

RUTH, FRANK P.—Age, 20 years. Enlisted, May 1, 1898, at Buffalo, to serve two years; mustered in as private, Co. C, May 17, 1898; mustered out with company, November 19, 1898, at Buffalo, N. Y.

RYAN, MAURICE A.—Age, 32 years Enlisted, May 1, 1898, at Buffalo, to serve two years; mustered in as private, Co. G, May 17, 1898; mustered out with company, November 19, 1898, at Buffalo, N. Y.

RYAN, MICHAEL J.—Age, 27 years. Enlisted, May 1, 1898, at Buffalo, to serve two years; mustered in as private, Co. K, May 17, 1898; mustered out with company, November 19, 1898, at Buffalo, N. Y.

RYAN, WILLIAM J.—Age, 24 years. Enlisted, May 1, 1898, at Buffalo, to serve two years; mustered in as corporal, Co. L, May 17, 1898; returned to ranks, July 14, 1898; mustered out with company, November 19, 1898, at Buffalo, N. Y.

RYDER, ARCHIE C.—Age, 24 years. Enlisted, May 1, 1898, at Buffalo, to serve two years; mustered in as private, Co A, May 17, 1898; mustered out with company, November 19, 1898, at Buffalo, N. Y.

SABINE, MARSHALL D.—Age, 26 years. Enlisted, May 1, 1898, at Buffalo, to serve two years; mustered in as sergeant, Co. A, May 17, 1898; promoted quartermaster-sergeant, September 1, 1898; first sergeant, October 19, 1898; mustered out with company, November 19, 1898, at Buffalo, N. Y.

SAGER, EDWARD.—Age, 22 years. Enlisted, May 1, 1898, at Buffalo, to serve two years; mustered in as corporal, Co. D, May 17, 1898; promoted sergeant, September 3, 1898; mustered out with company, November 19, 1898, at Buffalo, N. Y.

SAISBURY, ERNEST S.—Age, — years. Enlisted, June 17, 1898, at Buffalo, to serve two years; mustered in as private, Co. M, same date; mustered out with company, November 19, 1898, at Buffalo, N. Y.

SALOW, GEORGE.—Age, 22 years. Enlisted, May 1, 1898, at Buffalo, to serve two years; mustered in as private, Co. H, May 17, 1898; mustered out with company, November 19, 1898, at Buffalo, N. Y.

SALVADOR, BERNHARD.—Age, — years. Enlisted, June 14, 1898, at Buffalo, to serve two years; mustered in as private, Co. D, same date; mustered out with company, November 19, 1898, at Buffalo, N. Y.

SALZMAN, ORLANDO.—Age, 26 years. Enlisted, May 1, 1898, at Buffalo, to serve two years; mustered in as wagoner, Co. K, May 17, 1898; mustered out with company, November 19, 1898, at Buffalo, N. Y.

SARGENT, HARRY B.—Age, 25 years. Enlisted, May 1, 1898, at Buffalo, to serve two years; mustered in as sergeant, Co. M, May 17, 1898; mustered out with company, November 19, 1898, at Buffalo, N. Y.

SATTEL, JR., JOHN G.—Age, 24 years. Enlisted, May 1, 1898, at Buffalo, to serve two years; mustered in as private, Co. D, May 17, 1898; mustered out with company, November 19, 1898, at Buffalo, N. Y.

SAUER, ADAM.—Age, — years. Enlisted, June 24, 1898, at Buffalo, to serve two years; mustered in as private, Co. D, same date; transferred to band, June 29, 1898; mustered out with band, November 19, 1898, at Buffalo, N. Y.

SAUNDERS, JOHN.—Age, 21 years. Enlisted, May 1, 1898, at Jamestown, to serve two years; mustered in as private, Co. E, May 17, 1898; mustered out with company, November 19, 1898, at Buffalo, N. Y.

SAUSNER, FRANK J.—Age, 23 years. Enlisted, May 13, 1898, at Camp Black, to serve two years; mustered in as private, Co. E, May 17, 1898; mustered out with company, November 19, 1898, at Buffalo, N. Y.

SAUSS, JOHN.—Age, — years. Enlisted, June 18, 1898, at Buffalo, to serve two years; mustered in as private, Co. B, same date; mustered out with company, November 19, 1898, at Buffalo, N. Y.

SAVAGE, GEORGE.—Age, — years. Enlisted, June 14, 1898, at Buffalo, to serve two years; mustered in as private, Co. H, same date; mustered out with company, November 19, 1898, at Buffalo, N. Y.

SCHAIFER, ALOYSIUS J.—Age, 22 years.   Enlisted, May 1, 1898, at Buffalo, to serve two years; mustered in as private, Co. A. May 17, 1898; promoted corporal, June 22, 1898; mustered out with company, November 19, 1898, at Buffalo, N. Y.

SCHANLY, JR., FREDERICK G.—Age, — years. Enlisted, June 16, 1898, at Buffalo, to serve two years; mustered in as private, Co. D, same date; mustered out with company, November 19, 1898, at Buffalo, N. Y.

SCHATZ, JOHN.—Age, 29 years. Enlisted, May 1, 1898, at Buffalo, to serve two years; mustered in as private, Co. L, May 17, 1898; mustered out with company, November 19, 1898, at Buffalo, N. Y.

SCHAUS, JAMES P.—Age, — years. Enlisted, June 18, 1898, at Buffalo, to serve two years; mustered in as private, Co. A, same date; mustered out with company, November 19, 1898, at Buffalo, N. Y.

SCHAUSS, HENRY.—Age, — years. Enlisted, July 1, 1898, at Buffalo, to serve two years; mustered in as private, Co. E, same date; mustered out with company, November 19, 1898, at Buffalo, N. Y.

SCHEMBS, GEORGE H.—Age, — years.   Enlisted, June 14, 1898, at Buffalo, to serve two years; mustered in as private, Co. K, same date; mustered out with company, November 19, 1898, at Buffalo, N. Y.

SCHEN, HENRY.—Age, 21 years. Enlisted, May 1, 1898, at Buffalo, to serve two years; mustered in as private, Co. A, May 17, 1898; mustered out with company, November 19, 1898, at Buffalo, N. Y.

SCHENCK, JOHN H.—Age, 39 years. Enlisted, May 10, 1898, at Buffalo, to serve two years; mustered in as private, Co. L, May 17, 1898; promoted corporal, July 13, 1898; mustered out with company, November 19, 1898, at Buffalo, N. Y.

SCHEVENGBECK, JR., LOUIS.—Age, 21 years. Enlisted, May 1, 1898, at Buffalo, to serve two years; mustered in as private, Co. D, May 17, 1898; mustered out with company, November 19, 1898, at Buffalo, N. Y.

SCHICK, HENRY J.—Age, 31 years. Enlisted, May 1, 1898, at Buffalo, to serve two years; mustered in as first sergeant, Co. H, May 17, 1898; mustered out with company, November 19, 1898, at Buffalo, N. Y.

SCHILLING, GEORGE.—Age, — years. Enlisted, June 29, 1898, at Buffalo, to serve two years; mustered in as private, Co. H, same date; mustered out with company, November 19, 1898, at Buffalo, N. Y.

SCHMIDT, GEORGE S.—Age, 33 years. Enlisted, May 1, 1898, at Buffalo, to serve two years; mustered in as private, Co. L, May 17, 1898; mustered out with company, November 19, 1898, at Buffalo, N. Y.

SCHMIDT, OSCAR.—Age, — years. Enlisted, June 21, 1898, at Buffalo, to serve two years; mustered in as private, Co. F, same date; mustered out with company, November 19, 1898, at Buffalo, N. Y.

SCHOLLER, CHARLES J.—Age, 19 years. Enlisted, May 1, 1898, at Buffalo, to serve two years; mustered in as musician, Co. C, May 17, 1898; mustered out with company, November 19, 1898, at Buffalo, N. Y.

SCHONBERG, JOHN.—Age, — years. Enlisted, June 27, 1898, at Buffalo, to serve two years; mustered in as private, Co. L, same date; mustered out with company, November 19, 1898, at Buffalo, N. Y.

SCHOOLEY, JAMES A.—Age, — years. Enlisted, June 21, 1898, at Buffalo, to serve two years; mustered in as private, Co H, same date; mustered out with company, November 19, 1898, at Buffalo, N. Y.

SCHOSEK, ROBERT A.—Age, — years. Enlisted, June 13, 1898, at Buffalo, to serve two years; mustered in as private, Co. K, same date; mustered out with company, November 19, 1898, at Buffalo, N. Y.

SCHOTT, JOHN P.—Age, 21 years. Enlisted, May 1, 1898, at Buffalo, to serve two years; mustered in as private, Co. K, May 17, 1898; mustered out with company, November 19, 1898, at Buffalo, N. Y.

SCHRETTENBOUNER, GEORGE A.—Age, — years. Enlisted, June 14, 1898, at Buffalo, to serve two years; mustered in as private, Co. C, same date; mustered out with company, November 19, 1898, at Buffalo, N. Y.

SCHRIDER, FRED.—Age, 24 years. Enlisted, May 1, 1898, at Buffalo, to serve two years; mustered in as musician, Co. K, May 17, 1898; discharged for disability, July 21, 1898, at Camp Alger, near Dunn Loring, Va.

SCHUERMANN, ADOLF F.—Age, 19 years. Enlisted, May 1, 1898, at Buffalo, to serve two years; mustered in as private, Co. G, May 17, 1898; mustered out with company, November 19, 1898, at Buffalo, N. Y.

SCHULTZ, BERNARD.—Age, 28 years. Enlisted, May 1, 1898, at Buffalo, to serve two years; mustered in as private, Co. C, May 17, 1898; mustered out with company, November 19, 1898, at Buffalo, N. Y.

SCHULTZ, FRED.—Age, 23 years. Enlisted, May 1, 1898, at Buffalo, to serve two years; mustered in as private, Co. M, May 17, 1898; mustered out with company, November 19, 1898, at Buffalo, N. Y.

SCHULTZ, HERMAN.—Age, — years. Enlisted, June 14, 1898, at Buffalo, to serve two years; mustered in as private, Co. H, same date; mustered out with company, November 19, 1898, at Buffalo, N. Y.

SCHULTZ, THOMAS A.—Age, 22 years. Enlisted, May 1, 1898, at Buffalo, to serve two years; mustered in as private, Co. L, May 17, 1898; mustered out with company, November 19, 1898, at Buffalo, N. Y.

SCHUMACKER, JOHN.—Age, — years. Enlisted, June 13, 1898, at Buffalo, to serve two years; mustered in as private, Co. F, same date; mustered out with company, November 19, 1898, at Buffalo, N. Y.

SCHUNK, JACOB C.—Age, 28 years. Enlisted, May 1, 1898, at Buffalo, to serve two years; mustered in as private, Co. K, May 17, 1898; mustered out with company, November 19, 1898, at Buffalo, N. Y.

SCHUTT, GEORGE.—Age, — years. Enlisted, June 27, 1898, at Buffalo, to serve two years; mustered in as private, Co. I, same date; mustered out with company, November 19, 1898, at Buffalo, N. Y.

SCHUYLER, FRED J.—Age, 28 years. Enlisted, May 1, 1898, at Buffalo, to serve two years; mustered in as private, Co. G, May 17, 1898; mustered out with company, November 19, 1898, at Buffalo, N. Y.

SCHWAN, JOHN.—Age, 30 years. Enlisted, May 1, 1898, at Buffalo, to serve two years; mustered in as private, Co B, May 17, 1898; mustered out with company, November 19, 1898, at Buffalo, N. Y.

SCHWARTZ, FRANK.—Age, 22 years. Enlisted, May 1, 1898, at Buffalo, to serve two years; mustered in as private, Co. M, May 17, 1898; mustered out with company, November 19, 1898, at Buffalo, N. Y.

SCHWARTZENBERG, FRANK.—Age, 22 years. Enlisted, May 1, 1898, at Buffalo, to serve two years; mustered in as private, Co. K, May 17, 1898; mustered out with company, November 19, 1898, at Buffalo, N. Y.

SCHWARTZENHOLTZ, WILLIAM F.—Age, — years. Enlisted, June 18, 1898, at Buffalo, to serve two years; mustered in as private, Co. I, same date; discharged, October 20, 1898, to enlist in United States Army.

SCOTT, WALLACE.—Age, 24 years. Enlisted, May 1, 1898, at Buffalo, to serve two years; mustered in as private, Co. G, May 17, 1898; mustered out with company, November 19, 1898, at Buffalo, N. Y.

SCOVILLE, HARRY E.—Age, 36 years. Enlisted, May 1, 1898, at Buffalo, to serve two years; mustered in as corporal, Co. K, May 17, 1898; promoted sergeant, June 29, 1898; mustered out with company, November 19, 1898, at Buffalo, N. Y.

SCRIBNER, JAMES WARD.—Age, 30 years. Enrolled, May 1, 1898, at Buffalo, to serve two years; mustered in as first lieutenant and battalion adjutant, May 17, 1898; mustered out with regiment, November 19, 1898, at Buffalo, N. Y.; commissioned first lieutenant and battalion adjutant, May 17, 1898, with rank from same date, original.

SCRIPTURE, FRED A.—Age, 21 years. Enlisted, May 1, 1898, at Buffalo, to serve two years; mustered in as private, Co. C, May 17, 1898; mustered out with company, November 19, 1898, at Buffalo, N. Y.

SEABERG, CHARLES.—Age, 32 years. Enlisted, May 1, 1898, at Buffalo, to serve two years; mustered in as private, Co. M, May 17, 1898; mustered out with company, November 19, 1898, at Buffalo, N. Y.

SEGELHURST, GEORGE E.—Age, 21 years. Enlisted, May 1, 1898, at Buffalo, to serve two years; mustered in as corporal, Co. L, May 17, 1898; mustered out with company, November 19, 1898, at Buffalo, N. Y.

SEIBERT, GEORGE L.—Age, — years. Enlisted, June 14, 1898, at Buffalo, to serve two years; mustered in as private, Co. A, same date; mustered out with company, November 19, 1898, at Buffalo, N. Y.

SELBY, JOHN C.—Age, — years. Enlisted, June 16, 1898, at Buffalo, to serve two years; mustered in as private, Co. G, same date; mustered out with company, November 19, 1898, at Buffalo, N. Y.

SENDZIROUSKI, FRANK.—Age, 24 years. Enlisted, May 1, 1898, at Buffalo, to serve two years; mustered in as private, Co. D, May 17, 1898; mustered out with company, November 19, 1898, at Buffalo, N. Y.

SENF, MICHAEL.—Age, — years. Enlisted, June 14, 1898, at Buffalo, to serve two years; mustered in as private, Co. G, same date; mustered out with company, November 19, 1898, at Buffalo, N. Y.

SHANNON, WELLINGTON M.—Age, — years. Enlisted, June 24, 1898, at Buffalo, to serve two years; mustered in as private, Co. K, same date; transferred to band, June 29, 1898; mustered out with band, November 19, 1898, at Buffalo, N. Y.

SHAW, WILLIAM E.—Age, 33 years. Enlisted, May 11, 1898, at Buffalo, to serve two years; mustered in as private, Co. H, May 17, 1898; promoted corporal, July 25, 1898; mustered out with company, November 19, 1898, at Buffalo, N. Y.

SHEA, WILLIAM J.—Age, 26 years. Enlisted, May 1, 1898, at Buffalo, to serve two years; mustered in as private, Co. C, May 17, 1898; mustered out with company, November 19, 1898, at Buffalo, N. Y.

SHELDON, EDWARD M.—Age, 25 years. Enlisted, May 1, 1898, at Buffalo, to serve two years; mustered in as sergeant, Co. L, May 17, 1898; mustered out with company, November 19, 1898, at Buffalo, N. Y.

SHELDON, FRANCIS E.—Age, 25 years. Enlisted, May 1, 1898, at Buffalo, to serve two years; mustered in as sergeant, Co. L, May 17, 1898; mustered out with company, November 19, 1898, at Buffalo, N. Y.

SHERMAN, JOHN.—Age, — years. Enlisted, June 14, 1898, at Buffalo, to serve two years; mustered in as private, Co. F, same date; mustered out with company, November 19, 1898, at Buffalo, N. Y.

SHERRIE, CHARLES H.—Age, 42 years. Enlisted, May 1, 1898, at Buffalo, to serve two years; mustered in as private, Co. B, May 17, 1898; promoted quartermaster-sergeant, June 1, 1898; mustered out with company, November 19, 1898, at Buffalo, N. Y.

SHERWOOD, GEORGE.—Age, — years. Enlisted, June 29, 1898, at Buffalo, to serve two years; mustered in as private, Co. L, same date; mustered out with company, November 19, 1898, at Buffalo, N. Y.

SHINE, JAMES J.—Age, 35 years. Enlisted, May 1, 1898, at Buffalo, to serve two years; mustered in as private, Co. F, May 17, 1898; mustered out with company, November 19, 1898, at Buffalo, N. Y.

SICKMAN, CHARLES W.—Age, 42 years.   Enlisted, May 1, 1898, at Buffalo, to serve two years; mustered in as sergeant-major, May 17, 1898; mustered out with regiment, November 19, 1898, at Buffalo, N. Y.

SIEBOLD, WILLIAM O.—Age, 27 years.   Enlisted, May 1, 1898, at Buffalo, to serve two years; mustered in as sergeant, Co. H, May 17, 1898; mustered out with company, November 19, 1898, at Buffalo, N. Y.

SIKORA, WILLIAM.—Age, 19 years.   Enlisted, May 1, 1898, at Buffalo, to serve two years; mustered in as private, Co. F, May 17, 1898; mustered out with company, November 19, 1898, at Buffalo, N. Y.

SIMON, GEORGE A.—Age, 24 years.   Enlisted, May 1, 1898, at Buffalo, to serve two years; mustered in as private, Co. F, May 17, 1898; mustered out with company, November 19, 1898, at Buffalo, N. Y.

SIMON, JACOB J.—Age, — years.   Enlisted, June 24, 1898, at Buffalo, to serve two years; mustered in as private, Co. E, same date; transferred to band, June 29, 1898; mustered out with band, November 19, 1898, at Buffalo, N. Y.

SINCLAR, FRANK W.—Age, 18 years.   Enlisted, May 1, 1898, at Buffalo, to serve two years; mustered in as musician, Co. B, May 17, 1898; mustered out with company, November 19, 1898, at Buffalo, N. Y.

SLATER, CHARLES H.—Age, 21 years.   Enlisted, May 1, 1898, at Buffalo, to serve two years; mustered in as private, Co. D, May 17, 1898; mustered out with company, November 19, 1898, at Buffalo, N. Y.

SLATER, DANIEL A.—Age, 24 years.   Enlisted, May 1, 1898, at Buffalo, to serve two years; mustered in as private, Co. D, May 17, 1898; mustered out with company, November 19, 1898, at Buffalo, N. Y.

SLATER, EDWARD D.—Age, 21 years.   Enlisted, May 1, 1898, at Buffalo, to serve two years; mustered in as private, Co. M, May 17, 1898; mustered out with company, November 19, 1898, at Buffalo, N. Y.

SLATER, OTTO.—Age, 22 years. Enlisted, May 1, 1898, at Buffalo, to serve two years; mustered in as private, Co. D, May 17, 1898; mustered out with company, November 19, 1898, at Buffalo, N. Y.

SLEYS, CHARLES.—Age, 21 years. Enlisted, May 1, 1898, at Buffalo, to serve two years; mustered in as corporal, Co. I, May 17, 1898; promoted sergeant, July 12, 1898; mustered out with company, November 19, 1898, at Buffalo, N. Y.

SLOCUM, HERBERT G.—Age, — years. Enlisted, June 13, 1898, at Buffalo, to serve two years; mustered in as private, Co. I, same date; mustered out with company, November 19, 1898, at Buffalo, N. Y.

SMALL, GEORGE W.—Age, 20 years. Enlisted, May 1, 1898, at Buffalo, to serve two years; mustered in as artificer, Co. A, May 17, 1898; mustered out with company, November 19, 1898, at Buffalo, N. Y.

SMITH, ALFRED B.—Age, 19 years. Enlisted, May 1, 1898, at Buffalo, to serve two years; mustered in as private, Co. D, May 17, 1898; mustered out with company, November 19, 1898, at Buffalo, N. Y.

SMITH, ALLEN L.—Age, 22 years. Enlisted, May 1, 1898, at Buffalo, to serve two years; mustered in as private Co. H, May 17, 1898; mustered out with company, November 19, 1898, at Buffalo, N. Y.

SMITH, ARTHUR.—Age, — years. Enlisted, June 29, 1898, at Buffalo, to serve two years; mustered in as private, Co. L, same date; discharged, November 9, 1898.

SMITH, CHESTER G.—Age, 27 years. Enlisted, May 1, 1898, at Buffalo, to serve two years; mustered in as private, Co. C, May 17, 1898; promoted corporal, July 1, 1898; mustered out with company, November 19, 1898, at Buffalo, N. Y.

SMITH, EUGENE ALFRED.—Age, 33 years. Enrolled, May 1, 1898, at Buffalo, to serve two years; mustered in as major, May 17, 1898; mustered out with regiment, November 19, 1898, at Buffalo, N. Y.; commissioned major, May 17, 1898, with rank from same date, original.

SMITH, FRANCIS S.—Age, 29 years. Enlisted, May 1, 1898, at Buffalo, to serve two years; mustered in as private, Co. K, May 17, 1898; mustered out with company, November 19, 1898, at Buffalo, N. Y.

SMITH, FRANK.—Age, 21 years. Enlisted, May 1, 1898, at Buffalo, to serve two years; mustered in as private, Co. M, May 17, 1898; mustered out with company, November 19, 1898, at Buffalo, N. Y.

SMITH, FRANK E.—Age, — years. Enlisted, June 16, 1898, at Buffalo, to serve two years; mustered in as private, Co. K, same date; mustered out with company, November 19, 1898, at Buffalo, N. Y.

SMITH, FRANK H.—Age, 27 years. Enlisted, May 1, 1898, at Buffalo, to serve two years; mustered in as wagoner, Co. A, May 17, 1898; mustered out with company, November 19, 1898, at Buffalo, N. Y.

SMITH, GEORGE.—Age, 22 years. Enlisted, May 1, 1898, at Buffalo, to serve two years; mustered in as private, Co. K, May 17, 1898; mustered out with company, November 19, 1898, at Buffalo, N. Y.

SMITH, GEORGE D.—Age, 25 years. Enlisted, May 1, 1898, at Buffalo, to serve two years; mustered in as private, Co. D, May 17, 1898; mustered out with company, November 19, 1898, at Buffalo, N. Y.

SMITH, HARRY J.—Age, 29 years. Enrolled, May 1, 1898, at Buffalo, to serve two years; mustered in as second lieutenant, Co. B, May 17, 1898; mustered out with company, November 19, 1898, at Buffalo, N. Y.; commissioned second lieutenant, May 17, 1898, with rank from same date, original.

SMITH, HARRY W.—Age, 19 years. Enlisted, May 1, 1898, at Buffalo, to serve two years; mustered in as private, Co. G, May 17, 1898; mustered out with company, November 19, 1898, at Buffalo, N. Y.

SMITH, HENRY E.—Age, 32 years. Enlisted, May 1, 1898, at Buffalo, to serve two years; mustered in as private, Co. H, May 17, 1898; promoted corporal, July 25, 1898; mustered out with company, Novemebr 19, 1898, at Buffalo, N. Y.

SMITH, JAMES B.—Age, 22 years. Enlisted, May 1, 1898, at Buffalo, to serve two years; mustered in as private, Co. D, May 17, 1898; discharged for disability, July 18, 1898, at Camp Alger, near Dunn Loring, Va.

SMITH, J. O. FAL.—Age, 28 years. Enlisted, May 1, 1898, at Buffalo, to serve two years; mustered in as private, Co. L, May 17, 1898; mustered out with company, November 19, 1898, at Buffalo, N. Y.

SMITH, JOHN F.—Age, 19 years. Enlisted, May 1, 1898, at Buffalo, to serve two years; mustered in as private. Co. I, May 17, 1898; mustered out with company, November 19, 1898, at Buffalo, N. Y.

SMITH, JOSEPH.—Age, 24 years. Enlisted, May 1, 1898, at Buffalo, to serve two years; mustered in as private, Co. F, May 17, 1898; mustered out with company, November 19, 1898, at Buffalo, N. Y.

SMITH, LOUIS.—Age, 23 years. Enlisted, May 1, 1898, at Jamestown, to serve two years; mustered in as private, Co. E, May 17, 1898; mustered out with company, November 19, 1898, at Buffalo, N. Y.

SMITH, MICHAEL.—Age, — years. Enlisted, June 16, 1898, at Buffalo, to serve two years; mustered in as private, Co. B, same date; mustered out with company, November 19, 1898, at Buffalo, N. Y.

SMITH, PRESTON R.—Age, 27 years. Enlisted, May 1, 1898, at Buffalo, to serve two years; mustered in as private, Co. M, May 17, 1898; promoted corporal, July 1, 1898; mustered out with company, November 19, 1898, at Buffalo, N. Y.

SMITH, R. PORTER.—Age, 23 years. Enlisted, May 1, 1898, at Buffalo, to serve two years; mustered in as private, Co. L, May 17, 1898; promoted corporal, July 9, 1898; mustered out with company, November 19, 1898, at Buffalo, N. Y.

SMITH, WILLIAM.—Age, 22 years. Enlisted, May 1, 1898, at Buffalo, to serve two years; mustered in as private, Co. H, May 17, 1898; mustered out with company, November 19, 1898, at Buffalo, N. Y.

SMITH, WILLIAM D.—Age, 38 years. Enlisted, May 1, 1898, at Buffalo, to serve two years; mustered in as private, Co. K, May 17, 1898; promoted corporal, September 3, 1898; mustered out with company, November 19, 1898, at Buffalo, N. Y.

SNOOK, SIMEON.—Age, 20 years. Enlisted, May 1, 1898, at Buffalo, to serve two years; mustered in as private, Co. F, May 17, 1898; mustered out with company, November 19, 1898, at Buffalo, N. Y.

SNYDER, EDWARD C.—Age, 31 years. Enlisted, May 1, 1898, at Buffalo, to serve two years; mustered in as private, Co. I, May 17, 1898; mustered out with company, November 19, 1898, at Buffalo, N. Y.

SNYDER, JOHN A.—Age, — years. Enlisted, June 14, 1898, at Buffalo, to serve two years; mustered in as private, Co. C, same date; mustered out with company, November 19, 1898, at Buffalo, N. Y.

SNYDER, LEE.—Age, 22 years. Enlisted, May 1, 1898, at Buffalo, to serve two years; mustered in as private, Co. B, May 17, 1898; mustered out with company, November 19, 1898, at Buffalo, N. Y.

SODERBERG, CHARLES G.—Age, — years. Enlisted, June 20, 1898, at Buffalo, to serve two years; mustered in as private, Co. E, same date; mustered out with company, November 19, 1898, at Buffalo, N. Y.

SODERHOLM, GUST F.—Age, 23 years. Enlisted, May 1, 1898, at Buffalo, to serve two years; mustered in as private, Co. C, May 17, 1898; mustered out with company, November 19, 1898, at Buffalo, N. Y.

SOMERS, GEORGE B.—Age, 26 years. Enlisted, May 1, 1898, at Buffalo, to serve two years; mustered in as musician, Co. G, May 17, 1898; mustered out with company, November 19, 1898, at Buffalo, N. Y.

SOMMERFELT, HENRY C.—Age, — years. Enlisted, June 20, 1898, at Buffalo, to serve two years; mustered in as private, Co. L, same date; mustered out with company, November 19, 1898, at Buffalo, N. Y.

SORBER, WALTER H.—Age, 28 years. Enlisted, May 1, 1898, at Buffalo, to serve two years; mustered in as corporal, Co. I, May 17, 1898; mustered out with company, November 19, 1898, at Buffalo, N. Y.

SOUERS, JOHN J.—Age, 29 years. Enlisted, May 1, 1898, at Buffalo, to serve two years; mustered in as private, Co. A, May 17, 1898; discharged for disability, October 7, 1898, at Buffalo, N. Y.

SOUTHWORTH, EMERY F.—Age, 25 years. Enrolled, May 1, 1898, at Buffalo, to serve two years; mustered in as second lieutenant, Co. F, May 17, 1898; mustered out with company, November 19, 1898, at Buffalo, N. Y.; commissioned second lieutenant, May 17, 1898, with rank from same date, original.

SOUTHWORTH, JOHN C.—Age, 20 years. Enlisted, May 1, 1898, at Buffalo, to serve two years; mustered in as corporal, Co. F, May 17, 1898; mustered out with company, November 19, 1898, at Buffalo, N. Y.

SOWERS, FREDERICK M.—Age, — years. Enlisted, June 13, 1898, at Buffalo, to serve two years; mustered in as private, Co. D, same date; deserted, August 9, 1898, at Camp Alger, near Dunn Loring, Va.

SPADE, CHARLES F.—Age, 22 years. Enlisted, May 1, 1898, at Buffalo, to serve two years; mustered in as private, Co. F, May 17, 1898; appointed artificer, August 20, 1898; mustered out with company, November 19, 1898, at Buffalo, N. Y.

SPANG, WILLIAM F.—Age, — years. Enlisted, June 13, 1898, at Buffalo, to serve two years; mustered in as private, Co. F, same date; mustered out with company, November 19, 1898, at Buffalo, N. Y.

SPARFIELD, FREDERICK H.—Age, — years. Enlisted, June 16, 1898, at Buffalo, to serve two years; mustered in as private, Co. D, same date; mustered out with company, November 19, 1898, at Buffalo, N. Y.

SPARFIELD, WALTER J.—Age, — years. Enlisted, June 17, 1898, at Buffalo, to serve two years; mustered in as private, Co. D, same date; mustered out with company, November 19, 1898, at Buffalo, N. Y.

SPARKS, WILLIAM K.—Age, 23 years. Enlisted, May 1, 1898, at Buffalo, to serve two years; mustered in as private, Co. I, May 17, 1898; mustered out with company, November 19, 1898, at Buffalo, N. Y.

SPECHT, GEORGE E.—Age, — years. Enlisted, July 1, 1898, at Buffalo, to serve two years; mustered in as private, Co. D, same date; mustered out with company, November 19, 1898, at Buffalo, N. Y.

SPENCER, WILLIAM J.—Age, 28 years. Enlisted, May 1, 1898, at Buffalo, to serve two years; mustered in as private, Co. L, May 17, 1898; promoted corporal, July 9, 1898; mustered out with company, November 19, 1898, at Buffalo, N. Y.

SPOTH, JOHN.—Age, 19 years. Enlisted, May 1, 1898, at Buffalo, to serve two years; mustered in as private, Co. H, May 17, 1898; mustered out with company, November 19, 1898, at Buffalo, N. Y.

SPRAGUE, ELMER E.—Age, 30 years. Enlisted, May 1, 1898, at Jamestown, to serve two years; mustered in as private, Co. E, May 17, 1898; transferred to Hospital Corps, United States Army, June 22, 1898; to Co. E, September 29, 1898; mustered out with company, November 19, 1898, at Buffalo, N. Y.

SQUIRES, WILLIAM J.—Age, 34 years. Enlisted, May 1, 1898, at Buffalo, to serve two years; mustered in as private, Co. C, May 17, 1898; mustered out with company, November 19, 1898, at Buffalo, N. Y.

STANDART, COURTLAND H.—Age, 22 years. Enlisted, May 1, 1898, at Buffalo, to serve two years; mustered in as private, Co. G, May 17, 1898; mustered out with company, November 19, 1898, at Buffalo, N. Y.

STANGER, JACOB G.—Age, 29 years. Enlisted, May 1, 1898, at Buffalo, to serve two years; mustered in as wagoner, Co. I, May 17, 1898; mustered out with company, November 19, 1898, at Buffalo, N. Y.

STANLEY, FREDERICK A.—Age, — years. Enlisted, June 15, 1898, at Buffalo, to serve two years; mustered in as private, Co. E, same date; mustered out with company, November 19, 1898, at Buffalo, N. Y.

STAUFFENBERGER, PHILLIP.—Age, 24 years. Enlisted, May 1, 1898, at Buffalo, to serve two years; mustered in as private, Co. H, May 17, 1898; mustered out with company, November 19, 1898, at Buffalo, N. Y.

STEELE, CHARLES.—Age, 22 years. Enlisted, May 1, 1898, at Buffalo, to serve two years; mustered in as artificer, Co. G, May 17, 1898; mustered out with company, November 19, 1898, at Buffalo, N. Y.

STEGER, CHARLES F.—Age, 23 years. Enlisted, May 1, 1898, at Buffalo, to serve two years; mustered in as corporal, Co. A, May 17, 1898; mustered out with company, November 19, 1898, at Buffalo, N. Y.

STEPAN, GEORGE.—Age, — years. Enlisted, June 13, 1898, at Buffalo, to serve two years; mustered in as private, Co. D, same date; mustered out with company, November 19, 1898, at Buffalo, N. Y.

STERLING, ALFRED P.—Age, — years. Enlisted, June 13, 1898, at Buffalo, to serve two years; mustered in as private, Co. M, same date; appointed artificer, July 1, 1898; mustered o it with company, November 19, 1898, at Buffalo, N. Y.

STEWART, ROBERT.—Age, 22 years. Enlisted, May 1, 1898, at Buffalo, to serve two years; mustered in as private, Co. M, May 17, 1898; promoted corporal, July 1, 1898; mustered out with company, November 19, 1898, at Buffalo, N. Y.

STIFEL, FRED.—Age, — years. Enlisted, June 17, 1898, at Buffalo, to serve two years; mustered in as private, Co. M, same date; mustered out with company, November 19, 1898, at Buffalo, N. Y.

STIKER, RAYMOND F.—Age, 30 years. Enlisted, May 1, 1898, at Buffalo, to serve two years; mustered in as private, Co. B, May 17, 1898; promoted corporal, June 23, 1898; mustered out with company, November 19, 1898, at Buffalo, N. Y.

STILES, CHARLES W.—Age, — years. Enlisted, June 27, 1898, at Buffalo, to serve two years; mustered in as private, Co. L, same date; discharged, October 29, 1898, at Buffalo, N. Y.,

STINES, JOSEPH F.—Age, 31 years. Enlisted, May 13, 1898, at Camp Black, to serve two years; mustered in as private, Co. B, May 17, 1898; mustered out with company, November 19, 1898, at Buffalo, N. Y.

ST. JAMES, ALFRED.—Age, 21 years. Enlisted, May 12, 1898, at Camp Black, to serve two years; mustered in as private, Co. B, May 17, 1898; mustered out with company, November 19, 1898, at Buffalo, N. Y.

ST. JOHN, JAMES A.—Age, 21 years. Enlisted, May 1, 1898, at Buffalo, to serve two years; mustered in as private, Co. A, May 17, 1898; mustered out with company, November 19, 1898, at Buffalo, N. Y.

STONE, EDWARD C.—Age, — years. Enlisted, June 20, 1898, at Buffalo, to serve two years; mustered in as private, Co. I, same date; mustered out with company, November 19, 1898, at Buffalo, N. Y.

STONE, JOHN N.—Age, 36 years. Enlisted, May 1, 1898, at Jamestown, to serve two years; mustered in as private, Co. E, May 17, 1898; mustered out with company, November 19, 1898, at Buffalo, N. Y.

STORCK, HERMAN C.—Age, 28 years. Enlisted, May 1, 1898, at Buffalo, to serve two years; mustered in as private, Co. C, May 17, 1898; promoted corporal, May 22, 1898; mustered out with company, November 19, 1898, at Buffalo, N. Y.

STRAHL, CHARLES W.—Age, — years. Enlisted, June 13, 1898, at Buffalo, to serve two years; mustered in as private, Co. A, same date; mustered out with company, November 19, 1898, at Buffalo, N. Y.

STRAUCH, EDWARD A.—Age, 21 years. Enlisted, May 1, 1898, at Buffalo, to serve two years; mustered in as private, Co. A, May 17, 1898; mustered out with company, November 19, 1898, at Buffalo, N. Y.

STRIEBICH, JR., JOHN.—Age, — years. Enlisted, June 18, 1898, at Buffalo, to serve two years; mustered in as private, Co. A, same date; mustered out with company, November 19, 1898, at Buffalo, N. Y.

STRINGER, EDWARD G.—Age, 21 years.   Enlisted, May 1, 1898, at Buffalo, to serve two years; mustered in as private, Co. I, May 17, 1898; mustered out with company, November 19, 1898, at Buffalo, N. Y.

STROMDAHL, CHARLES J.—Age, 26 years.   Enlisted, May 1, 1898, at Jamestown, to serve two years; mustered in as private, Co. E, May 17, 1898; mustered out with company, November 19, 1898, at Buffalo, N. Y.

STRONG, EDGERTON B.—Age, — years.   Enlisted, June 17, 1898, at Buffalo, to serve two years; mustered in as private, Co. C, same date; mustered out with company, November 19, 1898, at Buffalo, N. Y.

STUART, CHARLES R.—Age, 27 years.   Enlisted, May 1, 1898, at Buffalo, to serve two years; mustered in as private, Co. G, May 17, 1898; mustered out with company, November 19, 1898, at Buffalo, N. Y.

SUGNET, CHARLES F.—Age, 25 years.   Enlisted, May 13, 1898, at Camp Black, to serve two years; mustered in as private, Co. L, May 17, 1898; mustered out with company, November 19, 1898, at Buffalo, N. Y.

SULLY, GEORGE U.—Age, 24 years.   Enlisted, May 1, 1898, at Buffalo, to serve two years; mustered in as private, Co. B, May 17, 1898; promoted corporal, June 1, 1898; mustered out with company, November 19, 1898, at Buffalo, N. Y.

SUMMEY, ALBERT E.—Age, 25 years.   Enlisted, May 1, 1898, at Buffalo, to serve two years; mustered in as hospital steward, May 17, 1898; mustered out with regiment, November 19, 1898, at Buffalo, N. Y.

SUNDBURGH, CHARLES J. L.—Age, — years.   Enlisted, June 13, 1898, at Buffalo, to serve two years; mustered in as private, Co. F, same date; transferred to Co. K, as musician, August 7, 1898; mustered out with company, November 19, 1898, at Buffalo, N. Y.

SUNDELL, THEODORE J. T.—Age, 27 years.   Enlisted, May 1, 1898, at Jamestown, to serve two years; mustered in as private, Co. E, May 17, 1898; mustered out with company, November 19, 1898, at Buffalo, N. Y.

SUNDHOLM, HERBERT A.—Age, 23 years. Enlisted, May 1, 1898, at Jamestown, to serve two years; mustered in as musician, Co. E, May 17, 1898; mustered out with company, November 19, 1898, at Buffalo, N. Y.

SWAN, GEORGE A.—Age, 19 years. Enlisted, May 1, 1898, at Buffalo, to serve two years; mustered in as private, Co. H, May 17, 1898; mustered out with company, November 19, 1898, at Buffalo, N. Y.

SWANSON, AUGUST.—Age, — years. Enlisted, June 13, 1898, at Buffalo, to serve two years; mustered in as private, Co. H, same date; mustered out with company, November 19, 1898, at Buffalo, N. Y.

SWEET, FRED D.—Age, 26 years. Enlisted, May 1, 1898, at Jamestown, to serve two years; mustered in as private, Co. E, May 17, 1898; mustered out with company, November 19, 1898, at Buffalo, N. Y.

SYKES, EDWARD J.—Age, — years. Enlisted, June 13, 1898, at Buffalo, to serve two years; mustered in as private, Co. L, same date; mustered out with company, November 19, 1898, at Buffalo, N. Y.

SYMONDS, EUGENE M.—Age, 25 years. Enlisted, May 1, 1898, at Buffalo, to serve two years; mustered in as private, Co. C, May 17, 1898; promoted corporal, July 1, 1898; mustered out with company, November 19, 1898, at Buffalo, N. Y.

SZCZEPANIAK, JOSEPH.—Age, 21 years. Enlisted, May 1, 1898, at Buffalo, to serve two years; mustered in as private, Co. H, May 17, 1898; mustered out with company, November 19, 1898, at Buffalo, N. Y.

TACKMAN, LOUIS.—Age, 36 years. Enlisted, May 1, 1898, at Buffalo, to serve two years; mustered in as private, Co. H, May 17, 1898; appointed artificer, August 1, 1898; mustered out with company, November 19, 1898, at Buffalo, N. Y.

TADE, JR., JOHN.—Age, — years. Enlisted, June 14, 1898, at Buffalo, to serve two years; mustered in as private, Co. H, same date; mustered out with company, November 19, 1898, at Buffalo, N. Y.

TANNER, DORSEY B.—Age, 21 years. Enlisted, May 1, 1898, at Buffalo, to serve two years; mustered in as private, Co. K, May 17, 1898; mustered out with company, November 19, 1898, at Buffalo, N. Y.

TARRANT, ALFRED P.—Age, 21 years. Enlisted, May 1, 1898, at Buffalo, to serve two years; mustered in as corporal, Co. G, May 17, 1898; returned to ranks, July 30, 1898; mustered out with company, November 19, 1898, at Buffalo, N. Y.

TARRANT, ALLEN A.—Age, 21 years. Enlisted, May 1, 1898, at Buffalo, to serve two years; mustered in as corporal, Co. G, May 17, 1898; mustered out with company, November 19, 1898, at Buffalo, N. Y.

TAYLOR, GEORGE.—Age, 27 years. Enlisted, May 1, 1898, at Buffalo, to serve two years; mustered in as private, Co. G, May 17, 1898; mustered out with company, November 19, 1898, at Buffalo, N. Y.

TAYLOR, LOUIS O.—Age, 22 years. Enlisted, May 1, 1898, at Buffalo, to serve two years; mustered in as private, Co. L, May 17, 1898; died of cerebral meningitis, June 6, 1898, in Fort Myer Hospital, Va.

TAYLOR, PAUL E.—Age, — years. Enlisted, June 13, 1898, at Buffalo, to serve two years; mustered in as private, Co. L, same date; transferred to Hospital Corps, United States Army, June 28, 1898; to Co. B, September 4, 1898; to Hospital Corps, United States Army, September 10, 1898, at Fort Columbus, New York Harbor.

TAYLOR, WILLIAM.—Age, 25 years. Enlisted, May 1, 1898, at Buffalo, to serve two years; mustered in as private, Co. I, May 17, 1898; mustered out with company, November 19, 1898, at Buffalo, N. Y.

TEMPLETON, EDWARD C.—Age, 24 years. Enlisted, May 1, 1898, at Jamestown, to serve two years; mustered in as private, Co. E, May 17, 1898; mustered out with company, November 19, 1898, at Buffalo, N. Y.

TER DOEST, HENRY J.—Age, — years. Enlisted, June 13, 1898, at Buffalo, to serve two years; mustered in as private, Co. G, same date; mustered out with company, November 19, 1898, at Buffalo, N. Y.

THEET, HENRY.—Age, 22 years. Enlisted, May 1, 1898, at Buffalo, to serve two years; mustered in as artificer, Co. H, May 17, 1898; returned to ranks, August 1, 1898; mustered out with company, November 19, 1898, at Buffalo, N. Y.

THEETGE, JOHN E.—Age, 22 years. Enlisted, May 1, 1898, at Buffalo, to serve two years; mustered in as private, Co. G, May 17, 1898; mustered out with company, November 19, 1898, at Buffalo, N. Y.

THOMAS, BENJAMIN H.—Age, 23 years. Enlisted, May 1, 1898, at Buffalo, to serve two years; mustered in as private, Co. C, May 17, 1898; promoted corporal, July 1, 1898; returned to ranks, August 10, 1898; mustered out with company, November 19, 1898, at Buffalo, N. Y. .

THOMAS, GEORGE.—Age, 28 years. Enlisted, May 1, 1898, at Buffalo, to serve two years; mustered in as private, Co. A, May 17, 1898; mustered out with company, November 19, 1898, at Buffalo, N. Y.

THOMPSON, WILLIAM.—Age, 25 years. Enlisted, May 1, 1898, at Buffalo, to serve two years; mustered in as private, Co. C, May 17, 1898; mustered out with company, November 19, 1898, at Buffalo, N. Y.

THOMPSON, WILLIAM C.—Age, 29 years. Enlisted, May 1, 1898, at Buffalo, to serve two years; mustered in as private, Co. A, May 17, 1898; mustered out with company, November 19, 1898, at Buffalo, N. Y.

THOMSON, WALTER A.—Age, 22 years. Enlisted, May 1, 1898, at Buffalo, to serve two years; mustered in as private, Co. L, May 17, 1898; mustered out with company, November 19, 1898, at Buffalo, N. Y.

THORNE, MARVIN.—Age, 25 years. Enlisted, May 1, 1898, at Buffalo, to serve two years; mustered in as private, Co. B, May 17, 1898; promoted corporal, June 23, 1898; mustered out with company, November 19, 1898, at Buffalo, N. Y.

THROBALD, GEORGE S.—Age, — years. Enlisted, June 27, 1898, at Buffalo, to serve two years; mustered in as private, Co. M, same date; transferred to band, June 29, 1898; mustered out with band, November 19, 1898, at Buffalo, N. Y.

THUNELL, JOHN.—Age, 21 years. Enlisted, May 1, 1898, at Buffalo, to serve two years; mustered in as private, Co. I, May 17, 1898; mustered out with company, November 19, 1898, at Buffalo, N. Y.

THUR, JR., CHARLES J.—Age, 23 years. Enlisted, May 1, 1898, at Buffalo, to serve two years; mustered in as corporal, Co. D, May 17, 1898; mustered out with company, November 19, 1898, at Buffalo, N. Y.

TIERNEY, EDWIN W.—Age, 23 years. Enlisted, May 1, 1898, at Buffalo, to serve two years; mustered in as private, Co. F, May 17, 1898; mustered out with company, November 19, 1898, at Buffalo, N. Y.

TOLSINA, NELSON B.—Age, 27 years. Enlisted, May 1, 1898, at Buffalo, to serve two years; mustered in as corporal, Co. A, May 17, 1898; mustered out with company, November 19, 1898, at Buffalo, N. Y.

TOWER, WILLARD O.—Age, 21 years. Enlisted, May 1, 1898, at Buffalo, to serve two years; mustered in as private, Co. B, May 17, 1898; transferred to Co. M, May 18, 1898; to Hospital Corps, United States Army, June 1, 1898; to Co. B, September 2, 1898; mustered out with company, November 19, 1898, at Buffalo, N. Y.

TOWN, WILLIAM A.—Age, 27 years. Enlisted, May 1, 1898, at Buffalo, to serve two years; mustered in as private, Co. K, May 17, 1898; mustered out with company, November 19, 1898, at Buffalo, N. Y.

TOWSLEY, JR., JOHN H.—Age, 37 years. Enlisted, May 1, 1898, at Jamestown, to serve two years; mustered in as private, Co. E, May 17, 1898; promoted quartermaster-sergeant, July 21, 1898; mustered out with company, November 19, 1898, at Buffalo, N. Y.

TROMTER, HARRY.—Age, 21 years. Enlisted, May 12, 1898, at Buffalo, to serve two years; mustered in as private, Co. H, May 17, 1898; mustered out with company, November 19, 1898, at Buffalo, N. Y.

TROST, JOSEPH.—Age, 21 years.   Enlisted, May 1, 1898, at
Buffalo, to serve two years; mustered in as private, Co. G, May
17, 1898; mustered out with company, November 19, 1898, at
Buffalo, N. Y.

TROUTON, WILLIAM.—Age, 22 years.   Enlisted, May 1, 1898,
at Buffalo, to serve two years; mustered in as corporal, Co. H,
May 17, 1898; returned to ranks, June 23, 1898; mustered out
with company, November 19, 1898, at Buffalo, N. Y.

TRUMPLER, AUGUST.—Age, 22 years.   Enlisted, May 1, 1898,
at Buffalo, to serve two years; mustered in as private, Co. H,
May 17, 1898; mustered out with company, November 19, 1898,
at Buffalo, N. Y.

TRUMPPHELLER, JOHN.—Age, — years.   Enlisted, June 13,
1898, at Buffalo, to serve two years; mustered in as private, Co.
F, same date; mustered out with company, November 19, 1898,
at Buffalo, N. Y.

TUERK, EDWARD P.—Age, 19 years.   Enlisted, May 1, 1898,
at Buffalo, to serve two years; mustered in as private, Co. G,
May 17, 1898; mustered out with company, November 19, 1898,
at Buffalo, N. Y.

TURNBULL, JOHN M.—Age, 29 years.   Enlisted, May 1, 1898,
at Buffalo, to serve two years; mustered in as private, Co. D,
May 17, 1898; promoted corporal, July 7, 1898; mustered out
with company, November 19, 1898, at Buffalo, N. Y.

TURNELL, HENNING D.—Age, — years.   Enlisted, June 15,
1898, at Buffalo, to serve two years; mustered in as private,
Co. E, same date; died of fever, September 24, 1898, at Women's
Christian Association Hospital, Jamestown, N. Y.

TURNER, HOMER M.—Age, 27 years.   Enlisted, May 1, 1898, at
Buffalo, to serve two years; mustered in as private, Co. M, May
17, 1898; mustered out with company, November 19, 1898, at
Buffalo, N Y.

ULRICH, GEORGE.—Age, 21 years.   Enlisted, May 1, 1898, at
Buffalo, to serve two years; mustered in as private, Co. D, May
17, 1898; appointed musician, no date; mustered out with company, November 19, 1898, at Buffalo, N. Y.

UNBEHAUN, ALFRED J.—Age, 19 years. Enlisted, May 1, 1898, at Buffalo, to serve two years; mustered in as private, Co. F, May 17, 1898; promoted corporal, September 3, 1898; mustered out with company, November 19, 1898, at Buffalo, N. Y.

UNGER, WILLIAM.—Age, — years. Enlisted, June 14, 1898, at Buffalo, to serve two years; mustered in as private, Co. D, same date; mustered out with company, November 19, 1898, at Buffalo, N. Y.

UPTON, GEORGE B.—Age, — years. Enlisted, June 22, 1898, at Buffalo, to serve two years; mustered in as private, Co. F, same date; promoted corporal, June 28, 1898; mustered out with company, November 19, 1898, at Buffalo, N. Y.

VALENTINE, GEORGE G.—Age, — years. Enlisted, June 16, 1898, at Buffalo, to serve two years; mustered in as private, Co. K, same date; mustered out with company, November 19, 1898, at Buffalo, N. Y.

VALENTINE, GEORGE J.—Age, — years. Enlisted, June 13, 1898, at Buffalo, to serve two years; mustered in as private, Co. F, same date; mustered out with company, November 19, 1898, at Buffalo, N. Y.

VANLINTON, GEORGE F.—Age, 24 years. Enlisted, May 1, 1898, at Buffalo, to serve two years; mustered in as private, Co. M, May 17, 1898; mustered out with company, November 19, 1898, at Buffalo, N. Y.

VAN VALKENBURG, LEE.—Age, — years. Enlisted, June 13, 1898, at Buffalo, to serve two years; mustered in as private, Co. L, same date; mustered out with company, November 19, 1898, at Buffalo, N. Y.

VARLEY, JAMES.—Age, 21 years. Enlisted, May 1, 1898, at Jamestown, to serve two years; mustered in as private, Co. E, May 17, 1898; mustered out with company, November 19, 1898, at Buffalo, N. Y.

VARLEY, JAMES S.—Age, 21 years. Enlisted, May 1, 1898, at Buffalo, to serve two years; mustered in as private, Co. K, May 17, 1898; promoted corporal, September 3, 1898; mustered out with company, November 19, 1898, at Buffalo, N. Y.

VARNER, PHILIP.—Age, 28 years. Enlisted, May 1, 1898, at Buffalo, to serve two years; mustered in as private, Co. I, May 17, 1898; promoted corporal, August 3, 1898; mustered out with company, November 19, 1898, at Buffalo, N. Y.

VATERLAUS, JOHN H.—Age, — years. Enlisted, June 16, 1898, at Buffalo, to serve two years; mustered in as private, Co. A, same date; mustered out with company, November 19, 1898, at Buffalo, N. Y.

VESPER, HUGO J.—Age, — years. Enlisted, June 16, 1898, at Buffalo, to serve two years; mustered in as private, Co. G, same date; promoted sergeant, June 18, 1898; mustered out with company, November 19, 1898, at Buffalo, N. Y.

VIGNERON, EUGENE J.—Age, 22 years. Enlisted, May 1, 1898, at Buffalo, to serve two years; mustered in as private, Co. I, May 17, 1898; promoted corporal, July 12, 1898; mustered out with company, November 19, 1898, at Buffalo, N. Y.

VOGEL, JOHN J.—Age, 24 years. Enlisted, May 1, 1898, at Buffalo, to serve two years; mustered in as private, Co. G, May 17, 1898; promoted corporal, June 29, 1898; mustered out with company, November 19, 1898, at Buffalo, N. Y.

VOGEL, LOUIS G.—Age, 21 years. Enlisted, May 1, 1898, at Buffalo, to serve two years; mustered in as sergeant, Co. K, May 17, 1898; mustered out with company, November 19, 1898, at Buffalo, N. Y.

WAGER, JOHN M.—Age, — years. Enlisted, June 13, 1898, at Buffalo, to serve two years; mustered in as private, Co. G, same date; mustered out with company, November 19, 1898, at Buffalo, N. Y.

WAGNER, ADAM.—Age, 24 years. Enlisted, May 1, 1898, at Buffalo, to serve two years; mustered in as private, Co. D, May 17, 1898; mustered out with company, November 19, 1898, at Buffalo, N. Y.

WAGNER, GEORGE W.—Age, — years. Enlisted, June 13, 1898, at Buffalo, to serve two years; mustered in as private, Co. A, same date; mustered out with company, November 19, 1898, at Buffalo, N. Y.

WAGNER, GOTTLIEB.—Age, 25 years. Enlisted, May 12, 1898. at Buffalo, to serve two years; mustered in as private, Co. H, May 17, 1898; mustered out with company, November 19, 1898, at Buffalo, N. Y.

WAGNER, WILLIAM.—Age, 19 years. Enlisted, May 1, 1898, at Buffalo, to serve two years; mustered in as private, Co. H, May 17, 1898; mustered out with company, November 19, 1898, at Buffalo, N. Y.

WAHL, EDWARD J. G.—Age, 20 years. Enlisted, May 1, 1898, at Buffalo, to serve two years; mustered in as private, Co. F, May 17, 1898; mustered out with company, November 19, 1898, at Buffalo, N. Y.

WALDO, FRANK S.—Age, 22 years. Enlisted, May 1, 1898, at Buffalo, to serve two years; mustered in as sergeant, Co. L, May 17, 1898; mustered out with company, November 19, 1898, at Buffalo, N. Y.

. WALDROFF, GEORGE H.—Age, 22 years. Enlisted, May 1, 1898, at Buffalo, to serve two years; mustered in as private, Co. H, May 17, 1898; mustered out with company, November 19, 1898, at Buffalo, N. Y.

WALICH, ANTHONY H.—Age, 23 years. Enlisted, May 1, 1898, at Buffalo, to serve two years; mustered in as private, Co. M, May 17, 1898; mustered out with company, November 19, 1898, at Buffalo, N. Y.

WALKER, ARCHIE H.—Age, — years. Enlisted, June 13, 1898, at Buffalo, to serve two years; mustered in as private, Co. B, same date; mustered out with company, November 19, 1898, at Buffalo, N. Y.

WALKER, JR., HENRY.—Age, — years. Enlisted, June 25, 1898, at Buffalo, to serve two years; mustered in as private, Co. L, same date; mustered out with company, November 19, 1898, at Buffalo, N. Y.

WALL, JULIES D.—Age, 18 years. Enlisted, May 1, 1898, at Buffalo, to serve two years; mustered in as private, Co. A, May 17, 1898; mustered out with company, November 19, 1898, at Buffalo, N. Y.

WALLACE, ALBERT M.—Age, — years. Enlisted, June 13, 1898, at Buffalo, to serve two years; mustered in as private, Co. G, same date; mustered out with company, November 19, 1898, at Buffalo, N. Y.

WALLACE, GEORGE B.—Age, 23 years. Enlisted, May 1, 1898, at Buffalo, to serve two years; mustered in as private, Co. B, May 17, 1898; mustered out with company, November 19, 1898, at Buffalo, N. Y.

WALLACE, ROBERT D.—Age, 24 years. Enlisted, May 1, 1898, at Buffalo, to serve two years; mustered in as private, Co. D, May 17, 1898; mustered out with company, November 19, 1898, at Buffalo, N. Y.

WALSH, EDWARD P.—Age, 36 years. Enlisted, May 1, 1898, at Jamestown, to serve two years; mustered in as corporal, Co. E, May 17, 1898; mustered out with company, November 19, 1898, at Buffalo, N. Y.

WALSH, JOHN.—Age, — years. Enlisted, June 13, 1898, at Buffalo, to serve two years; mustered in as private, Co. B, same date; mustered out with company, November 19, 1898, at Buffalo, N. Y.

WALTER, STEPHEN E.—Age, 27 years. Enlisted, May 1, 1898, at Buffalo, to serve two years; mustered in as private, Co. G, May 17, 1898; mustered out with company, November 19, 1898, at Buffalo, N. Y.

WALTERS, LOUIS W.—Age, — years. Enlisted, June 14, 1898, at Buffalo, to serve two years; mustered in as private, Co. I, same date; mustered out with company, November 19, 1898, at Buffalo, N. Y.

WARNER, NATHANIEL H.—Age, 28 years. Enlisted, May 1, 1898, at Buffalo, to serve two years; mustered in as private, Co. C, May 17, 1898; died of typhoid fever, August 30, 1898, at Buffalo, N. Y.

WARNER, RICHARD.—Age, 19 years. Enlisted, May 1, 1898, at Buffalo, to serve two years; mustered in as private, Co. M, May 17, 1898; discharged for disability, July 14, 1898, at Camp Alger, near Dunn Loring, Va.

WATSON, JAMES F.—Age, 21 years. Enlisted, May 1, 1898, at Buffalo, to serve two years; mustered in as private, Co. C, May 17, 1898; mustered out with company, November 19, 1898, at Buffalo, N. Y.

WAYHORN, JOHN.—Age, 23 years. Enlisted, May 1, 1898, at Buffalo, to serve two years; mustered in as private, Co. B, May 17, 1898; mustered out with company, November 19, 1898, at Buffalo, N. Y.

WEBB, JAMES B.—Age, 37 years. Enrolled, May 1, 1898, at Buffalo, to serve two years; mustered in as first lieutenant, Co. H, May 17, 1898; mustered out with company, November 19, 1898, at Buffalo, N. Y.; subsequent service as first lieutenant, Forty-sixth Regiment, United States Volunteer Infantry; commissioned first lieutenant, May 17, 1898, with rank from same date, original.

WEBBER, LAWRENCE.—Age, — years. Enlisted, June 13, 1898, at Buffalo, to serve two years; mustered in as private, Co. G, same date; mustered out with company, November 19, 1898, at Buffalo, N. Y.

WEBER, HENRY.—Age, 21 years. Enlisted, May 1, 1898, at Buffalo, to serve two years; mustered in as private, Co. L, May 17, 1898; mustered out with company, November 19, 1898, at Buffalo, N. Y.

WEBER, WILLIAM H.—Age, 30 years. Enlisted, May 1, 1898, at Buffalo, to serve two years; mustered in as private, Co. B, May 17, 1898; mustered out with company, November 19, 1898, at Buffalo, N. Y.

WEBORG, EDWIN.—Age, 19 years. Enlisted, May 16, 1898, at Camp Black, to serve two years; mustered in as musician, Co. K, May 17, 1898; mustered out with company, November 19, 1898, at Buffalo, N. Y.

WEBORG, FRANK C.—Age, 24 years. Enlisted, May 1, 1898, at Jamestown, to serve two years; mustered in as private, Co. E, May 17, 1898; mustered out with company, November 19, 1898, at Buffalo, N. Y.

WEBSTER, ALFRED L.—Age, 27 years. Enlisted, May 1, 1898, at Buffalo, to serve two years; mustered in as private. Co. L, May 17, 1898; mustered out with company, November 19, 1898, at Buffalo, N. Y.

WEBSTER, MATHEW.—Age, 21 years. Enlisted, May 1, 1898, at Camp Black, to serve two years; mustered in as musician, Co. E, May 17, 1898; mustered out with company, November 19, 1898, at Buffalo, N. Y

WEED, JAMES W.—Age, 26 years. Enlisted, May 1, 1898, at Jamestown, to serve two years; mustered in as private, Co. E, May 17, 1898; transferred to Signal Corps, United States Army, June 25, 1898.

WEGE, HENRY.—Age, 30 years. Enlisted, May 1, 1898, at Buffalo, to serve two years; mustered in as corporal, Co. F, May 17, 1898; mustered out with company, November 19, 1898, at Buffalo, N. Y.

WEICKEL, DANIEL J.—Age, 23 years. Enlisted, May 1, 1898, at Buffalo, to serve two years; mustered in as private, Co. M, May 17, 1898; mustered out with company, November 19, 1898, at Buffalo, N. Y.

WEIDNER, MAX.—Age, 21 years. Enlisted, May 1, 1898, at Buffalo, to serve two years; mustered in as private, Co. M, May 17, 1898; mustered out with company, November 19, 1898, at Buffalo, N. Y.

WEIGAND, GEORGE A.—Age, 20 years. Enlisted, May 1, 1898, at Buffalo, to serve two years; mustered in as sergeant, Co. H, May 17, 1898; mustered out with company, November 19, 1898, at Buffalo, N. Y.

WEIMANN, JOSEPH L.—Age, 20 years. Enlisted, May 1, 1898, at Buffalo, to serve two years; mustered in as private, Co. B, May 17, 1898; mustered out with company, November 19, 1898, at Buffalo, N. Y.

WEINBERG, BENJAMIN N.—Age, 22 years. Enlisted, May 1, 1898, at Buffalo, to serve two years; mustered in as private, Co. B, May 17, 1898; mustered out with company, November 19, 1898, at Buffalo, N. Y., as Benjaman M. Weinberg.

WEINHEIMER, CHARLES C.—Age, 23 years. Enlisted, May 1, 1898, at Buffalo, to serve two years; mustered in as private, Co. M, May 17, 1898; mustered out with company, November 19, 1898, at Buffalo, N. Y.

WEINSHEIMER, GEORGE W.—Age, 20 years. Enlisted, May 1, 1898, at Buffalo, to serve two years; mustered in as private, Co. H, May 17, 1898; mustered out with company, November 19, 1898, at Buffalo, N. Y.

WEIRIECH, HENRY J.—Age, 21 years. Enlisted, May 12, 1898, at Buffalo, to serve two years; mustered in as private, Co. M, May 17, 1898; mustered out with company, November 19, 1898, at Buffalo, N. Y.

WEIS, ADAM.—Age, — years. Enlisted, June 24, 1898, at Buffalo, to serve two years; mustered in as private, Co. F, same date; transferred to band, June 29, 1898; mustered out with band, November 19, 1898, at Buffalo, N. Y.

WELCH, JR., SAMUEL M.—Age, 47 years. Enrolled, May 1, 1898, at Buffalo, to serve two years; mustered in as colonel, May 17, 1898; mustered out with regiment, November 19, 1898, at Buffalo, N. Y.; commissioned colonel, April 30, 1898, with rank from same date, original.

WELCHLIN, CHARLES.—Age, 28 years. Enlisted, May 1, 1898, at Buffalo, to serve two years; mustered in as private, Co. K, May 17, 1898; discharged for disability, August 16, 1898, at Camp Alger, near Dunn Loring, Va.

WELLER, CHARLES O.—Age, 28 years. Enlisted, May 1, 1898, at Buffalo, to serve two years; mustered in as private, Co. K, May 17, 1898; promoted corporal, June 29, 1898; mustered out with company, November 19, 1898, at Buffalo, N. Y.

WEPPMAN, CHARLES.—Age, — years. Enlisted, June 29, 1898, at Buffalo, to serve two years; mustered in as private, Co. L, same date; mustered out with company, November 19, 1898, at Buffalo, N. Y.

WERNER, JOHN.—Age, — years. Enlisted, June 21, 1898, at Buffalo, to serve two years; mustered in as private, Co. K, same date; promoted corporal, June 29, 1898; mustered out with company, November 19, 1898, at Buffalo, N. Y.

WESOLEK, MICHAEL.—Age, 23 years. Enlisted, May 1, 1898, at Buffalo, to serve two years; mustered in as private, Co. I, May 17, 1898; discharged for disability, July 14, 1898, at Camp Alger, near Dunn Loring, Va.

WESTON, HARRY D.—Age, — years. Enlisted, June 22, 1898, at Buffalo, to serve two years; mustered in as private, Co. F, same date; mustered out with company, November 19, 1898, at Buffalo, N. Y.

WESTPHAL, FRED.—Age, 21 years. Enlisted, May 1, 1898, at Buffalo, to serve two years; mustered in as private, Co. K, May 17, 1898; mustered out with company, November 19, 1898, at Buffalo, N. Y.

WEYAND, EDWARD C.—Age, — years. Enlisted, June 15, 1898, at Buffalo, to serve two years; mustered in as private, Co. A, same date; mustered out with company, November 19, 1898, at Buffalo, N. Y.

WEYAND, HENRY A.—Age, 20 years. Enlisted, May 1, 1898, at Buffalo, to serve two years; mustered in as private, Co. B, May 17, 1898; mustered out with company, November 19, 1898, at Buffalo, N. Y.

WHEELER, ALBERT W.—Age, 32 years. Enlisted, May 1, 1898, at Buffalo, to serve two years; mustered in as private, Co. B, May 17, 1898; promoted corporal, June 23, 1898; mustered out with company, November 19, 1898, at Buffalo, N. Y.

WHITE, CARL.—Age, 21 years. Enlisted, May 1, 1898, at Buffalo, to serve two years; mustered in as private, Co. K, May 17, 1898; mustered out with company, November 19, 1898, at Buffalo, N. Y.

WHITE, HARRY L.—Age, — years. Enlisted, June 15, 1898, at Buffalo, to serve two years; mustered in as private, Co. K, same date; mustered out with company, November 19, 1898, at Buffalo, N. Y.

WHITE, JOHN.—Age, — years. Enlisted, June 29, 1898, at Buffalo, to serve two years; mustered in as private, Co. G, same date; mustered out with company, November 19, 1898, at Buffalo, N. Y.

WHITE, SEYMOUR P.—Age, 24 years. Enrolled, May 1, 1898, at Buffalo, to serve two years; mustered in as first lieutenant, Co. M, May 17, 1898; mustered out with company, November 19, 1898, at Buffalo, N. Y.; commissioned first lieutenant, May 17, 1898, with rank from same date, original.

WHITE, SYDNEY W.—Age, 22 years. Enlisted, May 1, 1898, at Buffalo, to serve two years; mustered in as private, Co. K, May 17, 1898; mustered out with company, November 19, 1898, at Buffalo, N. Y.

WHITNEY, DESHLER.—Age, 19 years. Enlisted, May 4, 1898, at Camp Black, to serve two years; mustered in as private, Co. G, May 17, 1898; mustered out with company, November 19, 1898, at Buffalo, N. Y.

WHITNEY, JAMES.—Age, — years. Enlisted, June 13, 1898, at Buffalo, to serve two years; mustered in as private, Co. D, same date; mustered out with company, November 19, 1898, at Buffalo, N. Y.

WILBER, GEORGE B.—Age, 28 years. Enlisted, May 1, 1898, at Buffalo, to serve two years; mustered in as private, Co. B, May 17, 1898; mustered out with company, November 19, 1898, at Buffalo, N. Y.

WILCOX, CLARENCE R.—Age, 19 years. Enlisted, May 1, 1898, at Jamestown, to serve two years; mustered in as private, Co. E, May 17, 1898; mustered out with company, November 19, 1898, at Buffalo, N. Y.

WILCOX, GEORGE.—Age, 21 years. Enlisted, May 1, 1898, at Buffalo, to serve two years; mustered in as private, Co. B, May 17, 1898; promoted corporal, June 23, 1898; mustered out with company, November 19, 1898, at Buffalo, N. Y.

WILKESON, EDWARD S. W.—Age, 27 years. Enlisted, May 1, 1898, at Buffalo, to serve two years; mustered in as private, Co. G, May 17, 1898; promoted corporal, August 24, 1898; mustered out with company, November 19, 1898, at Buffalo, N. Y.

WILKS, CHARLES.—Age, 30 years. Enlisted, May 1, 1898, at Buffalo, to serve two years; mustered in as private, Co. I, May 17, 1898; mustered out with company, November 19, 1898, at Buffalo, N. Y.

WILLARD, LOUIS G.—Age, — years. Enlisted, June 15, 1898, at Buffalo, to serve two years; mustered in as private, Co. E, same date; mustered out with company, November 19, 1898, at Buffalo, N. Y.

WILLAX, ANTHONY.—Age, 28 years. Enlisted, May 13, 1898, at Camp Black, to serve two years; mustered in as private, Co. L, May 17, 1898; mustered out with company, November 19, 1898, at Buffalo, N. Y.

WILLIAMS, GORDON.—Age, 21 years. Enlisted, May 1, 1898, at Buffalo, to serve two years; mustered in as private, Co. K, May 17, 1898; mustered out with company, November 19, 1898, at Buffalo, N. Y.

WILLOUGHBY, MATTHEW.—Age, 28 years. Enlisted, May 1, 1898, at Buffalo, to serve two years; mustered in as private, Co. L, May 17, 1898; mustered out with company, November 19, 1898, at Buffalo, N. Y.

WILSON, FRED H.—Age, 34 years. Enrolled, May 1, 1898, at Jamestown, to serve two years; mustered in as second lieutenant, Co. E, May 17, 1898; as first lieutenant, July 16, 1898; mustered out with company, November 19, 1898, at Buffalo, N. Y.; commissioned second lieutenant, May 17, 1898, with rank from same date, original; first lieutenant, July 8, 1898, with rank from same date, vice Johnson, promoted captain.

WILSON, GUILFORD REED.—Age, 43 years. Enrolled, May 1, 1898, at Buffalo, to serve two years; mustered in as first lieutenant and regimental quartermaster, May 17, 1898; mustered out with regiment, November 19, 1898, at Buffalo, N. Y.; commissioned captain and regimental quartermaster, May 17, 1898, with rank from same date, original.

WILSON, ROBERT H.—Age, 23 years. Enlisted, May 1, 1898, at Buffalo, to serve two years; mustered in as private, Co. A, May 17, 1898; mustered out with company, November 19, 1898, at Buffalo, N. Y.

WILSON, WALTER M.—Age, 22 years. Enlisted, May 1, 1898, at Buffalo, to serve two years; mustered in as private, Co. D, May 17, 1898; promoted sergeant, June 8, 1898; mustered out with company, November 19, 1898, at Buffalo, N. Y.

WILSON, WILLIAM.—Age, 30 years. Enlisted, May 1, 1898, at Buffalo, to serve two years; mustered in as private, Co. F, May 17, 1898; dishonorably discharged, August 5, 1898.

WINSON, GEORGE G.—Age, — years. Enlisted, June 15, 1898, at Buffalo, to serve two years; mustered in as private, Co. E, same date; mustered out with company, November 19, 1898, at Buffalo, N. Y.

WINTER, JULIAS.—Age, 27 years. Enlisted, May 1, 1898, at Buffalo, to serve two years; mustered in as private, Co. C, May 17, 1898; promoted corporal, October 19, 1898; mustered out with company, November 19, 1898, at Buffalo, N. Y.

WINTERS, GEORGE J.—Age, 31 years. Enlisted, May 1, 1898, at Buffalo, to serve two years; mustered in as artificer, Co. M, May 17, 1898; returned to ranks, at own request, June 30, 1898; mustered out with company, November 19, 1898, at Buffalo, N. Y.

WIPPERMAN, LOUIS.—Age, 21 years. Enlisted, May 1, 1898, at Buffalo, to serve two years; mustered in as corporal, Co. K, May 17, 1898; mustered out with company, November 19, 1898, at Buffalo, N. Y.

WIRGES, WILLIAM A.—Age, — years. Enlisted, June 24, 1898, at Buffalo, to serve two years; mustered in as private, Co. B, same date; transferred to band, June 29, 1898; mustered out with band, November 19, 1898, at Buffalo, N. Y.

WISSER, WILLIAM C.—Age, 24 years. Enlisted, May 1, 1898, at Buffalo, to serve two years; mustered in as private. Co. C, May 17, 1898; mustered out with company, November 19, 1898, at Buffalo, N. Y.

WITT, WILLIAM.—Age, 19 years. Enlisted, May 1, 1898, at Buffalo, to serve two years; mustered in as private, Co. F, May 17, 1898; mustered out with company, November 19, 1898, at Buffalo, N. Y.

WITTLIEF, AUGUST.—Age, — years. Enlisted, June 20, 1898, at Buffalo, to serve two years; mustered in as private, Co. L, same date; mustered out with company, November 19, 1898, at Buffalo, N. Y.

WOLF, FRANK M.—Age, 24 years. Enlisted, May 1, 1898, at Buffalo, to serve two years; mustered in as private, Co. B, May 17, 1898; mustered out with company, November 19, 1898, at Buffalo, N. Y.

WOLFF, ERNEST.—Age, 21 years. Enlisted, May 12, 1898, at Buffalo, to serve two years; mustered in as private, Co. H, May 17, 1898; mustered out with company, November 19, 1898, at Buffalo, N. Y.

WOLFF, OTTO W.—Age, 23 years. Enlisted, May 1, 1898, at Buffalo, to serve two years; mustered in as private, Co. D, May 17, 1898; promoted corporal, July 7, 1898; mustered out with company, November 19, 1898, at Buffalo, N. Y.

WOLFFSOHN, SAMUEL S.—Age, 30 years. Enlisted, May 1, 1898, at Buffalo, to serve two years; mustered in as private, Co. F, May 17, 1898; mustered out with company, November 19, 1898, at Buffalo, N. Y.

WOOD, GARNER.—Age, 24 years. Enlisted, May 1, 1898, at Buffalo, to serve two years; mustered in as private, Co. F, May 17, 1898; promoted corporal, June 28, 1898; mustered out with company, November 19, 1898, at Buffalo, N. Y.

WOOD, JOSIAH LE VERN.—Age, 24 years. Enlisted, May 1, 1898, at Buffalo, to serve two years; mustered in as private, Co. K, May 17, 1898; mustered out with company, November 19, 1898, at Buffalo, N. Y.

WOOD, WILLIAM E.—Age, — years. Enlisted, June 13, 1898, at Buffalo, to serve two years; mustered in as private, Co. B, same date; mustered out with company, November 19, 1898, at Buffalo, N. Y.

WOODWARD, CLYDE.—Age, 23 years. Enlisted, May 1, 1898, at Buffalo, to serve two years; mustered in as private, Co. G, May 17, 1898; mustered out with company, November 19, 1898, at Buffalo, N. Y.

WOODS, GEORGE M.—Age, 26 years. Enlisted, May 1, 1898, at Buffalo, to serve two years; mustered in as private, Co. G, May 17, 1898: mustered out with company, November 19, 1898, at Buffalo, N. Y.

WORDEN, HARRY.—Age, 35 years. Enlisted, May 1, 1898, at Buffalo, to serve two years; mustered in as corporal, Co. B, May 17, 1898; returned to ranks, no date; mustered out with company, November 19, 1898, at Buffalo, N. Y.

WORTMAN, EDWIN S.—Age, 21 years. Enlisted, May 1, 1898, at Buffalo, to serve two years; mustered in as private, Co. C, May 17, 1898; mustered out with company, November 19, 1898, at Buffalo, N. Y.

WORTMAN, JOSEPH.—Age, 25 years. Enlisted, May 1, 1898, at Buffalo, to serve two years; mustered in as private, Co. D, May 17, 1898; mustered out with company, November 19, 1898, at Buffalo, N. Y.

WRIGHT, CHARLES J.—Age, — years. Enlisted, June 20, 1898, at Buffalo, to serve two years; mustered in as private, Co. E, same date; mustered out with company, November 19, 1898, at Buffalo, N. Y.

YAEGER, JOSEPH.—Age, 20 years. Enlisted, May 1, 1898, at Buffalo, to serve two years; mustered in as private, Co. K, May 17, 1898; mustered out with company, November 19, 1898, at Buffalo, N. Y.

YAX, FRANK H.—Age, 21 years. Enlisted, May 1, 1898, at Buffalo, to serve two years; mustered in as private, Co. L, May 17, 1898; mustered out with company, November 19, 1898, at Buffalo, N. Y.

YEAMES, HERBERT H.—Age, 23 years. Enlisted, May 1, 1898, at Buffalo, to serve two years; mustered in as private, Co. A, May 17, 1898; mustered out with company, November 19, 1898, at Buffalo, N. Y.

YORK, GEORGE G.—Age, 26 years. Enlisted, May 1, 1898, at Jamestown, to serve two years; mustered in as corporal, Co. E, May 17, 1898; mustered out with company, November 19, 1898, at Buffalo, N. Y.

ZAHN, SIMON.—Age, 27 years. Enlisted, May 1, 1898, at Buffalo, to serve two years; mustered in as sergeant, Co. K, May 17, 1898; mustered out with company, November 19, 1898, at Buffalo, N. Y.

ZANG, PETER.—Age, 26 years. Enlisted, May 1, 1898, at Buffalo, to serve two years; mustered in as private, Co. C, May 17, 1898; mustered out with company, November 19, 1898, at Buffalo, N. Y.

ZAWADGKI, LOUIS.—Age, — years. Enlisted, June 16, 1898, at Buffalo, to serve two years; mustered in as private, Co. G, same date; mustered out with company, November 19, 1898, at Buffalo, N. Y.

ZEISE, OSWALD O.—Age, — years. Enlisted, June 16, 1898, at Buffalo, to serve two years; mustered in as private, Co. G, same date; mustered out with company, November 19, 1898, at Buffalo, N. Y.

ZIEGLER, WILLIAM.—Age, 23 years. Enlisted, May 1, 1898, at Buffalo, to serve two years; mustered in as corporal, Co F, May 17, 1898; mustered out with company, November 19, 1898, at Buffalo, N. Y.

ZIEMANN, GUSTAV A. R.—Age, 24 years. Enlisted as sergeant, May 1, 1898, at Buffalo, to serve two years; mustered in as second lieutenant, Co. D, May 17, 1898; mustered out with company, November 19, 1898, at Buffalo, N. Y.; commissioned second lieutenant, May 17, 1898, with rank from same date, original.

ZIMMER, HENRY J.—Age, 21 years. Enlisted, May 12, 1898, at Buffalo, to serve two years; mustered in as private, Co. M, May 17, 1898; mustered out with company, November 19, 1898, at Buffalo, N. Y.

ZIMMER, JOSEPH J.—Age, — years. Enlisted, June 22, 1898, at Buffalo, to serve two years; mustered in as private, Co. K, same date; mustered out with company, November 19, 1898, at Buffalo, N. Y.

ZIMMER, WILLIAM.—Age, 23 years. Enlisted, May 1, 1898, at Buffalo, to serve two years; mustered in as private, Co. C, May 17, 1898; mustered out with company, November 19, 1898, at Buffalo, N. Y.

ZIMMERMAN, CHARLES W.—Age, 22 years. Enlisted, May 1, 1898, at Buffalo, to serve two years; mustered in as private, Co. F, May 17, 1898; mustered out with company, November 19, 1898, at Buffalo, N. Y.

ZIMMEST, GEORGE J.—Age, — years. Enlisted, June 13, 1898, at Buffalo, to serve two years; mustered in as private, Co. D, same date; mustered out with company, November 19, 1898, at Buffalo, N. Y.

ZRENNER, JOSEPH H.—Age, 24 years. Enlisted, May 1, 1898, at Buffalo, to serve two years; mustered in as private, Co. C, May 17, 1898; mustered out with company, November 19, 1898, at Buffalo, N. Y.

ZULASKEE, NICHOLAS.—Age, 24 years. Enlisted, May 1, 1898, at Buffalo, to serve two years; mustered in as private, Co. I, May 17, 1898; mustered out with company, November 19, 1898, at Buffalo, N. Y.

Lightning Source UK Ltd.
Milton Keynes UK
UKHW052332090219
336872UK00005BA/482/P